GLEIM®

12TH EDITION

COST/MANAGERIAL ACCOUNTING

EXAM QUESTIONS & EXPLANATIONS

by

Irvin N. Gleim, Ph.D., CPA, CIA, CMA, CFM

with the assistance of
Grady M. Irwin, J.D.

Gleim Publications, Inc.
PO Box 12848
University Station
Gainesville, Florida 32604
(800) 87-GLEIM or (800) 874-5346
(352) 375-0772
Website: www.gleim.com
Email: admin@gleim.com

For updates to the first printing of the twelfth edition of ***Cost/Managerial Accounting Exam Questions and Explanations***

Go To: www.gleim.com/updates

Or: Email update@gleim.com with **MAN EQE 12-1** in the subject line. You will receive our current update as a reply.

Updates are available until the next edition is published.

ISSN: 1092-4205
ISBN: 978-1-61854-180-2

First Printing: July 2018

ACKNOWLEDGMENTS

Material from Uniform Certified Public Accountant Examination questions and unofficial answers, Copyright © 1969-2018 by the American Institute of Certified Public Accountants, Inc., is reprinted and/or adapted with permission.

The authors appreciate and thank The Institute of Internal Auditors, Inc., for permission to use the Institute's Certified Internal Auditor Examination questions, Copyright © 1976-2018, by The Institute of Internal Auditors, Inc.

The authors also appreciate and thank the Institute of Certified Management Accountants of the Institute of Management Accountants (formerly the National Association of Accountants) for permission to use questions from past CMA examinations, Copyright © 1973-2018 by the Institute of Management Accountants.

The authors appreciate questions contributed by the following individuals: K. Boze, J.W. Ferry, R. Gruber, F. Mayne, L.J. McCarthy, K. Putnam, J.B. Romal, C.J. Skender, and A. Wilson. Each question submitted by these individuals can be noted by viewing the question source, which appears in the first line of its answer explanation in the column to the right of the question.

Environmental Statement -- This book is printed on recyclable, environmentally friendly groundwood paper, sourced from certified sustainable forests and produced either TCF (totally chlorine-free) or ECF (elementally chlorine-free).

ABOUT THE AUTHOR

Irvin N. Gleim is Professor Emeritus in the Fisher School of Accounting at the University of Florida and is a member of the American Accounting Association, Academy of Legal Studies in Business, American Institute of Certified Public Accountants, Association of Government Accountants, Florida Institute of Certified Public Accountants, The Institute of Internal Auditors, and the Institute of Management Accountants. He has had articles published in the *Journal of Accountancy*, *The Accounting Review*, and *The American Business Law Journal* and is author/coauthor of numerous accounting books, aviation books, and CPE courses.

REVIEWERS AND CONTRIBUTORS

Garrett W. Gleim, B.S., CGMA, received a Bachelor of Science degree from the University of Pennsylvania, The Wharton School. He also holds a CPA certificate issued by the State of Delaware. Mr. Gleim coordinated the production staff, reviewed the manuscript, and provided production assistance throughout the project.

Grady M. Irwin, J.D., is a graduate of the University of Florida College of Law, and he has taught in the University of Florida College of Business. Mr. Irwin provided substantial editorial assistance throughout the project.

Yiqian Zhao, MAcc., CPA, CIA, is a graduate of the Fisher School of Accounting at the University of Florida. Ms. Zhao participated in the technical editing of the manuscript.

A PERSONAL THANKS

This manual would not have been possible without the extraordinary effort and dedication of Jacob Bennett, Julie Cutlip, Ethan Good, Blaine Hatton, Kelsey Hughes, Fernanda Martinez, Bree Rodriguez, Teresa Soard, Justin Stephenson, Joanne Strong, Elmer Tucker, and Candace Van Doren, who typed the entire manuscript and all revisions and drafted and laid out the diagrams, illustrations, and cover for this book.

The authors also appreciate the production and editorial assistance of Sirene Dagher, Jessica Hatker, Kristen Hennen, Belea Keeney, Katie Larson, Diana León, Bryce Owen, Jake Pettifor, Shane Rapp, Drew Sheppard, and Alyssa Thomas.

The authors also appreciate the critical reading assistance of Matthew Blockus, Felix Chen, Corey Connell, Dean Kingston, Melissa Leonard, Monica Metz, Kelly Meyer, Timothy Murphy, Cristian Prieto, Crystal Quach, Martin Salazar, and Diana Weng.

Finally, we appreciate the encouragement, support, and tolerance of our families throughout this project.

IF YOU HAVE QUESTIONS

Gleim has an efficient and effective way for users to submit an inquiry and receive a response regarding Gleim materials directly through their Test Prep. This system also allows you to view your Q&A session in your Gleim Personal Classroom.

Questions regarding the information in the Introduction (study suggestions, studying plans, exam specifics) should be emailed to personalcounselor@gleim.com.

Questions concerning orders, prices, shipments, or payments should be sent via email to customerservice@gleim.com and will be promptly handled by our competent and courteous customer service staff.

For technical support, you may use our automated technical support service at www.gleim.com/support, email us at support@gleim.com, or call us at (800) 874-5346.

TABLE OF CONTENTS

DETAILED TABLE OF CONTENTS

PREFACE FOR ACCOUNTING STUDENTS

The purpose of this book is to help you understand cost/managerial accounting concepts and procedures and their applications. These skills will enable you to perform better on your undergraduate exams, as well as look ahead to (and prepare for) professional certification exams (e.g., CIA, CMA, CPA, and EA).

One of the major benefits of this book is comprehensive coverage of cost/managerial accounting topics. Accordingly, when you use this book to help prepare for cost/managerial accounting courses and exams, you are assured of covering virtually all topics that can reasonably be expected to be studied in typical college or university courses. See Appendix A for a comprehensive list of cross-references.

The signature Gleim answer and explanation format is designed to facilitate effective study and learning. The Gleim EQE Test Prep is packed with features that allow you to customize quizzes to focus on the areas with the biggest opportunity for improvement and review detailed answer explanations for questions you missed.

The majority of the questions in this book are from past CIA, CMA, and CPA exams. Although a citation for the source of each question is provided, some have been modified to accommodate changes in professional pronouncements, to clarify questions, and/or to emphasize an accounting concept or its application. In addition, hundreds of publisher-written questions test areas covered in current textbooks but not directly tested on accounting certification exams to help you better prepare for your accounting coursework.

Note that this study manual should not be relied upon exclusively to prepare for the professional exams. You should primarily use review systems specifically developed for each exam. The Gleim CIA, CMA, CPA, and EA Review Systems are up-to-date and comprehensively cover all material necessary for successful completion of these exams. Further descriptions of these exams and our review materials are provided in the Introduction. To obtain any of these materials, order online at www.gleim.com or call us at (800) 874-5346.

Thank you for your interest in this book. We deeply appreciate the many letters and suggestions received from accounting students and educators during the past years, as well as from CIA, CMA, CPA, and EA candidates. Please go to www.gleim.com/feedbackMAN to share your suggestions on how we can improve this edition.

Please read the Introduction carefully. It is short but very important.

Good Luck on Your Exams,

Irvin N. Gleim

July 2018

GLEIM® EXAM PREP
Exceptional Coverage. Extraordinary Results.™
GLEIM
LOVES
STUDENTS
Save 20% with our student discount!
800.874.5346 | gleim.com/students

INTRODUCTION

This innovative accounting text provides students with a well-organized, extensive collection of multiple-choice questions covering the topics taught in typical cost and managerial accounting courses.

The Gleim *Exam Questions and Explanations* (EQE) series will help you to pretest yourself before class to determine whether you are strong or weak in the assigned area. Then test yourself after class to reinforce the concepts. The questions in these books cover **all** topics in your related courses, so you will encounter few questions on your exams for which you will not be well prepared.

The titles and organization of Study Units 1 through 18 are based on the current cost/managerial accounting textbooks listed in Appendix A, which contains a comprehensive cross-reference of your textbook to Gleim study units and subunits. If you are using a textbook that is not included in our list or if you have any suggestions on how we can improve these cross-references to make them more useful, please submit your request/feedback at www.gleim.com/crossreferences/MAN or email them to MANcrossreferences@gleim.com.

FEATURES

The Gleim EQE series will ensure your understanding of each topic you study in your courses with access to the largest bank of exam questions (including thousands from past certification exams) that is widely used by professors. This series provides immediate feedback on your study effort while you take your practice tests.

- Each book or EQE Test Prep question bank contains over 1,000 multiple-choice questions with correct and incorrect answer explanations and can be used in two or more classes.
- Exhaustive cross-references are presented for all related textbooks so that you can easily determine which group of questions pertains to a given chapter in your textbook.
- Questions taken directly from professional certification exams demonstrate the standards to which you will be held as a professional accountant and help prepare you for certification exams later.
- Titles include Auditing & Systems, Cost/Managerial Accounting, Financial Accounting, Federal Tax, and Business Law & Legal Studies. They thoroughly cover the topics you are presented with while pursuing your accounting degree. Go to www.gleim.com/eqe for more details.

After graduation, you will compete with graduates from schools across the country in the accounting job market. Make sure you measure up to standards that are as demanding as the standards of your counterparts at other schools. These standards will be tested on professional certification exams.

USE OF SUBUNITS

Each study unit of this book is divided into subunits to portion overwhelming topics into more manageable, bite-size learning components.

Topics and questions may overlap among subunits. The number of questions offers comprehensive coverage but does not present an insurmountable task. We define each subunit narrowly enough to cover a single topic but broadly enough to prevent questions from being repetitive.

QUESTION SOURCES

Past CIA, CMA, and CPA exams and sample questions are the primary sources of questions included in this study guide.

In addition, Gleim Exam Prep prepares questions (coded in this text as *Publisher, adapted*) based on the content of accounting textbooks, regulations, and other authoritative literature. Professionals and professors from schools around the country also have contributed to provide a more thorough and the largest bank of questions. See page ii for a list of their names.

The source of each question appears in the first line of its answer explanation in the column to the right of the question. Summary of source codes:

CIA	Certified Internal Auditor Examination
CMA	Certified Management Accountant Examination
CPA	Uniform Certified Public Accountant Examination
Publisher	EQE MAN author
Individual's name	Name of professional or professor who contributed the question

If you, your professor, or your classmates wish to submit questions, we will consider using them in future editions. Please email questions you develop, complete with answers and explanations, to professor.relations@gleim.com.

Writing and analyzing multiple-choice questions is an excellent way to prepare yourself for your exams. We will make every effort to consider, edit, and use questions you submit. However, we ask that you send us only serious, complete, carefully considered efforts.

MULTIPLE-CHOICE QUESTIONS

The major advantage of multiple-choice questions is their ability to cover a large number of topics with little time and effort in comparison to essay questions and/or computational problems.

The advantage of multiple-choice questions over true/false questions is that they require more analysis and result in a lower score for those with little or no knowledge.

Students and professors both like multiple-choice questions. Students find them relatively easy to answer because only one of the answer choices needs to be selected. Professors like them because they are easy to grade and much more material can be tested in the same period of time. Most professors also will ask students to complete essays or computational questions.

Note that the detailed Gleim answer explanations also can help students prepare for the inevitable essay questions.

ANSWER EXPLANATIONS ALONGSIDE THE QUESTIONS

The format of our book presents multiple-choice questions side by side with their answer explanations. The example below is from the CMA exam.

The use of standard costs in the budgeting process signifies that an organization has most likely implemented a

A. Flexible budget.

B. Capital budget.

C. Zero-based budget.

D. Static budget.

Answer (A) is correct. *(CMA, adapted)*

REQUIRED: The budget most likely implemented by a company that uses standard costs.

DISCUSSION: A flexible budget is a series of budgets prepared for various levels of sales and production. Another view is that it is based on cost formulas, or standard costs. Thus, the cost formulas are fed into the computerized budget program along with the actual level of sales or production. The result is a budget created for the actual level of activity.

Answer (B) is incorrect. A capital budget is a means of evaluating long-term investments and has nothing to do with standard costs. Answer (C) is incorrect. A zero-based budget is a planning process in which each manager must justify a department's entire budget each year. The budget is built from the base of zero each year. Answer (D) is incorrect. A static budget is for one level of activity. It can be based on expected actual or standard costs.

This format is designed to make studying more efficient by eliminating the need to turn pages back and forth from questions to answers.

Be careful, however. Do not misuse this format by consulting the answers before you have answered the questions. Misuse of the readily available answers will give you a false sense of security and will result in poor performance on your actual exams.

STUDY SUGGESTIONS

The emphasis in the next few pages is on developing strategies, approaches, and procedures to learn and retain the material in less time.

Using Tests to Study

Tests, especially quizzes and midterms, provide feedback on your study and test-taking procedures. It is extremely important to identify your opportunities for improvement on quizzes and tests at the beginning of the term so you can take corrective action on subsequent tests, including your final exam.

When your test is returned, determine how you did relative to the rest of your class and your professor's grading standards. Next, analyze your relative performance between types of questions (essay vs. multiple-choice) and types of subject matter (topics or study units). The objective is to identify the areas where you can improve.

Using Multiple-Choice Questions to Study

Experts on testing continue to favor multiple-choice questions as a valid means of evaluating various levels of knowledge. Using these questions to study for academic exams is an important tool not only for obtaining good grades, but also for long-range preparation for certification and professional exams. The following suggestions will help you study in conjunction with each Gleim *Exam Questions and Explanations* book and EQE Test Prep (visit www.gleim.com/students):

1. Locate the study unit that contains questions on the topic you are currently studying. Each *Exam Questions and Explanations* book and EQE Test Prep contains cross-references to the tables of contents of the most commonly used textbooks.
2. Work through a series of questions, selecting the answers you think are correct. Follow the Gleim multiple-choice question-answering technique outlined in the next section of this introduction.

3. **If you are using the Gleim book, do not consult the answer or answer explanations on the right side of the page until after you have chosen and written down an answer.**
    a. It is crucial that you cover the answer explanations and intellectually commit yourself to an answer. This method will help you understand the concept much better, even if you answered the question incorrectly. Our EQE Test Prep prevents you from consulting the answer, which allows you to study in an exam-like environment.
4. Study the explanations to the correct and incorrect answer choices for each question you answered incorrectly. In addition to learning and understanding the concept tested, analyze **why** you missed the question. Reasons for missing questions include

    - Misreading the requirement (stem)
    - Not understanding what is required
    - Making a math error
    - Applying the wrong rule or concept
    - Being distracted by one or more of the answers
    - Incorrectly eliminating answers from consideration
    - Not having any knowledge of the topic tested
    - Employing bad intuition when guessing

    Studying the important concepts that we provide in our answer explanations will help you understand the principles to the point that you can answer that question (or any other like it) successfully.
5. Identify your weaknesses in answering multiple-choice questions and take corrective action (before you take a test). The EQE Test Prep provides a detailed performance analysis.

    The analysis will show your weaknesses (areas needing more study) and also your strengths (areas of confidence). You can improve your performance on multiple-choice questions both by increasing your percentage of correct answers and by decreasing the time spent per question.

Multiple-Choice Question-Answering Technique

The following series of steps is suggested for answering multiple-choice questions. The important point is that you need to devote attention to and develop **the technique that works for you**. Personalize and practice your answering technique on questions in this study guide. Begin now to develop **your** control system.

1. **Budget your time.**
    a. We make this point with emphasis – **finish your exam before time expires**.
    b. Calculate the time allowed for each multiple-choice question after you have allocated time to the other questions (e.g., essays) on the exam. If 20 multiple-choice questions are allocated 40 minutes on your exam, you should spend a little under 2 minutes per question (always budget extra time for transferring answers to answer sheets, interruptions, etc.).
    c. Before beginning a series of multiple-choice questions, write the starting time on the exam near the first question.
    d. As you work through the questions, check your time. Assuming a time allocation of 120 minutes for 60 questions, you are fine if you worked 5 questions in 9 minutes. If you spent 11 minutes on 5 questions, you need to speed up. Remember that your goal is to answer all questions and achieve the maximum score possible.
2. **Answer the items in consecutive order.**
    a. Do **not** agonize over any one item. Stay within your time budget.
    b. Mark any questions you are unsure of and return to them later as time allows.
    c. Never leave a question unanswered **if** you will not be penalized for incorrect answers. Make your best guess in the time allowed.

3. **For each multiple-choice question,**
   a. **Ignore the answer choices.** Do not allow the answer choices to affect your reading of the question.
      1) If four answer choices are presented, three of them are incorrect. These incorrect choices are called **distractors** for good reason. Often, distractors are written to appear correct at first glance.
      2) In computational items, distractors are carefully calculated so they are the result of common mistakes. Be careful and double-check your computations if time permits.
   b. **Read the question carefully** to determine the precise requirement.
      1) Focusing on what is required enables you to ignore extraneous information and to proceed directly to determining the correct answer.
         a) Be especially careful to note when the requirement is an **exception**; e.g., "Which of the following items is **not** included in manufacturing overhead?"
   c. **Determine the correct answer** before looking at the answer choices.
   d. **Read the answer choices carefully.**
      1) Even if the first answer appears to be the correct choice, do **not** skip the remaining answer choices. Questions often ask for the "best" choice provided. Thus, each choice requires your consideration.
      2) Treat each answer choice as a true/false question as you analyze it.
   e. **Select the best answer.**
      1) If you are uncertain, guess intelligently (see "If You Don't Know the Answer" below). Improve on your 25% chance of getting the correct answer with blind guessing.
      2) For many multiple-choice questions, two answer choices can be eliminated with minimal effort, thereby increasing your educated guess to a 50-50 proposition.
4. **Transfer your answers to the answer sheet**, if one is provided.
   a. Make sure you are within your time budget so you will be able to perform this vital step in an unhurried manner.
   b. Do not wait to transfer answers until the very end of the exam session because you may run out of time.
   c. Double-check that you have transferred the answers correctly; e.g., recheck every 5th or 10th answer from your test paper to your answer sheet to ensure that you have not fallen out of sequence.

If You Don't Know the Answer

If the exam you are taking does not penalize incorrect answers, you should make an educated guess. First, rule out answers that you think are incorrect. Second, speculate on what the examiner is looking for and/or the rationale behind the question. Third, select the best answer or guess between equally appealing answers. Mark the question with a "?" in case you have time to return to it for further analysis.

If you cannot make an educated guess, read the stem and each answer, and pick the best or most intuitive answer. It's just a guess! Do **not** look at the previous answer to try to detect an answer. Answers are usually random, and it is possible to have four or more consecutive questions with the same answer letter, e.g., answer (B).

NOTE: Do not waste time beyond the amount you budgeted for each question. Move forward and stay on or ahead of schedule.

Examination Summary

	CPA (Certified Public Accountant)	CIA (Certified Internal Auditor)*	CMA (Certified Management Accountant)	EA (IRS Enrolled Agent)
Sponsoring Organization	American Institute of Certified Public Accountants	Institute of Internal Auditors	Institute of Certified Management Accountants	Internal Revenue Service
Contact Information	www.aicpa.org (888) 777-7077	www.theiia.org (407) 937-1111	www.imanet.org (800) 638-4427	www.irs.gov (313) 234-1280
Exam Parts	Auditing and Attestation (4 hrs.) Business Environment and Concepts (4 hrs.) Financial Accounting and Reporting (4 hrs.) Regulation (4 hrs.)	1 – Essentials of Internal Auditing (2.5 hrs.) 2 – Practice of Internal Auditing (2 hrs.) 3 – Business Knowledge for Internal Auditing (2 hrs.)	1 – Financial Reporting, Planning, Performance, and Control (4 hrs.) 2 – Financial Decision Making (4 hrs.)	1 – Individuals (3.5 hrs.) 2 – Businesses (3.5 hrs.) 3 – Representation, Practices, and Procedures (3.5 hrs.)
Exam Format	AUD: 72 multiple-choice questions 8 TBS BEC: 62 multiple-choice questions 4 TBS 3 written communications FAR: 66 multiple-choice questions 8 TBS REG: 76 multiple-choice questions 8 TBS	Part 1: 125 multiple-choice questions Parts 2 and 3: 100 multiple-choice questions	Parts 1 and 2: 100 multiple-choice questions 2 essays	Parts 1, 2, and 3: 100 multiple-choice questions
Avg. Pass Rate	AUD – 49% BEC – 53% FAR – 44% REG – 47%	Pass rates are not yet available for the reorganized exam.	1 – 40% 2 – 50%	1 – 61% 2 – 64% 3 – 86%
Testing Windows	January-March 10 April-June 10 July-September 10 October-December 10	On demand throughout the year	January-February May-June September-October	May-February (e.g., 5/01/2018-2/28/2019)
Resources	gleimcpa.com	gleimcia.com	gleimcma.com	gleimea.com
Available Prep Course Student Discounts	Up to 20%	Up to 20%	Up to 20%	Up to 10%

*Reflects the information for the reorganized 2019 exam.

ACCOUNTING CERTIFICATION PROGRAMS--OVERVIEW

The CPA (Certified Public Accountant) exam is the grandparent of all professional accounting exams. Its origin was in the 1896 public accounting legislation of New York. In 1917, the American Institute of CPAs (AICPA) began to prepare and grade a uniform CPA exam. It is currently used to measure the technical competence of those applying to be licensed as CPAs in all 50 states, Guam, Puerto Rico, the Virgin Islands, the District of Columbia, the Commonwealth of the Northern Mariana Islands, and an ever-expanding list of international locations.

The CIA (Certified Internal Auditor), CMA (Certified Management Accountant), and EA (IRS Enrolled Agent) exams are relatively new certification programs compared to the CPA. The CMA exam was first administered in 1972 and the first CIA exam in 1974. The EA exam dates back to 1959. Why were these other exams initially created? Generally, the requirements of the CPA designation instituted by the boards of accountancy (especially the necessity for public accounting experience) led to the development of the CIA and CMA programs, which allow for professionals to show proficiency in specific job functions. The EA designation is available for persons specializing in tax.

The table of selected CPA, CIA, CMA, and EA exam data on the preceding page provides an overview of these accounting exams.

ACCOUNTING CERTIFICATION PROGRAMS--PURPOSE

The primary purpose of professional exams is to measure the technical competence of candidates. Competence includes technical knowledge, the ability to apply such knowledge with good judgment, comprehension of professional responsibility, and ethical considerations. Additionally, the nature of these exams (low pass rate, broad and rigorous coverage, etc.) has several very important effects:

1. Candidates are forced to learn all of the material that should have been presented and learned in a good accounting education program.
2. Relatedly, candidates must integrate the topics and concepts that are presented in individual courses in accounting education programs.
3. The content of each exam provides direction to accounting education programs; i.e., what is tested on the exams will be taught to accounting students.

Certification is important to professional accountants because it provides

1. Participation in a recognized professional group
2. An improved professional training program arising out of the certification program
3. Recognition among peers for attaining the professional designation
4. An extra credential to enhance career opportunities
5. The personal satisfaction of attaining a recognized degree of competency

These reasons hold true in the accounting field due to wide recognition of the CPA designation. Accountants and accounting students are often asked whether they are CPAs when people learn they are accountants. Thus, there is considerable pressure for accountants to become **certified.**

A newer development is multiple certifications, which are important for the same reasons as initial certification. Accounting students and recent graduates should look ahead and obtain multiple certifications to broaden their career opportunities.

The CIA and CMA are now globally recognized certifications, making them appealing designations for multi-national companies.

When to Sit for the Certification Exams

Sit for all exams as soon as you can. Candidates are allowed to sit for the exam and then complete the requirements within a certain time period. The CIA program allows full-time students in their senior year to sit for the exam, and the CMA program offers a 7-year window for submission of educational credentials. The CIA and CMA exams are offered at a reduced fee for students. The requirements for the CPA vary by jurisdiction, but many state boards allow candidates to sit for the exam before they have completed the required hours. However, you will not be certified until you have met all requirements.

Register to take the parts of each exam that best match up to the courses you are currently taking. For example, if you are taking a Business Law course and a Federal Tax course this semester, schedule your CPA Regulation date for the week after classes end.

Dual certification can greatly enhance your career. Visit www.gleim.com/cmablog to find out why the CPA and CMA is an especially beneficial combination and to learn the steps on how to achieve dual certification.

Steps to Passing Certification Exams

1. Become knowledgeable about the exam you will be taking, and determine which part you will take first.
2. Purchase the complete Gleim Review System to thoroughly prepare yourself. Commit to systematic preparation for the exam as described in our review materials.
3. Communicate with your Personal Counselor to design a study plan that meets your needs. Call (800) 874-5346 or email personalcounselor@gleim.com.
4. Apply for membership in the exam's governing body and/or in the certification program as required.
5. Register online to take the desired part of the exam.
6. Schedule your test with the testing center in the location of your choice.
7. Work systematically through each study unit in the Gleim Review System.
8. Sit for and PASS the exam. Gleim guarantees success!
9. Email or call Gleim with your comments on our study materials and how well they prepared you for the exam.
10. Enjoy your career, pursue multiple certifications (CPA, CIA, CMA, EA, etc.), and recommend Gleim to others who are also taking these exams. Stay up-to-date on your Continuing Professional Education requirements with Gleim CPE.

STUDY UNIT ONE
OVERVIEW AND TERMINOLOGY

Cost/managerial accounting has evolved due to changes in the environment and the needs of organizations. Competition requires greater efficiency to provide better **customer value**. For this purpose, information must be obtained about all activities in the value chain that affect product cost. An emphasis only on manufacturing no longer suffices. Moreover, **quality and time** are now viewed as competitive weapons. Prompt delivery of reliable (defect-free) products and services requires financial and nonfinancial information about quality and time. Given the current trend of rapid technological change and shorter **product life cycles**, new products and services must be delivered more quickly, and managers must react flexibly to change. Thus, accounting systems must emphasize quality, cost, and time.

Advances in technology and reductions in its cost have made more sophisticated accounting systems feasible and permitted automation of production. For example, **computer-integrated manufacturing** provides (1) real-time monitoring, control, and reporting; (2) better quality and scheduling; (3) lower inventories and costs; and (4) small-lot production of customized goods. A related factor is the emergence of **just-in-time (JIT)** production. Demand pulls units through production, and each operation's output consists only of what is demanded by the next operation. Inventory is reduced or eliminated, output should be defect-free, and processes must be reorganized and improved.

Still another change is the growth of the **service sector**. Service entities also face competitive pressures, and the deregulation of services (banking, telecommunications, etc.) has increased competition. Accordingly, new methods are increasingly applied or adapted to service entities.

Responses to these changes have created a need for better methods of obtaining accounting information. One result is **activity-based management**. It is based on (1) **activity-based costing (ABC)** and (2) **process value analysis**. ABC provides more detailed and precise cost assignments by emphasizing the many activities that cause consumption of resources (costs). Process value analysis is a systematic understanding of the activities involved in making a product or rendering a service. It identifies those that add value and those that may be eliminated.

Despite many fundamental changes, traditional cost/managerial accounting remains the core of the body of knowledge presented in textbooks and tested on professional examinations. Consequently, this book addresses the most commonly tested subject matter while providing comprehensive coverage of more recent developments.

A committee of the Institute of Management Accountants issues **Statements on Management Accounting (SMAs)** to provide authoritative (but not mandatory) guidance. Also, the IMA has issued the *IMA Statement of Ethical Professional Practice*. It is in Appendix D.

QUESTIONS

1.1 Cost/Managerial Accounting

1.1.1. Management accounting differs from financial accounting in that financial accounting is

A. More oriented toward the future.

B. Primarily concerned with external financial reporting.

C. Primarily concerned with nonquantitative information.

D. Heavily involved with decision analysis and implementation of decisions.

Answer (B) is correct. *(Publisher, adapted)*

REQUIRED: The concept that applies more to financial than to management accounting.

DISCUSSION: Financial accounting is primarily concerned with historical accounting, i.e., traditional financial statements, and with external financial reporting to creditors and shareholders. Management accounting applies primarily to the planning and control of organizational operations, considers nonquantitative information, and is usually less precise.

Answer (A) is incorrect. Management accounting is future oriented. Answer (C) is incorrect. Financial accounting is primarily concerned with quantitative information. Answer (D) is incorrect. Decision analysis and implementation are characteristics of management accounting.

1.1.2. Which one of the following is least likely to be an objective of a cost accounting system?

A. Product costing.

B. Department efficiency.

C. Inventory valuation.

D. Sales commission determination.

Answer (D) is correct. *(CMA, adapted)*

REQUIRED: The item that is the least likely to be an objective of a cost accounting system.

DISCUSSION: A cost accounting system has numerous objectives, including product costing, assessing departmental efficiency, inventory valuation, income determination, and planning, evaluating, and controlling operations. Determining sales commissions is not an objective of a cost accounting system because such commissions are based on sales, not costs.

Answer (A) is incorrect. Product costing is an objective of a cost accounting system. Answer (B) is incorrect. Department efficiency is an objective of a cost accounting system. Answer (C) is incorrect. Inventory valuation is an objective of a cost accounting system.

1.1.3. Management should implement a different or more expensive accounting system only when

A. The cost of the system exceeds the benefits.

B. Management thinks it appropriate.

C. The board of directors dictates a change.

D. The benefits of the system exceed the cost.

Answer (D) is correct. *(Publisher, adapted)*

REQUIRED: The reason for using a different or more expensive accounting system.

DISCUSSION: Changing to a different or more expensive accounting system requires cost-benefit analysis. Changes should be undertaken only if the benefits of the proposed change exceed its cost.

Answer (A) is incorrect. Implementing a system in which cost exceeds benefits is economically irrational. Answer (B) is incorrect. Cost-benefit analysis should not be ignored. An accounting system should be selected on an objective basis. Answer (C) is incorrect. Dictation of a change by the board of directors implies a system selection on an other than objective basis.

1.1.4. Companies characterized by the production of heterogeneous products will most likely use which of the following methods for the purpose of averaging costs and providing management with unit cost data?

A. Process costing.

B. Job-order costing.

C. Direct costing.

D. Absorption costing.

Answer (B) is correct. *(CIA, adapted)*

REQUIRED: The method of averaging costs and providing management with unit cost data if products are heterogeneous.

DISCUSSION: The job-order cost system of accounting is appropriate when products have varied characteristics or when identifiable groupings are possible, e.g., batches of certain styles or types of furniture. The unique aspect of job-order costing is the identification of costs to specific units or a particular job.

Answer (A) is incorrect. Process costing accounts for continuous processing of homogeneous products. Answer (C) is incorrect. Direct (variable) costing includes only variable manufacturing costs in unit cost. Answer (D) is incorrect. Absorption costing includes all manufacturing costs in unit cost.

1.1.5. Which is the best description of traditional cost accounting?

A. The entire general ledger and subsidiary ledgers and related journals, etc., of a manufacturer.

B. The general ledger and subsidiary accounts and related records, etc., used to accumulate the costs of goods or services provided by an entity.

C. The accounts used to determine the costs of goods sold by an entity.

D. All of the journals, ledgers, records, and financial statements used by an entity to record, classify, summarize, and report economic activity.

Answer (B) is correct. *(Publisher, adapted)*

REQUIRED: The best description of traditional cost accounting.

DISCUSSION: Cost accounting includes all of the accounts and records used to accumulate the cost of goods and services provided by an entity. For a retailer, the inventory accounts, i.e., accounts for the costs of goods purchased from others for resale, serve this function. For a manufacturer or servicer, goods and services are created by the entity, not purchased from others. The means of accounting for such costs is a cost accounting system.

Answer (A) is incorrect. The general ledger and subsidiary ledgers have many financial accounting functions besides the accumulation of cost data. Answer (C) is incorrect. A retailer uses only inventory and cost of goods sold accounts to determine cost of goods sold. For a manufacturer, other accounts are used in the costing system, such as work-in-process and finished goods. Answer (D) is incorrect. The accounting system in general includes all of the journals, ledgers, records, and financial statements.

1.1.6. Cost and managerial accounting systems are goods in the economic sense and, as such, their benefits must exceed their costs. When managerial accounting systems change, the cost that is frequently ignored is the cost of

A. Educating users.

B. Gathering and analyzing data.

C. Training accounting staff.

D. Preparing reports.

Answer (A) is correct. *(Publisher, adapted)*

REQUIRED: The cost typically ignored in cost-benefit analysis of proposed changes in accounting systems.

DISCUSSION: Managers (users) must be willing and able to use new accounting systems. Accordingly, they should be encouraged to participate in the design and implementation of the new system. Otherwise, they may not understand or want to use the new information.

Answer (B) is incorrect. The costs of gathering and analyzing data are direct costs of changing managerial accounting systems and are usually considered. Answer (C) is incorrect. Training costs for staff are usually considered. Answer (D) is incorrect. Report preparation is explicitly considered in systems development.

1.1.7. An accounting system that collects financial and operating data on the basis of the underlying nature and extent of the cost drivers is

A. Direct costing.

B. Activity-based costing.

C. Cycle-time costing.

D. Variable costing.

Answer (B) is correct. *(CMA, adapted)*

REQUIRED: The accounting system that collects data on the basis of cost drivers.

DISCUSSION: An activity-based costing (ABC) system identifies the causal relationship between the incurrence of cost and the underlying activities that cause those costs. Under an ABC system, costs are applied to products on the basis of resources consumed (drivers).

Answer (A) is incorrect. Direct costing is a system that treats fixed costs as period costs; in other words, production costs consist only of variable costs, while fixed costs are expensed as incurred. Answer (C) is incorrect. Cycle time is the period from the time a customer places an order to the time that product is delivered. Answer (D) is incorrect. Variable costing is the same as direct costing, which expenses fixed costs as incurred.

1.1.8. The primary reason for adopting total quality management is to achieve

A. Greater customer satisfaction.

B. Reduced delivery time.

C. Reduced delivery charges.

D. Greater employee participation.

Answer (A) is correct. *(CIA, adapted)*

REQUIRED: The primary reason for adopting TQM.

DISCUSSION: TQM is an integrated system that identifies internal and external customers and establishes their requirements. The ultimate (external) customer is best served when internal customers are also well served.

Answer (B) is incorrect. Reduced delivery time is just one factor that increases customer satisfaction. Answer (C) is incorrect. Reduced delivery charges is just one factor that increases customer satisfaction. Answer (D) is incorrect. Increased employee participation is necessary to achieve TQM, but it is not the primary purpose for establishing the program.

1.1.9. Companies characterized by the production of basically homogeneous products will most likely use which of the following methods for the purpose of averaging costs and providing management with unit-cost data?

A. Job-order costing.

B. Direct costing.

C. Absorption costing.

D. Process costing.

Answer (D) is correct. *(CIA, adapted)*

REQUIRED: The method of averaging costs and providing management with unit cost data used by companies with homogeneous products.

DISCUSSION: Like products that are mass produced should be accounted for using process costing techniques to assign costs to products. Costs are accumulated by departments or cost centers rather than by jobs, work-in-process is stated in terms of equivalent units, and unit costs are established on a departmental basis. Process costing is an averaging process that calculates the average cost of all units.

Answer (A) is incorrect. Job-order costing is employed when manufacturing involves different (heterogeneous) products. Answer (B) is incorrect. Direct costing includes only variable manufacturing costs in unit cost. It may be used whether products are homogeneous or heterogeneous and with either process or job-order costing. Answer (C) is incorrect. Absorption costing includes all manufacturing costs as part of the cost of a finished product. It may be used whether products are homogeneous or heterogeneous and with either process or job-order costing.

1.1.10. Just-in-time manufacturing practices are based in part on the belief that

A. High inventory levels provide greater flexibility in production scheduling.

B. Attempting to reduce inventory to a consistently low level can lead to "panic" situations.

C. Goods should be "pulled" through the production process, not "pushed."

D. Beefed-up internal control in the central warehouse can greatly enhance productivity in the production areas.

Answer (C) is correct. *(Publisher, adapted)*

REQUIRED: The concept that is part of the philosophy of just-in-time manufacturing.

DISCUSSION: Just-in-time (JIT) manufacturing is a pull system; items are pulled through production by current demand, not pushed through by anticipated demand as in traditional manufacturing setups.

Answer (A) is incorrect. Under the JIT philosophy, high inventory levels often mask production problems. Answer (B) is incorrect. Attempting to reduce inventory to a consistently low level is a core objective of JIT. Answer (D) is incorrect. Under JIT, central warehouses are often eliminated.

1.1.11. The perpetual inventory method

A. Includes only variable manufacturing costs in the product cost calculation.

B. Requires a physical inventory count to determine amounts of inventories used or remaining.

C. Maintains a continuous record of transactions affecting the inventory balances.

D. Includes manufacturing and nonmanufacturing costs in inventory.

Answer (C) is correct. *(Publisher, adapted)*

REQUIRED: The difference between the perpetual and periodic inventory methods.

DISCUSSION: Perpetual inventory records provide for continuous record keeping of the quantities of inventory (and possibly unit costs or total costs). Perpetual inventory records can be maintained either in units or in units and dollars. This method requires a journal entry every time items are added to or taken from inventory.

Answer (A) is incorrect. Variable costing treats all fixed costs as period costs. It may be applied in either a perpetual or a periodic system. Answer (B) is incorrect. The periodic inventory system relies on physical counts to determine quantities. Answer (D) is incorrect. Only manufacturing costs are included in inventory.

1.1.12. Controllers ordinarily are not responsible for

A. Preparation of tax returns.

B. Reporting to government.

C. Protection of assets.

D. Investor relations.

Answer (D) is correct. *(Publisher, adapted)*

REQUIRED: The activity for which controllers usually are not responsible.

DISCUSSION: Controllers are usually in charge of budgets, accounting, accounting reports, and related controls. Treasurers are most often involved with control over cash, receivables, short-term investments, financing, and insurance. Thus, treasurers rather than controllers are concerned with investor relations.

Answer (A) is incorrect. The preparation of tax returns is a typical responsibility of the controller. Answer (B) is incorrect. External reporting is a function of the controller. Answer (C) is incorrect. The accounting system helps to safeguard assets.

1.1.13. The treasury function usually is not responsible for

A. Financial reporting.

B. Short-term financing.

C. Cash custody and banking.

D. Credit extension and collection of bad debts.

Answer (A) is correct. *(Publisher, adapted)*

REQUIRED: The function usually not performed by the treasurer.

DISCUSSION: Treasurers are usually concerned with investing cash and near-cash assets, the provision of capital, investor relations, insurance, etc. But controllers are responsible for the reporting and accounting activities of an organization, including financial reporting.

Answer (B) is incorrect. Short-term financing lies within the normal range of a treasurer's functions. Answer (C) is incorrect. The treasurer has custody of assets. Answer (D) is incorrect. Credit operations are often within the treasurer's purview.

1.1.14. Which professional organization represents management accountants in the United States?

A. The American Institute of Certified Public Accountants (AICPA).

B. The Institute of Internal Auditors (IIA).

C. The Institute of Certified Management Accountants (ICMA).

D. The Institute of Management Accountants (IMA).

Answer (D) is correct. *(Publisher, adapted)*

REQUIRED: The professional organization representing management accountants in the U.S.

DISCUSSION: The primary purpose of the IMA is to enhance the professionalism of management accountants. Membership is open to all persons interested in management accounting. Unlike the AICPA, which restricts membership to CPAs, the IMA does not require a member to have a CMA certificate.

Answer (A) is incorrect. The AICPA primarily represents the public accounting profession. Answer (B) is incorrect. The IIA represents internal auditors. Answer (C) is incorrect. The ICMA is a division of the IMA that administers the Certified Management Accountant (CMA) program.

1.1.15. The professional certification program most suited for one interested in a career in management accounting leads to which of the following designations?

A. CCP.

B. CIA.

C. CISA.

D. CMA.

Answer (D) is correct. *(Publisher, adapted)*

REQUIRED: The professional certification program most appropriate for a career in management accounting.

DISCUSSION: The Certified Management Accountant (CMA) program is administered by the IMA through the ICMA. The CMA certificate is awarded to those who pass two 4-hour examinations on (1) financial reporting, planning, performance, and control, and (2) financial decision making.

Answer (A) is incorrect. The Certified Computing Professional (CCP) designation is issued by the Association of IT Professionals (AITP). Answer (B) is incorrect. The Certified Internal Auditor (CIA) program is offered by The Institute of Internal Auditors (IIA). Answer (C) is incorrect. The Information Systems Audit and Control Association (ISACA) offers the Certified Information Systems Auditor (CISA) certificate.

1.2 Cost Definitions

1.2.1. Life-cycle costing

A. Is sometimes used as a basis for cost planning and product pricing.

B. Includes only manufacturing costs incurred over the life of the product.

C. Includes only manufacturing cost, selling expense, and distribution expense.

D. Emphasizes cost savings opportunities during the manufacturing cycle.

Answer (A) is correct. *(CMA, adapted)*

REQUIRED: The true statement about life-cycle costing.

DISCUSSION: Life-cycle costing estimates a product's revenues and expenses over its expected life cycle. This approach is especially useful when revenues and related costs do not occur in the same periods. It emphasizes the need to price products to cover all costs, not just those for production. Hence, costs are determined for all value-chain categories: upstream (R&D, design), manufacturing, and downstream (marketing, distribution, and customer service). The result is to highlight upstream and downstream costs in the cost planning process that often receive insufficient attention.

Answer (B) is incorrect. The life-cycle model includes the upstream (R&D and design) and downstream (marketing, distribution, and customer service) elements of the value chain as well as manufacturing costs. Answer (C) is incorrect. The life-cycle model includes the upstream (R&D and design) and downstream (marketing, distribution, and customer service) elements of the value chain as well as manufacturing costs. Answer (D) is incorrect. Life-cycle costing emphasizes the significance of locked-in costs, target costing, and value engineering for pricing and cost control. Thus, cost savings at all stages of the life cycle are important.

1.2.2. One of the purposes of standard costs is to

A. Simplify costing procedures and expedite cost reports.

B. Replace budgets and budgeting.

C. Serve as a basis for product costing for external reporting purposes.

D. Eliminate accounting for under- or overapplied manufacturing overhead at the end of the period.

Answer (A) is correct. *(CPA, adapted)*

REQUIRED: The purpose of standard costs.

DISCUSSION: A standard cost system differentiates the expected cost from the actual cost, thus identifying deviations from expected (attainable) results on a routine basis. One of the purposes of standard costs is to simplify costing procedures and expedite cost reports.

Answer (B) is incorrect. Standard costs are used to prepare budgets. Answer (C) is incorrect. Standard costs cannot be used for external reporting if material variances exist. Answer (D) is incorrect. Standard costs help measure over- and underapplied overhead.

1.2.3. The relevance of a particular cost to a decision is determined by

A. Riskiness of the decision.

B. Number of decision variables.

C. Amount of the cost.

D. Potential effect on the decision.

Answer (D) is correct. *(CMA, adapted)*

REQUIRED: The determinant of relevance of a particular cost to a decision.

DISCUSSION: Relevance is the capacity of information to make a difference in a decision by helping users of that information to predict the outcomes of events or to confirm or correct prior expectations. Thus, relevant costs are expected future costs that vary with the action taken. All other costs are constant and therefore have no effect on the decision.

1.2.4. Incremental cost is

A. The difference in total costs that results from selecting one choice instead of another.

B. The profit forgone by selecting one choice instead of another.

C. A cost that continues to be incurred in the absence of activity.

D. A cost common to all choices in question and not clearly or feasibly allocable to any of them.

Answer (A) is correct. *(CMA, adapted)*

REQUIRED: The definition of incremental cost.

DISCUSSION: Incremental cost is the difference in total cost between two courses of action. Incremental cost is also referred to as differential cost.

Answer (B) is incorrect. Opportunity cost is the profit forgone by selecting one choice instead of another. Answer (C) is incorrect. A fixed cost is incurred even though no output is produced. Answer (D) is incorrect. Common or joint costs are not allocable among the possible choices.

1.2.5. A company will produce 20,000 units of product A at a unit variable cost of $7 and a unit selling price of $13. Fixed costs are $40,000. However, the company will still have 40% idle capacity. The company can use this idle capacity to produce 6,000 units of a different product B, which it can sell for $7 per unit. The incremental variable cost of producing a unit of B is $6. Present fixed costs that will be allocated to B amount to $10,000. To decide whether to produce B, the company should use

A. Differential cost analysis.

B. Information economics.

C. Regression analysis.

D. Markov chain analysis.

Answer (A) is correct. *(CIA, adapted)*

REQUIRED: The method to determine whether idle capacity should be used to produce another product.

DISCUSSION: Nonroutine decisions involve such questions as whether to make or buy or accept a special order. These decisions should be made in part on the basis of relevant costs. Analysis of differential costs is therefore essential. The difference between the relevant costs of two decision choices is differential (incremental) cost.

Answer (B) is incorrect. Information economics applies to cost-benefit analysis of obtaining information for decision making. Answer (C) is incorrect. Regression analysis attempts to find an equation describing the change in a dependent variable related to a change in an independent variable. Answer (D) is incorrect. Markov analysis is useful when a problem involves a variety of states of nature, and the probability of moving from one state to another is dependent only upon the current state.

1.2.6. Conversion costs do not include

A. Depreciation.

B. Direct materials.

C. Indirect labor.

D. Indirect materials.

Answer (B) is correct. *(CMA, adapted)*

REQUIRED: The components not included in conversion costs.

DISCUSSION: Conversion costs are necessary to convert materials into finished products. They include all manufacturing costs, for example, direct labor and manufacturing overhead, other than direct materials.

Answer (A) is incorrect. Depreciation is a manufacturing overhead cost and therefore is a conversion cost. Answer (C) is incorrect. Indirect labor is a manufacturing overhead cost and therefore is a conversion cost. Answer (D) is incorrect. Indirect materials are manufacturing overhead costs and therefore are conversion costs.

1.2.7. Joint costs are costs of

A. Products requiring the services of two or more processing departments.

B. A product from a common process that has relatively little sales value and only a small effect on profit.

C. Production that are combined in the overhead account.

D. Two or more products produced from a common process.

Answer (D) is correct. *(Publisher, adapted)*

REQUIRED: The definition of joint costs.

DISCUSSION: Joint costs are the common costs of producing two or more inseparable products up to the point at which they become separable (the split-off point). The products are then sold as identifiably separate products or are processed further.

Answer (A) is incorrect. The costs accumulated in prior processing steps are considered materials costs for purposes of subsequent processing. Answer (B) is incorrect. Common products with relatively little sales value are by-products, e.g., woodchips from a sawmill. Joint cost is usually not allocated to them. Answer (C) is incorrect. Indirect costs are combined in the overhead account.

1.2.8. Controllable costs

A. Arise from periodic appropriation decisions and have no well-specified function relating inputs to outputs.

B. Are primarily subject to the influence of a given manager of a given responsibility center for a given time span.

C. Arise from having property, plant, and equipment, and a functioning organization.

D. Result specifically from a clear-cut measured relationship between inputs and outputs.

Answer (B) is correct. *(CIA, adapted)*

REQUIRED: The definition of controllable costs.

DISCUSSION: Controllable costs can be changed by action taken at the appropriate management (responsibility) level. Controllability is determined at different levels of the organization and is not inherent in the nature of a given cost. For example, an outlay for new machinery may be controllable to the division vice president but noncontrollable to a plant manager or lower-level manager.

Answer (A) is incorrect. Periodic appropriation decisions that have no well-specified function relating inputs to outputs apply to discretionary costs. Answer (C) is incorrect. Property, plant, and equipment costs are committed costs. Answer (D) is incorrect. Engineered costs result from a measured relationship between inputs and outputs.

1.2.9. When a decision is made in an organization, it is selected from a group of alternative courses of action. The loss associated with choosing the alternative that does not maximize the benefit is the

A. Net realizable value.

B. Expected value.

C. Opportunity cost.

D. Incremental cost.

Answer (C) is correct. *(CMA, adapted)*

REQUIRED: The loss associated with choosing the option that does not maximize the benefit.

DISCUSSION: Opportunity cost is the maximum benefit obtainable from the next best alternative use of a resource. It is the benefit forgone by not selecting that option.

Answer (A) is incorrect. Net realizable value is the value of an asset net of any disposal costs. Answer (B) is incorrect. Expected value is a probabilistically weighted average of potential outcomes. Answer (D) is incorrect. An incremental cost is the additional cost of selecting one option rather than another.

1.2.10. Which one of the following costs would be relevant in short-term decision making?

A. Incremental fixed costs.

B. All costs of inventory.

C. Total variable costs that are the same in the considered alternatives.

D. Costs of fixed assets to be used in the alternatives.

Answer (A) is correct. *(CMA, adapted)*

REQUIRED: The cost relevant to short-term decision making.

DISCUSSION: Relevant costs are future costs that differ among the options. Incremental or differential cost is the difference in total cost between two decisions. Consequently, incremental fixed cost is a relevant cost.

Answer (B) is incorrect. Inventory costs may not always differ among options. Answer (C) is incorrect. Costs that do not vary are not relevant to the decision process. Answer (D) is incorrect. The costs of fixed assets may be relevant or irrelevant depending upon whether they vary with the choice made.

1.2.11. Conversion cost pricing

A. Places minimal emphasis on the cost of materials used in manufacturing a product.

B. Could be used when the customer furnishes the material used in manufacturing a product.

C. Places heavy emphasis on indirect costs and disregards consideration of direct costs.

D. Places heavy emphasis on direct costs and disregards consideration of indirect costs.

Answer (B) is correct. *(CMA, adapted)*

REQUIRED: The true statement about conversion cost pricing.

DISCUSSION: Conversion costs consist of direct labor and manufacturing overhead, the costs of converting materials into finished goods. Normally, a company does not consider only conversion costs in making pricing decisions, but if the customer were to furnish the materials, conversion cost pricing would be appropriate.

Answer (A) is incorrect. Conversion cost pricing does not place any emphasis on materials cost. Answer (C) is incorrect. Direct labor is an element of conversion costs. Answer (D) is incorrect. Manufacturing overhead is an indirect cost that is an element of conversion costs.

Questions 1.2.12 through 1.2.17 are based on the following information.

Huron Industries has developed two new products but has only enough plant capacity to introduce one product during the current year. The following data will assist management in deciding which product should be selected.

Huron's fixed overhead includes rent and utilities, equipment depreciation, and supervisory salaries. Selling and administrative expenses are not allocated to products.

	Product A	Product B
Raw materials	$ 44.00	$ 36.00
Machining @ $12/hr.	18.00	15.00
Assembly @ $10/hr.	30.00	10.00
Variable overhead @ $8/hr.	36.00	18.00
Fixed overhead @ $4/hr.	18.00	9.00
Total cost	$ 146.00	$ 88.00
Suggested selling price	$ 169.95	$ 99.98
Actual R&D costs	$240,000	$175,000
Proposed advertising and promotion costs	$500,000	$350,000

1.2.12. For Huron's Product A, the unit costs for raw materials, machining, and assembly represent

A. Conversion costs.

B. Separable costs.

C. Prime costs.

D. Common costs.

Answer (C) is correct. *(CMA, adapted)*

REQUIRED: The type of cost represented by materials, machining, and assembly.

DISCUSSION: Direct materials and direct labor (such as machining and assembly) are a manufacturer's prime costs.

Answer (A) is incorrect. Conversion costs consist of direct labor and overhead. Answer (B) is incorrect. Separable costs are incurred beyond the point at which jointly produced items become separately identifiable. Answer (D) is incorrect. Common costs (joint costs) are incurred in the production of two or more inseparable products up to the point at which the products become separable.

1.2.13. The difference between the $99.98 suggested selling price for Huron's Product B and its total unit cost of $88.00 represents the unit's

A. Contribution margin ratio.

B. Gross profit.

C. Contribution.

D. Gross profit margin ratio.

Answer (B) is correct. *(CMA, adapted)*

REQUIRED: The difference between selling price and unit cost.

DISCUSSION: Gross profit is the difference between sales price and the full absorption cost of goods sold.

Answer (A) is incorrect. Contribution margin ratio is the ratio of contribution margin (sales – variable costs) to sales. Answer (C) is incorrect. Contribution (margin) is the difference between unit selling price and unit variable costs. Fixed costs are not considered. Answer (D) is incorrect. The gross profit margin ratio equals gross profit divided by sales.

1.2.14. The total overhead cost of $27.00 for Huron's Product B is a

A. Carrying cost.

B. Sunk cost.

C. Mixed cost.

D. Committed cost.

Answer (C) is correct. *(CMA, adapted)*

REQUIRED: The nature of total overhead.

DISCUSSION: A mixed cost is a combination of fixed and variable elements. The total overhead cost is mixed because it contains both fixed and variable overhead.

Answer (A) is incorrect. A carrying cost is the cost of carrying inventory; examples are insurance and rent. Answer (B) is incorrect. A sunk cost is a past cost or a cost that the entity has irrevocably committed to incur. Answer (D) is incorrect. A committed cost results when an entity holds fixed assets.

1.2.15. Research and development costs for Huron's two new products are

A. Conversion costs.

B. Sunk costs.

C. Relevant costs.

D. Avoidable costs.

Answer (B) is correct. *(CMA, adapted)*

REQUIRED: The nature of R&D costs.

DISCUSSION: Before they are incurred, R&D costs are often considered to be discretionary. However, Huron's R&D costs have already been incurred. Thus, they are sunk costs. A sunk cost is a past cost or a cost that the entity has irrevocably committed to incur. Because it is unavoidable, it is not relevant to future decisions.

Answer (A) is incorrect. Conversion costs (direct labor and manufacturing overhead) are incurred to convert materials into a finished product. Answer (C) is incorrect. Relevant costs are expected future costs that vary with the action taken. Answer (D) is incorrect. Avoidable costs may be eliminated by not engaging in an activity or by performing the activity more efficiently.

1.2.16. The advertising and promotion costs for the product selected by Huron will be

A. Discretionary costs.

B. Opportunity costs.

C. Prime costs.

D. Incremental costs.

Answer (A) is correct. *(CMA, adapted)*

REQUIRED: The nature of advertising and promotion costs.

DISCUSSION: A discretionary cost (a managed or program cost) results from a periodic decision about the total amount to be spent. It is also characterized by uncertainty about the relationship between input and the value of the related output. Examples are advertising and R&D costs.

Answer (B) is incorrect. An opportunity cost is the benefit provided by the best alternative use of a particular resource. Answer (C) is incorrect. Prime costs are the costs incurred for direct materials and direct labor. Answer (D) is incorrect. Incremental costs are the differences in costs between two decision choices.

1.2.17. The costs included in Huron's fixed overhead are

A. Joint costs.

B. Committed costs.

C. Opportunity costs.

D. Prime costs.

Answer (B) is correct. *(CMA, adapted)*

REQUIRED: The nature of fixed overhead.

DISCUSSION: Committed costs are those for which management has made a long-term commitment. They typically result when a firm holds fixed assets. Examples include long-term lease payments and depreciation. Committed costs are typically fixed costs.

Answer (A) is incorrect. Joint (common) costs are incurred in the production of two or more inseparable products up to the point at which they become separable. Answer (C) is incorrect. An opportunity cost is the benefit provided by the best alternative use of a particular resource. Answer (D) is incorrect. Prime costs are composed of direct material and direct labor costs.

1.3 Cost of Goods Manufactured and Sold

1.3.1. Glen Company has the following data pertaining to the year ended December 31:

Purchases	$450,000
Beginning inventory	170,000
Ending inventory	210,000
Freight-in	50,000
Freight-out	75,000

How much is the cost of goods sold for the year?

A. $385,000

B. $460,000

C. $485,000

D. $535,000

Answer (B) is correct. *(CPA, adapted)*

REQUIRED: The cost of goods sold for the year.

DISCUSSION: Freight-in is the cost of receiving inventory and is a product cost. Freight-out is the cost of shipping products to customers and should be treated as a selling expense (period cost). Thus, COGS is $460,000.

Beginning inventory		$170,000
Purchases	$450,000	
Freight-in	50,000	500,000
Goods available		$670,000
Ending inventory		(210,000)
Cost of goods sold		$460,000

Answer (A) is incorrect. Freight-out should be excluded from ending inventory. Answer (C) is incorrect. Freight-in, not freight-out, should be included in the cost of goods available. Answer (D) is incorrect. Freight-out should not be added to the cost of goods available.

1.3.2. The following information appeared in the accounting records of a retail store for the previous year:

Sales	$300,000
Purchases	140,000
Inventories	
January 1	70,000
December 31	100,000
Sales commissions	10,000

The gross margin was

A. $190,000

B. $180,000

C. $160,000

D. $150,000

Answer (A) is correct. *(CPA, adapted)*

REQUIRED: The gross margin.

DISCUSSION: The gross margin (profit) equals sales minus cost of goods sold. The cost of goods sold equals beginning inventory, plus purchases, minus ending inventory. Consequently, the gross margin is $190,000 [$300,000 – ($70,000 + $140,000 – $100,000)].

Answer (B) is incorrect. Sales commissions ($10,000) are deducted from the gross margin in arriving at net operating income. They are not included in cost of goods sold. Answer (C) is incorrect. The difference between sales and purchases is $160,000, but an adjustment to purchases must also be made for the change in inventory. Answer (D) is incorrect. The result of including sales commissions in costs of goods sold and not making an adjustment for the inventory change is $150,000.

Questions 1.3.3 through 1.3.6 are based on the following information.

Madtack Company's beginning and ending inventories for the month of November are

	November 1	November 30
Direct materials	$ 67,000	$ 62,000
Work-in-process	145,000	171,000
Finished goods	85,000	78,000

Production data for the month of November follows:

Direct labor	$200,000
Actual manufacturing overhead	132,000
Direct materials purchased	163,000
Transportation in	4,000
Purchase returns and allowances	2,000

Madtack uses one overhead control account and charges overhead to production at 70% of direct labor cost. The company does not formally recognize over- or underapplied overhead until year end.

1.3.3. Madtack Company's prime cost for November is

A. $370,000

B. $363,000

C. $170,000

D. $368,000

Answer (A) is correct. *(CMA, adapted)*

REQUIRED: The definition and calculation of prime cost.

DISCUSSION: Prime costs, consisting of direct materials and direct labor, are calculated as follows:

Beginning direct materials inventory	$ 67,000
Plus: Purchases	163,000
Plus: Transportation in	4,000
Minus: Purchase returns	(2,000)
Direct materials available for use	$232,000
Minus: Ending direct materials inventory	(62,000)
Direct materials used	$170,000
Plus: Direct labor	200,000
Prime costs	$370,000

Answer (B) is incorrect. The amount of $363,000 incorporates the change in finished goods inventories. Answer (C) is incorrect. The amount of $170,000 equals the materials used. Answer (D) is incorrect. The amount of $368,000 omits purchase returns and transportation in.

1.3.4. Madtack Company's total manufacturing cost for November is

A. $502,000

B. $503,000

C. $363,000

D. $510,000

Answer (D) is correct. *(CMA, adapted)*

REQUIRED: The total manufacturing costs.

DISCUSSION: Total manufacturing costs consist of direct materials, direct labor, and manufacturing overhead. Total prime costs were $370,000 ($170,000 direct materials + $200,000 direct labor). Overhead applied was $140,000 ($200,000 DL × 70%). Therefore, total manufacturing cost is $510,000 ($370,000 prime costs + $140,000 overhead applied).

Answer (A) is incorrect. The amount of $502,000 is based on actual overhead. Answer (B) is incorrect. The amount of $503,000 includes the change in finished goods inventories. Answer (C) is incorrect. The amount of $363,000 excludes overhead but includes the change in finished goods inventory.

1.3.5. Madtack Company's cost of goods transferred to finished goods inventory for November is

A. $469,000

B. $477,000

C. $495,000

D. $484,000

Answer (D) is correct. *(CMA, adapted)*

REQUIRED: The cost of goods transferred to finished goods inventory during the month.

DISCUSSION: Total manufacturing costs are adjusted for the change in work-in-process to calculate the cost of goods transferred. Total manufacturing cost was $510,000, so the cost of goods transferred (COGM) is $484,000 ($510,000 + $145,000 BWIP – $171,000 EWIP).

Answer (A) is incorrect. The amount of $469,000 uses actual overhead and adjusts the amounts for the change in finished goods inventory. Answer (B) is incorrect. The amount of $477,000 includes the change in finished goods inventory in the calculation. Answer (C) is incorrect. The amount of $495,000 uses materials purchased rather than materials used and also fails to adjust properly for transportation in.

1.3.6. Madtack Company's net charge to overhead control for the month of November is

A. $8,000 debit, overapplied.

B. $8,000 debit, underapplied.

C. $8,000 credit, overapplied.

D. $8,000 credit, underapplied.

Answer (C) is correct. *(CMA, adapted)*

REQUIRED: The net charge to the overhead control account for the month.

DISCUSSION: The overhead control account would have been debited for $132,000 of actual overhead. Credits would have totaled $140,000 representing 70% of direct labor costs of $200,000. Hence, the $140,000 credit exceeds the $132,000 debit. Overhead was overapplied by $8,000.

Answer (A) is incorrect. An overapplication of overhead is represented by a credit in the overhead control account. Answer (B) is incorrect. The overhead was overapplied for the month. Answer (D) is incorrect. The overhead was overapplied for the month.

1.3.7. The following cost data were taken from the records of a manufacturing company:

Depreciation on factory equipment	$ 1,000
Depreciation on sales office	500
Advertising	7,000
Freight-out (shipping)	3,000
Wages of production workers	28,000
Raw materials used	47,000
Sales salaries and commissions	10,000
Factory rent	2,000
Factory insurance	500
Materials handling	1,500
Administrative salaries	2,000

Based upon this information, the manufacturing cost incurred during the year was

A. $78,500

B. $80,000

C. $80,500

D. $83,000

Answer (B) is correct. *(CIA, adapted)*

REQUIRED: The amount of manufacturing cost.

DISCUSSION: Manufacturing costs include direct labor, direct materials, and any other indirect costs (overhead) connected with production. Selling and administrative costs (e.g., depreciation on sales office, freight-out, sales salaries, and commissions, advertising, and administrative salaries) are not included. Thus, manufacturing cost is $80,000.

Production wages	$28,000
Raw materials used	47,000
Factory rent	2,000
Factory insurance	500
Factory depreciation	1,000
Materials handling	1,500
	$80,000

Answer (A) is incorrect. The materials handling cost ($1,500) also must be added. Answer (C) is incorrect. Sales office depreciation ($500) should be excluded. Answer (D) is incorrect. Freight-out ($3,000) is a selling cost and should be excluded.

1.3.8. The following information pertains to the manufacturing activities of Griss Co. during the month just ended:

Beginning work-in-process (BWIP)	$12,000
Ending work-in-process (EWIP)	10,000
Cost of goods manufactured (COGM)	97,000
Direct materials issued to production	20,000

Factory overhead is assigned at 150% of direct labor cost. What was the direct labor cost incurred?

A. $30,000

B. $30,800

C. $45,000

D. $50,000

Answer (A) is correct. *(CPA, adapted)*

REQUIRED: The direct labor cost.

DISCUSSION: The calculation of COGM can be used to calculate direct labor:

$$\begin{aligned} \$12{,}000 \text{ BWIP} + \$20{,}000 \text{ DM} + \\ \text{DL} + 1.5\text{DL OH} - \$10{,}000 \text{ EWIP} &= \$97{,}000 \text{ COGM} \\ 2.5 \text{ DL} &= \$75{,}000 \\ \text{DL} &= \$30{,}000 \end{aligned}$$

Answer (B) is incorrect. The amount of $30,800 results from ignoring BWIP and EWIP. Answer (C) is incorrect. The amount of $45,000 equals factory overhead assigned. Answer (D) is incorrect. The amount of $50,000 equals $75,000 divided by 1.5.

1.3.9. What is the nature of work-in-process?

A. Inventory.

B. Cost of goods sold.

C. Productivity.

D. Nominal.

Answer (A) is correct. *(Publisher, adapted)*

REQUIRED: The nature of work-in-process.

DISCUSSION: Work-in-process is inventory. All the manufacturing costs charged to work-in-process this period and those remaining in the account from last period (BWIP) are allocated between goods that are completed and goods that are incomplete at year-end (EWIP). However, the costs of abnormal spoilage will be removed and charged to a loss account.

Answer (B) is incorrect. COGS is cost of goods manufactured adjusted for the change in finished goods inventory. Thus, it is an expense (nominal) account. Answer (C) is incorrect. Productivity is a nonsense term in this context. Answer (D) is incorrect. An inventory account is a real account.

1.3.10. Theoretically, cash discounts permitted on purchased raw materials should be

A. Added to other income, whether taken or not.

B. Added to other income, only if taken.

C. Deducted from inventory, whether taken or not.

D. Deducted from inventory, only if taken.

Answer (C) is correct. *(CPA, adapted)*

REQUIRED: The treatment of purchase discounts.

DISCUSSION: Cash discounts on purchases should be treated as reductions in the invoiced prices of specific purchases so that goods available for sale reflect net purchase prices. Any discounts not taken are recorded as losses in the income statement. The net method is preferable to recording inventories and payables at gross amounts because the net amounts are the most accurate exchange prices. Moreover, it measures management's stewardship by recording as financing charges any discounts not taken.

Answer (A) is incorrect. Cash discounts are never added to other income. Answer (B) is incorrect. Cash discounts are never added to other income. Answer (D) is incorrect. Deducting only discounts taken (the gross method) is theoretically inferior.

1.3.11. For a retailer, the income statement includes cost of goods sold. Cost of goods sold is, in effect, purchases adjusted for changes in inventory. For a manufacturer, purchases is replaced by

A. Inventory.

B. Cost of goods manufactured.

C. Finished goods.

D. Cost of goods sold.

Answer (B) is correct. *(Publisher, adapted)*

REQUIRED: The manufacturer's account equivalent to purchases.

DISCUSSION: Instead of purchasing goods and services for resale, a manufacturer produces goods and services for sale. Accordingly, the cost of goods manufactured (COGM) account is similar to the purchases account. Cost of goods sold (COGS) is equal to the beginning inventory of finished goods, plus COGM, minus the ending inventory of finished goods. COGM includes the costs of labor, materials, and overhead for goods completed within the current period and transferred to finished goods inventory.

Answer (A) is incorrect. Manufacturing and retailing companies have inventory accounts. Answer (C) is incorrect. The finished goods account of a manufacturer is similar to the merchandise inventory (goods held for resale) of a retailer. Answer (D) is incorrect. COGS is purchases or COGM adjusted for changes in inventory.

1.4 Variable vs. Fixed Costs

1.4.1. The difference between variable costs and fixed costs is

A. Variable costs per unit fluctuate and fixed costs per unit remain constant.

B. Variable costs per unit are fixed over the relevant range and fixed costs per unit are variable.

C. Total variable costs are variable over the relevant range and fixed in the long term, while fixed costs never change.

D. Variable costs per unit change in varying increments, while fixed costs per unit change in equal increments.

Answer (B) is correct. *(CMA, adapted)*

REQUIRED: The difference between variable and fixed costs.

DISCUSSION: Fixed costs remain unchanged within the relevant range for a given period despite fluctuations in activity, but per unit fixed costs do change as the level of activity changes. Thus, fixed costs are fixed in total but vary per unit as activity changes. Total variable costs vary directly with activity. They are fixed per unit, but vary in total.

Answer (A) is incorrect. Variable costs are fixed per unit; they do not fluctuate. Fixed costs per unit change as production changes. Answer (C) is incorrect. All costs are variable in the long term. Answer (D) is incorrect. Unit variable costs are fixed in the short term.

1.4.2. The difference between the sales price and total variable costs is

A. Gross operating profit.

B. Net profit.

C. The breakeven point.

D. The contribution margin.

Answer (D) is correct. *(CMA, adapted)*

REQUIRED: The difference between sales price and total variable costs.

DISCUSSION: The contribution margin is calculated by subtracting all variable costs from sales revenue. It represents the portion of sales that is available for covering fixed costs and profit.

Answer (A) is incorrect. Gross operating profit is the net result after deducting all manufacturing costs from sales, including both fixed and variable costs. Answer (B) is incorrect. Net profit is the remainder after deducting from revenue all costs, both fixed and variable. Answer (C) is incorrect. The breakeven point is the level of sales that equals the sum of fixed and variable costs.

1.4.3. A company has always used the full cost of its product as the starting point in the pricing of that product. The price set by competitors and the demand for the company's only product, the Widget, have never been predictable. Lately, the company's market share has been increasing as it continues to lower its price, but total revenues have not changed significantly relative to the gain in sales volume. The likely reason for the stability of total revenues is the

A. Variable cost component of the full cost.

B. Unstable contribution margin.

C. Fixed cost component of the full cost.

D. Drop in the incremental cost of the units in the increased sales volume.

Answer (C) is correct. *(CIA, adapted)*

REQUIRED: The likely reason for stability of total revenue given full costing, a lower price, and greater volume.

DISCUSSION: Fixed costs are fixed in total at different activity levels. Thus, unit fixed cost will vary inversely with the activity level. The use of full cost pricing results in a lowering of unit fixed cost used as a basis for unit price as sales increase. The consequence is a reduction of the unit sales price (assuming a constant unit profit margin is maintained). Total revenues may remain approximately the same as sales volume increases.

Answer (A) is incorrect. Variable cost per unit remains the same at all activity levels. Answer (B) is incorrect. An unstable contribution margin would affect total revenues. Answer (D) is incorrect. Incremental cost is lower because of the decline in unit fixed cost.

1.4.4. Unit fixed costs

A. Are constant per unit regardless of units produced or sold.

B. Are determined by dividing total fixed costs by a denominator such as production or sales volume.

C. Vary directly with the activity level when stated on a per-unit basis.

D. Include both fixed and variable elements.

Answer (B) is correct. *(Publisher, adapted)*

REQUIRED: The true statement about unit fixed costs.

DISCUSSION: A unit fixed cost is equal to total fixed costs divided by an appropriate denominator or activity level. The resulting average or unit fixed cost must be used with extreme caution in decision making.

Answer (A) is incorrect. Variable costs are constant per unit. Answer (C) is incorrect. Unit fixed costs vary inversely with activity. Answer (D) is incorrect. The question relates only to unit fixed costs.

1.4.5. Jago Co. has two products that use the same manufacturing facilities and cannot be subcontracted. Each product has sufficient orders to utilize the entire manufacturing capacity. For short-run profit maximization, Jago should manufacture the product with the

A. Lower total manufacturing costs for the manufacturing capacity.

B. Lower total variable manufacturing costs for the manufacturing capacity.

C. Greater gross profit per hour of manufacturing capacity.

D. Greater contribution margin per hour of manufacturing capacity.

Answer (D) is correct. *(CPA, adapted)*

REQUIRED: The product that will maximize short-run profit.

DISCUSSION: Fixed costs do not vary in the short run. Consequently, the appropriate decision criterion considers revenues and variable costs only, for example, contribution margin per hour of manufacturing capacity (contribution margin = sales revenue – variable costs).

Answer (A) is incorrect. The appropriate decision criterion considers revenues and variable costs only. Answer (B) is incorrect. The appropriate decision criterion considers revenues and variable costs only. Answer (C) is incorrect. The appropriate decision criterion considers revenues and variable costs only.

1.4.6. Which one of the following is true regarding a relevant range?

A. Total variable costs will not change.

B. Total fixed costs will not change.

C. Actual fixed costs usually fall outside the relevant range.

D. The relevant range cannot be changed after being established.

Answer (B) is correct. *(CMA, adapted)*

REQUIRED: The true statement about a relevant range.

DISCUSSION: The relevant range is the range of activity over which unit variable costs and total fixed costs are constant.

Answer (A) is incorrect. Variable costs will change in total, but unit variable costs will be constant across the relevant range. Answer (C) is incorrect. Actual fixed costs should not vary greatly from budgeted fixed costs for the relevant range. Answer (D) is incorrect. The relevant range can change whenever production activity changes; the relevant range is merely an assumption used for budgeting and control purposes.

1.4.7. Depreciation based on the number of units produced is classified as what type of cost?

A. Out-of-pocket.

B. Marginal.

C. Variable.

D. Fixed.

Answer (C) is correct. *(CPA, adapted)*

REQUIRED: The cost resulting from depreciation based on the number of units produced.

DISCUSSION: A variable cost is uniform per unit but, in total, fluctuates in direct proportion to changes in the related activity or volume. Thus, a per-unit depreciation charge is a variable cost.

Answer (A) is incorrect. The purchase of an asset, not the subsequent depreciation, is an out-of-pocket cost. Answer (B) is incorrect. A marginal cost is incurred by producing or selling an additional or partial unit. Marginal costs include materials, labor, etc. Answer (D) is incorrect. Total fixed costs do not fluctuate with activity levels. They are not based on units produced.

1.4.8. Depreciation based on the straight-line method is classified as what type of cost?

A. Out-of-pocket.

B. Marginal.

C. Variable.

D. Fixed.

Answer (D) is correct. *(J.W. Ferry)*

REQUIRED: The classification of depreciation when it is based on the straight-line method.

DISCUSSION: A fixed cost is unchanged over a given time period regardless of the related level of production activity. Straight-line depreciation is classified as fixed because it is correlated with the passage of time, not the level of activity.

Answer (A) is incorrect. Payment for an asset, not the subsequent depreciation, is an out-of-pocket cost. Answer (B) is incorrect. A marginal cost is incurred by producing or selling an additional or partial unit. Answer (C) is incorrect. Variable costs fluctuate with activity levels. For example, depreciation based on the units-of-production method is a variable cost.

1.4.9. Which one of the following categories of cost is most likely not considered a component of fixed factory overhead?

A. Rent.

B. Property taxes.

C. Depreciation.

D. Power.

Answer (D) is correct. *(CMA, adapted)*

REQUIRED: The item of cost most likely not considered a component of fixed factory overhead.

DISCUSSION: A fixed cost is one that remains unchanged within the relevant range for a given period despite fluctuations in activity. Such items as rent, property taxes, depreciation, and supervisory salaries are normally fixed costs because they do not vary with changes in production. Power costs, however, are at least partially variable because they increase as usage increases.

Answer (A) is incorrect. Rent is an example of fixed factory overhead. Answer (B) is incorrect. Property taxes are an example of fixed factory overhead. Answer (C) is incorrect. Depreciation is an example of fixed factory overhead.

1.4.10. Costs that increase as the volume of activity decreases within the relevant range are

A. Average costs per unit.

B. Average variable costs per unit.

C. Total fixed costs.

D. Total variable costs.

Answer (A) is correct. *(CIA, adapted)*

REQUIRED: The costs that increase as the volume of activity decreases within the relevant range.

DISCUSSION: As production levels decrease, total fixed costs must be allocated over fewer units. This increase in average fixed costs per unit increases total average cost per unit.

Answer (B) is incorrect. Average variable costs per unit remain constant as the volume of activity decreases. Answer (C) is incorrect. Total fixed costs are constant within the relevant range. Answer (D) is incorrect. Total variable costs decrease as volume decreases.

1.4.11. When the number of units manufactured increases, the most significant change in average unit cost will be reflected as

A. An increase in the nonvariable element.

B. A decrease in the variable element.

C. A decrease in the nonvariable element.

D. An increase in the semivariable element.

Answer (C) is correct. *(CIA, adapted)*

REQUIRED: The most significant change in average unit cost when the number of units manufactured increases.

DISCUSSION: As production increases or decreases, the most significant change in the average unit cost will occur in the nonvariable (fixed) element. When production increases, the average cost of the nonvariable element per unit will decrease because total fixed cost is constant.

Answer (A) is incorrect. The nonvariable (fixed) element varies indirectly with production level. Fixed cost per unit decreases with an increase in the production level. Answer (B) is incorrect. The variable element per unit is assumed to remain constant for changes in the production level within the relevant range. Answer (D) is incorrect. The semivariable element decreases to the extent it consists of fixed costs and remains constant to the extent it includes variable costs.

1.4.12. Quo Co. rented a building to Hava Fast Food. Each month Quo receives a fixed rental amount plus a variable rental amount based on Hava's sales for that month. As sales increase, so does the variable rental amount but at a reduced rate. Which of the following curves reflects the monthly rentals under the agreement?

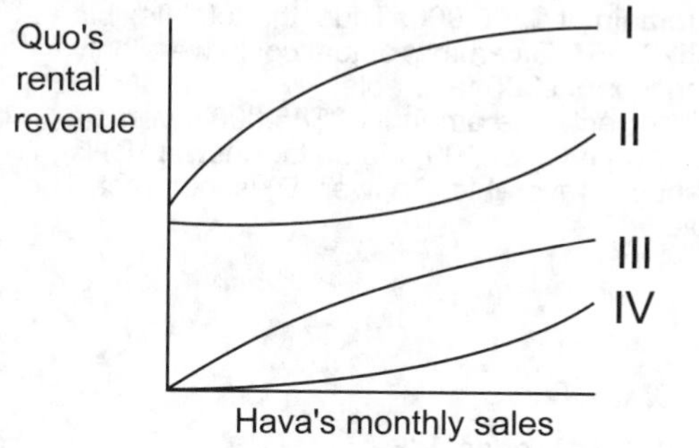

A. I

B. II

C. III

D. IV

Answer (A) is correct. *(CPA, adapted)*

REQUIRED: The nature of fixed and variable costs.

DISCUSSION: Fixed cost remains unchanged within the relevant range for a given period despite fluctuations in activity, but variable costs vary directly with the activity. Because a portion of the rental revenue is a fixed cost, it will never be zero regardless of sales. Because the total variable cost increases at a reduced rate as sales increase, the per-unit variable cost decreases. Furthermore, as sales increase over time, the rental revenue increases at a diminishing amount as represented by Curve I.

Answer (B) is incorrect. Curve II depicts a fixed component and a variable component that is increasing at an increasing rate. Answer (C) is incorrect. Curve III depicts only the variable component. Answer (D) is incorrect. Curve IV depicts a purely variable cost that is increasing at an increasing rate.

1.4.13. The following data were collected from the records of the shipping department of a company:

Month	Units Shipped	Cost of Shipping Supplies
1	7,000	$35,000
2	5,000	25,000
3	3,000	14,900
4	13,000	65,000
5	11,000	55,200
6	10,000	50,200
7	15,000	74,900

The cost of shipping supplies is most likely to be a

A. Variable cost.

B. Fixed cost.

C. Step cost.

D. Semi-fixed cost.

Answer (A) is correct. *(CIA, adapted)*

REQUIRED: The character of the cost of shipping supplies.

DISCUSSION: Variable costs are constant per unit but fluctuate in total with activity or volume (the rate of use of capacity). The cost per unit for shipping supplies is relatively constant at about $5, so this cost is variable.

Answer (B) is incorrect. Total fixed costs do not change within the relevant range. Thus, the per-unit fixed cost declines as production increases. Answer (C) is incorrect. A step cost is fixed over a relatively small range of activity but increases by a discrete amount (a step) as activity increases. For example, the cost of one direct labor hour is the same regardless of the output generated during that hour. But the cost increases by a discrete amount (the hourly rate) when the activity level is increased by one step (an hour). If the steps are small enough, the cost is essentially variable. As the steps increase, however, the cost may be classified as semi-fixed or fixed. Answer (D) is incorrect. The cost is variable. It changes over relatively small steps of activity.

1.4.14. Assuming all manufacturing costs for finished goods are known, which of the following statements explains why the accountant's unit cost used in inventory valuation for the annual financial statements would differ from the economist's marginal unit cost?

A. The company used LIFO or FIFO assumptions to compute inventory cost.

B. Accounting information that is based on historical manufacturing costs ignores current cost trends.

C. The economist's definition of marginal cost excludes a provision for profit per unit.

D. The manufacturing cost per unit reflected in financial statements includes fixed costs.

Answer (D) is correct. *(CIA, adapted)*

REQUIRED: The difference between the economist's marginal cost and the accountant's unit cost.

DISCUSSION: The economist's marginal cost equals the cost to produce one additional unit, and no fixed costs are included in the computation. It is the equivalent of the accountant's unit variable cost, an incremental unit cost. However, the accountant's unit cost for financial statement purposes includes an allocation of fixed costs.

Answer (A) is incorrect. The cost flow assumption is separate from the assumption of which costs are included. Answer (B) is incorrect. Variable costs are stated at current-period prices. Answer (C) is incorrect. Both accountants and economists usually exclude profit from inventory unit costs.

1.4.15. A manufacturing firm planned to manufacture and sell 100,000 units of product during the year at a variable cost per unit of $4.00 and a fixed cost per unit of $2.00. The firm fell short of its goal and only manufactured 80,000 units at a total incurred cost of $515,000. The firm's manufacturing cost variance was

A. $85,000 favorable.

B. $35,000 unfavorable.

C. $5,000 favorable.

D. $5,000 unfavorable.

Answer (C) is correct. *(CMA, adapted)*

REQUIRED: The manufacturing cost variance.

DISCUSSION: The firm planned to produce 100,000 units at $6 each ($4 variable + $2 fixed cost), or a total of $600,000, consisting of $400,000 of variable costs and $200,000 of fixed costs. Total production was only 80,000 units at a total cost of $515,000. The flexible budget for a production level of 80,000 units includes variable costs of $320,000 (80,000 units × $4). Fixed costs would remain at $200,000. Thus, the total flexible budget costs are $520,000. Given that actual costs were only $515,000, the variance is $5,000 favorable.

Answer (A) is incorrect. The amount of $85,000 favorable is based on a production level of 100,000 units. Answer (B) is incorrect. The variance is favorable. Answer (D) is incorrect. The variance is favorable.

1.5 Product vs. Period Costs

1.5.1. Inventoriable costs

A. Include only the prime costs of manufacturing a product.

B. Include only the conversion costs of manufacturing a product.

C. Are expensed when products become part of finished goods inventory.

D. Are regarded as assets before the products are sold.

Answer (D) is correct. *(CMA, adapted)*

REQUIRED: The true statement about inventoriable costs.

DISCUSSION: Product (inventoriable) costs are capitalized as part of inventory. But period costs are expensed as they are incurred and are not capitalized as assets. Under an absorption costing system, inventoriable costs include variable and fixed costs of production. Under variable costing, inventoriable costs include only variable production costs.

Answer (A) is incorrect. Overhead costs and prime costs (direct materials and labor) are included in inventory. Answer (B) is incorrect. Materials costs also are included. Answer (C) is incorrect. Inventory costs are expensed when the goods are sold, not when they are transferred to finished goods.

1.5.2. Internal auditors must often distinguish between product costs and period costs. Product costs are properly assigned to inventory when incurred. Period costs are always expensed in the same period in which they are incurred. Which of the following items is a product cost for a manufacturing company?

A. Insurance on the corporate headquarters building.

B. Property taxes on a factory.

C. Depreciation on salespersons' automobiles.

D. Salary of a sales manager.

Answer (B) is correct. *(CIA, adapted)*

REQUIRED: The item that is a product cost for a manufacturer.

DISCUSSION: For a manufacturer, product costs include direct materials, direct labor, and manufacturing overhead. Property taxes on a factory are a product cost because they are included in overhead.

Answer (A) is incorrect. Insurance on the corporate headquarters building is not a cost of production and is therefore a period cost. Answer (C) is incorrect. Depreciation on salespersons' automobiles is a selling cost, which is a period cost. Answer (D) is incorrect. The salary of a sales manager is a selling cost.

1.5.3. West Co.'s manufacturing costs for the month just ended were as follows:

Direct materials and direct labor	$700,000
Other variable manufacturing costs	100,000
Depreciation of factory building and manufacturing equipment	80,000
Other fixed manufacturing overhead	18,000

What amount should be considered product cost for external reporting purposes?

A. $700,000

B. $800,000

C. $880,000

D. $898,000

Answer (D) is correct. *(CPA, adapted)*

REQUIRED: The product cost for external reporting purposes.

DISCUSSION: According to GAAP, absorption (full) costing is required for external reporting purposes. Absorption costing includes fixed and variable factory overhead in product cost. Direct materials and direct labor are other elements of product cost. Consequently, the total product cost is $898,000 ($700,000 + $100,000 + $80,000 + $18,000).

Answer (A) is incorrect. The other variable (presumably overhead) costs and the fixed factory overhead (including depreciation on plant assets) should be inventoried. Answer (B) is incorrect. The depreciation and the other fixed factory overhead are product costs. Answer (C) is incorrect. The other fixed factory overhead is also a product cost.

1.5.4. Which one of the following best describes direct labor?

A. A prime cost.

B. A period cost.

C. A product cost.

D. Both a product cost and a prime cost.

Answer (D) is correct. *(CMA, adapted)*

REQUIRED: The best description of direct labor.

DISCUSSION: Direct labor is a product cost and a prime cost. Product costs are incurred to produce units of output and are deferred to future periods to the extent that output is not sold. Prime costs are the direct cost of manufacturing, for example, direct materials and direct labor.

Answer (A) is incorrect. Direct labor also is a product cost. Answer (B) is incorrect. A period cost is expensed when incurred. Direct labor cost is inventoriable. Answer (C) is incorrect. Direct labor also is a prime cost.

1.5.5. All costs related to the manufacturing function in a company are

A. Prime costs.

B. Direct costs.

C. Product costs.

D. Conversion costs.

Answer (C) is correct. *(CIA, adapted)*

REQUIRED: The classification of costs related to the manufacturing function.

DISCUSSION: Product costs are the costs of producing the product. Thus, product costs include the costs of the factors of production identifiable with the product, which usually include direct materials, direct labor, and manufacturing (not general) overhead. Manufacturing overhead includes fixed and variable elements. Product costs are inventoried until the product is sold, at which time they are expensed.

Answer (A) is incorrect. Prime costs are direct materials costs plus direct labor costs. Answer (B) is incorrect. Direct costs are directly traceable to a single cost objective. Manufacturing costs can be indirect or direct. Answer (D) is incorrect. Conversion costs are direct labor costs plus manufacturing overhead costs.

1.5.6. Following are Mill Co.'s production costs for the month just ended:

Direct materials	$100,000
Direct labor	90,000
Factory overhead	4,000

What amount of costs should be traced to specific products in the production process?

A. $194,000

B. $190,000

C. $100,000

D. $90,000

Answer (B) is correct. *(CPA, adapted)*

REQUIRED: The amount of direct costs.

DISCUSSION: Direct materials and direct labor can feasibly be identified with the production of specific goods. Factory overhead cannot be traced to a specific product but is allocated to all products produced. Thus, the amount of costs traceable to specific products in the production process equals $190,000 ($100,000 + $90,000).

Answer (A) is incorrect. This amount includes factory overhead. Answer (C) is incorrect. This amount excludes direct labor. Answer (D) is incorrect. This amount excludes direct materials.

1.5.7. Period costs

A. Are always expensed in the same period in which they are incurred.

B. Vary from one period to the next.

C. Remain unchanged over a given period of time.

D. Are associated with the periodic inventory method.

Answer (A) is correct. *(CIA, adapted)*

REQUIRED: The true statement about period costs.

DISCUSSION: Period costs are expensed as incurred. They are not identifiable with a product and are not inventoried. Period costs may be classified as either revenue expenditures or capital expenditures. Revenue expenditures, e.g., advertising and officers' salaries, are recognized in the income statement in the period the costs are incurred because they usually do not benefit future periods. Period costs classified as capital expenditures, e.g., depreciation, are initially recorded as assets and then expensed as they are consumed, used, or disposed of.

Answer (B) is incorrect. Whether a cost varies from period to period does not determine whether it is a period cost or product cost. Answer (C) is incorrect. Period costs can be either fixed or variable. Answer (D) is incorrect. The periodic inventory system is a method of maintaining inventory records.

1.5.8. Which of the following are usually considered period costs?

	A	B	C	D
Direct labor			X	X
Direct materials		X		X
Sales materials	X	X	X	
Advertising costs	X	X		
Indirect factory materials				X
Indirect labor				X
Sales commissions	X	X	X	
Factory utilities		X		X
Administrative supplies expense	X	X	X	
Administrative labor	X	X	X	X
Depreciation on administration building	X	X	X	X
Cost of research on customer demographics	X	X	X	

A. A.

B. B.

C. C.

D. D.

Answer (A) is correct. *(CIA, adapted)*

REQUIRED: The items usually considered period costs.

DISCUSSION: Period costs are expensed as incurred. They are not identifiable with a product and are not inventoried. Period costs may be classified as either revenue expenditures or capital expenditures. Revenue expenditures, e.g., advertising and officers' salaries, are recognized in the income statement in the period the costs are incurred because they usually do not benefit future periods. Period costs classified as capital expenditures, e.g., depreciation, are initially recorded as assets and then expensed as they are consumed, used, or disposed of. Accordingly, all the items listed are period costs except for the direct materials, direct labor, and the manufacturing overhead items.

Answer (B) is incorrect. Direct materials and factory utilities are product costs. Answer (C) is incorrect. Direct labor is a product cost, and advertising costs are period costs. Answer (D) is incorrect. Direct labor, direct materials, indirect factory materials, indirect labor, and factory utilities are product costs. Sales materials, advertising costs, sales commissions, supplies expense, and demographic research costs are period costs.

1.5.9. In a traditional manufacturing operation, direct costs would normally include

A. Machine repairs in an automobile factory.

B. Electricity in an electronics plant.

C. Wood in a furniture factory.

D. Commissions paid to sales personnel.

Answer (C) is correct. *(CIA, adapted)*

REQUIRED: The direct cost in a traditional manufacturing operation.

DISCUSSION: Direct costs are readily identifiable with and attributable to specific units of production. Wood is a raw material (a direct cost) of furniture.

Answer (A) is incorrect. Machine repairs in an automobile factory are usually an overhead (indirect) cost. Answer (B) is incorrect. Electricity in an electronics plant is usually an overhead (indirect) cost. Answer (D) is incorrect. Sales commissions are period costs. They are neither direct nor indirect costs of products.

1.5.10. A fixed cost that would be considered a direct cost is

A. A cost accountant's salary when the cost object is a unit of product.

B. The rental cost of a warehouse to store inventory when the cost object is the Purchasing Department.

C. A production supervisor's salary when the cost object is the Production Department.

D. Board of directors' fees when the cost object is the Marketing Department.

Answer (C) is correct. *(CMA, adapted)*

REQUIRED: The fixed cost that is direct.

DISCUSSION: A direct cost can be specifically associated with a single cost object in an economically feasible way. Thus, a production supervisor's salary can be directly associated with the department (s)he supervises.

Answer (A) is incorrect. A cost accountant's salary cannot be directly associated with a single product. Cost accountants work with many different products during a pay period. Answer (B) is incorrect. Warehouse rent is not directly traceable to the Purchasing Department. Other departments have influence over the level of inventories stored. Answer (D) is incorrect. Directors' fees cannot be directly associated with the Marketing Department. Directors provide benefits to all departments within a corporation.

1.5.11. Which one of the following costs is classified as a period cost?

A. The wages of the workers on the shipping docks who load completed products onto outgoing trucks.

B. The wages of a worker paid for idle time resulting from a machine breakdown in the molding operation.

C. The payments for employee (fringe) benefits paid on behalf of the workers in the manufacturing plant.

D. The wages paid to workers for rework on defective products.

Answer (A) is correct. *(CIA, adapted)*

REQUIRED: The cost classified as a period cost.

DISCUSSION: Period costs are expensed when incurred. They are not inventoriable because they are not sufficiently identifiable with specific production. The wages of the truck loaders are not associated with production and therefore should be classified as a selling expense and period cost.

Answer (B) is incorrect. The cost of idle time is a manufacturing overhead item and thus a product cost. Answer (C) is incorrect. Fringe benefits for manufacturing workers are treated as direct labor or manufacturing overhead, both of which are product costs. Answer (D) is incorrect. The cost of rework is a manufacturing overhead item (product cost).

1.5.12. For product costing purposes, the cost of production overtime caused by equipment failure that represents idle time plus the overtime premium should be classified as a(n)

A. Indirect cost.

B. Direct cost.

C. Controllable cost.

D. Discretionary cost.

Answer (A) is correct. *(CIA, adapted)*

REQUIRED: The classification of the cost of production overtime caused by equipment failure.

DISCUSSION: Indirect cost is not directly traceable to specific units of production. It is a component of overhead. The overtime premium (the excess of the overtime pay rate over the regular rate, multiplied by total overtime hours) and idle time are considered indirect costs and overhead. Their occurrence usually results from an abnormal volume of work. Accordingly, they are assigned to all units produced.

Answer (B) is incorrect. The overtime premium (even for direct labor) and idle time are indirect costs. Answer (C) is incorrect. Controllable cost is not relevant to product costing per se but to responsibility accounting. Answer (D) is incorrect. Discretionary costs, such as advertising, are period costs.

1.5.13. The salary of the line supervisor in the assembly division of an automobile company should be included in

A. Conversion costs.

B. Opportunity costs.

C. General and administrative costs.

D. Prime costs.

Answer (A) is correct. *(CIA, adapted)*

REQUIRED: The costs in which the salary of a line supervisor in the assembly division should be included.

DISCUSSION: Conversion costs include direct labor and manufacturing overhead. They are the costs of converting raw materials into finished products. Manufacturing overhead normally includes indirect labor expense, supplies expense, and other production facility expenses, such as plant depreciation and plant supervisors' salaries. The line supervisor's salary is a manufacturing overhead cost and should be included in conversion costs.

Answer (B) is incorrect. Opportunity cost is the maximum benefit forgone using a scarce resource for a given purpose. Answer (C) is incorrect. General and administrative costs are period costs and not inventoriable or identifiable with a particular product. Answer (D) is incorrect. Prime cost equals direct materials plus direct labor, i.e., those costs directly attributable to a product.

1.5.14. Indirect materials are a

	Conversion Cost	Manufacturing Cost	Prime Cost
A.	Yes	Yes	Yes
B.	Yes	Yes	No
C.	No	Yes	Yes
D.	No	No	No

Answer (B) is correct. *(J.W. Ferry)*

REQUIRED: The classification of indirect material cost.

DISCUSSION: Indirect materials are a manufacturing cost and a conversion cost. Indirect materials are a manufacturing cost that cannot be directly identified with a specific unit of production and is therefore part of manufacturing overhead. Conversion cost consists of direct labor and manufacturing overhead. Prime cost consists of direct materials and direct labor.

Answer (A) is incorrect. Indirect materials are not a prime cost. Answer (C) is incorrect. Indirect materials are a conversion cost but not a prime cost. Answer (D) is incorrect. Indirect materials are a conversion cost and a manufacturing cost.

1.5.15. The fixed portion of the semivariable cost of electricity for a manufacturing plant is a

	Conversion Cost	Product Cost
A.	No	No
B.	No	Yes
C.	Yes	Yes
D.	Yes	No

Answer (C) is correct. *(CPA, adapted)*

REQUIRED: The classification(s) of fixed electricity cost for a manufacturer.

DISCUSSION: Electricity costs in a manufacturing plant are a part of manufacturing overhead. Manufacturing overhead is both a conversion cost and a product cost.

Answer (A) is incorrect. The fixed portion of a semivariable cost is a conversion cost and a product cost. Answer (B) is incorrect. The fixed portion of a semivariable cost also is a conversion cost. Answer (D) is incorrect. The fixed portion of a semivariable cost is also a product cost.

1.5.16. The wages of the factory janitorial staff should be classified as

A. Manufacturing overhead cost.

B. Direct labor cost.

C. Period cost.

D. Prime cost.

Answer (A) is correct. *(CIA, adapted)*

REQUIRED: The classification of the wages of the factory janitorial staff.

DISCUSSION: Manufacturing overhead normally includes indirect labor expense, supplies expense, and other production facility expenses, such as plant depreciation, taxes, and plant supervisors' salaries. It includes all manufacturing costs except for direct materials and direct labor. Janitorial costs are not directly traceable to specific units of production. Thus, they are indirect labor costs included in fixed manufacturing overhead and are inventoried as a product cost.

Answer (B) is incorrect. Direct labor costs are directly traceable to specific units of production. Answer (C) is incorrect. Period costs are any costs that are not inventoriable. Answer (D) is incorrect. Prime cost equals direct materials cost plus direct labor cost.

1.6 Professional Responsibility

1.6.1. The *IMA Statement of Ethical Professional Practice* includes an integrity standard. It requires an IMA member to

A. Refrain from conduct that prejudices the ability to perform duties ethically.

B. Report any relevant information that could influence users of financial statements.

C. Disclose confidential information when authorized by his or her firm or required under the law.

D. Refuse gifts from anyone.

Answer (A) is correct. *(Publisher, adapted)*

REQUIRED: The action required of an IMA member by the integrity standard.

DISCUSSION: One of the responsibilities of an IMA member under the integrity standard is not to engage in any conduct that would prejudice carrying out duties ethically. Other responsibilities under this standard relate to (1) mitigating conflicts of interest, (2) abstaining from engaging in activities that discredit the profession, and (3) contributing to a positive ethical culture and placing the integrity of the profession above personal interests.

Answer (B) is incorrect. The credibility standard requires provision of all relevant information that could reasonably be expected to influence an intended user's understanding of reports, analyses, and recommendations. Answer (C) is incorrect. The confidentiality standard requires that information be kept confidential except when disclosure is authorized or legally required. Answer (D) is incorrect. The integrity standard does not specifically require a member to refuse gifts.

1.6.2. *IMA Statement of Ethical Professional Practice* requires an IMA member to follow the established policies of the organization when faced with an ethical conflict. If these policies do not resolve the conflict, the member should

A. Consult the board of directors immediately.

B. Discuss the problem with the immediate superior if (s)he is involved in the conflict.

C. Communicate the problem to authorities outside the organization.

D. Contact the next higher managerial level if initial presentation to the immediate superior does not resolve the conflict.

Answer (D) is correct. *(CIA, adapted)*

REQUIRED: The proper action when organizational policies do not resolve an ethical conflict.

DISCUSSION: In these circumstances, the problem should be discussed with the immediate superior unless (s)he is involved. In that case, initial presentation should be to the next higher managerial level. If the problem is not satisfactorily resolved after initial presentation, the question should be submitted to the next higher level.

Answer (A) is incorrect. This course of action would be appropriate only for the chief executive officer or for his or her immediate subordinate when the CEO is involved in the conflict. Answer (B) is incorrect. The proper action would be to present the matter to the next higher managerial level. Answer (C) is incorrect. Such action is inappropriate unless legally required.

1.6.3. The controller is responsible for directing the budgeting process. In this role, the controller has significant influence with executive management as individual department budgets are modified and approved. For the current year, the controller was instrumental in the approval of a particular line manager's budget without modification, even though significant reductions were made to the budgets submitted by other line managers. As a token of appreciation, the line manager in question has given the controller a gift certificate for a popular local restaurant. In considering whether or not to accept the certificate, the controller should refer to which section of *IMA Statement of Ethical Professional Practice*?

A. Competence.

B. Confidentiality.

C. Integrity.

D. Credibility.

Answer (C) is correct. *(CMA, adapted)*

REQUIRED: The ethical standard relevant to the controller's acceptance of a gift from a line manager.

DISCUSSION: The integrity standard requires an IMA member to "refrain from engaging in any conduct that would prejudice carrying out duties ethically."

Answer (A) is incorrect. The competence standard pertains to an IMA member's responsibility to maintain his or her professional skills and knowledge. It also pertains to the performance of activities in accordance with relevant laws, regulations, and technical standards. Answer (B) is incorrect. The confidentiality standard applies to an IMA member's responsibility not to disclose or use the firm's confidential information. Answer (D) is incorrect. The credibility standard requires that (1) information be communicated "fairly and objectively" and (2) all information that could reasonably influence users be disclosed.

1.6.4. If an IMA member has a problem in identifying unethical behavior or resolving an ethical conflict, the first action (s)he should normally take is to

A. Consult the board of directors.

B. Discuss the problem with his or her immediate superior.

C. Notify the appropriate law enforcement agency.

D. Resign from the company.

Answer (B) is correct. *(Publisher, adapted)*

REQUIRED: The proper ethical behavior by an IMA member.

DISCUSSION: *IMA Statement of Ethical Professional Practice* states that the member should first discuss an ethical problem with his or her immediate superior. If the superior is involved, the problem should be taken initially to the next higher managerial level.

Answer (A) is incorrect. The board would be consulted initially only if the immediate superior is the chief executive officer and that person is involved in the ethical conflict. Answer (C) is incorrect. An IMA member should keep information confidential except when disclosure is authorized or legally required. Answer (D) is incorrect. Resignation is a last resort.

1.6.5. According to the *IMA Statement of Ethical Professional Practice*, a member has a responsibility to recognize and help manage risk. Under which standard of ethical conduct would this responsibility be included?

A. Competence.

B. Confidentiality.

C. Integrity.

D. Credibility.

Answer (A) is correct. *(CMA, adapted)*

REQUIRED: The standard of ethical conduct related to the responsibility to recognize professional limitations.

DISCUSSION: The competence standard requires an IMA member to provide decision support information and recommendations that are accurate, clear, concise, and timely. It also requires a member to recognize and help manage risk.

Answer (B) is incorrect. The confidentiality standard states an IMA member's responsibility not to disclose or use the firm's confidential information. Answer (C) is incorrect. The integrity standard applies to conflicts of interest, avoidance of acts discreditable to the profession, refraining from activities that prejudice the ability to carry out duties ethically, and contributing to a positive ethical culture. Answer (D) is incorrect. The credibility standard requires that (1) information be communicated "fairly and objectively" and (2) all information that could reasonably influence users be disclosed.

1.6.6. Integrity is an ethical requirement for all IMA members. One aspect of integrity requires

A. Performance of professional duties in accordance with relevant laws.

B. Avoidance of apparent conflicts of interest.

C. Refraining from using confidential information for unethical or illegal advantage.

D. Maintenance of an appropriate level of professional leadership and expertise.

Answer (B) is correct. *(Publisher, adapted)*

REQUIRED: The aspect of the integrity requirement.

DISCUSSION: According to the *IMA Statement of Ethical Professional Practice*, IMA members must "mitigate actual conflicts of interest. Regularly communicate with business associates to avoid apparent conflicts of interest. Advise all parties of any potential conflicts of interest."

Answer (A) is incorrect. Performance of professional duties in accordance with relevant laws is an aspect of the competence requirement. Answer (C) is incorrect. Refraining from using confidential information for unethical or illegal advantage is an aspect of the confidentiality requirement. Answer (D) is incorrect. Maintenance of an appropriate level of professional leadership and expertise is an aspect of the competence requirement.

1.6.7. Which ethical standard is most clearly violated if an IMA member knows of information that could mislead users but does not report the deficiency?

A. Competence.

B. Legality.

C. Credibility.

D. Confidentiality.

Answer (C) is correct. *(Publisher, adapted)*

REQUIRED: The ethical standard most clearly violated when an IMA member does not report information that is misleading to users.

DISCUSSION: The credibility standard in the *IMA Statement of Ethical Professional Practice* requires, among other things, that all relevant information that could reasonably influence users be provided.

Answer (A) is incorrect. The competence standard pertains to, among other things, the member's responsibility to maintain an appropriate level of leadership and expertise. Answer (B) is incorrect. Legality is not addressed in the *IMA Statement of Ethical Professional Practice*. Answer (D) is incorrect. The confidentiality standard relates to, among other things, the IMA member's responsibility not to disclose or use the firm's confidential information inappropriately.

1.6.8. The *IMA Statement of Ethical Professional Practice* includes a competence standard. It requires an IMA member to

A. Report information, whether favorable or unfavorable.

B. Enhance his or her skills.

C. Call the IMA's helpline to ask about application of the *Statement* to an ethical issue.

D. Discuss, with subordinates, their responsibilities regarding the disclosure and use of confidential information about the firm.

Answer (B) is correct. *(Publisher, adapted)*

REQUIRED: The action required of an IMA member by the competence standard.

DISCUSSION: One of the responsibilities of an IMA member under the competence standard is to maintain an appropriate level of professional leadership and expertise by enhancing knowledge and skills.

Answer (A) is incorrect. The credibility standard requires an IMA member to communicate information fairly and objectively. Answer (C) is incorrect. One of the suggestions in the "Resolving Ethical Issues" section is to use the IMA's anonymous helpline. Answer (D) is incorrect. The confidentiality standard requires an IMA member to inform all relevant parties about appropriate use of confidential information and to monitor to ensure compliance.

1.6.9. In accordance with the *IMA Statement of Ethical Professional Practice*, a member who fails to perform professional duties in accordance with relevant standards is acting contrary to which one of the following standards?

A. Competence.

B. Confidentiality.

C. Integrity.

D. Credibility.

Answer (A) is correct. *(CMA, adapted)*

REQUIRED: The ethical standard violated by an IMA member who fails to perform professional duties in accordance with relevant standards.

DISCUSSION: One of the responsibilities of an IMA member under the competence standard is to "maintain an appropriate level of professional leadership and expertise by enhancing knowledge and skills." (S)he also must "perform professional duties in accordance with relevant laws, regulations, and technical standards." The third requirement is to "provide decision support information and recommendations that are accurate, clear, concise, and timely." This requirement also extends to recognition and management of risks.

Answer (B) is incorrect. The confidentiality standard applies to an IMA member's responsibility not to disclose or use the firm's confidential information inappropriately. Answer (C) is incorrect. The integrity standard applies to mitigating conflicts of interest, avoiding acts discreditable to the profession, refraining from activities that prejudice the ability to carry out duties ethically, contributing to a positive ethical culture, and placing integrity of the profession above personal interests. Answer (D) is incorrect. The credibility standard requires an IMA member to "communicate professional limitations or other constraints that would preclude responsible judgment or successful performance of an activity." The credibility standard also addresses (1) communicating information fairly and objectively; (2) providing all relevant information that could influence a user's understanding; and (3) reporting delays or deficiencies in information, timeliness, processing, or controls.

STUDY UNIT TWO
JOB COSTING

A **job costing system** accumulates costs by specific job. This method is appropriate when producing products with individual characteristics or when identifiable groupings are possible, e.g., ships or jewelry. **Direct costs** (direct materials and direct labor) are recorded at the actual amounts incurred, but **manufacturing overhead** is recorded using an estimated rate. Overhead costs are applied to (absorbed by) each job based on a predetermined application rate for the period. At the end of the period, overhead may have been overapplied or underapplied. Output that does not meet the quality standards for salability is **spoilage**. **Normal spoilage**, a product cost, is expected in the ordinary course of production. **Abnormal spoilage**, a period cost, exceeds the amount expected in the ordinary course. Common measures used to assign costs to products and services are **actual costing** and normal costing. Both assign direct costs based on actual costs. But **normal costing** applies overhead based on predetermined rates and the actual usage of the base used to assign the costs.

Below is the **cost flow** among accounts for a manufacturer (not a retailer, which purchases its inventory). It is substantially the same in job and process costing.

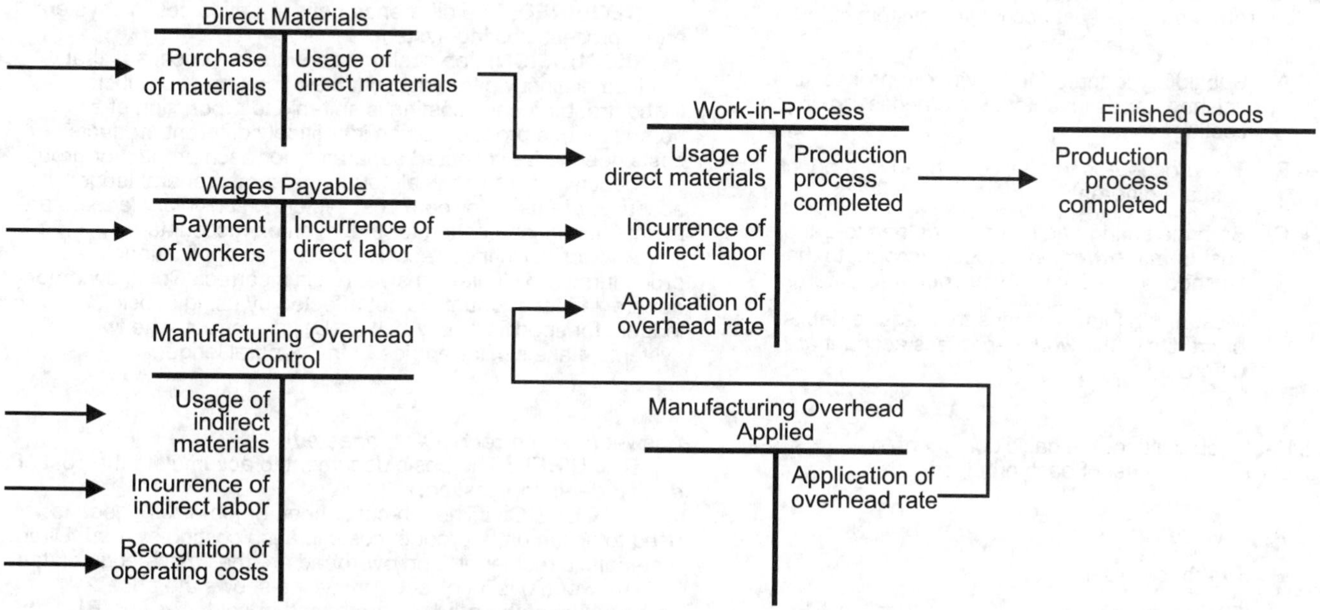

Indirect production costs (overhead) are assigned using predetermined rates. The denominator of a rate is capacity. **Practical capacity** is the maximum at which output is produced efficiently. It includes idle time resulting from holidays, downtime, etc., but not inadequate sales demand. **Theoretical capacity** is the level at which output is maximized assuming perfect efficiency. **Normal capacity** is required for GAAP reporting. It is expected production under normal conditions over a period of years or seasons (ASC 330-10-30-3).

QUESTIONS

2.1 When to Use Job Costing

2.1.1. Two basic costing systems for assigning costs to products or services are job costing and process costing. These two costing systems are usually viewed as being on opposite ends of a spectrum. The fundamental criterion employed to determine whether job costing or process costing should be employed is

A. Proportion of direct (traceable) costs expended to produce the product or service.

B. Number of cost pools employed to allocate the indirect costs to the product or service.

C. Type of bases used in allocating the indirect cost pools to the product or service.

D. The nature and amount of the product or service brought to the marketplace for customer consumption.

Answer (D) is correct. *(CIA, adapted)*

REQUIRED: The criterion for determining whether process or job costing is used.

DISCUSSION: Job costing is used if resources are expended to bring a distinct, identifiable product or service to the market. An entity is providing heterogeneous products or services that are often customized for the consumer. Process costing is used when masses of identical or similar units of product or services are provided for general consumer use.

Answer (A) is incorrect. The proportion of direct costs does not affect the selection of a costing system. Answer (B) is incorrect. The number of cost pools does not affect the selection of a costing system. Answer (C) is incorrect. The type of allocation bases does not affect the selection of a costing system.

2.1.2. A nonmanufacturing organization may use

A. Job-order costing but not process costing.

B. Process costing but not job-order costing.

C. Either job-order or process costing.

D. Neither job-order costing nor process costing.

Answer (C) is correct. *(CPA, adapted)*

REQUIRED: The appropriate method(s) of cost accumulation in a nonmanufacturing organization.

DISCUSSION: A nonmanufacturing entity may use either cost accumulation procedure. For example, banks frequently use process costing for certain departments and job costing for others. Public accounting firms ordinarily use job costing.

2.1.3. How does a job costing accounting system differ from a process cost accounting system?

A. Subsidiary ledgers for the work-in-process and finished goods inventories are necessary in job costing.

B. The procedures to apply overhead to product cost are different.

C. Both the timing and nature of entries to transfer cost from the work-in-process account to the finished goods inventory account are different.

D. Most of the journal entries that require debits or credits to the work-in-process account are different.

Answer (A) is correct. *(Publisher, adapted)*

REQUIRED: The difference between a job costing system and a process costing system.

DISCUSSION: Job costing accounts for processes that produce distinctly different products or groups of products. By contrast, process costing is suitable to production of a homogeneous product. Given identifiably different products, costs need to be collected separately for each product or group of products. Accordingly, although the same general ledger accounts are used for both cost systems, subsidiary ledgers are maintained in job costing for the inventory accounts.

Answer (B) is incorrect. The overhead application procedures are similar. Answer (C) is incorrect. Cost flow among general ledger accounts is not affected by using subsidiary ledgers for specific jobs. Answer (D) is incorrect. The two systems make similar entries to the general ledger.

2.1.4. In job costing, the basic document to accumulate the cost of each order is the

A. Invoice.

B. Purchase order.

C. Requisition sheet.

D. Job-cost sheet.

Answer (D) is correct. *(CPA, adapted)*

REQUIRED: The basic document to accumulate the cost of each order in job costing.

DISCUSSION: The job-cost sheet, or job-order sheet, is used to accumulate product costs in a job costing system. Direct materials, direct labor, and overhead are the costs accumulated.

Answer (A) is incorrect. An invoice shows the price and quantity of the product purchased or sold. Answer (B) is incorrect. The purchase order states the specifications, quantities, and prices of items to be purchased. Answer (C) is incorrect. A requisition sheet is an internal document used by production to request materials or other resources from another department.

2.1.5. In a manufacturing environment, job cost accounting systems and process cost accounting systems differ in the way

A. Costs are assigned to production runs and the number of units for which costs are averaged.

B. Orders are taken and the number of units in the orders.

C. Product profitability is determined and compared with planned costs.

D. Processes can be accomplished and the number of production runs that may be performed in a year.

Answer (A) is correct. *(CIA, adapted)*

REQUIRED: The way job cost and process cost accounting systems differ.

DISCUSSION: A cost system determines the manufacturing cost to be expensed (because output was sold) and the portion to be deferred (because output was still on hand). Process costing is used for continuous process output of units that are relatively homogeneous (e.g., oil refining and automobile production). Job costing is used to account for the cost of specific jobs or projects when output is heterogeneous. The difference is often overemphasized. Job costing simply requires subsidiary ledgers (to keep track of the specific jobs) for the same work-in-process and finished goods accounts that are basic to process costing.

Answer (B) is incorrect. How orders are taken is irrelevant to whether job or process costing is used. Answer (C) is incorrect. Profit is determined in the same way in both job and process costing. Answer (D) is incorrect. The cost system is not necessarily related to the manufacturing processes.

2.1.6. A company services office equipment. Some customers bring their equipment to the company's service shop; other customers prefer to have the company's service personnel come to their offices to repair their equipment. The most appropriate costing method for the company is

A. A job costing system.

B. An activity-based costing system.

C. A process costing system.

D. An operation costing system.

Answer (A) is correct. *(CIA, adapted)*

REQUIRED: The appropriate costing method for a service entity.

DISCUSSION: Job costing systems accumulate costs for tasks or projects that are unique and nonrepetitive. An entity that services office equipment is interested in identifying the costs applicable to each customer each service call.

Answer (B) is incorrect. ABC identifies the activities that affect costs and uses a separate driver for each activity to assign costs to cost objects. It may be used with job or process costing. Answer (C) is incorrect. Process costing applies to homogeneous products mass produced in continuous production runs. Answer (D) is incorrect. Operation costing is a hybrid of job and process costing.

2.1.7. A new advertising agency serves a wide range of clients including manufacturers, restaurants, service businesses, department stores, and other retail establishments. The accounting system the advertising agency has most likely adopted for its record keeping in accumulating costs is

A. Job costing.

B. Operation costing.

C. Relevant costing.

D. Process costing.

Answer (A) is correct. *(CIA, adapted)*

REQUIRED: The most likely accounting system adopted by a company with a wide range of clients.

DISCUSSION: Job costing is used by organizations whose products or services are readily identified by individual units or batches. The advertising agency accumulates its costs by client. Job costing is the most appropriate system for this type of nonmanufacturing firm.

Answer (B) is incorrect. Operation costing most likely is used by a manufacturer producing goods that have common characteristics plus some individual characteristics. Answer (C) is incorrect. Relevant costing refers to expected future costs that are considered in decision making. Answer (D) is incorrect. Process costing is used when an entity mass produces a homogeneous product continuously.

2.1.8. Which method of measuring the costs to be assigned to products or services uses budgeted rates for direct costs but applies those rates to the actual quantities of the inputs?

A. Actual costing.

B. Normal costing.

C. Extended costing.

D. Standard costing.

Answer (C) is correct. *(Publisher, adapted)*

REQUIRED: The cost measurement method that uses budgeted rates for direct costs but applies those rates to the actual quantities of the inputs.

DISCUSSION: Extended costing assigns both direct costs (such as labor and materials) and overhead to cost objects by using budgeted rates. The direct cost assigned equals the budgeted rate times the actual amount of the direct-cost input. The overhead assigned equals the budgeted rate times the actual amount of whichever driver or other base is used for cost assignment purposes. The use of budgeted rates for overhead as well as direct costs may be helpful to avoid fluctuations during the year. It is also helpful when some direct costs, such as direct labor, may not be known until year-end.

Answer (A) is incorrect. Actual costing uses only actual direct and overhead costs. Answer (B) is incorrect. Normal costing uses budgeted rates only for overhead costs. Answer (D) is incorrect. Standard costing applies budgeted rates to the standard (not actual) inputs allowed.

2.2 Cost Flow among Accounts

2.2.1. The work-in-process account is

A. Neither a real nor a nominal account.

B. An inventory account indicating the beginning and ending inventory of goods being processed.

C. A hybrid account (both a real and a nominal account).

D. A nominal account to which overhead costs are charged as incurred and credited as these costs are charged to production.

Answer (B) is correct. *(Publisher, adapted)*

REQUIRED: The nature of work-in-process.

DISCUSSION: Work-in-process is an inventory account to which direct materials, direct labor, and manufacturing overhead costs are charged as they are incurred in the production process. The sum of these costs plus the cost of BWIP is the total production cost to be accounted for in any one period. The total is assigned to goods completed during the period, i.e., to finished goods and to EWIP. Work-in-process may also be credited for abnormal spoilage.

Answer (A) is incorrect. Work-in-process is a real account. Answer (C) is incorrect. Work-in-process is an inventory account. Answer (D) is incorrect. Manufacturing overhead is a real account that pools overhead costs as incurred.

2.2.2. The debits in work-in-process are BWIP, direct labor, direct materials, and manufacturing overhead. The account should be credited for production that is completed and sent to finished goods inventory. The balance is

A. Zero.

B. EWIP (credit).

C. EWIP (debit).

D. Total production costs to be accounted for.

Answer (C) is correct. *(Publisher, adapted)*

REQUIRED: The composition of the balance of work-in-process after the account is credited for goods produced.

DISCUSSION: The sum of the debits to WIP equals total production costs. Ignoring possible spoilage, production consists either of completed goods or of those still in process. Accordingly, after the account is credited for the cost of goods completed and transferred to the FG inventory, the debit balance in the account is EWIP.

Answer (A) is incorrect. The balance is zero only if no EWIP exists. Answer (B) is incorrect. EWIP is credited when completed units are transferred but should never have a credit balance. Answer (D) is incorrect. Total production costs to be accounted for include finished goods as well as EWIP.

2.2.3. In a traditional job-order cost system, the issuance of indirect materials to a production department increases

A. Stores control.

B. Work-in-process control.

C. Factory overhead control.

D. Factory overhead applied.

Answer (C) is correct. *(CPA, adapted)*

REQUIRED: The account that increases when supplies are issued to a production department.

DISCUSSION: As overhead is incurred, factory overhead control is debited and accounts payable, supplies, etc., are credited. When overhead is applied, work-in-process is debited and factory overhead applied is credited. The difference between the debited and credited amounts is over- or underapplied overhead.

Answer (A) is incorrect. Stores control decreases (i.e., is credited). Answer (B) is incorrect. Work-in-process increases (with a debit) when overhead is applied. Answer (D) is incorrect. Factory overhead applied increases (with a credit) when overhead is applied, not when it is incurred.

2.2.4. What is the journal entry to record the purchase of materials on account?

A.	Raw materials inventory	XXX	
	Accounts payable		XXX
B.	Accounts payable	XXX	
	Raw materials inventory		XXX
C.	Accounts receivable	XXX	
	Accounts payable		XXX
D.	Raw materials inventory	XXX	
	Cash		XXX

Answer (A) is correct. *(Publisher, adapted)*

REQUIRED: The journal entry to record the purchase of materials on account.

DISCUSSION: The correct entry to record a purchase of materials on account is to increase the appropriate asset and liability accounts. Materials are charged to an inventory; the corresponding liability is accounts payable. The asset account(s) could be stores control and/or supplies or a number of other accounts. Also, subsidiary ledgers may be used to account for various individual items (a perpetual inventory system). The term "control" implies that a subsidiary ledger is being used.

Answer (B) is incorrect. The entry to record the return of materials to suppliers debits accounts payable and credits raw materials inventory. Answer (C) is incorrect. This entry reclassifies credit balances in accounts receivable as liabilities or debit balances in accounts payable as assets. Answer (D) is incorrect. This entry would record the purchase of materials for cash.

2.2.5. In a job-order cost system, the use of direct materials previously purchased usually is recorded as an increase in

A. Work-in-process control.

B. Manufacturing overhead control.

C. Manufacturing overhead applied.

D. Stores control.

Answer (A) is correct. *(CPA, adapted)*

REQUIRED: The account increased by the use of direct materials already on hand.

DISCUSSION: The purchase of direct materials requires a debit to (an increase in) direct materials inventory (stores control). This account is credited and work-in-process control is debited when direct materials are issued to a production department.

Answer (B) is incorrect. Manufacturing overhead control is debited (increased) when indirect, not direct, materials are issued. Answer (C) is incorrect. Manufacturing overhead applied is increased (credited) only when overhead is charged to work-in-process at a predetermined rate based on an appropriate activity base. Answer (D) is incorrect. Stores control is increased when direct materials are purchased.

2.2.6. A direct labor overtime premium should be charged to a specific job when the overtime is caused by the

A. Increased overall level of activity.

B. Customer's requirement for early completion of the job.

C. Management's failure to include the job in the production schedule.

D. Management's requirement that the job be completed before the annual factory vacation closure.

Answer (B) is correct. *(CPA, adapted)*

REQUIRED: The circumstances in which a direct labor overtime premium should be charged to a specific job.

DISCUSSION: A direct labor overtime premium equals the excess of the overtime pay rate over the regular rate, multiplied by total overtime hours. It is ordinarily considered an indirect cost, charged to overhead, and thereby allocated to all jobs. The reason is that the association of an overhead premium with a specific job may be attributable solely to random scheduling. Accordingly, the incurrence of the premium is usually regarded as a function of an abnormally large production volume, that is, as a condition affecting all jobs. However, if the premium directly results from the demands of a specific job, it should be charged as a direct cost to that job.

Answer (A) is incorrect. An overtime premium arising from increased overall activity is an indirect cost charged to overhead. Answer (C) is incorrect. Management's scheduling omission is a random factor. In such a case, the overtime premium is not caused by the demands of the specific job omitted. Answer (D) is incorrect. Assuming all jobs are to be completed prior to the closing, no specific job is the cause of the premium.

2.2.7. Under a job-order system of cost accounting, the dollar amount of the general ledger entry involved in the transfer of inventory from work-in-process to finished goods is the sum of the costs charged to all jobs

A. Started in process during the period.

B. In process during the period.

C. Completed and sold during the period.

D. Completed during the period.

Answer (D) is correct. *(CPA, adapted)*

REQUIRED: The costs included in the general ledger entry to transfer inventory to finished goods.

DISCUSSION: The entry to transfer inventory from WIP to FG is to debit finished goods and credit work-in-process. The amount of the entry is the sum of the costs (irrespective of the period in which they were incurred) charged to all jobs completed during the period.

Answer (A) is incorrect. The sum of the costs of jobs started in process during the period does not include the cost of goods started in a prior period and completed in this period. Also, it includes EWIP. Answer (B) is incorrect. The sum of the costs of jobs in process during the period includes the cost of EWIP. Answer (C) is incorrect. The sum of the costs of jobs completed and sold excludes the cost of goods completed but not yet sold.

2.2.8. In job-order costing, payroll taxes paid by the employer for manufacturing employees are usually accounted for as

A. Direct labor.

B. Manufacturing overhead.

C. Indirect labor.

D. Administrative costs.

Answer (A) is correct. *(CPA, adapted)*

REQUIRED: The accounting for employer payroll taxes.

DISCUSSION: Employer taxes on manufacturing payroll and fringe benefits (e.g., pensions and insurance) paid to manufacturing employees are treated as direct labor costs. The justification is that payroll taxes and fringe benefits are necessary to obtain such labor. The IMA in Statement of Management Accounting 4C, *Definition and Measurement of Direct Labor Cost*, supports this position.

Answer (B) is incorrect. Accounting for employer payroll taxes as direct labor costs is preferable, although some entities treat these costs as overhead. Answer (C) is incorrect. Indirect labor is a component of manufacturing overhead. Answer (D) is incorrect. Administrative costs are period costs.

2.2.9. In a job-order cost system, direct labor costs usually are recorded initially as an increase in

A. Manufacturing overhead applied.

B. Manufacturing overhead control.

C. Finished goods control.

D. Work-in-process control.

Answer (D) is correct. *(CPA, adapted)*

REQUIRED: The account to which direct labor is first charged in a job-order cost system.

DISCUSSION: Direct labor costs are inventoriable costs. They are initially debited to the work-in-process control account.

Answer (A) is incorrect. Direct labor costs are not part of applied manufacturing overhead. Answer (B) is incorrect. Direct labor cost is not included in actual manufacturing overhead. Answer (C) is incorrect. In a job-order cost system, direct labor is initially charged to WIP control. When the goods are finished, direct labor cost will be transferred from WIP control to finished goods control.

2.2.10. In a job-order cost system, the application of manufacturing overhead is usually reflected in the general ledger as an increase in

A. Manufacturing overhead control.

B. Finished goods control.

C. Work-in-process control.

D. Cost of goods sold.

Answer (C) is correct. *(CPA, adapted)*

REQUIRED: The account that is increased when overhead is applied in a job-order cost system.

DISCUSSION: The entry to record the application of manufacturing overhead to specific jobs is to charge WIP control and credit manufacturing overhead applied using a predetermined overhead rate. The effect is to increase the WIP control account.

Answer (A) is incorrect. Manufacturing overhead control increases when actual manufacturing overhead costs are incurred. Answer (B) is incorrect. Finished goods control increases only when goods are completed. Answer (D) is incorrect. Cost of goods sold is increased only when products are sold.

2.2.11. A company experienced a machinery breakdown on one of its production lines. As a consequence of the breakdown, manufacturing fell behind schedule, and a decision was made to schedule overtime to return manufacturing to schedule. Which one of the following methods is the proper way to account for the overtime paid to the direct laborers?

A. The overtime hours times the sum of the straight-time wages and overtime premium would be charged entirely to manufacturing overhead.

B. The overtime hours times the sum of the straight-time wages and overtime premium would be treated as direct labor.

C. The overtime hours times the overtime premium would be charged to repair and maintenance expense, and the overtime hours times the straight-time wages would be treated as direct labor.

D. The overtime hours times the overtime premium would be charged to manufacturing overhead, and the overtime hours times the straight-time wages would be treated as direct labor.

Answer (D) is correct. *(CIA, adapted)*

REQUIRED: The proper way to account for the overtime paid to the direct laborers.

DISCUSSION: Direct labor costs are wages paid to labor that can feasibly be specifically identified with the production of finished goods. Factory overhead consists of all costs, other than direct materials and direct labor, that are associated with the manufacturing process. Thus, straight-time wages would be treated as direct labor; however, because the overtime premium cost is a cost that should be borne by all production, the overtime hours times the overtime premium should be charged to manufacturing overhead.

Answer (A) is incorrect. The straight-time wages times the overtime hours should still be treated as direct labor. Answer (B) is incorrect. Only the straight-time wages times the overtime hours is charged to direct labor. Answer (C) is incorrect. Labor costs are not related to repairs and maintenance expense.

2.2.12. What is the entry to record completion of a particular product or group of products?

A.	Finished goods	XXX	
	Cost of goods sold		XXX
B.	Work-in-process	XXX	
	Finished goods		XXX
C.	Finished goods	XXX	
	Work-in-process		XXX
D.	Cost of goods sold	XXX	
	Work-in-process		XXX

Answer (C) is correct. *(Publisher, adapted)*

REQUIRED: The entry to record completion of a job.

DISCUSSION: The entry to record completion of a job is to charge finished goods inventory and credit WIP for the amounts of actual direct materials and actual direct labor used and of manufacturing overhead applied.

Answer (A) is incorrect. A debit to FG and a credit to COGS is the reverse of the entry to expense inventory that is sold. Answer (B) is incorrect. A debit to WIP and a credit to FG reverses the entry to transfer cost of goods finished from WIP to FG. Answer (D) is incorrect. All items sold are charged to FG inventory before being transferred to COGS. No entries should transfer costs directly from WIP to COGS.

2.3 Application of Overhead

2.3.1. In a job cost system, manufacturing overhead is

	An Indirect Cost of Jobs	A Necessary Element of Production
A.	No	Yes
B.	No	No
C.	Yes	Yes
D.	Yes	No

Answer (C) is correct. *(CPA, adapted)*
REQUIRED: The nature of factory overhead.
DISCUSSION: Factory overhead consists of indirect manufacturing costs that cannot be traced to specific units but are necessarily incurred as part of the production process. Examples are depreciation, utilities expense, insurance, and supervisors' salaries. Factory overhead is usually allocated to products based upon the level of activity during the period, e.g., direct labor hours or machine hours.

2.3.2. Which of the following items is not included in (charged to) manufacturing overhead?

A. Depreciation and supplies.
B. Costs of service departments.
C. Costs of marketing departments.
D. Costs of maintenance departments.

Answer (C) is correct. *(Publisher, adapted)*
REQUIRED: The item not charged to manufacturing overhead.
DISCUSSION: Marketing costs, for example, salaries of sales personnel, sales commissions, and advertising, are period costs and are expensed as incurred. They cannot be assigned to the product because these marketing costs are not associated with the manufacturing process.
Answer (A) is incorrect. Depreciation and supplies are indirectly associated with manufacturing and are assigned to products through the overhead account. Answer (B) is incorrect. Service department costs are indirectly associated with manufacturing and are assigned to products through the overhead account. Answer (D) is incorrect. Maintenance costs are indirectly associated with manufacturing and are assigned to products through the overhead account.

2.3.3. Many companies recognize three major categories of costs of manufacturing a product. These are direct materials, direct labor, and overhead. Which of the following is an overhead cost in the production of an automobile?

A. The cost of small tools used in mounting tires on each automobile.
B. The cost of the tires on each automobile.
C. The cost of the laborers who place tires on each automobile.
D. The delivery costs for the tires on each automobile.

Answer (A) is correct. *(CIA, adapted)*
REQUIRED: The overhead cost in the production of an automobile.
DISCUSSION: The cost of small tools used in mounting tires cannot be identified solely with the manufacture of a specific automobile. This cost should be treated as factory overhead because it is identifiable with the production process.
Answer (B) is incorrect. Tire costs are readily and directly identifiable with each automobile and, thus, are direct materials costs. Answer (C) is incorrect. The cost of the laborers who place tires on each automobile is readily and directly identifiable with each automobile. Hence, it is a direct labor cost. Answer (D) is incorrect. Delivery costs are readily and directly identifiable with the tires delivered. Thus, they are direct materials costs.

2.3.4. During the current accounting period, a manufacturing company purchased $70,000 of raw materials, of which $50,000 of direct materials and $5,000 of indirect materials were used in production. The company also incurred $45,000 of total labor costs and $20,000 of other manufacturing overhead costs. An analysis of the work-in-process control account revealed $40,000 of direct labor costs. Based upon the above information, what is the total amount accumulated in the overhead control account?

A. $25,000
B. $30,000
C. $45,000
D. $50,000

Answer (B) is correct. *(CIA, adapted)*
REQUIRED: The total amount accumulated in the overhead control account.
DISCUSSION: Overhead consists of all costs, other than direct materials and direct labor, that are associated with the manufacturing process. The overhead control account should have the following costs:

Indirect materials	$ 5,000
Indirect labor ($45,000 – $40,000)	5,000
Other overhead	20,000
Total overhead	$30,000

Answer (A) is incorrect. The amount of $25,000 excludes the indirect materials. Answer (C) is incorrect. The amount of $45,000 is the total labor cost. Answer (D) is incorrect. The amount of $50,000 is the direct materials cost.

2.3.5. Annual overhead application rates are used to

A. Budget overhead.

B. Smooth seasonal variability of overhead costs.

C. Simulate seasonal variability of activity levels.

D. Treat overhead as period costs.

Answer (B) is correct. *(Publisher, adapted)*

REQUIRED: The reason for annual overhead application rates.

DISCUSSION: Annual overhead application rates smooth seasonal variability of overhead costs and activity levels. If overhead were applied to the product as incurred, the overhead rate per unit in most cases would vary considerably from week to week or month to month. The purpose of an annual overhead application rate is to simulate constant overhead throughout the year.

Answer (A) is incorrect. Overhead must be budgeted before a rate can be calculated. Answer (C) is incorrect. Overhead application rates are used to smooth seasonal variability of overhead costs. Answer (D) is incorrect. An overhead rate applies overhead to the product.

2.3.6. There are several alternative denominator measures for applying overhead. Which is not commonly used?

A. Direct labor hours.

B. Direct labor cost.

C. Machine hours.

D. Sales value of product produced.

Answer (D) is correct. *(Publisher, adapted)*

REQUIRED: The denominator measure not appropriate for applying overhead.

DISCUSSION: Overhead in traditional systems normally is applied to production according to an allocation base, such as direct labor hours, direct labor cost, or machine hours. An allocation base is an indirect measure, but it should have a relatively close correlation with the incurrence of overhead. The sales value of the product produced is not a variable with a causal relationship to the incurrence of overhead.

Answer (A) is incorrect. Direct labor hours is an appropriate base when overhead is incurred uniformly by all types of employees. Answer (B) is incorrect. Direct labor cost often is used as a base in labor-intensive industries. Answer (C) is incorrect. Machine hours is a frequently used base in capital-intensive industries.

2.3.7. Units of production is an appropriate method of assigning overhead when

A. Several well-differentiated products are manufactured.

B. Direct labor costs are low.

C. Only one product is manufactured.

D. The manufacturing process is complex.

Answer (C) is correct. *(CMA, adapted)*

REQUIRED: The situation in which units of production is an appropriate method of assigning overhead.

DISCUSSION: Assigning overhead on the basis of the number of units produced is usually not appropriate. Costs should be assigned on the basis of some plausible relationship between the cost object and the incurrence of the cost, preferably cause and effect. Overhead costs, however, may be incurred regardless of the level of production. Nevertheless, if a firm manufactures only one product, this method may be acceptable because all costs are to be charged to the single product.

Answer (A) is incorrect. The number of units of production may have no logical relationship to overhead when several different products are made. Answer (B) is incorrect. A low level of direct labor costs means that fixed overhead is substantial, and appropriate cost drivers should be used to make the assignment. If drivers cannot be feasibly identified, an appropriate indirect measure should be chosen. Answer (D) is incorrect. A complex manufacturing process is likely to have many cost drivers, and overhead preferably should be allocated on the basis of what drives (causes) the costs.

2.3.8. In a capital-intensive industry, which is most likely to be an appropriate basis for applying overhead?

A. Direct labor hours.

B. Direct labor cost.

C. Machine hours.

D. Sales value of product produced.

Answer (C) is correct. *(Publisher, adapted)*

REQUIRED: The most appropriate basis for applying overhead in a capital-intensive industry.

DISCUSSION: In capital-intensive industries, the amount of overhead probably is related more to machine hours than to either direct labor hours or direct labor cost.

Answer (A) is incorrect. Direct labor hours is a more appropriate basis for applying overhead in a labor-intensive industry. Answer (B) is incorrect. Direct labor cost is often used as a base in labor-intensive industries. Answer (D) is incorrect. The sales value of product produced is virtually never an appropriate base on which to allocate overhead.

2.3.9. In a labor-intensive industry in which more overhead (service, support, more expensive equipment, etc.) is incurred by the more highly skilled and paid employees, what denominator measure is most likely to be appropriate for applying overhead?

A. Direct labor hours.

B. Direct labor cost.

C. Machine hours.

D. Sales value of product produced.

Answer (B) is correct. *(Publisher, adapted)*

REQUIRED: The most appropriate basis for applying overhead in a labor-intensive industry.

DISCUSSION: In labor-intensive industries, overhead is traditionally assigned on the basis of labor time. However, if more overhead is incurred by the more highly skilled and paid employees, the overhead rate should be based upon direct labor cost rather than direct labor hours.

Answer (A) is incorrect. Direct labor hours is appropriate when overhead is incurred uniformly by all types of employees. Answer (C) is incorrect. Machine hours is an appropriate base when overhead varies with machine time used. Answer (D) is incorrect. Sales value is virtually never an appropriate base for assigning overhead.

2.3.10. Practical capacity as a plant capacity concept

A. Assumes all personnel and equipment will operate at peak efficiency and total plant capacity will be used.

B. Does not consider idle time caused by inadequate sales demand.

C. Includes consideration of idle time caused by both limited sales orders and human and equipment inefficiencies.

D. Is the production volume that is necessary to meet sales demand for the next year.

Answer (B) is correct. *(CMA, adapted)*

REQUIRED: The true statement about practical capacity.

DISCUSSION: Practical capacity is the maximum level at which output is produced efficiently. It includes consideration of idle time resulting from holidays, downtime, change-over time, etc., not from inadequate sales demand.

Answer (A) is incorrect. Theoretical capacity assumes all personnel and equipment operate at peak efficiency and total plant capacity is used. Answer (C) is incorrect. Practical capacity ignores demand. Answer (D) is incorrect. The production volume to meet sales demand may be more or less than practical capacity.

2.3.11. Carley Products has no work-in-process or finished goods inventories at year end. The balances of Carley's accounts include the following:

Cost of goods sold	$2,040,000
General selling and administrative expenses	900,000
Sales	3,600,000
Manufacturing overhead control	700,000
Manufacturing overhead applied	648,000

Carley's pretax income for the year is

A. $608,000

B. $660,000

C. $712,000

D. $1,508,000

Answer (A) is correct. *(CMA, adapted)*

REQUIRED: The pretax income assuming an overhead application difference.

DISCUSSION: The pretax income is equal to sales minus cost of goods sold, general selling and administrative expenses, and underapplied manufacturing overhead (the excess of actual overhead over the amount applied).

Sales	$3,600,000
Cost of goods sold	(2,040,000)
Underapplied overhead	(52,000)
Gross margin	$1,508,000
GS&A expenses	(900,000)
Income before income taxes	$ 608,000

Answer (B) is incorrect. The amount of $660,000 is the result of failing to subtract the underapplied overhead. Answer (C) is incorrect. The amount of $712,000 is the pretax income assuming $52,000 of overhead was overapplied and therefore added in the calculation of the gross margin. Answer (D) is incorrect. The amount of $1,508,000 is the gross margin.

2.3.12. Effective cost capacity management

A. Minimizes the value delivered to customers.

B. Maximizes required future investments.

C. Matches the firm's resources with market opportunities.

D. Is limited to eliminating short-term worth.

Answer (C) is correct. *(Publisher, adapted)*

REQUIRED: The true statement about effective cost capacity management.

DISCUSSION: Maximizing the value created within an organization starts with understanding the nature and capabilities of all of the entity's resources (capacity), which may be defined from different perspectives. Managing capacity cost starts when a product or process is first envisioned. It continues through the subsequent disposal of resources downstream. Effective capacity cost management requires supporting effective matching of a firm's resources with current and future market opportunities.

Answer (A) is incorrect. Effective capacity management maximizes value delivered to customers. Answer (B) is incorrect. Effective capacity management minimizes required future investment. Answer (D) is incorrect. Effective capacity management minimizes waste in the short, intermediate, and long run.

2.3.13. The denominator of the overhead application rate can be based on one of several production capacities. Which results in the lowest expected over- or underapplied overhead?

A. Theoretical capacity.

B. Expected capacity.

C. Normal capacity.

D. Practical capacity.

Answer (B) is correct. *(Publisher, adapted)*

REQUIRED: The production capacity resulting in the lowest expected over- or underapplied overhead.

DISCUSSION: If actual output differs from the predetermined capacity level, a volume variance occurs. This variance equals the over- or underapplied overhead. The expected volume is that predicted for the period. Thus, the use of expected capacity as a denominator should result in the lowest expected over- or underapplied overhead.

Answer (A) is incorrect. Theoretical capacity is the maximum capacity assuming continuous operations with no holidays, downtime, etc. Answer (C) is incorrect. Normal capacity is an average expected capacity over a series of years. It varies from the expected capacity on a year-by-year basis. Answer (D) is incorrect. Practical capacity is theoretical capacity adjusted downward for holidays, maintenance time, etc. It is very difficult to attain.

2.3.14. Which measure of capacity applies the least amount of overhead to units of production?

A. Theoretical capacity.

B. Expected capacity.

C. Normal capacity.

D. Practical capacity.

Answer (A) is correct. *(Publisher, adapted)*

REQUIRED: The measure of capacity that applies the least overhead to production.

DISCUSSION: The larger the denominator in the overhead application rate, the smaller the rate and the lower the cost assigned to the product. Theoretical capacity, the absolute capacity during continuous operations, ignoring holidays, maintenance time, etc., provides the largest denominator.

Answer (B) is incorrect. Expected capacity is less than theoretical capacity. Answer (C) is incorrect. Normal capacity is less than theoretical capacity. Answer (D) is incorrect. Practical capacity is less than theoretical capacity.

2.3.15. Accounting for manufacturing overhead costs involves averaging in

	Job Costing	Process Costing
A.	Yes	No
B.	Yes	Yes
C.	No	Yes
D.	No	No

Answer (B) is correct. *(CPA, adapted)*

REQUIRED: The accounting system(s) using average manufacturing overhead costs.

DISCUSSION: Overhead consists of costs other than direct materials and labor that are averaged over the entire period, usually a year, based upon an estimated output level. The total of the estimated indirect costs is divided by the base used for cost assignment, e.g., direct labor hours, and assigned to the product based upon the actual output level. Consequently, manufacturing overhead costs are averaged in both job costing and process costing systems.

2.3.16. During an accounting period, which production account is debited and credited many times?

A. Manufacturing overhead applied.

B. Manufacturing overhead control.

C. Both.

D. Neither.

Answer (D) is correct. *(Publisher, adapted)*

REQUIRED: The overhead account(s) with numerous debits and credits.

DISCUSSION: When both manufacturing overhead control and manufacturing overhead applied are used, all overhead incurred is debited to the control account and all overhead applied is credited to manufacturing overhead applied.

Answer (A) is incorrect. The only debits to manufacturing overhead applied are to close the account at the end of the period and to correct errors. Answer (B) is incorrect. The only credits to manufacturing overhead control are to close the account at the end of the period and to correct errors. Answer (C) is incorrect. Neither account is debited and credited frequently.

2.3.17. When the amount of overapplied factory overhead is significant, the entry to close overapplied factory overhead will most likely require

A. A debit to cost of goods sold.

B. Debits to cost of goods sold, finished goods inventory, and work-in-process inventory.

C. A credit to cost of goods sold.

D. Credits to cost of goods sold, finished goods inventory, and work-in-process inventory.

Answer (D) is correct. *(CIA, adapted)*

REQUIRED: The most likely entry to close overapplied factory overhead.

DISCUSSION: Under a normal costing system, overhead is applied to all jobs worked on during the period at a predetermined rate. Because cost of goods sold, finished goods inventory, and work-in-process inventory all relate to these jobs, each should be adjusted by its proportionate share of over- or underapplied overhead. This apportionment may be based on either the percentage of total overhead (theoretically preferable) or the percentage of total cost. The entry to close overapplied overhead requires credits to these three accounts.

2.3.18. Cox Company found that the differences in product costs resulting from the application of predetermined overhead rates rather than actual overhead rates were immaterial even though actual production was substantially less than planned production. The most likely explanation is that

A. Overhead was composed chiefly of variable costs.

B. Several products were produced simultaneously.

C. Fixed manufacturing overhead was a significant cost.

D. Costs of overhead items were substantially higher than anticipated.

Answer (A) is correct. *(CPA, adapted)*
REQUIRED: The likely explanation for a small difference between applied and actual overhead.
DISCUSSION: Total variable overhead costs change in proportion to changes in the activity level. Total fixed costs do not. For the difference between applied and actual overhead to be immaterial when actual production is substantially less than planned production, overhead costs must be composed chiefly of variable costs.
Answer (B) is incorrect. For overhead application purposes, the simultaneous production of several products is similar to producing one product. Answer (C) is incorrect. If fixed manufacturing overhead had been significant, a material difference would have arisen. Answer (D) is incorrect. If actual costs are substantially higher than anticipated, overhead will be underapplied by a substantial amount.

2.3.19. A job-order cost system uses a predetermined factory overhead rate based on expected volume and expected fixed cost. At the end of the year, underapplied overhead might be explained by which of the following situations?

	Actual Volume	Actual Fixed Costs
A.	Greater than expected	Greater than expected
B.	Greater than expected	Less than expected
C.	Less than expected	Greater than expected
D.	Less than expected	Less than expected

Answer (C) is correct. *(CPA, adapted)*
REQUIRED: The situations resulting in underapplied overhead.
DISCUSSION: If too little fixed overhead is applied at the predetermined rate (expected fixed cost ÷ expected volume), the result is underapplied overhead (actual factory overhead exceeds overhead applied). If the actual and expected fixed costs are the same, but the actual volume is less than the expected (denominator) volume, overhead will be underapplied. If the actual volume equals expected volume but actual fixed costs exceed the expected (numerator) fixed costs, overhead is likewise underapplied.

2.3.20. Assuming two overhead accounts are used, what is the entry to close them and to charge underapplied overhead to cost of goods sold?

		Dr	Cr
A.	Cost of goods sold	XXX	
	Finished goods		XXX
B.	Manufacturing OH applied	XXX	
	Manufacturing OH control		XXX
	Cost of goods sold		XXX
C.	Cost of goods sold	XXX	
	Manufacturing OH applied		XXX
D.	Cost of goods sold	XXX	
	Manufacturing OH applied	XXX	
	Manufacturing OH control		XXX

Answer (D) is correct. *(Publisher, adapted)*
REQUIRED: The journal entry to close the overhead accounts and to charge underapplied overhead to COGS.
DISCUSSION: Although not theoretically sound, total under- or overapplied overhead is often debited (credited) to COGS. The correct entry to close the overhead accounts and to charge underapplied overhead to COGS is to debit the manufacturing overhead applied account for the amount of overhead applied for the period and to credit manufacturing overhead control for the amount of overhead actually incurred for the period. The amount actually incurred exceeds the amount of overhead applied because overhead is underapplied. The difference is the amount charged to COGS.
Answer (A) is incorrect. A debit to COGS and a credit to finished goods expenses inventoried costs related to items sold. Answer (B) is incorrect. The entry to close the overhead accounts credits COGS when overhead has been overapplied. Answer (C) is incorrect. Debiting COGS and crediting overhead applied does not close the overhead accounts.

2.3.21. The following information is available from the records of a manufacturing company that applies manufacturing overhead based on direct labor hours:

Estimated overhead cost	$500,000
Estimated labor hours	200,000
Actual overhead cost	$515,000
Actual labor hours	210,000

Based on this information, manufacturing overhead is

A. Underapplied by $9,524.

B. Overapplied by $10,000.

C. Overapplied by $15,000.

D. Overapplied by $40,750.

Answer (B) is correct. *(CIA, adapted)*
REQUIRED: The amount of manufacturing overhead based on direct labor hours.
DISCUSSION: Applied overhead equals the actual labor hours (210,000) times the estimated application rate ($500,000 ÷ 200,000 DLH = $2.50 per direct labor hour), or $525,000. This amount is $10,000 ($525,000 – $515,000 actual cost) higher than the actual overhead cost incurred. Thus, overhead was overapplied by $10,000.
Answer (A) is incorrect. The amount of $9,524 (underapplied) results from treating the actual overhead and labor hours as the estimated values and vice versa. Answer (C) is incorrect. The excess of actual over estimated overhead is $15,000. Answer (D) is incorrect. The amount of $40,750 (overapplied) results from treating actual overhead as the estimated value and vice versa.

2.3.22. Mason Co. uses a job-order cost system and applies manufacturing overhead to jobs using a predetermined overhead rate based on direct-labor dollars. The rate for the current year is 200% of direct-labor dollars. This rate was calculated last year and will be used throughout the current year. Mason had one job, No. 150, in process at the beginning of the month with raw materials costs of $2,000 and direct-labor costs of $3,000. During the month, raw materials and direct labor added to jobs were as follows:

	No. 150	No. 151	No. 152
Raw materials	$ --	$4,000	$1,000
Direct labor	1,500	5,000	2,500

Actual manufacturing overhead for the month was $20,000. During the month, Mason completed Job Nos. 150 and 151. For the month, manufacturing overhead was

A. Overapplied by $4,000.

B. Underapplied by $7,000.

C. Underapplied by $2,000.

D. Underapplied by $1,000.

Answer (C) is correct. *(CPA, adapted)*

REQUIRED: The under- or overapplied manufacturing overhead.

DISCUSSION: Mason incurred direct-labor costs of $9,000 ($1,500 Job 150 + $5,000 Job 151 + $2,500 Job 152). Hence, overhead applied was $18,000 ($9,000 × 200%). The amount underapplied was $2,000 ($20,000 actual OH – $18,000).

Answer (A) is incorrect. Overhead would have been overapplied by $4,000 if the direct-labor costs in beginning work-in-process had been treated as incurred during the month. Answer (B) is incorrect. Overhead would have been underapplied by $7,000 if Job 152 had been ignored. Answer (D) is incorrect. Overhead would have been underapplied by $1,000 if the direct-labor costs in beginning work-in-process had been treated as incurred during the month and if Job 152 had been ignored.

2.3.23. Worley Company has underapplied overhead of $45,000 for the year. Before disposition of the underapplied overhead, selected year-end balances from Worley's accounting records were

Sales	$1,200,000
Cost of goods sold	720,000
Direct materials inventory	36,000
Work-in-process inventory	54,000
Finished goods inventory	90,000

Under Worley's cost accounting system, over- or underapplied overhead is assigned to appropriate inventories and COGS based on year-end balances. In its year-end income statement, Worley should report COGS of

A. $682,500

B. $684,000

C. $757,500

D. $765,000

Answer (C) is correct. *(CPA, adapted)*

REQUIRED: The amount of cost of goods sold after allocation of underapplied overhead.

DISCUSSION: The assignment of underapplied overhead increases COGS. The underapplied overhead of $45,000 for the year should be assigned on a pro rata basis to work-in-process ($54,000), finished goods ($90,000), and COGS ($720,000). The sum of these three items is $864,000. Thus, $37,500 should be assigned to COGS [($720,000 ÷ $864,000) × $45,000]. COGS after assignment is $757,500 ($37,500 + $720,000). The remaining $7,500 should be assigned proportionately to work-in-process and finished goods.

Answer (A) is incorrect. The appropriate COGS balance if overhead was overapplied by $45,000 and $37,500 was assigned to COGS is $682,500. Answer (B) is incorrect. The COGS balance if overhead was overapplied by $45,000 and direct materials inventory was incorrectly included in the denominator of the ratio used to assign overhead is $684,000. Answer (D) is incorrect. Debiting the full amount of underapplied overhead ($45,000) to COGS results in $765,000.

2.3.24. Schneider, Inc., had the following information relating to Year 1:

Budgeted manufacturing overhead	$74,800
Actual manufacturing overhead	$78,300
Applied manufacturing overhead	$76,500
Estimated direct labor hours	44,000

If Schneider decides to use the actual results from Year 1 to determine the Year 2 overhead rate, what is the Year 2 overhead rate?

A. $1.700

B. $1.738

C. $1.740

D. $1.780

Answer (C) is correct. *(R. Gruber)*

REQUIRED: The overhead rate for Year 2 using Year 1 data.

DISCUSSION: The Year 1 overhead rate was $1.70 ($74,800 budgeted overhead ÷ 44,000 estimated DLH). Because applied manufacturing overhead equals actual DLH times the overhead rate, the actual direct labor hours for Year 1 were 45,000 ($76,500 ÷ $1.70). Thus, the overhead rate for Year 2 is $1.74 ($78,300 actual Year 1 overhead ÷ 45,000 actual Year 1 DLH).

Answer (A) is incorrect. The amount of $1.700 was the Year 1 rate. Answer (B) is incorrect. The amount of $1.738 equals Year 1 applied overhead divided by estimated (not actual) Year 1 hours. Answer (D) is incorrect. The amount of $1.780 (rounded) equals actual Year 1 overhead divided by estimated Year 1 hours.

2.3.25. At the beginning of the year, Smith, Inc., budgeted the following:

Units	10,000
Sales	$100,000
Total variable expenses	60,000
Total fixed expenses	20,000
Manufacturing overhead:	
Variable	30,000
Fixed	10,000

There were no beginning inventories. At the end of the year, no work was in process, total manufacturing overhead incurred was $39,500, and underapplied manufacturing overhead was $1,500. Manufacturing overhead was applied on the basis of budgeted unit production. How many units were produced this year?

A. 10,250

B. 10,000

C. 9,875

D. 9,500

Answer (D) is correct. *(Publisher, adapted)*

REQUIRED: The number of units produced given various overhead data.

DISCUSSION: Given actual overhead of $39,500 and underapplied overhead of $1,500, overhead applied was $38,000 ($39,500 – $1,500). Overhead is applied at the rate of $4 per unit ($40,000 budgeted overhead ÷ 10,000 budgeted units). Accordingly, 9,500 units were produced ($38,000 applied overhead ÷ $4 per unit application rate).

Answer (A) is incorrect. The amount of 10,250 units would have been produced if overhead had been overapplied by $1,500 [($39,500 + $1,500) ÷ $4]. Answer (B) is incorrect. The amount of 10,000 units is the result of dividing budgeted, not applied, overhead by the application rate. Answer (C) is incorrect. The amount of 9,875 units would have been produced if $39,500 had been the amount of applied overhead.

2.3.26. A company manufactures plastic products for the home and restaurant market. The company also does contract work for other customers and uses a job-order costing system. The flexible budget covering next year's expected range of output is

Direct labor hours	50,000	80,000	110,000
Machine hours	40,000	64,000	88,000
Variable OH costs	$100,000	$160,000	$220,000
Fixed OH costs	150,000	150,000	150,000
Total OH costs	$250,000	$310,000	$370,000

A predetermined overhead rate based on direct labor hours is used to apply total overhead. Management has estimated that 100,000 direct labor hours will be used next year. The predetermined overhead rate per direct labor hour to be used to apply total overhead to the individual jobs next year is

A. $3.36

B. $3.50

C. $3.70

D. $3.88

Answer (B) is correct. *(CIA, adapted)*

REQUIRED: The predetermined overhead rate per direct labor hour.

DISCUSSION: The predetermined overhead rate is calculated by dividing the total fixed overhead by the activity level to arrive at a unit fixed overhead cost that is added to the unit variable overhead cost. The unit variable overhead rate is the same at each activity level. Thus, the predetermined overhead rate is $3.50 [($150,000 FOH ÷ 100,000 hrs.) + ($220,000 VOH ÷ 110,000 hrs.)].

Answer (A) is incorrect. The amount of $3.36 per direct labor hour is based on use of an activity level of 110,000 direct labor hours to determine the fixed overhead rate. Answer (C) is incorrect. The amount of $3.70 is the result of assuming that $220,000 of variable overhead will be incurred for 100,000 (not 110,000) direct labor hours. Answer (D) is incorrect. The amount of $3.88 (rounded) results from using an activity level of 80,000 direct labor hours to determine the fixed overhead rate.

2.3.27. Application rates for manufacturing overhead best reflect anticipated fluctuations in sales over a cycle of years when they are computed under the concept of

A. Maximum capacity.

B. Normal capacity.

C. Practical capacity.

D. Expected actual capacity.

Answer (B) is correct. *(CPA, adapted)*

REQUIRED: The concept of capacity for best applying overhead over a cycle of years.

DISCUSSION: Normal capacity is the output level that will approximate demand over a period of years that includes seasonal, cyclical, and trend variations. Deviations in one year will be offset in other years.

Answer (A) is incorrect. Maximum (theoretical or ideal) capacity is the level at which output is maximized assuming perfectly efficient operations at all times. This level is impossible to maintain and results in underapplied overhead. Answer (C) is incorrect. Practical capacity is the maximum level at which output is produced efficiently. It usually also results in underapplied overhead. Answer (D) is incorrect. Expected actual capacity is a short-run output level. It minimizes under- or overapplied overhead but does not provide a consistent basis for assigning overhead cost. Per-unit overhead fluctuates because of short-term changes in the expected production level.

Questions 2.3.28 through 2.3.32 are based on the following information. Baehr Company is a manufacturing company with a fiscal year that runs from July 1 to June 30. The company uses a job costing system for its production costs. A predetermined overhead rate based upon direct labor hours is used to apply overhead to individual jobs. A flexible budget of overhead costs was prepared for the fiscal year as shown below.

Direct labor hours	100,000	120,000	140,000
Variable overhead costs	$325,000	$390,000	$455,000
Fixed overhead costs	216,000	216,000	216,000
Total overhead	$541,000	$606,000	$671,000

Although the annual ideal capacity is 150,000 direct labor hours, company officials have determined 120,000 direct labor hours to be normal capacity for the year.

The information presented below is for November. Jobs 83-50 and 83-51 were completed during November.

Inventories November 1:	
Raw materials and supplies	$ 10,500
Work-in-process (Job 83-50)	54,000
Finished goods	112,500
Purchases of raw materials and supplies:	
Raw materials	$135,000
Supplies	15,000
	$150,000

Materials and supplies requisitioned for production:	
Job 83-50	$ 45,000
Job 83-51	37,500
Job 83-52	25,500
Supplies	12,000
	$120,000

Factory direct labor hours:	
Job 83-50	3,500
Job 83-51	3,000
Job 83-52	2,000
	8,500

Labor costs:	
Direct labor wages	$51,000
Indirect labor wages (4,000 hours)	15,000
Supervisory salaries	6,000
	$72,000

Building occupancy costs (heat, light, depreciation, etc.):	
Factory facilities	$6,500
Sales offices	1,500
Administrative offices	1,000
	$9,000

Factory equipment costs:	
Power	$4,000
Repairs and maintenance	1,500
Depreciation	1,500
Other	1,000
	$8,000

2.3.28. Assume Baehr's predetermined overhead rate is $4.50 per direct labor hour. Actual manufacturing overhead incurred during November was

A. $38,000

B. $41,500

C. $47,500

D. $50,500

Answer (C) is correct. *(CMA, adapted)*

REQUIRED: The actual manufacturing overhead incurred during the period.

DISCUSSION: Actual manufacturing overhead incurred during November consisted of equipment costs, factory facilities costs, indirect labor wages and supervisory salaries ($15,000 + $6,000), and supplies requisitioned for production.

Equipment costs	$ 8,000
Factory facilities costs	6,500
Indirect labor wages and supervisory salaries	21,000
Supplies	12,000
Actual overhead	$47,500

Answer (A) is incorrect. The amount of $38,000 includes the building occupancy costs of the sales and administrative offices, but it does not include the cost of the supplies requisitioned for production. Answer (B) is incorrect. The amount of $41,500 does not include the supervisory salaries. Answer (D) is incorrect. The amount of $50,500 includes the actual purchase cost of supplies of $15,000 instead of the cost of the supplies requisitioned for production of $12,000.

2.3.29. Assume the predetermined overhead rate is $4.50 per direct labor hour. The manufacturing overhead costs applied to Job 83-52 during November were

A. $9,000
B. $21,000
C. $46,500
D. $8,000

Answer (A) is correct. *(CMA, adapted)*

REQUIRED: The manufacturing overhead costs applied to an incomplete job at the end of the period.

DISCUSSION: The overhead rate is given as $4.50 per hour. Job 83-52 incurred 2,000 direct labor hours resulting in $9,000 ($4.50 × 2,000 DLH) of overhead applied to that job in November.

Answer (B) is incorrect. The amount of $21,000 includes the direct labor cost for November for Job 83-52 of $12,000. Answer (C) is incorrect. The total cost for November for Job 83-52 is $46,500. Answer (D) is incorrect. The amount of $8,000 applies an overhead rate of $4.00 per DLH instead of the given rate of $4.50.

2.3.30. Assume the predetermined overhead rate is $4.50 per direct labor hour. The total cost of Job 83-50 is

A. $81,750
B. $135,750
C. $142,750
D. $146,750

Answer (B) is correct. *(CMA, adapted)*

REQUIRED: The total cost for a job begun in a prior period and completed currently.

DISCUSSION: Job 83-50 was completed during November after having been started in a previous period (BWIP was $54,000). During the period, $45,000 in materials costs was added. Also, direct labor was incurred at the rate of $6.00 per hour ($51,000 ÷ 8,500 total DLH). Direct labor cost for November for Job 83-50 was thus $21,000 ($6.00 × 3,500 DLH). Overhead applied was $15,750 (given overhead rate of $4.50 × 3,500 DLH). Total cost was $135,750 ($54,000 + $45,000 + $21,000 + $15,750).

Answer (A) is incorrect. The amount of $81,750 omits beginning work-in-process. Answer (C) is incorrect. The amount of $142,750 applies one-third, or $7,000 [($15,000 + $6,000) ÷ 3], of the indirect labor wages and supervisory salaries to the total cost of Job 83-50. Answer (D) is incorrect. The amount of $146,750 applies one-third, or $7,000, of the indirect labor wages and supervisory salaries, and one-third, or $4,000 ($12,000 ÷ 3), of the supplies requisitioned for production to the total cost of Job 83-50.

2.3.31. Assume Baehr's predetermined overhead rate is $4.50 per direct labor hour. The total amount of overhead applied to jobs during November was

A. $29,250
B. $38,250
C. $47,250
D. $56,250

Answer (B) is correct. *(CMA, adapted)*

REQUIRED: The total overhead applied to jobs during the current period.

DISCUSSION: During November, 8,500 direct labor hours were incurred. The overhead application rate is given as $4.50 per hour. Thus, the total overhead applied was $38,250 ($4.50 × 8,500 DLH).

Answer (A) is incorrect. The amount of $29,250 subtracts the $9,000 of building occupancy costs from the total overhead applied of $38,250. Answer (C) is incorrect. The amount of $47,250 adds the $9,000 of building occupancy costs to the total overhead applied of $38,250. Answer (D) is incorrect. The amount of $56,250 reallocates November's portion of $18,000 ($216,000 ÷ 12) of fixed overhead costs to the total overhead applied of $38,250. The overhead rate, however, takes fixed and variable overhead costs into account.

2.3.32. The best predetermined overhead rate to be used to apply overhead to individual jobs during Baehr's fiscal year is

A. $3.25 per DLH.
B. $4.79 per DLH.
C. $5.05 per DLH.
D. $5.41 per DLH.

Answer (C) is correct. *(CMA, adapted)*

REQUIRED: The predetermined rate to apply overhead to individual jobs.

DISCUSSION: The predetermined overhead rate is the estimated total overhead divided by the direct labor hours at normal capacity. The normal capacity for the year is 120,000 hours, and related overhead costs are $606,000. The overhead rate is therefore $5.05 ($606,000 ÷ 120,000 hours).

Answer (A) is incorrect. The amount of $3.25 per DLH only takes the variable overhead costs into account for the normal capacity of 120,000 hours. Answer (B) is incorrect. The amount of $4.79 per DLH is the overhead rate for a capacity of 140,000 direct labor hours. Answer (D) is incorrect. The amount of $5.41 per DLH is the overhead rate for a capacity of 100,000 direct labor hours.

2.3.33. Regan Company operates its factory on a two-shift basis and pays a late-shift differential of 15%. Regan also pays a premium of 50% for overtime work. Because Regan manufactures only for stock, the cost system provides for uniform direct-labor hourly charges for production done without regard to shift worked or work done on an overtime basis. Overtime and late-shift differentials are included in Regan's factory overhead application rate. The May payroll for production workers is as follows:

Wages at base direct-labor rates	$325,000
Shift differentials	25,000
Overtime premiums	10,000

For the month of May, what amount of direct labor should Regan charge to work-in-process?

A. $325,000

B. $335,000

C. $350,000

D. $360,000

Answer (A) is correct. *(CPA, adapted)*

REQUIRED: The amount of direct labor given shift pay differentials and overtime premiums.

DISCUSSION: Regan's cost system provides for uniform direct hourly charges for production done without regard to shift work or work done on an overtime basis. The shift pay differentials and overtime premiums are included in factory overhead. Accordingly, both the $25,000 and $10,000 amounts should be charged to overhead, and $325,000 should be charged to the WIP account as direct labor.

Answer (B) is incorrect. The amount of $335,000 includes overtime premiums. Answer (C) is incorrect. The amount of $350,000 includes shift differentials. Answer (D) is incorrect. The amount of $360,000 includes both the shift differentials and overtime premiums.

2.4 Work-in-Process Account Calculations

2.4.1. Under Pick Co.'s job costing system, manufacturing overhead is applied to work-in-process using a predetermined annual overhead rate. During January, Pick's transactions included the following:

Direct materials issued to production	$ 90,000
Indirect materials issued to production	8,000
Manufacturing overhead incurred	125,000
Manufacturing overhead applied	113,000
Direct labor costs	107,000

Pick had neither beginning nor ending work-in-process inventory. What was the cost of jobs completed in January?

A. $302,000

B. $310,000

C. $322,000

D. $330,000

Answer (B) is correct. *(CPA, adapted)*

REQUIRED: The cost of jobs completed.

DISCUSSION: Given no beginning or ending work-in-process, the cost of jobs completed equals the sum of direct materials, direct labor, and manufacturing overhead applied. Indirect materials costs are charged to overhead control and are not included in the amount transferred from work-in-process to finished goods except to the extent they are reflected in applied overhead. The difference between overhead incurred and overhead applied, if material, is assigned to finished goods, cost of goods sold, and ending work-in-process ($0 in this case). Thus, the cost of jobs completed was $310,000 ($90,000 + $113,000 + $107,000).

Answer (A) is incorrect. The amount of $302,000 results from subtracting indirect materials from the cost of jobs completed. Answer (C) is incorrect. The amount of $322,000 is based on overhead incurred. Answer (D) is incorrect. The amount of $330,000 includes indirect materials and overhead incurred but excludes overhead applied.

2.4.2. The Childers Company manufactures widgets. During the fiscal year just ended, the company incurred prime cost of $1.5 million and conversion cost of $1.8 million. Overhead is applied at the rate of 200% of direct labor cost. How much of the above costs represent direct materials cost?

A. $1,500,000

B. $300,000

C. $900,000

D. $600,000

Answer (C) is correct. *(A. Wilson)*

REQUIRED: The calculation of direct materials costs for the fiscal year just ended.

DISCUSSION: Prime cost is the sum of direct materials and direct labor costs. Conversion cost is the sum of direct labor and overhead costs.

$$\begin{aligned} OH &= 200\% \times DL \\ DL + OH &= \$1{,}800{,}000 \\ DL + 2DL &= \$1{,}800{,}000 \\ DL &= \$600{,}000 \\ DM + DL &= \$1{,}500{,}000 \\ DM + \$600{,}000 &= \$1{,}500{,}000 \\ DM &= \$900{,}000 \end{aligned}$$

Answer (A) is incorrect. The amount of $1,500,000 is the prime cost, including both direct materials and direct labor costs. Answer (B) is incorrect. The difference between conversion cost and prime cost is $300,000. Answer (D) is incorrect. Direct labor costs are equal to $600,000.

2.4.3. A manufacturer employs a job-order cost system. All jobs ordinarily pass through all three production departments, and Job 101 and Job 102 were completed during the current month.

Production Departments	Direct Labor Rate	Manufacturing Overhead Application Rates
Department 1	$12.00	150% of direct materials cost
Department 2	18.00	$8.00 per machine hour
Department 3	15.00	200% of direct labor cost

	Job 101	**Job 102**	**Job 103**
BWIP	$25,500	$32,400	$ - 0 -
DM:			
Department 1	$40,000	$26,000	$58,000
Department 2	3,000	5,000	14,000
Department 3	- 0 -	- 0 -	- 0 -
DL:			
Department 1	500	400	300
Department 2	200	250	350
Department 3	1,500	1,800	2,500
MH:			
Department 1	- 0 -	- 0 -	- 0 -
Department 2	1,200	1,500	2,700
Department 3	150	300	200

The cost of completed Job 101 is

A. $131,500

B. $189,700

C. $202,600

D. $215,200

Answer (D) is correct. *(CIA, adapted)*

REQUIRED: The cost of completed Job 101.

DISCUSSION: The cost of completed Job 101 includes all direct costs, applied overhead from each department, and the beginning WIP inventory. Consequently, total cost is $215,200 {($40,000 + $3,000) DM + [(500 × $12) + (200 × $18) + (1,500 × $15)] DL + [($40,000 DM cost in Dept. 1 × 150%) + (1,200 MH in Dept. 2 × $8) + ($15 × 1,500 DLH in Dept. 3 × 200%)] OH + $25,500 BWIP}.

Answer (A) is incorrect. The amount of $131,500 excludes the costs from Departments 2 and 3. Answer (B) is incorrect. The amount of $189,700 excludes the beginning WIP inventory balance. Answer (C) is incorrect. The amount of $202,600 excludes direct materials from Department 2 and direct labor from Departments 1 and 2.

2.4.4. Ajax Corporation transferred $72,000 of materials to its production department in February and incurred $37,000 of conversion costs ($22,000 of direct labor and $15,000 of overhead). At the beginning of the period, $14,000 of inventory (direct materials and conversion costs) was in process. At the end of the period, $18,000 of inventory was in process. What was the cost of goods manufactured?

A. $105,000

B. $109,000

C. $123,000

D. $141,000

Answer (A) is correct. *(Publisher, adapted)*

REQUIRED: The cost of goods manufactured for the period.

DISCUSSION: The sum of BWIP, direct materials, direct labor, and overhead, minus the cost of goods not completed during the period (EWIP), is the cost of goods manufactured.

BWIP	$ 14,000
Materials	72,000
Conversion costs	37,000
Minus EWIP	(18,000)
COGM	$105,000

Answer (B) is incorrect. The amount of $109,000 is the actual cost for the current period. BWIP should be added and EWIP subtracted to arrive at COGM. Answer (C) is incorrect. The $18,000 in EWIP was not subtracted from the total cost of $123,000. Answer (D) is incorrect. The $18,000 of EWIP was added to (not subtracted from) the total costs incurred.

2.4.5. Lucy Sportswear manufactures a specialty line of T-shirts using a job-order cost system. During March, the following costs were incurred in completing Job ICU2: direct materials, $13,700; direct labor, $4,800; administrative, $1,400; and selling, $5,600. Overhead was applied at the rate of $25 per machine hour, and Job ICU2 required 800 machine hours. If Job ICU2 resulted in 7,000 good shirts, the cost of goods sold per unit would be

A. $6.50

B. $6.30

C. $5.70

D. $5.50

Answer (D) is correct. *(CMA, adapted)*

REQUIRED: The cost of goods sold per unit.

DISCUSSION: Cost of goods sold is based on the manufacturing costs incurred in production but does not include selling or general and administrative expenses. Manufacturing costs equal $38,500 [$13,700 DM + $4,800 DL + (800 hours × $25) OH]. Thus, per-unit cost is $5.50 ($38,500 ÷ 7,000 units).

Answer (A) is incorrect. The amount of $6.50 includes selling and administrative expenses. Answer (B) is incorrect. Including selling costs results in cost of goods sold per unit of $6.30. Answer (C) is incorrect. Including administrative expenses results in cost of goods sold per unit of $5.70.

2.4.6. The work-in-process of Parrott Corporation increased $11,500 from the beginning to the end of November. Costs incurred during November included $12,000 for direct materials, $63,000 for direct labor, and $21,000 for overhead. What was the cost of goods manufactured during November?

A. $75,000

B. $84,500

C. $96,000

D. $107,500

Answer (B) is correct. *(Publisher, adapted)*

REQUIRED: The cost of goods manufactured.

DISCUSSION: Because the work-in-process inventory increased by $11,500 from the beginning to the end of November, not all of the $96,000 in costs incurred during the period was transferred out. Consequently, the cost of goods manufactured must have been $84,500 ($12,000 DM + $63,000 DL + $21,000 OH – $11,500).

Answer (A) is incorrect. The amount of $75,000 equals the sum of direct materials and direct labor. Answer (C) is incorrect. The amount of $96,000 equals the costs incurred during the period. Answer (D) is incorrect. The amount of $107,500 equals the costs incurred during the period plus $11,500.

2.4.7. Birk Co. uses a job-order cost system. The following debits (credit) appeared in Birk's work-in-process account for the month just ended:

April	Description	Amount
1	Balance	$ 4,000
30	Direct materials	24,000
30	Direct labor	16,000
30	Factory overhead	12,800
30	To finished goods	(48,000)

Birk applies overhead to production at a predetermined rate of 80% of direct labor cost. Job No. 5, the only job still in process at month end, has been charged with direct labor of $2,000. What was the amount of direct materials charged to Job No. 5?

A. $3,000

B. $5,200

C. $8,800

D. $24,000

Answer (B) is correct. *(CPA, adapted)*

REQUIRED: The amount of direct materials in ending work-in-process.

DISCUSSION: Total debits to WIP are $56,800 ($4,000 + $24,000 + $16,000 + $12,800). Given a credit of $48,000 for finished goods, EWIP is $8,800 ($56,800 – $48,000). Of this amount, $2,000 is direct labor and $1,600 ($2,000 × 80%) is overhead. Thus, the amount of direct materials charged to Job No. 5 was $5,200 ($8,800 – $2,000 – $1,600).

Answer (A) is incorrect. The amount of $3,000 is not meaningful in this context. Answer (C) is incorrect. The amount of $8,800 is the total EWIP credit. Answer (D) is incorrect. The amount of $24,000 is the debit for direct materials during the month.

2.4.8. Lucas Co. has a job-order cost system. For the month of April, the following debits (credits) appeared in the general ledger account, work-in-process:

April		
1	Balance	$ 24,000
30	Direct materials	80,000
30	Direct labor	60,000
30	Factory overhead	54,000
30	To finished goods	(200,000)

Lucas applies overhead to production at a predetermined rate of 90% based on direct labor cost. Job No. 100, the only job still in process at the end of April, has been charged with factory overhead of $4,500. The amount of direct materials charged to Job No. 100 was

A. $18,000

B. $8,500

C. $5,000

D. $4,500

Answer (B) is correct. *(CPA, adapted)*

REQUIRED: The amount of direct materials charged to the only job in process at the end of the period.

DISCUSSION: The ending balance in the WIP account is $18,000 ($24,000 + $80,000 + $60,000 + $54,000 – $200,000). This amount equals the $218,000 sum of all debits to the account minus the $200,000 credit. The $18,000 balance consists of materials, labor, and overhead for Job No. 100. Overhead is given as $4,500 (90% of direct labor cost). Direct labor is thus $5,000 ($4,500 ÷ .90), and the amount of direct materials is $8,500 ($18,000 – $5,000 DL – $4,500 OH).

Answer (A) is incorrect. The ending balance in the WIP account is $18,000. Answer (C) is incorrect. The direct labor cost of Job No. 100 is $5,000. Answer (D) is incorrect. The amount of factory overhead charged to Job No. 100 is $4,500.

Questions 2.4.9 and 2.4.10 are based on the following information.

Kaden Corp. has two divisions -- Ace and Bow. Ace has a job costing system and manufactures machinery on special order for unrelated customers. Bow has a process cost system and manufactures Product Zee, which is sold to Ace as well as to unrelated companies. Ace's work-in-process account at April 30 included the following:

Balance, April 1	$ 24,000
Direct materials (including transferred-in cost)	80,000
Direct labor	60,000
Manufacturing overhead	54,000
Transferred to finished goods	(200,000)

Ace applies manufacturing overhead at 90% of direct labor cost. Job No. 125, which was the only job in process at April 30, has been charged with manufacturing overhead of $4,500. Bow's cost to manufacture Product Zee is $3.00 per unit, which is sold to Ace for $5.00 per unit and to unrelated customers for $6.00 per unit.

2.4.9. Direct materials (including transferred-in cost) charged to Job No. 125 amounted to

A. $5,000

B. $8,500

C. $13,500

D. $18,000

Answer (B) is correct. *(CPA, adapted)*

REQUIRED: The amount of direct materials in EWIP.

DISCUSSION: The EWIP consists of direct materials, direct labor, and overhead. EWIP is

BWIP	$ 24,000
DM	80,000
DL	60,000
OH	54,000
COGM	(200,000)
EWIP	$ 18,000

Because manufacturing overhead is applied at 90% of direct labor cost and manufacturing overhead was $4,500 on Job No. 125, direct labor cost charged to Job No. 125 is $5,000 ($4,500 ÷ .9). Direct materials charged therefore equaled $8,500 ($18,000 EWIP – $4,500 OH – $5,000 DL).

Answer (A) is incorrect. DL is equal to $5,000 ($4,500 ÷ .9). Answer (C) is incorrect. The amount of $13,500 is the total of DL and DM (prime costs). Answer (D) is incorrect. The amount of $18,000 is the total cost charged to Job No. 125.

2.4.10. How much is the transfer price for Product Zee?

A. $2.00

B. $3.00

C. $5.00

D. $6.00

Answer (C) is correct. *(CPA, adapted)*

REQUIRED: The transfer price of Product Zee.

DISCUSSION: The transfer price is the price at which an item is sold in intraentity transactions. This price usually is less than the market price, but it may, at times, be set at a price equal to or greater than market to achieve overall corporate objectives. The transfer price is given as $5.00.

Answer (A) is incorrect. The amount of $2.00 is the difference between the transfer price of $5.00 to Ace and Bow's cost of $3.00 to manufacture Product Zee. Answer (B) is incorrect. The amount of $3.00 is Bow's cost to manufacture Product Zee. Answer (D) is incorrect. The amount of $6.00 is the sale price to unrelated customers.

2.4.11. If the COGS for the Cole Manufacturing Co. is $105,000 and FG inventory decreased by $9,000 during the year, what was the year-end COGM?

A. $9,000

B. $96,000

C. $105,000

D. $114,000

Answer (B) is correct. *(Publisher, adapted)*

REQUIRED: The cost of goods manufactured given a decline in the finished goods inventory.

DISCUSSION: The cost of goods manufactured is the cost of goods sold minus the inventory decrease during the year. Inventory decreased by $9,000. Thus, $96,000 ($105,000 – $9,000) of the cost related to goods manufactured during the period.

Answer (A) is incorrect. The inventory change is $9,000. Answer (C) is incorrect. The COGS is $105,000. Answer (D) is incorrect. The amount of $114,000 is the sum of COGS ($105,000) and the FG inventory decrease ($9,000).

Questions 2.4.12 and 2.4.13 are based on the following information. Blum Corp. manufactures plastic-coated metal clips. The information below was among Blum's year-end manufacturing costs.

<u>Wages</u>	
Machine operators	$200,000
Maintenance workers	30,000
Factory supervisors	90,000
<u>Materials Used</u>	
Metal wire	$500,000
Lubricant for oiling machinery	10,000
Plastic coating	380,000

2.4.12. Blum's year-end direct labor amounted to

A. $200,000

B. $230,000

C. $290,000

D. $320,000

Answer (A) is correct. *(CPA, adapted)*

REQUIRED: The amount of direct labor costs for the accounting period.

DISCUSSION: Direct labor cost consists of the labor costs incurred for those employees who work on the actual production of the product. In this problem, only the machine operators' wages ($200,000) are considered direct labor. The wages of the factory supervisors and maintenance workers are indirect labor and therefore part of manufacturing overhead.

Answer (B) is incorrect. Maintenance workers' wages should not be included. Answer (C) is incorrect. Factory supervisors' wages should not be included. Answer (D) is incorrect. The wages of the factory supervisors and maintenance workers should not be included.

2.4.13. Blum's year-end direct materials amounted to

A. $890,000

B. $880,000

C. $510,000

D. $500,000

Answer (B) is correct. *(CPA, adapted)*

REQUIRED: The amount of direct materials costs for the accounting period.

DISCUSSION: Direct materials are part of the product. Given that plastic-coated metal clips are being made, only the plastic coating and metal wire ($880,000) used to make the clips are considered direct materials. All other supplies, including lubricant for oiling the machinery, are part of manufacturing overhead.

Answer (A) is incorrect. The lubricant for oiling machinery is not a direct material. Answer (C) is incorrect. The plastic coating but not the lubricant should be included as a direct material. Answer (D) is incorrect. The plastic coating should also be included as a direct material.

2.4.14. Luna Co.'s year-end manufacturing costs were as follows:

Direct materials and direct labor	$500,000
Depreciation of manufacturing equipment	70,000
Depreciation of factory building	40,000
Janitor's wages for cleaning factory premises	15,000

How much of these costs should be inventoried for external reporting purposes?

A. $625,000

B. $610,000

C. $585,000

D. $500,000

Answer (A) is correct. *(CPA, adapted)*

REQUIRED: The computation of inventory costs for external reporting purposes.

DISCUSSION: Inventoriable costs are directly related to the product including direct materials, direct labor, manufacturing overhead, and any other expenses necessary to produce the product. All the costs listed are inventoriable:

Prime costs	$500,000
Depreciation of equipment	70,000
Depreciation of building	40,000
Janitor's wages	15,000
Total inventoriable costs	$625,000

Answer (B) is incorrect. The janitor's wages of $15,000 should be included. Answer (C) is incorrect. Depreciation of the factory building ($40,000) should be included. Answer (D) is incorrect. Depreciation of the manufacturing equipment, depreciation of the factory building, and the janitor's wages should be included.

Questions 2.4.15 and 2.4.16 are based on the following information. Hamilton Company uses job-order costing. Manufacturing overhead is applied to production at a predetermined rate of 150% of direct labor cost. Any over- or underapplied overhead is closed to the cost of goods sold account at the end of each month. Additional information is available as follows:

- Job 101 was the only job in process at January 31, with accumulated costs as follows:

Direct materials	$4,000
Direct labor	2,000
Applied manufacturing overhead	3,000
Total manufacturing costs	$9,000

- Jobs 102, 103, and 104 were started during February.
- Direct materials requisitions for February totaled $26,000.
- Direct labor cost of $20,000 was incurred for February.
- Actual manufacturing overhead was $32,000 for February.
- The only job still in process on February 28 was Job 104, with costs of $2,800 for direct materials and $1,800 for direct labor.

2.4.15. The cost of goods manufactured for February was

A. $77,700

B. $78,000

C. $79,700

D. $85,000

Answer (A) is correct. *(CPA, adapted)*

REQUIRED: The cost of goods manufactured (COGM).

DISCUSSION: COGM is the sum of the costs in BWIP and all the costs incurred during the period minus the costs in EWIP. The calculation of COGM uses applied overhead ($30,000 = $20,000 DL cost × 150%). The $7,300 in EWIP includes $2,800 for direct materials, $1,800 for direct labor, and $2,700 for applied overhead (at 150% of DL cost).

BWIP	$ 9,000
Direct labor	20,000
Applied overhead	30,000
Direct materials	26,000
EWIP	(7,300)
COGM	$77,700

Answer (B) is incorrect. The amount of $78,000 does not reflect BWIP and EWIP and is based on actual manufacturing overhead. Answer (C) is incorrect. Actual manufacturing overhead of $32,000 was used. Answer (D) is incorrect. EWIP was not subtracted.

2.4.16. Over- or underapplied manufacturing overhead should be closed to the cost of goods sold account at February 28 in the amount of

A. $700 overapplied.

B. $1,000 overapplied.

C. $1,700 underapplied.

D. $2,000 underapplied.

Answer (D) is correct. *(CPA, adapted)*

REQUIRED: The amount of over- or underapplied manufacturing overhead closed to COGS.

DISCUSSION: The amount of over- or underapplied overhead is the difference between the actual overhead incurred and the overhead applied. The amount of overhead applied was $30,000 ($20,000 DL cost × 150%). The amount of overhead incurred was $32,000. Consequently, underapplied overhead of $2,000 ($32,000 actual – $30,000 applied) should be closed to COGS.

Answer (A) is incorrect. The amount of $700 overapplied equals applied overhead in EWIP minus the difference between actual February overhead and overhead applied in February. Answer (B) is incorrect. The $3,000 of applied manufacturing overhead in BWIP should not be used in determining the current month's over- or underapplied overhead. Answer (C) is incorrect. The amounts of applied overhead in BWIP and EWIP should not be used in calculating the current month's over- or underapplied overhead.

Questions 2.4.17 through 2.4.20 are based on the following information. The T-accounts below provide selected data about a company's financial results for the year.

Materials Inventory

	Debit	Credit	
Jan. 1 bal.	$22,500	?	Credits
Debits	75,000		
Dec. 31 bal.	$18,000		

Work-in-Process

	Debit	Credit	
Jan. 1 bal.	$ 52,500	$282,000	Credits
Direct mat.	72,000		
Direct labor	90,000		
Overhead	112,500		
Dec. 31 bal.	$?		

Finished Goods

	Debit	Credit	
Jan. 1 bal.	$90,000	?	Credits
Debits	?		
Dec. 31 bal.	$72,000		

Manufacturing Wages Payable

	Debit	Credit	
Debits	$100,500	$66,000	Jan. 1 bal.
		99,000	Credits

Manufacturing Overhead

	Debit	Credit	
Debits	$111,000	?	Credits

Cost of Goods Sold

	Debit	Credit	
Debits	?		Credits

2.4.17. The amount of over- (under-) applied overhead is

A. $(10,500)
B. $(1,500)
C. $1,500
D. $10,500

Answer (C) is correct. *(Publisher, adapted)*

REQUIRED: The amount of over- (under-) applied overhead.

DISCUSSION: Applied overhead is the amount debited to WIP and credited to overhead control. Actual overhead is debited to overhead control. Thus, overhead was overapplied by $1,500 ($112,500 applied – $111,000 actual).

Answer (A) is incorrect. The amount of $(10,500) is a nonsense number. Answer (B) is incorrect. The amount of $(1,500) indicates that the overhead was underapplied. Answer (D) is incorrect. The amount of $10,500 is a nonsense number.

2.4.18. The amount of indirect materials in the manufacturing overhead account is

A. $4,500
B. $7,500
C. $12,000
D. $18,000

Answer (B) is correct. *(Publisher, adapted)*

REQUIRED: The amount of indirect materials in the manufacturing overhead account.

DISCUSSION: Materials inventory included direct and indirect materials, and total credits to the account were $79,500 ($22,500 beginning balance + $75,000 total debits – $18,000 ending balance). Given that $72,000 of direct materials were transferred to WIP, $7,500 ($79,500 – $72,000) of indirect materials must have been debited to manufacturing overhead.

Answer (A) is incorrect. The amount of $4,500 is the decrease in the materials balance. Answer (C) is incorrect. The amount of $12,000 is a nonsense number. Answer (D) is incorrect. The amount of $18,000 is the ending balance of materials.

2.4.19. The cost of goods sold is

A. $300,000
B. $282,000
C. $274,500
D. $372,000

Answer (A) is correct. *(Publisher, adapted)*

REQUIRED: The cost of goods sold.

DISCUSSION: The total of credits to finished goods equals the total of debits to COGS, and the total of credits to WIP ($282,000) equals the total of debits to finished goods during the period. Consequently, the total of credits to finished goods, that is, COGS, must have been $300,000 ($90,000 beginning FG + $282,000 total debits to FG during the period – $72,000 ending FG).

Answer (B) is incorrect. The amount of $282,000 equals the total credits to WIP. Answer (C) is incorrect. The amount of $274,500 is the total of direct materials, direct labor, and applied overhead debited to WIP during the period. Answer (D) is incorrect. The amount of $372,000 is the sum of beginning FG and the total transferred from WIP.

2.4.20. The ending balance in work-in-process consists of jobs started this period. Overhead is 125% of direct labor, and the direct labor cost component of EWIP is $10,000. How much are EWIP, the direct materials cost component, and the manufacturing overhead component?

	Ending WIP	Materials	Overhead
A.	$52,500	$30,000	$12,500
B.	$45,000	$27,000	$8,000
C.	$45,000	$22,500	$12,500
D.	$57,500	$22,500	$8,000

Answer (C) is correct. *(Publisher, adapted)*

REQUIRED: The EWIP, direct materials cost, and manufacturing overhead.

DISCUSSION: EWIP is $45,000 ($52,500 BWIP + $72,000 DM + $90,000 DL + $112,500 applied OH – $282,000 total credits). Given that the direct labor component is $10,000, the overhead component must be $12,500 ($10,000 × 1.25), and the direct materials component must be $22,500 ($45,000 – $10,000 – $12,500).

Answer (A) is incorrect. The amount of $52,500 is the BWIP. The amount of $30,000 for materials is based on the assumption that EWIP is $52,500. Answer (B) is incorrect. The amount of $27,000 for direct materials is based on the assumption that overhead is $8,000. Answer (D) is incorrect. The amount of $57,500 equals EWIP ($45,000) plus overhead ($12,500). The amount of $8,000 multiplied by 125% equals $10,000 (direct labor).

2.4.21. Tillman Corporation uses a job costing system and has two production departments, M and A. Budgeted manufacturing costs for the year are

	Dept. M	Dept. A
Direct materials	$700,000	$100,000
Direct labor	200,000	800,000
Manufacturing overhead	600,000	400,000

The actual materials and labor costs charged to Job No. 432 during the year were as follows:

Direct materials		$25,000
Direct labor:		
Dept. M	$ 8,000	
Dept. A	12,000	20,000

Tillman applies manufacturing overhead to production orders on the basis of direct labor cost using separate departmental rates predetermined at the beginning of the year based on the annual budget. The total annual manufacturing costs associated with Job No. 432 should be

A. $50,000

B. $55,000

C. $65,000

D. $75,000

Answer (D) is correct. *(CPA, adapted)*

REQUIRED: The total manufacturing costs associated with a job if overhead is based on direct labor cost applied using departmental rates.

DISCUSSION: Total manufacturing costs consist of materials, labor, and overhead. Materials and labor are given; overhead rates are to be determined for each department. Departmental rates are calculated by dividing departmental manufacturing overhead by direct labor costs.

$$\text{Dept. M} = \frac{\$600{,}000}{\$200{,}000} = \$3 \text{ per } \$1 \text{ of DLC}$$

$$\text{Dept. A} = \frac{\$400{,}000}{\$800{,}000} = \$0.50 \text{ per } \$1 \text{ of DLC}$$

For Job No. 432:

Dept. M overhead	=	$3 × $8,000	=	$24,000
Dept. A overhead	=	$0.50 × $12,000	=	$ 6,000

Thus, total manufacturing costs for Job No. 432 equal $75,000 ($25,000 materials + $20,000 labor + $24,000 M overhead + $6,000 A overhead).

Answer (A) is incorrect. The amount of $50,000 omits materials costs. Answer (B) is incorrect. The amount of $55,000 results from applying a single departmental overhead rate of $0.50 per direct labor dollar. Answer (C) is incorrect. The amount of $65,000 results from applying a single departmental overhead rate of $1.00 per direct labor dollar [($600,000 + $400,000) total annual overhead ÷ ($200,000 + $800,000) total annual direct labor cost].

Question 2.4.22 is based on the following information. Paradise Company budgets on an annual basis for its fiscal year. The following beginning and ending inventory levels (in units) are planned for the fiscal year of July 1 through June 30:

	July 1	June 30
Direct material*	40,000	50,000
Work-in-process	10,000	20,000
Finished goods	80,000	50,000

* Two units of direct material are needed to produce each unit of finished product.

2.4.22. If 500,000 complete units were to be manufactured during the fiscal year by Paradise Company, the number of units of direct materials to be purchased is

A. 1,000,000 units.

B. 1,020,000 units.

C. 1,010,000 units.

D. 990,000 units.

Answer (C) is correct. *(CMA, adapted)*

REQUIRED: The number of units of materials to be purchased at a given production level.

DISCUSSION: The total materials needed for production will be 1,000,000 units (500,000 units × 2 units of materials). Because Paradise Company planned to have beginning direct materials inventory (July 1) of 40,000 units and ending direct materials inventory (June 30) of 50,000 units, materials inventory is expected to increase by 10,000 units. Thus, materials purchases will be 1,010,000 units.

Answer (A) is incorrect. The total needed for production is 1,000,000 units. Answer (B) is incorrect. The number of units in materials is not doubled. Answer (D) is incorrect. The number of 990,000 units is less than the amount used in production.

2.5 Journal Entries

2.5.1. The Herron Company has a gross payroll of $2,000 per day based on a normal 40-hour work-week. Withholdings for income taxes amount to $200 per day. Gross payroll consists of $1,200 direct labor, $400 indirect labor, $280 selling expenses, and $120 administrative expenses each day. Assuming the weekly payroll and employer payroll taxes payable (but not employees' withholdings) have already been accrued, what is the journal entry to record the payment of the weekly payroll?

A.

Accrued payroll	$5,000	
Cash		$5,000

B.

Accrued payroll	$10,000	
Cash		$8,330
Employees' income taxes payable		1,000
Employees' FICA taxes payable		670

C.

Accrued payroll	$10,000	
Cash		$8,330
Work-in-process		1,670

D.

Work-in-process	$6,000	
Manufacturing overhead	2,900	
Selling and administrative expense	2,000	
Accrued payroll		$10,000
Employer payroll taxes payable		900

Answer (B) is correct. *(Publisher, adapted)*

REQUIRED: The journal entry to record the payment of the weekly payroll.

DISCUSSION: (1) Accrued payroll should be debited for the balance in the account, (2) cash should be debited for the actual amount of cash disbursed, (3) employees' income taxes payable should be credited for the amount of taxes withheld from the employees' paychecks, and (4) employees' FICA taxes payable and other liabilities should be credited for the amount of FICA taxes and other items withheld from the employees' paychecks. Income taxes of $200 per day ($1,000 per week) should be withheld from the employees for income taxes payable. An amount also should be withheld for the employees' portion of FICA taxes. In this case, the assumption must be made that the amount is $670, although no basis for the calculation is given. Employees' FICA taxes payable should be recognized, and no other entry given will satisfy the requirement. But if the employee withholdings had been recognized as liabilities when the payroll was accrued, the entry would be to debit the payroll liability and credit cash for $8,330.

Answer (A) is incorrect. The amount of cash paid is $8,330 (not $5,000). Furthermore, employee taxes payable are not recorded. Answer (C) is incorrect. Employee tax withholding liabilities, not WIP, are credited. Answer (D) is incorrect. Debits to WIP, OH control, and expense accounts, with credits to various payables, record the payroll liability rather than its payment.

2.5.2. ABC Company estimates its total vacation costs for the year to be $360,000. Direct labor costs are $180,000 monthly, and indirect labor costs are $45,000. ABC has chosen to accrue vacation costs monthly instead of recognizing them as incurred. Select the journal entry to record payroll and accrue the estimated vacation costs for the month of January.

A.

Work-in-process	$180,000	
Manufacturing OH control	75,000	
Est. liability for vacation pay		$ 30,000
Accrued payroll		225,000

B.

Wage expense	$225,000	
Accrued payroll		$225,000

C.

Vacation expense	$300,000	
Accrued payroll		$300,000

D.

Work-in-process	$225,000	
Accrued payroll		$225,000

Answer (A) is correct. *(Publisher, adapted)*

REQUIRED: The journal entry to accrue estimated vacation costs for the month of January.

DISCUSSION: (1) Work-in-process should be debited for direct labor incurred, (2) manufacturing overhead control should be debited for indirect labor and estimated vacation costs [$45,000 + ($360,000 ÷ 12)], (3) estimated liability for vacation pay should be credited for 1/12 of the annual expected cost of $360,000, and (4) accrued payroll should be credited for the gross payroll (total due to employees including their deductions). The liability for vacation pay should be debited for any vacation pay taken. Total vacation costs for the year are estimated to be $360,000. The explanation assumes that the annual cost is divided by 12 to arrive at a monthly cost of $30,000. More sophisticated approaches are available, e.g., accruing vacation costs in proportion to total labor expense.

Answer (B) is incorrect. (1) Direct labor should be charged to WIP, (2) manufacturing OH control should be debited for indirect labor and estimated vacation costs, and (3) estimated liability for vacation pay should be credited for 1/12 of its annual expected cost. Answer (C) is incorrect. Direct labor and indirect labor should be charged to WIP and manufacturing OH control, respectively. A credit also should be made for the estimated liability for vacation pay, and accrued payroll should be credited for $225,000. Answer (D) is incorrect. WIP should be debited for direct labor, and manufacturing OH control should be debited for indirect labor and estimated vacation costs. Estimated liability for vacation pay and accrued payroll should be credited.

2.5.3. What is the journal entry for the purchase of $500 of direct materials and $250 of supplies for cash?

A.

Supplies and materials	$750	
Accounts payable		$750

B.

Work-in-process	$500	
Manufacturing overhead	250	
Accounts payable		$750

C.

Stores control	$750	
Cash		$750

D.

Work-in-process	$750	
Cash		$750

Answer (C) is correct. *(Publisher, adapted)*

REQUIRED: The journal entry for the cash purchase of materials and supplies.

DISCUSSION: The correct entry to record the purchase of materials and supplies is to debit the stores control account for the combined cost of the materials and supplies ($750) and to credit cash.

Answer (A) is incorrect. Cash, not a payable, is credited. Answer (B) is incorrect. The supplies and materials were purchased with cash. Also, the materials and supplies are not debited to WIP and manufacturing overhead, respectively, until they are used or transferred out of storage. Answer (D) is incorrect. Materials is charged to WIP only when put into production. Supplies are charged to overhead when used.

2.5.4. Ajax Candy Company has a gross payroll of $75,000 per month consisting of $65,000 of direct labor and $10,000 of indirect manufacturing labor. Assume that the tax rate on employers is .8% for federal unemployment, 1.55% for state unemployment, and 7.65% for Social Security benefits, a total payroll tax rate of 10%. What is the journal entry to accrue the monthly payroll and payroll taxes?

A.

Salary expense	$75,000	
Accrued wages		$75,000

B.

Salary expense	$82,500	
Accrued wages		$75,000
Accrued payroll tax		7,500

C.

Work-in-process	$65,000	
Manufacturing OH control	17,500	
Accrued payroll		$75,000
Employer payroll taxes payable		7,500

D.

Work-in-process	$7,500	
Accrued payroll taxes payable		$7,500

Answer (C) is correct. *(Publisher, adapted)*

REQUIRED: The journal entry to accrue payroll taxes.

DISCUSSION: (1) Work-in-process should be debited for the amount of direct labor costs, (2) manufacturing overhead should be debited for the amount of indirect labor costs plus the employer payroll tax ($10,000 + $7,500), (3) accrued payroll should be credited for the amount of total direct and indirect labor costs, and (4) employer's payroll taxes payable should be credited for the amount of the payroll tax (.10 × $75,000 = $7,500).

Answer (A) is incorrect. Payroll taxes are not considered, and payroll is not being charged to WIP (for direct labor costs) and manufacturing OH (for indirect labor costs). Answer (B) is incorrect. Payroll must be charged to WIP for direct labor costs and manufacturing OH for indirect labor costs. Answer (D) is incorrect. (1) WIP should be debited for the amount of direct labor costs, (2) manufacturing OH should be debited for the amount of indirect labor costs plus the employer payroll taxes, (3) accrued payroll should be credited for the amount of total direct and indirect labor costs, and (4) taxes payable should be credited for 10% of the total wages.

2.5.5. What is the journal entry to record Legal Corporation's payment of state unemployment taxes for $600 if the tax has been accrued?

A. State unemployment taxes payable	$600	
Cash		$600
B. State unemployment taxes payable	$600	
Accrued payroll		$600
C. Manufacturing overhead	$600	
State unemployment taxes payable		$600
D. Accrued payroll	$600	
Cash		$600

Answer (A) is correct. *(Publisher, adapted)*

REQUIRED: The journal entry to record payment of state unemployment taxes.

DISCUSSION: The correct journal entry to record the payment of accrued state unemployment taxes is to debit state unemployment taxes payable and credit cash for the amount of state unemployment taxes paid.

Answer (B) is incorrect. Cash is credited when a liability is paid. Answer (C) is incorrect. Debiting overhead and crediting a payable is the entry to accrue an expense, not record payment. Answer (D) is incorrect. The question indicates that a tax liability, not accrued payroll, had been credited.

2.5.6. If $200 of direct materials and $125 of supplies were issued to work-in-process, which of the following entries is correct?

A. Work-in-process	$325	
Materials		$200
Supplies		125
B. Work-in-process	$125	
Overhead control	200	
Materials		$200
Supplies		125
C. Work-in-process	$200	
Overhead control	125	
Stores control		$325
D. Materials and supplies	$325	
Stores control		$325

Answer (C) is correct. *(Publisher, adapted)*

REQUIRED: The entry to record the issuance of direct materials and supplies.

DISCUSSION: The cost of direct materials should be debited to the WIP account as the materials are used in the production of goods. The cost of supplies should be debited to manufacturing overhead control as the supplies are used because their use cannot be identified with particular products. The credit should be to stores control or, if used, separate direct materials and supplies accounts.

Answer (A) is incorrect. Supplies are charged to overhead as they are used. Answer (B) is incorrect. The overhead and WIP amounts are reversed. Answer (D) is incorrect. Direct materials and supplies transferred out of stores control are debited to WIP and overhead control, respectively.

2.5.7. If $29,000 of manufacturing overhead costs have been incurred and $25,000 of manufacturing overhead has been applied, which of the following entries closes the overhead accounts and prorates the underapplied overhead among the relevant accounts? (Of the $25,000 applied, $2,500 is still in EWIP, and $5,000 is still in finished goods as part of unsold inventory.)

A. Cost of goods sold	$ 1,333	
Finished goods	1,333	
Work-in-process	1,334	
Overhead control	25,000	
Overhead applied		$29,000
B. Cost of goods sold	$ 2,800	
Finished goods	800	
Work-in-process	400	
Overhead applied	25,000	
Overhead control		$29,000
C. Cost of goods sold	$ 2,000	
Finished goods	1,500	
Work-in-process	500	
Overhead applied	25,000	
Overhead summary		$29,000
D. Overhead applied	$29,000	
Overhead control		$25,000
Cost of goods sold		2,000
Finished goods		1,500
Work-in-process		500

Answer (B) is correct. *(Publisher, adapted)*

REQUIRED: The entry that closes the overhead accounts and prorates the underapplied overhead.

DISCUSSION: Overhead applied has a credit balance. Thus, the closing entry must include a debit to the account. The reverse is true of the control account. In this case, only 10% of the $25,000 overhead applied remains in the WIP account ($2,500 ÷ $25,000). Accordingly, 10% of the $4,000 of underapplied overhead should be charged to work-in-process ($4,000 × 10%). Finished goods contains 20% ($5,000 ÷ $25,000) of the already applied overhead. Accordingly, $800 ($4,000 × 20%) should be charged to finished goods. The remaining 70% of applied overhead has been charged to cost of goods sold. Thus, 70% of the underapplied overhead ($2,800) should be charged to cost of goods sold. Proration based on the amounts of applied overhead in the inventory accounts is preferable, but the assignment is sometimes made on a total cost basis.

Answer (A) is incorrect. The proration should be 70%, 20%, and 10%, respectively, not 33%, 33%, and 34%. Also, the credit should be to overhead control. Answer (C) is incorrect. The proration should be 70%, 20%, and 10%, respectively, not 50%, 37.5%, and 12.5%. Also, the credit should be to overhead control. Answer (D) is incorrect. The amounts are wrong, and the entry is reversed.

2.5.8. What is the correct journal entry if $5,000 of direct labor and $1,250 of indirect labor were incurred?

A. Work-in-process	$6,250	
Accrued payroll		$6,250
B. Work-in-process	$5,000	
Overhead control	1,250	
Accrued payroll		$6,250
C. Work-in-process	$6,250	
Overhead control	1,250	
Accrued payroll		$6,250
Applied overhead		1,250
D. Payroll expense	$6,250	
Accrued payable		$6,250

Answer (B) is correct. *(Publisher, adapted)*

REQUIRED: The journal entry to record the incurrence of direct and indirect labor.

DISCUSSION: The WIP account is debited for the $5,000 direct labor cost. The $1,250 of indirect labor is debited to manufacturing overhead control because the labor cannot be identified with a particular product. For example, general maintenance is a cost of production that cannot be allocated to specific products. The liability of $6,250 also must be recognized. Accounting for payroll taxes is assumed to be done when the payroll is paid by debiting accrued payroll and crediting cash and the employee withholding liabilities.

Answer (A) is incorrect. The indirect labor should be debited to overhead. Answer (C) is incorrect. Only $5,000 goes to WIP. The remaining $1,250 is debited to overhead. Answer (D) is incorrect. Manufacturing labor costs must be inventoried rather than expensed.

2.5.9. The completion of Job #21, with total costs of $4,900, results in which of the following entries?

A. Finished goods	$4,900	
Work-in-process		$4,900
B. Finished goods	$4,900	
Job #21		$4,900
C. Cost of goods available	$4,900	
Work-in-process		$4,900
D. Work-in-process	$4,900	
Finished goods		$4,900

Answer (A) is correct. *(Publisher, adapted)*

REQUIRED: The entry to record the completion of a job.

DISCUSSION: During production, all the labor, material, and overhead are charged to WIP. Upon completion, the account must be credited for the total cost of the job. Thus, WIP is credited and finished goods is debited for $4,900. Upon sale, the cost is transferred from finished goods to COGS.

Answer (B) is incorrect. In the general ledger, the credit is to WIP rather than a specific subsidiary account, although subsidiary ledgers or job-cost cards exist for the WIP and the FG accounts. Answer (C) is incorrect. The cost of goods available account does not exist. Cost of goods available for sale is the sum of beginning inventories plus purchases or COGM. Answer (D) is incorrect. Finished goods should be debited and WIP credited.

2.5.10. A company manufactures pipes and uses a job-order costing system. During May, the following jobs were started (no other jobs were in process) and the following costs were incurred:

	Job X	Job Y	Job Z	Total
Direct materials requisitioned	$10,000	$20,000	$15,000	$45,000
Direct labor	5,000	4,000	2,500	11,500
	$15,000	$24,000	$17,500	$56,500

In addition, manufacturing overhead of $300,000 and direct labor costs of $150,000 were estimated to be incurred during the year. Actual overhead of $24,000 was incurred in May; overhead is applied on the basis of direct labor dollars. If only Job X and Job Z were completed during the month, the appropriate entry to record the initiation of all jobs would be

A. Work-in-process	$79,500	
Direct materials		$45,000
Direct labor		11,500
Applied man. overhead		23,000
B. Work-in-process	$80,500	
Direct materials		$45,000
Direct labor		11,500
Manufacturing overhead		24,000
C. Work-in-process	$80,500	
Direct materials		$45,000
Direct labor		11,500
Applied man. overhead		24,000
D. Direct labor	$11,500	
Direct materials	45,000	
Work-in-process		$56,000

Answer (A) is correct. *(CIA, adapted)*

REQUIRED: The entry to record work-in-process for the month.

DISCUSSION: Work-in-process is debited for the direct materials, direct labor, and manufacturing overhead charged to jobs initiated during the month. Materials and labor are given as $45,000 and $11,500, respectively. Overhead applied is calculated by multiplying the predetermined rate by the activity base. The $2 rate ($300,000 ÷ $150,000) times the $11,500 activity base equals overhead applied (charged to WIP), or $23,000.

Answer (B) is incorrect. The incurrence of overhead is reflected by a debit to manufacturing overhead and credits to various accounts. Answer (C) is incorrect. The amount of overhead applied is $23,000, not $24,000. Answer (D) is incorrect. Direct materials, direct labor, and applied manufacturing overhead should be credited and WIP debited.

2.5.11. If the year's overhead costs incurred are $29,000, and $25,000 in costs have been applied to the product, what is the appropriate closing entry (assuming separate accounts and no proration)?

A.	Cost of goods sold	$ 4,000	
	Overhead applied	25,000	
	Overhead control		$29,000
B.	Overhead control	$25,000	
	Cost of goods sold	4,000	
	Overhead applied		$29,000
C.	Cost of goods sold	$29,000	
	Overhead applied		$29,000
D.	Work-in-process	$29,000	
	Overhead control		$29,000

Answer (A) is correct. *(Publisher, adapted)*

REQUIRED: The journal entry to close actual overhead and applied overhead without proration.

DISCUSSION: When separate overhead control and overhead applied accounts are used, all overhead incurred is charged to the overhead control account. As overhead is applied, it is credited to overhead applied. Accordingly, the entry to close these accounts is to debit the applied account and credit the control account. Given no proration, the difference is taken directly to COGS. Material differences should be prorated among the WIP, FG, and COGS accounts. The proration should be in proportion to the amount of the current period's overhead already applied to the accounts.

Answer (B) is incorrect. Overhead control should be credited. Answer (C) is incorrect. Overhead applied should not be closed in entirety to COGS. Answer (D) is incorrect. Debiting WIP and crediting overhead control is the correct entry to apply overhead for the entire period if overhead applied had been credited.

2.5.12. What is the journal entry to record the application of $500 of indirect labor when two overhead accounts are used?

A.	Job #21	$500	
	Overhead control		$500
B.	Work-in-process	$500	
	Overhead control		$500
C.	Payroll payable	$500	
	Overhead control (Job #21)		$500
D.	Work-in-process	$500	
	Overhead applied		$500

Answer (D) is correct. *(Publisher, adapted)*

REQUIRED: The journal entry to record the application of indirect labor.

DISCUSSION: Indirect labor is debited to overhead control when incurred. Applied overhead is debited in the general ledger to WIP, not to a specific subsidiary account. The credit is to overhead applied (or to overhead control when one overhead account is used).

Answer (A) is incorrect. The debit should be to a general ledger account, and the credit should be to overhead applied when two overhead accounts are used. Answer (B) is incorrect. The credit should be to overhead applied when two overhead accounts are used. Answer (C) is incorrect. The debit to payroll payable indicates payment of a liability, not the recognition of indirect labor expense. The credit should be to overhead applied when two overhead accounts are used.

STUDY UNIT THREE
ACTIVITY-BASED COSTING

Activity-based costing (ABC) is a response to the significant increase in the incurrence of indirect costs resulting from the rapid advance of technology. ABC is a refinement of traditional costing systems (job or process costing). These traditional (volume-based) systems involve (1) accumulating costs in general ledger accounts (utilities, taxes, etc.), (2) using a single cost pool to combine the costs in all the related accounts, (3) selecting a single driver to use for the entire indirect cost pool, and (4) allocating the indirect cost pool to final cost objects.

Activity-based systems involve (1) identifying organizational **activities** that constitute overhead, (2) assigning the **costs of resources** consumed by the activities, and (3) assigning the **costs of activities** to final cost objects.

Activities are classified in a hierarchy according to the level of the production process at which they occur: (1) **unit-level** activities, (2) **batch-level** activities, (3) **product-sustaining** (or service-sustaining) activities, and (4) **facility-sustaining** activities.

After identification of activities, the next step in implementing an ABC system is to assign the costs of resources to the activities (**first-stage** allocation). A separate accounting system may be necessary to track resource costs separately from the general ledger. After identification of resources, **resource drivers** are designated to allocate resource costs to the activity cost pools. Resource drivers are measures of the resources consumed by an activity.

The final step in implementing an ABC system is allocating the amounts in the activity cost pools to final cost objects **(second-stage allocation)**. Costs are reassigned to final-stage (or, if intermediate cost objects are used, next-stage) cost objects on the basis of activity drivers. **Activity drivers** are measures of the demands made on an activity by next-stage cost objects, such as the number of parts in a product used to measure an assembly activity.

A **cost object** may be a job, product, process, activity, service, or anything else for which a cost measure is desired. **Intermediate** cost objects temporarily accumulate costs as the cost pools move from their originating points to the final cost objects. For example, work-in-process is an intermediate cost object, and finished salable goods are final cost objects.

A difficulty in applying ABC is that, although the first three levels of activities pertain to specific products or services, facility-level activities do not. Thus, facility-level costs are not accurately assignable to products or services. The theoretically sound solution may be to treat these costs as **period costs**. Nevertheless, organizations that apply ABC ordinarily assign them to products or services to obtain a full-absorption cost suitable for external financial reporting in accordance with GAAP.

For a glossary of activity accounting terms developed by the Consortium for Advanced Management, International (CAM-I), see Appendix C.

CAM-I
6836 Bee Cave, Suite 256
Austin, TX 78746
www.cam-i.org

The approach of the CAM-I is more complex than that found in most cost/managerial accounting textbooks. It provides a coherent and comprehensive set of terms for ABC/M. However, readers should understand that textbook usage in this field is nonstandard. Accordingly, this book attempts to provide a sense of the range of terminology used in practice.

QUESTIONS

3.1 Activity-Based Costing (ABC)

3.1.1. Activity-based costing (ABC) has become increasingly more feasible because of technological advances that allow managers to obtain better and more timely information at a relatively low cost. For this reason, a manufacturer is considering using bar-code identification for recording information on parts used by the manufacturer. A reason to use bar codes rather than other means of identification is to ensure that

A. The movement of all parts is recorded.

B. The movement of parts is easily and quickly recorded.

C. Vendors use the same part numbers.

D. Vendors use the same identification methods.

Answer (B) is correct. *(CIA, adapted)*

REQUIRED: The reason to use bar codes.

DISCUSSION: Bar-code scanning is a form of optical character recognition. Bar codes are a series of bars of different widths that represent critical information about the item. They can be read and the information can be recorded instantly using a scanner. Thus, bar coding records the movement of parts with minimal labor costs.

Answer (A) is incorrect. Any identification method may fail to record the movement of some parts. Answer (C) is incorrect. Each vendor has its own part-numbering scheme. Answer (D) is incorrect. Each vendor has its own identification method, although vendors in the same industry often cooperate to minimize the number of bar-code systems they use.

3.1.2. Which of the following is true about activity-based costing?

A. It should not be used with process or job costing.

B. It can be used only with process costing.

C. It can be used only with job costing.

D. It can be used with either process or job costing.

Answer (D) is correct. *(CPA, adapted)*

REQUIRED: The true statement about ABC.

DISCUSSION: Activity-based costing may be used by manufacturing, service, or retailing entities and in job or process costing systems.

Answer (A) is incorrect. Activity-based costing may be used with either process or job costing. Answer (B) is incorrect. Activity-based costing may be used with either process or job costing. Answer (C) is incorrect. Activity-based costing may be used with either process or job costing.

3.1.3. Unlike the traditional full-absorption cost system, activity-based costing (ABC) assigns

A. Costs to individual products based only on nonfinancial variables.

B. Costs to individual projects based on various activities involved.

C. Overhead to individual products based on some common measure of production volume.

D. Only costs that can be directly traced to individual products.

Answer (B) is correct. *(CIA, adapted)*

REQUIRED: The nature of ABC.

DISCUSSION: ABC determines the activities that relate to the incurrence of costs. First-stage allocation assigns the costs of resources to activity cost pools using resource drivers (causes of resource consumption by activities). Second-stage allocation then assigns the accumulated costs to cost objects on the basis of activity drivers (measures of demands on activities by next-stage cost objects).

Answer (A) is incorrect. Both financial and nonfinancial cost drivers are used in ABC. Answer (C) is incorrect. Traditional full-absorption costing assigns overhead to individual products based on some common measure of production volume. Answer (D) is incorrect. Both traditional full-absorption costing and ABC assign indirect costs to products.

3.1.4. Multiple or departmental overhead rates are considered preferable to a single or plantwide overhead rate when

A. Manufacturing is limited to a single product flowing through identical departments in a fixed sequence.

B. Various products are manufactured that do not pass through the same departments or use the same manufacturing techniques.

C. Cost drivers, such as direct labor, are the same over all processes.

D. Individual cost drivers cannot accurately be determined with respect to cause-and-effect relationships.

Answer (B) is correct. *(CMA, adapted)*

REQUIRED: The situation in which multiple or departmental overhead rates are considered preferable.

DISCUSSION: Multiple rates are appropriate when a process differs substantially among departments or when products do not go through all departments or all processes. The trend in cost accounting is toward activity-based costing, which divides production into numerous activities and identifies the cost driver(s) most relevant to each. The result is a more accurate tracing of costs.

Answer (A) is incorrect. One rate may be cost beneficial when a single product proceeds through homogeneous processes. Answer (C) is incorrect. If cost drivers are the same for all processes, multiple rates are unnecessary. Answer (D) is incorrect. Individual cost drivers for all relationships must be known to use multiple application rates.

3.1.5. Process value analysis is a key component of activity-based management that links product costing and

A. Reduction of the number of cost pools.

B. Continuous improvement.

C. Accumulation of heterogeneous cost pools.

D. Overhead rates based on broad averages.

Answer (B) is correct. *(Publisher, adapted)*

REQUIRED: The element of process value analysis.

DISCUSSION: Design of an ABC system starts with process value analysis, a comprehensive understanding of how an organization generates its output. It involves a determination of which activities that use resources are value-adding or nonvalue-adding and how the latter may be reduced or eliminated. This linkage of product costing and continuous improvement of processes is activity-based management (ABM). It encompasses driver analysis, activity analysis, and performance measurement.

Answer (A) is incorrect. ABC tends to increase the number of cost pools and drivers used. Answer (C) is incorrect. ABC's philosophy is to accumulate homogeneous cost pools. Thus, the cost elements in a pool should be consumed by cost objects in proportion to the same driver. Homogenizing cost pools minimizes broad averaging of costs that have different drivers. Answer (D) is incorrect. ABC's philosophy is to accumulate homogeneous cost pools. Thus, the cost elements in a pool should be consumed by cost objects in proportion to the same driver. Homogenizing cost pools minimizes broad averaging of costs that have different drivers.

3.1.6. A basic assumption of activity-based costing (ABC) is that

A. All manufacturing costs vary directly with units of production.

B. Products or services require the performance of activities, and activities consume resources.

C. Only costs that respond to unit-level drivers are product costs.

D. Only variable costs are included in activity cost pools.

Answer (B) is correct. *(CPA, adapted)*

REQUIRED: The basic assumption of ABC.

DISCUSSION: ABC identifies activities needed to provide products or services, assigns costs to those activities, and then reassigns costs to the products or services based on their consumption of activities. ABC helps to manage costs by providing more detailed analyses of costs than traditional methods. It also facilitates cost reduction by determining what activities do and do not add value to the product or service.

Answer (A) is incorrect. ABC does not assume that units produced is a cost driver for all manufacturing costs. Answer (C) is incorrect. Activities and their drivers may be classified as unit-level, batch-level, product-level, and facility-level. The first three levels pertain to specific products or services. Thus, costs at these levels are accurately assignable to those products or services. Furthermore, although facility-level activities do not pertain to specific products or services, organizations that apply ABC customarily assign them to products or services to obtain a full-absorption cost suitable for external financial reporting in accordance with GAAP. Answer (D) is incorrect. ABC recognizes that some fixed costs are product costs.

3.1.7. Because of changes that are occurring in the basic operations of many firms, all of the following represent trends in the way indirect costs are allocated except

A. Treating direct labor as an indirect manufacturing cost in an automated factory.

B. Using throughput time as an application base to increase awareness of the costs associated with lengthened throughput time.

C. Preferring plant-wide application rates that are applied to machine hours rather than incurring the cost of detailed allocations.

D. Using several machine cost pools to measure product costs on the basis of time in a machine center.

Answer (C) is correct. *(CMA, adapted)*

REQUIRED: The item not a trend in the way indirect costs are being allocated.

DISCUSSION: With the automation of factories and the corresponding emphasis on activity-based costing (ABC), companies are finding new ways of allocating indirect factory overhead. One change is that plant-wide application rates are being used less often because a closer matching of costs with cost drivers provides better information to management. ABC results in a more accurate application of indirect costs because it provides more refined data. Instead of a single cost goal for a process, a department, or even an entire plant, an indirect cost pool is established for each identified activity. The related cost driver, the factor that changes the cost of the activity, also is identified.

Answer (A) is incorrect. Computerization has decreased the amount of direct labor to the point that some companies are treating direct labor as an indirect factory overhead cost. Answer (B) is incorrect. Throughput time (the rate of production over a stated time), clearly drives (influences) costs. Answer (D) is incorrect. Multiple cost pools are preferable. They permit a better matching of indirect costs with cost drivers.

Questions 3.1.8 through 3.1.10 are based on the following information. A company has identified the following overhead costs and cost drivers for the coming year:

Overhead Item	Cost Driver	Budgeted Cost	Budgeted Activity Level
Machine setup	Number of setups	$ 20,000	200
Inspection	Number of inspections	130,000	6,500
Material handling	Number of material moves	80,000	8,000
Engineering	Engineering hours	50,000	1,000
Total		$280,000	

The following information was collected on three jobs that were completed during the year:

	Job 101	Job 102	Job 103
Direct materials	$5,000	$12,000	$8,000
Direct labor	$2,000	$ 2,000	$4,000
Units completed	100	50	200
Number of setups	1	2	4
Number of inspections	20	10	30
Number of material moves	30	10	50
Engineering hours	10	50	10

Budgeted direct labor cost was $100,000, and budgeted direct material cost was $280,000.

3.1.8. If the company uses activity-based costing, compute the cost of each unit of Job 102.

A. $340

B. $392

C. $440

D. $520

Answer (A) is correct. *(CIA, adapted)*

REQUIRED: The cost per unit of Job 102 under ABC.

DISCUSSION: The overhead costs for the activities are $100 per setup, $20 per inspection, $10 per material move, and $50 per engineering hour. Setups, inspections, material moves, and engineering hours are the respective activity cost drivers. Thus, overhead assigned to Job 102 is $3,000 [(2 setups × $100) + (10 inspections × $20) + (10 material moves × $10) + (50 engineering hours × $50)]. The production cost of Job 102 is $17,000 ($12,000 DM + $2,000 DL + $3,000 OH), and the cost per unit is $340 ($17,000 ÷ 50).

Answer (B) is incorrect. The amount of $392 assumes overhead is assigned based on direct labor cost. Answer (C) is incorrect. The amount of $440 assumes overhead assigned is $8,000. Answer (D) is incorrect. The amount of $520 assumes overhead is assigned based on direct materials cost.

3.1.9. If the company uses activity-based costing, how much overhead cost should be assigned to Job 101?

A. $1,300

B. $2,000

C. $5,000

D. $5,600

Answer (A) is correct. *(CIA, adapted)*

REQUIRED: The overhead assigned to Job 101 under activity-based costing (ABC).

DISCUSSION: ABC assigns overhead costs more precisely than traditional methods. It identifies the activities associated with the incurrence of costs, determines each activity cost driver, and assigns cost accordingly. The overhead costs for the activities are $100 per setup, $20 per inspection, $10 per material move, and $50 per engineering hour. The overhead assigned to Job 101 is therefore $1,300 [(1 setup × $100) + (20 inspections × $20) + (30 material moves × $10) + (10 engineering hours × $50)].

Answer (B) is incorrect. The amount of $2,000 equals the overhead assigned to Job 103. Answer (C) is incorrect. The amount of $5,000 equals the assigned overhead using direct materials cost as a base. Answer (D) is incorrect. The amount of $5,600 equals 2% ($2,000 DL cost ÷ $100,000 budgeted annual DL cost) of budgeted overhead.

3.1.10. The company prices its products at 140% of cost. If the company uses activity-based costing, the price of each unit of Job 103 would be

A. $98

B. $100

C. $116

D. $140

Answer (A) is correct. *(CIA, adapted)*

REQUIRED: The price to charge per unit of Job 103.

DISCUSSION: The costs per job for the activities are $100 per setup, $20 per inspection, $10 per material move, and $50 per engineering hour. Setups, inspections, material moves, and engineering hours are the respective activity cost drivers. Overhead assigned to Job 103 is $2,000 [(4 setups × $100) + (30 inspections × $20) + (50 material moves × $10) + (10 engineering hours × $50)]. Thus, the production cost of Job 103 is $14,000 ($8,000 DM + $4,000 DL + $2,000 OH), the cost per unit is $70 ($14,000 ÷ 200), and the price is $98 ($70 × 140%).

Answer (B) is incorrect. The amount of $100 is the unit cost if overhead is assigned based on direct materials cost. Answer (C) is incorrect. The amount of $116 is the unit cost if overhead is assigned based on direct labor cost. Answer (D) is incorrect. The amount of $140 assumes cost is $100.

3.1.11. A cosmetics manufacturer has used a traditional cost accounting system to apply quality control costs uniformly to all products at a rate of 14.5% of direct labor cost. Monthly direct labor cost for makeup is $27,500. In an attempt to distribute quality control costs more equitably, the manufacturer is considering activity-based costing. The monthly data shown in the chart below have been gathered for makeup.

Activity	Cost Driver	Cost Rates	Quantity of Makeup
Incoming material inspection	Type of material	$11.50 per type	12 types
In-process inspection	Number of units	$0.14 per unit	17,500 units
Product certification	Per order	$77 per order	25 orders

The monthly quality control cost assigned to makeup using activity-based costing (ABC) is

A. $88.64 per order.

B. $525.50 lower than the cost using the traditional system.

C. $8,500.50

D. $525.50 higher than the cost using the traditional system.

Answer (D) is correct. *(CMA, adapted)*

REQUIRED: The monthly quality control cost assigned using activity-based costing.

DISCUSSION: ABC identifies the causal relationship between the incurrence of cost and activities, determines the drivers of the activities, establishes cost pools related to the drivers and activities, and assigns costs to ultimate cost objects on the basis of the demands (resources or drivers consumed) placed on the activities by those cost objects. Hence, ABC assigns overhead costs based on multiple allocation bases or cost drivers. Under the traditional, single-base system, the amount allocated is $3,987.50 ($27,500 × 14.5%). Under ABC, the amount allocated is $4,513 [(12 × $11.50) + (17,500 × $.14) + (25 × $77)], or $525.50 more than under the traditional system.

Answer (A) is incorrect. The ABC assignment of $4,513 is at a rate of $180.52 for each of the 25 orders. Answer (B) is incorrect. ABC yields a higher allocation. Answer (C) is incorrect. The total is $4,513 on the ABC basis.

3.1.12. Gram Co. develops computer programs to meet customers' special requirements. How should Gram categorize payments to employees who develop these programs?

	Direct Costs	Value-Adding Costs
A.	Yes	Yes
B.	Yes	No
C.	No	No
D.	No	Yes

Answer (A) is correct. *(CPA, adapted)*

REQUIRED: The proper categorization of costs.

DISCUSSION: Direct costs may be defined as those that can be specifically associated with a single cost object and can be assigned to it in an economically feasible manner. Wages paid to labor that can be identified with a specific finished good are direct costs. Value-adding costs may be defined as the costs of activities that cannot be eliminated without reducing the quality, responsiveness, or quantity of the output required by a customer or by an organization. Hopefully, the amounts paid to programmers add value to computer programs.

Answer (B) is incorrect. The activities performed by programmers add value to computer programs. Thus, the payments to employees who develop these programs are considered value-adding costs. Answer (C) is incorrect. Payments to programmers are both direct costs and value-adding costs of computer programs. Answer (D) is incorrect. Wages paid to labor that can be identified with a specific finished good are direct costs. Accordingly, payments to employees who develop computer programs are direct costs.

Questions 3.1.13 and 3.1.14 are based on the following information.

Zeta Company is preparing its annual profit plan. As part of its analysis of the profitability of individual products, the controller estimates the amount of overhead that should be allocated to the individual product lines from the information given in the next column:

	Wall Mirrors	Specialty Windows
Units produced	25	25
Material moves per product line	5	15
Direct labor hours per unit	200	200
Budgeted materials handling costs		$50,000

3.1.13. Under a costing system that allocates overhead on the basis of direct labor hours, Zeta Company's materials handling costs allocated to one unit of wall mirrors would be

A. $1,000

B. $500

C. $2,000

D. $5,000

Answer (A) is correct. *(CMA, adapted)*

REQUIRED: The amount of materials handling costs allocated to one unit of wall mirrors when direct labor hours is the activity base.

DISCUSSION: If direct labor hours are used as the allocation base, the $50,000 of costs is allocated over 400 hours of direct labor. Multiplying the 25 units of each product times 200 hours results in 5,000 labor hours for each product, or a total of 10,000 hours. Dividing $50,000 by 10,000 hours results in a cost of $5 per direct labor hour. Multiplying 200 hours times $5 results in an allocation of $1,000 of overhead per unit of product.

Answer (B) is incorrect. The amount of $500 is the allocation based on number of material moves. Answer (C) is incorrect. The amount of $2,000 assumes that all the overhead is allocated to the wall mirrors. Answer (D) is incorrect. The amount of $5,000 assumes overhead of $250,000.

3.1.14. Under activity-based costing (ABC), Zeta's materials handling costs allocated to one unit of wall mirrors would be

A. $1,000

B. $500

C. $1,500

D. $2,500

Answer (B) is correct. *(CMA, adapted)*

REQUIRED: The amount of materials handling costs allocated to one unit of wall mirrors under ABC.

DISCUSSION: An activity-based costing (ABC) system allocates overhead costs on the basis of some causal relationship between the incurrence of cost and activities. Because the moves for wall mirrors constitute 25% (5 ÷ 20) of total moves, the mirrors should absorb 25% of the total materials handling costs. Thus, $12,500 ($50,000 × 25%) is allocated to mirrors. The remaining $37,500 is allocated to specialty windows. Dividing the $12,500 by 25 units produces a cost of $500 per unit of mirrors.

Answer (A) is incorrect. The amount of $1,000 uses direct labor as the allocation basis. Answer (C) is incorrect. The amount of $1,500 is the allocation per unit of specialty windows. Answer (D) is incorrect. The amount of $2,500 is not based on the number of material moves.

3.1.15. Factory Company makes two products, X and Z. X is being introduced this period, and Z has been in production for 2 years. For the period about to begin, 1,000 units of each product are to be manufactured. Assume that the only relevant overhead item is the cost of engineering change orders; that X and Z are expected to require eight and two change orders, respectively; that X and Z are expected to require 2 and 3 machine hours, respectively; and that the cost of a change order is $600. If Factory applies engineering change order costs on the basis of machine hours, the cross-subsidy per unit arising from this peanut-butter costing approach is

A. $1.20

B. $2.40

C. $3.60

D. $4.80

Answer (B) is correct. *(Publisher, adapted)*

REQUIRED: The cross-subsidy per unit.

DISCUSSION: The inaccurate averaging or spreading of indirect costs over products or service units that use different amounts of resources is called peanut-butter costing. Peanut-butter costing results in product-cost cross-subsidization, the condition in which the miscosting of one product causes the miscosting of other products. The total change order cost is $6,000 [(8 + 2) × $600], the cost per machine hour is $1.20 {$6,000 ÷ [(2 hours × 1,000 units) + (3 hours × 1,000 units)]}. The unit costs assigned X and Z are

	X	Z
Unit costs assigned on machine-hour basis	$2.40 ($1.20 × 2 hours)	$3.60 ($1.20 × 3 hours)
Unit costs assigned directly on charge-order basis	$4.80 [(8 orders × $600) ÷ 1,000 units]	$1.20 [(2 orders × $600) ÷ 1,000 units]

Thus, the unit amount by which machine-hour-based assignment overcosts Z and undercosts X (the cross-subsidy) is $2.40 ($3.60 – $1.20 or $4.80 – $2.40).

Answer (A) is incorrect. The unit cost per machine hour or the unit cost directly attributable to Z is $1.20. Answer (C) is incorrect. The unit cost assigned to Z on the machine-hour basis is $3.60. Answer (D) is incorrect. The unit cost assigned to X on a direct-tracing basis is $4.80.

Questions 3.1.16 and 3.1.17 are based on the following information.

Believing that its traditional cost system may be providing misleading information, Farragut Manufacturing is considering an activity-based costing (ABC) approach. It now employs a traditional cost system and has been applying its manufacturing overhead on the basis of machine hours.

Farragut plans on using 50,000 direct labor hours and 30,000 machine hours in the coming year. The following data show the manufacturing overhead that is budgeted.

Activity	Cost Driver	Budgeted Activity	Budgeted Cost
Material handling	No. of parts handled	6,000,000	$ 720,000
Setup costs	No. of setups	750	315,000
Machining costs	Machine hours	30,000	540,000
Quality control	No. of batches	500	225,000
Total manufacturing overhead cost:			$1,800,000

Cost, sales, and production data for one of Farragut's products for the coming year are as follows:

Prime costs:	
Direct material cost per unit	$4.40
Direct labor cost per unit .05 DLH @ $15.00/DLH	.75
Total prime cost	$5.15
Sales and production data:	
Expected sales	20,000 units
Batch size	5,000 units
Setups	2 per batch
Total parts per finished unit	5 parts
Machine hours required	80 MH per batch

3.1.16. If Farragut uses the traditional cost system, the cost per unit for this product for the coming year would be

A. $5.39

B. $5.44

C. $6.11

D. $6.95

Answer (C) is correct. *(CIA, adapted)*

REQUIRED: The unit cost under traditional costing.

DISCUSSION: Given that manufacturing overhead is applied on the basis of machine hours, the overhead rate is $60 per hour ($1,800,000 ÷ 30,000) or $.96 per unit [(80 machine hours per batch × $60) ÷ 5,000 units per batch]. Accordingly, the unit full cost is $6.11 ($5.15 unit prime cost + $.96).

Answer (A) is incorrect. The amount of $5.39 assumes that 80 machine hours are required for the total production of 20,000 units. Answer (B) is incorrect. The amount of $5.44 is based on the machining overhead rate ($18). Answer (D) is incorrect. The amount of $6.95 is based on the direct labor hour manufacturing overhead rate.

3.1.17. If Farragut employs an activity-based costing system, the cost per unit for the product described for the coming year would be

A. $6.00

B. $6.08

C. $6.21

D. $6.30

Answer (D) is correct. *(CIA, adapted)*

REQUIRED: The unit cost under the ABC system.

DISCUSSION: Materials handling cost per part is $.12 ($720,000 ÷ 6,000,000), cost per setup is $420 ($315,000 ÷ 750), machining cost per hour is $18 ($540,000 ÷ 30,000), and quality cost per batch is $450 ($225,000 ÷ 500). Hence, total manufacturing overhead applied is $22,920 [(5 parts per unit × 20,000 units × $.12) + (4 batches × 2 setups per batch × $420) + (4 batches × 80 machine hours per batch × $18) + (4 batches × $450)]. The total unit cost is $6.296 [$5.15 prime cost + ($22,920 ÷ 20,000 units) overhead].

Answer (A) is incorrect. The amount of $6.00 assumes one setup per batch and 80 total machine hours. Answer (B) is incorrect. The amount of $6.08 assumes that only 80 machine hours were used. Answer (C) is incorrect. The amount of $6.21 assumes one setup per batch.

Questions 3.1.18 through 3.1.21 are based on the following information.

Alaire Corporation manufactures several different types of printed circuit boards; however, two of the boards account for the majority of the company's sales. The first of these boards, a television (TV) circuit board, has been a standard in the industry for several years. The market for this type of board is competitive and therefore price-sensitive. Alaire plans to sell 65,000 of the TV boards next year at a price of $150 per unit. The second high-volume product, a personal computer (PC) circuit board, is a recent addition to Alaire's product line. Because the PC board incorporates the latest technology, it can be sold at a premium price; plans include the sale of 40,000 PC boards at $300 per unit.

Alaire's management group is meeting to discuss strategies, and the current topic of conversation is how to spend the sales and promotion dollars for next year. The sales manager believes that the market share for the TV board could be expanded by concentrating Alaire's promotional efforts in this area. In response to this suggestion, the production manager said, "Why don't you go after a bigger market for the PC board? The cost sheets that I get show that the contribution from the PC board is more than double the contribution from the TV board. I know we get a premium price for the PC board; selling it should help overall profitability."

Alaire uses a standard cost system, and the following data apply to the TV and PC boards:

	TV Board	PC Board
Direct materials	$80	$140
Direct labor	1.5 hours	4 hours
Machine time	.5 hours	1.5 hours

Variable factory overhead is applied on the basis of direct labor hours. For next year, variable factory overhead is budgeted at $1,120,000, and direct labor hours are estimated at 280,000. The hourly rates for machine time and direct labor are $10 and $14, respectively. Alaire applies a materials handling charge at 10% of materials cost; this materials handling charge is not included in variable factory overhead. Total expenditures for materials are budgeted at $10,600,000.

Ed Welch, Alaire's controller, believes that, before the management group proceeds with the discussion about allocating sales and promotional dollars to individual products, they should consider the activities involved in their production. As Welch explained to the group, "Activity-based costing integrates the cost of all activities, known as cost drivers, into individual product costs rather than including these costs in overhead pools." Welch has prepared the schedule shown below to help the management group understand this concept.

"Using this information," Welch explained, "we can calculate an activity-based cost for each TV board and each PC board and then compare it with the standard cost we have been using. The only cost that remains the same for both cost methods is the cost of direct materials. The cost drivers will replace the direct labor, machine time, and overhead costs in the standard cost."

Budgeted Cost		Cost Driver	Annual Activity for Cost Driver
Materials overhead:			
Procurement	$ 400,000	Number of parts	4,000,000 parts
Production scheduling	220,000	Number of boards	110,000 boards
Packaging and shipping	440,000	Number of boards	110,000 boards
	$1,060,000		
Variable overhead:			
Machine setup	$ 446,000	Number of setups	278,750 setups
Hazardous waste disposal	48,000	Pounds of waste	16,000 pounds
Quality control	560,000	Number of inspections	160,000 inspections
General supplies	66,000	Number of boards	110,000 boards
	$1,120,000		
Manufacturing:			
Machine insertion	$1,200,000	Number of parts	3,000,000 parts
Manual insertion	4,000,000	Number of parts	1,000,000 parts
Wave soldering	132,000	Number of boards	110,000 boards
	$5,332,000		

Required per unit	TV Board	PC Board
Parts	25	55
Machine insertions	24	35
Manual insertions	1	20
Machine setups	2	3
Hazardous waste	.02 lb.	.35 lb.
Inspections	1	2

3.1.18. On the basis of standard costs, the total contribution budgeted for the TV board is

A. $1,950,000

B. $2,275,000

C. $2,340,000

D. $2,470,000

Answer (A) is correct. *(Publisher, adapted)*

REQUIRED: The total contribution budgeted for the TV board on a standard cost basis.

DISCUSSION: As calculated below, the budgeted standard unit cost of a TV board is $120. This amount includes $6 of variable overhead [1.5 DLH × ($1,120,000 total VOH ÷ 280,000 DLH)]. Given a unit price of $150, the unit contribution margin is therefore $30. Total budgeted contribution is $1,950,000 (65,000 budgeted units × $30 UCM).

Direct materials	$ 80
DM handling (10% × $80)	8
Direct labor (1.5 hr. × $14)	21
Machine time (.5 hr. × $10)	5
Variable overhead (1.5 hr. × $4)	6
Budgeted unit cost	$120

Answer (B) is incorrect. The amount of $2,275,000 excludes the cost of machine time (65,000 units × $5 = $325,000). Answer (C) is incorrect. The amount of $2,340,000 excludes the variable overhead (65,000 units × $6 = $390,000). Answer (D) is incorrect. The amount of $2,470,000 excludes the direct materials handling cost (65,000 units × $8 = $520,000).

3.1.19. On the basis of activity-based costing (ABC), the total contribution budgeted for the TV board is

A. $1,594,000

B. $1,950,000

C. $2,037,100

D. $2,557,100

Answer (D) is correct. *(Publisher, adapted)*

REQUIRED: The total contribution budgeted for the TV board on an ABC basis.

DISCUSSION: As calculated below, the budgeted activity-based unit cost of a TV board is $110.66. Given a unit price of $150, the unit contribution margin is $39.34. Total budgeted contribution is $2,557,100 (65,000 budgeted units × $39.34 UCM).

Direct materials	$ 80.00
Procurement [25 parts × ($400,000 ÷ 4,000,000 parts)]	2.50
Scheduling ($220,000 ÷ 110,000 boards)	2.00
Packaging and shipping ($440,000 ÷ 110,000 boards)	4.00
Setups [($446,000 ÷ 278,750 setups) × 2 setups]	3.20
Waste disposal [($48,000 ÷ 16,000 lb.) × .02]	.06
Quality control ($560,000 ÷ 160,000 inspections)	3.50
General supplies ($66,000 ÷ 110,000 boards)	.60
Machine insertion [24 parts × (1,200,000 ÷ 3,000,000 parts)]	9.60
Manual insertion ($4,000,000 ÷ 1,000,000 parts)	4.00
Soldering ($132,000 ÷ 110,000 boards)	1.20
Budgeted ABC unit cost	$110.66

Answer (A) is incorrect. The amount of $1,594,000 is the CM for the PC board based on an ABC calculation. Answer (B) is incorrect. The amount of $1,950,000 is the CM for the TV board based on a standard-cost calculation. Answer (C) is incorrect. The amount of $2,037,100 erroneously includes $8 per board for materials handling (65,000 units × $8 = $520,000).

3.1.20. Refer to the information on the preceding page(s). On the basis of standard costs, the total contribution budgeted for the PC board is

A. $3,000,000

B. $2,960,000

C. $2,920,000

D. $2,360,000

Answer (D) is correct. *(Publisher, adapted)*

REQUIRED: The total contribution budgeted for the PC board on a standard cost basis.

DISCUSSION: As calculated below, the budgeted standard unit cost of a PC board is $241. This amount includes $16 of variable overhead [4 DLH × ($1,120,000 total VOH ÷ 280,000 DLH)]. Given a unit price of $300, the unit contribution margin is $59. Consequently, total budgeted contribution is $2,360,000 ($59 × 40,000 units).

Direct materials	$140
DM handling (10% × $140)	14
Direct labor (4 hr. × $14)	56
Machine time (1.5 hr. × $10)	15
Variable overhead (4 hr. × $4)	16
Budgeted unit cost	$241

Answer (A) is incorrect. The amount of $3,000,000 excludes the variable overhead (40,000 units × $16 = $640,000). Answer (B) is incorrect. The amount of $2,960,000 excludes the cost of machine time (40,000 units × $15 = $600,000). Answer (C) is incorrect. The amount of $2,920,000 excludes the direct materials handling cost (40,000 units × $14 = $560,000).

3.1.21. Refer to the information on the preceding page(s). On the basis of activity-based costs, the total contribution budgeted for the PC board is

A. $1,594,000

B. $1,950,000

C. $2,360,000

D. $2,557,100

Answer (A) is correct. *(Publisher, adapted)*

REQUIRED: The total contribution budgeted for the PC board on an ABC basis.

DISCUSSION: As calculated below, the budgeted activity-based unit cost of a PC board is $260.15. Given a unit price of $300, the unit contribution margin is $39.85. Total budgeted contribution is $1,594,000 (40,000 units × $39.85 UCM).

Direct materials	$140.00
Procurement [55 parts × ($400,000 ÷ 4,000,000 parts)]	5.50
Scheduling ($220,000 ÷ 110,000 boards)	2.00
Packaging and shipping ($440,000 ÷110,000 boards)	4.00
Setups [($446,000 ÷ 278,750 setups) × 3 setups]	4.80
Waste disposal [$48,000 ÷ 16,000 lb.) × .35]	1.05
Quality control [($560,000 ÷ 160,000 inspections) × 2]	7.00
General supplies ($66,000 ÷ 110,000 boards)	.60
Machine insertions [35 × ($1,200,000 ÷ 3,000,000 parts)]	14.00
Manual insertions [20 × ($4,000,000 ÷ 1,000,000 parts)]	80.00
Soldering ($132,000 ÷ 110,000 boards)	1.20
Budgeted ABC unit cost	$260.15

Answer (B) is incorrect. The amount of $1,950,000 is the CM for the TV board based on a standard-cost calculation. Answer (C) is incorrect. The amount of $2,360,000 is the CM for the PC board based on a standard-cost calculation. Answer (D) is incorrect. The amount of $2,557,100 is the CM for the TV board based on an ABC calculation.

3.1.22. In an activity-based costing (ABC) system, cost reduction is accomplished by identifying and eliminating

	All Cost Drivers	Nonvalue-Adding Activities
A.	No	No
B.	Yes	Yes
C.	No	Yes
D.	Yes	No

Answer (C) is correct. *(CPA, adapted)*

REQUIRED: The means of reducing costs in ABC.

DISCUSSION: An ABC system determines activities associated with the incurrence of costs and then accumulates a cost pool for each activity. It then identifies the driver(s) used to trace those costs to such cost objects as products or services. A driver is a factor that causes a change in a cost. Activities that do not add customer value are identified and eliminated to the extent possible. A clear understanding of what causes a cost (the driver) helps eliminate the nonvalue-adding activities. However, all drivers cannot be eliminated.

3.1.23. An assisted-living facility provides services in the form of residential space, meals, and other occupant assistance (OOA) to its occupants. The facility currently uses a traditional cost accounting system that charges each occupant a daily rate equal to the facility's annual cost of providing residential space, meals, and OOA divided by total occupant days. However, an activity-based costing (ABC) analysis has revealed that occupants' use of OOA varies substantially. This analysis determined that occupants could be grouped into three categories (low, moderate, and high usage of OOA) and that the activity driver of OOA should be nursing hours. The driver of the residential space and meals is occupant days. The following quantitative information was also provided:

Occupant Category	Annual Occupant Days	Annual Nursing Hours
Low usage	36,000	90,000
Medium usage	18,000	90,000
High usage	6,000	120,000
	60,000	300,000

The total annual cost of OOA was $7.5 million, and the total annual cost of providing residential space and meals was $7.2 million. Accordingly, the ABC analysis indicates that the daily costing rate for providing residential space, meals, and OOA should be

A. $182.50 for occupants in the low-usage category.

B. $145.00 for occupants in the medium-usage category.

C. $245.00 for occupants in the high-usage category.

D. $620.00 for all occupants.

Answer (A) is correct. *(Publisher, adapted)*

REQUIRED: The true statement about daily costing rates based on an ABC analysis.

DISCUSSION: This service organization produces three "products" (the three occupant categories), and the "units produced" equal occupant days. According to the ABC analysis, production involves two activities: (1) provision of residential space and meals and (2) OOA. The drivers of these activities are occupant days and nursing hours, respectively. Thus, the cost pool rate for the first activity (residential space and meals) is $120 per occupant day ($7,200,000 ÷ 60,000 days), and the cost pool rate for the second activity (OOA) is $25 ($7,500,000 ÷ 300,000 hours). The total cost for providing services to occupants in the low-usage category is $6,570,000 [($120 × 36,000 days) + ($25 × 90,000 hours)]. The daily cost rate for these occupants is therefore $182.50 ($6,570,000 ÷ 36,000 occupant days).

Answer (B) is incorrect. The sum of the cost pool rates equals $145.00 ($120 + $25). Answer (C) is incorrect. The rate per day for medium-usage occupants equals $245. Answer (D) is incorrect. The rate per day for high-usage occupants is $620.

3.1.24. In an activity-based costing system, what should be used to assign a department's manufacturing overhead costs to products produced in varying lot sizes?

A. A single cause-and-effect relationship.

B. Multiple cause-and-effect relationships.

C. Relative net sales values of the products.

D. A product's ability to bear cost allocations.

Answer (B) is correct. *(CPA, adapted)*

REQUIRED: The basis for assigning overhead in an ABC system.

DISCUSSION: Instead of using a single allocation base for overhead, an ABC system determines the multiple activities associated with the incurrence of costs and then accumulates a cost pool for each activity using the appropriate activity base (cost driver). Consequently, overhead is assigned based on the multiple cause-and-effect relationships between activities and their cost drivers.

3.1.25. What is the normal effect on the numbers of cost pools and cost assignment bases when an activity-based cost (ABC) system replaces a traditional cost system?

	Cost Pools	Cost Assignment Bases
A.	No effect	No effect
B.	Increase	No effect
C.	No effect	Increase
D.	Increase	Increase

Answer (D) is correct. *(CPA, adapted)*

REQUIRED: The effect on cost pools and allocation bases of changing to ABC.

DISCUSSION: In an ABC system, cost assignment is more precise than in traditional systems because activities rather than functions or departments are defined as cost objects. This structure permits assignment to more cost pools and the identification of a driver specifically related to each. A driver is a factor that causes a change in a cost. Thus, an ABC system uses more cost pools and cost assignment bases than a traditional system.

3.1.26. Activities, their drivers, and their costs may be classified as unit-level, batch-level, product-level, and facility-level. If activity-based costing (ABC) information is prepared for internal purposes, which costs are most likely to be treated as period costs?

A. Unit-level.

B. Batch-level.

C. Product-level.

D. Facility-level.

Answer (D) is correct. *(Publisher, adapted)*

REQUIRED: The level of costs in an ABC analysis most likely to be treated as period costs.

DISCUSSION: A difficulty in applying ABC is that, although the first three levels of activities pertain to specific products or services, facility-level activities do not. Thus, facility-level costs are not accurately assignable to products. The theoretically sound solution may be to treat these costs as period costs. Nevertheless, organizations that apply ABC ordinarily assign them to products to obtain a full absorption cost suitable for external financial reporting in accordance with GAAP. However, for internal purposes, facility-level costs should be treated as period costs to avoid distorting decisions about cost efficiency, pricing, and profitability.

Answer (A) is incorrect. Unit-level costs relate to particular products (or services). Answer (B) is incorrect. Batch-level costs relate to particular products (or services). Answer (C) is incorrect. Product-level costs relate to particular products (or services).

STUDY UNIT FOUR
COST-VOLUME-PROFIT ANALYSIS

Cost-volume-profit (CVP) analysis (**breakeven** analysis) (1) predicts the relationships among revenues, variable costs, and fixed costs at various production levels and (2) determines the probable effects of changes in unit volume, sales price, revenue (sales) mix, etc. **CVP variables** include (1) revenue as a function of price per unit and quantity produced, (2) fixed costs, (3) variable cost per unit or as a percentage of revenues, and (4) profit per unit or as a percentage of revenues. Also, CVP **assumptions** are made. Costs and revenues are deemed to be predictable and linear over the relevant range of activity and specified time span. For example, price reductions are not necessary to increase revenues, and no learning-curve effect reduces unit variable labor cost at higher output levels. Thus, a relevant range exists in which the relationships are true for a given time span. Within these limits, all costs are either fixed or variable relative to a given cost object, and the time value of money is ignored. Total variable costs change proportionally with the activity level, but unit variable costs and total fixed costs are constant over the relevant range. Unit sales prices and market conditions also are constant, and the revenue mix does not change. Volume of output is the sole **revenue driver** and **cost driver**, and any change in inventory is immaterial. Accordingly, the **breakeven point** is the output at which total revenues equal total costs. Another key concept is the **unit contribution margin (UCM)**, which is unit selling price minus unit variable cost. It is the contribution from the sale of one unit to cover fixed costs (and possibly a targeted operating income).

Under **activity-based costing (ABC)**, some costs fixed under CVP vary with (1) unit-based and (2) nonunit-based drivers. For example, they may vary with batch-level drivers (number of orders, pounds of materials, etc.) and product (service)-sustaining drivers (product testing, product design, etc.). But facility-sustaining costs are fixed because they should not be added to products. The total ABC cost is the sum of (1) fixed cost, (2) unit-level variable cost (units sold × unit variable cost), (3) batch-level costs (batch-level driver × cost per driver), and (4) product (service)-sustaining costs (product-sustaining driver × cost per driver).

QUESTIONS

4.1 Concepts

4.1.1. At the breakeven point, the contribution margin equals total

A. Variable costs.

B. Sales revenues.

C. Selling and administrative costs.

D. Fixed costs.

Answer (D) is correct. *(CPA, adapted)*

REQUIRED: The amount of contribution margin at the breakeven point.

DISCUSSION: No profit or loss occurs at the breakeven point. Thus, operating income equals zero, and fixed cost must equal the contribution margin (total revenue – total variable cost).

Answer (A) is incorrect. Variable costs are used to determine the contribution margin. Answer (B) is incorrect. Sales revenues are used to determine the contribution margin. Answer (C) is incorrect. Selling and administrative costs may be fixed or variable.

4.1.2. Cost-volume-profit (CVP) analysis allows management to determine the relative profitability of a product by

A. Highlighting potential bottlenecks in the production process.

B. Keeping fixed costs to an absolute minimum.

C. Determining the contribution margin per unit and the projected profits at various levels of production.

D. Assigning costs to a product in a manner that maximizes the contribution margin.

Answer (C) is correct. *(CPA, adapted)*

REQUIRED: The purpose of CVP analysis.

DISCUSSION: CVP analysis studies the relationships among sales volume, sales price, fixed costs, variable costs, and profit. It allows management to determine the unit contribution margin (UCM), that is, the difference between unit sales price and unit variable cost. The UCM is used to project the breakeven point (BEP) as well as profits at various levels of production.

Answer (A) is incorrect. CVP analysis does not control physical production. Answer (B) is incorrect. CVP analysis does not control production costs. Answer (D) is incorrect. CVP analysis is a means of estimating profitability at various sales levels rather than accounting for costs.

4.1.3. Cost-volume-profit (CVP) analysis is a key factor in many decisions, including choice of product lines, pricing of products, marketing strategy, and use of productive facilities. A calculation used in a CVP analysis is the breakeven point. Once the breakeven point has been reached, operating income will increase by the

A. Gross margin per unit for each additional unit sold.

B. Contribution margin per unit for each additional unit sold.

C. Fixed costs per unit for each additional unit sold.

D. Variable costs per unit for each additional unit sold.

Answer (B) is correct. *(CMA, adapted)*

REQUIRED: The amount by which operating income will increase once the breakeven point has been reached.

DISCUSSION: At the breakeven point, total revenue equals total fixed costs plus the variable costs incurred at that level of production. Beyond the breakeven point, each unit sale will increase operating income by the unit contribution margin (unit sales price – unit variable cost) because fixed cost will already have been recovered.

Answer (A) is incorrect. The gross margin equals sales price minus cost of goods sold, including fixed cost. Answer (C) is incorrect. All fixed costs have been covered at the breakeven point. Answer (D) is incorrect. Operating income will increase by the unit contribution margin, not the unit variable cost.

4.1.4. Which of the following is a characteristic of a contribution income statement?

A. Fixed and variable expenses are combined as one line.

B. Fixed expenses are listed separately from variable expenses.

C. Fixed and variable manufacturing costs are combined as one line item, but fixed operating expenses are shown separately from variable operating expenses.

D. Fixed and variable operating expenses are combined as one line item, but fixed manufacturing expenses are shown separately from variable manufacturing expenses.

Answer (B) is correct. *(CIA, adapted)*

REQUIRED: The characteristic of a contribution income statement.

DISCUSSION: A contribution income statement emphasizes the distinction between fixed and variable costs. Thus, fixed manufacturing costs and other fixed costs are separated from variable manufacturing costs and other variable costs. The basic categories in the contribution income statement are variable costs, contribution margin, fixed costs, and operating income.

4.1.5. The method of cost accounting that lends itself to breakeven analysis is

A. Variable costing.
B. Standard costing.
C. Absolute costing.
D. Absorption costing.

Answer (A) is correct. *(CPA, adapted)*
REQUIRED: The method of cost accounting used in breakeven analysis.
DISCUSSION: Variable costs are emphasized in breakeven analysis. Total revenue minus the total variable costs equals the contribution margin, a key concept in breakeven analysis.
Answer (B) is incorrect. Standard costs may be fixed or variable. Breakeven analysis emphasizes variable costs. Answer (C) is incorrect. The term absolute cost accounting is not meaningful in this context. Answer (D) is incorrect. Absorption costs also include fixed costs. Breakeven analysis emphasizes variable costs.

4.1.6. Cost-volume-profit relationships that are curvilinear may be analyzed linearly by considering only

A. Fixed and semivariable costs.
B. Relevant fixed costs.
C. Relevant variable costs.
D. A relevant range of volume.

Answer (D) is correct. *(CPA, adapted)*
REQUIRED: The circumstances in which curvilinear CVP relationships may be analyzed linearly.
DISCUSSION: CVP analysis is assumed to be linear over a relevant range of activity (volume). Over the relevant range, total fixed costs and unit variable costs are assumed to be constant.
Answer (A) is incorrect. The range of volume (activity), not costs, must be limited to analyze curvilinear CVP relationships. Answer (B) is incorrect. The linear approximation of a curvilinear CVP relationship is achieved not by limiting the costs considered but by restricting analysis to a given range of activity. Answer (C) is incorrect. A CVP analysis of a curvilinear relationship is performed by restricting the level of activity to a relevant range.

4.1.7. When an organization is operating above the breakeven point, the degree or amount that sales may decline before losses are incurred is called the

A. Residual income rate.
B. Marginal rate of return.
C. Margin of safety.
D. Target (hurdle) rate of return.

Answer (C) is correct. *(CMA, adapted)*
REQUIRED: The rate or amount that sales may decline before losses are incurred.
DISCUSSION: The margin of safety is the excess of budgeted revenues over breakeven revenues. It is considered in sensitivity analysis.
Answer (A) is incorrect. Residual income is the excess of earnings over an imputed charge for the given investment base. Answer (B) is incorrect. A marginal rate of return is the return on the next investment. Answer (D) is incorrect. A target or hurdle rate of return is the required rate of return. It is also known as the discount rate or the opportunity cost of capital.

4.1.8. The dollar amount of revenues needed to attain a desired income is calculated by dividing the contribution margin ratio (CMR) into

A. Fixed cost.
B. Desired income.
C. Desired income plus fixed costs.
D. Desired income less fixed costs.

Answer (C) is correct. *(CPA, adapted)*
REQUIRED: The formula to calculate the amount of revenues resulting in a desired income.
DISCUSSION: Breakeven analysis treats the desired income in the same way as fixed costs. The CMR {[(revenues – variable costs) ÷ revenues] or (UCM ÷ unit selling price)} is divided into the sum of fixed costs and desired profit.
Answer (A) is incorrect. The result is the breakeven point, not the revenues needed to earn a desired income. Answer (B) is incorrect. Fixed costs must be added to desired income. Answer (D) is incorrect. Fixed costs must be added to desired income.

4.1.9. The breakeven point in units increases when unit costs

A. Increase and sales price remains unchanged.
B. Decrease and sales price remains unchanged.
C. Remain unchanged and sales price increases.
D. Decrease and sales price increases.

Answer (A) is correct. *(CMA, adapted)*
REQUIRED: The event that causes the breakeven point in units to increase.
DISCUSSION: A BEP ratio can be increased either by raising the numerator or lowering the denominator. The breakeven point in units is calculated by dividing fixed costs by the unit contribution margin. If selling price is constant and costs increase, the unit contribution margin decreases. The effect is to decrease the denominator and increase the ratio.
Answer (B) is incorrect. A decrease in costs decreases the breakeven point. The unit contribution margin increases. Answer (C) is incorrect. An increase in the selling price also increases the unit contribution margin, resulting in a lower breakeven point. Answer (D) is incorrect. The unit contribution margin is increased by a cost decrease and a sales price increase, resulting in a lower breakeven point.

4.1.10. Del Co. has fixed costs of $100,000 and breakeven sales of $800,000. What is its projected profit at $1,200,000 sales?

A. $50,000

B. $150,000

C. $200,000

D. $400,000

Answer (A) is correct. *(CPA, adapted)*

REQUIRED: The projected profit at a given sales level.

DISCUSSION: Del's contribution margin ratio (CMR) can be calculated as follows:

BEP in dollars	=	Fixed costs ÷ CMR
BEP in dollars × CMR	=	Fixed costs
CMR	=	Fixed costs ÷ BEP in dollars
	=	$100,000 ÷ $800,000
	=	12.5%

Thus, at sales of $1,200,000, contribution margin is $150,000 ($1,200,000 × 12.5%), and profit is $50,000 ($150,000 contribution margin – $100,000 fixed costs).

Answer (B) is incorrect. This amount is the contribution margin. Answer (C) is incorrect. This amount is the profit of $50,000 plus a contribution margin of $150,000. Answer (D) is incorrect. This amount results from subtracting the breakeven amount from total projected sales.

4.1.11. A company's breakeven point in sales dollars may be affected by equal percentage increases in both selling price and variable cost per unit (assume all other factors are constant within the relevant range). The equal percentage changes in selling price and variable cost per unit will cause the breakeven point in sales dollars to

A. Decrease by less than the percentage increase in selling price.

B. Decrease by more than the percentage increase in the selling price.

C. Increase by the percentage change in variable cost per unit.

D. Remain unchanged.

Answer (D) is correct. *(CIA, adapted)*

REQUIRED: The effect of equal percentage changes in selling price and variable cost on the breakeven point in sales dollars.

DISCUSSION: The BEP in sales dollars is equal to total fixed costs divided by the CMR, and the CMR equals unit contribution margin divided by unit price. Equal percentage changes in the CMR numerator and denominator leave the overall ratio unaffected. Algebraically, this can be shown as follows:

If CM ÷ Price = CMR, then (1.1 × CM) ÷ (1.1 × Price) = CMR.

With CMR unchanged, the ratio of fixed costs to CMR is unchanged.

4.1.12. Product Cott has sales of $200,000, a contribution margin of 20%, and a margin of safety of $80,000. What is Cott's fixed cost?

A. $16,000

B. $24,000

C. $80,000

D. $96,000

Answer (B) is correct. *(CPA, adapted)*

REQUIRED: The fixed cost amount.

DISCUSSION: Sales minus the margin of safety equals the breakeven point ($200,000 – $80,000 = $120,000). Fixed costs equal the contribution margin at the breakeven point, so fixed costs are $24,000 ($120,000 × 20%).

Answer (A) is incorrect. The amount of $16,000 is 20% of the margin of safety. Answer (C) is incorrect. The amount of $80,000 is the margin of safety. Answer (D) is incorrect. Variable costs at the breakeven point equals $96,000 [($200,000 – $80,000) × (1– .20)].

4.1.13. A cost-volume-profit model developed in a dynamic environment determined that the estimated parameters used may vary between limits. Subsequent testing of the model with respect to all possible values of the estimated parameters is termed

A. A sensitivity analysis.

B. Statistical estimation.

C. Statistical hypothesis testing.

D. A time-series study.

Answer (A) is correct. *(CIA, adapted)*

REQUIRED: The term for subsequent testing of a model with respect to all possible values of the parameters.

DISCUSSION: Sensitivity analysis permits measurement of the effects of errors in certainty equivalents. They are estimated amounts developed by the best means available and assumed for purposes of a given decision model to be certain. The model then may be evaluated by changing certain data variables (certainty equivalents) critical to the success of the entity and observing the outcomes. This analysis allows quantification of the effects of forecasting or prediction errors and identification of the most critical variables.

Answer (B) is incorrect. Statistical estimation involves the estimation of parameters. Answer (C) is incorrect. Statistical hypothesis testing calculates the conditional probability that both the hypothesis is true and the sample results have occurred. Answer (D) is incorrect. A time-series study involves forecasting data over time.

4.1.14. In preparing a cost-volume-profit analysis for his candle manufacturing business, Joe Stark is considering raising his prices $1.00 per candle. Stark is worried about the impact the increase will have on his revenues from craft fairs. Stark is concerned about the

A. Elasticity of demand.

B. Substitution effect.

C. Nature of supply.

D. Maximization of utility.

Answer (A) is correct. *(CMA, adapted)*

REQUIRED: The concept related to the effect of a price increase on sales.

DISCUSSION: As prices increase, total revenue may increase or decrease depending on the price elasticity of demand (percentage change in quantity demanded ÷ percentage change in price). If demand is elastic (elasticity > 1.0), a price increase tends to reduce total revenues. If demand is inelastic, a price increase tends to raise total revenues.

Answer (B) is incorrect. The substitution effect is implicit in the concept of elasticity. The fewer substitutes, the less elastic is the demand for a good. Answer (C) is incorrect. In CVP analysis, the nature of the supply curve is not considered. Answer (D) is incorrect. Utility theory is implicit in the concept of elasticity. If demand is elastic, consumers derive less utility from paying a higher price.

4.2 Assumptions

4.2.1. In calculating the breakeven point for a multiproduct company, which of the following assumptions are commonly made when variable costing is used?

I. Sales volume equals production volume.

II. Variable costs are constant per unit.

III. A given sales mix is maintained for all volume changes.

A. I and II.

B. I and III.

C. II and III.

D. I, II, and III.

Answer (D) is correct. *(CPA, adapted)*

REQUIRED: The assumptions used in breakeven analysis.

DISCUSSION: Cost-volume-profit analysis assumes that costs and revenues are linear over the relevant range. It further assumes that total fixed costs and unit variable costs are constant. Thus, total variable costs are directly proportional to volume. CVP analysis also assumes that there is no material change in inventory (sales = production) and that the mix of products is constant (or that only one product is produced).

Answer (A) is incorrect. The sales mix is deemed to be constant. Answer (B) is incorrect. Unit variable cost is assumed to be constant. Answer (C) is incorrect. The assumption is that inventories do not change.

4.2.2. Breakeven analysis assumes over the relevant range that

A. Total costs are linear.

B. Fixed costs are nonlinear.

C. Variable costs are nonlinear.

D. Selling prices are nonlinear.

Answer (A) is correct. *(CPA, adapted)*

REQUIRED: The assumption underlying cost-volume-profit analysis.

DISCUSSION: Breakeven analysis assumes that the cost and revenue factors used in the formula are linear and do not fluctuate with volume. Hence, fixed costs are deemed to be fixed over the relevant range of volume, and variable cost per unit remains constant as volume changes within the relevant range.

Answer (B) is incorrect. Fixed costs are assumed to be constant in breakeven analysis. Answer (C) is incorrect. Variable costs per unit are constant and therefore linear in breakeven analysis. Answer (D) is incorrect. The selling price is assumed to be linear in breakeven analysis.

4.2.3. Cost-volume-profit analysis assumes that over the relevant range

A. Variable costs are nonlinear.

B. Fixed costs are nonlinear.

C. Selling prices are unchanged.

D. Total costs are unchanged.

Answer (C) is correct. *(CPA, adapted)*

REQUIRED: The assumption underlying CVP analysis.

DISCUSSION: CVP analysis assumes that unit selling price, total fixed costs, and unit variable cost are constant within the relevant range. Accordingly, unit contribution margin, marginal revenue, and marginal cost also are constant.

Answer (A) is incorrect. All costs are assumed to be linear. Total variable cost changes by a constant amount with each change in volume. Answer (B) is incorrect. Fixed costs are constant. Answer (D) is incorrect. Total costs vary directly with volume.

4.2.4. An assembly plant accumulates its variable and fixed manufacturing overhead costs in a single cost pool, which is then applied to work in process using a single application base. The assembly plant management wants to estimate the magnitude of the total manufacturing overhead costs for different volume levels of the application activity base using a flexible budget formula. If there is an increase in the application activity base that is within the relevant range of activity for the assembly plant, which one of the following relationships regarding variable and fixed costs is true?

A. The variable cost per unit is constant, and the total fixed costs decrease.

B. The variable cost per unit is constant, and the total fixed costs increase.

C. The variable cost per unit and the total fixed costs remain constant.

D. The variable cost per unit increases, and the total fixed costs remain constant.

Answer (C) is correct. *(CIA, adapted)*

REQUIRED: The effect on variable and fixed costs of a change in activity within the relevant range.

DISCUSSION: Total variable cost changes when changes in the activity level occur within the relevant range. The cost per unit for a variable cost, however, is constant for all activity levels within the relevant range. Thus, if the activity volume increases within the relevant range, total variable costs will increase. A fixed cost does not change when volume changes occur in the activity level within the relevant range. If the activity volume increases within the relevant range, total fixed costs will remain unchanged.

4.2.5. Cost-volume-profit analysis assumes that over the relevant range total

A. Revenues are linear.

B. Costs are unchanged.

C. Variable costs are nonlinear.

D. Fixed costs are nonlinear.

Answer (A) is correct. *(CPA, adapted)*

REQUIRED: The assumption underlying CVP analysis.

DISCUSSION: CVP analysis assumes that (1) all costs and revenues are linear and (2) unit price is constant within the relevant range. Consequently, total revenues are represented on a CVP chart by a line of constant positive slope (constant marginal revenue) beginning at the origin. This point corresponds to zero volume and zero revenue.

Answer (B) is incorrect. Total fixed costs but not total variable costs are constant. Thus, total costs increase in direct proportion to volume. Answer (C) is incorrect. Variable costs are linear. Answer (D) is incorrect. Fixed costs are constant.

4.2.6. Cost-volume-profit analysis assumes that over the relevant range

A. Total fixed costs are nonlinear.

B. Total costs are unchanged.

C. Unit variable costs are unchanged.

D. Unit revenues are nonlinear.

Answer (C) is correct. *(CPA, adapted)*

REQUIRED: The assumption underlying CVP analysis.

DISCUSSION: CVP analysis assumes that (1) unit selling price and unit variable costs are constant within the relevant range and (2) costs and revenues are linear.

Answer (A) is incorrect. Costs are linear. Answer (B) is incorrect. Total costs vary with production level. Answer (D) is incorrect. Revenues are linear.

4.3 High-Low Calculations

4.3.1. The least exact method for separating fixed and variable costs is

A. The least squares method.

B. Computer simulation.

C. The high-low method.

D. Matrix algebra.

Answer (C) is correct. *(Publisher, adapted)*

REQUIRED: The least exact method of estimating fixed and variable costs proportions.

DISCUSSION: The fixed and variable portions of mixed costs may be estimated by identifying the highest and the lowest costs within the relevant range. The difference in cost divided by the difference in activity is the variable rate. Once the variable rate is found, the fixed portion is determinable. The high-low method is a simple approximation of the mixed cost formula. The costs of using more sophisticated methods sometimes outweigh the incremental accuracy achieved. In these cases, the high-low method is sufficient.

Answer (A) is incorrect. The least squares method is a sophisticated method of identifying the fixed and variable costs. Answer (B) is incorrect. A computer simulation is a more exact method of separating fixed and variable costs. Answer (D) is incorrect. Matrix algebra is a precise method of separating fixed and variable costs.

4.3.2. Day Mail Order Co. applied the high-low method of cost estimation to customer order data for the first 4 months of the current year. What is the estimated variable order-filling cost component per order?

Month	No. of Orders	Cost
January	1,200	$ 3,120
February	1,300	3,185
March	1,800	4,320
April	1,700	3,895
	6,000	$14,520

A. $2.00

B. $2.42

C. $2.48

D. $2.50

Answer (A) is correct. *(CPA, adapted)*

REQUIRED: The estimated variable order-filling cost.

DISCUSSION: The high-low method estimates unit variable cost by dividing the difference in costs at the highest and lowest levels of activity by the differences in activity. The difference between the highest and lowest amounts of orders was 600 (1,800 – 1,200). Given a cost differential of $1,200 ($4,320 – $3,120), the estimated unit variable cost is $2.00 ($1,200 ÷ 600).

Answer (B) is incorrect. The total cost per unit is $2.42 ($14,520 ÷ 6,000). Answer (C) is incorrect. The sum of the highest cost and the lowest cost ($7,440) divided by the sum of highest orders and lowest orders equals $2.48. Answer (D) is incorrect. The average of the per-order cost of the high and low costs equals $2.50.

4.3.3. Jackson, Inc., is preparing a flexible budget for next year and requires a breakdown of the cost of steam used in its factory into the fixed and variable elements. The following data on the cost of steam used and direct labor hours worked are available for the last 6 months of this year:

Month	Cost of Steam	Direct Labor Hours
July	$ 15,850	3,000
August	13,400	2,050
September	16,370	2,900
October	19,800	3,650
November	17,600	2,670
December	18,500	2,650
Total	$101,520	16,920

Assuming that Jackson uses the high-low method of analysis, the estimated variable cost of steam per direct labor hour is

A. $4.00

B. $5.42

C. $5.82

D. $6.00

Answer (A) is correct. *(CPA, adapted)*

REQUIRED: The variable cost per direct labor hour.

DISCUSSION: The high-low method estimates variable cost by dividing the difference in costs incurred at the highest and lowest observed levels of activity by the difference in activity. The highest level of activity is 3,650 hours in October, and the lowest is 2,050 hours in August. The variable cost is found by dividing the change in cost by the change in activity (direct labor hours).

$$\frac{\$19,800 - \$13,400}{3,650 - 2,050} = \frac{\$6,400 \text{ cost}}{1,600 \text{ DLH}} = \$4.00/\text{DLH}$$

Answer (B) is incorrect. The amount of $5.42 is the cost per direct labor hour of the highest-cost month (October), which includes fixed costs as well as variable costs. Answer (C) is incorrect. The high-low method divides the difference in (not the sum of) costs by the difference in (not the sum of) hours between the months of highest and lowest activity to determine the variable cost per direct labor hour. Answer (D) is incorrect. The total 6-month cost of steam divided by the 6-month total of direct labor hours equals $6 per direct labor hour.

4.4 Basic Breakeven Problems

4.4.1. A company is concerned about its operating performance, as summarized below:

Revenues ($12.50 per unit)	$300,000
Variable costs	180,000
Operating loss	(40,000)

How many additional units should have been sold in order for the company to break even in Year 8?

A. 32,000

B. 24,000

C. 16,000

D. 8,000

Answer (D) is correct. *(CIA, adapted)*

REQUIRED: The additional units that should have been sold to break even.

DISCUSSION: The contribution margin ratio is 40% [($300,000 – $180,000 VC) ÷ $300,000 revenues]. Thus, the UCM is $5 ($12.50 unit SP × 40%), and the additional units that should have been sold equaled 8,000 ($40,000 NOL ÷ $5 UCM).

Answer (A) is incorrect. The breakeven sales volume is 32,000. Answer (B) is incorrect. The actual unit sales volume is 24,000. Answer (C) is incorrect. The amount of 16,000 treats the operating loss as operating income.

Questions 4.4.2 and 4.4.3 are based on the following information. Data available for the current year are presented below.

	Whole Company	Division 1	Division 2
Variable manufacturing cost of goods sold	$ 400,000	$220,000	$180,000
Unallocated costs (e.g., president's salary)	100,000		
Fixed costs controllable by division managers (e.g., advertising, engineering supervision costs)	90,000	50,000	40,000
Net revenue	1,000,000	600,000	400,000
Variable selling and administrative costs	130,000	70,000	60,000
Fixed costs controllable by others (e.g., depreciation, insurance)	120,000	70,000	50,000

4.4.2. Based upon the information presented above, the contribution margin for the company was

A. $400,000

B. $470,000

C. $530,000

D. $600,000

Answer (B) is correct. *(CIA, adapted)*

REQUIRED: The contribution margin for the company.

DISCUSSION: Contribution margin is sales minus variable costs. Direct costing considers only variable costs as product costs, so contribution margin appears in a direct costing income statement. Absorption costing treats both variable and fixed costs as product costs. Thus, variable costs are not stated separately, and contribution margin would not appear in the income statement. Accordingly, the CM is $470,000 ($1,000,000 net revenues – $400,000 variable COGS – $130,000 variable S&A costs).

Answer (A) is incorrect. The total variable manufacturing cost of goods sold is $400,000. Contribution margin equals net revenue minus variable costs. Answer (C) is incorrect. The total variable costs for the year is $530,000. Contribution margin equals net revenue minus variable costs. Answer (D) is incorrect. Variable selling and administrative costs must also be subtracted from net revenue in determining contribution margin.

4.4.3. The contribution by Division 1 was

A. $190,000

B. $260,000

C. $310,000

D. $380,000

Answer (A) is correct. *(CIA, adapted)*

REQUIRED: The contribution by Division 1.

DISCUSSION: The contribution margin for Division 1 is $310,000 ($600,000 net revenue – $290,000 total variable costs). The contribution controllable by Division 1's manager is $260,000 ($310,000 CM – $50,000 controllable fixed cost). The total contribution by Division 1 equals its net revenue minus all costs traceable to it. Thus, the total contribution is $190,000 ($260,000 controllable contribution – $70,000 allocated but controllable by others).

Answer (B) is incorrect. The contribution controllable by the Division 1 manager is $260,000. Answer (C) is incorrect. The contribution margin for Division 1 is $310,000. Answer (D) is incorrect. Net revenue minus variable manufacturing costs equals $380,000.

4.4.4. The following information relates to a corporation, which produced and sold 50,000 units during a recent accounting period:

Sales	$850,000
Manufacturing costs:	
Fixed	210,000
Variable	140,000
Selling and administrative costs:	
Fixed	300,000
Variable	45,000
Income tax rate	40%

For the next accounting period, if production and sales are expected to be 40,000 units, the company should anticipate a contribution margin per unit of

A. $1.86

B. $3.10

C. $7.30

D. $13.30

Answer (D) is correct. *(CMA, adapted)*

REQUIRED: The contribution margin per unit.

DISCUSSION: Unit contribution margin is the difference between unit selling price and unit variable cost. Unit selling price is $17 ($850,000 ÷ 50,000 units), and unit variable cost is $3.70 [($140,000 variable manufacturing cost + $45,000 variable S&A cost) ÷ 50,000 units sold]. Accordingly, unit contribution margin is $13.30 ($17 – $3.70).

Answer (A) is incorrect. This is an after-tax amount based on the inclusion of all fixed costs in the calculation. Answer (B) is incorrect. This amount is erroneously based on the inclusion of all fixed costs in the calculation of the UCM. Answer (C) is incorrect. Including the $300,000 of fixed S&A costs in the calculation of the UCM results in $7.30.

4.4.5. At annual sales of $900,000, the Ebo product has the following unit sales price and costs:

Sales price	$20
Prime cost	6
Manufacturing overhead:	
Variable	1
Fixed	7
Selling & admin. costs:	
Variable	1
Fixed	3
Total costs	(18)
Profit	$ 2

What is Ebo's breakeven point in units?

A. 25,000

B. 31,500

C. 37,500

D. 45,000

Answer (C) is correct. *(CPA, adapted)*

REQUIRED: The breakeven point in units.

DISCUSSION: The breakeven point in units is equal to the fixed costs divided by the unit contribution margin (UCM). The number of units sold was 45,000 ($900,000 revenues ÷ $20 unit sales price). Total fixed costs were thus $450,000 [(45,000 units × ($7 FOH + $3 FS&A)]. The UCM equals unit sales price minus unit variable cost ($20 – $6 – $1 – $1 = $12). Thus, the breakeven point in units is 37,500 ($450,000 fixed costs ÷ $12 UCM).

Answer (A) is incorrect. The amount of 25,000 does not include the prime cost in variable expenses for the calculation of the unit contribution margin. Answer (B) is incorrect. The breakeven point is calculated by dividing fixed costs by the unit contribution margin. The unit contribution margin is the unit selling price minus the unit variable cost. Answer (D) is incorrect. Dividing the fixed costs of $450,000 by the unit fixed costs of $10 ($7 FOH + $3 FS&A) does not equal the breakeven point.

4.4.6. A manufacturer is considering dropping a product line. It currently produces a multi-purpose woodworking clamp in a simple manufacturing process that uses special equipment. Variable costs amount to $6.00 per unit. Fixed overhead costs, exclusive of depreciation, have been allocated to this product at a rate of $3.50 a unit and will continue whether or not production ceases. Depreciation on the special equipment amounts to $20,000 a year. Fixed costs are $18,000. The clamp has a selling price of $10 a unit. Ignoring tax effects, the minimum number of units that would have to be sold in the current year to break even on a cash flow basis is

A. 4,500 units.

B. 5,000 units.

C. 20,000 units.

D. 36,000 units.

Answer (A) is correct. *(CMA, adapted)*

REQUIRED: The breakeven point in units on a cash flow basis.

DISCUSSION: The BEP in units is equal to fixed costs divided by the unit contribution margin ($10 unit selling price – $6 unit variable cost). Hence, the number of units that must be sold to break even on continuation of the product line is 4,500 [$18,000 fixed costs ÷ ($10 – $6)]. Fixed overhead allocated is not considered in this calculation because it is not a cash flow element, and will continue regardless of the decision.

Answer (B) is incorrect. The BEP is equal to the salvage value (not depreciation) divided by the UCM of $4 ($10 – $6). Depreciation is a non-cash flow element, and therefore should not be considered in the cash flow breakeven point calculation. Answer (C) is incorrect. The BEP is equal to the salvage value (not depreciation) divided by the UCM of $4 ($10 – $6). Depreciation is a non-cash flow element, and therefore should not be considered in the cash flow breakeven point calculation. Answer (D) is incorrect. Unit fixed costs should not be subtracted in determining the unit contribution margin. The fixed costs will continue regardless so they are not included in the calculation. Therefore, the $18,000 salvage value will be divided by the $4 unit contribution margin in determining the cash flow breakeven point in units.

4.4.7. A company with $280,000 of fixed costs has the following data:

	Product A	Product B
Sales price per unit	$5	$6
Variable costs per unit	$3	$5

Assume three units of A are sold for each unit of B sold. How much will sales be in dollars of product B at the breakeven point?

A. $200,000

B. $240,000

C. $280,000

D. $840,000

Answer (B) is correct. *(CIA, adapted)*

REQUIRED: The breakeven point for B in sales dollars.

DISCUSSION: The breakeven point equals fixed costs divided by unit contribution margin. The composite unit contribution margin for A and B is $7 {[3 units of A × ($5 – $3)] + [1 unit of B × ($6 – $5)]}. Thus, 40,000 composite units ($280,000 ÷ $7), including 40,000 units of B, are sold at the breakeven point. Hence, sales of B at the breakeven point equal $240,000 (40,000 units × $6).

Answer (A) is incorrect. Applying product A's price results in $200,000 (40,000 × $5). Answer (C) is incorrect. Fixed costs equal $280,000. Answer (D) is incorrect. Product A sales and product B sales at the breakeven point equals $840,000.

4.4.8. The following information pertains to Syl Co.:

Sales	$800,000
Variable costs	160,000
Fixed costs	40,000

What is Syl's breakeven point in sales dollars?

A. $200,000

B. $160,000

C. $50,000

D. $40,000

Answer (C) is correct. *(CPA, adapted)*

REQUIRED: The breakeven point in sales dollars.

DISCUSSION: The breakeven point in sales dollars is the fixed costs divided by the contribution margin ratio. Variable costs equal 20% of sales ($160,000 ÷ $800,000). Hence, the contribution margin ratio is 80%, and the breakeven point in dollars is $50,000 ($40,000 FC ÷ 80%).

Answer (A) is incorrect. The sum of FC and VC at the $800,000 sales level is $200,000. Answer (B) is incorrect. VC at the $800,000 sales level is $160,000. Answer (D) is incorrect. The FC is $40,000.

4.4.9. Two companies are expected to have annual sales of 1,000,000 decks of playing cards next year. Estimates for next year are presented below:

	Company 1	Company 2
Selling price per deck	$3.00	$3.00
Cost of paper per deck	.62	.65
Printing ink per deck	.13	.15
Labor per deck	.75	1.25
Variable overhead per deck	.30	.35
Fixed costs	$960,000	$252,000

Given these data, which of the following responses is true?

	Breakeven Point in Units for Company 1	Breakeven Point in Units for Company 2	Volume in Units at Which Profits of Company 1 and Company 2 Are Equal
A.	800,000	420,000	1,180,000
B.	800,000	420,000	1,000,000
C.	533,334	105,000	1,000,000
D.	533,334	105,000	1,180,000

Answer (A) is correct. *(CIA, adapted)*

REQUIRED: The breakeven points and the indifference point for the companies.

DISCUSSION: Company 1's unit contribution margin is $1.20 ($3 – $.62 – $.13 – $.75 – $.30) and Company 2's is $.60 ($3 – $.65 – $.15 – $1.25 – $.35). The BEP in units is found by dividing the fixed costs by the UCM. Thus, Company 1's is 800,000 ($960,000 ÷ $1.20) and Company 2's is 420,000 ($252,000 ÷ $ .60). The volume at which profits are equal occurs when the difference between total revenue and total cost is also the same. Company 1 has a per unit cost of $1.80 ($.62 + .13 + .75 + .30) and Company 2 has a per unit cost of $2.40 ($.65 +.15 + 1.25 + .35). Both charge $3 per deck, so total revenue for the two companies at the indifference volume (U) will be equal. Consequently, total costs should also be equal.

$$U(\$.62 + .13 + .75 + .30) + \$960{,}000 = U(\$.65 + .15 + 1.25 + .35) + \$252{,}000$$
$$\$1.80U + \$960{,}000 = \$2.40U + \$252{,}000$$
$$\$.60U = \$708{,}000$$
$$U = 1{,}180{,}000$$

4.4.10. Two companies produce and sell the same product in a competitive industry. Thus, the selling price of the product for each company is the same. Company 1 has a contribution margin ratio of 40% and fixed costs of $25 million. Company 2 is more automated, making its fixed costs 40% higher than those of Company 1. Company 2 also has a contribution margin ratio that is 30% greater than that of Company 1. By comparison, Company 1 will have the <List A> breakeven point in terms of dollar sales volume and will have the <List B> dollar profit potential once the indifference point in dollar sales volume is exceeded.

	List A	List B
A.	Lower	Lesser
B.	Lower	Greater
C.	Higher	Lesser
D.	Higher	Greater

Answer (A) is correct. *(CIA, adapted)*

REQUIRED: The breakeven points and dollar profit potentials for two manufacturers.

DISCUSSION: Company 1's breakeven point is lower because its fixed costs are lower. Company 1's breakeven point is $62,500,000 ($25,000,000 ÷ 40%). Company 2's breakeven point is $67,307,692 [($25,000,000 × 1.4) ÷ (40% × 1.3)]. If X equals the unit sales price, the indifference point, at which dollar profits are equal, is $83,333,333 ($25,000,000 + .60X = $35,000,000 + .48X). Beyond the indifference point, Company 1's profits are lower than Company 2's because Company 2 has a higher contribution margin ratio.

4.4.11. A company has the opportunity to increase annual sales by $100,000 by selling to a new, riskier group of customers. Based on sales, the uncollectible expense is expected to be 15%, and collection costs will be 5%. The company's manufacturing and selling expenses are 70% of sales, and its effective tax rate is 40%. If the company accepts this opportunity, after-tax profit will increase by

A. $4,000

B. $6,000

C. $9,000

D. $10,000

Answer (B) is correct. *(CMA, adapted)*

REQUIRED: The increase in after-tax profit as a result of an increase in sales.

DISCUSSION: The company's manufacturing and selling costs exclusive of bad debts equal 70% of sales. Hence, the gross profit on the $100,000 increase in sales will be $30,000 ($100,000 × 30%). The increase in after-tax profit is calculated as follows:

Increase in gross profit	$30,000
Less: Uncollectible accounts ($100,000 × 15%)	(15,000)
Less: Collection costs ($100,000 × 5%)	(5,000)
Increase in pre-tax income	$10,000
Less: Income tax expense ($10,000 × 40%)	(4,000)
Increase in after-tax income	$ 6,000

Answer (A) is incorrect. The amount of $4,000 is the tax expense on the increased income. Answer (C) is incorrect. The amount of $9,000 does not include collection costs in calculating income. Answer (D) is incorrect. The amount of $10,000 does not include the effect of taxes.

4.4.12. A company manufactures a single product. Estimated cost data regarding this product and other information for the product and the company are as follows:

Sales price per unit	$40
Total variable production cost per unit	$22
Sales commission (on sales)	5%
Fixed costs and expenses:	
Manufacturing overhead	$5,598,720
General and administrative	$3,732,480
Effective income tax rate	40%

The number of units the company must sell in the coming year in order to reach its breakeven point is

A. 388,800 units.

B. 518,400 units.

C. 583,200 units.

D. 972,000 units.

Answer (C) is correct. *(CIA, adapted)*

REQUIRED: The number of units to reach the breakeven point.

DISCUSSION: The breakeven point is determined by dividing total fixed costs by the unit contribution margin. The total fixed costs are $9,331,200 ($5,598,720 manufacturing overhead + $3,732,480 general and administrative). The contribution margin is $16.00 ($40 sales price – $22 variable production cost – $2.00 commission). Thus, the breakeven point is 583,200 units ($9,331,200 ÷ $16).

Answer (A) is incorrect. Not subtracting the variable costs per unit from sales price results in 388,800 units. Answer (B) is incorrect. This number of units does not reflect the sales commissions in the total variable costs. Answer (D) is incorrect. Including taxes in the total variable costs results in 972,000 units, which understates the unit contribution margin.

4.4.13. A manufacturer sells its sole product for $10 per unit, with a unit contribution margin of $6. The fixed manufacturing cost rate per unit is $2 based on a denominator capacity of 1 million units, and fixed marketing costs are $1.5 million. If 900,000 units are produced, the absorption-costing breakeven point in units sold is

A. 425,000 units.

B. 583,333 units.

C. 900,000 units.

D. 1,000,000 units.

Answer (A) is correct. *(Publisher, adapted)*

REQUIRED: The absorption-costing breakeven point in units sold.

DISCUSSION: The absorption-costing breakeven point in units sold equals the sum of (1) the total fixed costs and (2) the product of the fixed manufacturing cost application rate and the difference between the BEP in units sold (X) and units produced, with the sum divided by the UCM. Thus, the absorption-costing breakeven point in units sold can be calculated as follows:

$$X = \frac{(\$2 \times 1{,}000{,}000 \text{ denominator capacity}) + \$1{,}500{,}000 + \$2(X - 900{,}000)}{\$6}$$

$$X = \frac{\$3{,}500{,}000 + \$2X - \$1{,}800{,}000}{\$6}$$

$$\$6X = \$1{,}700{,}000 + \$2X$$
$$X = 425{,}000$$

Answer (B) is incorrect. The variable-costing BEP is 583,333 units. Answer (C) is incorrect. The actual production level is 900,000 units. Answer (D) is incorrect. The capacity used to calculate the fixed overhead application rate is 1,000,000 units.

4.4.14. A not-for-profit social agency provides home health care assistance to as many patients as possible. Its budgeted appropriation (X) for next year must cover fixed costs of $5 million, and the annual per-patient cost (Y) of its services. However, the agency is preparing for a possible 10% reduction in its appropriation that will lower the number of patients served from 5,000 to 4,000. The reduced appropriation and the annual per-patient cost equal

	Reduced Appropriation	Per-Patient Annual Cost
A.	$5,000,000	$4,000
B.	$8,333,333	$833
C.	$9,000,000	$1,000
D.	$10,000,000	$5,000

Answer (C) is correct. *(Publisher, adapted)*

REQUIRED: The reduced appropriation and the annual per-patient cost.

DISCUSSION: This question applies CVP analysis in a not-for-profit context in which the agency wishes to assist as many people as possible. Thus, a breakeven point must be calculated. Total revenue (the appropriation) equals fixed cost plus the product of unit variable cost (per-patient annual cost) and the number of patients who can be assisted given the available resources. The following are simultaneous equations stated in the two unknowns:

$$X - 5{,}000Y = \$5{,}000{,}000$$
$$.9X - 4{,}000Y = \$5{,}000{,}000$$

Because X must equal 5,000Y + $5,000,000, the second equation may be solved as follows for the per-patient annual cost (Y):

$$.9(5{,}000Y + \$5{,}000{,}000) - 4{,}000Y = \$5{,}000{,}000$$
$$4{,}500Y + \$4{,}500{,}000 - 4{,}000Y = \$5{,}000{,}000$$
$$500Y = \$500{,}000$$
$$Y = \$1{,}000$$

Accordingly, the budgeted appropriation (X) must be $10,000,000 [(5,000 × $1,000) VC + $5,000,000 FC], and the reduced appropriation must be $9,000,000 ($10,000,000 × 90%).

Answer (A) is incorrect. The fixed cost is $5,000,000 and the number served given a reduced appropriation is 4,000. Answer (B) is incorrect. These amounts are the appropriation and per-patient annual cost, respectively, for the next year that result from a 10% increase in the appropriation of the current year instead of a 10% decrease in the next year's appropriation. Answer (D) is incorrect. The budgeted appropriation is $10,000,000 and the number of people it would serve is 5,000.

4.5 Calculating the Effects of Changes in CVP Variables

4.5.1. Lake Co. has just increased its direct labor wage rates. All other budgeted costs and revenues were unchanged. How did this increase affect Lake's budgeted breakeven point and budgeted margin of safety?

	Budgeted Breakeven Point	Budgeted Margin of Safety
A.	Increase	Increase
B.	Increase	Decrease
C.	Decrease	Decrease
D.	Decrease	Increase

Answer (B) is correct. *(CPA, adapted)*

REQUIRED: The effect on the breakeven point and margin of safety of an increase in direct labor cost.

DISCUSSION: The BEP is the sales volume at which total revenue equals total cost. The margin of safety is the excess of budgeted sales over the breakeven volume. Given that all other costs and revenues are constant, an increase in direct labor cost will increase the BEP and decrease the margin of safety.

4.5.2. A retail company determines its selling price by marking up variable costs 60%. In addition, the company uses frequent selling price markdowns to stimulate sales. If the markdowns average 10%, what is the company's contribution margin ratio?

A. 27.5%

B. 30.6%

C. 37.5%

D. 41.7%

Answer (B) is correct. *(CIA, adapted)*

REQUIRED: The contribution margin ratio.

DISCUSSION: The contribution margin equals revenues minus variable costs. The CMR equals the UCM divided by the selling price. Because the company determines its selling price by marking up variable costs of 60% and variable costs average $10 per unit, the average selling price is $16 (1.60 × $10). However, the 10% markdown implies that the actual average selling price is $14.40 (.90 × $16). The CMR is therefore 30.6% [($14.40 – $10.00) ÷ $14.40].

Answer (A) is incorrect. Omitting markdowns from the denominator results in 27.5%. Answer (C) is incorrect. Ignoring markdowns results in 37.5%. Answer (D) is incorrect. Omitting markdowns from the numerator results in 41.7%.

4.5.3. Which of the following would decrease unit contribution margin the most?

A. A 15% decrease in selling price.

B. A 15% increase in variable expenses.

C. A 15% decrease in variable expenses.

D. A 15% decrease in fixed expenses.

Answer (A) is correct. *(CMA, adapted)*

REQUIRED: The change in a CVP variable causing the greatest decrease in UCM.

DISCUSSION: Unit contribution margin (UCM) equals unit selling price minus unit variable costs. It can be decreased by either lowering the price or raising the variable costs. As long as UCM is positive, a given percentage change in selling price must have a greater effect than an equal but opposite percentage change in variable cost. The example below demonstrates this point.

Original:	UCM = SP – UVC
	= $100 – $50
	= $50
Lower Selling Price:	UCM = (SP × .85) – UVC
	= $85 – $50
	= $35
Higher Variable Cost:	UCM = SP – (UVC × 1.15)
	= $100 – $57.50
	= $42.50

Since $35 < $42.50, the lower selling price has the greater effect.

Answer (B) is incorrect. A 15% increase in variable expenses will not decrease the CM as much as a 15% decrease in sales price. Answer (C) is incorrect. A decrease in variable expenses would increase UCM. Answer (D) is incorrect. Fixed expenses have no effect on the contribution margin.

4.5.4. The contribution margin increases when revenues remain the same and

A. Variable cost per unit decreases.

B. Variable cost per unit increases.

C. Fixed costs decrease.

D. Fixed costs increase.

Answer (A) is correct. *(CPA, adapted)*

REQUIRED: The cause of an increased CM when revenues remain constant.

DISCUSSION: CM equals revenues minus variable costs. With constant revenues, an increase in the CM may occur if the variable costs decrease.

Answer (B) is incorrect. When variable cost per unit increases, CM decreases if revenues and price remain the same. Answer (C) is incorrect. The CM does not vary with fixed costs. Answer (D) is incorrect. The CM does not vary with fixed costs.

4.5.5. A company has $450,000 per year of fixed production costs, of which $150,000 are noncash outlays. The variable cost per unit is $15, and the unit selling price is $25. The breakeven volume in sales units for this company would be

A. 18,000 units.

B. 30,000 units.

C. 45,000 units.

D. 60,000 units.

Answer (C) is correct. *(CIA, adapted)*

REQUIRED: The breakeven volume in sales units.

DISCUSSION: The breakeven volume in sales units equals fixed costs divided by the unit contribution margin (unit price – unit variable cost). Consequently, the breakeven point is 45,000 units [$450,000 ÷ ($25 – $15)].

Answer (A) is incorrect. Dividing fixed costs by unit price results in 18,000 units. Answer (B) is incorrect. Fixed costs divided by unit variable cost equals 30,000 units. Answer (D) is incorrect. Adding $150,000 to the fixed costs results in 60,000 units.

4.5.6. If the fixed costs attendant to a product increase while variable costs and sales price remain constant, what will happen to contribution margin (CM) and breakeven point (BEP)?

	CM	BEP
A.	Increase	Decrease
B.	Decrease	Increase
C.	Unchanged	Increase
D.	Unchanged	Unchanged

Answer (C) is correct. *(CPA, adapted)*

REQUIRED: The effect of an increase in fixed costs on the CM and the BEP.

DISCUSSION: The BEP in units is equal to fixed costs divided by the UCM (unit selling price – variable cost per unit). Consequently, an increase in fixed costs has no effect on the CM but causes the BEP to increase; that is, more units must be sold to cover the increased fixed costs.

Answer (A) is incorrect. Contribution margin is not affected by a change in fixed costs. Also, the BEP will increase. Answer (B) is incorrect. Contribution margin is not affected by a change in fixed costs. Answer (D) is incorrect. The BEP will increase. More units must be sold to cover the increased fixed costs.

4.5.7. A company has sales of $500,000, variable costs of $300,000, and operating income of $150,000. If the company increased the sales price per unit by 10%, reduced fixed costs by 20%, and left variable cost per unit unchanged, what would be the new breakeven point in sales dollars?

A. $88,000

B. $100,000

C. $110,000

D. $125,000

Answer (A) is correct. *(CIA, adapted)*

REQUIRED: The new breakeven point in sales dollars.

DISCUSSION: The breakeven point in sales dollars is equal to total fixed costs divided by the contribution margin ratio. Fixed costs are $50,000 ($500,000 sales – $300,000 variable costs – $150,000 operating income). If sales increase by 10% ($500,000 × 1.10 = $550,000) and fixed costs decrease by 20% ($50,000 × .80 = $40,000), the new contribution margin is 45.45% [($550,000 – $300,000) ÷ $550,000]. The new breakeven point can be calculated as follows:

BEP in dollars = Fixed costs ÷ CMR
= $40,000 ÷ .4545
= $88,000

Answer (B) is incorrect. Ignoring the 10% sales price increase results in $100,000. Answer (C) is incorrect. Ignoring the 20% decrease in fixed costs results in $110,000. Answer (D) is incorrect. Ignoring the changes in sales price and fixed costs results in $125,000.

4.5.8. The contribution margin per unit is the difference between the selling price and the variable cost per unit, and the contribution margin ratio is the ratio of the unit contribution margin to the selling price per unit. If the selling price and the variable cost per unit both increase 10% and fixed costs do not change, what is the effect on the contribution margin per unit and the contribution margin ratio?

A. Both remain unchanged.

B. Both increase.

C. Contribution margin per unit increases, and the contribution margin ratio remains unchanged.

D. Contribution margin per unit increases, and the contribution margin ratio decreases.

Answer (C) is correct. *(CPA, adapted)*

REQUIRED: The effect on the UCM and CMR of an equal percentage increase in the selling price and unit variable cost.

DISCUSSION: UCM equals selling price minus variable costs. Thus, equal percentage increases in the selling price and the variable cost per unit cause a proportionate increase in the UCM. The CMR equals the UCM divided by the selling price. If the selling price and variable cost per unit increase in the same proportion, the CMR is unchanged. For example, if SP is $20 and the unit variable cost is $10, the CMR is 50%. If the selling price and unit variable cost are increased by 10% to $22 and $11, respectively, the CMR remains 50%.

4.5.9. The most likely strategy to reduce the breakeven point would be to

A. Increase both the fixed costs and the contribution margin.

B. Decrease both the fixed costs and the contribution margin.

C. Decrease the fixed costs and increase the contribution margin.

D. Increase the fixed costs and decrease the contribution margin.

Answer (C) is correct. *(CPA, adapted)*

REQUIRED: The strategy to reduce the breakeven point.

DISCUSSION: A ratio can be reduced either by decreasing the numerator or increasing the denominator. The breakeven point in units equals fixed costs divided by the unit contribution margin. The breakeven point in sales dollars is the fixed costs divided by the contribution margin ratio. Because fixed costs are in the numerator and the contribution margin is in the denominator, decreasing the fixed costs and increasing the contribution margin reduces the breakeven point.

Answer (A) is incorrect. Increasing the fixed costs increases the breakeven point. Answer (B) is incorrect. Decreasing the contribution margin increases the breakeven point. Answer (D) is incorrect. Increasing fixed costs and decreasing the contribution margin increases the breakeven point.

4.5.10. Which of the following will result in raising the breakeven point?

A. A decrease in the variable cost per unit.

B. An increase in the semivariable cost per unit.

C. An increase in the contribution margin per unit.

D. A decrease in income tax rates.

Answer (B) is correct. *(CIA, adapted)*

REQUIRED: The change in a CVP factor that will raise the breakeven point.

DISCUSSION: An increase in semivariable costs consists of either higher fixed cost, higher variable cost, or both. An increase in either will raise the BEP. If fixed costs increase, more units must be sold to cover the greater fixed costs. If variable costs increase, the unit contribution margin will decrease and again more units must be sold to cover the fixed costs.

Answer (A) is incorrect. If other factors are constant, an increase in sales price or a decrease in unit variable cost increases the unit contribution margin and lowers the BEP. Answer (C) is incorrect. An increase in the unit contribution margin lowers the BEP. Answer (D) is incorrect. If income taxes are taken into account, they are treated as variable costs. A decrease in variable costs lowers the BEP.

4.5.11. An enterprise sells three chemicals: petrol, septine, and tridol. Petrol is the company's most profitable product; tridol is the least profitable. Which one of the following events will definitely decrease the firm's overall breakeven point for the upcoming accounting period?

A. The installation of new computer-controlled machinery and subsequent layoff of assembly-line workers.

B. A decrease in tridol's selling price.

C. An increase in the overall market for septine.

D. An increase in anticipated sales of petrol relative to sales of septine and tridol.

Answer (D) is correct. *(CMA, adapted)*

REQUIRED: The event that will decrease the firm's overall breakeven point.

DISCUSSION: Since petrol is the company's most profitable product, it has a higher unit contribution margin than septine and tridol. Thus, an increase in sales of petrol relative to the other products will result in a higher weighted-average unit contribution margin and a lower breakeven point (fixed costs ÷ weighted-average UCM).

Answer (A) is incorrect. The acquisition of new machinery will result in greater fixed costs and thus a higher breakeven point. Answer (B) is incorrect. A decrease in selling price reduces the unit contribution margin, which in turn increases the breakeven point. Answer (C) is incorrect. The effect of an increase in the market for septine cannot be determined. The facts given do not indicate whether its unit contribution margin is greater or less than the weighted-average unit contribution margin for all the products.

4.5.12. A company increased the selling price of its product from $1.00 to $1.10 a unit when total fixed costs increased from $400,000 to $480,000 and variable cost per unit remained unchanged. How will these changes affect the breakeven point?

A. The breakeven point in units will be increased.

B. The breakeven point in units will be decreased.

C. The breakeven point in units will remain unchanged.

D. The effect cannot be determined from the information given.

Answer (D) is correct. *(CPA, adapted)*

REQUIRED: The effect on the BEP of an increase in selling price and fixed costs.

DISCUSSION: The breakeven point in units equals fixed costs divided by the UCM (selling price – variable costs). To determine the new breakeven point, the variable cost per unit, the total fixed costs, and the new selling price per unit must be known. The increase in selling price lowers the breakeven point and the increase in fixed costs raises it. Thus, the net effect of these changes cannot be determined when variable costs are not known.

4.5.13. A company is contemplating marketing a new product. Fixed costs will be $800,000 for production of 75,000 units or less and $1,200,000 if production exceeds 75,000 units. The variable cost ratio is 60% for the first 75,000 units. Variable costs will decrease to 50% of sales for units in excess of 75,000. If the product is expected to sell for $25 per unit, how many units must the company sell to break even?

A. 120,000

B. 111,000

C. 96,000

D. 80,000

Answer (B) is correct. *(Publisher, adapted)*

REQUIRED: The breakeven point in units with changing fixed and variable cost behavior patterns.

DISCUSSION: The BEP in units is equal to fixed cost divided by the difference between unit selling price and unit variable cost (the unit contribution margin). At less than 75,000 units, fixed costs are $800,000 and UCM is $10 [$25 – ($25 × 60%)]. At this UCM, 80,000 units ($800,000 ÷ $10) must be sold, but this volume is not within the relevant range. At any production level greater than 75,000 units, total fixed costs are $1,200,000 but there are two UCM layers. The first 75,000 units sold will produce a contribution margin of $750,000 (75,000 × $10). Hence, another $450,000 ($1,200,000 – $750,000) must be contributed. The UCM is $12.50 [$25 – ($25 × 50%)] for units in excess of 75,000, and 36,000 ($450,000 ÷ $12.50) additional units must be sold. Total unit sales at the BEP are 111,000 (75,000 + 36,000).

Answer (A) is incorrect. Only the first 75,000 units have a UCM of $10. Additional units in excess of 75,000 have a UCM of $12.50. Answer (C) is incorrect. The first 75,000 units have a UCM of only $10. Answer (D) is incorrect. Production of units in excess of 75,000 units will increase fixed costs from $800,000 to $1,200,000.

Questions 4.5.14 through 4.5.16 are based on the following information. MultiFrame Company has the following revenue and cost budgets for the two products it sells:

	Plastic Frames	Glass Frames
Sales price	$10.00	$15.00
Direct materials	(2.00)	(3.00)
Direct labor	(3.00)	(5.00)
Fixed overhead	(3.00)	(4.00)
Net income per unit	$ 2.00	$ 3.00
Budgeted unit sales	100,000	300,000

The budgeted unit sales equal the current unit demand, and total fixed overhead for the year is budgeted at $975,000. Assume that the company plans to maintain the same proportional mix. In numerical calculations, MultiFrame rounds to the nearest cent and unit.

4.5.14. The total number of units MultiFrame needs to produce and sell to break even is

A. 150,000 units.

B. 354,545 units.

C. 177,273 units.

D. 300,000 units.

Answer (A) is correct. *(CMA, adapted)*

REQUIRED: The total units sold at the breakeven point.

DISCUSSION: The calculation of the breakeven point is to divide the fixed costs by the contribution margin per unit. This determination is more complicated for a multi-product firm. If the same proportional product mix is maintained, one unit of plastic frames is sold for every three units of glass frames. Accordingly, a composite unit consists of four frames: one plastic and three glass. For plastic frames, the unit contribution margin is $5 ($10 – $2 – $3). For glass frames, the unit contribution margin is $7 ($15 – $3 – $5). Thus, the composite unit contribution margin is $26 ($5 + $7 + $7 + $7), and the breakeven point is 37,500 packages ($975,000 FC ÷ $26). Because each composite unit contains four frames, the total units sold equal 150,000.

Answer (B) is incorrect. The total units sold at the breakeven point is 150,000. Answer (C) is incorrect. The total units sold at the breakeven point is 150,000. Answer (D) is incorrect. The total units sold at the breakeven point is 150,000.

4.5.15. The total number of units needed to break even if the budgeted direct labor costs were $2 for plastic frames instead of $3 is

A. 154,028 units.

B. 144,444 units.

C. 156,000 units.

D. 146,177 units.

Answer (B) is correct. *(CMA, adapted)*

REQUIRED: The breakeven point in units if labor costs for the plastic frames are reduced.

DISCUSSION: If the labor costs for the plastic frames are reduced by $1, the composite unit contribution margin will be $27 {($10 – $2 – $2) + [($15 – $3 – $5) × 3]}. Hence, the new breakeven point is 144,444 units [4 units × ($975,000 FC ÷ $27)].

Answer (A) is incorrect. The new breakeven point is 144,444 units. Answer (C) is incorrect. The new breakeven point is 144,444 units. Answer (D) is incorrect. The new breakeven point is 144,444 units.

4.5.16. The total number of units needed to break even if sales were budgeted at 150,000 units of plastic frames and 300,000 units of glass frames with all other costs remaining constant is

A. 171,958 units.

B. 418,455 units.

C. 153,947 units.

D. 365,168 units.

Answer (C) is correct. *(CMA, adapted)*

REQUIRED: The total number of units needed to break even if the product mix is changed.

DISCUSSION: The unit contribution margins for plastic frames and glass frames are $5 ($10 – $2 – $3) and $7 ($15 – $3 – $5), respectively. If the number of plastic frames sold is 50% of the number of glass frames sold, a composite unit will contain one plastic frame and two glass frames. Thus, the composite unit contribution margin will be $19 ($5 + $7 + $7), and the breakeven point in units will be 153,947 [3 units × ($975,000 ÷ $19)].

Answer (A) is incorrect. The breakeven point in units will be 153,947. Answer (B) is incorrect. The breakeven point in units will be 153,947. Answer (D) is incorrect. The breakeven point in units will be 153,947.

4.6 Targeted Income

Questions 4.6.1 and 4.6.2 are based on the following information. A company that sells its single product for $40 per unit had after-tax net income for the past year of $1,188,000 after applying an effective tax rate of 40%. The projected costs for manufacturing and selling its single product in the coming year are listed below.

Variable costs per unit:	
Direct material	$ 5.00
Direct labor	4.00
Manufacturing overhead	6.00
Selling and administrative costs	3.00
Total variable cost per unit	$18.00
Annual fixed operating costs:	
Manufacturing overhead	$6,200,000
Selling and administrative costs	3,700,000
Total annual fixed cost	$9,900,000

4.6.1. The dollar sales volume required in the coming year to earn the same after-tax net income as the past year is

A. $20,160,000

B. $21,600,000

C. $23,400,000

D. $26,400,000

Answer (B) is correct. *(CIA, adapted)*

REQUIRED: The dollar sales volume required in the coming year to earn the same after-tax net income as the past year.

DISCUSSION: The desired after-tax net income is $1,188,000 (the past year's amount). Given a 40% tax rate, the pretax equivalent is $1,980,000 [$1,188,000 ÷ (1.0 – .40)]. Pretax net income equals dollar sales (unit sales × $40), minus total fixed costs, minus total variable costs (unit sales × unit variable cost). Hence, the contribution margin (sales – variable costs) is equated with the sum of fixed costs and the targeted pretax net income. Unit sales (S) equal 540,000, and sales dollars equal $21,600,000 (540,000 units × $40).

$$\begin{aligned} \$40\text{ S} - \$9{,}900{,}000 - \$18\text{ S} &= \$1{,}980{,}000 \\ \$22\text{ S} &= \$11{,}880{,}000 \\ \text{S} &= 540{,}000\text{ units} \end{aligned}$$

Answer (A) is incorrect. Not adjusting after-tax net income to pretax net income results in $20,160,000. Answer (C) is incorrect. Adjusting after-tax net income by dividing by the tax rate rather than one minus the tax rate results in $23,400,000. Answer (D) is incorrect. Equating the sum of the desired pretax net income and total fixed costs with total variable costs instead of the contribution margin results in $26,400,000.

4.6.2. The company has learned that a new direct material is available that will increase the quality of its product. The new material will increase the direct material costs by $3 per unit. The company will increase the selling price of the product to $50 per unit and increase its marketing costs by $1,575,000 to advertise the higher-quality product. The number of units the company has to sell in order to earn a 10% before-tax return on sales would be

A. 337,500 units.

B. 346,875 units.

C. 425,000 units.

D. 478,125 units.

Answer (D) is correct. *(CIA, adapted)*

REQUIRED: The number of units the company has to sell to earn a 10% before-tax return on sales.

DISCUSSION: Pretax net income (10% of dollar sales) equals dollar sales (unit sales × $50), minus total fixed costs (increased by $1,575,000 of marketing costs), minus total variable costs (increased by $3 per unit). Unit sales (S) therefore equal 478,125 units.

$$\begin{aligned} .10(\$50\text{ S}) &= \$50\text{ S} - (\$9{,}900{,}000 + \$1{,}575{,}000) - (\$18 + \$3)\text{S} \\ \$24\text{ S} &= \$11{,}475{,}000 \\ \text{S} &= 478{,}125\text{ units} \end{aligned}$$

Answer (A) is incorrect. Using the wrong sign for the pretax net income results in 337,500 units. Answer (B) is incorrect. Subtracting, not adding, the incremental marketing costs to determine total fixed costs results in 346,875 units. Answer (C) is incorrect. Failing to adjust for the increase in direct materials costs results in 425,000 units.

Questions 4.6.3 and 4.6.4 are based on the following information. A wholesale distributing company has budgeted its before-tax profit to be $643,500 for Year 3. The company is preparing its annual budget for Year 4 and has accumulated the following data:

Year 4 Data	
Projected annual revenues	$6,000,000
Variable costs as a percent of revenues:	
Cost of merchandise	30%
Sales commissions	5%
Shipping expenses	10%
Annual fixed operating costs:	
Selling expenses	$ 772,200
Administrative expenses	$1,801,800

4.6.3. If the wholesale distributing company wants to earn the same before-tax operating income in Year 4 as budgeted for Year 3, the annual revenues would not be the projected $6 million but would have to be

A. $4,950,000

B. $5,362,500

C. $5,850,000

D. $7,150,000

Answer (C) is correct. *(CIA, adapted)*

REQUIRED: The revenues needed to earn a given before-tax operating income.

DISCUSSION: The contribution margin ratio is 55% (100% – 30% variable cost for merchandise – 5% variable cost for sales commissions – 10% variable cost for shipping). Thus, the necessary revenues equal the sum of the fixed costs and the desired before-tax operating income, divided by the CMR, or $5,850,000 [($772,200 + $1,801,800 + $643,500) ÷ 55%].

Answer (A) is incorrect. The amount of $4,950,000 results from using a 65% contribution margin, which incorrectly excludes the 10% variable cost for shipping. Answer (B) is incorrect. The amount of $5,362,500 results from using a 60% contribution margin, which incorrectly excludes the 5% variable cost for sales commissions. Answer (D) is incorrect. The amount of $7,150,000 results from using a 45% contribution margin, which is the sum of the variable cost percentages.

4.6.4. Using the original $6 million projection, the wholesale distributing company's margin of safety in terms of revenues for Year 4 would be

A. $82,500

B. $150,000

C. $280,000

D. $1,320,000

Answer (D) is correct. *(CIA, adapted)*

REQUIRED: The margin of safety.

DISCUSSION: The margin of safety equals the difference between the projected Year 4 revenues and the breakeven point. The projected revenues equal $6 million. The breakeven point equals the annual fixed operating costs of $2,574,000 ($772,200 + $1,801,800) divided by the contribution margin ratio of 55% (100% – 30% – 5% – 10%), or $4,680,000. The margin of safety is $1,320,000 ($6,000,000 – $4,680,000).

Answer (A) is incorrect. The amount of $82,500 equals the difference between the before-tax operating income for Year 4 and Year 3. Answer (B) is incorrect. The amount of $150,000 equals the difference between projected Year 4 revenues and the revenues required to earn the same before-tax operating income in Year 4 as in Year 3. Answer (C) is incorrect. The amount of $280,000 equals the difference between the projected revenues for Year 4 and the breakeven point based on a 45% contribution margin ratio.

4.6.5. In using cost-volume-profit analysis to calculate expected unit sales, which of the following should be added to fixed costs in the numerator?

A. Predicted operating loss.

B. Predicted operating income.

C. Unit contribution margin.

D. Variable costs.

Answer (B) is correct. *(CPA, adapted)*

REQUIRED: The addition to fixed costs when calculating expected unit sales.

DISCUSSION: CVP analysis can be used to restate the equation for target net income to determine the required level of unit sales.

$$\text{Target unit volume} = \frac{\text{Fixed costs} + \text{Target operating income}}{\text{UCM}}$$

Answer (A) is incorrect. Predicted operating loss is subtracted from fixed costs, not added. Answer (C) is incorrect. Unit contribution margin is the denominator. Answer (D) is incorrect. Variable costs are a component of unit contribution margin.

Questions 4.6.6 through 4.6.8 are based on the following information. The data below pertain to the forecasts of XYZ Company for the upcoming year.

	Total Cost	Unit Cost
Sales (40,000 units)	$1,000,000	$25
Raw materials	160,000	4
Direct labor	280,000	7
Manufacturing overhead:		
Variable	80,000	2
Fixed	360,000	
Selling and general expenses:		
Variable	120,000	3
Fixed	225,000	

4.6.6. In forecasting purchases of inventory for XYZ Company, all of the following are useful except

A. Knowledge of the behavior of business cycles.

B. Internal allocations of costs to different segments of the firm.

C. Information on the seasonal variations in demand.

D. Econometric modeling.

Answer (B) is correct. *(CIA, adapted)*

REQUIRED: The item not useful for forecasting inventory purchases.

DISCUSSION: Internal accounting allocations of costs to different segments of the firm are arbitrary assignments of already incurred costs that are irrelevant to forecasting the firm's purchases.

Answer (A) is incorrect. Knowing the behavior of business cycles can be valuable when forecasting the required purchases of inventory. Answer (C) is incorrect. Understanding seasonal variations in demand for the product can be valuable when forecasting the required purchases of inventory. Answer (D) is incorrect. Using econometric models can be valuable when forecasting the required purchases of inventory.

4.6.7. How many units does XYZ Company need to produce and sell to make a before-tax profit of 10% of sales?

A. 65,000 units.

B. 36,562 units.

C. 90,000 units.

D. 25,000 units.

Answer (C) is correct. *(CIA, adapted)*

REQUIRED: The number of units to produce and sell to meet a profit goal.

DISCUSSION: Revenue minus variable and fixed expenses equals net income. If X equals unit sales, revenue equals \$25X, total variable expenses equal \$16X (\$4 + \$7 + \$2 + \$3), total fixed expenses equal \$585,000 (\$360,000 + \$225,000), and net income equals 10% of revenue. Hence, X equals 90,000 units.

$$\begin{aligned} \$25X - \$16X - \$585{,}000 &= \$25X \times 10\% \\ 6.5X &= \$585{,}000 \\ X &= 90{,}000 \text{ units} \end{aligned}$$

Answer (A) is incorrect. The breakeven point is 65,000 units. Answer (B) is incorrect. It produces a net loss. Answer (D) is incorrect. The amount of 25,000 is the excess of the required units over the breakeven point.

4.6.8. Assuming that XYZ Company sells 80,000 units, what is the maximum that can be paid for an advertising campaign while still breaking even?

A. $135,000

B. $1,015,000

C. $535,000

D. $695,000

Answer (A) is correct. *(CIA, adapted)*

REQUIRED: The maximum that can be paid for an advertising campaign while still breaking even.

DISCUSSION: The company will break even when net income equals zero. Net income is equal to revenue minus variable expenses and fixed expenses, including advertising. Thus, if X equals advertising cost, the equation is

$$\begin{aligned} (80{,}000)(\$25) - (80{,}000)(\$16) - \$585{,}000 - X &= 0 \\ \$2{,}000{,}000 - \$1{,}280{,}000 - \$585{,}000 - X &= 0 \\ X &= \$135{,}000 \end{aligned}$$

4.6.9. Based on potential sales of 500 units per year, a new product has estimated traceable costs of $990,000. What is the target price to obtain a 15% profit margin on sales?

A. $2,329

B. $2,277

C. $1,980

D. $1,935

Answer (A) is correct. *(CPA, adapted)*

REQUIRED: The target price.

DISCUSSION: Costs of the product must be 85% of sales to achieve a 15% profit on sales. Thus, sales must be $1,164,706 ($990,000 ÷ .85). The price per unit is $2,329 ($1,164,706 ÷ 500).

Answer (B) is incorrect. The amount of $2,277 results from multiplying $990,000 by 1.15 and dividing by 500 units. Answer (C) is incorrect. The cost per unit is $1,980 ($990,000 ÷ 500 units). Answer (D) is incorrect. The amount of $1,935 is 85% of $2,277.

Questions 4.6.10 and 4.6.11 are based on the following information.

Delphi Company has developed a new product that will be marketed for the first time during the next fiscal year. Although the Marketing Department estimates that 35,000 units could be sold at $36 per unit, Delphi's management has allocated only enough manufacturing capacity to produce a maximum of 25,000 units of the new product annually. The fixed costs associated with the new product are budgeted at $450,000 for the year, which includes $60,000 for depreciation on new manufacturing equipment.

Data associated with each unit of product are presented as follows. Delphi is subject to a 40% income tax rate.

Direct material	$ 7.00
Direct labor	3.50
Manufacturing overhead	4.00
Variable manufacturing cost	$14.50
Selling expenses	1.50
Total variable cost	$16.00

4.6.10. The maximum after-tax profit that can be earned by Delphi Company from sales of the new product during the next fiscal year is

A. $30,000

B. $50,000

C. $110,000

D. $66,000

Answer (A) is correct. *(CMA, adapted)*

REQUIRED: The maximum after-tax income.

DISCUSSION: Delphi's breakeven point is 22,500 units ($450,000 fixed costs ÷ $20 UCM). The unit contribution margin (UCM) is $20 ($36 selling price – $16 unit variable costs). At the breakeven point, all fixed costs have been recovered. Hence, pretax profit equals the unit contribution margin times unit sales in excess of the breakeven point, or $50,000 [(25,000 unit sales – 22,500 BEP) × $20 UCM]. After-tax profit is $30,000 [$50,000 × (1.0 – .40)].

Answer (B) is incorrect. The amount of $50,000 is the pre-tax profit. Answer (C) is incorrect. The amount of $110,000 fails to include depreciation as a fixed cost and ignores income taxes. Answer (D) is incorrect. The amount of $66,000 fails to include depreciation as a fixed cost.

4.6.11. Delphi Company's management has stipulated that it will not approve the continued manufacture of the new product after the next fiscal year unless the after-tax profit is at least $75,000 the first year. The unit selling price to achieve this target profit must be at least

A. $37.00

B. $36.60

C. $34.60

D. $39.00

Answer (D) is correct. *(CMA, adapted)*

REQUIRED: The unit selling price to achieve a targeted after-tax profit.

DISCUSSION: If X represents the necessary selling price, 25,000 equals maximum sales volume, $16 is the variable cost per unit, $450,000 is the total fixed cost, and $125,000 [$75,000 target after-tax profit ÷ (1.0 – .40)] is the desired pre-tax profit, the following formula may be solved to determine the requisite unit price:

$$\begin{aligned} 25{,}000(X - \$16) - \$450{,}000 &= \$125{,}000 \\ 25{,}000X - \$400{,}000 - \$450{,}000 &= \$125{,}000 \\ 25{,}000X &= \$975{,}000 \\ X &= \$39 \end{aligned}$$

Answer (A) is incorrect. The amount of $37.00 does not consider income taxes. Answer (B) is incorrect. The amount of $36.60 excludes depreciation. Answer (C) is incorrect. The amount of $34.60 does not include depreciation or taxes.

Questions 4.6.12 through 4.6.14 are based on the following information. Bruell Electronics Co. is developing a new product, surge protectors for high-voltage electrical flows. The cost information below relates to the product:

	Unit Costs
Direct materials	$3.25
Direct labor	4.00
Distribution	.75

The company will also be absorbing $120,000 of additional fixed costs associated with this new product. A corporate fixed charge of $20,000 currently absorbed by other products will be allocated to this new product.

4.6.12. If the selling price is $14 per unit, the breakeven point in units (rounded to the nearest hundred) for surge protectors is

A. 8,500 units.

B. 10,000 units.

C. 15,000 units.

D. 20,000 units.

Answer (D) is correct. *(CMA, adapted)*

REQUIRED: The breakeven point in units.

DISCUSSION: The breakeven point in units for a new product equals total additional fixed costs divided by the unit contribution margin. Unit variable costs total $8 ($3.25 + $4.00 + $.75). Thus, UCM is $6 ($14 unit selling price – $8 unit variable cost), and the breakeven point is 20,000 units ($120,000 ÷ $6).

Answer (A) is incorrect. A breakeven point of 8,500 units ignores variable costs. Answer (B) is incorrect. The breakeven point is 20,000 units when the contribution margin is $6 per unit. Answer (C) is incorrect. This number of units equals fixed costs divided by unit variable cost.

4.6.13. How many surge protectors (rounded to the nearest hundred) must Bruell Electronics sell at a selling price of $14 per unit to gain $30,000 additional income before taxes?

A. 10,700 units.

B. 12,100 units.

C. 20,000 units.

D. 25,000 units.

Answer (D) is correct. *(CMA, adapted)*

REQUIRED: The number of units to be sold to generate a targeted pre-tax income.

DISCUSSION: The number of units to be sold to generate a specified pre-tax income equals the sum of total fixed costs and the targeted pre-tax income, divided by the unit contribution margin. Unit variable costs total $8 ($3.25 + $4.00 + $.75), and UCM is $6 ($14 unit selling price – $8). Thus, the desired unit sales level equals 25,000 units [($120,000 + $30,000) ÷ $6].

Answer (A) is incorrect. The number of 10,700 units is based on a UCM equal to selling price. Answer (B) is incorrect. A contribution margin of $6 per unit necessitates sales of 25,000 units to produce a $30,000 before-tax profit. Answer (C) is incorrect. The number of 20,000 units is the breakeven point.

4.6.14. How many surge protectors (rounded to the nearest hundred) must Bruell Electronics sell at a selling price of $14 per unit to increase after-tax income by $30,000? Bruell Electronics' effective income tax rate is 40%.

A. 10,700 units.

B. 12,100 units.

C. 20,000 units.

D. 28,300 units.

Answer (D) is correct. *(CMA, adapted)*

REQUIRED: The number of units to be sold to generate a specified after-tax income.

DISCUSSION: The number of units to be sold to generate a specified pre-tax income equals the sum of total fixed costs and the targeted pre-tax income, divided by the unit contribution margin. Given a desired after-tax income of $30,000 and a tax rate of 40%, the targeted pre-tax income must be $50,000 [$30,000 ÷ (1.0 – .40)]. Unit variable costs total $8 ($3.25 + $4.00 + $.75), and UCM is $6 ($14 unit selling price – $8). Hence, the desired unit sales level is 28,333 [($120,000 + $50,000) ÷ $6]. Rounded to the nearest hundred, the answer is 28,300 units.

Answer (A) is incorrect. The number of 10,700 units is based on a UCM equal to the selling price and $30,000 of pretax income. Answer (B) is incorrect. A $6 UCM necessitates sales of 28,300 units to produce a $30,000 after-tax profit. Answer (C) is incorrect. The number of 20,000 units is the breakeven point.

4.6.15. A controller developed the following direct-costing income statement for Year 1:

			Per Unit
Sales (150,000 units at $30)		$ 4,500,000	$30
Variable costs:			
Direct materials	$1,050,000		$ 7
Direct labor	1,500,000		10
Mfg. overhead	300,000		2
Selling & mktg.	300,000		2
		(3,150,000)	(21)
Contribution margin		$ 1,350,000	$ 9
Fixed costs:			
Mfg. overhead	$ 600,000		$ 4
Selling & mktg.	300,000		2
		(900,000)	(6)
Operating income		$ 450,000	$ 3

The controller based the next year's budget on the assumption that fixed costs, unit sales, and the sales price would remain as they were in Year 1, but with operating income being reduced to $300,000. By July of Year 2, the controller was able to predict that unit sales would increase over Year 1 levels by 10%. Based on the Year 2 budget and the new information, the predicted Year 2 operating income would be

A. $300,000

B. $330,000

C. $420,000

D. $585,000

Answer (C) is correct. *(CIA, adapted)*

REQUIRED: The projected net income given constant FC and sales price and different estimates of unit sales.

DISCUSSION: Since fixed costs, unit sales, and sales price are projected to remain the same, and operating income will be reduced, the variable costs must increase. If the July Year 2 prediction that unit sales will increase by 10% from 150,000 to 165,000 is based on the budgeted FC, sales price, and VC, predicted operating income can be calculated as follows:

Contribution margin – Fixed costs = Operating income
CM – FC = $ 300,000
CM – $900,000 = $ 300,000
CM = $1,200,000

Budgeted UCM = $1,200,000 ÷ 150,000 units = $8

Total CM = 165,000 units × $8 = $1,320,000
FC = (900,000)
Operating income = $ 420,000

Answer (A) is incorrect. This amount is the projected net income before the increase in sales. Answer (B) is incorrect. The amount of $330,000 takes into account a 10% increase in fixed costs to $990,000 when the fixed costs did not increase. Answer (D) is incorrect. The UCM for Year 2 is $8 per unit, not $9.

4.6.16. A company, which is subject to a 40% income tax rate, had the following operating data for the period just ended:

Selling price per unit	$ 60
Variable cost per unit	22
Fixed costs	504,000

Management plans to improve the quality of its sole product by (1) replacing a component that costs $3.50 with a higher-grade unit that costs $5.50 and (2) acquiring a $180,000 packing machine. The company will depreciate the machine over a 10-year life with no estimated salvage value by the straight-line method of depreciation. If the company wants to earn after-tax income of $172,800 in the upcoming period, it must sell

A. 19,300 units.

B. 21,316 units.

C. 22,500 units.

D. 23,800 units.

Answer (C) is correct. *(CMA, adapted)*

REQUIRED: The number of units to be sold to generate a targeted after-tax profit given that variable costs and fixed costs increase.

DISCUSSION: The units to be sold equal fixed costs plus the desired pretax profit, divided by the unit contribution margin. In the preceding year, the unit contribution margin is $38 ($60 selling price – $22 unit variable cost). That amount will decrease by $2 to $36 in the upcoming year because of use of a higher-grade component. Fixed costs will increase from $504,000 to $522,000 as a result of the $18,000 ($180,000 ÷ 10 years) increase in fixed costs attributable to depreciation on the new machine. Dividing the $172,800 of desired after-tax income by 60% (the complement of the tax rate) produces a desired before-tax income of $288,000. Hence, the breakeven point in units is 22,500 [($522,000 + $288,000) ÷ $36].

Answer (A) is incorrect. The number of 19,300 units does not take income taxes into consideration. Answer (B) is incorrect. The number of 21,316 units fails to consider the increased variable costs from the introduction of the higher-priced component. Answer (D) is incorrect. The number of 23,800 units does not take income taxes into consideration, and it includes the entire cost of the new machine as a fixed cost.

4.6.17. The following information is taken from Wampler Co.'s current-year contribution income statement:

Sales	$200,000
Contribution margin	120,000
Fixed costs	90,000
Income taxes	12,000

What was Wampler's margin of safety?

A. $50,000

B. $150,000

C. $168,000

D. $182,000

Answer (A) is correct. *(CPA, adapted)*

REQUIRED: The margin of safety.

DISCUSSION: The margin of safety is the excess of sales over breakeven sales. Thus, income taxes are not relevant because the margin of safety is a pretax amount. Sales are given ($200,000). Breakeven sales in dollars can be calculated as follows:

Breakeven sales = Fixed costs ÷ Contr. margin ratio
= $90,000 ÷ ($120,000 ÷ $200,000)
= $90,000 ÷ 0.6
= $150,000

The margin of safety is thus $50,000 ($200,000 sales – $150,000 BE sales).

Answer (B) is incorrect. The amount of $150,000 equals breakeven sales. Answer (C) is incorrect. Breakeven sales do not equal $32,000 ($200,000 sales – $168,000). Answer (D) is incorrect. Breakeven sales do not equal $18,000 ($200,000 sales – $182,000).

4.7 Multiproduct (Service) Breakeven

4.7.1. Bjax Corporation has a separate production line for each of two products: A and B. Product A has a contribution margin of $4 per unit, Product B has a contribution margin of $5 per unit, and the corporation's nonvariable expenses of $200,000 are unchanged regardless of volume. Under these conditions, which of the following statements will always be applicable?

A. At a sales volume in excess of 25,000 units of A and 25,000 units of B, operations will be profitable.

B. The ratio of net profit to total sales for B will be larger than for A.

C. The contribution margin per unit of direct materials is lower for A than for B.

D. Income will be maximized if B only is sold.

Answer (A) is correct. *(CIA, adapted)*

REQUIRED: The statement that is always true given contribution margins and fixed costs for two products.

DISCUSSION: If Bjax Corporation has a sales volume in excess of 25,000 units of A and 25,000 units of B, operations will always be profitable. Given Product A's contribution margin of $4 per unit, sales of 25,000 units will yield a contribution margin of $100,000. The contribution margin per unit for Product B is given as $5; therefore, sales of 25,000 units will yield a contribution margin of $125,000. The total contribution margin for the two products is $225,000 ($100,000 + $125,000). Fixed costs are $200,000. Thus, operating income is at least $25,000.

Answer (B) is incorrect. No information is given about net profit or total sales. Answer (C) is incorrect. No information is given on direct materials. Answer (D) is incorrect. If only B is sold, the income made from A is lost. Each product can be produced without affecting the other.

4.7.2. Von Stutgatt International's breakeven point is 8,000 racing bicycles and 12,000 five-speed bicycles. If the selling price and variable costs are $570 and $200 for a racer and $180 and $90 for a five-speed, respectively, what is the weighted-average contribution margin?

A. $90

B. $202

C. $230

D. $370

Answer (B) is correct. *(J.B. Romal)*

REQUIRED: The weighted-average contribution margin.

DISCUSSION: The contribution margin is selling price minus variable costs. The CM for a racer is $370 ($570 – $200), and the CM for a five-speed is $90 ($180 – $90). The sales mix is 40% racers [8,000 ÷ (8,000 + 12,000)] and 60% five-speeds [12,000 ÷ (8,000 + 12,000)]. Thus, the weighted-average CM is $202 [($370 × 40%) + ($90 × 60%)].

Answer (A) is incorrect. The CM for a five-speed is $90. Answer (C) is incorrect. The amount of $230 is a simple average. Answer (D) is incorrect. The CM for a racer is $370.

Questions 4.7.3 through 4.7.8 are based on the following information. The officers of Bradshaw Company are reviewing the profitability of the company's four products and the potential effects of several proposals for varying the product mix. An excerpt from the income statement and other data follow:

	Totals	Product P	Product Q	Product R	Product S
Revenues	$62,600	$10,000	$18,000	$12,600	$22,000
Cost of goods sold	44,274	4,750	7,056	13,968	18,500
Gross profit	$18,326	$ 5,250	$10,944	$ (1,368)	$ 3,500
Operating expenses	12,012	1,990	2,976	2,826	4,220
Income before income taxes	$ 6,314	$ 3,260	$ 7,968	$ (4,194)	$ (720)
Units sold		1,000	1,200	1,800	2,000
Sales price per unit		$10.00	$15.00	$7.00	$11.00
Variable cost of goods sold per unit		2.50	3.00	6.50	6.00
Variable operating expenses per unit		1.17	1.25	1.00	1.20

Each of the following proposals is to be considered independently of the other proposals. Consider only the product changes stated in each proposal; the activity of other products remains stable. Ignore income taxes.

4.7.3. If Product R is discontinued, the effect on income will be

A. $4,194 increase.

B. $900 increase.

C. $1,368 increase.

D. $12,600 decrease.

Answer (B) is correct. *(CPA, adapted)*

REQUIRED: The effect on income if one product in a mix is discontinued.

DISCUSSION: If Product R is discontinued, the effect will be a $900 increase in income. Fixed costs are assumed to remain the same. The variable costs per unit of R are $7.50 ($6.50 + $1.00). Given that the sales price per unit is $7.00, the negative UCM is $.50 ($7.00 – $7.50). Based on sales of 1,800 units, the loss is $900. Discontinuing the R product line will therefore increase income by $900.

Answer (A) is incorrect. A $4,194 increase assumes that the fixed costs associated with Product R would also be eliminated. Answer (C) is incorrect. A $1,368 increase assumes that the operating expenses are all fixed expenses. Answer (D) is incorrect. The revenue generated by Product R is $12,600.

4.7.4. If Product R is discontinued and a consequent loss of customers causes a decrease of 200 units in sales of Q, the total effect on income will be

A. $15,600 decrease.

B. $1,250 decrease.

C. $2,044 increase.

D. $2,866 increase.

Answer (B) is correct. *(CPA, adapted)*

REQUIRED: The effect on income if discontinuing one product also decreases sales of another product.

DISCUSSION: If R is discontinued, the effect on income is a $900 increase. Fixed costs are assumed to remain the same. The variable costs per unit of R are $7.50 ($6.50 + $1.00). Given that the sales price per unit is $7.00, the negative UCM is $.50 ($7.00 – $7.50). Based on sales of 1,800 units, the loss is $900. Discontinuing the R product line will therefore increase income by $900. Q's UCM is $10.75 ($15 SP – $3 – $1.25). Hence, a 200-unit decrease results in a reduction in income of $2,150 (200 × $10.75). The net effect is a decrease in income of $1,250 ($2,150 loss – $900 gain).

Answer (A) is incorrect. The decrease in sales is $15,600. Answer (C) is incorrect. The total effect on income is a decrease. Answer (D) is incorrect. The total effect on income is a decrease.

4.7.5. If the sales price of R is increased to $8 with a decrease in the number of units sold to 1,500, the effect on income will be

A. $2,199 decrease.

B. $600 decrease.

C. $750 increase.

D. $1,650 increase.

Answer (D) is correct. *(CPA, adapted)*

REQUIRED: The effect on income if the sales price of a product increases and sales volume declines.

DISCUSSION: If 1,500 units of R are sold at $8, the unit contribution margin is $.50 ($8.00 – $6.50 – $1.00 = $.50), and the total contribution margin is $750. R currently has a negative CM of $900. The net effect is an increase in income of $1,650 ($750 CM + recovery of the $900 negative CM).

Answer (A) is incorrect. The old unit price did not cover variable units. Thus, if the new unit sales price exceeds the unit variable costs, the income effect must be an increase. Answer (B) is incorrect. The old unit price did not cover variable units. Thus, if the new unit sales price exceeds the unit variable costs, the income effect must be an increase. Answer (C) is incorrect. The amount of $750 is the CM on sales of 1,500 units of R at $8 per unit.

4.7.6. The plant in which R is produced can be used to produce a new product, T. Total variable costs and expenses per unit of T are $8.05, and 1,600 units can be sold at $9.50 each. If T is introduced and R is discontinued, the total effect on income will be

A. $3,220 increase.

B. $2,600 increase.

C. $2,320 increase.

D. $1,420 increase.

Answer (A) is correct. *(CPA, adapted)*

REQUIRED: The effect on income when a new product is introduced and an old one discontinued.

DISCUSSION: If 1,600 units of T can be sold at $9.50 each, the unit contribution margin (UCM) is $1.45 ($9.50 – $8.05), and the total CM is $2,320 (1,600 × $1.45). Product R currently contributes a negative CM of $900. Thus, the net effect of discontinuing R and introducing T is a $3,220 increase in income ($2,320 + $900).

Answer (B) is incorrect. The increase in sales is $2,600. Answer (C) is incorrect. The total CM for Product T is $2,320. Answer (D) is incorrect. The $900 of negative CM from R should be added to, not subtracted from, the CM generated by producing T.

4.7.7. Production of P can be doubled by adding a second shift, but higher wages must be paid, increasing the variable cost of goods sold to $3.50 for each additional unit. If the 1,000 additional units of P can be sold at $10 each, the total effect on income will be

A. $10,000 increase.

B. $6,500 increase.

C. $5,330 increase.

D. $2,260 increase.

Answer (C) is correct. *(CPA, adapted)*

REQUIRED: The effect on income if additional units can be produced and variable manufacturing costs increase.

DISCUSSION: The sale of the 1,000 additional units at a price of $10 and a variable cost of $3.50 results in a UCM of $5.33 ($10 – $3.50 – $1.17). If 1,000 additional units are sold, the effect on net income will be a $5,330 increase (1,000 × $5.33).

Answer (A) is incorrect. The increase in revenue is $10,000. Answer (B) is incorrect. A $6,500 increase does not consider the $1.17 variable operating expense per unit. Answer (D) is incorrect. The amount of $2,260 equals the current income before taxes of $3,260 for 1,000 units of P minus the $1,000 increase in variable costs.

4.7.8. Part of the plant in which P is produced can easily be adapted to the production of S, but changes in quantities may make changes in sales prices advisable. If production of P is reduced to 500 units (to be sold at $12 each) and production of S is increased to 2,500 units (to be sold at $10.50 each), the total effect on income will be

A. $1,515 decrease.

B. $2,540 decrease.

C. $4,165 increase.

D. $6,330 decrease.

Answer (A) is correct. *(CPA, adapted)*

REQUIRED: The effect on income if the production and prices of two products change.

DISCUSSION: The new and old contribution margins can be calculated as follows:

New CM			
P	500 × ($12.00 – $3.67)	=	$ 4,165
S	2,500 × ($10.50 – $7.20)	=	8,250
			$12,415
Old CM			
P	1,000 × ($10.00 – $3.67)	=	$ 6,330
S	2,000 × ($11.00 – $7.20)	=	7,600
			$13,930

The loss in income is thus $1,515 ($12,415 new – $13,930 old).

Answer (B) is incorrect. The total income of P and S is $2,540. Answer (C) is incorrect. The new CM of P of $4,165. Answer (D) is incorrect. The old CM of P is $6,330.

4.7.9. A company must decide which one of the following four products to manufacture:

Product	Sales Price	Variable Cost	Direct Labor Hours per Unit
M	$10	$ 7	1.5
N	20	12	2.0
O	5	2	0.5
P	8	4	1.0

Which product will result in the highest contribution margin per hour?

A. M.

B. N.

C. O.

D. P.

Answer (C) is correct. *(CIA, adapted)*

REQUIRED: The product with the highest contribution margin per hour.

DISCUSSION: Contribution margin equals price minus variable cost. The contribution margins of M, N, O, and P are $3 ($10 – $7), $8 ($20 – $12), $3 ($5 – $2), and $4 ($8 – $4), respectively. However, the contribution margins per hour are $2 ($3 ÷ 1.5), $4 ($8 ÷ 2.0), $6 ($3 ÷ 0.5), and $4 ($4 ÷ 1.0), respectively. Consequently, O has the highest contribution margin per hour.

Answer (A) is incorrect. Product M has a CM per hour of $2.00 [($10 – $7) ÷ 1.5], whereas product O's is $6.00 [($5 – $2) ÷ 0.5]. Answer (B) is incorrect. Product N has the highest contribution margin, but product O has the highest contribution margin per hour. Answer (D) is incorrect. Product P has a CM per hour of $4.00 [($8 – $4) ÷ 1.0], but O's is $6.00 [($5 – $2) ÷ 0.5].

Questions 4.7.10 and 4.7.11 are based on the following information. The data below pertain to two types of products manufactured by Cobb Corp. Fixed costs total $300,000 annually. The expected mix in units is 60% for product Y and 40% for product Z.

	Per Unit	
	Sales Price	Variable Costs
Product Y	$120	$ 70
Product Z	500	200

4.7.10. How much is Cobb's breakeven point in units?

A. 857

B. 1,111

C. 2,000

D. 2,459

Answer (C) is correct. *(CPA, adapted)*

REQUIRED: The BEP in units for a two-product firm.

DISCUSSION: The BEP in units is equal to fixed costs divided by the unit contribution margin (UCM). The weighted-average UCM is $150, calculated as follows:

	Product Y	Product Z
Sales price	$120	$500
Minus: Variable costs	(70)	(200)
Contribution margin	$ 50	$300
Times: Mix ratio	× 60%	× 40%
Weighted contribution margin	$ 30	$120

The BEP is 2,000 units ($300,000 fixed costs ÷ $150 UCM).

Answer (A) is incorrect. The amount of 857 units assumes a $350 weighted-average CM. Answer (B) is incorrect. The amount of 1,111 units results from dividing fixed costs by the sum of unit variable costs for Y and Z. Answer (D) is incorrect. The amount of 2,459 units results from dividing fixed costs by the weighted-average variable costs.

4.7.11. How much is Cobb's breakeven point in dollars?

A. $300,000

B. $400,000

C. $420,000

D. $544,000

Answer (D) is correct. *(CPA, adapted)*

REQUIRED: The BEP in dollars for a two-product firm.

DISCUSSION: The BEP in units is equal to fixed costs divided by the unit contribution margin (UCM). The weighted-average UCM is $150, calculated as follows:

	Product Y	Product Z
Sales price	$120	$500
Minus: Variable costs	(70)	(200)
Contribution margin	$ 50	$300
Times: Mix ratio	× 60%	× 40%
Weighted contribution margin	$ 30	$120

The BEP in units is 2,000 units ($300,000 fixed costs ÷ $150 UCM). The revenue (sales) mix will include 1,200 units of Y (2,000 × 60%) and 800 units of Z (2,000 × 40%). Hence, the BEP in dollars will be $544,000 [(1,200 × $120) + (800 × $500)].

Answer (A) is incorrect. The amount of fixed costs is $300,000. Answer (B) is incorrect. This figure is equal to 800 units of Z times $500. Answer (C) is incorrect. This figure equals the sum of the UCMs of Y and Z ($50 + $300 = $350) times 1,200 units.

Questions 4.7.12 through 4.7.14 are based on the following information.

Moorehead Manufacturing Company produces two products for which the data presented to the right have been tabulated. Fixed manufacturing cost is applied at a rate of $1.00 per machine hour. The sales manager has had a $160,000 increase in the budget allotment for advertising and wants to apply the money to the most profitable product. The products are not substitutes for one another in the eyes of the company's customers.

Per Unit	XY-7	BD-4
Selling price	$4.00	$3.00
Variable manufacturing cost	2.00	1.50
Fixed manufacturing cost	.75	.20
Variable selling cost	1.00	1.00

4.7.12. Suppose the sales manager chooses to devote the entire $160,000 to increased advertising for XY-7. The minimum increase in sales units of XY-7 required to offset the increased advertising is

A. 640,000 units.

B. 160,000 units.

C. 128,000 units.

D. 80,000 units.

Answer (B) is correct. *(CMA, adapted)*

REQUIRED: The minimum increase in sales units to offset increased advertising costs.

DISCUSSION: The contribution margin (CM) for XY-7 is $1 per unit ($4 selling price – $3 unit variable cost). Thus, 160,000 units of XY-7 will generate an additional $160,000 of CM, which is sufficient to cover the increase in advertising costs.

Answer (A) is incorrect. This number of units would be the result if the UCM for XY-7 were $.25 instead of $1.00 (640,000 × $.25 = $160,000). Fixed manufacturing costs are not included in determining UCM. Answer (C) is incorrect. This number of units implies a $1.25 UCM. Variable selling costs are included and fixed manufacturing costs are not included in determining UCM. Answer (D) is incorrect. This number of units implies a $2.00 UCM. The correct UCM of $1.00 is found by subtracting all variable costs from the selling price.

4.7.13. Suppose the sales manager chooses to devote the entire $160,000 to increased advertising for BD-4. The minimum increase in sales dollars of BD-4 required to offset the increased advertising would be

A. $160,000

B. $320,000

C. $960,000

D. $1,600,000

Answer (C) is correct. *(CMA, adapted)*

REQUIRED: The minimum increase in sales dollars to offset increased advertising costs.

DISCUSSION: Sales dollars must increase sufficiently to cover the $160,000 increase in advertising. The unit contribution margin for BD-4 is $.50 ($3 selling price – $2.50 variable costs), and the CMR is 1/6 (UCM ÷ $3 selling price). Dividing the $160,000 by 1/6 gives the sales dollars necessary to generate a CM of $960,000 ($160,000 ÷ 1/6 = $960,000).

Answer (A) is incorrect. A $1 increase in sales does not result in a $1 increase in profits. Variable costs of producing the units must be deducted in order to determine the contribution margin derived from each unit sold. Answer (B) is incorrect. The number 320,000 is the number of sales units, not sales dollars, needed to offset the increased advertising costs. Answer (D) is incorrect. Fixed manufacturing costs are not included in determining unit contribution margin.

4.7.14. Suppose Moorehead has only 100,000 machine hours that can be made available to produce additional units of XY-7 and BD-4. If the potential increase in sales units for either product resulting from advertising is far in excess of this production capacity, which product should be advertised and what is the estimated increase in contribution margin earned?

A. Product XY-7 should be produced, yielding a contribution margin of $75,000.

B. Product XY-7 should be produced, yielding a contribution margin of $133,333.

C. Product BD-4 should be produced, yielding a contribution margin of $187,500.

D. Product BD-4 should be produced, yielding a contribution margin of $250,000.

Answer (D) is correct. *(CMA, adapted)*

REQUIRED: The more profitable product and the estimated increase in contribution margin.

DISCUSSION: The machine hours are a scarce resource that must be allocated to the product(s) in a proportion that maximizes the total CM. Given that potential additional sales of either product are in excess of production capacity, only the product with the greater CM per unit of scarce resource should be produced. XY-7 requires .75 hours; BD-4 requires .2 hours of machine time (given fixed manufacturing cost applied at $1 per machine hour of $.75 for XY-7 and $.20 for BD-4).

XY-7 has a CM of $1.33 per machine hour ($1 UCM ÷ .75 hours), and BD-4 has a CM of $2.50 per machine hour ($.50 ÷ .2 hours). Thus, only BD-4 should be produced, yielding a CM of $250,000 (100,000 × $2.50). The key to the analysis is CM per unit of scarce resource.

Answer (A) is incorrect. Product XY-7 actually has a CM of $133,333, which is lower than the $250,000 CM for product BD-4. Answer (B) is incorrect. Product BD-4 has a higher CM at $250,000. Answer (C) is incorrect. Product BD-4 has a CM of $250,000.

Questions 4.7.15 and 4.7.16 are based on the following information. A company sells two products, X and Y. The sales mix consists of a composite unit of 2 units of X for every 5 units of Y (2:5). Fixed costs are $49,500. The unit contribution margins for X and Y are $2.50 and $1.20, respectively.

4.7.15. Considering the company as a whole, the number of composite units to break even is

A. 1,650 composite units.

B. 4,500 composite units.

C. 8,250 composite units.

D. 22,500 composite units.

Answer (B) is correct. *(CIA, adapted)*

REQUIRED: The composite breakeven point.

DISCUSSION: The composite breakeven point for a multiproduct firm is computed by dividing total fixed costs by a composite contribution margin.

Composite contribution margin = 2($2.50) + 5($1.20) = $11

BEP = $49,500 ÷ $11 = 4,500 composite units

Answer (A) is incorrect. The contribution margin for the ratio of each product should be added, not multiplied, in determining the composite contribution margin. Answer (C) is incorrect. The result if the composite unit consisted only of five units of Y would be 8,250 [$49,500 ÷ (5 × $1.20)]. Answer (D) is incorrect. The number of units of Y in 4,500 composite units is 22,500.

4.7.16. If the company had an operating income of $22,000, the unit sales must have been

	Product X	Product Y
A.	5,000	12,500
B.	13,000	32,500
C.	23,800	59,500
D.	28,600	71,500

Answer (B) is correct. *(CIA, adapted)*

REQUIRED: The computation of unit sales given profit.

DISCUSSION: Composite unit sales can be determined by adding profit to fixed costs and dividing by the $11 composite CM. The composite CM for X and Y is $11 [(2 × $2.50) + (5 × $1.20)]. To earn an operating income of $22,000, 6,500 composite units must be sold [($49,500 FC + $22,000 profit) ÷ $11]. Thus, 13,000 units (2 × 6,500) of product X and 32,500 units (5 × 6,500) of product Y must have been sold.

Answer (A) is incorrect. Selling 5,000 units of X and 12,500 units of Y would result in a $22,000 loss. Answer (C) is incorrect. Selling 23,800 units of X and 59,500 units of Y would result in an operating income of $81,400. Answer (D) is incorrect. Selling 28,600 units of X and 71,500 units of Y would result in an operating income of $107,800.

4.8 Activity-Based Costing

Questions 4.8.1 through 4.8.4 are based on the following information. Cinnabar Corp. manufactures one product. Its total fixed costs calculated according to traditional cost-volume-profit (CVP) analysis and activity-based costing (ABC) equal $300,000 and $100,000, respectively. Unit selling price is $40, and unit-based variable cost per unit is $20. In addition, total cost also varies with one batch-level and one product-sustaining driver. Relevant information about nonunit-based drivers includes the following:

	Batch-Level Driver	Product-Sustaining Driver
Cost per driver	$2,000	$60
Quantity of driver	40	2,000

4.8.1. According to traditional CVP analysis, how many units must be sold to generate operating income of $30,000?

A. 5,000

B. 6,500

C. 16,500

D. 21,500

Answer (C) is correct. *(Publisher, adapted)*

REQUIRED: The unit sales needed to generate specified operating income under traditional CVP methods.

DISCUSSION: Using traditional CVP methods, the sum of fixed costs and the targeted (pretax) operating income is divided by the unit contribution margin (unit price – unit variable cost). Consequently, the units required to be sold to generate operating income of $30,000 equal 16,500 [($300,000 + $30,000) ÷ ($40 – $20)].

Answer (A) is incorrect. Assuming that fixed costs equal $100,000 and omitting targeted operating income results in 5,000. Answer (B) is incorrect. Assuming that fixed costs equal $100,000 results in 6,500. Answer (D) is incorrect. Assuming that fixed costs equal $400,000 results in 21,500.

4.8.2. According to ABC analysis, how many units must be sold to generate operating income of $30,000?

A. 10,500

B. 12,500

C. 15,000

D. 16,500

Answer (D) is correct. *(Publisher, adapted)*

REQUIRED: The unit sales needed to generate specified operating income using ABC.

DISCUSSION: Under ABC, the sum of fixed costs, the batch-level costs, the product-sustaining costs, and the targeted (pretax) operating income is divided by the unit contribution margin (unit price – unit variable cost). Batch-level costs equal $80,000 (40 × $2,000), and product-sustaining costs equal $120,000 (2,000 × $60). Thus, the units required to be sold equal 16,500 [($100,000 + $80,000 + $120,000 + $30,000) ÷ ($40 – $20)]. This result is the same reached using traditional CVP methods. The sum of fixed costs, batch-level costs, and product-sustaining costs is the same as fixed costs determined without regard to ABC. The reason is that some fixed costs have been reclassified as nonunit-based variable costs. However, the results of the two methods may differ significantly if activity levels and costs of the nonunit-based drivers change.

Answer (A) is incorrect. Omitting the product-sustaining costs from the calculation results in 10,500. Answer (B) is incorrect. Omitting the batch-level costs from the calculation results in 12,500. Answer (C) is incorrect. The breakeven point in units is 15,000.

4.8.3. Assume that Cinnabar's product is redesigned. The result is that unit-based variable cost per unit is reduced to $16. If fixed costs are assumed to remain at $300,000 and operating income of $30,000 is desired, how many units must be sold according to traditional CVP analysis?

A. 11,250

B. 12,500

C. 13,750

D. 16,500

Answer (C) is correct. *(Publisher, adapted)*

REQUIRED: The unit sales to generate specified operating income under traditional CVP analysis if unit-based variable costs are decreased.

DISCUSSION: The sum of fixed costs and the targeted (pretax) operating income is divided by the new unit contribution margin ($40 – $16 = $24). Thus, the units required to be sold under the traditional approach equal 13,750 [($300,000 + $30,000) ÷ $24].

Answer (A) is incorrect. Subtracting targeted operating income from the fixed costs results in 11,250. Answer (B) is incorrect. The breakeven point in units is 12,500. Answer (D) is incorrect. Assuming no change in the unit-based variable cost per unit results in 16,500.

4.8.4. Assume that an ABC analysis of the effects of the redesign of the product mentioned in the fact pattern unexpectedly revealed an increase in the batch-level cost per driver to $2,400 and in the quantity of the product-sustaining driver to 2,600. According to ABC analysis, how many units must be sold to break even if fixed costs are unchanged?

A. 15,800

B. 13,750

C. 17,600

D. 16,500

Answer (C) is correct. *(Publisher, adapted)*

REQUIRED: The unit sales needed to generate specified operating income using ABC given certain changes in the variables.

DISCUSSION: Under ABC, the sum of the fixed cost, the batch-level cost, the product-sustaining cost, and the targeted (pretax) operating income is divided by the unit contribution margin. Batch-level costs increase to $96,000 (40 × $2,400), and product-sustaining costs increase to $156,000 (2,600 × $60). Thus, the units required to be sold equal 17,600 [($100,000 + $96,000 + $156,000) ÷ ($40 – $20)].

Answer (A) is incorrect. Assuming that the quantity of the product-sustaining driver is unchanged results in 15,800. Answer (B) is incorrect. The amount calculated based on the traditional CVP analysis is 13,750, which assumed $300,000 of fixed costs and a unit-based variable cost per unit of $16. Answer (D) is incorrect. The amount calculated before the redesign is 16,500.

STUDY UNIT FIVE
BUDGETING

A **budget** is a quantitative plan used to (1) communicate objectives, (2) motivate employees, (3) control activities, and (4) evaluate performance. The annual budget based on an organization's objectives usually combines financial, quantitative, and qualitative measures. **Strategic budgeting** is long-range planning based on the strengths and weaknesses of the organization and assessed risks. The influences of internal and external factors are evaluated to derive the best strategy.

A **budget manual** includes a planning calendar and distribution instructions for all budget schedules. The calendar is the schedule of activities for the development of the budget. It includes dates indicating when information is to be provided to others by each source.

The **operating budget** sequence is the part of the **master budget** process that begins with the sales budget and culminates in the pro forma income statement. Its emphasis is on obtaining and using resources. The **production budget** (for a manufacturer) is based on the sales forecast in units, adjusted for inventory change. It is prepared for each department and is used to plan when items will be produced.

The **financial budget** sequence includes the capital budget, cash budget, and pro forma financial statements. It emphasizes obtaining the funds to purchase operating assets. The **capital budget** may be prepared more than a year in advance to allow sufficient time to plan financing of major expenditures. The **cash budget** is vital because an entity must have adequate cash at all times. But it cannot be prepared until other budgets are complete. Because the effects of a shortage are severe, cash budgets are prepared annually, quarterly, monthly, and weekly.

After the individual budgets are complete, budgeted financial statements are prepared. They are **pro forma** because they are prepared before actual activities begin. The **pro forma income statement** culminates the operating budget sequence. It is used to decide whether budgeted activities will result in acceptable income. The **pro forma balance sheet** is prepared using the cash and capital budgets and the pro forma income statement. Along with the pro forma statement of cash flows, it culminates the financial budget sequence. The **pro forma statement of cash flows** classifies cash flows stemming from operating, investing, or financing activities.

A **fixed (static) budget** is based on one level of activity. A **flexible budget** is a series of budgets prepared for many levels of activity so that actual performance can be compared with the appropriate budgeted level. In traditional systems, flexible budgets are usually prepared based on one cost driver or measure of activity. In an **activity-based** system, flexible budgets use multiple cost drivers. Moreover, the driver analysis and the flexible budget amounts depend on the cost hierarchy (unit-level, batch-level, product- or service-sustaining, and facility-sustaining).

The following is the **budget cycle** for a manufacturer that includes all elements of the value chain:

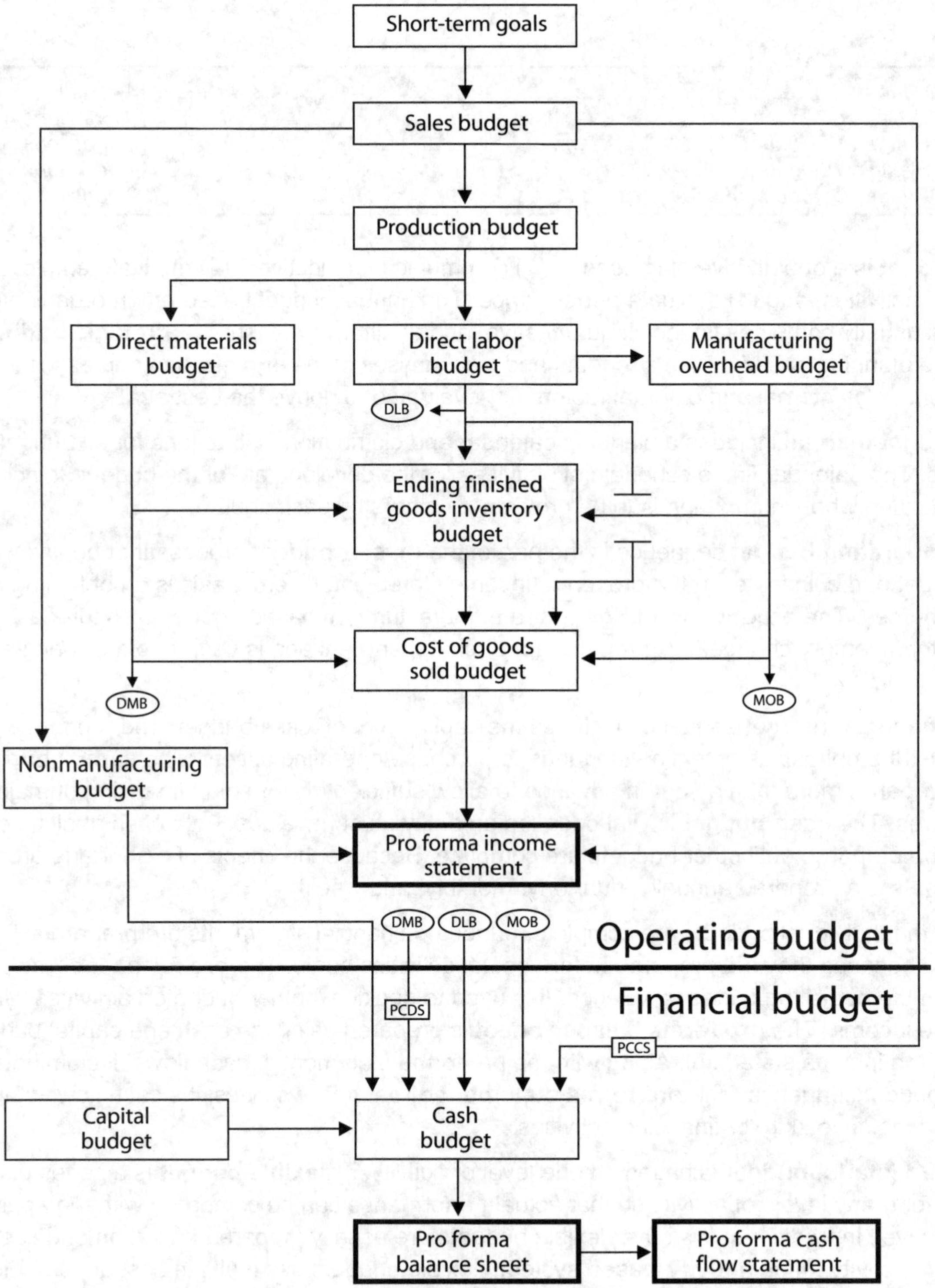

*PCCS = Projected cash collections schedule
PCDS = Projected cash disbursements schedule

QUESTIONS

5.1 Budget Concepts

5.1.1. Which one of the following best describes the role of top management in the budgeting process? Top management

A. Should be involved only in the approval process.

B. Lacks the detailed knowledge of the daily operations and should limit their involvement.

C. Needs to be involved, including using the budget process to communicate goals.

D. Needs to separate the budgeting process and the business planning process into two separate processes.

Answer (C) is correct. *(CMA, adapted)*

REQUIRED: The best description of top management's role in the budgeting process.

DISCUSSION: Among other things, the budget is a tool by which management can communicate goals to lower-level employees. It is also a tool for motivating employees to reach those goals. For the budget to function in these communication and motivating roles, top management must be involved in the process. This involvement does not extend to dictating the exact numerical contents of the budget since top management lacks a detailed knowledge of daily operations.

Answer (A) is incorrect. Top managers can use the budget for motivational and communication purposes; they should do more than merely sign off on the finished document. Answer (B) is incorrect. Top managers should be involved in the budget process even though they lack detailed knowledge of daily operations; the budget can still communicate company objectives and goals. Answer (D) is incorrect. The budget process is a part of the overall planning process.

5.1.2. The major objectives of any budget system are to

A. Define responsibility centers, provide a framework for performance evaluation, and promote communication and coordination among organization segments.

B. Define responsibility centers, facilitate the fixing of blame for missed budget predictions, and ensure goal congruence between superiors and subordinates.

C. Foster the planning of operations, provide a framework for performance evaluation, and promote communication and coordination among organization segments.

D. Foster the planning of operations, facilitate the fixing of blame for missed budget predictions, and ensure goal congruence between superiors and subordinates.

Answer (C) is correct. *(CIA, adapted)*

REQUIRED: The major objectives of any budget system.

DISCUSSION: A budget is a realistic plan for the future expressed in quantitative terms. The process of budgeting forces a company to establish goals, determine the resources necessary to achieve those goals, and anticipate future difficulties in their achievement. A budget is also a control tool because it establishes standards and facilitates comparison of actual and budgeted performance. Because a budget establishes standards and accountability, it motivates good performance by highlighting the work of effective managers. Moreover, the nature of the budgeting process fosters communication of goals to company subunits and coordination of their efforts. Budgeting activities by entities within the company must be coordinated because they are interdependent. Thus, the sales budget is a necessary input to the formulation of the production budget. In turn, production requirements must be known before purchases and expense budgets can be developed, and all other budgets must be completed before preparation of the cash budget.

5.1.3. Which one of the following is not considered to be a benefit of participative budgeting?

A. Individuals at all organizational levels are recognized as being part of the team; this results in greater support of the organization.

B. The budget estimates are prepared by those in direct contact with various activities.

C. Managers are more motivated to reach the budget objectives since they participated in setting them.

D. When managers set the final targets for the budget, senior management need not be concerned with the overall profitability of current operations.

Answer (D) is correct. *(CMA, adapted)*

REQUIRED: The item that is not considered to be a benefit of participative budgeting.

DISCUSSION: One of the behavioral considerations of budgeting is the extent of participation in the process by managers at all levels within the organization. Managers are more motivated to achieve budgeted goals when they are involved in budget preparation. A broad level of participation usually leads to greater support for the budget and the entity as a whole, as well as a greater understanding of what is to be accomplished. Advantages of a participative budget include greater accuracy of budget estimates. Managers with immediate operational responsibility for activities have a better understanding of what results can be achieved and at what costs. Also, managers cannot blame unrealistic objectives as an excuse for not achieving budget expectations when they have helped to establish those objectives. Despite the involvement of lower level managers, senior management must still participate in the budget process to ensure that the combined objectives of the various departments are consistent with profitability objectives of the company.

Answer (A) is incorrect. Participative budgeting promotes teamwork. Answer (B) is incorrect. A participative budget involves those most directly affected. Answer (C) is incorrect. A participative budget is a powerful motivator.

5.1.4. The budget that describes the long-term position and objectives of an entity within its environment is the

A. Capital budget.

B. Operating budget.

C. Cash management budget.

D. Strategic budget.

Answer (D) is correct. *(CMA, adapted)*

REQUIRED: The budget that describes the long-term position and objectives of an entity.

DISCUSSION: Strategic budgeting is a form of long-range planning based on identifying and specifying organizational objectives. The strengths and weaknesses of the organization are evaluated and risk levels are assessed. The influences of environmental factors are forecast to derive the best strategy for reaching the organization's objectives.

Answer (A) is incorrect. Capital budgeting involves evaluating specific long-term investment decisions. Answer (B) is incorrect. The operating budget is a short-range management tool. Answer (C) is incorrect. Cash management is a short-range consideration related to liquidity.

5.1.5. The process of creating a formal plan and translating goals into a quantitative format is

A. Process costing.

B. Activity-based costing.

C. Budgeting.

D. Variance analysis.

Answer (C) is correct. *(CMA, adapted)*

REQUIRED: The term for the process of creating a formal plan and translating goals into a quantitative format.

DISCUSSION: A budget is a realistic plan for the future expressed in quantitative terms. It is also a planning tool. Budgeting facilitates control and communication and also provides motivation to employees.

Answer (A) is incorrect. Process costing determines the cost of manufactured products. Answer (B) is incorrect. ABC is a means of product costing that emphasizes activities as basic cost objects. Answer (D) is incorrect. Variance analysis compares actual costs with planned costs.

5.1.6. Budgetary slack can best be described as

A. The elimination of certain expenses to enhance budgeted income.

B. The planned overestimation of budgeted expenses.

C. A plug number used to achieve a preset level of operating income.

D. The planned underestimation of budgeted expenses.

Answer (B) is correct. *(CMA, adapted)*

REQUIRED: The meaning of budgetary slack.

DISCUSSION: A budget is a control that, among other things, establishes a performance standard. The natural reaction of a manager whose efforts are to be judged is to negotiate for a less stringent performance measure. Over-estimation of expenses, that is, incorporation of slack into the budget, is a means of avoiding an unfavorable variance from expectations. However, this practice is wasteful and may lead to inaccurate performance appraisal.

Answer (A) is incorrect. Including slack in a budget is the opposite of enhancing budgeted income. Answer (C) is incorrect. Slack is not a plug number but an overestimation of expenses. Answer (D) is incorrect. Slack is the overestimation of expenses.

5.1.7. The goals and objectives upon which an annual profit plan is most effectively based are

A. Financial measures such as net income, return on investment, and earnings per share.

B. Quantitative measures such as growth in unit sales, number of employees, and manufacturing capacity.

C. Qualitative measures of organizational activity such as product innovation leadership, product quality levels, and product safety.

D. A combination of financial, quantitative, and qualitative measures.

Answer (D) is correct. *(CMA, adapted)*

REQUIRED: The objectives upon which an annual profit plan is most effectively based.

DISCUSSION: Objectives vary with the organization's type and stage of development. Broad objectives should be established at the top and restated in more specific terms as they are communicated downward in a means-end hierarchy. Each subunit may have its own specific objectives. A conflict sometimes exists in determining organizational objectives. For example, customer service may be one objective, but profitability or return on investment may be a conflicting objective. Thus, the annual profit plan is usually based on a combination of financial, quantitative, and qualitative measures.

Answer (A) is incorrect. More than financial measures are needed to prepare a profit plan. Long-term quality measures also must be considered. Answer (B) is incorrect. Quantitative measures are insufficient if financial measures are not considered. Answer (C) is incorrect. Qualitative measures are insufficient if financial measures are not considered.

5.1.8. The use of budgetary slack does not allow the preparer to

A. Be flexible under unexpected circumstances.

B. Increase the probability of achieving budgeted performance.

C. Use the budget to control subordinate performance.

D. Blend personal goals with organizational goals.

Answer (C) is correct. *(CMA, adapted)*

REQUIRED: The function prevented by budgetary slack.

DISCUSSION: Managers often try to incorporate slack into a budget to provide flexibility when unexpected costs arise. In such cases, the preparer can still achieve budgeted performance even though costs are higher than actually expected. However, the existence of slack in a budget does not allow the best possible control of employee performance. Control involves comparison of performance with a standard. If the standard is inaccurate, the value of the comparison is diminished.

Answer (A) is incorrect. Slack increases flexibility when unforeseen circumstances arise. Answer (B) is incorrect. Lowering the standard of performance increases the probability of achieving budgetary objectives. Answer (D) is incorrect. The existence of slack increases the likelihood that a manager will receive the personal rewards that follow from meeting the expectations of superiors.

5.1.9. From the perspective of corporate management, the use of budgetary slack

A. Increases the effectiveness of the corporate planning process.

B. Increases the ability to identify potential budget weaknesses.

C. Encourages the use of effective corrective actions.

D. Increases the likelihood of inefficient resource allocation.

Answer (D) is correct. *(CMA, adapted)*

REQUIRED: The perspective of corporate management on the use of budgetary slack.

DISCUSSION: Budgetary slack increases the probability that budgeted performance will be achieved. However, resources may not be efficiently used because the manager responsible for meeting budgetary objectives will have less incentive to minimize costs.

Answer (A) is incorrect. Slack decreases the effectiveness of planning. A budget with significant slack does not reflect the best estimate of future results. Answer (B) is incorrect. Weaknesses will be overlooked if total costs are within prearranged limits, and this effect is more likely if slack is included in the budget. Answer (C) is incorrect. Corrective actions (such as hiring a new manager) may not occur as quickly if slack is included in a budget.

5.1.10. A company's product has an expected 4-year life cycle from research, development, and design through its withdrawal from the market. Budgeted costs are

Upstream costs (R&D, design)	$2,000,000
Manufacturing costs	3,000,000
Downstream costs (marketing, distribution, customer service)	1,200,000
After-purchase costs	1,000,000

The company plans to produce 200,000 units and price the product at 125% of the whole-life unit cost. Thus, the budgeted unit selling price is

A. $15

B. $31

C. $36

D. $45

Answer (D) is correct. *(Publisher, adapted)*

REQUIRED: The unit selling price.

DISCUSSION: Whole-life costs include after-purchase costs (operating, support, repair, and disposal) incurred by customers as well as life-cycle costs (R&D, design, manufacturing, marketing, distribution, and research). Hence, the budgeted unit whole-life cost is $36 [($2,000,000 + $3,000,000 + $1,200,000 + $1,000,000) ÷ 200,000 units], and the budgeted unit selling price is $45 ($36 × 125%).

Answer (A) is incorrect. The budgeted unit manufacturing cost is $15. Answer (B) is incorrect. The budgeted unit life-cycle cost is $31. Answer (C) is incorrect. The budgeted unit whole-life cost is $36.

5.1.11. A manufacturer has prepared quarterly budgets for the next 12 months. These budgets anticipate steady decreases in the unit costs of a new product. Accordingly, if unit costs for the fourth quarter are materially lower than those for the first quarter, but an unfavorable variance is reported, the company is most likely using

A. Kaizen budgeting.

B. Activity-based budgeting.

C. Life-cycle budgeting.

D. Whole-life budgeting.

Answer (A) is correct. *(Publisher, adapted)*

REQUIRED: The type of budgeting used by an entity that anticipates continuous improvement.

DISCUSSION: The Japanese term kaizen means continuous improvement. Kaizen budgeting assumes the continuous improvement of products and processes, usually by many small innovations rather than major changes. It requires estimates of the effects of improvements and the costs of their implementation. Kaizen budgeting is based not on the existing system but on changes yet to be made, and budget targets cannot be reached unless those improvements occur. Accordingly, an unfavorable variance may occur even if improvements occur because their magnitude is less than that budgeted.

Answer (B) is incorrect. Activity-based budgeting stresses identification of activities and driver analysis rather than functions and spending categories. Answer (C) is incorrect. The essence of life-cycle budgeting is accounting for costs at all stages in the value chain. Answer (D) is incorrect. Whole-life costs include customers' after-purchase costs as well as life-cycle costs.

5.1.12. All types of organizations can benefit from budgeting. A major difference between governmental budgeting and business budgeting is that

A. Business budgeting is required by the SEC.

B. Governmental budgeting is usually done on a zero base.

C. Business budgeting can be used to measure progress in achieving company objectives, whereas governmental budgeting cannot be used to measure progress in achieving objectives.

D. Governmental budgeting usually reflects the legal limits on proposed expenditures.

Answer (D) is correct. *(CMA, adapted)*

REQUIRED: The major difference between governmental and business budgeting.

DISCUSSION: A governmental budget is a legal document adopted in accordance with procedures specified by applicable laws. It must be complied with by the administrators of the governmental unit for which the budget is prepared. The effectiveness and efficiency of governmental efforts are difficult to measure in the absence of the profit-centered activity that characterizes business operations. Thus, the use of budgets in the appropriation process is of major importance.

Answer (A) is incorrect. Business budgeting is not mandated by the SEC or any other organization. Answer (B) is incorrect. Few governments (if any) actually use a zero-base budgeting system. Answer (C) is incorrect. In some instances, governmental budgeting can be used to measure progress in achieving objectives. For example, the objective may be to expend all appropriated funds.

5.1.13. A systemized approach known as zero-based budgeting (ZBB)

A. Presents the plan for only one level of activity and does not adjust to changes in the level of activity.

B. Presents a statement of expectations for a period of time but does not present a firm commitment.

C. Divides the activities of individual responsibility centers into a series of packages that are prioritized.

D. Classifies budget requests by activity and estimates the benefits arising from each activity.

Answer (C) is correct. *(CMA, adapted)*

REQUIRED: The true statement about zero-based budgeting.

DISCUSSION: Zero-based budgeting is a planning process in which each manager must justify a department's entire budget every year (or period). Different levels of service (work effort) are evaluated for each activity, measures of work and performance are established, and activities are ranked (prioritized) according to their importance to the entity. For each budgetary unit, decision packages are prepared that describe various levels of service that may be provided, including at least one level lower than the current one.

Answer (A) is incorrect. A static budget does not adjust for changes in activity levels. Answer (B) is incorrect. ZBB does present a firm commitment. Answer (D) is incorrect. Each activity is prepared as a series of packages.

5.1.14. The budgeting tool or process in which estimates of revenues and expenses are prepared for each product beginning with the product's research and development phase and traced through to its customer support phase is a(n)

A. Master budget.

B. Activity-based budget.

C. Zero-base budget.

D. Life-cycle budget.

Answer (D) is correct. *(CMA, adapted)*

REQUIRED: The budget tool that estimates a product's revenues and expenses from R&D through customer support.

DISCUSSION: A life-cycle budget estimates a product's revenues and expenses over its expected life cycle. This approach is especially useful when revenues and related costs do not occur in the same periods. It emphasizes the need to budget revenues to cover all costs, not just those for production. Thus, costs are determined for all value-chain categories: (1) upstream (R&D, design), (2) manufacturing, and (3) downstream (marketing, distribution, and customer service). The result is to highlight upstream and downstream costs that often receive insufficient attention.

Answer (A) is incorrect. A master budget summarizes all of an entity's budgets and plans. Answer (B) is incorrect. An activity-based budget emphasizes the costs of activities, the basic cost objects in activity-based costing. Answer (C) is incorrect. A zero-base budget requires each manager to justify his or her subunit's entire budget each year.

5.2 Types of Budgets

5.2.1. Which of the following is normally included in the financial budget of a firm?

A. Direct materials budget.

B. Selling expense budget.

C. Budgeted balance sheet.

D. Sales budget.

Answer (C) is correct. *(Publisher, adapted)*

REQUIRED: The item normally included in the financial budget.

DISCUSSION: The financial budget normally includes (1) the capital budget, (2) the cash budget, (3) the budgeted balance sheet, and (4) the budgeted statement of cash flows.

Answer (A) is incorrect. The direct materials budget is included in the production budget. Answer (B) is incorrect. The selling expense budget is included in the operating budget. Answer (D) is incorrect. The sales budget is included in the operating budget.

5.2.2. The basic difference between a master budget and a flexible budget is that a master budget is

A. Based on one specific level of production, and a flexible budget can be prepared for any production level within a relevant range.

B. Only used before and during the budget period, and a flexible budget is only used after the budget period.

C. Based on a fixed standard, whereas a flexible budget allows management latitude in meeting goals.

D. For an entire production facility, whereas a flexible budget is applicable to single departments only.

Answer (A) is correct. *(CPA, adapted)*

REQUIRED: The basic difference between a master budget and a flexible budget.

DISCUSSION: A flexible budget allows adjustment of the budget to the actual level of activity before comparing the budgeted activity with actual results. The master budget contains estimates by management from all functional areas based on one level of production. Thus, the basic difference is that a flexible budget can be prepared for any production level within a relevant range, but the master budget is based on one level of production.

Answer (B) is incorrect. Flexible budgets are adjusted during the budget period. Answer (C) is incorrect. Master budgets, not flexible budgets, recognize the organization's objectives. Answer (D) is incorrect. Flexible budgets are applicable to the entire production facility.

5.2.3. All of the following are considered operating budgets except the

A. Sales budget.

B. Materials budget.

C. Production budget.

D. Capital budget.

Answer (D) is correct. *(CMA, adapted)*

REQUIRED: The budget that is not considered a part of the operating budget.

DISCUSSION: The operating budget consists of all budgets that concern normal operating activities, including the sales budget, production budget, materials budget, direct labor budget, and factory overhead budget. The capital expenditures budget, which outlines needs for new capital investment, is not a part of normal operations.

Answer (A) is incorrect. The sales budget is part of the operating budget. Answer (B) is incorrect. The direct materials budget is part of the operating budget. Answer (C) is incorrect. The production budget is part of the operating budget.

5.2.4. Which one of the following statements regarding selling and administrative budgets is most accurate?

A. Selling and administrative budgets are usually optional.

B. Selling and administrative budgets are fixed in nature.

C. Selling and administrative budgets are difficult to allocate by month and are best presented as one number for the entire year.

D. Selling and administrative budgets need to be detailed in order that the key assumptions can be better understood.

Answer (D) is correct. *(CMA, adapted)*

REQUIRED: The most accurate statement about selling and administrative budgets.

DISCUSSION: Sales and administrative budgets are prepared after the sales budget. Like the other budgets, they constitute prospective information based on the preparer's assumptions about conditions expected to exist and actions expected to be taken.

Answer (A) is incorrect. Selling and administrative budgets are no more optional than any other component of the master budget. Answer (B) is incorrect. Selling and administrative budgets have both variable and fixed components. Answer (C) is incorrect. Selling and administrative budgets should be prepared on the same basis as the remainder of the budget, typically on at least a monthly basis.

5.2.5. When sales volume is seasonal in nature, certain items in the budget must be coordinated. The three most significant items to coordinate in budgeting seasonal sales volume are

A. Direct labor hours, work-in-process inventory, and sales volume.

B. Production volume, finished goods inventory, and sales volume.

C. Raw material inventory, direct labor hours, and manufacturing overhead costs.

D. Raw material inventory, work-in-process inventory, and production volume.

Answer (B) is correct. *(CMA, adapted)*

REQUIRED: The three most significant items to coordinate in budgeting seasonal sales.

DISCUSSION: The most important items that need to be coordinated in a seasonal business are sales volume and production. The sales budget is the basis for other budgets. The sales projection determines how much needs to be purchased and produced. In turn, projected sales and production (or purchases) must be coordinated with existing quantities on hand (inventory) and with amounts to be held in the future. If a manufacturer faces sharp variations in demand, this coordination becomes especially crucial.

Answer (A) is incorrect. Direct labor and work-in-process are less directly significant to the desired coordination. Answer (C) is incorrect. Direct labor, raw materials, and overhead are less directly significant to the desired coordination. Answer (D) is incorrect. Raw materials and work-in-process are less directly significant to the desired coordination.

5.2.6. There are various budgets within the master budget cycle. One of these budgets is the production budget. Which one of the following best describes the production budget?

A. It summarizes all discretionary costs.

B. It includes required direct labor hours.

C. It includes required material purchases.

D. It is calculated from the desired ending inventory and the sales forecast.

Answer (D) is correct. *(CMA, adapted)*

REQUIRED: The best description of a production budget.

DISCUSSION: A production budget is based on sales forecasts, in units, with adjustments for beginning and ending inventories. It is used to plan when items will be produced.

Answer (A) is incorrect. Discretionary costs are not related to production. Answer (B) is incorrect. The direct labor budget is prepared after the production budget. Answer (C) is incorrect. The materials purchases budget is prepared after the production budget.

5.2.7. Which one of the following items is the last schedule to be prepared in the normal budget preparation process?

A. Cash budget.

B. Cost of goods sold budget.

C. Manufacturing overhead budget.

D. Selling expense budget.

Answer (A) is correct. *(CMA, adapted)*

REQUIRED: The last schedule prepared.

DISCUSSION: The last schedule prepared before the financial statements is the cash budget. The cash budget is a schedule of estimated cash collections and payments. The various operating budgets and the capital budget are inputs to the cash budgeting process.

Answer (B) is incorrect. The cost of goods sold budget provides information necessary to prepare the cash budget. Answer (C) is incorrect. The manufacturing overhead budget provides information necessary to prepare the cash budget. Answer (D) is incorrect. The selling expense budget provides information necessary to prepare the cash budget.

5.2.8. Which one of the following items would have to be included for a company preparing a schedule of cash receipts and disbursements for Calendar Year 1?

A. A purchase order issued in December Year 1 for items to be delivered in February Year 2.

B. Dividends declared in November Year 1 to be paid in January Year 2 to shareholders of record as of December Year 1.

C. The amount of uncollectible customer accounts for Year 1.

D. The borrowing of funds from a bank on a note payable taken out in June Year 1 with an agreement to pay the principal and interest in June Year 2.

Answer (D) is correct. *(CMA, adapted)*

REQUIRED: The item included in a cash budget for Year 1.

DISCUSSION: A schedule of cash receipts and disbursements (cash budget) should include all cash inflows and outflows during the period without regard to the accrual accounting treatment of the transactions. Thus, it should include all checks written and all sources of cash, including borrowings. A borrowing from a bank in June Year 1 should appear as a cash receipt for Year 1.

Answer (A) is incorrect. The cash disbursement presumably will not occur until Year 2. Answer (B) is incorrect. The cash flow will not occur until dividends are paid in Year 2. Answer (C) is incorrect. Bad debt expense is a noncash item.

5.2.9. Pro forma financial statements are part of the budgeting process. Normally, the last pro forma statement prepared is the

A. Capital expenditure plan.

B. Income statement.

C. Statement of cost of goods sold.

D. Statement of cash flows.

Answer (D) is correct. *(CMA, adapted)*

REQUIRED: The last pro forma financial statement prepared.

DISCUSSION: The statement of cash flows is usually the last of the listed items prepared. All other elements of the budget process must be completed before it can be developed.

Answer (A) is incorrect. The capital expenditure plan must be prepared before the cash budget. Cash may be needed to pay for capital purchases. Answer (B) is incorrect. The income statement must be prepared before the statement of cash flows, which reconciles net income and net operating cash flows. Answer (C) is incorrect. Cost of goods sold is included in the income statement, which is an input to the statement of cash flows.

5.3 Budgetary Control

5.3.1. Which one of the following organizational policies is most likely to result in undesirable managerial behavior?

A. Joe Walk, the chief executive officer of Eagle Rock Brewery, wrote a memorandum to his executives stating, "Operating plans are contracts, and they should be met without fail."

B. The budgeting process at Madsen Manufacturing starts with operating managers providing goals for their respective departments.

C. Fullbright Lighting holds quarterly meetings of departmental managers to consider possible changes in the budgeted targets due to changing conditions.

D. At Fargo Transportation, managers are expected to provide explanations for variances from the budget in their departments.

Answer (A) is correct. *(CMA, adapted)*

REQUIRED: The organizational policy most likely to result in undesirable managerial behavior.

DISCUSSION: Control is the process of making certain that plans are achieving the desired objectives. A budget is one of the most common control devices. It is a plan for the future, not a contract. To interpret a budget or other plan to be as inflexible as a contract may encourage a manager to act contrary to the entity's best interests.

Answer (B) is incorrect. Participatory budgeting obtains the support of those involved and is likely to foster desirable behavior. Answer (C) is incorrect. Changing budget targets as conditions change results in setting fairer performance goals. Answer (D) is incorrect. Allowing managers to provide explanations for variances does nothing to cause undesirable behavior. If explanations are acceptable, no reason exists to manipulate statements.

5.3.2. Kallert Manufacturing currently uses the company budget as a planning tool only. Management has decided to use budgets for control purposes also. To implement this change, the management accountant must

A. Organize a budget committee and appoint a budget director.

B. Report daily to operating management all deviations from plan.

C. Synchronize the budgeting and accounting system with the organizational structure.

D. Develop forecasting procedures.

Answer (C) is correct. *(CMA, adapted)*

REQUIRED: The action required to use a planning budget for control purposes.

DISCUSSION: A budget is a means of control because it sets cost guidelines with which actual performance can be compared. The feedback provided by comparison of actual and budgeted performance reveals whether a manager has used assets efficiently. If a budget is to be used for control purposes, however, the accounting system must be designed to produce information required for control. Moreover, the budgeting and accounting system must be related to the organizational structure so that variances are assigned to the proper individuals.

Answer (A) is incorrect. A budget director and committee are needed even if a budget is to be used only for planning. Answer (B) is incorrect. Daily reporting is usually not necessary. Also, reporting all deviations is not cost effective. Answer (D) is incorrect. The entity already should be using forecasting procedures if the budget is used as a planning tool.

5.3.3. A planning calendar in budgeting is the

A. Calendar period covered by the budget.

B. Schedule of activities for the development and adoption of the budget.

C. Calendar period covered by the annual budget and the long-range plan.

D. Sales forecast by months in the annual budget period.

Answer (B) is correct. *(CMA, adapted)*

REQUIRED: The definition of a budget planning calendar.

DISCUSSION: The budget planning calendar is the schedule of activities for the development and adoption of the budget. It should include a list of dates indicating when specific information is to be provided by each information source to others. The preparation of a master budget usually takes several months. For instance, many firms start the budget for the next calendar year some time in September in hopes of having it completed by December 1. Because all of the individual departmental budgets are based on forecasts prepared by others and the budgets of other departments, it is essential to have a planning calendar to ensure the proper integration of the entire process.

Answer (A) is incorrect. The period covered by the budget precedes the events in the planning calendar. Answer (C) is incorrect. The period covered by the budget precedes the events in the planning calendar. Answer (D) is incorrect. The planning calendar is not associated with sales.

5.3.4. A continuous (rolling) budget

A. Presents planned activities for a period but does not present a firm commitment.

B. Presents the plan for only one level of activity and does not adjust to changes in the level of activity.

C. Presents the plan for a range of activity so that the plan can be adjusted for changes in activity.

D. Drops the current month or quarter and adds a future month or quarter as the current month or quarter is completed.

Answer (D) is correct. *(CMA, adapted)*

REQUIRED: The true statement about a continuous budget.

DISCUSSION: A continuous budget is revised on a regular (continuous) basis. Typically, a budget is extended for another month or quarter in accordance with new data as the current month or quarter ends. For example, if the budget is for 12 months, a budget for the next 12 months will be available continuously as each month ends.

Answer (A) is incorrect. A continuous budget is a firm (but not a contractual) commitment. Answer (B) is incorrect. A continuous budget can be for various levels of activity. A static budget is prepared for only one level of activity. Answer (C) is incorrect. A flexible budget presents plans for a range of activity so that adjustments can be made as conditions change.

5.3.5. A budget manual, which enhances the operation of a budget system, is most likely to include

A. A chart of accounts.

B. Distribution instructions for budget schedules.

C. Employee hiring policies.

D. Documentation of the accounting system software.

Answer (B) is correct. *(CMA, adapted)*

REQUIRED: The item normally included in a budget manual.

DISCUSSION: A budget manual describes how a budget is to be prepared. Items usually included in a budget manual are a planning calendar and distribution instructions for all budget schedules. Distribution instructions are important because, once a schedule is prepared, other departments within the organization will use the schedule to prepare their own budgets. Without distribution instructions, someone who needs a particular schedule may be overlooked.

Answer (A) is incorrect. A chart of accounts is included in the accounting manual. Answer (C) is incorrect. Employee hiring policies are not needed for budget preparation. They are already available in the human resources manual. Answer (D) is incorrect. Software documentation is not needed in the budget preparation process.

5.4 Flexible Budgets

5.4.1. When preparing a performance report for a cost center using flexible budgeting techniques, the planned cost column should be based on the

A. Budgeted amount in the original budget prepared before the beginning of the year.

B. Actual amount for the same period in the preceding year.

C. Budget adjusted to the actual level of activity for the period being reported.

D. Budget adjusted to the planned level of activity for the period being reported.

Answer (C) is correct. *(CMA, adapted)*

REQUIRED: The basis for the planned cost column in a flexible budget performance report.

DISCUSSION: If a report is to be used for performance evaluation, the planned cost column should be based on the actual level of activity for the period. The ability to adjust amounts for varying activity levels is the primary advantage of flexible budgeting.

Answer (A) is incorrect. The static budget amount is not useful for comparison purposes. The budget for the actual activity level achieved is more important. Answer (B) is incorrect. Prior-year figures are not useful if activity levels are different. Answer (D) is incorrect. A budget based on planned activity level is not as meaningful as one based on actual activity level.

5.4.2. Which one of the following statements regarding the difference between a flexible budget and a static budget is true?

A. A flexible budget primarily is prepared for planning purposes, while a static budget is prepared for performance evaluation.

B. A flexible budget provides cost allowances for different levels of activity, whereas a static budget provides costs for one level of activity.

C. A flexible budget includes only variable costs, whereas a static budget includes only fixed costs.

D. A flexible budget is established by operating management, while a static budget is determined by top management.

Answer (B) is correct. *(CMA, adapted)*

REQUIRED: The difference between a flexible and a static budget.

DISCUSSION: A flexible budget provides cost allowances for different levels of activity, but a static budget provides costs for only one level of activity. Thus, a flexible budget conceptually is a series of budgets prepared for many different levels of activity.

Answer (A) is incorrect. Both budgets are prepared for both planning and performance evaluation purposes. Answer (C) is incorrect. Both budgets include both fixed and variable costs. Answer (D) is incorrect. Either budget can be established by any level of management.

5.4.3. Which one of the following budgeting methodologies would be most appropriate for a firm facing a significant level of uncertainty in unit sales volumes for next year?

A. Top-down budgeting.

B. Life-cycle budgeting.

C. Static budgeting.

D. Flexible budgeting.

Answer (D) is correct. *(CMA, adapted)*

REQUIRED: The budgeting methodology most appropriate for a firm facing significant uncertainty about unit sales volumes.

DISCUSSION: Flexible budgeting consists of preparing a series of budgets for many levels of sales. A flexible budget is designed to allow adjustment of the budget to the actual level of activity before comparing the budgeted activity with actual results.

Answer (A) is incorrect. Top-down budgeting entails imposition of a budget by top management on lower-level employees. It is the antithesis of participatory budgeting. Answer (B) is incorrect. Life-cycle budgeting estimates a product's revenues and costs for each link in the value chain from R&D and design to production, marketing, distribution, and customer service. The product life cycle ends when customer service is withdrawn. Answer (C) is incorrect. A static budget is for only one level of activity.

5.4.4. The difference between the actual amounts and the flexible budget amounts for the actual output achieved is the

A. Production volume variance.

B. Flexible budget variance.

C. Sales volume variance.

D. Standard cost variance.

Answer (B) is correct. *(CMA, adapted)*

REQUIRED: The term for the difference between the actual amounts and the flexible budget amounts.

DISCUSSION: A flexible budget is prepared at the end of the budget period when the actual results are available. A flexible budget reflects the revenues that should have been earned and costs that should have been incurred given the achieved levels of production and sales. The difference between the flexible budget and actual figures is known as the flexible budget variance.

Answer (A) is incorrect. The production volume variance equals under- or overapplied fixed overhead. Answer (C) is incorrect. The sales volume variance is the difference between the flexible budget amount and the static budget amount. Answer (D) is incorrect. A standard cost variance is not necessarily based on a flexible budget.

5.4.5. The use of standard costs in the budgeting process signifies that an organization has most likely implemented a

A. Flexible budget.

B. Capital budget.

C. Zero-based budget.

D. Static budget.

Answer (A) is correct. *(CMA, adapted)*

REQUIRED: The budget most likely implemented by a company that uses standard costs.

DISCUSSION: A flexible budget is a series of budgets prepared for various levels of sales and production. Another view is that it is based on cost formulas, or standard costs. Thus, the cost formulas are fed into the computerized budget program along with the actual level of sales or production. The result is a budget created for the actual level of activity.

Answer (B) is incorrect. A capital budget is a means of evaluating long-term investments and has nothing to do with standard costs. Answer (C) is incorrect. A zero-based budget is a planning process in which each manager must justify a department's entire budget each year. The budget is built from the base of zero each year. Answer (D) is incorrect. A static budget is for one level of activity. It can be based on expected actual or standard costs.

5.4.6. A difference between standard costs used for cost control and budgeted costs

A. Can exist because standard costs must be determined after the budget is completed.

B. Can exist because standard costs represent what costs should be, whereas budgeted costs represent expected actual costs.

C. Can exist because budgeted costs are historical costs, whereas standard costs are based on engineering studies.

D. Cannot exist because they should be the same amounts.

Answer (B) is correct. *(CMA, adapted)*

REQUIRED: The true statement about the difference between standard costs and budgeted costs.

DISCUSSION: Standard costs are predetermined, attainable unit costs. Standard cost systems isolate deviations (variances) of actual from expected costs. One advantage of standard costs is that they facilitate flexible budgeting. Accordingly, standard and budgeted costs should not differ when standards are currently attainable. However, in practice, budgeted (estimated actual) costs may differ from standard costs when operating conditions are not expected to reflect those anticipated when the standards were developed.

Answer (A) is incorrect. Standard costs are determined independently of the budget. Answer (C) is incorrect. Budgeted costs are expected future costs, not historical costs. Answer (D) is incorrect. Budgeted and standard costs should in principle be the same, but in practice they will differ when standard costs are not expected to be currently attainable.

5.4.7. A flexible budget is appropriate for

A. Control of fixed factory overhead but not direct materials and direct labor.

B. Control of direct materials and direct labor but not selling and administrative expenses.

C. Any level of activity, regardless of range.

D. Control of direct labor and direct materials but not fixed factory overhead.

Answer (D) is correct. *(CMA, adapted)*

REQUIRED: The appropriate use of a flexible budget.

DISCUSSION: A flexible budget is actually a series of several budgets prepared for many levels of operating activity. A flexible budget is designed to allow adjustment of the budget to the actual level of activity before comparing the budgeted activity with actual results. This flexibility is important if costs vary with the activity level. Thus, a flexible budget is particularly appropriate for control of direct labor and direct materials (both variable costs) but is not necessary for control of fixed factory overhead. By definition, overhead costs do not change as activity levels change.

Answer (A) is incorrect. A flexible budget is not necessary for control of costs that will be the same at all levels of activity. Answer (B) is incorrect. Flexible budgets are useful for controlling variable costs, including variable selling and administrative costs. Answer (C) is incorrect. A flexible budget is prepared for a specific range of activity levels.

5.5 Budget Computations

5.5.1. A company's budget contains the following information:

	Units
Beginning finished goods inventory	85
Beginning work-in-process in equivalent units	10
Desired ending finished goods inventory	100
Desired ending work-in-process in equivalent units	40
Projected sales	1,800

How many equivalent units should the company plan to produce?

A. 1,800

B. 1,565

C. 1,815

D. 1,845

Answer (D) is correct. *(CMA, adapted)*

REQUIRED: The equivalent units to produce in the coming year.

DISCUSSION: The finished units needed are calculated as follows:

Needed for sales	1,800
Needed for ending inventory	100
Total finished units needed	1,900
Less: Beginning inventory	(85)
Finished units needed	1,815

The units to be produced are calculated as follows:

Finished units needed	1,815
Needed for ending inventory	40
Total units in process	1,855
Less: Beginning WIP inventory	(10)
Units to be produced	1,845

Answer (A) is incorrect. The amount of 1,800 equals projected unit sales. Answer (B) is incorrect. Units needed for sales minus all inventory amounts equals 1,565. Answer (C) is incorrect. Finished units needed equals 1,815.

5.5.2. Based on past experience, a company has developed the following budget formula for estimating its shipping expenses. The company's shipments average 12 lbs. per shipment:

Shipping costs = \$16,000 + (\$0.50 × lbs. shipped)

The planned activity and actual activity regarding orders and shipments for the current month are given in the following schedule:

	Plan	Actual
Sales orders	800	780
Shipments	800	820
Units shipped	8,000	9,000
Sales	\$120,000	\$144,000
Total pounds shipped	9,600	12,300

The actual shipping costs for the month amounted to \$21,000. The appropriate monthly flexible budget allowance for shipping costs for the purpose of performance evaluation would be

A. \$20,680

B. \$20,920

C. \$20,800

D. \$22,150

Answer (D) is correct. *(CMA, adapted)*

REQUIRED: The appropriate budgeted amount for shipping costs when 12,300 pounds are shipped.

DISCUSSION: The flexible budget formula is

Shipping costs = \$16,000 + (\$0.50 × lbs. shipped)

Therefore, to determine the flexible budget amount, multiply the actual pounds shipped (12,300) times the standard cost (\$0.50) to arrive at a total expected variable cost of \$6,150. Adding the variable cost to \$16,000 of fixed cost produces a budget total of \$22,150.

Answer (A) is incorrect. The amount of \$20,680 is based on the actual number of sales orders, rather than on pounds shipped. Answer (B) is incorrect. The amount of \$20,920 is based on the number of shipments, not the number of pounds shipped. Answer (C) is incorrect. The amount of \$20,800 is based on planned pounds shipped of 9,600, not actual pounds shipped of 12,300.

5.5.3. Mien Co. is budgeting sales of 53,000 units of product Nous for next month. The manufacture of one unit of Nous requires 4 kilos of chemical Loire. During the month, Mien plans to reduce the inventory of Loire by 50,000 kilos and increase the finished goods inventory of Nous by 6,000 units. There is no Nous work-in-process inventory. How many kilos of Loire is Mien budgeting to purchase next month?

A. 138,000

B. 162,000

C. 186,000

D. 238,000

Answer (C) is correct. *(CPA, adapted)*

REQUIRED: The number of kilos budgeted for purchase.

DISCUSSION: Projected sales of 53,000 units and a 6,000-unit increase in inventory require production of 59,000 units. Thus, 236,000 (59,000 × 4) kilos of Loire are needed for production. Mien intends to reduce the inventory of Loire by 50,000 kilos, so 186,000 (236,000 – 50,000) kilos must be purchased.

Answer (A) is incorrect. Since 236,000 kilos are needed [(53,000 + 6,000) × 4] and Mien intends to reduce inventory by 50,000 units, 186,000 kilos must be purchased (236,000 – 50,000). Answer (B) is incorrect. The amount of 162,000 does not consider the 6,000-unit increase in the finished goods inventory of Nous. Answer (D) is incorrect. Since 236,000 kilos are needed [(53,000 + 6,000) × 4] and Mien intends to reduce inventory by 50,000 units, 186,000 kilos must be purchased (236,000 – 50,000).

5.5.4. A company has budgeted sales for the upcoming quarter as follows:

	January	February	March
Units	15,000	18,000	16,500

The ending finished goods inventory for each month equals 50% of the next month's budgeted sales. Additionally, 3 pounds of raw materials is required for each finished unit produced. The ending raw materials inventory for each month equals 200% of the next month's production requirements. If the raw materials cost $4.00 per pound and must be paid for in the month purchased, the budgeted raw materials purchases (in dollars) for January are

A. $216,000

B. $207,000

C. $198,000

D. $180,000

Answer (A) is correct. *(CIA, adapted)*

REQUIRED: The budgeted direct materials purchases.

DISCUSSION: The budgeted amount of direct materials purchases is computed as follows:

	January	February
Sales (finished units)	15,000	18,000
Desired ending FG inventory	9,000	8,250
Estimated beginning FG inventory	(7,500)	(9,000)
Production requirements (units)	16,500	17,250
Direct materials per finished unit	× 3	× 3
Direct materials required for production	49,500	51,750
Desired ending direct materials inventory (2.0 × 51,750)	103,500	
Total requirements	153,000	
Est. beginning direct materials inventory (2.0 × 49,500)	(99,000)	
Purchases (pounds)	54,000	

Budgeted direct materials purchases for January therefore are $216,000 (54,000 units × $4).

Answer (B) is incorrect. The amount of $207,000 equals materials required for February's production. Answer (C) is incorrect. The amount of $198,000 equals materials required for January's production. Answer (D) is incorrect. The amount of $180,000 equals materials required for January's sales.

5.5.5. Barnes Corporation expected to sell 150,000 board games during the month of November, and the company's master budget contained the following data related to the sale and production of these games:

Revenue	$2,400,000
Cost of goods sold:	
Direct materials	675,000
Direct labor	300,000
Variable overhead	450,000
Contribution	$ 975,000
Fixed overhead	250,000
Fixed selling and administration	500,000
Operating income	$ 225,000

Actual sales during November were 180,000 games. Using a flexible budget, the company expects the operating income for the month of November to be

A. $225,000

B. $270,000

C. $420,000

D. $510,000

Answer (C) is correct. *(CMA, adapted)*

REQUIRED: The expected operating income based on a flexible budget at a given production level.

DISCUSSION: Revenue of $2,400,000 reflects a unit selling price of $16 ($2,400,000 ÷ 150,000 games). The contribution margin is $975,000, or $6.50 per game ($975,000 ÷ 150,000 games). Increasing sales will result in an increased contribution margin of $195,000 (30,000 games × $6.50). Assuming no additional fixed costs, net income will increase to $420,000 ($225,000 originally reported + $195,000).

Answer (A) is incorrect. The net income before the increase in sales is $225,000. Answer (B) is incorrect. Net income was originally $1.50 per game. The $270,000 amount simply extrapolates that amount to sales of 180,000 games. Answer (D) is incorrect. The amount of $510,000 results from treating variable overhead as a fixed cost. Variable overhead is a $3 component ($450,000 ÷ 150,000 units) of unit variable cost.

5.5.6. A cash budget is being prepared for the purchase of Toyi, a merchandise item. Budgeted data are

Cost of goods sold for upcoming year	$300,000
Accounts payable, beginning of upcoming year	20,000
Inventory, beginning of upcoming year	30,000
Inventory, end of upcoming year	42,000

Purchases will be made in 12 equal monthly amounts and paid for in the following month. What is the budgeted cash payment for purchases of Toyi?

A. $295,000

B. $300,000

C. $306,000

D. $312,000

Answer (C) is correct. *(CPA, adapted)*

REQUIRED: The budgeted cash payment for purchases.

DISCUSSION: Purchases equal cost of goods sold, plus ending inventory, minus beginning inventory, or $312,000 ($300,000 + $42,000 – $30,000). Purchases are made evenly throughout the year at a rate of $26,000 per month ($312,000 ÷ 12). Given that 11 payments will be made in the upcoming year for that year's purchases, the total cash payment will be $306,000 [(11 × $26,000) + $20,000 beginning accounts payable balance].

Answer (A) is incorrect. The budgeted cash payment is $306,000. Answer (B) is incorrect. The cost of goods sold is $300,000. Answer (D) is incorrect. The amount of purchases is $312,000. Because purchases will be paid for in the following month, only the first 11 monthly payments will be made in the upcoming year and the December payment will be made the following year.

5.5.7. Rolling Wheel purchases bicycle components in the month prior to assembling them into bicycles. Assembly is scheduled 1 month prior to budgeted sales. Rolling Wheel pays 75% of component costs in the month of purchase and 25% of the costs in the following month. Component costs included in budgeted cost of sales are

April	May	June	July	August
$5,000	$6,000	$7,000	$8,000	$8,000

What is Rolling Wheel's budgeted cash payments for components in May?

A. $5,750

B. $6,750

C. $7,750

D. $8,000

Answer (C) is correct. *(CPA, adapted)*

REQUIRED: The budgeted cash payments for purchases.

DISCUSSION: Because the components are purchased 1 month prior to assembly and assembled 1 month prior to sale, there is a total of 2-month lag time. In April, Rolling Wheel purchases June materials. Thus, it needs to pay 75% of the June cost in April and 25% of the June cost in May. In May, Rolling Wheel purchases July material. Thus, it needs to pay 75% of the July cost (for the materials purchased for production in July) in May and 25% of the July cost in June. Thus, the budgeted cash payments in May = (25% × $7,000) + (75% × $8,000) = $7,750.

	March	April	May
Purchase	75% × $6,000 (for May production)	75% × $7,000 (for June production)	75% × $8,000 (for July production)
Assembly	$25% × $5,000 (for April production)	25% × $6,000 (for May production)	25% × $7,000 (for June production)
Total	$5,750	$6,750	$7,750

Answer (A) is incorrect. The amount of $5,750 equals the budgeted cash payments for components in March. Answer (B) is incorrect. The amount of $6,750 equals the budgeted cash payments for components in April. Answer (D) is incorrect. The amount of $8,000 equals the budgeted cash payments for components in June.

5.5.8. A company is preparing its cash budget for the coming month. All sales are made on account. Given the following:

	Beginning Balances	Budgeted Amounts
Cash	$ 50,000	
Accounts receivable	180,000	
Sales		$800,000
Cash disbursements		780,000
Depreciation		25,000
Ending accounts receivable balance		210,000

What is the expected cash balance of the company at the end of the coming month?

A. $15,000

B. $40,000

C. $45,000

D. $70,000

Answer (B) is correct. *(CIA, adapted)*

REQUIRED: The expected cash balance of the company at the end of the coming month.

DISCUSSION: Collections on account equal beginning accounts receivable of $180,000, plus sales on account of $800,000, minus budgeted ending accounts receivable of $210,000, or $770,000. The beginning cash balance of $50,000, plus cash collections on account of $770,000, minus budgeted cash disbursements of $780,000 equals $40,000. Depreciation of $25,000 is excluded because it is a noncash expense.

Answer (A) is incorrect. The amount of $15,000 includes depreciation expense which should be excluded because it is a noncash expense. Answer (C) is incorrect. The amount of $770,000 ($180,000 + $800,000 – $210,000), not $800,000, was the amount of cash collected for receivables. Also, the $25,000 of depreciation should not be deducted because it is a noncash expense. Answer (D) is incorrect. The amount of $770,000 ($180,000 + $800,000 – $210,000), not $800,000, was the amount of cash collected for receivables.

Questions 5.5.9 and 5.5.10 are based on the following information.

The operating results in summarized form for a retail computer store for Year 5 are

Revenue:	
Hardware sales	$4,800,000
Software sales	2,000,000
Maintenance contracts	1,200,000
Total revenue	$8,000,000
Costs and expenses:	
Cost of hardware sales	$3,360,000
Cost of software sales	1,200,000
Marketing expenses	600,000
Customer maintenance costs	640,000
Administration expenses	1,120,000
Total costs and expenses	$6,920,000
Operating income	$1,080,000

The computer store is in the process of formulating its operating budget for Year 6 and has made the following assumptions:

- The selling prices of hardware are expected to increase 10%, but there will be no selling price increases for software or maintenance contracts.
- Hardware unit sales are expected to increase 5% with a corresponding 5% growth in the number of maintenance contracts; growth in units software sales is estimated at 8%.
- The cost of hardware and software is expected to increase 4%.
- Marketing expenses will be increased 5% in the coming year.
- Three technicians will be added to the customer maintenance operations in the coming year, increasing the customer maintenance costs by $120,000.
- Administrative costs will be held at the same level.

5.5.9. The retail computer store's budgeted total revenue for Year 6 would be

A. $8,804,000

B. $8,460,000

C. $8,904,000

D. $8,964,000

Answer (D) is correct. *(CIA, adapted)*

REQUIRED: The budgeted total revenue for Year 6.

DISCUSSION: Hardware selling prices are expected to increase by 10% and unit volume by 5%. Thus, hardware revenue should be $5,544,000 ($4,800,000 sales in Year 5 × 1.10 × 1.05). Given that unit sales of software are expected to increase by 8%, software revenue should increase to $2,160,000 ($2,000,000 sales in Year 5 × 1.08). The number of maintenance contracts is expected to increase by 5%, so maintenance contracts revenue should increase to $1,260,000 ($1,200,000 sales in Year 5 × 1.05). Budgeted revenue therefore should be $8,964,000 ($5,544,000 + $2,160,000 + $1,260,000).

Answer (A) is incorrect. The amount of $8,804,000 omits the growth in software sales. Answer (B) is incorrect. The amount of $8,460,000 omits the increase in the selling price of hardware. Answer (C) is incorrect. The amount of $8,904,000 omits the growth in maintenance contracts.

5.5.10. The retail computer store's budgeted total costs and expenses for the coming year would be

A. $7,252,400

B. $7,526,960

C. $7,558,960

D. $7,893,872

Answer (B) is correct. *(CIA, adapted)*

REQUIRED: The budgeted total costs and expenses for Year 6.

DISCUSSION: Hardware unit sales are expected to increase by 5%, and the cost of hardware is expected to increase by 4%. Thus, the cost of hardware sales should be $3,669,120 ($3,360,000 costs in Year 5 × 1.05 × 1.04). Software unit sales are expected to increase by 8%, and the cost of software is expected to increase by 4%. Accordingly, the cost of software sales should be $1,347,840 ($1,200,000 cost in Year 5 × 1.08 × 1.04). Marketing expense should increase to $630,000 ($600,000 in Year 5 × 1.05) and customer maintenance costs to $760,000 ($640,000 in Year 5 + $120,000). Administrative costs are expected to remain at $1,120,000. Consequently, total costs and expenses should be $7,526,960 ($3,669,120 + $1,347,840 + $630,000 + $760,000 + $1,120,000).

Answer (A) is incorrect. The amount of $7,252,400 omits the increase in hardware and software cost of sales attributable to the volume increase. Answer (C) is incorrect. Increasing customer maintenance costs by 5% before the $120,000 for technicians was added results in $7,558,960. Answer (D) is incorrect. The amount of $7,893,872 includes an additional 10% increase for hardware cost of sales.

Questions 5.5.11 and 5.5.12 are based on the following information. A company produces a product that requires 2 pounds of a raw material. It is forecast that there will be 6,000 pounds of raw material on hand at the end of June. At the end of any given month, the company wishes to have 30% of next month's raw material requirements on hand. The company has budgeted production of the product for July, August, September, and October to be 10,000, 12,000, 13,000, and 11,000 units, respectively. As of June 1, the raw material sells for $1.00 per pound.

5.5.11. The cost of inventory is determined using the last-in, first-out (LIFO) method. If the price of raw material increases 10% as of June 30, what will be the effect of this increase on the cost of purchases from July to September?

A. $600 increase.

B. $7,060 increase.

C. $9,200 increase.

D. $60 increase.

Answer (B) is correct. *(CIA, adapted)*

REQUIRED: The effect of an increase in the price of the direct material on the cost of purchases.

DISCUSSION: The amount of purchases can be calculated as follows:

	BI		Current Requirements		Purchases		EI
July	6,000	–	20,000	+	21,200	=	7,200
August	7,200	–	24,000	+	24,600	=	7,800
September	7,800	–	26,000	+	24,800	=	6,600
					70,600 lbs.		

The current requirement for each month is the budgeted production multiplied by the materials needed per product (2 pounds). Ending inventory is 30% of budgeted production for the next month times the materials needed for each product. Purchases equals the sum of current requirements and ending inventory, minus beginning inventory. Thus, the effect of the change in price is to increase the cost of purchases by $7,060 (70,600 pounds × $1 per pound × 10%).

Answer (A) is incorrect. The amount of $600 equals 10% of the ending inventory in June. Answer (C) is incorrect. The amount of $9,200 equals $.10 times the pounds required for production from July through October. Answer (D) is incorrect. The amount of $60 results from taking the difference between June and September ending inventory and multiplying it by $.10.

5.5.12. In the month of September, raw material purchases and ending inventory, respectively, will be (in pounds):

A. 24,800 and 6,600.

B. 32,600 and 6,600.

C. 13,000 and 3,900.

D. 24,800 and 3,900.

Answer (A) is correct. *(CIA, adapted)*

REQUIRED: The total (in pounds) of direct materials purchases and ending inventory for September.

DISCUSSION: The ending inventory equals 6,600 pounds [(11,000 units × 2 pounds) required in October × 30%]. The requirements for September equal 26,000 pounds (13,000 units × 2 pounds), and the beginning inventory is 7,800 pounds (26,000 pounds × 30%). Thus, September purchases equal 24,800 pounds (26,000 pounds currently required + 6,600 pounds EI – 7,800 pounds BI).

Answer (B) is incorrect. Adding beginning inventory to purchases results in 32,600. Answer (C) is incorrect. The budgeted production in units is 13,000, and the number of units that can be produced using the ending inventory of direct materials for August is 3,900. Answer (D) is incorrect. The number of units that can be produced using the ending inventory of direct materials for August is 3,900.

Questions 5.5.13 and 5.5.14 are based on the following information.

The Raymar Company is preparing its cash budget for the months of April and May. The firm has established a $200,000 line of credit with its bank at a 12% annual rate of interest on which borrowings for cash deficits must be made in $10,000 increments. There is no outstanding balance on the line of credit loan on April 1. Principal repayments are to be made in any month in which there is a surplus of cash. Interest is to be paid monthly. If there are no outstanding balances on the loans, Raymar will invest any cash in excess of its desired end-of-month cash balance in U.S. Treasury bills. Raymar intends to maintain a minimum balance of $100,000 at the end of each month by either borrowing for deficits below the minimum balance or investing any excess cash. Expected monthly collection and disbursement patterns are shown in the column to the right.

- Collections: 50% of the current month's sales budget and 50% of the previous month's sales budget.
- Accounts Payable Disbursements: 75% of the current month's accounts payable budget and 25% of the previous month's accounts payable budget.
- All other disbursements occur in the month in which they are budgeted.

Budget Information

	March	April	May
Sales	$40,000	$50,000	$100,000
Accounts payable	30,000	40,000	40,000
Payroll	60,000	70,000	50,000
Other disbursements	25,000	30,000	10,000

5.5.13. In April, Raymar's budget will result in

A. $45,000 in excess cash.

B. A need to borrow $50,000 on its line of credit for the cash deficit.

C. A need to borrow $100,000 on its line of credit for the cash deficit.

D. A need to borrow $90,000 on its line of credit for the cash deficit.

Answer (C) is correct. *(CMA, adapted)*

REQUIRED: The effect on cash at the end of April.

DISCUSSION: April's cash collections are $45,000 [($50,000 April sales × 50%) + ($40,000 March sales × 50%)]. Disbursements for accounts payable are $37,500 [($40,000 April payables × 75%) + ($30,000 March payables × 25%)]. In addition to the accounts payable disbursements, payroll and other disbursements will require an additional $100,000. Thus, total disbursements are estimated to be $137,500. The net negative cash flow (amount to be borrowed) is $92,500 ($137,500 – $45,000). Because the line of credit must be drawn upon in $10,000 increments, the loan must be for $100,000.

Answer (A) is incorrect. Cash receipts equal $45,000. Answer (B) is incorrect. The cash deficit is $92,500 without borrowing. Answer (D) is incorrect. A loan of only $90,000 leaves $2,500 below the desired ending cash balance.

5.5.14. In May, Raymar will be required to

A. Repay $20,000 principal and pay $1,000 interest.

B. Repay $90,000 principal and pay $100 interest.

C. Pay $900 interest.

D. Borrow an additional $20,000 and pay $1,000 interest.

Answer (D) is correct. *(CMA, adapted)*

REQUIRED: The transaction required in May.

DISCUSSION: The entity must borrow $100,000 in April, so interest must be paid in May at the rate of 1% per month (12% annual rate). Consequently, interest expense is $1,000 ($100,000 × 1%). May receipts are $75,000 [($100,000 May sales × 50%) + ($50,000 April sales × 50%)]. Disbursements in May are $40,000 [($40,000 May payables × 75%) + ($40,000 April payables × 25%)]. In addition to the May accounts payable disbursements, payroll and other disbursements are $60,000, bringing total disbursements to $101,000 ($60,000 + $40,000 + $1,000). Thus, disbursements exceed receipts by $26,000 ($101,000 – $75,000). However, cash has a beginning balance of $7,500 ($100,000 April loan – $92,500 negative cash flow for April using the collections and disbursements information given). As a result, an additional $18,500 must be borrowed to eliminate the cash deficit. Given the requirement that loans be in $10,000 increments, the May loan must be for $20,000.

Answer (A) is incorrect. No funds are available to repay the loan. May receipts are less than May disbursements. Answer (B) is incorrect. No funds are available to repay the loan. May receipts are less than May disbursements. Answer (C) is incorrect. The 1% interest is calculated on a $100,000 loan, not a $90,000 loan.

Questions 5.5.15 through 5.5.17 are based on the following information.

Rokat Corporation is a manufacturer of tables sold to schools, restaurants, hotels, and other institutions. The table tops are manufactured by Rokat, but the table legs are purchased from an outside supplier. The Assembly Department takes a manufactured table top and attaches the four purchased table legs. It takes 20 minutes of labor to assemble a table. The company follows a policy of producing enough tables to ensure that 40% of next month's sales are in the finished goods inventory. Rokat also purchases sufficient direct materials inventory to ensure that direct materials inventory is 60% of the following month's scheduled production.

Rokat's sales budget in units for the next quarter is as follows:

July	2,300
August	2,500
September	2,100

Rokat's ending inventories in units for June 30 are

Finished goods	1,900
Direct materials (legs)	4,000

5.5.15. The number of tables to be produced by Rokat during August is

A. 2,300 tables.

B. 2,340 tables.

C. 1,400 tables.

D. 1,900 tables.

Answer (B) is correct. *(CMA, adapted)*

REQUIRED: The number of tables to be produced.

DISCUSSION: The company will need 2,500 finished units for August sales. In addition, 840 units (2,100 September unit sales × 40%) should be in inventory at the end of August. August sales plus the desired ending inventory equals 3,340 units. Of these units, 40% of August's sales, or 1,000 units, should be available from beginning inventory. Consequently, production in August should be 2,340 units.

Answer (A) is incorrect. The number of tables to be produced in July is 2,300. Answer (C) is incorrect. The amount of 1,400 tables is based on July's beginning inventory, sales, and ending inventory. Answer (D) is incorrect. July's beginning inventory equals 1,900 tables.

5.5.16. Assume Rokat's required production for August and September is 1,600 and 1,800 units, respectively, and the July 31 direct materials inventory is 4,200 units. The number of table legs to be purchased in August is

A. 6,520 legs.

B. 9,400 legs.

C. 2,200 legs.

D. 6,400 legs.

Answer (A) is correct. *(CMA, adapted)*

REQUIRED: The number of table legs to be purchased.

DISCUSSION: The August production of 1,600 units will require 6,400 table legs. September's production of 1,800 units will require 7,200 table legs. Thus, inventory at the end of August should be 4,320 legs (7,200 legs × 60%). The total of legs needed during August is 10,720 (6,400 + 4,320), of which 4,200 are available from the July 31 ending inventory. The remaining 6,520 legs must be purchased during August.

Answer (B) is incorrect. The amount of 9,400 legs is based on an ending inventory of 100% of September's production. Answer (C) is incorrect. Failing to consider the legs needed for the ending inventory results in 2,200 legs. Answer (D) is incorrect. The amount needed for August production is 6,400 legs.

5.5.17. Assume that Rokat Corporation will produce 1,800 units in the month of September. How many employees will be required for the Assembly Department? (Fractional employees are acceptable since employees can be hired on a part-time basis. Assume a 40-hour week and a 4-week month.)

A. 15 employees.

B. 3.75 employees.

C. 60 employees.

D. 600 employees.

Answer (B) is correct. *(CMA, adapted)*

REQUIRED: The number of employees required.

DISCUSSION: Each unit requires 20 minutes of assembly time, or 1/3 of an hour. The assembly of 1,800 units will therefore require 600 hours of labor (1,800 × 1/3). At 40 hours per week for 4 weeks, each employee will work 160 hours during the month. Thus, 3.75 employees (600 ÷ 160) are needed.

Answer (A) is incorrect. This number of employees assumes production occurs in a single 40-hour week. Answer (C) is incorrect. This number of employees assumes that each leg requires 20 minutes to assemble and that production occurs in a single 40-hour week. Answer (D) is incorrect. This number of employees is the number of hours needed, not the number of employees.

Questions 5.5.18 through 5.5.20 are based on the following information. Super Drive, a computer disk storage and back-up company, uses accrual accounting. The company's Statement of Financial Position for the year ended November 30 is as follows:

Super Drive
Statement of Financial Position
as of November 30

Assets		Liabilities and Stockholders' Equity	
Cash	$ 52,000	Accounts payable	$ 175,000
Accounts receivable, net	150,000	Common stock	900,000
Inventory	315,000	Retained earnings	442,000
Property, plant, and equipment	1,000,000	Total liabilities and stockholders' equity	$1,517,000
Total assets	$1,517,000		

Additional information regarding Super Drive's operations include the following:

- Sales are budgeted at $520,000 for December and $500,000 for January of the next year.
- Collections are expected to be 60% in the month of sale and 40% in the month following the sale.
- Eighty percent of the disk drive components are purchased in the month prior to the month of sale, and 20% are purchased in the month of sale. Purchased components are 40% of the cost of goods sold.
- Payment for the components is made in the month following the purchase.
- Cost of goods sold is 80% of sales.

5.5.18. Super Drive's budgeted cash collections for the month of December are

A. $208,000

B. $520,000

C. $402,000

D. $462,000

Answer (D) is correct. *(CMA, adapted)*

REQUIRED: The budgeted cash collections for the month of December.

DISCUSSION: Collections are expected to be 60% in the month of sale and 40% in the month following the sale. Thus, collections in December consist of the $150,000 of receivables at November 30, plus 60% of December sales. Total collections are therefore $462,000 [$150,000 + ($520,000 × 60%)].

Answer (A) is incorrect. The amount of $208,000 equals 40% of December sales. Answer (B) is incorrect. Total sales are not collected in the month of sale. Answer (C) is incorrect. The amount of $402,000 represents only 60% of receivables but 100% of receivables will be collected.

5.5.19. Super Drive's projected balance in accounts payable on December 31 is

A. $161,280

B. $326,400

C. $166,400

D. $416,000

Answer (A) is correct. *(CMA, adapted)*

REQUIRED: The projected balance in accounts payable on December 31.

DISCUSSION: Payments are made in the month following purchase. The balance in accounts payable on November 30 is $175,000; this amount will be paid in December. The account is credited for purchases of a portion of components to be used for sales in December (20% of December components) and for sales in January (80% of January components). Cost of goods sold is 80% of sales, and components are 40% of cost of goods sold. Thus, December component needs are $166,400 ($520,000 sales × 80% × 40%), and January component needs are $160,000 ($500,000 sales × 80% × 40%). The December purchases of December component needs equal $33,280 ($166,400 × 20%). December purchases of January component needs are $128,000 ($160,000 × 80%). Hence, the total of December purchases (ending balance in accounts payable) equals $161,280 ($33,280 + $128,000).

Answer (B) is incorrect. The sum of the component needs for December and January equals $326,400. Answer (C) is incorrect. December component needs equals $166,400. Answer (D) is incorrect. Cost of sales for December equals $416,000.

5.5.20. Super Drive's projected gross profit for the month ending December 31 is

A. $416,000

B. $104,000

C. $134,000

D. $536,000

Answer (B) is correct. *(CMA, adapted)*

REQUIRED: The projected gross profit for December.

DISCUSSION: Given that cost of goods sold is 80% of sales, gross profit is 20% of sales. Consequently, pro forma gross profit is $104,000 ($520,000 × 20%).

Answer (A) is incorrect. Cost of goods sold is $416,000 (80% of sales). Answer (C) is incorrect. The amount of $134,000 equals 20% of the sum of November receivables and December sales. Answer (D) is incorrect. Gross profit cannot be greater than sales.

5.5.21. Cook Co.'s total costs of operating five sales offices last year were $500,000, of which $70,000 represented fixed costs. Cook has determined that total costs are significantly influenced by the number of sales offices operated. Last year's costs and number of sales offices can be used as the bases for predicting annual costs. What would be the budgeted cost for the coming year if Cook were to operate seven sales offices?

A. $700,000

B. $672,000

C. $602,000

D. $586,000

Answer (B) is correct. *(CPA, adapted)*

REQUIRED: The budgeted cost for the coming year if Cook were to operate seven sales offices.

DISCUSSION: Using the formula $y = a + bx$, y is the total budgeted cost, a is the fixed costs, b is the variable cost per unit, and x is the number of budgeted sales offices. The fixed costs are $70,000, the variable cost per unit is $86,000 [($500,000 – $70,000) ÷ 5], and the number of budgeted sales offices is 7. Thus, the budgeted cost for the coming year assuming seven sales offices is $672,000 [$70,000 + (7 × $86,000)].

Answer (A) is incorrect. The amount of $700,000 assumes the total costs are variable. Answer (C) is incorrect. The amount of $602,000 excludes fixed costs. Answer (D) is incorrect. The amount of $586,000 is last year's total costs plus the per-unit variable cost.

5.5.22. An entity has the following cost components for 100,000 units of product for the year:

Direct materials	$200,000
Direct labor	100,000
Manufacturing overhead	200,000
Selling and administrative expense	150,000

All costs are variable except for $100,000 of manufacturing overhead and $100,000 of selling and administrative expenses. The total costs to produce and sell 110,000 units for the year are

A. $650,000

B. $715,000

C. $695,000

D. $540,000

Answer (C) is correct. *(CMA, adapted)*

REQUIRED: The flexible budget costs for producing and selling a given quantity.

DISCUSSION: Direct materials unit costs are strictly variable at $2 ($200,000 ÷ 100,000 units). Similarly, direct labor has a variable unit cost of $1 ($100,000 ÷ 100,000 units). The $200,000 of manufacturing overhead for 100,000 units is 50%. The variable unit cost is $1. Selling costs are $100,000 fixed and $50,000 variable for production of 100,000 units, and the variable unit selling expenses is $.50 ($50,000 ÷ 100,000 units). The total unit variable cost is therefore $4.50 ($2 + $1 + $1 + $.50). Fixed costs are $200,000. At a production level of 110,000 units, variable costs are $495,000 (110,000 units × $4.50). Hence, total costs are $695,000 ($495,000 + $200,000).

Answer (A) is incorrect. The cost at a production level of 100,000 units is $650,000. Answer (B) is incorrect. The amount of $715,000 assumes a variable unit cost of $6.50 with no fixed costs. Answer (D) is incorrect. Total costs are $695,000 based on a unit variable cost of $4.50 each.

5.5.23. National Warehousing is constructing a corporate planning model. Cash sales are 30% of the company's sales, with the remainder subject to the following collection pattern:

One month after sale	60%
Two months after sale	30
Three months after sale	8
Uncollectible	2

If S_n is defined as total sales in month n, which one of the following expressions correctly describes National's collections on account in any given month?

A. $0.6S_{n-1} + 0.3S_{n-2} + 0.08S_{n-3}$

B. $0.42S_{n+1} + 0.21S_{n+2} + 0.056S_{n+3}$

C. $0.42S_{n-1} + 0.21S_{n-2} + 0.056S_{n-3}$

D. $0.42S_{n-1} + 0.21S_{n-2} + 0.056S_{n-3} – 0.014S_n$

Answer (C) is correct. *(CMA, adapted)*

REQUIRED: The equation that describes collections on account.

DISCUSSION: Because the entity will collect 30% of its sales at the time of sale, only 70% is on account. Of this amount, (1) 60% is collected in the month after the sale, (2) 30% in the second month, and (3) 8% in the third month. Thus, the collections in any given month will be (1) 42% (60% × 70% total sales) of the previous month's sales (S_{n-1}), (2) 21% (30% × 70%) of the second preceding month's sales (S_{n-2}), and (3) 5.6% (8% × 70%) of the third preceding month's sales (S_{n-3}).

Answer (A) is incorrect. Cash sales are 30% of total sales. Answer (B) is incorrect. The previous month's sales are represented by (S_{n-1}), the second preceding month's sales are represented by (S_{n-2}), etc. Answer (D) is incorrect. The uncollectible sales should not be deducted from the collections on account.

Questions 5.5.24 through 5.5.28 are based on the following information. Superflite expects April sales of its deluxe model airplane, the C-14, to be 402,000 units at $11 each. Each C-14 requires three purchased components shown below.

	Purchase Cost	Number Needed for Each C-14 Unit
A-9	$0.50	1
B-6	0.25	2
D-28	1.00	3

Manufacturing direct labor and variable overhead per unit of C-14 totals $3.00. Fixed manufacturing overhead is $1.00 per unit at a production level of 500,000 units. Superflite plans the following beginning and ending inventories for the month of April and uses standard absorption costing for valuing inventory.

Part No.	Units at April 1	Units at April 30
C-14	12,000	10,000
A-9	21,000	9,000
B-6	32,000	10,000
D-28	14,000	6,000

5.5.24. Superflite's C-14 production budget for April should be based on the manufacture of

A. 390,000 units.

B. 400,000 units.

C. 402,000 units.

D. 424,000 units.

Answer (B) is correct. *(CMA, adapted)*

REQUIRED: The number of units upon which the production budget should be based.

DISCUSSION: Sales are expected to be 402,000 units in April. The beginning inventory is 12,000 units, and the ending inventory is expected to be 10,000 units, a decline in inventory of 2,000 units. Thus, the budget should be based on production of 400,000 units (402,000 units to be sold – 12,000 units BI + 10,000 units EI).

Answer (A) is incorrect. Not considering the need to produce for ending inventory results in 390,000 units. Answer (C) is incorrect. Sales for the month equals 402,000 units. A portion of these sales will come from the beginning inventory. Answer (D) is incorrect. The sum of sales and beginning and ending inventories is 424,000 units.

5.5.25. Without prejudice to your response to any other question, assume for this question that Superflite plans to manufacture 400,000 units in April. The book value of the planned April 30 inventories is

A. $53,000

B. $83,000

C. $93,000

D. $128,500

Answer (C) is correct. *(CMA, adapted)*

REQUIRED: The carrying amount of planned ending inventories.

DISCUSSION: The 9,000 units of A-9 are measured at $0.50 each, or $4,500 in total. The 10,000 units of B-6 at $0.25 each total $2,500. The 6,000 units of D-28 cost $1 each and total $6,000. The 10,000 units of the finished product, C-14, are measured as follows:

Direct materials:	A-9	(1 × $0.50)	=	$0.50
	B-6	(2 × $0.25)	=	0.50
	D-28	(3 × $1)	=	3.00
Labor and variable overhead				3.00
Fixed overhead				1.00
Total standard cost				$8.00

At a standard cost of $8 each, the 10,000 units of C-14 total $80,000. Adding the four inventory items ($4,500 + $2,500 + $6,000 + $80,000) results in total budgeted April 30 inventory of $93,000.

Answer (A) is incorrect. Failing to include the cost of the direct materials in the finished product results in $53,000. Answer (B) is incorrect. The amount of $83,000 omits the fixed overhead. Answer (D) is incorrect. The carrying amount of the beginning inventories is $128,500.

5.5.26. Without prejudice to your response to any other question, assume for this question that Superflite plans to manufacture 400,000 units in April. Superflite's April budget for the purchase of A-9 should be

A. 379,000 units.

B. 388,000 units.

C. 402,000 units.

D. 412,000 units.

Answer (B) is correct. *(CMA, adapted)*

REQUIRED: The purchases budget for component A-9.

DISCUSSION: Each of the 400,000 units to be produced in April requires one unit of A-9, a total requirement of 400,000 units. In addition, ending inventory is expected to be 9,000 units. Thus, 409,000 units must be supplied during the month. Of these, 21,000 are available in the beginning inventory. Subtracting the 21,000 beginning inventory from 409,000 leaves 388,000 to be purchased.

Answer (A) is incorrect. Failing to consider the 9,000 units in the ending inventory results in 379,000 units. Answer (C) is incorrect. Sales for the month equal 402,000 units. Answer (D) is incorrect. Adding the decline in inventory of 12,000 to production needs instead of subtracting it results in 412,000.

5.5.27. Without prejudice to your response to any other question, assume for this question that Superflite plans to manufacture 400,000 units in April. The total April budget for all purchased components should be

A. $1,580,500

B. $1,600,000

C. $1,608,000

D. $1,700,000

Answer (A) is correct. *(CMA, adapted)*

REQUIRED: The total purchases budget.

DISCUSSION: Each of the 400,000 units to be produced in April requires one unit of A-9, a total requirement of 400,000 units. In addition, ending inventory should be 9,000 units. Thus, 409,000 units must be supplied. Of these, 21,000 are available in the beginning inventory. Subtracting the 21,000 beginning inventory from 409,000 leaves 388,000 to be purchased. At $0.50 each, these 388,000 units will cost $194,000. The inventory of component B-6 declines by 22,000 units. Subtracting this number from the 800,000 units (2 × 400,000 units of C-14) needed for production leaves 778,000 to be purchased at $0.25 each, a total of $194,500. The inventory of component D-28 declines by 8,000 units. Subtracting this number from the 1,200,000 units needed for production (each product requires three units of D-28) leaves 1,192,000 to be purchased at $1 each. The total cost of the components to be purchased equals $1,580,500.

Answer (B) is incorrect. Assuming an extra purchase for ending inventories results in $1,600,000. Answer (C) is incorrect. Adding the beginning and ending inventories results in $1,608,000. Answer (D) is incorrect. The amount of $1,700,000 is based on a misstatement of the number of components needed.

5.5.28. Without prejudice to your response to any other question, assume for this question that Superflite plans to manufacture 400,000 units in April. Superflite's budgeted gross margin for April is

A. $1,105,500

B. $1,200,000

C. $1,206,000

D. $1,608,000

Answer (C) is correct. *(CMA, adapted)*

REQUIRED: The gross margin.

DISCUSSION: Given sales of 402,000 units at $11 each, total revenue is $4,422,000. The standard cost of these units is $8. This is calculated as (1 × $0.50) + (2 × $0.25) + (3 × $1.00) + $3.00 + $1.00. Multiplying $8 times 402,000 units results in a cost of goods sold of $3,216,000. Subtracting cost of goods sold from revenues produces a budgeted gross margin of $1,206,000. Underabsorbed fixed overhead is normally ignored in budgeted monthly financial statements because it is based on an annual average and is offset by year end.

Answer (A) is incorrect. Gross margin is based on a unit price of $11, a unit cost of $8, and unit sales of 402,000. Answer (B) is incorrect. The amount of $1,200,000 is based on production volume, not sales volume. Answer (D) is incorrect. The amount of $1,608,000 is the cost of sales minus the direct materials included in cost of sales.

5.5.29. RedRock Company uses flexible budgeting for cost control. RedRock produced 10,800 units of product during October, incurring indirect materials costs of $13,000. Its master budget for the year reflected indirect materials costs of $180,000 at a production volume of 144,000 units. A flexible budget for October production would reflect indirect materials costs of

A. $13,000

B. $13,500

C. $13,975

D. $11,700

Answer (B) is correct. *(CMA, adapted)*

REQUIRED: The flexible budget amount of indirect materials cost for the month.

DISCUSSION: The cost of indirect materials for 144,000 units was expected to be $180,000. Consequently, the unit cost of indirect materials is $1.25 ($180,000 ÷ 144,000). Multiplying the $1.25 unit cost times the 10,800 units produced results in an expected total indirect materials cost of $13,500.

Answer (A) is incorrect. The actual cost of indirect materials in October is $13,000. Answer (C) is incorrect. The amount of $13,975 is not the flexible budget cost for indirect materials. Answer (D) is incorrect. The amount of $11,700 is not the flexible budget cost for indirect materials.

STUDY UNIT SIX
ABSORPTION VS. VARIABLE COSTING

The difference between absorption and variable costing is in the treatment of the fixed portion of manufacturing overhead. **Absorption costing** (full costing) includes all costs of manufacturing, both variable and fixed, in product cost. This method is required under GAAP and for federal income tax purposes. **Variable costing** assigns only variable manufacturing costs to products. This method is not permitted for external reporting, although it is very useful for managerial purposes. Variable costing also is known as contribution margin reporting. It emphasizes the margin available to cover fixed costs. Variable costing sometimes is called direct costing, but this term is misleading because indirect costs still must be allocated, not traced, to the product. The effects of these different treatments of fixed overhead are apparent in the comparative income statements presented below, prepared using identical cost data:

Absorption Costing (Required under GAAP)			Variable Costing (For Internal Reporting Only)		
Sales		**$8,000**	**Sales**		**$8,000**
Beginning inventory	$ 0		Beginning inventory	$ 0	
Mfg. costs -- variable and fixed	7,500		Variable manufacturing costs	4,500	
Goods available for sale	$7,500		Goods available for sale	$4,500	
Minus: Ending inventory	(1,500)		Minus: Ending inventory	(900)	
Absorption cost of goods sold		(6,000)	**Variable cost of goods sold**		(3,600)
			Variable S&A expenses		(200)
Gross margin		**$2,000**	**Contribution margin**		**$4,200**
			Fixed overhead		(3,000)
S&A exp. -- variable and fixed		(800)	Fixed S&A expenses		(600)
Operating income		**$1,200**	**Operating income**		**$ 600**

Absorption and variable costing are two points on a continuum of possible inventory costing methods. At one extreme is **superabsorption costing**, which treats costs from all links in the value chain as inventoriable. At the other extreme is **supervariable (throughput) costing**, which treats direct materials as the only product cost.

The derivation of the contribution margin is an important element in the variable-costing income statement. It indicates how much sales contribute to covering fixed costs and providing a profit. Accordingly, variable costing provides a better measure than absorption costing of the relative profitability of individual products, product lines, territories, or customers. It provides information about cost-volume-profit (CVP) relationships (Study Unit 4). This information is the primary objective of variable costing.

QUESTIONS

6.1 Variable Costing

6.1.1. Which of the following is a term more descriptive of the type of cost accounting often called direct costing?

A. Out-of-pocket costing.

B. Variable costing.

C. Relevant costing.

D. Prime costing.

Answer (B) is correct. *(CPA, adapted)*
REQUIRED: The term that best describes direct costing.
DISCUSSION: Variable costing is the more accurate term. Variable (direct) costing considers only variable manufacturing costs to be product costs, i.e., inventoriable. These costs include variable manufacturing overhead, an indirect cost.
Answer (A) is incorrect. Out-of-pocket costs require immediate expenditure. Answer (C) is incorrect. Relevant costs vary with alternative decisions. Answer (D) is incorrect. Prime costs include only direct labor and direct materials costs (i.e., no variable manufacturing overhead).

6.1.2. Which of the following is an argument against the use of variable costing?

A. Absorption costing overstates the balance sheet value of inventories.

B. Variable manufacturing overhead is a period cost.

C. Fixed manufacturing overhead is difficult to allocate properly.

D. Fixed manufacturing overhead is necessary for the production of a product.

Answer (D) is correct. *(CIA, adapted)*
REQUIRED: The argument against the use of variable costing.
DISCUSSION: Variable costing treats fixed manufacturing costs as period costs, but absorption costing accumulates them as product costs. If product costs are all manufacturing costs incurred to produce output, fixed manufacturing overhead should be inventoried because it is necessary for production. The counter argument in favor of variable costing is that fixed manufacturing overhead is more closely related to capacity to produce than to the production of individual units. Internal reporting for cost behavior analysis is more useful if it concentrates on production of units.
Answer (A) is incorrect. Variable costing arguably understates inventory. Answer (B) is incorrect. Variable manufacturing overhead is a product cost under any cost system. Answer (C) is incorrect. The difficulty of allocating fixed manufacturing overhead is an argument against absorption costing.

6.1.3. In the application of variable costing as a cost-allocation process in manufacturing,

A. Variable direct costs are treated as period costs.

B. Nonvariable indirect costs are treated as product costs.

C. Variable indirect costs are treated as product costs.

D. Nonvariable direct costs are treated as product costs.

Answer (C) is correct. *(CIA, adapted)*
REQUIRED: The true statement about variable costing.
DISCUSSION: Variable costing considers only variable manufacturing costs to be product costs. Variable indirect costs included in variable overhead are therefore treated as inventoriable. Fixed costs are considered period costs and are expensed as incurred.
Answer (A) is incorrect. Variable manufacturing costs, whether direct (direct materials and direct labor) or indirect (variable overhead), are accounted for as product costs, not period costs. Answer (B) is incorrect. Nonvariable indirect costs are treated as period costs in variable costing. Answer (D) is incorrect. In variable costing, nonvariable direct costs are treated as period costs, not product costs.

6.1.4. A basic tenet of variable costing is that period costs should be currently expensed. What is the rationale behind this procedure?

A. Period costs are uncontrollable and should not be charged to a specific product.

B. Period costs are usually immaterial in amount, and the cost of assigning them to specific products will outweigh the benefits.

C. Allocation of period costs is arbitrary at best and could lead to erroneous decisions by management.

D. Because period costs will occur whether or not production occurs, it is improper to allocate these costs to production and defer a current cost of doing business.

Answer (D) is correct. *(CPA, adapted)*
REQUIRED: The rationale for the variable costing method.
DISCUSSION: Fixed costs are a basic expense of doing business. They are incurred to continue operating the business regardless of production levels. Accordingly, they are not controllable in the short run and should not be deferred.
Answer (A) is incorrect. Period costs are controllable at higher levels of management in the long run. Answer (B) is incorrect. Period costs are usually material. Answer (C) is incorrect. Although the allocation of period costs may be arbitrary, the more basic rationale behind variable costing is the lack of controllability in the short run.

6.1.5. Using the variable costing method, which of the following costs are assigned to inventory?

	Variable Selling and Administrative Costs	Variable Factory Overhead Costs
A.	Yes	Yes
B.	Yes	No
C.	No	No
D.	No	Yes

Answer (D) is correct. *(CPA, adapted)*

REQUIRED: The costs assigned to inventory.

DISCUSSION: Under variable costing, only variable manufacturing costs (not variable selling, general, and administrative costs) are assigned to inventory. Variable factory overhead is a variable manufacturing cost. Thus, it is assigned to inventory.

Answer (A) is incorrect. Variable selling and administrative costs are not assigned to inventory. Answer (B) is incorrect. Variable factory overhead costs are assigned to inventory, and variable selling and administrative costs are not. Answer (C) is incorrect. Only variable factory overhead costs are assigned to inventory.

6.1.6. The costing method that is properly classified for both external and internal reporting purposes is

		External Reporting	Internal Reporting
A.	Activity-based costing	No	Yes
B.	Job costing	No	Yes
C.	Variable costing	No	Yes
D.	Process costing	No	No

Answer (C) is correct. *(CMA, adapted)*

REQUIRED: The costing method that is properly classified for both internal and external reporting purposes.

DISCUSSION: Activity-based costing, job costing, process costing, and standard costing all can be used for both internal and external purposes. Variable costing is not acceptable under GAAP for external reporting purposes because it treats fixed manufacturing costs as period costs.

Answer (A) is incorrect. Activity-based costing, job costing, process costing, and standard costing can be used for internal and external purposes. Variable costing is not acceptable under GAAP for external reporting purposes because it treats fixed manufacturing costs as period costs. Answer (B) is incorrect. Job costing is acceptable for external reporting purposes. Answer (D) is incorrect. Process costing is acceptable for external reporting purposes.

6.1.7. Cay Co.'s fixed manufacturing overhead costs for the month just ended totaled $100,000, and variable selling costs totaled $80,000. Under variable costing, how should these costs be classified?

	Period Costs	Product Costs
A.	$0	$180,000
B.	$80,000	$100,000
C.	$100,000	$80,000
D.	$180,000	$0

Answer (D) is correct. *(CPA, adapted)*

REQUIRED: The classification of fixed manufacturing overhead and variable selling costs.

DISCUSSION: Product costs are incurred to produce units of output, and they are expensed when the product is sold. Such costs include direct materials, direct labor, and factory (not general and administrative) overhead. Period costs are charged to expense as incurred because they are not identifiable with a product. Variable (also called direct) costing considers only variable manufacturing costs to be product costs. Fixed manufacturing costs and fixed and variable selling costs are considered period costs and are expensed as incurred. Thus, the entire $180,000 ($100,000 + $80,000) is classified as period costs.

Answer (A) is incorrect. The fixed overhead and selling costs are not identifiable with a product. Answer (B) is incorrect. The fixed overhead is not identifiable with a product. Answer (C) is incorrect. The selling costs are not identifiable with a product.

6.1.8. Which of the following must be known about a production process to institute a variable costing system?

A. The variable and fixed components of all costs related to production.

B. The controllable and noncontrollable components of all costs related to production.

C. Standard production rates and times for all elements of production.

D. Contribution margin and breakeven point for all goods in production.

Answer (A) is correct. *(CPA, adapted)*

REQUIRED: The elements needed to institute a variable costing system.

DISCUSSION: Variable costing considers only variable manufacturing costs to be product costs, i.e., inventoriable. Fixed manufacturing costs are treated as period costs. Thus, one need only be able to determine the variable and fixed manufacturing costs to institute a variable costing system.

Answer (B) is incorrect. Even fixed costs are controllable in the long run. Answer (C) is incorrect. Standard costing is not necessary to institute variable costing. Actual costs may be used. Answer (D) is incorrect. Selling prices as well as variable and fixed costs must be known to calculate the contribution margin and breakeven point.

6.1.9. What costs are treated as product costs under variable costing?

A. Only direct costs.

B. Only variable production costs.

C. All variable costs.

D. All variable and fixed manufacturing costs.

Answer (B) is correct. *(CPA, adapted)*

REQUIRED: The costs allocated to product under variable costing.

DISCUSSION: Product costs under variable costing include direct materials, direct labor, and variable factory overhead. Each is a variable production cost.

Answer (A) is incorrect. Variable factory overhead must also be included. Answer (C) is incorrect. Only variable production costs, not variable selling and administrative costs, are product costs in variable costing. Answer (D) is incorrect. Absorption costing, not variable costing, includes all variable and fixed production costs.

6.1.10. Under the variable-costing concept, unit product cost would most likely be increased by

A. A decrease in the remaining useful life of factory machinery depreciated on the units-of-production method.

B. A decrease in the number of units produced.

C. An increase in the remaining useful life of factory machinery depreciated on the sum-of-the-years'-digits method.

D. An increase in the commission paid to salesmen for each unit sold.

Answer (A) is correct. *(CPA, adapted)*

REQUIRED: The change most likely to increase unit product cost under variable costing.

DISCUSSION: Variable costing considers only variable manufacturing costs to be product costs. Fixed manufacturing costs are period costs. Units-of-production depreciation is included in variable manufacturing overhead. Thus, a decrease in the remaining useful life of machinery increases unit product cost.

Answer (B) is incorrect. Variable costs per unit remain constant. Answer (C) is incorrect. SYD depreciation affects fixed, not variable, manufacturing overhead. Answer (D) is incorrect. Commissions are a selling expense. It is a period cost, not a product cost.

6.1.11. In an income statement prepared as an internal report using the variable costing method, which of the following terms should appear?

	Gross Profit (Margin)	Operating Income
A.	Yes	Yes
B.	Yes	No
C.	No	No
D.	No	Yes

Answer (D) is correct. *(CPA, adapted)*

REQUIRED: The income classification for a variable-costing income statement.

DISCUSSION: Gross profit (margin) is selling price minus COGS. The computation of COGS takes into account fixed manufacturing overhead in inventory. Absorption costing calculates gross profit. Variable costing treats fixed manufacturing overhead as an expense in the period of incurrence. In variable costing, the contribution margin (sales – variable costs) is calculated, not a gross profit (margin). Both methods, however, compute operating income on their income statements.

Answer (A) is incorrect. The variable-costing income statement does not report gross profit. Answer (B) is incorrect. The variable-costing income statement does not report gross profit, but it does include operating income. Answer (C) is incorrect. The variable-costing income statement does include operating income.

6.1.12. In an income statement prepared as an internal report using the variable costing method, variable selling and administrative expenses are

A. Not used.

B. Treated the same as fixed selling and administrative expenses.

C. Used in the computation of operating income but not in the computation of the contribution margin.

D. Used in the computation of the contribution margin.

Answer (D) is correct. *(CPA, adapted)*

REQUIRED: The treatment of variable selling and administrative expenses in an income statement based on variable costing.

DISCUSSION: In a variable costing income statement, the contribution margin equals sales minus all variable costs, which include the variable selling and administrative expenses as well as variable manufacturing costs (direct materials, direct labor, and variable factory overhead). Operating income equals the contribution margin minus all fixed costs.

Answer (A) is incorrect. Variable selling and administrative expenses are included in the determination of the contribution margin. Answer (B) is incorrect. Fixed selling and administrative expenses are subtracted from the contribution margin to arrive at operation income. Answer (C) is incorrect. Variable selling and administrative expenses are used in the computation of the contribution margin.

6.1.13. In an income statement prepared using the variable-costing method, fixed factory overhead would

A. Not be used.

B. Be used in the computation of operating income but not in the computation of the contribution margin.

C. Be used in the computation of the contribution margin.

D. Be treated the same as variable factory overhead.

Answer (B) is correct. *(CPA, adapted)*

REQUIRED: The treatment of fixed factory overhead in an income statement based on variable costing.

DISCUSSION: Under the variable-costing method, the contribution margin equals sales minus variable expenses. Fixed selling and administrative costs and fixed factory overhead are deducted from the contribution margin to arrive at operating income. Thus, fixed costs are included only in the computation of operating income.

Answer (A) is incorrect. Fixed factory overhead is deducted from the contribution margin to determine operating income. Answer (C) is incorrect. Only variable expenses are used in the computation of the contribution margin. Answer (D) is incorrect. Variable factory overhead is included in the computation of contribution margin and fixed factory overhead is not.

6.1.14. When using a variable costing system, the contribution margin (CM) discloses the excess of

A. Revenues over fixed costs.

B. Projected revenues over the breakeven point.

C. Revenues over variable costs.

D. Variable costs over fixed costs.

Answer (C) is correct. *(CPA, adapted)*

REQUIRED: The definition of contribution margin (CM) in a variable costing system.

DISCUSSION: Contribution margin is the difference between revenues and variable costs. No distinction is made between variable product costs and variable selling costs; both are deducted from revenue to arrive at CM.

Answer (A) is incorrect. CM is the excess of total revenue over total variable costs, not over fixed costs. Answer (B) is incorrect. Projected revenues over the breakeven point is the projected net income. Answer (D) is incorrect. CM is the excess of total revenue over total variable costs, not variable costs over fixed costs.

6.1.15. Which of the following statements is true for a firm that uses variable costing?

A. The cost of a unit of product changes because of changes in number of units manufactured.

B. Profits fluctuate with sales.

C. An idle facility variation is calculated.

D. Product costs include variable administrative costs.

Answer (B) is correct. *(CMA, adapted)*

REQUIRED: The true statement about variable costing.

DISCUSSION: In a variable costing system, only the variable costs are recorded as product costs. All fixed costs are expensed in the period incurred. Because changes in the relationship between production levels and sales levels do not cause changes in the amount of fixed manufacturing cost expensed, profits more directly follow the trends in sales.

Answer (A) is incorrect. Changing unit costs based on different levels of production is a characteristic of absorption costing systems. Answer (C) is incorrect. An idle facility variation is calculated in absorption costing. Answer (D) is incorrect. Neither variable nor absorption costing includes administrative costs in inventory.

6.2 Absorption vs. Variable Costing

6.2.1. In a company, products pass through some or all of the production departments during manufacturing, depending upon the product being manufactured. Direct material and direct labor costs are traced directly to the products as they flow through each production department. Manufacturing overhead is assigned in each department using separate departmental manufacturing overhead rates. The inventory costing method that the manufacturing company is using in this situation is

A. Absorption costing.

B. Activity-based costing.

C. Backflush costing.

D. Variable costing.

Answer (A) is correct. *(CIA, adapted)*

REQUIRED: The appropriate inventory costing method.

DISCUSSION: Absorption costing inventories all direct manufacturing costs and both variable and fixed manufacturing overhead (indirect) costs.

Answer (B) is incorrect. Activity-based costing develops cost pools for activities and allocates those costs to cost objects based on the drivers of the activities. Answer (C) is incorrect. A backflush costing system applies costs based on output. Answer (D) is incorrect. Variable costing excludes fixed manufacturing overhead costs from inventoriable costs and treats them as period costs.

6.2.2. Absorption costing and variable costing are two different methods of assigning costs to units produced. Of the four cost items listed below, identify the one that is not correctly accounted for as a product cost.

	Part of Product Cost under	
	Absorption Cost	Variable Cost
A. Manufacturing supplies	Yes	Yes
B. Insurance on factory	Yes	No
C. Direct labor costs	Yes	Yes
D. Packaging and shipping costs	Yes	Yes

Answer (D) is correct. *(CMA, adapted)*

REQUIRED: The cost not correctly accounted for.

DISCUSSION: Under absorption costing, all manufacturing costs, both fixed and variable, are treated as product costs. Under variable costing, only variable costs of manufacturing are inventoried as product costs. Fixed manufacturing costs are expensed as period costs. Packaging and shipping costs are not product costs under either method because they are incurred after the goods have been manufactured. Instead, they are included in selling and administrative expenses for the period.

Answer (A) is incorrect. Manufacturing supplies are variable costs inventoried under both methods. Answer (B) is incorrect. Factory insurance is a fixed manufacturing cost inventoried under absorption costing but written off as a period cost under variable costing. Answer (C) is incorrect. Direct labor cost is a product cost under both methods.

6.2.3. Dowell Co. manufactures a wooden item. Which of the following is included with the inventoriable cost under absorption costing and excluded from the inventoriable cost under variable costing?

A. Cost of electricity used to operate production machinery.

B. Straight-line depreciation on factory equipment.

C. Cost of scrap pieces of lumber.

D. Wages of assembly-line personnel.

Answer (B) is correct. *(CPA, adapted)*

REQUIRED: The cost inventoried under absorption costing but not variable costing.

DISCUSSION: Under variable costing, all direct labor, direct materials, and variable overhead costs are handled in precisely the same manner as in absorption costing. Only fixed factory overhead costs are treated differently. Absorption costing treats fixed factory overhead as a product cost. Variable costing treats variable factory overhead as a product cost but fixed factory overhead as an expense of the accounting period (as are fixed and variable selling, general, and administrative expenses). Straight-line depreciation on factory equipment is an item of fixed factory overhead because it will not vary with output within the relevant range. Accordingly, it will be inventoried under absorption costing and expensed under variable costing.

Answer (A) is incorrect. The cost of electricity used to operate production machinery is a variable factory overhead cost and is therefore treated similarly under absorption and variable costing. Answer (C) is incorrect. Scrap is a direct material, so its accounting treatment is not dependent on whether absorption or variable costing is used. Answer (D) is incorrect. The two methods account for direct labor cost in the same way.

6.2.4. A company manufactures a single product for its customers by contracting in advance of production. Thus, the company produces only units that will be sold by the end of each period. For the last period, the following data were available:

Sales	$40,000
Direct materials	9,050
Direct labor	6,050
Rent (9/10 factory, 1/10 office)	3,000
Depreciation on factory equipment	2,000
Supervision (2/3 factory, 1/3 office)	1,500
Salespeople's salaries	1,300
Insurance (2/3 factory, 1/3 office)	1,200
Office supplies	750
Advertising	700
Depreciation on office equipment	500
Interest on loan	300

The gross margin percentage (rounded) was

A. 41%

B. 44%

C. 46%

D. 51%

Answer (C) is correct. *(CIA, adapted)*

REQUIRED: The gross margin percentage given sales and cost data.

DISCUSSION: The gross margin percentage equals gross profit (sales – COGS) divided by sales. Sales are given as $40,000, and expenses included in cost of goods sold are listed below:

Sales		$40,000
Cost of goods sold:		
Direct materials	$9,050	
Direct labor	6,050	
Rent ($3,000 × 9/10)	2,700	
Depreciation	2,000	
Supervision ($1,500 × 2/3)	1,000	
Insurance ($1,200 × 2/3)	800	(21,600)
Gross margin		$18,400

The gross margin percentage is 46% ($18,400 ÷ $40,000). Office expenses are usually general and administrative expenses, which are period rather than product costs.

Answer (A) is incorrect. The gross margin percentage of 41 results from including sales salaries and advertising expenses in the calculation. Answer (B) is incorrect. The gross margin percentage of 44 results from including 100% of the rent and supervision expenses. Answer (D) is incorrect. The gross margin percentage of 51 results from omitting depreciation on manufacturing equipment from the calculation.

6.2.5. Lynn Manufacturing Co. prepares income statements using both standard absorption and standard variable costing methods. For the month just ended, unit standard costs were unchanged from the previous month. In the month just ended, the only beginning and ending inventories were finished goods of 5,000 units. How would Lynn's ratios using absorption costing compare with those using variable costing?

	Current Ratio	Return on Equity
A.	Same	Same
B.	Same	Smaller
C.	Greater	Same
D.	Greater	Smaller

Answer (D) is correct. *(CPA, adapted)*

REQUIRED: The effect on the current ratio and the return on shareholders' equity of using absorption costing rather than variable costing.

DISCUSSION: Absorption costing includes fixed factory overhead in finished goods inventory. Variable costing does not. Thus, the current ratio is higher under absorption costing. The current ratio equals current assets (including inventory) divided by current liabilities. When production equals sales and costs do not change, the two methods result in the same net income. Because inventory (and therefore retained earnings) is greater under absorption costing, return on equity is smaller than under variable costing.

Answer (A) is incorrect. The current ratio is higher and return on equity is lower. Answer (B) is incorrect. The current ratio is higher. Answer (C) is incorrect. The return on equity is lower.

6.2.6. Using absorption costing, fixed manufacturing overhead costs are best described as

A. Direct period costs.

B. Indirect period costs.

C. Direct product costs.

D. Indirect product costs.

Answer (D) is correct. *(CIA, adapted)*

REQUIRED: The manufacturing overhead costs under absorption costing.

DISCUSSION: Using absorption costing, fixed manufacturing overhead is included in inventoriable (product) costs. Fixed manufacturing overhead costs are indirect costs because they cannot be directly traced to specific units produced.

Answer (A) is incorrect. Fixed manufacturing overhead costs are neither direct nor period costs. Answer (B) is incorrect. Fixed manufacturing overhead costs are not period costs. Answer (C) is incorrect. Fixed manufacturing overhead costs are not direct costs.

6.2.7. The Blue Company has failed to reach its planned activity level during its first 2 years of operation. The following table shows the relationship among units produced, sales, and normal activity for these years and the projected relationship for Year 3. All prices and costs have remained the same for the last 2 years and are expected to do so in Year 3. Income has been positive in both Year 1 and Year 2.

	Units Produced	Sales	Planned Activity
Year 1	90,000	90,000	100,000
Year 2	95,000	95,000	100,000
Year 3	90,000	90,000	100,000

Because Blue Company uses an absorption costing system, gross margin for Year 3 should be

A. Greater than Year 1.

B. Greater than Year 2.

C. Equal to Year 1.

D. Equal to Year 2.

Answer (C) is correct. *(CIA, adapted)*

REQUIRED: The true interperiod gross margin relationship.

DISCUSSION: Gross margin equals sales minus COGS (BI + COGM – EI). An absorption costing system applies fixed as well as variable manufacturing overhead to products. Because Blue's production has always been less than planned activity, fixed manufacturing overhead was underapplied each year. Thus, Blue must have debited underapplied fixed manufacturing overhead (an unfavorable production volume variance) each year to COGS, WIP, and FG. Because production always equaled sales, however, no inventories existed at any year end, and each annual underapplication should have been debited entirely to COGS. Consequently, the gross margins for Years 1 and 3 must be the same because the gross revenue and COGS were identical for the two periods.

Answer (A) is incorrect. The gross margins for Years 1 and 3 are equal. Answer (B) is incorrect. The greater sales volume in Year 2 should have produced a greater gross margin than in Year 1 or 3. Answer (D) is incorrect. The greater sales volume in Year 2 should have produced a greater gross margin than in Year 1 or 3.

6.2.8. A manufacturing company prepares income statements using both absorption and variable costing methods. At the end of a period, actual sales revenues, total gross profit, and total contribution margin approximated budgeted figures, whereas net income was substantially greater than the budgeted amount. There were no beginning or ending inventories. The most likely explanation of the net income increase is that, compared to budget, actual

A. Manufacturing fixed costs had increased.

B. Selling and administrative fixed expenses had decreased.

C. Sales prices and variable costs had increased proportionately.

D. Sales prices had declined proportionately less than variable costs.

Answer (B) is correct. *(CPA, adapted)*

REQUIRED: The most likely reason that net income exceeded budgeted net income.

DISCUSSION: Gross margin equals sales minus cost of goods sold. The cost of goods sold equals the cost of goods manufactured (direct materials, direct labor, and variable and fixed manufacturing overhead) adjusted for the change in inventory. Given that sales and gross margin approximated budgeted amounts, the excess of net income must be attributable to a decrease in fixed selling and administrative expenses. The contribution margin (sales – all variable expenses) also approximated budget, so the net income increase could not be the result of a decrease in variable expenses. Consequently, a decrease in fixed selling and administrative expenses must be the cause of the net income decline.

Answer (A) is incorrect. An increase in actual manufacturing fixed costs would have caused a decrease in NI and a decrease in absorption costing gross margin. Answer (C) is incorrect. A proportionate increase in sales prices and variable costs would increase gross margin and gross profit. Answer (D) is incorrect. Less of a decline in sales prices than in variable costs would increase gross margin and gross profit.

6.2.9. In an income statement prepared as an internal report, total fixed costs normally are shown separately under

	Absorption Costing	Variable Costing
A.	No	No
B.	No	Yes
C.	Yes	Yes
D.	Yes	No

Answer (B) is correct. *(CPA, adapted)*

REQUIRED: The income statement(s) in which total fixed costs are normally shown separately.

DISCUSSION: In a variable-costing income statement, all variable costs are deducted from sales revenue to arrive at the contribution margin. Total fixed costs are then deducted from the contribution margin to determine operating income. In an absorption-costing income statement, fixed factory overhead included in the cost of goods sold is deducted from sales revenue in the calculation of the gross margin. Other fixed costs are among the amounts subtracted from the gross margin to determine operating income.

Answer (A) is incorrect. Total fixed costs are shown separately under variable costing. Answer (C) is incorrect. Total fixed costs are not shown separately under absorption costing. Answer (D) is incorrect. Total fixed costs are normally shown separately under variable costing but not under absorption costing.

6.2.10. A company pays bonuses to its managers based on operating income. The company uses absorption costing, and overhead is applied on the basis of direct labor hours. To increase bonuses, the managers may do all of the following except

A. Produce those products requiring the most direct labor.

B. Defer expenses such as maintenance to a future period.

C. Increase production schedules independent of customer demands.

D. Decrease production of those items requiring the most direct labor.

Answer (D) is correct. *(CMA, adapted)*

REQUIRED: The action that will not increase bonuses based on operating income.

DISCUSSION: Under an absorption costing system, income can be manipulated by producing more products than are sold because more fixed manufacturing overhead will be allocated to the ending inventory. When inventory increases, some fixed costs are capitalized rather than expensed. Decreasing production, however, will result in lower income because more of the fixed manufacturing overhead will be expensed in the current period.

Answer (A) is incorrect. Producing more of the products requiring the most direct labor will permit more fixed overhead to be capitalized in the inventory account. Answer (B) is incorrect. Deferring expenses such as maintenance will increase income in the current period (but may result in long-range losses caused by excessive downtime). Answer (C) is incorrect. Increasing production without a concurrent increase in demand applies more fixed costs to inventory.

6.2.11. The management of a company computes net income using both absorption and variable costing. This year, the net income under the variable-costing approach was greater than the net income under the absorption-costing approach. This difference is most likely the result of

A. A decrease in the variable marketing expenses.

B. An increase in the finished goods inventory.

C. Sales volume exceeding production volume.

D. Inflationary effects on overhead costs.

Answer (C) is correct. *(CIA, adapted)*

REQUIRED: The reason net income is greater under variable costing than absorption costing.

DISCUSSION: Absorption costing (full costing) is the accounting method that considers all manufacturing costs as product costs. These costs include variable and fixed manufacturing costs, whether direct or indirect. However, variable costing treats fixed manufacturing overhead as a period cost instead of charging it to the product (inventory). Thus, when sales exceed production, the absorption costing method recognizes fixed manufacturing overhead inventoried in a prior period. Variable costing does not. Accordingly, net income under variable costing is greater than net income under absorption costing.

Answer (A) is incorrect. A change in a variable period cost will affect absorption and variable costing in the same way. Answer (B) is incorrect. If the beginning inventory is less than the ending finished goods inventory, absorption costing assigns more fixed overhead costs to the balance sheet and less to the cost of goods sold on the income statement than does variable costing. Answer (D) is incorrect. Inflationary effects usually affect both absorption and variable costing in the same way.

6.2.12. Net profit under absorption costing may differ from net profit determined under variable costing. This difference equals the change in the quantity of all units

A. In inventory times the relevant fixed costs per unit.

B. Produced times the relevant fixed costs per unit.

C. In inventory times the relevant variable cost per unit.

D. Produced times the relevant variable cost per unit.

Answer (A) is correct. *(CPA, adapted)*

REQUIRED: The calculation of the difference in net profit between absorption costing and variable costing.

DISCUSSION: Variable costing treats all fixed costs as period costs. Absorption costing treats fixed costs as product costs. The difference in net profit equals the fixed manufacturing cost per unit times the change in the number of units in inventory (assuming a constant per-unit fixed manufacturing cost).

Answer (B) is incorrect. The effect of units sold must be considered. Answer (C) is incorrect. The effects of units sold and the assigned fixed costs must be considered. Answer (D) is incorrect. The effects of units sold and the assigned fixed costs must be considered.

6.2.13. A company's net income recently increased by 30% while its inventory increased to equal a full year's sales requirements. Which of the following accounting methods would be most likely to produce the favorable income results?

A. Absorption costing.

B. Direct costing.

C. Variable costing.

D. Standard direct costing.

Answer (A) is correct. *(CIA, adapted)*

REQUIRED: The method likely to produce favorable income when inventory increases.

DISCUSSION: Inventory increases when production exceeds sales. In absorption costing, fixed costs that are expensed under variable costing are deferred to future periods. If an entity has very high fixed costs and a relatively low contribution margin, income may be increased by producing in excess of sales.

Answer (B) is incorrect. Direct costing is a synonym for variable costing. Answer (C) is incorrect. Variable costing does not record fixed costs in inventory. Thus, it does not have the same effects on income as absorption costing. Answer (D) is incorrect. Use of standard costs does not change the income effects of direct (variable) costing.

6.2.14. When comparing absorption costing with variable costing, which of the following statements is not true?

A. Absorption costing enables managers to increase operating profits in the short run by increasing inventories.

B. When sales volume is more than production volume, variable costing will result in higher operating profit.

C. A manager who is evaluated based on variable costing operating profit would be tempted to increase production at the end of a period in order to get a more favorable review.

D. Under absorption costing, operating profit is a function of both sales volume and production volume.

Answer (C) is correct. *(CIA, adapted)*

REQUIRED: The false statement comparing absorption costing and variable costing.

DISCUSSION: Absorption (full) costing is the accounting method that considers all manufacturing costs as product costs. These costs include variable and fixed manufacturing costs whether direct or indirect. Variable (direct) costing considers only variable manufacturing costs to be product costs, i.e., inventoriable. Fixed manufacturing costs are considered period costs and are expensed as incurred. If production is increased without increasing sales, inventories will rise. However, all fixed costs associated with production will be an expense of the period under variable costing. Thus, this action will not artificially increase profits and improve the manager's review.

Answer (A) is incorrect. Increasing inventories increases absorption costing profit as a result of capitalizing fixed factory overhead. Answer (B) is incorrect. When sales volume exceeds production, inventories decline. Thus, fixed factory overhead expensed will be greater under absorption costing. Answer (D) is incorrect. Under variable costing, operating profit is a function of sales. Under absorption costing, it is a function of sales and production.

6.2.15. Fleet, Inc., manufactured 700 units of Product A, a new product, during the year. Product A's variable and fixed manufacturing costs per unit were $6.00 and $2.00, respectively. The inventory of Product A on December 31 consisted of 100 units. There was no inventory of Product A on January 1. What would be the change in the dollar amount of inventory on December 31 if variable costing were used instead of absorption costing?

A. $800 decrease.

B. $200 decrease.

C. $0

D. $200 increase.

Answer (B) is correct. *(CPA, adapted)*

REQUIRED: The difference in inventory using variable rather than absorption costing.

DISCUSSION: Given an inventory increase of 100 units during the year and the fixed manufacturing cost per unit of $2.00, $200 (100 units × $2.00) of overhead would be deferred using absorption costing but expensed immediately using variable costing. Thus, variable-costing inventory would be $200 less than absorption costing.

Answer (A) is incorrect. The total increase in inventories for the year is $800. Answer (C) is incorrect. The cost per unit will differ. Fixed manufacturing costs are a product cost under absorption costing and a period cost under variable costing. Answer (D) is incorrect. Inventory will decrease.

6.2.16. Given the following information, the total contribution margin is

Sales revenue	$5,000
Variable cost of goods sold	2,700
Full cost of goods sold	2,900
Fixed selling and admin. expenses	1,100
Variable selling and admin. expenses	800

A. $1,500

B. $2,100

C. $3,900

D. $4,200

Answer (A) is correct. *(CIA, adapted)*

REQUIRED: The total contribution margin.

DISCUSSION: Contribution margin equals sales revenue minus all variable costs. Thus, the total contribution margin is calculated as follows:

Sales	$5,000
Variable cost of goods sold	(2,700)
Variable selling and admin. exps.	(800)
Contribution margin	$1,500

Answer (B) is incorrect. The gross margin is $2,100. Answer (C) is incorrect. The amount of $3,900 equals revenue minus fixed selling and administrative expenses. Answer (D) is incorrect. The amount of $4,200 equals revenue minus variable selling and administrative expenses.

6.3 Calculations

Questions 6.3.1 and 6.3.2 are based on the following information. Noth, Inc., manufactures and sells a single product. Planned and actual production in the current year, its first year of operation, was 100,000 units. Planned and actual costs in the current year were as follows:

	Manufacturing	Nonmanufacturing
Variable	$600,000	$500,000
Fixed	400,000	300,000

Noth sold 85,000 units of product in the current year at a selling price of $30 per unit.

6.3.1. Using absorption costing, Noth's operating income in the current year would be

A. $750,000

B. $900,000

C. $975,000

D. $1,020,000

Answer (B) is correct. *(CIA, adapted)*

REQUIRED: The absorption-costing operating income.

DISCUSSION: Under absorption costing, the product cost includes cell production costs, whether variable or fixed. Unit product cost under absorption costing is $10 ($1,000,000 ÷ 100,000 units produced). Operating income is calculated as follows:

Revenue (85,000 units × $30)		$2,550,000
Cost of goods sold (85,000 units × $10)		(850,000)
Gross margin		$1,700,000
Nonmanufacturing costs:		
Variable	$500,000	
Fixed	300,000	(800,000)
Absorption-basis operating income		$ 900,000

Answer (A) is incorrect. The amount of $750,000 equals absorption-costing net income minus ending inventory (15,000 units × $10). Answer (C) is incorrect. The amount of $975,000 treats the variable nonmanufacturing costs as manufacturing costs. Answer (D) is incorrect. The amount of $1,020,000 assumes that all costs are manufacturing costs.

6.3.2. Using variable costing, Noth's operating income in the current year would be

A. $750,000

B. $840,000

C. $915,000

D. $975,000

Answer (B) is correct. *(CIA, adapted)*

REQUIRED: The variable-costing operating income.

DISCUSSION: Under variable costing, the product cost includes only variable manufacturing costs. All fixed costs are expensed in the period incurred. Unit product cost under variable costing is $6 ($600,000 ÷ 100,000 units produced).

Revenue (85,000 units × $30)	$2,550,000
Variable cost of goods sold (85,000 units × $6)	(510,000)
Variable nonmanufacturing costs	(500,000)
Contribution margin	$1,540,000
Fixed costs	(700,000)
Variable-basis operating income	$ 840,000

Answer (A) is incorrect. The amount of $750,000 equals variable costing net income minus ending inventory (15,000 units × $6). Answer (C) is incorrect. The amount of $915,000 treats all variable costs as manufacturing costs. Answer (D) is incorrect. The amount of $975,000 treats all variable costs and fixed manufacturing costs as product costs.

Questions 6.3.3 through 6.3.6 are based on the following information. Peterson Company's records for the year ended December 31 show that no finished goods inventory existed at January 1 and no work was in process at the beginning or end of the year.

Net sales		$1,400,000
Manufacturing costs:	Variable	630,000
	Fixed	315,000
Operating expenses:	Variable	98,000
	Fixed	140,000
Units manufactured		70,000
Units sold		60,000

6.3.3. What is Peterson's finished goods inventory cost at December 31 under the variable costing method?

A. $90,000

B. $104,000

C. $105,000

D. $135,000

Answer (A) is correct. *(CPA, adapted)*

REQUIRED: The finished goods inventory cost.

DISCUSSION: Variable costing considers only variable manufacturing costs as product costs. Fixed manufacturing costs are considered period costs. The total variable manufacturing cost is given as $630,000. For the 70,000 units produced, unit cost was $9.00 ($630,000 ÷ 70,000 units). If EI is 10,000 units (70,000 produced – 60,000 sold), total cost of FG inventory is $90,000 (10,000 units × $9).

Answer (B) is incorrect. Variable operating expenses should not be included in COGM. Answer (C) is incorrect. This figure equals 10,000 units times $630,000 divided by 60,000 units. Answer (D) is incorrect. The inventory balance under absorption costing is $135,000.

6.3.4. What would be Peterson's finished goods inventory cost at December 31 under the absorption costing method?

A. $90,000

B. $104,000

C. $105,000

D. $135,000

Answer (D) is correct. *(Publisher, adapted)*

REQUIRED: The finished goods inventory cost under absorption costing.

DISCUSSION: Absorption costing treats variable and fixed manufacturing costs as product costs. Unit cost of goods manufactured equals the sum of the variable ($630,000) and fixed ($315,000) costs, divided by the number of units manufactured (70,000), or $13.50 per unit. Given that 10,000 units remain in inventory (70,000 produced – 60,000 sold), EI is $135,000.

Answer (A) is incorrect. The finished goods inventory cost under variable costing is $90,000. Answer (B) is incorrect. Variable operating expenses should not be included in COGM. Furthermore, fixed costs of manufacturing need to be included in the calculation of EI. Answer (C) is incorrect. The amount of $105,000 equals 10,000 units times $630,000 divided by 60,000 units.

6.3.5. Under the absorption costing method, Peterson's operating income for the year is

A. $217,000

B. $307,000

C. $352,000

D. $374,500

Answer (C) is correct. *(CPA, adapted)*

REQUIRED: The operating income.

DISCUSSION: In absorption costing, the unit costs include both fixed and variable manufacturing costs. Fixed manufacturing costs are given as $315,000. For the 70,000 units produced, unit cost was $13.50 [($630,000 + $315,000) ÷ 70,000].

Sales	$1,400,000
COGS (60,000 × $13.50)	(810,000)
Gross margin	$ 590,000
Operating expenses:	
Variable	(98,000)
Fixed	(140,000)
Operating income	$ 352,000

Answer (A) is incorrect. If all units manufactured are sold, the operating income is $217,000. Answer (B) is incorrect. The operating income under variable costing is $307,000. Answer (D) is incorrect. Units manufactured, not units sold, should be the denominator in determining the unit cost of inventory.

6.3.6. Under the variable costing method, Peterson's operating income for the year is

A. $217,000

B. $307,000

C. $352,000

D. $762,000

Answer (B) is correct. *(Publisher, adapted)*

REQUIRED: The operating income.

DISCUSSION: In variable costing, the unit COGS includes only the variable manufacturing costs, which were $9.00 per unit ($630,000 ÷ 70,000 units). The income statement follows:

Sales	$1,400,000
COGS (60,000 × $9)	(540,000)
Variable operating expenses	(98,000)
Contribution margin	$ 762,000
Fixed costs:	
Manufacturing	(315,000)
Operating	(140,000)
Variable-costing operating income	$ 307,000

Answer (A) is incorrect. The amount of $217,000 is the operating income if all units manufactured were sold. Answer (C) is incorrect. The operating income under absorption costing is $352,000. Answer (D) is incorrect. The contribution margin is $762,000.

Questions 6.3.7 and 6.3.8 are based on the following information. Kirklin Co., a manufacturer operating at 95% of capacity, has been offered a new order at $7.25 per unit requiring 15% of capacity. No other use of the 5% current idle capacity can be found. However, if the order were accepted, the subcontracting for the required 10% additional capacity would cost $7.50 per unit.

The variable cost of production for Kirklin on a per-unit basis follows:

Materials	$3.50
Labor	1.50
Variable overhead	1.50
	$6.50

6.3.7. In applying the contribution margin approach to evaluating whether to accept the new order, assuming subcontracting, what is Kirklin's average variable cost per unit?

A. $6.83

B. $7.17

C. $7.25

D. $7.50

Answer (B) is correct. *(CIA, adapted)*

REQUIRED: The average variable unit cost of the order.

DISCUSSION: Variable cost is equal to the direct costs associated with a product, an order, or other decision. In this case, one-third of the order has a variable cost of $6.50, and two-thirds of the order has a variable cost of $7.50. Thus, the average variable cost is $7.17 [($6.50 × 1/3) + ($7.50 × 2/3)].

Answer (A) is incorrect. The amount of $6.83 assumes two-thirds of the order is produced at $6.50 per unit and one-third at $7.50 per unit. Answer (C) is incorrect. The sales price per unit of the new order is $7.25. Answer (D) is incorrect. The unit cost above 100% capacity is $7.50.

6.3.8. Assuming the average variable cost per unit of the new order is $7.17, Kirklin's expected contribution margin per unit of the new order is

A. $.08

B. $.25

C. $.33

D. $.42

Answer (A) is correct. *(CIA, adapted)*

REQUIRED: The unit contribution margin of the new order.

DISCUSSION: The unit contribution margin of the new order is the selling price of $7.25 minus the average variable cost. The average variable cost is $7.17. Accordingly, the unit contribution margin on the order is $.08.

Answer (B) is incorrect. A $.25 contribution margin assumes a cost per unit of $7.00. Answer (C) is incorrect. The contribution margin is determined by subtracting the average variable cost ($7.17) from the unit sales price ($7.25). Answer (D) is incorrect. The contribution margin is determined by subtracting the average variable cost ($7.17) from the unit sales price ($7.25).

6.3.9. During May, Roy Co. produced 10,000 units of Product X. Costs incurred by Roy during May:

Direct materials	$10,000
Direct labor	20,000
Variable manufacturing overhead	5,000
Variable selling and general expenses	3,000
Fixed manufacturing overhead	9,000
Fixed selling and general expenses	4,000
Total	$51,000

Under absorption costing, Product X's unit cost was

A. $5.10

B. $4.40

C. $3.80

D. $3.50

Answer (B) is correct. *(CPA, adapted)*

REQUIRED: The product's unit cost under absorption costing.

DISCUSSION: The absorption-basis per-unit cost of Product X can be calculated as follows:

Direct materials	$10,000
Direct labor	20,000
Variable overhead	5,000
Fixed overhead	9,000
Total manufacturing costs	$44,000
Units produced	÷ 10,000
Cost per unit	$ 4.40

Answer (A) is incorrect. Unit cost under absorption costing does not include variable or fixed selling and general expenses. Answer (C) is incorrect. The amount of $3.80 includes variable selling and general expenses but not fixed manufacturing overhead. Answer (D) is incorrect. The unit cost under variable costing is $3.50.

Questions 6.3.10 and 6.3.11 are based on the following information. Presented are Valenz Company's records for the current fiscal year ended November 30:

Direct materials used	$300,000
Direct labor	100,000
Variable manufacturing overhead	50,000
Fixed manufacturing overhead	80,000
Selling and admin. costs -- variable	40,000
Selling and admin. costs -- fixed	20,000

6.3.10. If Valenz Company uses variable costing, the inventoriable costs for the fiscal year are

A. $400,000

B. $450,000

C. $490,000

D. $530,000

Answer (B) is correct. *(CMA, adapted)*

REQUIRED: The inventoriable costs using the variable costing.

DISCUSSION: Under variable costing, the only costs that are capitalized are the variable costs of manufacturing. These include

Direct materials used	$300,000
Direct labor	100,000
Variable overhead	50,000
Total inventoriable costs	$450,000

Answer (A) is incorrect. The amount of $400,000 does not include $50,000 of variable overhead. Answer (C) is incorrect. The $40,000 of variable selling and administrative costs should not be included in the inventoriable costs. Answer (D) is incorrect. The inventoriable cost under absorption (full) costing is $530,000.

6.3.11. Using absorption (full) costing, inventoriable costs for Valenz are

A. $400,000

B. $450,000

C. $530,000

D. $590,000

Answer (C) is correct. *(CMA, adapted)*

REQUIRED: The inventoriable costs using the absorption costing.

DISCUSSION: The absorption method is required for financial statements prepared according to GAAP. It charges all costs of production to inventories. The variable cost of materials ($300,000), direct labor ($100,000), variable overhead ($50,000), and fixed overhead ($80,000) are included. They total $530,000.

Answer (A) is incorrect. Not including $80,000 of fixed overhead and $50,000 of variable overhead results in $400,000. Answer (B) is incorrect. The inventoriable cost under variable costing is $450,000. Answer (D) is incorrect. Selling and administrative costs are not inventoriable using absorption (full) costing.

Questions 6.3.12 and 6.3.13 are based on the following information. Osawa, Inc., planned and actually manufactured 200,000 units of its single product during its first year of operations. Variable manufacturing costs were $30 per unit of product. Planned and actual fixed manufacturing costs were $600,000, and selling and administrative costs totaled $400,000. Osawa sold 120,000 units of product at a selling price of $40 per unit.

6.3.12. Osawa's operating income using absorption (full) costing is

A. $200,000

B. $440,000

C. $600,000

D. $840,000

Answer (B) is correct. *(CMA, adapted)*

REQUIRED: The operating income under absorption costing.

DISCUSSION: Because production equaled planned output, and fixed costs equaled the budgeted amount, fixed overhead was not over- or under-applied. Also, planned fixed overhead equaled the actual amount. Thus, no fixed overhead variances had to be accounted for. Osawa applied $600,000 of fixed overhead, or $3 per unit ($600,000 ÷ 200,000 units), to its output. The unit cost of the 80,000 (200,000 – 120,000 sold) units in ending inventory is therefore $33 ($30 VC + $3 FC). Absorption costing net income is computed as follows:

Sales (120,000 units × $40)		$4,800,000
Variable production costs (200,000 units × $30)	$6,000,000	
Fixed production costs	600,000	
Total production costs	$6,600,000	
Ending inventory (80,000 units × $33)	(2,640,000)	
Cost of goods sold		(3,960,000)
Gross profit		$ 840,000
Selling and administrative expenses		(400,000)
Operating income		$ 440,000

Answer (A) is incorrect. The amount of $200,000 is the operating income under variable costing. Answer (C) is incorrect. The amount of $600,000 is the operating income that results from capitalizing $240,000 fixed manufacturing costs and $160,000 of selling and administrative costs (the $160,000 is incorrect because all selling and administrative costs should be expensed). Answer (D) is incorrect. The amount of $840,000 is the gross profit under absorption costing, i.e., before selling and administrative expenses.

6.3.13. Osawa's operating income for the year using variable costing is

A. $200,000

B. $440,000

C. $800,000

D. $600,000

Answer (A) is correct. *(CMA, adapted)*

REQUIRED: The operating income under variable costing.

DISCUSSION: The contribution margin from manufacturing (sales – variable costs) is $10 ($40 – $30) per unit sold, or $1,200,000 (120,000 units × $10). The fixed costs of manufacturing ($600,000) and selling and administrative costs ($400,000) are deducted from the contribution margin to arrive at an operating income of $200,000. The difference between the absorption income of $440,000 and the $200,000 of variable costing income is attributable to capitalization of the fixed manufacturing costs under the absorption method. Because 40% of the goods produced are still in inventory (80,000 ÷ 200,000), 40% of the $600,000 in fixed costs, or $240,000, was capitalized under the absorption method. That amount was expensed under the variable costing method.

Answer (B) is incorrect. The amount of $440,000 is the operating income under absorption costing. Answer (C) is incorrect. The amount of $800,000 is the operating income if fixed costs of manufacturing are not deducted. Answer (D) is incorrect. The amount of $600,000 is the operating income that results from capitalizing 40% of both fixed manufacturing costs and selling and administrative costs.

Questions 6.3.14 through 6.3.17 are based on the following information.

The annual flexible budget below was prepared for use in making decisions relating to Crump Company's Product X:

	100,000 Units	150,000 Units	200,000 Units
Sales volume	$800,000	$1,200,000	$1,600,000
Manufacturing costs:			
Variable	$300,000	$ 450,000	$ 600,000
Fixed	200,000	200,000	200,000
Total mfg.	$500,000	$ 650,000	$ 800,000
Selling and other expenses:			
Variable	$200,000	$ 300,000	$ 400,000
Fixed	160,000	160,000	160,000
Total S&A	$360,000	$ 460,000	$ 560,000
Income (or loss)	$ (60,000)	$ 90,000	$ 240,000

The 200,000-unit budget has been adopted and will be used for allocating fixed manufacturing costs to units of Product X. At the end of the first 6 months, the following information is available:

	Units
Production completed	120,000
Sales	60,000

All fixed costs are budgeted and incurred uniformly throughout the year, and all costs incurred coincide with the budget. Over- and underapplied fixed manufacturing costs are deferred until year end. Annual sales have the following seasonal pattern:

	Portion of Annual Sales
First quarter	10%
Second quarter	20%
Third quarter	30%
Fourth quarter	40%

6.3.14. The amount of fixed manufacturing costs applied to Product X during the first 6 months under absorption costing is

A. Overapplied by $20,000.

B. Equal to the fixed costs incurred.

C. Underapplied by $40,000.

D. Underapplied by $80,000.

Answer (A) is correct. *(CPA, adapted)*

REQUIRED: The true statement about the amount of applied manufacturing overhead.

DISCUSSION: Under absorption costing, fixed manufacturing overhead is applied based on the number of units produced. Fixed manufacturing overhead equals $200,000. Given that production is budgeted at 200,000 units, the fixed manufacturing overhead rate is $1 per unit. Production completed in the first 6 months equals 120,000 units, so $120,000 of overhead was applied. Because all costs incurred coincide with the budget, only $100,000 [$200,000 × (6/12)] of the budgeted fixed manufacturing overhead was incurred. Consequently, manufacturing overhead is overapplied by $20,000 ($120,000 – $100,000).

Answer (B) is incorrect. An amount of $100,000 was incurred and $120,000 was applied. Answer (C) is incorrect. Fixed manufacturing overhead is applied based on units produced, not units sold. Answer (D) is incorrect. The amount of $80,000 equals annual fixed manufacturing overhead minus the amount applied to 120,000 units.

6.3.15. Crump's reported operating income (or loss) for the first 6 months under absorption costing is

A. $160,000

B. $0

C. $40,000

D. $(40,000)

Answer (C) is correct. *(CPA, adapted)*

REQUIRED: The operating income (loss) under the absorption costing method.

DISCUSSION: Variable manufacturing cost is $3 per unit, and fixed manufacturing cost is $1 per unit. Selling price is $8 per unit ($1,600,000 ÷ 200,000 units). The variable selling expenses are $2 per unit ($400,000 ÷ 200,000 units). The fixed selling expenses equal $80,000 for the 6-month period (50% of the $160,000 annual selling expense).

Revenue (60,000 units × $8)	$480,000
Cost of goods sold	(240,000)
Gross margin	$240,000
Variable selling expenses	(120,000)
Fixed selling expenses	(80,000)
Absorption-basis operating income	$ 40,000

Answer (A) is incorrect. The variable selling expense ($120,000) was not subtracted. Answer (B) is incorrect. Zero is the variable costing operating income. Answer (D) is incorrect. An operating income of $40,000, not a loss, should be reported.

6.3.16. Crump's reported operating income (or loss) for the first 6 months under variable costing is

A. $180,000

B. $40,000

C. $0

D. $(180,000)

Answer (C) is correct. *(CPA, adapted)*

REQUIRED: The operating income (loss) under the variable costing method.

DISCUSSION: Sales are 60,000 units at $8, variable manufacturing cost is $3 per unit, variable selling cost is $2 per unit, and fixed costs are 50% of the annual amounts.

Revenue (60,000 units × $8)	$480,000
Cost of goods sold	(180,000)
Variable selling expenses	(120,000)
Fixed manufacturing expenses	(100,000)
Fixed selling expenses	(80,000)
Variable-basis operating income	$ 0

Answer (A) is incorrect. The contribution margin is $180,000. Answer (B) is incorrect. The absorption-costing operating income is $40,000. Answer (D) is incorrect. The amount of $(180,000) results from subtracting the annual fixed costs.

6.3.17. Assuming that 90,000 units of Product X were sold during the first 6 months and that this is to be used as a basis, Crump's revised budget estimate for the total number of units to be sold during this year is

A. 360,000

B. 240,000

C. 200,000

D. 300,000

Answer (D) is correct. *(CPA, adapted)*

REQUIRED: The annual sales budget based on the first 6 months of the year.

DISCUSSION: To calculate the revised annual sales budget based on the first 6 months of the year, the number of units sold during the first 6 months (90,000) and their proportion of the annual sales must be considered. The 90,000 units of Product X sold during the first 6 months represent 30% of annual sales (10% first quarter + 20% second quarter), so annual sales are 300,000 units (90,000 ÷ .30).

Answer (A) is incorrect. The revised estimate of sales for the year is 300,000 units. Answer (B) is incorrect. The revised estimate of sales for the year is 300,000 units. Answer (C) is incorrect. The original annual sales budget is 200,000 units. The sales estimate needs to be revised using the actual sales information for the first 6 months of the year.

6.3.18. During the month just ended, Vane Co. produced and sold 10,000 units of a product. Manufacturing and selling costs incurred were as follows:

Direct materials and direct labor	$400,000
Variable manufacturing overhead	90,000
Fixed manufacturing overhead	20,000
Variable selling costs	10,000

The product's unit cost under variable (direct) costing was

A. $49

B. $50

C. $51

D. $52

Answer (A) is correct. *(CPA, adapted)*

REQUIRED: The product's unit cost under direct (variable) costing.

DISCUSSION: Variable (direct) costing includes variable manufacturing costs only: direct materials, direct labor, and variable manufacturing overhead. Fixed manufacturing overhead and selling expenses are treated as period costs. Hence, the unit cost is $49 [($400,000 + $90,000) ÷ 10,000 units].

Answer (B) is incorrect. Variable selling costs ($1 per unit) of $50 should not be included. Answer (C) is incorrect. Unit cost under absorption costing is $51. Answer (D) is incorrect. Unit cost under variable (direct) costing does not include fixed manufacturing overhead or variable selling costs.

Questions 6.3.19 through 6.3.25 are based on the following information.

Valyn Corporation employs an absorption costing system for internal reporting purposes; however, the company is considering using variable costing. Data regarding Valyn's planned and actual operations for the calendar year are presented below.

	Planned Activity	Actual Activity
Beginning finished goods inventory in units	35,000	35,000
Sales in units	140,000	125,000
Production in units	140,000	130,000

The planned per-unit cost figures shown in the schedule were based on the estimated production and sale of 140,000 units for the year. Valyn uses a predetermined manufacturing overhead rate for applying manufacturing overhead to its product; thus, a combined manufacturing overhead rate of $9.00 per unit was employed for absorption costing purposes. Any over- or underapplied manufacturing overhead is closed to the cost of goods sold account at the end of the reporting year.

	Planned Costs Per Unit	Planned Costs Total	Incurred Costs
Direct materials	$12.00	$1,680,000	$1,560,000
Direct labor	9.00	1,260,000	1,170,000
Variable manufacturing overhead	4.00	560,000	520,000
Fixed manufacturing overhead	5.00	700,000	715,000
Variable selling expenses	8.00	1,120,000	1,000,000
Fixed selling expenses	7.00	980,000	980,000
Variable administrative expenses	2.00	280,000	250,000
Fixed administrative expenses	3.00	420,000	425,000
Total	$50.00	$7,000,000	$6,620,000

The beginning finished goods inventory for absorption costing purposes was valued at the previous year's planned unit manufacturing cost, which was the same as the current year's planned unit manufacturing cost. There are no work-in-process inventories at either the beginning or the end of the year. The planned and actual unit selling price for the current year was $70.00 per unit.

6.3.19. Valyn Corporation's total fixed costs expensed this year on the absorption costing basis were

A. $2,095,000

B. $2,000,000

C. $2,055,000

D. $2,030,000

Answer (A) is correct. *(CMA, adapted)*

REQUIRED: The total fixed costs under the absorption costing basis.

DISCUSSION: Under the absorption method, all selling and administrative fixed costs are charged to the current period. Accordingly, $980,000 of selling expenses and $425,000 of actual fixed administrative expenses were expensed during the year. The fixed manufacturing costs must be calculated after giving consideration to the increase in inventory during the period (some fixed costs were capitalized) and to the underapplied overhead. The beginning finished goods inventory included 35,000 units, each of which had absorbed $5 of fixed manufacturing overhead. Each unit produced during the year also absorbed $5 of fixed manufacturing overhead. Given that 125,000 of those units were sold, cost of goods sold was debited for $625,000 of fixed overhead (125,000 units × $5). At year end, the underapplied overhead was also added to cost of goods sold. Because production was expected to be 140,000 units, the overhead application rate for the $700,000 of planned fixed manufacturing overhead was $5 per unit. Only 130,000 units were manufactured. Thus, $650,000 (130,000 units × $5) of overhead was applied to units in process. Because inventory increased from 35,000 to 40,000 units (35,000 BI + 130,000 produced – 125,000 sold), $25,000 (5,000-unit increase × $5) of the applied fixed manufacturing overhead for the period was inventoried, not expensed. Actual overhead was $715,000, so the underapplied overhead was $65,000 ($715,000 – $650,000). This amount was charged to cost of goods sold at year end. The total of the fixed costs expensed was therefore $2,095,000 ($980,000 selling expenses + $425,000 administrative expenses + $625,000 standard manufacturing overhead costs of units sold + $65,000 underapplied overhead).

6.3.20. The value of Valyn Corporation's actual ending finished goods inventory on the absorption costing basis was

A. $900,000

B. $1,200,000

C. $1,220,000

D. $1,350,000

Answer (B) is correct. *(CMA, adapted)*

REQUIRED: The actual finished goods ending inventory using absorption costing.

DISCUSSION: Under the absorption method, unit cost is $30 ($12 direct materials + $9 direct labor + $4 variable overhead + $5 fixed overhead). Given beginning inventory of 35,000 units, the ending inventory equals 40,000 units (35,000 BI + 130,000 produced – 125,000 sold). Thus, ending inventory was $1,200,000 (40,000 units × $30).

6.3.21. The value of Valyn Corporation's actual ending finished goods inventory on the variable costing basis was

A. $1,200,000

B. $1,170,000

C. $1,000,000

D. $715,000

Answer (C) is correct. *(CMA, adapted)*

REQUIRED: The actual finished goods ending inventory.

DISCUSSION: Using variable costing, the unit cost of ending inventory is $25 ($12 direct materials + $9 direct labor + $4 variable overhead). Given beginning inventory of 35,000 units, the ending inventory equals 40,000 units (35,000 BI + 130,000 produced – 125,000 sold). Thus, ending inventory was $1,000,000 (40,000 units × $25).

Answer (A) is incorrect. The amount of $1,200,000 is the actual ending finished goods inventory on the absorption costing basis. Answer (B) is incorrect. The amount of $1,170,000 is the incurred cost of direct labor. Answer (D) is incorrect. The amount of $715,000 is the incurred cost of fixed manufacturing overhead.

6.3.22. Valyn Corporation's actual manufacturing contribution margin calculated on the variable costing basis was

A. $4,375,000

B. $5,250,000

C. $5,500,000

D. $5,625,000

Answer (D) is correct. *(CMA, adapted)*

REQUIRED: The actual contribution margin on the variable costing basis.

DISCUSSION: At $70 per unit, actual sales revenue was $8,750,000 for 125,000 units. Actual variable costs of manufacturing were $25 per unit ($12 + $9 + $4). The unit costs incurred for the actual production level of 130,000 units were the same as the unit costs for a planned production level of 140,000 units. These unit costs were the same for units manufactured in both the current and previous year. For example, total planned direct materials cost for 140,000 units was $1,680,000, or $12 per unit. The incurred unit cost was also $12 ($1,560,000 ÷ 130,000 units). Thus, total variable manufacturing cost was $3,125,000 (125,000 units × $25). Consequently, manufacturing contribution margin was $5,625,000 ($8,750,000 – $3,125,000).

Answer (A) is incorrect. The amount of $4,375,000 is the sum of variable selling and administrative manufacturing costs planned for actual activity. Answer (B) is incorrect. The amount of $5,250,000 is the contribution margin for sales of 140,000 units. Answer (C) is incorrect. The amount of $5,500,000 is the contribution margin for sales of 130,000 units.

6.3.23. Valyn Corporation's absorption costing operating income was

A. Higher than variable costing operating income because actual production exceeded actual sales.

B. Lower than variable costing operating income because actual production exceeded actual sales.

C. Lower than variable costing operating income because actual production was less than planned production.

D. Lower than variable costing operating income because actual sales were less than planned sales.

Answer (A) is correct. *(CMA, adapted)*

REQUIRED: The true statement comparing absorption costing and variable costing income.

DISCUSSION: Absorption costing results in a higher income figure than variable costing whenever production exceeds sales because absorption costing capitalizes some fixed factory overhead as part of inventory. These costs are expensed during the period incurred under variable costing. Consequently, variable costing recognizes greater expenses and lower income when production exceeds sales. The reverse is true when sales exceed production. In that case, the absorption method results in a lower income because some fixed costs of previous periods absorbed by the beginning inventory are expensed in the current period as cost of goods sold. Variable costing income is never burdened with fixed costs of previous periods.

Answer (B) is incorrect. An increase in inventory results in a higher income under absorption costing. Answer (C) is incorrect. The important relationship is between actual production and actual sales, not between actual and planned production. Answer (D) is incorrect. Planned sales do not determine actual income.

6.3.24. The total variable cost currently expensed by Valyn Corporation on the variable costing basis was

A. $4,375,000

B. $4,900,000

C. $4,290,000

D. $4,550,000

Answer (A) is correct. *(CMA, adapted)*

REQUIRED: The total variable cost expensed under the variable costing method.

DISCUSSION: The unit variable manufacturing cost was $25 ($12 direct materials + $9 direct labor + $4 variable overhead). Other variable costs included selling expenses ($8 per unit) and administrative expenses ($2 per unit). The unit selling and administrative costs actually incurred for sales of 125,000 units were the same as the planned unit costs. For example, actual unit variable selling expense was $8 ($1,000,000 ÷ 125,000 units sold), which equaled the planned unit cost. Thus, total unit variable cost was $35 ($25 + $8 + $2). The total expensed was $4,375,000 (125,000 units sold × $35).

6.3.25. Refer to the information on the preceding page(s). The difference between Valyn Corporation's operating income calculated on the absorption costing basis and calculated on the variable costing basis was

A. $65,000

B. $25,000

C. $40,000

D. $75,000

Answer (B) is correct. *(CMA, adapted)*

REQUIRED: The difference between absorption costing and variable costing income.

DISCUSSION: The difference is caused by the capitalization of some of the fixed manufacturing overhead. When inventories increase during the period, the absorption method capitalizes that overhead and transfers it to future periods. The variable costing method expenses it in the current period. Inventories increased by 5,000 units during the period, and each of those units would have included $5 of fixed manufacturing overhead under absorption costing. Accordingly, $25,000 of fixed manufacturing overhead would have been capitalized. Recognizing $25,000 of fixed costs in the balance sheet instead of the income statement results in a $25,000 difference in income between the two costing methods.

Answer (A) is incorrect. The amount of $65,000 assumes unit fixed overhead of $13 ($5 fixed overhead + $8 variable selling expense). Answer (C) is incorrect. The amount of $40,000 assumes unit fixed overhead of $8. Answer (D) is incorrect. The amount of $75,000 assumes unit fixed overhead of $15.

6.3.26. A manufacturing company employs variable costing for internal reporting and analysis purposes. However, it converts its records to absorption costing for external reporting. The Accounting Department always reconciles the two operating income figures to assure that no errors have occurred in the conversion. The fixed manufacturing overhead cost per unit was based on the planned level of production of 480,000 units. Financial data for the year are presented below:

	Budget	Actual
Sales (in units)	495,000	510,000
Production (in units)	480,000	500,000

	Variable Costing	Absorption Costing
Variable costs	$10.00	$10.00
Fixed manufacturing overhead	0.00	6.00
Total unit manufacturing costs	$10.00	$16.00

The difference between the operating income calculated under the variable costing method and the operating income calculated under the absorption costing method would be

A. $57,600

B. $60,000

C. $90,000

D. $120,000

Answer (B) is correct. *(CIA, adapted)*

REQUIRED: The difference between variable costing and absorption costing operating income.

DISCUSSION: The difference between variable costing and absorption costing is that the former treats fixed manufacturing overhead as a period cost. The latter method treats it as a product cost. Given that sales exceeded production, both methods expense all fixed manufacturing overhead incurred during the year. However, 10,000 units (510,000 sales – 500,000 production) manufactured in a prior period were also sold. These units presumably were recorded at $10 under variable costing and $16 under absorption costing. Consequently, absorption costing operating income is $60,000 (10,000 units × $6) less than that under variable costing.

Answer (A) is incorrect. The amount of $57,600 equals 10,000 units times $5.76 per unit (total budgeted fixed manufacturing overhead ÷ 500,000 units). Answer (C) is incorrect. The amount of $90,000 is the difference between planned sales (495,000 units) and actual sales (510,000 units), times the fixed manufacturing overhead per unit ($6). Answer (D) is incorrect. The amount of $120,000 is the volume variance under absorption costing.

6.3.27. Keller Company, a manufacturer of rivets, uses absorption costing. Keller's manufacturing costs were as follows:

Direct materials and direct labor	$800,000
Depreciation of machines	100,000
Rent for factory building	60,000
Electricity to run machines	35,000

How much of these costs should be inventoried?

A. $800,000

B. $835,000

C. $935,000

D. $995,000

Answer (D) is correct. *(CPA, adapted)*

REQUIRED: The amount of costs inventoried.

DISCUSSION: Under absorption costing, the inventoried costs consist of all direct materials, direct labor, and manufacturing overhead. Manufacturing overhead includes depreciation, factory rent, and power for the machines. Thus, the total cost to be inventoried is $995,000 ($800,000 + $100,000 + $60,000 + $35,000).

Answer (A) is incorrect. Inventoriable costs also include all manufacturing overhead. Answer (B) is incorrect. Inventoriable costs under absorption costing include the depreciation of machines ($100,000) and the factory rent ($60,000). Answer (C) is incorrect. Rent for the factory building ($60,000) is inventoriable.

Questions 6.3.28 and 6.3.29 are based on the following information. A and B are autonomous divisions of a corporation. They have no beginning or ending inventories, and the number of units produced is equal to the number of units sold. The following is financial information relating to the two divisions:

	A	B
Sales	$150,000	$400,000
Other revenue	10,000	15,000
Direct materials	30,000	65,000
Direct labor	20,000	40,000
Variable manufacturing overhead	5,000	15,000
Fixed manufacturing overhead	25,000	55,000
Variable S&A expense	15,000	30,000
Fixed S&A expense	35,000	60,000
Central corporate expenses (allocated)	12,000	20,000

6.3.28. What is the total contribution to corporate profits generated by Segment A before allocation of central corporate expenses?

A. $18,000

B. $20,000

C. $30,000

D. $90,000

Answer (C) is correct. *(CIA, adapted)*

REQUIRED: The total contribution to profits by A.

DISCUSSION: Segment A's total contribution to corporate profits includes everything except the central corporate expense allocation. Thus, the total contribution is $30,000 ($150,000 sales + $10,000 other revenue – $30,000 direct materials – $20,000 direct labor – $5,000 variable overhead – $25,000 fixed overhead – $15,000 variable S&A expense – $35,000 fixed S&A expense).

Answer (A) is incorrect. The amount of $18,000 is the result of subtracting the central corporate expenses. Answer (B) is incorrect. The amount of $20,000 is the result of excluding other revenue. Answer (D) is incorrect. The amount of $90,000 is the result of not subtracting the fixed costs.

6.3.29. What is the contribution margin of Segment B?

A. $150,000

B. $205,000

C. $235,000

D. $265,000

Answer (D) is correct. *(CIA, adapted)*

REQUIRED: The contribution margin of B.

DISCUSSION: The contribution margin equals revenue minus variable costs. Thus, Segment B's contribution margin is $265,000 ($400,000 sales + $15,000 other revenue – $65,000 direct materials – $40,000 direct labor – $15,000 variable overhead – $30,000 variable S&A expense).

Answer (A) is incorrect. The amount of $150,000 is the result of subtracting fixed costs. Answer (B) is incorrect. The amount of $205,000 is the result of subtracting fixed S&A costs. Answer (C) is incorrect. The amount of $235,000 is the result of subtracting fixed S&A costs but not variable S&A costs.

STUDY UNIT SEVEN
STANDARD COSTS AND VARIANCES

Standard costs are budgeted unit costs. Establishing standards is necessary to know when actual costs differ significantly from target or standard costs. Because of the effects of fixed costs, standard costing is most effective in a flexible budgeting system. When actual costs and standard costs differ, a favorable (unfavorable) **variance** results when actual costs are lower (higher) than standard costs. Variance analysis is the basis of a performance evaluation based on a budget. A favorable variance increases income and an unfavorable variance decreases income. **Static budget variances** are the differences between the static budget and the actual results for the period. **Flexible budget variances** are the differences between actual results and flexible budget amounts based on actual output. **Sales-volume variances** are the differences between flexible budget amounts and static budget amounts.

The total flexible budget variance for **direct materials** consists of (1) a price variance and (2) an efficiency (quantity or usage) variance. The **price variance** formula is AQ × (AP – SP). For better control, the materials price variance should be isolated at the time of purchase. The **efficiency variance** formula is (AQ – SQ) × SP. The total flexible budget variance for **direct labor** also consists of a rate variance and an efficiency (usage) variance. The efficiency variance for direct materials or direct labor can be divided into a mix variance and a yield variance. The **mix variance** equals the actual total quantity of inputs times the difference between (1) the standard price (rate) at the standard mix of inputs and (2) the standard price (rate) at the actual mix of inputs. The formula for the mix variance is ATQ × (SPSM – SPAM). The **yield variance** equals the standard price (rate) at the standard mix times the difference between (1) the actual total quantity of inputs and (2) the standard total quantity of inputs. The formula for the yield variance is (STQ – ATQ) × SPSM.

In a four-way analysis, a manufacturer's **total overhead variance** has two variable and two fixed components.

- The **variable** component consists of (1) a spending variance and (2) an efficiency variance.
- The **fixed** component consists of (1) a spending variance and (2) a production-volume variance.

Variable Overhead Variances

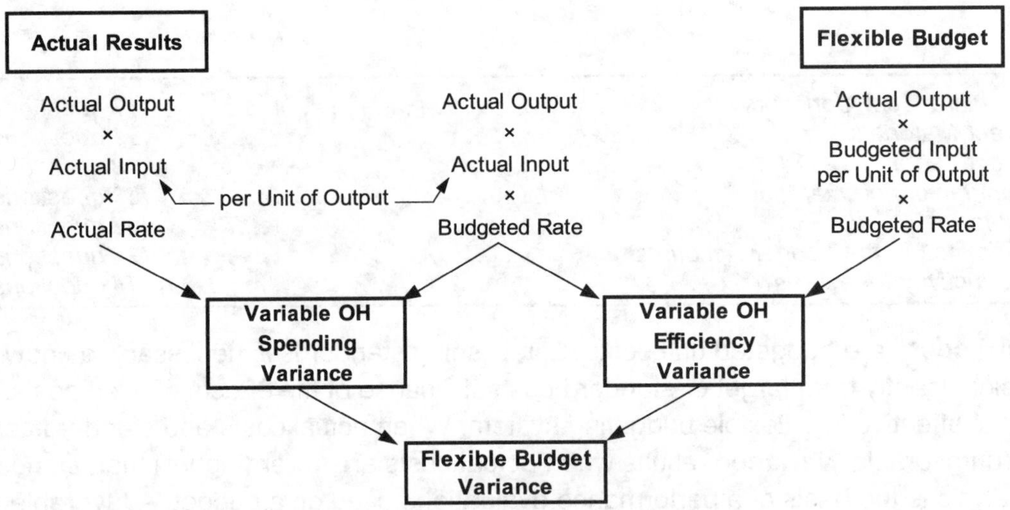

Fixed Overhead Variances

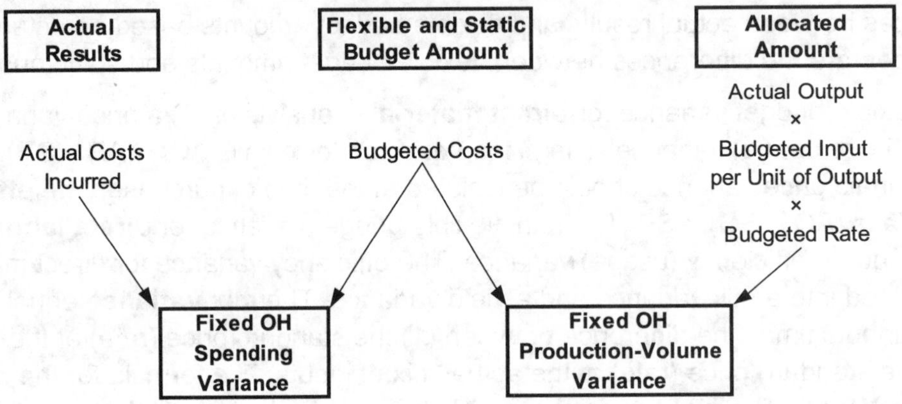

QUESTIONS

7.1 Standard Cost Concepts

7.1.1. A standard-cost system may be used in

A. Job-order costing but not process costing.
B. Either job-order costing or process costing.
C. Process costing but not job-order costing.
D. Neither process costing nor job-order costing.

Answer (B) is correct. *(CPA, adapted)*

REQUIRED: The cost accumulation system(s) that may use standard costing.

DISCUSSION: A standard-cost system assigns standard (predetermined) costs to the product. It then compares expected with actual cost. This comparison allows deviations (i.e., variances) from expected results to be identified and investigated. A standard-cost system can be used in both job-order and process costing systems to isolate variances.

7.1.2. When a manager is concerned with monitoring total cost, total revenue, and net profit conditioned upon the level of productivity, an accountant would normally recommend

	Flexible Budgeting	Standard Costing
A.	Yes	Yes
B.	Yes	No
C.	No	Yes
D.	No	No

Answer (A) is correct. *(CPA, adapted)*

REQUIRED: The technique(s) for monitoring cost, revenue, and profit given different levels of activity.

DISCUSSION: A flexible budget is a set of static budgets prepared in anticipation of varying levels of activity. It permits evaluation of actual results when actual and expected production differ. Setting cost standards facilitates preparation of a flexible budget. For example, a standard unit variable cost is useful in determining the total variable cost for a given output.

7.1.3. A difference between standard costs used for cost control and the budgeted costs of the same manufacturing effort can exist because

A. Standard costs represent what costs should be, whereas budgeted costs are expected actual costs.

B. Budgeted costs are historical costs, whereas standard costs are based on engineering studies.

C. Budgeted costs include some slack, whereas standard costs do not.

D. Standard costs include some slack, whereas budgeted costs do not.

Answer (A) is correct. *(CMA, adapted)*

REQUIRED: The difference between standard costs and budgeted costs.

DISCUSSION: In the long run, these costs should be the same. In the short run, however, they may differ because standard costs represent what costs should be, whereas budgeted costs are expected actual costs. Budgeted costs may vary widely from standard costs in certain months, but, for an annual budget period, the amounts should be similar.

Answer (B) is incorrect. Standard costs are not necessarily determined by engineering studies. Answer (C) is incorrect. Standard costs are usually based on currently attainable standards applicable when a process is under control. They are set without regard to variances or slack. Answer (D) is incorrect. Budgeted costs include expected deviations from the standards.

7.1.4. When standard costs are used in a process costing system, how, if at all, are equivalent units of production (EUP) involved or used in the cost report at standard?

A. Equivalent units are not used.

B. Equivalent units are computed using a special approach.

C. The actual equivalent units are multiplied by the standard cost per unit.

D. The standard equivalent units are multiplied by the actual cost per unit.

Answer (C) is correct. *(CPA, adapted)*

REQUIRED: The way equivalent units are used in a standard cost report.

DISCUSSION: A process costing system accounts for continuous production of homogeneous goods. EUP are calculated to determine how many complete units could have been produced, given no BWIP and no EWIP. For example, if 100 units in EWIP are 40% complete, the same amount of work could have produced 40 complete units. To determine the cost of the units produced, these EUP are multiplied by the standard cost per unit.

Answer (A) is incorrect. Equivalent units are used to calculate costs. Answer (B) is incorrect. Equivalent units are calculated in the regular manner. Answer (D) is incorrect. Standard EUP is a nonsense term.

7.1.5. The sales volume variance equals

A. A static budget amount minus a flexible budget amount.

B. Actual operating income minus flexible budget operating income.

C. Budgeted unit price minus actual unit price, times the actual units produced.

D. Budgeted unit price times the difference between actual inputs and expected inputs for the actual output level achieved.

Answer (A) is correct. *(Publisher, adapted)*

REQUIRED: The definition of the sales volume variance.

DISCUSSION: The sales volume variance assumes that, if unit prices and costs and total fixed costs are constant, the only variable is the sales activity level. Thus, the difference between a given static budget amount and the corresponding flexible budget amount is the sales volume variance.

Answer (B) is incorrect. Flexible budget operating income minus actual operating income is the flexible budget variance (flexible budget amount for the actual activity – actual result) for operating income. Answer (C) is incorrect. Budgeted unit price minus actual unit price, times the actual units produced, is the price or rate variance. Answer (D) is incorrect. Budgeted unit price times the difference between actual inputs and expected inputs for the actual activity level achieved is a quantity or efficiency variance.

7.1.6. The difference between the actual costs incurred and the costs that should have been incurred given the actual output achieved is the

A. Production volume variance.

B. Flexible budget variance.

C. Sales volume variance.

D. Standard cost variance.

Answer (B) is correct. *(CMA, adapted)*

REQUIRED: The term for the difference between the actual amounts and the flexible budget amounts.

DISCUSSION: A flexible budget is a series of several budgets prepared for many levels of activity. A flexible budget allows adjustment of the budget to the actual level before comparing the budgeted and actual results. The difference between the flexible budget and actual amounts is the flexible budget variance.

Answer (A) is incorrect. The production volume variance equals under- or overapplied fixed manufacturing overhead. Answer (C) is incorrect. The sales volume variance is the difference between the flexible budget amount and the static budget amount. Answer (D) is incorrect. A standard cost variance is not necessarily based on a flexible budget.

7.1.7. Companies in what type of industry may use a standard cost system for cost control?

	Mass Production Industry	Service Industry
A.	Yes	Yes
B.	Yes	No
C.	No	No
D.	No	Yes

Answer (A) is correct. *(CPA, adapted)*

REQUIRED: The types of industry that may use a standard cost system.

DISCUSSION: A standard cost system assigns a predetermined unit amount to output. It is applicable to both job-order and process costing systems and to service as well as mass production industries. For example, a standard labor cost may be developed for the labor involved in a service activity.

7.1.8. The flexible budget variance in operating income is

A. Actual operating income minus flexible budget operating income.

B. Budgeted unit price times the difference between actual inputs and budgeted inputs for the actual activity level achieved.

C. A flexible budget amount minus a static budget amount.

D. Actual unit price minus budgeted unit price, times the actual units produced.

Answer (A) is correct. *(Publisher, adapted)*

REQUIRED: The definition of the flexible budget variance in operating income.

DISCUSSION: The flexible budget variance in operating income is the difference in operating income between actual results and the flexible budget. The flexible budget is based on standard costs and the actual activity level. Deviations from that budget should be explained by changes in any of the items in the flexible budget except the activity level, for example, revenues, variable costs, contribution margin, and fixed costs.

Answer (B) is incorrect. Budgeted unit price times the difference between actual inputs and budgeted inputs for the actual activity level achieved is an efficiency variance. Answer (C) is incorrect. A flexible budget amount minus a static budget amount is a volume variance. Answer (D) is incorrect. Actual unit price minus budgeted unit price, times the actual units produced, is a price variance.

7.1.9. In analyzing company operations, the controller of the corporation found a $250,000 favorable flexible-budget revenue variance. The variance was calculated by comparing the actual results with the flexible budget. This variance can be wholly explained by

A. The total flexible budget variance.

B. The total sales volume variance.

C. The total static budget variance.

D. Changes in unit selling prices.

Answer (D) is correct. *(CMA, adapted)*

REQUIRED: The cause of a favorable flexible-budget revenue variance.

DISCUSSION: Variance analysis can be used to judge the effectiveness of selling departments. If a firm's sales differ from the amount budgeted, the difference may be attributable to either the sales price variance or the sales volume (quantity) variance. Changes in unit selling prices may account for the entire variance if the actual quantity sold is equal to the quantity budgeted. None of the revenue variance is attributed to the sales volume variance because no such variance exists when a flexible budget is used. The flexible budget is based on the level of sales at actual volume.

Answer (A) is incorrect. The total flexible budget variance includes items other than revenue. Answer (B) is incorrect. The sales volume variance represents the change in contribution margin caused by a difference between actual and budgeted units sold. However, given a flexible budget, there is no difference between budgeted and actual units sold. By definition, a flexible budget's volume is identical to actual volume. Answer (C) is incorrect. The total static budget variance includes many items other than revenue.

7.1.10. The best basis upon which cost standards should be set to measure controllable production inefficiencies is

A. Engineering standards based on ideal performance.

B. Normal capacity.

C. Recent average historical performance.

D. Engineering standards based on attainable performance.

Answer (D) is correct. *(CMA, adapted)*

REQUIRED: The best basis upon which cost standards should be set.

DISCUSSION: Standards must be accepted by those who will carry them out if they are to have maximum effectiveness. Subordinates should believe that standards are both fair and achievable. Otherwise, they may tend to sabotage, ignore, or circumvent them.

Answer (A) is incorrect. Employees may not cooperate with standards based on ideal performance. Attainable standards are usually better for motivational purposes. Answer (B) is incorrect. Normal capacity may not suffice to control production inefficiencies. Answer (C) is incorrect. Historical performance may not always be a guide to future performance, and standards should be based on anticipated future conditions.

7.1.11. Which of the following is a purpose of standard costing?

A. Determine breakeven production level.

B. Control costs.

C. Eliminate the need for subjective decisions by management.

D. Allocate cost with more accuracy.

Answer (B) is correct. *(CPA, adapted)*

REQUIRED: The purpose of standard costing.

DISCUSSION: Standard costing isolates the variances between predetermined costs and actual costs. It allows management to measure performance and to correct inefficiencies, thereby helping to control costs.

Answer (A) is incorrect. A standard costing system is not needed to perform breakeven CVP analysis. Answer (C) is incorrect. Standard costs are used by management as an aid in decision making. Answer (D) is incorrect. Standard costing does not allocate costs more accurately, especially when variances exist.

7.1.12. Which one of the following statements about ideal standards is false?

A. Ideal standards are also called theoretical or maximum-efficiency standards.

B. Ideal standards do not make provisions for workers with different degrees of experience and skill levels.

C. Ideal standards make no allowance for waste, spoilage, and machine breakdowns.

D. Ideal standards can be used for cash budgeting or product costing.

Answer (D) is correct. *(CMA, adapted)*

REQUIRED: The false statement about ideal standards.

DISCUSSION: Ideal (perfect, theoretical, or maximum-efficiency) standards are standard costs set for production under optimal conditions. They are based on the work of the most skilled workers with no allowance for waste, spoilage, machine breakdowns, or other downtime. Ideal standards can have positive behavioral implications if workers are motivated to strive for excellence, for example, in a Total Quality Management (TQM) environment. However, they are not in wide use because they can have negative behavioral effects if the standards are impossible to attain. Ideal standards ordinarily are replaced by currently attainable standards for cash budgeting, product costing, and budgeting departmental performance. Otherwise, accurate financial planning is impossible.

Answer (A) is incorrect. Ideal standards are perfection standards. Answer (B) is incorrect. Ideal standards are based solely on the most efficient workers. Answer (C) is incorrect. Ideal standards assume optimal conditions.

7.1.13. Which one of the following statements pertaining to practical standards is false?

A. Practical standards can be used for product costing and cash budgeting.

B. A firm using practical standards has no reason to make any midyear adjustments to the production standards if an old machine is replaced by a newer, faster machine.

C. Under practical standards, exceptions from standards are less likely; consequently, managers will be better able to practice management by exception.

D. Practical standards are more likely to be attained by workers making diligent efforts.

Answer (B) is correct. *(CMA, adapted)*

REQUIRED: The false statement about practical standards.

DISCUSSION: Practical (currently attainable) standards may be defined as the performance that is reasonably expected to be achieved with an allowance for normal spoilage, waste, and downtime. An alternative interpretation is that practical standards represent possible but difficult to attain results. But practical standards need to be adjusted if working conditions change.

Answer (A) is incorrect. Practical standards are more appropriate than ideal standards for purposes of cash budgeting, product costing, and departmental performance budgeting. Under one interpretation of the term, practical standards are the expected results. Answer (C) is incorrect. Practical standards reflect expectations or at least standards that are more likely to be attainable than ideal standards. Consequently, unfavorable variances indicate that operations have not been normally efficient and effective. Answer (D) is incorrect. Practical standards reflect either reasonable expectations or at least possible results attainable with very efficient operations.

7.1.14. Listed below are four names for different kinds of standards associated with a standard cost system. Which one describes the labor costs that should be incurred under efficient operating conditions?

A. Ideal.

B. Basic.

C. Maximum-efficiency.

D. Currently attainable.

Answer (D) is correct. *(CPA, adapted)*

REQUIRED: The type of cost incurred under efficient operations.

DISCUSSION: Currently attainable standards apply to the efficient operation of labor and resources. They are difficult but possible to achieve.

Answer (A) is incorrect. Ideal standards are impossible to achieve. For example, they include no waste. Answer (B) is incorrect. Basic standards is a nonsense concept in this context. Answer (C) is incorrect. Maximum-efficiency (ideal) standards are not readily achievable.

7.1.15. Which of the following factors should not be considered when deciding whether to investigate a variance?

A. Magnitude of the variance.

B. Trend of the variances over time.

C. Likelihood that an investigation will eliminate future occurrences of the variance.

D. Whether the variance is favorable or unfavorable.

Answer (D) is correct. *(CIA, adapted)*

REQUIRED: The factor not relevant in deciding whether to investigate a variance.

DISCUSSION: A variance shows a deviation of actual results from the expected or budgeted results. All significant variances should be investigated, whether favorable or unfavorable.

Answer (A) is incorrect. Only significant variances should be investigated. Also, the benefits of each step in the entire standard-cost process must be cost effective. Benefits should exceed costs. Answer (B) is incorrect. The trend of variances over time should be considered. A negative variance that has been getting progressively smaller may not need investigating, whereas a variance that is increasing should be investigated promptly. Answer (C) is incorrect. The objective of variance investigation is pinpointing responsibility and taking corrective action toward eliminating variances.

7.1.16. Standard costing will produce the same income before extraordinary items as actual costing when standard cost variances are assigned to

A. Work-in-process and finished goods inventories.

B. An income or expense account.

C. Cost of goods sold and inventories.

D. Cost of goods sold.

Answer (C) is correct. *(CPA, adapted)*

REQUIRED: The account(s) to which the standard cost variances should be allocated.

DISCUSSION: Assigning variances to cost of goods sold and inventories (proration) based on production and sales for the period effectively converts standard costing to actual costing. This conversion is necessary for external reporting purposes when the amounts involved are material.

Answer (A) is incorrect. A substantial portion of the variance usually needs to be allocated to COGS. Answer (B) is incorrect. Standard cost variances need to be allocated to cost of goods sold and inventories. Answer (D) is incorrect. The variance also needs to be allocated to the inventory account.

7.1.17. The budget for a given cost during a given period was $80,000. The actual cost for the period was $72,000. Considering these facts, the plant manager has done a better-than-expected job in controlling the cost if

A. The cost is variable and actual production was 90% of budgeted production.

B. The cost is variable and actual production equaled budgeted production.

C. The cost is variable and actual production was 80% of budgeted production.

D. The cost is a discretionary fixed cost and actual production equaled budgeted production.

Answer (B) is correct. *(CPA, adapted)*

REQUIRED: The circumstances in which the plant manager has done a better-than-expected job.

DISCUSSION: When comparing actual job performance with the budget, the deviations must be noted and compared with the appropriate budget that would have been in effect had perfect information been available. In this case, if the cost is variable and actual production matched the budgeted production, $80,000 is the expected actual cost. Given that the actual cost was $72,000, the plant manager has done a good job in controlling the cost.

Answer (A) is incorrect. If the cost is variable and actual production was 90% of budgeted production, the plant manager has merely met the standard ($80,000 × 90% = $72,000). Answer (C) is incorrect. If the cost is variable and actual production was 80% of budgeted production, the plant manager has done a less-than-adequate job in controlling the cost assuming a standard of $64,000 (80% of $80,000). Answer (D) is incorrect. The question does not state whether the discretionary fixed cost was controlled by the plant manager.

7.2 Direct Materials

7.2.1. If a company follows a practice of isolating variances as soon as possible, the appropriate time to isolate and recognize a direct materials price variance is when

A. Materials are issued.

B. Materials are purchased.

C. Materials are used in production.

D. The purchase order originates.

Answer (B) is correct. *(CPA, adapted)*

REQUIRED: The earliest appropriate time to isolate a direct materials price variance.

DISCUSSION: The time of purchase is the most appropriate moment to recognize a price variance. Analysis at that time permits the earliest possible examination of variances.

Answer (A) is incorrect. Time elapses between purchase and issuance of materials. Thus, the earliest time to recognize price variances is upon purchase. Answer (C) is incorrect. A materials price variance can be recognized at purchase. Answer (D) is incorrect. The transaction has not occurred when the purchase order originates.

7.2.2. In a standard cost system, the materials price variance is obtained by multiplying the

A. Actual price by the difference between actual quantity used and standard quantity used.

B. Actual quantity purchased by the difference between standard price and actual price.

C. Standard price by the difference between expected quantity and budgeted quantity.

D. Standard quantity used by the difference between actual price and standard price.

Answer (B) is correct. *(CPA, adapted)*

REQUIRED: The method used to compute the materials price variance.

DISCUSSION: The materials price variance is the portion of the flexible budget variance attributable entirely to a difference in purchased input unit cost. If it is recognized at the time of purchase, it is calculated by multiplying the actual quantity purchased (AQP) by the difference between standard price (SP) and actual price (AP) [AQP × (SP – AP)].

Answer (A) is incorrect. The product of actual price and the difference between actual quantity used and standard quantity used is not a defined variance. Answer (C) is incorrect. The product of standard price and the difference between expected quantity and budgeted quantity is the sales volume variance. Answer (D) is incorrect. The materials price variance is the actual quantity of input purchased times the difference between the standard price of materials and the actual price.

7.2.3. The materials mix variance equals

A. (Inputs allowed – inputs used) × budgeted weighted-average materials unit price for the planned mix.

B. (Budgeted weighted-average labor rate for planned mix – budgeted weighted-average labor rate for actual mix) × inputs used.

C. (Inputs allowed – inputs used) × budgeted weighted-average labor rate for the planned mix.

D. (Budgeted weighted-average materials unit cost for planned mix – budgeted weighted-average materials unit cost for actual mix) × inputs used.

Answer (D) is correct. *(Publisher, adapted)*

REQUIRED: The definition of the materials mix variance.

DISCUSSION: Materials yield and mix variances are the components of the materials efficiency variance. They are useful only if certain classes or types of materials can be substituted for each other. The materials mix variance is calculated to isolate the effects of the change in the mix of materials used. Thus, it equals the materials actually used times the difference between (1) the budgeted weighted-average materials unit cost for the planned mix and (2) the budgeted weighted-average unit cost for the actual mix. Because substitutability of materials may not be possible in every situation, the materials mix variance is suitable for analysis only when the manager has some control over the composition of the mix.

Answer (A) is incorrect. The materials yield variance equals (inputs allowed – inputs used) × budgeted weighted-average materials unit price for the planned mix. Answer (B) is incorrect. The labor mix variance equals (budgeted weighted-average labor rate for planned mix – budgeted weighted-average labor rate for actual mix) × inputs used. Answer (C) is incorrect. The labor yield variance equals (inputs allowed – inputs used) × budgeted weighted-average labor rate for the planned mix.

7.2.4. Under a standard cost system, the materials efficiency variances are the responsibility of

A. Production and industrial engineering.

B. Purchasing and industrial engineering.

C. Purchasing and sales.

D. Sales and industrial engineering.

Answer (A) is correct. *(CMA, adapted)*

REQUIRED: The function(s) responsible for the materials efficiency (quantity) variance.

DISCUSSION: The materials efficiency variance is the difference between actual and standard quantities used in production, times the standard price. An unfavorable materials efficiency variance is usually caused by wastage, shrinkage, or theft. Thus, it may be the responsibility of the production department because excess usage would occur while the materials are in that department. In addition, industrial engineering may play a role because it is responsible for design of the production process.

Answer (B) is incorrect. Purchasing rarely can control the materials efficiency variance. Answer (C) is incorrect. Sales has no effect on the materials efficiency variance. Answer (D) is incorrect. Sales has no effect on the materials efficiency variance.

7.2.5. Price variances and efficiency variances can be key to the performance measurement within a company. In evaluating the performance within a company, a materials efficiency variance can be caused by all of the following except the

A. Performance of the workers using the material.

B. Actions of the purchasing department.

C. Design of the product.

D. Sales volume of the product.

Answer (D) is correct. *(CMA, adapted)*

REQUIRED: The item not a cause of a materials efficiency variance.

DISCUSSION: An unfavorable materials quantity or usage (efficiency) variance can be caused by a number of factors, including waste, shrinkage, theft, poor performance by production workers, nonskilled workers, or the purchase of below-standard-quality materials by the purchasing department. Changes in product design can also affect the quantity of materials used. Sales volume of the product should not be a contributing factor to a materials efficiency variance.

Answer (A) is incorrect. Worker performance is a possible cause of a materials efficiency variance. Answer (B) is incorrect. Purchasing department actions are possible causes of a materials efficiency variance. Answer (C) is incorrect. Product design is a possible cause of a materials efficiency variance.

7.2.6. A favorable materials price variance coupled with an unfavorable materials usage variance most likely results from

A. Machine efficiency problems.

B. Product mix production changes.

C. The purchase and use of higher-than-standard quality materials.

D. The purchase of lower than standard quality materials.

Answer (D) is correct. *(CMA, adapted)*

REQUIRED: The cause of a favorable materials price variance coupled with an unfavorable materials usage variance.

DISCUSSION: A favorable materials price variance is the result of paying less than the standard price for materials. An unfavorable materials usage variance is the result of using an excessive quantity of materials. If a purchasing manager were to buy substandard materials to achieve a favorable price variance, an unfavorable quantity variance could result from using an excessive amount of poor quality materials.

Answer (A) is incorrect. Machine efficiency problems do not explain the price variance. Answer (B) is incorrect. A change in product mix does not explain the price variance. Answer (C) is incorrect. Materials of higher-than-standard quality are more likely to cause an unfavorable price variance and a favorable quantity variance.

7.2.7. The standard direct materials cost to produce a unit of Lem is 4 meters of materials at $2.50 per meter. During May, 4,200 meters of materials costing $10,080 were purchased and used to produce 1,000 units of Lem. What was the materials price variance for May?

A. $400 favorable.

B. $420 favorable.

C. $80 unfavorable.

D. $480 unfavorable.

Answer (B) is correct. *(CPA, adapted)*

REQUIRED: The material price variance.

DISCUSSION: The actual price paid for materials during May ($10,080 actual cost ÷ 4,200 meters used) is $2.40 per meter. The materials price variance equals the actual quantity of materials purchased and used, times the difference between the actual price of materials and the standard price. The materials price variance for the month can be calculated as follows:

Materials price variance	=	AQ × (SP – AP)
	=	4,200 meters × ($2.50 – $2.40)
	=	4,200 meters × .10
	=	$420 favorable

Answer (A) is incorrect. The amount of $400 favorable assumes use of the standard quantity, not the actual quantity purchased. Answer (C) is incorrect. The amount of $80 is the difference between the actual cost of 4,200 meters and the standard cost of 4,000 meters. Answer (D) is incorrect. The amount of $480 unfavorable equals $2.40 actual unit cost times 200 meters (4,200 – 4,000).

7.2.8. Under a standard cost system, the materials price variances are usually the responsibility of the

A. Production manager.

B. Cost accounting manager.

C. Sales manager.

D. Purchasing manager.

Answer (D) is correct. *(CMA, adapted)*

REQUIRED: The individual responsible for the materials price variance.

DISCUSSION: The materials price variance is the difference between the standard price and the actual price paid for materials. This variance is usually the responsibility of the purchasing department. Thus, the purchasing manager has an incentive to obtain the best price possible.

Answer (A) is incorrect. The production manager has no control over the price paid for materials. Answer (B) is incorrect. The cost accounting manager has no control over the price paid for materials. Answer (C) is incorrect. The sales manager has no control over the price paid for materials.

Questions 7.2.9 through 7.2.11 are based on the following information. ChemKing uses a standard costing system in the manufacture of its single product. The 35,000 units of direct materials purchased and used cost $105,000, and two units of direct materials are required to produce one unit of final product. In November, the company produced 12,000 units of product. The flexible budget for materials was $60,000, and the unfavorable static budget variance was $35,000.

7.2.9. ChemKing's standard price for one unit of material is

A. $2.50

B. $3.00

C. $5.00

D. $6.00

Answer (A) is correct. *(CMA, adapted)*

REQUIRED: The standard price for one unit of direct materials.

DISCUSSION: Given that the flexible budget was $60,000, the actual units of output produced was 12,000, and the standard number of inputs per unit of output was 2, the standard unit cost for direct materials must be $2.50 [($60,000 flexible budget ÷ 12,000 units produced) ÷ 2 units of direct materials].

Answer (B) is incorrect. The amount of $3.00 is the actual cost per unit of direct materials. Answer (C) is incorrect. The amount of $5.00 is the total standard cost of direct materials for each unit of finished product. Answer (D) is incorrect. The amount of $6.00 is the actual cost of direct materials per unit of finished product.

7.2.10. ChemKing's direct materials quantity variance was

A. $17,500 unfavorable.

B. $27,500 unfavorable.

C. $33,000 unfavorable.

D. $45,000 unfavorable.

Answer (B) is correct. *(CMA, adapted)*

REQUIRED: The direct materials quantity variance for the month.

DISCUSSION: The materials quantity variance is the portion of the flexible budget variance attributable entirely to a difference in the number of inputs required to generate a unit of output. It can be calculated by multiplying the difference between the standard quantity of inputs for the achieved level of production and quantity actually used, times the standard unit price. The standard quantity is derived by multiplying the actual number of outputs by the standard number of inputs per unit of output (12,000 × 2 = 24,000). Thus, the materials quantity variance is $27,500 U [(24,000 – 35,000) × $2.50]

Answer (A) is incorrect. The amount of $17,500 unfavorable is the materials price variance. Answer (C) is incorrect. The amount of $33,000 unfavorable results from using the actual input unit price of $3.00 rather than the standard price of $2.50. Answer (D) is incorrect. The amount of $45,000 unfavorable is the flexible budget variance.

7.2.11. The number of outputs planned for in ChemKing's static budget was

A. 9,600 units.

B. 11,667 units.

C. 12,000 units.

D. 14,000 units.

Answer (D) is correct. *(CMA, adapted)*

REQUIRED: The units of output in the static budget.

DISCUSSION: The static budget variance ($35,000 unfavorable) is the total variance to be explained. It can be calculated as the difference between the actual results and the static budget. If the actual costs incurred for direct materials were $35,000 worse (i.e., higher) than were planned for in the static budget, the static budget must have been $70,000 ($105,000 – $35,000). The budgeted level of output was therefore 14,000 units ($70,000 ÷ 2 standard units of input per output ÷ $2.50 standard input unit price).

Answer (A) is incorrect. The amount of 9,600 units results from using the actual units of input per output (2.916666) instead of the standard (2). Answer (B) is incorrect. The amount of 11,667 units results from using the actual input unit price of $3.00 instead of the standard price of $2.50. Answer (C) is incorrect. The amount of 12,000 units is the actual level of output.

Questions 7.2.12 and 7.2.13 are based on the following information. Soard, Inc., manufactures a product that has the direct materials standard cost presented below. Budgeted and actual information for the current month for the manufacture of the finished product and the purchase and use of the direct materials is also presented.

Standard cost for direct materials: 1.60 lb. @ $2.50 per lb.

	Budget	Actual
Finished goods (in units)	30,000	32,000
Direct materials usage (in pounds)	?	51,000
Direct materials purchases (in pounds)	48,000	50,000
Total cost of direct materials purchases	?	$120,000

7.2.12. Soard's direct materials price variance for the current month is

A. $7,500 unfavorable.

B. $7,500 favorable.

C. $500 favorable.

D. $8,000 favorable.

Answer (B) is correct. *(CIA, adapted)*

REQUIRED: The direct materials price variance for the current period.

DISCUSSION: The direct materials price variance is the portion of the flexible budget variance attributable entirely to a difference in input unit cost. It is calculated by multiplying the actual inputs consumed in production times the difference between the standard unit cost for inputs and the actual unit cost [AQ × (SP – AP)]. The actual unit cost equals the total spent on materials divided by the number of units used ($120,000 ÷ 51,000 = $2.35294). Thus, the price variance is $7,500 favorable [51,000 × ($2.50 – $2.35294)].

Answer (A) is incorrect. The $7,500 variance is favorable. Answer (C) is incorrect. The amount of $500 favorable is the quantity variance. Answer (D) is incorrect. The amount of $8,000 favorable is the flexible budget variance.

7.2.13. Soard's direct materials efficiency variance for the current month is

A. $500 favorable.

B. $8,000 favorable.

C. $7,500 favorable.

D. $8,000 unfavorable.

Answer (A) is correct. *(CIA, adapted)*

REQUIRED: The direct materials efficiency variance.

DISCUSSION: The direct materials efficiency variance is the portion of the flexible budget variance attributable entirely to a difference in the number of inputs required to generate a unit of output. It is calculated by multiplying the difference between the standard quantity of inputs for the achieved level of production and the quantity actually used, times the standard unit price. The standard quantity equals the actual number of outputs times the standard number of inputs per unit of output (32,000 × 1.6 = 51,200). The materials efficiency (quantity) variance is therefore $500 F [(51,200 – 51,000) × $2.50].

Answer (B) is incorrect. The amount of $8,000 favorable is the flexible budget variance. Answer (C) is incorrect. The amount of $7,500 favorable is the price variance. Answer (D) is incorrect. The amount of $8,000 unfavorable is the sales volume variance.

7.2.14. The efficiency variance for either direct labor or materials can be divided into

A. Spending variance and yield variance.

B. Yield variance and price variance.

C. Volume variance and mix variance.

D. Yield variance and mix variance.

Answer (D) is correct. *(CMA, adapted)*

REQUIRED: The components into which a direct labor or materials efficiency variance can be divided.

DISCUSSION: A direct labor or materials efficiency variance is calculated by multiplying the difference between standard and actual usage times the standard cost per unit of input. The efficiency variances can be divided into yield and mix variances. Mix and yield variances are calculated only when the production process involves combining several materials or classes of labor in varying proportions (when substitutions are allowable in combining resources).

Answer (A) is incorrect. A spending variance is not the same as an efficiency variance. Answer (B) is incorrect. A price variance is not the same as an efficiency variance. Answer (C) is incorrect. A volume variance is based on fixed costs, and an efficiency variance is based on variable costs.

7.2.15. The materials yield variance equals

A. (Inputs allowed – inputs used) × budgeted weighted-average materials unit price for the planned mix.

B. (Budgeted weighted-average labor rate for planned mix – budgeted weighted-average labor rate for actual mix) × inputs used.

C. (Inputs allowed – inputs used) × budgeted weighted-average labor rate for the planned mix.

D. (Budgeted weighted-average materials unit cost for planned mix – budgeted weighted-average materials unit cost for actual mix) × inputs used.

Answer (A) is correct. *(Publisher, adapted)*

REQUIRED: The definition of materials yield variance.

DISCUSSION: The yield variance is the difference between actual input and the standard input allowed, times the budgeted weighted-average unit price. The materials yield variance is a calculation based on the assumption that the standard mix was maintained in producing a given output.

Answer (B) is incorrect. The labor mix variance equals (budgeted weighted-average labor rate for planned mix – budgeted weighted-average labor rate for actual mix) × inputs used. Answer (C) is incorrect. The labor yield variance equals (inputs allowed – inputs used) × budgeted weighted-average labor rate for the planned mix. Answer (D) is incorrect. The materials mix variance equals (budgeted weighted-average materials unit cost for planned mix – budgeted weighted-average materials unit cost for actual mix) × inputs used.

7.2.16. A company reported a significant materials efficiency variance for the month of January. All of the following are possible explanations for this variance except

A. Cutting back preventive maintenance.

B. Inadequately training and supervising the labor force.

C. Processing a large number of rush orders.

D. Producing more units than planned for in the master budget.

Answer (D) is correct. *(CIA, adapted)*

REQUIRED: The item that is not a reason for a significant materials efficiency variance.

DISCUSSION: Producing more units than planned in the master budget results in a favorable production volume variance. Accordingly, applied fixed manufacturing overhead exceeds the budgeted amount. However, a materials efficiency variance (the difference between the actual and standard input for the given unit output) does not necessarily result because production is greater than expected.

Answer (A) is incorrect. Poorly functioning machines is an obvious cause of waste and spoilage. Answer (B) is incorrect. An inadequately trained and supervised labor force is an obvious cause of waste and spoilage. Answer (C) is incorrect. Rush orders disrupt the manufacturing process by interfering with normal work routines. These disruptions adversely affect each of the manufacturing processes, including the efficient use of material, labor, and overhead.

7.2.17. If the materials flexible budget variance for a given operation is favorable, why must this variance be further evaluated as to price and usage?

A. There is no need to further evaluate the total materials variance if it is favorable.

B. Generally accepted accounting principles require that all variances be analyzed in three stages.

C. All variances must appear in the annual report to equity owners for proper disclosure.

D. Determining price and usage variances allows management to evaluate the efficiency of the purchasing and production functions.

Answer (D) is correct. *(CPA, adapted)*

REQUIRED: The reason for evaluating a favorable variance as to price and usage.

DISCUSSION: A standard cost system differentiates predetermined cost from actual cost, which allows deviations to be identified. An overall variance may include both unfavorable and favorable components. Separately analyzing the components of a variance results in more useful information. Thus, the price variance is used to evaluate the purchasing department, and the usage variance identifies production inefficiencies.

Answer (A) is incorrect. All material variances should be investigated, regardless of the direction of the variance. Answer (B) is incorrect. GAAP do not require standard costing. Answer (C) is incorrect. Variances usually are not reported to third parties and do not appear in the annual report.

7.2.18. Which department is customarily held responsible for an unfavorable materials usage variance?

A. Quality control.

B. Purchasing.

C. Engineering.

D. Production.

Answer (D) is correct. *(CPA, adapted)*

REQUIRED: The department usually responsible for an unfavorable materials usage variance.

DISCUSSION: Responsibility for variances should have some relationship to the decision and control processes used. Materials usage should be the primary responsibility of the production management personnel.

Answer (A) is incorrect. Quality control is responsible for quality standards, not material usage during production. Answer (B) is incorrect. Purchasing usually is responsible for a materials price variance. Answer (C) is incorrect. Engineering is responsible for design, engineering, and quality standards.

7.2.19. When items are transferred from stores to production, an accountant debits work-in-process and credits materials accounts. During production, a materials quantity variance may occur. The materials quantity variance is debited for an unfavorable variance and credited for a favorable variance. The intent of variance entries is to provide

A. Accountability for materials lost during production.

B. A means of safeguarding assets in the custody of the system.

C. Compliance with GAAP.

D. Information for use in controlling the cost of production.

Answer (D) is correct. *(CIA, adapted)*

REQUIRED: The intent of variance entries.

DISCUSSION: One step in the control process is measurement of actual results against standards. For example, the standard quantity of materials for a given output is established prior to production. If the actual materials usage exceeds the standard, the variance is unfavorable and corrective action may be needed.

Answer (A) is incorrect. Accountability is adequately established by the inventory entries. Answer (B) is incorrect. Variance entries cannot safeguard assets, they can only provide information for use in controlling the cost of production. Answer (C) is incorrect. Internal cost accounting information need not comply with GAAP.

7.2.20. At the end of its fiscal year, Graham Co. had several substantial variances from standard variable manufacturing costs. The one that should be allocated between inventories and cost of sales is the one attributable to

A. Additional cost of raw material acquired under a speculative purchase contract.

B. A breakdown of equipment.

C. Overestimates of production volume for the period resulting from failure to predict an unusual decline in the market for the company's product.

D. Increased labor rates won by the union as a result of a strike.

Answer (D) is correct. *(CPA, adapted)*

REQUIRED: The standard variable manufacturing cost variance allocated to inventory and COGS.

DISCUSSION: A standard cost system differentiates the predetermined cost from the actual cost. Thus, deviations are identified. Increased wages are a part of doing business and usually increase the cost of the items made and sold.

Answer (A) is incorrect. Gains and losses on speculation are not product costs. Answer (B) is incorrect. During a breakdown, variable manufacturing costs should not be incurred. Answer (C) is incorrect. A volume variance relates to fixed rather than variable manufacturing costs.

7.2.21. The standard unit cost is used in the calculation of which of the following variances?

	Materials Price Variance	Materials Usage Variance
A.	No	No
B.	No	Yes
C.	Yes	No
D.	Yes	Yes

Answer (D) is correct. *(CPA, adapted)*

REQUIRED: The variance(s) using standard unit costs.

DISCUSSION: The materials price variance is isolated at either the time of purchase or use in production. It is calculated by multiplying the actual quantity of units purchased (or used) by the difference between actual price and standard price. The materials quantity (usage) variance is calculated by multiplying the difference between (1) the standard quantity of units (the actual output times the standard number of inputs per unit of output) and (2) the actual quantity of units consumed, times standard price. Thus, the standard unit cost is used to compute both the materials price variance and the materials quantity variance.

7.3 Direct Labor

7.3.1. A debit balance in the direct labor efficiency variance account indicates that

A. Standard hours exceed actual hours.

B. Actual hours exceed standard hours.

C. Standard rate and standard hours exceed actual rate and actual hours.

D. Actual rate and actual hours exceed standard rate and standard hours.

Answer (B) is correct. *(CPA, adapted)*

REQUIRED: The cause of a debit balance in the labor efficiency variance account.

DISCUSSION: A debit balance indicates an unfavorable labor efficiency variance. Actual hours exceed standard hours.

Answer (A) is incorrect. If standard hours exceed actual, the result is a credit balance. Answer (C) is incorrect. If standard rate and standard hours exceed actual rate and actual hours, the result is a credit balance in the labor efficiency and the labor rate variance. Answer (D) is incorrect. If actual rate and actual hours exceed standard rate and standard hours, the result is a debit balance in the labor efficiency and the labor rate variance.

7.3.2. An unfavorable direct labor efficiency variance could be caused by a(n)

A. Unfavorable variable overhead spending variance.

B. Unfavorable direct materials usage variance.

C. Unfavorable fixed overhead volume variance.

D. Favorable variable overhead spending variance.

Answer (B) is correct. *(CMA, adapted)*

REQUIRED: The possible cause of an unfavorable direct labor efficiency variance.

DISCUSSION: An unfavorable direct labor efficiency variance indicates that actual hours exceeded standard hours. Too many hours may have been used because of inefficiency on the part of employees, excessive coffee breaks, machine down-time, inadequate materials, or materials of poor quality that required excessive rework. An unfavorable direct materials usage variance might be related to an unfavorable labor efficiency variance. Working on a greater quantity of direct materials may require more direct labor time.

Answer (A) is incorrect. The variable overhead spending variance may be affected by, but does not affect, a direct labor efficiency variance. It equals the difference between actual variable overhead, which includes indirect but not direct labor, and the variable overhead applied based on the standard rate and the actual activity level, which may or may not be measured in direct labor hours. Thus, the effect of an unfavorable direct labor efficiency variance is to decrease an unfavorable variable overhead spending variance or to increase a favorable variable overhead spending variance. Answer (C) is incorrect. The fixed overhead volume variance does not affect, and is not affected by, a direct labor efficiency variance. It equals the difference between budgeted fixed overhead and the fixed overhead applied based on the standard rate and the standard input (e.g., direct labor) allowed for the actual output. Answer (D) is incorrect. The variable overhead spending variance may be affected by, but does not affect, a direct labor efficiency variance. It equals the difference between actual variable overhead, which includes indirect but not direct labor, and the variable overhead applied based on the standard rate and the actual activity level, which may or may not be measured in direct labor hours. Thus, the effect of an unfavorable direct labor efficiency variance is to decrease an unfavorable variable overhead spending variance or to increase a favorable variable overhead spending variance.

7.3.3. Which of the following unfavorable variances is directly affected by the relative position of a production process on a learning curve?

A. Materials mix.

B. Materials price.

C. Labor rate.

D. Labor efficiency.

Answer (D) is correct. *(CPA, adapted)*

REQUIRED: The variance affected by the learning curve.

DISCUSSION: The efficiency of employees varies with how long they have been performing the particular task. Thus, more experienced employees are expected to be more efficient, which affects the labor efficiency variance.

Answer (A) is incorrect. The learning curve has little correlation with materials mix variances. Answer (B) is incorrect. A materials price variance is primarily the result of external factors. Answer (C) is incorrect. The labor rate variance should not be affected by the learning curve.

7.3.4. Under a standard cost system, direct labor price variances are usually not attributable to

A. Union contracts approved before the budgeting cycle.

B. Labor rate predictions.

C. The use of a single average standard rate.

D. The assignment of different skill levels of workers than planned.

Answer (A) is correct. *(CMA, adapted)*

REQUIRED: The factor that usually does not affect the direct labor price variance.

DISCUSSION: The direct labor price (rate) variance is the actual hours worked times the difference between the standard rate and the actual rate paid. This difference may be attributable to (1) a change in labor rates since the establishment of the standards, (2) using a single average standard rate despite different rates earned among different employees, (3) assigning higher-paid workers to jobs estimated to require lower-paid workers (or vice versa), or (4) paying hourly rates, but basing standards on piecework rates (or vice versa). The difference should not be caused by a union contract approved before the budgeting cycle because such rates would have been incorporated into the standards.

Answer (B) is incorrect. Predictions about labor rates may have been inaccurate. Answer (C) is incorrect. Using a single average standard rate may lead to variances if some workers are paid more than others and the proportions of hours worked differ from estimates. Answer (D) is incorrect. Assigning higher paid (and higher skilled) workers to jobs not requiring such skills leads to an unfavorable variance.

7.3.5. How is labor rate variance computed?

A. The difference between standard and actual rates times standard hours.

B. The difference between standard and actual hours times actual rate.

C. The difference between standard and actual rates times actual hours.

D. The difference between standard and actual hours times the difference between standard and actual rates.

Answer (C) is correct. *(CPA, adapted)*

REQUIRED: The formula for computing the labor rate variance.

DISCUSSION: The labor rate variance is the difference between the standard and the actual rates times the actual hours: AQ × (SP – AP).

Answer (A) is incorrect. The actual hours must be used to determine the labor rate variance. Answer (B) is incorrect. The difference between standard and actual hours times actual rate gives no useful variances. Answer (D) is incorrect. The difference between standard and actual hours, times the difference between standard and actual rates, is the rate or usage variance in three-way analysis of labor variances (not widely used).

7.3.6. Excess direct labor wages resulting from overtime premium will be disclosed in which type of variance?

A. Yield.

B. Quantity.

C. Labor efficiency.

D. Labor rate.

Answer (D) is correct. *(CPA, adapted)*

REQUIRED: The variance that reflects overtime premiums.

DISCUSSION: A standard cost system distinguishes the predetermined cost from the actual cost. Thus, deviations can be identified. Depending on the circumstances, the premium paid for overtime hours may be treated as overhead or as a direct labor cost. In the second case, it increases the labor rate and is reflected in the labor rate variance.

7.3.7. On the diagram below, the line OW represents the standard labor cost at any output volume expressed in direct labor hours. Point S indicates the actual output at standard cost, and Point A indicates the actual hours and actual cost required to produce S.

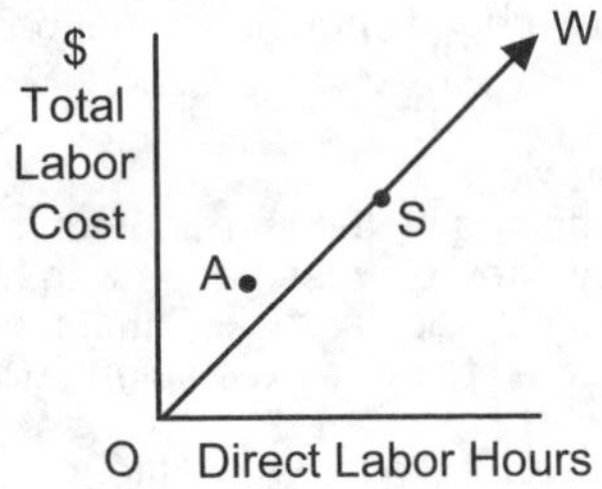

Which of the following variances are favorable or unfavorable?

	Rate Variance	Efficiency Variance
A.	Favorable	Unfavorable
B.	Favorable	Favorable
C.	Unfavorable	Unfavorable
D.	Unfavorable	Favorable

Answer (D) is correct. *(CPA, adapted)*

REQUIRED: The nature of the direct labor variances.

DISCUSSION: Point S is to the right of Point A. Consequently, the standard direct labor hours allowed for the actual output exceeded the actual hours required, and the labor efficiency (quantity or usage) variance is favorable. Point A is above the line OW. Thus, the actual hourly rate must have been greater than the standard rate, and the labor rate (price) variance is unfavorable. But the total labor variance is favorable because Point S (total standard labor cost of the actual output) is higher than Point A (total actual labor cost).

Answer (A) is incorrect. The rate variance is unfavorable and the efficiency variance is favorable. Answer (B) is incorrect. The rate variance is unfavorable. Answer (C) is incorrect. The efficiency variance is favorable.

7.3.8. Tub Co. uses a standard cost system. The following information pertains to direct labor for product B for the month of October:

Standard hours allowed for actual production	2,000
Actual rate paid per hour	$8.40
Standard rate per hour	$8.00
Labor efficiency variance	$1,600 U

What were the actual hours worked?

A. 1,800

B. 1,810

C. 2,190

D. 2,200

Answer (D) is correct. *(CPA, adapted)*

REQUIRED: The actual hours worked.

DISCUSSION: The labor efficiency variance is the difference between the standard hours and the actual hours worked, times the standard wage rate.

$$(SQ - AQ) \times SP = \text{Labor efficiency variance}$$
$$(2{,}000 \text{ hours} - AQ) \times \$8 = -\$1{,}600$$
$$\$16{,}000 - \$8AQ = -\$1{,}600$$
$$-\$8AQ = -\$17{,}600$$
$$AQ = 2{,}200 \text{ hours}$$

Answer (A) is incorrect. The amount of 1,800 results from treating the variance as favorable. Answer (B) is incorrect. The amount of 1,810 results from treating the variance as favorable and using the actual rate per hour. Answer (C) is incorrect. The amount of 2,190 results from using the actual rate per hour.

Questions 7.3.9 and 7.3.10 are based on the following information. The standard direct labor cost to produce 1 pound of output for Noth Company is presented below. Related data regarding the planned and actual production activities for the current month for the company are also given below. (DLH = Direct Labor Hours)

Direct Labor Standard: .4 DLH @ $12.00 per DLH	
Planned production	15,000 pounds
Actual production	15,500 pounds
Actual direct labor costs (6,250 DLH)	$75,250

7.3.9. Noth Company's direct labor rate variance for the current month would be

A. $10 unfavorable.

B. $240 unfavorable.

C. $248 unfavorable.

D. $250 unfavorable.

Answer (D) is correct. *(CIA, adapted)*

REQUIRED: The direct labor rate variance.

DISCUSSION: The direct labor rate variance equals the actual direct labor hours times the difference between the standard direct labor rate and the actual direct labor rate, or $250 unfavorable {6,250 DLH × [$12 – ($75,250 ÷ 6,250 DLH)]}.

Answer (A) is incorrect. The amount of $10 unfavorable is the difference between the planned direct labor hours and the actual direct labor hours times the difference between the standard direct labor rate and the actual direct labor rate. Answer (B) is incorrect. The amount of $240 unfavorable is the planned direct labor hours times the difference between the standard direct labor rate and the actual direct labor rate. Answer (C) is incorrect. The amount of $248 unfavorable is the direct labor hours allowed for actual production times the difference between the standard direct labor rate and the actual direct labor rate.

7.3.10. Noth Company's direct labor efficiency variance for the current month would be

A. $600 unfavorable.

B. $602 unfavorable.

C. $2,400 unfavorable.

D. $3,000 unfavorable.

Answer (A) is correct. *(CIA, adapted)*

REQUIRED: The direct labor efficiency variance.

DISCUSSION: The direct labor efficiency variance equals the difference between the direct labor hours allowed for the output achieved and the actual hours worked, times the standard direct labor rate, or $600 unfavorable {[(.4 DLH × 15,500 pounds) – 6,250 DLH worked] × $12}.

Answer (B) is incorrect. The amount of $602 unfavorable equals the actual direct labor rate times the difference between the direct labor hours allowed for the output achieved and the actual hours worked, an undefined variance. Answer (C) is incorrect. The amount of $2,400 unfavorable is the sales volume variance. Answer (D) is incorrect. The amount of $3,000 unfavorable equals the standard direct labor rate times the difference between the direct labor hours allowed for the planned production and the actual hours worked, an undefined variance.

Questions 7.3.11 through 7.3.15 are based on the following information.

Landeau Manufacturing Company budgeted 1,000 units of output for the fiscal year ending June 30. Standard labor rates and standard hours allowed for the budgeted output in April are

	Standard DL Rate per Hour	Standard DLH Allowed for Output
Labor class III	$8.00	500
Labor class II	7.00	500
Labor class I	5.00	500

The wage rates for each labor class increased on January 1 under the terms of a new union contract. The standard wage rates were not revised.

The actual unit output was 1,100. The actual direct labor hours (DLH) and the actual direct labor rates for April were as follows:

	Actual Rate	Actual DLH
Labor class III	$8.50	550
Labor class II	7.50	650
Labor class I	5.40	375

7.3.11. Landeau's direct labor rate variance is

A. $750 U.

B. $825 U.

C. $750 F.

D. $1,575 U.

Answer (A) is correct. *(Publisher, adapted)*

REQUIRED: The direct labor rate variance.

DISCUSSION: The rate variance is the actual quantity of labor hours times the difference between the actual and standard prices (rates).

Class III:	550 × ($8.00 – $8.50)	=	550 × ($0.50)	=	$275 U
Class II:	650 × ($7.00 – $7.50)	=	650 × ($0.50)	=	$325 U
Class I:	375 × ($5.00 – $5.40)	=	375 × ($0.40)	=	$150 U
Direct labor rate variance					$750 U

Answer (B) is incorrect. The amount of $825 U is an erroneous amount derived from reversing the sign of the direct labor yield variance. Answer (C) is incorrect. The direct labor rate variance is unfavorable. The actual rates exceed the standard rates. Answer (D) is incorrect. The amount of $1,575 U is the total direct labor variance.

7.3.12. Landeau's direct labor efficiency variance is

A. $750 U.

B. $825 F.

C. $1,575 U.

D. $175 F.

Answer (D) is correct. *(Publisher, adapted)*

REQUIRED: The direct labor efficiency variance.

DISCUSSION: The labor efficiency variance equals the difference between the flexible budget amount and the actual hours times the standard rate. The flexible budget amount equals the actual output times the standard hours per unit of output, times the weighted-average standard rate at the standard mix. Standard hours allowed are 1.5 per unit (1,500 hours ÷ 1,000 units). The weighted-average standard rate at the standard mix (SRSM) is $6.667 ($10,000 ÷ 1,500 hours).

Standard DL Rate per Hour		Standard DLH per Unit		
$8.00	×	500	=	$ 4,000
7.00	×	500	=	3,500
5.00	×	500	=	2,500
Static budget labor cost				$10,000

Flexible budget = (1,100 units actual output × 1.5 standard hours per unit × $6.667 SRSM)
= (1,650 budgeted inputs × $6.667 SRSM)
= $11,000

	Actual DLH		Standard DL Rate per Hour		
Class III:	550	×	$8.00	=	$ 4,400
Class II:	650	×	7.00	=	4,550
Class I:	375	×	5.00	=	1,875
				=	$10,825
Labor efficiency variance				=	$11,000 – $10,825
				=	$175 F

Answer (A) is incorrect. The amount of $750 U is the direct labor rate variance. Answer (B) is incorrect. The direct labor efficiency variance is $175 F. Answer (C) is incorrect. The amount of $1,575 U is the total labor variance.

7.3.13. Landeau's labor mix variance is

A. $216.67 U.

B. $325.00 U.

C. $733.33 U.

D. $625.00 F.

Answer (B) is correct. *(Publisher, adapted)*

REQUIRED: The labor mix variance.

DISCUSSION: The labor mix variance equals the actual total quantity of inputs times the difference between (1) the weighted-average standard rate for the standard mix (SRSM) and (2) the weighted-average standard rate for the actual mix (SRAM). The weighted-average standard rate at the standard mix (SRSM) is $6.667 ($10,000 ÷ 1,500 hours).

Standard DL Rate per Hour		Standard DLH per Unit		
$8.00	×	500	=	$ 4,000
7.00	×	500	=	3,500
5.00	×	500	=	2,500
Static budget labor cost				$10,000

Actual total hours × SRSM = 1,575 × $6.667
= $10,500

The actual total hours times the SRAM is $10,825.

	Actual DLH		Standard DL Rate per Hour		
Class III:	550	×	$8.00	=	$ 4,400
Class II:	650	×	7.00	=	4,550
Class I:	375	×	5.00	=	1,875
				=	$10,825
Labor efficiency variance				=	$10,500 – $10,825
				=	$325 U

Answer (A) is incorrect. The amount of $216.67 U equals actual hours of class II labor times the difference between the standard rate for that class and the weighted-average standard rate. Answer (C) is incorrect. The amount of $733.33 U equals actual hours of class III labor times the difference between the standard rate for that class and the weighted-average standard rate. Answer (D) is incorrect. The amount of $625.00 F equals actual hours of class I labor times the difference between the standard rate for that class and the weighted-average standard rate.

7.3.14. Landeau's total direct labor variance is

A. $1,575 U.

B. $750 U.

C. $325 U.

D. $500 F.

Answer (A) is correct. *(Publisher, adapted)*

REQUIRED: The total direct labor variance.

DISCUSSION: The total labor variance equals the static budget labor cost minus the actual labor cost.

Class III:	500 × $8.00	=	$ 4,000
Class II:	500 × $7.00	=	3,500
Class I:	500 × $5.00	=	2,500
Static budget labor cost			$10,000
Class III:	550 × $8.50	=	$ 4,675
Class II:	650 × $7.50	=	4,875
Class I:	375 × $5.40	=	2,025
Actual labor cost			$11,575

The $1,575 variance ($10,000 – $11,575) is unfavorable because actual exceeded static budget.

Answer (B) is incorrect. The amount of $750 U is the direct labor rate variance. Answer (C) is incorrect. The amount of $325 U is the labor mix variance. Answer (D) is incorrect. The amount of $500 F is the labor yield variance.

7.3.15. Refer to the information on the preceding page(s).Landeau's labor yield variance is

A. $500 F.

B. $750 U.

C. $175 F.

D. $1,500 U.

Answer (A) is correct. *(Publisher, adapted)*

REQUIRED: The labor yield variance.

DISCUSSION: The labor yield variance equals the weighted-average standard rate at the standard mix (SRSM) times the difference between (1) the actual total quantity and (2) the standard total quantity of labor hours. Standard hours allowed is 1.5 per unit (1,500 hours ÷ 1,000 units). The weighted-average standard rate at the standard mix (SRSM) is $6.667 ($10,000 ÷ 1,500 hours).

Standard DL Rate per Hour		Standard DLH per Unit		
$8.00	×	500	=	$ 4,000
7.00	×	500	=	3,500
5.00	×	500	=	2,500
Static budget labor cost				$10,000

Actual total hours × SRSM = 1,575 × $6.667
= $10,500

Standard total hours × SRSM = (1,100 × 1.5) × $6.667
= 1,650 × $6.667
= $11,000

Labor yield variance = $11,000 – $10,500
= $500 F

Answer (B) is incorrect. The amount of $750 U is the direct labor rate variance. Answer (C) is incorrect. The amount of $175 F is the direct labor efficiency variance. Answer (D) is incorrect. The amount of 1,500 is not a dollar amount. It is the total standard DLH allowed for the output.

7.3.16. Which of the following is the most probable reason a company would experience an unfavorable labor rate variance and a favorable labor efficiency variance?

A. The mix of workers assigned to the particular job was heavily weighted toward the use of higher-paid, experienced individuals.

B. The mix of workers assigned to the particular job was heavily weighted toward the use of new, relatively low-paid unskilled workers.

C. Because of the production schedule, workers from other production areas were assigned to assist in this particular process.

D. Defective materials caused more labor to be used to produce a standard unit.

Answer (A) is correct. *(CPA, adapted)*

REQUIRED: The probable reason for an unfavorable labor rate variance and a favorable labor efficiency variance.

DISCUSSION: More experienced people may perform more efficiently, but they are usually paid more.

Answer (B) is incorrect. The use of unskilled workers may result in an unfavorable labor efficiency variance. But the labor rate variance is favorable because they are paid less. Answer (C) is incorrect. The use of untrained workers who are paid at unbudgeted amounts may result in both an unfavorable labor efficiency variance and an unfavorable labor rate variance. Answer (D) is incorrect. Defective materials are not likely to cause an unfavorable labor rate variance.

7.3.17. Yola Co. manufactures one product with a standard direct labor cost of 4 hours at $12.00 per hour. During June, 1,000 units were produced using 4,100 hours at $12.20 per hour. The unfavorable direct labor efficiency variance was

A. $1,220

B. $1,200

C. $820

D. $400

Answer (B) is correct. *(CPA, adapted)*

REQUIRED: The amount of an unfavorable direct labor efficiency variance.

DISCUSSION: The labor efficiency variance is the difference between the standard hours and the actual hours worked, times the standard wage rate.

Labor efficiency variance = (SQ – AQ) × SP
= (4,000 hours – 4,100 hours) × $12
= (–100 hours) × $12
= $1,200 unfavorable

Answer (A) is incorrect. Using the actual labor rate results in $1,220. Answer (C) is incorrect. The labor rate variance is $820. Answer (D) is incorrect. The difference between the direct labor efficiency variance and the cost difference ($0.20) times the standard hours is $400.

7.3.18. Information on Hanley's direct labor costs for the month of January is as follows:

Actual direct labor rate	$7.50
Standard direct labor hours allowed	11,000
Actual direct labor hours	10,000
Direct labor rate variance – favorable	$5,500

The standard direct labor rate in January was

A. $6.95

B. $7.00

C. $8.00

D. $8.05

Answer (D) is correct. *(CPA, adapted)*

REQUIRED: The standard direct labor rate for the month.

DISCUSSION: The labor rate variance, actual hours, and actual rate are given. Thus, the standard rate can be derived using the following formula:

$$\begin{aligned} AQ \times (SP - AP) &= \text{Labor rate variance} \\ 10{,}000 \times (SP - \$7.50) &= \$5{,}500 \text{ F} \\ 10{,}000SP - \$75{,}000 &= \$5{,}500 \\ 10{,}000SP &= \$80{,}500 \\ SP &= \$8.05 \end{aligned}$$

Answer (A) is incorrect. The amount of $6.95 treats the $0.55 variance per unit as unfavorable. Answer (B) is incorrect. Actual hours, not standard hours, are used to determine the standard rate. Furthermore, the favorable variance should be added, not subtracted, in calculating the standard rate. Answer (C) is incorrect. Actual hours, not standard hours, should be used in determining the standard rate.

7.3.19. Sullivan Corporation's direct labor costs for the month of March were as follows:

Standard direct labor hours	42,000
Actual direct labor hours	40,000
Direct labor rate variance – favorable	$8,400
Standard direct labor rate per hour	$6.30

What was Sullivan's total direct labor payroll for the month of March?

A. $243,600

B. $252,000

C. $264,600

D. $260,400

Answer (A) is correct. *(CPA, adapted)*

REQUIRED: The direct labor payroll for March.

DISCUSSION: Given the labor rate variance, actual hours, and standard rate, the total payroll amount can be derived by substituting into the formula and solving.

$$\begin{aligned} AQ \times (SP - AP) &= \text{Labor rate variance} \\ 40{,}000 \times (\$6.30 - AP) &= \$8{,}400 \text{ F} \\ \$252{,}000 - 40{,}000AP &= \$8{,}400 \\ 40{,}000AP &= \$243{,}600 \end{aligned}$$

The amount paid for direct labor is 40,000 times the actual rate, or $243,600.

Answer (B) is incorrect. The amount of $252,000 equals actual hours times the standard rate. Answer (C) is incorrect. The amount of $264,600 equals standard hours times the standard rate. Answer (D) is incorrect. The favorable rate variance should be subtracted from the payroll calculated at the standard rate for the actual hours.

7.3.20. The labor yield variance equals

A. (Inputs allowed – inputs used) × budgeted weighted-average materials unit price for the planned mix.

B. (Budgeted weighted-average labor rate for planned mix – budgeted weighted-average labor rate for actual mix) × inputs used.

C. (Inputs allowed – inputs used) × budgeted weighted-average labor rate for the planned mix.

D. (Budgeted weighted-average materials unit cost for planned mix – budgeted weighted-average materials unit cost for actual mix) × inputs used.

Answer (C) is correct. *(Publisher, adapted)*

REQUIRED: The definition of the labor yield variance.

DISCUSSION: The labor yield variance isolates the effect of using more or fewer total units of labor. The labor rate and the mix of labor inputs are constant. The labor yield variance equals the difference between the actual units of labor used and the standard units allowed for the actual output, times the standard weighted-average labor rate.

Answer (A) is incorrect. The materials yield variance equals (inputs allowed – inputs used) × budgeted weighted-average materials unit price for the planned mix. Answer (B) is incorrect. The labor mix variance equals (budgeted weighted-average labor rate for planned mix – budgeted weighted-average labor rate for actual mix) × inputs used. Answer (D) is incorrect. The materials mix variance equals (budgeted weighted-average materials unit cost for planned mix – budgeted weighted-average materials unit cost for actual mix) × inputs used.

7.3.21. The labor mix variance equals

A. (Inputs allowed – inputs used) × budgeted weighted-average materials unit price for the planned mix.

B. (Budgeted weighted-average labor rate for planned mix – budgeted weighted-average labor rate for actual mix) × inputs used.

C. (Inputs allowed – inputs used) × budgeted weighted-average labor rate for the planned mix.

D. (Budgeted weighted-average materials unit cost for planned mix – budgeted weighted-average materials unit cost for actual mix) × inputs used.

Answer (B) is correct. *(Publisher, adapted)*

REQUIRED: The definition of the labor mix variance.

DISCUSSION: The labor mix variance isolates the effect of using different proportions of classes of labor. It equals the units of labor input actually used times the difference between the budgeted weighted-average labor rate for the planned mix and the budgeted weighted-average labor rate for the actual mix.

Answer (A) is incorrect. The materials yield variance equals (inputs allowed – inputs used) × budgeted weighted-average materials unit price for the planned mix. Answer (C) is incorrect. The labor yield variance equals (inputs allowed – inputs used) × budgeted weighted-average labor rate for the planned mix. Answer (D) is incorrect. The materials mix variance equals (budgeted weighted-average materials unit cost for planned mix – budgeted weighted-average materials unit cost for actual mix) × inputs used.

7.3.22. The difference between the actual labor rate multiplied by the actual hours worked and the standard labor rate multiplied by the standard labor hours is the

A. Total labor variance.

B. Labor rate variance.

C. Labor usage variance.

D. Labor efficiency variance.

Answer (A) is correct. *(CPA, adapted)*

REQUIRED: The variance defined by the difference between total actual labor costs and total standard costs allowed.

DISCUSSION: The total actual labor cost equals the actual labor rate times the actual labor hours. The total standard cost for good output equals the standard rate times the standard hours allowed. The total labor rate variance is the difference between the total actual labor costs and the total standard labor costs.

Answer (B) is incorrect. The labor rate variance is AQ × (SP – AP). Answer (C) is incorrect. The labor usage variance is (SQ – AQ) × SP. Answer (D) is incorrect. The labor efficiency variance is the same as the labor usage variance: (SQ – AQ) × SP.

7.3.23. The following direct labor information pertains to the manufacture of product Glu:

Time required to make one unit	2 direct labor hours
Number of direct workers	50
Number of productive hours per week, per worker	40
Weekly wages per worker	$500
Workers' benefits treated as direct labor costs	20% of wages

What is the standard direct labor cost per unit of product Glu?

A. $30

B. $24

C. $15

D. $12

Answer (A) is correct. *(CPA, adapted)*

REQUIRED: The standard direct labor cost per unit.

DISCUSSION: The hourly wage per worker is $12.50 ($500 ÷ 40 hrs.). The direct labor cost per hour is $15 [$12.50 × (1.0 + benefits equal to 20% of wages)]. Consequently, the standard direct labor cost per unit is $30 ($15 × 2 hrs.).

Answer (B) is incorrect. The weekly wages and benefits per worker ($500 × 1.2) should be divided by 40 hours per week, not by 50 workers. Answer (C) is incorrect. This amount is the DL cost per hour. Two DL hours are required per unit. Answer (D) is incorrect. The weekly wages and benefits per worker ($500 × 1.2) should be divided by 40 hours per week, not by 50 workers. Furthermore, 2 DL hours are required per unit.

7.4 Manufacturing Overhead

7.4.1. Differences in product costs resulting from the application of actual overhead rates rather than predetermined overhead rates could be immaterial if

A. Production is not stable.

B. Fixed manufacturing overhead is a significant cost.

C. Several products are produced simultaneously.

D. Overhead is composed only of variable costs.

Answer (D) is correct. *(CPA, adapted)*

REQUIRED: The circumstance in which the difference between actual and predetermined overhead rates may be immaterial.

DISCUSSION: Actual overhead and predetermined amounts of overhead are most likely to be similar if overhead is composed primarily of variable costs. In principle, unit variable overhead should fluctuate little with the activity level.

Answer (A) is incorrect. Fluctuating production levels could cause significant differences between actual and applied fixed manufacturing overhead. Fixed manufacturing overhead per unit changes with the activity level. Answer (B) is incorrect. Fluctuating production levels could cause significant differences between actual and applied fixed manufacturing overhead. Fixed manufacturing overhead per unit changes with the activity level. Answer (C) is incorrect. A change in the product mix may cause significant differences between the predetermined and actual manufacturing overhead rates.

7.4.2. The variance in an absorption costing system that measures the departure from the denominator level of activity that was used to set the fixed overhead rate is the

A. Spending variance.

B. Efficiency variance.

C. Production volume variance.

D. Flexible budget variance.

Answer (C) is correct. *(CMA, adapted)*

REQUIRED: The difference between actual production and the denominator level of production.

DISCUSSION: A denominator level of activity must be used to establish the standard cost (application rate) for fixed overhead. The production volume variance is the difference between budgeted fixed costs and the standard cost per unit of input times the standard units of input allowed for the actual production.

Answer (A) is incorrect. The fixed overhead spending variance is the difference between actual fixed costs and budgeted costs. Answer (B) is incorrect. The efficiency variance is applicable to variable overhead. Answer (D) is incorrect. The flexible budget variance is the difference between actual and budgeted amounts in a flexible budget.

7.4.3. Which one of the following variances is of least significance from a behavioral control perspective?

A. Unfavorable direct materials quantity variance amounting to 20% of the quantity allowed for the output attained.

B. Unfavorable direct labor efficiency variance amounting to 10% more than the budgeted hours for the output attained.

C. Favorable direct labor rate variance resulting from an inability to hire experienced workers to replace retiring workers.

D. Fixed overhead volume variance resulting from management's decision midway through the fiscal year to reduce its budgeted output by 20%.

Answer (D) is correct. *(CMA, adapted)*

REQUIRED: The variance of least significance from a behavioral control perspective.

DISCUSSION: Most variances are of significance to someone who is responsible for that variance. However, a fixed overhead volume variance is often not the responsibility of anyone other than top management. The fixed overhead volume variance equals the difference between budgeted fixed overhead and the amount applied (standard input allowed for the actual output × standard rate). It can be caused by economic downturns, labor strife, bad weather, or a change in planned output. Thus, a fixed overhead volume variance resulting from a top management decision to reduce output has fewer behavioral implications than other variances.

Answer (A) is incorrect. An unfavorable direct materials quantity variance affects production management and possibly the purchasing function. It may indicate an inefficient use of materials or the use of poor quality materials. Answer (B) is incorrect. An unfavorable direct labor efficiency variance reflects upon production workers who have used too many hours. Answer (C) is incorrect. A favorable direct labor rate variance related to hiring is a concern of the human resources function. The favorable rate variance might be more than offset by an unfavorable direct labor efficiency variance or a direct materials quantity variance (if waste occurred).

Questions 7.4.4 through 7.4.6 are based on the following information. Dori Castings, a job-order shop, uses a full-absorption, standard-cost system to account for its production costs. The O/H costs are applied on a direct-labor-hour basis.

7.4.4. Dori's choice of a production volume as a denominator for calculating its factory O/H rate has

A. An effect on the variable factory O/H rate for applying costs to production.

B. No effect on the fixed factory O/H budget variance.

C. No effect on the fixed factory O/H production volume variance, nor the variable O/H spending variance.

D. No effect on the overall (net) fixed factory O/H variance.

Answer (B) is correct. *(CMA, adapted)*

REQUIRED: The effect of using production volume as the denominator in calculating the factory O/H rate.

DISCUSSION: The use of a production volume as the denominator in calculating the factory O/H rate has no effect on the fixed factory O/H budget variance. This variance is the difference between actual fixed costs and budgeted (lump sum) fixed costs.

Answer (A) is incorrect. By definition, the total variable factory O/H varies with the activity level, but total fixed O/H and unit variable O/H do not. Answer (C) is incorrect. The fixed factory O/H production volume variance is the difference between budgeted fixed O/H and fixed O/H applied based on the predetermined rate. Answer (D) is incorrect. The overall (net) fixed factory O/H variance is the difference between the actual fixed O/H and the fixed O/H applied based on the predetermined rate.

7.4.5. A production volume variance will exist for Dori in a month when

A. Production volume differs from sales volume.

B. Actual direct labor hours differ from standard allowed direct labor hours.

C. The fixed factory O/H applied on the basis of standard allowed direct labor hours differs from actual fixed factory O/H.

D. The fixed factory O/H applied on the basis of standard allowed direct labor hours differs from the budgeted fixed factory O/H.

Answer (D) is correct. *(CMA, adapted)*

REQUIRED: The definition of a production volume variance.

DISCUSSION: A fixed O/H production volume variance is the difference between the budgeted fixed factory O/H and the O/H applied based on a predetermined rate and standard direct labor hours allowed for the actual output.

Answer (A) is incorrect. Sales volume is irrelevant. Answer (B) is incorrect. The difference between actual direct labor hours and standard direct labor hours allowed is the basis of the variable O/H efficiency variance. Answer (C) is incorrect. The difference between fixed factory O/H applied on the basis of standard allowed direct labor hours and the budgeted fixed factory O/H defines the total fixed O/H variance.

7.4.6. The amount of fixed factory O/H that Dori will apply to finished production is the

A. Actual direct labor hours times the standard fixed factory O/H rate per direct labor hour.

B. Standard allowed direct labor hours for the actual units of finished output times the standard fixed factory O/H rate per direct labor hour.

C. Standard units of output for the actual direct labor hours worked times the standard fixed factory O/H rate per unit of output.

D. Actual fixed factory O/H cost per direct labor hour times the standard allowed direct labor hours.

Answer (B) is correct. *(CMA, adapted)*

REQUIRED: The fixed factory O/H application basis.

DISCUSSION: Fixed factory O/H in a standard costing system is applied to the product based on the predetermined O/H rate multiplied by the standard hours allowed for the actual output. Thus, the applied fixed factory O/H is limited to the standard amount.

Answer (A) is incorrect. The standard hours allowed for the actual units of finished output is used, not the AH. Answer (C) is incorrect. The O/H application is not based on units of production for the AH. Answer (D) is incorrect. The applied fixed factory O/H is limited to the standard amount determined using the standard O/H rate per DL hour, not the actual O/H cost per DL hour.

7.4.7. Variable overhead is applied on the basis of standard direct labor hours. If, for a given period, the direct labor efficiency variance is unfavorable, the variable overhead efficiency variance will be

A. Favorable.

B. Unfavorable.

C. Zero.

D. The same amount as the direct labor efficiency variance.

Answer (B) is correct. *(CMA, adapted)*

REQUIRED: The effect on the variable overhead efficiency variance.

DISCUSSION: If variable overhead is applied to production on the basis of direct labor hours, both the variable overhead efficiency variance and the direct labor efficiency variance will be calculated on the basis of the same number of hours. If the direct labor efficiency variance is unfavorable, the overhead efficiency variance will also be unfavorable because both variances are based on the difference between standard and actual direct labor hours worked.

7.4.8. The fixed factory overhead application rate is a function of a predetermined activity level. If standard hours allowed for good output equal this predetermined activity level for a given period, the volume variance will be

A. Zero.

B. Favorable.

C. Unfavorable.

D. Either favorable or unfavorable, depending on the budgeted overhead.

Answer (A) is correct. *(CPA, adapted)*

REQUIRED: The volume variance when standard hours allowed for good output equal the predetermined activity.

DISCUSSION: The volume variance is the difference between the amount of fixed overhead applied and the amount budgeted. Thus, given no difference between the predetermined activity level and the standard input allowed for the actual output, no variance occurs.

Answer (B) is incorrect. A favorable volume variance means standard input allowed for the actual output exceeds the predetermined (budgeted) amount. Answer (C) is incorrect. An unfavorable volume variance means that standard input allowed for the actual output is less than the amount budgeted. Answer (D) is incorrect. No variance occurs.

7.4.9. Which of the following standard costing variances would be least controllable by a production supervisor?

A. Overhead volume.

B. Overhead efficiency.

C. Labor efficiency.

D. Materials usage.

Answer (A) is correct. *(CPA, adapted)*

REQUIRED: The variance least controllable by a production supervisor.

DISCUSSION: The production volume variance measures the effect of not operating at the budgeted activity level. This variance can be caused by, for example, insufficient sales or a labor strike. These events are out of the production supervisor's control. Thus, the production volume variance is the least controllable by a production supervisor.

Answer (B) is incorrect. The variable manufacturing overhead efficiency variance is wholly attributable to variable overhead. Answer (C) is incorrect. The efficiency of employees affects the labor efficiency variance. Answer (D) is incorrect. The materials usage variance is typically influenced most by activities within the production department.

7.4.10. Baby Frames, Inc., evaluates manufacturing overhead in its factory by using variance analysis. The following information applies to the month of May:

	Actual	Budgeted
Number of frames manufactured	19,000	20,000
Variable overhead costs	$4,100	$2 per direct labor hour
Fixed overhead costs	$22,000	$20,000
Direct labor hours	2,100 hours	0.1 hour per frame

What is the fixed overhead spending variance?

A. $1,000 favorable.

B. $1,000 unfavorable.

C. $2,000 favorable.

D. $2,000 unfavorable.

Answer (D) is correct. *(CPA, adapted)*

REQUIRED: The fixed overhead spending variance.

DISCUSSION: The fixed overhead spending variance is the difference between the amount budgeted for fixed manufacturing overhead costs and the actual costs incurred. The fixed overhead spending variance is thus $2,000 unfavorable ($20,000 budgeted – $22,000 actual).

Answer (A) is incorrect. The fixed overhead spending variance is unfavorable. Answer (B) is incorrect. The fixed overhead spending variance is $2,000. Answer (C) is incorrect. Actual costs exceed budgeted costs, causing the $2,000 variance to be unfavorable.

Questions 7.4.11 and 7.4.12 are based on the following information. The diagram below depicts a manufacturing overhead flexible budget line DB and standard overhead application line OA for White Company. Activity is expressed in machine hours, with Point V indicating the standard hours required for the actual output in September. Point S indicates the actual machine hours (inputs) and actual costs in September.

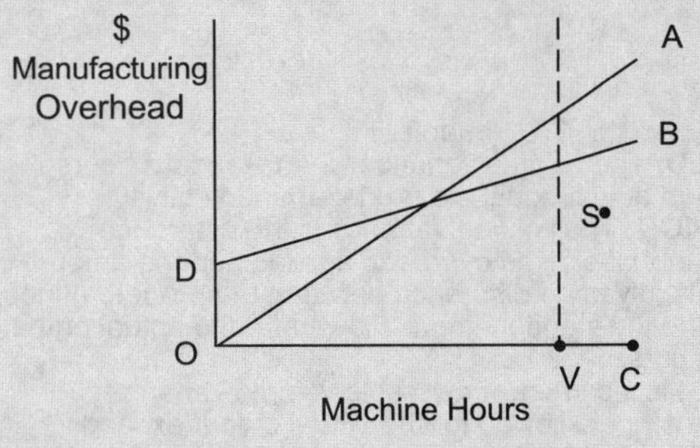

7.4.11. Are the following manufacturing overhead variances favorable or unfavorable for White Company?

	Volume (Capacity) Variance	Efficiency Variance
A.	Favorable	Favorable
B.	Favorable	Unfavorable
C.	Unfavorable	Favorable
D.	Unfavorable	Unfavorable

Answer (B) is correct. *(CPA, adapted)*

REQUIRED: The nature of the volume and efficiency variances.

DISCUSSION: The production volume variance (fixed manufacturing overhead budgeted – fixed manufacturing overhead applied) is favorable when actual activity exceeds the budgeted level, that is, when fixed overhead applied exceeds the amount budgeted. Line OA (standard overhead applied) is above line DB (the flexible budget) at Point V. Thus, total overhead applied exceeded the amount budgeted at activity level V. Because variable overhead applied equals the flexible-budget amount at all activity levels within the relevant range, the difference between OA and DB is solely the result of the volume variance. Fixed overhead costs applied equaled the flexible-budget amount at the intersection of OA and DB, which is to the left of V. Accordingly, at all points on OA to the right of the intersection, the volume variance is favorable. The efficiency variance (budgeted variable overhead rate × the difference between actual hours and the standard hours allowed) is unfavorable because Point S (actual hours) is to the right of Point V (standard hours allowed).

7.4.12. White's budgeted total variable manufacturing overhead cost for C machine hours is

A. AB.

B. BC.

C. AC minus DO.

D. BC minus DO.

Answer (D) is correct. *(CPA, adapted)*

REQUIRED: The budgeted total variable manufacturing overhead cost for C machine hours.

DISCUSSION: DB is the flexible budget line for total overhead. At O (zero machine hours), budgeted variable overhead is zero. Thus, DO must equal the fixed overhead cost. At C, BC represents total budgeted overhead, and BC minus DO must therefore equal the budgeted total variable overhead.

Answer (A) is incorrect. AB is the overapplied fixed overhead for C hours. Answer (B) is incorrect. BC is the total budgeted overhead for C hours. Answer (C) is incorrect. AC minus DO is the sum of the budgeted variable overhead for C hours and the overapplied fixed overhead.

7.4.13. Under the two-variance method for analyzing manufacturing overhead, the difference between the actual manufacturing overhead and the manufacturing overhead applied to production is the

A. Controllable variance.

B. Net overhead variance.

C. Efficiency variance.

D. Volume variance.

Answer (B) is correct. *(CPA, adapted)*

REQUIRED: The difference between the actual manufacturing overhead and manufacturing overhead applied.

DISCUSSION: The net overhead variance is the difference between the sum of actual fixed and variable overhead and the sum of the fixed and variable overhead applied (total overhead rate × the standard input allowed for the actual output).

Answer (A) is incorrect. The controllable (budget) variance is the difference between actual total overhead incurred and budgeted overhead at the standard input allowed. Answer (C) is incorrect. The efficiency variance is not separately calculated in two-way analysis. Answer (D) is incorrect. The volume variance is the difference between budgeted fixed overhead and the amount applied.

7.4.14. If overhead is applied on the basis of units of output, the variable overhead efficiency variance will be

A. Zero.

B. Favorable, if output exceeds the budgeted level.

C. Unfavorable, if output is less than the budgeted level.

D. A function of the direct labor efficiency variance.

Answer (A) is correct. *(CMA, adapted)*

REQUIRED: The effect on the variable overhead efficiency variance.

DISCUSSION: The variable overhead efficiency variance equals the product of the variable overhead application rate and the difference between the standard input for the actual output and the actual input. Hence, the variance will be zero if variable overhead is applied on the basis of units of output because the difference between actual and standard input cannot be recognized.

Answer (B) is incorrect. The variance will be zero. Answer (C) is incorrect. The variance will be zero. Answer (D) is incorrect. The correlation between the variable overhead and direct labor efficiency variances occurs only when overhead is applied on the basis of direct labor.

7.4.15. Under the two-variance method for analyzing overhead, which of the following variances consists of both variable and fixed overhead elements?

	Controllable (Budget) Variance	Volume Variance
A.	Yes	Yes
B.	Yes	No
C.	No	No
D.	No	Yes

Answer (B) is correct. *(CPA, adapted)*

REQUIRED: The variance(s), if any, including both fixed and variable O/H elements.

DISCUSSION: Two-way overhead variance analysis combines the two spending variances and the one efficiency variance into the controllable (budget) variance. It thus contains both variable and fixed overhead elements. The volume variance under two-way analysis consists entirely of the fixed overhead volume variance.

7.4.16. Under the two-variance method for analyzing manufacturing overhead, which of the following is used in the computation of the controllable (budget) variance?

	Budget Allowance Based on Actual Hours	Budget Allowance Based on Standard Hours
A.	Yes	Yes
B.	Yes	No
C.	No	No
D.	No	Yes

Answer (D) is correct. *(CPA, adapted)*

REQUIRED: The item(s), if any, used in the computation of the controllable (budget) variance.

DISCUSSION: In two-way analysis, the total manufacturing overhead variance equals the production volume variance (total fixed overhead cost budgeted – fixed overhead applied based on standard input allowed for the actual output) and the controllable (budget) variance [total actual overhead – (lump-sum fixed overhead budgeted + variable overhead based on the standard rate and the standard input allowed for the actual output)]. Thus, the budget allowance based on standard, not actual, hours is used in the computation of the controllable (budget) variance.

7.4.17. Under the three-variance method for analyzing manufacturing overhead, the difference between the actual manufacturing overhead and the manufacturing overhead applied to production is the

A. Net manufacturing overhead variance.

B. Controllable variance.

C. Efficiency variance.

D. Spending variance.

Answer (A) is correct. *(CPA, adapted)*

REQUIRED: The difference between the actual manufacturing overhead and the manufacturing overhead applied.

DISCUSSION: Three-way analysis calculates spending, efficiency, and production volume variances. However, regardless of whether two-, three-, or four-way analysis is used, the net overhead variance is the difference between actual total overhead and the total applied to the product.

Answer (B) is incorrect. The controllable (flexible budget) variance is calculated in two-way analysis. Answer (C) is incorrect. The efficiency variance is calculated in three- or four-way analysis. Answer (D) is incorrect. In three-way analysis, the spending variance is the difference between (1) actual total overhead and (2) the sum of budgeted fixed overhead and the variable overhead based on the actual input at the standard rate. It combines the variable overhead spending and the fixed overhead spending variances used in four-way analysis.

7.4.18. Under the three-variance method for analyzing manufacturing overhead, the difference between the actual manufacturing overhead and the budget allowance based on actual input is the

A. Efficiency variance.

B. Spending variance.

C. Volume variance.

D. Idle capacity variance.

Answer (B) is correct. *(CPA, adapted)*

REQUIRED: The difference between the actual manufacturing overhead and the budget allowance based on actual input.

DISCUSSION: In three-way analysis, the spending variance is the difference between (1) actual total overhead and (2) the sum of budgeted (lump-sum) fixed overhead and the variable overhead based on the actual input at the standard rate. It combines the variable overhead spending and the fixed overhead spending variances used in four-way analysis.

Answer (A) is incorrect. The efficiency variance equals the standard rate for variable overhead times the difference between actual input and the standard input. Answer (C) is incorrect. The production volume (idle capacity) variance is the difference between the budgeted (lump-sum) fixed overhead and the amount applied. Answer (D) is incorrect. The production volume (idle capacity) variance is the difference between the budgeted (lump-sum) fixed overhead and the amount applied.

7.4.19. Under the three-variance method for analyzing manufacturing overhead, which of the following is used in the computation of the spending variance?

	Actual Manufacturing Overhead	Budget Allowance Based on Actual Input
A.	No	Yes
B.	No	No
C.	Yes	No
D.	Yes	Yes

Answer (D) is correct. *(CPA, adapted)*

REQUIRED: The components of the spending variance.

DISCUSSION: In three-way analysis, the spending variance is the difference between actual total manufacturing overhead and the sum of budgeted (lump-sum) fixed overhead and the variable overhead based on the actual input at the standard rate. It combines the variable overhead spending and the fixed overhead spending variances used in four-way analysis.

7.4.20. During the month just ended, a department's fixed overhead standard costing system reported unfavorable spending and volume variances. The activity level selected for allocating overhead to the product was based on 80% of practical capacity. If 100% of practical capacity had been selected instead, how would the reported unfavorable spending and volume variances be affected?

	Spending Variance	Volume Variance
A.	Increased	Unchanged
B.	Increased	Increased
C.	Unchanged	Increased
D.	Unchanged	Unchanged

Answer (C) is correct. *(CPA, adapted)*

REQUIRED: The effects on unfavorable spending and volume variances of increasing the budgeted activity level.

DISCUSSION: The fixed overhead spending variance equals the actual costs incurred minus the budgeted amount. Thus, the spending variance is not affected by the denominator level of the overhead application driver. However, the volume variance equals the budgeted amount minus the amount applied. Because the fixed overhead applied depends on the activity level of the driver used for application, a change in the denominator affects the volume variance. If the denominator increases, the application rate and the amount applied decrease, causing the variance to increase.

7.4.21. Union Company uses a standard cost accounting system. The following factory overhead and production data are available for August:

Standard fixed overhead rate per DLH	$1
Standard variable overhead rate per DLH	$4
Budgeted monthly DLH	40,000
Actual DLH worked	39,500
Standard DLH allowed for actual production	39,000
Overall overhead variance – favorable	$2,000

The applied factory overhead for August should be

A. $195,000

B. $197,000

C. $197,500

D. $199,500

Answer (A) is correct. *(CPA, adapted)*

REQUIRED: The applied manufacturing overhead for the month.

DISCUSSION: The applied overhead equals the standard direct hours allowed for actual production multiplied by the total standard overhead rate per hour.

39,000 × ($4 VOH + $1 FOH) = $195,000

Answer (B) is incorrect. The amount of $197,000 includes the $2,000 favorable overhead variance. This variance should not be added to the $195,000 applied overhead. Answer (C) is incorrect. The actual DLH worked were used to determine the applied FO when the standard DLH allowed for actual production should have been used. Answer (D) is incorrect. The actual DLH worked were used instead of the standard DLH allowed. Furthermore, the $2,000 favorable overhead variance should not be included.

7.4.22. Peters Company uses a flexible budget system and prepared the following information for the year:

Percent of capacity	80%	90%
Direct labor hours	24,000	27,000
Variable manufacturing overhead	$48,000	$54,000
Fixed manufacturing overhead	$108,000	$108,000
Total manufacturing overhead rate per DLH	$6.50	$6.00

Peters operated at 80% of capacity during the year but applied manufacturing overhead based on the 90% capacity level. Assuming that actual manufacturing overhead was equal to the budgeted amount for the attained capacity, what is the amount of overhead variance for the year?

A. $6,000 overabsorbed.

B. $6,000 underabsorbed.

C. $12,000 overabsorbed.

D. $12,000 underabsorbed.

Answer (D) is correct. *(CPA, adapted)*

REQUIRED: The manufacturing overhead variance for the year.

DISCUSSION: The total overhead variance is calculated by determining the difference between the actual overhead and applied overhead. Given that actual overhead was equal to the budgeted amount for the attained capacity, the only variance was caused by under- or overabsorption of fixed overhead. The fixed overhead rate at the 90% activity level is $4 ($108,000 fixed overhead ÷ 27,000 DLH). Given that the actual activity level achieved was 80% and that 24,000 standard hours were allowed, $96,000 (24,000 × $4.00) of fixed overhead was absorbed. Thus, underabsorbed (underapplied) fixed overhead was $12,000 ($108,000 – $96,000).

Answer (A) is incorrect. The amount of $6,000 overabsorbed is the difference in variable overhead at the 80% and 90% levels. Answer (B) is incorrect. The amount of $6,000 underabsorbed is the difference in variable overhead at the 80% and 90% levels. Answer (C) is incorrect. The overhead variance for the year is $12,000 underabsorbed, not overabsorbed.

7.4.23. Nil Co. uses a predetermined factory overhead application rate based on direct labor cost. For the year ended December 31, Nil's budgeted factory overhead was $600,000, based on a budgeted volume of 50,000 direct labor hours, at a standard direct labor rate of $6 per hour. Actual factory overhead amounted to $620,000, with actual direct labor cost of $325,000. For the year, overapplied factory overhead was

A. $20,000

B. $25,000

C. $30,000

D. $50,000

Answer (C) is correct. *(CPA, adapted)*

REQUIRED: The overapplied factory overhead for the period.

DISCUSSION: Nil Co. applies factory overhead using a predetermined overhead rate, based on direct labor cost. Overhead was budgeted for $600,000 based on a budgeted labor cost of $300,000 ($6 × 50,000 hrs.). Thus, $2 of overhead was applied for each $1 of labor. Given actual labor cost of $325,000, $650,000 ($2 × $325,000) of overhead was applied during the period. Actual overhead was $620,000, so $30,000 ($650,000 – $620,000) was overapplied.

Answer (A) is incorrect. The difference between budgeted and actual factory overhead is $20,000. Answer (B) is incorrect. The difference between budgeted direct labor costs and actual direct labor costs is $25,000. Answer (D) is incorrect. The difference between the applied factory overhead and the budgeted amount is $50,000.

7.4.24. The company's master budget shows straight-line depreciation on factory equipment of $258,000. The master budget was prepared at an annual production volume of 103,200 units of product. This production volume is expected to occur uniformly throughout the year. During September, the company produced 8,170 units of product, and the accounts reflected actual depreciation on factory machinery of $20,500. The company controls manufacturing costs with a flexible budget. The flexible budget amount for depreciation on factory machinery for September would be

A. $19,475

B. $20,425

C. $20,500

D. $21,500

Answer (D) is correct. *(CMA, adapted)*

REQUIRED: The amount of depreciation expense shown on the flexible budget for the month.

DISCUSSION: Since depreciation is a fixed cost, that cost will be the same each month regardless of production. Therefore, the budget for September would show depreciation of $21,500 ($258,000 annual depreciation × 1/12).

Answer (A) is incorrect. Depreciation is a fixed cost that will be the same each month regardless of production. The budget for September would show depreciation of $21,500 ($258,000 × 1/12). Answer (B) is incorrect. The amount of $20,425 is based on the units-of-production method. Answer (C) is incorrect. The amount shown in the accounts is $20,500.

7.4.25. Universal Company uses a standard cost system and prepared the following budget at normal capacity for the month of January:

Direct labor hours	24,000
Variable manufacturing overhead	$48,000
Fixed manufacturing overhead	$108,000
Total manufacturing overhead per DLH	$6.50

Actual data for January were as follows:

Direct labor hours worked	22,000
Total manufacturing overhead	$147,000
Standard DLH allowed for capacity attained	21,000

Using the two-way analysis of overhead variances, what is the budget (controllable) variance for January?

A. $3,000 favorable.

B. $13,500 unfavorable.

C. $9,000 favorable.

D. $10,500 unfavorable.

Answer (A) is correct. *(CPA, adapted)*

REQUIRED: The controllable (budget) variance.

DISCUSSION: In two-way analysis, the flexible budget (controllable) variance is the total manufacturing overhead variance not attributable to the production-volume variance. The total overhead variance equals the difference between (1) actual total overhead and (2) the overhead applied based on the standard input allowed for the actual output, or $10,500 unfavorable [$147,000 actual – ($6.50 × 21,000 DLH) applied]. The production-volume variance (budgeted fixed overhead – amount applied) is $13,500 unfavorable {$108,000 budgeted – [($108,000 ÷ 24,000 DLH) × 21,000 DLH]}. Thus, the controllable variance must be $3,000 favorable ($13,500 unfavorable – $10,500 unfavorable).

Answer (B) is incorrect. The amount of $13,500 unfavorable is the production volume variance. Answer (C) is incorrect. The amount of $9,000 favorable equals the difference between total actual overhead and overhead budgeted at normal capacity. Answer (D) is incorrect. The amount of $10,500 unfavorable equals the total overhead variance.

7.4.26. Margolos, Inc., ends the month with a volume variance of $6,360 unfavorable. If budgeted fixed manufacturing overhead was $480,000, overhead was applied on the basis of 32,000 budgeted machine hours, and budgeted variable manufacturing overhead was $170,000, what were the standard machine hours allowed (SH) for the month's actual output?

A. 32,424

B. 32,000

C. 31,687

D. 31,576

Answer (D) is correct. *(J.B. Romal)*

REQUIRED: The standard machine hours allowed.

DISCUSSION: The production volume variance (VV) results from the difference between budgeted fixed manufacturing overhead and the amount applied at the standard rate based on the standard input allowed for actual output. The variance is unfavorable if the budgeted amount exceeds the applied amount. The overhead rate is $15 per machine hour ($480,000 ÷ 32,000).

$$
\begin{aligned}
VV &= \text{Budgeted} - \text{Applied} \\
\$6,360 &= \$480,000 - (\$15 \times SH) \\
\$15 \times SH &= \$480,000 - \$6,360 \\
SH &= \$473,640 \div \$15 \\
SH &= 31,576
\end{aligned}
$$

Answer (A) is incorrect. The amount of 32,424 assumes the variance is favorable. Answer (B) is incorrect. The amount of 32,000 is the amount of budgeted hours. Answer (C) is incorrect. The amount of 31,687 assumes budgeted fixed overhead is $650,000 ($480,000 + $170,000).

Questions 7.4.27 and 7.4.28 are based on the following information. Tiny Tykes Corporation had the following activity relating to its fixed and variable overhead for the month of July:

Actual costs	
Fixed overhead	$120,000
Variable overhead	80,000
Flexible budget (Standard input allowed for actual output achieved × budgeted rate)	
Variable overhead	90,000
Applied (Standard input allowed for actual output achieved × budgeted rate)	
Fixed overhead	125,000
Variable overhead spending variance	2,000 F
Production volume variance	5,000 U

7.4.27. If the budgeted rate for applying variable overhead was $20 per direct labor hour, how efficient or inefficient was Tiny Tykes Corporation in terms of using direct labor hours as an activity base?

A. 100 direct labor hours inefficient.

B. 100 direct labor hours efficient.

C. 400 direct labor hours inefficient.

D. 400 direct labor hours efficient.

Answer (D) is correct. *(CMA, adapted)*

REQUIRED: The efficiency variance stated in terms of direct labor hours.

DISCUSSION: The variable overhead spending and efficiency variances are the components of the total variable overhead variance. Given that actual variable overhead was $80,000 and the variable overhead based on the budgeted rate was $90,000, the total variance is $10,000 favorable. If the overhead spending variance is $2,000 favorable, the efficiency variance must be $8,000 favorable ($10,000 total – $2,000 spending). At a rate of $20 per hour, this variance is equivalent to 400 direct labor hours ($8,000 ÷ $20).

Answer (A) is incorrect. The variances are favorable.
Answer (B) is incorrect. The number of 100 direct labor hours are equivalent to the spending variance (100 hours × $20 = $2,000).
Answer (C) is incorrect. The variances are favorable.

7.4.28. Tiny Tykes' fixed overhead efficiency variance is

A. $3,000 favorable.

B. $3,000 unfavorable.

C. $5,000 favorable.

D. Never a meaningful variance.

Answer (D) is correct. *(CMA, adapted)*

REQUIRED: The fixed overhead efficiency variance.

DISCUSSION: Variable overhead variances can be subdivided into spending and efficiency components. However, fixed overhead variances do not have an efficiency component because fixed costs, by definition, are not related to changing levels of output. Fixed overhead variances are typically subdivided into a budget (or fixed overhead spending) variance and a volume variance.

Questions 7.4.29 through 7.4.31 are based on the following information. Patie Company uses a standard FIFO, process-cost system to account for its only product, Mituea. Patie has found that direct machine hours (DMH) provide the best estimate of the application of O/H. Four (4) standard direct machine hours are allowed for each unit. Using simple linear regression analysis in the form y = a + b(DMH), given that (a) equals fixed costs and (b) equals variable costs, Patie has developed the following O/H budget for a normal activity level of 100,000 direct machine hours:

ITEM (y)	a	b
Supplies		$ 0.50
Indirect Labor	$ 54,750	6.50
Depreciation -- Plant and Equipment	27,000	
Property Taxes and Insurance	32,300	
Repairs and Maintenance	14,550	1.25
Utilities	3,400	4.75
Total O/H	$132,000	$13.00

Actual fixed O/H incurred was $133,250, and actual variable O/H was $1,225,000. Patie produced 23,500 equivalent units during the year using 98,700 direct machine hours.

7.4.29. What is Patie's standard overhead rate?

A. $13.00 per DMH.

B. $11.68 per DMH.

C. $1.32 per DMH.

D. $14.32 per DMH.

Answer (D) is correct. *(L.J. McCarthy)*

REQUIRED: The standard overhead rate.

DISCUSSION: The total overhead equation is

y = $132,000 + ($13 × DMH)

This equation is derived by adding individual overhead items. The fixed portion needs to be converted to a rate by dividing it by normal capacity. Thus, the fixed overhead rate is $1.32 ($132,000 ÷ 100,000). To calculate the total overhead rate, the fixed rate is added to the variable rate. Thus, the total overhead rate per DMH is $14.32 ($1.32 + $13.00).

Answer (A) is incorrect. The amount of $13.00 per DMH is the variable overhead rate per machine hour. Answer (B) is incorrect. The amount of $11.68 per DMH equals $13 minus $1.32. Answer (C) is incorrect. The amount of $1.32 per DMH is the fixed overhead rate per machine hour.

7.4.30. If Patie produced 23,500 equivalent units during the year using 98,700 direct machine hours, how much overhead should be applied to production?

A. $1,413,384

B. $1,432,000

C. $1,346,080

D. $1,222,000

Answer (C) is correct. *(L.J. McCarthy)*

REQUIRED: The standard overhead applied to production.

DISCUSSION: Overhead is applied using the standard activity allowed for actual production. The standard activity allowed is the standard activity per equivalent unit times the actual production, or 94,000 hours (4 DMH × 23,500). The overhead applied is $1,346,080 (94,000 × $14.32).

Answer (A) is incorrect. The amount of $1,413,384 is based on 98,700 actual DMH. Answer (B) is incorrect. The amount of $1,432,000 is for the original 100,000 DMH budgeted. Answer (D) is incorrect. Fixed overhead costs also should be included.

7.4.31. Assuming Patie's actual fixed overhead incurred was $133,250 and actual variable overhead incurred was $1,225,000, what is the total overhead variance?

A. $12,170 unfavorable.

B. $12,170 favorable.

C. $55,134 unfavorable.

D. $55,134 favorable.

Answer (A) is correct. *(L.J. McCarthy)*

REQUIRED: The total overhead variance for the year.

DISCUSSION: The total overhead variance is the difference between applied overhead and the actual overhead. Overhead is applied using the standard activity allowed for actual production. The standard activity allowed is the standard activity per equivalent unit times the actual production, or 94,000 hours (4 DMH × 23,500). The overhead applied is $1,346,080 (94,000 × $14.32). The actual overhead is $1,358,250 ($133,250 + $1,225,000). Thus, the underapplied overhead is $12,170 U ($1,358,250 – $1,346,080).

Answer (B) is incorrect. The variance is unfavorable. Answer (C) is incorrect. The variance of $55,134 unfavorable is based on the actual DMH. Answer (D) is incorrect. The variance is unfavorable.

7.4.32. A company uses flexible budgeting for the control of costs. The company's annual master budget includes $324,000 for fixed production supervisory salaries at a volume of 180,000 units. Supervisory salaries are expected to be incurred uniformly throughout the year. During the month of September, 15,750 units were produced, and production supervisory salaries incurred were $28,000. A performance report for September would reflect a budget variance of

A. $350 favorable.

B. $350 unfavorable.

C. $1,000 unfavorable.

D. $1,000 favorable.

Answer (C) is correct. *(CMA, adapted)*

REQUIRED: The budget variance given budgeted and actual fixed costs and sales.

DISCUSSION: The budget (spending) variance for fixed O/H equals actual minus budgeted fixed O/H. The $324,000 cost of supervisory salaries is fixed and is incurred at $27,000 per month. Thus, the variance is the difference between actual costs of $28,000 and the budgeted costs of $27,000, or $1,000 unfavorable.

Answer (A) is incorrect. Supervisor salaries are expected to be incurred uniformly through the year; thus, supervisor salaries are based on time, not units produced. Answer (B) is incorrect. Supervisor salaries are expected to be incurred uniformly through the year; thus, supervisor salaries are based on time, not units produced. Answer (D) is incorrect. The actual O/H ($28,000) was greater than the budgeted O/H ($324,000 ÷ 12 months = $27,000); therefore, the variance is unfavorable.

7.4.33. The following information is available from the Tyro Company:

Actual manufacturing overhead	$15,000
Fixed overhead expenses, actual	$7,200
Fixed overhead expenses, budgeted	$7,000
Actual hours	3,500
Standard hours	3,800
Variable overhead rate per DLH	$2.50

Assuming that Tyro uses a three-way analysis of overhead variances, what is the spending variance?

A. $750 favorable.

B. $750 unfavorable.

C. $950 favorable.

D. $200 unfavorable.

Answer (A) is correct. *(CPA, adapted)*

REQUIRED: The spending variance assuming a three-way variance analysis.

DISCUSSION: The spending variance ($750 favorable) is the difference between the actual total manufacturing overhead ($15,000) and the budgeted amount for the actual input [$7,000 + (3,500 × $2.50) = $ 15,750].

Answer (B) is incorrect. The spending variance is favorable. Answer (C) is incorrect. The amount of $950 favorable is based on actual fixed overhead. Answer (D) is incorrect. The amount of $200 unfavorable is the fixed overhead spending (budget) variance.

7.5 Sales

7.5.1. The sales quantity variance is partly a function of the unit contribution margin (UCM). It equals

A. Actual units × (budgeted weighted-average UCM for planned mix – budgeted weighted-average UCM for actual mix).

B. (Actual units – master budget units) × budgeted weighted-average UCM for the planned mix.

C. Budgeted market share percentage × (actual market size in units – budgeted market size in units) × budgeted weighted-average UCM.

D. (Actual market share percentage-budgeted market share percentage) × actual market size in units × budgeted weighted-average UCM.

Answer (B) is correct. *(Publisher, adapted)*

REQUIRED: The definition of the sales quantity variance.

DISCUSSION: The sales volume variance equals the difference between the flexible budget contribution margin for the actual volume and that included in the master budget. Its components are the sales quantity and sales mix variances. The sales quantity variance focuses on the firm's aggregate results. It assumes a constant product mix and an average contribution margin for the composite unit. It equals the difference between actual and budgeted unit total sales, times the budgeted weighted-average UCM for the planned mix.

Answer (A) is incorrect. This equation defines the sales mix variance. Answer (C) is incorrect. This equation defines the market size variance. Answer (D) is incorrect. This equation defines the market share variance.

7.5.2. The sales volume variance is partly a function of the unit contribution margin (UCM). For a single-product company, it is

A. The difference between actual and master budget sales volume, times actual UCM.

B. The difference between flexible budget and actual sales volume, times master budget UCM.

C. The difference between flexible budget and master budget sales volume, times actual UCM.

D. The difference between flexible budget and master budget sales volume, times master budget UCM.

Answer (D) is correct. *(CIA, adapted)*

REQUIRED: The definition of sales volume variance.

DISCUSSION: For a single-product company, the sales volume variance is the difference between the actual and budgeted sales quantities times the budgeted UCM. If the company sells two or more products, the difference between the actual and budgeted product mixes must be considered. In that case, the sales volume variance equals the difference between (1) actual total unit sales times the budgeted weighted-average UCM for the actual mix and (2) budgeted total unit sales times the budgeted weighted-average UCM for the planned mix.

Answer (A) is incorrect. Budgeted, not actual, UCM is used to calculate this variance. Answer (B) is incorrect. The flexible budget volume is the actual volume, resulting in a zero variance. Answer (C) is incorrect. Budgeted, not actual, UCM is used to calculate this variance.

7.5.3. The sales mix variance is partly a function of the unit contribution margin (UCM). It equals

A. Actual units × (budgeted weighted-average UCM for planned mix – budgeted weighted-average UCM for actual mix).

B. (Actual units – master budget units) × budgeted weighted-average UCM for planned mix.

C. Budgeted market share percentage × (actual market size in units – budgeted market size in units) × budgeted weighted-average UCM.

D. (Actual market share percentage – budgeted market share percentage) × actual market size in units × budgeted weighted-average UCM.

Answer (A) is correct. *(Publisher, adapted)*

REQUIRED: The definition of the sales mix variance.

DISCUSSION: The sales mix variance may be viewed as a sum of variances. For each product in the mix, the difference between actual units sold and its budgeted percentage of the actual total unit sales is multiplied by the budgeted UCM for the product. The results are added to determine the mix variance. An alternative is to multiply total actual units sold by the difference between the budgeted weighted-average UCM for the planned mix and that for the actual mix.

Answer (B) is incorrect. This equation defines the sales quantity variance. Answer (C) is incorrect. This equation defines the market size variance. Answer (D) is incorrect. This equation defines the market share variance.

7.5.4. The market size variance is partly a function of the unit contribution margin (UCM). It equals

A. Actual units × (budgeted weighted-average UCM for planned mix – budgeted weighted-average UCM for actual mix).

B. (Actual units – master budget units) × budgeted weighted-average UCM for the planned mix.

C. Budgeted market share percentage × (actual market size in units – budgeted market size in units) × budgeted weighted-average UCM.

D. (Actual market share percentage – budgeted market share percentage) × actual market size in units × budgeted weighted-average UCM.

Answer (C) is correct. *(Publisher, adapted)*

REQUIRED: The definition of the market size variance.

DISCUSSION: The components of the sales quantity variance are the market size variance and the market share variance. The market size variance gives an indication of the change in contribution margin caused by a change in the market size. The market size and market share variances are relevant to industries in which total level of sales and market share are known, e.g., the automobile industry. The market size variance measures the effect of changes in an industry's sales on an individual company, and the market share variance analyzes the impact of a change in market share.

Answer (A) is incorrect. This equation defines the sales mix variance. Answer (B) is incorrect. This equation defines the sales quantity variance. Answer (D) is incorrect. This equation defines the market share variance.

7.5.5. In the budgeted profit-volume chart below, EG represents a two-product company's profit path. EH and HG represent the profit paths of products #1 and #2, respectively.

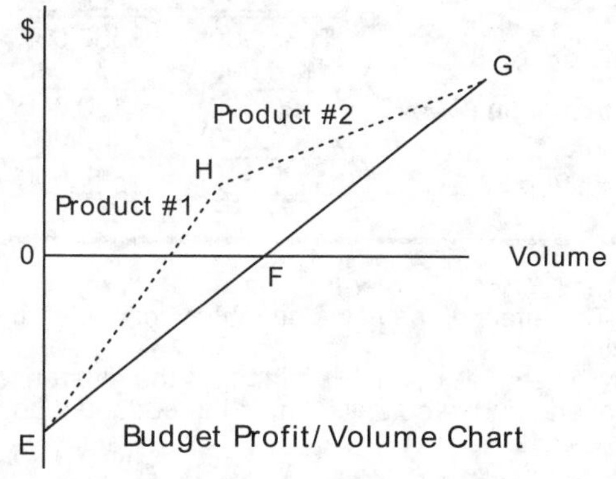

Sales prices and cost behavior were as budgeted, actual total sales equaled budgeted sales, and there were no inventories. Actual profit was greater than budgeted profit. Which product had actual sales in excess of budget, and what margin does OE divided by OF represent?

	Product with Excess Sales	OE ÷ OF
A.	#1	Contribution margin
B.	#1	Gross margin
C.	#2	Contribution margin
D.	#2	Gross margin

Answer (A) is correct. *(CPA, adapted)*

REQUIRED: The product with actual sales over budget and the significance of OE divided by OF.

DISCUSSION: Sales prices and total unit sales volume were as budgeted, costs expected to be fixed or variable behaved as anticipated, and no inventories existed. Thus, the excess of actual over budgeted profit must be attributable to a favorable sales mix, that is, to selling more units of the product with the higher UCM and fewer units of the product with the lower UCM. The profit path of product #1 has a steeper slope (contribution per unit of volume) than that for product #2. Consequently, product #1 had a higher UCM than product #2. Because a favorable sales mix variance arises from selling more of the product with the higher UCM, given that total unit sales equaled the budgeted amount, the sales of product #1 must have exceeded the budget.

Given that EG is the company's profit path, OE must represent the loss at zero sales volume. No variable costs are incurred at this volume, so OE must equal total fixed costs. OF is the unit sales volume at which no profit is earned or loss incurred (the breakeven point). At the breakeven point, the total contribution margin [(unit price – unit variable cost) × unit sales] equals the fixed costs. Accordingly, OE (fixed costs) divided by OF (unit sales) must equal the UCM.

Answer (B) is incorrect. OE divided by OF is the UCM. Answer (C) is incorrect. Product #1 had actual sales in excess of the budget. Answer (D) is incorrect. OE divided by OF is the UCM, and product #1 had actual sales in excess of the budget.

7.5.6. For a company that produces more than one product, the sales volume variance can be divided into which two of the following additional variances?

A. Sales price variance and flexible budget variance.

B. Sales mix variance and sales price variance.

C. Sales quantity variance and sales mix variance.

D. Sales mix variance and production volume variance.

Answer (C) is correct. *(CMA, adapted)*

REQUIRED: The components of the sales volume variance.

DISCUSSION: The sales volume variance can be divided into the sales quantity variance and the sales mix variance. The sales quantity variance is the change in contribution margin caused by the difference between actual and budgeted volume, assuming that budgeted sales mix, unit variable costs, and unit sales prices are constant. Thus, it equals the sales volume variance when the sales mix variance is zero. In a multiproduct firm, the sales mix variance is a variance caused by a sales mix that differs from that budgeted. For example, even when the sales quantity is exactly as budgeted, an unfavorable sales mix variance can be caused by greater sales of a low-contribution product at the expense of lower sales of a high-contribution product.

7.5.7. The market share variance is partly a function of the unit contribution margin (UCM). It equals

A. Actual units × (budgeted weighted-average UCM for planned mix – budgeted weighted-average UCM for actual mix).

B. (Actual units – master budget units) × budgeted weighted-average UCM for the planned mix.

C. Budgeted market share percentage × (actual market size in units – budgeted market size in units) × budgeted weighted-average UCM.

D. (Actual market share percentage – budgeted market share percentage) × actual market size in units × budgeted weighted-average UCM.

Answer (D) is correct. *(Publisher, adapted)*

REQUIRED: The definition of the market share variance.

DISCUSSION: The market share variance gives an indication of the amount of contribution margin gained (forgone) because of a change in the market share.

Answer (A) is incorrect. This equation defines the sales mix variance. Answer (B) is incorrect. This equation defines the sales quantity variance. Answer (C) is incorrect. This equation defines the market size variance.

Questions 7.5.8 through 7.5.12 are based on the following information.

Folsom Fashions sells a line of women's dresses. Folsom's performance report for November follows.

The company uses a flexible budget to analyze its performance and to measure the effect on operating income of the various factors affecting the difference between budgeted and actual operating income.

	Actual	Budget
Dresses sold	5,000	6,000
Sales	$235,000	$300,000
Variable costs	(145,000)	(180,000)
Contribution margin (CM)	90,000	120,000
Fixed costs	(84,000)	(80,000)
Operating income	$ 6,000	$ 40,000

7.5.8. The effect of the sales quantity variance on Folsom's contribution margin for November is

A. $30,000 unfavorable.

B. $18,000 unfavorable.

C. $20,000 unfavorable.

D. $15,000 unfavorable.

Answer (C) is correct. *(CMA, adapted)*

REQUIRED: The effect of the sales quantity variance on the contribution margin.

DISCUSSION: The sales quantity variance is the difference between the actual and budgeted units, times the budgeted unit CM.

$$(5{,}000 - 6{,}000) \times \frac{\$120{,}000}{6{,}000} = \$20{,}000 \text{ U}$$

Answer (A) is incorrect. The difference between the actual and budgeted contribution margins is $30,000. Answer (B) is incorrect. The difference between actual and budgeted unit sales times the actual unit CM equals $18,000. Answer (D) is incorrect. The sales price variance is $15,000.

7.5.9. What additional information is needed for Folsom to calculate the dollar impact of a change in market share on operating income for November?

A. Folsom's budgeted market share and the budgeted total market size.

B. Folsom's budgeted market share, the budgeted total market size, and average market selling price.

C. Folsom's budgeted market share and the actual total market size.

D. Folsom's actual market share and the actual total market size.

Answer (C) is correct. *(CMA, adapted)*

REQUIRED: The additional information necessary for a market share variance calculation.

DISCUSSION: A change in market share reflects a change in relative competitiveness. To isolate the effect on operating income of an increase or a decrease in market share, the company must know its budgeted and actual market shares, the actual size of the market for November, and the budgeted weighted-average unit contribution margin. Such computations may help Folsom to determine whether its decline in sales resulted from a loss of competitiveness or a shrinkage of the market.

Answer (A) is incorrect. Folsom needs to know the actual total market size. Answer (B) is incorrect. Folsom needs to know the actual total market size. Answer (D) is incorrect. Folsom needs to know the budgeted market share.

7.5.10. The retailer's sales price variance for November is

A. $30,000 unfavorable.

B. $18,000 unfavorable.

C. $20,000 unfavorable.

D. $15,000 unfavorable.

Answer (D) is correct. *(CMA, adapted)*

REQUIRED: The amount of the sales price variance for the month.

DISCUSSION: The sales price variance is the actual number of units sold (5,000), times the difference between budgeted selling price ($300,000 ÷ 6,000) and actual selling price ($235,000 ÷ 5,000).

$$(\$50 - \$47) \times 5{,}000 = \$15{,}000 \text{ U}$$

Answer (A) is incorrect. The difference between the actual and budgeted contribution margins is $30,000. Answer (B) is incorrect. The difference between actual and budgeted unit sales times the actual unit CM equals $18,000. Answer (C) is incorrect. The sales quantity variance is $20,000.

7.5.11. Folsom's variable cost flexible budget variance for November is

A. $5,000 favorable.

B. $5,000 unfavorable.

C. $4,000 favorable.

D. $4,000 unfavorable.

Answer (A) is correct. *(CMA, adapted)*

REQUIRED: The variable cost flexible budget variance.

DISCUSSION: The variable cost flexible budget variance is equal to the difference between actual variable costs and the product of the actual quantity sold and the budgeted unit variable cost ($180,000 ÷ 6,000 = $30).

($30 × 5,000) – $145,000 = $5,000 F

Answer (B) is incorrect. The variance is favorable. Answer (C) is incorrect. The amount of the fixed cost variance is $4,000. Answer (D) is incorrect. The amount of the fixed cost variance is $4,000.

7.5.12. Folsom's fixed cost variance for November is

A. $5,000 favorable.

B. $5,000 unfavorable.

C. $4,000 favorable.

D. $4,000 unfavorable.

Answer (D) is correct. *(CMA, adapted)*

REQUIRED: The fixed cost variance for the month.

DISCUSSION: The fixed cost variance equals the difference between actual fixed costs and budgeted fixed costs.

$84,000 – $80,000 = $4,000 U

Answer (A) is incorrect. The variable cost variance is $5,000. Answer (B) is incorrect. The variable cost variance is $5,000. Answer (C) is incorrect. The variance is unfavorable.

7.5.13. The gross profit of Reade Company for each of the years ended December 31, Year 9 and Year 8, was as follows:

	Year 9	Year 8
Sales	$792,000	$800,000
Cost of goods sold	(464,000)	(480,000)
Gross profit	$328,000	$320,000

Assuming that Year 9 selling prices were 10% lower, what was the decrease in gross profit caused by the change in selling prices?

A. $8,000

B. $72,000

C. $79,200

D. $88,000

Answer (D) is correct. *(CPA, adapted)*

REQUIRED: The change in gross profit given a reduction in selling price.

DISCUSSION: With a 10% decrease in prices in Year 9, that year's sales were 90% of the amount at Year 8 prices. Dividing Year 9 sales of $792,000 by 90% gives $880,000 of sales at Year 8 prices. Thus, sales and gross profit were $88,000 ($880,000 – $792,000) lower because of the 10% decrease in selling price.

Answer (A) is incorrect. The amount of $8,000 is the decrease in sales from the preceding year. Answer (B) is incorrect. The amount of $72,000 is the Year 8 sales multiplied by 90% and then by 10%. Answer (C) is incorrect. The amount of $79,200 is 10% of Year 9 sales.

7.5.14. Teezer Co. bundles three of its software products into a package that sells for $540. The following are the stand-alone unit selling prices and manufacturing costs and the rankings for incremental allocation purposes of the three products in the package:

	Price	Cost	Ranking for Incremental Allocation
Item A	$360	$60	1
Item B	$240	$48	2
Item C	$120	$24	3

What is the difference between the unit revenue allocated to Item B using the incremental method and the amount allocated using the stand-alone method based on unit selling prices?

A. $270

B. $180

C. $90

D. $0

Answer (D) is correct. *(Publisher, adapted)*

REQUIRED: The difference between the unit revenue allocated to Item B using the incremental method and the amount allocated using the stand-alone method based on unit selling prices.

DISCUSSION: Given that Item B is second in the revenue-allocation sequence, it will receive $180 ($540 unit price of the package – $360 unit price of the primary product) under the incremental method. It will also receive $180 {[$240 unit price of B ÷ ($360 + $240 + $120)] × $540} under the stand-alone method based on unit selling prices. Thus, the difference is $0 ($180 – $180).

Answer (A) is incorrect. The amount of $270 is allocated to A under the stand-alone method. Answer (B) is incorrect. The amount of $180 is allocated to B under either method. Answer (C) is incorrect. The amount of $90 is allocated to C under the stand-alone method. It is also the difference between the amounts allocated to C under the two methods. The incremental allocation to C is $0.

Questions 7.5.15 and 7.5.16 are based on the following information.

Clear Plus, Inc., manufactures and sells boxes of pocket protectors. The static master budget and the actual results for May appear in the opposite column.

	Actual	Static Budget
Unit sales	12,000	10,000
Sales	$132,000	$100,000
Variable costs of sales	(70,800)	(60,000)
Contribution margin	61,200	40,000
Fixed costs	(32,000)	(30,000)
Operating income	$ 29,200	$ 10,000

7.5.15. The operating income for Clear Plus using a flexible budget for May is

A. $12,000

B. $19,200

C. $30,000

D. $18,000

Answer (D) is correct. *(CMA, adapted)*

REQUIRED: The flexible budget operating income.

DISCUSSION: A flexible budget is prepared after the budget period has ended and actual sales and costs are known. Assuming that unit sales price ($100,000 ÷ 10,000 units = $10), variable costs of sales ($60,000 ÷ 10,000 unit = $6), and total fixed costs ($30,000) do not change, a flexible budget may be prepared for the actual sales level (12,000 units). Hence, the budgeted contribution margin (sales – variable costs of sales) equals $48,000 [(12,000 units × $10) – (12,000 units × $6)]. The operating income is therefore $18,000 ($48,000 CM – $30,000 FC).

Answer (A) is incorrect. Assuming that all costs are variable results in $12,000. Answer (B) is incorrect. The amount of $19,200 is based on actual variable costs. Answer (C) is incorrect. The amount of $30,000 is based on actual sales revenues.

7.5.16. Which one of the following statements concerning Clear Plus's actual results for May is correct?

A. The flexible budget variance is $8,000 favorable.

B. The sales price variance is $32,000 favorable.

C. The sales volume variance is $8,000 favorable.

D. The flexible budget variable cost variance is $10,800 unfavorable.

Answer (C) is correct. *(CMA, adapted)*

REQUIRED: The true statement about the actual results.

DISCUSSION: The sales volume variance is the change in contribution margin caused by the difference between the actual and budgeted volume. It equals the budgeted unit contribution margin times the difference between actual and expected volume, or $8,000 [(12,000 – 10,000) × ($10 – $6)]. The sales volume variance is favorable because actual sales exceeded budgeted sales.

Answer (A) is incorrect. The flexible budget variance is $11,200 favorable ($29,200 actual operating income – $18,000 flexible budget operating income). Answer (B) is incorrect. The sales price variance is $12,000 [$132,000 actual sales – (12,000 units sold × $10)]. Answer (D) is incorrect. The total projected variable costs at the actual sales level equal $72,000 (12,000 units × $6). Thus, the variable cost variance is $1,200 favorable ($72,000 – $70,800 actual).

7.5.17. Actual and budgeted information about the sales of a product are presented for June as follows.

	Actual	Budget
Units	8,000	10,000
Sales revenue	$92,000	$105,000

The sales price variance for June was

A. $8,000 favorable.

B. $10,000 favorable.

C. $10,000 unfavorable.

D. $10,500 unfavorable.

Answer (A) is correct. *(CIA, adapted)*

REQUIRED: The sales price variance for the month.

DISCUSSION: The sales price variance is the difference between actual price and budgeted price, times actual units. Actual price was $11.50 ($92,000 ÷ 8,000). Budgeted price was $10.50 ($105,000 ÷ 10,000). Sales price variance is therefore $8,000 [8,000 actual units × ($11.50 – $10.50)]. The variance is favorable because actual sales price was greater than budgeted sales price.

Answer (B) is incorrect. The sales price variance is based on the actual units sold rather than the budgeted sales. Answer (C) is incorrect. The sales price variance is the difference between the $11.50 actual sales price ($92,000 ÷ 8,000) and the $10.50 budgeted sales price ($105,000 ÷ 10,000), times the 8,000 units sold. Answer (D) is incorrect. The sales price variance is the difference between the $11.50 actual sales price ($92,000 ÷ 8,000) and the $10.50 budgeted sales price ($105,000 ÷ 10,000), times the 8,000 units sold.

Questions 7.5.18 through 7.5.20 are based on the following information. The following are the relevant data for calculating sales variances for Fortuna Co., which sells its sole product in two countries:

	Gallia	Helvetica	Total
Budgeted selling price per unit	$6.00	$10.00	NA
Budgeted variable cost per unit	(3.00)	(7.50)	NA
Budgeted contribution margin per unit	$3.00	$ 2.50	NA
Budgeted unit sales	300	200	500
Budgeted mix percentage	60%	40%	100%
Actual units sold	260	260	520
Actual selling price per unit	$6.00	$ 9.50	NA

7.5.18. The sales volume variance for the two countries is

A. $130 U.

B. $120 U.

C. $30 F.

D. $150 U.

Answer (C) is correct. *(Publisher, adapted)*

REQUIRED: The sales volume variance for sales in multiple countries.

DISCUSSION: The sales volume variance in Gallia is $120 U [$3.00 budgeted UCM × (260 actual units sold – 300 budgeted unit sales)]. The sales volume variance in Helvetica is $150 F [$2.50 budgeted UCM × (260 actual units sold – 200 budgeted unit sales)]. Thus, the two-country sales volume variance is $30 F ($150 F – $120 U).

Answer (A) is incorrect. The two-country sales price variance is $130 U. Answer (B) is incorrect. The sales volume variance for sales in Gallia is $120 U. Answer (D) is incorrect. The sales volume variance for sales in Helvetica is $150 F.

7.5.19. The sales quantity variance for the two countries is

A. $156 U.

B. $30 F.

C. $56 F.

D. $100 F.

Answer (C) is correct. *(Publisher, adapted)*

REQUIRED: The sales quantity variance for sales in multiple countries.

DISCUSSION: The sales quantity variance in Gallia is $36 F {[(520 actual total units sold × .6 budgeted percentage) – 300 budgeted unit sales] × $3 budgeted UCM}. The sales quantity variance in Helvetica is $20 F {[(520 actual total units sold × .4 budgeted percentage) – 200 budgeted unit sales] × $2.50 budgeted UCM}. Thus, the multiple-country sales quantity variance is $56 F ($36 F + $20 F).

Answer (A) is incorrect. The sales mix variance in Gallia is $156 U. Answer (B) is incorrect. The two-country sales volume variance is $30 F. Answer (D) is incorrect. The combined sales price and sales volume variance is $100 F.

7.5.20. The sales mix variance for the two countries is

A. $156 U.

B. $26 U.

C. $56 F.

D. $150 F.

Answer (B) is correct. *(Publisher, adapted)*

REQUIRED: The sales mix variance for sales in multiple countries.

DISCUSSION: The sales mix variance in Gallia is $156 U {[260 actual units sold – (520 actual total units sold × .6 budgeted percentage)] × $3 budgeted UCM}. The sales mix variance in Helvetica is $130 F {[260 actual units sold – (520 actual total units sold × .4 budgeted percentage)] × $2.50 budgeted UCM}. Thus, the multiple-country sales mix variance is $26 U ($156 U – $130 F).

Answer (A) is incorrect. The sales mix variance in Gallia is $156 U. Answer (C) is incorrect. The two-country sales quantity variance is $56 F. Answer (D) is incorrect. The sales volume variance in Helvetica is $150 F.

7.5.21. The variance that arises solely because the quantity actually sold differs from the quantity budgeted to be sold is

A. Static budget variance.

B. Master budget increment.

C. Sales mix variance.

D. Sales volume variance.

Answer (D) is correct. *(CMA, adapted)*

REQUIRED: The variance that arises solely when actual sales differ from budgeted sales.

DISCUSSION: If a firm's sales differ from the amount budgeted, the difference could be attributable either to the sales price variance or the sales volume variance. The sales volume variance is the change in contribution margin caused by the difference between the actual and budgeted sales volumes.

Answer (A) is incorrect. A static budget variance is the difference between actual costs or revenues and those budgeted on a static budget. Answer (B) is incorrect. A master budget increment is an increase in a budgeted figure on the firm's master budget. Answer (C) is incorrect. The sales mix variance is caused when a company's actual sales mix is different from the budgeted sales mix.

7.5.22. The following exhibit reflects a summary of performance for a single item of a retail store's inventory for April.

	Actual Results	Flexible Budget Variances	Flexible Budget	Static (Master) Budget
Sales (units)	11,000	--	11,000	12,000
Revenue (sales)	$208,000	$12,000 U	$220,000	$240,000
Variable costs	121,000	11,000 U	110,000	120,000
Contribution margin	$ 87,000	$23,000 U	$110,000	$120,000
Fixed costs	72,000	--	72,000	72,000
Operating income	$ 15,000	$23,000 U	$ 38,000	$ 48,000

The sales volume variance is

A. $1,000 F.

B. $10,000 U.

C. $11,000 F.

D. $12,000 U.

Answer (B) is correct. *(CIA, adapted)*

REQUIRED: The sales volume variance.

DISCUSSION: The sales volume variance is the difference between the flexible budget contribution margin and the static (master) budget contribution margin. Its components are the sales quantity and sales mix variances. The contribution margin is used rather than operating income because fixed costs are the same in both budgets. Unit sales price and variable cost are held constant so as to isolate the effect of the difference in unit sales volume. Because the flexible budget contribution margin ($110,000) is less than the master budget amount ($120,000), the variance ($10,000) is unfavorable.

Answer (A) is incorrect. The sales volume variance is the difference between the flexible budget contribution margin ($110,000) and the master budget amount ($120,000). The $10,000 variance is unfavorable because the flexible budget amount is less than the master budget contribution margin. Answer (C) is incorrect. The difference between actual and flexible variable costs is $11,000. The sales volume variance is the difference between the flexible budget contribution margin ($110,000) and the master budget amount ($120,000). The $10,000 variance is unfavorable because the flexible budget amount is less than the master budget contribution margin. Answer (D) is incorrect. The difference between the flexible budget revenue ($220,000) and the actual revenue ($208,000) is $12,000. The sales volume variance is measured as the difference between the flexible budget contribution margin and the master budget contribution margin.

7.6 Variances in the Ledger Accounts

7.6.1. How should a usage variance that is significant in amount be treated at the end of an accounting period?

A. Reported as a deferred charge or credit.

B. Allocated among work-in-process inventory, finished goods inventory, and cost of goods sold.

C. Charged or credited to cost of goods manufactured.

D. Allocated among cost of goods manufactured, finished goods inventory, and cost of goods sold.

Answer (B) is correct. *(CPA, adapted)*

REQUIRED: The treatment of a usage variance at the end of a period.

DISCUSSION: Allocating a variance among work-in-process, finished goods, and cost of goods sold properly matches the variance with the items produced. This procedure adjusts the respective accounts, which are expressed in terms of standard costs, to actual costs.

Answer (A) is incorrect. Some of the variance should be allocated to cost of goods sold. Answer (C) is incorrect. The cost of goods manufactured is the cost of the goods transferred from WIP to finished goods, not a balance at year end. Answer (D) is incorrect. The cost of goods manufactured is the cost of the goods transferred from WIP to finished goods, not a balance at year end.

Questions 7.6.2 through 7.6.4 are based on the following information. Alpha Company paid janitors $5 per hour to clean the production area. It initially set the standard cost of janitorial work at $4.50 per hour, and 530 hours were worked by the janitors.

7.6.2. What is the proper journal entry to account for this expense for the month of June if 530 hours were worked by the janitors?

A. Salaries expense	$2,650	
Payroll		$2,650
B. Variable overhead control	$2,650	
Variable overhead		
Variable overhead applied		$2,650
C. Variable overhead control	$2,650	
Payroll payable		$2,650
D. Variable overhead applied	$2,650	
Payroll payable		$2,650

Answer (C) is correct. *(Publisher, adapted)*

REQUIRED: The journal entry to record the actual variable overhead incurred.

DISCUSSION: The entry to record actual variable overhead incurred ($5 × 530 hours = $2,650) is to debit the variable overhead control account. A corresponding credit is made to accounts payable or any other appropriate account.

Answer (A) is incorrect. Actual indirect production costs are debited to overhead control. Answer (B) is incorrect. Overhead application is usually based on standard rates and a given activity base, not amounts actually incurred. Overhead is applied by crediting overhead control (or a separate applied overhead account) and debiting WIP. Answer (D) is incorrect. Variable overhead is debited to variable overhead control, not variable overhead applied.

7.6.3. What is the appropriate entry to record the application of the 530 hours worked by the janitors?

A. Work-in-process	$2,385	
Variable overhead applied		$2,385
B. Work-in-process	$2,385	
Variable overhead control		$2,385
C. Variable overhead control	$ 265	
Work-in-process	2,385	
Variable overhead applied		$2,650
D. Cost of goods sold	$2,385	
Variable overhead applied		$2,385

Answer (A) is correct. *(Publisher, adapted)*

REQUIRED: The journal entry to record the application of variable overhead.

DISCUSSION: The entry to record the application of variable overhead is to debit the WIP account and enter a corresponding credit to the variable overhead applied account for the amount of overhead computed using the predetermined overhead rate (530 × $4.50 = $2,385).

Answer (B) is incorrect. Overhead control is debited for overhead incurred. Answer (C) is incorrect. The overhead application is at $4.50, not $5.00, per hour. Answer (D) is incorrect. The goods to which these costs apply are in process.

7.6.4. What entry accounts for the recognition of the variance that occurred? Assume that this was the only variable overhead variance.

A. Variable overhead applied	$2,650	
Variance summary		$ 265
Variable overhead control		2,385
B. Variable overhead applied	$2,385	
Variable overhead spending variance	265	
Variable overhead control		$2,650
C. Variable overhead applied	$2,385	
Variable overhead efficiency variance	265	
Variable overhead control		$2,650
D. Variable overhead control	$2,385	
Variable spending variance	265	
Variable overhead applied		$2,650

Answer (B) is correct. *(Publisher, adapted)*

REQUIRED: The journal entry to record the isolation of the variance.

DISCUSSION: The spending variance is recognized by a debit, given that more was spent for that activity than was estimated. The entry to record the unfavorable variable overhead spending variance is to debit the variable overhead spending variance account for the appropriate amount. The variable overhead applied account is debited for its balance. The variable overhead control account is credited for its balance. These entries result in a zero balance in both the applied and the control accounts assuming no variable overhead efficiency variance.

Answer (A) is incorrect. The variance is a debit to a spending variance account, not a credit to a variance summary. Answer (C) is incorrect. The variance is a spending variance resulting from the excess of an actual cost over a standard cost, not an efficiency variance. Answer (D) is incorrect. Variable overhead applied is debited and variable overhead control is credited to close out the accounts.

7.6.5. To adjust finished goods inventory for external reporting purposes to reflect the difference between direct costing and absorption costing, which of the following journal entries may be made?

A. Finished goods inventory adjustment account	XXX	
Fixed overhead		XXX
B. Work-in-process	XXX	
Fixed overhead		XXX
C. Fixed overhead	XXX	
Work-in-process		XXX
D. Finished goods	XXX	
Work-in-process		XXX

Answer (A) is correct. *(Publisher, adapted)*

REQUIRED: The entry to adjust finished goods inventory for external reporting purposes.

DISCUSSION: The journal entry to record the adjustment of FG inventory for external reporting purposes is to debit the FG inventory adjustment account for the desired amount and to credit fixed overhead. To avoid alteration of the inventory accounts, the adjustment is taken to an adjustment account.

Answer (B) is incorrect. The entry is an adjustment to WIP. Answer (C) is incorrect. Costs are not transferred from WIP to overhead. Answer (D) is incorrect. The entry represents the transfer of completed units to FG.

7.6.6. Company Z uses a standard cost system that carries materials at actual price until they are transferred to the WIP account. In project A, 500 units of X were used at a cost of $10 per unit. Standards require 450 units to complete this project. The standard price is established at $9 per unit. What is the proper journal entry?

A. Work-in-process	$4,950	
DM price variance	500	
DM efficiency variance		$ 450
Inventory		5,000
B. Work-in-process	$5,950	
DM price variance		$ 500
DM efficiency variance		450
Inventory		5,000
C. Work-in-process	$4,050	
DM price variance	500	
DM efficiency variance	450	
Inventory		$5,000
D. Work-in-process	$5,000	
Inventory		$5,000

Answer (C) is correct. *(Publisher, adapted)*

REQUIRED: The journal entry to record direct materials issued and related variances.

DISCUSSION: The entry to record direct materials used is to debit WIP at standard prices and standard quantities (450 units × $9 = $4,050). In this question, all direct materials variances are recorded at the time WIP is charged. The materials price variance and the materials efficiency variance must be calculated. The project used more units at a higher price than estimated, so both variances are unfavorable (debits). The materials efficiency variance is $450 U [(500 – 450) × $9]. The materials price variance is $500 U [500 units × ($10 – $9)]. Inventory is credited for the actual prices and actual quantities (500 × $10 = $5,000).

Answer (A) is incorrect. The unfavorable DM efficiency variance should be a debit. Answer (B) is incorrect. The unfavorable DM price and efficiency variances should be debits. Answer (D) is incorrect. The entry fails to record the variances.

7.6.7. Given a favorable variable overhead efficiency variance of $1,600 and an unfavorable spending variance of $265, what is the closing entry?

A. Income summary	$1,335	
VOH spending variance	265	
VOH efficiency variance		$1,600
B. Variance summary	$1,865	
Cost of goods sold		$1,865
C. VOH efficiency variance	$1,600	
VOH spending variance		$ 265
Income summary		1,335
D. VOH efficiency variance	$1,600	
VOH spending variance	265	
Income summary		$1,865

Answer (C) is correct. *(Publisher, adapted)*

REQUIRED: The journal entry to close an unfavorable variable overhead spending variance and a favorable variable overhead efficiency variance.

DISCUSSION: The entry to record the closing of an unfavorable variable overhead spending variance and a favorable variable overhead efficiency variance is to debit the second and credit the first. A favorable net variance of $1,335 is the result ($1,600 F – $265 U = $1,335 F). The net favorable variance is credited to income summary (or allocated among COGS and the inventories).

Answer (A) is incorrect. The net variance is favorable and should be credited to income summary. Answer (B) is incorrect. The entry does not close the variance accounts. Moreover, the net variance is $1,335. Answer (D) is incorrect. The spending variance is unfavorable and was initially debited. Closing the account therefore requires a credit.

7.6.8. Omega Company would have applied $31,500 of fixed manufacturing overhead if capacity usage had equaled the master budget. Given that 2,000 standard hours were allowed for the actual output, that actual fixed manufacturing overhead equaled the budgeted amount, and that overhead was applied at a rate of $15 per hour, what is the entry to close the fixed manufacturing overhead accounts?

A.

Fixed overhead control	$30,000	
Production volume variance	1,500	
Fixed overhead applied		$31,500

B.

Cost of goods sold	$31,500	
Fixed overhead control		$31,500

C.

Work-in-process	$30,000	
Overhead price variance	1,500	
Fixed overhead applied		$31,500

D.

Fixed overhead applied	$30,000	
Production volume variance	1,500	
Fixed overhead control		$31,500

Answer (D) is correct. *(Publisher, adapted)*

REQUIRED: The year-end journal entry to close the fixed overhead accounts.

DISCUSSION: The entry is to debit fixed overhead applied and credit fixed overhead control for their respective balances. The difference is attributable solely to the production volume variance because the spending variance is zero (actual fixed manufacturing overhead = the budgeted amount). The volume variance is unfavorable because fixed overhead is underapplied. The underapplication (the unfavorable volume variance debited) is $1,500 [$31,500 budgeted fixed manufacturing overhead – (2,000 hours × $15 per hour)].

Answer (A) is incorrect. The normal balances in the overhead applied and overhead control accounts are a credit and a debit, respectively. Thus, the closing entries must be the reverse. Answer (B) is incorrect. The fixed overhead applied account must be closed with a debit entry. Answer (C) is incorrect. The entry does not close the overhead accounts.

7.6.9. If a project required 50 hours to complete at a cost of $10 per hour but should have taken only 45 hours at a cost of $12 per hour, what is the proper entry to record the costs?

A.

Work-in-process	$540	
DL efficiency variance	60	
DL price variance		$100
Accrued payroll		500

B.

Wage expense	$440	
DL efficiency variance	60	
Accrued payroll		$500

C.

Work-in-process	$460	
DL price variance	100	
DL efficiency variance		$ 60
Accrued payroll		500

D.

Work-in-process	$500	
Accrued payroll		$500

Answer (A) is correct. *(Publisher, adapted)*

REQUIRED: The journal entry to record accrued payroll and labor cost variances.

DISCUSSION: The entry to record accrued payroll is to debit WIP at the standard wage rate times the standard number of hours and to credit accrued payroll for the actual payroll dollar amount. The project required more hours but a lower wage rate than estimated. Thus, the labor efficiency variance is unfavorable (a debit), and the labor price variance is favorable (a credit).

Labor eff. var. (50 – 45)	× $12	=	$ 60 U
Labor price var. ($12 – $10)	× 50	=	$100 F

Answer (B) is incorrect. The entry omits the price variance and fails to inventory the labor costs. Answer (C) is incorrect. The entry is appropriate if the hourly rate is greater than estimated, but hours worked were less. Answer (D) is incorrect. The labor variances must be recognized.

7.6.10. What is the normal year-end treatment of immaterial variances recognized in a cost accounting system using standard costs?

A. Reclassified to deferred charges until all related production is sold.

B. Allocated among cost of goods manufactured and ending work-in-process inventory.

C. Closed to cost of goods sold in the period in which they arose.

D. Capitalized as a cost of ending finished goods inventory.

Answer (C) is correct. *(CPA, adapted)*

REQUIRED: The normal year-end treatment of immaterial variances accumulated in a standard cost system.

DISCUSSION: Normally, all immaterial variances are closed to COGS in the period in which they arose. This process is simpler than allocating the variance among the inventories and COGS.

Answer (A) is incorrect. Immaterial variances cannot be said to provide future benefit. Answer (B) is incorrect. If allocated, the allocation should be to EWIP, FG inventory, and COGS in proportion to the relative flow of goods. However, for cost-benefit reasons, only material variances are usually allocated in this manner. Answer (D) is incorrect. Immaterial variances should be closed to cost of goods sold, not capitalized, in the period in which they arose.

7.6.11. Assume price variances are recorded at the time of purchase. What is the journal entry to record a direct materials price variance if materials are purchased at $5 per unit for $650 and their standard price is $4 per unit?

A. Inventory	$650	
Accounts payable		$650
B. Inventory	$520	
DM price variance	130	
Accounts payable		$650
C. Inventory	$520	
Work-in-process	130	
Cash		$650
D. Finished goods	$520	
DM price variance	130	
Cash		$650

Answer (B) is correct. *(Publisher, adapted)*

REQUIRED: The journal entry to record a direct materials price variance at the time of purchase.

DISCUSSION: The entry at the time of purchase is to debit inventory for $520, which is the actual quantity purchased ($650 ÷ $5 per unit = 130 units) times the standard unit price ($4). Accounts payable is credited for $650 (actual quantity × actual price). The difference between the actual and standard prices is the price variance. Because the actual price exceeded the standard, the price variance is debited for the difference. The price variance is $130 [130 units × ($5 – $4)] unfavorable.

Answer (A) is incorrect. The entry assumes the price variance is not recorded at time of purchase. Answer (C) is incorrect. The variance should be charged to a separate account, not WIP. Answer (D) is incorrect. Materials should be debited to inventory.

7.6.12. Assume price variances are recorded at the time of purchase. Materials are purchased at $5 per unit for $650, and their standard price is $4 per unit. What is the journal entry if all materials purchased were used to complete a project that should normally require 100 units?

A. Work-in-process	$650	
DM price variance		$130
Inventory		520
B. Work-in-process	$520	
DM price variance	130	
Inventory		$650
C. DM efficiency variance	$130	
Work-in-process	520	
Inventory		$650
D. Work-in-process	$400	
DM efficiency variance	120	
Inventory		$520

Answer (D) is correct. *(Publisher, adapted)*

REQUIRED: The journal entry to record the direct materials used.

DISCUSSION: The entry to record direct materials used is to debit WIP for the standard quantity requisitioned times the standard unit price (100 units × $4/unit = $400). The actual quantity purchased is 130 units ($650 ÷ 5). Inventory is credited for the actual quantity requisitioned times the standard unit price, or $520 (130 × $4). When actual quantity used exceeds standard quantity allowed, an unfavorable direct materials efficiency variance results. The variance account should be debited for the $120 difference (30 extra units × $4 standard unit cost).

Answer (A) is incorrect. An efficiency (not price) variance should be debited (not credited). Answer (B) is incorrect. The entry records an unfavorable price, not quantity, variance. Answer (C) is incorrect. The entry confuses the amounts of the price and efficiency variances.

7.6.13. Which of the following is not an acceptable treatment of manufacturing overhead variances at an interim reporting date?

A. Apportion the total only among work-in-process and finished goods inventories on hand at the end of the interim reporting period.

B. Apportion the total only between that part of the current period's production remaining in inventories at the end of the period and that part sold during the period.

C. Carry forward the total to be offset by opposite balances in later periods.

D. Charge or credit the total to the cost of goods sold during the period.

Answer (A) is correct. *(CPA, adapted)*

REQUIRED: The unacceptable treatment of manufacturing overhead variances at an interim reporting date.

DISCUSSION: Overhead variances may be deferred, debited or credited to COGS, or apportioned among inventories and COGS. To apportion the total only between WIP and FG would not allocate a proper proportion to COGS.

Answer (B) is incorrect. Allocating the variance among COGS and inventories is the usual process for material variances. Answer (C) is incorrect. Purchase price variances or volume or capacity variances that are planned and expected to be absorbed by the end of the annual period ordinarily should be deferred at interim reporting dates. Answer (D) is incorrect. Charging or crediting the variance to COGS is appropriate when the variance is immaterial.

7.6.14. If a manufacturing overhead volume variance exists at an interim reporting date, what is an appropriate treatment?

A. Allocate the variance to work-in-process and finished goods inventories.

B. Allocate the variance to that part of the current period's production remaining in inventories at the end of the period and the deferred variance account.

C. Carry forward the variance as a deferred charge or credit.

D. Charge or credit the variance to the cost of goods completed this period.

Answer (C) is correct. *(Publisher, adapted)*

REQUIRED: The treatment of a manufacturing overhead volume variance at an interim date.

DISCUSSION: Purchase price variances or volume or capacity variances that are planned and expected to be absorbed by the end of the annual period should ordinarily be deferred at interim reporting dates.

Answer (A) is incorrect. An allocation should include COGS. Answer (B) is incorrect. An allocation should include COGS. Answer (D) is incorrect. Charging or crediting the variance to COGS is appropriate when the variance is immaterial.

7.7 Productivity Measures

7.7.1. Productivity is defined as the ratio of outputs of a production process to the inputs that are used. Consider a process that currently produces 2,000 units of output with 500 hours of labor per day. This process can be redesigned to produce 2,520 units of output requiring 600 labor hours per day. The percentage change in productivity from redesigning the process is

A. 5%

B. 10%

C. 20%

D. 26%

Answer (A) is correct. *(CIA, adapted)*

REQUIRED: The percentage change in productivity after a process change.

DISCUSSION: Before redesign, productivity equaled 4 units per hour (2,000 units ÷ 500 hours). After redesign, productivity equaled 4.2 units per hour (2,520 units ÷ 600 hours). Thus, the percentage change in productivity was 5% [(4.2 – 4.0) ÷ 4.0].

Answer (B) is incorrect. A 10% change requires output of 2,640 units. Answer (C) is incorrect. The percentage of 20 is the percentage change in labor hours per day. Answer (D) is incorrect. The percentage of 26 is the percentage change in units of output per day.

7.7.2. A manufacturing cell's partial productivity can be measured using data on

A. Inventory shrinkage.

B. Inventory turnover.

C. Direct materials usage.

D. Scrap.

Answer (C) is correct. *(CIA, adapted)*

REQUIRED: The data used in measuring a manufacturing cell's partial productivity.

DISCUSSION: A partial productivity measure may be stated as the ratio of output to the quantity of a single factor of production (e.g., materials, labor, or capital). Partial productivity measures, for example, the number of finished units per direct labor hour or per pound of direct materials, are useful when compared over time among different factories or with benchmarks. A partial productivity measure comparing results over time determines whether the actual relationship between inputs and outputs has improved or deteriorated.

Answer (A) is incorrect. Inventory shrinkage measures the effectiveness of internal control. Answer (B) is incorrect. Inventory turnover measures the efficiency of asset usage. Answer (D) is incorrect. Scrap is neither an input nor a good output.

Questions 7.7.3 and 7.7.4 are based on the following information. Fabro, Inc., produced 1,500 units of Product RX-6 last week. The inputs to the production process for Product RX-6 were:

- 450 pounds of Material A at a cost of $1.50 per pound
- 300 pounds of Material Z at a cost of $2.75 per pound
- 300 labor hours at a cost of $15.00 per hour

7.7.3. What is the total factor productivity for Product RX-6?

A. 2.00 units per pound.

B. 5.00 units per hour.

C. 0.25 units per dollar input.

D. 0.33 units per dollar input.

Answer (C) is correct. *(CMA, adapted)*

REQUIRED: The total factor productivity.

DISCUSSION: Total factor productivity equals units of output divided by the cost of all inputs. It varies with output levels, input prices, input quantities, and input mix. Thus, the total factor productivity equals 0.25 units per dollar input {1,500 units ÷ [(450 pounds of A × $1.50) + (300 pounds of Z × $2.75) + (300 hours × $15)]}.

Answer (A) is incorrect. The total factor productivity is measured in units of output per dollar of input. Answer (B) is incorrect. The total factor productivity is measured in units of output per dollar of input. Answer (D) is incorrect. This answer is based only on labor costs. All input costs should be included.

7.7.4. What is the best productivity measure for the first-line supervisor in Fabro, Inc.'s production plant?

A. 5.00 units per labor hour.

B. $2.00 per pound.

C. 0.33 units per dollar input.

D. $15.00 per labor hour.

Answer (A) is correct. *(CMA, adapted)*

REQUIRED: The best productivity measure for the first-line supervisor in the production plant.

DISCUSSION: A first-line supervisor's primary job is employee supervision, so his or her productivity should be measured on the basis of output per labor hour. Thus, 5 units per labor hour expended (1,500 units ÷ 300 labor hours) measures productivity based on the factor over which the first-line supervisor has the most control.

Answer (B) is incorrect. A first-line supervisor normally does not control the price paid for either materials or labor. Answer (C) is incorrect. The first-line supervisor does not control the prices paid for materials or labor. Accordingly, output per dollar of input is not a meaningful measure. Answer (D) is incorrect. A first-line supervisor normally does not control the price paid for either materials or labor.

STUDY UNIT EIGHT
NONROUTINE DECISIONS

Nonroutine decisions often are made using **incremental** (differential or marginal) analysis. The quantitative analysis emphasizes the ways in which costs and benefits vary with the option chosen. Thus, the focus is on **relevant costs**. Incremental costing is used to make decisions about (1) whether to accept a special order, (2) whether to make or buy a product, (3) pricing, (4) choosing a product mix, (5) adding or dropping product lines, (6) selling or processing units further, (7) acquiring or disposing of an organizational segment, or (8) selecting a market channel. Incremental cost analysis requires caution. Many nonquantitative factors must be considered, including whether (1) special price concessions violate price discrimination statutes, (2) government contract pricing regulations apply, (3) sales to a special customer affect sales in the firm's regular market, (4) regular customers will learn of a special price and demand equal terms, and (5) sales in other product lines will decline because a product line was discontinued.

Certain cost terms are common in decision analysis. An **avoidable** cost can be saved by not selecting an option. An **imputed** cost requires no dollar outlay and is not recognized in the accounting records. But it must be considered in an investment decision because it is an economic cost. An **opportunity** cost is imputed. It is the benefit forgone by not selecting the next best use of scarce resources. A **postponable** cost may be delayed with little effect on current operations. Routine maintenance is an example. A **relevant** cost should be considered because it is a future cost that varies with the option chosen. A **sunk** cost cannot be avoided because the expenditure has occurred or an irrevocable decision to incur the cost has been made. Sunk costs are irrelevant because they do not vary with the option selected.

QUESTIONS

8.1 Basic Concepts

8.1.1. Which one of the following is most relevant to a manufacturing equipment replacement decision?

A. Original cost of the old equipment.

B. Disposal price of the old equipment.

C. Gain or loss on the disposal of the old equipment.

D. A lump-sum write-off amount from the disposal of the old equipment.

Answer (B) is correct. *(CMA, adapted)*

REQUIRED: The item most relevant to a manufacturing equipment replacement decision.

DISCUSSION: Management decision analysis is based on the concept of relevant costs. Relevant costs differ among decision choices. Thus, incremental or differential costs are always relevant. Because they were incurred in the past, historical costs, such as the original cost of the equipment, are not relevant. Similarly, any gain or loss on the old equipment is not relevant because this amount is based on the historical cost. However, the disposal price of the old equipment is relevant because it involves a future cash inflow that will not occur unless the equipment is disposed of.

Answer (A) is incorrect. The original cost of the old equipment is a sunk cost with no relevance to future decision making. Answer (C) is incorrect. Gain or loss is based on historical cost, which is a sunk cost. Answer (D) is incorrect. A lump-sum write-off of a sunk cost is not relevant to a future decision.

8.1.2. Relevant or differential cost analysis

A. Takes all variable and fixed costs into account to analyze decision alternatives.

B. Considers only variable costs as they change with each decision alternative.

C. Considers the change in reported net income for each alternative to arrive at the optimum decision for the company.

D. Considers all variable and fixed costs as they change with each decision alternative.

Answer (D) is correct. *(CMA, adapted)*

REQUIRED: The true statement about relevant or differential cost analysis.

DISCUSSION: Relevant cost analysis considers only those costs that differ among decision options. Both fixed and variable costs are considered if they vary with the option selected.

Answer (A) is incorrect. All costs are not considered. Answer (B) is incorrect. Fixed costs also are considered if they differ among options. Answer (C) is incorrect. Cost differences are evaluated.

8.1.3. The relevance of a particular cost to a decision is determined by the

A. Size of the cost.

B. Riskiness of the decision.

C. Potential effect on the decision.

D. Accuracy and verifiability of the cost.

Answer (C) is correct. *(CMA, adapted)*

REQUIRED: The factor that determines whether a cost is relevant to a particular decision.

DISCUSSION: Managerial decisions should be based on the relevant revenues and costs. A particular cost or revenue is relevant if it varies with the option chosen. Thus, a relevant cost or revenue can affect the decision made.

Answer (A) is incorrect. The size of the cost is irrelevant if the cost does not affect the decision process. Answer (B) is incorrect. The riskiness of the decision is irrelevant if the cost does not affect the decision process. Answer (D) is incorrect. Some estimate must be considered regardless of its accuracy and verifiability.

8.1.4. The term that refers to costs incurred in the past that are not relevant to a future decision is

A. Discretionary cost.

B. Full absorption cost.

C. Underallocated indirect cost.

D. Sunk cost.

Answer (D) is correct. *(CMA, adapted)*

REQUIRED: The past costs not relevant to a future decision.

DISCUSSION: A sunk cost cannot be avoided because it represents an expenditure that has already been made or an irrevocable decision to incur the cost.

Answer (A) is incorrect. A discretionary cost is characterized by uncertainty about the input-output relationship; advertising and research are examples. Answer (B) is incorrect. Full absorption costing includes in production costs materials, labor, and both fixed and variable overhead. Answer (C) is incorrect. Underallocated indirect cost is a cost that has not yet been charged to production.

8.1.5. Total unit costs are

A. Relevant for cost-volume-profit analysis.

B. Irrelevant in marginal analysis.

C. Independent of the cost system used to generate them.

D. Needed for determining product contribution.

Answer (B) is correct. *(CMA, adapted)*

REQUIRED: The true statement about total unit costs.

DISCUSSION: Marginal (incremental or differential) analysis determines the differences in costs among decision choices. Total unit costs are not relevant in marginal analysis because of the inclusion of costs that may not vary among the possible choices considered. In marginal analysis, only the incremental costs are relevant.

Answer (A) is incorrect. Fixed and variable costs behave differently and therefore receive different treatment in CVP analysis. Answer (C) is incorrect. Total unit costs are a product of the system used to calculate them. Answer (D) is incorrect. Only variable costs are needed to determine product contribution.

8.1.6. A decision-making concept, described as "the contribution to income that is forgone by not using a limited resource for its best alternative use," is called

A. Marginal cost.

B. Incremental cost.

C. Potential cost.

D. Opportunity cost.

Answer (D) is correct. *(CMA, adapted)*

REQUIRED: The contribution to income forgone by not using a limited resource for its best alternative use.

DISCUSSION: Opportunity cost is the profit forgone by selecting one choice instead of another. It is the benefit provided by the best alternative use of a scarce resource.

Answer (A) is incorrect. Marginal cost is the incremental cost of producing one additional unit. Answer (B) is incorrect. Incremental cost is the increase in costs between one option and another. Answer (C) is incorrect. Potential cost is the cost that may be incurred in the future.

Questions 8.1.7 and 8.1.8 are based on the following information. Management accountants are frequently asked to analyze various decision situations including the following:

I. The cost of a special device that is necessary if a special order is accepted
II. The cost proposed annually for the plant service for the grounds at corporate headquarters
III. Joint production costs incurred, to be considered in a sell-at-split versus a process-further decision
IV. The costs of alternative uses of plant space, to be considered in a make-or-buy decision
V. The cost of obsolete inventory acquired several years ago, to be considered in a keep-versus-disposal decision

8.1.7. The costs described in situations I and IV are

A. Prime costs.

B. Discretionary costs.

C. Relevant costs.

D. Differential costs.

Answer (C) is correct. *(CMA, adapted)*

REQUIRED: The costs involved in special-order and make-or-buy decisions.

DISCUSSION: The costs of alternative uses of plant space to be considered in a make-or-buy decision and the cost of a special device necessary for acceptance of a special order are relevant. Relevant costs are future costs that are expected to vary with the action taken. Other costs have no effect on the decision.

Answer (A) is incorrect. Prime costs are direct materials and direct labor costs. Answer (B) is incorrect. Discretionary costs have an uncertain input-output relationship. Advertising and research are examples. Answer (D) is incorrect. Differential cost (incremental cost) is the difference in total cost between two decisions.

8.1.8. The costs described in situations III and V are

A. Prime costs.

B. Sunk costs.

C. Discretionary costs.

D. Relevant costs.

Answer (B) is correct. *(CMA, adapted)*

REQUIRED: The previously incurred costs.

DISCUSSION: Sunk costs are unavoidable. They are the results of past irrevocable decisions and have no relevance to future decisions. Joint production costs are irrelevant to deciding whether to sell at split-off or to process further. Similarly, the costs of obsolete inventory are irrelevant to future decisions. Thus, these are sunk costs.

Answer (A) is incorrect. Prime costs are direct materials and direct labor costs. Answer (C) is incorrect. Discretionary costs have an uncertain input-output relationship. Answer (D) is incorrect. Relevant costs are future costs that are expected to vary with the action taken.

8.1.9. The term relevant cost applies to all the following decision situations except the

A. Acceptance of a special order.

B. Determination of a product price.

C. Replacement of equipment.

D. Addition or deletion of a product line.

Answer (B) is correct. *(CMA, adapted)*

REQUIRED: The decision to which relevant cost does not apply.

DISCUSSION: Relevant costs are expected future costs that vary with the action taken. All other costs are assumed to be constant and thus have no effect on the decision. Relevant costing is not applicable to determining a product price because this decision involves an evaluation of, among other things, demand, competitors' actions, and desired profit margin.

Answer (A) is incorrect. Relevant cost is an important decision tool with regard to acceptance of a special order. Answer (C) is incorrect. Relevant cost is an important decision tool with regard to replacement of equipment. Answer (D) is incorrect. Relevant cost is an important decision tool with regard to an addition or deletion of a product line.

8.1.10. In a manufacturing environment, the best short-term profit-maximizing approach is to

A. Maximize unit gross profit times the number of units sold.

B. Minimize variable costs per unit times the number of units produced.

C. Minimize fixed overhead cost per unit by producing at full capacity.

D. Maximize contribution per unit times the number of units sold.

Answer (D) is correct. *(CMA, adapted)*

REQUIRED: The best short-term profit-maximizing approach in a manufacturing environment.

DISCUSSION: In the short run, the best approach is to maximize the contribution margin [(price – unit variable cost) × units sold]. Fixed costs can be ignored. The important consideration is the total contribution margin available to cover fixed costs and contribute to profits.

Answer (A) is incorrect. A long-term strategy is to maximize gross profit, which is calculated after subtracting fixed costs. Answer (B) is incorrect. Minimizing total variable cost ignores the effect of selling price on profit maximization. Answer (C) is incorrect. In the short run, fixed overhead does not change and is therefore not relevant.

8.1.11. In a decision analysis situation, which one of the following costs is not likely to contain a variable cost component?

A. Labor.

B. Overhead.

C. Depreciation.

D. Selling.

Answer (C) is correct. *(CMA, adapted)*

REQUIRED: The cost not likely to have a variable component.

DISCUSSION: Most costs either are variable or have a mix of fixed and variable components. For example, labor and materials are primarily variable. Their amounts fluctuate with the relevant cost drivers. Selling expenses and overhead costs can be either fixed or variable. Depreciation, however, is strictly a fixed cost in a decision analysis because it requires no cash outlay. Instead, the initial acquisition of the long-lived asset requires the cash outlay.

Answer (A) is incorrect. Labor costs are either variable or mixed. Answer (B) is incorrect. Overhead costs are either variable or mixed. Answer (D) is incorrect. Selling costs are either variable or mixed.

8.2 Insourcing vs. Outsourcing (Make or Buy)

8.2.1. A company's approach to an insourcing vs. outsourcing decision

A. Depends on whether the company is operating at or below normal volume.

B. Involves an analysis of avoidable costs.

C. Should use absorption (full) costing.

D. Should use activity-based costing.

Answer (B) is correct. *(CMA, adapted)*

REQUIRED: The true statement about a company's approach to a make-or-buy decision.

DISCUSSION: Available resources should be used as efficiently as possible before outsourcing. If the total relevant costs of production are less than the cost to buy the item, it should be produced in-house. The relevant costs are those that can be avoided.

Answer (A) is incorrect. Whether operations are at normal volume is less important than the amount of idle capacity. The company is less likely to buy if it has sufficient unused capacity. Answer (C) is incorrect. Total costs (absorption costing) are not as important as relevant costs. Answer (D) is incorrect. Activity-based costing is used to allocate fixed overhead. Fixed overhead is not relevant in an insourcing vs. outsourcing decision unless it is avoidable.

8.2.2. Costs relevant to an insourcing vs. outsourcing decision include variable manufacturing costs as well as

A. Avoidable fixed costs.

B. Factory depreciation.

C. Property taxes.

D. Factory management costs.

Answer (A) is correct. *(CMA, adapted)*

REQUIRED: The costs included in the analysis of insourcing vs. outsourcing decisions.

DISCUSSION: Relevant costs are anticipated costs that will vary among the choices available. If two courses of action share some costs, those costs are not relevant because they will be incurred regardless of the decision made. Relevant costs include fixed costs that could be avoided if the items were purchased from an outsider.

Answer (B) is incorrect. Depreciation should not be considered unless it can be avoided. Answer (C) is incorrect. Property taxes are not affected by the decision and are therefore not relevant unless the decision to buy leads to sale of the property. Answer (D) is incorrect. Factory management costs are not affected by the decision and are therefore not relevant unless the decision to buy reduces the number of factory managers.

8.2.3. In an insourcing vs. outsourcing decision, the decision process favors the use of total costs rather than unit costs. The reason is that

A. Unit cost may be calculated based on different volumes.

B. Irrelevant costs may be included in the unit amounts.

C. Allocated costs may be included in the unit amounts.

D. All of the answers are correct.

Answer (D) is correct. *(Publisher, adapted)*

REQUIRED: The advantage(s) of using total costs in an insourcing vs. outsourcing analysis.

DISCUSSION: Unit costs should be used with extreme care. In each situation, they may be calculated based on a different volume level from that anticipated, so comparability may be lost. Irrelevant costs included in the unit cost should be disregarded; only relevant costs should be included in the analysis. Allocated costs should also be ignored, and only the relevant costs that will change with the option chosen should be considered.

8.2.4. What is the opportunity cost of making a component part in a factory given no alternative use of the capacity?

A. The variable manufacturing cost of the component.

B. The total manufacturing cost of the component.

C. The total variable cost of the component.

D. Zero.

Answer (D) is correct. *(CMA, adapted)*

REQUIRED: The opportunity cost of making a component if there is no alternative use for the factory.

DISCUSSION: Opportunity cost is the benefit forgone by not selecting the best alternative use of scarce resources. The opportunity cost is zero when no alternative use for the production facility is available.

8.2.5. In an insourcing vs. outsourcing situation, which of the following qualitative factors is usually considered?

A. Special technology.

B. Skilled labor.

C. Special materials requirements.

D. All of the answers are correct.

Answer (D) is correct. *(Publisher, adapted)*

REQUIRED: The qualitative factor(s) affecting an insourcing vs. outsourcing decision.

DISCUSSION: Special technology may be available either within or outside the firm that relates to the particular product. The firm may possess necessary skilled labor or the supplier may. Special materials requirements may also affect the decision process because one supplier may have monopolized a key component. Another factor to be considered is that assurance of quality control is often a reason for making rather than buying.

8.2.6. Laurel Corporation has its own cafeteria with the following annual costs:

Food	$100,000
Labor	75,000
Overhead	110,000
Total	$285,000

The overhead is 40% fixed. Of the fixed overhead, $25,000 is the salary of the cafeteria supervisor. The remainder of the fixed overhead has been allocated from total company overhead. Assuming the cafeteria supervisor will remain and the corporation will continue to pay his or her salary, the maximum cost the corporation will be willing to pay an outside firm to service the cafeteria is

A. $285,000

B. $175,000

C. $219,000

D. $241,000

Answer (D) is correct. *(CMA, adapted)*

REQUIRED: The maximum that could be paid.

DISCUSSION: Given that overhead is 40% fixed, $66,000 ($110,000 × 60%) is variable, and $44,000 is fixed. Of the latter amount, $25,000 is attributable to the supervisor's salary. The $19,000 remainder is allocated from total company overhead and is unavoidable. Assuming the company will continue to pay the supervisor's salary if an outside firm services the cafeteria, the total fixed overhead is not an avoidable (incremental) cost. Thus, the total avoidable cost of the cafeteria's operation is $241,000 ($100,000 food + $75,000 labor + $66,000 VOH). This amount is the savings from hiring an outside firm. Accordingly, it is also the maximum that the corporation should be willing to pay the outside firm.

Answer (A) is incorrect. The amount of $285,000 is greater than the avoidable cost of operating the cafeteria. Answer (B) is incorrect. The company can pay more than $175,000. Its overhead costs are avoidable. Answer (C) is incorrect. The company can pay more than $219,000.

8.2.7. When applying the cost-benefit approach to a decision, the primary criterion is how well management goals will be achieved in relation to costs. Costs include all expected

A. Variable costs for the courses of action but not expected fixed costs because only the expected variable costs are relevant.

B. Incremental out-of-pocket costs as well as all expected continuing costs that are common to all the alternative courses of action.

C. Future costs that differ among the alternative courses of action plus all qualitative factors that cannot be measured in numerical terms.

D. Historical and future costs relative to the courses of action including all qualitative factors that cannot be measured in numerical terms.

Answer (C) is correct. *(CIA, adapted)*

REQUIRED: The costs included in cost-benefit analysis.

DISCUSSION: The analysis of a make-or-buy decision is based on relevant costs. If costs do not vary with the option chosen, they are irrelevant. Moreover, the decision may be based on nonquantitative factors, for example, the desire to maintain a relationship with a vendor or to assume control over development of a product.

Answer (A) is incorrect. Variable and fixed costs may be relevant or irrelevant. Answer (B) is incorrect. Expected incremental out-of-pocket expenses should be considered, but common costs should not. Answer (D) is incorrect. Historical costs are not relevant to cost-benefit analysis because they are sunk costs.

8.2.8. A company manufactures components for use in producing one of its finished products. When 12,000 units are produced, the full cost per unit is $35, separated as follows:

Direct materials	$ 5
Direct labor	15
Variable overhead	10
Fixed overhead	5

A supplier has offered to sell 12,000 components to the company for $37 each. If the company accepts the offer, some of the facilities currently being used to manufacture the components can be rented as warehouse space for $40,000. However, $3 of the fixed overhead currently applied to each component would have to be covered by the company's other products. What is the differential cost to the company of purchasing the components from the supplier?

A. $8,000

B. $20,000

C. $24,000

D. $44,000

Answer (B) is correct. *(CIA, adapted)*

REQUIRED: The differential cost of purchasing the components.

DISCUSSION: Differential (incremental) cost is the difference in total cost between two decisions. The relevant costs do not include unavoidable costs, such as the $3 of fixed overhead. It would cost the company an additional $20,000 to purchase, rather than manufacture, the components.

Purchase price (12,000 × $37)	$444,000
Minus: Rental income	(40,000)
Net cost to purchase	$404,000
Cost to manufacture (12,000 × $32)	(384,000)
Cost differential	$ 20,000

Answer (A) is incorrect. The amount of $8,000 assumes that $3 of fixed overhead is avoidable. Answer (C) is incorrect. The amount of $24,000 compares the full cost of manufacturing with cost to purchase. Answer (D) is incorrect. The amount of $44,000 ignores the opportunity cost.

8.2.9. Listed below are a company's monthly unit costs to manufacture and market a particular product.

Manufacturing costs:	
Direct materials	$2.00
Direct labor	2.40
Variable indirect	1.60
Fixed indirect	1.00
Marketing costs:	
Variable	2.50
Fixed	1.50

The company must decide to continue making the product or buy it from an outside supplier. The supplier has offered to make the product at the same level of quality that the company can make it. Fixed marketing costs would be unaffected, but variable marketing costs would be reduced by 30% if the company were to accept the proposal. What is the maximum amount per unit that the company can pay the supplier without decreasing operating income?

A. $8.50

B. $6.75

C. $7.75

D. $5.25

Answer (B) is correct. *(CMA, adapted)*

REQUIRED: The maximum amount paid to an outside supplier without decreasing operating income.

DISCUSSION: The key to this question is, what costs will the company avoid if it buys from the outside supplier? It will no longer incur the $2.00 of direct materials, nor the $2.40 of direct labor, nor the $1.60 of variable overhead, nor $0.75 ($2.50 × 30%) of the variable marketing costs (regardless of whether the company makes or buys, it will still incur 70% of the variable marketing costs). The firm will therefore avoid costs of $6.75 ($2.00 + $2.40 + $1.60 + $0.75). Hence, it will at least break even by paying no more than $6.75.

Answer (A) is incorrect. The amount of $8.50 assumes that all variable marketing costs are avoidable. Answer (C) is incorrect. The amount of $7.75 assumes that fixed manufacturing costs of $1 are avoidable. Answer (D) is incorrect. The amount of $5.25 results from subtracting the savings in marketing costs ($0.75) from the manufacturing savings ($6.00).

Question 8.2.10 is based on the following information.

A business needs a computer application that can be either developed internally or purchased. Suitable software from a vendor costs $29,000. Minor modifications and testing can be conducted by the systems staff as part of their regular workload.

If the software is developed internally, a systems analyst would be assigned full time, and a contractor would assume the analyst's responsibilities. The hourly rate for the regular analyst is $25. The hourly rate for the contractor is $22. The contractor would occupy an empty office. The office has 100 square feet, and occupancy cost is $45 per square foot.

Other related data are as follows. Computer time is charged using predetermined rates. The organization has sufficient excess computer capacity for either software development or modification/testing of the purchased software.

	Internal Development	Purchased Software
Systems analyst time in hours		
Development	1,000	N/A
Modifications and testing	N/A	40
Computer charges	$800	$250
Additional hardware purchases	$3,200	N/A
Incidental supplies	$500	$200

8.2.10. Based solely on the cost figures presented, the cost of developing the computer application will be

A. $3,500 less than acquiring the purchased software package.

B. $500 less than acquiring the purchased software package.

C. $1,550 more than acquiring the purchased software package.

D. $3,550 more than acquiring the purchased software package.

Answer (A) is correct. *(CIA, adapted)*

REQUIRED: The comparison of the costs of developing and purchasing software.

DISCUSSION: Development cost equals the cost of the outside contractor plus the costs for hardware and supplies. Computer charges are transfer prices and do not require additional expenditures, given idle capacity. The relevant cost of supplies is $300 ($500 – $200 cost if the software is purchased). The contractor's use of an otherwise idle office is not relevant. Thus, the relevant cost of development is $25,500 [($22 hourly cost of the contractor × 1,000 hours) + $3,200 hardware purchases + $300 incremental cost of supplies]. This amount is $3,500 lower than the $29,000 cost of purchase. A systems analyst's work on the new software is not relevant because the analyst's compensation would be incurred even if the software were purchased.

Answer (B) is incorrect. The contractor is not paid $25 per hour. Answer (C) is incorrect. Computer charges of $550 and $4,500 in occupancy charges should not be included. Answer (D) is incorrect. The contractor is not paid $25 per hour, and 40 hours of modification and testing, $550 of the computer charges, and the occupancy costs are irrelevant.

8.2.11. Which of the following qualitative factors favors the buy choice in an insourcing vs. outsourcing decision?

A. Maintaining a long-run relationship with suppliers is desirable.

B. Quality control is critical.

C. Idle capacity is available.

D. All of the answers are correct.

Answer (A) is correct. *(Publisher, adapted)*

REQUIRED: The qualitative factor(s) favoring buying in an insourcing vs. outsourcing decision.

DISCUSSION: The maintenance of long-run relationships with suppliers may become paramount in a make-or-buy decision. Abandoning long-run supplier relationships may cause difficulty in obtaining needed parts when terminated suppliers find it advantageous not to supply parts in the future.

Answer (B) is incorrect. If quality is important, one can ordinarily control it better in one's own plant. Answer (C) is incorrect. The availability of idle capacity more likely favors the decision to make. Answer (D) is incorrect. The importance of quality control and the availability of idle capacity are qualitative factors favoring the make choice in an insourcing versus outsourcing decision.

Questions 8.2.12 through 8.2.14 are based on the following information. Richardson Motors uses 10 units of Part No. T305 each month in the production of large diesel engines. The cost to manufacture one unit of T305 is presented as follows:

Direct materials	$ 2,000
Materials handling (20% of direct materials cost)	400
Direct labor	16,000
Manufacturing overhead (150% of direct labor)	24,000
Total manufacturing cost	$42,400

Materials handling, which is not included in manufacturing overhead, represents the direct variable costs of the receiving department that are applied to direct materials and purchased components on the basis of their cost. Richardson's annual manufacturing overhead budget is one-third variable and two-thirds fixed. Simpson Castings, one of Richardson's reliable vendors, has offered to supply T305 at a unit price of $30,000.

8.2.12. If Richardson Motors purchases the ten T305 units from Simpson Castings, the capacity Richardson used to manufacture these parts would be idle. Should Richardson decide to purchase the parts from Simpson, the out-of-pocket cost per unit of T305 would

A. Decrease $6,400.

B. Increase $3,600.

C. Increase $9,600.

D. Decrease $12,400.

Answer (C) is correct. *(CMA, adapted)*

REQUIRED: The effect on out-of-pocket cost per unit if the parts are purchased from an outside supplier.

DISCUSSION: The out-of-pocket cost of making the part equals the total manufacturing cost minus the fixed overhead, or $26,400 {$42,400 – [(2 ÷ 3) × $24,000]}. The cost of the component consists of the $30,000 purchase price plus the $6,000 (20% of cost) of variable receiving costs, or a total of $36,000. Thus, unit out-of-pocket cost would increase by $9,600 if the components were purchased.

Answer (A) is incorrect. Assuming all of the overhead is variable results in $6,400. Answer (B) is incorrect. Overlooking the $6,000 of receiving costs for purchased components results in $3,600. Answer (D) is incorrect. The difference between the full cost of making the part and the price of the component is $12,400.

8.2.13. Assume Richardson Motors is able to rent all idle capacity for $50,000 per month. If Richardson decides to purchase the 10 units from Simpson Castings, Richardson's monthly cost for T305 would

A. Decrease $14,000.

B. Increase $46,000.

C. Decrease $64,000.

D. Increase $96,000.

Answer (B) is correct. *(CMA, adapted)*

REQUIRED: The total change in monthly cost if components are purchased and idle capacity is rented.

DISCUSSION: The out-of-pocket cost of making the part equals the total manufacturing cost minus the fixed overhead, or $26,400 {$42,400 – [(2 ÷ 3) × $24,000]}. The cost of the component consists of the $30,000 purchase price plus the $6,000 (20% of cost) of variable receiving costs, or a total of $36,000. Thus, unit out-of-pocket cost would increase by $9,600 if the components were purchased.

For 10 components, the total cost increase would be $96,000, but the $50,000 rental would reduce the net increase to $46,000.

Answer (A) is incorrect. Overlooking the $6,000 per unit of receiving costs for purchased components results in $14,000. Answer (C) is incorrect. Assuming all overhead is variable and ignoring rental revenue results in $64,000. Answer (D) is incorrect. Overlooking the rental revenue results in $96,000.

8.2.14. Assume the rental opportunity does not exist and Richardson Motors could use the idle capacity to manufacture another product that would contribute $104,000 per month. If Richardson chooses to manufacture the ten T305 units in order to maintain quality control, Richardson's opportunity cost is

A. $68,000

B. $88,000

C. $8,000

D. $(96,000)

Answer (C) is correct. *(CMA, adapted)*

REQUIRED: The opportunity cost of manufacturing components when facilities could otherwise be used to produce $104,000 per month.

DISCUSSION: The out-of-pocket cost of making the part equals the total manufacturing cost minus the fixed overhead, or $26,400 {$42,400 – [(2 ÷ 3) × $24,000]}. The cost of the component consists of the $30,000 purchase price plus the $6,000 (20% of cost) of variable receiving costs, or a total of $36,000. Thus, unit out-of-pocket cost would increase by $9,600 if the components were purchased.

For 10 units, the additional cost of purchasing is $96,000. However, the net effect of purchasing is a gain of $8,000 ($104,000 contribution from making another product – $96,000). Opportunity cost is the benefit from the next best alternative use of the resources. Hence, the company's opportunity cost of making the part is $8,000.

Answer (A) is incorrect. This amount overlooks the $6,000 per unit of receiving costs for purchased components. Answer (B) is incorrect. This amount assumes only one-third of the overhead is fixed. Answer (D) is incorrect. This amount ignores the $104,000 income from alternative production.

Questions 8.2.15 and 8.2.16 are based on the following information. Regis Company manufactures plugs used in its manufacturing cycle at a cost of $36 per unit that includes $8 of fixed overhead. Regis needs 30,000 of these plugs annually, and Orlan Company has offered to sell these units to Regis at $33 per unit. If Regis decides to purchase the plugs, $60,000 of the annual fixed overhead applied will be eliminated, and the company may be able to rent the facility previously used for manufacturing the plugs.

8.2.15. If Regis Company purchases the plugs but does not rent the unused facility, the company would

A. Save $3.00 per unit.

B. Lose $6.00 per unit.

C. Save $2.00 per unit.

D. Lose $3.00 per unit.

Answer (D) is correct. *(CMA, adapted)*

REQUIRED: The amount saved or lost if the company purchases the item but does not rent out the unused facility.

DISCUSSION: Exclusive of the fixed overhead, the unit cost of making the plugs is $28 ($36 total cost – $8 fixed OH). Purchasing the plugs will avoid $2 per unit of fixed overhead ($60,000 OH applied ÷ 30,000 units). Accordingly, $6 per unit of fixed overhead is unavoidable, and the relevant (avoidable) unit cost of making the plugs is $30 [$36 total cost – ($8 fixed OH – $2 avoidable cost)]. The purchase option therefore results in a $3-per-unit loss ($33 purchase price – $30 relevant cost).

Answer (A) is incorrect. A $3.00 savings is the difference between the current cost of $36.00 per unit and the purchase price of $33.00 per unit. It does not take into account the relevant costs. Answer (B) is incorrect. The fixed overhead per unit that is unavoidable is $6.00. Answer (C) is incorrect. The fixed overhead per unit that will be eliminated by purchasing is $2.00.

8.2.16. If the plugs are purchased and the facility rented, Regis Company wishes to realize $100,000 in savings annually. To achieve this goal, the minimum annual rent on the facility must be

A. $10,000

B. $40,000

C. $70,000

D. $190,000

Answer (D) is correct. *(CMA, adapted)*

REQUIRED: The minimum annual rent on the abandoned facility to achieve a targeted annual savings.

DISCUSSION: If Regis purchases the plugs, Regis will still incur fixed costs per unit of $6 [$8 – ($60,000 ÷ $30,000)], however, since these costs are committed (sunk costs), they are not relevant to this decision. Thus, the relevant cost per unit will be $30 ($36 cost – $6 fixed cost per unit). Without regard to rental of idle production capacity, the company will lose $3 per unit ($33 purchase price – $30 relevant cost) by purchasing the plugs. The total annual loss will be $90,000 (30,000 units × $3). Consequently, to achieve the targeted savings, the minimum annual rent must be $190,000 ($90,000 loss from purchasing + $100,000 targeted savings).

Questions 8.2.17 and 8.2.18 are based on the following information. Geary Manufacturing has assembled the data appearing in the next column pertaining to two products. Past experience has shown that the unavoidable fixed manufacturing overhead included in the cost per machine hour averages $10. Geary has a policy of filling all sales orders, even if it means purchasing units from outside suppliers. Total machine capacity is 50,000 hours.

	Blender	Electric Mixer
Direct materials	$ 6	$11
Direct labor	4	9
Manufacturing overhead at $16 per hour	16	32
Cost if purchased from an outside supplier	20	38
Annual demand (units)	20,000	28,000

8.2.17. With all other things constant, if Geary Manufacturing is able to reduce the direct materials for an electric mixer to $6 per unit, the company should

A. Produce 25,000 electric mixers and purchase all other units as needed.

B. Produce 20,000 blenders and 15,000 electric mixers, and purchase all other units as needed.

C. Produce 20,000 blenders and purchase all other units as needed.

D. Purchase all units as needed.

Answer (A) is correct. *(CMA, adapted)*

REQUIRED: The optimal strategy if direct materials costs for a product are reduced.

DISCUSSION: Reducing unit direct materials cost for mixers from $11 to $6 decreases unit variable cost to $27 ($6 DM + $9 DL + $12 VOH) and increases the cost savings of making a mixer from $6 to $11, or $5.50 per hour ($11 ÷ 2 hours per unit). Given a cost savings per hour for blenders of $4, the company can minimize total variable cost by making 25,000 mixers (50,000 hours capacity ÷ 2). Total variable cost will be $1,189,000 [(25,000 mixers × $27) + (3,000 mixers × $38) + (20,000 blenders × $20)].

Answer (B) is incorrect. Producing 20,000 blenders and 15,000 mixers results in a total variable cost of $1,219,000. Answer (C) is incorrect. Producing 20,000 blenders results in a total variable cost of $1,384,000. Answer (D) is incorrect. The variable cost of making these items is less than the cost of purchase.

8.2.18. If 50,000 machine hours are available and Geary Manufacturing desires to follow an optimal strategy, it should

A. Produce 25,000 electric mixers and purchase all other units as needed.

B. Produce 20,000 blenders and 15,000 electric mixers, and purchase all other units as needed.

C. Produce 20,000 blenders and purchase all other units as needed.

D. Produce 28,000 electric mixers and purchase all other units as needed.

Answer (B) is correct. *(CMA, adapted)*

REQUIRED: The optimal strategy with respect to producing or purchasing two products.

DISCUSSION: Sales (20,000 blenders and 28,000 mixers) and total revenue are constant, so the strategy is to minimize total variable cost. Each blender requires 1 machine hour ($16 OH ÷ $16 per hour), and each mixer requires 2 machine hours ($32 OH ÷ $16 per hour). For blenders, the unit variable cost is $16 [$6 DM + $4 DL + ($16 – $10) VOH]. For each blender made, the company saves $4 ($20 – $16), or $4 ($4 ÷ 1 hour) per unit of the constrained resource. The unit variable cost to make a mixer is $32 [$11 DM + $9 DL + ($32 – $10 × 2) VOH]. The savings is $6 per mixer ($38 – $32), or $3 ($6 ÷ 2 hours) per unit of the constrained resource. Thus, as many blenders as possible should be made. If 20,000 hours (20,000 units × 1 hour) are used for blenders, 30,000 hours are available for 15,000 mixers. Total variable cost is $1,294,000 [(20,000 blenders × $16) + (15,000 mixers × $32) + (13,000 mixers × $38)].

Answer (A) is incorrect. Producing 25,000 mixers results in a total variable cost of $1,314,000. Answer (C) is incorrect. Producing 20,000 blenders and no mixers increases costs by $90,000 (15,000 units × $6). Answer (D) is incorrect. The company can produce at most 25,000 mixers.

8.2.19. A company needs special gears. The machinery to make the gears can be rented for $100,000 for 1 year, but the company can buy the gears and avoid the rental cost. Because the demand for the gears may be high (0.6 probability) or low (0.4 probability) and contribution margins vary, the company prepared the following decision tree:

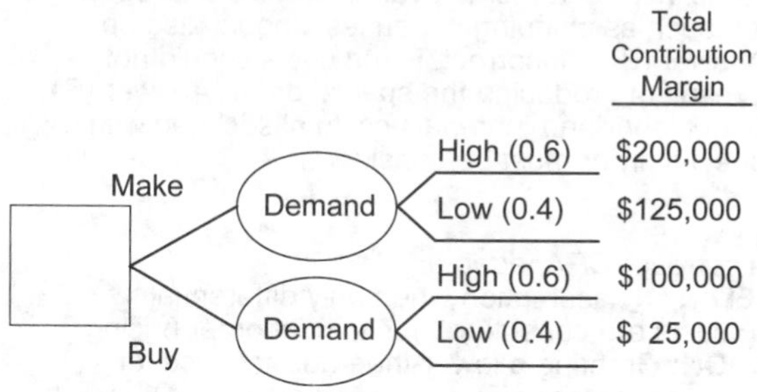

Which of the following statements is true?

A. The expected value of making is $20,000.

B. The expected value of buying is $70,000.

C. Making the gears is the best choice.

D. Buying the gears is the best choice.

Answer (B) is correct. *(CIA, adapted)*
REQUIRED: The true statement about a decision tree.
DISCUSSION: The expected value of buying the gears is

.6	×	$100,000	=	$60,000
.4	×	$ 25,000	=	10,000
				$70,000

Answer (A) is incorrect. The expected value to make the gears is $70,000 [(.6 × $200,000) + (.4 × $125,000) – $100,000 machine rental]. Answer (C) is incorrect. Making the gears gives the same expected value as buying the gears, although the projected CMs for the make decision are higher than those for the buy decision. Answer (D) is incorrect. Making the gears gives the same expected value as buying the gears, although the projected CMs for the make decision are higher than those for the buy decision.

8.3 Special Order

8.3.1. A company manufactures a product that is sold for $37.95. It uses an absorption cost system. Plant capacity is 750,000 units annually, but normal volume is 500,000 units. Costs at normal volume are given below.

	Unit Cost	Total Cost
Direct materials	$ 9.80	$ 4,900,000
Direct labor	4.50	2,250,000
Manufacturing overhead	12.00	6,000,000
Selling and administrative: Variable	2.50	1,250,000
Fixed	4.20	2,100,000
Total cost	$33.00	$16,500,000

Fixed manufacturing overhead is budgeted at $4,500,000. A customer has offered to purchase 100,000 units at $25.00 each to be packaged in large cartons, not the normal individual containers. It will pick up the units in its own trucks. Thus, variable selling and administrative expenses will decrease by 60%. The company should compare the total revenue to be derived from this order with the total relevant costs of

A. $1,830,000

B. $1,880,000

C. $2,930,000

D. $3,150,000

Answer (A) is correct. *(CIA, adapted)*
REQUIRED: The total relevant costs of the special order.
DISCUSSION: The necessary assumptions are that all fixed costs and the unit variable costs of direct materials, direct labor, and variable manufacturing overhead are not affected by the special order. Thus, the fixed costs are not relevant. The unit costs of direct materials and direct labor are given as $9.80 and $4.50, respectively. The unit variable overhead cost is $3.00 [($6,000,000 total overhead – $4,500,000 total fixed overhead) ÷ 500,000 units normal volume]. The unit variable selling and administrative cost is $1.00 [$2.50 × (1.0 – .6)]. Consequently, the total relevant cost of the special order is $1,830,000 [100,000 units × ($9.80 + $4.50 + $3.00 + $1.00)].

Answer (B) is incorrect. Variable manufacturing overhead per unit is determined by using normal volume, not plant capacity, as the denominator level. Answer (C) is incorrect. The total relevant cost of the special order is $1,830,000 [100,000 units × ($9.80 + $4.50 + $3.00 + $1.00)]. Answer (D) is incorrect. Fixed selling and administrative expenses of $4.20 per unit should not be included. Furthermore, variable manufacturing overhead of $3 per unit, not total manufacturing overhead of $12 per unit, should be used in the calculation of relevant costs.

8.3.2. Production of a special order will increase gross profit when the additional revenue from the special order is greater than

A. The direct materials and labor costs in producing the order.

B. The fixed costs incurred in producing the order.

C. The indirect costs of producing the order.

D. The marginal cost of producing the order.

Answer (D) is correct. *(CIA, adapted)*

REQUIRED: The circumstances in which increased gross profit will result from a special order.

DISCUSSION: Gross profit will increase if the incremental or marginal cost of producing the order is less than the marginal revenue. Marginal cost equals the relevant variable costs assuming fixed costs are not affected by the special order.

Answer (A) is incorrect. Indirect variable costs of producing a special order, such as shipping expenses, should also be considered. Answer (B) is incorrect. Fixed costs should not increase as a result of producing the special order. Answer (C) is incorrect. Direct labor and materials costs associated with producing a special order must be considered.

8.3.3. When only differential manufacturing costs are taken into account for special-order pricing, an essential assumption is that

A. Manufacturing fixed and variable costs are linear.

B. Selling and administrative fixed and variable costs are linear.

C. Acceptance of the order will not affect regular sales.

D. Acceptance of the order will not cause unit selling and administrative variable costs to increase.

Answer (C) is correct. *(CPA, adapted)*

REQUIRED: The assumption when only differential manufacturing costs are considered for special-order pricing.

DISCUSSION: Granting a lower-than-normal price for a special order has potential effects on regular sales. Other customers may demand the same price. Thus, the decision to consider only differential (marginal) manufacturing costs should be based on a determination that all other costs are not relevant. The other costs should not vary with the option chosen.

Answer (A) is incorrect. Manufacturing costs need not be linear. The analysis of a special order considers total marginal costs. Consequently, the unit variable costs and total fixed costs need not be constant, and any changes need not be in direct proportion to the measure of activity. Answer (B) is incorrect. The assumption is that selling and administrative costs are not relevant. Thus, whether they are linear also is irrelevant. Answer (D) is incorrect. The assumption is that acceptance of the order will not cause total selling and administrative costs to change.

8.3.4. When considering a special order that will enable a company to make use of currently idle capacity, which of the following costs is irrelevant?

A. Materials.

B. Depreciation.

C. Direct labor.

D. Variable overhead.

Answer (B) is correct. *(CPA, adapted)*

REQUIRED: The irrelevant cost when a special order permits use of idle capacity.

DISCUSSION: Because depreciation is expensed whether or not the the special order is accepted, it is irrelevant to the decision. Only the variable costs are relevant.

Answer (A) is incorrect. Materials are relevant to a decision whether to accept a special order. Answer (C) is incorrect. Direct labor is relevant to a decision whether to accept a special order. Answer (D) is incorrect. Variable overhead is relevant to a decision whether to accept a special order.

8.3.5. Which of the following cost allocation methods is used to determine the lowest price that can be quoted for a special order that will use idle capacity within a production area?

A. Job order.

B. Process.

C. Variable.

D. Standard.

Answer (C) is correct. *(CPA, adapted)*

REQUIRED: The most appropriate cost allocation method for determining the lowest price for a special order.

DISCUSSION: If idle capacity exists, the lowest feasible price for a special order is one covering the variable cost. Variable costing considers fixed cost to be a period cost, not a product cost. Fixed costs are not relevant to short-term inventory costing with idle capacity because the fixed costs will be incurred whether or not any production occurs. Any additional revenue in excess of the variable costs will decrease losses or increase profits.

Answer (A) is incorrect. Job order is a cost accumulation procedure that may treat fixed costs as product costs. Answer (B) is incorrect. The process method is a cost accumulation procedure that may treat fixed costs as product costs. Answer (D) is incorrect. Standard costing attempts to measure deviations from expected costs.

Questions 8.3.6 through 8.3.8 are based on the following information. Kator Co. is a manufacturer of industrial components. One of their products that is used as a subcomponent in auto manufacturing is KB-96. This product has the following financial structure per unit:

Selling price	$150
Direct materials	$ 20
Direct labor	15
Variable manufacturing overhead	12
Fixed manufacturing overhead	30
Shipping and handling	3
Fixed selling and administrative	10
Total costs	$ 90

8.3.6. Kator Co. has received a special, one-time order for 1,000 KB-96 parts. Assuming Kator has excess capacity, the minimum price that is acceptable for this one-time special order is in excess of

A. $47

B. $50

C. $60

D. $77

Answer (B) is correct. *(CMA, adapted)*

REQUIRED: The minimum acceptable price.

DISCUSSION: A company must cover the incremental costs of a special order when it has excess capacity. The incremental costs for product KB-96 are $50 ($20 direct materials + $15 direct labor + $12 variable overhead + $3 shipping and handling). The fixed costs will not change as a result of the special order, so they are not relevant. Thus, any price in excess of $50 per unit is acceptable.

Answer (A) is incorrect. The amount of $47 ignores the shipping and handling costs. Answer (C) is incorrect. The amount of $60 includes fixed selling and administrative costs. Answer (D) is incorrect. The amount of $77 includes fixed manufacturing overhead but omits shipping and handling costs.

8.3.7. During the next year, KB-96 sales are expected to be 10,000 units. All of the costs will remain the same except that fixed manufacturing overhead will increase by 20% and direct materials will increase by 10%. The selling price per unit for next year will be $160. Based on this data, the contribution margin from KB-96 for next year will be

A. $620,000

B. $750,000

C. $1,080,000

D. $1,110,000

Answer (C) is correct. *(CMA, adapted)*

REQUIRED: The contribution margin for next year.

DISCUSSION: Contribution margin equals sales minus variable costs. All variable costs will remain the same except that direct materials will increase to $22 per unit (1.1 × $20). Thus, total unit variable costs will be $52 ($22 + $15 + $12 + $3), and the contribution margin will be $1,080,000 [10,000 units ($160 unit selling price – $52)].

Answer (A) is incorrect. The amount of $620,000 includes all fixed costs. Answer (B) is incorrect. The amount of $750,000 includes all manufacturing costs. Answer (D) is incorrect. The amount of $1,110,000 assumes that the fixed costs and shipping and handling are the only relevant costs.

8.3.8. Kator Co. has received a special, one-time order for 1,000 KB-96 parts. Assume that Kator is operating at full capacity and that the contribution margin of the output that would be displaced by the special order is $10,000. Using the original data, the minimum price that is acceptable for this one-time special order is in excess of

A. $60

B. $70

C. $87

D. $100

Answer (A) is correct. *(CMA, adapted)*

REQUIRED: The minimum acceptable price.

DISCUSSION: Given no excess capacity, the price must cover the incremental costs. The incremental costs for KB-96 equal $50 ($20 direct materials + $15 direct labor + $12 variable overhead + $3 shipping and handling). Opportunity cost is the benefit of the next best alternative use of scarce resources. Because acceptance of the special order would cause the company to forgo a contribution margin of $10,000, that amount must be reflected in the price. Hence, the minimum unit price is $60 [$50 unit incremental cost + ($10,000 lost CM ÷ 1,000 units)].

Answer (B) is incorrect. The amount of $70 includes fixed selling and administrative costs. Answer (C) is incorrect. The amount of $87 includes fixed manufacturing overhead but omits shipping and handling costs. Answer (D) is incorrect. The amount of $100 is based on full absorption cost.

8.3.9. Clay Co. has considerable excess manufacturing capacity. A special job order's cost sheet includes the following applied manufacturing overhead costs:

Fixed costs	$21,000
Variable costs	33,000

The fixed costs include a normal $3,700 allocation for in-house design costs, although no in-house design will be done. Instead, the job will require the use of external designers costing $7,750. What is the total amount to be included in the calculation to determine the minimum acceptable price for the job?

A. $36,700

B. $40,750

C. $54,000

D. $58,050

Answer (B) is correct. *(CPA, adapted)*

REQUIRED: The total amount to be included in the calculation to determine the minimum acceptable price.

DISCUSSION: Given excess capacity, neither increased fixed costs nor opportunity costs are incurred by accepting the special order. Thus, the marginal cost of the order (the minimum acceptable price) is $40,750 ($33,000 variable costs + $7,750 cost of external design).

Answer (A) is incorrect. The amount of $36,700 equals variable costs plus the in-house design costs. Answer (C) is incorrect. The amount of $54,000 equals the fixed costs plus the variable costs. Answer (D) is incorrect. The amount of $58,050 equals the fixed costs, plus the variable costs, minus the in-house design costs, plus the external design costs.

8.4 Other Nonroutine Decisions

8.4.1. An entity has developed and patented a new laser disc reading device that will be marketed internationally. Which of the following factors should the entity consider in pricing the device?

I. Quality of the new device

II. Life of the new device

III. Customers' relative preference for quality compared with price

A. I and II only.

B. I and III only.

C. II and III only.

D. I, II, and III.

Answer (D) is correct. *(CPA, adapted)*

REQUIRED: The factors considered when pricing a new product.

DISCUSSION: Product pricing is a function of consumer demand, competitive factors, and the seller's cost structure and profit objectives. Thus, the seller must consider the trade-off between the price and quality effects on demand. A better-quality product, for example, one with a relatively long useful life, is more costly to produce and therefore sells for a higher price, which in turn reduces the amount demanded.

Answer (A) is incorrect. The customers' preference is also important when determining the price of a product. Answer (B) is incorrect. The life of the product should also be considered when pricing a product. Answer (C) is incorrect. The quality of a product is important when determining how much to charge for it.

8.4.2. If a U.S. manufacturer's price in the U.S. market is below an appropriate measure of costs and the seller has a reasonable prospect of recovering the resulting loss in the future through higher prices or a greater market share, the seller has engaged in

A. Collusive pricing.

B. Dumping.

C. Predatory pricing.

D. Price discrimination.

Answer (C) is correct. *(Publisher, adapted)*

REQUIRED: The pricing strategy characterized by charging a price that is below an appropriate measure of costs when the seller reasonably expects to recover the loss through higher prices or a greater market share.

DISCUSSION: Predatory pricing is intentionally pricing below cost to eliminate competition and reduce supply. Federal statutes and many state laws prohibit the practice. The U.S. Supreme Court has held that pricing is predatory when two conditions are met: (1) The seller's price is below "an appropriate measure of its costs," and (2) it has a reasonable prospect of recovering the resulting loss through higher prices or greater market share.

Answer (A) is incorrect. Collusive pricing involves a conspiracy to set higher prices. Answer (B) is incorrect. Dumping is defined under U.S. law as sale by a non-U.S. company in the U.S. market of a product below its market value in the country where it was produced. Such sale is illegal if it threatens material injury to a U.S. industry. Answer (D) is incorrect. Price discrimination entails charging different prices to different customers for essentially the same product if the effect is to lessen competition substantially; to tend to create a monopoly; or to injure, destroy, or prevent competition.

8.4.3. When a multiproduct plant operates at full capacity, quite often decisions must be made as to which products to emphasize. These decisions are frequently made with a short-run focus. In making such decisions, managers should select products with the highest

A. Sales price per unit.

B. Individual unit contribution margin.

C. Sales volume potential.

D. Contribution margin per unit of the constraining resource.

Answer (D) is correct. *(CMA, adapted)*

REQUIRED: The products to be made in the short run.

DISCUSSION: In the short run, many costs are fixed. Hence, contribution margin (revenues – all variable costs) becomes the best measure of profitability. Moreover, certain resources are also fixed. Accordingly, when deciding which products to produce at full capacity, the criterion should be the contribution margin per unit of the most constrained resource. This approach maximizes total contribution margin.

Answer (A) is incorrect. The highest sales price does not consider costs and constraints. Answer (B) is incorrect. The product with the highest UCM may require greater usage of the constrained resource than another product contributing a lesser amount per unit. Answer (C) is incorrect. The highest sales volume does not consider costs and constraints.

8.4.4. A company manufactures jet engines on a cost-plus basis. The cost of a particular jet engine the company manufactures is shown as follows:

Direct materials	$200,000
Direct labor	150,000
Overhead:	
Supervisor's salary	20,000
Fringe benefits on direct labor	15,000
Depreciation	12,000
Rent	11,000
Total cost	$408,000

If production of this engine were discontinued, the production capacity would be idle, and the supervisor would be laid off. When asked to bid on the next contract for this engine, the minimum unit price that the company should bid is

A. $408,000

B. $365,000

C. $397,000

D. $385,000

Answer (D) is correct. *(CMA, adapted)*

REQUIRED: The minimum unit price that should be bid.

DISCUSSION: The company will need to cover its variable costs and any other incremental costs. Thus, direct materials ($200,000), direct labor ($150,000), the supervisor's salary ($20,000), and fringe benefits on direct labor ($15,000) are the incremental unit costs of manufacturing the engines. The breakeven price is therefore $385,000 ($200,000 + $150,000 + $20,000 + $15,000).

Answer (A) is incorrect. Depreciation and rent are allocated costs that will be incurred even if the contract is lost. Answer (B) is incorrect. The supervisor's salary will have to be covered. The $20,000 salary is an avoidable cost. Answer (C) is incorrect. Depreciation is a cost that cannot be avoided.

8.4.5. A company produces and sells three products:

	C	J	P
Sales	$200,000	$150,000	$125,000
Separable (product) fixed costs	60,000	35,000	40,000
Allocated fixed costs	35,000	40,000	25,000
Variable costs	95,000	75,000	50,000

The company lost its lease and must move to a smaller facility. As a result, total allocated fixed costs will be reduced by 40%. However, one product must be discontinued. The expected net income after the appropriate product has been discontinued is

A. $10,000

B. $15,000

C. $20,000

D. $25,000

Answer (D) is correct. *(CIA, adapted)*

REQUIRED: The expected net income after eliminating the appropriate product to maximize profits.

DISCUSSION: Product P should be eliminated because it has the smallest product margin.

	C	J	P	Total
Sales	$200,000	$150,000	$125,000	$475,000
Variable costs	95,000	75,000	50,000	220,000
Contribution margin	$105,000	$ 75,000	$ 75,000	$255,000
Separable (product) fixed costs	60,000	35,000	40,000	135,000
Product margin	$ 45,000	$ 40,000	$ 35,000	$120,000
Allocated fixed costs				100,000
Net income				$ 20,000

After discontinuing P, total product margin is $85,000 ($45,000 + $40,000), and total allocated fixed costs are $60,000 [($35,000 + $40,000 + $25,000) × (1.0 – 0.4)]. Hence, expected net income is $25,000 ($85,000 – $60,000).

Answer (A) is incorrect. The amount of $10,000 is 40% of net income after eliminating product P. Answer (B) is incorrect. The amount of $15,000 is net income if product C is eliminated. Answer (C) is incorrect. The amount of $20,000 is net income if product J is eliminated.

8.4.6. A company has 7,000 obsolete toys carried in inventory at a manufacturing cost of $6 per unit. If the toys are reworked for $2 per unit, they could be sold for $3 per unit. If the toys are scrapped, they could be sold for $1.85 per unit. Which alternative is more desirable (rework or scrap), and what is the total dollar amount of the advantage of that alternative?

A. Scrap, $5,950.

B. Rework, $36,050.

C. Scrap, $47,950.

D. Rework, $8,050.

Answer (A) is correct. *(CIA, adapted)*

REQUIRED: The total dollar amount of the advantage of the more desirable option.

DISCUSSION: The original manufacturing cost of $6 per unit is a sunk cost that is not relevant to this decision. The relevant costs are the amounts that must be expended now. Thus, selling the toys for scrap has a $5,950 advantage because rework produces an additional $7,000 [($3 – $2) × 7,000], but the alternative generates an additional $12,950 (7,000 × $1.85).

Answer (B) is incorrect. The original manufacturing cost of $6 should not be added to the sales price. Answer (C) is incorrect. The original manufacturing cost of $6 should not be added to the sales price. Answer (D) is incorrect. The amount of $8,050 (rework) does not include the cost of the rework.

8.4.7. A tailor estimates that 60,000 special zippers will be used in the manufacture of men's jackets during the next year. A zipper supplier has quoted a price of $.60 per zipper. The tailor would prefer to purchase 5,000 units per month, but the supplier is unable to guarantee this delivery schedule. To ensure availability of these zippers, the tailor is considering the purchase of all 60,000 units at the beginning of the year. Assuming the tailor can invest cash at 8%, the tailor's opportunity cost of purchasing the 60,000 units at the beginning of the year is

A. $1,320

B. $1,440

C. $2,640

D. $36,000

Answer (A) is correct. *(CMA, adapted)*

REQUIRED: The opportunity cost of purchasing the total annual requirement at the beginning of the year.

DISCUSSION: The cost of 60,000 zippers is $36,000 (60,000 × $.60). The monthly cost is $3,000 (5,000 × $.60). The company would like to purchase the items monthly, so it will invest at least $3,000 in January. Accordingly, the zippers to be used in January will be purchased at the first of the year even if no special purchase is made. Thus, the incremental advance purchase is only $33,000. Because the alternative arrangement involves a constant monthly expenditure of $3,000, the incremental investment declines by that amount each month (for example, January $36,000 – $3,000 = $33,000; February $33,000 – $3,000 = $30,000 . . . ; December $3,000 – $3,000 = $0). The result is that the average incremental investment for the year is $16,500 ($33,000 ÷ 2), and the opportunity cost of purchasing 60,000 units at the beginning of the year is $1,320 ($16,500 × 8%).

Answer (B) is incorrect. The amount of $1,440 is 8% of $18,000 ($36,000 ÷ 2). Answer (C) is incorrect. The amount of $2,640 equals 8% of $33,000. Answer (D) is incorrect. The amount of $36,000 equals the price of the zippers.

8.4.8. Briar Co. signed a government construction contract providing for a formula price of actual cost plus 10%. In addition, Briar was to receive one-half of any savings resulting from the formula price's being less than the target price of $2.2 million. Briar's actual costs incurred were $1,920,000. How much should Briar receive from the contract?

A. $2,060,000

B. $2,112,000

C. $2,156,000

D. $2,200,000

Answer (C) is correct. *(CPA, adapted)*

REQUIRED: The amount received from a cost-plus contract.

DISCUSSION: The formula price is 110% of actual cost, or $2,112,000 ($1,920,000 × 110%), a savings of $88,000 on the $2,200,000 target price. Accordingly, the amount received should be $2,156,000 {$2,112,000 + [($2,200,000 – $2,112,000) × 50%]}.

Answer (A) is incorrect. The amount of $2,060,000 equals actual costs plus 50% of the excess of the target price over actual costs. Answer (B) is incorrect. The amount of $2,112,000 is the formula price. Answer (D) is incorrect. The amount of $2,200,000 is the target price.

Questions 8.4.9 and 8.4.10 are based on the following information. Whitehall Corporation produces chemicals used in the cleaning industry. During the previous month, Whitehall incurred $300,000 of joint costs in producing 60,000 units of AM-12 and 40,000 units of BM-36. Whitehall uses the units-of-production method to allocate joint costs. Currently, AM-12 is sold at split-off for $3.50 per unit. Flank Corporation has approached Whitehall to purchase all of the production of AM-12 after further processing. The further processing will cost Whitehall $90,000.

8.4.9. Concerning AM-12, which one of the following alternatives is most advantageous?

A. Whitehall should process further and sell to Flank if the total selling price per unit after further processing is greater than $3.00, which covers the joint costs.

B. Whitehall should continue to sell at split-off unless Flank offers at least $4.50 per unit after further processing, which covers Whitehall's total costs.

C. Whitehall should process further and sell to Flank if the total selling price per unit after further processing is greater than $5.00.

D. Whitehall should process further and sell to Flank if the total selling price per unit after further processing is greater than $5.25, which maintains the same gross profit percentage.

Answer (C) is correct. *(CMA, adapted)*

REQUIRED: The most advantageous processing and selling alternative.

DISCUSSION: The unit price of the product at the split-off point is known to be $3.50, so the joint costs are irrelevant. The additional unit cost of further processing is $1.50 ($90,000 ÷ 60,000 units). Consequently, the unit price must be at least $5.00 ($3.50 opportunity cost + $1.50).

Answer (A) is incorrect. The joint costs are irrelevant. Answer (B) is incorrect. The unit price must cover the $3.50 opportunity cost plus the $1.50 of additional costs. Answer (D) is incorrect. Any price greater than $5 will provide greater profits, in absolute dollars, even though the gross profit percentage declines.

8.4.10. Assume that Whitehall Corporation agreed to sell AM-12 to Flank Corporation for $5.50 per unit after further processing. During the first month of production, Whitehall sold 50,000 units with 10,000 units remaining in inventory at the end of the month. With respect to AM-12, which one of the following statements is true?

A. The operating profit last month was $50,000, and the inventory value is $15,000.

B. The operating profit last month was $50,000, and the inventory value is $45,000.

C. The operating profit last month was $125,000, and the inventory value is $30,000.

D. The operating profit last month was $200,000, and the inventory value is $30,000.

Answer (B) is correct. *(CMA, adapted)*

REQUIRED: The operating profit and inventory value after specified sales of a product.

DISCUSSION: Joint costs are allocated based on units of production. Accordingly, the unit joint cost allocated to AM-12 is $3.00 [$300,000 ÷ (60,000 units of AM-12 + 40,000 units of BM-36)]. The unit cost of AM-12 is therefore $4.50 [$3.00 joint cost + ($90,000 additional cost ÷ 60,000 units)]. Total inventory value is $45,000 (10,000 units × $4.50), and total operating profit is $50,000 [50,000 units sold × ($5.50 unit price – $4.50 unit cost)].

Answer (A) is incorrect. The $3 unit joint cost should be included in the inventory value. Answer (C) is incorrect. The $1.50 unit additional cost should be included in total unit cost. Answer (D) is incorrect. The $3 unit joint cost should be included in the cost of goods sold, and inventory should include the $1.50 unit additional cost.

Questions 8.4.11 through 8.4.13 are based on the following information. Condensed monthly operating income data for Korbin, Inc., for May follows:

	Urban Store	Suburban Store	Total
Sales	$80,000	$120,000	$200,000
Variable costs	32,000	84,000	116,000
Contribution margin	$48,000	$ 36,000	$ 84,000
Direct fixed costs	20,000	40,000	60,000
Store segment margin	$28,000	$ (4,000)	$ 24,000
Common fixed cost	4,000	6,000	10,000
Operating income	$24,000	$ (10,000)	$ 14,000

Additional information regarding Korbin's operations follows:

- One-fourth of each store's direct fixed costs would continue if either store is closed.
- Korbin allocates common fixed costs to each store on the basis of sales dollars.
- Management estimates that closing the Suburban Store would result in a 10% decrease in the Urban Store's sales, while closing the Urban Store would not affect the Suburban Store's sales.
- The operating results for May are representative of all months.

8.4.11. A decision by Korbin to close the Suburban Store would result in a monthly increase (decrease) in Korbin's operating income of

A. $(10,800)

B. $(6,000)

C. $(1,200)

D. $4,000

Answer (A) is correct. *(CMA, adapted)*

REQUIRED: The effect on operating income of closing the Suburban Store.

DISCUSSION: If the Suburban Store is closed, one-fourth of its direct fixed costs will continue. Thus, the segment margin that should be used to calculate the effect of its closing on Korbin's operating income is $6,000 {$36,000 contribution margin – [$40,000 direct fixed costs × (1.0 – .25)]}. In addition, the sales (and contribution margin) of the Urban Store will decline by 10% if the Suburban store closes. A 10% reduction in Urban's $48,000 contribution margin will reduce income by $4,800. Accordingly, the effect of closing the Suburban Store is to decrease operating income by $10,800 ($6,000 + $4,800).

Answer (B) is incorrect. The amount of $(6,000) overlooks the decline in profitability at the Urban Store. Answer (C) is incorrect. The amount of $(1,200) assumes that the effect on the Urban Store is a $4,800 increase in contribution margin. Answer (D) is incorrect. Profits will decline.

8.4.12. Korbin is considering a promotional campaign at the Suburban Store that would not affect the Urban Store. Increasing annual promotional expense at the Suburban Store by $60,000 in order to increase this store's sales by 10% would result in a monthly increase (decrease) in Korbin's operating income during the year (rounded) of

A. $(5,000)

B. $(1,400)

C. $487

D. $7,000

Answer (B) is correct. *(CMA, adapted)*

REQUIRED: The effect on monthly income of an advertising campaign.

DISCUSSION: The $60,000 advertising campaign will increase direct fixed costs by $5,000 per month ($60,000 ÷ 12). Sales and contribution margin will also increase by 10%. Hence, the contribution margin for the Suburban Store will increase by $3,600 ($36,000 × 10%), and income will decline by $1,400 ($5,000 – $3,600).

Answer (A) is incorrect. The amount of $(5,000) is the monthly advertising cost. Answer (C) is incorrect. The contribution margin of the Suburban Store will increase by $3,600, which is $1,400 less than the increased advertising cost. Answer (D) is incorrect. The amount of $7,000 omits the 10% increase in variable costs from the calculation.

8.4.13. One-half of the Suburban Store's dollar sales are from items sold at variable cost to attract customers to the store. Korbin is considering the deletion of these items, a move that would reduce the Suburban Store's direct fixed expenses by 15% and result in a 20% loss of Suburban Store's remaining sales volume. This change would not affect the Urban Store. A decision by Korbin to eliminate the items sold at cost would result in a monthly increase (decrease) in Korbin's operating income of

A. $(5,200)

B. $(1,200)

C. $(7,200)

D. $2,000

Answer (B) is correct. *(CMA, adapted)*

REQUIRED: The effect on monthly income of eliminating sales made at variable cost.

DISCUSSION: If 50% of the Suburban Store's sales are at variable cost, its contribution margin (sales – variable costs) must derive wholly from sales of other items. However, eliminating sales at variable cost reduces other sales by 20%. Thus, the effect is to reduce the contribution margin to $28,800 ($36,000 × .8). Moreover, fixed costs will be reduced by 15% to $34,000 ($40,000 × .85). Consequently, the new segment margin is $(5,200) ($34,000 direct fixed costs – $28,800 contribution margin), a decrease of $1,200 [$(5,200) – $(4,000)].

Answer (A) is incorrect. The amount of $(5,200) is the new segment margin. Answer (C) is incorrect. The amount of $(7,200) is the reduction in the Suburban Store's contribution margin. Answer (D) is incorrect. Operating income must decrease.

8.4.14. Data regarding four different products manufactured by an organization are presented as follows. Direct material and direct labor are readily available from the respective resource markets. However, the manufacturer is limited to a maximum of 3,000 machine hours per month.

	Products			
	A	B	C	D
Unit price	$15	$18	$20	$25
Variable cost	7	11	10	16

Units Produced per Machine Hour:
A: 3
B: 4
C: 2
D: 3

The product that is the most profitable for the manufacturer in this situation is

A. Product A.

B. Product B.

C. Product C.

D. Product D.

Answer (B) is correct. *(CIA, adapted)*

REQUIRED: The product that is the most profitable for the manufacturer.

DISCUSSION: When resources are limited, maximum profits are achieved by maximizing the dollar contribution margin per limited or constraining factor. In this situation, machine hours are the constraining factor. Product B has a contribution margin per machine hour of $28 [4 × ($18 – $11)], which is greater than that of Product A [3 × ($15 – $7) = $24], Product C [2 × ($20 – $10) = $20], or Product D [3 × ($25 – $16) = $27].

Answer (A) is incorrect. Product A has the greatest contribution margin ratio (53%) but a lower CM per hour than B. Answer (C) is incorrect. Product C has a greater dollar unit contribution margin ($10) but a lower CM per hour than B. Answer (D) is incorrect. Product D has the greatest selling price per unit ($25) but a lower CM per hour than B.

8.4.15. An oil well has been drilled. The cost of site preparation was $10,000. Drilling costs were $90,000. Once drilled, the well may or may not be completed. If completed, the costs are $40,000 to fracture the underground formation (enabling the oil to flow freely) and $30,000 for production casing pipe and other costs to put the well into production. If the well is completed, the present value of recoverable oil is $130,000. The well should be

A. Completed because the net benefit is $50,000.

B. Completed because the net benefit is $60,000.

C. Not completed because the overall loss will be $40,000.

D. Not completed because the overall loss will be $30,000.

Answer (B) is correct. *(K. Putnam)*

REQUIRED: The decision whether to invest and the net benefit or overall loss.

DISCUSSION: The costs relevant to the well completion decision are the incremental costs of $70,000 ($40,000 + $30,000). Incremental revenues equal the $130,000 present value of recoverable oil. Accordingly, the net benefit of completing the well is $60,000 ($130,000 – $70,000).

Answer (A) is incorrect. The $10,000 site preparation cost is an irrelevant sunk cost in the decision whether to complete the well. Answer (C) is incorrect. Although the overall loss on the well is $40,000, the decision whether to complete the well should rely only on future costs and revenues. The site preparation costs of $10,000 and drilling costs of $90,000 are sunk costs and should be ignored. Answer (D) is incorrect. The drilling costs of $90,000 are sunk costs and should be ignored.

8.5 Comprehensive

Questions 8.5.1 through 8.5.7 are based on the following information.

The Ashley Co. manufactures and sells a household product marketed through direct mail and advertisements in home improvement and gardening magazines. Although similar products are available in hardware and department stores, none are as effective as Ashley's model.

The company uses a standard cost system in its manufacturing accounting. The standards have not undergone a thorough review in the past 18 months. The general manager has seen no need for such a review because

- The materials quality and unit costs were fixed by a 3-year purchase commitment signed in July, Year 1.
- A 3-year labor contract had been signed in July, Year 1.
- There have been no significant variations from standard costs for the past three quarters.

The standard cost for the product, as established in July, Year 1, is presented below:

Materials (.75 lb. at $1 per lb.)	$0.75
Direct labor (.3 hr. at $4 per hour)	1.20
Overhead (.3 hr. at $7 per hour)	2.10
Standard manufacturing cost per unit	$4.05

The standard for overhead costs was developed from the following budgeted costs based upon an activity level of 1 million units (300,000 direct labor hours):

Variable manufacturing overhead	$ 600,000
Fixed manufacturing overhead	1,500,000
Total manufacturing overhead	$2,100,000

The earnings statement and the factory costs for the first quarter of Year 3 are presented in the opposite column. The first quarter results indicate that Ashley probably will achieve its sales goal of 1.2 million units for the current year. A total of 320,000 units were manufactured during the first quarter to increase inventory levels needed to support the growing sales volume.

ACTION Hardware, a national chain, recently asked Ashley to manufacture and sell a slightly modified version of the product that ACTION will distribute through its stores.

ACTION has offered to buy a minimum quantity of 200,000 units each year over the next 3 years and has offered to pay $4.10 for each unit, F.O.B. shipping point.

The Ashley management is interested in the proposal because it represents a new market. The company has adequate capacity to meet the production requirements. However, in addition to the possible financial results of taking the order, Ashley must consider carefully the other consequences of this departure from its normal practices. The president asked an assistant to the general manager to make an estimate of the financial aspects of the proposal for the first 12 months.

The assistant recommended that the order not be accepted and presented the analysis shown below to support the recommendation.

Sales Proposal of ACTION Hardware
First 12 Months' Results

Proposed sales (200,000 at $4.10)	$820,000
Estimated costs and expenses	
Manufacturing (200,000 at $4.05)	$810,000
Sales salaries	10,000
Administrative salaries	20,000
Total estimated costs	$840,000
Net loss	$ (20,000)

Note: None of our regular selling costs are included because this is a new market. However, a 16.6% increase in sales and administrative salaries has been incorporated because sales volume will increase by that amount.

Ashley Co.
First Quarter Earnings
Period Ended March 31, Year 3

Sales (300,000 units)		$2,700,000
Cost of goods sold		
Standard cost of goods	$1,215,000	
Variation from standard costs	12,000	(1,227,000)
Gross profit		$1,473,000
Operating expenses		
Selling		
Advertising	$ 200,000	
Mailing list costs	175,000	
Postage	225,000	
Salaries	60,000	
Administrative		
Salaries	120,000	
Office rent	45,000	
Total operating expenses		(825,000)
Income before taxes		$ 648,000
Income taxes (45%)		(291,600)
Net income		$ 356,400

Ashley Co.
Factory Costs
For the Quarter Ended March 31, Year 3

Materials	$ 266,000
Direct labor	452,000
Variable manufacturing overhead	211,000
Fixed manufacturing overhead	379,000
Total manufacturing costs	$1,308,000
Minus: Standard cost of goods manufactured	$1,296,000
Unfavorable variation from standard cost	$ 12,000

8.5.1. The financial analysis prepared by the general manager's assistant is

A. Deficient in that the contribution margin is not calculated.

B. Deficient in that the sales projections are not realistic.

C. Deficient in that current changes in standard costs are recognized.

D. Adequately prepared.

Answer (A) is correct. *(Publisher, adapted)*

REQUIRED: The deficiency in the financial analysis.

DISCUSSION: A primary deficiency in the financial analysis is that no contribution margin is calculated. The analysis uses a full standard cost approach to determine the profitability of a special project. Special projects should be evaluated based upon their incremental costs and benefits.

Answer (B) is incorrect. The sales projection is based on the buyer's minimum purchase quantity. Answer (C) is incorrect. A deficiency in the analysis is that current changes are not reflected. Answer (D) is incorrect. An adequate financial analysis should include CM data.

8.5.2. A determination should be made regarding fixed manufacturing costs. This determination involves

A. Anticipation of a decrease because of the allocation of fixed costs to include the special order.

B. Anticipation of an increase because of the increased volume incurred as a result of the special order.

C. No consideration of fixed manufacturing costs.

D. Consideration of administrative and sales salaries.

Answer (B) is correct. *(Publisher, adapted)*

REQUIRED: The necessary determination regarding fixed manufacturing costs.

DISCUSSION: The additional financial data needed for a more comprehensive analysis include an analysis of fixed manufacturing costs for any incremental increases as a result of increased volume. The special order may be such a significant proportion of the total manufacturing capacity that it will increase fixed costs in a step pattern.

Answer (A) is incorrect. The special order does not decrease fixed costs. Only incremental increases in fixed costs are allocated to the special order. Answer (C) is incorrect. A possible increase in fixed costs should be considered. Answer (D) is incorrect. Administrative and sales salaries are not fixed manufacturing costs.

8.5.3. Revisions of standards should be made for

A. Variable overhead.

B. Labor and materials.

C. Variable overhead and labor.

D. Variable overhead, labor, and materials.

Answer (D) is correct. *(Publisher, adapted)*

REQUIRED: The item(s) needing revision of standards.

DISCUSSION: Revisions of standards are appropriate for variable overhead, direct labor, and direct materials. These components have not been reviewed in the past 18 months. They may have undergone significant change within this period, and additional change may be predicted in the immediate future.

Answer (A) is incorrect. Revision of the standards also should be made for labor and materials. Answer (B) is incorrect. Revision of the standards also should be made for variable overhead. Answer (C) is incorrect. Revision of the standards also should be made for materials.

8.5.4. Assume that the manufacturing costs incurred in the first quarter reflect the anticipated costs for the ACTION special purchase. What is the expected materials cost per unit?

A. $.75

B. $1.00

C. $.83

D. $.80

Answer (C) is correct. *(Publisher, adapted)*

REQUIRED: The expected materials cost per unit for the special purchase.

DISCUSSION: The expected materials cost per unit based on the manufacturing costs incurred in the first quarter equals the materials cost in the first quarter divided by the number of units. The manufacturing cost in the first quarter for materials was $266,000, and 320,000 units were manufactured. Thus, the unit materials cost equals $.83 (rounded).

Answer (A) is incorrect. The amount of $.75 is the standard cost of materials for the product as established in July Year 1. Answer (B) is incorrect. The amount of $1.00 is the standard cost per pound of materials as established in July Year 1. Answer (D) is incorrect. The unit materials cost equals the materials cost for the first quarter divided by the quantity manufactured in the first quarter.

8.5.5. Refer to the information on the preceding page(s). Assume that the manufacturing costs incurred in the first quarter reflect the anticipated costs for the ACTION special purchase. What is the total expected direct labor cost of this purchase?

A. $240,000

B. $452,000

C. $282,000

D. $200,000

Answer (C) is correct. *(Publisher, adapted)*

REQUIRED: The total expected direct labor cost for the special purchase.

DISCUSSION: The total expected direct labor cost equals the expected direct labor cost per unit multiplied by the anticipated number of units. Based on the incurred costs in the first quarter of $452,000 and the 320,000 units manufactured, the unit direct labor cost equals $1.41 (rounded). The proposed purchase is of 200,000 units. Thus, the expected direct labor cost equals $282,000 (200,000 × $1.41).

Answer (A) is incorrect. The amount of $240,000 was calculated using the standard cost of direct labor of $1.20 instead of using the unit direct labor cost of $1.41. Answer (B) is incorrect. The amount of $452,000 is the direct labor cost incurred in the first quarter. Answer (D) is incorrect. The amount of $200,000 is the minimum quantity of units, not dollar labor cost.

8.5.6. Refer to the information on the preceding page(s). Assume that the first quarter factory costs incurred reflect the anticipated costs for the ACTION special purchase. What is the expected variable overhead cost per unit?

A. $2.10

B. $1.50

C. $.60

D. $.66

Answer (D) is correct. *(Publisher, adapted)*

REQUIRED: The expected variable overhead cost per unit for the special purchase.

DISCUSSION: The expected variable overhead cost per unit based on the first quarter production equals the variable manufacturing overhead cost incurred divided by the number of units manufactured. Accordingly, $211,000 divided by 320,000 units equals $.66 (rounded).

Answer (A) is incorrect. The amount of $2.10 is the total standard unit manufacturing overhead. Answer (B) is incorrect. The amount of $1.50 is the standard unit fixed manufacturing overhead. Answer (C) is incorrect. The amount of $.60 is the standard unit variable manufacturing overhead.

8.5.7. Refer to the information on the preceding page(s). Assume that the actual cost relationships in the quarter ended March 31, Year 3, relevant to this decision about the sales proposal of ACTION Hardware are valid. What is the manufacturing contribution margin?

A. $580,000

B. $240,000

C. $820,000

D. $10,000

Answer (B) is correct. *(Publisher, adapted)*

REQUIRED: The manufacturing contribution margin based on the cost data for the first quarter.

DISCUSSION: The manufacturing CM is calculated by subtracting incremental manufacturing costs from the proposed sales. Assuming that the actual cost relationships for the quarter ended March 31 are valid, the per-unit costs incurred during the quarter must be used to determine the CM. The unit cost for materials is .83 ($266,000 materials in the first quarter ÷ 320,000 units manufactured), the unit cost for labor is 1.41 ($452,000 direct labor cost in the first quarter ÷ 320,000 units manufactured), and the unit cost for variable manufacturing overhead is .66 ($211,000 variable manufacturing overhead in the first quarter ÷ 320,000 units). The manufacturing CM is calculated as follows:

Proposed sales (200,000 × $4.10)		$820,000
Incremental manufacturing costs:		
Materials (200,000 × $.83)	$166,000	
Labor (200,000 × $1.41)	282,000	
Variable overhead (200,000 × $.66)	132,000	(580,000)
Manufacturing CM		$240,000

Answer (A) is incorrect. The amount of $580,000 is the total of the incremental manufacturing costs. Answer (C) is incorrect. The proposed sales are $820,000. Answer (D) is incorrect. The amount of $10,000 is the estimated sales salaries expense for the first 12 months.

Questions 8.5.8 through 8.5.10 are based on the following information.

Ignore taxes when answering these questions. ABC Company produces and sells a single product called Kleen. Annual production capacity is 100,000 machine hours. It takes 1 machine hour to produce a unit of Kleen. Annual demand for Kleen is expected to remain at 80,000 units. The selling price is expected to remain at $10 per unit. Cost data for producing and selling Kleen are presented to the right:

Variable costs (per unit):	
Direct materials	$1.50
Direct labor	2.50
Variable overhead	0.80
Variable selling	2.00
Fixed costs (per year):	
Fixed overhead	$100,000.00
Fixed selling and administrative	50,000.00

8.5.8. ABC Company has 2,000 units of Kleen that were partially damaged in storage. It can sell these units through regular channels at reduced prices. These 2,000 units will be valueless unless sold this way. Sale of these units will not affect regular sales of Kleen. The relevant unit cost for determining the minimum selling price for these units is

A. $6.80

B. $6.00

C. $4.00

D. $2.00

Answer (D) is correct. *(CIA, adapted)*

REQUIRED: The relevant unit cost for determining the minimum selling price for damaged units.

DISCUSSION: The unit cost relevant to determining the minimum selling price for the damaged units is the incremental cost that will be incurred. Thus, the relevant unit cost is variable selling cost, or $2.00. The other costs are considered to be sunk (irrelevant) costs because they have already been incurred.

Answer (A) is incorrect. The amount of $6.80 is the total variable cost per unit. Answer (B) is incorrect. Direct materials and direct labor costs are sunk costs and therefore should not be considered. Answer (C) is incorrect. The amount of $4.00 is the prime cost per unit.

8.5.9. MNO Company offers to make and ship 25,000 units of Kleen directly to ABC Company's customers. If ABC Company accepts this offer, it will continue to produce and ship the remaining 55,000 units. ABC's fixed manufacturing overhead will drop to $90,000. Its fixed selling and administrative expenses will remain unchanged. Variable selling expenses will drop to $0.80 per unit for the 25,000 units produced and shipped by MNO company. What is the maximum amount per unit that ABC Company should pay MNO Company for producing and shipping the 25,000 units?

A. $6.80

B. $6.40

C. $5.60

D. $5.20

Answer (B) is correct. *(CIA, adapted)*

REQUIRED: The maximum unit amount that should be paid for producing and shipping the units.

DISCUSSION: The maximum amount per unit that should be paid is the savings by not making the product.

Variable manufacturing costs [25,000 × ($1.50 + $2.50 + $0.80)]	$120,000
Fixed overhead ($100,000 – $90,000)	10,000
Variable selling costs [25,000 × ($2.00 – $0.80)]	30,000
Total cost savings	$160,000
Units	÷ 25,000
Cost savings per unit	$ 6.40

Answer (A) is incorrect. The amount of $6.80 is the total variable cost per unit. Answer (C) is incorrect. The amount of $5.60 does not include the unit variable overhead cost of $.80. Answer (D) is incorrect. The amount of $5.20 does not include variable selling costs of $30,000.

8.5.10. ABC Company receives a one-time special order for 5,000 units of Kleen. Acceptance of this order will not affect the regular sales of 80,000 units. Variable selling costs for each of these 5,000 units will be $1.00. What is the differential cost to ABC Company of accepting this special order?

A. $39,000

B. $34,000

C. $30,250

D. $29,000

Answer (D) is correct. *(CIA, adapted)*

REQUIRED: The differential cost of accepting a special order.

DISCUSSION: Differential (incremental) costs change as a result of changes in operations or objectives. The differential cost per unit includes all variable manufacturing costs and variable selling costs. Thus, the differential cost per unit is $5.80 ($1.50 + $2.50 + $.80 + $1.00). The total differential cost is $29,000 (5,000 × $5.80).

Answer (A) is incorrect. The amount of $39,000 results from including $3.00 of variable selling costs per unit. Answer (B) is incorrect. The amount of $34,000 includes variable selling costs per unit of $2.00. Answer (C) is incorrect. The differential cost equals the 5,000 special-order units times a unit variable cost of $5.80.

Questions 8.5.11 through 8.5.18 are based on the following information.

Jenco, Inc., manufactures a combination fertilizer and weedkiller under the name Fertikil. This is the only product Jenco produces. Fertikil is sold nationwide through normal marketing channels to retail nurseries and garden stores.

Taylor Nursery plans to sell a similar fertilizer and weedkiller compound through its regional nursery chain under its own private label. Taylor has asked Jenco to submit a bid for a 25,000-pound order of the private brand compound. Although the chemical composition of the Taylor compound differs from Fertikil, the manufacturing process is very similar.

The Taylor compound will be produced in 1,000-pound lots. Each lot will require 60 direct labor hours and the following chemicals:

Chemicals	Quantity in Pounds
CW-3	400
JX-6	300
MZ-8	200
BE-7	100

The first three chemicals (CW-3, JX-6, MZ-8) are all used in the production of Fertikil. BE-7 was used in a compound that Jenco has discontinued. This chemical was not sold or discarded because it does not deteriorate and storage facilities have been adequate. Jenco can sell BE-7 at the prevailing market price minus $.10 per pound selling and handling expenses.

Jenco also has on hand a chemical called CN-5 that was manufactured for use in another product no longer produced. CN-5, which cannot be used in Fertikil, can be substituted for CW-3 on a one-for-one basis without affecting the quality of the Taylor compound. The quantity of CN-5 in inventory has a salvage value of $500.

Inventory and cost data for the chemicals that can be used to produce the Taylor compound are

Raw Materials	Pounds in Inventory	Actual Price per Pound When Purchased	Current Market Price per Pound
CW-3	22,000	$ .80	$ .90
JX-6	5,000	.55	.60
MZ-8	8,000	1.40	1.60
BE-7	4,000	.60	.65
CN-5	5,500	.75	(salvage)

The current direct labor rate is $7 per hour. The manufacturing overhead rate is established at the beginning of the year and is applied consistently throughout the year using direct labor hours (DLH) as the base. The predetermined overhead rate for the current year, based on a two-shift capacity of 400,000 total DLH with no overtime, is as follows:

Variable manufacturing overhead	$2.25 per DLH
Fixed manufacturing overhead	3.75 per DLH
Combined rate	$6.00 per DLH

Jenco's production manager reports that the existing equipment and facilities are adequate to manufacture the Taylor compound. However, Jenco is within 800 hours of its two-shift capacity this month before it must schedule overtime. If need be, the Taylor compound can be produced on regular time by shifting a portion of Fertikil production to overtime. Jenco's rate for overtime hours is one-and-one-half the regular pay rate, or $10.50 per hour. There is no allowance for any overtime premium in the manufacturing overhead rate.

Jenco's standard markup policy for new products is 25% of full manufacturing cost.

8.5.11. If Jenco bids this month for the special one-time order of 25,000 pounds, the total direct labor cost is

A. $10,500

B. $12,950

C. $16,250

D. $2,450

Answer (B) is correct. *(Publisher, adapted)*

REQUIRED: The total direct labor cost for the one-time order.

DISCUSSION: Given that 25 (25,000 pounds ÷ 1,000-pound lots) lots are produced, each requiring 60 direct labor hours, 1,500 hours are necessary. This one-time order requires 800 hours scheduled during regular time and 700 remaining hours of overtime. Thus, overtime is a relevant cost for this order. Total direct labor cost equals $12,950 [(1,500 DLH × $7) + (700 DLH × $3.50 hourly overtime premium)].

Answer (A) is incorrect. The amount of $10,500 does not include overtime cost of $2,450. Answer (C) is incorrect. Total direct labor cost equals $12,950. Answer (D) is incorrect. The amount of $2,450 is the overtime premium cost for this order.

8.5.12. If Jenco bids this month for the special one-time order of 25,000 pounds, the total overhead cost used for this decision is

A. $5,625

B. $9,000

C. $3,375

D. $5,825

Answer (C) is correct. *(Publisher, adapted)*

REQUIRED: The total overhead cost for the one-time order.

DISCUSSION: The total overhead cost used for this decision includes the variable overhead only. The fixed overhead is not relevant to this one-time order. A total of 1,500 direct labor hours is used (25 lots × 60 DLH per lot). The variable overhead rate is $2.25 per hour. Thus, $3,375 of total overhead is relevant to this decision (1,500 DLH × $2.25). The overtime premium is direct labor cost, not a part of overhead, because it is attributable to a particular job.

Answer (A) is incorrect. The amount of $5,625 is total fixed overhead. Answer (B) is incorrect. The amount of $9,000 includes total fixed overhead of $5,625. Answer (D) is incorrect. The amount of $5,825 equals the variable overhead plus the overtime premium.

8.5.13. The total variable cost of the special order for this month is

A. $21,800

B. $40,375

C. $31,375

D. $34,750

Answer (D) is correct. *(Publisher, adapted)*

REQUIRED: The total variable cost of the special order.

DISCUSSION: The total variable cost of the special order is the sum of direct materials, direct labor, and overhead. The cost of materials is $18,425 ($500 + $4,050 + $4,500 + $8,000 + $1,375). Overtime is a relevant cost of this order appropriately included in the total direct labor cost $12,950 [(1,500 DLH × $7) + (700 DLH × $3.50 hourly overtime premium)]. The special order does not increase fixed overhead costs and is not a continuing product that should contribute to fixed overhead. Thus, fixed overhead is not relevant.

Total direct materials cost	$18,425
Direct labor	12,950
Variable overhead	3,375
Total cost of special order	$34,750

Answer (A) is incorrect. The amount of $21,800 does not include $12,950 of direct labor cost. Answer (B) is incorrect. The amount of $40,375 includes fixed overhead. Answer (C) is incorrect. The amount of $31,375 omits variable overhead.

8.5.14. What is the total direct materials cost for recurring 25-lot orders?

A. $18,425

B. $21,500

C. $26,425

D. $23,125

Answer (D) is correct. *(Publisher, adapted)*

REQUIRED: The total direct materials cost for the recurring orders.

DISCUSSION: The total direct materials cost for recurring orders includes the regular price of each product times the number of pounds. The substitution of CN-5 is no longer possible because Jenco's supply was exhausted in the first special batch.

CW-3:	10,000 lbs.× $.90/lb.	$ 9,000
JX-6:	7,500 lbs.× $.60/lb.	4,500
MZ-8:	5,000 lbs.× $1.60/lb.	8,000
BE-7:	2,500 lbs.× $.65/lb.	1,625
Total direct materials cost		$23,125

Answer (A) is incorrect. The amount of $18,425 is the total direct materials cost for the special one-time order of 25,000 pounds of the private brand. Answer (B) is incorrect. The amount of $21,500 does not include direct materials cost of $1,625 for BE-7. Answer (C) is incorrect. The total direct materials cost for recurring 25-lot orders is $23,125.

8.5.15. What is the total overhead costs for recurring 25-lot orders?

A. $5,625

B. $9,000

C. $3,375

D. $7,500

Answer (B) is correct. *(Publisher, adapted)*

REQUIRED: The total overhead costs for recurring orders.

DISCUSSION: The total overhead costs for recurring orders should include variable and fixed overhead because a continuing product should contribute to fixed overhead as well as cover all variable costs. The overhead charge is

1,500 DLH × $6/DLH = $9,000

Answer (A) is incorrect. The amount of $5,625 is the fixed overhead cost. Answer (C) is incorrect. The amount of $3,375 is the variable overhead cost. Answer (D) is incorrect. The total overhead costs for recurring 25-lot orders are $9,000.

8.5.16. What is the full cost of the one-time special order of 25,000 pounds?

A. $18,425

B. $12,950

C. $55,906

D. $40,375

Answer (D) is correct. *(Publisher, adapted)*

REQUIRED: The full cost of the one-time special order.

DISCUSSION: The full cost is the variable cost plus fixed overhead. Fixed overhead is $3.75 per DLH, and 1,500 hours are required.

Direct materials	$18,425
Direct labor	12,950
Variable overhead	3,375
Fixed overhead ($3.75/DLH × 1,500 DLH)	5,625
Total cost of special order	$40,375

Answer (A) is incorrect. The amount of $18,425 is the total direct materials cost. Answer (B) is incorrect. The amount of $12,950 is the direct labor cost. Answer (C) is incorrect. The total cost of the special order is $40,375.

8.5.17. Refer to the information on the preceding page(s). If Jenco bids this month for the special one-time order of 25,000 pounds of the private brand, the special order's total direct materials cost is

A. $17,050

B. $18,425

C. $14,375

D. $10,425

Answer (B) is correct. *(Publisher, adapted)*

REQUIRED: The direct materials cost for the one-time order.

DISCUSSION: The special order requires three chemicals used in manufacturing the main product (CW-3, JX-6, MZ-8). Relevant costs are the current market prices. Chemicals not used in current production (BE-7 and CN-5) have relevant costs equal to their value to the firm. The order requires 10,000 pounds (400 lbs. per lot × 25) of CW-3. However, the 5,500 pounds of CN-5 can be substituted on a one-for-one basis at a total cost of $500 (salvage). The cost of the 4,500 pounds of CW-3 (10,000 – 5,500) is $4,050 (4,500 × $.90). The cost of JX-6 is $4,500 (300 lbs. × 25 lots × $.60). The cost of MZ-8 is $8,000 (200 lbs. × 25 lots × $1.60). The cost of BE-7 is $1,375 [100 lbs. × 25 lots × ($.65 – $.10)]. Thus, the total direct materials cost is $18,425 ($500 + $4,050 + $4,500 + $8,000 + $1,375).

Answer (A) is incorrect. The amount of $17,050 does not include the direct materials cost of $1,375 for chemical BE-7. Answer (C) is incorrect. The amount of $14,275 omits the cost of $4,050 for chemical CW-3. Answer (D) is incorrect. The amount of $10,425 omits the cost of $800 for chemical MZ-8.

8.5.18. Refer to the information on the preceding page(s). What is the total direct labor cost for recurring 25-lot orders, assuming that 60% of each order can be completed during regular hours?

A. $12,600

B. $10,500

C. $16,500

D. $18,225

Answer (A) is correct. *(Publisher, adapted)*

REQUIRED: The direct labor cost for recurring orders given capacity overflow.

DISCUSSION: For recurring orders, the total direct labor cost equals direct labor hours times the standard rate, with adjustments for any overtime caused by the recurring orders. If 60% of a batch (1,500 DLH × .6 = 900 DLH) can be completed during regular time, the remaining 600 DLH directly incur overtime. The overtime premium is therefore a relevant cost of the new product.

Regular time (1,500 DLH × $7.00 per DLH)	$10,500
Overtime premium (600 DLH × $3.50 per DLH)	2,100
Total direct labor cost	$12,600

Answer (B) is incorrect. The amount of $10,500 does not include $2,100 of overtime premium. Answer (C) is incorrect. The total direct labor cost is $12,600. Answer (D) is incorrect. The total direct labor cost is $12,600.

Page Intentionally Left Blank

Questions 8.5.19 through 8.5.22 are based on the following information.

Framar, Inc., manufactures machinery to customer specifications. It operated at about 75% of practical capacity during the year. The operating results for the most recent fiscal year are presented below.

Framar, Inc.
Income Statement
For the Year Ended September 30
(000 omitted)

Sales		$25,000
Minus: Sales commissions		(2,500)
Net sales		$22,500
Expenses		
Direct materials		$ 6,000
Direct labor		7,500
Manufacturing O/H-variable		
Supplies	$ 625	
Indirect labor	1,500	
Power	125	2,250
Manufacturing O/H-fixed		
Supervision	$ 500	
Depreciation	1,000	1,500
Corporate administration		750
Total expenses		$18,000
Net income before taxes		$ 4,500
Income taxes (40%)		(1,800)
Net income		$ 2,700

Top management has developed the pricing formula presented below. It is based upon the operating results achieved during the most recent fiscal year. The relationships used in the formula are expected to continue during the next fiscal year. The company expects to operate at 75% of practical capacity during the next fiscal year.

APA, Inc., has asked Framar to bid on some custom-designed machinery. Framar used the formula to develop a price and submitted a bid of $165,000. The calculations are given next to the pricing formula shown below.

Details of Formula		APA Bid Calculations
Estimated direct materials cost	$XXX	$ 29,200
Estimated direct labor cost	XXX	56,000
Estimated manufacturing O/H calculated at 50% of DL	XXX	28,000
Estimated corporate O/H calculated at 10% of DL	XXX	5,600
Estimated total costs excluding sales commissions	$XXX	$118,800
Add 25% for profits and taxes	XXX	29,700
Suggested price (with profits) before sales commissions	$XXX	$148,500
Suggested total price equal to suggested price divided by .9 to adjust for 10% sales commissions	$XXX	$165,000

8.5.19. What is the contribution margin if the bid is accepted?

A. $102,000

B. $63,300

C. $27,900

D. $46,500

Answer (D) is correct. *(Publisher, adapted)*

REQUIRED: The CM if the bid is accepted.

DISCUSSION: The CM equals the gross revenue minus any variable costs. Variable costs include the sales commission, direct materials, direct labor, and variable manufacturing overhead. Variable manufacturing overhead for the most recent fiscal year was 30% of direct labor ($2,250 ÷ $7,500). The cost relationships are expected to continue.

Submitted bid		$165,000
Minus: Sales commission (10%)		(16,500)
Net sales		$148,500
Minus variable costs:		
Direct materials	$29,200	
Direct labor	56,000	
Variable mfg. overhead (30% of direct labor)	16,800	(102,000)
Contribution margin		$ 46,500

Answer (A) is incorrect. The amount of $102,000 is the total variable costs. Answer (B) is incorrect. Variable manufacturing overhead of $16,800 should be subtracted from net sales. Answer (C) is incorrect. The amount of $27,900 is the increase in net income if the bid is accepted.

8.5.20. If the bid is accepted, what is the increase in net income?

A. $27,900

B. $46,500

C. $63,300

D. $148,500

Answer (A) is correct. *(Publisher, adapted)*

REQUIRED: The net increase in income if the bid is accepted.

DISCUSSION: The CM for the APA job is $46,500. It increases net income, assuming the fixed costs are incurred even if the bid is rejected. The increase in net income equals the CM minus income taxes at a rate of 40%, or $27,900 [$46,500 × (1.0 – .4)].

Answer (B) is incorrect. The amount of $46,500 is the contribution margin if the bid is accepted. Answer (C) is incorrect. Variable manufacturing overhead of $16,800 also should be subtracted from sales to arrive at the CM. Answer (D) is incorrect. The amount of $148,500 is the total net sales.

8.5.21. Should Framar manufacture the machinery for a counteroffer of $127,000?

A. Yes, net income will increase by $7,380.

B. Yes, net income will increase by $12,300.

C. No, net income will decrease by $12,700.

D. None of the answers are correct.

Answer (A) is correct. *(Publisher, adapted)*

REQUIRED: The appropriate decision as to whether the job should be accepted at a lower price.

DISCUSSION: Acceptance of the counteroffer of $127,000 results in a net increase in income. The incremental revenue exceeds the incremental costs.

Counteroffer	$127,000
Sales commission (10%)	(12,700)
Net sales	$114,300
Variable manufacturing costs	(102,000)
Contribution margin	$ 12,300
Income taxes (40%)	(4,920)
Increase in net income	$ 7,380

Answer (B) is incorrect. The amount of $12,300 is the contribution margin of the counteroffer. Answer (C) is incorrect. The amount of $12,700 is the sales commission. Answer (D) is incorrect. Net income increases by $7,380.

8.5.22. What is the lowest price Framar can charge for this machinery without reducing its net income after taxes?

A. $114,300

B. $127,000

C. $113,333

D. $102,000

Answer (C) is correct. *(Publisher, adapted)*

REQUIRED: The lowest price without reducing net income after taxes.

DISCUSSION: The lowest price for the machinery is the total incremental cost associated with the job. It should recover the variable manufacturing costs and the sales commission. Variable manufacturing cost is $102,000, and the sales commission is 10%. Consequently, the minimum sales price is $113,333 [$102,000 ÷ (1.0 – 10%)].

Answer (A) is incorrect. A price of $114,300 results in a $522 increase in net income. Answer (B) is incorrect. A price of $127,000 results in a $7,380 increase in net income. Answer (D) is incorrect. A price of $102,000 results in a $10,200 decrease in income.

Questions 8.5.23 through 8.5.28 are based on the following information.

National Industries is a diversified corporation with separate and distinct operating divisions. Each division's performance is evaluated on the basis of total dollar profits and return on divisional investment.

The WindAir Division manufactures and sells air-conditioning units. The coming year's budgeted income statement, based upon a sales volume of 15,000 units, appears below.

WindAir Division
Budgeted Income Statement
For the Next Fiscal Year

	Per Unit	Total (000 omitted)
Sales revenue	$400	$6,000
Manufacturing costs		
Compressor	$ 70	$1,050
Other materials	37	555
Direct labor	30	450
Variable overhead	45	675
Fixed overhead	32	480
Total manufacturing costs	$214	$3,210
Gross margin	$186	$2,790
Operating expenses		
Variable selling	$ 18	$ 270
Fixed selling	19	285
Fixed administrative	38	570
Total operating expenses	$ 75	$1,125
Net income before taxes	$111	$1,665

WindAir's division manager believes sales can be increased if the unit selling price of the air conditioners is reduced. A market research study conducted by an independent firm indicates that a 5% reduction in the selling price ($20) will increase sales volume by 16%, or 2,400 units. WindAir has sufficient production capacity to manage this increased volume with no increase in fixed costs.

WindAir currently uses a compressor in its units that it purchases from an outside supplier at a cost of $70 per compressor. The division manager of WindAir has approached the manager of the Compressor Division regarding the sale of a compressor unit to WindAir. The Compressor Division currently manufactures and sells a unit exclusively to outside firms that is similar to the unit used by WindAir. The specifications of the WindAir compressor are slightly different, which will reduce the Compressor Division's materials costs by $1.50 per unit. In addition, the Compressor Division will not incur any variable selling costs for the units sold to WindAir. The manager of WindAir wants all of the compressors it uses to come from one supplier and has offered to pay $50 for each compressor unit.

The Compressor Division has the capacity to produce 75,000 units. The coming year's budgeted income statement for the Compressor Division is shown below and is based upon a sales volume of 64,000 units without considering WindAir's proposal.

Compressor Division
Budgeted Income Statement
For the Next Fiscal Year

	Per Unit	Total (000 omitted)
Sales revenue	$100	$6,400
Manufacturing costs		
Materials	$ 12	$ 768
Direct labor	8	512
Variable overhead	10	640
Fixed overhead	11	704
Total manufacturing costs	$ 41	$2,624
Gross margin	$ 59	$3,776
Operating expenses		
Variable selling	$ 6	$ 384
Fixed selling	4	256
Fixed administrative	7	448
Total operating expenses	$ 17	$1,088
Net income before taxes	$ 42	$2,688

8.5.23. What is WindAir's current unit contribution margin on air conditioners?

A. $111

B. $125

C. $200

D. $186

Answer (C) is correct. *(Publisher, adapted)*

REQUIRED: The unit contribution margin on air-conditioning units.

DISCUSSION: All the manufacturing costs are variable except $32 of fixed overhead per unit. Variable selling expenses equal $18. Thus, total variable costs are $200 ($214 – $32 + $18). The current UCM therefore is $200 ($400 unit selling price – $200 unit variable costs).

Answer (A) is incorrect. The amount of $111 is the net income before taxes. Answer (B) is incorrect. WindAir's current contribution margin on air conditioners is $200. Answer (D) is incorrect. The amount of $186 is the gross margin per unit.

8.5.24. What is the effect on WindAir's net income if it acquires the compressors from an outside source and reduces the price by 5%?

A. $132,000

B. $55,200

C. $76,800

D. $214,320

Answer (A) is correct. *(Publisher, adapted)*

REQUIRED: The change in net income given a price reduction and increased sales.

DISCUSSION: The total CM before the price decrease is $3,000,000 (15,000 units × $200 per unit). Given the price reduction, the unit CM decreases from $200 to $180 because the selling price declines by $20 ($400 × 5%). The units sold increase by 2,400 to 17,400. The new CM is $3,132,000 (17,400 units × $180 new UCM). CM therefore increases by $132,000 ($3,132,000 – $3,000,000).

8.5.25. As a result of decreasing selling price from $400 to $380, sales increase by 2,400 units at a unit contribution margin of $180. This increase in contribution margin attributable to greater sales

A. Must be adjusted for the $480,000 of fixed costs.

B. Must be adjusted for the loss of the $20 unit contribution margin for 15,000 units previously budgeted.

C. Must be adjusted for the incremental fixed manufacturing overhead (2,400 units × $32).

D. Is the change in pretax income.

Answer (B) is correct. *(Publisher, adapted)*

REQUIRED: The effect of the increase in the contribution margin due to increased sales.

DISCUSSION: The increased sales result in a volume variance of $432,000 favorable (2,400 units × $180). The change in sales occurs because of a lower price that creates a sales price variance (15,000 units currently budgeted × $20 per unit = $300,000 unfavorable). Thus, the decrease in price must be considered in addition to the increase in volume.

Answer (A) is incorrect. Fixed costs do not change with the increase in volume within the relevant range. Answer (C) is incorrect. Fixed costs do not change with the increase in volume within the relevant range. Answer (D) is incorrect. The $432,000 sales volume variance must be decreased by the $300,000 sales price variance.

8.5.26. What is the effect on the Compressor Division's net income of the sale to WindAir of 17,400 compressors if some external sales must be lost?

A. Decrease net income $35,500.

B. Decrease net income $129,800.

C. Decrease net income $59,000.

D. Increase net income $22,000.

Answer (A) is correct. *(Publisher, adapted)*

REQUIRED: The gain (loss) on the internal sale of a component given a set price and reduction of external sales.

DISCUSSION: If the Compressor Division sells all 17,400 units to WindAir, its external sales decline to 57,600 (75,000 maximum capacity – 17,400 sales to WindAir). To determine UCM, materials costs decrease by $1.50 for internal sales. No variable selling expenses are incurred.

Unit Contribution Margin	Outside Sales	WindAir Sales
Selling price	$100	$50.00
Variable costs		
Direct materials	$ 12	$10.50
Direct labor	8	8.00
Overhead	10	10.00
Selling expenses	6	-0-
Total variable costs	$ 36	$28.50
Unit contribution margin	$ 64	$21.50

The loss of the contribution from the sale of 6,400 units (64,000 – 57,600) that would otherwise be sold to outsiders is $409,600 (6,400 × $64). The sale to WindAir contributes $374,100 (17,400 × $21.50). The net result is a reduction in net income of $35,000 ($409,600 – $374,100).

8.5.27. If National Industries requires the Compressor Division to sell 17,400 compressors to WindAir, how much is the effect on the corporation's pretax earnings?

A. $(409,600)

B. $722,100

C. $312,500

D. $(215,400)

Answer (C) is correct. *(Publisher, adapted)*

REQUIRED: The net effect on corporate earnings of buying parts internally.

DISCUSSION: The net effect is the cost savings from use of an internally manufactured part minus the loss of contribution from sales to outsiders.

Outside purchase price	$ 70.00
Compressor Division's variable cost to produce	(28.50)
Savings per unit	$ 41.50
Number of units	× 17,400.00
Total cost savings	$722,100.00
Compressor Division's CM loss from sales to outsiders (6,400 × $64)	(409,600.00)
Increase in pretax net income	$312,500.00

Answer (A) is incorrect. The amount of $(409,600) is Compressor Division's CM loss from sales to WindAir by not selling to outside customers. Answer (B) is incorrect. The amount of $722,100 is the total cost savings of using the internally manufactured part. Answer (D) is incorrect. The increase in pretax net income is $312,500.

8.5.28. Refer to the information on the preceding page(s). What is the effect of decreasing the sales price 10% to increase sales by 4,500 units?

	Contribution Margin	Net Income Before Taxes
A.	$120,000	$(480,000)
B.	$120,000	$120,000
C.	$720,000	$120,000
D.	$720,000	$720,000

Answer (B) is correct. *(Publisher, adapted)*

REQUIRED: The effect of decreasing selling price to increase unit sales.

DISCUSSION: The 10% price decrease ($400 × 10%) lowers the UCM from $200 to $160. The additional 4,500 units sold increase the total contribution margin by $720,000 (4,500 × $160). The decrease in sales price reduces the contribution margin by $600,000 (15,000 × $40). The net effect on the contribution margin and net income (the fixed costs do not change) is $120,000 favorable ($720,000 F – $600,000 U).

Answer (A) is incorrect. Net income before taxes is $120,000. Answer (C) is incorrect. The net effect on the contribution margin is an increase of $120,000. Answer (D) is incorrect. The increase in the total contribution margin from the additional unit sales volume is $720,000.

STUDY UNIT NINE
RESPONSIBILITY ACCOUNTING, PERFORMANCE MEASUREMENT, AND TRANSFER PRICING

A **responsibility accounting system** assigns revenues, costs, and invested capital to responsibility centers. It requires assignment of responsibility to particular managers for the execution of particular plans, measurement of results, and comparison of the results with the plans.

A responsibility system should encourage the efficient achievement of goals. Thus, managerial control should promote **goal congruence** and **managerial effort**. One means of attaining goal congruence is to harmonize the measures used to evaluate managers with the measures used in top management's decision models.

Congruence of managerial and organizational goals requires (1) assigning responsibility for activities, (2) delegating the authority to do necessary tasks, (3) establishing accountability and the degree of control, and (4) measuring and evaluating performance. **Responsibility** is the obligation to perform. **Authority** is the power to direct and require performance from others. **Accountability** is the liability for failure to meet the obligation. **Controllability** is the extent to which a manager can influence activities. Performance theoretically should be evaluated only on the basis of factors controllable by the manager. But controllability and responsibility are rarely coextensive. A responsibility accounting system establishes subunits called **responsibility centers**. Each manager has authority over, and is responsible and accountable for, defined activities. A **cost** center is responsible for costs only. A **revenue** center is responsible for revenues but not costs other than marketing. A **profit** center is responsible for revenues and expenses. An **investment** center is responsible for revenues, expenses, and invested capital. A **service** center provides support to other subunits.

The trend in performance evaluation is the **balanced scorecard**. It is a report that relates **critical success factors (CSFs)** to measures of performance. CSFs are measurable financial and nonfinancial elements of performance that are vital to competitive advantage. CSFs are identified by a **SWOT** analysis that addresses internal factors (strengths and weaknesses) and external factors (opportunities and threats). The firm's greatest strengths are its **core competencies**.

Accounting based performance measures include (1) return on investment, (2) residual income, and (3) economic value added.

Return on investment (ROI) equals some measure of income divided by some measure of investment. The DuPont approach defines ROI as return on sales (Income ÷ Revenues) times investment turnover (Revenues ÷ Investment).

Residual income (RI) is the excess of operating income over a target return on invested capital. Projects with a positive residual income should be accepted.

Economic value added (EVA) is the formula for residual income adjusted for the opportunity cost of capital. EVA equals after-tax operating income [earnings before interest and taxes × (1.0 – the tax rate)], minus the product of (1) the after-tax weighted-average cost of capital and (2) an investment base equal to total assets minus current liabilities.

In **decentralization**, decision making occurs at as low of a level as possible. The premise is that a local manager can make better decisions than a centralized manager. Decentralization typically reflects larger companies that are divided into multiple segments. In most organizations, a mixture of centralization and decentralization is used.

Transfer prices are amounts charged by one segment of an entity for goods and services it provides to another segment. The issue is determining a price that motivates the seller and the buyer to achieve the same goals. Common methods include (1) variable cost, (2) full cost, (3) market price, and (4) negotiation. The minimum price that a seller is willing to accept is the sum of the incremental cost of producing the unit plus the opportunity cost of selling the unit internally. The opportunity cost of selling internally varies depending on whether (1) an external market for the product exists and (2) the seller has excess capacity.

QUESTIONS

9.1 Basis of a Responsibility System

9.1.1. An effective managerial control system has favorable motivational effects. Which of the following are aspects of motivation?

	Managerial Effort	Goal Congruence
A.	No	No
B.	No	Yes
C.	Yes	Yes
D.	Yes	No

Answer (C) is correct. *(Publisher, adapted)*

REQUIRED: The aspect(s), if any, of motivation.

DISCUSSION: A managerial control system should encourage the efficient achievement of organizational objectives. Thus, goal congruence and managerial effort are aspects of motivation. All managers should be motivated to expend the necessary effort to reach common goals.

9.1.2. Goal congruence is most likely to be promoted when

A. An entity uses a cost-based transfer price.

B. A manager of a retail store is charged imputed interest on inventory.

C. Percentage return on investment rather than residual income is used to measure managerial performance.

D. An annual accrual accounting measure is used to evaluate a manager who makes capital investment decisions.

Answer (B) is correct. *(Publisher, adapted)*

REQUIRED: The circumstances in which goal congruence is most likely to be promoted.

DISCUSSION: If the measure of the retail store manager's performance does not consider opportunity costs, for example, the cost of financing inventory, (s)he may be tempted to make suboptimal decisions about inventory amounts. For example, excessive inventory may minimize the costs for which the manager is responsible while increasing the costs for which (s)he is not.

Answer (A) is incorrect. A cost-based transfer price may provide no incentive to minimize cost. Answer (C) is incorrect. The organization may be better served if a manager maximizes an absolute dollar amount rather than a rate of return. Answer (D) is incorrect. The accrual return on investment in the first years of a capital project may be very low even though it has a positive net present value.

9.1.3. To make goal setting effective and worthwhile, the goals should be

A. Just beyond what subordinates are likely to reach.

B. Qualitative and approximate.

C. Based on superior performers' output.

D. Specific, objective, and verifiable.

Answer (D) is correct. *(CIA, adapted)*

REQUIRED: The nature of desirable goals.

DISCUSSION: Effective goal setting requires a sufficient knowledge of employees' jobs to set specific, objective, verifiable goals. Employees also must understand how goal-oriented performance is measured.

Answer (A) is incorrect. Employees become discouraged if goals cannot be met. Answer (B) is incorrect. Goals should be quantitative and specific. They should not be too abstract. Answer (C) is incorrect. Not all employees are superior. Employees are discouraged by unreachable goals. Goals should be based on an employee's skills and capacity for improvement.

9.1.4. The extent to which a manager can influence organizational activities is

A. Authority.

B. Responsibility.

C. Accountability.

D. Controllability.

Answer (D) is correct. *(Publisher, adapted)*

REQUIRED: The extent to which a manager can influence organizational activities.

DISCUSSION: Controllability is the extent to which a manager can influence activities and related revenues, costs, or other items. In principle, controllability is proportionate to, but not coextensive with, responsibility.

Answer (A) is incorrect. Authority is the power to direct and exact performance from others. It includes the right to prescribe the means and methods by which work will be done. Answer (B) is incorrect. Responsibility is the obligation to perform. Answer (C) is incorrect. Accountability is the liability for failure to meet the obligation.

9.1.5. In a well-run organization, a manager may have responsibility for activities that (s)he cannot influence significantly. This arrangement may be justified because of the

A. Manager's knowledge about the activities and the potential for behavioral change.

B. Manager's knowledge about the activities but not the potential for behavioral change.

C. Improvement in managerial morale, effort, and performance.

D. Improvement in managerial morale and the potential for behavioral change.

Answer (A) is correct. *(Publisher, adapted)*

REQUIRED: The reason(s) for assigning responsibility without control.

DISCUSSION: A manager who does not control an activity may nevertheless be well informed about it. Thus, a purchasing agent may be able to explain price variances even though (s)he cannot control them. Moreover, if a manager is accountable solely for activities over which (s)he has extensive influence, the manager may develop too narrow a focus. For example, the manager of a cost center may make decisions based only on cost efficiency and ignore overall effectiveness goals. Extending the manager's responsibility to profits without changing his or her level of control may encourage desirable behavior congruent with overall goals.

Answer (B) is incorrect. Favorable behavioral change may justify assigning responsibility without control. Answer (C) is incorrect. If responsibility exceeds a manager's influence, the result may be reduced morale, a decline in managerial effort, and poor performance. Answer (D) is incorrect. If responsibility exceeds a manager's influence, the result may be reduced morale, a decline in managerial effort, and poor performance.

9.1.6. A segment of an organization is referred to as a service center if it has

A. Responsibility for developing markets and selling the output of the organization.

B. Responsibility for combining the raw materials, direct labor, and other factors of production into a final output.

C. Authority to make decisions affecting the major determinants of profit including the power to choose its markets and sources of supply.

D. Authority to provide specialized support to other units within the organization.

Answer (D) is correct. *(CMA, adapted)*

REQUIRED: The definition of a service center.

DISCUSSION: A service center exists primarily and sometimes solely to provide specialized support to other units within the organization. Service centers are usually operated as cost centers.

Answer (A) is incorrect. A service center has no responsibility for developing markets or selling. Answer (B) is incorrect. A production center is engaged in manufacturing. Answer (C) is incorrect. A profit center can choose its markets and sources of supply.

9.1.7. The least complex segment or area of responsibility for which costs are allocated is a(n)

A. Profit center.

B. Investment center.

C. Contribution center.

D. Cost center.

Answer (D) is correct. *(CMA, adapted)*

REQUIRED: The least complex segment or area of responsibility for which costs are allocated.

DISCUSSION: A cost center is a responsibility center that is accountable only for costs. The cost center is the least complex type of segment because it has no responsibility for revenues or investments.

Answer (A) is incorrect. A profit center is a segment responsible for both revenues and costs. A profit center has the authority to make decisions concerning markets and sources of supply. Answer (B) is incorrect. An investment center is a responsibility center that is accountable for revenues (markets), costs (sources of supply), and invested capital. Answer (C) is incorrect. A contribution center is responsible for revenues and variable costs, but not invested capital.

9.1.8. Which of the following techniques would be best for evaluating the management performance of a department that is operated as a cost center?

A. Return on assets ratio.

B. Return on investment ratio.

C. Payback method.

D. Variance analysis.

Answer (D) is correct. *(CIA, adapted)*

REQUIRED: The best method for evaluating a cost center.

DISCUSSION: A cost center is a responsibility center that is responsible for costs only. Of the alternatives given, variance analysis is the only one that can be used in a cost center. Variance analysis involves comparing actual costs with predicted or standard costs.

Answer (A) is incorrect. Return on assets cannot be computed for a cost center. The manager is not responsible for revenue (return) or the assets available. Answer (B) is incorrect. Return on investment cannot be computed for a cost center. The manager is not responsible for revenue (return) or the assets available. Answer (C) is incorrect. The payback method is a means of evaluating alternative investment proposals.

9.1.9. Responsibility accounting defines an operating center that is responsible for revenue and costs as a(n)

A. Profit center.

B. Revenue center.

C. Division.

D. Operating unit.

Answer (A) is correct. *(CMA, adapted)*

REQUIRED: The name given to a responsibility center that is responsible for both revenue and costs.

DISCUSSION: A profit center is responsible for both revenues and costs, whereas a cost center is responsible only for costs.

Answer (B) is incorrect. A revenue center is responsible only for revenues, not costs. Answer (C) is incorrect. A division can be any type of responsibility center. Answer (D) is incorrect. An operating unit can be organized as any type of center.

9.1.10. The basic purpose of a responsibility accounting system is

A. Budgeting.

B. Motivation.

C. Authority.

D. Variance analysis.

Answer (B) is correct. *(CMA, adapted)*

REQUIRED: The basic purpose of a responsibility accounting system.

DISCUSSION: The basic purpose of a responsibility accounting system is to motivate management to perform in a manner consistent with overall company objectives. The assignment of responsibility implies that some revenues and costs can be changed through effective management. The system should have certain controls that provide for feedback reports indicating deviations from expectations. Higher-level management may focus on those deviations for either reinforcement or correction.

Answer (A) is incorrect. Budgeting is an element of a responsibility accounting system, not the basic purpose. Answer (C) is incorrect. Authority is an element of a responsibility accounting system, not the basic purpose. Answer (D) is incorrect. Analysis of variances is an element of a responsibility accounting system, not the basic purpose.

9.1.11. Decentralized firms can delegate authority and yet retain control and monitor managers' performance by structuring the organization into responsibility centers. Which one of the following organizational segments is most like an independent business?

A. Revenue center.

B. Profit center.

C. Cost center.

D. Investment center.

Answer (D) is correct. *(CMA, adapted)*

REQUIRED: The organizational segment most like an independent business.

DISCUSSION: An investment center is the organizational type most like an independent business because it is responsible for its own revenues, costs incurred, and capital invested. The other types of centers do not incorporate all three elements.

Answer (A) is incorrect. A revenue center is responsible only for revenue generation, not for costs or capital investment. Answer (B) is incorrect. A profit center is responsible for revenues and costs but not for invested capital. Answer (C) is incorrect. A cost center is evaluated only on the basis of costs incurred. It is not responsible for revenues or invested capital.

9.1.12. A successful responsibility accounting reporting system is dependent upon

A. The correct allocation of controllable variable costs.

B. Identification of the management level at which all costs are controllable.

C. The proper delegation of responsibility and authority.

D. A reasonable separation of costs into their fixed and variable components since fixed costs are not controllable and must be eliminated from the responsibility report.

Answer (C) is correct. *(CMA, adapted)*

REQUIRED: The factor upon which a successful responsibility accounting system is dependent.

DISCUSSION: Managerial performance ideally should be evaluated only on the basis of those factors controllable by the manager. Managers may control revenues, costs, or investments in resources. However, controllability is not an absolute. More than one manager may be able to influence a cost, and managers may be accountable for some costs they do not control. In practice, given the difficulties of determining the locus of controllability, responsibility may be assigned on the basis of knowledge about the incurrence of a cost rather than the ability to control it. Accordingly, a successful system is dependent upon the proper delegation of responsibility and the commensurate authority.

Answer (A) is incorrect. Fixed costs also may be controllable, and some costs not controllable may need to be assigned. Answer (B) is incorrect. Knowledge about the incurrence of a cost rather than controllability may in practice be an appropriate basis for delegation of responsibility. Answer (D) is incorrect. Fixed costs can be controllable.

9.1.13. Costs are accumulated by a responsibility center for control purposes when using

	Job-Order Costing	Process Costing
A.	Yes	Yes
B.	Yes	No
C.	No	No
D.	No	Yes

Answer (A) is correct. *(CPA, adapted)*

REQUIRED: The product costing method that uses responsibility centers to accumulate costs.

DISCUSSION: A responsibility center is a subunit (part or segment) of an organization whose manager is accountable for a specified set of activities. Both job-order costing and process costing may accumulate their costs by responsibility centers.

9.1.14. Controllable revenue would be included in a performance report for a

	Profit Center	Cost Center
A.	No	No
B.	No	Yes
C.	Yes	No
D.	Yes	Yes

Answer (C) is correct. *(CPA, adapted)*

REQUIRED: The responsibility center(s), if any, that include(s) controllable revenue in a performance report.

DISCUSSION: A profit center is a segment of a company responsible for both revenues and expenses. A profit center has the authority to make decisions concerning markets (revenues) and sources of supply (costs).

9.1.15. The following is a summarized income statement of Carr Co.'s profit center No. 43 for the month just ended:

Contribution margin		$70,000
Period expenses:		
Manager's salary	$20,000	
Facility depreciation	8,000	
Corporate expense allocation	5,000	(33,000)
Profit center income		$37,000

Which of the following amounts would most likely be subject to the control of the profit center's manager?

A. $70,000

B. $50,000

C. $37,000

D. $33,000

Answer (A) is correct. *(CPA, adapted)*

REQUIRED: The amount most likely subject to the control of the profit center's manager.

DISCUSSION: A profit center is a segment of a company responsible for both revenues and expenses. A profit center has the authority to make decisions concerning markets (revenues) and sources of supply (costs). However, the profit center's manager does not control his or her own salary, investment, and the resulting costs (e.g., depreciation of plant assets), or expenses incurred at the corporate level. Consequently, profit center No. 43 is most likely able to control its $70,000 contribution margin (sales – variable costs) but not the other items in the summarized income statement.

Answer (B) is incorrect. The profit center's manager does not control his or her $20,000 salary. Answer (C) is incorrect. The profit center's manager does not control the listed period expenses and therefore does not control the profit center's income. Answer (D) is incorrect. The listed period expenses ($33,000) are not controlled by the profit center.

9.1.16. A segment of an organization is an investment center if it has

A. Authority to make decisions affecting the major determinants of profit, including the power to choose its markets and sources of supply.

B. Authority to make decisions affecting the major determinants of profit, including the power to choose its markets and sources of supply and significant control over the amount of invested capital.

C. Authority to make decisions over the most significant costs of operations, including the power to choose the sources of supply.

D. Responsibility for developing markets for, and selling the output of, the organization.

Answer (B) is correct. *(CMA, adapted)*

REQUIRED: The nature of an investment center.

DISCUSSION: In investment centers, managers are responsible for all activities, including costs, revenues, and investments. An investment center is a profit center with significant control over the amount of capital invested. This control extends to (1) investments such as receivables and property, plant, and equipment and (2) entry into new markets.

Answer (A) is incorrect. A profit center is responsible for controlling expenses and generating revenues. Answer (C) is incorrect. A cost center has authority over the sources of supply but not of revenues or investments. Answer (D) is incorrect. A revenue center is responsible for developing markets and selling the firm's products.

9.2 Responsibility Accounting

9.2.1. In a responsibility accounting system, a feedback report that focuses on the difference between budgeted amounts and actual amounts is an example of

A. Management by exception.

B. Assessing blame.

C. Granting rewards to successful managers.

D. Ignoring other variables for which the budgeted goals were met.

Answer (A) is correct. *(Publisher, adapted)*

REQUIRED: The term for feedback reports that focus on differences between budgeted and actual amounts.

DISCUSSION: A responsibility accounting system should have certain controls that provide for feedback reports indicating deviations from expectations. Management may then focus on those deviations (exceptions) for either reinforcement or correction.

Answer (B) is incorrect. The responsibility accounting system should not be used exclusively to assess blame. Answer (C) is incorrect. The responsibility accounting system should not be used exclusively to give rewards. Answer (D) is incorrect. Feedback reports concentrate on deviations, but not to the total exclusion of other budgeted variables.

9.2.2. Making segment disclosures is an advantage to a company because it

A. Facilitates evaluation of company management by providing data on particular segments.

B. Eliminates the interdependence of segments.

C. Masks the effect of intersegment transfers.

D. Provides competitors with comparative information on the company's performance.

Answer (A) is correct. *(CIA, adapted)*

REQUIRED: The reason that making segment disclosures is an advantage.

DISCUSSION: Segment reporting is an aspect of responsibility accounting. It facilitates evaluation of company management and of the quality of the economic investment in particular segments.

Answer (B) is incorrect. Interdependence of segments is not affected by reporting methods. Answer (C) is incorrect. Masking the effects of intersegment transfers is a disadvantage of segment reporting. Answer (D) is incorrect. Providing information to competitors is a disadvantage of segment reporting.

9.2.3. If a manufacturing company uses responsibility accounting, which one of the following items is least likely to appear in a performance report for a manager of an assembly line?

A. Supervisory salaries.

B. Materials.

C. Repairs and maintenance.

D. Equipment depreciation.

Answer (D) is correct. *(CMA, adapted)*

REQUIRED: The item least likely to appear in a performance report for the manager of an assembly line.

DISCUSSION: Responsibility accounting holds managers responsible only for factors under their control. The depreciation of equipment will probably not appear on the performance report of an assembly-line manager because the manager usually has no control over the investment in the equipment.

Answer (A) is incorrect. The manager of an assembly line is likely to be responsible for the salaries of supervisors, which is to some degree controllable by the manager. Answer (B) is incorrect. The manager of an assembly line is likely to be responsible for the materials, which is to some degree controllable by the manager. Answer (C) is incorrect. The manager of an assembly line is likely to be responsible for the repairs and maintenance, which is to some degree controllable by the manager.

Question 9.2.4 is based on the following information. A and B are autonomous divisions of a corporation. They have no beginning or ending inventories, and the number of units produced is equal to the number of units sold. Following is financial information relating to the two divisions.

	A	B
Sales	$150,000	$400,000
Other revenue	10,000	15,000
Direct materials	30,000	65,000
Direct labor	20,000	40,000
Variable factory overhead	5,000	15,000
Fixed factory overhead	25,000	55,000
Variable S&A expense	15,000	30,000
Fixed S&A expense	35,000	60,000
Central corporate expenses (allocated)	12,000	20,000

9.2.4. What is the contribution margin of Division B?

A. $150,000

B. $205,000

C. $235,000

D. $265,000

Answer (D) is correct. *(CIA, adapted)*

REQUIRED: The contribution margin of B.

DISCUSSION: The contribution margin equals revenue minus variable costs. Division B's contribution margin is $265,000 ($400,000 sales + $15,000 other revenue – $65,000 direct materials – $40,000 direct labor – $15,000 variable overhead – $30,000 variable S&A expense).

Answer (A) is incorrect. The amount of $150,000 is the result of subtracting fixed costs. Answer (B) is incorrect. The amount of $205,000 is the result of subtracting fixed S&A costs. Answer (C) is incorrect. The amount of $235,000 is the result of subtracting fixed S&A costs but not variable S&A costs.

9.2.5. The receipt of raw materials used in the manufacture of products and the shipping of finished goods to customers is under the control of the warehouse supervisor, whose time is spent approximately 60% on receiving and 40% on shipping activities. Separate staffs for these operations are employed. The labor-related costs for the warehousing function are as follows:

Warehouse supervisor's salary	$ 40,000
Receiving clerks' wages	75,000
Shipping clerks' wages	55,000
Employee benefit costs (30% of wage and salary costs)	51,000
	$221,000

The company employs a responsibility accounting system for performance-reporting purposes. Costs are classified as period or product costs. What is the total of labor-related costs reported as product costs under the control of the warehouse supervisor?

A. $97,500

B. $128,700

C. $130,000

D. $221,000

Answer (A) is correct. *(CIA, adapted)*

REQUIRED: The total labor-related costs listed as product costs under the control of the warehouse supervisor.

DISCUSSION: The responsibility accounting report should list only the costs over which the warehousing supervisor exercises control or significant influence. The supervisor's salary therefore should be excluded because it is controlled by the warehouse supervisor's superior. Moreover, only the product costs are to be considered. These exclude the shipping clerks' wages and fringe benefits because they are period costs (shipping is a selling expense). Thus, the only product cost under the control of the warehouse supervisor is the receiving clerks' wages ($75,000) and the related fringe benefits (.3 × $75,000 = $22,500), or a total of $97,500.

Answer (B) is incorrect. Sixty percent of the warehouse supervisor's salary is included. None of the supervisor's salary should be included because it is controlled by the supervisor's superior. Answer (C) is incorrect. The shipping clerks' wages are periodic selling costs and therefore are not included. Also, the receiving clerks' benefits should be included on the responsibility accounting report. Answer (D) is incorrect. Neither the warehouse supervisor's salary nor any of the shipping clerks' wages and benefits should be included on the responsibility accounting report.

9.2.6. When using a contribution margin format for internal reporting purposes, the major distinction between segment manager performance and segment performance is

A. Unallocated fixed costs.

B. Direct variable costs of producing the product.

C. Direct fixed costs controllable by the segment manager.

D. Direct fixed costs controllable by others.

Answer (D) is correct. *(CMA, adapted)*

REQUIRED: The major distinction between segment manager performance and segment performance.

DISCUSSION: The performance of the segment is judged on all costs assigned to it, but the segment manager is only judged on costs that he or she can control. Some fixed costs are imposed on segments by the organization's upper management, and they are thus beyond the segment manager's control. These direct costs controllable by others make up the difference between segment manager performance and segment performance.

Answer (A) is incorrect. Unallocated fixed costs do not affect either performance measure. Answer (B) is incorrect. Direct variable costs affect both performance measures. Answer (C) is incorrect. Direct fixed costs controllable by the segment manager affect both performance measures.

9.2.7. A company plans to implement a bonus plan based on segment performance. In addition, it plans to convert to a responsibility accounting system for segment reporting. The following costs are included in the segment performance reports prepared under the current system. They are being reviewed to determine whether they should be included in the responsibility accounting segment reports:

I. Corporate administrative costs allocated on the basis of net segment sales.

II. Personnel costs assigned on the basis of the number of employees in each segment.

III. Fixed computer facility costs divided equally among each segment.

IV. Variable computer operational costs charged to each segment based on actual hours used times a predetermined standard rate; any variable cost efficiency or inefficiency remains in the computer department.

The only item that logically could be included in the segment performance reports prepared on a responsibility accounting basis is the

A. Corporate administrative costs.

B. Personnel costs.

C. Fixed computer facility costs.

D. Variable computer operational costs.

Answer (D) is correct. *(CIA, adapted)*

REQUIRED: The item included in the segment performance reports prepared on a responsibility accounting basis.

DISCUSSION: The variable computer cost can be included. The segments are charged for actual usage, which is under each segment's control. The predetermined standard rate is set at the beginning of the year and is known by the segment managers. Moreover, the efficiencies and inefficiencies of the computer department are not passed on to the segments. Both procedures promote a degree of control by the segments.

Answer (A) is incorrect. Corporate administrative costs should be excluded from the performance report. The segments have no control over their incurrence or the allocation basis. The allocation depends upon the segment sales (controllable) as well as the sales of other segments (uncontrollable). Answer (B) is incorrect. The segments have no control over the incurrence of personnel costs or the method of assignment, which depends upon the number of employees in the segment (controllable) in proportion to the total number of employees in all segments (not controllable). Answer (C) is incorrect. The segments have no control over fixed computer facility costs, and the equal assignment is arbitrary and bears no relation to usage.

9.2.8. Managers are most likely to accept allocations of common costs based on

A. Cause and effect.

B. Ability to bear.

C. Fairness.

D. Benefits received.

Answer (A) is correct. *(Publisher, adapted)*

REQUIRED: The criterion most likely to result in acceptable allocations of common costs.

DISCUSSION: The difficulty with common costs is that they are indirect costs whose allocation may be arbitrary. A direct cause-and-effect relationship between a common cost and the actions of the cost object to which it is allocated is desirable. Such a relationship promotes acceptance of the allocation by managers who perceive the fairness of the procedure. But identification of cause and effect may not be feasible.

Answer (B) is incorrect. Allocation using an ability-to-bear criterion punishes successful managers and rewards underachievers. Answer (C) is incorrect. Fairness is an objective rather than a criterion. Moreover, fairness may be interpreted differently by different managers. Answer (D) is incorrect. The benefits-received criterion is preferable when a cause-effect relationship cannot be feasibly identified.

9.2.9. A management decision may be beneficial for a given profit center but not for the entire company. From the overall company viewpoint, this decision leads to

A. Sub-optimization.

B. Centralization.

C. Goal congruence.

D. Maximization.

Answer (A) is correct. *(CPA, adapted)*

REQUIRED: The effect when a decision benefits a profit center but not the company.

DISCUSSION: Sub-optimization occurs when one segment takes an action that benefits itself but not the entity as a whole.

Answer (B) is incorrect. Centralization describes the extent to which decision-making authority is dispersed in an organization. Answer (C) is incorrect. Goal congruence occurs when the goals of subordinates and the organization are shared. Answer (D) is incorrect. Maximization is the quantitative or qualitative achievement of the best results by choosing an action.

9.2.10. Which one of the following companies is likely to experience dysfunctional motivation on the part of its managers due to its allocation methods?

A. To allocate depreciation of forklifts used by workers at its central warehouse, Company A uses predetermined amounts calculated on the basis of the long-term average use of the services provided.

B. Company B uses the sales revenue of its various divisions to allocate costs connected with the upkeep of its headquarters building. It also uses ROI to evaluate the divisional performances.

C. Company C does not allow its service departments to pass on their cost overruns to the production departments.

D. Company D's MIS is operated out of headquarters and serves its various divisions. The allocation of the MIS-related costs to its divisions is limited to costs the divisions will incur if they were to outsource their MIS needs.

Answer (B) is correct. *(CMA, adapted)*

REQUIRED: The company most likely to experience dysfunctional motivation on the part of its managers.

DISCUSSION: Managerial performance ordinarily should be evaluated only on the basis of those factors controllable by the manager. If a manager is allocated costs that (s)he cannot control, dysfunctional motivation can result. In the case of allocations, a cause-and-effect basis should be used. Allocating the costs of upkeep on a headquarters building on the basis of sales revenue is arbitrary because cost may have no relationship to divisional sales revenues. Consequently, divisional ROI is reduced by a cost over which a division manager has no control. Furthermore, the divisions with the greatest sales are penalized by receiving the greatest allocation.

Answer (A) is incorrect. Allocating depreciation on the basis of long-term average use is a reasonable basis of allocation. This basis is controllable by the division managers and reflects a causal relationship. Answer (C) is incorrect. A service department's cost overruns may not be attributable to any activities of production departments. Answer (D) is incorrect. Market-based allocations of costs of services are reasonable applications of the cause-and-effect principle.

9.2.11. A large corporation allocates the costs of its headquarters staff to its decentralized divisions. The best reason for this allocation is to

A. More accurately measure divisional operating results.

B. Improve divisional management's morale.

C. Remind divisional managers that common costs exist.

D. Discourage any use of central support services.

Answer (C) is correct. *(Publisher, adapted)*

REQUIRED: The best reason for allocating headquarters costs.

DISCUSSION: The allocation reminds managers that support costs exist and that the managers would incur these costs if their operations were independent. The allocation also reminds managers that profit center earnings must cover some amount of support costs.

Answer (A) is incorrect. An arbitrary allocation may skew operating results. Answer (B) is incorrect. The allocation may create resentment and conflict. Answer (D) is incorrect. Efficient use of central support services should be encouraged.

9.2.12. Which measures would be useful in evaluating the performance of a manufacturing system?

I. Throughput time

II. Total setup time for machines/total production time

III. Number of rework units/total number of units completed

A. I and II only.

B. II and III only.

C. I and III only.

D. I, II, and III.

Answer (D) is correct. *(CPA, adapted)*

REQUIRED: The measures useful in evaluating the performance of a manufacturing system.

DISCUSSION: Throughput time is the average amount of time required to convert raw materials into finished goods ready to be shipped. Total setup time as a percentage of total production time provides valuable information for scheduling. The number of rework items as a percentage of total number of units completed provides efficiency and quality control data. These are all important factors in evaluating the performance of a manufacturing system.

9.2.13. Many measures of performance are based on accounting information. For example, a manager may be evaluated based on return on investment (income ÷ investment). Accordingly, the basis for stating this measure is dollars. Assume that ROI is the chosen measure, and investment is defined as total assets. Comparability problems are most likely when the attribute used to calculate total assets is

A. Current cost.

B. Current disposal price.

C. Historical cost.

D. Present value.

Answer (C) is correct. *(Publisher, adapted)*

REQUIRED: The attribute most likely to create comparability problems.

DISCUSSION: Historical cost creates comparability issues. Returns on significantly depreciated assets may be higher than those on newer assets that have been acquired using inflated dollars. Thus, otherwise similarly situated managers may report different operating results. Moreover, managers may be reluctant to replace aging assets.

Answer (A) is incorrect. Current cost is an attempt to remedy the theoretical deficiencies of historical cost by presenting more accurate balance sheet measures. Answer (B) is incorrect. Current disposal price is an attempt to remedy the theoretical deficiencies of historical cost by presenting more accurate balance sheet measures. Answer (D) is incorrect. Present value is an attempt to remedy the theoretical deficiencies of historical cost by presenting more accurate balance sheet measures.

9.2.14. An entity's decision-making model for capital budgeting is based on the net present value of discounted cash flows. The same entity's managerial performance evaluation model is based on annual divisional return on investment. Which of the following is true?

A. Managers are likely to maximize the measures in the decision-making model.

B. Managers are likely to maximize the measures in the performance evaluation model.

C. Managers have an incentive to accept a project with a positive net present value that initially has a negative effect on net income.

D. The use of models with different criteria promotes goal congruence.

Answer (B) is correct. *(Publisher, adapted)*

REQUIRED: The true statement about use of different models for decision making and managerial evaluation.

DISCUSSION: Effective management control requires performance measurement and feedback. This process affects allocation of resources to subunits. It also affects decisions about managers' compensation, advancement, and future assignments. Furthermore, evaluating their performance motivates managers to optimize the measures in the performance evaluation model. However, that model may be inconsistent with the entity's model for decision making.

Answer (A) is incorrect. Self-interest is an incentive to maximize the measures used in performance evaluation. Answer (C) is incorrect. A manager evaluated on the basis of annual ROI has an interest in maximizing short-term net income, not long-term NPV. Answer (D) is incorrect. The models should be synchronized so that the goals of the entity and the manager are congruent.

9.2.15. Which of the following criteria would be most useful to a sales department manager in evaluating the performance of the manager's customer-service group?

A. The customer is always right.

B. Customer complaints should be processed promptly.

C. Employees should maintain a positive attitude when dealing with customers.

D. All customer inquiries should be answered within 7 days of receipt.

Answer (D) is correct. *(CIA, adapted)*

REQUIRED: The criterion most useful for evaluating a customer-service group.

DISCUSSION: A criterion that requires all customer inquiries to be answered within 7 days of receipt permits accurate measurement of performance. The quantitative and specific nature of the appraisal using this standard avoids the vagueness, subjectivity, and personal bias that may afflict other forms of personnel evaluations.

Answer (A) is incorrect. Customer orientation is difficult to quantify. Answer (B) is incorrect. The standard specified is vague. Answer (C) is incorrect. No measure of a positive attitude has been specified for the employee.

9.2.16. Using the balanced scorecard approach, an organization evaluates managerial performance based on

A. A single ultimate measure of operating results, such as residual income.

B. Multiple financial and nonfinancial measures.

C. Multiple nonfinancial measures only.

D. Multiple financial measures only.

Answer (B) is correct. *(Publisher, adapted)*

REQUIRED: The nature of the balanced scorecard approach.

DISCUSSION: The trend in managerial performance evaluation is the balanced scorecard approach. Multiple measures of performance permit a determination as to whether a manager is achieving certain objectives at the expense of others that may be equally or more important. These measures may be financial or nonfinancial and usually include items with four perspectives: (1) financial; (2) customer satisfaction; (3) internal business processes; and (4) learning and growth.

Answer (A) is incorrect. The balanced scorecard approach uses multiple measures. Answer (C) is incorrect. The balanced scorecard approach uses financial and nonfinancial measures. Answer (D) is incorrect. The balanced scorecard approach uses financial and nonfinancial measures.

9.2.17. A major problem in comparing profitability measures among companies is the

A. Lack of general agreement over which profitability measure is best.

B. Differences in the size of the companies.

C. Differences in the accounting methods used by the companies.

D. Differences in the dividend policies of the companies.

Answer (C) is correct. *(CMA, adapted)*

REQUIRED: The major problem in profitability comparisons.

DISCUSSION: The use of different accounting methods impairs comparability. Consequently, financial statements must be adjusted to permit interentity comparisons.

Answer (A) is incorrect. Even if a general agreement is reached, different accounting methods still impair comparability. Answer (B) is incorrect. Differences in the size of entities do not directly affect the measure of profitability to the same extent as the choice of accounting principles. Answer (D) is incorrect. Differences in dividend policies do not directly affect the measure of profitability to the same extent as the choice of accounting principles.

9.2.18. Faced with 3 years of steadily decreasing profits despite increased sales and a growing economy, which of the following is the healthiest course of action for a chief executive officer to take?

A. Set a turnaround goal of significantly increasing profits within 2 months. Set clear short-term objectives for each operating unit that, together, should produce the turnaround.

B. Reduce staff by 10% in every unit.

C. Classify all job functions as either (1) adding value in the eyes of the customer (such as production and sales) or (2) not adding value in the eyes of the customer (such as accounting and human resources). Reduce staff in the non-value-adding functions by 20%.

D. Implement a plan to encourage innovation at all levels. Use early retirement and reemployment programs to trim staff size.

Answer (D) is correct. *(CIA, adapted)*

REQUIRED: The healthiest course of action given decreasing profits despite increasing sales.

DISCUSSION: The characteristics of organizational decline are (1) greater centralization, (2) lack of long-term planning, (3) reduced innovation, (4) scapegoating, (5) resistance to change, (6) high turnover of competent leaders, (7) low morale, (8) nonprioritized downsizing, and (9) conflict. Reversing these characteristics is the key to reversing organizational decline, for example, by encouraging innovation in all aspects of the organization's activities and by redeploying personnel.

Answer (A) is incorrect. Two characteristics of organizational decline are increased centralization of decision making and lack of long-term planning. The exclusive emphasis on short-term results is likely to be counterproductive. Answer (B) is incorrect. Another characteristic of organizational decline is nonprioritized downsizing. By itself, downsizing rarely changes an entity's results. Answer (C) is incorrect. Reducing staff disproportionately in control functions could have disastrous consequences.

9.2.19. A company, which has many branch stores, has decided to benchmark one of its stores for the purpose of analyzing the accuracy and reliability of branch store financial reporting. Which one of the following is the most likely measure to be included in a financial benchmark?

A. High turnover of employees.

B. High level of employee participation in setting budgets.

C. High amount of bad debt write-offs.

D. High number of suppliers.

Answer (C) is correct. *(CIA, adapted)*

REQUIRED: The most likely measure to be included in a financial benchmark.

DISCUSSION: High bad debt write-offs could indicate fraud, which compromises the accuracy and reliability of financial reports. Bad debt write-offs may result from recording fictitious sales.

Answer (A) is incorrect. Turnover of employees is not a financial benchmark. Answer (B) is incorrect. Employee participation in setting budgets is not a financial benchmark. Answer (D) is incorrect. The number of suppliers is not a financial benchmark.

9.2.20. The segment margin of the Wire Division of a manufacturer should not include

A. Net sales of the Wire Division.

B. Fixed selling expenses of the Wire Division.

C. Variable selling expenses of the Wire Division.

D. The Wire Division's fair share of the salary of the manufacturer's president.

Answer (D) is correct. *(CMA, adapted)*

REQUIRED: The item not included in a statement showing segment margin.

DISCUSSION: Segment margin is the contribution margin for a segment of a business minus fixed costs. It is a measure of long-run profitability. Thus, an allocation of the corporate officers' salaries should not be included in segment margin because they are neither variable costs nor fixed costs that can be rationally allocated to the segment. Other items that are often not allocated include corporate income taxes, interest, company-wide R&D expenses, and central administration costs.

Answer (A) is incorrect. Sales of the division would appear on the statement. Answer (B) is incorrect. The division's fixed selling expenses are separable fixed costs. Answer (C) is incorrect. Variable costs of the division are included.

Questions 9.2.21 through 9.2.24 are based on the following information. Buscemi Company makes its single product, XY, using highly automated procedures that require little direct labor. The product XY results from processing component XX. Conversion costs include direct labor and all manufacturing costs except those for direct materials (the costs of XX). Conversion costs are deemed to be fixed because they are constant regardless of the number of components processed. They can be changed only by changing capacity. Marketing, sales, and research and development costs are not significant in comparison with the other costs and therefore are not separately reported.

Total assets and their composition were essentially unchanged during the two periods for which the following information is available:

	Year 1	Year 2
Units of XY manufactured and sold (work-in process is zero)	600,000	690,000
Unit sales price of XY	\$40	\$37
Units of component XX processed	1,800,000	1,740,000
Unit cost of component XX	\$1.20	\$1.26
Processing capacity (units of component XX)	2,250,000	2,100,000
Conversion cost ÷ units of capacity	\$3.90	\$3.95

9.2.21. What is the change in operating income (OI) from Year 1 to Year 2?

A. \$1,977,600

B. \$1,530,000

C. \$(480,000)

D. \$(447,600)

Answer (A) is correct. *(Publisher, adapted)*

REQUIRED: The change in OI.

DISCUSSION: OI equals revenues minus costs. For Year 1, OI equals \$13,065,000 [(600,000 units XY × \$40 unit sales price) – (1,800,000 units XX × \$1.20 unit DM cost) – (2,250,000 capacity units × \$3.90 unit CC)]. For Year 2, OI equals \$15,042,600 [(690,000 units XY × \$37 unit sales price) – (1,740,000 units XX × \$1.26 unit DM cost) – (2,100,000 capacity units × \$3.95 unit CC)]. Consequently, OI increased by \$1,977,600 (\$15,042,600 OI Year 2 – \$13,065,000 OI Year 1).

Answer (B) is incorrect. The amount of \$1,530,000 is the increase in revenues. Answer (C) is incorrect. The amount of \$(480,000) is the decrease in conversion costs. Answer (D) is incorrect. The amount of \$(447,600) is the decrease in total costs.

9.2.22. What amount of the change in operating income (OI) from Year 1 to Year 2 resulted solely from the change in unit sales?

A. \$3,600,000

B. \$3,330,000

C. \$3,276,000

D. \$324,000

Answer (C) is correct. *(Publisher, adapted)*

REQUIRED: The change in OI resulting solely from the change in unit sales.

DISCUSSION: The growth element of the change in OI reflects the changes from one period to the next in revenues and costs resulting solely from the change in unit sales, holding the previous period's input and output prices and input-output relationships constant. The revenue portion of the growth element is \$3,600,000 [\$40 Year 1 unit sales price × (690,000 units sold in Year 2 – 600,000 units sold in Year 1)]. The cost portion of the growth element is {[1,800,000 units DM processed in Year 1 × (690,000 units sold in Year 2 ÷ 600,000 units sold in Year 1)] – 1,800,000 units in Year 1} × \$1.20 unit DM cost in Year 1. This cost is calculated using the Year 1 input price and the Year 1 input-units-of-XX-to-output-units-of-XY relationship. Thus, the growth element of the change in OI is \$3,276,000 (\$3,600,000 revenue increase – \$324,000 cost increase). The cost portion of the change in unit sales contains no amount for conversion costs because they are fixed for a given capacity. The actual capacity for Year 1 (2,250,000 units of XX) was sufficient to process Year 2 output (690,000 units of XY) at the Year 1 input-output ratio (1,800,000 units of XX ÷ 600,000 units of XY), so no additional capacity cost is required.

Answer (A) is incorrect. The amount of \$3,600,000 is the revenue portion of the growth element. Answer (B) is incorrect. The amount of \$3,330,000 is the revenue portion of the growth element calculated using Year 2's unit sales price. Answer (D) is incorrect. The amount of \$324,000 is the cost portion of the growth element.

9.2.23. What amount of the change in operating income (OI) from Year 1 to Year 2 resulted solely from the changes in input and output prices?

A. $(2,070,000)

B. $(2,182,500)

C. $(2,194,200)

D. $(2,306,700)

Answer (D) is correct. *(Publisher, adapted)*

REQUIRED: The change in OI resulting solely from changes in input and output prices.

DISCUSSION: The price-recovery element of the change in OI reflects the changes from one period to the next in revenues and costs resulting solely from changes in input and output prices, holding the current period's unit sales and the previous period's input-output relationships constant. The revenue portion of the price-recovery element is $(2,070,000) [690,000 units sold in Year 2 × ($37 Year 2 unit sales price – $40 Year 1 unit sales price)]. The direct-materials cost portion of the price-recovery element is $124,200 {[1,800,000 units DM processed in Year 1 × (690,000 units sold in Year 2 ÷ 600,000 units sold in Year 1)] × ($1.26 DM cost in Year 2 – $1.20 DM cost in Year 1)}. The conversion-cost portion of the price-recovery element is $112,500 [2,250,000 units of capacity in Year 1 × ($3.95 cost per unit of capacity in Year 2 – $3.90 cost per unit of capacity in Year 1)]. Accordingly, the price-recovery element of the change in OI is $(2,306,700), which equals the sum of a $2,070,000 revenue decrease, a $124,200 increase in direct-materials costs, and a $112,500 increase in conversation (capacity) costs.

Answer (A) is incorrect. A $2,070,00 decrease omits the effects of the increases in input prices. Answer (B) is incorrect. A $2,182,500 decrease omits the effect of the increase in the unit direct materials cost. Answer (C) is incorrect. A $2,194,200 decrease omits the effect of the increase in the unit conversion (capacity) cost.

9.2.24. What amount of the change in operating income (OI) from Year 1 to Year 2 resulted solely from changes in input-output relationships?

A. $2,306,700

B. $1,008,300

C. $981,000

D. $592,500

Answer (B) is correct. *(Publisher, adapted)*

REQUIRED: The changes in OI resulting solely from changes in input-output relationships.

DISCUSSION: The productivity element of the change in OI reflects the changes from one period to the next in costs resulting solely from changes in input-output relationships. Thus, it equals the difference between the inputs that would have been required in the previous period and those actually used in the current period to generate the current period's output, multiplied by the current period's input price, holding all other factors constant. The direct-materials cost portion of the productivity element is $(415,800) {1,740,000 units DM processed in Year 2 – [1,800,000 units DM processed in Year 1 × (690,000 units sold in Year 2 ÷ 600,000 units sold in Year 1)]} × $1.26 DM cost in Year 2. The conversion-cost portion of the productivity element is $(592,500) [(2,100,000-unit capacity in Year 2 – 2,250,000-unit capacity in Year 1) × $3.95]. (NOTE: Conversion cost is fixed as long as capacity does not change. Moreover, because Year 1 capacity was sufficient to produce Year 2 as well as Year 1 output at the Year 1 input-output ratio, it may be used in this computation. However, conversion cost decreases from Year 1 to Year 2 with the reduction in capacity.) Accordingly, the productivity element of the change in OI is a cost reduction of $1,008,300 ($415,800 + $592,500).

Answer (A) is incorrect. The absolute amount of the price-recovery element of the change in OI is $2,306,700. Answer (C) is incorrect. The amount of $981,000 results from using the Year 1 input prices. Answer (D) is incorrect. The amount of $592,500 is the conversion-cost portion of the productivity element of the change in OI.

9.2.25. X Company manufactures product XC on one machine, but only in response to customer orders. For the upcoming year, 50 orders are expected, but the range of possible orders is from 20 to 80. Each order consists of 800 units and requires 80 hours of manufacturing time. The machine's annual capacity is 4,800 hours. If orders are processed in the sequence in which they are received, average manufacturing cycle time is

A. 80 hours.

B. 120 hours.

C. 200 hours.

D. 280 hours.

Answer (D) is correct. *(Publisher, adapted)*

REQUIRED: The average manufacturing cycle time.

DISCUSSION: Assuming that (1) order arrivals are consistent with a Poisson distribution and (2) processing is in the sequence of arrivals (a first-in, first-out assumption), the formula below is used to calculate average waiting time in the production facility. Waiting time is the average time from when an order is received by production to the time it is set up and processed (ANO = periodic average number of orders, OMT = order manufacturing time, and PC = periodic capacity):

$$\begin{aligned}\text{Avg. waiting time} &= \text{ANO} \times \text{OMT}^2 \div 2[\text{PC} - (\text{ANO} \times \text{OMT})]\\ &= 50 \times (80)^2 \div 2[4{,}800 - (50 \times 80)]\\ &= 50 \times 6{,}400 \div 2 \times (4{,}800 - 4{,}000)\\ &= 320{,}000 \div 1{,}600\\ &= 200\end{aligned}$$

Average manufacturing cycle time is therefore 280 hours (200 hours average waiting time + 80 hours manufacturing time).

Answer (A) is incorrect. The order manufacturing time is 80 hours. Answer (B) is incorrect. The average waiting time minus order manufacturing time is 120 hours. Answer (C) is incorrect. The average waiting time is 200 hours.

Questions 9.2.26 and 9.2.27 are based on the following information.

Wolk Corporation is a highly automated manufacturing firm. The vice president of finance has decided that traditional standards are inappropriate for performance measures in an automated environment. Labor is insignificant in terms of the total cost of production and tends to be fixed, material quality is considered more important than minimizing material cost, and customer satisfaction is the number one priority. As a result, delivery performance measures have been chosen to evaluate performance.

The following information is considered typical of the time involved to complete orders.

• Wait time:	
- From order being placed to start of production	10.0 days
- From start of production to completion	5.0 days
• Inspection time	1.5 days
• Process time	3.0 days
• Move time	2.5 days

9.2.26. What is the manufacturing cycle efficiency for this order?

A. 25.0%

B. 13.6%

C. 37.5%

D. 33.3%

Answer (A) is correct. *(CMA, adapted)*

REQUIRED: The manufacturing cycle efficiency.

DISCUSSION: Manufacturing cycle efficiency is the quotient of (1) the time required for value-added production divided by (2) total manufacturing cycle time (throughput time or velocity of production). Cycle time is the time elapsed from when an order is ready for production (is received by the manufacturing facility) until it is completed. For this order, the total manufacturing cycle time is 12 days (5.0 + 1.5 + 3.0 + 2.5), and the manufacturing cycle efficiency is 25% (3 days of processing ÷ 12).

Answer (B) is incorrect. The amount of 13.6% includes the 10 days prior to production in the denominator, a period not included in the calculation of manufacturing cycle efficiency. Answer (C) is incorrect. Inspection time and move time should be included in the denominator. Answer (D) is incorrect. The amount of 33.3% equals inspection and move time divided by the manufacturing cycle time.

9.2.27. What is the delivery cycle time for this order?

A. 7 days.

B. 12 days.

C. 15 days.

D. 22 days.

Answer (D) is correct. *(CMA, adapted)*

REQUIRED: The delivery cycle time.

DISCUSSION: The delivery cycle time is defined as the entire time from receipt of the order until delivery of the order. This period equals 22 days (10.0 + 5.0 + 1.5 + 3.0 + 2.5).

Answer (A) is incorrect. Seven days excludes the wait time. Answer (B) is incorrect. Twelve days ignores the 10 days of the waiting period prior to the start of production. Answer (C) is incorrect. Fifteen days incorporates the wait time but not the production periods.

9.2.28. When evaluating projects, breakeven time is best described as

A. Annual fixed costs ÷ monthly contribution margin.

B. Project investment ÷ annual net cash inflows.

C. The point where cumulative cash inflows on a project equal total cash outflows.

D. The point at which discounted cumulative cash inflows on a project equal discounted total cash outflows.

Answer (D) is correct. *(CMA, adapted)*

REQUIRED: The definition of breakeven time.

DISCUSSION: Breakeven time is a capital budgeting tool that is widely used to evaluate the rapidity of new product development. It is the period required for the discounted cumulative cash inflows for a project to equal the discounted cumulative cash outflows. The concept is similar to the payback period, but it is more sophisticated because it incorporates the time value of money. It also differs from the payback method because the period covered begins at the outset of a project, not when the initial cash outflow occurs.

Answer (A) is incorrect. It is related to breakeven point, not breakeven time. Answer (B) is incorrect. The payback period equals investment divided by annual undiscounted net cash inflows. Answer (C) is incorrect. The payback period is the period required for total undiscounted cash inflows to equal total undiscounted cash outflows.

9.3 Profit Center Performance

9.3.1. A firm earning a profit can increase its return on investment by

A. Increasing sales revenue and operating expenses by the same dollar amount.

B. Decreasing sales revenues and operating expenses by the same percentage.

C. Increasing investment and operating expenses by the same dollar amount.

D. Increasing sales revenues and operating expenses by the same percentage.

Answer (D) is correct. *(CMA, adapted)*

REQUIRED: The means by which a profitable firm can increase its ROI.

DISCUSSION: ROI equals income divided by invested capital. If a firm is profitable, increasing sales and expenses by the same percentage increases ROI. For example, if a company has sales of $100 and expenses of $80, its net income is $20. Given invested capital of $100, ROI is 20% ($20 ÷ $100). If sales and expenses both increase 10% to $110 and $88, respectively, net income increases to $22. ROI then is 22% ($22 ÷ $100).

Answer (A) is incorrect. Increasing sales and expenses by the same dollar amount does not change income or ROI. Answer (B) is incorrect. Decreasing revenues and expenses by the same percentage reduces income and ROI. Answer (C) is incorrect. Increasing investment and operating expenses by the same dollar amount reduces ROI. The higher investment increases the denominator, and the increased expenses reduce the numerator.

9.3.2. Which denominator used in the return on investment (ROI) formula is criticized because it combines the effects of operating decisions made at one organizational level with financing decisions made at another organizational level?

A. Total assets employed.

B. Shareholders' equity.

C. Working capital plus other assets.

D. Total assets available.

Answer (B) is correct. *(CMA, adapted)*

REQUIRED: The ROI denominator.

DISCUSSION: ROI equals income divided by invested capital. The denominator may be defined in various ways, e.g., (1) total assets available, (2) assets employed, (3) working capital plus other assets, and (4) shareholders' equity. If shareholders' equity (total assets – total liabilities) is chosen, a portion of long-term liabilities must be allocated to the investment center to determine the manager's resource base. One problem with this definition of the resource base is that, although it has the advantage of emphasizing return to owners, it reflects decisions at different levels of the entity: (1) short-term liabilities incurred by the responsibility center (operating decisions) and (2) long-term liabilities controlled at the corporate level (long-term financing decisions).

Answer (A) is incorrect. Total assets employed reflects an assumption that the subunit manager does not influence the resource base (denominator of the ROI calculation). Answer (C) is incorrect. Working capital plus other assets reflects the assumption that the manager controls short-term credit. However, no corporate-level decision to allocate long-term liabilities to subunits is necessary. Answer (D) is incorrect. Total assets available reflects an assumption that the subunit manager does not influence the resource base (denominator of the ROI calculation).

9.3.3. Which one of the following statements pertaining to the return on investment (ROI) as a performance measurement is false?

A. When the average age of assets differs substantially across segments of a business, the use of ROI may not be appropriate.

B. ROI relies on financial measures that are capable of being independently verified, while other forms of performance measures are subject to manipulation.

C. The use of ROI may lead managers to reject capital investment projects that can be justified by using discounted cash flow models.

D. The use of ROI can make it undesirable for a skillful manager to take on troubleshooting assignments such as those involving turning around unprofitable divisions.

Answer (B) is correct. *(CMA, adapted)*

REQUIRED: The false statement about ROI as a performance measure.

DISCUSSION: ROI is calculated by dividing a segment's income by the invested capital. Thus, ROI can be manipulated by falsifying income or invested capital.

Answer (A) is incorrect. ROI can be misleading when the quality of the investment base differs among segments. Answer (C) is incorrect. Managers may reject projects that are profitable (a return greater than the cost of capital) but decrease ROI. For example, the manager of a segment with a 15% ROI may not want to invest in a new project with a 10% ROI, even though the cost of capital might be only 8%. Answer (D) is incorrect. The use of ROI does not reflect the relative difficulty of tasks undertaken by managers.

9.3.4. Which one of the following items would most likely not be incorporated into the calculation of a division's investment base when using the residual income approach for performance measurement and evaluation?

A. Fixed assets employed in division operations.

B. Land being held by the division as a site for a new plant.

C. Division inventories when division management exercises control over the inventory levels.

D. Division accounts payable when division management exercises control over the amount of short-term credit used.

Answer (B) is correct. *(CMA, adapted)*

REQUIRED: The item most likely not incorporated into the calculation of a division's investment base.

DISCUSSION: An evaluation of an investment center is based upon the return on the investment base. These assets include plant and equipment, inventories, and receivables. However, land not in use will most likely not be included in the investment base. Total assets in use rather than total assets available is preferable when the investment center has been forced to carry idle assets.

Answer (A) is incorrect. Fixed operating assets are controlled by the division manager and contribute to profits. Answer (C) is incorrect. Inventories are operating assets that contribute to profits and are controlled by the division manager. Answer (D) is incorrect. The level of accounts payable is an operating decision that should be considered in the evaluation of the division manager.

9.3.5. Most firms use return on investment (ROI) to evaluate the performance of investment center managers. If top management wishes division managers to use all assets without regard to financing, the denominator in the ROI calculation will be

A. Total assets available.

B. Total assets employed.

C. Working capital plus other assets.

D. Shareholders' equity.

Answer (A) is correct. *(CMA, adapted)*

REQUIRED: The ROI denominator if managers use all assets without regard to financing.

DISCUSSION: ROI equals return (income) divided by invested capital. Invested capital may be defined in various ways, for example, as (1) total assets available, (2) total assets employed, (3) working capital plus other assets (current liabilities are subtracted from total assets to exclude the assets provided by short-term creditors), and (4) shareholders' equity (a portion of long-term as well as short-term liabilities must be allocated to determine the manager's resource base). Total assets available assumes the manager uses all assets without regard to financing.

Answer (B) is incorrect. Total assets employed excludes idle assets. Answer (C) is incorrect. Deducting current liabilities reflects the manager's control over short-term credit. Answer (D) is incorrect. Shareholders' equity is determined by subtracting total liabilities from total assets. Thus, this measure also considers financing.

9.3.6. When evaluating a profit center or an investment center, top management should concentrate on

A. Dollar sales.

B. Net income.

C. Profit percentages.

D. Return on investment.

Answer (D) is correct. *(Publisher, adapted)*

REQUIRED: The focus of management when evaluating an investment center.

DISCUSSION: Each investment center of a business should be evaluated based upon return on investment. ROI is comparable to calculations made both within and outside a particular organization. Management may review all investment opportunities available. In essence, net income is stated as a proportion of investment capital (resources required).

9.3.7. Return on investment (ROI) is a very popular measure employed to evaluate the performance of corporate segments because it incorporates all of the major ingredients of profitability (revenue, cost, investment) into a single measure. Under which one of the following combinations of actions regarding a segment's revenues, costs, and investment would a segment's ROI always increase?

	Revenues	Costs	Investment
A.	Increase	Decrease	Increase
B.	Decrease	Decrease	Decrease
C.	Increase	Increase	Increase
D.	Increase	Decrease	Decrease

Answer (D) is correct. *(CIA, adapted)*

REQUIRED: The responsibility center(s) that include controllable revenues in their performance reports.

DISCUSSION: An increase in revenue and a decrease in costs will increase the ROI numerator. A decrease in investment will decrease the denominator. The ROI must increase in this situation.

9.3.8. The following information pertains to Bala Co. for the year ended December 31:

Sales	$600,000
Income	100,000
Capital investment	400,000

Which of the following equations should be used to compute Bala's return on investment?

A. (4/6) × (6/1) = ROI.

B. (6/4) × (1/6) = ROI.

C. (4/6) × (1/6) = ROI.

D. (6/4) × (6/1) = ROI.

Answer (B) is correct. *(CPA, adapted)*

REQUIRED: The equation used to compute ROI.

DISCUSSION: ROI equals capital turnover (sales ÷ investment) times the profit margin (income ÷ sales). Thus, Bala's ROI can be represented by [($600,000 ÷ $400,000) × ($100,000 ÷ $600,000)].

Answer (A) is incorrect. The ROI yielded is 400%, which is the reciprocal of the true ROI of 25%. Answer (C) is incorrect. Capital turnover is sales divided by investment, not investment divided by sales. Answer (D) is incorrect. Profit margin is income divided by sales, not sales divided by income.

9.3.9. The following information pertains to Quest Co.'s Gold Division for the year just ended:

Sales	$311,000
Variable cost	250,000
Traceable fixed costs	50,000
Average invested capital	40,000
Imputed interest rate	10%

Quest's return on investment was

A. 10.00%

B. 13.33%

C. 27.50%

D. 30.00%

Answer (C) is correct. *(CPA, adapted)*

REQUIRED: The return on investment.

DISCUSSION: Quest's return on investment can be calculated as follows:

ROI = Operating income ÷ Average invested capital
= ($311,000 – $250,000 – $50,000) ÷ $40,000
= $11,000 ÷ $40,000
= 27.5%

Answer (A) is incorrect. The amount of 10.00% is the imputed interest rate. Answer (B) is incorrect. A 13.33% ROI would result from a net income of $5,332. Answer (D) is incorrect. A 30.00% ROI would result from a net income of $12,000.

9.3.10. The following selected data pertain to the Darwin Division of Beagle Co. for the year just ended:

Sales	$400,000
Operating income	40,000
Capital turnover	4
Imputed interest rate	10%

What was Darwin's residual income for the year?

A. $0

B. $4,000

C. $10,000

D. $30,000

Answer (D) is correct. *(CPA, adapted)*

REQUIRED: The residual income for Darwin.

DISCUSSION: Residual income equals operating income minus a target return on invested capital. Since the capital turnover equals sales divided by average invested capital, average invested capital is $100,000 ($400,000 sales ÷ 4 capital turnover). Residual income can now be calculated as follows:

Residual income = Operating income – Target return on invested capital
= $40,000 – ($100,000 × 10%)
= $40,000 – $10,000
= $30,000

Answer (A) is incorrect. Residual income is $30,000. Answer (B) is incorrect. Operating income times the imputed interest rate is $4,000. Answer (C) is incorrect. The target return on invested capital is $10,000.

9.3.11. Listed below is selected financial information for the Western Division of the Hinzel Company for last year.

Account	Amount (thousands)
Average working capital	$ 625
General and administrative expenses	75
Net sales	4,000
Average plant and equipment	1,775
Cost of goods sold	3,525

If Hinzel treats the Western Division as an investment center for performance measurement purposes, what is the before-tax return on investment (ROI) for last year?

A. 34.78%

B. 22.54%

C. 19.79%

D. 16.67%

Answer (D) is correct. *(CMA, adapted)*
REQUIRED: The before-tax ROI for an investment center.
DISCUSSION: An investment center's ROI is its operating income divided by its average invested capital. The Western Division's operating income is $400 ($4,000 sales – $3,525 cost of goods sold – $75 general expenses). Given average plant and equipment of $1,775 and average working capital of $625, the total average invested capital is $2,400. ROI is thus 16.67% ($400 ÷ $2,400).
Answer (A) is incorrect. Subtracting working capital from plant and equipment in calculating the net investment results in 34.78%. Answer (B) is incorrect. The percentage of 22.54% does not include average working capital in the total for the net investment. Answer (C) is incorrect. Not subtracting general and administrative expenses in the calculation of before-tax profit results in 19.79%.

9.3.12. Residual income is a performance evaluation that is used in conjunction with, or instead of, return on investment (ROI). In many cases, residual income is preferred to ROI because

A. Residual income is a measure over time, while ROI represents the results for one period.

B. Residual income concentrates on maximizing absolute dollars of income rather than a percentage return as with ROI.

C. The imputed interest rate used in calculating residual income is more easily derived than the target rate that is compared to the calculated ROI.

D. Average investment is employed with residual income while year-end investment is employed with ROI.

Answer (B) is correct. *(CIA, adapted)*
REQUIRED: The reason for preferring residual income to ROI.
DISCUSSION: Residual income equals earnings in excess of a minimum desired return. Thus, it is measured in dollars. If performance is evaluated using ROI, a manager may reject a project that exceeds the minimum return if the project will decrease overall ROI. For example, given a target rate of 20%, a project with an ROI of 22% might be rejected if the current ROI is 25%.
Answer (A) is incorrect. Residual income and ROI are the results for a single period. Answer (C) is incorrect. The target rate for ROI is the same as the imputed interest rate used in the residual income calculation. Answer (D) is incorrect. The same investment base should be used to calculate residual income and ROI.

9.3.13. James Webb is the general manager of the Industrial Product Division, and his performance is measured using the residual income method. Webb is reviewing the following forecasted information for his division for next year:

Category	Amount (thousands)
Working capital	$ 1,800
Revenue	30,000
Plant and equipment	17,200

If the imputed interest charge is 15% and Webb wants to achieve a residual income target of $2,000,000, what will costs (cost of goods sold and other operating expenses) have to be in order to achieve the target?

A. $9,000,000

B. $10,800,000

C. $25,150,000

D. $25,690,000

Answer (C) is correct. *(CMA, adapted)*
REQUIRED: The maximum costs consistent with meeting a residual income target.
DISCUSSION: Residual income is the excess of operating income over a targeted amount equal to an imputed interest charge on invested capital. If a manager has $19,000,000 of invested capital ($17,200,000 of plant and equipment + $1,800,000 of working capital), a 15% imputed interest charge equals $2,850,000. Adding $2,000,000 of residual income to the imputed interest results in a target profit of $4,850,000. This profit can be achieved if costs are $25,150,000 ($30,000,000 revenue – $4,850,000 profit).
Answer (A) is incorrect. Costs of $9,000,000 result in a residual income greater than $2,000,000. Answer (B) is incorrect. Costs of $10,800,000 result in a residual income greater than $2,000,000. Answer (D) is incorrect. Subtracting working capital from plant and equipment in determining invested capital results in $25,690,000.

9.3.14. A computer service center had the following operating statistics for the month:

Sales	$450,000
Operating income	25,000
Net profit after taxes	8,000
Total assets	500,000
Shareholders' equity	200,000
Cost of capital	6%

Based on the above information, which one of the following statements is true? The computer service center has a

A. Return on investment of 4%.

B. Residual income of $(5,000).

C. Return on investment of 1.6%.

D. Residual income of $(22,000).

Answer (B) is correct. *(CMA, adapted)*

REQUIRED: The true statement about the company's performance.

DISCUSSION: Return on investment is commonly calculated by dividing pretax income by total assets available. Residual income is the excess of the return on investment over a targeted amount equal to an imputed interest charge on invested capital. The rate used is ordinarily the weighted-average cost of capital. Some companies measure managerial performance in terms of the amount of residual income rather than the percentage return on investment. Because the computer service center has assets of $500,000 and a cost of capital of 6%, it must earn $30,000 on those assets to cover the cost of capital. Given that operating income was only $25,000, it had a negative residual income of $5,000.

Answer (A) is incorrect. Although the firm's return on equity investment was 4%, its return on all funds invested was 5% ($25,000 pretax operating income ÷ $500,000). Answer (C) is incorrect. ROI is commonly based on before-tax income. Answer (D) is incorrect. The amount of $(22,000) equals the difference between net profit after taxes and targeted income.

9.3.15. Economic value added (EVA) is a measure of managerial performance. EVA equals

A. Net income after interest and taxes – (the weighted-average cost of capital × total assets).

B. [Earnings before interest and taxes × (1.0 – the tax rate)] – [the weighted-average cost of capital × (total assets – current liabilities)].

C. Earnings before interest and taxes – residual income.

D. After-tax operating income – interest on debt – dividends paid.

Answer (B) is correct. *(Publisher, adapted)*

REQUIRED: The definition of EVA.

DISCUSSION: Economic value added (EVA) is a more specific version of residual income. It equals after-tax operating income [earnings before interest and taxes × (1.0 – the tax rate)], minus the product of the after-tax weighted-average cost of capital and an investment base equal to total assets minus current liabilities. EVA is the business unit's true economic profit primarily because a charge for the cost of equity capital is implicit in the cost of capital. The cost of equity is an opportunity cost, that is, the return that could have been obtained on the best alternative investment of similar risk. Thus, the EVA measures the marginal benefit obtained by using resources in a particular way. It determines whether a segment of a business is increasing shareholder value.

Answer (A) is incorrect. Interest should not be subtracted twice. The WACC includes interest. Answer (C) is incorrect. EVA is a specific way of calculating residual income. Answer (D) is incorrect. The EVA calculation subtracts an opportunity cost of equity capital, not an actual cost.

9.3.16. Valecon Co. reported the following information for the year just ended:

	Segment A	Segment B	Segment C
Pre-tax operating income	$ 4,000,000	$ 2,000,000	$3,000,000
Current assets	4,000,000	3,000,000	4,000,000
Long-term assets	16,000,000	13,000,000	8,000,000
Current liabilities	2,000,000	1,000,000	1,500,000

If the applicable income tax rate and after-tax weighted-average cost of capital for each segment are 30% and 10%, respectively, the segment with the highest economic value added (EVA) is

A. Segment A.

B. Segment B.

C. Segment C.

D. Not determinable from this information.

Answer (C) is correct. *(Publisher, adapted)*

REQUIRED: The segment with the highest economic value added.

DISCUSSION: EVA equals after-tax operating income minus the product of the after-tax weighted-average cost of capital and an investment base equal to total assets minus current liabilities. Thus, the EVA for Segment C is $1,050,000 {[$3,000,000 × (1.0 – .3)] – [.10 × ($4,000,000 + $8,000,000 – $1,500,000)]}.

Answer (A) is incorrect. The EVA for Segment A is $1,000,000. Answer (B) is incorrect. The EVA for Segment B is $(100,000). Answer (D) is incorrect. The EVAs are determinable.

Questions 9.3.17 and 9.3.18 are based on the following information. Dzyubenko Co. reported these data at year end:

Pre-tax operating income	$ 4,000,000
Current assets	4,000,000
Long-term assets	16,000,000
Current liabilities	2,000,000
Long-term liabilities	5,000,000

The long-term debt has an interest rate of 8%, and its fair value equaled its book value at year-end. The fair value of the equity capital is $2 million greater than its book value. Dzyubenko's income tax rate is 25%, and its cost of equity capital is 10%.

9.3.17. What is the weighted-average cost of capital (WACC) to be used in the economic value added (EVA) calculation?

A. 8.0%

B. 8.89%

C. 9%

D. 10%

Answer (C) is correct. *(Publisher, adapted)*

REQUIRED: The WACC to be used in an EVA calculation.

DISCUSSION: The WACC is an after-tax rate determined using the fair values of the sources of long-term funds. Thus, the appropriate cost of debt is 6% [.08 × (1.0 – .25 tax rate)] because interest is tax deductible. However, the given cost of equity capital (10%) is not adjusted because distributions to shareholders are not deductible. The fair value of long-term debt is given as $5 million. The carrying amount of equity must be $13 million ($20 million of assets – $7 million of liabilities), and its fair value is $15 million ($13 million + $2 million). Accordingly, the WACC is 9%:

$$\text{WACC} = \frac{(.06 \times \$5 \text{ million FV of LT debt}) + (10\% \times \$15 \text{ million FV of equity})}{(\$5 \text{ million} + \$15 \text{ million})}$$

$$= \frac{\$300{,}000 + \$1.5 \text{ million}}{\$20 \text{ million}}$$

$$= .09$$

Answer (A) is incorrect. The pre-tax cost of debt is 8.0%. Answer (B) is incorrect. The amount of 8.89% is based on the book value of equity. Answer (D) is incorrect. The cost of equity is 10%.

9.3.18. The EVA is

A. $1,380,000

B. $1,620,000

C. $1,830,000

D. $3,000,000

Answer (A) is correct. *(Publisher, adapted)*

REQUIRED: The EVA.

DISCUSSION: EVA equals after-tax operating income minus the product of the after-tax WACC and an investment base equal to total assets minus current liabilities.

$$\text{WACC} = \frac{(.06 \times \$5 \text{ million FV of LT debt}) + (10\% \times \$15 \text{ million FV of equity})}{(\$5 \text{ million} + \$15 \text{ million})}$$

$$= \frac{\$300{,}000 + \$1.5 \text{ million}}{\$20 \text{ million}}$$

$$= .09$$

Thus, EVA is $1,380,000 {[$4 million × (1.0 – .25)] – [.09 after-tax WACC × ($20 million total assets – $2 million current liabilities)]}.

Answer (B) is incorrect. The amount of $1,620,000 is the required return on the investment base. Answer (C) is incorrect. The amount of $1,830,000 is based on the assumption that $13 million is the investment base. Answer (D) is incorrect. The amount of $3,000,000 is the after-tax operating income.

Questions 9.3.19 through 9.3.21 are based on the following information. Semibar Co. reports net income of $651,000. The information for the year just ended is also available:

	January 1	December 31
Equity	$4,200,000	$4,480,000
Share price	$25	$30
Shares outstanding	400,000	400,000
Cost of equity	10%	10%
Dividends per share		$1.00

9.3.19. Semibar's equity value creation is

A. $630,000

B. $231,000

C. $210,000

D. $203,000

Answer (C) is correct. *(Publisher, adapted)*

REQUIRED: The equity value creation.

DISCUSSION: The equity spread measures equity value creation by multiplying beginning equity capital by the difference between the return on equity (net income ÷ average equity) and the percentage cost of equity.

$$\text{EVC} = \$4{,}200{,}000 \times \left[\frac{\$651{,}000}{(\$4{,}200{,}000 + \$4{,}480{,}000) \div 2} - 10\%\right]$$

$$= \$4{,}200{,}000 \times \left(\frac{\$651{,}000}{\$4{,}340{,}000} - 10\%\right)$$

$$= \$4{,}200{,}000 \times (15\% - 10\%)$$

$$= \$210{,}000$$

Answer (A) is incorrect. The amount of $630,000 results from failing to subtract the cost of equity. Answer (B) is incorrect. The amount of $231,000 results from using beginning equity in the denominator rather than average equity. Answer (D) is incorrect. The amount of $203,000 results from using ending equity in both places in the formula rather than beginning and average equity, respectively.

9.3.20. The market value added (MVA) is

A. $2,000,000

B. $1,720,000

C. $400,000

D. $280,000

Answer (B) is correct. *(Publisher, adapted)*

REQUIRED: The market value added.

DISCUSSION: MVA is the difference between the market value of equity (shares outstanding × share price) and the equity supplied by shareholders. Thus , MVA equals $1,720,000 {[($30 × 400,000 shares) – $4,480,000 SE at 12/31] – [($25 × 400,000 shares) – $4,200,000 SE at 1/1]}.

Answer (A) is incorrect. The amount of $2,000,000 equals 400,000 shares times the increase in the share price. Answer (C) is incorrect. Dividends paid is $400,000. Answer (D) is incorrect. The increase in equity is $280,000.

9.3.21. The total shareholder return is

A. 24%

B. 20%

C. 16.67%

D. 4%

Answer (A) is correct. *(Publisher, adapted)*

REQUIRED: The total shareholder return.

DISCUSSION: The total shareholder return is the sum of the change in the share price and dividends per share, divided by the initial stock price. It equals 24% {[($30 – $25) + $1] ÷ $25}.

Answer (B) is incorrect. The amount of 20% is based on a denominator equal to the ending share price. Answer (C) is incorrect. The amount of 16.67% ignores dividends and is based on a denominator equal to the ending share price. Answer (D) is incorrect. The amount of 4% ignores the share price change.

9.3.22. Maplewood Industries wants its division managers to concentrate on improving profitability. The performance evaluation measures that are most likely to encourage this behavior are

A. Dividends per share, return on equity, and times interest earned.

B. Turnover of operating assets, gross profit margin, and return on equity.

C. Return on operating assets, the current ratio, and the debt-to-equity ratio.

D. Turnover of operating assets, dividends per share, and times interest earned.

Answer (B) is correct. *(CMA, adapted)*

REQUIRED: The performance evaluation measures most likely to motivate managers to improve profitability.

DISCUSSION: To improve profitability, managers should concentrate on those activities over which they have control. Thus, a division manager should seek (1) increased turnover of operating assets, (2) higher gross profit margin, and (3) greater return on equity.

Answer (A) is incorrect. A division manager does not control dividends or times interest earned. Answer (C) is incorrect. A division manager does not control the debt-to-equity ratio. Answer (D) is incorrect. A division manager does not control dividends or times interest earned.

9.3.23. The imputed interest rate used in the residual income approach to performance evaluation can best be described as the

A. Average lending rate for the year being evaluated.

B. Historical weighted-average cost of capital for the company.

C. Target return on investment set by the company's management.

D. Average return on investments for the company over the last several years.

Answer (C) is correct. *(CMA, adapted)*

REQUIRED: The true statement about the imputed interest rate used in the residual income approach to performance evaluation.

DISCUSSION: Residual income is the excess of operating income over a targeted amount equal to an imputed interest charge on invested capital. The rate used ordinarily is set as a target return by management but is often equal to the weighted average cost of capital.

Answer (A) is incorrect. The cost of equity capital also must be included in the imputed interest rate. Answer (B) is incorrect. The current weighted-average cost of capital must be used. Answer (D) is incorrect. The rate should be based on cost of capital, not investment returns of preceding years.

9.4 Decentralization and Transfer Pricing

9.4.1. The primary difference between centralization and decentralization is

A. Separate offices for all managers.

B. Geographical separation of divisional headquarters and central headquarters.

C. The extent of freedom of decision making by many levels of management.

D. The relative size of the firm.

Answer (C) is correct. *(Publisher, adapted)*

REQUIRED: The primary difference between centralization and decentralization.

DISCUSSION: The primary distinction is in the degree of freedom of decision making by managers at many levels. In decentralization, decision making is at as low a level as possible. The premise is that the local manager can make more informed decisions than a centralized manager. Centralization assumes decision making must be consolidated so that activities throughout the organization may be more effectively coordinated. In most organizations, a mixture of these approaches is best.

Answer (A) is incorrect. Whether all managers have separate offices is a trivial issue. Answer (B) is incorrect. Geographical separation is possible in a centralized environment. Answer (D) is incorrect. Relative size is a secondary factor in determining whether to centralize.

9.4.2. Which of the following is most likely to be a disadvantage of decentralization?

A. Lower-level employees will develop less rapidly than in a centralized organization.

B. Lower-level employees will complain of not having enough to do.

C. Top management will have less time available to devote to unique problems.

D. Lower-level managers may make conflicting decisions.

Answer (D) is correct. *(CIA, adapted)*

REQUIRED: The item most likely to be a disadvantage of decentralization.

DISCUSSION: The disadvantages of decentralization include (1) a tendency to focus on short-run results to the detriment of the long-term health of the entity, (2) an increased risk of loss of control by top management, (3) the increased difficulty of coordinating interdependent units, and (4) less cooperation and communication among competing decentralized unit managers.

Answer (A) is incorrect. Decentralization encourages development of lower-level managers. They have greater responsibilities and authority. Answer (B) is incorrect. More tasks are delegated to lower-level employees. Answer (C) is incorrect. Top managers make fewer operating decisions.

9.4.3. The CEO of a rapidly growing high-technology firm has exercised centralized authority over all corporate functions. Because the company now operates in four states, the CEO is considering the advisability of decentralizing operational control over production and sales. Which of the following conditions probably will result from and be a valid reason for decentralizing?

A. Greater local control over compliance with federal regulations.

B. More efficient use of headquarters staff officials and specialists.

C. Quicker and better operating decisions.

D. Greater economies in purchasing.

Answer (C) is correct. *(CIA, adapted)*

REQUIRED: The condition that is a valid reason for decentralizing.

DISCUSSION: Decentralization results in greater speed in making operating decisions because they are made by lower-level managers instead of being referred to top management. The quality of operating decisions also should be enhanced, assuming proper training of managers. Those closest to the problems should be the most knowledgeable about them.

Answer (A) is incorrect. Compliance with governmental regulations is probably more easily achieved by centralization. A disadvantage of decentralization is the difficulty of assuring uniform action by units of the entity that have substantial autonomy. Answer (B) is incorrect. Decentralization may result in duplication of efforts, resulting in less efficient use of headquarters staff officials and specialists. Answer (D) is incorrect. Decentralization usually results in a duplication of purchasing efforts.

9.4.4. Which of the following is not a cost of decentralization?

A. Dysfunctional decision making owing to disagreements of managers regarding overall goals and subgoals of the individual decision makers.

B. A decreased understanding of the overall goals of the organization.

C. Increased costs for developing the information system.

D. Decreased costs of corporate-level staff services and management talent.

Answer (D) is correct. *(Publisher, adapted)*

REQUIRED: The item not a cost of decentralization.

DISCUSSION: The costs of centralized staff may actually decrease under decentralization. But the corporate staff and the various services they provide may have to be duplicated in various divisions, thereby increasing overall costs. Suboptimal decisions may result from disharmony among organizational goals, subgoals of the division, and the individual goals of managers. The overall goals of the firm may more easily be misunderstood because individual managers may not have a top manager's perspective. Moreover, the information system necessary for adequate reporting in a decentralized mode tends to duplication, which increases costs.

Answer (A) is incorrect. Dysfunctional decision making is a cost of decentralization. Answer (B) is incorrect. A decreased understanding of the overall goals of an organization is a cost of decentralization. Answer (C) is incorrect. Increased costs for developing the information system is a cost of decentralization.

9.4.5. Which one of the following will not occur in an organization that gives managers throughout the organization maximum freedom to make decisions?

A. Individual managers regarding the managers of other segments as they do external parties.

B. Two divisions of the organization having competing models that aim for the same market segments.

C. Delays in securing approval for the introduction of new products.

D. Greater knowledge of the marketplace and improved service to customers.

Answer (C) is correct. *(CMA, adapted)*

REQUIRED: The event not occurring in a decentralized organization.

DISCUSSION: Decentralization is beneficial because it creates greater responsiveness to the needs of local customers, suppliers, and employees. Managers at lower levels are more knowledgeable about local markets and the needs of customers, etc. A decentralized organization also is more likely to respond flexibly and quickly to changing conditions, for example, by expediting the introduction of new products. Furthermore, greater authority enhances managerial morale and development. Disadvantages of decentralization include duplication of effort and lack of goal congruence.

Answer (A) is incorrect. When segments are autonomous, other segments are regarded as external parties, e.g., as suppliers, customers, or competitors. Answer (B) is incorrect. Autonomous segments may have the authority to compete in the same markets. Answer (D) is incorrect. Decentralizing decision making results in improved service. The managers closest to customers are making decisions about customer service.

9.4.6. The price that one division of a company charges another division for goods or services provided is called the

A. Market price.

B. Transfer price.

C. Outlay price.

D. Distress price.

Answer (B) is correct. *(CIA, adapted)*

REQUIRED: The price that one division of a company charges another for goods or services provided.

DISCUSSION: A transfer price is the price charged by one segment of an organization for a product or service supplied to another segment of the same organization.

Answer (A) is incorrect. Market price is an approach to determine a transfer price. Answer (C) is incorrect. Outlay price is an approach to determine a transfer price. Answer (D) is incorrect. Distress price is an approach to determine a transfer price.

9.4.7. The most fundamental responsibility center affected by the use of market-based transfer prices is a(n)

A. Production center.

B. Investment center.

C. Cost center.

D. Profit center.

Answer (D) is correct. *(CMA, adapted)*

REQUIRED: The most fundamental responsibility center affected by the use of market-based transfer prices.

DISCUSSION: Transfer prices are often used by profit centers and investment centers. Profit centers are the more fundamental of these two centers because investment centers are responsible not only for revenues and costs but also for invested capital.

Answer (A) is incorrect. A production center may be a cost center, a profit center, or even an investment center. Transfer prices are not used in a cost center. Transfer prices are used to compute profitability, but a cost center is responsible only for cost control. Answer (B) is incorrect. An investment center is not as fundamental as a profit center. Answer (C) is incorrect. Transfer prices are not used in a cost center.

9.4.8. Transfer pricing should encourage goal congruence and managerial effort. In a decentralized organization, it should also encourage autonomous decision making. Managerial effort is

A. The desire and the commitment to achieve a specific goal.

B. The sharing of goals by supervisors and subordinates.

C. The extent to which individuals have the authority to make decisions.

D. The extent of the attempt to accomplish a specific goal.

Answer (D) is correct. *(Publisher, adapted)*

REQUIRED: The definition of managerial effort.

DISCUSSION: Managerial effort is the extent to which a manager attempts to accomplish a goal. Managerial effort may include psychological as well as physical commitment to a goal.

Answer (A) is incorrect. Motivation is the desire and the commitment to achieve a specific goal. Answer (B) is incorrect. Goal congruence is the sharing of goals by supervisors and subordinates. Answer (C) is incorrect. Autonomy is the extent to which individuals have the authority to make decisions.

9.4.9. Goal congruence is

A. The desire and the commitment to achieve a specific goal.

B. The sharing of goals by supervisors and subordinates.

C. The extent to which individuals have the authority to make decisions.

D. The extent of the attempt to accomplish a specific goal.

Answer (B) is correct. *(Publisher, adapted)*

REQUIRED: The definition of goal congruence.

DISCUSSION: Goal congruence is agreement on the goals of the organization or the segment by supervisors and subordinates. Performance is assumed to be optimized when the parties understand that personal and segmental goals should be consistent with those of the organization.

Answer (A) is incorrect. Motivation is the desire and the commitment to achieve a specific goal. Answer (C) is incorrect. Autonomy is the extent to which individuals have the authority to make decisions. Answer (D) is incorrect. Managerial effort is the extent of the attempt to accomplish a specific goal.

9.4.10. Motivation is

A. The desire and the commitment to achieve a specific goal.

B. The sharing of goals by supervisors and subordinates.

C. The extent to which individuals have the authority to make decisions.

D. The extent of the attempt to accomplish a specific goal.

Answer (A) is correct. *(Publisher, adapted)*

REQUIRED: The definition of motivation.

DISCUSSION: Motivation is the desire to attain a specific goal (goal congruence) and the commitment to accomplish the goal (managerial effort). Managerial motivation is therefore a combination of managerial effort and goal congruence.

Answer (B) is incorrect. Goal congruence is the sharing of goals by supervisors and subordinates. Answer (C) is incorrect. Autonomy is the extent to which individuals have the authority to make decisions. Answer (D) is incorrect. Managerial effort is the extent of the attempt to accomplish a specific goal.

9.4.11. A proposed transfer price may be based upon the outlay cost. Outlay cost plus opportunity cost is the

A. Retail price.

B. Price representing the cash outflows of the supplying division plus the contribution to the supplying division from an outside sale.

C. Price usually set by an absorption-costing calculation.

D. Price set by charging for variable costs plus a lump sum or an additional markup, but less than full markup.

Answer (B) is correct. *(Publisher, adapted)*

REQUIRED: The definition of outlay cost plus opportunity cost.

DISCUSSION: At this price, the supplying division is indifferent as to whether it sells internally or externally. Outlay cost plus opportunity cost therefore represents a minimum acceptable price for a seller. However, no transfer price formula is appropriate in all circumstances.

Answer (A) is incorrect. The retail price is the definition of the market price, assuming an arm's-length transaction. Answer (C) is incorrect. Full cost is the price usually set by an absorption-costing calculation. Answer (D) is incorrect. The variable-cost-plus price is the price set by charging for variable costs plus a lump sum or an additional markup, but less than full markup.

9.4.12. A proposed transfer price may be a cost-plus price. Variable-cost-plus price is the price

A. On the open market.

B. Representing the cash outflows of the supplying division plus the contribution to the supplying division from an outside sale.

C. Usually set by an absorption-costing calculation.

D. Set by charging for variable costs plus a lump sum or an additional markup, but less than full markup.

Answer (D) is correct. *(Publisher, adapted)*

REQUIRED: The definition of variable-cost-plus price.

DISCUSSION: The variable-cost-plus price is the price set by charging for variable cost plus either a lump sum or an additional markup but less than the full markup price. This permits top management to enter the decision process and dictate that a division transfer at variable cost plus some appropriate amount.

Answer (A) is incorrect. The price on the open market is the definition of the market price. Answer (B) is incorrect. Outlay cost plus opportunity cost is the price representing the cash outflows of the supplying division plus the contribution to the supplying division from an outside sale. Answer (C) is incorrect. The full-cost price is the price usually set by an absorption-costing calculation.

9.4.13. A proposed transfer price may be based upon the full-cost price. Full-cost price is the price

A. On the open market.

B. Representing the cash outflows of the supplying division plus the contribution to the supplying division from an outside sale.

C. Usually set by an absorption-costing calculation.

D. Set by charging for variable costs plus a lump sum or an additional markup, but less than full markup.

Answer (C) is correct. *(Publisher, adapted)*

REQUIRED: The definition of full-cost price.

DISCUSSION: Full-cost price is the price usually set by an absorption-costing calculation and includes materials, labor, and a full allocation of manufacturing O/H. This full-cost price may lead to dysfunctional behavior by the supplying and receiving divisions, e.g., purchasing from outside sources at a slightly lower price that is substantially above the variable costs of internal production.

Answer (A) is incorrect. The market price is the price on the open market. Answer (B) is incorrect. The outlay cost plus opportunity cost is the price representing the cash outflows of the supplying division plus the contribution to the supplying division from an outside sale. Answer (D) is incorrect. The variable-cost-plus price is the price set by charging for variable costs plus a lump sum or an additional markup, but less than full markup.

9.4.14. A large manufacturing company has several autonomous divisions that sell their products in perfectly competitive external markets as well as internally to the other divisions of the company. Top management expects each of its divisional managers to take actions that will maximize the organization's goals as well as their own goals. Top management also promotes a sustained level of management effort of all of its divisional managers. Under these circumstances, for products exchanged between divisions, the transfer price that will generally lead to optimal decisions for the manufacturing company would be a transfer price equal to the

A. Full cost of the product.

B. Full cost of the product plus a markup.

C. Variable cost of the product plus a markup.

D. Market price of the product.

Answer (D) is correct. *(CIA, adapted)*

REQUIRED: The optimal transfer price.

DISCUSSION: A market-based transfer price promotes goal congruence and sustained management effort. It is also consistent with divisional autonomy. A market transfer price is most appropriate when (1) the market is competitive, (2) interdivisional dependency is low, and (3) buying in the market involves no marginal costs or benefits.

Answer (A) is incorrect. A transfer price at full cost means that the seller does not make a profit. In addition, the seller may be forgoing profits that could be obtained by selling to outside customers. Thus, full-cost transfer prices can lead to suboptimal decisions. Answer (B) is incorrect. A transfer price at full cost plus markup results in no incentive for the seller to control its costs. Thus, a sustained level of management effort may not be maintained. Answer (C) is incorrect. A transfer price at variable cost plus markup has the same weaknesses as full cost plus markup.

9.4.15. A limitation of transfer prices based on actual cost is that they

A. Charge inefficiencies to the department that is transferring the goods.

B. Can lead to suboptimal decisions for the company as a whole.

C. Must be adjusted by some markup.

D. Lack clarity and administrative convenience.

Answer (B) is correct. *(CIA, adapted)*

REQUIRED: The limitation of transfer prices based on actual cost.

DISCUSSION: The optimal transfer price of a selling division should be set at a point that will have the most desirable economic effect on the firm as a whole while at the same time continuing to motivate the management of every division to perform efficiently. Setting the transfer price based on actual costs rather than standard costs would give the selling division little incentive to control costs.

Answer (A) is incorrect. Inefficiencies are charged to the buying department. Answer (C) is incorrect. By definition, cost-based transfer prices are not adjusted by some markup. Answer (D) is incorrect. Cost-based transfer prices provide the advantages of clarity and administrative convenience.

9.4.16. A firm has intracompany service transfers from Division Core, a cost center, to Division Pro, a profit center. Under stable economic conditions, which of the following transfer prices is likely to be most conducive to evaluating whether both divisions have met their responsibilities?

A. Actual cost.

B. Standard variable cost.

C. Actual cost plus markup.

D. Negotiated price.

Answer (B) is correct. *(CPA, adapted)*

REQUIRED: The transfer price likely to be most useful for evaluating both divisions.

DISCUSSION: A cost center is responsible for costs only. A profit center is responsible for costs and revenues. Hence, the transfer from the cost center must, by definition, be at a cost-based figure. The transfer should be at standard variable cost so as to isolate any variance resulting from Core's operations. Assuming fixed costs are not controllable in the short run, the relevant variance is the difference between actual cost and the standard variable cost.

Answer (A) is incorrect. Actual cost is not appropriate for a transfer price from a cost center to a profit center. Answer (C) is incorrect. As a cost center, Core will use cost as a transfer price. Answer (D) is incorrect. As a cost center, Core will use cost as a transfer price.

9.4.17. The Eastern division sells goods internally to the Western division of the same company. The quoted external price in industry publications from a supplier near Eastern is $200 per ton plus transportation. It costs $20 per ton to transport the goods to Western. Eastern's actual market cost per ton to buy the direct materials to make the transferred product is $100. Actual per-ton direct labor is $50. Other actual costs of storage and handling are $40. The company president selects a $220 transfer price. This is an example of

A. Market-based transfer pricing.

B. Cost-based transfer pricing.

C. Negotiated transfer pricing.

D. Cost plus 20% transfer pricing.

Answer (A) is correct. *(CIA, adapted)*

REQUIRED: The type of transfer price.

DISCUSSION: The optimal transfer price of a selling division should be set at a point that will have the most desirable economic effect on the firm as a whole while at the same time continuing to motivate the management of every division to perform efficiently. Because the $220 transfer price selected is based on the quoted external price (market), it is an example of market-based transfer pricing.

Answer (B) is incorrect. The cost-based price is $210 ($100 + $50 + $40 + $20). Answer (C) is incorrect. No negotiations occurred. Answer (D) is incorrect. Cost plus 20% equals $252 ($210 × 1.20).

9.4.18. Which of the following is the most significant disadvantage of a cost-based transfer price?

A. Requires internally developed information.

B. Imposes market effects on company operations.

C. Requires externally developed information.

D. May not promote long-term efficiencies.

Answer (D) is correct. *(CIA, adapted)*

REQUIRED: The most significant disadvantage of a cost-based transfer price.

DISCUSSION: A cost-based transfer price is charged in an intraentity transaction that covers only the selling subunit's costs. However, by ignoring relevant alternative market prices, an entity may pay more than is necessary to produce goods and services internally.

Answer (A) is incorrect. Internally developed information should be developed whether or not transfer prices are used. Answer (B) is incorrect. The market affects operations when the transfer price is a market price. Answer (C) is incorrect. Externally developed information is needed for a market-based transfer price.

9.4.19. Which of the following is not true about international transfer prices for a multinational firm?

A. Allows firms to attempt to minimize worldwide taxes.

B. Allows the firm to evaluate each division.

C. Provides each division with a profit-making orientation.

D. Allows firms to correctly price products in each country in which it operates.

Answer (D) is correct. *(CIA, adapted)*

REQUIRED: The false statement about international transfer prices.

DISCUSSION: The calculation of transfer prices in the international arena must be systematic. A scheme for calculating transfer prices for a firm may correctly price the firm's product in Country A but not in Country B. The product may be overpriced in Country B, causing sales to be lower than anticipated; or, the product may be underpriced in Country B, and the authorities may allege that the firm is dumping its product there.

Answer (A) is incorrect. Properly chosen transfer prices allow firms to attempt to minimize worldwide taxes by producing various parts of the products in different countries and strategically transferring the parts at various systematically calculated prices. Answer (B) is incorrect. Properly chosen transfer prices allocate revenues and expenses to divisions in various countries. These numbers are used as part of the input for the performance evaluation of each division. Answer (C) is incorrect. Transfer prices motivate division managers to buy parts and products (from either internal or external suppliers) at the lowest possible prices and to sell their products (to either internal or external customers) at the highest possible prices. Hence, each division has a profit making orientation.

9.4.20. A company has two divisions, A and B, each operated as a profit center. A charges B $35 per unit for each unit transferred to B. Other data follow:

A's variable cost per unit	$ 30
A's fixed costs	10,000
A's annual sales to B	5,000 units
A's sales to outsiders	50,000 units

A is planning to raise its transfer price to $50 per unit. Division B can purchase units at $40 each from outsiders, but doing so would idle A's facilities now committed to producing units for B. Division A cannot increase its sales to outsiders. From the perspective of the company as a whole, from whom should Division B acquire the units, assuming B's market is unaffected?

A. Outside vendors.

B. Division A, but only at the variable cost per unit.

C. Division A, but only until fixed costs are covered, then from outside vendors.

D. Division A, despite the increased transfer price.

Answer (D) is correct. *(CIA, adapted)*

REQUIRED: The purchasing decision benefiting the entity as a whole.

DISCUSSION: Opportunity costs are $0 because A's facilities would be idle if B did not purchase from A. Assuming fixed costs are not affected by the decision, the intraentity sale is preferable from the overall perspective because A's $30 variable unit cost is less than the outside vendor's price of $40.

Answer (A) is incorrect. Outside purchase increases the entity's cost of sales by $10 per unit. Answer (B) is incorrect. The transfer price is irrelevant to the decision. It does not affect overall profits. Answer (C) is incorrect. The initial issue is covering variable rather than fixed costs.

9.4.21. The Alpha Division of a company, which is operating at capacity, produces and sells 1,000 units of a certain electronic component in a perfectly competitive market. Revenue and cost data are as follows:

Sales	$50,000
Variable costs	34,000
Fixed costs	12,000

The minimum transfer price that should be charged to the Beta Division of the same company for each component is

A. $12

B. $34

C. $46

D. $50

Answer (D) is correct. *(CIA, adapted)*

REQUIRED: The minimum transfer price that should be charged to another division of the same company.

DISCUSSION: In a perfectly competitive market, market price ordinarily is the appropriate transfer price. Because the market price is objective, using it avoids waste and maximizes efficiency. In a perfectly competitive market, the market price equals the minimum transfer price, the sum of outlay cost and opportunity cost. Outlay cost is the variable cost per unit, or $34 ($34,000 ÷ 1,000). Opportunity cost is the contribution margin forgone, or $16 ($50 – $34). Thus, the minimum transfer price is $50 ($34 + $16).

Answer (A) is incorrect. Given that Alpha Division has no idle capacity, the transfer price to Beta should be the market price of $50 per unit. Answer (B) is incorrect. The opportunity cost needs to be included. Answer (C) is incorrect. The minimum transfer price equals outlay (variable) costs plus opportunity cost, not variable costs plus fixed costs.

Questions 9.4.22 through 9.4.24 are based on the following information.

Parkside, Inc., has several divisions that operate as decentralized profit centers. Parkside's Entertainment Division manufactures video arcade equipment using the products of two of Parkside's other divisions. The Plastics Division manufactures plastic components, one type that is made exclusively for the Entertainment Division, while other less complex components are sold to outside markets. The products of the Video Cards Division are sold in a competitive market; however, one video card model is also used by the Entertainment Division.

The actual costs per unit used by the Entertainment Division are presented below.

	Plastic Components	Video Cards
Direct material	$1.25	$2.40
Direct labor	2.35	3.00
Variable overhead	1.00	1.50
Fixed overhead	.40	2.25
Total cost	$5.00	$9.15

The Plastics Division sells its commercial products at full cost plus a 25% markup and believes the proprietary plastic component made for the Entertainment Division would sell for $6.25 per unit on the open market. The market price of the video card used by the Entertainment Division is $10.98 per unit.

9.4.22. A per-unit transfer price from the Video Cards Division to the Entertainment Division at full cost, $9.15, would

A. Allow evaluation of both divisions on a competitive basis.

B. Satisfy the Video Cards Division's profit desire by allowing recovery of opportunity costs.

C. Provide no profit incentive for the Video Cards Division to control or reduce costs.

D. Encourage the Entertainment Division to purchase video cards from an outside source.

Answer (C) is correct. *(CMA, adapted)*

REQUIRED: The negative effect of a full-cost transfer price.

DISCUSSION: The use of full (absorption) cost ensures that the selling division will not incur a loss and provides more incentive to the buying division to buy internally than does use of market price. However, there is no motivation for the seller to control production cost since all costs can be passed along to the buying division.

Answer (A) is incorrect. Evaluating the seller is difficult if it can pass along all costs to the buyer. Answer (B) is incorrect. Transfers at full cost do not allow for a seller's profit. Answer (D) is incorrect. A full-cost transfer is favorable to the buyer. It is lower than the market price.

9.4.23. Assume that the Entertainment Division is able to purchase a large quantity of video cards from an outside source at $8.70 per unit. The Video Cards Division, having excess capacity, agrees to lower its transfer price to $8.70 per unit. This action would

A. Optimize the profit goals of the Entertainment Division while subverting the profit goals of Parkside, Inc.

B. Allow evaluation of both divisions on the same basis.

C. Subvert the profit goals of the Video Cards Division while optimizing the profit goals of the Entertainment Division.

D. Optimize the overall profit goals of Parkside, Inc.

Answer (D) is correct. *(CMA, adapted)*

REQUIRED: The impact of lowering the transfer price to match an outside seller's price.

DISCUSSION: If the selling division has excess capacity, it should lower its transfer price to match the outside offer. This decision optimizes the profits of the company as a whole by allowing for use of capacity that would otherwise be idle.

Answer (A) is incorrect. This action is congruent with the goals of Parkside. The use of idle capacity enhances profits. Answer (B) is incorrect. The transfer is at a loss (relative to full cost) to the selling division, although the company as a whole will benefit. Answer (C) is incorrect. The buying division is indifferent as to whether to purchase internally or externally.

9.4.24. Assume that the Plastics Division has excess capacity and it has negotiated a transfer price of $5.60 per plastic component with the Entertainment Division. This price will

A. Cause the Plastics Division to reduce the number of commercial plastic components it manufactures.

B. Motivate both divisions as estimated profits are shared.

C. Encourage the Entertainment Division to seek an outside source for plastic components.

D. Demotivate the Plastics Division causing mediocre performance.

Answer (B) is correct. *(CMA, adapted)*

REQUIRED: The effect of using a negotiated transfer price that is greater than full cost but less than market price.

DISCUSSION: Given that the seller has excess capacity, transfers within the company entail no opportunity cost. Accordingly, the transfer at the negotiated price will improve the performance measures of the selling division. Purchasing internally at below the market price also benefits the buying division, so the motivational purpose of transfer pricing is achieved. The goal congruence purpose is also achieved because the internal transaction benefits the company.

Answer (A) is incorrect. This arrangement creates no disincentive for the selling division. It will make a profit on every unit transferred. Answer (C) is incorrect. The market price charged by outside sources is higher than the negotiated price. Answer (D) is incorrect. Given idle capacity, selling at any amount in excess of variable cost should motivate the selling division.

9.4.25. An appropriate transfer price between two divisions of a manufacturer can be determined from the following data:

Fabricating Division:	
Market price of subassembly	$50
Variable cost of subassembly	$20
Excess capacity (in units)	1,000
Assembling Division:	
Number of units needed	900

What is the natural bargaining range for the two divisions?

A. Between $20 and $50.

B. Between $50 and $70.

C. Any amount less than $50.

D. $50 is the only acceptable price.

Answer (A) is correct. *(CMA, adapted)*

REQUIRED: The natural bargaining range for the transfer price.

DISCUSSION: An ideal transfer price should permit each division to operate independently and achieve its goals while functioning in the overall best interest of the firm. The production capacity of the selling division is always a consideration in setting transfer price. If Fabricating had no excess capacity, it would charge Assembling the regular market price. However, since Fabricating has excess capacity of 1,000 units, negotiation is possible because any transfer price greater than the variable cost of $20 would absorb some of the fixed costs and result in increased divisional profits. Thus, any price between $20 and $50 is acceptable to Fabricating. Any price under $50 is acceptable to Assembling because that is the price that would be paid to an outside supplier.

Answer (B) is incorrect. Assembling would not pay more than the market price of $50. Answer (C) is incorrect. Fabricating will not be willing to accept less than its variable cost of $20. Answer (D) is incorrect. Fabricating should be willing to accept any price between $20 and $50.

9.4.26. Division A of a company is currently operating at 50% capacity. It produces a single product and sells all its production to outside customers for $13 per unit. Variable costs are $7 per unit, and fixed costs are $6 per unit at the current production level. Division B, which currently purchases this product from an outside supplier for $12 per unit, would like to purchase the product from Division A. Division A will operate at 80% capacity to meet outside customers' and Division B's demand. What is the minimum price that Division A should charge Division B for this product?

A. $7.00 per unit.

B. $9.60 per unit.

C. $12.00 per unit.

D. $13.00 per unit.

Answer (A) is correct. *(CIA, adapted)*

REQUIRED: The minimum price that should be charged by one division of a company to another.

DISCUSSION: From the seller's perspective, the price should reflect at least its incremental cash outflow (outlay cost) plus the contribution from an outside sale (opportunity cost). Because A has idle capacity, the opportunity cost is $0. Thus, the minimum price Division A should charge Division B is $7.00.

Answer (B) is incorrect. The minimum that should be charged is $7.00. Since Division A has idle capacity, the minimum transfer price should recover variable costs ($7.00). Answer (C) is incorrect. Division A should not include any fixed costs in their transfer price because Division A has idle capacity. Answer (D) is incorrect. Since Division A has idle capacity, the minimum transfer price should recover Division A's variable (outlay) costs.

9.5 Comprehensive

Questions 9.5.1 through 9.5.13 are based on the following information.

	Segment A	Segment B	Segment C	Segment D
Net income	$ 5,000	--	--	$ 90,000
Sales	60,000	$750,000	$135,000	1,800,000
Investment	24,000	500,000	45,000	--
Net income as % of sales	--	--	--	--
Turnover of investment	--	--	--	--
ROI	--	--	20%	7.5%
Minimum ROI--dollars	--	--	--	$ 120,000
Minimum ROI--%	20%	6%	--	--
Residual income	--	--	$ 2,250	--

9.5.1. For Segment B, net income as a percentage of sales is

A. 8%

B. 6.67%

C. 4%

D. 10%

Answer (C) is correct. *(Publisher, adapted)*

REQUIRED: The net income as a percentage of sales.

DISCUSSION: Residual income was zero, indicating that net income was equal to the minimum dollar ROI. Given a 6% minimum ROI as a percentage of investment, net income equals $30,000 (6% × $500,000 investment). Net income ($30,000) divided by sales ($750,000) equals 4%.

Answer (A) is incorrect. Net income as a percentage of sales is calculated by dividing net income by the sales of Segment B. Answer (B) is incorrect. The net income as a percentage of sales for Segment C is 6.67%. Answer (D) is incorrect. The minimum ROI percentage for Segment D is 10%.

9.5.2. For Segment C, net income as a percentage of sales is

A. 5%

B. 6.67%

C. 4%

D. 20%

Answer (B) is correct. *(Publisher, adapted)*

REQUIRED: The net income as a percentage of sales.

DISCUSSION: Net income as a percentage of sales is the ROI divided by turnover of investment. The turnover of the investment is sales ($135,000) divided by the investment ($45,000), or 3. Thus, net income is 6.67% (20% ÷ 3) as a percentage of sales for Segment C.

Answer (A) is incorrect. The net income as a percentage of sales for Segment D is 5%. Answer (C) is incorrect. The net income as a percentage of sales for Segment B is 4%. Answer (D) is incorrect. The ROI for Segment C is 20%.

9.5.3. For Segment A, ROI is

A. 6%

B. 20%

C. 20.8%

D. 7.5%

Answer (C) is correct. *(Publisher, adapted)*

REQUIRED: The ROI for Segment A.

DISCUSSION: ROI is equal to net income divided by investment. Net income equals $5,000. Investment equals $24,000. Consequently, ROI equals 20.8%.

Answer (A) is incorrect. The ROI for Segment B is 6%. Answer (B) is incorrect. The ROI for Segment C is 20%. Answer (D) is incorrect. The ROI for Segment D is 7.5%.

9.5.4. For Segment B, ROI is

A. 6%

B. 20.8%

C. 20%

D. 7.5%

Answer (A) is correct. *(Publisher, adapted)*

REQUIRED: The ROI for Segment B.

DISCUSSION: Residual income is given as zero. Thus, the actual ROI is the same as the minimum percentage ROI of 6%.

Answer (B) is incorrect. The ROI for Segment A is 20.8%. Answer (C) is incorrect. The ROI for Segment C is 20%. Answer (D) is incorrect. The ROI for Segment D is 7.5%.

9.5.5. For Segment C, the turnover of investment is

A. 3

B. 1.5

C. 2.5

D. 4

Answer (A) is correct. *(Publisher, adapted)*

REQUIRED: The turnover of investment for Segment C.

DISCUSSION: The turnover of investment for Segment C is calculated by dividing sales by investment. Given sales of $135,000 and investment of $45,000, Segment C's turnover of investment is 3.

Answer (B) is incorrect. The turnover of investment for Segment B is 1.5. Answer (C) is incorrect. The turnover of investment for Segment A is 2.5. Answer (D) is incorrect. The turnover of investment is calculated by dividing sales by investment.

9.5.6. For Segment D, the turnover of investment is

A. 3

B. 1.5

C. 2.5

D. 4

Answer (B) is correct. *(Publisher, adapted)*

REQUIRED: The turnover of investment for Segment D.

DISCUSSION: The turnover of investment for Segment D is determined by dividing sales by investment. For Segment D, net income ($90,000) as a percentage of sales ($1,800,000) equals 5%. ROI is given as 7.5%. Dividing net income as a percentage of sales (5%) into ROI (7.5%) gives a turnover of investment of 1.5.

Answer (A) is incorrect. The turnover of investment for Segment C is 3. Answer (C) is incorrect. The turnover of investment for Segment A is 2.5. Answer (D) is incorrect. The turnover of investment is calculated by dividing sales by investment.

9.5.7. For Segment A, the minimum dollar ROI is

A. $30,000

B. $6,750

C. $4,800

D. $120,000

Answer (C) is correct. *(Publisher, adapted)*

REQUIRED: The minimum rate of return in dollars for Segment A.

DISCUSSION: The minimum ROI in dollars equals the amount of the investment times the minimum rate of return percentage. The amount of the investment is $24,000. The minimum rate of return percentage is 20%. Accordingly, the minimum ROI in dollars is $4,800.

Answer (A) is incorrect. The minimum dollar ROI for Segment B is $30,000. Answer (B) is incorrect. The minimum dollar ROI for Segment C is $6,750. Answer (D) is incorrect. The minimum dollar ROI for Segment D is $120,000.

9.5.8. For Segment B, the minimum dollar ROI is

A. $30,000

B. $6,750

C. $4,800

D. $120,000

Answer (A) is correct. *(Publisher, adapted)*

REQUIRED: The minimum rate of return in dollars for Segment B.

DISCUSSION: The minimum ROI in dollars equals the amount of the investment times the minimum rate of return percentage. The amount of the investment is $500,000. The minimum rate of return percentage is given as 6%. Thus, the minimum ROI in dollars equals $30,000.

Answer (B) is incorrect. The minimum dollar ROI for Segment C is $6,750. Answer (C) is incorrect. The minimum dollar ROI for Segment A is $4,800. Answer (D) is incorrect. The minimum dollar ROI for Segment D is $120,000.

9.5.9. For Segment C, the minimum dollar ROI is

A. $30,000

B. $6,750

C. $4,800

D. $120,000

Answer (B) is correct. *(Publisher, adapted)*

REQUIRED: The minimum rate of return in dollars for Segment C.

DISCUSSION: The minimum ROI in dollars equals the minimum ROI percentage times the investment. The investment was $45,000. Neither the minimum percentage nor the minimum ROI is known. However, the ROI percentage (20%) and the investment ($45,000) are known. Thus, net income is $9,000. Given residual income of $2,250, the minimum ROI in dollars must have been $6,750 ($9,000 – $2,250).

Answer (A) is incorrect. The minimum dollar ROI for Segment B is $30,000. Answer (C) is incorrect. The minimum dollar ROI for Segment A is $4,800. Answer (D) is incorrect. The minimum dollar ROI for Segment D is $120,000.

9.5.10. Assume that the minimum dollar ROI is $6,750 for Segment C. The minimum percentage of ROI is

A. 20%

B. 6%

C. 15%

D. 10%

Answer (C) is correct. *(Publisher, adapted)*

REQUIRED: The minimum percentage of ROI for Segment C.

DISCUSSION: The minimum percentage of ROI in Segment C equals the minimum dollar ROI divided by the investment. The minimum dollar ROI is $6,750. Consequently, the minimum percentage ROI is 15% ($6,750 ÷ $45,000).

Answer (A) is incorrect. The minimum ROI percentage for Segment A is 20%. Answer (B) is incorrect. The minimum ROI percentage for Segment B is 6%. Answer (D) is incorrect. The minimum ROI percentage for Segment D is 10%.

9.5.11. Refer to the information on the preceding page(s). In Segment D, the minimum percentage of ROI is

A. 20%

B. 6%

C. 15%

D. 10%

Answer (D) is correct. *(Publisher, adapted)*

REQUIRED: The minimum percentage of ROI for Segment D.

DISCUSSION: The minimum percentage of ROI for Segment D is the minimum ROI in dollars ($120,000) divided by the investment, which must be calculated. The ROI is given as 7.5%. The net income ($90,000) as a percentage of sales ($1,800,000) equals 5%. The turnover of investment (ROI ÷ net income as a percentage of sales) is 1.5. Given turnover of 1.5 and sales of $1,800,000, investment must have been $1,200,000. The minimum percentage ROI is $120,000 divided by the $1,200,000 investment, or 10%.

Answer (A) is incorrect. The minimum ROI percentage for Segment A is 20%. Answer (B) is incorrect. The minimum ROI percentage for Segment B is 6%. Answer (C) is incorrect. The minimum ROI percentage for Segment C is 15%.

9.5.12. Refer to the information on the preceding page(s). In Segment A, the residual income is

A. $200

B. $12,000

C. $(30,000)

D. $4,800

Answer (A) is correct. *(Publisher, adapted)*

REQUIRED: The residual income for Segment A.

DISCUSSION: Segment A's residual income equals to the net income ($5,000) minus the minimum ROI in dollars. Minimum ROI in dollars equals the minimum ROI percentage (20%) times the investment ($24,000), or $4,800. Residual income is therefore $200.

Answer (B) is incorrect. The amount of $12,000 is the minimum ROI percentage multiplied by sales. Answer (C) is incorrect. The amount of $(30,000) is the residual income for Segment D. Answer (D) is incorrect. The amount of $4,800 equals the minimum ROI in dollars.

9.5.13. Refer to the information on the preceding page(s). In Segment D, the residual income is

A. $2,250

B. $9,000

C. $(30,000)

D. $0

Answer (C) is correct. *(Publisher, adapted)*

REQUIRED: The residual income for Segment D.

DISCUSSION: The minimum ROI in dollars is given as $120,000 and net income is given as $90,000. Thus, residual income equals net income of $90,000 minus minimum ROI in dollars of $120,000, or $(30,000). Segment D did not achieve its minimum ROI and therefore has a negative residual income.

Answer (A) is incorrect. The residual income for Segment C is $2,250. Answer (B) is incorrect. The amount of $9,000 is 7.5% of $120,000. Answer (D) is incorrect. The amount of $0 assumes that net income is $120,000.

Questions 9.5.14 through 9.5.18 are based on the following information.

Oslo Co.'s industrial photo-finishing division, Rho, incurred the following costs and expenses during the year just ended:

	Variable	Fixed
Direct materials	$200,000	
Direct labor	150,000	
Factory overhead	70,000	$42,000
General, selling, and administrative	30,000	48,000
Totals	$450,000	$90,000

During the year, Rho produced 300,000 units of industrial photo prints, which were sold for $2.00 each. Oslo's investment in Rho was $500,000 and $700,000 at January 1 and December 31, respectively. Oslo normally imputes interest on investments at 15% of average invested capital.

9.5.14. Assume that net operating income was $60,000 and that average invested capital was $600,000. For the year ended December 31, Rho's residual income (loss) was

A. $150,000

B. $60,000

C. $(45,000)

D. $(30,000)

Answer (D) is correct. *(CPA, adapted)*

REQUIRED: The residual income (loss).

DISCUSSION: Rho's residual income can be calculated as follows:

Residual income = Operating income – Target return on invested capital
= $60,000 – ($600,000 × 15%)
= $60,000 – $90,000
= $30,000 loss

Answer (A) is incorrect. The target return on invested capital should not be added to net operating income. Answer (B) is incorrect. The target return on invested capital needs to be deducted from net operating income. Answer (C) is incorrect. This figure is based on a 17.5% imputed interest.

9.5.15. For the year ended December 31, Rho's return on average investment was

A. 15.0%

B. 10.0%

C. 8.6%

D. (5.0%)

Answer (B) is correct. *(CPA, adapted)*

REQUIRED: The return on average investment.

DISCUSSION: Rho's return on average investment can be calculated as follows:

ROI = Operating income ÷ Average invested capital
= [(300,000 units × $2) – $450,000 – $90,000] ÷ [($500,000 + $700,000) ÷ 2]
= $60,000 ÷ $600,000
= 10%

Answer (A) is incorrect. Fifteen percent is the imputed rate. Answer (C) is incorrect. This figure results from operating income divided by the year-end invested capital of $700,000. Answer (D) is incorrect. This percentage equals the residual loss ($30,000) divided by average invested capital.

9.5.16. How many industrial photo-print units did Rho have to sell during the year to break even?

A. 180,000

B. 120,000

C. 90,000

D. 60,000

Answer (A) is correct. *(CPA, adapted)*

REQUIRED: The breakeven point in units.

DISCUSSION: The breakeven point in units is total fixed costs divided by the unit contribution margin (UCM). The UCM is the selling price minus variable costs per unit. Variable costs per unit equal $1.50 ($450,000 ÷ 300,000 units). Thus, the UCM equals $0.50 ($2 – $1.50). Dividing the $90,000 of fixed costs by the $0.50 UCM yields a breakeven point of 180,000 units.

Answer (B) is incorrect. Selling 120,000 units results in a loss of $0.25 per unit. Answer (C) is incorrect. Selling 90,000 units results in a loss of $0.50 per unit. Answer (D) is incorrect. Selling 60,000 units results in a loss of $1 per unit.

9.5.17. For the year ended December 31, Rho's contribution margin was

A. $250,000

B. $180,000

C. $150,000

D. $60,000

Answer (C) is correct. *(CPA, adapted)*

REQUIRED: The contribution margin.

DISCUSSION: The contribution margin equals sales of $600,000 (300,000 units × $2) minus variable costs of $450,000, or $150,000.

Answer (A) is incorrect. Contribution margin is sales minus total variable costs. Answer (B) is incorrect. All variable costs, including general, selling, and administrative, need to be deducted from sales to determine contribution margin. Answer (D) is incorrect. Fixed costs are not subtracted to determine contribution margin.

9.5.18. Assume the variable cost per unit was $1.50. Based on Rho's financial data and an estimated production of 350,000 units of industrial photo-prints for the following year, Rho's estimated total costs and expenses for the following year will be

A. $525,000

B. $540,000

C. $615,000

D. $630,000

Answer (C) is correct. *(CPA, adapted)*

REQUIRED: The estimated total costs and expenses given an increase in production.

DISCUSSION: Over the relevant range, fixed costs will not fluctuate. The variable cost per unit was $1.50. Thus, total costs and expenses will be

Variable (350,000 units × $1.50)	$525,000
Fixed	90,000
Total costs and expenses	$615,000

Answer (A) is incorrect. Fixed costs must be considered in determining total costs and expenses. Answer (B) is incorrect. The amount of $540,000 is the total costs and expenses for the year just ended, based on a production of 300,000 units. Answer (D) is incorrect. Within the relevant range, fixed costs are constant at $90,000.

Questions 9.5.19 through 9.5.24 are based on the following information. The information was presented as part of Question 6 on Part 4 of the December 1981 CMA examination.

PortCo Products is a divisionalized furniture manufacturer. The divisions are autonomous segments, with each division being responsible for its own sales, costs of operations, working capital management, and equipment acquisition. Each division serves a different market in the furniture industry. Because the markets and products of the divisions are so different, there have never been any transfers between divisions.

The Commercial Division manufactures equipment and furniture that are purchased by the restaurant industry. The division plans to introduce a new line of counter and chair units that feature a cushioned seat for the counter chairs. John Kline, the division manager, has discussed the manufacturing of the cushioned seat with Russ Fiegel of the Office Division. They both believe a cushioned seat currently made by the Office Division for use on its deluxe office stool could be modified for use on the new counter chair. Consequently, Kline has asked Russ Fiegel for a price for 100-unit lots of the cushioned seat. The following conversation took place about the price to be charged for the cushioned seats:

Fiegel: "John, we can make the necessary modifications to the cushioned seat easily. The raw materials used in your seat are slightly different and should cost about 10% more than those used in our deluxe office stool. However, the labor time should be the same because the seat fabrication operation basically is the same. I would price the seat at our regular rate -- full cost plus 30% markup."

Kline: "That's higher than I expected, Russ. I was thinking that a good price would be your variable manufacturing costs. After all, your capacity costs will be incurred regardless of this job."

Fiegel: "John, I'm at capacity. By making the cushion seats for you, I'll have to cut my production of deluxe office stools. Of course, I can increase my production of economy office stools. The labor time freed by not having to fabricate the frame or assemble the deluxe stool can be shifted to the frame fabrication and assembly of the economy office stool. Fortunately, I can switch my labor force between these two models of stools without any loss of efficiency. As you know, overtime is not a feasible alternative in our community. I'd like to sell it to you at variable cost, but I have excess demand for both products. I don't mind changing my product mix to the economy model if I get a good return on the seats I make for you. Here are my standard costs for the two stools and a schedule of my manufacturing overhead."

Kline: "I guess I see your point, Russ, but I don't want to price myself out of the market. Maybe we should talk to Corporate to see if they can give us any guidance."

Office Division
Standard Costs and Prices

	Deluxe Office Stool		Economy Office Stool
Raw materials			
Framing	$ 8.15		$ 9.76
Cushioned seat			
Padding	2.40		--
Vinyl	4.00		--
Molded seat (purchased)	--		6.00
Direct labor			
Frame fabrication (.5 × $7.50/DLH)	3.75	(.5 × $7.50/DLH)	3.75
Cushion fabrication (.5 × $7.50/DLH)	3.75		--
Assembly* (.5 × $7.50/DLH)	3.75	(.3 × $7.50/DLH)	2.25
Manufacturing overhead (1.5 DLH × $12.80/DLH)	19.20	(.8DLH × $12.80/DLH)	10.24
Total standard cost	$45.00		$32.00
Selling price (30% markup)	$58.50		$41.60

*Attaching seats to frames and attaching rubber feet.

Office Division
Manufacturing Overhead Budget

Overhead Item	Nature	Amount
Supplies	Variable–at current market prices	$ 420,000
Indirect labor	Variable	375,000
Supervision	Nonvariable	250,000
Power	Use varies with activity; rates are fixed	180,000
Heat and light	Nonvariable–light is fixed regardless of production while heat/air conditioning varies with fuel charges	140,000
Property taxes and insurance taxes	Nonvariable–any change in amounts/rates is independent of production	200,000
Depreciation	Fixed dollar total	1,700,000
Employee benefits	20% of supervision, direct and indirect labor	575,000
	Total overhead	$3,840,000
	Capacity in DLH	÷ 300,000
	Overhead rate/DLH	$12.80

9.5.19. What amount of employee benefit is associated with direct labor costs?

A. $675,000

B. $75,000

C. $450,000

D. $500,000

Answer (C) is correct. *(Publisher, adapted)*

REQUIRED: The amount of employee benefits that is associated with direct labor costs.

DISCUSSION: To find the amount associated with direct labor, 20% of supervision and indirect labor costs are subtracted from total employee benefits {$575,000 – [($250,000 + $375,000) × 20%]}, or $450,000.

Answer (A) is incorrect. Total employee benefits should be reduced by 20% of supervision and indirect labor costs to determine the benefits associated with direct labor costs. Answer (B) is incorrect. The amount of $75,000 is the result of subtracting 80% of supervision and indirect labor costs from total employee benefits. Answer (D) is incorrect. Supervision costs also need to be subtracted.

9.5.20. What is the variable manufacturing overhead rate?

A. $7.80/hr.

B. $11.25/hr.

C. $5.17/hr.

D. $5.00/hr.

Answer (D) is correct. *(Publisher, adapted)*

REQUIRED: The variable manufacturing overhead rate.

DISCUSSION: Total variable overhead is calculated as follows. (Heat or air conditioning costs are excluded. They vary with fuel charges and therefore with production levels.)

	Total
Supplies	$ 420,000
Indirect labor	375,000
Power	180,000
Employee benefits:	
20% direct labor	450,000
20% indirect labor	75,000
Total	$1,500,000

This total is divided by the capacity in DLH (300,000) to arrive at a variable overhead rate of $5 per DLH.

Answer (A) is incorrect. The rate of $7.80/hr. is the fixed manufacturing overhead rate per direct labor hour. Answer (B) is incorrect. The variable manufacturing overhead rate is determined by dividing variable expenses (supplies, indirect labor, power, and direct and indirect labor benefits) by direct labor hours. Answer (C) is incorrect. The rate of $5.17/hr. incorrectly includes supervision benefits of $50,000.

9.5.21. What is the transfer price per 100-unit lot based on variable manufacturing costs to produce the modified cushioned seat?

A. $1,329

B. $1,869

C. $789

D. $1,986

Answer (A) is correct. *(Publisher, adapted)*

REQUIRED: The transfer price based on the variable manufacturing cost.

DISCUSSION: The variable manufacturing cost to produce a 100-unit lot is 100 times the sum of direct materials, direct labor, and variable overhead per seat.

Cushion materials		
Padding	$2.40	
Vinyl	4.00	
Total cushion materials	$6.40	
Cost increase 10% (given)	×1.10	
Cost of cushioned seat		$ 7.04
Cushion fabrication labor ($7.50/DLH × .5 DLH)		3.75
Variable overhead ($5.00/DLH × .5 DLH)		2.50
Total variable cost per cushioned seat		$13.29

The appropriate transfer price for a 100-unit lot is thus $1,329 ($13.29 unit variable cost × 100).

Answer (B) is incorrect. The transfer price plus the opportunity cost of $540 is $1,869. Answer (C) is incorrect. The transfer price minus the opportunity cost of $540 is $789. Answer (D) is incorrect. The transfer price based on the variable manufacturing costs is $1,329.

9.5.22. Refer to the information on the preceding page(s). What is the fixed manufacturing overhead rate?

A. $7.80/hr.

B. $11.25/hr.

C. $5.17/hr.

D. $5.00/hr.

Answer (A) is correct. *(Publisher, adapted)*

REQUIRED: The fixed manufacturing overhead rate.

DISCUSSION: Total fixed overhead is calculated as follows:

Supervision	$ 250,000
Heat and light	140,000
Property taxes and insurance	200,000
Depreciation	1,700,000
Benefits (20% of supervision)	50,000
Total fixed overhead	$2,340,000

This total is divided by the 300,000-hour level of activity to arrive at an hourly rate of $7.80.

Answer (B) is incorrect. The fixed manufacturing overhead rate is determined by dividing fixed expenses (supervision, heat and light, property taxes and insurance, depreciation, and supervision benefits) by direct labor hours. Answer (C) is incorrect. The rate of $5.17/hr. incorrectly includes supervision benefits of $50,000. Answer (D) is incorrect. The rate of $5.00/hr. is the variable manufacturing overhead rate per hour.

9.5.23. Refer to the information on the preceding page(s). How many economy office stools can be produced with the labor hours currently used to make 100 deluxe stools?

A. 187

B. 125

C. 100

D. 150

Answer (B) is correct. *(Publisher, adapted)*

REQUIRED: The economy stools that can be produced in the time spent to make a specified amount of deluxe stools.

DISCUSSION: The labor hours used in cushion fabrication are used to make the modified cushioned seat. Thus, the labor time freed by not making deluxe stools equals the frame fabrication and assembly time only. The number of economy stools that can be produced is 125.

Labor hours to make 100 deluxe stools (1.5 × 100)	150 hr.
Minus: Labor hours to make 100 cushioned seats (cushion fabrication .5 × 100)	(50) hr.
Labor hours available for economy stool	100 hr.
Labor hours to make one economy stool	÷ .8 hr.
Stools produced by extra labor in economy stool production (100 ÷ .8 hr.)	125 stools

Answer (A) is incorrect. The number of economy stools that can be made in 150 hours is 187. Answer (C) is incorrect. The number of hours available is 100. Answer (D) is incorrect. The number of hours required to make 100 deluxe stools before considering the hours required to make 100 cushioned seats is 150.

9.5.24. Refer to the information on the preceding page(s).When computing the opportunity cost for the deluxe office stool, what is the contribution margin per unit produced?

A. $25.20

B. $15.84

C. $45.00

D. $33.30

Answer (A) is correct. *(Publisher, adapted)*

REQUIRED: The contribution margin per unit of the deluxe office stool.

DISCUSSION: The contribution margin per unit equals the selling price minus the variable costs. Variable costs per unit for the deluxe office stool equal $33.30, and the selling price is $58.50. Thus, the contribution margin is $25.20 per unit ($58.50 – $33.30). The total standard cost is $45.00, which includes $11.70 of fixed overhead (1.5 hr. × $7.80), and the variable costs are $33.30 ($45.00 – $11.70).

Answer (B) is incorrect. The contribution margin of the economy office stool is $15.84. Answer (C) is incorrect. The total standard cost is $45.00. Answer (D) is incorrect. The variable cost subtracted from the sales price to yield the contribution margin is $33.30.

STUDY UNIT TEN
PROCESS COSTING

Process costing applies to homogeneous products that are processed in the same way and are assigned similar amounts of costs. It differs from **job costing**, which accounts for products that are not subject to the same processes.

Process costing uses a general ledger work-in-process account for each production department and averages costs for all units. Job costing uses a subsidiary ledger for each job and attaches specific costs to each product. The simplified diagram below illustrates the cost flows.

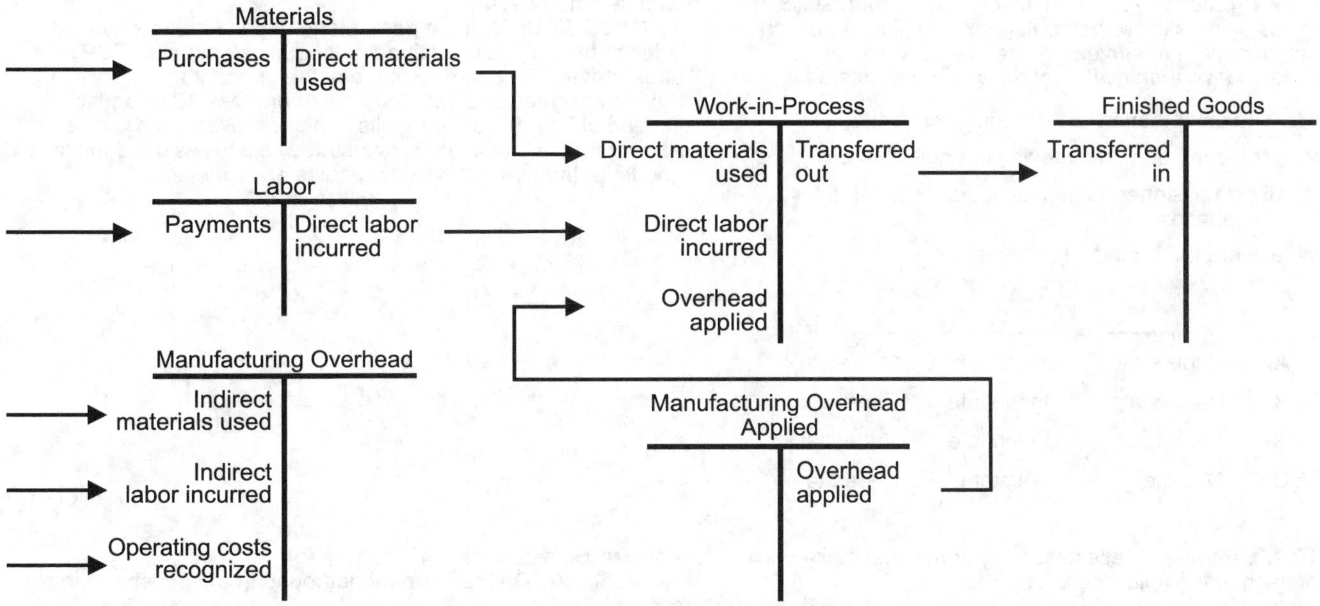

When units are unfinished, they are restated as **equivalent units of production (EUP)**. An EUP is the set of inputs required to make one physical unit. The EUP conversion determines (1) the equivalent units based on the percentage of completion and (2) the per-unit cost separately for (a) materials and (b) conversion cost. Conversion costs are assumed to be uniformly incurred, and transferred-in costs are always 100% complete.

Either of two cost flow assumptions for calculating **unit-average costs** may be used.

Weighted-average:

$$\frac{\text{Costs incurred during period + Costs in BWIP}}{\text{EUP transferred out + EUP in EWIP}}$$

First-in, first-out (FIFO):

$$\frac{\text{Costs incurred during period}}{\text{EUP transferred out + (EUP in EWIP − EUP in BWIP)}}$$

A simpler alternative to the FIFO and weighted-average methods is the **standard costing** method covered in Study Unit 7.

Operation costing is appropriate when similar products are produced in different models or styles or otherwise have distinctive traits. It is a hybrid of job costing and process costing. Operation costing accumulates total conversion costs and determines a unit conversion cost for each operation. This procedure is similar to overhead assignment. However, direct materials costs are charged specifically to products as in job costing. More work-in-process accounts are needed because one is required for each operation. Operation costing is used by firms that produce batches of similar units that are subject to selected processing steps (operations). Different batches may pass through different sets of operations, but all units are processed identically within a given operation. Operation costing also may be appropriate when different materials are processed through the same basic operations, such as the woodworking, finishing, and polishing of different product lines of furniture, and for such items as clothes, shoes, electronics, and jewelry.

QUESTIONS

10.1 Basic Process Costing

10.1.1. An error was made in the computation of the percentage of completion of the current year's ending work-in-process (EWIP) inventory. The error resulted in assigning a lower percentage of completion to each component of the inventory than actually was the case. Consequently, the following were misstated:

1. The computation of total equivalent units
2. The computation of costs per equivalent unit
3. Costs assigned to cost of goods completed for the period

What were the effects of the error?

	1	2	3
A.	Understate	Overstate	Overstate
B.	Understate	Understate	Overstate
C.	Overstate	Understate	Understate
D.	Overstate	Overstate	Understate

Answer (A) is correct. *(CPA, adapted)*
REQUIRED: The effects of understating the percentage of completion of EWIP.
DISCUSSION: If the percentage of completion assigned is lower than actually attained, total equivalent units (EUP) are understated. For example, if the actual percentage is 75%, but 50% is assigned and 100 units are in process, EUP equals 50 instead of 75. This error results in higher (overstated) costs per equivalent unit and higher (overstated) costs assigned to finished goods for the period (assuming costs are constant).

10.1.2. A true process costing system could make use of each of the following except

A. Standard costs.
B. Individual lots.
C. Variable costing.
D. Responsibility accounting.

Answer (B) is correct. *(CPA, adapted)*
REQUIRED: The element not found in a process costing system.
DISCUSSION: Process costing is used for mass and continuous production processes. It assigns unit costs on the basis of the average costs of all units. A job costing system is appropriate when producing individual, differentiable jobs, batches, or units (lots).
Answer (A) is incorrect. Standard costs can be used in both process and job costing. Answer (C) is incorrect. Variable costing can be used in both process and job costing. Answer (D) is incorrect. Responsibility accounting can be used in both process and job costing.

10.1.3. A corporation manufactures two brands of barbed wire fencing for sale to wholesalers and large ranchers. Which of the following would be the best type of costing system for such a company to use?

A. EOQ system.

B. Job costing.

C. Process system.

D. Retail inventory system.

Answer (C) is correct. *(CIA, adapted)*

REQUIRED: The costing system used by a manufacturer of two brands of one product.

DISCUSSION: Process costing is used for mass production of a standardized product on a continuous basis. Costs are assigned to large groups of similar items, and average unit costs are calculated.

Answer (A) is incorrect. An EOQ system is an inventory control. Answer (B) is incorrect. Job costing is used when products are heterogeneous. Each job (customer) is a separate cost center. Answer (D) is incorrect. The retail method converts ending inventory stated at retail to cost. It is not used by a manufacturer.

10.1.4. Which of the following characteristics applies to process costing but not to job costing?

A. Identifiable batches of production.

B. Equivalent units of production (EUP).

C. Averaging process.

D. Use of standard costs.

Answer (B) is correct. *(CPA, adapted)*

REQUIRED: The item that applies only to process costing.

DISCUSSION: EUP are calculated in process costing. EUP allow WIP to be stated in terms of completed units, a step not necessary in job costing, which assigns costs individually to each job. Stating WIP in terms of EUP permits calculation of average unit costs for mass-produced homogeneous goods.

Answer (A) is incorrect. Job costing is used for identifiable batches of production. Answer (C) is incorrect. Process costing and job costing use an averaging process. Answer (D) is incorrect. Standard costs can be used with either costing method.

10.1.5. A valid reason for using predetermined overhead rates for process costing is

A. The unrepresentative unit cost that will otherwise result when total factory overhead fluctuates significantly from period to period.

B. The noncomparability of the degree of completion of units in work-in-process from 1 month to the next when predetermined rates are not used.

C. The noncomparability of FIFO and weighted-average equivalent units of production for overhead when predetermined rates are not used.

D. The difference in transfer prices that will occur between two different plants of a company when predetermined rates are not used.

Answer (A) is correct. *(CIA, adapted)*

REQUIRED: The reason for using predetermined overhead rates.

DISCUSSION: Predetermined overhead rates are used for costing purposes to minimize the effect of fluctuating overhead from period to period. These fluctuations may be caused by seasonal factors or other causes of variability. If not annualized or normalized, these fluctuations result in significantly different unit costs for the same products in different periods.

Answer (B) is incorrect. Predetermined overhead rates are not used in calculating the degree of completion of work-in-process. Answer (C) is incorrect. Predetermined overhead rates are not used in calculating the equivalent units of production. Answer (D) is incorrect. Predetermined overhead rates may result in transfer prices that less accurately measure the actual costs of products internally produced in comparison with those externally purchased.

10.1.6. An equivalent unit of direct materials or conversion cost is equal to

A. The amount of direct materials or conversion cost necessary to complete one unit of production.

B. A unit of work-in-process inventory.

C. The amount of direct materials or conversion cost necessary to start a unit of production in work-in-process.

D. Fifty percent of the direct materials or conversion cost of a unit of finished goods inventory (assuming a linear production pattern).

Answer (A) is correct. *(CPA, adapted)*

REQUIRED: The definition of EUP.

DISCUSSION: EUP measure the amount of work performed in each production phase in terms of fully processed units during a given period. Incomplete units are restated as the equivalent amount of completed units. The calculation is made separately for direct materials and conversion cost (direct labor and overhead).

Answer (B) is incorrect. A unit of WIP inventory is not completed; an EUP is equal to one completed unit. Answer (C) is incorrect. An EUP is the amount of direct materials and conversion cost to complete, not start, a unit. Answer (D) is incorrect. An EUP is the amount of direct materials and conversion cost to complete 100%, not 50%, of a unit.

10.1.7. In the computation of manufacturing cost per equivalent unit, the weighted-average method of process costing considers

A. Current costs only.

B. Current costs plus cost of beginning work-in-process inventory.

C. Current costs plus cost of ending work-in-process inventory.

D. Current costs minus cost of beginning work-in-process inventory.

Answer (B) is correct. *(CPA, adapted)*

REQUIRED: The costs used in the weighted-average method.

DISCUSSION: The weighted-average method of process costing combines the costs of work done in the previous period and the current period. Thus, the cost of the EUP is equal to the current cost (current period) plus the cost of BWIP (previous period).

Answer (A) is incorrect. The FIFO method considers only current costs. Answer (C) is incorrect. The costs are being counted twice. The costs in EWIP are already included in current costs. Answer (D) is incorrect. BWIP costs are added to, not subtracted from, the current costs in the weighted-average method.

10.1.8. In developing a predetermined factory overhead application rate for use in a process costing system, which of the following could be used in the numerator and denominator?

	Numerator	Denominator
A.	Actual factory overhead	Actual machine hours
B.	Actual factory overhead	Estimated machine hours
C.	Estimated factory overhead	Actual machine hours
D.	Estimated factory overhead	Estimated machine hours

Answer (D) is correct. *(CPA, adapted)*

REQUIRED: The possible numerator and denominator of a predetermined manufacturing overhead rate.

DISCUSSION: The predetermined overhead rate is calculated by dividing the estimated overhead (the numerator) by the estimated amount of the activity base (the denominator). The latter may be direct labor hours, direct labor dollars, machine hours, or some other reasonable base.

Answer (A) is incorrect. Actual amounts of overhead and machine hours are not known. Answer (B) is incorrect. Estimated overhead must be used in the numerator. Answer (C) is incorrect. Estimated machine hours must be used in the denominator.

10.1.9. The completion of goods is recorded as a decrease in work-in-process control when using

	Job Costing	Process Costing
A.	Yes	No
B.	Yes	Yes
C.	No	Yes
D.	No	No

Answer (B) is correct. *(CPA, adapted)*

REQUIRED: The costing system(s) in which work-in-process control is decreased when goods are completed.

DISCUSSION: The cost flow among accounts in process costing is similar to that for job costing. Both use the basic general ledger accounts, for example, materials control, work-in-process control, manufacturing overhead control, finished goods control, and cost of goods sold. Consequently, each system credits (decreases) work-in-process control and debits (increases) finished goods control when goods are completed.

10.1.10. In a process cost system, the application of manufacturing overhead usually is recorded as an increase in

A. Cost of goods sold.

B. Work-in-process inventory control.

C. Manufacturing overhead control.

D. Finished goods inventory control.

Answer (B) is correct. *(CPA, adapted)*

REQUIRED: The account in which the application of manufacturing overhead is recorded in a process costing system.

DISCUSSION: The principal distinction between process costing and job costing is that the latter uses subsidiary WIP and finished goods ledgers to account for separate jobs. However, the same general ledger accounts are used in both systems, and cost flow among accounts also is the same. Both systems increase (debit) work-in-process (a general ledger account) to record applied overhead and other production costs.

Answer (A) is incorrect. COGS is debited (increased) when finished goods are sold. Answer (C) is incorrect. Overhead control is debited (increased) when actual overhead is incurred. Answer (D) is incorrect. Finished goods control is debited (increased) when goods are completed.

10.2 Operation Costing

10.2.1. Operation costing is appropriate for products that are

A. Unique.

B. Produced in batches or production runs.

C. Homogeneous.

D. Related to food and beverage industries.

Answer (B) is correct. *(Publisher, adapted)*

REQUIRED: The kind of product appropriate for operation costing.

DISCUSSION: Operation costing is used when different groups of products are subject to some but not all of the same processing steps (operations). Every unit passing through a given operation is processed in the same way, and conversion costs are accumulated by operation. Direct materials costs are accumulated by batch.

Answer (A) is incorrect. Job costing is used for unique products. Answer (C) is incorrect. Process costing is used for homogeneous products. Answer (D) is incorrect. Food and beverage products may be unique or homogeneous and may be produced in jobs, lots, or batches.

10.2.2. An operation costing system is

A. Identical to a process costing system except that actual cost is used for manufacturing overhead.

B. The same as a process costing system except that materials costs are assigned on the basis of batches of production.

C. The same as a job costing system except that materials are accounted for in the same way as they are in a process costing system.

D. A system in which manufacturing activities are finely divided into individual, discrete steps or operations.

Answer (B) is correct. *(CMA, adapted)*

REQUIRED: The definition of operation costing.

DISCUSSION: Operation costing is a hybrid of job and process costing systems that assigns materials costs on the basis of batches of production. It is used by manufacturers of goods that undergo some similar and some dissimilar processes. Operation costing accumulates total conversion costs and determines a unit conversion cost for each operation. However, direct materials costs are charged specifically to products or batches as in job costing systems.

Answer (A) is incorrect. Operation costing differs from process costing in the treatment of materials. Answer (C) is incorrect. Operation costing differs from process costing in the treatment of materials. Answer (D) is incorrect. Conversion costs are accumulated by operations, not by separate steps. Thus, operation may be synonymous with department or process.

10.2.3. Operation costing is a product costing system best described as

A. Job costing.

B. The cost accounting system designed for hospitals.

C. Process costing.

D. A blend of job costing and process costing.

Answer (D) is correct. *(Publisher, adapted)*

REQUIRED: The best description of operation costing.

DISCUSSION: Operation costing is a hybrid of job costing and process costing. As in process costing, a single average unit conversion cost is applied to units passing through an operation. Direct materials costs are applied to the individual batches in the same manner as in job costing. It is used to account for the costs of batch processing of relatively large numbers of similar units in individual production runs.

Answer (A) is incorrect. Operation costing is a hybrid form of job costing and process costing. Answer (B) is incorrect. Operation costing was developed for batch processing operations. Answer (C) is incorrect. Operation costing is a hybrid form of job costing and process costing.

10.2.4. Three commonly employed systems for product costing are job-order costing, operation costing, and process costing. Match the type of production environment with the costing method used.

	Job-Order Costing	Operation Costing	Process Costing
A.	Auto repair	Clothing manufacturing	Oil refining
B.	Loan processing	Drug manufacturing	Custom printing
C.	Custom printing	Paint manufacturing	Paper manufacturing
D.	Engineering design	Auto assembly	Motion picture production

Answer (A) is correct. *(CIA, adapted)*

REQUIRED: The match of the types of production environments with the costing methods.

DISCUSSION: Job-order costing is appropriate when producing products with unique characteristics. Process costing should be used to assign costs to similar products that are mass-produced on a continuous basis. Operation costing is a hybrid of job-order and process costing systems. It is used by manufacturers of goods that undergo some similar and some dissimilar processes. Thus, job-order costing is appropriate for auto repair, operation costing for clothing manufacturing, and process costing for oil refining.

Answer (B) is incorrect. Job-order costing is used for custom printing. Answer (C) is incorrect. Process costing is used for paint manufacturing. Answer (D) is incorrect. Motion picture production requires job-order costing.

10.3 Transferred-in Costs

10.3.1. What are transferred-in costs in a process costing system?

A. Labor costs incurred for transferring employees from another department within the same plant instead of hiring temporary workers from the outside.

B. Costs of the output of a previous internal process that is subsequently used in a succeeding internal process.

C. Supervisory salaries that are transferred from an overhead cost center to a production cost center.

D. Ending work-in-process inventory of a previous process that will be used in a succeeding process.

Answer (B) is correct. *(CPA, adapted)*

REQUIRED: The definition of transferred-in costs.

DISCUSSION: Transferred-in costs are the costs of the output of a previous internal process that is subsequently used in a succeeding internal process. Transferred-in costs are similar to direct materials costs added at the beginning of the process.

Answer (A) is incorrect. The costs of employees transferred from another department are not product costs attached to units when they were transferred in from a preceding internal process. Answer (C) is incorrect. The costs of supervisory salaries transferred from an overhead cost center to a production cost center are not product costs attached to units transferred in from a preceding internal process. Answer (D) is incorrect. Another department's EWIP has not yet been transferred.

10.3.2. In a process costing system, how is the unit cost affected in a production cost report when direct materials are added in a department subsequent to the first department and the added materials result in additional units?

A. The first department's unit cost is increased, which necessitates an adjustment of the transferred-in unit cost.

B. The first department's unit cost is decreased, which necessitates an adjustment of the transferred-in unit cost.

C. The first department's unit cost is increased, which does not necessitate an adjustment of the transferred-in unit cost.

D. The first department's unit cost is decreased, which does not necessitate an adjustment of the transferred-in unit cost.

Answer (B) is correct. *(CPA, adapted)*

REQUIRED: The effect of adding direct materials in a subsequent department, thereby creating additional units.

DISCUSSION: If additional units are created in a process (e.g., by adding direct materials in a subsequent department), the number of equivalent units increases. The unit cost also decreases because the total transferred-in cost is constant. Thus, an adjustment of the transferred-in unit cost is necessary.

Answer (A) is incorrect. As additional units are created, the number of equivalent units increases, and the unit cost decreases. Answer (C) is incorrect. As additional units are created, the number of equivalent units increases, and the unit cost decreases. Also, a retroactive adjustment of the transferred-in unit cost is necessary. Answer (D) is incorrect. A retroactive adjustment of the transferred-in unit cost is necessary when more units are subsequently created.

10.3.3. Purchased direct materials are added in the second department of a three-department process. This addition increases the number of units produced in the second department and will

A. Always change the direct labor cost percentage in the ending work-in-process inventory.

B. Never cause an adjustment to the unit cost transferred in from the first department.

C. Always increase total unit costs.

D. Always decrease total ending work-in-process inventory.

Answer (A) is correct. *(CPA, adapted)*

REQUIRED: The effect of adding materials in a subsequent department, thereby creating more units.

DISCUSSION: When direct materials are added to the production process in the second department, thereby increasing the number of units produced, more units are available to absorb the direct labor and overhead costs. Accordingly, the labor and overhead cost percentages are reduced (relative to direct materials cost).

Answer (B) is incorrect. If work done in a subsequent department increases the units produced in a previous department, an adjustment of the transferred-in unit cost is necessary. Answer (C) is incorrect. As the number of units produced increases, the unit cost of production usually decreases. Answer (D) is incorrect. Although the number of units has increased and unit cost has decreased, total inventory is not affected.

10.3.4. In a production cost report using process costing, transferred-in costs are similar to

A. Direct materials added at a point during the process.

B. Conversion costs added during the process.

C. Costs transferred to the next process.

D. Costs included in beginning inventory.

Answer (A) is correct. *(CPA, adapted)*

REQUIRED: The type of cost most similar to transferred-in costs.

DISCUSSION: Transferred-in costs are similar to materials added at a point during the process. Both attach to (become part of) the product at that point, which is usually the beginning of the process. Computations for transferred-in costs are usually separate from those for other direct materials costs and conversion costs.

Answer (B) is incorrect. Conversion costs (direct labor and overhead) are usually continuously added throughout the process. Answer (C) is incorrect. Transferred-out costs are those attached to completed units. Answer (D) is incorrect. The beginning inventory of a period (the ending inventory of the prior period) usually includes direct materials costs and conversion costs.

10.3.5. Purchased direct materials are added in the second department of a three-department process. This addition does not increase the number of units produced in the second department and will

A. Not change the dollar amount transferred to the next department.

B. Decrease total ending work-in-process inventory.

C. Increase the factory overhead portion of the ending work-in-process inventory.

D. Increase total unit cost.

Answer (D) is correct. *(CPA, adapted)*

REQUIRED: The effect of adding direct materials in a subsequent department given constant production.

DISCUSSION: Adding materials to a production process without changing the number of units produced increases the unit cost. The numerator (total cost) increases while the denominator (total units) remains the same.

Answer (A) is incorrect. If purchased materials are added to the process, the cost will be added to the total cost transferred to the next department. Answer (B) is incorrect. The unit cost, and therefore the cost of EWIP, increases when materials are added. Answer (C) is incorrect. Materials cost is separate from overhead.

10.3.6. How do transferred-in costs differ from direct materials?

A. They usually consist of the basic units being produced.

B. They are of greater value than most other materials added.

C. They are greater in value than the value of all other materials added.

D. They are added at the beginning of the process, unlike other direct materials.

Answer (A) is correct. *(Publisher, adapted)*

REQUIRED: The reason transferred-in costs are distinguished from other types of direct materials.

DISCUSSION: Usually, transferred-in costs pertain to the units of production that move from one process to another. Thus, they are the basic units being produced. Direct materials are added to the basic units during processing.

Answer (B) is incorrect. Value is not an issue in differentiating transferred-in costs from direct materials. Answer (C) is incorrect. Value is not an issue in differentiating transferred-in costs from direct materials. Answer (D) is incorrect. Direct materials may be added at the beginning of a process and, conceivably, the transferred-in materials (i.e., basic units) could be added to the process after the direct materials are processed.

10.4 Equivalent Units of Production (EUP)

10.4.1. Equivalent units of production are used in process accounting to

A. Measure the efficiency of the production process.

B. Establish standard costs.

C. Provide a means of assigning cost to partially completed units.

D. Allocate overhead to production.

Answer (C) is correct. *(Publisher, adapted)*

REQUIRED: The purpose of calculating equivalent units of production (EUP).

DISCUSSION: EUP are used to allocate cost to incomplete goods. Thus, if 50% of the direct materials have been added to 100 units in process, 50 EUP of materials have been produced. Similarly, if 30% of the conversion costs has been incurred for 1,000 units, 300 EUP have been produced.

Answer (A) is incorrect. EUP are calculated to allocate production costs, not to measure production efficiency. Answer (B) is incorrect. EUP are calculated to allocate production costs, not to measure production efficiency. Answer (D) is incorrect. Overhead is usually assigned based on a measure of activity, e.g., labor cost or machine hours.

10.4.2. EUP analysis is usually applied to

A. Direct materials and conversion costs.

B. Direct materials costs only.

C. Conversion costs only.

D. Overhead costs.

Answer (A) is correct. *(Publisher, adapted)*

REQUIRED: The costs relevant to EUP analysis.

DISCUSSION: EUP analysis is usually done separately for direct materials and conversion costs. A production process may use several types of materials, e.g., transferred-in cost plus additional materials. Several conversion activities may be required as well. Thus, the percentage of completion is rarely the same for both costs.

Answer (B) is incorrect. EUP analysis usually is applied to direct materials costs. Answer (C) is incorrect. EUP analysis usually is applied to conversion costs. Answer (D) is incorrect. Overhead is part of conversion costs.

10.4.3. The following information pertains to a company's Finishing Department operations in May.

	Units	% Completion
Work-in-process, May 1	2,000	40%
Units started during May	10,000	
Units completed and transferred to FG	8,000	
Work-in-process, May 31	?	25%

Materials are added at the end of the process, and conversion costs are incurred evenly throughout the process. The equivalent units of materials added during May were

A. 8,000

B. 8,200

C. 9,100

D. 10,000

Answer (A) is correct. *(CIA, adapted)*

REQUIRED: The equivalent units of materials added in May.

DISCUSSION: Given that the materials are added at the end of the process, no equivalent units of materials are included in beginning or ending work-in-process. Thus, the EUP for materials equal the 8,000 units [(2,000 × 100%) + (8,000 – 2,000) + (4,000 × 0%)] transferred out during May.

Answer (B) is incorrect. The amount of 8,200 equals the equivalent units of conversion costs for May. Answer (C) is incorrect. The amount of 9,100 equals the EUP for conversion costs that result from reversing the degrees of completion for beginning and ending work-in-process. Answer (D) is incorrect. The amount of 10,000 equals the EUP if the materials were added at the beginning of the process.

10.4.4. In process 2, material G is added when a batch is 60% complete. Ending work-in-process units, which are 50% complete, would be included in the computation of equivalent units for

	Conversion Costs	Material G
A.	Yes	No
B.	No	Yes
C.	No	No
D.	Yes	Yes

Answer (A) is correct. *(CPA, adapted)*

REQUIRED: The computation(s) of EUP that include ending work-in-process.

DISCUSSION: Conversion costs (direct labor and manufacturing overhead) are the costs of transforming direct materials into finished products. If EWIP is 50% complete, it is presumably 50% complete as to conversion costs (all costs other than direct materials). But if material G is added only at the 60% point, no equivalent units of G have been produced. Thus, EWIP is included in the computation of EUP of conversion costs but not material G.

Answer (B) is incorrect. EWIP is included in the computation for conversion costs but not material G. Answer (C) is incorrect. EWIP is included in the computation for conversion costs. Answer (D) is incorrect. EWIP is not included in the computation of EUP of material G.

10.4.5. Separate equivalent units calculations often are not made for

A. Conversion costs.

B. Transferred-in costs.

C. Direct materials costs.

D. Direct labor costs.

Answer (D) is correct. *(Publisher, adapted)*

REQUIRED: The cost for which a separate EUP calculation often is not made.

DISCUSSION: Overhead in traditional costing systems is often applied on the basis of a direct labor activity base such as hours or cost. One EUP calculation is made for conversion costs (direct labor and overhead). No basis exists for separating these costs if they are incurred uniformly.

Answer (A) is incorrect. EUP must be calculated for conversion costs. Answer (B) is incorrect. Transferred-in costs usually are included at the beginning of the process. They consist of costs incurred in preceding departments and are therefore conceptually similar to direct materials. Thus, they are separate from other costs. Answer (C) is incorrect. Direct materials may be added at various points in the operation. Each kind of material should be the basis for a separate EUP calculation.

10.4.6. Kew Co. had 3,000 units in work-in-process at April 1 that were 60% complete as to conversion cost. During April, 10,000 units were completed. At April 30, the 4,000 units in work-in-process were 40% complete as to conversion cost. Direct materials are added at the beginning of the process. How many units were started during April?

A. 9,000

B. 9,800

C. 10,000

D. 11,000

Answer (D) is correct. *(CPA, adapted)*

REQUIRED: The number of units started in April.

DISCUSSION: The following physical flow formula may be used to calculate the unknown:

BWIP + Units started	=	Units completed + EWIP
3,000 + Units started	=	10,000 + 4,000
Units started	=	11,000

Answer (A) is incorrect. Units started in April equal units completed during April + EWIP – BWIP. Answer (B) is incorrect. Beginning work-in-process at April 1 is 3,000 (not 1,800) units, and the ending work-in-process at April 30 is 4,000 (not 1,600) units. Answer (C) is incorrect. During April, 10,000 units were completed (not started).

10.5 FIFO vs. Weighted-Average Assumption for EUP

10.5.1. FIFO requires separate costing of goods started last period and finished this period and goods started and completed this period. The weighted-average method does not. Which is the true statement about the cost of completed goods transferred under FIFO to the next production department or to finished goods inventory?

A. The two amounts are kept separate but are combined by the next department.

B. The two amounts are ultimately recorded in separate finished goods accounts.

C. The two amounts are considered combined as the goods are transferred.

D. The goods started and completed this period are transferred prior to those started last period and completed this period.

Answer (C) is correct. *(Publisher, adapted)*

REQUIRED: The true statement about the cost of completed goods transferred under FIFO.

DISCUSSION: Under FIFO, goods started last period and completed this period are differentiated from goods started and completed this period. The goods started last period but completed this period include the costs from last period as well as this period's costs to complete, whereas goods started and completed this period only include current costs. In the weighted-average method, the costs of the prior and current periods are averaged. When the goods are transferred to the next department or to finished goods under FIFO, however, they are considered transferred out at one average cost so that a multitude of layers of inventory is not created. This procedure is consistent with the basic concept of process costing.

Answer (A) is incorrect. If the cost of goods started last period and completed this period and the cost of goods started and completed this period are kept separate, separate layers will continue to multiply as the units of product are passed through additional WIP accounts. Thus, these costs are combined before transfer to the next department. Answer (B) is incorrect. If the cost of goods started last period and completed this period and the cost of goods started and completed this period are kept separate, separate layers will continue to multiply as the units of product are passed through additional WIP accounts. Thus, these costs are combined before transfer to the next department. Answer (D) is incorrect. Under FIFO, the goods that were started last period and completed this period are deemed to be completed first and transferred first.

10.5.2. In comparing the FIFO and weighted-average methods for calculating equivalent units

A. The FIFO method tends to smooth costs out more over time than the weighted-average method.

B. The weighted-average method is more precise than the FIFO method because the weighted-average method is based only on the work completed in the current period.

C. The two methods will give similar results even if physical inventory levels and production costs (material and conversion costs) fluctuate greatly from period to period.

D. The FIFO method is better than the weighted-average method for judging the performance in a period independently from performance in preceding periods.

Answer (D) is correct. *(CIA, adapted)*

REQUIRED: The true statement about the FIFO and weighted-average methods of calculating EUP.

DISCUSSION: The calculation of the cost per equivalent unit using the FIFO method separates the costs in one period from the costs of prior periods. Under the weighted-average method, the costs in the beginning work-in-process inventory are combined with current-period costs.

Answer (A) is incorrect. The weighted-average method tends to smooth costs over time. Answer (B) is incorrect. The FIFO method is more precise. It is based only on the work completed in the current period. Answer (C) is incorrect. The two methods provide dissimilar results when physical inventory levels and the production costs (materials and conversion costs) fluctuate greatly from period to period.

10.5.3. A process costing system was used for a department that began operations in January. Approximately the same number of physical units, at the same degree of completion, were in work-in-process at the end of both January and February. Monthly conversion costs are allocated between ending work-in-process and units completed. Compared with the FIFO method, would the weighted-average method use the same or a greater number of equivalent units to calculate the monthly allocations?

	Equivalent Units for Weighted-Average Compared with FIFO	
	January	February
A.	Same	Same
B.	Greater number	Greater number
C.	Greater number	Same
D.	Same	Greater number

Answer (D) is correct. *(CPA, adapted)*

REQUIRED: The comparison of equivalent units calculated under the FIFO and weighted-average methods.

DISCUSSION: The weighted-average method calculates EUP by adding the EUP in ending work-in-process (EWIP) to the total of all units completed during the period, regardless of when they were started. The FIFO method determines EUP by subtracting the work done on the beginning work-in-process (BWIP) in the prior period from the weighted-average total. If the number of EUP in BWIP is zero, as it was for the month of January, the two methods produce the same result. Otherwise, the weighted-average computation is greater.

Answer (A) is incorrect. The weighted-average method calculates the greater number of EUP except when the number of EUP in BWIP is zero. Answer (B) is incorrect. Both the FIFO and the weighted-average methods produce the same result for the first month of operations. Answer (C) is incorrect. The weighted-average total is greater for February and the same for January.

10.5.4. The units transferred in from the first department to the second department should be included in the computation of the equivalent units for the second department under which of the following methods of process costing?

	FIFO	Weighted-Average
A.	Yes	Yes
B.	Yes	No
C.	No	Yes
D.	No	No

Answer (A) is correct. *(CPA, adapted)*

REQUIRED: The cost flow method(s) that include(s) transferred-in costs in EUP calculations.

DISCUSSION: The units transferred from the first to the second department should be included in the computation of EUP for the second department regardless of the cost flow assumption used. The transferred-in units are considered materials added at the beginning of the period.

Answer (B) is incorrect. Units transferred in also should be included in the EUP computation under the weighted-average method. Answer (C) is incorrect. Units transferred in also should be included in the EUP computation under the FIFO method. Answer (D) is incorrect. Units transferred in should be included in the EUP computation under both methods.

10.5.5. In a given process costing system, the EUP are computed using the weighted-average method. With respect to conversion costs, the percentage of completion for the current period only is included in the calculation of the

	Beginning Work-in-Process Inventory	Ending Work-In-Process Inventory
A.	No	No
B.	No	Yes
C.	Yes	No
D.	Yes	Yes

Answer (B) is correct. *(CPA, adapted)*

REQUIRED: The in-process inventory(ies) in which conversion costs are calculated.

DISCUSSION: The weighted-average process costing method considers only the degree of completion of EWIP in the calculation of EUP. Because this method includes the costs incurred in the prior period for units in BWIP, EUP are equal to units completed and transferred out plus the EUP completed in EWIP.

Answer (A) is incorrect. The percentage of completion of the ending work-in-process inventory with regard to conversion costs is a factor in the calculation of EWIP under the weighted-average or FIFO method. Answer (C) is incorrect. The total units in beginning work-in-process inventory are used in the calculation of conversion costs. The percentage of completion of the ending work-in-process inventory is included in the calculation of conversion costs. Answer (D) is incorrect. Under the weighted-average method, the total units in beginning work-in-process inventory are used in the calculation of conversion costs. In effect, the BWIP is assumed to be 100% complete.

10.5.6. Assuming no beginning work-in-process (BWIP) inventory, and that the ending work-in-process (EWIP) inventory is 50% complete as to conversion costs, the number of equivalent units as to conversion costs would be

A. The same as the units completed.

B. The same as the units placed in process.

C. Less than the units completed.

D. Less than the units placed in process.

Answer (D) is correct. *(CPA, adapted)*

REQUIRED: The number of EUP as to conversion costs.

DISCUSSION: Given no BWIP, it is immaterial whether the FIFO or weighted-average method is used. Thus, conversion cost EUP equal the units that were started and completed this period plus the EUP in EWIP. Because the units in EWIP are 50% complete as to conversion costs, they will not be fully counted for purposes of determining EUP.

Answer (A) is incorrect. Given no BWIP, the only units completed were those started in the current period. Total EUP include these units plus the EUP in EWIP. Answer (B) is incorrect. Given no BWIP, conversion cost EUP equals units started if no EWIP exists. Answer (C) is incorrect. Conversion cost EUP include units completed plus work in EWIP.

10.5.7. Assuming no beginning work-in-process inventory, and that the ending work-in-process inventory is 100% complete as to materials costs, the number of equivalent units as to materials costs is

A. The same as the units placed in process.

B. The same as the units completed.

C. Less than the units placed in process.

D. Less than the units completed.

Answer (A) is correct. *(CPA, adapted)*

REQUIRED: The number of EUP as to materials costs.

DISCUSSION: Given no BWIP, whether the FIFO or weighted-average method is used is immaterial. Because EWIP is 100% complete as to materials costs, the EUP for materials costs are equal to the number of units placed in process (units in EWIP + units transferred to finished goods).

Answer (B) is incorrect. The number of EUP is equal to the units completed only if there is no EWIP. Answer (C) is incorrect. The number of EUP is less than the units placed in process when EWIP is less than 100% complete as to materials costs. Answer (D) is incorrect. The EUP must at least equal the number of units completed.

10.5.8. One approach to calculating EUP is to begin with the total work that could be done, i.e., the units in BWIP and those transferred in. Is another approach possible?

A. Yes, begin with the total work that could not be done, e.g., work already completed in BWIP.

B. Yes, begin with the total work that has been done (units transferred out and the completed EUP in EWIP).

C. Yes, begin with the total work that has been done (units transferred out and the EUP required to complete EWIP).

D. No, EUP may be calculated in only one way.

Answer (B) is correct. *(Publisher, adapted)*

REQUIRED: The alternate approach to computing EUP.

DISCUSSION: Total work that can be done is one starting point for computing EUP. Total work that can be done is the sum of the units in BWIP and those transferred in. In FIFO, only EUP to complete BWIP are added. Under the weighted-average method, the work done to date is included in addition to work in the current period. The EUP required to complete EWIP are subtracted from the total work that can be done. The other approach is to consider all the work done, i.e., to add the units transferred out to the units already completed in EWIP.

Answer (A) is incorrect. EUP calculations relate to work that was done. Answer (C) is incorrect. To compute the work that was done, the completed EUP in EWIP must be added. Answer (D) is incorrect. There are at least two methods to calculate EUP. Two of the methods are to begin with the total work that could be done and to begin with the total work that has been done.

Questions 10.5.9 through 10.5.12 are based on the following information. Nine concepts are listed below:

1. EUP to complete BWIP
2. EUP from last period in BWIP
3. Units transferred in
4. Total units transferred out
5. Units transferred out that were started and completed this period
6. Units transferred out that were started last period and completed this period
7. EUP to complete EWIP
8. EUP completed in EWIP
9. Total units in BWIP

10.5.9. What is a correct formula for weighted-average EUP?

A. 1 + 2 + 3 + 7

B. 2 + 4 – 8

C. 1 + 2 + 3 – 7

D. 4 + 5 + 6 + 8

Answer (C) is correct. *(Publisher, adapted)*

REQUIRED: The formula for weighted-average EUP.

DISCUSSION: Weighted-average EUP are computed as all the work that could have been done (the total units transferred in), minus work that was not done (the EUP required to complete EWIP). The formula is 1 + 2 + 3 – 7.

Answer (A) is incorrect. The EUP required to complete EWIP should be subtracted (not added). Answer (B) is incorrect. This formula (2 + 4 – 8) results in double counting. The work done last period in BWIP is also included in the total units transferred out. Answer (D) is incorrect. Units started and completed this period plus the units started last period and completed this period equal the total units transferred out.

10.5.10. What is another correct formula for weighted-average EUP?

A. 8 + 6 + 5

B. 8 + 4 + 2 + 1

C. 8 + 7 + 4 + 2

D. 8 + 6 + 5 – 2

Answer (A) is correct. *(Publisher, adapted)*

REQUIRED: The alternative formula for weighted-average EUP.

DISCUSSION: Another approach is to consider the total work that has been done. The total done is the sum of (1) the units started and completed this period, (2) those started last period and completed this period (total units transferred out), and (3) the EUP completed in EWIP (8 + 6 + 5).

Answer (B) is incorrect. The units in BWIP are included in the units transferred out. Answer (C) is incorrect. The work to complete WIP has not been done and should not be part of this period's EUP. Answer (D) is incorrect. This formula (8 + 6 + 5 – 2) is the formula for FIFO EUP.

10.5.11. What is the correct formula for FIFO EUP?

A. 1 + 3 – 7

B. 1 + 2 + 3

C. 1 + 4 – 7

D. 9 – 5 – 6

Answer (A) is correct. *(Publisher, adapted)*

REQUIRED: The formula for determining FIFO EUP.

DISCUSSION: One FIFO approach is to determine the EUP that could be produced in this period. The total work that can be done is that needed to finish BWIP and complete all the goods transferred in. The EUP needed to finish any EWIP should then be subtracted (1 + 3 – 7).

Answer (B) is incorrect. The work done last period in BWIP is not part of FIFO EUP, and the work completed this period is not subtracted. Answer (C) is incorrect. The EUP to complete BWIP are included in the total units transferred out. Answer (D) is incorrect. This formula (9 – 5 – 6) gives the number of physical units (not EUP) in EWIP.

10.5.12. What is another correct formula for FIFO EUP?

A. 8 + 4

B. 8 + 4 – 2

C. 8 + 7 + 6 + 5

D. 7 + 4 + 2 + 1

Answer (B) is correct. *(Publisher, adapted)*

REQUIRED: The alternative formula for FIFO EUP.

DISCUSSION: Another approach to computing FIFO EUP is to begin with the work that was done, which is the EUP completed in EWIP plus the units transferred out. Subtracting the work that had been done in the prior period gives the FIFO EUP (8 + 4 – 2).

Answer (A) is incorrect. EUP from last period in BWIP should be subtracted. Answer (C) is incorrect. This formula (8 + 7 + 6 + 5) includes the work needed to complete EWIP. Answer (D) is incorrect. BWIP is included in units transferred out.

Questions 10.5.13 and 10.5.14 are based on the following information. A manufacturing company employs a process cost system. The company's product passes through both Department 1 and Department 2 in order to be completed. Conversion costs are incurred uniformly throughout the process in Department 2. The direct material is added in Department 2 when conversion is 80% complete. This direct material is a preservative that does not change the volume. Spoiled units are discovered at the final inspection and are recognized then for costing purposes. The physical flow of units for the current month is presented below.

Beginning work-in-process in Department 2 (90% complete with respect to conversion costs)	14,000
Transferred in from Department 1	76,000
Completed and transferred to finished goods	80,000
Spoiled units – all normal	1,500
Ending work-in-process in Department 2 (60% complete with respect to conversion costs)	8,500

10.5.13. If the manufacturing company uses the weighted-average method, the equivalent units for direct materials in Department 2 for the current month would be

A. 67,500

B. 80,000

C. 81,500

D. 90,000

Answer (C) is correct. *(CIA, adapted)*

REQUIRED: The EUP for direct materials based on the weighted-average method.

DISCUSSION: The weighted-average method does not distinguish between work done currently and in the prior period. Assuming that (1) materials are added when units are 80% complete, (2) ending work-in-process is 60% complete, (3) goods are inspected when they are 100% complete, and (4) EUP are calculated for normal spoilage, the total weighted-average EUP for direct materials equal 81,500 (80,000 units transferred + 1,500 normally spoiled units).

Answer (A) is incorrect. The EUP for direct materials added in accordance with the FIFO method equal 67,500. Answer (B) is incorrect. Units transferred equal 80,000. Answer (D) is incorrect. The actual physical flow for the month is 90,000.

10.5.14. If the manufacturing company uses the FIFO (first-in, first-out) method, the equivalent units for conversion costs in Department 2 for the current month would be

A. 72,500

B. 74,000

C. 85,200

D. 86,600

Answer (B) is correct. *(CIA, adapted)*

REQUIRED: The EUP for conversion costs based on the FIFO method.

DISCUSSION: The FIFO method distinguishes between work done in the prior period and work done currently. The total FIFO EUP equal the work done currently on beginning work-in-process, plus the work done on ending work-in-process, plus all units started and completed currently. Thus, total FIFO EUP equal 74,000 {(14,000 units in BWIP × 10%) + (8,500 units in EWIP × 60%) + [(81,500 spoiled and transferred – 14,000 units in BWIP) × 100%]}.

Answer (A) is incorrect. The amount of 72,500 ignores spoilage. Answer (C) is incorrect. The amount of 85,200 includes 90% of the beginning work-in-process. Answer (D) is incorrect. The amount of 86,600 is based on the weighted-average method.

Questions 10.5.15 through 10.5.17 are based on the following information. The Cutting Department is the first stage of Mark Company's production cycle. BWIP for this department was 80% complete as to conversion costs. EWIP was 50% complete. Information as to conversion costs in the Cutting Department for January is presented below.

	Units	CC
WIP at January 1	25,000	$ 22,000
Units started and costs incurred during January	135,000	143,000
Units completed and transferred to next department during January	100,000	

10.5.15. Using the FIFO method, what was the conversion cost of WIP in the Cutting Department at January 31?

A. $22,000

B. $33,000

C. $39,000

D. $78,000

Answer (C) is correct. *(Publisher, adapted)*

REQUIRED: The FIFO conversion cost of EWIP.

DISCUSSION: Under the FIFO method, EUP for a period include only the work done that period and exclude any work done in a prior period. The total of conversion cost EUP for the period is calculated below.

	Units	Work Done in Current Period	CC (EUP)
BWIP	25,000	20%	5,000
Started & completed	75,000	100%	75,000
EWIP	60,000	50%	30,000
Total EUP			110,000

The total of the conversion costs for the period is given as $143,000. Dividing by total EUP of 110,000 gives a unit cost of $1.30. Thus, the conversion cost of the EWIP inventory is $39,000 (30,000 EUP in EWIP × $1.30).

Answer (A) is incorrect. The amount of $22,000 is the BWIP. Answer (B) is incorrect. The amount of $33,000 equals the unit conversion cost for the preceding period [$22,000 ÷ (25,000 × 80%)] times 30,000 EUP. Answer (D) is incorrect. The amount of $78,000 equals $1.30 times 60,000 units.

10.5.16. What is the per-unit conversion cost of goods started last period and completed this period?

A. $0.88

B. $1.10

C. $1.44

D. $1.30

Answer (C) is correct. *(Publisher, adapted)*

REQUIRED: The unit conversion cost of goods.

DISCUSSION: The total of the units started last period and completed this period is 25,000. These units were 80% completed at the start of the period, at a cost of $22,000. The cost to complete was $6,500 (5,000 EUP × $1.30). The total cost of $28,500 is divided by 25,000 to obtain the unit cost.

Answer (A) is incorrect. The amount of $0.88 does not consider the conversion cost of $6,500 to complete BWIP. Answer (B) is incorrect. The amount of $1.10 is the conversion cost per EUP for last period. Answer (D) is incorrect. The amount of $1.30 is the conversion cost per EUP for this period.

10.5.17. What is the unit conversion cost of goods started this period and completed this period using the weighted-average method?

A. $1.10

B. $1.14

C. $1.27

D. $1.30

Answer (C) is correct. *(Publisher, adapted)*

REQUIRED: The weighted-average unit conversion cost.

DISCUSSION: The weighted-average method combines the costs in BWIP and the current-period costs. Thus, it calculates total EUP as total units to account for minus the work yet to be done on EWIP. The total cost to account for is $165,000 ($22,000 BWIP + $143,000 current costs). Total units to account for are 160,000 (25,000 BWIP + 135,000 started in January), and units in EWIP 50% complete equal 60,000 (160,000 – 100,000 transferred). Thus, weighted-average EUP equal 130,000 [160,000 – (60,000 × 50%)], and the unit cost is $1.27 ($165,000 ÷ 130,000).

Answer (A) is incorrect. The amount of $1.10 is the conversion cost per EUP for last period. Answer (B) is incorrect. The amount of $1.14 is the unit conversion cost of goods started last period and completed this period. Answer (D) is incorrect. The amount of $1.30 is the current FIFO unit conversion cost.

10.5.18. On November 1, Yankee Company had 20,000 units of WIP in Department No. 1 which were 100% complete as to material costs and 20% complete as to conversion costs. During November, 160,000 units were started in Department No. 1 and 170,000 units were completed and transferred to Department No. 2. WIP on November 30 was 100% complete as to material costs and 40% complete as to conversion costs. By what amount would the equivalent units for conversion costs for the month of November differ if the FIFO method were used instead of the weighted-average method?

A. 20,000 decrease.

B. 16,000 decrease.

C. 8,000 decrease.

D. 4,000 decrease.

Answer (D) is correct. *(CPA, adapted)*

REQUIRED: The difference in EUP between the FIFO and the weighted-average methods.

DISCUSSION: The weighted-average method combines previous and current period work, while the FIFO method includes only the EUP for the work done in the current period. Thus, the difference is the EUP for BWIP.

Units in Department No. 1

BWIP (20%)	20,000	170,000	Transferred
Started	160,000		
		10,000	EWIP (40%)

Conversion Costs

Wtd.-Avg. EUP

Transferred	170,000
EWIP (10,000 × 40%)	4,000
Wtd.-Avg. EUP	174,000

FIFO EUP

Transferred:	16,000
BWIP (20,000 × 80%)	16,000
Started and completed	150,000
EWIP (10,000 × 40%)	4,000
FIFO EUP	170,000

The difference is that the weighted-average method includes the work done in the previous period (in the prior period, 20% of BWIP was completed). Accordingly, the difference is that weighted-average EUP is greater than FIFO EUP by 4,000 (20,000 × 20%).

Answer (A) is incorrect. The number of physical units in BWIP is 20,000. Answer (B) is incorrect. The number of EUP required to complete BWIP is 16,000. Answer (C) is incorrect. The number of EUP required to complete EWIP is 8,000.

10.6 FIFO EUP Calculations

10.6.1. Kerner Manufacturing uses a process cost system to manufacture laptop computers. The following information summarizes operations relating to laptop computer model #KJK20 during the quarter ending March 31:

	Units	Direct Materials
WIP inventory, January 1	100	$ 70,000
Started during the quarter	500	
Completed during the quarter	400	
WIP inventory, March 31	200	
Costs added during the quarter		$750,000

Beginning work-in-process inventory was 50% complete for direct materials. Ending work-in-process inventory was 75% complete for direct materials. Using the FIFO method, what were the equivalent units of production with regard to materials for the quarter ended March 31?

A. 450

B. 500

C. 550

D. 600

Answer (B) is correct. *(CPA, adapted)*

REQUIRED: The equivalent units of materials under FIFO.

DISCUSSION: Under the FIFO method, equivalent units are determined based only on work performed during the current period. They include work performed to complete BWIP, work on units started and completed during the period, and work done on EWIP. Thus, total FIFO EUP of materials are

BWIP	100 units	×	50%	=	50
Started and completed (400 – 100 in BWIP)	300 units	×	100%	=	300
EWIP	200 units	×	75%	=	150
Total EUP					500

Answer (A) is incorrect. The amount of 450 omits the 50 equivalent units of work on BWIP during the current period. Answer (C) is incorrect. The amount of 550 is based on the weighted-average method. Answer (D) is incorrect. The amount of 600 is the sum of the physical units completed plus the physical units in BWIP.

10.6.2. The Wilson Company manufactures the famous Ticktock watch on an assembly-line basis. January 1 work-in-process consisted of 5,000 units partially completed. During the month, an additional 110,000 units were started, and 105,000 units were completed. The ending work-in-process was 60% complete as to conversion costs. Conversion costs are added evenly throughout the process. The following conversion costs were incurred:

Beginning costs for work-in-process	$ 1,500
Total current conversion costs	273,920

The conversion costs assigned to ending work-in-process totaled $15,360 using the FIFO method of process costing. What was the percentage of completion as to conversion costs of the 5,000 units in BWIP?

A. 20%

B. 40%

C. 60%

D. 80%

Answer (D) is correct. *(A. Wilson)*

REQUIRED: The percentage completion of BWIP as to conversion costs.

DISCUSSION: Ending work-in-process consists of 10,000 (5,000 + 110,000 – 105,000) units 60% complete, or 6,000 EUP for conversion costs (10,000 × 60%). Conversion cost is $2.56 per unit ($15,360 ÷ 6,000 units). Total EUP for conversion costs for the month are 107,000 ($273,920 ÷ $2.56 per unit). Total EUP equal the sum of EUP to finish BWIP, units started and completed, and EUP in EWIP. Assuming that 100,000 units were started this period and completed, the amount of EUP for conversion costs added to BWIP this period is determined below:

107,000 EUP = BWIP + Units started & completed + EWIP
107,000 EUP = BWIP + 100,000 EUP + 6,000 EUP
BWIP = 1,000 EUP this period

Thus, BWIP consisted of 4,000 EUP (5,000 – 1,000) with respect to conversion costs. That is, it was 80% complete (4,000 ÷ 5,000).

Answer (A) is incorrect. Considering only the 1,000 EUP for conversion costs added to BWIP this period and dividing it by 5,000 units partially completed in beginning work-in-process results in 20% completion. Answer (B) is incorrect. BWIP consisted of 4,000 EUP for conversion costs that was 80% complete (4,000 ÷ 5,000). Answer (C) is incorrect. The EWIP is 60% complete.

10.6.3. A company produces plastic drinking cups and uses a process cost system. Cups go through three departments: mixing, molding, and packaging. During the month of June, the following information is known about the mixing department:

Work-in-process at June 1	10,000 units An average 75% complete
Units completed during June	140,000 units
Work-in-process at June 30	20,000 units An average 25% complete

Materials are added at two points in the process. Material A is added at the beginning of the process and Material B at the midpoint of the mixing process. Conversion costs are incurred uniformly throughout the mixing process. Assuming a FIFO costing flow, the equivalent units for Material A, Material B, and conversion costs, respectively, for the month of June (assuming no spoilage) are

A. 150,000, 130,000, and 137,500.

B. 150,000, 140,000, and 135,000.

C. 160,000, 130,000, and 135,000.

D. 160,000, 140,000, and 137,500.

Answer (A) is correct. *(CIA, adapted)*

REQUIRED: The EUP for Material A, Material B, and conversion costs.

DISCUSSION: The FIFO calculation considers only the work done in the current period. Given that A is added at the beginning of the process, the BWIP was complete with regard to A. Thus, assuming no spoilage, the EUP for A equaled 150,000 (140,000 units completed + 20,000 EWIP – 10,000 BWIP). B is added at the midpoint, so the units in BWIP, but not those in EWIP, had received B. The EUP for B were therefore 130,000 (140,000 units completed – 10,000 BWIP). The FIFO EUP for conversion costs were 137,500 [130,000 units started and completed + 2,500 EUP to complete BWIP (10,000 × 25%) + 5,000 EUP (20,000 × 25%) in EWIP].

Answer (B) is incorrect. The amount of 140,000 EUP for Material B includes the 10,000 units in BWIP in which Material B was added in a prior period. Furthermore, 135,000 (130,000 + 5,000) EUP for conversion costs does not consider the 2,500 EUP to complete BWIP. Answer (C) is incorrect. The amount of 160,000 (140,000 + 20,000) of EUP for Material A includes the 10,000 units in BWIP in which Material A was added in the previous period. Furthermore, 135,000 (130,000 + 5,000) EUP for conversion costs does not consider the 2,500 EUP to complete BWIP. Answer (D) is incorrect. The amount of 160,000 (140,000 + 20,000) of EUP for Material A includes the 10,000 units in BWIP in which Material A was added in the previous period. Furthermore, 140,000 EUP for Material B includes the 10,000 units in BWIP in which Material B was added in a prior period.

10.6.4. A company employs a process cost system using the first-in, first-out (FIFO) method. The product passes through both Department 1 and Department 2 in order to be completed. Units enter Department 2 upon completion in Department 1. Additional direct materials are added in Department 2 when the units have reached the 25% stage of completion with respect to conversion costs. Conversion costs are added proportionally in Department 2. The production activity in Department 2 for the current month was as follows:

Beginning work-in-process inventory (40% complete with respect to conversion costs)	15,000
Units transferred in from Department 1	80,000
Units completed and transferred to finished goods	85,000
Ending work-in-process inventory (20% complete with respect to conversion costs)	10,000

How many equivalent units for direct materials were added in Department 2 for the current month?

A. 70,000 units.

B. 80,000 units.

C. 85,000 units.

D. 95,000 units.

Answer (A) is correct. *(CIA, adapted)*

REQUIRED: The EUP for direct materials added in Department 2 for the current month.

DISCUSSION: Beginning inventory is 40% complete. Thus, direct materials have already been added. Ending inventory has not reached the 25% stage of completion, so direct materials have not yet been added to these units. Thus, the EUP for direct materials calculated on a FIFO basis are equal to the units started and completed in the current period (85,000 units completed – 15,000 units in BWIP = 70,000 units started and completed).

Answer (B) is incorrect. The amount transferred in from Department 1 was 80,000 total units. Answer (C) is incorrect. The EUP for direct materials calculated on a weighted-average basis equals 85,000. Answer (D) is incorrect. The sum of units transferred in from Department 1 and ending work-in-process inventory equals 90,000 units.

10.6.5. The following data pertain to a company's cracking-department operations in December:

	Units	Completion
Work-in-process, December 1	20,000	50%
Units started	170,000	
Units completed and transferred to the distilling department	180,000	
Work-in-process, December 31	10,000	50%

Materials are added at the beginning of the process, and conversion costs are incurred uniformly throughout the process. Assuming use of the FIFO method of process costing, the equivalent units of production (EUP) with respect to conversion performed during December were

A. 170,000

B. 175,000

C. 180,000

D. 185,000

Answer (B) is correct. *(CIA, adapted)*

REQUIRED: The EUP for conversion.

DISCUSSION: Under the FIFO method, EUP are determined based only on work performed during the current period. Thus, units in beginning work-in-process must be excluded.

	Conversion
Units transferred out	180,000
Add: EWIP (10,000 × 50%)	5,000
Total completed units	185,000
Less: BWIP (20,000 × 50%)	(10,000)
Equivalent units of production	175,000

Answer (A) is incorrect. The number of EUP of materials for the period is 170,000. Answer (C) is incorrect. The total amount of work done on the completed units is 180,000. Answer (D) is incorrect. The amount determined using the weighted-average method is 185,000.

10.6.6. The following data were provided by Boze Co.:

	Units	% Complete (Conversion)
BWIP	100	75%
Units started	10,000	
EWIP	150	40%

Assuming the FIFO method is used, what were the EUP for conversion costs?

A. 10,250

B. 10,040

C. 9,935

D. 9,910

Answer (C) is correct. *(K. Boze)*

REQUIRED: The EUP for conversion costs based on the FIFO assumption.

DISCUSSION: The FIFO method for EUP assumes the units in beginning inventory are finished first followed by the units started this period. In this period, BWIP required only 25% conversion to be complete, 9,850 units (10,000 started – 150 EWIP) were started and completed, and EWIP is only 40% complete as to conversion costs.

Finished BWIP	100 ×	.25	=	25
Units started and completed	9,850 ×	1.00	=	9,850
Conversion applied to EWIP	150 ×	.40	=	60
FIFO EUP				9,935

Answer (A) is incorrect. The amount of 10,250 (100 + 10,000 + 150) does not consider the percentage complete as to conversion costs. Also, EWIP is double counted. Answer (B) is incorrect. BWIP required only 25% conversion to be complete, 9,850 units were started and completed, and EWIP is only 40% complete as to conversion costs. Answer (D) is incorrect. The amount of 9,910 (9,850 + 60) does not consider the conversion costs required to complete BWIP.

10.7 Weighted-Average EUP Calculations

10.7.1. The following information pertains to Lap Co.'s Palo Division for the month just ended:

	Number of Units	Cost of Materials
Beginning work-in-process	15,000	$ 5,500
Started during the month	40,000	18,000
Units completed	42,500	
Ending work-in-process	12,500	

All materials are added at the beginning of the process. Using the weighted-average method, the cost per equivalent unit for materials is

A. $0.59

B. $0.55

C. $0.45

D. $0.43

Answer (D) is correct. *(CPA, adapted)*

REQUIRED: The cost per EUP for materials using the weighted-average method.

DISCUSSION: The weighted-average method does not distinguish between work done in the previous period and that done in the current period. Consequently, given that materials are added at the start of the process, the total EUP equal 55,000 (42,500 units completed + 12,500 units in EWIP), the total cost of materials is $23,500, and the cost per EUP for materials is $0.43 (rounded).

Answer (A) is incorrect. The amount of $0.59 results from deducting the units in BWIP from the total EUP. Answer (B) is incorrect. The amount of $0.55 is cost divided by units completed. Answer (C) is incorrect. The amount of $0.45 is based on the FIFO method.

10.7.2. A company uses weighted-average process costing for the product it manufactures. All direct materials are added at the beginning of production, and conversion costs are applied evenly during production. The following data apply to the past month:

Total units in beginning inventory (30% complete as to conversion costs)	1,500
Total units transferred to finished goods inventory	7,400
Total units in ending inventory (60% complete as to conversion costs)	2,300

Assuming no spoilage, equivalent units of production (EUP) with respect to conversion costs total

A. 8,330

B. 8,780

C. 9,230

D. 9,700

Answer (B) is correct. *(CIA, adapted)*

REQUIRED: The equivalent units of production for conversion costs.

DISCUSSION: The weighted-average method averages the work performed in the prior period with the work done in the current period. Thus, beginning work-in-process is left in the calculation (unlike FIFO).

	Conversion
Units transferred out	7,400
Add: EWIP (2,300 × 60%)	1,380
EUP	8,780

Answer (A) is incorrect. The EUP for conversion costs are 8,330 [8,780 weighted-average EUP – (1,500 units in BWIP × 30%)] if the FIFO method were used. Answer (C) is incorrect. Including 30% of BWIP in the total results in 9,230. Answer (D) is incorrect. The sum of the physical, not equivalent, units completed and in EWIP is 9,700.

10.7.3. Dex Co. had the following production for the month of June:

	Units
Work-in-process at June 1	10,000
Started during June	40,000
Completed and transferred to finished goods during June	33,000
Abnormal spoilage incurred	2,000
Work-in-process at June 30	15,000

Materials are added at the beginning of the process. As to conversion cost, the beginning work-in-process was 70% completed, and the ending work-in-process was 60% completed. Spoilage is detected at the end of the process. Using the weighted-average method, the equivalent units for June, with respect to conversion costs, were

A. 42,000

B. 44,000

C. 45,000

D. 50,000

Answer (B) is correct. *(CPA, adapted)*

REQUIRED: The EUP for conversion costs using the weighted-average method.

DISCUSSION: The weighted-average method averages BWIP costs and current costs. Thus, all the work completed this period, including that started last period, is included in EUP. Although its cost will be recognized as a loss rather than inventoried, abnormal spoilage is included in the EUP calculation. The spoiled units are 100% complete as to conversion costs because inspection for spoilage is at the end of the process. The EUP calculation for conversion costs is 44,000 [(33,000 units completed × 100%) + (2,000 units spoiled × 100%) + (15,000 units in EWIP × 60%)].

Answer (A) is incorrect. The amount of 42,000 (33,000 + 9,000) omits abnormal spoilage. Answer (C) is incorrect. The amount of 45,000 equals the sum of units completed, spoiled units, and BWIP. Answer (D) is incorrect. The amount of 50,000 equals units started plus units in BWIP.

10.7.4. The Wiring Department is the second stage of Flem Company's production cycle. On May 1, the BWIP contained 25,000 units 60% complete as to conversion costs. During May, 100,000 units were transferred in from the first stage of Flem's production cycle. On May 31, EWIP contained 20,000 units 80% complete as to conversion costs. Materials are added at the end of the process. Using the weighted-average method, the EUP on May 31 were

	Transferred-In Costs	Materials	Conversion Costs
A.	100,000	125,000	100,000
B.	125,000	105,000	105,000
C.	125,000	105,000	121,000
D.	125,000	125,000	121,000

Answer (C) is correct. *(CPA, adapted)*

REQUIRED: The EUP for materials, conversion costs, and transferred-in costs using the weighted-average method.

DISCUSSION: Materials are added at the end of the process, and conversion costs are assumed to be incurred uniformly. By definition, transferred-in costs always are 100% complete. The number of units completed equals 105,000 (25,000 BWIP + 100,000 transferred in – 20,000 EWIP).

	Units	T-I EUP	%	Mat. EUP	%	CC EUP
Completed	105	105	100	105	100	105
EWIP	20	20	0	--	80	16
EUP		125		105		121

Answer (A) is incorrect. Transferred-in costs and conversion costs of 100,000 EUP are the units transferred in from the first stage of Flem's production cycle. Materials of 125,000 EUP are the EUP for transferred-in costs. Answer (B) is incorrect. The 16,000 (20,000 × 80%) EUP in ending inventory should be included in the EUP calculation for conversion costs. Answer (D) is incorrect. The 20,000 units in ending inventory should not be included in the EUP calculation for materials.

10.7.5. A company manufactures a product that passes through two production departments: molding and assembly. Direct materials are added in the assembly department when conversion is 50% complete. Conversion costs are incurred uniformly. The activity in units for the assembly department during April is as follows:

	Units
Work-in-process inventory, April 1 (60% complete as to conversion costs)	5,000
Transferred in from molding department	32,000
Defective at final inspection (within normal limits)	2,500
Transferred out to finished goods inventory	28,500
Work-in-process inventory, April 30 (40% complete as to conversion costs)	6,000

The number of equivalent units for direct materials in the assembly department for April calculated on the weighted-average basis is

A. 26,000 units.

B. 28,500 units.

C. 31,000 units.

D. 34,000 units.

Answer (C) is correct. *(CIA, adapted)*

REQUIRED: The EUP for direct materials on the weighted-average basis.

DISCUSSION: The weighted-average approach averages the costs in beginning work-in-process with those incurred during the period. Accordingly, the degree of completion of the BWIP is ignored in computing the EUP for direct materials. Direct materials EUP therefore consist of units transferred to finished goods (28,500) and units that failed inspection (2,500), or 31,000. Ending work-in-process inventory has not reached the point at which materials are added.

Answer (A) is incorrect. The number of direct materials EUP calculated using the FIFO method is 26,000 (31,000 weighted-average EUP – 5,000 EUP in BWIP). Answer (B) is incorrect. The number of units transferred out to finished goods inventory is 28,500. Answer (D) is incorrect. The number of physical units minus the conversion work previously done on the BWIP is 34,000 [5,000 units in BWIP + 32,000 units transferred in – (5,000 units in BWIP × 60%)].

10.7.6. Roy Company manufactures Product X in a two-stage production cycle in Departments A and B. Materials are added at the beginning of the process in Department B. Roy uses the weighted-average method. BWIP (6,000 units) for Department B was 50% complete as to conversion costs. EWIP (8,000 units) was 75% complete. During February, 12,000 units were completed and transferred out of Department B. An analysis of the costs relating to WIP and production activity in Department B for February follows:

	Transferred-In Costs	Materials Costs	Conversion Costs
WIP, February 1:			
Costs attached	$12,000	$2,500	$1,000
Feb. activity:			
Costs added	29,000	5,500	5,000

The total cost per equivalent unit transferred out for February of Product X, rounded to the nearest penny, was

A. $2.75

B. $2.78

C. $2.82

D. $3.01

Answer (B) is correct. *(CPA, adapted)*

REQUIRED: The total cost per equivalent unit transferred out using the weighted-average method.

DISCUSSION: The total cost per equivalent unit transferred out is equal to the unit cost for transferred-in costs, materials costs, and conversion costs. Transferred-in costs are by definition 100% complete. Given that materials are added at the beginning of the process in Department B, all units are complete as to materials. Conversion costs are assumed to be uniformly incurred.

	Units	T-I	%	Mat.	%	CC
Completed	12	12	100	12	100	12
EWIP	8	8	100	8	75	6
EUP		20		20		18

Transferred-in:	($12,000 + $29,000) / 20,000 EUP	=	$2.05
Materials cost:	($2,500 + $5,500) / 20,000 EUP	=	.40
Conversion cost:	($1,000 + $5,000) / 18,000 EUP	=	.33
Total unit cost			$2.78

Answer (A) is incorrect. Unit conversion cost should be calculated using 18,000 EUP. Answer (C) is incorrect. Unit materials cost should be calculated using 20,000 EUP. Answer (D) is incorrect. Unit transferred-in cost should be calculated based on 18,000 EUP.

10.7.7. Information for the month of January concerning Department A, the first stage of Ogden Corporation's production cycle, is as follows:

	Materials	Conversion
BWIP	$ 8,000	$ 6,000
Current costs	40,000	32,000
Total costs	$ 48,000	$38,000
Equivalent units using weighted-average method	100,000	95,000
Average unit costs	$ 0.48	$ 0.40
Goods completed		90,000 units
EWIP		10,000 units

Materials are added at the beginning of the process. The ending work-in-process is 50% complete as to conversion costs. How would the total costs accounted for be distributed, using the weighted-average method?

	Goods Completed	Ending Work-In-Process
A.	$79,200	$6,800
B.	$79,200	$8,800
C.	$86,000	$0
D.	$88,000	$6,800

Answer (A) is correct. *(CPA, adapted)*
REQUIRED: The weighted-average distribution of total costs between goods completed and EWIP.
DISCUSSION: The weighted-average method combines the costs in BWIP with those for the current period. Materials are added at the beginning of the process, and conversion costs are assumed to be incurred uniformly. EUP and average-unit cost calculations were given.

Completed goods:	
Materials (90,000 × $.48)	$43,200
Conversion costs (90,000 × $.40)	36,000
Cost of completed goods	$79,200

Given that EWIP is 50% complete as to conversion costs, 5,000 (10,000 × 50%) equivalent units of conversion cost are in ending inventory.

EWIP:	
Materials (10,000 × $.48)	$ 4,800
Conversion costs (5,000 × $.40)	2,000
Cost of EWIP	$ 6,800

Answer (B) is incorrect. The amount of $8,800 is based on the assumption that EWIP is 100% complete as to conversion costs. Answer (C) is incorrect. The total to be distributed is $86,000. Of this amount, some portion must be assigned to EWIP. Answer (D) is incorrect. The amount of $88,000 is the sum of the costs of goods completed ($79,200) and EWIP ($8,800 if EWIP is 100% complete as to conversion costs).

10.7.8. During March, Bly Company's Department Y equivalent unit product costs, computed under the weighted-average method, were as follows:

Materials	$1
Conversion	3
Transferred-in	5

Materials are introduced at the end of the process in Department Y. There were 4,000 units (40% complete as to conversion costs) in WIP at March 31. The total costs assigned to the March 31 WIP inventory should be

A. $36,000
B. $28,800
C. $27,200
D. $24,800

Answer (D) is correct. *(CPA, adapted)*
REQUIRED: The total costs of EWIP using the weighted-average method.
DISCUSSION: The unit costs of EUP under weighted-average are given. EWIP consists of 4,000 units 40% complete as to conversion costs (1,600 EUP). Given also that materials are added at the end of the process, no materials cost is included in EWIP. Thus, the EWIP reflects only transferred-in costs and conversion costs.

Transferred-in (4,000 × $5)	$20,000
Conversion (1,600 × $3)	4,800
EWIP	$24,800

Answer (A) is incorrect. The total cost for 4,000 completed units is $36,000 ($20,000 + $12,000 + $4,000). Answer (B) is incorrect. Materials are not added until the end of the process. Answer (C) is incorrect. Conversion costs for 1,600 EUP (4,000 × 40%) in EWIP (not conversion costs to complete EWIP) should be added to transferred-in cost.

10.8 Comprehensive

Questions 10.8.1 through 10.8.5 are based on the following information. These data are based on the processing operations of HDG Enterprises. Assume that process conversion costs are uniform, but certain materials are added at different points in the process. Material 1 is added at the beginning of the process. The transferred-in costs are added at the 20% point in the process. Material 2 is added uniformly from the 50% to the 70% points in the process. Material 3 is added at the 75% point in the process, and Material 4 is added uniformly at the 90% to the 100% points in the process. The January BWIP was 10,000 units 60% complete, 60,000 units were added, and EWIP was 20,000 units 95% complete.

10.8.1. What was the number of Material 3 EUP for the month?

	FIFO	Weighted Average
A.	50,000	60,000
B.	60,000	60,000
C.	60,000	70,000
D.	70,000	70,000

Answer (D) is correct. *(Publisher, adapted)*

REQUIRED: The EUP for Material 3 for the month.

DISCUSSION: Material 3 is added at the 75% point in the process. None of Material 3 was in BWIP. Accordingly, it had to be added to the 10,000 units in BWIP and all the 60,000 units started this period because the EWIP was 95% complete. Accordingly, the month's Material 3 EUP are 70,000 units for both FIFO and weighted average.

Answer (A) is incorrect. The amount of 50,000 units of EUP for FIFO subtracts BWIP from the 60,000 units that were added, and 60,000 units for weighted average does not include BWIP. Answer (B) is incorrect. The amount of 60,000 units of EUP for FIFO and weighted average does not include Material 3 added for BWIP units. Answer (C) is incorrect. The amount of 60,000 units of EUP for FIFO does not include Material 3 added for BWIP.

10.8.2. What was the number of Material 1 EUP for the month?

	FIFO	Weighted Average
A.	50,000	60,000
B.	60,000	60,000
C.	60,000	70,000
D.	70,000	70,000

Answer (C) is correct. *(Publisher, adapted)*

REQUIRED: The EUP for Material 1 for the month.

DISCUSSION: Material 1 is added at the very beginning of the process. Accordingly, BWIP included 10,000 EUP for Material 1. During the period, 60,000 units were added. Thus, for FIFO, the EWIP is 60,000 EUP (current work done). For weighted average, it is 70,000 EUP (60,000 units added this period plus the 10,000 units in BWIP).

Answer (A) is incorrect. The amount of 50,000 units of EUP for FIFO subtracts BWIP from the 60,000 units that were added, and 60,000 units for weighted average does not include the BWIP. Answer (B) is incorrect. The amount of 60,000 units of EUP for weighted average does not include BWIP. Answer (D) is incorrect. The amount of 70,000 units of EUP for FIFO includes BWIP.

10.8.3. What was the number of conversion EUP for the month?

	FIFO	Weighted Average
A.	50,000	60,000
B.	63,000	69,000
C.	60,000	70,000
D.	53,000	59,000

Answer (B) is correct. *(Publisher, adapted)*

REQUIRED: The EUP for conversion for the month.

DISCUSSION: Under weighted average, the conversion EUP include the 50,000 units complete (10,000 BWIP, plus 60,000 started, minus 20,000 EWIP) plus the 19,000 EUP in EWIP (20,000 × 95%), or 69,000 EUP. For FIFO, the 69,000 EUP for weighted average is reduced by the 6,000 (10,000 units × 60%) of work completed in BWIP.

Answer (A) is incorrect. The amount of 50,000 units of EUP for FIFO equals the units completed, and 60,000 units for weighted average equals the units that were added. Answer (C) is incorrect. The amount of 60,000 units of EUP for FIFO equals the units that were added, and 70,000 units for weighted average equals the units that were added, plus BWIP. Answer (D) is incorrect. The amount of 53,000 units of EUP for FIFO is the conversion EUP for FIFO minus BWIP, and 59,000 units for weighted average is the conversion EUP for weighted average minus BWIP.

10.8.4. What was the number of Material 2 EUP for the month?

	FIFO	Weighted Average
A.	50,000	60,000
B.	60,000	70,000
C.	65,000	70,000
D.	63,000	67,000

Answer (C) is correct. *(Publisher, adapted)*

REQUIRED: The EUP for Material 2 for the month.

DISCUSSION: Material 2 is added uniformly from the 50% to the 70% portion of the process. Accordingly, of the 10,000 BWIP at the 60% completion point, only 5,000 EUP are in BWIP. Thus, an additional 5,000 units are added to BWIP. Also, Material 2 was added to all 60,000 units started during the period because EWIP is at the 95% point. Accordingly, EWIP should be 65,000 EUP for FIFO and 70,000 EUP for weighted average.

Answer (A) is incorrect. All of BWIP is subtracted from the 60,000 units added, and 60,000 units EUP for weighted average does not include BWIP. Answer (B) is incorrect. The amount of 60,000 units of EUP for FIFO does not include the 5,000 units of BWIP to which Material 2 was added. Answer (D) is incorrect. The amount of 63,000 units of EUP for FIFO is the conversion EUP for the month, and 67,000 units for weighted average is the weighted-average conversion EUP minus one-half of the FIFO conversion EUP in BWIP [69,000 – (.5 × 4,000)].

10.8.5. What was the number of Material 4 EUP for the month?

	FIFO	Weighted Average
A.	50,000	60,000
B.	60,000	60,000
C.	65,000	70,000
D.	70,000	70,000

Answer (B) is correct. *(Publisher, adapted)*

REQUIRED: The EUP for Material 4 for the month.

DISCUSSION: Material 4 is added uniformly between the 90% and the 100% point in the process. Accordingly, BWIP, which was 60% complete, has no Material 4. Thus, weighted-average and FIFO EUP are the same. All 50,000 units completed contain Material 4, plus 10,000 EUP in EWIP (half of the 20,000 EWIP because Material 4 is added uniformly between the 90% and 100% points).

Answer (A) is incorrect. The amount of 50,000 units of EUP for FIFO does not include the 10,000 units in EWIP that contain Material 4. Answer (C) is incorrect. The amount of 65,000 units of EUP for FIFO is the number of Material 2 EUP, and 70,000 units for weighted average includes the 10,000 units in EWIP that do not contain Material 4. Answer (D) is incorrect. The amount of 70,000 units of EUP for FIFO and weighted average includes the 10,000 units in EWIP that do not contain Material 4.

Questions 10.8.6 through 10.8.13 are based on the following information.

Kimbeth Manufacturing uses a process cost system to manufacture Dust Density Sensors for the mining industry. The following information pertains to operations for the month of May.

	Units
Beginning work-in-process inventory, May 1	16,000
Started in production during May	100,000
Completed production during May	92,000
Ending work-in-process inventory, May 31	24,000

The beginning inventory was 60% complete for materials and 20% complete for conversion costs. The ending inventory was 90% complete for materials and 40% complete for conversion costs.

Costs pertaining to the month of May are as follows:

- Beginning inventory costs are materials, $54,560; direct labor, $20,320; and overhead, $15,240.
- Costs incurred during May are materials used, $468,000; direct labor, $182,880; and overhead, $391,160.

10.8.6. Using the FIFO method, Kimbeth's equivalent unit cost of materials for May is

A. $4.12

B. $4.50

C. $4.60

D. $4.80

Answer (B) is correct. *(CMA, adapted)*

REQUIRED: The equivalent unit cost of materials under FIFO.

DISCUSSION: Under the FIFO method, EUP for materials equal 104,000 [(16,000 units in BWIP × 40%) + (76,000 units started and completed × 100%) + (24,000 units in EWIP × 90%)]. Consequently, the equivalent unit cost of materials is $4.50 ($468,000 total materials cost in May ÷ 104,000 EUP).

Answer (A) is incorrect. The amount of $4.12 is based on EUP calculated under the weighted-average method. Answer (C) is incorrect. The amount of $4.60 is the weighted-average cost per equivalent unit. Answer (D) is incorrect. The amount of $4.80 omits the 6,400 EUP added to beginning work-in-process.

10.8.7. Using the FIFO method, Kimbeth's equivalent unit conversion cost for May is

A. $5.65

B. $5.83

C. $6.00

D. $6.20

Answer (B) is correct. *(CMA, adapted)*

REQUIRED: The conversion cost per equivalent unit under FIFO.

DISCUSSION: Under the FIFO method, EUP for conversion costs equal 98,400 [(16,000 units in BWIP × 80%) + (76,000 units started and completed × 100%) + (24,000 units in EWIP × 40%)]. Conversion costs incurred during the current period equal $574,040 ($182,880 DL + $391,160 FOH). Hence, the equivalent unit cost for conversion costs is $5.83 ($574,040 ÷ 98,400).

Answer (A) is incorrect. The amount of $5.65 is based on EUP calculated under the weighted-average method. Answer (C) is incorrect. The amount of $6.00 is the cost per equivalent unit calculated under the weighted-average method. Answer (D) is incorrect. The amount of $6.20 results from combining conversion costs for May with those in beginning work-in-process and dividing by 98,400 EUP.

10.8.8. Using the first-in, first-out (FIFO) method, Kimbeth's equivalent units of production (EUP) for materials are

A. 97,600 units.

B. 104,000 units.

C. 107,200 units.

D. 108,000 units.

Answer (B) is correct. *(CMA, adapted)*

REQUIRED: The equivalent units of production for materials under FIFO.

DISCUSSION: Under FIFO, EUP are based solely on work performed during the current period. The EUP equal the sum of the work done on the beginning work-in-process inventory, units started and completed in the current period, and the ending work-in-process inventory. Because 92,000 units were completed during the period, 76,000 (92,000 – 16,000 in BWIP) must have been started and completed during the period. Thus, total EUP for May is calculated as follows:

Beginning WIP	[(100% – 60%) × 16,000 units]	6,400
Units started and completed	100% × 76,000 units	76,000
Ending WIP	90% × 24,000 units	21,600
	EUP =	104,000

Answer (A) is incorrect. The amount of 97,600 units omits the 6,400 EUP added to beginning work-in-process. Answer (C) is incorrect. The amount of 107,200 units assumes beginning work-in-process was 40% complete. Answer (D) is incorrect. The amount of 108,000 units equals the sum of the physical units in beginning work-in-process and the physical units completed.

10.8.9. Using the FIFO method, Kimbeth's equivalent units of production for conversion costs are

A. 85,600 units.

B. 88,800 units.

C. 95,200 units.

D. 98,400 units.

Answer (D) is correct. *(CMA, adapted)*

REQUIRED: The equivalent units of production for conversion costs under FIFO.

DISCUSSION: Under FIFO, EUP are based solely on work performed during the current period. The EUP equal the sum of the work done on the beginning work-in-process inventory, units started and completed in the current period, and the ending work-in-process inventory. Because 92,000 units were completed during the period, 76,000 (92,000 – 16,000 in BWIP) must have been started and completed during the period. Thus, total EUP for May is calculated as follows:

Beginning WIP	[(100% – 20%) × 16,000 units]	12,800
Units started and completed	100% × 76,000 units	76,000
Ending WIP	40% × 24,000 units	9,600
	EUP =	98,400

Answer (A) is incorrect. The amount of 85,600 units omits the work done on beginning work-in-process. Answer (B) is incorrect. The amount of 88,800 units omits the work done on ending work-in-process. Answer (C) is incorrect. The amount of 95,200 units assumes the beginning work-in-process was 40% complete as to conversion costs.

10.8.10. Using the FIFO method, Kimbeth's total cost of units in the ending work-in-process inventory at May 31 is

A. $153,168

B. $154,800

C. $155,328

D. $156,960

Answer (A) is correct. *(CMA, adapted)*

REQUIRED: The total cost of units in ending work-in-process under FIFO.

DISCUSSION: Under the FIFO method, EUP for materials equal 104,000 [(16,000 units in BWIP × 40%) + (76,000 units started and completed × 100%) + (24,000 units in EWIP × 90%)]. Consequently, the equivalent unit cost of materials is $4.50 ($468,000 total materials cost in May ÷ 104,000 EUP). EUP for materials in ending work-in-process equal 21,600 (24,000 × 90%). Thus, total FIFO materials cost is $97,200 (21,600 EUP × $4.50). Under the FIFO method, EUP for conversion costs equal 98,400 [(16,000 units in BWIP × 80%) + (76,000 units started and completed × 100%) + (24,000 units in EWIP × 40%)]. Conversion costs incurred during the current period equal $574,040 ($182,880 direct labor + $391,160 fixed overhead). Therefore, the equivalent unit cost for conversion costs is $5.83 ($574,040 ÷ 98,400). EUP for conversion costs in ending work-in-process equal 9,600 (24,000 × 40%). Total conversion costs are therefore $55,968 (9,600 EUP × $5.83). Consequently, total work-in-process costs are $153,168 ($97,200 + $55,968).

Answer (B) is incorrect. The amount of $154,800 is based on a FIFO calculation for materials and a weighted-average calculation for conversion costs. Answer (C) is incorrect. The amount of $155,328 is based on a weighted-average calculation for materials and a FIFO calculation for conversion costs. Answer (D) is incorrect. The amount of $156,960 is the weighted-average cost of ending work-in-process.

10.8.11. Using the weighted-average method, the total cost of the units in the ending work-in-process inventory at May 31 is

A. $153,168

B. $154,800

C. $155,328

D. $156,960

Answer (D) is correct. *(CMA, adapted)*

REQUIRED: The ending work-in-process under the weighted-average method.

DISCUSSION: The weighted-average costs per equivalent unit for materials and conversion costs are $4.60 and $6.00, respectively. EUP for materials in ending work-in-process equal 21,600 (24,000 × 90%). Thus total weighted-average materials cost is $99,360 ($4.60 × 21,600). EUP for conversion costs in ending work-in-process equal 9,600 (24,000 units × 40%). Total conversion costs are therefore $57,600 ($6.00 × 9,600 EUP). Consequently, total ending work-in-process costs are $156,960 ($99,360 + $57,600).

Answer (A) is incorrect. The amount of $153,168 is the FIFO cost of ending work-in-process. Answer (B) is incorrect. The amount of $154,800 is based on a FIFO calculation for materials and a weighted-average calculation for conversion costs. Answer (C) is incorrect. The amount of $155,328 is based on a weighted-average calculation for materials and a FIFO calculation for conversion costs.

10.8.12. Refer to the information on the preceding page(s). Using the weighted-average method, Kimbeth's equivalent unit cost of materials for May is

A. $4.12

B. $4.50

C. $4.60

D. $5.02

Answer (C) is correct. *(CMA, adapted)*

REQUIRED: The weighted-average equivalent unit cost for materials.

DISCUSSION: Under the weighted-average method, units in beginning WIP are treated as 100% complete and will produce EUP in the current period even though materials were added in the previous period. Because 92,000 units were completed during the period, 76,000 (92,000 – 16,000 BWIP) must have been started and completed during the year. Thus, total EUP for May is calculated as follows:

Beginning WIP	100% × 16,000 units	16,000
Units started and completed	100% × 76,000 units	76,000
Ending WIP	90% × 24,000 units	21,600
	EUP =	113,600

The total materials costs incurred during the period and accumulated in beginning work-in-process is $522,560 ($468,000 + $54,560). Thus, weighted-average unit cost is $4.60 ($522,560 ÷ 113,600 EUP).

Answer (A) is incorrect. The amount of $4.12 equals materials costs for May divided by weighted-average EUP. Answer (B) is incorrect. The amount of $4.50 is the equivalent unit cost based on the FIFO method. Answer (D) is incorrect. The amount of $5.02 is based on a FIFO calculation of equivalent units and a weighted-average calculation of costs.

10.8.13. Refer to the information on the preceding page(s). Using the weighted-average method, Kimbeth's equivalent unit conversion cost for May is

A. $5.65

B. $5.83

C. $6.00

D. $6.20

Answer (C) is correct. *(CMA, adapted)*

REQUIRED: The weighted-average conversion cost per equivalent unit.

DISCUSSION: Under the weighted-average method, units in beginning WIP are treated as 100% complete and will produce EUP in the current period even though materials were added in the previous period. Because 92,000 units were completed during the period, 76,000 (92,000 – 16,000 BWIP) must have been started and completed during the year. Thus, total EUP for May is calculated as follows:

Beginning WIP	100% × 16,000 units	16,000
Units started and completed	100% × 76,000 units	76,000
Ending WIP	40% × 24,000 units	9,600
	EUP =	101,600

The sum of the conversion costs accumulated in beginning work-in-process and incurred during the period is $609,600 ($20,320 + $15,240 + $182,880 + $391,160). Thus, the weighted-average unit cost is $6.00 ($609,600 ÷ 101,600 EUP).

Answer (A) is incorrect. The amount of $5.65 omits the conversion costs in beginning work-in-process. Answer (B) is incorrect. The amount of $5.83 is the equivalent unit conversion cost based on FIFO. Answer (D) is incorrect. The amount of $6.20 is based on a FIFO calculation of equivalent units and a weighted-average calculation of costs.

STUDY UNIT ELEVEN
COST ALLOCATION:
SUPPORT COSTS AND JOINT COSTS

Cost allocation assigns costs that cannot feasibly be directly traced to specific cost pools and cost objects. Examples are support department costs and joint costs.

Support (service) department costs are allocated to users. Such costs are part of overhead. Issues include whether to use (1) a single rate for variable and fixed costs or (2) separate rates and allocation bases. Another issue is whether to use (1) actual or budgeted costs and (2) actual or budgeted usage as an allocation base. The **direct method** allocates costs directly to the producing departments without recognition of services provided among the support departments. Allocations to production departments are based on their relative use of services. The **step (step-down) method** allocates support costs to other support departments. The allocation may begin with the costs of the support department that (1) provides the highest percentage of its total support to other support departments, (2) provides support to the greatest number of other support departments, or (3) incurs the greatest costs of support provided to other support departments. The costs of the other departments then are allocated, but no cost is assigned to departments whose costs already have been allocated. The process continues until all support costs are allocated. The **reciprocal method** recognizes all support among support departments. If all reciprocal support is recognized, linear algebra may be used to reach a solution.

Cost allocation also is necessary when two or more separate products are produced by one process from a common input. The outputs are **joint products**, and the costs incurred up to the split-off point are **joint costs** (common costs). Joint costs are allocated to joint products but not by-products. Costs incurred after split-off **(separable costs)** can be identified with a particular product. Among the methods used to allocate joint costs is the **physical-unit method**. It is based on a physical measure, e.g., volume, weight, or a linear measure. The **sales value at split-off method** uses the relative sales values of the separate products at split-off. The **estimated net-realizable-value (NRV) method** is based on final sales value minus separable costs. The **constant gross-margin percentage NRV method** allocates joint costs so that the percentage is the same for every product. If further processing is needed, the relative sales value is estimated by subtracting the additional costs from the final sales value to determine net realizable value.

By-products have relatively small total value and are produced simultaneously from a common process with products of greater value and quantity (joint products). The most cost-effective method for recognition of by-products is to account for their value at the time of sale as a reduction of the cost of goods sold or as a revenue.

The decision to **sell or process further** is made based on whether the incremental revenue from further processing exceeds the incremental cost. The joint cost of the product is irrelevant because it is a sunk cost.

QUESTIONS

11.1 Cost Allocation

11.1.1. Which of the following statements best describes cost allocation?

A. A company can maximize or minimize total company income by selecting different bases on which to allocate indirect costs.

B. A company should select an allocation base to raise or lower reported income on given products.

C. A company's total income will remain unchanged no matter how indirect costs are allocated.

D. A company should ordinarily allocate indirect costs randomly or based on an ability-to-bear criterion.

Answer (C) is correct. *(CPA, adapted)*

REQUIRED: The best statement about cost allocation.

DISCUSSION: Allocation is a distribution of costs that cannot be traced directly to the cost objects that are assumed to have caused them. The process involves (1) choosing a cost object, (2) determining the indirect (nontraceable) costs that should be assigned to the cost object, (3) deciding how costs are to be accumulated in cost pools prior to allocation, and (4) selecting the allocation base (not a driver). But it is not feasible to associate indirect costs directly with a given cost object. They must be allocated. However, how they are allocated has no effect on net income of the overall entity.

Answer (A) is incorrect. The method of allocation of indirect costs affects net income of individual segments but not net income of the overall entity. Answer (B) is incorrect. The allocation base should be the most representative of the usage of resources by cost objects. Answer (D) is incorrect. The allocation base should be the most representative of the use of resources by cost objects.

11.1.2. Allocation of support department costs to the production departments is necessary to

A. Control costs.

B. Determine overhead rates.

C. Maximize efficiency.

D. Measure use of plant capacity.

Answer (B) is correct. *(CMA, adapted)*

REQUIRED: The reason support department costs are allocated to production departments.

DISCUSSION: Support department costs are indirect costs allocated to production departments to determine overhead rates when the measurement of full (absorption) costs is desired. Overhead should be charged to production on an equitable basis to provide information useful for such purposes as (1) allocation of resources, (2) pricing, (3) measurement of profits, and (4) cost reimbursement.

Answer (A) is incorrect. Costs can be controlled by the support departments without allocation. However, allocation encourages cost control by the production departments. If the costs are allocated, managers have an incentive not to use support services indiscriminately. Answer (C) is incorrect. Allocation of costs has no effect on the efficiency of support services when the department that receives the allocation has no influence over the costs being controlled. Answer (D) is incorrect. Activity in the support departments is not a measure of the use of production plant capacity.

11.1.3. A computer company charges indirect manufacturing costs to a project at a fixed percentage of a cost pool. This project is covered by a cost-plus government contract. Which of the following is an appropriate guideline for determining how costs are assigned to the pool?

A. Establish separate pools for variable and fixed costs.

B. Assign prime costs and variable administrative costs to the same pool.

C. Establish a separate pool for each assembly line worker to account for wages.

D. Assign all manufacturing costs related to the project to the same pool.

Answer (A) is correct. *(CIA, adapted)*

REQUIRED: The best way to assign indirect manufacturing costs to cost pools.

DISCUSSION: Cost pools are accounts in which a variety of similar costs are accumulated prior to allocation to cost objects. The overhead account is a cost pool into which various types of overhead are accumulated prior to their allocation. Indirect manufacturing costs are an element of overhead allocated to a cost pool. Ordinarily, different allocation methods are applied to variable and fixed costs, thus requiring them to be separated. Establishing separate pools allows the determination of dual overhead rates. As a result, the assessment of capacity costs, the charging of appropriate rates to user departments, and the isolation of variances are facilitated.

Answer (B) is incorrect. Prime costs are direct costs, and variable administrative costs are period, not manufacturing, costs. The question inquires about indirect manufacturing costs. Answer (C) is incorrect. Establishing a separate pool for each assembly line worker to account for wages is not necessary under most cost allocation schemes. Answer (D) is incorrect. Different allocation methods are usually applied to variable costs and fixed costs.

11.1.4. The allocation of costs to particular cost objects allows a firm to analyze all of the following except

A. Whether a particular department should be expanded.

B. Why the sales of a particular product have increased.

C. Whether a product line should be discontinued.

D. Why a particular product should be purchased rather than manufactured in-house.

Answer (B) is correct. *(CMA, adapted)*

REQUIRED: The item that a firm will not be able to analyze as the result of allocating costs to particular cost objects.

DISCUSSION: Cost allocation is an internal matter that does not affect demand (except to the extent it results in a change in price).

Answer (A) is incorrect. Cost allocation permits a company to determine the profitability of a department and to make decisions relative to expanding or contracting its operations. Answer (C) is incorrect. Cost allocation permits a company to determine the profitability of a product line and to decide whether to discontinue that line. Answer (D) is incorrect. Make-or-buy decisions depend on cost analyses.

11.1.5. Costs are allocated to cost objects in many ways and for many reasons. Which one of the following is a purpose of cost allocation?

A. Evaluating revenue center performance.

B. Measuring income and assets for external reporting.

C. Budgeting cash and controlling expenditures.

D. Aiding in variable costing for internal reporting.

Answer (B) is correct. *(CMA, adapted)*

REQUIRED: The purpose of cost allocation.

DISCUSSION: Cost allocation is the process of assigning and reassigning costs to cost objects. It is used for those costs that cannot be directly associated with a specific cost object. Cost allocation is often used for purposes of measuring income and assets for external reporting purposes. Cost allocation is less meaningful for internal purposes because responsibility accounting systems emphasize controllability, a process often ignored in cost allocation.

Answer (A) is incorrect. A revenue center is evaluated on the basis of revenue generated, without regard to costs. Answer (C) is incorrect. Cost allocation is not necessary for cash budgeting and controlling expenditures. Answer (D) is incorrect. Allocations are not needed for variable costing, which concerns direct, not indirect, costs.

11.1.6. The allocation of general overhead costs to operating departments can be least justified in determining

A. Income of a product or functional unit.

B. Costs for short-term decisions.

C. Costs of products sold and remaining in inventory.

D. Costs for the federal government's cost-plus contracts.

Answer (B) is correct. *(CIA, adapted)*

REQUIRED: The inappropriate use of allocated cost data to operating departments.

DISCUSSION: In the short term, management decisions are based on incremental costs without regard to fixed overhead because it cannot be changed in the short term. Thus, the emphasis in the short term should be on controllable costs. For example, support department costs allocated as a part of overhead may not be controllable in the short term.

Answer (A) is incorrect. Determining the income of a product or functional unit requires absorption (full-cost) data. Answer (C) is incorrect. Determining the costs of products sold and remaining in inventory requires absorption (full-cost) data. Answer (D) is incorrect. Determining the costs for the federal government's cost-plus contracts requires absorption (full-cost) data.

11.1.7. Which of the following would be a reasonable basis for allocating the materials handling costs to the units produced in an activity-based costing system?

A. Number of production runs per year.

B. Number of components per completed unit.

C. Amount of time required to produce one unit.

D. Amount of overhead applied to each completed unit.

Answer (B) is correct. *(CIA, adapted)*

REQUIRED: The reasonable basis for allocating the materials handling costs to the units produced.

DISCUSSION: The cost driver of an indirect cost ordinarily is the cost allocation base. The costs in a homogenous cost pool have the same cause-and-effect relationship with this base. The number of components in a finished product is an appropriate allocation base because it has a causal relationship with the amount of materials handling costs.

Answer (A) is incorrect. The number of production runs per year is related to batch costs and not to individual unit costs. Answer (C) is incorrect. The amount of time required to produce one unit is the traditional basis for allocating overhead costs to the units produced when the production process is labor-intensive. Answer (D) is incorrect. The amount of overhead applied to each completed unit is not an allocation basis but the result of the allocation process when determining product costs.

11.1.8. Cost objects

A. May be intermediate if the costs charged are later reallocated to another cost object.

B. May be final if the cost object is the job, product, or process itself.

C. Should be logically linked with the cost pool.

D. All of the answers are correct.

Answer (D) is correct. *(Publisher, adapted)*

REQUIRED: The true statement(s) about cost objects.

DISCUSSION: Cost objects are the intermediate and final dispositions of cost pools. Cost objects may be intermediate as cost pools move from their originating points to the final cost objects. They may be final, e.g., a job, activity, product, or process itself, and should be logically related to the cost pool, preferably on a cause-and-effect basis.

Answer (A) is incorrect. Cost objects may be intermediate. Answer (B) is incorrect. Cost objects may be final. Answer (C) is incorrect. Cost objects should be logically related to the cost pool.

11.2 Support Department Costs

11.2.1. The method for allocating service department costs that best recognizes the mutual services rendered to other service departments is the

A. Dual-rate allocation method.

B. Direct allocation method.

C. Step-down allocation method.

D. Simultaneous-equations method.

Answer (D) is correct. *(CIA, adapted)*

REQUIRED: The method for allocating support department costs.

DISCUSSION: The simultaneous-equations (reciprocal) method recognizes mutual services rendered among support departments. This method allocates each support department's costs among the departments providing mutual services before reallocation to other users.

Answer (A) is incorrect. The dual-rate allocation method may not recognize reciprocal services among support departments. Answer (B) is incorrect. The direct allocation method allocates the cost of support departments directly to the production departments without any intermediate allocations to other support departments. Answer (C) is incorrect. The step-down allocation method allows for partial recognition of reciprocity of services among support departments.

11.2.2. Several methods are used to allocate support department costs to the production departments. The method that recognizes support provided by one department to another but does not allow for two-way allocation of costs among support departments is the

A. Direct method.

B. Linear method.

C. Reciprocal method.

D. Step-down method.

Answer (D) is correct. *(CMA, adapted)*

REQUIRED: The allocation method that recognizes one-way but not two-way support department cost allocation.

DISCUSSION: The direct method allocates all support department costs to production departments without recognizing any services provided by one support department to another. The step-down (step) method is a sequential process that allocates support costs among support as well as production departments. However, after a department's costs have been allocated, no allocations are made to it. The reciprocal method uses simultaneous equations to recognize mutual services.

Answer (A) is incorrect. The direct method does not make allocations to other support departments. Answer (B) is incorrect. The term linear method is not meaningful in this context. Answer (C) is incorrect. The reciprocal method recognizes reciprocal interdepartmental support activities.

11.2.3. The variable costs of support departments most likely should be allocated to production departments by using

A. Actual short-run output based on predetermined rates.

B. Actual short-run output based on actual rates.

C. The support department's expected costs of long-run capacity.

D. The support department's actual costs based on actual use of services.

Answer (A) is correct. *(Publisher, adapted)*

REQUIRED: The most likely basis for allocating variable support costs to production departments.

DISCUSSION: The usual method of overhead allocation of variable support department costs to production departments is to multiply the actual usage of the production department by the predetermined rate. This basis establishes the user department's responsibility for the actual usage at the predetermined rate.

Answer (B) is incorrect. The actual rate may differ substantially from the estimated rate, and the production department usually has no control over the actual rate. Answer (C) is incorrect. The capacity costs of the support department should be allocated by a fixed overhead rate or lump-sum charge based upon the capacity needs of the production department. Answer (D) is incorrect. User departments do not influence support department costs.

11.2.4. The fixed costs of support departments should be allocated to production departments based on

A. Actual short-run use based on predetermined rates.

B. Actual short-run units based on actual rates.

C. The support department's expected costs of long-run capacity.

D. The support department's actual costs based on actual use of services.

Answer (C) is correct. *(Publisher, adapted)*

REQUIRED: The appropriate basis for allocating fixed support costs to production departments.

DISCUSSION: The fixed costs of support departments should be allocated to production departments in lump-sum amounts on the basis of the support department's budgeted costs of long-term capacity to serve. This basis allows the production department to (1) budget the capacity needed from the support departments and (2) agree on the assessment of costs. Analysis of actual results permits evaluation of the support departments' ability to provide the estimated volume of service.

11.2.5. The step-down method of support department cost allocation often begins with allocation of the costs of the support department that

A. Provides the greatest percentage of its support to the production departments.

B. Provides the greatest percentage of its support to other support departments.

C. Provides the greatest total output of support.

D. Has the highest total costs among the support departments.

Answer (B) is correct. *(CIA, adapted)*

REQUIRED: The basis for determining the order of step-down allocation.

DISCUSSION: The step-down method may start with the department that renders the highest percentage of its total support to other support departments. It then progresses in descending order to the support department rendering the least percentage of its support to the other support departments. An alternative is to begin with the department that renders the highest dollar value of support to other support departments. A third possibility is to begin with the department that provides support to the greatest number of other support departments.

Answer (A) is incorrect. The step-down method may start with the department that provides the highest percentage of its total support to other support (not production) departments. Answer (C) is incorrect. Beginning with the support department with the greatest output is not customary. Answer (D) is incorrect. Beginning with the support department with the highest costs is not customary.

11.2.6. Which overhead allocation methods do not charge support department costs to a support department after its costs have been allocated?

A. Reciprocal and direct methods.

B. Step-down and reciprocal methods.

C. Direct and step-down methods.

D. Simultaneous solution and reciprocal methods.

Answer (C) is correct. *(Publisher, adapted)*

REQUIRED: The cost allocation methods in which no costs can be charged to a support department after its own costs have been allocated.

DISCUSSION: Under the direct method, support department costs are not allocated to other support departments. Under the step-down method, support department costs are allocated to other support departments but no reallocation occurs.

Answer (A) is incorrect. The reciprocal method allocates support department costs among support departments providing reciprocal services. This method requires reallocation and the use of simultaneous equations. Answer (B) is incorrect. The reciprocal method allocates support department costs among support departments providing reciprocal services. This method requires reallocation and the use of simultaneous equations. Answer (D) is incorrect. The simultaneous solution method is a synonym for the reciprocal method.

11.2.7. In allocating factory service department costs to producing departments, which one of the following items would most likely be used as an activity base?

A. Units of product sold.

B. Salary of service department employees.

C. Units of electric power consumed.

D. Direct materials usage.

Answer (C) is correct. *(CMA, adapted)*

REQUIRED: The item most likely used as an activity base when allocating factory service department costs.

DISCUSSION: Service department costs are considered part of factory overhead and should be allocated to the production departments that use the services. A basis reflecting cause and effect should be used to allocate service department costs. For example, the number of kilowatt hours used by each producing department is probably the best allocation base for electricity costs.

Answer (A) is incorrect. Making allocations on the basis of units sold may not meet the cause-and-effect criterion. Answer (B) is incorrect. The salary of service department employees is the cost allocated, not a basis of allocation. Answer (D) is incorrect. Making allocations on the basis of materials usage may not meet the cause-and-effect criterion.

Questions 11.2.8 through 11.2.10 are based on the following information. A company has two support departments, Power and Maintenance, and two production departments, Machining and Assembly. All costs are regarded as strictly variable. For September, the following information is available:

	Support Departments		Production Departments	
	Power	Maintenance	Machining	Assembly
Direct costs	$62,500	$40,000	$25,000	$15,000
Actual activity:				
Kilowatt hrs.		50,000	150,000	50,000
Maintenance hours	250		1,125	1,125

11.2.8. If the company uses the direct method for allocating support department costs to production departments, what dollar amount of Power Department cost will be allocated to the Machining Department for September?

A. $37,500

B. $15,625

C. $39,062.50

D. $46,875

Answer (D) is correct. *(CIA, adapted)*

REQUIRED: The cost allocated under the direct method.

DISCUSSION: Under the direct method, support department costs are allocated directly to the producing departments without recognition of support provided to other service departments. Allocation of support department costs is made only to production departments based on their relative use of support, in this case, kilowatt hours. Thus, the cost allocated to the Machining Department is $46,875 [$62,500 × (150,000 ÷ 200,000)].

Answer (A) is incorrect. The amount of $37,500 results from allocating the cost based on total kilowatt hours used by support and production departments. Answer (B) is incorrect. The amount of $15,625 is the amount allocated to the Assembly Department. Answer (C) is incorrect. The amount of $39,062.50 results from allocating the cost based on direct costs for each production department.

11.2.9. If the company uses the direct method for allocating support department costs to production departments, what dollar amount of Power Department cost will be allocated to the Maintenance Department for September?

A. $12,500

B. $15,625

C. $8,000

D. $0

Answer (D) is correct. *(CIA, adapted)*

REQUIRED: The cost allocated under the direct method.

DISCUSSION: Under the direct method, support department costs are allocated directly to the producing departments without recognition of support provided to other support departments. Allocation of support department costs is made only to production departments based on their relative use of services. Thus, none of the cost is allocated to the Maintenance Department.

11.2.10. Assume the company uses the sequential or step method for allocating support department costs to production departments. The company begins with the support department that receives the least support from other support departments. What dollar amount of Power Department costs will be allocated to the Maintenance Department for September?

A. $0

B. $12,500

C. $6,250

D. $8,000

Answer (B) is correct. *(CIA, adapted)*

REQUIRED: The cost allocated using the step method.

DISCUSSION: Under the step method, support costs are allocated to producing departments and to other support departments. This method does not reallocate any cost to the departments whose costs already have been allocated. Thus, Power Department costs are allocated first because the Maintenance Department receives relatively more support from the Power Department. The Power Department cost allocated to the Maintenance Department is $12,500 [$62,500 × (50,000 ÷ 250,000)]. This allocation is based on the total kilowatt hours used by all departments (support and production).

Answer (A) is incorrect. Under the step method, support costs are allocated to both production and support departments. Answer (C) is incorrect. The amount of $6,250 results from allocating Power Department costs based on maintenance hours used. Answer (D) is incorrect. The amount of $8,000 results from allocating the Maintenance Department's direct costs to itself based on kilowatt hours used.

11.2.11. A company has two production and two support departments that are housed in the same building. The most reasonable basis for allocating building costs (rent, insurance, maintenance, security) to the production and support departments is

A. Direct labor hours.

B. Number of employees.

C. Square feet of floor space occupied.

D. Direct materials cost.

Answer (C) is correct. *(CIA, adapted)*

REQUIRED: The most reasonable basis for allocating building costs to the production and support departments.

DISCUSSION: Allocation of indirect costs should be systematic and rational, that is, based on a variable strongly correlated with the incurrence of cost by the cost object. Thus, building costs (rent, insurance, maintenance, and security) are related closely to the square feet of floor space occupied by each department.

Answer (A) is incorrect. Direct labor hours clearly are less related to the incurrence of building costs than square footage. Answer (B) is incorrect. The number of employees is more appropriate for allocating personnel department costs. Answer (D) is incorrect. Direct materials cost clearly is less related to the incurrence of building costs than square footage.

Questions 11.2.12 and 11.2.13 are based on the following information. The Power and Maintenance Departments of a manufacturing company are support departments that provide support to each other as well as to the organization's two production departments, Plating and Assembly. The manufacturing company employs separate departmental manufacturing overhead rates for the two production departments requiring the allocation of the support department costs to the two manufacturing departments. Square footage of area served is used to allocate the Maintenance Department costs, and percentage of power usage is used to allocate the Power Department costs. Department costs and operating data are as follows:

	Support Departments		Production Departments	
	Power	Maintenance	Plating	Assembly
Costs:				
Labor	$ 60,000	$180,000		
Overhead	1,440,000	540,000		
Total costs	$1,500,000	$720,000		
Operating Data:				
Square feet	6,000	1,500	6,000	24,000
Percent of usage:				
Long-run capacity		5%	60%	35%
Expected actual use		4%	70%	26%

11.2.12. The allocation method that would provide this manufacturer with the theoretically best allocation of support department costs would be

A. A dual-rate allocation method allocating variable cost on expected actual usage and fixed costs on long-run capacity usage.

B. The step-down allocation method.

C. The direct allocation method.

D. The reciprocal (or linear algebra) allocation method.

Answer (D) is correct. *(CIA, adapted)*

REQUIRED: The best support cost allocation method.

DISCUSSION: The reciprocal method theoretically is the best allocation method. By recognizing the mutual support provided among all support departments, it acknowledges all sources of cost.

Answer (A) is incorrect. Dual rates may be used with any allocation method. Answer (B) is incorrect. The step-down method provides only for partial recognition of support provided by other support departments. Answer (C) is incorrect. The direct method does not recognize the services rendered by other support departments.

11.2.13. Assume that the manufacturing company employs the step-down allocation method to allocate support department costs. If it allocates the cost of the Maintenance Department first, then the amount of the Maintenance Department's costs that are directly allocated to the Plating Department would be

A. $144,000

B. $120,000

C. $115,200

D. $90,000

Answer (B) is correct. *(CIA, adapted)*

REQUIRED: The amount of maintenance costs directly allocated to the Plating Department under the step-down method.

DISCUSSION: The allocation base is 36,000 square feet (6,000 + 6,000 + 24,000). Plating's share is one-sixth (6,000 ÷ 36,000) of the total cost of maintenance services, or $120,000 ($720,000 ÷ 6).

Answer (A) is incorrect. The amount of $144,000 is the allocation based on the direct method. Answer (C) is incorrect. The amount of $115,200 is based on the total square footage of the entire plant. Answer (D) is incorrect. The amount of $90,000 results from allocating overhead costs only.

Questions 11.2.14 through 11.2.18 are based on the following information. The managers of Rochester Manufacturing are discussing ways to allocate the cost of service departments, such as Quality Control and Maintenance, to the production departments. To aid them in this discussion, the controller has provided the following information:

	Quality Control	Maintenance	Machining	Assembly	Total
Budgeted overhead costs before allocation	$350,000	$200,000	$400,000	$300,000	$1,250,000
Budgeted machine hours	--	--	50,000	--	50,000
Budgeted direct labor hours	--	--	--	25,000	25,000
Budgeted hours of service:					
Quality Control	--	7,000	21,000	7,000	35,000
Maintenance	10,000	--	18,000	12,000	40,000

11.2.14. If Rochester uses the direct method of allocating service department costs, the total service costs allocated to the assembly department would be

A. $80,000

B. $87,500

C. $120,000

D. $167,500

Answer (D) is correct. *(CMA, adapted)*

REQUIRED: The total service costs allocated to the Assembly Department using the direct method.

DISCUSSION: Under the direct method, service department costs are allocated directly to the production departments, with no allocation to other service departments. The total budgeted hours of service by the Quality Control Department to the two production departments is 28,000 (21,000 + 7,000). Given that the Assembly Department is expected to use 25% (7,000 ÷ 28,000) of the total hours budgeted for the production departments, it will absorb 25% of total quality control costs ($350,000 × 25% = $87,500). The total budgeted hours of service by the Maintenance Department to the production departments is 30,000 (18,000 + 12,000). The Assembly Department is expected to use 40% (12,000 ÷ 30,000) of the total maintenance hours budgeted for the production departments. Thus, the Assembly Department will be allocated 40% of the $200,000 of maintenance costs, or $80,000. The total service department costs allocated to the Assembly Department is $167,500 ($87,500 + $80,000).

11.2.15. If Rochester uses the step-down method of allocating service costs beginning with quality control, the maintenance costs allocated to the assembly department would be

A. $70,000

B. $108,000

C. $162,000

D. $200,000

Answer (B) is correct. *(CMA, adapted)*

REQUIRED: The maintenance costs allocated to the Assembly Department if the step-down method is applied beginning with quality control costs.

DISCUSSION: The step-down method allocates service costs to both service and production departments but does not involve reciprocal allocations among service departments. Accordingly, Quality Control will receive no allocation of maintenance costs. The first step is to allocate quality control costs to the Maintenance Department. Maintenance is expected to use 20% (7,000 ÷ 35,000) of the available quality control hours and will be allocated $70,000 ($350,000 × 20%) of quality control costs. Thus, total allocable maintenance costs equal $270,000 ($70,000 + $200,000). The Assembly Department is estimated to use 40% (12,000 ÷ 30,000) of the available maintenance hours. Consequently, it will be allocated maintenance costs of $108,000 ($270,000 × 40%).

11.2.16. Using the direct method, the total amount of overhead allocated to each machine hour at Rochester would be

A. $2.40

B. $5.25

C. $8.00

D. $15.65

Answer (D) is correct. *(CMA, adapted)*

REQUIRED: The total overhead allocated to each machine hour.

DISCUSSION: Machining uses 75% (21,000 ÷ 28,000) of the total quality control hours and 60% (18,000 ÷ 30,000) of the total maintenance hours budgeted for the production departments. Under the direct method, it will therefore be allocated $262,500 ($350,000 × 75%) of quality control costs and $120,000 ($200,000 × 60%) of maintenance costs. In addition, Machining is expected to incur another $400,000 of overhead costs. Thus, the total estimated Machining overhead is $782,500 ($262,500 + $120,000 + $400,000), and the overhead cost per machine hour is $15.65 ($782,500 ÷ 50,000 hours).

11.2.17. If Rochester decides not to allocate service costs to the production departments, the overhead allocated to each direct labor hour in the Assembly Department would be

A. $3.20

B. $3.50

C. $12.00

D. $16.00

Answer (C) is correct. *(CMA, adapted)*

REQUIRED: The overhead cost per direct labor hour in the Assembly Department if no support costs are allocated to production departments.

DISCUSSION: With no allocation of service department costs, the only overhead applicable to the Assembly Department is the $300,000 budgeted for that department. Hence, the overhead cost applied per direct labor hour will be $12 ($300,000 budgeted overhead ÷ 25,000 hours).

11.2.18. If Rochester uses the reciprocal method of allocating service costs, the total amount of quality control costs (rounded to the nearest dollar) to be allocated to the other departments would be

A. $284,211

B. $336,842

C. $350,000

D. $421,053

Answer (D) is correct. *(CMA, adapted)*

REQUIRED: The total quality control costs to be allocated to the other departments using the reciprocal method.

DISCUSSION: The reciprocal method involves mutual allocations of service costs among service departments. For this purpose, a system of simultaneous equations is necessary. The total costs for the Quality Control Department consist of $350,000 plus 25% (10,000 hours ÷ 40,000 hours) of maintenance costs. The total costs for the Maintenance Department equal $200,000 plus 20% (7,000 hours ÷ 35,000 hours) of quality control costs. These relationships can be expressed by the following equations:

$$Q = \$350,000 + .25M$$
$$M = \$200,000 + .2Q$$

To solve for Q, the second equation can be substituted into the first as follows:

$$Q = \$350,000 + .25(\$200,000 + .2Q)$$
$$Q = \$350,000 + \$50,000 + .05Q$$
$$.95Q = \$400,000$$
$$Q = \$421,053$$

11.2.19. Parat College allocates support department costs to its individual schools using the step method. Information for May is as follows:

	Support Departments	
	Maintenance	Power
Costs incurred	$99,000	$54,000
Service percentages provided to:		
Maintenance	--	10%
Power	20%	--
School of Education	30%	20%
School of Technology	50%	70%
	100%	100%

What is the amount of May support department costs allocated to the School of Education?

A. $40,500

B. $42,120

C. $46,100

D. $49,125

Answer (C) is correct. *(CPA, adapted)*

REQUIRED: The amount of support department costs allocated.

DISCUSSION: The step method allocates service costs to other service departments as well as to production departments but does not provide for reciprocal allocations. In this case, the process should begin with Maintenance because it has the higher total costs and provides a higher percentage of services to the other service department. However, after these costs are allocated, no Power costs are allocated to Maintenance. They are allocated as follows:

	Maint.	Power	School of Ed.	School of Tech.
Allocation of M	($99,000)	$19,800	$29,700	$49,500
		54,000		
Allocation of P		(73,800)	16,400*	57,400**
			$46,100	

* $73,800 × [20% ÷ (20% + 70%)] = $16,400

** $73,800 × [70% ÷ (20% + 70%)] = $57,400

Answer (A) is incorrect. The amount of $40,500 equals 30% of $99,000 plus 20% of $54,000. Answer (B) is incorrect. The step method results in an allocation of $46,100. Answer (D) is incorrect. The amount of $49,125 results from using the direct method.

Questions 11.2.20 through 11.2.27 are based on the following information. Barnes Company has two support departments and three production departments, each producing a separate product. For a number of years, Barnes has allocated the costs of the support departments to the production departments on the basis of the annual sales revenue dollars. In a recent audit report, the internal auditor stated that the distribution of support department costs on the basis of annual sales dollars would lead to support inequities. The auditor recommended that maintenance and engineering hours be used as a better support cost allocation basis. For illustrative purposes, the following information was appended to the audit report:

	Support Departments		Production Departments		
	Maintenance	Engineering	Product A	Product B	Product C
Maintenance hours used		400	800	200	200
Engineering hours used	400		800	400	400
Department direct costs	$12,000	$54,000	$80,000	$90,000	$50,000

11.2.20. After applying the simultaneous equations (reciprocal) method, what is the total Engineering Department cost to be allocated?

A. $12,000

B. $54,000

C. $57,000

D. $60,000

Answer (D) is correct. *(CIA, adapted)*

REQUIRED: The total cost to be allocated.

DISCUSSION: The reciprocal method uses simultaneous equations. Solving the following simultaneous equations indicates that Engineering's total cost to be allocated is $60,000. Total maintenance hours equal 1,600 (400 + 800 + 200 + 200), of which 400, or 25%, are used by Engineering. Total engineering hours equal 2,000, of which 400, or 20%, are used by Maintenance.

M = Maintenance Department's total cost
E = Engineering Department's total cost
$M = \$12,000 + .2E$
$E = \$54,000 + .25M$
$E = \$54,000 + .25 \times (\$12,000 + .2E)$
$E = \$60,000$

Answer (A) is incorrect. The amount of $12,000 equals the original maintenance costs. Answer (B) is incorrect. None of the maintenance costs have been allocated to Engineering. Answer (C) is incorrect. The amount of $57,000 results from using the step-down method and beginning with the Maintenance Department.

11.2.21. After applying the simultaneous equations (reciprocal) method, assume that the Engineering Department's total cost to be allocated is $60,000. How much of this cost is allocated to Departments A, B, and C?

A. $48,000

B. $54,000

C. $60,000

D. $66,000

Answer (A) is correct. *(Publisher, adapted)*

REQUIRED: The total engineering costs allocated to the production departments.

DISCUSSION: The Engineering Department's $60,000 in costs is allocated based on the denominator of 2,000 total hours (400 + 800 + 400 + 400).

Dept. A: $60,000 × (800 ÷ 2,000)	=	$24,000
Dept. B: $60,000 × (400 ÷ 2,000)	=	12,000
Dept. C: $60,000 × (400 ÷ 2,000)	=	12,000
Total		$48,000

Answer (B) is incorrect. The amount of $54,000 is the amount allocated to Departments A, B, and C under the direct method. Answer (C) is incorrect. The amount of $60,000 is the total to be allocated. Answer (D) is incorrect. The amount of $66,000 is the total support cost incurred.

11.2.22. Assume that the Engineering Department's total cost to be allocated is $60,000 after applying the simultaneous equations (reciprocal) method. What is the total Maintenance Department cost to be allocated?

A. $24,000

B. $18,000

C. $22,500

D. $12,000

Answer (A) is correct. *(Publisher, adapted)*

REQUIRED: The Maintenance Department's total cost to be allocated.

DISCUSSION: Substituting the Engineering Department's $60,000 of total cost into the equation for maintenance costs,

$E = \$60,000$
$M = \$12,000 + .2E$
$M = \$12,000 + \$12,000 = \$24,000$

Answer (B) is incorrect. The amount of $18,000 is the amount allocated to the production departments. Answer (C) is incorrect. The amount of $22,500 equals $12,000 (costs incurred) plus 20% (400 ÷ 2,000) of engineering costs incurred. Answer (D) is incorrect. The amount of $12,000 equals the maintenance costs actually incurred.

11.2.23. Assume that the Maintenance Department's total cost to be allocated is $24,000. Under the reciprocal method, what portion of Maintenance Department cost is allocated to Department A?

A. 800 ÷ 1,600

B. 800 ÷ 1,200

C. 200 ÷ 1,200

D. 200 ÷ 1,600

Answer (A) is correct. *(Publisher, adapted)*

REQUIRED: The portion of maintenance expense allocated to Department A under the reciprocal method.

DISCUSSION: The Maintenance Department's total cost to be allocated in accordance with the reciprocal method is $24,000. Of this amount, 50% (800 ÷ 1,600) is allocated to A, 12.5% (200 ÷ 1,600) to B, and 12.5% (200 ÷ 1,600) to C. Thus, $18,000 ($24,000 × 75%) of maintenance cost is allocated to Departments A, B, and C, but only $12,000 was actually incurred.

Answer (B) is incorrect. The denominator should be the total maintenance hours (1,600). Answer (C) is incorrect. The denominator should be the total maintenance hours (1,600), and the numerator should be the hours provided to Department A (800). Answer (D) is incorrect. The numerator should be the hours provided to Department A (800).

11.2.24. Assume that maintenance costs are allocated first because the Maintenance Department provides a greater percentage of its total support to the other support department. Using the step-down method of cost allocation, how much maintenance cost is allocated to the Engineering Department?

A. $6,000

B. $3,000

C. $1,500

D. $0

Answer (B) is correct. *(Publisher, adapted)*

REQUIRED: The maintenance cost allocated to Engineering using the step-down method.

DISCUSSION: Under the step-down or sequential method, the service departments are allocated in order from the one that provides the most service to other service departments down to the one that provides the least service. Thus, maintenance costs are allocated to the Engineering Department, but engineering costs are not allocated to the Maintenance Department. Accordingly, $3,000 [$12,000 of costs incurred × (400 ÷ 1,600)] is allocated to the Engineering Department.

Answer (A) is incorrect. The maintenance cost allocated to the Engineering Department using the reciprocal method is $6,000. Answer (C) is incorrect. The amount of $1,500 equals the maintenance cost allocated to Department B. Answer (D) is incorrect. No costs are allocated under the direct method.

11.2.25. Assume that maintenance costs are allocated first because the Maintenance Department provides a greater percentage of its total support to the other support department. Using the step-down method of cost allocation, what amount of maintenance cost is allocated to Department B?

A. $1,500

B. $6,000

C. $3,000

D. $15,750

Answer (A) is correct. *(Publisher, adapted)*

REQUIRED: The maintenance cost allocated to Department B using the step-down method.

DISCUSSION: Under the step-down method of cost allocation, the proportion of hours of maintenance provided to Department B (200 ÷ 1,600) determines B's share of the maintenance cost. Thus, the allocation is $1,500 [$12,000 × (200 ÷ 1,600)].

Answer (B) is incorrect. The amount of $6,000 is the maintenance cost allocated to Department A using the step-down method. Answer (C) is incorrect. The amount of $3,000 is the total maintenance cost allocated to B and C. Answer (D) is incorrect. The amount of $15,750 is the total of maintenance and engineering costs allocated to B under the step-down method.

11.2.26. Assume that maintenance costs are allocated first because the Maintenance Department provides a greater percentage of its total support to the other support department. Using the step-down method of cost allocation, what amount of engineering costs is allocated to the Maintenance Department?

A. $12,000

B. $10,800

C. $3,000

D. $0

Answer (D) is correct. *(Publisher, adapted)*

REQUIRED: The engineering costs allocated to Maintenance under the step-down method.

DISCUSSION: Under the step-down method, after a department's costs have been allocated to subsequent departments, no reallocation to that department is made. Thus, no engineering costs are reallocated to the Maintenance Department.

Answer (A) is incorrect. The amount of $12,000 equals the maintenance costs actually incurred. Answer (B) is incorrect. The amount of $10,800 assumes that engineering costs are allocated first. Answer (C) is incorrect. The amount of $3,000 is the maintenance cost allocated to the Engineering Department under the step-down method.

11.2.27. Refer to the information on the preceding page(s). Assume that maintenance costs are allocated first because the Maintenance Department provides a greater percentage of its total support to the other support department. Using the step-down method of cost allocation, what amount of engineering cost is allocated to Department C?

A. $6,000

B. $28,500

C. $14,250

D. $0

Answer (C) is correct. *(Publisher, adapted)*

REQUIRED: The engineering costs allocated to Department C using the step-down method.

DISCUSSION: Using the step-down method, the total engineering costs allocated to Department C equal the actual engineering costs ($54,000) plus $3,000 [$12,000 × (400 ÷ 1,600)] of maintenance costs allocated to engineering, times the proportion of engineering hours used by Department C. Thus, the allocation is $14,250 [($54,000 + $3,000) × (400 ÷ 1,600)].

Answer (A) is incorrect. The amount of $6,000 is the maintenance cost allocated to Department A using the step-down method. Answer (B) is incorrect. The amount of $28,500 is the allocation to Department A. Answer (D) is incorrect. The amount of $0 is the allocation to the Maintenance Department.

Questions 11.2.28 and 11.2.29 are based on the following information. Longstreet Company's Photocopying Department provides photocopy services for both Departments A and B and has prepared its total budget using the following information for next year:

Fixed costs	$100,000
Available capacity	4,000,000 pages
Budgeted usage	
Department A	1,200,000 pages
Department B	2,400,000 pages
Variable cost	$0.03 per page

11.2.28. Assume that Longstreet uses the single-rate method of cost allocation and the allocation base is budgeted usage. How much photocopying cost will be allocated to Department B in the budget year?

A. $72,000

B. $122,000

C. $132,000

D. $138,667

Answer (D) is correct. *(CMA, adapted)*

REQUIRED: The service cost allocated to Department B using a single rate based on budgeted usage.

DISCUSSION: Department B is budgeted to use 66 2/3% of total production (2,400,000 ÷ 3,600,000), so it should be allocated fixed costs of $66,667 ($100,000 × 66 2/3%). The variable cost allocation is $72,000 (2,400,000 pages × $.03 per page), and the total allocated is therefore $138,667 ($66,667 + $72,000).

Answer (A) is incorrect. The amount of $72,000 is the variable cost allocation. Answer (B) is incorrect. The amount of $122,000 assumes that fixed costs are allocated equally between A and B. Answer (C) is incorrect. The amount of $132,000 assumes fixed costs are allocated at a per-page rate based on available capacity ($100,000 ÷ 4,000,000 pages = $.025 per page), not on budgeted usage ($100,000 ÷ 3,600,000 pages = $.0278 per page).

11.2.29. Assume that Longstreet uses the dual-rate cost allocation method, and the allocation basis is budgeted usage for fixed costs and actual usage for variable costs. How much cost would be allocated to Department A during the year if actual usage for Department A is 1,400,000 pages and actual usage for Department B is 2,100,000 pages?

A. $42,000

B. $72,000

C. $75,333

D. $82,000

Answer (C) is correct. *(CMA, adapted)*

REQUIRED: The service cost allocated to Department A if a dual-rate allocation method is used.

DISCUSSION: Based on budgeted usage, Department A should be allocated 33 1/3% [1,200,000 pages ÷ (1,200,000 pages + 2,400,000 pages)] of fixed costs, or $33,333 ($100,000 × 33 1/3%). The variable costs are allocated at $.03 per unit for 1,400,000 pages, or $42,000. The sum of the fixed and variable elements is $75,333.

Answer (A) is incorrect. The amount of $42,000 equals the variable costs allocated to Department A. Answer (B) is incorrect. The amount of $72,000 is the allocation to Department B using a single rate. Answer (D) is incorrect. The amount of $82,000 assumes fixed costs are allocated at a per-page rate based on actual usage ($100,000 ÷ 3,500,000 pages = $.0286 per page).

Questions 11.2.30 and 11.2.31 are based on the following information. Fabricating and Finishing are the two production departments of Ewell Company. Building Operations and Information Services are service departments that provide support to the two production departments as well as to each other. Ewell uses departmental overhead rates in the two production departments to allocate the service department costs to the production departments. Square footage is used to allocate Building Operations, and computer time is used to allocate Information Services. The costs of the service departments and relevant operating data for the departments are as follows:

	Building Operations	Information Services	Fabricating	Finishing
Costs:				
Labor and benefit costs	$200,000	$ 300,000		
Other traceable costs	350,000	900,000		
Total	$550,000	$1,200,000		
Operating Data:				
Square feet occupied	5,000	10,000	16,000	24,000
Computer time (in hours)	200		1,200	600

11.2.30. If Ewell employs the direct method to allocate the costs of the service departments, then the amount of Building Operations costs allocated to Fabricating would be

A. $140,000

B. $160,000

C. $176,000

D. $220,000

Answer (D) is correct. *(CIA, adapted)*

REQUIRED: The amount of building operations costs allocated to Fabricating under the direct method.

DISCUSSION: The direct method does not allocate service costs to other service departments. Hence, the allocation base is the square footage in the two production departments. Fabricating's share is 40% (16,000 ÷ 40,000) of the total cost incurred by Building Operations, or $220,000 ($550,000 × 40%).

Answer (A) is incorrect. The amount of $140,000 is 40% of other traceable costs. Answer (B) is incorrect. The amount of $160,000 assumes an allocation base of 55,000 square feet. Answer (C) is incorrect. The amount of $176,000 assumes an allocation base of 50,000 square feet, the base that would be used under the step method if the costs of Building Operations are allocated first.

11.2.31. If Ewell employs the step method to allocate the costs of the service departments and if Information Services costs are allocated first, then the total amount of service department costs (Information Services and Building Operations) allocated to Finishing would be

A. $657,000

B. $681,600

C. $730,000

D. $762,000

Answer (D) is correct. *(CIA, adapted)*

REQUIRED: The total service department costs allocated to Finishing under the step method.

DISCUSSION: The step method of service department cost allocation is a sequential (but not a reciprocal) process. These costs are allocated to other service departments as well as to users. The process usually begins with the service department that renders the greatest percentage of its services to other service departments. If the $1,200,000 of Information Services costs is allocated first, the allocation base is 2,000 computer hours (200 + 1,200 + 600). Thus, $120,000 [$1,200,000 × (200 ÷ 2,000)] will be allocated to Building Operations and $360,000 [$1,200,000 × (600 ÷ 2,000)] to Finishing. The total of the Building Operations costs to be allocated to production equals $670,000 ($550,000 + $120,000). The allocation base will be 40,000 square feet because no costs are allocated back to Information Services. Accordingly, the total of service costs allocated to Finishing equals $762,000 {$360,000 + [$670,000 × (24,000 ÷ 40,000)]}.

Answer (A) is incorrect. The amount of $657,000 results from allocating Building Operations costs first. Also, the Information Services costs are allocated using total computer hours. Answer (B) is incorrect. The amount of $681,600 results from allocating Building Operations costs to Information Services. Answer (C) is incorrect. The amount of $730,000 allocates the costs of both service departments according to the direct method rather than the step method.

11.3 Introduction to Joint Costs

11.3.1. If a company obtains two salable products from the refining of one ore, the refining process should be accounted for as a(n)

A. Mixed cost process.

B. Joint process.

C. Extractive process.

D. Reduction process.

Answer (B) is correct. *(CPA, adapted)*

REQUIRED: The type of costing process in which two products are refined from one direct material.

DISCUSSION: When two or more separate products are produced by a common manufacturing process from a common input, the outputs from the process are joint products. The joint costs of two or more joint products with significant values generally are allocated to the joint products based upon the products' net realizable values at the point they became separate.

Answer (A) is incorrect. Mixed costs have fixed and variable components. Answer (C) is incorrect. Extractive process is a technical manufacturing term and has no special meaning in cost accounting. Answer (D) is incorrect. Reduction process is a technical manufacturing term and has no special meaning in cost accounting.

11.3.2. Joint costs are useful for

A. Setting the selling price of a product.

B. Determining whether to continue producing an item.

C. Evaluating management by means of a responsibility reporting system.

D. Determining inventory cost for accounting purposes.

Answer (D) is correct. *(CIA, adapted)*

REQUIRED: The usefulness of joint costs in cost accounting.

DISCUSSION: Joint costs are useful for inventory costing when two or more identifiable products emerge from a common production process. The joint costs of production must be allocated on some basis, such as relative sales value.

Answer (A) is incorrect. Items such as additional processing costs, competitive conditions in sales markets, and the relative contribution margins of all products derived from the common process must be considered in setting selling prices. Answer (B) is incorrect. Items such as additional processing costs, competitive conditions in sales markets, and the relative contribution margins of all products derived from the common process must be considered in determining whether to continue producing an item. Answer (C) is incorrect. Management of one department may have no control over joint costs.

11.3.3. Which of the following components of production are allocable as joint costs when a single manufacturing process produces several salable products?

A. Direct materials, direct labor, and overhead.

B. Direct materials and direct labor only.

C. Direct labor and overhead only.

D. Overhead and direct materials only.

Answer (A) is correct. *(CPA, adapted)*

REQUIRED: The components allocable as joint costs.

DISCUSSION: Joint costs are those costs incurred prior to the split-off point to produce two or more goods manufactured simultaneously by a single process or series of processes. Joint costs, which include direct materials, direct labor, and overhead, are not separately identifiable and must be allocated to the individual joint products.

Answer (B) is incorrect. Joint costs also include overhead. Answer (C) is incorrect. Joint costs also include direct materials. Answer (D) is incorrect. Joint costs also include direct labor.

11.3.4. Which of the following is not a method to allocate joint costs?

A. Estimated net realizable value.

B. Physical units.

C. Relative profitability.

D. Sales value at split-off.

Answer (C) is correct. *(Publisher, adapted)*

REQUIRED: The method not used to allocate joint costs.

DISCUSSION: Several methods may be used to allocate joint production costs, including (1) the quantitative (physical-unit) method, based on some physical measure such as volume, weight, or a linear measure; (2) the relative sales-value method, based on the sales values at split-off or estimated NRV; (3) the weighted-average method, based on a predetermined standard or index of production; and (4) the constant gross margin NRV method. Relative profitability cannot be used to allocate joint costs because the method of joint cost allocation determines profitability.

Answer (A) is incorrect. Relative sales value is used to allocate joint costs. Answer (B) is incorrect. A physical measure, e.g., weight, volume, or linear measure, is used to allocate joint costs. Answer (D) is incorrect. Sales value at split-off is used to allocate joint costs.

11.3.5. One hundred pounds of raw material W is processed into 60 pounds of X and 40 pounds of Y. Joint costs are $135. X is sold for $2.50 per pound, and Y can be sold for $3.00 per pound or processed further into 30 pounds of Z (10 pounds are lost in the second process) at an additional cost of $60. Each pound of Z can then be sold for $6.00. What is the effect on profits of further processing product Y into product Z?

A. $60 increase.

B. $30 increase.

C. No change.

D. $60 decrease.

Answer (C) is correct. *(CPA, adapted)*

REQUIRED: The effect on profits of further processing of a product.

DISCUSSION: The joint costs of $135 do not vary with the option chosen. Without further processing of product Y, revenue equals $270 [(60 lbs × $2.50) + (40 lbs × $3.00)], and net revenue equals $135 ($270 – $135). If product Y is processed further into product Z, revenue equals $330 [(60 lbs × $2.50) + (30 lbs × $6.00)]. This additional processing is at an incremental cost of $60, resulting in net revenue of $135 ($330 – $135 – $60). Hence, further processing results in no increase or decrease in net revenue.

Answer (A) is incorrect. The additional cost of $60 must be considered in evaluating the profit effect of processing product Y into product Z. Answer (B) is incorrect. A greater sales amount is obtained by processing product Y into product Z with an additional cost of $60, creating the same profit under each process. Answer (D) is incorrect. The profit effect is the same whether or not product Y is processed into product Z.

11.3.6. A joint process is a manufacturing operation yielding two or more identifiable products from the resources employed in the process. The two characteristics that identify a product generated from this type of process as a joint product are that it

A. Is identifiable as an individual product only upon reaching the split-off point, and it has relatively minor sales value when compared to the other products.

B. Is identifiable as an individual product before the production process, and it has relatively significant physical volume when compared with the other products.

C. Is identifiable as an individual product only upon reaching the split-off point, and it has relatively significant sales value when compared with the other products.

D. Has relatively significant physical volume when compared with the other products, and it can be sold immediately without any additional processing.

Answer (C) is correct. *(CIA, adapted)*

REQUIRED: The two characteristics of a joint product.

DISCUSSION: Joint products are two or more separate products generated by a common process from a common input that are not separable prior to the split-off point. Moreover, in contrast with by-products, they have significant sales values in relation to each other either before or after additional processing.

Answer (A) is incorrect. A joint product has relatively significant sales value when compared with the other products. A by-product is identifiable as an individual product only upon reaching the split-off point, and it has relatively minor sales value when compared to the other products. Answer (B) is incorrect. Products that are separately identifiable before the production process are not classified as joint products. Furthermore, physical volume has nothing to do with determining a joint product. Some joint products with significant physical volume may not have significant sales value. Answer (D) is incorrect. Products do not have to be salable at the split-off point to be considered joint products. Many joint products must be processed after the split-off point before they can be sold.

11.3.7. The principal disadvantage of using the physical quantity method of allocating joint costs is that

A. Costs assigned to inventories may have no relationship to value.

B. Physical quantities may be difficult to measure.

C. Additional processing costs affect the allocation base.

D. Joint costs, by definition, should not be separated on a unit basis.

Answer (A) is correct. *(CMA, adapted)*

REQUIRED: The principal disadvantage of using the physical quantity method of allocating joint costs.

DISCUSSION: Joint costs are most often assigned on the basis of relative sales values or net realizable values. Basing allocations on physical quantities, such as pounds, gallons, etc., is usually not desirable because the costs assigned may have no relationship to value. When large items have low selling prices and small items have high selling prices, the large items might always sell at a loss when physical quantities are used to allocate joint costs.

Answer (B) is incorrect. Physical quantities are usually easy to measure. Answer (C) is incorrect. Additional processing costs will have no more effect on the allocation of joint costs based on physical quantities than any other base. Answer (D) is incorrect. The purpose of allocating joint costs, under any method, is to separate such costs on a unit basis.

11.3.8. Which of the following is(are) often subject to further processing in order to be salable?

	By-Products	Scrap
A.	No	No
B.	No	Yes
C.	Yes	Yes
D.	Yes	No

Answer (D) is correct. *(CPA, adapted)*

REQUIRED: The item(s) often requiring further processing to be salable.

DISCUSSION: Scrap and by-products often are similar physically and are accounted for in the same way. Scrap might even be considered a by-product of a manufacturing process. However, by-products usually have a greater sales value than scrap. Also, scrap rarely is processed further.

11.3.9. A company produces two main products and a by-product out of a joint process. The ratio of output quantities to input quantities of direct material used in the joint process remains consistent from month to month. The company has employed the physical-volume method to allocate joint production costs to the two main products. The net realizable value of the by-product is used to reduce the joint production costs before the joint costs are allocated to the main products. Data regarding the company's operations for the current month are presented in the chart below. During the month, the company incurred joint production costs of $2,520,000. The main products are not marketable at the split-off point and, thus, have to be processed further.

	First Main Product	Second Main Product	By-Product
Monthly output in pounds	90,000	150,000	60,000
Selling price per pound	$30	$14	$2
Separable process costs	$540,000	$660,000	

The amount of joint production cost that the company would allocate to the Second Main Product by using the physical-volume method to allocate joint production costs would be

A. $1,200,000

B. $1,260,000

C. $1,500,000

D. $1,575,000

Answer (C) is correct. *(CMA, adapted)*

REQUIRED: The joint cost allocated to the Second Main Product based on physical volume.

DISCUSSION: The joint cost to be allocated is $2,400,000 [$2,520,000 total joint cost – (60,000 pounds of the by-product) × $2]. Accordingly, the joint cost to be allocated to the Second Main Product on a physical-volume basis is $1,500,000 {[150,000 pounds ÷ (90,000 pounds + 150,000 pounds) × $2,400,000]}.

Answer (A) is incorrect. The amount of $1,200,000 assumes that the by-product is charged with a portion of the net joint cost. Answer (B) is incorrect. The amount of $1,260,000 assumes that the by-product is charged with a portion of the gross joint cost. Answer (D) is incorrect. The amount of $1,575,000 does not deduct by-product NRV from the joint cost.

11.4 Relative Sales Value

11.4.1. For purposes of allocating joint costs to joint products, the sales price at point of sale, reduced by cost to complete after split-off, is assumed to be equal to the

A. Joint costs.

B. Total costs.

C. Net sales value at split-off.

D. Sales price less a normal profit margin at point of sale.

Answer (C) is correct. *(CPA, adapted)*

REQUIRED: The assumption about the sales price at point of sale, reduced by cost to complete after split-off.

DISCUSSION: The relative sales value method is the most frequently used method to allocate joint costs to joint products. It allocates joint costs based upon the products' proportion of total sales revenue. For joint products salable at the split-off point, the relative sales value is the selling price at split-off. However, if further processing is needed, the relative sales value is approximated by subtracting the additional anticipated processing costs from the final sales value to arrive at the estimated net sales value at split-off.

Answer (A) is incorrect. Joint costs are computed up to the split-off point. Answer (B) is incorrect. Total costs include the cost to complete after split-off. Answer (D) is incorrect. The normal profit margin does not necessarily equal the cost to complete after split-off.

11.4.2. For purposes of allocating joint costs to joint products, the relative sales-value method could be used in which of the following situations?

	No Costs Beyond Split-off	Costs Beyond Split-off
A.	Yes	Yes
B.	Yes	No
C.	No	Yes
D.	No	No

Answer (A) is correct. *(CPA, adapted)*

REQUIRED: The situation(s) in which the relative sales-value method could be used to allocate joint costs.

DISCUSSION: The relative sales-value method is used to allocate joint costs to the separate products at the split-off point. Joint costs are allocated based upon each product's proportion of total sales revenue. For joint products salable at the split-off point, the relative sales value is the selling price at split-off. If further processing is needed, the relative sales value is approximated by subtracting additional processing costs from the final sales value.

11.4.3. The method of accounting for joint product costs that will produce the same gross profit rate for all products is the

A. Relative sales-value method.

B. Physical-measure method.

C. Actual costing method.

D. Services-received method.

Answer (A) is correct. *(CPA, adapted)*

REQUIRED: The method resulting in the same gross profit rate for all joint products.

DISCUSSION: The relative sales-value method produces the same gross profit as a percentage of sales value at split-off (or estimated NRV at split-off) for each product. The reason is that it allocates joint costs in proportion to sales values. However, the assumption is that no beginning or ending inventories or separable costs exist.

Answer (B) is incorrect. Physical measure may not be related to the fair value of separate products. Answer (C) is incorrect. The actual cost of each product cannot be determined. Answer (D) is incorrect. Services received has no meaning in joint product costing.

11.4.4. Actual sales values at the split-off point for joint products Y and Z are not known. For purposes of allocating joint costs to products Y and Z, the relative sales value at split-off method is used. An increase in the costs beyond split-off occurs for Product Z, while those of Product Y remain constant. If the selling prices of finished products Y and Z remain constant, the percentage of the total joint costs allocated to Product Y and Product Z will

A. Decrease for Product Y and Product Z.

B. Decrease for Product Y and increase for Product Z.

C. Increase for Product Y and Product Z.

D. Increase for Product Y and decrease for Product Z.

Answer (D) is correct. *(CPA, adapted)*

REQUIRED: The effect on the allocation of joint costs, given an increase in separable costs beyond split-off for one product.

DISCUSSION: The actual sales values of products Y and Z at the split-off point are not known. However, these values may be approximated by calculating the estimated net realizable values (final sales values – separable costs). Assuming constant selling prices and increasing costs for product Z, the net realizable value at split-off for Z must necessarily be decreasing. The relative sales value method allocates joint costs in accordance with the ratio of each joint product's sales value at split-off to the total sales value at split-off for all joint products. Therefore, the costs allocated to Z must be decreasing, while the costs allocated to Y are increasing.

11.4.5. Lowe Co. manufactures products A and B from a joint process. Sales value at split-off was $700,000 for 10,000 units of A and $300,000 for 15,000 units of B. Using the sales value at split-off approach, joint costs properly allocated to A were $140,000. Total joint costs were

A. $98,000

B. $200,000

C. $233,333

D. $350,000

Answer (B) is correct. *(CPA, adapted)*

REQUIRED: The total joint costs given the joint costs properly allocated to one product.

DISCUSSION: The relative sales value is a cost allocation method that allocates joint costs in proportion to the relative sales value of the individual products. Total sales value is $1,000,000 ($700,000 for A + $300,000 for B). The $140,000 of joint costs allocated to product A was 70% ($700,000 ÷ $1,000,000) of total joint costs. The calculation for total joint costs (Y) is

$$.7Y = \$140{,}000$$
$$Y = \$140{,}000 \div .7$$
$$Y = \$200{,}000$$

Answer (A) is incorrect. This figure is 70% of the $140,000 joint cost allocated to A. To arrive at total joint costs, $140,000 needs to be divided by 70%. Answer (C) is incorrect. Total joint costs are determined by dividing the joint costs allocated to A by A's percentage of sales value at split-off. Answer (D) is incorrect. Total joint costs are based on sales value, not units produced.

11.4.6.

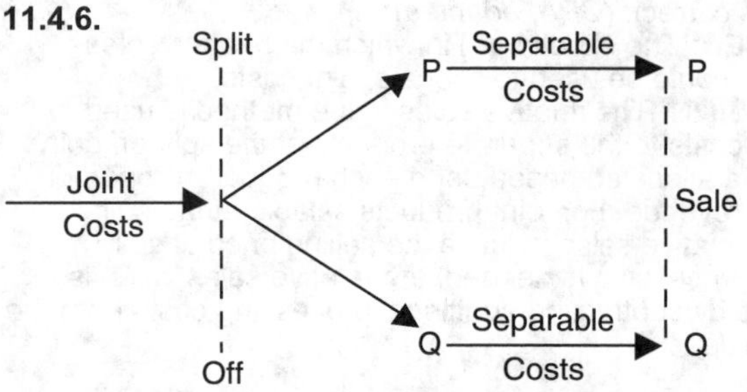

The diagram represents the production and sales relationships of joint products P and Q. Joint costs are incurred until split-off; then separable costs are incurred in refining each product. Market values of P and Q at split-off are used to allocate joint costs. If the market value of P at split-off increases and all other costs and selling prices remain unchanged, then the gross margin of

	P	Q
A.	Increases	Decreases
B.	Increases	Increases
C.	Decreases	Decreases
D.	Decreases	Increases

Answer (D) is correct. *(CPA, adapted)*

REQUIRED: The effects on the gross margins of joint products if the market value of one product at split-off increases while other costs and prices are constant.

DISCUSSION: The allocation of joint costs to P and Q is in accordance with their relative sales values at split-off. If P's market value at split-off increases, its allocation of joint costs will increase and Q's will decrease. Given that other costs and final selling prices are constant, P's gross margin (final sales revenue – cost of goods sold, which includes the allocation of joint costs) decreases and Q's increases.

11.4.7. A company processes a raw material into products F1, F2, and F3. Each ton of raw material produces five units of F1, two units of F2, and three units of F3. Joint processing costs to the split-off point are $15 per ton. Further processing results in the following per-unit figures:

	F1	F2	F3
Additional processing costs per unit	$28	$30	$25
Selling price per unit	30	35	35

If joint costs are allocated based on the net realizable value of finished product, what proportion of joint costs should be allocated to F1?

A. 20%

B. 30%

C. 33 1/3%

D. 50%

Answer (A) is correct. *(CIA, adapted)*

REQUIRED: The proportion of joint costs that should be allocated to product F1.

DISCUSSION: To determine the proportion of joint costs to be allocated to F1, the NRVs of the three products must be calculated. NRV per unit is selling price minus additional processing costs.

F1: 5 × ($30 – $28) = $10
F2: 2 × ($35 – $30) = 10
F3: 3 × ($35 – $25) = 30
$50

The joint costs allocated to F1 equal 20% ($10 ÷ $50).

Answer (B) is incorrect. The proportion of selling price attributable to F1 is 30%. Answer (C) is incorrect. Joint costs are not divided equally among the three products. Answer (D) is incorrect. The proportion of based physical units attributable to F1 is 50%.

11.4.8. A processing department produces joint products Ajac and Bjac, each of which incurs separable production costs after split-off. Information concerning a batch produced at a $60,000 joint cost before split-off follows:

Product	Separable Costs	Sales Value
Ajac	$ 8,000	$ 80,000
Bjac	22,000	40,000
	$30,000	$120,000

What is the joint cost assigned to Ajac if costs are assigned using the relative net realizable value?

A. $16,000

B. $40,000

C. $48,000

D. $52,000

Answer (C) is correct. *(CPA, adapted)*

REQUIRED: The joint cost assigned to Ajac if costs are assigned based on relative NRV.

DISCUSSION: The NRV of Ajac is $72,000 ($80,000 – $8,000), and the NRV of Bjac is $18,000 ($40,000 – $22,000). Thus, the joint cost assigned to Ajac if costs are assigned based on relative NRV is $48,000 {$60,000 × [$72,000 ÷ ($72,000 + $18,000)]}.

Answer (A) is incorrect. This amount results from allocating joint costs on the basis of separable costs. Answer (B) is incorrect. This amount ignores the separable costs. Answer (D) is incorrect. This amount equals the joint cost minus the separable costs of Ajac.

11.4.9. A cheese company produces natural cheese from cow's milk. As a result of the process, a secondary product, whey, is produced in the proportion of one pound for each pound of cheese. The following are the standards for 1,000 pounds of milk:

Input: 1,000 pounds of milk at $.20/pound
40 hours of labor at $10/hour
Overhead applied equaling 100% of direct labor cost

Output: 450 pounds of cheese
450 pounds of whey

The following prices and demand are expected:

	Price per Pound	Demand in Pounds
Cheese	$2.00	450
Whey	.80	375

Given that the company allocates common costs on the basis of NRVs, the allocated common costs per 1,000 pounds of milk (rounded) are

	Cheese	Whey
A.	$450	$150
B.	$500	$500
C.	$714	$286
D.	$750	$250

Answer (D) is correct. *(CIA, adapted)*

REQUIRED: The common cost allocation.

DISCUSSION: The relative sales-value method allocates costs in proportion to the relative sales value of the individual products. The total common costs are

Milk (1,000 lb. × $.20)	$ 200	
Labor (40 hr. × $10)	400	
Overhead (1.0 × $400 DL cost)	400	
Common costs	$1,000	
Sales value:		
Cheese (450 × $2)	$ 900	75%
Whey (375 × $.80)	300	25%
Total	$1,200	
Cost to cheese ($1,000 × 75%)	$ 750	
Cost to whey ($1,000 × 25%)	250	
Total allocated	$1,000	

If only 375 pounds of whey can be sold, the other 75 pounds are worthless and are not allocated any common cost.

Answer (A) is incorrect. Allocations of $450 to cheese and $150 to whey result from omitting overhead from total common costs. Answer (B) is incorrect. An allocation of $500 to both cheese and whey is based on output in pounds. Answer (C) is incorrect. Allocations of $714 to cheese and $286 to whey are based on relative unit sales prices.

11.4.10. Andy Company manufactures products N, P, and R from a joint process. The following information is available:

	N	P	R	Total
Units produced	12,000	?	?	24,000
Joint costs	$ 48,000	?	?	$120,000
Sales value at split-off	?	?	$50,000	$200,000
Additional costs if processed further	$ 18,000	$14,000	$10,000	$ 42,000
Sales value if processed further	$110,000	$90,000	$60,000	$260,000

Assuming that joint product costs are allocated using the relative sales value at split-off approach, what was the sales value at split-off for products N and P?

	Product N	Product P
A.	$66,000	$56,000
B.	$80,000	$70,000
C.	$98,000	$84,000
D.	$150,000	$50,000

Answer (B) is correct. *(CPA, adapted)*

REQUIRED: The relative sales value at split-off of two joint products.

DISCUSSION: The relative sales-value method allocates joint costs in proportion to the relative sales value of the individual products.

	Sales Value	Weighting Factor	Joint Cost Allocated
N	X	(X ÷ 200) × $120,000	$ 48,000
P	Y		?
R	$ 50,000	(50 ÷ 200) × $120,000	?
	$200,000		$120,000

X is calculated below from the information given. If 40% of the cost is allocated to product N, the sales value of N must be 40% of the total sales value.

$$(X \div \$200{,}000) \times \$120{,}000 = \$48{,}000$$
$$X \div \$200{,}000 = .4$$
$$X = \$80{,}000$$

Y is equal to the difference between total sales value at split-off ($200,000) and the sales value for products N and P ($80,000 + $50,000), or $70,000.

Answer (A) is incorrect. The total costs of N and P are $66,000 and $56,000, respectively. Answer (C) is incorrect. The total sales value at split-off of N and P must be $150,000. Answer (D) is incorrect. The total sales value at split-off of N and P is $150,000, and $50,000 is the sales value of R at split-off.

11.4.11. Ashwood Company manufactures three main products, F, G, and W, from a joint process. Joint costs are allocated on the basis of relative sales value at split-off. Additional information for June production activity follows:

	F	G	W	Total
Units produced	50,000	40,000	10,000	100,000
Joint costs	?	?	?	$450,000
Sales value at split-off	$420,000	$270,000	$60,000	$750,000
Additional costs if processed further	$ 88,000	$ 30,000	$12,000	$130,000
Sales value if processed further	$538,000	$320,000	$78,000	$936,000

Assuming that the 10,000 units of W were processed further and sold for $78,000, what was Ashwood's gross profit on this sale?

A. $21,000

B. $28,500

C. $30,000

D. $36,000

Answer (C) is correct. *(CPA, adapted)*

REQUIRED: The gross profit on the sale of a joint product that is processed beyond split-off.

DISCUSSION: The relative sales-value at split-off method allocates joint costs in proportion to the relative sales value of the individual products. The total sales value at split-off is $750,000.

	Sales Value	Weighting Factor	Joint Cost Allocated
W	$60,000	(60 ÷ 750) × $450,000	$36,000

The joint cost allocated at split-off is thus $36,000. The units are processed further at a cost of $12,000 and sold for $78,000. The gross profit is thus $30,000 ($78,000 – $36,000 – $12,000).

Answer (A) is incorrect. This figure uses units produced (10,000 units of W ÷ 100,000 total units) as a weighting factor. Answer (B) is incorrect. This figure uses sales value if processed further ($78,000 W ÷ $936,000 total) as a weighting factor. Answer (D) is incorrect. The joint cost allocated to W is $36,000.

Questions 11.4.12 and 11.4.13 are based on the following information.

Petro-Chem, Inc., is a small company that acquires high-grade crude oil from low-volume production wells owned by individuals and small partnerships. The crude oil is processed in a single refinery into Two Oil, Six Oil, and impure distillates. Petro-Chem does not have the technology or capacity to process these products further and sells most of its output each month to major refineries. There were no beginning inventories of finished goods or work-in-process on November 1. The production costs and output of Petro-Chem for November are shown in the next column.

Crude oil acquired and placed in production	$5,000,000
Direct labor and related costs	2,000,000
Manufacturing overhead	3,000,000

Production and sales

- Two Oil, 300,000 barrels produced; 80,000 barrels sold at $20 each
- Six Oil, 240,000 barrels produced; 120,000 barrels sold at $30 each
- Distillates, 120,000 barrels produced and sold at $15 each

11.4.12. The portion of the joint production costs assigned to Six Oil based upon physical output is

A. $3,636,000

B. $3,750,000

C. $1,818,000

D. $7,500,000

Answer (A) is correct. *(CMA, adapted)*

REQUIRED: The joint production costs assigned to Six Oil based on physical output.

DISCUSSION: The total production costs incurred are $10,000,000, consisting of crude oil of $5,000,000, direct labor of $2,000,000, and overhead of $3,000,000. The total physical output was 660,000 barrels, consisting of 300,000 barrels of Two Oil, 240,000 barrels of Six Oil, and 120,000 barrels of distillates. Thus, the allocation (rounded) is $3,636,000 {$10,000,000 × [240,000 ÷ (300,000 + 240,000 + 120,000)]}.

Answer (B) is incorrect. The amount of $3,750,000 is based on the physical quantity of units sold, not units produced. Answer (C) is incorrect. The amount of $1,818,000 is the amount that would be assigned to distillates. Answer (D) is incorrect. Six Oil does not compose 75% of the total output in barrels.

11.4.13. The portion of the joint production costs assigned to Two Oil based upon the relative sales value of output is

A. $4,800,000

B. $4,000,000

C. $2,286,000

D. $2,500,000

Answer (B) is correct. *(CMA, adapted)*

REQUIRED: The joint production costs assigned to a product based on relative sales value.

DISCUSSION: The total production costs incurred are $10,000,000, consisting of crude oil of $5,000,000, direct labor of $2,000,000, and overhead of $3,000,000. The total value of the output is as follows:

Two Oil (300,000 × $20)	$ 6,000,000
Six Oil (240,000 × $30)	7,200,000
Distillates (120,000 × $15)	1,800,000
Total sales value	$15,000,000

Because Two Oil composes 40% of the total sales value ($6,000,000 ÷ $15,000,000), it will be assigned 40% of the $10,000,000 of joint costs, or $4,000,000.

Answer (A) is incorrect. The amount of $4,800,000 is the amount that would be assigned to Six Oil. Answer (C) is incorrect. The amount of $2,286,000 is based on the relative sales value of units sold. Answer (D) is incorrect. The amount of $2,500,000 is based on the physical quantity of barrels sold.

11.4.14. Warfield Corporation manufactures products C, D, and E from a joint process. Joint costs are allocated on the basis of relative sales value at split-off. Additional information is presented below.

	C	D	E	Total
Units produced	6,000	4,000	2,000	12,000
Joint costs	$ 72,000	?	?	$120,000
Sales value at split-off	?	?	$30,000	$200,000
Additional costs if processed further	$ 14,000	$10,000	$ 6,000	$ 30,000
Sales value if processed further	$140,000	$60,000	$40,000	$240,000

How much of the joint costs should Warfield allocate to product D?

A. $24,000
B. $28,800
C. $30,000
D. $32,000

Answer (C) is correct. *(CPA, adapted)*
REQUIRED: The joint costs allocated to product D.
DISCUSSION: Given that total joint costs are $120,000 and total sales value at split-off is $200,000, the ratio of joint costs to sales value is 60% ($120,000 ÷ $200,000). The joint costs of product C are $72,000. Thus, C's sales value at split-off is $120,000 ($72,000 ÷ 60%). If product C's sales value is $120,000, D's sales value is $50,000 ($200,000 – $30,000 E – $120,000 C). Accordingly, the joint costs of product D are $30,000, which is 60% of D's $50,000 sales value at split-off.
Answer (A) is incorrect. The $48,000 of joint costs to be allocated to products D and E should be allocated based on relative sales values at split-off, not allocated equally between products D and E. Answer (B) is incorrect. The joint cost allocation is based on sales value at split-off, not on sales value if processed further. Furthermore, the allocation is based on total sales values of products C, D, and E, not just products D and E. Answer (D) is incorrect. The $48,000 of joint costs to be allocated to products D and E should be allocated based on relative sales values at split-off, not on units produced. Furthermore, the allocation is based on total sales values of products C, D, and E, not just products D and E.

11.5 By-Products

11.5.1. In accounting for by-products, the value of the by-product may be recognized at the time of

	Production	Sale
A.	Yes	Yes
B.	Yes	No
C.	No	No
D.	No	Yes

Answer (A) is correct. *(CPA, adapted)*
REQUIRED: The timing of recognition of by-products.
DISCUSSION: Practice with regard to recognizing by-products in the accounts is not uniform. The most cost-effective method for the initial recognition of by-products is to account for their value at the time of sale as a reduction in the joint cost or as a revenue. The alternative is to recognize the net realizable value at the time of production, a method that results in the recording of by-product inventory.

11.5.2. A manufacturing company properly classifies and accounts for one product as a by-product rather than as a main product because it

A. Can never be developed into a main product by this or any other manufacturer.
B. Has no sales value to the manufacturing company.
C. Has low physical volume when compared with the other main products.
D. Has low sales value when compared with the main products.

Answer (D) is correct. *(CIA, adapted)*
REQUIRED: The reason a product is classified as a by-product.
DISCUSSION: By-products are products of relatively small total value that are produced simultaneously from a common manufacturing process with products of greater value and quantity.
Answer (A) is incorrect. A by-product can be developed into a main product. Answer (B) is incorrect. By-products have sales value to the manufacturer. Answer (C) is incorrect. The physical volume of the by-product can be significant.

11.5.3. By-products may have which of the following characteristics?

	Zero Costs Beyond Split-off	Additional Costs Beyond Split-off
A.	No	No
B.	No	Yes
C.	Yes	Yes
D.	Yes	No

Answer (C) is correct. *(CPA, adapted)*
REQUIRED: The characteristic(s) of by-products.
DISCUSSION: By-products are joint products that have minor sales values compared with the sales values of the main product(s). To be salable, by-products may or may not require additional processing beyond the split-off point. Thus, the incurrence of separable costs beyond the split-off point may or may not be required.

11.5.4. For the purposes of cost accumulation, which of the following are identifiable as different individual products before the split-off point?

	By-Products	Joint Products
A.	Yes	Yes
B.	Yes	No
C.	No	No
D.	No	Yes

Answer (C) is correct. *(CPA, adapted)*

REQUIRED: The products identifiable before the split-off point.

DISCUSSION: In a joint production process, at the split-off point, neither by-products nor joint products are separately identifiable as individual products. Joint costs up to the split-off point are usually related to both joint products and by-products. After split-off, additional (separable) costs can be traced and charged to the individual products. By-products usually do not receive an allocation of joint costs.

11.5.5. Under an acceptable method of costing by-products, inventory costs of the by-product are based on the portion of the joint production cost allocated to the by-product

A. But any subsequent processing cost is debited to the cost of the main product.

B. But any subsequent processing cost is debited to revenue of the main product.

C. Plus any subsequent processing cost.

D. Minus any subsequent processing cost.

Answer (C) is correct. *(CPA, adapted)*

REQUIRED: The true statement about inventory costs of by-products.

DISCUSSION: By-product is a term for one or more products of relatively small total value that are produced simultaneously with a product of greater value and quantity, normally called the main product. One method of accounting for by-products is to recognize them in inventory as they are produced. These inventory costs of the by-products may be based on an allocation of some portion of joint costs plus any subsequent processing costs.

Answer (A) is incorrect. Subsequent processing costs must be assigned to by-products. Answer (B) is incorrect. Subsequent processing costs must be assigned to by-products. Answer (D) is incorrect. Subsequent processing costs are added to the inventory costs of the by-product.

11.5.6. Under an acceptable method of costing by-products, inventory costs of a by-product are based on the portion of the joint production cost allocated to a by-product plus any subsequent processing cost. Why was joint cost allocated to by-products?

A. They were treated as joint products even though they presumably met the definition of by-products because of their small relative sales values.

B. All by-products must be allocated some portion of joint costs.

C. Such allocation is required by the Cost Accounting Standards Board (CASB).

D. The by-products produced a loss.

Answer (A) is correct. *(Publisher, adapted)*

REQUIRED: The explanation of the allocation of joint cost to by-products.

DISCUSSION: The usual treatment of by-products is to account for their revenues or net realizable values as a reduction in cost or as a revenue item without allocation of joint costs. However, if joint cost is allocated to by-products, they are treated as joint products even though their relative values are small.

Answer (B) is incorrect. Allocation of joint cost to by-products is not required by GAAP. Answer (C) is incorrect. Allocation of joint cost to by-products is not required by the CASB. Answer (D) is incorrect. No information is given indicating that the by-products' subsequent processing resulted in a loss.

11.5.7. The main issues for accounting recognition of by-products are similar to those for

A. Joint products.

B. Scrap.

C. Product costs.

D. Main products.

Answer (B) is correct. *(Publisher, adapted)*

REQUIRED: The item that involves accounting issues similar to those for by-products.

DISCUSSION: Scrap and by-products usually are similar, both physically and for accounting purposes. Scrap might even be considered a by-product of a manufacturing process. However, joint cost almost never is allocated to scrap, but joint cost may be allocated to by-products. The main issue is whether to recognize scrap or by-products at the time of production or at the time of sale. Another issue is whether to treat the recognized amounts as contra costs or as revenues.

Answer (A) is incorrect. The timing of recognition is usually not an issue for joint (main) products. Answer (C) is incorrect. Product costs are by definition inventoriable. The value of by-products may or may not be inventoried. Answer (D) is incorrect. The timing of recognition is usually not an issue for joint (main) products.

Questions 11.5.8 through 11.5.12 are based on the following information. Earl Corporation manufactures a product that gives rise to a by-product called Zafa. The only costs associated with Zafa are selling costs of $1 for each unit sold. Earl accounts for Zafa sales first by deducting its separable costs from such sales and then by deducting this net amount from cost of sales of the major product. This year, 1,000 units of Zafa were sold at $4 each.

11.5.8. If Earl changes its method of accounting for Zafa sales by recording the net amount as additional sales revenue, Earl's gross margin will

A. Be unaffected.

B. Increase by $3,000.

C. Decrease by $3,000.

D. Increase by $4,000.

Answer (A) is correct. *(CPA, adapted)*

REQUIRED: The effect on gross margin of changing the treatment of by-product sales.

DISCUSSION: The gross margin equals sales minus cost of sales. Before the change, the net amount was subtracted from cost of sales (i.e., it increased the gross margin). After the change, the net amount is added to regular sales with no additional increase in cost of goods sold. Thus, the gross margin is the same.

11.5.9. If Earl changes its method of accounting for Zafa sales by recording the net amount as other income, Earl's gross margin will

A. Be unaffected.

B. Increase by $3,000.

C. Decrease by $3,000.

D. Decrease by $4,000.

Answer (C) is correct. *(CPA, adapted)*

REQUIRED: The effect on gross margin of accounting for by-product sales as other income.

DISCUSSION: Sales revenue minus cost of goods sold is gross margin. If the net revenue from the by-product is recorded as other income rather than subtracted from cost of goods sold, the gross margin decreases by $3,000 [1,000 × ($4 sales – $1 COGS)].

Answer (A) is incorrect. Gross margin is affected. Answer (B) is incorrect. The gross margin decreases by $3,000. Answer (D) is incorrect. The gross amount of Zafa sales is $4,000.

11.5.10. If Earl records the net realizable value of Zafa as inventory as it is produced, what will the per-unit value be?

A. $1

B. $2

C. $3

D. $4

Answer (C) is correct. *(Publisher, adapted)*

REQUIRED: The unit net realizable value.

DISCUSSION: The NRV is selling price minus cost to complete and cost to dispose. The selling price of Zafa is $4, and the selling costs are $1. Given no completion or additional processing costs, unit net realizable value is $3.

Answer (A) is incorrect. The selling cost is $1. Answer (B) is incorrect. The unit net realizable value is $3. Answer (D) is incorrect. The selling price of Zafa is $4.

11.5.11. Earl sold 1,000 units of Zafa. Assuming that 1,500 units were produced for the year and that net realizable value is recorded as inventory, Earl's net income will increase by

A. $6,000

B. $4,500

C. $3,000

D. $1,500

Answer (B) is correct. *(Publisher, adapted)*

REQUIRED: The change in net income if 1,500 units are produced and inventory is valued at net realizable value.

DISCUSSION: If the 1,500 units of the by-product are recognized at the time of production, net income must increase by $4,500 ($3 unit NRV × 1,500). Ending inventory of Zafa reduces cost of sales, and by-product revenue either decreases costs or increases other income.

Answer (A) is incorrect. The amount of $6,000 is the potential gross revenue from Zafa. Answer (C) is incorrect. The amount of $3,000 is the net revenue from sales of 1,000 units. Answer (D) is incorrect. The amount of $1,500 equals 1,500 units times the $1 unit selling cost.

11.5.12. If Earl records Zafa inventory at net realizable value as it is produced this year, what is the profit recognized next year on a sale of 500 units?

A. $0

B. $500

C. $1,000

D. $1,500

Answer (A) is correct. *(Publisher, adapted)*

REQUIRED: The profit from the sale of inventory measured at net realizable value.

DISCUSSION: Because net realizable value is selling price minus completion and disposal cost, the sale results in no profit. The sale of 500 units of Zafa measured at $3 per unit produces no profit ($4 unit selling price – $3 inventory cost – $1 selling cost = $0).

Answer (B) is incorrect. The amount of $500 equals 500 units times the $1 selling cost. Answer (C) is incorrect. The amount of $1,000 is the selling cost of 1,000 units. Answer (D) is incorrect. The amount of $1,500 is the $3 inventory cost multiplied by the 500 units sold.

11.5.13. If the values of by-products are recorded as produced, why should they be recorded at net realizable value minus normal profit?

A. To permit a sales profit to be recognized upon sale.

B. To be valued at the lower of cost or market.

C. To control the loss upon sale.

D. To recognize a profit when the inventory value is recorded.

Answer (A) is correct. *(Publisher, adapted)*

REQUIRED: The reason by-products should be measured at net realizable value minus normal profit.

DISCUSSION: If inventory is measured at NRV minus normal profit, recognition of normal profit is deferred until sale of the product. This treatment also results in a more conservative measure of inventory.

Answer (B) is incorrect. NRV minus normal profit may be greater than cost. Answer (C) is incorrect. Measurement at NRV minus normal profit implies that some profit is to be recognized upon sale. Answer (D) is incorrect. If a cost is credited for the value of the inventory, no profit is recognized when inventory is recorded at NRV minus normal profit.

11.5.14. Mig Co., which began operations in the month just ended, produces gasoline and a gasoline by-product. The following information is available pertaining to sales and production for the month:

Total production costs to split-off point	$120,000
Gasoline sales	270,000
By-product sales	30,000
Gasoline ending inventory	15,000
Additional by-product costs:	
Marketing	10,000
Production	15,000

Mig accounts for the by-product at the time of production. What was Mig's cost of sales for gasoline and the by-product?

	Gasoline	By-Product
A.	$105,000	$25,000
B.	$115,000	$15,000
C.	$108,000	$37,000
D.	$100,000	$0

Answer (D) is correct. *(CPA, adapted)*

REQUIRED: The cost of sales for both the gasoline and the by-product.

DISCUSSION: If the by-product is accounted for at the time of production, by-product inventory is recorded at its selling price (or net realizable value in this case, given separable by-product costs) because by-products usually do not receive an allocation of joint costs. Thus, the by-product's cost of sales is zero. Assuming sales of the by-product reduced joint costs, the cost of sales of the gasoline was $100,000 ($120,000 cost to split-off – $30,000 sales of the by-product + $25,000 additional by-product costs – $15,000 EI).

Answer (A) is incorrect. This amount is the result of subtracting the ending gasoline inventory from total production costs to split-off point, and $25,000 equals the additional by-product costs. Answer (B) is incorrect. This amount ignores the $15,000 ending inventory. Answer (C) is incorrect. Allocating joint costs to by-products based on relative sales value is not cost effective, and by-product cost of sales should be zero.

Questions 11.5.15 through 11.5.19 are based on the following information.

Atlas Foods produces the following three supplemental food products simultaneously through a refining process costing $93,000.

The joint products, Alfa and Betters, have a final selling price of $4 per pound and $10 per pound, respectively, after additional processing costs of $2 per pound of each product are incurred after the split-off point. Morefeed, a by-product, is sold at the split-off point for $3 per pound.

Alfa	10,000 pounds of Alfa, a popular but relatively rare grain supplement having a caloric value of 4,400 calories per pound
Betters	5,000 pounds of Betters, a flavoring material high in carbohydrates with a caloric value of 11,200 calories per pound
Morefeed	1,000 pounds of Morefeed, used as a cattle feed supplement with a caloric value of 1,000 calories per pound

11.5.15. Assuming Atlas Foods inventories Morefeed, the by-product, the joint cost to be allocated to Alfa using the net realizable value method is

A. $3,000

B. $30,000

C. $31,000

D. $60,000

Answer (B) is correct. *(CMA, adapted)*

REQUIRED: The joint cost allocated to a joint product based on net realizable values if the by-product is inventoried.

DISCUSSION: The NRV at split-off for each of the joint products are as follows:

	Selling Price Per Pound		Additional Processing Cost Per Pound		NRV Per Unit		Units of Output		Total NRV
Alfa	$ 4	–	$2	=	$2	×	10,000 lbs.	=	$20,000
Betters	$10	–	$2	=	$8	×	5,000 lbs.	=	$40,000

The 1,000 pounds of Morefeed has a split-off value of $3 per pound, or $3,000. Assuming that Morefeed (a by-product) is inventoried (recognized in the accounts when produced) and treated as a reduction of joint costs, the allocable joint cost is $90,000 ($93,000 – $3,000). The total net realizable value of the main products is $60,000 ($20,000 Alfa + $40,000 Betters). The allocation to Alfa is $30,000 [$90,000 × ($20,000 ÷ $60,000)].

Answer (A) is incorrect. The value of the by-product is $3,000. Answer (C) is incorrect. Failing to adjust the joint processing cost for the value of the by-product results in $31,000. Answer (D) is incorrect. The amount allocated to Betters is $60,000.

11.5.16. Assuming Atlas Foods inventories Morefeed, the by-product, the joint cost to be allocated to Alfa, using the physical quantity method is

A. $3,000

B. $30,000

C. $31,000

D. $60,000

Answer (D) is correct. *(CMA, adapted)*

REQUIRED: The joint cost allocated to Alfa based on the physical quantity method if the by-product is inventoried.

DISCUSSION: Joint cost is $93,000 and Morefeed has a split-off value of $3,000 (1,000 pounds × $3 split-off value per pound). Assuming the latter amount is treated as a reduction in joint cost, the allocable joint cost is $90,000. The total physical quantity (volume) of the two joint products is 15,000 pounds (10,000 Alfa + 5,000 Betters). Hence, $60,000 of the net joint costs [(10,000 ÷ 15,000) × $90,000] should be allocated to Alfa.

Answer (A) is incorrect. The amount of $3,000 is the value of the by-product. Answer (B) is incorrect. The amount of $30,000 is based on the net realizable value method. Answer (C) is incorrect. The amount of $31,000 is based on the net realizable value method and fails to adjust the joint processing cost for the value of the by-product.

11.5.17. Assuming Atlas Foods inventories Morefeed, the by-product, the joint cost to be allocated to Betters using the weighted-quantity method based on caloric value per pound is

A. $39,208

B. $39,600

C. $40,920

D. $50,400

Answer (D) is correct. *(CMA, adapted)*

REQUIRED: The joint cost allocated to Betters based on weighted quantities if the by-product is inventoried.

DISCUSSION: Joint cost is $93,000 and Morefeed has a split-off value of $3,000 (1,000 pounds × $3 split-off value per pound). Assuming the latter amount is treated as a reduction in joint cost, the allocable joint cost is $90,000. The caloric value of Alfa is 44,000,000 (4,400 × 10,000 pounds), the caloric value of Betters is 56,000,000 (11,200 × 5,000 pounds), and the total is 100,000,000. Of this total volume, Alfa makes up 44% and Betters 56%. Thus, $50,400 ($90,000 × 56%) should be allocated to Betters.

Answer (A) is incorrect. The figure of $39,208 is the amount allocated to Alfa if the 1,000,000 calories attributable to Morefeed is included in the computation. Answer (B) is incorrect. The figure of $39,600 is the allocation to Alfa. Answer (C) is incorrect. The figure of $40,920 is the allocation to Alfa if the sales value of the by-product is not treated as a reduction of joint cost.

11.5.18. Assuming Atlas Foods inventories Morefeed, the by-product, and that it incurs no additional processing costs for Alfa and Betters, the joint cost to be allocated to Alfa using the gross market value method is

A. $36,000

B. $40,000

C. $41,333

D. $50,000

Answer (B) is correct. *(CMA, adapted)*

REQUIRED: The joint cost allocated to Alfa using the gross market value method if the by-product is inventoried.

DISCUSSION: The gross market value of Alfa is $40,000 (10,000 pounds × $4), Betters has a total gross value of $50,000 (5,000 pounds × $10), and Morefeed has a split-off value of $3,000. If the value of Morefeed is inventoried and treated as a reduction in joint cost, the allocable joint cost is $90,000 ($93,000 – $3,000). The total gross value of the two main products is $90,000 ($40,000 + $50,000). Of this total value, $40,000 should be allocated to Alfa [($40,000 ÷ $90,000) × $90,000].

Answer (A) is incorrect. The amount of $36,000 is based on 40%, not 4/9. Answer (C) is incorrect. The amount of $41,333 fails to adjust the joint cost by the value of the by-product. Answer (D) is incorrect. The amount of $50,000 is the joint cost allocated to Betters.

11.5.19. Assuming Atlas Foods does not inventory Morefeed, the by-product, the joint cost to be allocated to Betters using the net realizable value method is

A. $30,000

B. $31,000

C. $52,080

D. $62,000

Answer (D) is correct. *(CMA, adapted)*

REQUIRED: The joint cost allocated to a joint product based on net realizable values if the by-product is not inventoried.

DISCUSSION: The NRV of Alfa is $20,000, and the NRV of Betters is $40,000. If the joint cost is not adjusted for the value of the by-product, the amount allocated to Betters is $62,000 {$93,000 × [$40,000 ÷ ($20,000 + $40,000)]}.

Answer (A) is incorrect. The amount allocated to Alfa when the by-product is inventoried is $30,000. Answer (B) is incorrect. The amount allocated to Alfa when the by-product is not inventoried is $31,000. Answer (C) is incorrect. Assuming that a weighting method using caloric value is used results in $52,080.

11.6 Sell-or-Process-Further Decisions

11.6.1. There is a market for both product X and product Y. Which of the following costs and revenues would be most relevant in deciding whether to sell product X or process it further to make product Y?

A. Total cost of making X and the revenue from sale of X and Y.

B. Total cost of making Y and the revenue from sale of Y.

C. Additional cost of making Y, given the cost of making X, and additional revenue from Y.

D. Additional cost of making X, given the cost of making Y, and additional revenue from Y.

Answer (C) is correct. *(CIA, adapted)*

REQUIRED: The costs relevant to the decision to further process a product.

DISCUSSION: Incremental costs are the additional costs incurred for accepting one alternative rather than another. Questions involving incremental costing (sometimes called differential costing) decisions are based upon a variable costing analysis. The typical problem for which incremental cost analysis can be used involves two or more alternatives, for example, selling or processing further. Thus, the relevant costs and revenues are the marginal costs and marginal revenues.

Answer (A) is incorrect. The cost of making X is a sunk cost (irrelevant). In addition, only X or Y, not both, can be sold. Answer (B) is incorrect. Only the relevant, incremental costs are considered. Answer (D) is incorrect. Y is made only after X is completed.

11.6.2. In joint-product costing and analysis, which one of the following costs is relevant when deciding the point at which a product should be sold to maximize profits?

A. Separable costs after the split-off point.

B. Joint costs to the split-off point.

C. Sales salaries for the period when the units were produced.

D. Purchase costs of the materials required for the joint products.

Answer (A) is correct. *(CMA, adapted)*

REQUIRED: The cost relevant to deciding when a joint product should be sold.

DISCUSSION: Joint products are created from processing a common input. Joint costs are incurred prior to the split-off point and cannot be identified with a particular joint product. As a result, joint costs are irrelevant to the timing of sale. However, separable costs incurred after the split-off point are relevant because, if incremental revenues exceed the separable costs, products should be processed further, not sold at the split-off point.

Answer (B) is incorrect. Joint costs have no effect on the decision when to sell a product. Answer (C) is incorrect. Sales salaries for the production period do not affect the decision. Answer (D) is incorrect. Purchase costs are joint costs.

Questions 11.6.3 and 11.6.4 are based on the following information.

N-Air Corporation uses a joint process to produce three products: A, B, and C, all derived from one input. The company can sell these products at the point of split-off (end of the joint process) or process them further. The joint production costs during October were $10,000. N-Air allocates joint costs to the products in proportion to the relative physical volume of output. Additional information is presented in the opposite column.

			If Processed Further	
Product	Units Produced	Unit Sales Price at Split-off	Unit Sales Price	Unit Additional Cost
A	1,000	$4.00	$5.00	$ .75
B	2,000	2.25	4.00	1.20
C	1,500	3.00	3.75	.90

11.6.3. Assuming that all products were sold at the split-off point during October, the gross profit from the production process would be

A. $13,000

B. $10,000

C. $8,625

D. $3,000

Answer (D) is correct. *(CIA, adapted)*

REQUIRED: The gross profit from the production process if all products are sold at the split-off point.

DISCUSSION: If all products are sold at split-off, the gross profit is computed as follows:

Product A (1,000 × $4.00)	$ 4,000
Product B (2,000 × $2.25)	4,500
Product C (1,500 × $3.00)	4,500
Total sales	$13,000
Joint costs	(10,000)
Gross profit	$ 3,000

Answer (A) is incorrect. This amount is the total sales if all products are sold at split-off. Answer (B) is incorrect. This amount is the joint production cost during October. Answer (C) is incorrect. If all products were sold at split-off, total sales are determined by multiplying units produced by the unit sales price at split-off, not the unit sales price if processed further.

11.6.4. Assuming sufficient demand exists, N-Air could sell all the products at the prices previously mentioned at either the split-off point or after further processing. To maximize its profits, N-Air Corporation should

A. Sell product A at split-off and perform additional processing on products B and C.

B. Sell product B at split-off and perform additional processing on products C and A.

C. Sell product C at split-off and perform additional processing on products A and B.

D. Sell products A, B, and C at split-off.

Answer (C) is correct. *(CIA, adapted)*

REQUIRED: The product(s) that should be processed further to maximize profits.

DISCUSSION: To maximize profits, it must be determined whether each product's incremental revenues will exceed its incremental costs. Joint costs are irrelevant because they are sunk costs.

	A	B	C
Unit sales price if processed further	$5.00	$4.00	$3.75
Minus unit sales price at split-off	(4.00)	(2.25)	(3.00)
Incremental revenue per unit	$1.00	$1.75	$ .75
Minus incremental unit cost	(.75)	(1.20)	(.90)
Excess unit revenue over unit cost	$ .25	$ .55	$ (.15)

It is most profitable for N-Air to process products A and B further and to sell product C at the split-off point.

11.6.5. A firm produces two joint products (A and B) from one unit of raw material, which costs $1,000. Product A can be sold for $700 and product B can be sold for $500 at the split-off point. Alternatively, both A and/or B can be processed further and sold for $900 and $1,200, respectively. The additional processing costs are $100 for A and $750 for B. Should the firm process products A and B beyond the split-off point?

A. Both A and B should be processed further.

B. Only B should be processed further.

C. Only A should be processed further.

D. Neither product should be processed further.

Answer (C) is correct. *(CIA, adapted)*

REQUIRED: The best decision regarding additional processing.

DISCUSSION: The incremental costs ($100) for A are less than the incremental revenue ($200). However, the incremental costs of B ($750) exceed the incremental revenue ($700). Consequently, the firm should process A further and sell B at the split-off point.

11.6.6. Copeland, Inc., produces X-547 in a joint manufacturing process. The company is studying whether to sell X-547 at the split-off point or upgrade the product to become Xylene. The following information has been gathered:

I. Selling price per pound of X-547
II. Variable manufacturing costs of upgrade process
III. Avoidable fixed costs of upgrade process
IV. Selling price per pound of Xylene
V. Joint manufacturing costs to produce X-547

Which items should be reviewed when making the upgrade decision?

A. I, II, and IV.

B. I, II, III, and IV.

C. All items.

D. I, II, IV, and V.

Answer (B) is correct. *(CMA, adapted)*

REQUIRED: The items reviewed for a sell-or-process further decision.

DISCUSSION: Common, or joint, costs cannot be identified with a particular joint product. By definition, joint products have common costs until the split-off point. Costs incurred after the split-off point are separable costs. The decision to continue processing beyond split-off is made separately for each product. The costs relevant to the decision are the separable costs because they can be avoided by selling at the split-off point. They should be compared with the incremental revenues from processing further. Thus, items I (revenue from selling at split-off point), II (variable costs of upgrade), III (avoidable fixed costs of upgrade), and IV (revenue from selling after further processing) are considered in making the upgrade decision.

11.7 Journal Entries

Questions 11.7.1 through 11.7.4 are based on the following information.

Lares Confectioners, Inc., makes a candy bar called Rey that sells for $.50 per pound. The manufacturing process also yields a product known as Nagu. Without further processing, Nagu sells for $.10 per pound. With further processing, Nagu sells for $.30 per pound. During the month of April, total joint manufacturing costs up to the point of separation consisted of the charges to work-in-process presented in the opposite column.

Direct materials	$150,000
Direct labor	120,000
Manufacturing overhead	30,000

Production for the month was 394,000 pounds of Rey and 30,000 pounds of Nagu. To complete Nagu during the month of April and obtain a selling price of $.30 per pound, further processing of Nagu during April required the following additional costs:

Direct materials	$2,000
Direct labor	1,500
Manufacturing overhead	500

11.7.1. If the joint costs of $300,000 are allocated based on relative net realizable values, and Nagu is considered a joint product rather than a by-product, what are the journal entries for Nagu and Rey to record the cost allocation and subsequent processing to the point at which both are in finished goods inventory?

A.

	Debit	Credit
Finished goods (Rey)	$292,574	
Work-in-process (Nagu)	7,426	
Work-in-process (joint)		$300,000
Work-in-process (Nagu)	$ 4,000	
Direct materials		$ 2,000
Direct labor		1,500
Manufacturing overhead		500
Finished goods (Nagu)	$ 11,426	
Work-in-process (Nagu)		$ 11,426

B.

	Debit	Credit
Work-in-process (Nagu)	$ 4,000	
Direct materials		$ 2,000
Direct labor		1,500
Manufacturing overhead		500

C.

	Debit	Credit
Work-in-process (Nagu)	$ 4,967	
Work-in-process (joint)		$ 4,967
Work-in-process (Nagu)	$ 4,000	
Direct materials		$ 2,000
Direct labor		1,500
Manufacturing overhead		500

D.

	Debit	Credit
Finished goods (Rey)	$295,033	
Work-in-process (Nagu)	4,967	
Work-in-process (joint)		$300,000
Work-in-process (Nagu)	$ 4,000	
Direct materials		$ 2,000
Direct labor		1,500
Manufacturing overhead		500
Finished goods (Nagu)	$ 8,967	
Work-in-process (Nagu)		$ 8,967

Answer (A) is correct. *(Publisher, adapted)*

REQUIRED: The journal entries to record transfer of joint products to finished goods after joint cost allocation based on relative NRV.

DISCUSSION: The final sales value of Nagu is $9,000 (30,000 lb. × $.30). The cost of additional processing is $4,000 ($2,000 + $1,500 + $500). Its NRV is therefore $5,000. The sales value of Rey continues to be $197,000 (394,000 × $.50). Thus, the allocation of the $300,000 of common costs is $292,574 to Rey {[$197,000 ÷ ($197,000 + $5,000)] × $300,000} and $7,426 to Nagu {[$5,000 ÷ ($197,000 + $5,000)] × $300,000}. Consequently, the amount transferred to finished goods (Nagu) is the sum of the joint cost allocation and the additional processing costs ($7,426 + $4,000 = $11,426).

Answer (B) is incorrect. An entry that debits finished goods (Rey) for $292,574 and work-in-process (Nagu) for $7,426 with a corresponding credit to work-in-process (joint) for $300,000 should be included. Also, an entry that debits finished goods (Nagu) for $11,426 and credits work-in-process (Nagu) for $11,426 should be included as the sum of the joint cost allocation and the additional processing costs ($7,426 + $4,000 = $11,426). Answer (C) is incorrect. The entry to allocate joint costs should be debits to finished goods (Rey) for $292,574 and work-in-process (Nagu) for $7,426, with a corresponding credit to work-in-process (joint) for $300,000. The third entry is a debit to finished goods (Nagu) for $11,426 and a corresponding credit to work-in-process (Nagu) for $11,426. Answer (D) is incorrect. The entry to allocate joint costs should be debits to finished goods (Rey) for $292,574 and work-in-process (Nagu) for $7,426, with a corresponding credit to work-in-process (joint) for $300,000. The third entry should be a debit to finished goods (Nagu) for $11,426 with a corresponding credit to work-in-process (Nagu) for $11,426.

11.7.2. What are the journal entries for Nagu if it is processed further and transferred to finished goods, with joint costs being allocated between Rey and Nagu based on relative sales value at the split-off point?

A.

Work-in-process (Nagu)	$4,500	
Work-in-process (Rey)		$4,500
Work-in-process (Nagu)	$4,000	
Direct materials		$2,000
Direct labor		1,500
Manufacturing overhead		500
Finished goods (Nagu)	$8,500	
Work-in-process (Nagu)		$8,500

B.

Work-in-process (Nagu)	$8,500	
Work-in-process (Rey)		$8,500
Finished goods (Nagu)	$8,500	
Work-in-process (Nagu)		$8,500

C.

Finished goods (Nagu)	$8,500	
Work-in-process (Nagu)		$8,500

D.

Work-in-process (Rey)	$4,500	
Work-in-process (Nagu)		$4,500
Work-in-process (Rey)	$4,000	
Direct materials		$2,000
Direct labor		1,500
Manufacturing overhead		500
Finished goods (Rey)	$8,500	
Work-in-process (Rey)		$8,500

Answer (A) is correct. *(Publisher, adapted)*

REQUIRED: The journal entries for joint products and further processing.

DISCUSSION: The initial journal entry requires the joint costs to be allocated between Rey and Nagu based on relative sales value at split-off. Total joint costs are $300,000 ($150,000 raw materials + $120,000 direct labor + $30,000 manufacturing overhead). The ratio to calculate Nagu's joint costs is

$$\frac{\text{Sales value of Nagu}}{\text{Total sales value of Rey and Nagu}}$$

$$\frac{30{,}000 \text{ lb.} \times \$.10}{(394{,}000 \text{ lb.} \times \$.50) + (30{,}000 \text{ lb.} \times \$.10)}$$

$$= \frac{\$3{,}000}{\$200{,}000} = .015 \text{ joint cost ratio}$$

Nagu's share of the joint costs is $4,500 ($300,000 × .015), and the journal entry is a debit to WIP (Nagu) and a credit to WIP (Rey) for this amount. The next journal entry to reflect the cost of further processing of Nagu is to debit WIP (Nagu) and credit direct materials, direct labor, and manufacturing overhead for the additional costs incurred. The final journal entry is to transfer the WIP costs of $8,500 to finished goods.

11.7.3. What is the journal entry for Nagu if it is further processed as a by-product and recorded as inventory at net realizable value, which reduces Rey's manufacturing costs?

A.

By-product inventory (Nagu)	$3,000	
Work-in-process (Rey)		$3,000

B.

By-product inventory (Nagu)	$4,000	
Direct materials		$2,000
Direct labor		1,500
Manufacturing overhead		500

C.

Work-in-process (Rey)	$5,000	
Direct materials	2,000	
Direct labor	1,500	
Manufacturing overhead	500	
By-product inventory (Nagu)		$9,000

D.

By-product inventory (Nagu)	$9,000	
Direct materials		$2,000
Direct labor		1,500
Manufacturing overhead		500
Work-in-process (Rey)		5,000

Answer (D) is correct. *(Publisher, adapted)*

REQUIRED: The journal entry to transfer a by-product at net realizable value.

DISCUSSION: NRV is the selling price minus the cost necessary to process further. After further processing, the NRV of Nagu is $5,000 [(30,000 lb. × $.30 per lb.) – $2,000 materials – $1,500 DL – $500 O/H]. Thus, the journal entry is a debit to by-product inventory of Nagu for the selling price and corresponding credits to direct materials, direct labor, and manufacturing overhead. The final credit of $5,000 is to work-in-process (Rey), assuming that Rey is still in process.

11.7.4. Refer to the information on the preceding page(s). Select the proper journal entry for Nagu if it is recorded as inventory at sales value without further processing, with a corresponding reduction of Rey's manufacturing costs.

A. By-product inventory	$3,000	
Finished goods		$3,000
B. By-product inventory	$3,000	
Work-in-process		$3,000
C. Work-in-process	$3,000	
By-product inventory		$3,000
D. Cost of goods sold	$3,000	
By-product inventory		$3,000

Answer (B) is correct. *(Publisher, adapted)*

REQUIRED: The appropriate journal entry to record a by-product transfer.

DISCUSSION: To transfer a by-product at sales value with a corresponding reduction of manufacturing costs requires estimation of the sales value of the transferred item. The selling price of Nagu is $3,000 (30,000 lb. produced × $.10 per lb. incremental cost) without further processing. The sales value is to be accounted for as a reduction in manufacturing costs. Accordingly, the debit and credit are to by-product inventory and work-in-process, respectively, if Rey is still in process.

Answer (A) is incorrect. Work-in-process should be credited for $3,000 to reduce the manufacturing costs. Answer (C) is incorrect. By-product inventory should be debited and work-in-process should be credited for $3,000 to reduce manufacturing costs. Answer (D) is incorrect. By-product inventory should be debited and work-in-process should be credited for $3,000 to reduce manufacturing costs.

11.8 Comprehensive

Questions 11.8.1 and 11.8.2 are based on the following information. Pickett Manufacturing uses a joint production process that produces three products at the split-off point. Joint production costs during April were $720,000. Product information for April was as follows:

	Product		
	R	S	T
Units produced	2,500	5,000	7,500
Units sold	2,000	6,000	7,000
Sales prices:			
At split-off	$100	$80	$20
After further processing	$150	$115	$30
Costs to process after split-off	$150,000	$150,000	$100,000

11.8.1. Assume that all three products are main products and that they can be sold at the split-off point or processed further, whichever is economically beneficial to the company. What is Pickett's total cost of Product S in April if joint cost allocation is based on sales value at split-off?

A. $375,000

B. $390,000

C. $510,000

D. $571,463

Answer (C) is correct. *(CIA, adapted)*

REQUIRED: The total cost of Product S in April.

DISCUSSION: Total sales value at split-off is $800,000 [(2,500 × $100) + (5,000 × $80) + (7,500 × $20)]. Product S accounts for 50% (5,000 × $80 = $400,000) of the sales value and therefore $360,000 ($720,000 × 50%) of the joint costs. The total cost of Product S is $510,000 ($360,000 allocated costs + $150,000 differential costs).

Answer (A) is incorrect. The amount of $375,000 is the total cost of R. Answer (B) is incorrect. The amount of $390,000 is based on the physical units method of allocating the joint costs. Answer (D) is incorrect. The amount of $571,463 uses the sales value at split-off based on actual sales.

11.8.2. Assume that Product T is treated as a by-product and that the company accounts for the by-product at net realizable value as a reduction of joint cost. Assume also that Products S and T must be processed further before they can be sold. What is Pickett's total cost of Product R in April if joint cost allocation is based on net realizable values?

A. $220,370

B. $370,370

C. $374,630

D. $595,000

Answer (A) is correct. *(CIA, adapted)*

REQUIRED: The total cost of Product R for April.

DISCUSSION: The net realizable value (NRV) method is an appropriate method of allocation when products cannot be sold at split-off. Further processing of R, which is salable at split-off, is not economical because the cost of $150,000 exceeds the benefit [2,500 units × ($150 – $100) = $125,000]. Thus, R's NRV is $250,000 (2,500 units × $100 price at split-off). However, S and T must be processed further. S's NRV is $425,000 [(5,000 units × $115) – $150,000], and T's NRV is $125,000 [(7,500 units × $30) – $100,000]. Given that the NRV of T is a reduction of joint cost, the total joint cost to be allocated is therefore $595,000 ($720,000 – $125,000 NRV of T). Accordingly, based on the NRV method, the joint cost allocated to R is $220,370 {[$250,000 R's NRV ÷ ($250,000 R's NRV + $425,000 S's NRV)] × $595,000 allocable joint cost}. Because further processing of R is uneconomical, the total cost of R is $220,370.

Answer (B) is incorrect. The amount of $370,370 includes additional processing costs. Answer (C) is incorrect. The amount of $374,630 is the joint cost allocated to S. Answer (D) is incorrect. The amount of $595,000 is the allocable joint cost.

Questions 11.8.3 and 11.8.4 are based on the following information. Sonimad Sawmill manufactures two lumber products from a joint milling process. The two products developed are mine support braces (MSB) and unseasoned commercial building lumber (CBL). A standard production run incurs joint costs of $300,000 and results in 60,000 units of MSB and 90,000 units of CBL. Each MSB sells for $2 per unit, and each CBL sells for $4 per unit.

11.8.3. Assuming no further processing work is done after the split-off point, the amount of joint cost allocated to commercial building lumber (CBL) on a physical quantity allocation basis would be

A. $75,000

B. $180,000

C. $225,000

D. $120,000

Answer (B) is correct. *(CMA, adapted)*

REQUIRED: The joint cost allocated to CBL based on physical quantities.

DISCUSSION: Given 60,000 units of MSB and 90,000 units of CBL (a total of 150,000 units), CBL makes up 60% of the total quantity (90,000 ÷ 150,000). Thus, CBL should be charged with 60% of the joint costs ($300,000 × 60% = $180,000).

Answer (A) is incorrect. The amount of $75,000 is the joint cost allocated to MSB based on the relative sales-value method. Answer (C) is incorrect. The amount of $225,000 is the joint cost allocated to CBL based on the relative sales-value method. Answer (D) is incorrect. The amount of $120,000 is the joint cost allocated to MSB based on physical quantities.

11.8.4. If there are no further processing costs incurred after the split-off point, the amount of joint cost allocated to the mine support braces (MSB) on a relative sales-value basis would be

A. $75,000

B. $180,000

C. $225,000

D. $120,000

Answer (A) is correct. *(CMA, adapted)*

REQUIRED: The joint cost allocated to MSB based on the relative sales-value method.

DISCUSSION: At $2 each, the 60,000 units of MSB sell for $120,000. At $4 each, the 90,000 units of CBL sell for $360,000. Because 25% [$120,000 ÷ ($120,000 + $360,000)] of the total sales is produced by MSB, it should absorb 25% of the joint cost. Thus, $75,000 ($300,000 joint cost × 25%) is allocated to MSB.

Answer (B) is incorrect. The amount of $180,000 is the joint cost allocated to CBL based on physical quantities. Answer (C) is incorrect. The amount of $225,000 is the joint cost allocated to CBL based on the relative sales-value method. Answer (D) is incorrect. The amount of $120,000 is the joint cost allocated to MSB based on physical quantities.

Questions 11.8.5 through 11.8.10 are based on the following information.

Doe Corporation grows, processes, cans, and sells three main pineapple products – sliced pineapple, crushed pineapple, and pineapple juice. The outside skin is cut off in the Cutting Department and processed as animal feed. The skin is treated as a by-product. Doe's production process is as follows:

Pineapples first are processed in the Cutting Department. The pineapples are washed, and the outside skin is cut away. Then the pineapples are cored and trimmed for slicing. The three main products (sliced, crushed, juice) and the by-product (animal feed) are recognizable after processing in the Cutting Department. Each product is then transferred to a separate department for final processing.

The trimmed pineapples are forwarded to the Slicing Department where they are sliced and canned. Any juice generated during the slicing operation is packed in the cans with the slices.

The pieces of pineapple trimmed from the fruit are diced and canned in the Crushing Department. Again, the juice generated during this operation is packed in the can with the crushed pineapple.

The core and surplus pineapple generated from the Cutting Department are pulverized into a liquid in the Juicing Department. An evaporation loss equal to 8% of the weight of the good output produced in this department occurs as the juices are heated.

The outside skin is chopped into animal feed in the Feed Department.

The Doe Corporation uses the net-realizable-value (relative sales-value) method to assign costs of the joint process to its main products. The by-product is inventoried at its net realizable value. The NRV of the by-product reduces the joint costs of the main products.

A total of 270,000 pounds entered the Cutting Department during May. The schedule below shows the costs incurred in each department, the proportion by weight transferred to the four final processing departments, and the selling price of each product.

Doe uses the net-realizable-value method of determining inventory values for all products and by-products.

May Processing Data and Costs

Department	Costs Incurred	Proportion of Product by Weight Transferred to Departments	Selling Price per Pound of Final Product
Cutting	$60,000	--	None
Slicing	4,700	35%	$.60
Crushing	10,580	28	.55
Juicing	3,250	27	.30
Animal Feed	700	10	.10
Total	$79,230	100%	

11.8.5. What is the total amount of separable costs for the three main products?

A. $15,280

B. $18,530

C. $16,750

D. $12,280

Answer (B) is correct. *(Publisher, adapted)*

REQUIRED: The total amount of separable costs for the three main products.

DISCUSSION: Separable costs for the three main products are the sum of the costs to further process the items to a salable state. The incremental costs incurred in slicing, crushing, and juicing are given. They total $18,530 ($4,700 + $10,580 + $3,250). The incremental costs incurred for animal feed are not included because they are the separable costs for the by-product.

Answer (A) is incorrect. The amount of $15,280 includes only incremental costs incurred in slicing and crushing and should also include incremental costs of $3,250 incurred in juicing. Answer (C) is incorrect. The total amount of separable costs for the three main products is $18,530 ($4,700 slicing + $10,580 crushing + $3,250 juicing). Answer (D) is incorrect. The total amount of separable costs for the three main products is $18,530 ($4,700 slicing + $10,580 crushing + $3,250 juicing).

11.8.6. How many net pounds of pineapple juice were produced in May?

A. 72,900

B. 79,200

C. 64,525

D. 67,500

Answer (D) is correct. *(Publisher, adapted)*

REQUIRED: The net pounds of pineapple juice produced during the period.

DISCUSSION: The gross pounds of pineapple juice are 27% of the 270,000 total pounds entered into the various production units, or 72,900 pounds. Also, 8% of the good output is lost to evaporation. The net amount of pineapple juice is

$$
\begin{aligned}
X &= 72{,}900 - .08X \\
1.08X &= 72{,}900 \\
X &= 67{,}500 \text{ lb.}
\end{aligned}
$$

Answer (A) is incorrect. The gross pounds of pineapple juice is 72,900. Answer (B) is incorrect. The net amount of pineapple juice is 67,500 lb. (72,900 gross pounds ÷ 1.08). Answer (C) is incorrect. The net amount of pineapple juice is 67,500 lb. (72,900 gross pounds ÷ 1.08).

11.8.7. What is the net realizable value at the split-off point of pineapple slices?

A. $52,000

B. $56,700

C. $49,800

D. $39,200

Answer (A) is correct. *(Publisher, adapted)*

REQUIRED: The net realizable value at split-off of pineapple slices.

DISCUSSION: The net realizable value at the split-off point can be estimated as the final sales revenue minus separable costs for further processing. Sales value equals the pounds of slices (270,000 × 35% = 94,500) times the selling price ($.60 per pound), or $56,700. The separable costs are given as $4,700. Accordingly, the net realizable value at split-off is $52,000 ($56,700 – $4,700).

Answer (B) is incorrect. The amount of $56,700 is the sales revenue of the slices. Separable costs of $4,700 should be subtracted from $56,700 to arrive at the net realizable value at split-off of $52,000. Answer (C) is incorrect. The net realizable value of pineapple slices at the split-off point is $52,000, equal to $56,700 sales revenue minus $4,700 separable costs. Answer (D) is incorrect. The net realizable value of pineapple slices at the split-off point is $52,000, equal to $56,700 sales revenue minus $4,700 separable costs.

11.8.8. What is the total amount of joint costs for the Cutting Department to be assigned to each of the three main products in accordance with Doe's policy?

A. $60,000

B. $57,300

C. $58,000

D. $62,300

Answer (C) is correct. *(Publisher, adapted)*

REQUIRED: The total joint costs to be allocated to the main products.

DISCUSSION: The joint costs to be allocated to main products are the Cutting Department costs minus any net revenue from the by-product. The animal feed's net revenue is $2,000 [sales value of $2,700 (270,000 lb. × 10% × $.10/lb.) – separable costs of $700]. The balance of joint costs of $58,000 ($60,000 total joint costs – $2,000 net by-product revenue) must be allocated to the main products in proportion to their net realizable values.

Answer (A) is incorrect. The amount of $60,000 is the total joint costs. Answer (B) is incorrect. The amount of $57,300 results from subtracting animal feed sales value of $2,700 from $60,000 of total joint costs, instead of subtracting animal feed net by-product revenue of $2,000. Answer (D) is incorrect. The maximum joint costs to be allocated is $60,000.

11.8.9. Refer to the information on the preceding page(s). How much of the joint costs is allocated to crushed pineapple?

A. $30,160

B. $18,350

C. $9,860

D. $17,980

Answer (D) is correct. *(Publisher, adapted)*

REQUIRED: The joint costs allocated to crushed pineapple.

DISCUSSION: The weights are found as percentages of total pounds. The pounds produced in Slicing equal 94,500 (270,000 × 35%), and the production of Crushing is 75,600 (270,000 × 28%).

Product	Pounds Produced	Selling Price	Sales Revenue	Separable Costs
Slices	94,500	$.60	$ 56,700	$ 4,700
Crushed	75,600	.55	41,580	10,580
Juice	67,500*	.30	20,250	3,250
Totals			$118,530	$18,530

*The gross pounds of pineapple juice are 27% of the 270,000 total pounds entered into the various production units, or 72,900 pounds. Also, 8% of the good output is lost to evaporation. The net amount of pineapple juice is

$$X = 72{,}900 - .08X$$
$$1.08X = 72{,}900$$
$$X = 67{,}500 \text{ lb.}$$

	Net Realizable Value	
	Amount	Percent
Slices	$ 52,000	52%
Crushed	31,000	31%
Juice	17,000	17%
Totals	$100,000	100%

The joint costs to be allocated are $60,000 minus $2,000 net by-product revenue [sales value of $2,700 (270,000 lb. × 10% × $.10 per lb.) – separable costs of $700]. The joint costs allocated to crushed pineapple are $17,980 ($58,000 × 31%).

Answer (A) is incorrect. The amount of $30,160 is the amount allocated to sliced pineapple. Answer (B) is incorrect. The amount of $18,350 equals total separable costs. Answer (C) is incorrect. The amount of $9,860 is the joint cost allocated to pineapple juice.

11.8.10. Refer to the information on the preceding page(s). What is the gross margin for the pineapple juice?

A. $9,860

B. $7,140

C. $3,250

D. $20,250

Answer (B) is correct. *(Publisher, adapted)*

REQUIRED: The gross margin for pineapple juice.

DISCUSSION: Gross margin for pineapple juice equals the sales revenue minus the separable costs and the juice's allotted proportion of joint costs. The allotted amount of joint costs equals $9,860 ($58,000 total joint cost* × 17% allocation percentage**).

Sales revenue (67,500 lb. × $.30)	$20,250
Separable cost	(3,250)
Proportionate joint costs	(9,860)
Gross margin	$ 7,140

*The joint costs to be allocated are $60,000 minus $2,000 net by-product revenue [sales value of $2,700 (270,000 lb. × 10% × $.10 per lb.) – separable costs of $700].

**The weights are found as percentages of total pounds. The pounds produced in Slicing equal 94,500 (270,000 × 35%), and the production of Crushing is 75,600 (270,000 × 28%). The gross pounds of pineapple juice are 27% of the 270,000 total pounds entered into the various production units, or 72,900 pounds. Also, 8% of the good output is lost to evaporation. The net amount of pineapple juice is 67,500 pounds (72,900 ÷ 1.08).

Product	Pounds Produced	Selling Price	Sales Revenue	Separable Costs
Slices	94,500	$.60	$ 56,700	$ 4,700
Crushed	75,600	.55	41,580	10,580
Juice	67,500	.30	20,250	3,250
Totals			$118,530	$18,530

	Net Realizable Value Amount	Percent
Slices	$ 52,000	52%
Crushed	31,000	31%
Juice	17,000	17%
Totals	$100,000	100%

17% allocation percentage = 17,000 ÷ 100,000 = 17%

Answer (A) is incorrect. The amount of $9,860 is the joint cost allocated to the pineapple juice. Answer (C) is incorrect. The amount of $3,250 is the separable cost of the pineapple juice. Answer (D) is incorrect. The amount of $20,250 is the sales revenue for the pineapple juice. A gross margin of $7,140 is obtained by subtracting $3,250 separable cost and $9,860 joint cost from the sales revenue of $20,250.

Questions 11.8.11 and 11.8.12 are based on the following information. Sonimad Sawmill manufactures two lumber products from a joint milling process. The two products developed are mine support braces (MSB) and unseasoned commercial building lumber (CBL). A standard production run incurs joint costs of $300,000 and results in 60,000 units of MSB and 90,000 units of CBL. Each MSB sells for $2 per unit, and each CBL sells for $4 per unit. Continuing with the data provided above, assume the commercial building lumber is not marketable at split-off but must be further planed and sized at a cost of $200,000 per production run. During this process, 10,000 units are unavoidably lost; these spoiled units have no discernible value. The remaining units of commercial building lumber are salable at $10.00 per unit. The mine support braces, although salable immediately at the split-off point, are coated with a tar-like preservative that costs $100,000 per production run. The braces are then sold for $5 each.

11.8.11. Using the net-realizable-value (NRV) basis, the completed cost assigned to each unit of commercial building lumber would be

A. $2.92

B. $5.625

C. $2.50

D. $5.3125

Answer (D) is correct. *(CMA, adapted)*

REQUIRED: The completed cost assigned to each unit of commercial building lumber using the NRV method.

DISCUSSION: The first step is to compute the sales for each product. The 60,000 units of MSB will sell for $5 each after further processing at a cost of $100,000. Their NRV is $200,000 [(60,000 units × $5) – $100,000]. The 80,000 units of CBL sell for $10 each, or $800,000, after further processing. But to determine the NRV for CBL, the costs of this processing must be deducted from sales. Consequently, the NRV for CBL is $600,000 ($800,000 – $200,000). CBL therefore contributes 75% [$600,000 ÷ ($200,000 + $600,000)] of the realizable value and should bear an equal proportion of the $300,000 of joint costs, or $225,000. The total cost of CBL is $425,000 ($225,000 joint cost + $200,000 further processing costs), and the unit cost is $5.3125 ($425,000 ÷ 80,000).

Answer (A) is incorrect. The amount of $2.92 is the completed cost assigned to each MSB using the NRV method [($75,000 joint cost + $100,000 further processing costs) ÷ 60,000 units]. Answer (B) is incorrect. The amount of $5.625 is determined by using a sales price for MSB of $2.00 instead of $5.00, which is the sales price for MSB after further processing. Answer (C) is incorrect. The completed cost assigned to each unit of CBL using the NRV method is $5.3125 [80,000 units of CBL ÷ ($225,000 joint cost + $200,000 additional processing costs)].

11.8.12. If Sonimad Sawmill chose not to process the mine support braces beyond the split-off point, the contribution from the joint milling process would be

A. $120,000 higher.

B. $180,000 lower.

C. $100,000 higher.

D. $80,000 lower.

Answer (D) is correct. *(CMA, adapted)*

REQUIRED: The difference in contribution from the joint milling process if MSB are not processed further.

DISCUSSION: MSB sell for $120,000 (60,000 units × $2) at the split-off point. By processing further, the company earns $200,000 ($300,000 in sales – $100,000 in preservative costs). Thus, the contribution from the joint milling process would be $80,000 lower ($200,000 – $120,000) if MSB are sold at the split-off point.

Answer (A) is incorrect. The sales value at split-off is $120,000. Answer (B) is incorrect. The amount of $180,000 ignores the preservative costs. Answer (C) is incorrect. The cost of processing MSB further is $100,000.

STUDY UNIT TWELVE
QUALITY

Quality is a vital issue in a competitive world economy. Improving quality (1) increases demand (and market share) through heightened customer satisfaction, (2) significantly lowers costs, (3) creates goodwill, and (4) increases employee expertise. Quality has been defined in numerous ways. One approach focuses on the dimensions of quality: (1) performance, (2) aesthetics, (3) features, (4) reliability, (5) durability, (6) serviceability, (7) fitness of use, (8) perceived quality, and (9) conformance. The traditional view is that conforming products have characteristics within an acceptable range of values that includes a target value. The modern view is the **zero-defects** approach that seeks to eliminate all nonconforming output. An extension of this approach is **robust quality**. Its goal is to meet the target value in every case.

Total quality management (TQM) is a comprehensive approach that treats quality as a basic organizational function. TQM is the continuous pursuit of quality in every aspect of organizational activities through a philosophy of (1) doing it right the first time, (2) employee training and empowerment, (3) promotion of teamwork, (4) **continuous improvement** of **processes**, and (5) attention to satisfaction of internal and external customers. TQM (1) emphasizes the supplier's relationship with the customer, (2) identifies customer needs, and (3) recognizes that everyone in a process is at some time a customer or supplier of someone else, within or outside of the organization.

The **costs of quality** must be assessed in terms of relative costs and benefits. **Conformance** (control) costs include costs of prevention and costs of appraisal (financial measures of internal performance). **Prevention** costs result in high returns because preventing a problem is cheaper than finding and correcting it. **Appraisal** embraces such activities as inspection and testing of materials, in-process items, finished goods, and packaging. **Nonconformance (failure) costs** include internal failure costs (a financial measure of internal performance) and external failure costs (a financial measure of customer satisfaction). **Internal failure** costs occur when nonconforming products or services are detected before delivery. **External failure** costs are incurred after delivery because products or services are nonconforming or otherwise do not satisfy customers.

Spoiled goods cannot be reworked. Traditional systems distinguished between normal and abnormal spoilage because some spoilage was viewed as inevitable. However, rigorous approaches to quality regard normal spoilage as minimal or even nonexistent. Thus, all spoilage may be identified as abnormal. **Normal spoilage** occurs under normal, efficient operating conditions. It is uncontrollable in the short run and therefore should be expressed as a function of good output (treated as a product cost). Accordingly, normal spoilage is assigned to all good units in process costing systems. **Abnormal spoilage** is not expected to occur under normal, efficient operating conditions. The cost of abnormal spoilage should be separately identified and reported. Abnormal spoilage typically is treated as a period cost (a loss) because it is unusual.

Scrap consists of materials left over from production but still usable for other purposes. Scrap may be sold to outside customers, usually for a nominal amount, or used for a different process. Scrap is recorded at the time of production or at the time of sale. **Normal rework** costs common to all jobs are customarily debited to manufacturing overhead control, with credits to materials, wages payable, and overhead applied. If they relate to a specific job, they are debited to work-in-process for that job. Abnormal rework is debited to a loss account.

QUESTIONS

12.1 Quality

12.1.1. The International Organization for Standardization has developed the ISO 9000 quality standards. The standards for ring networks include fault management, configuration management, accounting management, security management, and performance monitoring. Which of the following controls is included in the performance-monitoring standards?

A. Reporting the failure of network fiber-optic lines.

B. Recording unauthorized access violations.

C. Compiling statistics on the number of times that application software is used.

D. Allocating network costs to system users of the network.

Answer (C) is correct. *(CIA, adapted)*

REQUIRED: The controls included in the ISO 9000 performance-monitoring standards.

DISCUSSION: The International Organization for Standardization consists of standards organizations from more than 150 countries. The ISO 9000 performance-monitoring standards pertain to management's ongoing assessment of the quality of performance over time. Recording software usage is a performance-monitoring control related to the extent and efficiency of network software use.

Answer (A) is incorrect. The failure of network fiber-optic lines is a fault management control. Answer (B) is incorrect. Recording unauthorized access violations is a security management control. Answer (D) is incorrect. Allocating network costs to system users of the network is an accounting management control.

12.1.2. A traditional quality control process in manufacturing consists of mass inspection of goods only at the end of a production process. A major deficiency of the traditional control process is that

A. It is expensive to do the inspections at the end of the process.

B. It is not possible to rework defective items.

C. It is not 100% effective.

D. It does not focus on improving the entire production process.

Answer (D) is correct. *(CIA, adapted)*

REQUIRED: The major deficiency of mass inspection of goods only at the end of production.

DISCUSSION: The process used to produce the goods is not thoroughly reviewed and evaluated for efficiency and effectiveness. A total quality management approach is superior because it focuses on continuous improvement in every aspect of organizational activities. Preventing defects and increasing efficiency by improving the production process raise quality standards and decrease costs.

Answer (A) is incorrect. Other quality control processes can also be expensive. Answer (B) is incorrect. Reworking defective items may be possible although costly. Answer (C) is incorrect. No quality control system will be 100% effective.

12.1.3. Total quality management (TQM) in a manufacturing environment is best exemplified by

A. Identifying and reworking production defects before sale.

B. Designing the product to minimize defects.

C. Performing inspections to isolate defects as early as possible.

D. Making machine adjustments periodically to reduce defects.

Answer (B) is correct. *(CIA, adapted)*

REQUIRED: The activity characteristic of TQM.

DISCUSSION: TQM emphasizes quality as a basic organizational function. TQM is the continuous pursuit of quality in every aspect of organizational activities. One of the basic principles of TQM is doing it right the first time. Thus, errors should be caught and corrected at the source, and quality should be built in (designed in) from the start.

12.1.4. One of the main reasons that implementation of a total quality management program works better through the use of teams is

A. Teams are more efficient and help an organization reduce its staffing.

B. Employee motivation is always higher for team members than for individual contributors.

C. Teams are a natural vehicle for sharing ideas, which leads to process improvement.

D. The use of teams eliminates the need for supervision, thereby allowing a company to reduce staffing.

Answer (C) is correct. *(CIA, adapted)*

REQUIRED: The reason that implementation of a TQM program works better through the use of teams.

DISCUSSION: TQM promotes teamwork by modifying or eliminating traditional (and rigid) vertical hierarchies and instead forming flexible groups of specialists. Quality circles, cross-functional teams, and self-managed teams are typical formats. Teams are an excellent vehicle for encouraging the sharing of ideas and removing process improvement obstacles.

Answer (A) is incorrect. Teams are often inefficient and costly. Answer (B) is incorrect. High motivation does not directly affect the process improvement that is the key to quality improvement. Answer (D) is incorrect. The use of teams with less supervision and reduced staffing may be by-products of TQM, but they are not ultimate objectives.

12.1.5. Focusing on customers, promoting innovation, learning new philosophies, driving out fear, and providing extensive training are all elements of a major change in organizations. These elements are aimed primarily at

A. Copying leading organizations to better compete with them.

B. Focusing on the total quality of products and services.

C. Being efficient and effective at the same time, in order to indirectly affect profits.

D. Managing costs of products and services better, in order to become the low-cost provider.

Answer (B) is correct. *(CIA, adapted)*

REQUIRED: The purpose of focusing on customers, promoting innovation, learning new philosophies, driving out fear, and providing extensive training.

DISCUSSION: TQM is a comprehensive approach to quality. It treats the pursuit of quality as a basic organizational function that is as important as production or marketing. TQM is the continuous pursuit of quality in every aspect of organizational activities through a philosophy of (1) doing it right the first time, (2) employee training and empowerment, (3) promotion of teamwork, (4) improvement of processes, and (5) attention to satisfaction of internal and external customers. TQM (1) emphasizes the supplier's relationship with the customer, (2) identifies customer needs, and (3) recognizes that everyone in a process is at some time a customer or supplier of someone else, either within or without the organization.

Answer (A) is incorrect. Competitive benchmarking is just one tool for implementing TQM. Answer (C) is incorrect. TQM emphasizes quality improvement, not profitability or cost reduction. Answer (D) is incorrect. TQM emphasizes quality improvement, not profitability or cost reduction.

12.1.6. One of the main reasons total quality management (TQM) can be used as a strategic weapon is that

A. The cumulative improvement from a company's TQM efforts cannot readily be copied by competitors.

B. Introducing new products can lure customers away from competitors.

C. Reduced costs associated with better quality can support higher shareholder dividends.

D. TQM provides a comprehensive planning process for a business.

Answer (A) is correct. *(CIA, adapted)*

REQUIRED: The reason TQM can be used as a strategic weapon.

DISCUSSION: Because TQM affects every aspect of the organization's activities, it permeates the organizational culture. Thus, the cumulative effect of TQM's continuous improvement process can attract and hold customers and cannot be duplicated by competitors.

Answer (B) is incorrect. New products can be quickly copied by competitors and therefore do not provide a sustained competitive advantage. Answer (C) is incorrect. TQM does not focus solely on cost reduction. Answer (D) is incorrect. TQM is only one tool of strategic management.

12.1.7. Under a total quality management (TQM) approach,

A. Measurement occurs throughout the process, and errors are caught and corrected at the source.

B. Quality control is performed by highly trained inspectors at the end of the production process.

C. Upper management assumes the primary responsibility for the quality of the products and services.

D. A large number of suppliers are used in order to obtain the lowest possible prices.

Answer (A) is correct. *(CIA, adapted)*

REQUIRED: The true statement about total quality management.

DISCUSSION: Total quality management emphasizes quality as a basic organizational function. TQM is the continuous pursuit of quality in every aspect of organizational activities. One of the basic tenets of TQM is doing it right the first time. Thus, errors should be caught and corrected at the source.

Answer (B) is incorrect. Total quality management emphasizes discovering errors throughout the process, not inspection of finished goods. Answer (C) is incorrect. All members of the organization assume responsibility for quality of the products and services. Answer (D) is incorrect. The total quality management philosophy recommends limiting the number of suppliers to create a strong relationship.

12.1.8. Which of the following is a characteristic of total quality management (TQM)?

A. Management by objectives.

B. On-the-job training by other workers.

C. Quality by final inspection.

D. Education and self-improvement.

Answer (D) is correct. *(CIA, adapted)*

REQUIRED: The characteristic of TQM.

DISCUSSION: Education and self-improvement are essential. Hence, continuous improvement should be everyone's primary career objective.

Answer (A) is incorrect. Management by objectives is a system with an aggressive pursuit of numerical quotas. Answer (B) is incorrect. Informal learning from coworkers serves to entrench bad work habits, while TQM stresses proper training of everyone. Answer (C) is incorrect. Quality by final inspection is unnecessary if quality is built in from the start.

12.1.9. In which of the following organizational structures does total quality management (TQM) work best?

A. Hierarchical.

B. Teams of people from the same specialty.

C. Teams of people from different specialties.

D. Specialists working individually.

Answer (C) is correct. *(CIA, adapted)*

REQUIRED: The structure in which TQM works best.

DISCUSSION: TQM advocates replacement of the traditional hierarchical structure with teams of people from different specialties. This change follows from TQM's emphasis on empowering employees and teamwork.

Answer (A) is incorrect. Hierarchical organization stifles TQM. Answer (B) is incorrect. TQM works best by bringing together specialists from different areas who can share contrasting perspectives. Answer (D) is incorrect. Teamwork is essential for TQM.

12.1.10. Which one of the following is not a characteristic of an innovative manufacturer?

A. Emphasis on continuous improvement.

B. Responsiveness to the changing manufacturing environment.

C. Emphasis on existing products.

D. Improved customer satisfaction through product quality.

Answer (C) is correct. *(CIA, adapted)*

REQUIRED: The item not a characteristic of innovative manufacturers.

DISCUSSION: Innovators are customer driven. Because customers demand ever better quality and competitors are attempting to provide that quality, continuous improvement (called kaizen by the Japanese) is essential. Thus, the flow of innovative products and services must be continuous. Simply emphasizing existing products is not an effective strategy for most organizations.

Answer (A) is incorrect. Continuous improvement is important for achieving and maintaining high levels of performance. Answer (B) is incorrect. More and more manufacturers are automating to (1) achieve high quality, (2) deliver customized products on time, (3) minimize inventory, and (4) increase flexibility. Answer (D) is incorrect. Customer satisfaction is the highest priority according to modern management practice.

12.1.11. The most important component of quality control is

A. Ensuring goods and services conform to the design specifications.

B. Satisfying upper management.

C. Conforming with ISO 9000 specifications.

D. Determining the appropriate timing of inspections.

Answer (A) is correct. *(CIA, adapted)*

REQUIRED: The most important component of quality control.

DISCUSSION: The intent of quality control is to ensure that goods and services conform to the design specifications. Whether the focus is on feedforward, feedback, or concurrent control, the emphasis is on ensuring product or service conformity.

Answer (B) is incorrect. Quality control emphasizes satisfying the customer, not upper management. Answer (C) is incorrect. Ensuring conformance with ISO 9000 specifications is a component of a compliance audit, not quality control. Answer (D) is incorrect. Determining the appropriate timing of inspections is only one step towards approaching quality control. Consequently, it is not the primary component of the quality control function.

12.1.12. Which of the following is a key to successful total quality management (TQM)?

A. Training quality inspectors.

B. Focusing intensely on the customer.

C. Creating appropriate hierarchies to increase efficiency.

D. Establishing a well-defined quality standard, then focusing on meeting it.

Answer (B) is correct. *(CIA, adapted)*

REQUIRED: The key to successful total quality management.

DISCUSSION: TQM emphasizes satisfaction of customers, both internal and external. TQM (1) considers the supplier's relationship with the customer, (2) identifies customer needs, and (3) recognizes that everyone in a process is at some time a customer or supplier of someone else, within or outside the organization. Thus, TQM (1) begins with external customer requirements, (2) identifies internal customer-supplier relationships and requirements, and (3) establishes requirements for external suppliers.

Answer (A) is incorrect. TQM de-emphasizes specialized quality inspectors. Answer (C) is incorrect. Centralization often needs to be reduced to implement a TQM process. Answer (D) is incorrect. TQM involves continuous improvement. After a standard is reached, continuous improvement requires its constant reevaluation.

12.1.13. If a company is customer-centered, its customers are defined as

A. Only people external to the company who have purchased something from the company.

B. Only people internal to the company who directly use its product.

C. Anyone external to the company and those internal who rely on its product to get their job done.

D. Everybody external to the company who is currently doing, or may in the future do, business with the company.

Answer (C) is correct. *(CIA, adapted)*

REQUIRED: The definition of customers if a firm is customer-centered.

DISCUSSION: One of the principles of TQM is customer orientation, whether the customer is internal or external. An internal customer is a member of the organization who relies on another member's work to accomplish his or her task.

12.1.14. Quality control circles are now used all over the world. They typically consist of a group of 5 to 10 employees who meet regularly. The primary goal of these circles is

A. To improve the quality of leadership in the organization.

B. To tap the creative problem-solving potential of every employee.

C. To improve communications between employees and managers by providing a formal communication channel.

D. To allow for the emergence of team leaders who can be targeted for further leadership development.

Answer (B) is correct. *(CIA, adapted)*

REQUIRED: The primary goal of quality control circles.

DISCUSSION: Quality control circles are used to obtain voluntary input from employees to promote problem solving. Potential benefits include (1) lower costs, (2) better employer-employee relations, and (3) greater employee commitment.

Answer (A) is incorrect. Improving the quality of leadership is not the primary goal of quality control circles. Answer (C) is incorrect. Improved communication is a by-product of quality control circles. Answer (D) is incorrect. The emergence of team leaders who can be chosen for further leadership development is a by-product of the quality control circles.

12.1.15. The four categories of costs associated with product quality costs are

A. External failure, internal failure, prevention, and carrying.

B. External failure, internal failure, prevention, and appraisal.

C. Warranty, product liability, training, and appraisal.

D. Warranty, product liability, prevention, and appraisal.

Answer (B) is correct. *(CMA, adapted)*

REQUIRED: The categories of product quality costs.

DISCUSSION: The four categories of quality costs are (1) prevention, (2) appraisal, (3) internal failure, and (4) external failure. Costs of prevention include attempts to avoid defective output, such as (1) employee training, (2) review of equipment design, (3) preventive maintenance, and (4) evaluation of suppliers. Appraisal includes quality control programs, inspection, and testing. Internal failure costs are incurred when detection of defective products occurs before shipment. They include costs of (1) scrap, (2) rework, (3) tooling changes, and (4) downtime. External failure costs are incurred after the product has been shipped. They include the costs associated with warranties, product liability, and loss of customer goodwill.

12.1.16. A company produced and sold 100,000 units of a component with a variable cost of $20 per unit. First-quality components have a selling price of $50. The component's specifications require its weight to be 20 kg. with a tolerance of ±1 kg. Unfortunately, 1,200 of the units produced failed the company's tolerance specifications. These 1,200 units were reworked at a cost of $12 per unit and sold as factory seconds at $45 each. Had the company had a quality assurance program in place such that all units produced conformed to specifications, the increase in the company's contribution margin from this component would have been

A. $14,400

B. $20,400

C. $21,600

D. $39,600

Answer (B) is correct. *(CIA, adapted)*

REQUIRED: The increase in the contribution margin if a quality assurance program had been established.

DISCUSSION: The loss per unit includes the cost of rework and the reduction in the selling price. Consequently, the increase in the contribution margin if all units meet specifications is $20,400 {1,200 × [$12 + ($50 – $45)]}.

Answer (A) is incorrect. The amount of $14,400 ignores the price reduction. Answer (C) is incorrect. The amount of $21,600 is the contribution from the 1,200 units at the original price, minus rework costs. Answer (D) is incorrect. The amount of $39,600 is the revenue from the 1,200 units at the reduced price, minus rework costs.

Questions 12.1.17 and 12.1.18 are based on the following information. Listed below are costs of quality that a manufacturing company has incurred throughout its operations. The company plans to prepare a report that classifies these costs into the following four categories: preventive costs, appraisal costs, internal failure costs, and external failure costs.

Cost Items	Amount
Design reviews	$275,000
Finished goods returned due to failure	55,000
Freight on replacement finished goods	27,000
Labor inspection during manufacturing	75,000
Labor inspection of raw materials	32,000
Manufacturing product-testing labor	63,000
Manufacturing rework labor and overhead	150,000
Materials used in warranty repairs	68,000
Process engineering	180,000
Product-liability claims	145,000
Product-testing equipment	35,000
Repairs to equipment due to breakdowns	22,000
Scheduled equipment maintenance	90,000
Scrap material	125,000
Training of manufacturing workers	156,000

12.1.17. The costs of quality that are incurred in detecting units of product that do not conform to product specifications are referred to as

A. Preventive costs.

B. Appraisal costs.

C. Internal failure costs.

D. External failure costs.

Answer (B) is correct. *(CIA, adapted)*

REQUIRED: The costs of quality incurred in detecting units that do not conform to specifications.

DISCUSSION: The categories of quality costs include conformance costs (prevention and appraisal) and nonconformance costs (internal failure and external failure). Appraisal costs embrace such activities as statistical quality control programs, inspection, and testing. Thus, the cost of detecting nonconforming products is an appraisal cost.

Answer (A) is incorrect. Prevention attempts to avoid defective output, e.g., by employee training, review of equipment design, preventive maintenance, and evaluation of suppliers. Answer (C) is incorrect. Internal failure costs are incurred when detection of defective products occurs before shipment, including scrap, rework, tooling changes, and downtime. Answer (D) is incorrect. External failure costs are incurred after shipment, including the costs associated with warranties, product liability, and loss of customer goodwill.

12.1.18. The dollar amount of the costs of quality classified as preventive costs for the manufacturing firm would be

A. $643,000

B. $701,000

C. $736,000

D. $768,000

Answer (B) is correct. *(CIA, adapted)*

REQUIRED: The preventive costs.

DISCUSSION: Prevention attempts to avoid defective output, e.g., by employee training, review of equipment design, preventive maintenance, and evaluation of suppliers. Accordingly, the preventive costs equal $701,000 ($275,000 design reviews + $180,000 process engineering + $90,000 scheduled maintenance + $156,000 training).

Answer (A) is incorrect. The amount of $643,000 omits scheduled equipment maintenance and includes labor inspection of raw materials (an appraisal cost). Answer (C) is incorrect. The amount of $736,000 includes the cost of product testing equipment (an appraisal cost). Answer (D) is incorrect. The amount of $768,000 includes the cost of product testing equipment and labor inspection of raw materials. Both costs are appraisal costs.

12.1.19. In a quality control program, which of the following is (are) categorized as internal failure costs?

I. Rework
II. Responding to customer complaints
III. Statistical quality control procedures

A. I only.
B. II only.
C. III only.
D. I, II, and III.

Answer (A) is correct. *(CPA, adapted)*
REQUIRED: The item(s) categorized as internal failure costs.
DISCUSSION: Internal failure costs are those incurred when detection of defective products occurs before shipment. Examples are scrap, rework, tooling changes, and downtime.

12.1.20. Management of a company is attempting to build a reputation as a world-class manufacturer of quality products. Which of the four costs would be the most damaging to its ability to build a reputation as a world-class manufacturer?

A. Prevention costs.
B. Appraisal costs.
C. Internal failure costs.
D. External failure costs.

Answer (D) is correct. *(CIA, adapted)*
REQUIRED: The cost most damaging to a manufacturer's reputation.
DISCUSSION: The entity must avoid external failures. If customers perceive its products to be of low quality, it will not have reputation as a world-class manufacturer. Thus, it should emphasize conformance (prevention and appraisal).
Answer (A) is incorrect. The entity must avoid shipment of poor quality products. Incurrence of prevention cost is preferable to external failure costs. Answer (B) is incorrect. The entity must avoid shipment of poor quality products. Incurrence of the costs of appraisal is preferable to external failure costs. Answer (C) is incorrect. The entity must avoid shipment of poor quality products. Incurrence of the costs of internal failure is preferable to external failure costs.

12.1.21. All of the following generally are included in a cost-of-quality report except

A. Warranty claims.
B. Design engineering.
C. Supplier evaluations.
D. Lost contribution margin.

Answer (D) is correct. *(CMA, adapted)*
REQUIRED: The item that does not normally appear in a cost-of-quality report.
DISCUSSION: A cost-of-quality report includes most costs related to quality, including the costs of (1) external failure, (2) internal failure, (3) prevention, and (4) appraisal. Lost contribution margins from poor product quality are external failure costs that normally do not appear on a cost-of-quality report because they are opportunity costs. Opportunity costs are not usually recorded by the accounting system, thereby understating the costs of poor quality.
Answer (A) is incorrect. The costs of warranty claims are readily measurable external failure costs recorded by the accounting system. Answer (B) is incorrect. The costs of design engineering are prevention costs that are usually included in cost-of-quality reports. Answer (C) is incorrect. The costs of supplier evaluations are prevention costs that are usually included in cost-of-quality reports.

12.1.22. Nonfinancial performance measures are important to engineering and operations managers in assessing the quality levels of their products. Which of the following indicators can be used to measure product quality?

I. Returns and allowances
II. Number and types of customer complaints
III. Production cycle time

A. I and II only.
B. I and III only.
C. II and III only.
D. I, II, and III.

Answer (A) is correct. *(CPA, adapted)*
REQUIRED: The indicators of product quality.
DISCUSSION: Nonfinancial performance measures, such as product quality, are useful for day-to-day control purposes. Examples (indicators) of nonfinancial performance measures include the following: outgoing quality level for each product line, returned merchandise, customer report card, competitive rank, and on-time delivery.

12.1.23. In Year 4, a manufacturing company instituted a total quality management (TQM) program producing the following report:

Summary Cost of Quality Report
(in thousands)

	Year 3	Year 4	% Change
Prevention costs	$ 200	$ 300	+50
Appraisal costs	210	315	+50
Internal failure costs	190	114	–40
External failure costs	1,200	621	–48
Total quality costs	$1,800	$1,350	–25

On the basis of this report, which one of the following statements is most likely true?

A. An increase in conformance costs resulted in a higher-quality product and a decrease in nonconformance costs.

B. An increase in inspection costs was solely responsible for the decrease in quality costs.

C. Quality costs such as scrap and rework decreased by 48%.

D. Quality costs such as returns and repairs under warranty decreased by 40%.

Answer (A) is correct. *(CMA, adapted)*

REQUIRED: The true statement about a report prepared by an entity adopting a TQM program.

DISCUSSION: TQM emphasizes the supplier's relationship with the customer and recognizes that everyone in a process is at some time a customer or supplier of someone else either within or outside the organization. The costs of quality include costs of conformance and costs of nonconformance. Costs of conformance include prevention costs and appraisal costs. Nonconformance costs are composed of internal failure costs and external failure costs. Conformance costs (prevention and appraisal) increased substantially. But the nonconformance costs (internal and external failure) decreased. Thus, the increase in conformance costs resulted in a higher-quality product.

Answer (B) is incorrect. Prevention costs also increased substantially, which could also have led to higher-quality products. Answer (C) is incorrect. Scrap and rework are internal failure costs, which decreased by 40%. Answer (D) is incorrect. Returns and repairs are external failure costs, which decreased by 48%.

12.1.24. Management of a company is attempting to build a reputation as a world-class manufacturer of quality products. Which of the following measures would not be used by the firm to measure quality?

A. The percentage of shipments returned by customers because of poor quality.

B. The number of parts shipped per day.

C. The number of defective parts per million.

D. The percentage of products passing quality tests the first time.

Answer (B) is correct. *(CIA, adapted)*

REQUIRED: The item not used for quality measurement.

DISCUSSION: The number of parts shipped per day is most likely to be used as a measure of the effectiveness and efficiency of shipping procedures, not the quality of the product. This measure does not consider how many of the parts are defective.

Answer (A) is incorrect. The percentage of shipments returned is a very useful direct measure of the number of unacceptable products. Answer (C) is incorrect. The number of defective parts per million, a simple and direct measure of poor quality, is likely to be used. Answer (D) is incorrect. The percentage of products passing quality tests the first time measures quality by the number of nondefective products.

12.1.25. Conformance is how well a product and its components meet applicable standards. According to the robust quality concept,

A. A certain percentage of defective units is acceptable.

B. Units are acceptable if their characteristics lie within an acceptable range of values.

C. The goal is for all units to be within specifications.

D. Every unit should reach a target value.

Answer (D) is correct. *(Publisher, adapted)*

REQUIRED: The true statement about robust quality.

DISCUSSION: The traditional view is that conforming products have characteristics within an acceptable specified range of values that includes a target value. This view also regards a certain percentage of defective (nonconforming) units as acceptable. The traditional view was superseded by the zero-defects approach that seeks to eliminate all nonconforming output. An extension of this approach is the robust quality concept. Its goal is to seeks the target value in every case. The reason is that hidden quality costs occur when output varies from the target even though the units are within specifications.

Answer (A) is incorrect. The traditional view of quality treats a certain number of defective units as acceptable. Moreover, a unit is deemed to be acceptable if it is within a range of specified values. Answer (B) is incorrect. The traditional view of quality treats a certain number of defective units as acceptable. Moreover, a unit is deemed to be acceptable if it is within a range of specified values. Answer (C) is incorrect. The robust quality concept is an extension of the zero-defects approach. The goal of robust quality is in every case to reach a target value, not merely a range of acceptable values.

12.1.26. Quality cost indices are often used to measure and analyze the cost of maintaining or improving the level of quality. Such indices are computed by dividing the total cost of quality over a given period by some measure of activity during that period (for example, sales dollars). The following cost data are available for a company for the month of March. The company's quality cost index is calculated using total cost of quality divided by sales dollars.

Sales	$400,000
Direct materials cost	100,000
Direct labor cost	80,000
Testing and inspection cost	6,400
Scrap and rework cost	16,800
Quality planning cost	2,800
Cost of customer complaints and returns	4,000

The quality cost index for March is

A. 7.5%

B. 6.5%

C. 22.0%

D. 5.9%

Answer (A) is correct. *(CIA, adapted)*

REQUIRED: The quality cost index for March.

DISCUSSION: The total cost of quality equals the sum of prevention costs (quality planning), appraisal costs (testing and inspection), internal failure costs (scrap and rework), and external failure costs (customer complaints and returns), or $30,000 ($2,800 + $6,400 + $16,800 + $4,000). The quality cost index equals the total costs of quality, divided by sales, times 100%. Thus, the quality cost index for March is 7.5% [($30,000 ÷ $400,000) × 100%].

Answer (B) is incorrect. The percentage of 6.5 does not include the $4,000 cost of customer complaints. Answer (C) is incorrect. The sum of direct labor and testing and inspection costs, divided by sales, equals 22.0%. Answer (D) is incorrect. The percentage of 5.9 does not include testing and inspection cost in quality costs.

12.1.27. According to current accounting literature, the dimensions of quality most likely include

	Perceived Quality	Aesthetics	Cost
A.	Yes	Yes	Yes
B.	Yes	Yes	No
C.	No	No	Yes
D.	No	No	No

Answer (B) is correct. *(Publisher, adapted)*

REQUIRED: The listed dimension(s), if any, of quality.

DISCUSSION: The dimensions of quality include (1) perceived quality, (2) aesthetics, (3) performance, (4) features, (5) reliability, (6) durability, (7) serviceability, (8) fitness of use, and (9) conformance. Perceived quality is the reputation of a product or service derived from customers' past experience with the provider. Aesthetics is the dimension of subjective judgments about the appearance of tangible products or of the facilities, personnel, etc., related to services. However, cost is not normally regarded as a separate dimension of quality. It may be a factor that influences the perception of quality, but it is not the sole factor. Moreover, cost does not relate to fitness for use. Thus, a cheaper product is not necessarily a lower-quality product.

12.1.28. The following information is available for Portia Co. for its past 2 fiscal years:

	Year 1	Year 2
Statistical process control	$ 70,000	$ 100,000
Quality audits	35,000	50,000
Training	40,000	80,000
Inspection and testing	100,000	150,000
Rework	90,000	50,000
Spoilage	80,000	55,000
Warranties	180,000	80,000
Estimated customer losses	800,000	450,000
Net sales	3,000,000	3,200,000

In its cost of quality report for Year 2, Portia will disclose that the ratio of

A. Conformance costs to total quality costs increased from 17.56% in Year 1 to 37.44% in Year 2.

B. Nonconformance costs to total quality costs increased from 62.56% in Year 1 to 82.44% in Year 2.

C. Nonconformance costs to net sales equaled 19.84% in Year 1.

D. Conformance costs to net sales equaled 8.17% in Year 2.

Answer (A) is correct. *(Publisher, adapted)*

REQUIRED: The true statement about quality cost ratios.

DISCUSSION: Conformance costs are the costs of prevention and appraisal, e.g., statistical process control, quality audits, training, inspection, and testing. These costs equal $245,000 ($70,000 + $35,000 + $40,000 + $100,000) in Year 1 and $380,000 ($100,000 + $50,000 + $80,000 + $150,000) in Year 2. Total quality costs for Years 1 and 2 are $1,395,000 ($245,000 + $90,000 + $80,000 + $180,000 + $800,000) and $1,015,000 ($380,000 + $50,000 + $55,000 + $80,000 + $450,000), respectively. Accordingly, the ratio of conformance costs to total quality costs increased from 17.56% ($245,000 ÷ $1,395,000) in Year 1 to 37.44% ($380,000 ÷ $1,015,000) in Year 2.

Answer (B) is incorrect. The ratio of nonconformance costs to total quality costs decreased from 82.44% in Year 1 to 62.56% in Year 2. Answer (C) is incorrect. The ratio of nonconformance costs to net sales equaled 38.33% in Year 1 and 19.84% in Year 2. Answer (D) is incorrect. The ratio of conformance costs to net sales equaled 8.17% in Year 1 and 11.88% in Year 2.

12.1.29. The Plan-Do-Check-Act (PDCA) Cycle is a quality tool devised by W.E. Deming. It is best described as

A. A management by fact approach to continuous improvement.

B. An ongoing evaluation of the practices of best-in-class organizations.

C. The translation of customer requirements into design requirements.

D. The responsibility of every employee, work group, department, or supplier to inspect the work.

Answer (A) is correct. *(Publisher, adapted)*

REQUIRED: The best description of PDCA.

DISCUSSION: PDCA is a management by fact or scientific method approach to continuous improvement. PDCA creates a process-centered environment because it involves (1) studying the current process, (2) collecting and analyzing data to identify causes of problems, (3) planning for improvement, and (4) deciding how to measure improvement (Plan). The plan is then implemented on a small scale if possible (Do). The next step is to determine what happened (Check). If the experiment was successful, the plan is fully implemented (Act). The cycle is then repeated using what was learned from the preceding cycle.

Answer (B) is incorrect. Competitive benchmarking is an ongoing evaluation of the practices of best-in-class organizations. Answer (C) is incorrect. Quality deployment is the translation of customer requirements into design requirements. Answer (D) is incorrect. The quality at the source concept emphasizes the responsibility of every employee, work group, department, or supplier to inspect the work.

12.1.30. Which of the following quality costs are nonconformance costs?

A. Systems development costs.

B. Costs of inspecting in-process items.

C. Environmental costs.

D. Costs of quality circles.

Answer (C) is correct. *(Publisher, adapted)*

REQUIRED: The nonconformance costs.

DISCUSSION: Nonconformance costs include internal and external failure costs. External failure costs include environmental costs, e.g., fines for violations of environmental laws and loss of customer goodwill.

Answer (A) is incorrect. Systems development costs are prevention (conformance) costs. Answer (B) is incorrect. Costs of inspecting in-process items are appraisal (conformance) costs. Answer (D) is incorrect. Costs of quality circles are prevention (conformance) costs.

12.1.31. Quality costing is similar in service and manufacturing entities. Nevertheless, the differences between these entities have certain implications for quality management. Thus,

A. Direct labor costs are usually a higher percentage of total costs in manufacturing entities.

B. External failure costs are relatively greater in service entities.

C. Quality improvements resulting in more efficient use of labor time are more likely to be accepted by employees in service entities.

D. Poor service is less likely to result in loss of customers than a faulty product.

Answer (B) is correct. *(Publisher, adapted)*

REQUIRED: The difference between service entities and manufacturers with quality implications.

DISCUSSION: External failure costs result when problems occur after delivery. They occur because products or services are nonconforming or otherwise do not satisfy customers. External failure costs for service entities are even more important than for manufacturers. Faulty goods sometimes may be reworked or replaced to a customer's satisfaction, but poor service tends to result in a loss of customers.

Answer (A) is incorrect. Direct labor costs usually are a higher percentage of total costs in service entities. Answer (C) is incorrect. Service activities are usually more labor intensive than in modern manufacturing. Thus, more efficient labor usage is more likely to be viewed as a threat to employee job security in service entities. Answer (D) is incorrect. Poor service is more likely to result in loss of customers than a faulty product.

12.1.32. According to the robust quality concept,

A. The minimum point on the total quality cost curve occurs when conformance cost per unit equals nonconformance cost per unit.

B. Improving quality requires tradeoffs among categories of quality costs.

C. Beyond some point, incurrence of prevention and appraisal costs is not cost beneficial.

D. Costs in all categories of quality costs may be reduced while improving quality.

Answer (D) is correct. *(Publisher, adapted)*

REQUIRED: The robust quality view about quality costs.

DISCUSSION: The optimal level of quality costs traditionally has been deemed to occur at the point where the conformance cost curve intercepts the nonconformance cost curve (the minimum point on the total cost curve). Thus, beyond some point, incurrence of prevention and appraisal costs is not cost beneficial. However, the robust quality view is that this relationship is not always true. Improving quality and reducing costs in each category may be possible if the most efficient prevention methods are applied. For example, selection of a supplier meeting high quality standards for defect rates and delivery times may reduce not only failure costs but also the prevention and appraisal costs incurred when supplier performance was less reliable.

12.1.33. A manufacturer that wants to improve its staging process compares its procedures against the check-in process for a major airline. Which of the following tools is the manufacturer using?

A. Total quality management.

B. Statistical process control.

C. Economic value added.

D. Benchmarking.

Answer (D) is correct. *(CPA, adapted)*

REQUIRED: The tool that the manufacturer is using in comparing its procedures to the check-in process of a major airline.

DISCUSSION: Benchmarking is a primary tool used in quality management. It is a means of helping organizations with productivity management and business process analysis. Benchmarking involves analysis and measurement of key outputs against those of the best organizations. This procedure also involves identifying the underlying key actions and causes that contribute to the performance difference. The benchmark need not be a competitor or even a similar entity. Process (function) benchmarking studies operations of organizations with similar processes regardless of industry. Thus, a comparison to procedures against the check-in process for a major airline is an example of benchmarking.

Answer (A) is incorrect. Total quality management is the continuous pursuit of quality in every aspect of organizational activities through a philosophy of doing it right the first time, employee training and empowerment, promotion of teamwork, improvement of processes, and attention to satisfaction of both internal and external customers. This tool is not helpful in comparing the processes of two companies in different industries. Answer (B) is incorrect. Statistical process control is used to monitor and measure the manufacturing process in real time. This tool is not helpful in comparing the processes of two companies in different industries. Answer (C) is incorrect. Economic value added is calculated using monetary amounts and is thus a financial performance measure. It is not a helpful tool in improving the staging process of a company.

12.2 Spoilage

12.2.1. A company produces stereo speakers for automobile manufacturers. The automobile manufacturers emphasize total quality control (TQC) in their production processes and reject approximately 3% of the stereo speakers received as being of unacceptable quality. The company inspects the rejected speakers to determine which ones should be reworked and which ones should be discarded. The discarded speakers are classified as

A. Waste.

B. Scrap.

C. Spoilage.

D. Rework costs.

Answer (C) is correct. *(CIA, adapted)*

REQUIRED: The classification of discarded units.

DISCUSSION: Spoilage consists of units of output that do not satisfy customer criteria for good units. Spoiled units are discarded or sold at lower prices (e.g., as seconds).

Answer (A) is incorrect. Waste is material that is lost, evaporates, or shrinks in a manufacturing process, or it is residue that has no measurable recovery value. Answer (B) is incorrect. Scrap is material residue from a manufacturing process that has measurable but relatively minor recovery value. Answer (D) is incorrect. Rework costs are incurred to make unacceptable units appropriate for sale or use.

12.2.2. Spoilage from a manufacturing process was discovered during an inspection of work in process. In a process costing system, the cost of the spoilage would be added to the cost of the good units produced if the spoilage is

	Abnormal	Normal
A.	No	Yes
B.	No	No
C.	Yes	Yes
D.	Yes	No

Answer (A) is correct. *(CPA, adapted)*

REQUIRED: The kind(s) of spoilage added to the cost of good units in a process-costing system.

DISCUSSION: Normal spoilage is the spoilage that occurs under normal operating conditions. It is essentially uncontrollable in the short run. Normal spoilage arises under efficient operations and is treated as a product cost. Abnormal spoilage is spoilage that is not expected to occur under normal, efficient operating conditions. Because of its unusual nature, abnormal spoilage is typically treated as a loss in the period in which it is incurred.

12.2.3. Normal spoilage is defined as

A. Spoilage that results from normal operations.

B. Uncontrollable waste as a result of a special production run.

C. Spoilage that arises under inefficient operations.

D. Controllable spoilage.

Answer (A) is correct. *(Publisher, adapted)*

REQUIRED: The definition of normal spoilage.

DISCUSSION: Normal spoilage occurs under normal operating conditions. It is essentially uncontrollable in the short run. Normal spoilage occurs when operations are efficient and is treated as a product cost.

Answer (B) is incorrect. If spoilage occurs as a result of a special production run, it is abnormal. Answer (C) is incorrect. Spoilage is abnormal if it occurs when operations are inefficient. Answer (D) is incorrect. If spoilage is controllable, it should be controlled under normal circumstances.

12.2.4. A manufacturing firm has a normal spoilage rate of 4% of the units inspected; anything over this rate is considered abnormal spoilage. Final inspection occurs at the end of the process. The firm uses the FIFO inventory flow assumption. The processing for the current month was as follows:

	Units
Beginning work-in-process inventory	24,600
Units entered into production	470,400
Good units completed	(460,800)
Units failing final inspection	(22,600)
Ending work-in-process inventory	11,600

The equivalent units assigned to normal and abnormal spoilage for the current month would be

	Normal Spoilage	Abnormal Spoilage
A.	18,432 units	4,168 units
B.	18,816 units	3,784 units
C.	19,336 units	3,264 units
D.	19,800 units	2,800 units

Answer (C) is correct. *(CIA, adapted)*

REQUIRED: The equivalent units assigned to normal and abnormal spoilage.

DISCUSSION: Normal spoilage equals 4% of the units inspected. The equivalent units of normal spoilage equal 19,336 [(460,800 units passing inspection + 22,600 units failing inspection) × .04]. The equivalent units of abnormal spoilage equal total spoiled units minus the units of normal spoilage, or 3,264 (22,600 total spoiled units – 19,336 normal spoilage).

Answer (A) is incorrect. Normal spoilage is 4% of the total goods inspected, not 4% of the completed units passing inspection. Answer (B) is incorrect. Normal spoilage is 4% of the units inspected, not of the units entering production. Answer (D) is incorrect. The amount of 19,800 equals 4% of total units to account for.

12.2.5. Forming Department is the first of a two-stage production process. Spoilage is identified when the units complete the forming process. Costs of spoiled units are assigned to units completed and transferred to the second department in the period spoilage is identified. The following concerns Forming's conversion costs:

Conversion	Units	Costs
Beginning work-in-process (50% complete)	2,000	$10,000
Units started during month	8,000	75,500
Spoilage-normal	500	
Units completed & transferred	7,000	
Ending work-in-process (80% complete)	2,500	

What was Forming's weighted-average conversion cost transferred to the second department?

A. $59,850

B. $64,125

C. $67,500

D. $71,250

Answer (C) is correct. *(CPA, adapted)*

REQUIRED: The conversion costs transferred to the second production department.

DISCUSSION: Under the weighted-average method, total equivalent units include the equivalent units transferred and the equivalent units in ending work-in-process. Because normal spoilage costs attach to the good output, the transferred costs equal the costs of both the good units and the spoiled units. Total conversion costs under the weighted-average method are $85,500 ($10,000 BWIP + $75,500 units started during month costs). Total equivalent units are 9,500 [7,000 good units transferred + (2,500 uninspected units in EWIP × 80%) + 500 completed units spoiled]. Accordingly, the conversion cost per equivalent unit is $9 ($85,500 ÷ 9,500), and total costs transferred are $67,500 [(7,000 good units transferred + 500 completed units spoiled) × $9].

Answer (A) is incorrect. The amount of $59,850 equals 7,000 units times $8.55 ($85,500 ÷ 10,000 units). Answer (B) is incorrect. The amount of $64,125 equals 7,500 units times $8.55 ($85,500 ÷ 10,000 units). Answer (D) is incorrect. The amount of $71,250 results from not calculating equivalent units for spoilage in determining unit conversion cost. It equals $9.50 times 7,500 units.

12.2.6. If a process has several inspection points, how should the costs of normal spoilage be accounted for?

A. Charged to the cost of goods completed during the period.

B. Assigned to EWIP and goods completed during the period based on their relative values.

C. Assigned to the good units passing through each inspection point.

D. Assigned to EWIP and goods completed during the period based on units.

Answer (C) is correct. *(Publisher, adapted)*

REQUIRED: The way to assign normal spoilage costs given several inspection points.

DISCUSSION: At each inspection point, the costs of normal spoilage should be assigned to the good units passing through the inspection point. Consequently, the cost of moving the good units to the inspection point includes the direct materials and conversion costs of the normally spoiled units as well as those of the good units.

Answer (A) is incorrect. Normal spoilage is assigned to good units as they pass through each inspection point, not just to goods completed during the period. Answer (B) is incorrect. Normal spoilage must be assigned to all good units as they pass through each inspection point. Answer (D) is incorrect. Normal spoilage is assigned to good units as they pass through each inspection point based on their relative values (not based on units).

12.2.7. In a process costing system in which normal spoilage is assumed to occur at the end of a process, the cost attributable to normal spoilage should be assigned to

A. Ending work-in-process inventory.

B. Cost of goods manufactured and ending work-in-process inventory in the ratio of units worked on during the period to units remaining in work-in-process inventory.

C. Cost of goods manufactured (transferred out).

D. A separate loss account in order to highlight production inefficiencies.

Answer (C) is correct. *(CPA, adapted)*

REQUIRED: The inventory to which normal spoilage is assigned when it occurs at the end of the process.

DISCUSSION: Normal spoilage is a product cost because it attaches to a product and is expensed when sold. When normal spoilage occurs at the end of the process, the product must be complete before the spoilage can be detected. Thus, all normal spoilage costs should be assigned to finished goods inventory.

Answer (A) is incorrect. The EWIP contains no spoiled units because spoilage does not occur until processing is complete. Answer (B) is incorrect. The EWIP contains no spoiled units because spoilage does not occur until processing is complete. Answer (D) is incorrect. Normal spoilage costs attach to the product because they are expected. Abnormal spoilage costs are charged to a separate loss account.

12.2.8. In a job costing system, $45,000 has been charged to a job ($25,000 of direct materials, $10,000 direct labor, and $10,000 applied overhead). The job yields 500 units of a product, of entity 100 are rejected as spoiled with no salvage value. The cost of the spoilage is determined to be $9,000. If the entity wishes to use this job as the basis for setting a spoilage standard for comparison with future work, the conceptually superior way to express the spoilage rate is

A. 20% of total inputs.

B. 25% of good outputs.

C. 90% of labor inputs.

D. 36% of material inputs.

Answer (B) is correct. *(F. Mayne)*

REQUIRED: The calculation of a normal spoilage rate to be used for future comparison.

DISCUSSION: Normal spoilage occurs under efficient operating conditions. It is uncontrollable in the short run and therefore should be expressed as a function of good output (treated as a product cost). The rate can be determined using the ratio of (1) the cost of spoiled units to (2) the cost of good units minus the cost of spoiled units. The ratio may also be stated in terms of units. Thus, the rate is 25% [$9,000 ÷ ($45,000 – $9,000)] or [100 units ÷ (500 – 100) units].

Answer (A) is incorrect. Normal spoilage is expressed as a function of good output. Answer (C) is incorrect. Normal spoilage is not directly related to labor. Answer (D) is incorrect. Normal spoilage is not directly related to materials.

12.2.9. Shrinkage should be accounted for as

A. Miscellaneous revenue.

B. An offset to overhead.

C. Reworked units.

D. Spoilage.

Answer (D) is correct. *(Publisher, adapted)*

REQUIRED: The accounting treatment of shrinkage.

DISCUSSION: Shrinkage consists of materials lost through the manufacturing process (e.g., heat, compression, etc.). It is accounted for in the same way as spoilage. If shrinkage is normal, it is a product cost. If it is abnormal, it is a period cost.

Answer (A) is incorrect. Shrinkage usually does not result in scrap or waste products that can be sold and accounted for as a revenue or a contra cost. Answer (B) is incorrect. Shrinkage usually does not result in scrap or waste products that can be sold and accounted for as a revenue or a contra cost. Answer (C) is incorrect. Reworked units are those reprocessed to produce good units.

12.2.10. Abnormal spoilage

A. Cannot occur when perfection standards are used.

B. Is not usually controllable by the production supervisor.

C. Results from unrealistic production standards.

D. Is not expected to occur under efficient operating conditions.

Answer (D) is correct. *(CIA, adapted)*

REQUIRED: The definition of abnormal spoilage.

DISCUSSION: Abnormal spoilage is spoilage that is not expected to occur under normal, efficient operating conditions. The cost of abnormal spoilage should be separately identified and reported to management. Abnormal spoilage is typically treated as a period cost (a loss) because of its unusual nature.

Answer (A) is incorrect. Perfection standards are based on perfect operating conditions, and negative deviation from such standards is expected. Answer (B) is incorrect. Abnormal spoilage may result from any of a variety of conditions or circumstances that are usually controllable by first-line supervisors. Answer (C) is incorrect. Abnormal spoilage may result from any of a variety of conditions or circumstances that are not necessarily related to standards.

12.2.11. A manufacturing firm may experience both normal and abnormal spoilage in its operations. The costs of both normal and abnormal spoilage are accounted for in the accounting records. The costs associated with any abnormal spoilage are

A. Assigned to the good units transferred to finished goods.

B. Assigned to the units transferred to finished goods and those remaining in work-in-process.

C. Charged to the manufacturing overhead control account.

D. Charged to a special abnormal spoilage loss account.

Answer (D) is correct. *(CIA, adapted)*

REQUIRED: The treatment of costs associated with abnormal spoilage.

DISCUSSION: Abnormal spoilage is a period cost that is separately reported in the income statement. Costs associated with abnormal spoilage are not inventoried and are therefore treated as a loss in the period of detection.

Answer (A) is incorrect. Assigning spoilage costs to finished goods is an appropriate method of accounting for normal spoilage traceable to a job or process. Answer (B) is incorrect. Assigning spoilage costs to finished goods and work-in-process is an appropriate method of accounting for normal spoilage traceable to a job or process, provided the units in process have passed the inspection point. Answer (C) is incorrect. Charging spoilage costs to manufacturing overhead is an appropriate method of accounting for normal spoilage in a job costing system, assuming the allowance for normal spoilage is included in the predetermined overhead rate.

12.2.12. What is a quantity of production report?

A. A report of the units completed this period compared with the preceding period, and a moving average of the number completed during the 12 preceding periods.

B. A report that states the units transferred into one or more manufacturing accounts during a period and the disposition of those units.

C. A cost of goods manufactured statement.

D. A report that lists and accounts for all debits to the manufacturing account during the period and the disposition of those costs.

Answer (B) is correct. *(Publisher, adapted)*

REQUIRED: The nature of a quantity of production report.

DISCUSSION: A quantity of production report indicates the disposition of the units in BWIP and those entering the process during the period: the units (1) completed, (2) spoiled, and (3) in EWIP.

Answer (A) is incorrect. The quantity of production report applies only the units transferred into and out of the process in the current period. Answer (C) is incorrect. The cost of goods manufactured statement reports the cost of goods completed rather than an accounting for all of the units in the process. Answer (D) is incorrect. A cost of production report relates the costs recorded in and transferred from the manufacturing account.

12.2.13. What is a cost of production report?

A. A report that lists and accounts for all debits to the manufacturing account during the period and the disposition of those costs.

B. A report that states the units transferred into one or more manufacturing accounts during a period and the disposition of those units.

C. A cost of goods manufactured statement.

D. A report that analyzes variances from standard costs and their allocation.

Answer (A) is correct. *(Publisher, adapted)*

REQUIRED: The nature of a cost of production report.

DISCUSSION: A cost of production report is a formal statement of the data in a manufacturing or work-in-process account or accounts. The debits in the account are added to determine the total cost for which the process is accountable. A listing presents the disposition of those costs.

Answer (B) is incorrect. A quantity of production report applies only to the units transferred into and out of the process in the current period. Answer (C) is incorrect. The cost of goods manufactured statement reports cost of goods completed, not the disposition of the costs incurred during the period. Answer (D) is incorrect. An analysis of standard cost variances report (1) identifies significant deviations from expectations and (2) reports the disposition (allocation) of the variances.

12.2.14. In its production process, Hern Corp., which does not use a standard cost system, incurred total production costs for the month of $90,000, of which Hern attributed $60,000 to normal spoilage and $30,000 to abnormal spoilage. Hern should account for this spoilage as

A. Period cost of $90,000.

B. Inventoriable cost of $90,000.

C. Period cost of $60,000 and inventoriable cost of $30,000.

D. Inventoriable cost of $60,000 and period cost of $30,000.

Answer (D) is correct. *(CPA, adapted)*

REQUIRED: The proper accounting for spoilage.

DISCUSSION: Normal spoilage arises under efficient operating conditions and is therefore a product cost. Abnormal spoilage is not expected to occur under efficient operating conditions. It is accounted for as a period cost. Thus, the normal spoilage of $60,000 is an inventoriable cost, and the abnormal spoilage of $30,000 is a period cost.

Questions 12.2.15 and 12.2.16 are based on the following information. Harper Co.'s Job 501 for the manufacture of 2,200 coats was completed during August at the unit costs presented as follows. Final inspection of Job 501 disclosed 200 spoiled coats, which were sold to a jobber for $6,000.

Direct materials	$20
Direct labor	18
Manufacturing overhead (includes an allowance of $1 for spoiled work)	18
	$56

12.2.15. Assume that spoilage loss is charged to all production during August. What would be the unit cost of the good coats produced on Job 501?

A. $57.50

B. $55.00

C. $56.00

D. $58.60

Answer (C) is correct. *(CPA, adapted)*

REQUIRED: The unit cost of goods produced when spoilage is charged to all production.

DISCUSSION: The unit cost of goods produced includes direct materials, direct labor, and manufacturing overhead. Given that the spoilage is included in the calculation of overhead, it must be considered normal and a product cost. Thus, the unit cost remains $56.

Answer (A) is incorrect. The amount of $57.50 is the unit cost for 2,000 units, assuming that $6,000 is subtracted from a total cost of $121,000 (2,200 units × $55). Answer (B) is incorrect. The amount of $55 excludes the $1 of overhead for spoiled work. Answer (D) is incorrect. The amount of $58.60 is the unit cost for 2,000 units that results from subtracting $6,000 from the total cost of the 2,200 units produced.

12.2.16. Assume that the spoilage loss is attributable to the exacting specifications of Job 501 and is charged to this specific job. What would be the unit cost of the good coats produced on Job 501?

A. $55.00

B. $57.50

C. $58.60

D. $61.60

Answer (B) is correct. *(CPA, adapted)*

REQUIRED: The unit cost of goods produced if the actual spoilage loss is charged to this job.

DISCUSSION: If the spoilage is charged to this specific job (rather than to manufacturing overhead), the spoilage allowance should be removed from the overhead rate. The overhead application rate decreases to $17 because this job's spoilage is not typical and is not averaged with other jobs. The costs of producing the 2,000 good coats include the costs incurred in the production of the 2,200 coats, minus the $6,000 received for the spoiled coats. The unit cost is the net cost of production divided by the number of good coats produced (2,000).

$$\frac{2{,}200\ (\$20 + \$18 + \$17) - \$6{,}000}{2{,}000} = \$57.50$$

Answer (A) is incorrect. The total production should be multiplied by $55 ($56 – $1 spoilage allowance). Furthermore, the $6,000 received for spoiled goods should be allocated over the 2,000 good units. Answer (C) is incorrect. The $1-per-unit spoilage allowance in overhead should be deducted. Answer (D) is incorrect. The $1-per-unit spoilage allowance in overhead should be deducted. Furthermore, the $6,000 received for spoiled goods should be allocated over the good units.

12.2.17. A department adds material at the beginning of a process and identifies defective units when the process is 40% complete. At the beginning of the period, there was no work in process. At the end of the period, the number of work-in-process units equaled the number of units transferred to finished goods. If all units in ending work in process were 66% complete, then ending work in process should be allocated

A. 50% of all normal defective unit costs.

B. 40% of all normal defective unit costs.

C. 50% of the material costs and 40% of the conversion costs of all normal defective unit costs.

D. None of the normal defective unit costs.

Answer (A) is correct. *(CPA, adapted)*

REQUIRED: The normal spoilage costs allocated to EWIP.

DISCUSSION: Inspection occurs when the units are 40% complete. Thus, EWIP, which is 66% complete, contains good units only. Because normal spoilage attaches to good units, and the units transferred to finished goods equal those in EWIP, the normal defective unit costs should be allocated 50% to EWIP and 50% to finished goods.

Answer (B) is incorrect. EWIP contains 50% of the good units produced. Answer (C) is incorrect. EWIP should be allocated 50% of all normal spoilage costs. Answer (D) is incorrect. Normal spoilage costs should be allocated to EWIP if it contains inspected units.

12.2.18. In manufacturing its products for the month just ended, Elk Co. incurred normal spoilage of $10,000 and abnormal spoilage of $12,000. How much spoilage cost should Elk charge as a period cost for the month?

A. $22,000

B. $12,000

C. $10,000

D. $0

Answer (B) is correct. *(CPA, adapted)*

REQUIRED: The spoilage charged as a period cost.

DISCUSSION: Normal spoilage occurs under efficient operating conditions and is therefore a product cost. Abnormal spoilage is not expected to occur under efficient operating conditions. It is accounted for as a period cost. Thus, the amount of spoilage charged as a period cost is the $12,000 related to abnormal spoilage.

Answer (A) is incorrect. The amount of $22,000 includes the normal spoilage ($10,000), which is a product cost. Answer (C) is incorrect. The $10,000 normal spoilage is a product cost. Answer (D) is incorrect. The abnormal spoilage ($12,000) is a period cost.

12.2.19. A company uses a job-order cost system in accounting for its manufacturing operations. Because its processes are labor oriented, it applies manufacturing overhead on the basis of direct labor hours (DLH). Normal spoilage is defined as 4% of the units passing inspection. The company includes a provision for normal spoilage cost in its budgeted manufacturing overhead and manufacturing overhead rate. Data regarding a job consisting of 30,000 units are presented below:

Volume Data:	
Good units passing inspection	28,500
Units failing inspection (spoiled)	1,500
Total units in job	30,000

Cost Data:	Per Unit	Total Cost
Direct materials	$ 18.00	$ 540,000
Direct labor (2 DLH at $16.00/DLH)	32.00	960,000
Manufacturing overhead (2 DLH at $30.00/DLH)	60.00	1,800,000
Total	$110.00	$3,300,000

The 1,500 units that failed inspection required .25 direct labor hours per unit to rework the units into good units. What is the proper charge to the loss from abnormal spoilage account?

A. $1,440

B. $4,140

C. $3,450

D. Zero.

Answer (B) is correct. *(CIA, adapted)*

REQUIRED: The proper charge to loss from abnormal spoilage account.

DISCUSSION: Normal spoilage equals 1,140 units (28,500 good units × 4%), so abnormal spoilage equals 360 units (1,500 total spoiled units – 1,140 units of normal spoilage). Given that .25 DLH is needed to rework a spoiled unit, the loss from abnormal spoilage is $4,140 {360 units × [($16 × .25) direct labor + ($30 × .25) manufacturing overhead]}.

Answer (A) is incorrect. The amount of $1,440 (360 units × $4.00) ignores the manufacturing overhead. Answer (C) is incorrect. The amount of $3,450 [300 units × ($4.00 + $7.50)] uses the wrong amount for abnormal spoilage. Answer (D) is incorrect. A loss should be charged for abnormal spoilage. Total spoilage exceeded the 4% normal rate.

12.2.20. The normal spoilage rate for a company is 5% of normal input. A current job consisted of 31,000 total units, of which 28,500 good units were produced and 2,500 units were defective. The amount of abnormal spoilage on this job is

A. 950 units.

B. 1,000 units.

C. 1,075 units.

D. 1,550 units.

Answer (B) is correct. *(CIA, adapted)*

REQUIRED: The amount of abnormal spoilage.

DISCUSSION: Normal input (input for the good units and normal spoilage) is calculated by dividing the good units produced by the proportion left after the normal spoiled units are removed, or 95% (100% – 5%). Thus, normal input is the input for 30,000 units (28,500 ÷ .95), normal spoilage is 1,500 units (30,000 – 28,500), and abnormal spoilage is the difference between total and normal spoilage [(31,000 – 28,500) – 1,500].

Answer (A) is incorrect. Total spoiled units minus 5% of 31,000 units equals 950 units. Answer (C) is incorrect. Total spoiled units minus 5% of 28,500 units equals 1,075 units. Answer (D) is incorrect. Taking 5% of 31,000 units equals 1,550 units.

12.2.21. During the month of May, a company completed 50,000 units costing $600,000, exclusive of spoilage allocation. Of these completed units, 25,000 were sold during the month. An additional 10,000 units, costing $80,000, were 50% complete at May 31. All units are inspected between the completion of manufacturing and transfer to finished goods inventory. Normal spoilage for the month was $20,000, and abnormal spoilage of $50,000 was also incurred during the month. The portion of total spoilage that should be charged against revenue in May is

A. $50,000

B. $20,000

C. $70,000

D. $60,000

Answer (D) is correct. *(CMA, adapted)*

REQUIRED: The portion of total spoilage that should be charged against revenue.

DISCUSSION: Normal spoilage is an inventoriable cost of production that is charged to cost of goods sold when the units are sold. Abnormal spoilage is a period cost recognized when incurred. The $50,000 of abnormal spoilage is therefore expensed during May. In addition, 50% of the normal spoilage is debited to cost of goods sold because 50% (25,000 ÷ 50,000) of the units completed were sold during the period. No spoilage is allocated to work-in-process because inspection occurs after completion. Thus, the normal spoilage expensed during the month is $10,000 ($20,000 × 50%). Total spoilage charged against revenue is $60,000 ($50,000 + $10,000).

Answer (A) is incorrect. The amount of $50,000 is abnormal spoilage. Answer (B) is incorrect. The amount of $20,000 equals normal spoilage for the month. Answer (C) is incorrect. The amount of $70,000 is the sum of normal spoilage and abnormal spoilage.

12.2.22. Assume 550 units were worked on during a period in which a total of 500 good units were completed. Normal spoilage consisted of 30 units; abnormal spoilage, 20 units. Total production costs were $2,200. The company accounts for abnormal spoilage separately on the income statement as loss due to abnormal spoilage. Normal spoilage is not accounted for separately. What is the cost of the good units produced?

A. $2,000

B. $2,080

C. $2,120

D. $2,200

Answer (C) is correct. *(CIA, adapted)*

REQUIRED: The cost of the good units produced given normal and abnormal spoilage.

DISCUSSION: Abnormal spoilage is not expected to occur under efficient operating conditions. Thus, abnormal spoilage is excluded from the cost of the good units. Thus, the total production cost of $2,200 is reduced by $80 [20 units × ($2,200 ÷ 550 total units)] to arrive at the $2,120 cost of good units.

Answer (A) is incorrect. The amount of $2,000 does not include the normal spoilage ($120). Answer (B) is incorrect. Normal spoilage ($120), not abnormal spoilage ($80), should be included in the cost of good units produced. Answer (D) is incorrect. The total production costs should be reduced by the abnormal spoilage ($80) to find the cost of good units produced.

12.3 Scrap and Rework

12.3.1. Scrap consists of

A. Defective units that may be used or sold.

B. Materials remaining from the production cycle but usable for purposes other than the original purpose.

C. Materials remaining from the production cycle but not usable for any purpose.

D. Finished goods that do not meet quality control standards and cannot be reworked.

Answer (B) is correct. *(Publisher, adapted)*

REQUIRED: The definition of scrap.

DISCUSSION: Scrap consists of materials left over from the production cycle but still usable for purposes other than those for which it was originally intended. Scrap may be sold to outside customers, usually for a nominal amount, or may be used for a different production process.

Answer (A) is incorrect. Scrap consists of materials that may not necessarily be defective. Answer (C) is incorrect. Waste consists of materials remaining from the production cycle but not usable for any purpose. Answer (D) is incorrect. Scrap consists of materials, not finished goods.

12.3.2. A product that does not meet quality control standards and needs to be reworked to be salable as either an irregular or a good product is classified as

A. Spoiled goods.

B. Defective goods.

C. Scrap.

D. Waste.

Answer (B) is correct. *(Publisher, adapted)*

REQUIRED: The classification of a product requiring rework to be salable.

DISCUSSION: Defective goods are products that have not met the quality control standards at the completion of the production process. Defective goods require rework to be salable as either an irregular item or a good product.

Answer (A) is incorrect. Spoiled goods are sold for salvage value or destroyed. Answer (C) is incorrect. Scrap consists of materials that may be used in a different production process or sold to outsiders. Answer (D) is incorrect. Waste has no further use.

12.3.3. During the month just ended, Delta Co. experienced scrap, normal spoilage, and abnormal spoilage in its manufacturing process. The cost of units produced includes

A. Scrap, but not spoilage.

B. Normal spoilage, but neither scrap nor abnormal spoilage.

C. Scrap and normal spoilage, but not abnormal spoilage.

D. Scrap, normal spoilage, and abnormal spoilage.

Answer (C) is correct. *(CPA, adapted)*

REQUIRED: The accounting for scrap and spoilage.

DISCUSSION: Scrap consists of direct material left over from the production process. It can either be sold, in which case it reduces factory overhead, or discarded, in which case it is absorbed into the cost of the good output. Normal spoilage occurs under normal operating conditions. Because it is expected under efficient operations, it is treated as a product cost. It is absorbed into the cost of the good output. Abnormal spoilage is not expected to occur under normal, efficient operating conditions. Abnormal spoilage is typically treated as a period cost (a loss).

Answer (A) is incorrect. Good units bear the cost of normal spoilage. Answer (B) is incorrect. Good units bear the cost of scrap. Answer (D) is incorrect. Good units do not bear the cost of abnormal spoilage.

12.3.4. The sale of scrap from a manufacturing process usually is recorded as a(n)

A. Decrease in factory overhead control.

B. Increase in factory overhead control.

C. Decrease in finished goods control.

D. Increase in finished goods control.

Answer (A) is correct. *(CPA, adapted)*

REQUIRED: The usual accounting for a sale of scrap.

DISCUSSION: The sale of scrap arising from a manufacturing process is usually recorded by crediting factory overhead control. The effect is to allocate the net cost of the scrap (historical cost – disposal proceeds) to the good units produced.

Answer (B) is incorrect. Factory overhead control is credited for the amounts realized upon sale, decreasing it. Answer (C) is incorrect. Crediting finished goods would not allocate the disposal value to all good units. Answer (D) is incorrect. Amounts received from the sale of scrap reduce the costs inventoried.

12.3.5. Rework costs should be regarded as a cost of quality in a manufacturing company's quality control program when they are

I. Caused by the customer.
II. Caused by internal failure.

A. I only.

B. II only.

C. Both I and II.

D. Neither I nor II.

Answer (B) is correct. *(CPA, adapted)*

REQUIRED: The proper classification of rework costs.

DISCUSSION: Internal failure costs are those incurred when detection of defective products occurs before shipment. Examples are scrap, rework, tooling changes, and downtime. The costs of external failure, e.g., warranty, product liability, and customer ill will, arise when problems occur after shipment.

Answer (A) is incorrect. Rework results from an internal failure and therefore cannot be caused by the customer. Answer (C) is incorrect. Rework results from an internal failure and therefore cannot be caused by the customer. Answer (D) is incorrect. Rework costs should be regarded as costs of quality in a manufacturing company's quality control program when caused by internal failure.

12.3.6. Some units of output failed to pass final inspection at the end of the manufacturing process. The production and inspection supervisors determined that the estimated incremental revenue from reworking the units exceeded the cost of rework. The rework of the defective units was authorized, and the following costs were incurred in reworking the units:

Materials requisitioned from stores:	
Direct materials	$ 5,000
Miscellaneous supplies	300
Direct labor	14,000

The manufacturing overhead budget includes an allowance for rework. The predetermined manufacturing overhead rate is 150% of direct labor cost. The account(s) to be charged and the appropriate charges for the rework cost would be

A. Work-in-process inventory control for $19,000.

B. Work-in-process inventory control for $5,000 and manufacturing overhead control for $35,300.

C. Overhead control for $19,300.

D. Overhead control for $40,300.

Answer (D) is correct. *(CIA, adapted)*

REQUIRED: The account(s) to be charged and the appropriate charges for the rework cost.

DISCUSSION: The rework charge for direct materials, indirect materials (supplies), direct labor, and overhead applied on the basis of direct labor cost is $40,300 [$5,000 + $300 + $14,000 + (1.5 × $14,000)]. If an allowance for rework is included in a manufacturing overhead budget, rework of defective units is spread over all jobs or batches as part of the predetermined overhead application rate. Thus, the debit is to overhead.

Answer (A) is incorrect. Overhead should be charged for direct materials, supplies, direct labor, and applied overhead incurred for rework. Answer (B) is incorrect. Overhead should be charged for direct materials, supplies, direct labor, and applied overhead incurred for rework. Answer (C) is incorrect. The amount of $19,300 excludes the predetermined manufacturing overhead.

12.3.7. Assuming the value of scrap sales is material, when is it not necessary to record the scrap in inventory as it is produced?

A. When it is sold regularly, e.g., daily, weekly, etc.

B. When the unit value fluctuates.

C. If it is recognized as miscellaneous revenue.

D. If it is recognized as an offset to overhead.

Answer (A) is correct. *(Publisher, adapted)*

REQUIRED: The circumstances in which a significant inventory of scrap need not be recorded.

DISCUSSION: If scrap is sold on a regular basis, e.g., daily, it should be recorded either as a contra cost or as a revenue. If it is not sold regularly and not recorded in inventory, income may be misstated.

Answer (B) is incorrect. Failure to record significant scrap can misstate income. Answer (C) is incorrect. The issue is timing the recognition of scrap, not the account used. Answer (D) is incorrect. The issue is timing the recognition of scrap, not the account used.

12.3.8. Hart Company incurred the following costs on Job 109 for the manufacture of 200 motors:

Original cost accumulation:	
Direct materials	$ 660
Direct labor	800
Overhead (150% of DL)	1,200
	$2,660
Direct costs of reworking 10 units:	
Direct materials	$ 100
Direct labor	160
	$ 260

The rework costs were attributable to the exacting specifications of Job 109, and the full rework costs were charged to this specific job. What is the cost per finished unit of Job 109?

A. $15.80

B. $14.60

C. $13.80

D. $13.30

Answer (A) is correct. *(CPA, adapted)*

REQUIRED: The cost per finished unit of a job, given rework costs.

DISCUSSION: The rework costs are attributable to the specifications of Job 109, so the full rework costs should be charged to this job. Accordingly, the cost of reworking the 10 units must include $260 of direct costs and an additional charge for overhead.

Original cost	$2,660
Rework direct costs	260
Rework overhead ($160 DL × 150%)	240
Job 109 total costs	$3,160
Divided by 200 motors	÷ 200
Job 109 unit cost	$15.80

Answer (B) is incorrect. The amount of $14.60 does not include the overhead for the rework. Answer (C) is incorrect. The amount of $13.80 excludes the overhead and direct labor costs of rework. Answer (D) is incorrect. The amount of $13.30 does not include the direct and overhead costs for the rework.

12.4 Comprehensive

Questions 12.4.1 through 12.4.8 are based on the following information.

Ranka Company manufactures high-quality leather products. The company's profits have declined during the past 9 months. Ranka has used unit cost data (which were developed 18 months ago) in planning and controlling its operations. In an attempt to isolate the causes of poor profit performance, management is investigating the manufacturing operations of each of its products.

One of Ranka's main products is fine leather belts. The belts are produced in a single, continuous process in the Bluett Plant. During the process, leather strips are sewn, punched, and dyed. Buckles are attached by rivets when the belts are 70% complete as to direct labor and overhead (conversion costs). The belts then enter a final finishing stage to conclude the process. Labor and overhead are applied continuously during the process.

The leather belts are inspected twice during the process: (1) right before the buckles are attached (70% point in the process) and (2) at the conclusion of the finishing stage (100% point in the process). Ranka uses the weighted-average method to calculate its unit costs.

The leather belts produced at the Bluett Plant sell wholesale for $9.95 each. Management wants to compare the current manufacturing costs per unit with the prices on the market for leather belts. Top management has asked the Bluett Plant to submit data on the cost of manufacturing the leather belts for the month of October. These data will be used to evaluate whether modifications in the production process should be initiated or whether an increase in the selling price of the belts is justified. The cost per equivalent unit being used for planning and control purposes is $5.35.

The work-in-process inventory consisted of 400 partially completed units on October 1. The belts were 25% complete as to conversion costs. The costs included in the inventory on October 1 were

Leather strips	$1,000
Conversion costs	300
Total	$1,300

During October, 7,600 leather strips were placed in production. A total of 6,800 good leather belts were completed. A total of 300 belts were identified as defective at the two inspection points -- 100 at the first inspection point (before buckle is attached) and 200 at the final inspection point (after finishing). This quantity of defective belts was considered normal. In addition, 200 belts were removed from the production line when the process was 40% complete as to conversion costs because they had been damaged as a result of a malfunction during the sewing operation. This malfunction was considered an unusual occurrence, so the spoilage was classified as abnormal. Defective (spoiled) units are not reprocessed and have zero salvage value. The work-in-process inventory on October 31 consisted of 700 belts 50% complete as to conversion costs.

The costs charged to production for October were

Leather strips	$20,600
Buckles	4,550
Conversion costs	20,700
Total	$45,850

12.4.1. What are the total equivalent units for the leather strips for the month?

A. 7,000

B. 8,000

C. 7,500

D. 7,800

Answer (B) is correct. *(Publisher, adapted)*

REQUIRED: The total EUP for leather strips.

DISCUSSION: Leather strip EUP are the total completed during the month, plus normal spoilage, plus abnormal spoilage, plus any work-in-process at month-end.

Completed during the month	6,800
Normal spoilage:	
1st inspection	100
2nd inspection	200
Abnormal spoilage	200
Work-in-process at 10/31	700
Total equivalent units	8,000

Answer (A) is incorrect. The amount of 7,000 excludes normal spoilage and EWIP. Answer (C) is incorrect. Normal and abnormal spoilage should be included. Answer (D) is incorrect. The amount of 7,800 excludes abnormal spoilage.

12.4.2. What is the cost per equivalent unit for the buckles?

A. $.65

B. $.67

C. $.64

D. $.59

Answer (A) is correct. *(Publisher, adapted)*

REQUIRED: The cost per EUP for buckles.

DISCUSSION: The buckles are attached when the belts are 70% complete, which is immediately after the first inspection. Thus, the 100 units of normal spoilage detected at the first inspection point did not have buckles and are not included in this EUP calculation. The cost per EUP for the buckles is the cost assigned to the buckles divided by the EUP. The 6,800 buckles added to belts completed during the month plus 200 units of normal spoilage identified at the second inspection point equal 7,000 EUP (the units in EWIP do not have buckles because they are only 50% complete). Given that $4,550 in costs is attributable to the 7,000 buckles, the cost per EUP is $.65 ($4,550 ÷ 7,000).

Answer (B) is incorrect. The amount of $.67 equals $4,550 divided by 6,800. Answer (C) is incorrect. The amount of $.64 equals $4,550 divided by 7,100. Answer (D) is incorrect. The amount of $.59 equals $4,550 divided by 7,700.

12.4.3. What is the total production cost to account for in October?

A. $45,850

B. $47,150

C. $52,150

D. $43,516

Answer (B) is correct. *(Publisher, adapted)*

REQUIRED: The total cost of production to account for.

DISCUSSION: Total BWIP cost is $1,300, and costs charged to production during the month are $45,850. Thus, the total cost to account for is $47,150. Alternatively, the cost can be calculated by adding each component.

Material ($1,000 + $20,600)	$21,600
Buckles	4,550
Conversion ($300 + $20,700)	21,000
Total costs	$47,150

Answer (A) is incorrect. The amount of $45,850 does not include the cost of BWIP ($1,300). Answer (C) is incorrect. The amount of $52,150 does not reflect the total of BWIP ($1,300) and the costs charged to production during the month ($45,850). Answer (D) is incorrect. The amount of $43,516 does not reflect the total cost of BWIP ($1,300) and the costs charged to production during the month ($45,850).

12.4.4. What is the total cost of normal spoilage?

A. $1,845

B. $1,566

C. $1,696

D. $2,460

Answer (C) is correct. *(Publisher, adapted)*

REQUIRED: The total cost of normal spoilage.

DISCUSSION: The cost of normal spoilage is equal to the sum of the products of the EUP attributable to normal spoilage and the EUP cost for each component.

Leather {300 EUP × [($1,000 + $20,600) ÷ 8,000 EUP]}	$ 810
Buckles [200 EUP × ($4,550 ÷ 7,000 EUP)]	130
Conversion {270 EUP* × [($300 + $20,700) ÷ 7,500 EUP]}	756
Total	$1,696

* Consists of 200 units 100% complete and 100 units 70% complete

Answer (A) is incorrect. The amount of $1,845 equals 300 spoiled units times $6.15 (total cost per EUP). Answer (B) is incorrect. Omitting the cost of spoiled buckles results in $1,566. Answer (D) is incorrect. The amount of $2,460 includes abnormal spoilage.

12.4.5. What is the total cost per equivalent unit?

A. $5.50

B. $6.33

C. $6.49

D. $6.15

Answer (D) is correct. *(Publisher, adapted)*

REQUIRED: The total cost per EUP.

DISCUSSION: The total cost per EUP is the sum of EUP costs for strips, buckles, and conversion. The 100 units of normal spoilage detected by the first inspection were 70% complete (70 EUP), and the 200 units of normal spoilage identified at the second inspection point were 100% complete. The 200 units of abnormal spoilage were 40% complete (80 EUP). EWIP was 50% complete.

	Leather Strips	Buckles	Conversion Cost
Completed during the month	6,800	6,800	6,800
Normal spoilage			
1st inspection	100	--	70
2nd inspection	200	200	200
Abnormal spoilage	200	--	80
WIP at 10/31	700	--	350
Equivalent units	8,000	7,000	7,500

Cost per EUP:	
Strips [($1,000 + $20,600) ÷ 8,000]	$2.70
Buckles ($4,550 ÷ 7,000)	.65
Conversion [($300 + $20,700) ÷ 7,500]	2.80
Total cost per EUP	$6.15

Answer (A) is incorrect. The amount of $5.50 does not include the unit cost for buckles ($.65). Answer (B) is incorrect. The amount of $6.33 excludes the EUP for leather strips related to spoilage. Answer (C) is incorrect. The amount of $6.49 excludes all EUP for spoilage.

12.4.6. Refer to the information on the preceding page(s). What is the total work-in-process as of October 31?

A. $1,890

B. $1,696

C. $4,305

D. $2,870

Answer (D) is correct. *(Publisher, adapted)*

REQUIRED: The total ending work-in-process inventory.

DISCUSSION: The cost of EWIP is equal to the EUP in each category times the appropriate unit cost. Leather strips, the only item in EI as of October 31, are 100% complete as to leather and 50% complete as to conversion.

Leather strips (700 × $2.70)	$1,890
Conversion (700 × .5 × $2.80)	980
Total	$2,870

Answer (A) is incorrect. The cost of conversion ($980) should be included. Answer (B) is incorrect. The cost of normal spoilage equals $1,696. Answer (C) is incorrect. The amount of $4,305 equals 700 units times $6.15 (total cost per EUP).

12.4.7. Refer to the information on the preceding page(s). What is the average cost per unit for finished goods?

A. $5.89

B. $6.40

C. $6.15

D. $6.51

Answer (B) is correct. *(Publisher, adapted)*

REQUIRED: The average cost per unit for finished goods.

DISCUSSION: The average cost for finished goods is the total cost of the good units completed plus the cost of normal spoilage, divided by the number of good units completed. The cost of good units completed is $41,820 (6,800 × $6.15 total cost per EUP). The cost of normal spoilage is $1,696. Thus, $43,516 ($41,820 + $1,696) is the total cost transferred, and the unit cost is $6.40 ($43,516 ÷ 6,800).

Answer (A) is incorrect. The total cost of production to be accounted for divided by total physical units equals $5.89. Answer (C) is incorrect. The total cost per EUP is $6.15. Answer (D) is incorrect. The amount of $6.51 includes abnormal spoilage in the numerator.

12.4.8. Refer to the information on the preceding page(s). If the 300 defective belts (normal spoilage) are repaired, and management wants to ensure the incremental costs do not exceed the cost of producing new units, how should the rework costs be accounted for?

A. As normal materials, labor, and overhead.

B. Charged only to those belts repaired.

C. Expensed as extraordinary.

D. Charged to overhead and spread over the cost of all products.

Answer (B) is correct. *(Publisher, adapted)*

REQUIRED: The appropriate accounting treatment to control rework costs.

DISCUSSION: To control rework, the costs of repairing 300 defective belts should be separated from other costs. The costs may flow through the WIP accounts but should be kept separate (like a specific job in job costing). An alternative is to use another WIP account for rework on a job lot basis. The effect is to prevent spending more for the rework than manufacturing a new product. Generally, manufacturers prefer to rework items rather than discard them.

Answer (A) is incorrect. If rework costs are accounted for as normal materials, labor, and overhead, the costs of rework are averaged with the costs of production. The result is to limit oversight of rework costs exceeding the costs of normal production. Answer (C) is incorrect. The rework costs should not be expensed as extraordinary. Moreover, extraordinary items are eliminated from GAAP. Answer (D) is incorrect. Charging the costs to overhead provides no effective control over rework costs.

Questions 12.4.9 and 12.4.10 are based on the following information.

Ramseur Company employs a process costing system for its two-department manufacturing operation using the first-in, first-out (FIFO) inventory method. When units are completed in Department 1, they are transferred to Department 2 for completion. Inspection takes place in Department 2 immediately before the direct materials are added, when the process is 70% complete with respect to conversion. The specific identification method is used to account for lost units.

The number of defective units (that is, those failing inspection) is usually below the normal tolerance limit of 4% of units inspected. Defective units have minimal value, and the company sells them without any further processing for whatever it can. Generally, the amount collected equals, or slightly exceeds, the transportation cost. A summary of the manufacturing activity for Department 2, in units for the current month, is presented below.

	Physical Flow (output units)
Beginning inventory (60% complete with respect to conversion)	20,000
Units transferred in from Department 1	180,000
Total units to account for	200,000
Units completed in Department 2 during the month	170,000
Units found to be defective at inspection	5,000
Ending inventory (80% complete with respect to conversion)	25,000
Total units accounted for	200,000

12.4.9. Ramseur's equivalent units for direct materials for the current month would be

A. 175,000 units.

B. 181,500 units.

C. 195,000 units.

D. 200,000 units.

Answer (C) is correct. *(CIA, adapted)*

REQUIRED: The equivalent units for direct materials for the current month.

DISCUSSION: Under the FIFO method, only work done in the current period is considered in the calculation. Direct materials are added when the units are 70% complete. Since beginning inventory is 60% complete with respect to conversion costs, no direct materials have been added yet. Thus, all materials will be added in the current period, which means 100% of the 20,000 beginning inventory units will be included in the calculation.

The units in ending inventory are 80% complete with respect to conversion. Since direct materials are added at 70%, all 25,000 units in ending inventory have had direct materials added and are 100% complete with respect to direct materials.

There are two more unit types we must account for: defective units and units that are started and completed in the current period. Inspection of the units takes place before direct materials are added, and if units are defective, then no direct materials will be added. Thus, defective units are not included in the calculation. Lastly, there are 150,000 units started and completed (170,000 units completed – 20,000 beginning inventory). The direct materials were added to these units in the current period, so they are included in the calculation.

Adding up all the units, we get 195,000 equivalent units for direct materials (20,000 beginning inventory + 25,000 ending inventory + 150,000 started and completed units).

Answer (A) is incorrect. The number of 175,000 units does not include 20,000 units from BWIP. Answer (B) is incorrect. The number of 181,500 units includes 150,000 units plus 40% of BWIP, 80% of EWIP, and 70% of the defective units. Answer (D) is incorrect. The number of 200,000 units includes 100% of the defective units.

12.4.10. The units that failed inspection during the current month would be classified by Ramseur as

A. Abnormal spoilage.

B. Normal scrap.

C. Normal reworked units.

D. Normal waste.

Answer (B) is correct. *(CIA, adapted)*

REQUIRED: The classification of units that failed inspection.

DISCUSSION: The units that failed inspection are classified as normal scrap because they have minimal value and can be sold without further reworking. The defective units are less than the 4% tolerance limit for normal spoilage (5,000 defective units ÷ 200,000 total units = 2.5%, < 4% tolerance limit). Scrap can be sold, disposed of, or reused.

Answer (A) is incorrect. Abnormal spoilage is not a normal result of efficient operations. In this case, the percentage of spoiled units is within the normal tolerance limit. Answer (C) is incorrect. Reworked units are defective units that require further processing for them to be sold. This company does not rework defective units. Answer (D) is incorrect. Waste has no monetary value and may have a disposal cost associated with it.

Questions 12.4.11 through 12.4.13 are based on the following information.

JC Company employs a process cost system. A unit of product passes through three departments -- molding, assembly, and finishing -- before it is complete. Finishing Department information for May follows:

	Units
Work-in-process inventory--May 1	1,400
Units transferred in from the Assembly Department	14,000
Units spoiled	700
Units transferred out to finished goods inventory	11,200

Raw materials are added at the beginning of the processing in the Finishing Department without changing the number of units being processed.

WIP was 70% complete as to conversion on May 1 and 40% complete as to conversion on May 31. All spoilage was discovered at final inspection before the units were transferred to finished goods; 560 of the units spoiled were within the limit considered normal.

The JC Company employs the weighted-average costing method. The equivalent units and the current costs per equivalent unit of production for each cost factor are as follows:

	EUP	Current Costs per EUP
Transferred-in	15,400	$5.00
Raw materials	15,400	1.00
Conversion cost	13,300	3.00
Total cost per EUP		$9.00

12.4.11. The cost of production transferred to the finished goods inventory is

A. $100,800

B. $105,840

C. $107,100

D. $102,060

Answer (B) is correct. *(CMA, adapted)*

REQUIRED: The weighted-average cost of production transferred to finished goods.

DISCUSSION: The costs assigned to finished goods inventory consist of the costs attached to the units transferred out plus the costs of normal spoilage (so the good units absorb the cost of normal spoilage). Because spoilage is detected at the end of the process, its unit cost ($9) is the same as the unit cost for good units. The cost of production transferred to finished goods is $105,840 [(11,200 good units + 560 normally spoiled units) × $9]. The remaining 140 units are abnormal spoilage and are written off as a period cost.

Answer (A) is incorrect. The amount of $100,800 does not include the cost of normal spoilage. Answer (C) is incorrect. The amount of $107,100 includes the cost of abnormal spoilage. Answer (D) is incorrect. The amount of $102,060 includes the cost of abnormal spoilage instead of normal spoilage.

12.4.12. The cost assigned to WIP on May 31 is

A. $28,000

B. $21,000

C. $25,200

D. $30,240

Answer (C) is correct. *(CMA, adapted)*

REQUIRED: The cost of EWIP using the weighted-average method.

DISCUSSION: To determine the cost assigned to EWIP, the EUP in EI must be calculated. BI plus units transferred in, minus the units completed and transferred, minus spoilage, equals EWIP of 3,500 units (1,400 + 14,000 – 11,200 – 700). Materials are added at the beginning of the process, and transferred-in costs are treated as if they were materials added at the beginning of the process. Because conversion is 40% complete, the EUP for conversion costs are 1,400 (3,500 × 40%).

Transferred-in (3,500 × $5)	$17,500
Materials (3,500 × $1)	3,500
Conversion cost (1,400 × $3)	4,200
EWIP costs	$25,200

Answer (A) is incorrect. The amount of $28,000 includes no materials cost and includes all of the conversion cost for the 3,500 units in WIP. Answer (B) is incorrect. Omitting conversion costs results in $21,000. Answer (D) is incorrect. The amount of $30,240 includes the cost of 560 spoiled units.

12.4.13. If the total costs of prior departments included in the WIP of the Finishing Department on May 1 amounted to $6,300, the total cost transferred in from the Assembly Department to the Finishing Department during May is

A. $70,000

B. $62,300

C. $70,700

D. $63,700

Answer (C) is correct. *(CMA, adapted)*

REQUIRED: The total costs transferred in during the period using the weighted-average method.

DISCUSSION: The total transferred-in cost is calculated by multiplying the transferred-in EUP by the cost per EUP (15,400 × $5 = $77,000). Given that $6,300 was included in the BWIP, the remainder ($77,000 – $6,300 = $70,700) must have been transferred in during the month.

Answer (A) is incorrect. The cost of units transferred in during May is $70,000. Answer (B) is incorrect. The total transferred-in costs equal $70,700 {[(1,400 + 14,000) × $5] – $6,300}. Answer (D) is incorrect. The transferred-in cost of BWIP (1,400 × $5) should be included.

STUDY UNIT THIRTEEN
CAPITAL BUDGETING

Capital budgeting plans expenditures for assets, the returns on which are expected to continue beyond 1 year. Capital budgeting decisions are long-term and relatively inflexible. Thus, accurate forecasting is needed. Choosing among investments requires a **ranking procedure**. The first step is to determine the asset cost or net investment. The second step is to calculate the periodic estimated cash flows. The third step is to relate the cash-flow benefits to their cost by using a method to evaluate the purchase. The fourth step is to rank the investments and choose the best. Present value and future value (time value of money) calculations are essential to capital budgeting. They are based on the **compound interest** concept that money in the future is worth less than the same amount today.

Methods for ranking investment proposals include those not based on the time value of money and those that are. The **payback period** is the number of years required to complete the return of the original investment (initial net investment ÷ periodic constant expected cash flow). The payback method also may be used with discounted cash flows. The **accounting rate of return** equals annual GAAP-based net operating income divided by the investment. The **profitability or excess present value** index is the ratio of the present value of future net cash inflows to the present value of the initial net investment.

Net present value (NPV) is the difference between the present values of the (1) net cash inflows and (2) net cash outflows. NPV is used when the discount rate is specified. The **internal rate of return (IRR)** is an interest rate calculated so that the NPV of the investment is zero. The NPV and IRR are best practices but assume that an investment decision is inflexible. However, some investments have **real options** that are not addressed in NPV and IRR models. For example, real options may include expanding future investment in a project or delaying investment. These options correspond to call options. Other real options include abandoning or reducing the scale of an investment. These options correspond to put options.

Capital budgeting is related to capital structure (permanent financing by long-term debt, preferred stock, and common shareholders' equity). **Financial leverage** is the relative amount of the fixed cost of capital, principally debt, in a capital structure. Leverage creates financial risk and relates directly to the cost of capital. The more leverage, the higher the financial risk, and the higher the cost of debt. The **degree of financial leverage (DFL)** is the percentage change in earnings available to common shareholders associated with a given percentage change in net operating income. **Operating leverage** is the extent to which production costs are fixed. The **degree of operating leverage (DOL)** is the percentage change in net operating income associated with a given percentage change in sales. The **degree of total leverage (DTL)** equals the DFL times the DOL.

In theory, an **optimal capital structure** exists. It minimizes the weighted-average cost of capital, maximizes the value of stock, and usually contains some (not 100%) debt. The **cost of capital** is the weighted average of the interest cost of debt (net of tax) and the implicit cost of equity capital to be invested. It is a required minimum return of a new long-term investment. The **weighted-average cost of capital** weights the percentage cost of each component by its percentage of the capital structure stated in terms of market values. The **cost of debt** equals the effective interest rate times one minus the marginal tax rate. The **cost of common stock (and retained earnings)** is the rate that investors can earn elsewhere on investments of comparable risk. But the **cost of new external common equity** is higher because of stock flotation costs. The **cost of preferred stock** equals the preferred dividend divided by the net issuance price.

One method of estimating the cost of common stock is the **capital asset pricing model (CAPM)**. It adds the risk-free rate to the product of (1) the beta coefficient (β) (a measure of the firm's risk) and (2) the difference between the market return and the risk-free rate. This **market risk premium** is the amount above the risk-free rate required to induce average investors to enter the market. The **dividend growth model** estimates the cost of common stock as equal to the next expected dividend per share divided by the market price, plus the expected constant growth rate.

QUESTIONS

13.1 General Concepts

13.1.1. Which one of the following is the best characteristic concerning the capital budget? The capital budget is a(n)

A. Plan to ensure that there are sufficient funds available for the operating needs of the company.

B. Exercise that sets the long-range goals of the company including the consideration of external influences caused by others in the market.

C. Plan that results in the cash requirements during the operating cycle.

D. Plan that assesses the long-term needs of the company for plant and equipment purchases.

Answer (D) is correct. *(CMA, adapted)*

REQUIRED: The true statement about the capital budget.

DISCUSSION: Capital budgeting is the process of planning expenditures for long-lived assets. It involves choosing among investment proposals using a ranking procedure. Evaluations are based on various measures involving the IRR.

Answer (A) is incorrect. Capital budgeting involves long-term investment needs, not immediate operating needs. Answer (B) is incorrect. Establishing long-term goals in the context of relevant factors in the environment is strategic planning. Answer (C) is incorrect. Cash budgeting determines operating cash flows. Capital budgeting evaluates the rate of return on specific investment alternatives.

13.1.2. During the year just ended, Deet Corp. experienced the following power outages:

Number of Outages per Month	Number of Months
0	3
1	2
2	4
3	3
	12

Each power outage results in out-of-pocket costs of $400. For $500 per month, Deet can lease an auxiliary generator to provide power during outages. If Deet leases an auxiliary generator for the current year, the estimated savings (or additional expenditures) would be

A. $(3,600)

B. $(1,200)

C. $1,600

D. $1,900

Answer (C) is correct. *(CPA, adapted)*

REQUIRED: The estimated savings from leasing a generator.

DISCUSSION: Assuming the power outages in Year 1 are repeated in Year 2, the number of outages will be 19 [(1 × 2) + (2 × 4) + (3 × 3)], and the cost will be $7,600 (19 × $400). The lease of the generator will cost $6,000 (12 × $500). Thus, the estimated savings is $1,600 ($7,600 – $6,000).

Answer (A) is incorrect. The cost of outages will be $7,600 (19 × $400) and the cost of leasing the generator will be $6,000 (12 × $500). Answer (B) is incorrect. The amount of $(1,200) assumes 12 power outages instead of 19. Answer (D) is incorrect. The amount of $1,900 assumes a savings of $100 per outage.

13.1.3. Of the following decisions, capital budgeting techniques would least likely be used in evaluating the

A. Acquisition of new aircraft by a cargo company.

B. Design and implementation of a major advertising program.

C. Trade for a star quarterback by a football team.

D. Adoption of a new method of allocating nontraceable costs to product lines.

Answer (D) is correct. *(CMA, adapted)*

REQUIRED: The decision least likely to be evaluated using capital budgeting.

DISCUSSION: Capital budgeting is the process of planning expenditures for investments on which the returns are expected to occur over a period of more than 1 year. Thus, capital budgeting applies to the acquisition or disposal of long-term assets and the financing ramifications of such decisions. The adoption of a new method of allocating nontraceable costs to product lines has no effect on a firm's cash flows, the acquisition of long-term assets, and financing. Thus, capital budgeting is irrelevant to such a decision.

Answer (A) is incorrect. A new aircraft is a long-term investment in a capital good. Answer (B) is incorrect. A major advertising program is a high cost investment with long-term effects. Answer (C) is incorrect. A star quarterback is a costly asset who is expected to have a substantial effect on the team's long-term profitability.

13.1.4. The capital budgeting model that is generally considered the best model for long-range decision making is the

A. Payback model.

B. Accounting rate of return model.

C. Unadjusted rate of return model.

D. Discounted cash flow model.

Answer (D) is correct. *(CMA, adapted)*

REQUIRED: The best capital budgeting model for long-range decision making.

DISCUSSION: The capital budgeting methods that are generally considered the best for long-range decision making are the internal rate of return and net present value methods. These are both discounted cash flow methods.

Answer (A) is incorrect. The payback method gives no consideration to the time value of money or to returns after the payback period. Answer (B) is incorrect. The accounting rate of return does not consider the time value of money. Answer (C) is incorrect. The unadjusted rate of return does not consider the time value of money.

13.1.5. Discounted cash flow concepts apply to

	Interest Factors	Risk
A.	Yes	Yes
B.	Yes	No
C.	No	Yes
D.	No	No

Answer (A) is correct. *(Publisher, adapted)*

REQUIRED: The concept(s) underlying the time value of money.

DISCUSSION: The time value of money relates to (1) the investment value of money and (2) the risk (uncertainty) inherent in any unperformed (executory) agreement. Thus, a dollar today is worth more than a dollar in the future, and the longer the wait for a dollar, the more uncertain the receipt is.

13.1.6. All of the following items are included in discounted cash flow analysis except

A. Future operating cash savings.

B. The current asset disposal price.

C. The future asset depreciation expense.

D. The tax effects of future asset depreciation.

Answer (C) is correct. *(CMA, adapted)*

REQUIRED: The item not included in discounted cash flow analysis.

DISCUSSION: Discounted cash flow analysis, using either the internal rate of return (IRR) or the net present value (NPV) method, is based on the time value of cash inflows and outflows. All future operating cash savings are considered, as well as the tax effects on cash flows of future depreciation charges. The cash proceeds of future asset disposals are likewise a necessary consideration. Depreciation expense is a consideration only to the extent that it affects the cash flows for taxes. Otherwise, depreciation is excluded from the analysis because it is a noncash expense.

Answer (A) is incorrect. Future operating cash savings is a consideration in discounted cash flow analysis. Answer (B) is incorrect. The current asset disposal price is a consideration in discounted cash flow analysis. Answer (D) is incorrect. The tax effects of future asset depreciation is a consideration in discounted cash flow analysis.

13.1.7. Which one of the following statements concerning cash flow determination for capital budgeting purposes is not correct?

A. Tax depreciation must be considered because it affects cash payments for taxes.

B. Book depreciation is relevant because it affects net income.

C. Sunk costs are not incremental flows and should not be included.

D. Proceeds from disposal of old equipment should be included in cash flow forecasts.

Answer (B) is correct. *(CMA, adapted)*

REQUIRED: The false statement about cash flow determination.

DISCUSSION: Tax depreciation is relevant to cash flow analysis because it affects the amount of income taxes that must be paid. However, book depreciation is not relevant because it does not affect the amount of cash generated by an investment.

Answer (A) is incorrect. It is a true statement relating to capital budgeting. Answer (C) is incorrect. It is a true statement relating to capital budgeting. Answer (D) is incorrect. It is a true statement relating to capital budgeting.

13.1.8. For the next 2 years, a lease is estimated to have an operating net cash inflow of $7,500 per annum, before adjusting for $5,000 per annum tax-basis lease amortization, and a 40% tax rate. The present value of an ordinary annuity of $1 per year at 10% for 2 years is 1.74. What is the lease's after-tax present value using a 10% discount factor?

A. $2,610

B. $4,350

C. $9,570

D. $11,310

Answer (D) is correct. *(CPA, adapted)*

REQUIRED: The after-tax present value of a lease.

DISCUSSION: The net present value of the lease is calculated as follows:

Annual operating cash inflow	$ 7,500
Annual income tax ($7,500 × 40%)	(3,000)
Depreciation tax shield ($5,000 × 40%)	2,000
Net annual after-tax cash flows	$ 6,500
Times: PV factor	× 1.74
Present value of net cash inflow	$11,310

Answer (A) is incorrect. The amount of $2,610 is the present value of $1,500. Answer (B) is incorrect. The amount of $4,350 is the present value of $2,500. Answer (C) is incorrect. The amount of $9,750 is the present value of $5,500.

13.1.9. An actuary has determined that a company should have $90 million accumulated in its pension fund 20 years from now for the fund to be able to meet its obligations. An interest rate of 8% is considered appropriate for all pension fund calculations. The company wishes to know how much it should contribute to the pension fund at the end of each of the next 20 years. Which set of instructions correctly describes the procedures necessary to compute the annual contribution?

A. Divide $90,000,000 by the factor for present value of an ordinary annuity.

B. Multiply $90,000,000 by the factor for present value of an ordinary annuity.

C. Divide $90,000,000 by the factor for future value of an ordinary annuity.

D. Multiply $90,000,000 by the factor for future value of an ordinary annuity.

Answer (C) is correct. *(CIA, adapted)*

REQUIRED: The instructions that describe the procedures for calculating the annual contribution.

DISCUSSION: The future value of an annuity equals the appropriate interest factor (for n periods at an interest rate of i), which is derived from standard tables, times the periodic payment. The $90 million amount is the future value of the funding payments. The amount of each funding payment can be calculated by dividing the future value of the funding payments by the interest factor for future value of an ordinary annuity for n equals 20 and i equals 8%.

Answer (A) is incorrect. The amount of $90,000,000 is a future value. The interest factor to be used for the division process should be a future value factor, not a present value factor. Answer (B) is incorrect. The amount of $90,000,000 is a future value. The factor to be used should be a future value factor. That factor should be used in a division, rather than a multiplication, process. Answer (D) is incorrect. The amount of $90,000,000 should be divided by the appropriate interest factor.

13.1.10. The discount rate ordinarily used in present value calculations is the

A. Federal Reserve rate.

B. Treasury bill rate.

C. Minimum desired rate of return set by the entity.

D. Prime rate.

Answer (C) is correct. *(Publisher, adapted)*

REQUIRED: The discount rate customarily used in present value calculations.

DISCUSSION: The discount rate most often used in present value calculations is the minimum desired rate of return as set by management. The NPV determined in this calculation is a first step in the decision process. It indicates how the project's return compares with the minimum desired rate of return.

Answer (A) is incorrect. The Federal Reserve rate may be considered. However, an entity sets its minimum desired rate of return in view of its needs. Answer (B) is incorrect. The Treasury bill rate may be considered. However, an entity sets its minimum desired rate of return in view of its needs. Answer (D) is incorrect. The prime rate may be considered. However, an entity sets its minimum desired rate of return in view of its needs.

Questions 13.1.11 through 13.1.13 are based on the following information.

Crown Corporation has agreed to sell some used computer equipment to Bob Parsons, one of the company's employees, for $5,000. Crown and Parsons have been discussing alternative financing arrangements for the sale. The information in the opposite column is pertinent to these discussions.

Present Value of an Ordinary Annuity of $1

Payments	5%	6%	7%	8%
1	0.952	0.943	0.935	0.926
2	1.859	1.833	1.808	1.783
3	2.723	2.673	2.624	2.577
4	3.546	3.465	3.387	3.312
5	4.329	4.212	4.100	3.993
6	5.076	4.917	4.767	4.623
7	5.786	5.582	5.389	5.206
8	6.463	6.210	5.971	5.747

13.1.11. Crown Corporation has offered to accept a $1,000 down payment and set up a note receivable for Bob Parsons that calls for a $1,000 payment at the end of each of the next 4 years. If Crown uses a 6% discount rate, the present value of the note receivable would be

A. $2,940

B. $4,465

C. $4,212

D. $3,465

Answer (D) is correct. *(CMA, adapted)*

REQUIRED: The present value of a note receivable that requires an equal payment at the end of each year.

DISCUSSION: The four equal payments are an ordinary annuity because they are due at the end of each period. Given a discount rate of 6%, the appropriate present value is 3.465. The present value is $3,465 ($1,000 payment × 3.465).

Answer (A) is incorrect. The amount of $2,940 assumes the note is payable in full at the end of the fourth year. Answer (B) is incorrect. The amount of $4,465 equals $1,000 times 3.465, plus $1,000. Answer (C) is incorrect. The amount of $4,212 equals $1,000 times 4.212.

13.1.12. Bob Parsons has agreed to the immediate down payment of $1,000 but would like the note for $4,000 to be payable in full at the end of the fourth year. Because of the increased risk associated with the terms of this note, Crown Corporation would apply an 8% discount rate. The present value of this note would be

A. $2,940

B. $3,312

C. $3,940

D. $2,557

Answer (A) is correct. *(CMA, adapted)*

REQUIRED: The present value of a note payable in full at the end of its term.

DISCUSSION: A present value table for a single future amount is not given, so the first step is to derive the appropriate discount factor from the table for the present value of an ordinary annuity. The factor for four payments at 8% is 3.312. The factor for three payments is 2.577. Consequently, the difference between the factors for 3 and 4 years is .735 (3.312 – 2.577). The present value of a single $4,000 payment in 4 years is therefore $2,940 ($4,000 × .735).

Answer (B) is incorrect. The amount of $3,312 equals $1,000 times 3.312. Answer (C) is incorrect. The amount of $3,940 equals $4,000 times .735, plus $1,000. Answer (D) is incorrect. The amount of $2,557 equals $1,000 times 2.557.

13.1.13. If Bob Parsons borrowed the $5,000 at 8% interest for 4 years from his bank and paid Crown Corporation the full price of the equipment immediately, Crown could invest the $5,000 for 3 years at 7%. The future value of this investment (rounded) would be

A. $6,297

B. $6,127

C. $6,553

D. $6,803

Answer (B) is correct. *(CMA, adapted)*

REQUIRED: The future value of an amount.

DISCUSSION: The present value of a future amount equals the amount times the appropriate interest factor. Thus, the future amount must equal the present value divided by the interest factor. The present value is given, and the interest factor for the present value of an amount can be derived from the table for the present value of an ordinary annuity. In this case, the factor is equal to the difference between the factors for three and two periods at the given interest rate of 7% (2.624 – 1.808 = .816). Accordingly, the future amount of $5,000 in 3 years given an interest rate of 7% is $6,127 ($5,000 present value ÷ .816).

Answer (A) is incorrect. The amount of $6,297 equals $5,000 divided by .794 (2.577 – 1.783). Answer (C) is incorrect. The amount of $6,553 equals $5,000 divided by .763 (3.387 – 2.624). Answer (D) is incorrect. The amount of $6,803 equals $5,000 divided by .735 (3.312 – 2.577).

13.1.14. Janet Taylor Casual Wear has $75,000 in a bank account as of December 31, Year 3. If the company plans on depositing $4,000 in the account at the end of each of the next 3 years (Year 4, Year 5, and Year 6) and all amounts in the account earn 8% per year, what will the account balance be at December 31, Year 6? Ignore the effect of income taxes.

	8% Interest Rate Factors	
Period	Future Value of $1	Future Value of an Annuity of $1
1	1.08	1.00
2	1.17	2.08
3	1.26	3.25
4	1.36	4.51

A. $87,000

B. $88,000

C. $96,070

D. $107,500

Answer (D) is correct. *(CMA, adapted)*

REQUIRED: The future value of an investment.

DISCUSSION: Both future value tables are used because the $75,000 already in the account is multiplied by the future value factor of 1.26 to determine the amount in 3 years, or $94,500. The three payments of $4,000 represent an ordinary annuity. Multiplying the three-period annuity factor (3.25) by the payment amount ($4,000) results in a future value of the annuity of $13,000. Adding the two elements results in a total account balance of $107,500 ($94,500 + $13,000).

Answer (A) is incorrect. The amount of $87,000 is in the account if interest were zero. Answer (B) is incorrect. The amount of $88,000 ignores the interest that would be earned on the $75,000 initial balance. Answer (C) is incorrect. The amount of $96,070 is available after 2 years (December 31, Year 5).

13.1.15. Which one of the following capital investment evaluation methods does not take the time value of money into consideration?

A. Net present value.

B. Discounted payback.

C. Internal rate of return.

D. Accounting rate of return.

Answer (D) is correct. *(CMA, adapted)*

REQUIRED: The capital investment evaluation method that does not discount cash flows.

DISCUSSION: The accounting rate of return (unadjusted rate of return or rate of return on the carrying amount) equals accounting net income divided by the required initial or average investment. The accounting rate of return ignores the time value of money.

Answer (A) is incorrect. The net present value is the sum of the present values of all the cash inflows and outflows associated with an investment. Answer (B) is incorrect. The discounted payback method calculates the payback period by determining the present values of the future cash flows. Answer (C) is incorrect. The internal rate of return is the discount rate at which the NPV is zero.

13.1.16. The length of time required to recover the initial cash outlay of a capital project is determined by using the

A. Discounted cash flow method.

B. Payback method.

C. Weighted net present value method.

D. Net present value method.

Answer (B) is correct. *(CMA, adapted)*

REQUIRED: The method of determining the time required to recover the initial cash outlay of a capital project.

DISCUSSION: The payback method measures the number of years required to complete the return of a project's original investment.

Answer (A) is incorrect. The discounted cash flow method computes a rate of return. Answer (C) is incorrect. The net present value method is based on discounted cash flows; the length of time to recover an investment is not the result. Answer (D) is incorrect. The net present value method is based on discounted cash flows; the length of time to recover an investment is not the result.

13.1.17. The internal rate of return (IRR) is the

A. Hurdle rate.

B. Rate of interest for which the net present value is greater than 1.0.

C. Rate of interest for which the net present value is equal to zero.

D. Rate of return generated from the operational cash flows.

Answer (C) is correct. *(CMA, adapted)*

REQUIRED: The true statement about the IRR.

DISCUSSION: The IRR is the interest rate at which the present value of the expected future cash inflows is equal to the present value of the cash outflows for a project. Thus, the IRR is the interest rate that will produce a net present value (NPV) equal to zero. The IRR method assumes that the cash flows will be reinvested at the internal rate of return.

Answer (A) is incorrect. The hurdle rate is a concept used to calculate the NPV of a project; it is determined by management prior to the analysis. Answer (B) is incorrect. The IRR is the rate of interest at which the NPV is zero. Answer (D) is incorrect. The IRR is a means of evaluating potential investment projects.

13.1.18. Pole Co. is investing in a machine with a 3-year life. The machine is expected to reduce annual cash operating costs by $30,000 in each of the first 2 years and by $20,000 in Year 3. Present values of an annuity of $1 at 14% are

Period 1	0.88
2	1.65
3	2.32

Using a 14% cost of capital, what is the present value of these future savings?

A. $59,600

B. $60,800

C. $62,900

D. $69,500

Answer (C) is correct. *(CPA, adapted)*

REQUIRED: The present value of an investment.

DISCUSSION: The annual savings are as follows:

Year 1	$30,000
Year 2	$30,000
Year 3	$20,000

Thus, the operating costs are reduced by a total amount of $80,000 from Year 1 to Year 3. Present value of an annuity of $1 is given. In order to use the given PV annuity factors to determine the NPV, the amount of cash savings must be the same for each PV factor. For the 3-year PV factor, there are savings of at least $20,000 in all three years; for the 2-year PV factor, $10,000 cash savings remain in Year 1 and Year 2 ($30,000 – $20,000). Therefore, the 3-year PV factor of 2.32 can be used to discount the $20,000 savings for Year 1 to Year 3; the 2-year PV factor of 1.65 can be used to discount the Year 1 and Year 2 savings of $10,000.

Using a 14% cost of capital and ignoring tax effects, the present value of the future savings can be calculated as follows:

PV of 3-year cash savings:	$20,000 × 2.32 =	$46,400
PV of 2-year cash savings:	$10,000 × 1.65 =	16,500
Net present value		$62,900

Answer (A) is incorrect. This amount equals the present value of a 3-year annuity for $30,000, minus $10,000. Answer (B) is incorrect. The present value of the future savings is $62,900. Answer (D) is incorrect. This amount equals the present value of a 2-year annuity for $30,000, plus $20,000.

13.1.19. The net present value method of capital budgeting assumes that cash flows are reinvested at

A. The risk-free rate.

B. The cost of debt.

C. The rate of return of the project.

D. The discount rate used in the analysis.

Answer (D) is correct. *(CMA, adapted)*

REQUIRED: The assumed rate at which cash flows are reinvested under the net present value (NPV) method.

DISCUSSION: The NPV method assumes that periodic cash inflows earned over the life of an investment are reinvested at the company's cost of capital (i.e., the discount rate used in the analysis). This is contrary to the assumption under the internal rate of return method, which assumes that cash inflows are reinvested at the internal rate of return. As a result of this difference, the two methods will occasionally give different rankings of investment alternatives.

Answer (A) is incorrect. The NPV method assumes that cash inflows are reinvested at the discount rate used in the NPV calculation. Answer (B) is incorrect. The cost of debt may or may not reflect the firm's actual cost of capital. Answer (C) is incorrect. The internal rate of return method assumes a reinvestment rate equal to the rate of return on the project.

13.1.20. The technique that reflects the time value of money and is calculated by dividing the present value of the future net after-tax cash inflows that have been discounted at the desired cost of capital by the initial cash outlay for the investment is called the

A. Capital rationing method.

B. Average rate of return method.

C. Profitability index method.

D. Accounting rate of return method.

Answer (C) is correct. *(CMA, adapted)*

REQUIRED: The method that divides the present value of future net cash inflows by the initial cash outlay.

DISCUSSION: The profitability index, also called the excess present value index, measures the ratio of the present value of a project's future net cash inflows to the original investment. If capital rationing is necessary, the profitability index allows management to identify the projects with the highest return per investment dollar.

Answer (A) is incorrect. Capital rationing is not a method but rather a condition that characterizes capital budgeting when insufficient capital is available to finance all profitable investment opportunities. Answer (B) is incorrect. The average rate of return method does not divide the future cash flows by the cost of the investment. Answer (D) is incorrect. The accounting rate of return does not recognize the time value of money.

Questions 13.1.21 through 13.1.24 are based on the following information. In order to increase production capacity, Gunning Industries is considering replacing an existing production machine with a new technologically improved machine effective January 1. The following information is being considered by Gunning Industries:

- The new machine would be purchased for $160,000 in cash. Shipping, installation, and testing would cost an additional $30,000.
- The new machine is expected to increase annual sales by 20,000 units at a sales price of $40 per unit. Incremental operating costs include $30 per unit in variable costs and total fixed costs of $40,000 per year.
- The investment in the new machine will require an immediate increase in working capital of $35,000. This cash outflow will be recovered after 5 years.
- Gunning uses straight-line depreciation for financial reporting and tax reporting purposes. The new machine has an estimated useful life of 5 years and zero salvage value.
- Gunning is subject to a 40% corporate income tax rate.

Gunning uses the net present value method to analyze investments and will employ the following factors and rates:

Period	Present Value of $1 at 10%	Present Value of an Ordinary Annuity of $1 at 10%
1	.909	.909
2	.826	1.736
3	.751	2.487
4	.683	3.170
5	.621	3.791

13.1.21. Gunning Industries' net cash outflow in a capital budgeting decision is

A. $190,000

B. $195,000

C. $204,525

D. $225,000

Answer (D) is correct. *(CMA, adapted)*

REQUIRED: The net cash outflow in a capital budgeting decision.

DISCUSSION: The machine costs $160,000 and will require $30,000 to install and test. In addition, the company will have to invest in $35,000 of working capital to support the production of the new machine. Thus, the total investment necessary is $225,000.

Answer (A) is incorrect. The amount of $190,000 ignores the investment in working capital. Answer (B) is incorrect. The amount of $195,000 ignores the $30,000 of shipping, installation, and testing costs. Answer (C) is incorrect. The amount of $204,525 is the present value of $225,000 at 10% for 1 year.

13.1.22. Gunning Industries' discounted annual depreciation tax shield for the year of replacement is

A. $13,817

B. $16,762

C. $20,725

D. $22,800

Answer (A) is correct. *(CMA, adapted)*

REQUIRED: The discounted annual depreciation tax shield.

DISCUSSION: Gunning uses straight-line depreciation. Thus, the annual charge is $38,000 [($160,000 + $30,000) ÷ 5 years], and the tax savings is $15,200 ($38,000 × 40%). That benefit will be received in 1 year, so the present value is $13,817 ($15,200 tax savings × .909 present value of $1 for 1 year at 10%).

Answer (B) is incorrect. The amount of $16,762 is greater than the undiscounted tax savings. Answer (C) is incorrect. The amount of $20,725 assumes a 60% tax rate (the complement of the actual 40% rate). Answer (D) is incorrect. The amount of $22,800 assumes a 60% tax rate and no discounting.

13.1.23. The overall discounted cash flow impact of Gunning Industries' working capital investment for the new production machine would be

A. $(7,959)

B. $(10,080)

C. $(13,265)

D. $(35,000)

Answer (C) is correct. *(CMA, adapted)*

REQUIRED: The overall discounted cash flow impact of the working capital investment.

DISCUSSION: The $35,000 of working capital requires an immediate outlay for that amount, but it will be recovered in 5 years. Thus, the net discounted cash outflow is $13,265 [$35,000 initial investment – ($35,000 future inflow × .621 PV of $1 for 5 years at 10%)].

Answer (A) is incorrect. The amount of $(7,959) assumes the initial investment and its return are reduced by applying a 40% tax rate. Answer (B) is incorrect. The amount of $(10,080) assumes the initial investment was discounted for 1 year. Answer (D) is incorrect. The amount of $(35,000) fails to consider that the $35,000 will be recovered (essentially in the form of a salvage value) after the fifth year.

13.1.24. The acquisition of the new production machine by Gunning Industries will contribute a discounted net-of-tax contribution margin of

A. $242,624

B. $303,280

C. $363,936

D. $454,920

Answer (D) is correct. *(CMA, adapted)*

REQUIRED: The discounted net-of-tax contribution margin from the new machine.

DISCUSSION: The new machine will increase sales by 20,000 units a year. The increase in the pretax total contribution margin will be $200,000 per year [20,000 units × ($40 SP – $30 VC)], and the annual increase in the after-tax contribution margin will be $120,000 [$200,000 × (1.0 – .4)]. The present value of the after-tax increase in the contribution margin over the 5-year useful life of the machine is $454,920 ($120,000 × 3.791 PV of an ordinary annuity for 5 years at 10%).

Answer (A) is incorrect. The amount of $242,624 deducts fixed costs from the pretax contribution margin and applies a 60% tax rate. Answer (B) is incorrect. The amount of $303,280 deducts fixed costs from the after-tax contribution margin before discounting. Answer (C) is incorrect. The amount of $363,936 deducts fixed costs from the contribution margin before calculating taxes and the present value.

13.1.25. Risk to a company is affected by both project variability and how project returns correlate with those of the company's prevailing business. Overall company risk will be lowest when a project's returns exhibit

A. Low variability and negative correlation.

B. Low variability and positive correlation.

C. High variability and positive correlation.

D. High variability and no correlation.

Answer (A) is correct. *(CIA, adapted)*

REQUIRED: The circumstance in which overall company risk will be lowest.

DISCUSSION: A common general definition is that risk is an investment with an unknown outcome but a known probability distribution of returns (a known mean and standard deviation). An increase in the standard deviation (variability) of returns is synonymous with an increase in the riskiness of a project. Risk is also increased when the project's returns are positively (directly) correlated with other investments in the firm's portfolio. Thus, risk increases when returns on all projects increase or decrease together. Consequently, the overall risk is decreased when projects have low variability and are negatively correlated (the diversification effect).

13.1.26. When the risks of the individual components of a project's cash flows are different, an acceptable procedure to evaluate these cash flows is to

A. Divide each cash flow by the payback period.

B. Compute the net present value of each cash flow using the firm's cost of capital.

C. Compare the internal rate of return from each cash flow to its risk.

D. Discount each cash flow using a discount rate that reflects the degree of risk.

Answer (D) is correct. *(CMA, adapted)*

REQUIRED: The acceptable procedure for evaluating cash flows when the risks of individual components of the project's cash flows are different.

DISCUSSION: Risk-adjusted discount rates can be used to evaluate capital investment options. If risks differ among various elements of the cash flows, then different discount rates can be used for different flows.

Answer (A) is incorrect. The payback period ignores both the varying risk and the time value of money. Answer (B) is incorrect. Using the cost of capital as the discount rate does not make any adjustment for the risk differentials among the various cash flows. Answer (C) is incorrect. Risk has to be incorporated into the company's hurdle rate to use the internal rate of return method with risk differentials.

13.1.27. Sensitivity analysis, if used with capital projects,

A. Is used extensively when cash flows are known with certainty.

B. Measures the change in the discounted cash flows when using the discounted payback method rather than the net present value method.

C. Is a "what-if" technique that asks how a given outcome will change if the original estimates of the capital budgeting model are changed.

D. Is a technique used to rank capital expenditure requests.

Answer (C) is correct. *(CMA, adapted)*

REQUIRED: The true statement about sensitivity analysis.

DISCUSSION: After a problem has been formulated into any mathematical model, it may be subjected to sensitivity analysis, which is a trial-and-error method used to determine the sensitivity of the estimates used. For example, forecasts of many calculated NPVs under various assumptions may be compared to determine how sensitive the NPV is to changing conditions. Changing the assumptions about a certain variable or group of variables may drastically alter the NPV, suggesting that the risk of the investment may be excessive.

Answer (A) is incorrect. Sensitivity analysis is useful when cash flows or other assumptions are uncertain. Answer (B) is incorrect. Sensitivity analysis can be used with any of the capital budgeting methods. Answer (D) is incorrect. Sensitivity analysis is not a ranking technique; it calculates results under varying assumptions.

13.1.28. When determining net present value in an inflationary environment, adjustments should be made to

A. Increase the discount rate only.

B. Increase the estimated cash inflows and increase the discount rate.

C. Decrease the estimated cash inflows and increase the discount rate.

D. Increase the estimated cash inflows and decrease the discount rate.

Answer (B) is correct. *(CMA, adapted)*

REQUIRED: The adjustment to determine NPV in an inflationary environment.

DISCUSSION: In an inflationary environment, nominal future cash flows should increase to reflect the decrease in the value of the unit of measure. Also, the investor should increase the discount rate to reflect the increased inflation premium arising from the additional uncertainty. Lenders require a higher interest rate in an inflationary environment.

13.1.29. Fast Freight, Inc., is planning to purchase equipment to make its operations more efficient. This equipment has an estimated life of 6 years. As part of this acquisition, a $75,000 investment in working capital is anticipated. In a discounted cash flow analysis, the investment in working capital

A. Should be amortized over the useful life of the equipment.

B. Should be treated as a recurring cash outflow over the life of the equipment.

C. Should be treated as an immediate cash outflow.

D. Should be treated as an immediate cash outflow recovered at the end of 6 years.

Answer (D) is correct. *(CMA, adapted)*

REQUIRED: The true statement about an investment in working capital related to an equipment purchase.

DISCUSSION: The investment in a new project includes more than the initial cost of new capital equipment. In addition, funds must be provided for increases in receivables and inventories. This investment in working capital is treated as an initial cost of the investment that is recovered in full as a cash inflow at the end of the project's life.

Answer (A) is incorrect. The investment in working capital is needed throughout the life of the investment. Answer (B) is incorrect. The investment occurs only at the start of the project. Answer (C) is incorrect. The initial investment is an initial recoverable cash outflow.

13.1.30. A company is expanding its manufacturing plant, which requires an investment of $4 million in new equipment and plant modifications. The company's sales are expected to increase by $3 million per year as a result of the expansion. Cash investment in current assets averages 30% of sales; accounts payable and other current liabilities are 10% of sales. What is the estimated total investment for this expansion?

A. $3.4 million.

B. $4.3 million.

C. $4.6 million.

D. $5.2 million.

Answer (C) is correct. *(CMA, adapted)*

REQUIRED: The estimated total cash investment.

DISCUSSION: The investment required includes increases in working capital (e.g., additional receivables and inventories resulting from the acquisition of a new manufacturing plant). The additional working capital is an initial cost of the investment, but one that will be recovered (i.e., it has a salvage value equal to its initial cost). The company can use current liabilities to fund assets to the extent of 10% of sales. Thus, the total initial cash outlay will be $4.6 million {$4 million + [(30% – 10%) × $3 million sales]}.

Answer (A) is incorrect. The amount of $3.4 million deducts the investment in working capital from the cost of equipment. Answer (B) is incorrect. The amount of $4.3 million equals $4 million plus 10% of $3 million. Answer (D) is incorrect. The amount of $5.2 million equals $4 million plus 30% of $4 million.

13.1.31. In equipment replacement decisions, which one of the following does not affect the decision-making process?

A. Current disposal price of the old equipment.

B. Operating costs of the old equipment.

C. Original fair value of the old equipment.

D. Operating costs of the new equipment.

Answer (C) is correct. *(CMA, adapted)*

REQUIRED: The irrelevant factor when making an equipment replacement decision.

DISCUSSION: All relevant costs should be considered when evaluating an equipment replacement decision. These include the initial investment in the new equipment, any required investment in working capital, the disposal price of the new equipment, the disposal price of the old equipment, the operating costs of the old equipment, and the operating costs of the new equipment. The original cost or fair value of the old equipment is a sunk cost and is irrelevant to future decisions.

Answer (A) is incorrect. The current disposal price of the old equipment should be considered when evaluating an equipment replacement decision. Answer (B) is incorrect. The operating costs of the old equipment should be considered when evaluating an equipment replacement decision. Answer (D) is incorrect. The operating costs of the new equipment should be considered when evaluating an equipment replacement decision.

13.2 Payback

13.2.1. Which of the following is a strength of the payback method?

A. It considers cash flows for all years of the project.

B. It distinguishes the sources of cash inflows.

C. It considers the time value of money.

D. It is easy to understand.

Answer (D) is correct. *(CPA, adapted)*

REQUIRED: The strength of the payback method.

DISCUSSION: The strength of the payback method is its simplicity. The payback period is the time required for undiscounted net cash inflows to equal the cost of initial investment.

Answer (A) is incorrect. The payback method ignores the effects of cash flows after the payback period. Answer (B) is incorrect. The payback method uses periodic cash flows. It does not distinguish the sources of the cash inflows. Answer (C) is incorrect. The time value of money is ignored.

13.2.2. A characteristic of the payback method (before taxes) is that it

A. Incorporates the time value of money.

B. Neglects total project profitability.

C. Uses accrual accounting inflows in the numerator of the calculation.

D. Uses the estimated expected life of the asset in the denominator of the calculation.

Answer (B) is correct. *(CMA, adapted)*

REQUIRED: The characteristic of the payback method.

DISCUSSION: The payback method calculates the number of years required to complete the return of the original investment. This measure is determined by dividing the net investment required by the average expected cash flow to be generated, resulting in the number of years required to recover the original investment. Payback is easy to calculate but has two principal problems: (1) It ignores the time value of money, and (2) it does not consider returns after the payback period. Thus, it ignores total project profitability.

Answer (A) is incorrect. The payback method does not incorporate the time value of money. Answer (C) is incorrect. The payback method uses the net investment in the numerator of the calculation. Answer (D) is incorrect. Payback uses the net annual cash inflows in the denominator of the calculation.

13.2.3. The bailout payback method

A. Incorporates the time value of money.

B. Equals the recovery period from normal operations.

C. Eliminates the disposal value from the payback calculation.

D. Measures the risk if a project is terminated.

Answer (D) is correct. *(CMA, adapted)*

REQUIRED: The true statement about the bailout payback method.

DISCUSSION: The payback period equals the net investment divided by the average expected cash flow, resulting in the number of years required to recover the original investment. The bailout payback incorporates the salvage value of the asset into the calculation. It determines the length of the payback period when the periodic cash inflows are combined with the salvage value. Hence, the method measures risk. The longer the payback period, the more risky the investment.

Answer (A) is incorrect. The bailout payback method does not consider the time value of money. Answer (B) is incorrect. The bailout payback includes salvage value as well as cash flow from operations. Answer (C) is incorrect. The bailout payback incorporates the disposal value in the payback calculation.

13.2.4. A machine costing $1,000 produces total cash inflows of $1,400 over 4 years. Determine the payback period given the following cash flows:

Year	After-Tax Cash Flows	Cumulative Cash Flows
1	$400	$ 400
2	300	700
3	500	1,200
4	200	1,400

A. 2 years.

B. 2.60 years.

C. 2.86 years.

D. 3 years.

Answer (B) is correct. *(CIA, adapted)*

REQUIRED: The payback period given the annual cash flows.

DISCUSSION: Because $700 is received in the first 2 years, only $300 is recovered in Year 3. The payback period is therefore 2.6 years [2 years + ($300 ÷ $500) of Year 3].

Answer (A) is incorrect. After 2 years, $300 ($1,000 – $700) remains to be recovered. Answer (C) is incorrect. The payback period is determined by adding 2 plus the percentage of Year 3 cash flows necessary to recover the balance of the $1,000 original investment. Answer (D) is incorrect. At the end of 3 years, $200 ($1,200 – $1,000) more than the original cost will have been recovered.

13.2.5. Jasper Company has a payback goal of 3 years on new equipment acquisitions. A new sorter is being evaluated that costs $450,000 and has a 5-year life. Straight-line depreciation will be used; no salvage is anticipated. Jasper is subject to a 40% income tax rate. To meet the company's payback goal, the sorter must generate reductions in annual cash operating costs of

A. $60,000

B. $100,000

C. $150,000

D. $190,000

Answer (D) is correct. *(CMA, adapted)*

REQUIRED: The cash savings that must be generated to achieve a targeted payback period.

DISCUSSION: Given a periodic constant cash flow, the payback period is calculated by dividing cost by the annual after-tax cash inflows, or cash savings. To achieve a payback period of 3 years, the annual increment in net cash inflow generated by the investment must be $150,000 ($450,000 ÷ 3-year targeted payback period). This amount equals the total reduction in cash operating costs minus related taxes. Depreciation is $90,000 ($450,000 ÷ 5 years). Because depreciation is a noncash deductible expense, it shields $90,000 of the cash savings from taxation. Accordingly, $60,000 ($150,000 – $90,000) of the additional net cash inflow must come from after-tax net income. At a 40% tax rate, $60,000 of after-tax income equals $100,000 ($60,000 ÷ 60%) of pre-tax income from cost savings, and the outflow for taxes is $40,000. Thus, the annual reduction in cash operating costs required is $190,000 ($150,000 additional net cash inflow required + $40,000 tax outflow).

Answer (A) is incorrect. The amount of $60,000 is after-tax net income from the cost savings. Answer (B) is incorrect. The amount of $100,000 is the pre-tax income from the cost savings. Answer (C) is incorrect. The amount of $150,000 ignores the impact of depreciation and income taxes.

13.2.6. Womark Company purchased a new machine on January 1 of this year for $90,000, with an estimated useful life of 5 years and a salvage value of $10,000. The machine will be depreciated using the straight-line method. The machine is expected to produce cash flow from operations, net of income taxes, of $36,000 a year in each of the next 5 years. The new machine's salvage value is $20,000 in Years 1 and 2, and $15,000 in Years 3 and 4. What will be the bailout period (rounded) for this new machine?

A. 1.4 years.

B. 2.2 years.

C. 1.9 years.

D. 3.4 years.

Answer (C) is correct. *(CPA, adapted)*

REQUIRED: The bailout period for an investment in a new machine.

DISCUSSION: The bailout period is the time required for the sum of the (1) cumulative net cash inflow and (2) salvage value to equal the original investment. During Years 1 and 2, cost minus salvage value is $70,000, and the annual net cash inflow is $36,000. Thus, the incremental amount to be recovered during Year 2 is $34,000 ($70,000 – $36,000). Interpolating in Year 2 therefore yields a bailout period of 1.9 years [1 + ($34,000 ÷ $36,000)].

Answer (A) is incorrect. Annual cash flows are $36,000, not $50,000. Answer (B) is incorrect. Cost minus salvage value in Year 2 is $70,000, not $80,000. Answer (D) is incorrect. The incremental amount to be recovered during Year 2 is $34,000, not $14,000.

13.2.7. An investment project is expected to yield $10,000 in annual revenues, will incur $2,000 in fixed costs per year, and requires an initial inventory of $5,000. Given a cost of goods sold of 60% of sales and ignoring taxes, what is the payback period in years?

A. 2.50

B. 5.00

C. 2.00

D. 1.25

Answer (A) is correct. *(CIA, adapted)*

REQUIRED: The payback period in years.

DISCUSSION: The payback period equals the original investment divided by the constant net cash inflow per year. Net cash inflow per year is $2,000 (see below), and the payback period is 2.5 years ($5,000 investment ÷ $2,000).

Annual revenue	$10,000
COGS (60%)	(6,000)
Cash flow before fixed costs	$ 4,000
Fixed costs	(2,000)
Annual net cash inflow	$ 2,000

Answer (B) is incorrect. The amount of 5.00 assumes a $10,000 investment. Answer (C) is incorrect. The amount of 2.00 assumes a $10,000 investment and a $5,000 constant annual net cash inflow. Answer (D) is incorrect. The amount of 1.25 equals $5,000 divided by $4,000.

13.2.8. Whatney Co. is considering the acquisition of a new, more efficient press. The cost of the press is $360,000, and the press has an estimated 6-year life with zero salvage value. Whatney uses straight-line depreciation for both financial reporting and income tax reporting purposes and has a 40% corporate income tax rate. In evaluating equipment acquisitions of this type, Whatney uses a goal of a 4-year payback period. To meet Whatney's desired payback period, the press must produce a minimum annual before-tax operating cash savings of

A. $90,000

B. $110,000

C. $114,000

D. $150,000

Answer (B) is correct. *(CMA, adapted)*

REQUIRED: The minimum annual before-tax operating cash savings yielding a specified payback period.

DISCUSSION: Payback is the number of years required to complete the return of the original investment. Given a periodic constant cash flow, the payback period equals net investment divided by the constant expected periodic after-tax cash flow. The desired payback period is 4 years, so the constant after-tax annual cash flow must be $90,000 ($360,000 ÷ 4). Assuming that the company has sufficient other income to permit realization of the full tax savings, depreciation of the machine will shield $60,000 ($360,000 ÷ 6) of income from taxation each year, an after-tax cash savings of $24,000 ($60,000 × 40%). Thus, the machine must generate an additional $66,000 ($90,000 – $24,000) of after-tax cash savings from operations. This amount is equivalent to $110,000 [$66,000 ÷ (1.0 – .4)] of before-tax operating cash savings.

Answer (A) is incorrect. The amount of $90,000 is the total desired annual after-tax cash savings. Answer (C) is incorrect. The amount of $114,000 results from adding, not subtracting, the $24,000 of tax depreciation savings to determine the minimum annual after-tax operating savings. Answer (D) is incorrect. The amount of $150,000 assumes that depreciation is not tax deductible.

13.3 Cost of Capital

13.3.1. A firm's optimal capital structure

A. Minimizes the firm's tax liability.

B. Minimizes the firm's risk.

C. Maximizes the firm's degree of financial leverage.

D. Maximizes the price of the firm's stock.

Answer (D) is correct. *(CIA, adapted)*

REQUIRED: The optimal capital structure.

DISCUSSION: In theory, the optimal capital structure is the permanent, long-term financing represented by long-term debt, preferred stock, and common stock. Capital structure differs from financial structure, which includes short-term debt plus the long-term accounts. The optimal capital structure minimizes the weighted-average cost of capital and maximizes the entity's value reflected in its stock price.

Answer (A) is incorrect. A high debt ratio minimizes taxes but might not maximize shareholder wealth. The risk may be unacceptable. Answer (B) is incorrect. A low debt ratio minimizes risk but might not maximize shareholder wealth. The potential return may be unacceptable. Answer (C) is incorrect. Maximum financial leverage results in excessive risk and therefore does not maximize shareholder wealth.

13.3.2. The firm's marginal cost of capital

A. Should be the same as the firm's rate of return on equity.

B. Is unaffected by the firm's capital structure.

C. Is inversely related to the firm's required rate of return used in capital budgeting.

D. Is a weighted average of the investors' required returns on debt and equity.

Answer (D) is correct. *(CMA, adapted)*

REQUIRED: The true statement about the marginal cost of capital.

DISCUSSION: The marginal cost of capital is the cost of the next dollar of capital. The marginal cost continually increases because the lower cost sources of funds are used first. The marginal cost represents a weighted average of both debt and equity capital.

Answer (A) is incorrect. If the cost of capital were the same as the rate of return on equity (which is usually higher than that of debt capital), there would be no incentive to invest. Answer (B) is incorrect. The marginal cost of capital is affected by the degree of debt in the firm's capital structure. Financial risk plays a role in the returns desired by investors. Answer (C) is incorrect. The rate of return used for capital budgeting purposes should be at least as high as the marginal cost of capital.

13.3.3. A firm seeking to optimize its capital budget has calculated its marginal cost of capital and projected rates of return on several potential projects. The optimal capital budget is determined by

A. Calculating the point at which marginal cost of capital meets the projected rate of return, assuming that the most profitable projects are accepted first.

B. Calculating the point at which average marginal cost meets average projected rate of return, assuming the largest projects are accepted first.

C. Accepting all potential projects with projected rates of return exceeding the lowest marginal cost of capital.

D. Accepting all potential projects with projected rates of return lower than the highest marginal cost of capital.

Answer (A) is correct. *(CIA, adapted)*

REQUIRED: The determinant of the optimal capital budget.

DISCUSSION: In economics, a basic principle is that a firm should increase output until marginal cost equals marginal revenue. Similarly, the optimal capital budget is determined by calculating the point at which marginal cost of capital (which increases as capital requirements increase) and marginal efficiency of investment (which decreases if the most profitable projects are accepted first) intersect.

Answer (B) is incorrect. The intersection of average marginal cost with average projected rates of return when the largest (not most profitable) projects are accepted first offers no meaningful capital budgeting conclusion. Answer (C) is incorrect. The optimal capital budget may exclude profitable projects as lower-cost capital goes first to projects with higher rates of return. Answer (D) is incorrect. Accepting projects with rates of return lower than the cost of capital is not rational.

13.3.4. An analysis of a company's planned equity financing using the Capital Asset Pricing Model (or Security Market Line) incorporates only the

A. Expected market earnings, the risk-free rate, and the beta coefficient.

B. Expected market earnings and the price-earnings ratio.

C. Risk-free rate, the price-earnings ratio, and the beta coefficient.

D. Risk-free rate and the dividend payout ratio.

Answer (A) is correct. *(CMA, adapted)*

REQUIRED: The components of the capital asset pricing model.

DISCUSSION: The capital asset pricing model adds the risk-free rate to the product of the market risk premium and the beta coefficient. The market risk premium is the amount above the risk-free rate (approximated by the U.S. treasury bond yield) that must be paid to induce investment in the market. The beta coefficient of an individual stock is the correlation between the price volatility of the stock market as a whole and the price volatility of the individual stock.

13.3.5.

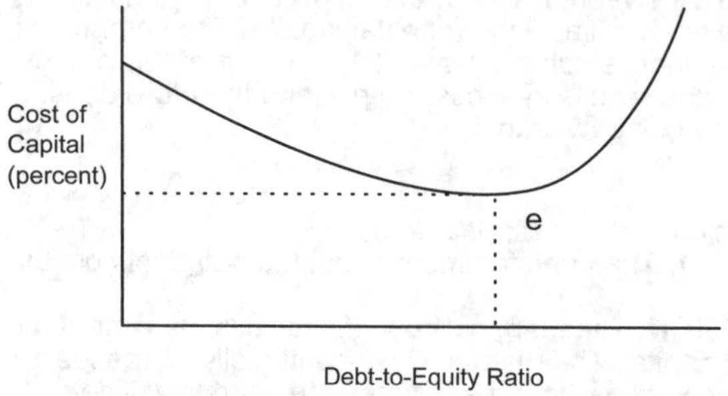

In referring to the graph of a firm's cost of capital, if e is the optimal position, which one of the following statements best explains the saucer or U-shaped curve?

A. The composition of debt and equity does not affect the firm's cost of capital.

B. The cost of capital is almost always favorably influenced by increases in financial leverage.

C. The cost of capital is almost always negatively influenced by increases in financial leverage.

D. Use of at least some debt financing will enhance the value of the firm.

Answer (D) is correct. *(CMA, adapted)*

REQUIRED: The best explanation of the U-shaped curve in a cost-of-capital graph.

DISCUSSION: The U-shaped curve indicates that the cost of capital is quite high when the debt-to-equity ratio is quite low. As debt increases, the cost of capital declines as long as the cost of debt is less than that of equity. Eventually, the decline in the cost of capital levels off because the cost of debt ultimately rises as more debt is used. Additional increases in debt (relative to equity) will then increase the cost of capital. The implication is that some debt is present in the optimal capital structure because the cost of capital initially declines when debt is added. However, a point is reached (e) at which debt becomes excessive and the cost of capital begins to rise.

Answer (A) is incorrect. The composition of the capital structure affects the cost of capital since the components have different costs. Answer (B) is incorrect. The cost of debt does not remain constant as financial leverage increases. Eventually, that cost also increases. Answer (C) is incorrect. Increased leverage is initially favorable.

13.3.6. Which of the changes in leverage would apply to a company that substantially increases its investment in fixed assets as a proportion of total assets and replaces some of its long-term debt with equity?

	Financial Leverage	Operating Leverage
A.	Increase	Decrease
B.	Decrease	Increase
C.	Increase	Increase
D.	Decrease	Decrease

Answer (B) is correct. *(CIA, adapted)*

REQUIRED: The change applicable when fixed assets and equity increase.

DISCUSSION: Leverage is the relative amount of fixed cost in a firm's overall cost structure. Leverage creates risk because fixed costs must be covered, regardless of the level of sales. Financial leverage arises from the use of a high level of debt in the firm's financing structure, revealed through amounts paid out for interest. An increase in equity decreases financial leverage. Operating leverage is based on the degree that fixed costs are used in the production process. An entity with a high percentage of fixed costs is riskier than a firm in the same industry that relies more on variable costs to produce. When fixed assets increase, operating leverage also increases.

13.3.7. A measure that describes the risk of an investment project relative to other investments in general is the

A. Coefficient of variation.

B. Beta coefficient.

C. Standard deviation.

D. Expected return.

Answer (B) is correct. *(CIA, adapted)*

REQUIRED: The measure of the risk of an investment relative to investments in general.

DISCUSSION: The required rate of return on equity capital in the capital asset pricing model is the risk-free rate (determined by government securities), plus the product of the market risk premium times the beta coefficient (beta measures the firm's risk). The market risk premium is the amount above the risk-free rate that will induce investment in the market. The beta coefficient of an individual stock is the correlation between the volatility (price variation) of the stock market and that of the price of the individual stock.

Answer (A) is incorrect. The coefficient of variation compares risk with expected return (standard deviation ÷ expected return). Answer (C) is incorrect. Standard deviation measures dispersion (risk) of project returns. Answer (D) is incorrect. Expected return does not describe risk.

13.3.8. A company's beta value has decreased because of a change in its marketing strategy. Consequently, the discount rate applied to expected cash flows of potential projects will be

A. Reduced.

B. Increased.

C. Unchanged.

D. Zero.

Answer (A) is correct. *(CIA, adapted)*

REQUIRED: The effect of a decrease in beta value on the discount rate applied to cash flows of potential projects.

DISCUSSION: The relationship between (1) a firm's beta value and (2) the discount rate applied to cash flows is positive. Thus, a decrease in beta reduces the discount rate.

Answer (B) is incorrect. The discount rate is reduced, not increased. Answer (C) is incorrect. The discount rate is reduced. Answer (D) is incorrect. A zero discount rate incorrectly suggests that future cash flows do not need to be discounted for evaluation purposes.

13.3.9. A company has made the decision to finance next year's capital projects through debt rather than additional equity. The benchmark cost of capital for these projects should be

A. The before-tax cost of new-debt financing.

B. The after-tax cost of new-debt financing.

C. The cost of equity financing.

D. The weighted-average cost of capital.

Answer (D) is correct. *(CIA, adapted)*

REQUIRED: The benchmark cost of capital.

DISCUSSION: A weighted average of the costs of all financing sources should be used, with the weights determined by the usual financing proportions. The terms of any financing raised at the time of initiating a particular project do not represent the cost of capital for the firm. When a firm achieves its optimal capital structure, the weighted-average cost of capital is minimized.

13.3.10. When a company increases its degree of financial leverage (DFL), the

A. Equity beta of the company falls.

B. Systematic risk of the company falls.

C. Systematic risk of the company rises.

D. Standard deviation of returns on the equity of the company rises.

Answer (D) is correct. *(CIA, adapted)*

REQUIRED: The effect of increasing the DFL.

DISCUSSION: The DFL (1) equals the percentage change in earnings available to common shareholders (2) divided by the percentage change in net operating income. When the DFL increases, fixed interest charges and risk increase. As a result, the variability of the returns to equity holders increases. Thus, the standard deviation of returns on equity increases.

Answer (A) is incorrect. An increase in the DFL increases the risk. Thus, beta rises. Beta is a measure of the volatility of a stock price relative to the average stock. Answer (B) is incorrect. Systematic risk, also known as market risk, is unrelated to the DFL. Systematic risk is not specific to an entity. It is the risk associated with an entity's stock that cannot be diversified because it is caused by factors that affect all stocks. Answer (C) is incorrect. Systematic risk, also known as market risk, is unrelated to the DFL.

13.3.11. If a company has a higher dividend-payout ratio, then, if all else is equal, it will have a

A. Higher marginal cost of capital.

B. Lower marginal cost of capital.

C. Higher investment opportunity schedule.

D. Lower investment opportunity schedule.

Answer (A) is correct. *(CIA, adapted)*

REQUIRED: The effect of a higher dividend-payout ratio.

DISCUSSION: The higher the dividend-payout ratio, the sooner retained earnings are exhausted and external financing must be obtained. Assuming the same investments are made, the result is a higher marginal cost of capital because lower-cost capital sources are used up earlier.

Answer (B) is incorrect. The marginal cost of capital is higher. Answer (C) is incorrect. The existence of investment opportunities is unrelated to the dividend payout. Answer (D) is incorrect. The existence of investment opportunities is unrelated to the dividend payout.

13.3.12. If two companies, company X and company Y, are alike in all respects except that company X employs more debt financing and less equity financing than company Y does, which of the following statements is true?

A. Company X has more net earnings variability than company Y.

B. Company X has more operating earnings variability than company Y.

C. Company X has less operating earnings variability than company Y.

D. Company X has less financial leverage than company Y.

Answer (A) is correct. *(CIA, adapted)*

REQUIRED: The true statement about debt and equity financing.

DISCUSSION: Given that X is more highly leveraged, it has greater fixed financing charges than Y. Interest payments are fixed financing charges, but common share dividends are not. As a result, X is more risky and therefore has a more volatile net income stream than Y, if other factors are constant.

Answer (B) is incorrect. The level of fixed financing charges does not affect operating income variability. Answer (C) is incorrect. The level of fixed financing charges does not affect operating income variability. Answer (D) is incorrect. X has greater, not less, financial leverage than Y. Greater use of debt financing means that a company has greater financial leverage.

13.3.13. A firm must select from among several methods of financing arrangements when meeting its capital requirements. To acquire additional growth capital while attempting to maximize earnings per share, a firm should normally

A. Attempt to increase both debt and equity in equal proportions, which preserves a stable capital structure and maintains investor confidence.

B. Select debt over equity initially, even though increased debt is accompanied by interest costs and a degree of risk.

C. Select equity over debt initially, which minimizes risk and avoids interest costs.

D. Discontinue dividends and use current cash flow, which avoids the cost and risk of increased debt and the dilution of EPS through increased equity.

Answer (B) is correct. *(CIA, adapted)*

REQUIRED: The financing arrangement to acquire additional growth capital and maximize EPS.

DISCUSSION: EPS ordinarily is higher if debt, not equity, is used to raise capital, provided that the entity is not over-leveraged. The reason is that the cost of debt is lower than the cost of equity because interest is tax deductible. However, higher EPS is offset by greater risk resulting from required interest costs, creditors' liens on the firm's assets, and the possibility of a proportionately lower EPS if sales fail to meet projections.

Answer (A) is incorrect. EPS is not a function of investor confidence and is not maximized by concurrent proportional increases in debt and equity. EPS is usually higher if debt is used instead of equity to raise capital, at least initially. Answer (C) is incorrect. Equity capital is initially more costly than debt. Answer (D) is incorrect. Using only current cash flow to raise capital is usually too conservative an approach for a growth-oriented entity. Management is expected to be willing to take acceptable risks to be competitive and attain an acceptable rate of growth.

13.3.14. The market value of a firm's outstanding common shares will be higher, everything else equal, if

A. Investors have a lower required return on equity.

B. Investors expect lower dividend growth.

C. Investors have longer expected holding periods.

D. Investors have shorter expected holding periods.

Answer (A) is correct. *(CIA, adapted)*

REQUIRED: The item resulting in a higher market value for common shares.

DISCUSSION: The dividend growth model often is used to calculate the cost of equity. The simplified formula is

$$R = \frac{D}{P} + G$$

R is the required rate of return, D is the next dividend, P is the stock's price, and G is the dividend growth rate. The equation is also used to determine the stock price.

$$P = \frac{D}{R - G}$$

Thus, when investors have a lower required return on equity, the denominator is smaller, which translates into a higher market value.

Answer (B) is incorrect. If investors expect lower dividend growth, the market value of common shares decreases. Answer (C) is incorrect. The expected holding periods of investors are not related to the market value of the common shares. Answer (D) is incorrect. The expected holding periods of investors are not related to the market value of the common shares.

13.3.15. Assume that nominal interest rates just increased substantially but that the expected future dividends for a company over the long run were not affected. As a result of the increase in nominal interest rates, the company's stock price should

A. Increase.

B. Decrease.

C. Stay constant.

D. Change, but in no obvious direction.

Answer (B) is correct. *(CIA, adapted)*

REQUIRED: The effect on a company's stock price of an increase in nominal interest rates.

DISCUSSION: The dividend growth model often is used to calculate the price of stock. R is the required rate of return, D is the next dividend, P is the stock's price, and G is the dividend growth rate.

$$P = \frac{D}{R - G}$$

Assuming that D and G are constant, an increase in R resulting from an increase in the nominal interest rate causes P to decrease.

13.3.16. The marginal cost of debt for a firm is defined as the interest rate on <List A> debt minus the <List B>.

	List A	List B
A.	New	Firm's marginal tax rate
B.	Outstanding	Firm's marginal tax rate
C.	New	Interest rate times the firm's marginal tax rate
D.	Outstanding	Interest rate times the firm's marginal tax rate

Answer (C) is correct. *(CIA, adapted)*

REQUIRED: The marginal cost of debt.

DISCUSSION: The marginal cost of debt must equal the cost of new debt minus the tax savings. Thus, marginal cost equals the cost of new debt times one minus the marginal tax rate, or $K_d (1 - T)$. This expression equals $K_d - K_d T$.

13.3.17. If k is the cost of debt and t is the marginal tax rate, the after-tax cost of debt, k_i, is best represented by the formula

A. $k_i = k \div t$

B. $k_i = k \div (1 - t)$

C. $k_i = k(t)$

D. $k_i = k(1 - t)$

Answer (D) is correct. *(CMA, adapted)*

REQUIRED: The formula representing the after-tax cost of debt.

DISCUSSION: The after-tax cost of debt is the cost of debt times the quantity one minus the tax rate. For example, the after-tax cost of a 10% bond is 7% [10% × (1 – 30%)] if the tax rate is 30%.

Answers (A) and (B) are incorrect. The after-tax cost of debt is the cost of debt times the quantity one minus the tax rate. Answers (B) and (B) are incorrect. The after-tax cost of debt is the cost of debt times the quantity one minus the tax rate. Answer (C) is incorrect. The cost of debt times the marginal tax rate equals the tax savings from issuing debt.

13.3.18. In accordance with the dividend growth model, the three elements needed to estimate the cost of equity capital for use in determining a firm's weighted-average cost of capital are

A. Current dividends per share, expected growth rate in dividends per share, and current book value per share of common stock.

B. Current earnings per share, expected growth rate in dividends per share, and current market price per share of common stock.

C. Current earnings per share, expected growth rate in earnings per share, and current book value per share of common stock.

D. Current dividends per share, expected growth rate in dividends per share, and current market price per share of common stock.

Answer (D) is correct. *(CMA, adapted)*

REQUIRED: The elements of the cost of equity when determining the weighted-average cost of capital.

DISCUSSION: The dividend growth model requires three elements to estimate the cost of equity capital: (1) dividends per share, (2) the expected constant growth rate in dividends per share, and (3) the market price of the stock. Accordingly, the cost of equity capital equals the dividend yield (dividends ÷ price) plus the growth rate.

Answer (A) is incorrect. Carrying amount per share is not a variable in the cost of equity capital. Answer (B) is incorrect. Current dividends, not current earnings, per share are a requirement for the formula. Answer (C) is incorrect. Carrying amount per share is not a variable in the cost of equity capital. Also, current dividends, not current earnings, per share are a requirement for the formula.

13.3.19. In general, it is more expensive for a company to finance with equity capital than with debt capital because

A. Long-term bonds have a maturity date and must therefore be repaid in the future.

B. Investors are exposed to greater risk with equity capital.

C. Equity capital is in greater demand than debt capital.

D. Dividends fluctuate to a greater extent than interest rates.

Answer (B) is correct. *(CMA, adapted)*

REQUIRED: The reason equity financing is more expensive than debt financing.

DISCUSSION: Providers of equity capital are exposed to more risk than are lenders because the firm is not obligated to pay them a return. Also, in case of liquidation, creditors are paid before equity investors. Thus, equity financing is more expensive than debt because equity investors require a higher return to compensate for the greater risk assumed.

Answer (A) is incorrect. The obligation to repay at a specific maturity date reduces the risk to investors and thus the required return. Answer (C) is incorrect. The demand for equity capital is directly related to its greater cost to the issuer. Answer (D) is incorrect. Dividends are based on managerial discretion and may rarely change; interest rates, however, fluctuate daily based upon market conditions.

13.3.20. All of the following are examples of imputed costs except

A. The stated interest paid on a bank loan.

B. The use of the firm's internal cash funds to purchase assets.

C. Assets that are considered obsolete that maintain a net book value.

D. Decelerated depreciation.

Answer (A) is correct. *(CMA, adapted)*

REQUIRED: The item not an imputed cost.

DISCUSSION: An imputed cost must be estimated. It exists but is not specifically stated and is the result of a process designed to recognize economic reality. An imputed cost may not require a dollar outlay formally recognized by the accounting system, but it is relevant to the decision-making process. For example, the stated interest on a bank loan is not an imputed cost because it is specifically stated and requires a dollar outlay. But the cost of using retained earnings as a source of capital is unstated and must be imputed.

Answer (B) is incorrect. The cost of internally generated funds is unstated. Answer (C) is incorrect. The cost of obsolete assets should be written off. Answer (D) is incorrect. Understated depreciation results in unstated costs.

13.3.21. Colt, Inc., is planning to use retained earnings to finance anticipated capital expenditures. The beta coefficient for Colt's stock is 1.15, the risk-free rate of interest is 8.5%, and the market return is estimated at 12.4%. If a new issue of common stock were used in this model, the flotation costs would be 7%. By using the capital asset pricing model (CAPM) equation [$R = RF + \beta \times (RM - RF)$], the cost of using retained earnings to finance the capital expenditures is

A. 13.21%

B. 12.99%

C. 12.40%

D. 14.26%

Answer (B) is correct. *(CMA, adapted)*

REQUIRED: The cost of using retained earnings to finance capital expenditures under the CAPM.

DISCUSSION: The CAPM determines the cost of capital by adding the risk-free rate to the product of the market risk premium and the beta coefficient (the beta coefficient is a measure of the firm's risk). The market risk premium is the amount in excess of the risk-free rate that investors must be paid to induce them to enter the market. The 7% flotation costs are not relevant because the entity does not plan to issue common stock. Thus, the cost of retained earnings is 12.99% [8.5% + 1.15 (12.4% – 8.5%)].

Answer (A) is incorrect. The percentage of 13.21 results from using 7% instead of 8.5%. Answer (C) is incorrect. The estimated market return is 12.4%. Answer (D) is incorrect. The percentage of 14.26 equals 1.15 times 12.4%.

Questions 13.3.22 and 13.3.23 are based on the following information. Carlisle Company currently sells 400,000 bottles of perfume each year. Each bottle costs $.84 to produce and sells for $1.00. Fixed costs are $28,000 per year. The firm has annual interest expense of $6,000, preferred stock dividends of $2,000 per year, and a 40% tax rate.

13.3.22. The degree of financial leverage for Carlisle Company is

A. 2.4

B. 1.78

C. 1.35

D. 1.2

Answer (C) is correct. *(CMA, adapted)*

REQUIRED: The degree of financial leverage.

DISCUSSION: The degree of financial leverage is the percentage change in earnings available to common shareholders that is associated with a given percentage change in net operating income. Operating income equals earnings before interest and taxes. The more financial leverage used, the greater the degree of financial leverage and the riskier the entity. An alternative formula for financial leverage divides EBIT by EBIT minus interest and preferred dividends (before tax effect). Earnings before interest and taxes equal $36,000 [$400,000 sales – ($.84 × 400,000 units) VC – $28,000 FC]. Using the second formula, the calculation is as follows:

$$\frac{\$36{,}000}{\$36{,}000 - \$6{,}000 - (\$2{,}000 \div .6)} = \frac{\$36{,}000}{\$26{,}667} = 1.35$$

Answer (A) is incorrect. A DFL of 2.4 is obtained by overstating the contribution margin or the fixed costs. Answer (B) is incorrect. A DFL of 1.78 is the degree of operating leverage, not financial leverage. Answer (D) is incorrect. A DFL of 1.2 is obtained by understating the $64,000 of contribution margin or understating the $28,000 of fixed costs.

13.3.23. If Carlisle Company did not have preferred stock, the degree of total leverage would

A. Decrease in proportion to a decrease in financial leverage.

B. Increase in proportion to an increase in financial leverage.

C. Remain the same.

D. Decrease but not be proportional to the decrease in financial leverage.

Answer (A) is correct. *(CMA, adapted)*

REQUIRED: The true statement about the degree of total leverage without preferred stock.

DISCUSSION: The degree of total leverage equals the degree of operating leverage times the degree of financial leverage. Thus, a decrease in either ratio results in a decrease in total leverage. Given no preferred stock, the DFL and the DTL are lower because the pretax income necessary to pay the preferred dividends [P ÷ (1 – t)] is subtracted from the denominator of the DFL.

Answer (B) is incorrect. The DTL decreases. Answer (C) is incorrect. The elimination of preferred stock changes the equation. Answer (D) is incorrect. The decrease is proportional.

13.3.24. The explicit cost of debt financing is the interest expense. The implicit cost(s) of debt financing is (are) the

A. Increase in the cost of debt as the debt-to-equity ratio increases.

B. Increases in the cost of debt and equity as the debt-to-equity ratio increases.

C. Increase in the cost of equity as the debt-to-equity ratio decreases.

D. Decrease in the weighted-average cost of capital as the debt-to-equity ratio increases.

Answer (B) is correct. *(CMA, adapted)*

REQUIRED: The implicit cost of debt financing.

DISCUSSION: Debt capital often appears to have a lower cost than equity because the implicit costs are not obvious. The implicit costs are attributable to the increased risk created by the additional debt burden. Thus, as the debt-to-equity ratio increases, the cost of debt and equity increases given the increased risk to shareholders and creditors from a higher degree of leverage. An explanation based on the marginal cost of capital and the marginal efficiency of investment leads to the same conclusion. Lower-cost capital sources are used first. Additional projects then must be undertaken with funds from higher-cost sources. Similarly, risk is increased because the most profitable investments are made initially, leaving the less profitable investments for the future.

Answer (A) is incorrect. Debt and equity sources increase in cost as leverage increases. Answer (C) is incorrect. Equity costs decline as leverage decreases. Answer (D) is incorrect. The weighted-average cost of capital will increase with increased leverage.

13.3.25. Newmass, Inc., paid a cash dividend to its common shareholders over the past 12 months of $2.20 per share. The current market value of the common stock is $40 per share, and investors are anticipating the common dividend to grow at a rate of 6% annually. The cost to issue new common stock will be 5% of the market value. Based on the dividend growth model, the cost of a new common stock issue will be

A. 11.50%

B. 11.79%

C. 11.83%

D. 12.14%

Answer (D) is correct. *(CMA, adapted)*

REQUIRED: The cost of equity financing using the dividend growth method.

DISCUSSION: The cost of equity using the dividend growth model equals the next dividend divided by the stock price, plus the constant growth rate in dividend. To account for flotation costs, the stock price is multiplied by one minus the flotation cost. Given that the next dividend is $2.332 ($2.20 × 1.06), the cost of new common stock is 12.14% ({$2.332 ÷ [$40 × (1 – .05)]} + .06).

Answer (A) is incorrect. The expected future dividend of $2.332 ($2.20 × 1.06) should be divided by the adjusted stock price (current market value – the cost of issuing the new common stock). Answer (B) is incorrect. The expected future dividend of $2.332 ($2.20 × 1.06) should be used in calculating the cost of the new common stock issue. Answer (C) is incorrect. The current stock price must be adjusted for the cost of issuing the new common stock.

13.3.26. A company, which has no current debt, has a beta of 0.95 for its common stock. Management is considering a change in the capital structure to 30% debt and 70% equity. This change would increase the beta on the stock to 1.05, and the after-tax cost of debt will be 7.5%. The expected return on equity is 16%, and the risk-free rate is 6%. Should the company's management proceed with the capital structure change?

A. No, because the cost of equity capital will increase.

B. Yes, because the cost of equity capital will decrease.

C. Yes, because the weighted-average cost of capital will decrease.

D. No, because the weighted-average cost of capital will increase.

Answer (C) is correct. *(CMA, adapted)*

REQUIRED: The correct decision regarding a proposed capital structure change and the reason for it.

DISCUSSION: The important consideration is whether the overall cost of capital will be lower for a given proposal. According to the Capital Asset Pricing Model, the change will result in a lower average cost of capital. For the existing structure, the cost of equity capital is 15.5% [6% + .95 (16% – 6%)]. Because the company has no debt, the average cost of capital is also 15.5%. Under the proposal, the cost of equity capital is 16.5% [6% + 1.05 (16% – 6%)], and the weighted average cost of capital is 13.8% [.3(.075) + .7(.165)]. Hence, the proposal of 13.8% should be accepted.

Answer (A) is incorrect. The average cost of capital needs to be considered. Answer (B) is incorrect. The average cost of capital needs to be considered. Answer (D) is incorrect. The weighted average cost of capital will decrease.

13.3.27. Osgood Products has announced that it plans to finance future investments so that the firm will achieve an optimum capital structure. Which one of the following corporate objectives is consistent with this announcement?

A. Maximize earnings per share.

B. Minimize the cost of debt.

C. Maximize the net worth of the firm.

D. Minimize the cost of equity.

Answer (C) is correct. *(CMA, adapted)*

REQUIRED: The consistent corporate objective.

DISCUSSION: Financial structure is the composition of the financing sources of the assets of a firm. Traditionally, the financial structure consists of current liabilities, long-term debt, retained earnings, and stock. For most firms, the optimum structure includes a combination of debt and equity. Debt is cheaper than equity, but excessive use of debt increases the firm's risk and drives up the weighted-average cost of capital.

Answer (A) is incorrect. The maximization of EPS may not always suggest the best capital structure. Answer (B) is incorrect. The minimization of debt cost may not be optimal; as long as the firm can earn more on debt capital than it pays in interest, debt financing may be indicated. Answer (D) is incorrect. Minimizing the cost of equity may signify overly conservative management.

13.3.28. A firm's new financing will be in proportion to the market value of its current financing shown below.

	Carrying Amount ($000 Omitted)
Long-term debt	$7,000
Preferred stock (100,000 shares)	1,000
Common stock (200,000 shares)	7,000

The firm's bonds are currently selling at 80% of par, generating a current market yield of 9%, and the corporation has a 40% tax rate. The preferred stock is selling at its par value and pays a 6% dividend. The common stock has a current market value of $40 and is expected to pay a $1.20 per share dividend this fiscal year. Dividend growth is expected to be 10% per year, and flotation costs are negligible. The firm's weighted-average cost of capital is (round calculations to tenths of a percent)

A. 13.0%

B. 8.13%

C. 9.6%

D. 9.0%

Answer (C) is correct. *(CMA, adapted)*

REQUIRED: The weighted-average cost of capital.

DISCUSSION: The first step is to determine the component costs of each form of capital. Multiplying the current yield of 9% times one minus the tax rate (1.0 – .40 = .60) results in an after-tax cost of debt of 5.4% (9% × .60). Since the preferred stock is trading at par, the component cost is 6% (the annual dividend rate). The component cost of common equity is calculated using the dividend growth model, which combines the dividend yield with the growth rate. Dividing the $1.20 dividend by the $40 market price produces a dividend yield of 3%. Adding the 3% dividend yield and the 10% growth rate gives a 13% component cost of common equity.

Once the costs of the three types of capital have been computed, the next step is to weight them according to their current market values. The market value of the long-term debt is 80% of its carrying amount, or $5,600,000 ($7,000,000 × 80%). The $1,000,000 of preferred stock is selling at par. The common stock has a current market value of $8,000,000 (200,000 shares × $40).

Long-term debt	$ 5,600,000	×	5.4%	=	$ 302,400
Preferred stock	1,000,000	×	6.0%	=	60,000
Common stock	8,000,000	×	13.0%	=	1,040,000
Totals	$14,600,000				$1,402,400

Thus, the weighted-average cost of capital is 9.6% ($1,402,000 ÷ $14,600,000).

Answer (A) is incorrect. The amount of 13.0% is the cost of equity. Answer (B) is incorrect. The amount of 8.13% is the simple average. Answer (D) is incorrect. The amount of 9.0% is based on carrying amounts.

13.3.29. A company's current capital structure is optimal, and the company wishes to maintain it.

Debt	25%
Preferred equity	5
Common equity	70

Management is planning to build a $75 million facility that will be financed according to this desired capital structure. Currently, $15 million of cash is available for capital expansion. The percentage of the $75 million that will come from a new issue of common stock is

A. 52.50%

B. 50.00%

C. 70.00%

D. 56.00%

Answer (D) is correct. *(CMA, adapted)*

REQUIRED: The percentage of the new financing needed that will come from a new issue of common stock.

DISCUSSION: Because $15 million is already available, the company must finance $60 million ($75 million – $15 million). Of this amount, 70%, or $42 million, should come from the issuance of common stock to maintain the current capital structure. The $42 million represents 56% of the total $75 million.

13.3.30. An optimal capital budget is determined by the point at which the marginal cost of capital is

A. Minimized.

B. Equal to the average cost of capital.

C. Equal to the rate of return on total assets.

D. Equal to the marginal rate of return on investment.

Answer (D) is correct. *(CIA, adapted)*

REQUIRED: The definition of an optimal capital budget.

DISCUSSION: According to microeconomic theory, an entity should produce until its marginal revenue equals its marginal cost. In capital budgeting terms, marginal revenue is the marginal rate of return on investment, and marginal cost is the marginal cost of capital (MCC). Thus, the entity should continue to invest until the cost of the last investment equals the return.

13.4 Net Present Value

13.4.1. The capital budgeting technique known as net present value uses

	Cash Flow over Life of Project	Time Value of Money
A.	No	Yes
B.	No	No
C.	Yes	No
D.	Yes	Yes

Answer (D) is correct. *(CPA, adapted)*

REQUIRED: The matters considered by the net present value technique.

DISCUSSION: The net present value method is a capital budgeting technique that consists of discounting the net after-tax cash flows over a project's life using the appropriate discount rate.

13.4.2. If a firm identifies (or creates) an investment opportunity with a present value <List A> its cost, the value of the firm and the price of its common stock will <List B>.

	List A	List B
A.	Greater than	Increase
B.	Greater than	Decrease
C.	Equal to	Increase
D.	Equal to	Decrease

Answer (A) is correct. *(CIA, adapted)*

REQUIRED: The effect of investment opportunities on the value of the entity and its stock price.

DISCUSSION: Investments with present values in excess of their costs (positive NPVs) that can be identified or created by the capital budgeting activities of the entity have a positive effect on entity value and on the price of the common stock of the entity. Accordingly, the more effective capital budgeting is, the higher the stock price.

Answer (B) is incorrect. Positive NPV investments increase, not decrease, entity value and share price. Answer (C) is incorrect. Investments with present values equal to their costs have a zero NPV and neither increase nor decrease entity value and share price. Answer (D) is incorrect. Investments with present values equal to their costs have a zero NPV and neither increase nor decrease entity value and share price.

13.4.3. A disadvantage of the net present value method of capital expenditure evaluation is that it

A. Is calculated using sensitivity analysis.

B. Computes the true interest rate.

C. Does not provide the true rate of return on investment.

D. Is difficult to apply because it uses a trial-and-error approach.

Answer (C) is correct. *(CMA, adapted)*

REQUIRED: The disadvantage of the NPV method.

DISCUSSION: The NPV is broadly defined as the excess of the present value of the estimated net cash inflows over the net cost of the investment. A discount rate has to be estimated by the person conducting the analysis. A disadvantage is that it does not provide the true rate of return for an investment, only that the rate of return is higher than a stipulated discount rate (which may be the cost of capital).

Answer (A) is incorrect. The ability to perform sensitivity analysis is an advantage of the NPV method. Answer (B) is incorrect. The NPV method does not compute the true interest rate. Answer (D) is incorrect. The IRR method, not the NPV method, uses a trial-and-error approach when cash flows are not identical from year to year.

13.4.4. Amster Corporation has not yet decided on its hurdle rate for use in the evaluation of capital budgeting projects. This lack of information will prohibit Amster from calculating a project's

	Accounting Rate of Return	Net Present Value	Internal Rate of Return
A.	No	No	No
B.	Yes	Yes	Yes
C.	No	Yes	Yes
D.	No	Yes	No

Answer (D) is correct. *(CMA, adapted)*

REQUIRED: The capital budgeting technique(s), if any, that require determination of a hurdle rate.

DISCUSSION: A hurdle rate is not necessary in calculating the accounting rate of return or the internal rate of return. However, the net present value cannot be calculated without knowing the company's hurdle rate.

13.4.5. The proper discount rate to use in calculating certainty equivalent net present value is the

A. Risk-adjusted discount rate.

B. Risk-free rate.

C. Cost of equity capital.

D. Cost of debt.

Answer (B) is correct. *(CMA, adapted)*

REQUIRED: The proper discount rate to use in calculating certainty equivalent net present value.

DISCUSSION: Rational investors choose projects that yield the best return given some level of risk. If an investor desires no risk, that is, an absolutely certain rate of return, the risk-free rate is used in calculating NPV. The risk-free rate is the return on a risk-free investment such as government bonds.

Answer (A) is incorrect. A risk-adjusted discount rate is not an absolutely certain rate of return. A discount rate is adjusted upward as the investment becomes riskier. Answer (C) is incorrect. The cost of equity capital does not equate to the certainty equivalence of a risk-free investment's return. Answer (D) is incorrect. The cost of debt capital does not equate to the certainty equivalence of a risk-free investment's return.

13.4.6. An advantage of the net present value method over the internal rate of return model in discounted cash flow analysis is that the net present value method

A. Computes a desired rate of return for capital projects.

B. Can be used when there is no constant rate of return required for each year of the project.

C. Uses a discount rate that equates the discounted cash inflows with the outflows.

D. Uses discounted cash flows whereas the internal rate of return model does not.

Answer (B) is correct. *(CMA, adapted)*

REQUIRED: The advantage of the NPV method over the IRR model.

DISCUSSION: The NPV method calculates the present values of estimated future net cash inflows and compares the total with the net cost of the investment. The cost of capital must be specified. If the NPV is positive, the project should be accepted. The IRR method computes the interest rate at which the NPV is zero. The IRR method is relatively easy to use when cash inflows are the same from one year to the next. However, when cash inflows differ from year to year, the IRR can be found only through the use of trial and error. In such cases, the NPV method is usually easier to apply. Also, the NPV method can be used when the rate of return required for each year varies. For example, a company might want to achieve a higher rate of return in later years when risk might be greater. Only the NPV method can incorporate varying levels of rates of return.

Answer (A) is incorrect. The IRR method calculates a rate of return. Answer (C) is incorrect. The IRR is the rate at which NPV is zero. Answer (D) is incorrect. Both methods discount cash flows.

13.4.7. A project's net present value, ignoring income tax considerations, is normally affected by the

A. Proceeds from the sale of the asset to be replaced.

B. Carrying amount of the asset to be replaced by the project.

C. Amount of annual depreciation on the asset to be replaced.

D. Amount of annual depreciation on fixed assets used directly on the project.

Answer (A) is correct. *(CPA, adapted)*

REQUIRED: The matter affecting net present value.

DISCUSSION: To compute a project's net present value, the initial investment is subtracted from the present value of the after-tax cash flows. The proceeds from the sale of the asset to be replaced reduce the initial investment.

Answer (B) is incorrect. The carrying amount of the asset to be replaced affects the gain or loss on the sale for tax purposes. Answer (C) is incorrect. The amount of annual depreciation on the asset to be replaced affects the carrying value. Answer (D) is incorrect. Annual depreciation of other assets, even if used directly, affects the taxable income. Ignoring income tax considerations, there is no effect on the project's net present value.

13.4.8. The use of an accelerated method instead of the straight-line method of depreciation in computing the net present value of a project has the effect of

A. Raising the hurdle rate necessary to justify the project.

B. Lowering the net present value of the project.

C. Increasing the present value of the depreciation tax shield.

D. Increasing the cash outflows at the initial point of the project.

Answer (C) is correct. *(CMA, adapted)*

REQUIRED: The effect on NPV of using an accelerated depreciation method.

DISCUSSION: Accelerated depreciation results in greater depreciation in the early years of an asset's life compared with the straight-line method. Thus, accelerated depreciation results in lower income tax expense in the early years of a project and higher income tax expense in the later years. By effectively deferring taxes, the accelerated method increases the present value of the depreciation tax shield.

Answer (A) is incorrect. The hurdle rate can be reached more easily as a result of the increased present value of the depreciation tax shield. Answer (B) is incorrect. The greater depreciation tax shield increases the NPV. Answer (D) is incorrect. Greater initial depreciation reduces the cash outflows for the taxes but has no effect on the initial cash outflows.

13.4.9. A firm has no capital rationing constraint and is analyzing many independent investment alternatives. The firm should accept all investment proposals

A. If debt financing is available for them.

B. That have positive cash flows.

C. That provide returns greater than the before-tax cost of debt.

D. That have a positive net present value.

Answer (D) is correct. *(CMA, adapted)*

REQUIRED: The investment proposals that should be accepted by a company with no capital rationing constraints.

DISCUSSION: A company should accept any investment proposal, unless some are mutually exclusive, that has a positive net present value or an internal rate of return greater than the company's desired rate of return.

Answer (A) is incorrect. The mere availability of financing is not the only consideration; more important is the cost of the financing, which must be less than the rate of return on the proposed investment. Answer (B) is incorrect. An investment with positive cash flows may be a bad investment due to the time value of money; cash flows in later years are not as valuable as those in earlier years. Answer (C) is incorrect. Returns should exceed the desired rate of return.

13.4.10. The NPV profiles for two mutually exclusive capital projects are shown in the graph below. Which statement is true?

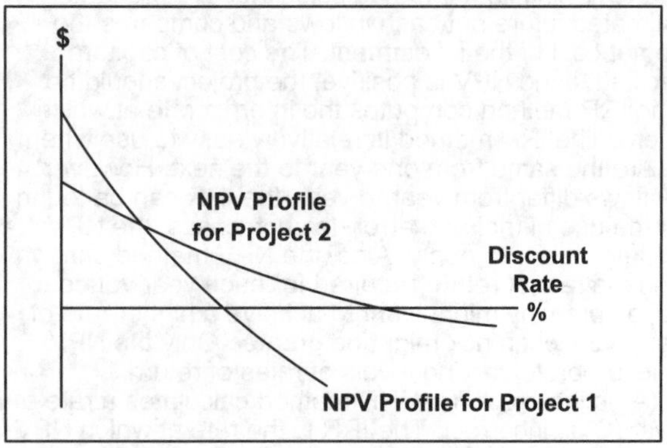

A. Project 2 has higher internal rate of return than Project 1.

B. Project 1 has a higher internal rate of return than Project 2.

C. Project 1 has a higher net present value than Project 2.

D. Project 2 has a higher net present value than Project 1.

Answer (A) is correct. *(Publisher, adapted)*

REQUIRED: The true statement about the NPV profiles of two mutually exclusive capital projects.

DISCUSSION: The NPV is the excess of the present value of the estimated cash inflows over the net cost of the investment. The internal rate of return is the discount rate at which the NPV profile crosses the horizontal axis. The NPV profile for Project 2 intersects the horizontal axis at a higher discount rate than does that for Project 1. Thus, Project 2 has a higher internal rate of return.

Answer (B) is incorrect. Project 1 has the lower internal rate of return. Answer (C) is incorrect. The profiles of Projects 1 and 2 intersect. To the left of the intersection point, Project 1 has a higher NPV. To the right of the intersection point, Project 2 has a higher NPV. Answer (D) is incorrect. The profiles of Projects 1 and 2 intersect. To the left of the intersection point, Project 1 has a higher NPV. To the right of the intersection point, Project 2 has a higher NPV.

13.4.11. The following data relate to two capital-budgeting projects of equal risk:

	Present Value of Cash Flows	
Period	Project A	Project B
0	$(10,000)	$(30,000)
1	4,550	13,650
2	4,150	12,450
3	3,750	11,250

Which of the projects will be selected using the profitability-index (PI) approach and the NPV approach?

	PI	NPV
A.	B	A
B.	Either	B
C.	Either	A
D.	B	B

Answer (B) is correct. *(CIA, adapted)*

REQUIRED: The projects selected using the profitability index and the net present value approaches.

DISCUSSION: The profitability index (PI) is the ratio of the present value of future net cash inflows to the net cash invested. In this case, the projects have the same index.

$$\frac{\$4{,}550 + \$4{,}150 + \$3{,}750}{\$10{,}000} = 1.245$$

$$\frac{\$13{,}650 + \$12{,}450 + \$11{,}250}{\$30{,}000} = 1.245$$

The NPV of a project is the excess of the present values of future cash inflows over the net cost of the investment. Project B is preferable under the NPV approach.

$$NPV_A = \$12{,}450 - \$10{,}000 = \$2{,}450$$

$$NPV_B = \$37{,}350 - \$30{,}000 = \$7{,}350$$

Questions 13.4.12 and 13.4.13 are based on the following information. The tax impact of equipment depreciation affects capital budgeting decisions. Currently, the Modified Accelerated Cost Recovery System (MACRS) is used as the depreciation method for most assets for tax purposes.

13.4.12. The MACRS method of depreciation for assets with 3, 5, 7, and 10-year recovery periods is most similar to which one of the following depreciation methods used for financial reporting purposes?

A. Straight-line.

B. Units-of-production.

C. Sum-of-the-years'-digits.

D. 200%-declining-balance.

Answer (D) is correct. *(CMA, adapted)*

REQUIRED: The financial accounting depreciation method most like MACRS for assets with recovery periods of less than 10 years.

DISCUSSION: MACRS for assets with lives of 10 years or less is based on the 200% declining-balance method of depreciation. Thus, an asset with a 3-year life would have a straight-line rate of 33-1/3%, or a double-declining-balance rate of 66-2/3%.

Answer (A) is incorrect. The straight-line method uses the same percentage each year during an asset's life, but MACRS uses various percentages. Answer (B) is incorrect. MACRS is unrelated to the units-of-production method. Answer (C) is incorrect. MACRS is unrelated to SYD depreciation.

13.4.13. When employing the MACRS method of depreciation in a capital budgeting decision, the use of MACRS as compared with the straight-line method of depreciation will result in

A. Equal total depreciation for both methods.

B. MACRS producing less total depreciation than straight line.

C. Equal total tax payments, after discounting for the time value of money.

D. MACRS producing more total depreciation than straight line.

Answer (A) is correct. *(CMA, adapted)*

REQUIRED: The effect on a capital budgeting decision of using MACRS depreciation instead of the straight-line method.

DISCUSSION: For tax purposes, straight-line depreciation is an alternative to the MACRS method. Both methods will result in the same total depreciation over the life of the asset; however, MACRS will result in greater depreciation in the early years of the asset's life because it is an accelerated method. Given that MACRS results in larger depreciation deductions in the early years, taxes will be lower in the early years and higher in the later years. Because the incremental benefits will be discounted over a shorter period than the incremental depreciation costs, MACRS is preferable to the straight-line method.

Answer (B) is incorrect. Both methods will produce the same total depreciation over the life of the asset. Answer (C) is incorrect. Both methods will produce the same total tax payments (assuming rates do not change). However, given that the tax payments will be lower in the early years under MACRS, discounting for the time value of money makes the straight-line alternative less advantageous. Answer (D) is incorrect. Both methods will produce the same total depreciation over the life of the asset.

13.4.14. Scott, Inc., is planning to invest $120,000 in a 10-year project. Scott estimates that the annual cash inflow, net of income taxes, from this project will be $20,000. Scott's desired rate of return on investments of this type is 10%. Information on present value factors is as follows:

	At 10%	At 12%
Present value of $1 for 10 periods	0.386	0.322
Present value of an annuity of $1 for 10 periods	6.145	5.650

Scott's expected rate of return on this investment is

A. Less than 10%, but more than 0%.

B. 10%

C. Less than 12%, but more than 10%.

D. 12%

Answer (C) is correct. *(CPA, adapted)*

REQUIRED: The approximate expected rate of return given the annual after-tax income, rate of return, and investment cost.

DISCUSSION: The initial investment of $120,000 provides a 10-year, $20,000 annuity net of income taxes. The present value of an ordinary annuity of $1 implicit in the relationship between the investment and the net annual cash inflow from the investment is 6.00 ($120,000 ÷ $20,000). Because 6.00 is between the annuity factors for 10% and 12%, the expected rate of return is greater than 10% but less than 12%.

13.4.15. The profitability index (present value index)

A. Represents the ratio of the discounted net cash outflows to cash inflows.

B. Is the relationship between the net discounted cash inflows less the discounted cash outflows divided by the discounted cash outflows.

C. Is calculated by dividing the discounted profits by the cash outflows.

D. Is the ratio of the discounted net cash flows to initial investment.

Answer (D) is correct. *(CMA, adapted)*

REQUIRED: The true statement about the profitability index.

DISCUSSION: The profitability index, also known as the excess present value index, is the ratio of discounted net cash flows to the initial investment. It is a variation of the NPV method that facilitates comparison of different-sized investments.

Answer (A) is incorrect. The cash inflows also are discounted in the profitability index. Answer (B) is incorrect. The denominator is the initial investment. Answer (C) is incorrect. The profitability index is based on cash flows, not profits.

13.4.16. If an investment project has a profitability index of 1.15, the

A. Project's internal rate of return is 15%.

B. Project's cost of capital is greater than its internal rate of return.

C. Project's internal rate of return exceeds its net present value.

D. Net present value of the project is positive.

Answer (D) is correct. *(CMA, adapted)*

REQUIRED: The meaning of a profitability index in excess of 1.0.

DISCUSSION: The profitability index (excess present value index) of an investment is the ratio of the present value of the future net cash flows (or only cash inflows) to the net initial investment. It is a variation of the NPV method that facilitates comparison of different-sized investments. A profitability index greater than 1.0 indicates a profitable investment, i.e., one that has a positive net present value.

Answer (A) is incorrect. The IRR is the discount rate at which the NPV is $0, which is also the rate at which the profitability index is 1.0. The IRR cannot be determined solely from the index. Answer (B) is incorrect. If the index is 1.15 and the discount rate is the cost of capital, the NPV is positive, and the IRR must be higher than the cost of capital. Answer (C) is incorrect. The IRR is a discount rate, whereas the NPV is an amount.

13.4.17. The profitability index approach to investment analysis

A. Fails to consider the timing of project cash flows.

B. Considers only the project's contribution to net income and does not consider cash flow effects.

C. Always yields the same accept/reject decisions for independent projects as the net present value method.

D. Always yields the same accept/reject decisions for mutually exclusive projects as the net present value method.

Answer (C) is correct. *(CMA, adapted)*

REQUIRED: The true statement about the profitability index.

DISCUSSION: The profitability index is the ratio of a discounted cash flow amount to the initial investment. It is a variation of the net present value (NPV) method and facilitates the comparison of different-sized investments. Because it is based on the NPV method, the profitability index yields the same decision as the NPV for independent projects. However, decisions may differ for mutually exclusive projects of different sizes.

Answer (A) is incorrect. The profitability index, like the NPV method, discounts cash flows based on the cost of capital. Answer (B) is incorrect. The profitability index is cash based. Answer (D) is incorrect. The NPV and the profitability index may yield different decisions if projects are mutually exclusive and of different sizes.

13.4.18. The treasurer of a firm has an opportunity to purchase a secured 15% mortgage with 5 years remaining for $10,000. If the firm purchases the mortgage, it will receive five annual payments of $3,000 each. If the treasurer wants no less than a 12% return on long-term cash investments, the NPV of the mortgage will be

Years:	1	2	3	4	5
Present value of $1 at 12%:	.89	.80	.71	.64	.57
Present value of $1 at 15%:	.87	.76	.66	.57	.50

A. $80

B. $830

C. $5,000

D. Not enough information.

Answer (B) is correct. *(CIA, adapted)*

REQUIRED: The NPV of a mortgage.

DISCUSSION: The NPV is equal to the sum of the discounted future cash inflows minus the required investment. Given that the entity receives $3,000 annually over the next 5 years, the present value of the cash inflows is the sum of the products of each year's 12% discount factor and $3,000. The discount rate used is the entity's rate of return, not the mortgage's rate of return.

[$3,000(.89 + .80 + .71 + .64 + .57)] = $10,830
$10,830 – Initial investment = NPV
$10,830 – $10,000 = $830
NPV = $830

Answer (A) is incorrect. The discount rate used should be the firm's rate of return (12%) and not the mortgage's rate of return (15%). Answer (C) is incorrect. The amount of $5,000 does not discount the annual payments. Answer (D) is incorrect. The NPV is $830.

13.4.19. Each of three mutually exclusive projects costs $200. Using the table provided, rank the projects in descending NPV order

Year	Present Value Interest Factor (10%)	Projects' Cash Flow A	B	C
1	.91	$300	$200	$ 0
2	.83	200	100	100
3	.75	100	0	100
4	.68	0	100	200
5	.62	0	200	300

A. A, B, C.

B. B, A, C.

C. C, B, A.

D. A, C, B.

Answer (D) is correct. *(CIA, adapted)*

REQUIRED: The NPVs ranked in descending order.

DISCUSSION: The NPV equals the sum of the discounted future cash flows minus the required investment.

	A	B	C
	$273	$182	$ 0
	166	83	83
	75	0	75
	0	68	136
	0	124	186
PV	$514	$457	$480
	(200)	(200)	(200)
NPV	$314	$257	$280

Answer (A) is incorrect. C has a greater NPV than B. Answer (B) is incorrect. B has the lowest NPV. Answer (C) is incorrect. A has a greater NPV than either B or C.

13.4.20. Oak Co. bought a machine that will depreciate on the straight-line basis over an estimated useful life of 7 years. The machine has no salvage value. Oak expects the machine to generate after-tax net cash inflows from operations of $110,000 in each of the 7 years. Oak's minimum rate of return is 12%. Information on present value factors is as follows:

Present value of $1 at 12% at the end of 7 periods	.452
Present value of an ordinary annuity of $1 at 12% for 7 periods	4.564

Assuming a positive net present value of $12,000, what was the cost of the machine?

A. $485,200

B. $490,040

C. $502,040

D. $514,040

Answer (B) is correct. *(CPA, adapted)*

REQUIRED: The cost of a machine given NPV data.

DISCUSSION: The original cost of the equipment can be calculated as follows:

PV of after-tax cash inflows ($110,000 × 4.564)	$502,040
Net present value	(12,000)
Cost of new equipment	$490,040

Answer (A) is incorrect. This amount equals 4.52 times $110,000, minus $12,000. Answer (C) is incorrect. This amount equals the present value of the series of after-tax net cash inflows over a 7-year period. Answer (D) is incorrect. This amount results from adding the NPV to, not subtracting it from, the present value of the series of after-tax net cash inflows over a 7-year period.

13.4.21. On January 1, a company invested in an asset with a useful life of 3 years. The company's expected rate of return is 10%. The cash flow and present and future value factors for the 3 years are as follows:

Year	Cash Inflow from the Asset	Present Value of $1 at 10%	Future Value of $1 at 10%
1	$ 8,000	.91	1.10
2	9,000	.83	1.21
3	10,000	.75	1.33

All cash inflows are assumed to occur at year end. If the asset generates a positive net present value of $2,000, what was the amount of the original investment?

A. $20,250

B. $22,250

C. $30,991

D. $33,991

Answer (A) is correct. *(CIA, adapted)*

REQUIRED: The original investment given NPV and PV and FV tables.

DISCUSSION: The NPV of a proposed investment is computed by subtracting the original investment from the present value of future cash flows. Accordingly, the original investment is

$$\begin{aligned} \$2{,}000 &= (\$8{,}000 \times .91) + (\$9{,}000 \times .83) \\ &\quad + (\$10{,}000 \times .75) - X \\ \$2{,}000 &= \$7{,}280 + \$7{,}470 + \$7{,}500 - X \\ X + \$2{,}000 &= \$22{,}250 \\ X &= \$20{,}250 \end{aligned}$$

Answer (B) is incorrect. The amount of $22,250 is the present value of future cash flows. Answer (C) is incorrect. The NPV of $2,000 needs to be subtracted from the present value of future cash flows ($22,250) to yield an original investment of $20,250. Answer (D) is incorrect. The NPV of $2,000 needs to be subtracted from the present value of future cash flows ($22,250) to yield an original investment of $20,250.

13.4.22. Garwood Company has purchased a machine that will be depreciated on the straight-line basis over an estimated useful life of 7 years with no salvage value. The machine is expected to generate cash flow from operations, net of income taxes, of $80,000 in each of the 7 years. Garwood's expected rate of return is 12%. Information on present value factors is as follows:

Present value of $1 at 12% for seven periods	0.452
Present value of an ordinary annuity of $1 at 12% for seven periods	4.564

Assuming a positive net present value of $12,720, what was the cost of the machine?

A. $240,400

B. $253,120

C. $352,400

D. $377,840

Answer (C) is correct. *(CPA, adapted)*

REQUIRED: The cost of the machine given after-tax cash flows, present value data, and a positive NPV.

DISCUSSION: The NPV is the excess of the present value of the future cash flows over the initial net investment. The after-tax annual cash flow is $80,000, and the present value of an ordinary annuity of $1 for 7 years at 12% is 4.564. The present value of the cash flows is $365,120 ($80,000 × 4.564). Given a positive NPV of $12,720, the cost of the machine must have been $352,400 ($365,120 – $12,720).

Answer (A) is incorrect. The total cash flows of $560,000 were multiplied by the present value of $1 at 12%. The present value factor of an ordinary annuity must be used in calculating this present value. Answer (B) is incorrect. The total cash flows of $560,000 were multiplied by the present value of $1 at 12%. The present value factor of an ordinary annuity must be used in calculating this present value. Furthermore, the positive NPV of $12,720 should be subtracted from the present value of the cash flows. Answer (D) is incorrect. The positive NPV of $12,720 needs to be subtracted, not added, to the present value.

13.5 Internal Rate of Return

13.5.1. The internal rate of return is

A. The discount rate at which the NPV of the cash flows is zero.

B. The breakeven borrowing rate for the project in question.

C. The yield or effective rate of interest quoted on long-term debt and other instruments.

D. All of the answers are correct.

Answer (D) is correct. *(Publisher, adapted)*

REQUIRED: The true statement(s) about internal rate of return.

DISCUSSION: The internal rate of return (IRR) is the discount rate at which the present value of the cash flows equals the original investment. Thus, the NPV of the project is zero at the IRR. The IRR is also the maximum borrowing cost the firm could afford to pay for a specific project (the breakeven rate). The IRR is similar to the yield or effective rate quoted in the business media.

13.5.2. Which of the following characteristics represent an advantage of the internal rate of return technique over the accounting rate of return technique in evaluating a project?

I. Recognition of the project's salvage value
II. Emphasis on cash flows
III. Recognition of the time value of money

A. I only.

B. I and II.

C. II and III.

D. I, II, and III.

Answer (C) is correct. *(CPA, adapted)*

REQUIRED: The advantage(s) of the IRR technique over the accounting rate of return technique.

DISCUSSION: A project's internal rate of return is the discount rate that equates the present value of the future cash flows with the initial cost of the investment. The accounting rate of return is calculated by dividing the increase in average annual accounting net income by the required investment. Thus, while both techniques take salvage value into consideration, accounting rate of return ignores cash flows and the time value of money.

13.5.3. If income tax considerations are ignored, how is depreciation handled by the following capital budgeting techniques?

	Internal Rate of Return	Accounting Rate of Return	Payback
A.	Excluded	Included	Excluded
B.	Included	Excluded	Included
C.	Excluded	Excluded	Included
D.	Included	Included	Included

Answer (A) is correct. *(CMA, adapted)*

REQUIRED: The manner in which depreciation is handled by each capital budgeting technique.

DISCUSSION: If taxes are ignored, depreciation is not a consideration in any of the methods based on cash flows because it is a non-cash expense. Thus, the internal rate of return, net present value, and payback methods would not consider depreciation because these methods are based on cash flows. However, the accounting rate of return employs accrual-basis net income of which depreciation is a component.

13.5.4. Polo Co. requires higher rates of return for projects with a life span greater than 5 years. Projects extending beyond 5 years must earn a higher specified rate of return. Which of the following capital budgeting techniques can readily accommodate this requirement?

	Internal Rate of Return	Net Present Value
A.	Yes	No
B.	No	Yes
C.	No	No
D.	Yes	Yes

Answer (D) is correct. *(CPA, adapted)*

REQUIRED: The capital budgeting technique(s) that can accommodate a higher desired rate of return for longer projects.

DISCUSSION: A project's internal rate of return is the discount rate at which its net present value is zero. A project's net present value is the excess of the present value of the expected future net cash inflows over the cost of the investment. Thus, both techniques can be readily adjusted for an increase in the desired return by changing the discount rate.

13.5.5. An organization is using capital budgeting techniques to compare two independent projects. It could accept one, both, or neither of the projects. Which of the following statements is true about the use of net-present-value (NPV) and internal-rate-of-return (IRR) methods for evaluating these two projects?

A. NPV and IRR criteria will always lead to the same accept or reject decision for two independent projects.

B. If the first project's IRR is higher than the organization's desired rate of return, the first project will be accepted but the second project will not.

C. If the NPV criterion leads to accepting or rejecting the first project, one cannot predict whether the IRR criterion will lead to accepting or rejecting the first project.

D. If the NPV criterion leads to accepting the first project, the IRR criterion will never lead to accepting the first project.

Answer (A) is correct. *(CIA, adapted)*

REQUIRED: The true statement about the NPV and IRR methods.

DISCUSSION: The NPV criterion is that the NPV is positive, and the IRR criterion is that the desired rate of return is less than the IRR. When the desired rate of return is less than the IRR, the NPV is positive. When it exceeds the IRR, the NPV is negative. Accordingly, when two projects are independent, the NPV and IRR criteria always result in the same accept or reject decision.

Answer (B) is incorrect. If the second project's IRR is higher than the first project's, the entity accepts the second project based on the IRR criterion. Answer (C) is incorrect. If the projects are independent, the NPV and IRR criteria indicate the same decision. Answer (D) is incorrect. If the projects are independent, the NPV and IRR criteria indicate the same decision.

13.5.6. Everything else being equal, the internal rate of return (IRR) of an investment project will be lower if

A. The investment cost is lower.

B. Cash inflows are received later in the life of the project.

C. Cash inflows are larger.

D. The project has a shorter payback period.

Answer (B) is correct. *(CIA, adapted)*

REQUIRED: The true statement about the IRR.

DISCUSSION: The IRR is the discount rate at which the net present value is zero. Because the present value of a dollar is higher the sooner it is received, projects with later cash flows have lower NPVs for any given discount rate than projects with earlier cash flows, if other factors are constant. Thus, projects with later cash flows will have a lower IRR.

Answer (A) is incorrect. The present value of the cash inflows is inversely related to the discount rate. If the discount rate is higher, the present value of the cash inflows is lower. If the investment cost is lower, a higher discount rate (the IRR) is required to set the net present value equal to zero. Answer (C) is incorrect. The larger the cash inflows, the higher the IRR is. Higher cash inflows have a higher present value at any given discount rate. A higher discount rate is required to set the net present value equal to zero. Answer (D) is incorrect. Projects with shorter payback periods have higher cash inflows early in the life of the project. Projects with earlier cash inflows have higher IRRs.

13.5.7. The rankings of mutually exclusive investments determined using the internal rate of return method (IRR) and the net present value method (NPV) may be different when

A. The lives of the multiple projects are equal and the size of the required investments are equal.

B. The required rate of return equals the IRR of each project.

C. The required rate of return is higher than the IRR of each project.

D. Multiple projects have unequal lives and the size of the investment for each project is different.

Answer (D) is correct. *(CMA, adapted)*

REQUIRED: The circumstances in which IRR and NPV rankings of mutually exclusive projects may differ.

DISCUSSION: The two methods ordinarily yield the same results, but differences can occur when the duration of the projects and the initial investments differ. The reason is that the IRR method assumes cash inflows from the early years will be reinvested at the internal rate of return. The NPV method assumes that early cash inflows are reinvested at the NPV discount rate.

Answer (A) is incorrect. The two methods will give the same results if the lives and required investments are the same. Answer (B) is incorrect. If the required rate of return equals the IRR, the two methods will yield the same decision. Answer (C) is incorrect. If the required rate of return is higher than the IRR, both methods will yield a decision not to acquire the investment.

13.5.8. If the net present value (NPV) of Project A is known to be higher than the NPV of Project B, it can be concluded that

A. The internal rate of return (IRR) of Project A will definitely be higher than the IRR of Project B.

B. The IRR of Project A will definitely be lower than the IRR of Project B.

C. The ranking of IRRs is indeterminate based on the information provided.

D. The payback period for Project A is definitely shorter than the payback period for Project B.

Answer (C) is correct. *(CIA, adapted)*

REQUIRED: The significance of a higher NPV.

DISCUSSION: The IRR is the discount rate at which the NPV is zero. The NPV is the present value of future cash flows minus the present value of the investment. Because of a possible difference in the scale of the projects and other factors, a higher NPV does not necessarily result in a higher IRR.

13.5.9. The payback reciprocal can be used to approximate a project's

A. Profitability index.

B. Net present value.

C. Accounting rate of return if the cash flow pattern is relatively stable.

D. Internal rate of return if the cash flow pattern is relatively stable.

Answer (D) is correct. *(CMA, adapted)*

REQUIRED: The item that can be approximated by a project's payback reciprocal.

DISCUSSION: The payback reciprocal (1 ÷ payback) has been shown to approximate the internal rate of return (IRR) when the periodic cash flows are equal and the life of the project is at least twice the payback period.

Answer (A) is incorrect. The payback reciprocal is not related to the profitability index. Answer (B) is incorrect. The payback reciprocal approximates the IRR, which is the rate at which the NPV is $0. Answer (C) is incorrect. The accounting rate of return is based on accrual-income based figures, not on discounted cash flows.

13.5.10. A weakness of the internal rate of return (IRR) approach for determining the acceptability of investments is that it

A. Does not consider the time value of money.

B. Is not a straightforward decision criterion.

C. Implicitly assumes that the firm is able to reinvest project cash flows at the firm's cost of capital.

D. Implicitly assumes that the firm is able to reinvest project cash flows at the project's internal rate of return.

Answer (D) is correct. *(CMA, adapted)*

REQUIRED: The weakness of the internal rate of return approach.

DISCUSSION: The IRR is the rate at which the discounted future cash flows equal the net investment (NPV = 0). One disadvantage of the method is that inflows from the early years are assumed to be reinvested at the IRR. This assumption may not be sound. Investments in the future may not earn as high a rate as is currently available.

Answer (A) is incorrect. The IRR method considers the time value of money. Answer (B) is incorrect. The IRR provides a straightforward decision criterion. Any project with an IRR greater than the firm's desired rate of return is acceptable. Answer (C) is incorrect. The IRR method implicitly assumes reinvestment at the IRR; the NPV method implicitly assumes reinvestment at the cost of capital.

13.5.11. A company's marginal cost of new capital (MCC) is 10% up to $600,000. MCC increases .5% for the next $400,000 and another .5% thereafter. Several proposed capital projects are under consideration, with projected cost and internal rates of return (IRR) as follows:

Project	Cost	IRR
A	$100,000	10.5%
B	300,000	14.0
C	450,000	10.8
D	350,000	13.5
E	400,000	12.0

What should the company's capital budget be?

A. $0

B. $1,050,000

C. $1,500,000

D. $1,600,000

Answer (B) is correct. *(CIA, adapted)*

REQUIRED: The capital budget.

DISCUSSION: The IRR is the discount rate at which the NPV (discounted net cash inflows – investment) of a project is zero. Thus, an investment should be acceptable if the IRR exceeds the desired rate of return. Projects B, D, and E, with a combined cost of $1,050,000, have the highest IRRs. Each is in excess of the maximum 11% cost of capital (10% + .5% + .5%). Because the combined cost of B, D, and E exceeds the level ($1,000,000) at which the desired rate of return rises to 11%, Projects A (10.5%) and C (10.8%) must be rejected using the IRR criterion.

Answer (A) is incorrect. Any projects with an IRR of 11% or greater should be accepted. Answer (C) is incorrect. The amount of $1,500,000 includes Project C. It should be rejected because its IRR of 10.8% is less than the 11% desired rate of return. Answer (D) is incorrect. The amount of $1,600,000 includes Projects A and C. They should be rejected because their respective IRRs are less than the 11% desired rate of return.

13.5.12. A project requires an initial cash investment of $10,000, and no other cash outflows are necessary. Cash inflows from the project over its 3-year life are $6,000 at the end of the first year, $5,000 at the end of the second year, and $2,000 at the end of the third year. The future value interest factors for an amount of $1 at the desired rate of return of 8% are

Period			
1	2	3	4
1.080	1.166	1.260	1.360

The present value interest factors for an amount of $1 for three periods are as follows:

Interest Rate				
8%	9%	10%	12%	14%
.794	.772	.751	.712	.675

The modified IRR (MIRR) for the project is closest to

A. 8%

B. 9%

C. 10%

D. 12%

Answer (D) is correct. *(Publisher, adapted)*

REQUIRED: The approximate MIRR.

DISCUSSION: The MIRR is the interest rate at which the present value of the cash outflows discounted at the desired rate of return equals the present value of the end value. The end value is the future value of the cash inflows assuming they are reinvested at the cost of capital. The present value of the outflows is $10,000 because no future outflows occur. The end value is $14,396 [($6,000 × 1.166) + ($5,000 × 1.08) + ($2,000 × 1.00)]. Accordingly, the present value of $1 interest factor for the rate at which the present value of the outflows equals the present value of the end value is .695 ($10,000 ÷ $14,396). This factor is closest to that for 12%.

13.5.13. Kern Co. is planning to invest in a 2-year project that is expected to yield cash flows from operations, net of income taxes, of $50,000 in the first year and $80,000 in the second year. Kern requires an internal rate of return of 15%. The present value of $1 for one period at 15% is 0.870 and for two periods at 15% is 0.756. The future value of $1 for one period at 15% is 1.150 and for two periods at 15% is 1.323. The maximum that Kern should invest immediately is

A. $81,670

B. $103,980

C. $130,000

D. $163,340

Answer (B) is correct. *(CPA, adapted)*

REQUIRED: The maximum investment given the desired IRR.

DISCUSSION: To be considered a worthwhile investment, a capital project must have a positive net present value, meaning the initial investment must not exceed the present value of the discounted future cash flows.

PV of 1st-year cash flows:	$50,000 × .870 =	$ 43,500
PV of 2nd-year cash flows:	$80,000 × .756 =	60,480
PV of future cash flows:		$103,980

For the project to be profitable, Kern must invest no more than $103,980.

Answer (A) is incorrect. The maximum that should be invested immediately is the present value of the two future cash flows. Answer (C) is incorrect. Future cash flows need to be discounted using the present value factors. Answer (D) is incorrect. The cash flows need to be discounted using the present value factors, not the future value factors.

Questions 13.5.14 and 13.5.15 are based on the following information. Jorelle Company's financial staff has been requested to review a proposed investment in new capital equipment. Applicable financial data is presented below. There will be no salvage value at the end of the investment's life and, due to realistic depreciation practices, it is estimated that the salvage value and net book value are equal at the end of each year. All cash flows are assumed to take place at the end of each year. For investment proposals, Jorelle uses a 12% after-tax target rate of return.

Investment Proposal

Year	Purchase Cost and Book Value	Annual Net After-Tax Cash Flows	Annual Net Income
0	$250,000	$ 0	$ 0
1	168,000	120,000	35,000
2	100,000	108,000	39,000
3	50,000	96,000	43,000
4	18,000	84,000	47,000
5	0	72,000	51,000

Discounted Factors for a 12% Rate of Return

Year	Present Value of $1.00 Received at the End of Each Period	Present Value of an Annuity of $1.00 Received at the End of Each Period
1	.89	.89
2	.80	1.69
3	.71	2.40
4	.64	3.04
5	.57	3.61
6	.51	4.12

13.5.14. The accounting rate of return on the average investment proposal is

A. 12.0%

B. 17.2%

C. 28.0%

D. 34.4%

Answer (D) is correct. *(CMA, adapted)*

REQUIRED: The accounting rate of return.

DISCUSSION: The accounting rate of return (unadjusted rate of return or book value rate of return) equals accounting net income divided by the required average investment. The accounting rate of return ignores the time value of money. The average income over 5 years is $43,000 per year [($35,000 + $39,000 + $43,000 + $47,000 + $51,000) ÷ 5]. Hence, the accounting rate of return is 34.4% [$43,000 ÷ ($250,000 ÷ 2)].

Answer (A) is incorrect. This percentage is the discount rate. Answer (B) is incorrect. This percentage equals $43,000 divided by $250,000. Answer (C) is incorrect. This percentage equals $35,000 divided by $125,000.

13.5.15. The net present value for the investment proposal is

A. $106,160

B. $(97,970)

C. $356,160

D. $96,560

Answer (A) is correct. *(CMA, adapted)*

REQUIRED: The NPV.

DISCUSSION: The NPV is the sum of the present values of all cash inflows and outflows associated with the proposal. If the NPV is positive, the proposal should be accepted. The NPV is determined by discounting each expected cash flow using the appropriate 12% interest factor for the present value of $1. Thus, the NPV is $106,160 [(.89 × $120,000) + (.80 × $108,000) + (.71 × $96,000) + (.64 × $84,000) + (.57 × $72,000) – (1.00 × $250,000)].

Answer (B) is incorrect. The amount of $(97,970) is based on net income instead of cash flows. Answer (C) is incorrect. The amount of $356,160 excludes the purchase cost. Answer (D) is incorrect. The amount of $96,560 equals average after-tax cash inflow times the interest factor for the present value of a 5-year annuity, minus $250,000.

Questions 13.5.16 and 13.5.17 are based on the following information. A firm with an 18% desired rate of return is considering the following projects (on January 1, Year 1):

	January 1, Year 1 Cash Outflow (000's Omitted)	December 31, Year 5 Cash Inflow (000's Omitted)	Project Internal Rate of Return
Project A	$3,500	$7,400	16%
Project B	4,000	9,950	?

Present Value of $1 Due at the End of "N" Periods

N	12%	14%	15%	16%	18%	20%	22%
4	.6355	.5921	.5718	.5523	.5158	.4823	.4230
5	.5674	.5194	.4972	.4761	.4371	.4019	.3411
6	.5066	.4556	.4323	.4104	.3704	.3349	.2751

13.5.16. Using the net-present-value (NPV) method, Project A's net present value is

A. $316,920

B. $23,140

C. $(265,460)

D. $(316,920)

Answer (C) is correct. *(CIA, adapted)*

REQUIRED: The net present value of Project A.

DISCUSSION: The cash inflow occurs 5 years after the cash outflow, and the NPV method uses the firm's desired rate of return of 18%. The present value of $1 due at the end of 5 years discounted at 18% is .4371. Thus, the NPV of Project A is $(265,460) [($7,400,000 cash inflow × .4371) – $3,500,000 cash outflow].

Answer (A) is incorrect. The amount of $316,920 discounts the cash inflow over a 4-year period. Answer (B) is incorrect. The amount of $23,140 assumes a 16% discount rate. Answer (D) is incorrect. The amount of $(316,920) discounts the cash inflow over a 4-year period and also subtracts the present value of the cash inflow from the cash outflow.

13.5.17. Project B's internal rate of return is closest to

A. 15%

B. 16%

C. 18%

D. 20%

Answer (D) is correct. *(CIA, adapted)*

REQUIRED: The percentage closest to Project B's internal rate of return.

DISCUSSION: The internal rate of return is the discount rate at which the NPV is zero. Consequently, the cash outflow equals the present value of the inflow at the internal rate of return. The present value of $1 factor for Project B's internal rate of return is therefore .4020 ($4,000,000 cash outflow ÷ $9,950,000 cash inflow). This factor is closest to the present value of $1 for 5 periods at 20%.

Answer (A) is incorrect. This percentage results in a positive NPV for Project B. Answer (B) is incorrect. This percentage is the approximate internal rate of return for Project A. Answer (C) is incorrect. This percentage is the company's cost of capital.

13.6 Cash Flow Calculations

13.6.1. A firm is replacing a grinder purchased 5 years ago for $15,000 with a new one costing $25,000 cash. The original grinder is being depreciated on a straight-line basis over 15 years to a zero salvage value; the firm will sell this old equipment to a third party for $6,000 cash. The new equipment will be depreciated on a straight-line basis over 10 years to a zero salvage value. Assuming a 40% marginal tax rate, the firm's net cash investment at the time of purchase if the old grinder is sold and the new one purchased is

A. $19,000

B. $15,000

C. $17,400

D. $25,000

Answer (C) is correct. *(CMA, adapted)*

REQUIRED: The net cash investment at the time of purchase of an old asset and the sale of a new one.

DISCUSSION: The old machine has a carrying amount of $10,000 [$15,000 cost – 5 ($15,000 cost ÷ 15 years) depreciation]. The loss on the sale is $4,000 ($10,000 – $6,000 cash received), and the tax savings from the loss is $1,600 ($4,000 × 40%). Thus, total inflows are $7,600. The only outflow is the $25,000 purchase price of the new machine. The net cash investment is therefore $17,400 ($25,000 – $7,600).

Answer (A) is incorrect. This figure overlooks the tax savings from the loss on the old machine. Answer (B) is incorrect. This figure is obtained by deducting the old book value from the purchase price. Answer (D) is incorrect. The net investment is less than $25,000 given sales proceeds from the old machine and the tax savings.

Questions 13.6.2 through 13.6.5 are based on the following information.

The following data pertain to a 4-year project being considered by Metro Industries:

- A depreciable asset that costs $1,200,000 will be acquired on January 1. The asset, which is expected to have a $200,000 salvage value at the end of 4 years, qualifies as 3-year property under the Modified Accelerated Cost Recovery System (MACRS).
- The new asset will replace an existing asset that has a tax basis of $150,000 and can be sold on the same January 1 for $180,000.
- The project is expected to provide added annual sales of 30,000 units at $20. Additional cash operating costs are: variable, $12 per unit; fixed, $90,000 per year.
- A $50,000 working capital investment that is fully recoverable at the end of the fourth year is required.

Metro is subject to a 40% income tax rate and rounds all computations to the nearest dollar. Assume that any gain or loss affects the taxes paid at the end of the year in which it occurred. The company uses the net present value method to analyze investments and will employ the following factors and rates.

Period	Present Value of $1 at 12%	Present Value of $1 Annuity at 12%	MACRS
1	0.89	0.89	33%
2	0.80	1.69	45
3	0.71	2.40	15
4	0.64	3.04	7

13.6.2. The discounted cash flow for the fourth year MACRS depreciation on the new asset is

A. $0

B. $17,920

C. $21,504

D. $26,880

Answer (C) is correct. *(CMA, adapted)*

REQUIRED: The discounted cash flow for the fourth year MACRS depreciation deduction on the new asset.

DISCUSSION: Tax law allows taxpayers to ignore salvage value when calculating depreciation under MACRS. Thus, the depreciation deduction is 7% of the initial $1,200,000 cost, or $84,000. At a 40% tax rate, the deduction will save the company $33,600 in taxes in the fourth year. The present value of this savings is $21,504 ($33,600 × 0.64 present value of $1 at 12% for four periods).

Answer (A) is incorrect. A tax savings will result in the fourth year from the MACRS deduction. Answer (B) is incorrect. The amount of $17,920 is based on a depreciation calculation in which salvage value is subtracted from the initial cost. Answer (D) is incorrect. The appropriate discount factor for the fourth period is 0.64, not 0.80.

13.6.3. The discounted, net-of-tax amount that relates to disposal of the existing asset is

A. $150,000

B. $169,320

C. $180,000

D. $190,680

Answer (B) is correct. *(CMA, adapted)*

REQUIRED: The discounted, net-of-tax amount relating to the disposal of the existing asset.

DISCUSSION: The cash inflow from the existing asset is $180,000, but that amount is subject to tax on the $30,000 gain ($180,000 – $150,000 tax basis). The tax on the gain is $12,000 ($30,000 × 40%). Because the tax will not be paid until year end, the discounted value is $10,680 ($12,000 × .89 PV of $1 at 12% for one period). Thus, the net-of-tax inflow is $169,320 ($180,000 – $10,680). NOTE: This asset was probably a Section 1231 asset, and any gain on sale qualifies for the special capital gain tax rates. Had the problem not stipulated a 40% tax rate, the capital gains rate would be used. An answer based on that rate is not among the options.

Answer (A) is incorrect. The amount of $150,000 is the tax basis of the asset. Answer (C) is incorrect. The amount of $180,000 ignores the impact of income taxes. Answer (D) is incorrect. The discounted present value of the income taxes is an outflow and is deducted from the inflow from the sale of the asset.

13.6.4. The expected incremental sales will provide a discounted, net-of-tax contribution margin over 4 years of

A. $57,600

B. $92,160

C. $273,600

D. $437,760

Answer (D) is correct. *(CMA, adapted)*

REQUIRED: The expected net-of-tax contribution margin over 4 years.

DISCUSSION: Additional annual sales are 30,000 units at $20 per unit. If variable costs are expected to be $12 per unit, the unit contribution margin is $8, and the total before-tax annual contribution margin is $240,000 (30,000 units × $8). The after-tax total annual contribution margin is $144,000 [$240,000 × (1.0 – .4)]. This annual increase in the contribution margin should be treated as an annuity. Thus, its present value is $437,760 ($144,000 × 3.04 PV of an annuity of $1 at 12% for four periods).

Answer (A) is incorrect. The amount of $57,600 multiplies the annual increase in contribution margin by the tax rate instead of the PV factor. Answer (B) is incorrect. The amount of $92,160 is based on only 1 year's results, not 4. Answer (C) is incorrect. The amount of $273,600 improperly includes fixed costs in the calculation of the contribution margin.

13.6.5. The overall discounted-cash-flow impact of the working capital investment on Metro's project is

A. $(2,800)

B. $(18,000)

C. $(50,000)

D. $(59,200)

Answer (B) is correct. *(CMA, adapted)*

REQUIRED: The overall discounted-cash-flow impact of the working capital investment.

DISCUSSION: The working capital investment is treated as a $50,000 outflow at the beginning of the project and a $50,000 inflow at the end of 4 years. Accordingly, the present value of the inflow after 4 years should be subtracted from the initial $50,000 outlay. The overall discounted-cash-flow impact of the working capital investment is $18,000 [$50,000 – ($50,000 × .64 PV of $1 at 12% for four periods)].

Answer (A) is incorrect. The firm will have its working capital tied up for 4 years, which results in a cost of $18,000 at 12% interest. Answer (C) is incorrect. The working capital investment is recovered at the end of the fourth year. Hence, the working capital cost of the project is the difference between $50,000 and the present value of $50,000 in 4 years. Answer (D) is incorrect. The answer cannot exceed $50,000, which is the amount of the cash outflow.

13.6.6. An entity is considering a 10-year capital investment project with forecasted revenues of $40,000 per year and forecasted cash operating expenses of $29,000 per year. The initial cost of the equipment for the project is $23,000, and the entity expects to sell the equipment for $9,000 at the end of the tenth year. The equipment will be depreciated over 7 years. The project requires a working capital investment of $7,000 at its inception and another $5,000 at the end of Year 5. Assuming a 40% marginal tax rate, the expected net cash flow from the project in the tenth year is

A. $32,000

B. $24,000

C. $20,000

D. $11,000

Answer (B) is correct. *(CMA, adapted)*

REQUIRED: The expected net cash flow from the project in the tenth year.

DISCUSSION: The project will have an $11,000 before-tax cash inflow from operations in the tenth year ($40,000 – $29,000). Also, $9,000 will be generated from the sale of the equipment. The entire $9,000 will be taxable because the basis of the asset was reduced to zero in the 7th year. Thus, taxable income will be $20,000 ($11,000 + $9,000), leaving a net after-tax cash inflow of $12,000 [$20,000 × (1.0 – .4)]. To this $12,000 must be added the $12,000 tied up in working capital ($7,000 + $5,000). The total net cash flow in the 10th year will therefore be $24,000.

Answer (A) is incorrect. The amount of $32,000 omits the $8,000 outflow for income taxes. Answer (C) is incorrect. Taxes will be $8,000, not $12,000. Answer (D) is incorrect. The amount of $11,000 is the net operating cash flow.

13.6.7. A company is analyzing a capital investment proposal for new equipment to produce a product over the next 8 years. The analyst is attempting to determine the appropriate "end-of-life" cash flows for the analysis. At the end of 8 years, the equipment must be removed from the plant and will have a net book value of zero, a tax basis of $75,000, a cost to remove of $40,000, and scrap salvage value of $10,000. The effective tax rate is 40%. What is the appropriate "end-of-life" cash flow related to these items that should be used in the analysis?

A. $45,000

B. $27,000

C. $12,000

D. $(18,000)

Answer (C) is correct. *(CMA, adapted)*

REQUIRED: The appropriate end-of-life cash flow related to the investment.

DISCUSSION: The tax basis of $75,000 and the $40,000 cost to remove can be written off. However, the $10,000 scrap value is a cash inflow. Thus, the taxable loss is $105,000 ($75,000 loss on disposal + $40,000 expense to remove – $10,000 of inflows). At a 40% tax rate, the $105,000 loss will produce a tax savings (inflow) of $42,000. The final cash flows will consist of an outflow of $40,000 (cost to remove) and inflows of $10,000 (scrap) and $42,000 (tax savings), or a net inflow of $12,000.

Answer (A) is incorrect. The amount of $45,000 ignores income taxes and assumes that the loss on disposal involves a cash inflow. Answer (B) is incorrect. The amount of $27,000 assumes that the loss on disposal involves a cash inflow. Answer (D) is incorrect. The amount of $(18,000) ignores the tax loss on disposal.

13.6.8. Doro Co. is considering the purchase of a $100,000 machine that is expected to result in a decrease of $25,000 per year in cash expenses after taxes. This machine, which has no residual value, has an estimated useful life of 10 years and will be depreciated on a straight-line basis. For this machine, the accounting rate of return based on initial investment will be

A. 10%

B. 15%

C. 25%

D. 35%

Answer (B) is correct. *(CPA, adapted)*

REQUIRED: The accounting rate of return based on initial investment.

DISCUSSION: The ARR is based on the accrual method and does not discount future cash flows. Accordingly, the ARR equals the decrease in annual cash expenses after taxes minus annual depreciation, divided by the initial investment. Annual straight-line depreciation is $10,000 [($100,000 cost – $0 salvage value) ÷ 10 years].

$$\text{ARR} = \frac{\$25{,}000 - \$10{,}000}{\$100{,}000} = 15\%$$

Answer (A) is incorrect. The depreciation rate per year is 10%. Answer (C) is incorrect. Depreciation must be subtracted from the $25,000 of cash expenses. Answer (D) is incorrect. Depreciation must be subtracted from, not added to, the $25,000 of cash expenses.

13.7 Comprehensive

Questions 13.7.1 through 13.7.4 are based on the following information.

An organization has four investment proposals with the following costs and expected cash inflows:

		Expected Cash Inflows		
Project	Cost	End of Year 1	End of Year 2	End of Year 3
A	Unknown	$10,000	$10,000	$10,000
B	$20,000	$ 5,000	$10,000	$15,000
C	$25,000	$15,000	$10,000	$ 5,000
D	$30,000	$20,000	Unknown	$20,000

Additional Information:

Discount Rate	Number of Periods	Present Value of $1 Due at the End of n Periods (PVIF)	Present Value of an Annuity of $1 per Period for n Periods (PVIFA)
5%	1	0.9524	0.9524
5%	2	0.9070	1.8594
5%	3	0.8638	2.7232
10%	1	0.9091	0.9091
10%	2	0.8264	1.7355
10%	3	0.7513	2.4869
15%	1	0.8696	0.8696
15%	2	0.7561	1.6257
15%	3	0.6575	2.2832

13.7.1. If Project A has an internal rate of return (IRR) of 15%, it has a cost of

A. $8,696

B. $22,832

C. $24,869

D. $27,232

Answer (B) is correct. *(CIA, adapted)*

REQUIRED: The cost of Project A given the IRR.

DISCUSSION: The IRR is the discount rate at which the NPV is zero, so the present value of the costs equals the present value of the cash inflows. At an IRR of 15%, the present value of the inflows (and therefore the present value of the costs) for Project A equals the constant annual inflow times the present value of an ordinary annuity of $1 for three periods at 15%. Thus, the cost of Project A is $22,832 ($10,000 × 2.2832).

Answer (A) is incorrect. The amount of $8,696 uses the present value interest factor for one period at 15%. Answer (C) is incorrect. The amount of $24,869 is obtained using a 10% discount rate. Answer (D) is incorrect. The amount of $27,232 is based on a 5% discount rate.

13.7.2. If the discount rate is 10%, the net present value (NPV) of Project B is

A. $4,079

B. $6,789

C. $9,869

D. $39,204

Answer (A) is correct. *(CIA, adapted)*

REQUIRED: The NPV of Project B given the discount rate.

DISCUSSION: The NPV is the present value of the cash inflows minus the cost of the project. The inflows for this project are not constant, so the individual cash flows may be discounted using the interest factors for the present value of $1 due at the end of a period discounted at 10%. The sum of these present values is $24,079 [($5,000 × .9091) + ($10,000 × .8264) + ($15,000 × .7513)]. Thus, the NPV is $4,079 ($24,079 – $20,000 cost).

Answer (B) is incorrect. The amount of $6,789 uses a 5% discount rate. Answer (C) is incorrect. The amount of $9,869 is the NPV of Project A at a 10% discount rate. Answer (D) is incorrect. The amount of $39,204 uses present value interest factors for annuities.

13.7.3. The payback period of Project C is

A. 0 years.

B. 1 year.

C. 2 years.

D. 3 years.

Answer (C) is correct. *(CIA, adapted)*

REQUIRED: The payback period for Project C.

DISCUSSION: The payback period is the time necessary to recover the investment. After 2 years, the cumulative cash inflows for Project C equal the initial investment outlay of $25,000.

Answer (A) is incorrect. The payback period is zero only if a project has no cost or provides immediate cash inflows at least equal to the investment outlay. Answer (B) is incorrect. After 1 year, the cumulative cash inflows for Project C are only $15,000. The initial investment outlay is $25,000. Answer (D) is incorrect. Project C pays back its initial investment outlay in only 2 years.

13.7.4. If the discount rate is 5% and the discounted payback period of Project D is exactly 2 years, then the Year 2 cash inflow for Project D is

A. $5,890

B. $10,000

C. $12,075

D. $14,301

Answer (C) is correct. *(CIA, adapted)*

REQUIRED: The Year 2 cash inflow for Project D.

DISCUSSION: The discounted payback period is the time required for discounted cash flows to recover the cost of the investment. Thus, the cost of Project D must equal the present value of the end-of-Year-1 cash inflow discounted at 5% plus the present value of the end-of-Year-2 cash inflow. The Year 2 cash inflow (X) is calculated as follows:

$$\begin{aligned} \$30{,}000 &= (\$20{,}000 \times .9524) + (X \times .9070) \\ X &= (\$30{,}000 - \$19{,}048) \div .9070 \\ X &= \$12{,}075 \end{aligned}$$

Answer (A) is incorrect. The amount of $5,890 uses present value interest factors for annuities. Answer (B) is incorrect. The amount of $10,000 is based on the regular payback period. Answer (D) is incorrect. The amount of $14,301 is obtained using a 10% discount rate.

Questions 13.7.5 through 13.7.7 are based on the following information. Capital Invest, Inc., uses a 12% hurdle rate for all capital expenditures and has done the following analysis for four projects for the upcoming year:

	Project 1	Project 2	Project 3	Project 4
Initial capital outlay	$200,000	$298,000	$248,000	$272,000
Annual net cash inflows				
Year 1	65,000	100,000	80,000	95,000
Year 2	70,000	135,000	95,000	125,000
Year 3	80,000	90,000	90,000	90,000
Year 4	40,000	65,000	80,000	60,000
Net present value	(3,798)	4,276	14,064	14,662
Profitability index	98%	101%	106%	105%
Internal rate of return	11%	13%	14%	15%

13.7.5. Which project(s) should Capital Invest undertake during the upcoming year, assuming it has no budget restrictions?

A. All of the projects.

B. Projects 1, 2, and 3.

C. Projects 2, 3, and 4.

D. Projects 1, 3, and 4.

Answer (C) is correct. *(CMA, adapted)*

REQUIRED: The project(s) undertaken assuming no budget restrictions.

DISCUSSION: A company using the NPV method should undertake all projects with a positive NPV, unless some of those projects are mutually exclusive. Given that Projects 2, 3, and 4 have positive NPVs, they should be undertaken. Project 1 has a negative NPV.

13.7.6. Which project(s) should Capital Invest undertake during the upcoming year if it has only $600,000 of funds available?

A. Projects 1 and 3.

B. Projects 2, 3, and 4.

C. Projects 2 and 3.

D. Projects 3 and 4.

Answer (D) is correct. *(CMA, adapted)*

REQUIRED: The project(s) undertaken given capital rationing.

DISCUSSION: Given that only $600,000 is available and that each project costs $200,000 or more, no more than two projects can be undertaken. Because Projects 3 and 4 have the greatest NPVs, profitability indexes, and IRRs, they are the projects in which the company should invest.

Answer (A) is incorrect. Project 1 has a negative NPV. Answer (B) is incorrect. This answer violates the $600,000 limitation. Answer (C) is incorrect. The combined NPV of Projects 2 and 3 is less than the combined NPV of Projects 3 and 4.

13.7.7. Which project(s) should Capital Invest undertake during the upcoming year if it has only $300,000 of capital funds available?

A. Project 1.

B. Projects 2, 3, and 4.

C. Projects 3 and 4.

D. Project 3.

Answer (D) is correct. *(CMA, adapted)*

REQUIRED: The project(s) undertaken given capital rationing.

DISCUSSION: Given that $300,000 is available and that each project costs $200,000 or more, only one project can be undertaken. Because Project 3 (NPV $14,004) has a positive NPV and the highest profitability index, it is the best investment among the given feasible options. The high profitability index means that the company will achieve the highest NPV per dollar of investment with Project 3. The profitability index facilitates comparison of different-sized investments. However, Project 4 has the higher NPV ($14,662).

Answer (A) is incorrect. Project 1 has a negative NPV. Answer (B) is incorrect. Choosing more than one project violates the $300,000 limitation. Answer (C) is incorrect. Choosing more than one project violates the $300,000 limitation.

Questions 13.7.8 through 13.7.10 are based on the following information.

A company purchased a new machine to stamp the company logo on its products. The cost of the machine was $250,000, and it has an estimated useful life of 5 years with an expected salvage value at the end of its useful life of $50,000. The company uses the straight-line depreciation method.

The new machine is expected to save $125,000 annually in operating costs. The company's tax rate is 40%, and it uses a 10% discount rate to evaluate capital expenditures.

Year	Present Value of $1	Present Value of an Ordinary Annuity of $1
1	.909	.909
2	.826	1.736
3	.751	2.487
4	.683	3.170
5	.621	3.791

13.7.8. What is the traditional payback period for the new stamping machine?

A. 2.00 years.

B. 2.63 years.

C. 2.75 years.

D. 2.94 years.

Answer (C) is correct. *(CIA, adapted)*

REQUIRED: The traditional payback period.

DISCUSSION: The traditional payback period is the number of years required to complete the return of the original investment. It equals the net investment divided by the average expected periodic net cash inflow. The periodic net cash inflow equals the $125,000 annual savings minus the additional taxes paid. This $125,000 increase in pretax income is reduced by an increase in depreciation of $40,000 [($250,000 cost – $50,000 salvage) ÷ 5 years]. Thus, taxes increase by $34,000 [($125,000 – $40,000) × 40%], and the after-tax periodic net cash inflow is $91,000 ($125,000 – $34,000). Accordingly, the payback period is 2.75 years ($250,000 ÷ $91,000).

Answer (A) is incorrect. The period of 2.00 years does not consider cash flows for taxes. Answer (B) is incorrect. The period of 2.63 years omits salvage value from the depreciation calculation. Answer (D) is incorrect. The period of 2.94 years treats depreciation as a negative cash flow and ignores taxes.

13.7.9. What is the accounting rate of return based on the average investment in the new stamping machine?

A. 20.4%

B. 34.0%

C. 40.8%

D. 51.0%

Answer (C) is correct. *(CIA, adapted)*

REQUIRED: The accounting rate of return based on the average investment.

DISCUSSION: The accounting rate of return equals annual after-tax net income divided by average investment. Annual after-tax net income equals $51,000 [($125,000 cost savings – $40,000 depreciation*) × (1.0 – 0.4)]. Consequently, the accounting rate of return equals 40.8% [$51,000 ÷ ($250,000 investment ÷ 2)].

*Depreciation = ($250,000 cost – $50,000 salvage) ÷ 5 years
= $40,000

Answer (A) is incorrect. The percentage of 20.4 is the accounting rate of return using the original investment. Answer (B) is incorrect. The percentage of 34.0 results from adding the salvage value to the original investment. Answer (D) is incorrect. The percentage of 51.0 assumes an average investment of $100,000.

13.7.10. What is the net present value (NPV) of the new stamping machine?

A. $125,940

B. $200,000

C. $250,000

D. $375,940

Answer (A) is correct. *(CIA, adapted)*

REQUIRED: The NPV of the machine.

DISCUSSION: The NPV is the excess of the present values of the estimated cash inflows over the net cost of the investment. The annual after-tax net cash inflow from the cost savings is $91,000. In the fifth year, the cash inflows also include the salvage value.

Year	Cash Flow Amounts	PV Factor	PV of Cash Flow
0	$(250,000)	1.000	$(250,000)
1	$91,000	.909	82,719
2	$91,000	.826	75,166
3	$91,000	.751	68,341
4	$91,000	.683	62,153
5	$91,000 + $50,000	.621	87,561
	Net present value		$125,940

Answer (B) is incorrect. The amount of $200,000 is the cost of the machine minus salvage value. Answer (C) is incorrect. The amount of $250,000 is the cost of the machine. Answer (D) is incorrect. The amount of $375,940 is the NPV of the machine plus its purchase price.

Questions 13.7.11 through 13.7.17 are based on the following information.

At the beginning of Year 6, Garrison Corporation is considering the replacement of an old machine that is currently being used. The old machine is fully depreciated but can be used by the corporation for an additional 5 years, that is, through Year 10. If Garrison decides to replace the old machine, Picco Company has offered to purchase it for $60,000 on the replacement date. The old machine would have no salvage value in Year 10.

If the replacement occurs, a new machine will be acquired from Hillcrest Industries on January 2, Year 6. The purchase price of $1 million for the new machine will be paid in cash at the time of replacement. Because of the increased efficiency of the new machine, estimated annual cash savings of $300,000 will be generated through Year 10, the end of its expected useful life. The new machine is not expected to have any salvage value at the end of Year 10.

All operating cash receipts, operating cash expenditures, and applicable tax payments and credits are assumed to occur at the end of the year. Garrison employs the calendar year for reporting purposes.

- Garrison requires all investments to earn a 12% after-tax rate of return to be accepted.
- Garrison is subject to a marginal income tax rate of 40% on all income and gains (losses).
- The new machine will have depreciation as follows:

Year	Depreciation
3	$ 250,000
4	380,000
5	370,000
	$1,000,000

Discount tables for several different interest rates that are to be used in any discounting calculations are given below.

Present Value of $1.00 Received at End of Period

Period	9%	12%	15%	18%	21%
1	.92	.89	.87	.85	.83
2	.84	.80	.76	.72	.68
3	.77	.71	.65	.61	.56
4	.71	.64	.57	.51	.47
5	.65	.57	.50	.44	.39

Present Value of an Annuity of $1.00 Received at the End of Each Period

Period	9%	12%	15%	18%	21%
1	.92	.89	.87	.85	.83
2	1.76	1.69	1.63	1.57	1.51
3	2.53	2.40	2.28	2.18	2.07
4	3.24	3.04	2.85	2.69	2.54
5	3.89	3.61	3.35	3.13	2.93

13.7.11. If Garrison requires investments to earn a 12% return, the NPV for replacing the old machine with the new machine is

A. $171,000

B. $136,400

C. $143,000

D. $83,000

Answer (C) is correct. *(CMA, adapted)*

REQUIRED: The NPV of the new machine.

DISCUSSION: The $300,000 of annual savings discounted at 12% has a present value of $1,083,000 ($300,000 × 3.61 PV of an ordinary annuity for five periods at 12%). The net cost of the new machine is the $1,000,000 purchase price minus the $60,000 cash inflow from the sale of the old machine, or $940,000. The resulting NPV is $143,000 ($1,083,000 present value of future savings – $940,000 cash outlay).

Answer (A) is incorrect. The $300,000 is an annual savings, which should be discounted at the present value of an annuity of $1 for five periods at 12%, or 3.61 ($300,000 × 3.61 = $1,083,000). The $300,000 annual savings should not be discounted using the present value of $1 for five periods at 12%, or .57 ($300,000 × .57 = $171,000). Furthermore, the properly discounted amount ($1,083,000) should be reduced by the net cash outlay ($1,000,000 – $60,000) for the new equipment. Answer (B) is incorrect. The NPV equals the present value of future cash savings minus net initial cash outlays. Answer (D) is incorrect. The cash inflows generated from the sale of old machinery should be added to the difference between the present value of cash inflows and the purchase price of new machinery.

13.7.12. Assume that Garrison is not subject to income taxes. The IRR, to the nearest percent, to replace the old machine is

A. 9%

B. 15%

C. 17%

D. 18%

Answer (D) is correct. *(CMA, adapted)*

REQUIRED: The rounded IRR for replacing the old machine.

DISCUSSION: The IRR is the discount rate at which the present value of the cash flows equals the original investment. Thus, the NPV of the project is zero at the IRR. The IRR also is the maximum borrowing cost for a specific project. The IRR is similar to the yield or effective rate quoted in the business media. The formula for the IRR involving an annuity equates the annual cash flow, times an unknown annuity factor, with the initial net investment ($940,000 = $300,000 × Factor). The solution of the equation gives a factor of 3.133, found in the 18% column on the five-period line.

13.7.13. Assume that Garrison is not subject to income taxes. The payback period to replace the old machine with the new machine is

A. 1.14 years.

B. 2.78 years.

C. 3.13 years.

D. 3.33 years.

Answer (C) is correct. *(CMA, adapted)*

REQUIRED: The payback period for the new machine.

DISCUSSION: The payback method determines the time for the investment dollars to be recovered by the annual net cash inflows. The time is computed by dividing the net investment by the average periodic net cash inflow. The initial net cash outlay divided by the annual cash savings equals 3.13 years ($940,000 ÷ $300,000).

Answer (A) is incorrect. The initial cash outlay divided by the annual cash savings equals 3.13, not 1.14. Answer (B) is incorrect. The initial cash outlay divided by the annual cash savings equals 3.13, not 2.78. Answer (D) is incorrect. The initial cash outlay is $940,000 ($1,000,000 outlay – $60,000 inflow).

13.7.14. Assume that Garrison is not subject to income taxes. The present value of the depreciation tax shield for Year 4 is

A. $182,400

B. $121,600

C. $109,440

D. $114,304

Answer (B) is correct. *(CMA, adapted)*

REQUIRED: The present value of the depreciation tax shield for the second year of the machine's life.

DISCUSSION: The applicable depreciation for Year 4 is $380,000. At a tax rate of 40%, the savings is $152,000 ($380,000 × 40%). Its present value is $121,600 ($152,000 × .80 PV of $1 for two periods at 12%).

Answer (A) is incorrect. The present value of the depreciation tax shield equals the present value of the product of Year 4 depreciation multiplied by the tax rate of 40%. Answer (C) is incorrect. The amount of $109,440 is the present value of the tax saving discounted at 18%, not the required 12%. Answer (D) is incorrect. The present value of the depreciation tax shield is the PV of $1 for two periods at 12% times the savings of $152,000 ($380,000 × 40%).

13.7.15. The present value of the after-tax cash flow associated with the salvage of the old machine is

A. $38,640

B. $36,000

C. $32,040

D. $27,960

Answer (A) is correct. *(CMA, adapted)*

REQUIRED: The present value of the after-tax cash flow associated with the salvage of the old machine.

DISCUSSION: The old machine is sold for $60,000, and the entire selling price is a taxable gain because the carrying amount is zero. At a 40% tax rate, the tax is $24,000. However, the tax is not paid until the end of the year. Discounting the tax payment results in a present value of $21,360 ($24,000 × .89). This amount is subtracted from the $60,000 selling price (not discounted because received immediately) to yield an after-tax NPV of $38,640.

Answer (B) is incorrect. The $24,000 tax payment to be paid at year end should be discounted using the present value factor of .89. Answer (C) is incorrect. The $60,000 payment received for the machinery is received immediately upon sale and therefore should not be discounted. Answer (D) is incorrect. Only the discounted amount of income tax should be subtracted from the $60,000 received for the machinery.

13.7.16. The present value of the annual after-tax cash savings that arise from the increased efficiency of the new machine throughout its life (calculated before consideration of any depreciation tax shield) is

A. $563,400

B. $375,600

C. $433,200

D. $649,800

Answer (D) is correct. *(CMA, adapted)*

REQUIRED: The present value of the annual after-tax cash savings from the new machine ignoring the tax shield.

DISCUSSION: The annual savings of $300,000 must be reduced by the 40% tax, so the net effect is an annual cash savings of $180,000 [(1 – .4) × $300,000]. The present value of the after-tax savings is therefore $649,800 ($180,000 × 3.61 PV of an ordinary annuity for five periods at 12%).

Answer (A) is incorrect. The amount of $563,400 is the present value of the annual after-tax cash savings discounted at 18%, not the firm's required 12%. Answer (B) is incorrect. The annual savings must be reduced by the 40% tax. It is achieved by multiplying annual savings by 1 – .4, not 1 – .6. Answer (C) is incorrect. The present value is the annual after-tax savings discounted at the PV of an ordinary annuity for five periods at 12%.

13.7.17. Refer to the information on the preceding page(s). If the new machine is expected to be sold for $80,000 on December 31, Year 3, the present value of the additional after-tax cash flow is

A. $18,240

B. $27,360

C. $45,600

D. $48,000

Answer (B) is correct. *(CMA, adapted)*

REQUIRED: The present value of the additional after-tax cash flow resulting from a future sale.

DISCUSSION: At the time of sale, the asset is fully depreciated, and any sale proceeds are fully taxable as a gain. Thus, the $80,000 taxable gain results in $32,000 of tax ($80,000 × .40), and the after-tax cash flow is $48,000. The present value is $27,360 ($48,000 × .57 PV of $1 for five periods at 12%).

Answer (A) is incorrect. The after-tax cash flow of $48,000, not the $32,000 of tax, should be discounted at the PV factor of $1 for five periods at 12%. Answer (C) is incorrect. The $32,000 of tax should be subtracted from the sale amount before discounting the after-tax cash flow. Answer (D) is incorrect. This amount is the after-tax cash inflow, which needs to be discounted to its PV.

Questions 13.7.18 through 13.7.20 are based on the following information. A company that annually reviews its investment opportunities and selects appropriate capital expenditures for the coming year is presented with two projects, called Project A and Project B. Best estimates indicate that the investment outlay for Project A is $30,000 and for Project B is $1 million. The projects are considered to be equally risky. Project A is expected to generate cash inflows of $40,000 at the end of each year for 2 years. Project B is expected to generate cash inflows of $700,000 at the end of the first year and $500,000 at the end of the second year. The company has a desired rate of return of 8%.

13.7.18. What is the net present value (NPV) of each project when the desired rate of return is zero?

	Project A	Project B
A.	$30,000	$1,000,000
B.	$50,000	$200,000
C.	$80,000	$1,200,000
D.	$110,000	$2,200,000

Answer (B) is correct. *(CIA, adapted)*

REQUIRED: The NPV of each project.

DISCUSSION: The NPV is the excess of the present value of estimated cash inflows over the net cost of the investment. At a zero desired rate of return, the NPV is the sum of a project's undiscounted cash flows. Thus, the NPV of Project A is $50,000 ($40,000 + $40,000 – $30,000), and the NPV of Project B is $200,000 ($700,000 + $500,000 – $1,000,000).

Answer (A) is incorrect. The amounts of $30,000 and $1,000,000 are the initial investment outlays for A and B, respectively. Answer (C) is incorrect. The amounts of $80,000 and $1,200,000 are the cash inflows for A and B, respectively. Answer (D) is incorrect. The amounts of $110,000 for Project A and $2,200,000 for Project B are calculated by adding the initial outlays to the sum of the cash inflows.

13.7.19. The internal rate of return of Project A, to the nearest full percentage point, is

A. 10%

B. 15%

C. 25%

D. 100%

Answer (D) is correct. *(CIA, adapted)*

REQUIRED: The IRR for Project A.

DISCUSSION: The IRR is the discount rate at which the NPV is zero. The IRR may be determined as follows if IRR is the internal rate of return, t is the time period, and n is the number of time periods:

$$\text{NPV} = \sum_{t=1}^{n} \frac{\text{Annual net cash inflow}}{(1 + \text{IRR})^t} - \text{Net investment}$$

Substituting in the expression above yields an IRR of 100%.

$$0 = \frac{\$40{,}000}{(1 + \text{IRR})} + \frac{\$40{,}000}{(1 + \text{IRR})^2} - \$30{,}000$$

IRR = 100%

Answer (A) is incorrect. Applying a discount rate of 10% results in a NPV of $69,421. Answer (B) is incorrect. Applying a discount rate of 15% results in a NPV of $65,028. Answer (C) is incorrect. Applying a discount rate of 25% results in a NPV of $57,600.

13.7.20. Net present value (NPV) and internal rate of return (IRR) differ in that

A. NPV assumes reinvestment of project cash flows at the desired rate of return, whereas IRR assumes reinvestment of project cash flows at the internal rate of return.

B. NPV and IRR make different accept or reject decisions for independent projects.

C. IRR can be used to rank mutually exclusive investment projects, but NPV cannot.

D. NPV is expressed as a percentage, while IRR is expressed as a dollar amount.

Answer (A) is correct. *(CIA, adapted)*

REQUIRED: The difference between NPV and IRR.

DISCUSSION: The NPV method is based on the assumption that cash inflows from the investment project can be reinvested at the desired rate of return. The IRR method is based on the assumption that cash flows from each project can be reinvested at the IRR for that particular project. This assumption is a weakness of the method. The desired rate of return is the appropriate reinvestment rate because it is the opportunity cost for a project at a given level of risk. The problem with the IRR method is that it assumes a higher discount rate even though a project may not have a greater level of risk.

Answer (B) is incorrect. NPV and IRR make consistent accept or reject decisions for independent projects. When NPV is positive, IRR exceeds the desired rate of return and the project is acceptable. Answer (C) is incorrect. The NPV method can be used to rank mutually exclusive projects, but IRR cannot. The reinvestment rate assumption causes IRR to make faulty project rankings under some circumstances. Answer (D) is incorrect. IRR is expressed as a percentage and NPV in dollar terms.

STUDY UNIT FOURTEEN
INVENTORY MANAGEMENT: TRADITIONAL AND MODERN APPROACHES

Traditional inventory management determines how much to have in stock, how much to order (or produce), and when to place the order (or begin production). **Minimizing the total cost** of inventory involves constant reevaluation of the tradeoffs among the four components of the total:

$$\text{Purchase costs} + \text{Carrying costs} + \text{Ordering costs} + \text{Stockout costs}$$

The **reorder point is calculated** as follows:

$$(\text{Average daily demand} \times \text{Lead time in days}) + \text{Safety stock}$$

The total **cost of carrying safety stock** has two components:

$$\text{Expected stockout cost} + \text{Carrying cost}$$

The **economic order quantity (EOQ)** model is a formula for determining the order quantity that minimizes the sum of ordering costs and carrying costs (assuming uniform demand, constant order or setup costs, and no quantity discounts)

$$\sqrt{\frac{2 \times \text{Fixed cost per purchase order} \times \text{Periodic demand}}{\text{Per unit carrying cost}}}$$

If a manufacturer knows exactly when materials are needed, orders can be placed so that they arrive no earlier than when actually needed. This **just-in-time (JIT)** approach relies on a supplier who is willing to be responsible for producing or storing the needed inventory and shipping it to arrive on time. JIT limits output to the demand (pull) of the subsequent operation. Reductions in inventory result in (1) less investment in idle assets; (2) reduction of storage space requirements; and (3) lower inventory taxes, pilferage, and obsolescence risks. The focus of quality control is the prevention of quality problems, so zero machine breakdowns (achieved through preventive maintenance) and zero defects are ultimate goals. Higher quality and lower inventory are complementary. JIT is based on a philosophy that combines purchasing, production, and inventory control. Minimization of inventory is a goal because many inventory-related activities are nonvalue-added. Indeed, carrying inventory is a symptom of correctable problems, such as poor quality, long cycle times, and lack of coordination with suppliers. JIT also includes changes in the production process itself.

Backflush costing often is used in a JIT system. It may delay entries to inventory until as late as the end of the period. Conventional systems track materials, work-in-process, and finished goods in sequence. The system provides comprehensive inventory control information and enables the calculation of variances. Backflush costing eliminates the sequential tracking of costs and calculation of variances. Transfer of goods, manufacture of goods, and use of materials are recorded only at the end of the period based on standard costs.

The **theory of constraints (TOC)** improves a process not by maximizing efficiency in every part of the process but by short-term focus on the constraints. Increasing the efficiency of processes that are not constraints merely creates backup. A TOC analysis (1) identifies the constraint (bottleneck), (2) determines the most profitable product mix given the constraint, (3) maximizes product flow through the constraint, (4) increases capacity at the constraint, and (5) redesigns the process to reduce total cycle time (receipt of order to shipment). A basic principle is that short-term profit maximization requires maximizing the throughput (contribution) margin through the constraint. **Throughput costing** (supervariable costing) recognizes only direct materials-related costs (purchase and handling) as variable and relevant to the throughput margin. All other manufacturing costs are ignored because they are fixed in the short term.

QUESTIONS

14.1 Inventory Fundamentals

14.1.1. Economic order quantity models and two-bin systems are commonly used controls for a company's materials function. Those controls primarily relate to what part of the cycle?

A. Materials requirements.

B. Raw materials acceptance.

C. Physical storage.

D. Product distribution.

Answer (A) is correct. *(CIA, adapted)*

REQUIRED: The part of the inventory cycle to which EOQ and two-bin systems are related.

DISCUSSION: Each method helps determine need by controlling, monitoring, or analyzing the quantity of materials to purchase. The EOQ model determines the order quantity that minimizes the sum of ordering and carrying costs. Once the reorder point is established, a two-bin system may be used to signal the time to reorder when perpetual records are not kept. An inventory item is divided into two groups. When the first group is depleted, the order is placed, and the second group protects against stockout until replenishment.

Answer (B) is incorrect. Materials acceptance is not part of the control cycle to which EOQ models and two-bin systems are related. Answer (C) is incorrect. Physical storage is not part of the control cycle to which EOQ models and two-bin systems are related. Answer (D) is incorrect. Product distribution is not part of the control cycle to which EOQ models and two-bin systems are related.

14.1.2. Which inventory costing system results in the best inventory turnover ratio in a period of rising prices?

A. LIFO.

B. FIFO.

C. Weighted average.

D. Perpetual.

Answer (A) is correct. *(Publisher, adapted)*

REQUIRED: The inventory costing system with the best inventory turnover ratio in a period of rising prices.

DISCUSSION: The inventory turnover ratio equals cost of sales divided by average inventory. A high inventory turnover ratio is preferable because it indicates better usage of inventory. The ratio can be increased by increasing cost of sales or decreasing average inventory. In a period of rising prices, LIFO provides a lower inventory valuation because cost of sales includes the higher costs of more recently purchased goods, and inventory consists of the previously purchased, lower cost goods.

Answer (B) is incorrect. FIFO costing results in higher inventory measures when prices are rising. Answer (C) is incorrect. Weighted-average costing results in higher inventory measures when prices are rising. Answer (D) is incorrect. Perpetual is an approach toward inventory record keeping, not an inventory costing system.

14.1.3. Order-filling costs, as opposed to order-getting costs, include all but which of the following items?

A. Credit check of new customers.

B. Packing and shipping of sales orders.

C. Collection of payments for sales orders.

D. Mailing catalogs to current customers.

Answer (D) is correct. *(CMA, adapted)*

REQUIRED: The variable not affecting order-filling costs.

DISCUSSION: Order-filling costs include the costs necessary to prepare and ship the order, including the resulting payment process. Thus, (1) clerical processing, (2) credit checking, (3) packing, (4) shipping, and (5) collecting payments are phases of the order-filling cycle. Mailing catalogs to current customers is an order-getting cost.

Answer (A) is incorrect. Credit checking of new customers, a clerical processing task, is an order-filling cost. Answer (B) is incorrect. The costs incurred to pack and ship orders are order-filling costs. Answer (C) is incorrect. The costs incurred in billing and in collecting payments for orders are order-filling costs.

14.1.4. In forecasting purchases of inventory for a firm, all of the following are useful except

A. Knowledge of the behavior of business cycles.

B. Internal allocations of costs to different segments of the firm.

C. Information on the seasonal variations in demand.

D. Econometric modeling.

Answer (B) is correct. *(CIA, adapted)*

REQUIRED: The item not useful in forecasting purchases.

DISCUSSION: Internal allocations of costs relate to costs already incurred, that is, to sunk costs. Sunk costs are not relevant to decision making, for example, to forecasting future purchases.

Answer (A) is incorrect. In time series analysis, the cyclical fluctuation in business activity is usually incorporated as an index number in the forecasting model. Answer (C) is incorrect. In time series analysis, the seasonal variation is usually incorporated as an index number in the forecasting model. Answer (D) is incorrect. An econometric model is an application of statistical methods to economic problems. Such a model is used as a forecasting tool.

14.1.5. A two-bin inventory order system is a

A. Constant order-cycle system.

B. Red-line system.

C. Constant order-quantity system.

D. Computerized control system.

Answer (C) is correct. *(Publisher, adapted)*

REQUIRED: The nature of a two-bin inventory order system.

DISCUSSION: A two-bin order system divides inventory into two quantities. Inventory is reordered when the items in the first bin are used up. Essentially, the second bin provides for a safety stock plus the quantity used during the lead time before receiving the reorder. The amount of the inventory in the first bin is a constant quantity. Thus, the two-bin procedure is a constant order-quantity system because the same amount is ordered each time.

Answer (A) is incorrect. The constant order-cycle is a system in which inventory is ordered on a uniform time cycle, and the quantity varies. Answer (B) is incorrect. In a red-line system, a red line is drawn inside an inventory bin to indicate the reorder point. Answer (D) is incorrect. A two-bin system is a manual system.

14.1.6. Which condition justifies accepting a low inventory turnover ratio?

A. High carrying costs.

B. High stockout costs.

C. Short inventory order lead times.

D. Low inventory order costs.

Answer (B) is correct. *(Publisher, adapted)*

REQUIRED: The condition that justifies acceptance of a low inventory turnover ratio.

DISCUSSION: The inventory turnover ratio equals cost of sales divided by average inventory. High stockout costs justify maintaining relatively large inventory levels. For example, if major customers are lost because of stockouts, the higher costs of maintaining a large safety stock are acceptable.

Answer (A) is incorrect. High carrying costs encourage more frequent orders of smaller quantities, which result in lower average inventory levels and a higher inventory turnover ratio. Answer (C) is incorrect. Short lead times encourage more frequent orders of smaller quantities, which result in lower average inventory levels and a higher inventory turnover ratio. Answer (D) is incorrect. Low order costs encourage more frequent orders of smaller quantities, which result in lower average inventory levels and a higher inventory turnover ratio.

14.1.7. Napier Company's budgeted sales and budgeted cost of sales for the coming year are $126 million and $72 million, respectively. Short-term interest rates are expected to average 10%. If Napier can increase inventory turnover from its current level of nine times per year to a level of 12 times per year, its cost savings in the coming year are expected to be

A. $150,000

B. $200,000

C. $350,000

D. $600,000

Answer (B) is correct. *(CMA, adapted)*

REQUIRED: The cost savings from increasing inventory turnover.

DISCUSSION: If budgeted cost of sales for the coming year is $72 million, and inventory turns over nine times during the year, the average investment in inventory is $8 million ($72,000,000 ÷ 9). If the inventory turnover increases to 12 times per year, the average investment in inventory is only $6 million ($72,000,000 ÷ 12), a decrease of $2 million. Given an interest rate of 10%, the savings are $200,000 per year.

Answer (A) is incorrect. The amount of $150,000 is based on gross profit, not cost of sales. Answer (C) is incorrect. The amount of $350,000 is based on sales, not cost of sales. Answer (D) is incorrect. The amount of $600,000 is 10% of $6 million.

Questions 14.1.8 and 14.1.9 are based on the following information. Inventory management requires a firm to balance the quantity of inventory on hand for operations with the investment in inventory. Two cost categories of concern in inventory management are carrying costs and order costs.

14.1.8. The carrying costs associated with inventory management include

A. Insurance costs, shipping costs, storage costs, and obsolescence.

B. Storage costs, handling costs, capital invested, and obsolescence.

C. Purchasing costs, shipping costs, set-up costs, and quantity discounts lost.

D. Obsolescence, set-up costs, capital invested, and purchasing costs.

Answer (B) is correct. *(CMA, adapted)*

REQUIRED: The items included in carrying costs.

DISCUSSION: Carrying costs include storage costs, handling costs, insurance costs, interest on capital invested, and obsolescence.

Answer (A) is incorrect. Shipping costs are ordering costs, not carrying costs. Answer (C) is incorrect. It states various ordering (or manufacturing) costs. Answer (D) is incorrect. The set-up costs for a production run are equivalent to ordering costs. Additionally, purchasing costs are considered costs of ordering.

14.1.9. The order costs associated with inventory management include

A. Insurance costs, purchasing costs, shipping costs, and obsolescence.

B. Obsolescence, setup costs, quantity discounts lost, and storage costs.

C. Quantity discounts lost, storage costs, handling costs, and interest on capital invested.

D. Purchasing costs, shipping costs, setup costs, and quantity discounts lost.

Answer (D) is correct. *(CMA, adapted)*

REQUIRED: The items included in order costs.

DISCUSSION: Order costs include (1) purchasing costs, (2) shipping costs, (3) setup costs for a production run, and (4) quantity discounts lost.

Answer (A) is incorrect. Insurance costs are carrying costs. Answer (B) is incorrect. Obsolescence and storage costs are carrying costs. Answer (C) is incorrect. Storage costs, handling costs, and interest on capital invested are carrying costs.

14.1.10. The control of order-filling costs

A. Can be accomplished through the use of flexible budget standards.

B. Is related to pricing decisions, sales promotion, and customer reaction.

C. Is not crucial because the costs are typically fixed and not subject to frequent changes.

D. Is not crucial because the order-filling routine is entrenched and external influences are minimal.

Answer (A) is correct. *(CMA, adapted)*

REQUIRED: The true statement about the control of order-filling costs.

DISCUSSION: Order-filling costs can be controlled by the same method used in other cost control systems. Thus, flexible budgeting can be used to control order-filling costs.

Answer (B) is incorrect. The control of order-filling costs may be only indirectly related to pricing decisions, sales promotion, and customer reaction. Answer (C) is incorrect. Order-filling costs may change frequently. Answer (D) is incorrect. The order-filling routine should be dynamic and flexible enough to adjust for changes in volume, etc.

14.1.11. Which of the following will not affect the budgeting of order-getting costs?

A. Market research and tests.

B. Location of distribution warehouses.

C. Policies and actions of competitors.

D. Sales promotion policies.

Answer (B) is correct. *(CMA, adapted)*

REQUIRED: The variable not affecting order-getting costs.

DISCUSSION: Order-getting costs are necessary to obtain a particular order. Thus, budgeting and planning should emphasize (1) market research, (2) competitor analysis, (3) promotion policies, (4) general economic conditions, and (5) all related policies and decisions affecting the organization up to the time of the order. The location of distribution warehouses is an order-filling cost consideration.

Answer (A) is incorrect. Market research and tests are necessary to get orders. Answer (C) is incorrect. Being familiar with the policies and actions of competitors is necessary to get orders. Answer (D) is incorrect. Sales promotion policies are necessary to get orders.

14.2 Economic Order Quantity (EOQ)

14.2.1. The purpose of the economic order quantity model is to

A. Minimize the safety stock.

B. Minimize the sum of the order costs and the holding costs.

C. Minimize the inventory quantities.

D. Minimize the sum of the demand costs and the backlog costs.

Answer (B) is correct. *(CIA, adapted)*

REQUIRED: The purpose of the EOQ model.

DISCUSSION: The EOQ model is deterministic. It calculates the ideal order (or production lot) quantity given (1) specified periodic demand, (2) the cost per order or production run, and (3) the periodic cost of carrying one unit in stock. The model minimizes the sum of inventory carrying costs and either ordering or production setup costs.

Answer (A) is incorrect. The basic EOQ model does not include safety stock. Answer (C) is incorrect. In the EOQ model, costs, not quantities, are minimized. Answer (D) is incorrect. Quantity demanded is a variable in the model, but order costs, not demand costs, are relevant. Backlogs are customer orders that cannot be filled immediately because of stockouts. Backlog costs are not quantified in the model.

14.2.2. Which of the following is used in determining the economic order quantity (EOQ)?

A. Regression analysis.

B. Calculus.

C. Markov process.

D. Queuing theory.

Answer (B) is correct. *(CIA, adapted)*

REQUIRED: The method for determining the EOQ.

DISCUSSION: The primary business application of differential calculus is to identify the maxima or minima of curvilinear functions. In business and economics, these are the points of revenue or profit maximization (maxima) or cost minimization (minima). The EOQ results from differentiating the total cost with regard to order quantity.

Answer (A) is incorrect. Regression analysis is used to fit a linear trend line to a dependent variable based on one or more independent variables. Answer (C) is incorrect. Markov process models are used to study the evolution of certain systems over repeated trials. Answer (D) is incorrect. Queuing theory is a waiting-line method used to balance desirable service levels and the cost of providing more service.

14.2.3. The economic order quantity (EOQ) formula can be adapted in order for a firm to determine the optimal mix between cash and marketable securities. The EOQ model assumes all of the following except that

A. The cost of a transaction is independent of the dollar amount of the transaction and interest rates are constant over the short run.

B. An opportunity cost is associated with holding cash, beginning with the first dollar.

C. The total demand for cash is known with certainty.

D. Cash flow requirements are random.

Answer (D) is correct. *(CMA, adapted)*

REQUIRED: The assumption not made in the EOQ model.

DISCUSSION: The EOQ formula is a deterministic model that requires a known demand for inventory or, in this case, the amount of cash needed. Thus, the cash flow requirements cannot be random. The model also assumes a given carrying (interest) cost and a flat transaction cost for converting marketable securities to cash, regardless of the amount withdrawn.

Answer (A) is incorrect. The EOQ model assumes that (1) the cost of a transaction is independent of the dollar amount of the transaction, and (2) interest rates are constant over the short run. Answer (B) is incorrect. The EOQ model assumes an opportunity cost is associated with holding cash, beginning with the first dollar. Answer (C) is incorrect. The EOQ model assumes that the total demand for cash is certain.

14.2.4. Ardmore Industries is in the process of reviewing its inventory and production policies. The company often has an excess supply of some products and shortages of other products needed for planned production runs. The method that Ardmore should use to establish its inventory policies regarding these products is

A. Linear programming.

B. Regression analysis.

C. Economic production quantity analysis.

D. Contribution margin analysis.

Answer (C) is correct. *(CMA, adapted)*

REQUIRED: The quantitative method that should be used for planning inventory policy.

DISCUSSION: The economic order quantity (EOQ) model can be used to establish inventory policy. In the case of a manufacturer, the EOQ model is called economic production quantity analysis. The objective of the model is to minimize the total of inventory holding costs and the costs of production runs (e.g., setup costs).

Answer (A) is incorrect. Linear programming is used to maximize profits or minimize costs given resource constraints. Answer (B) is incorrect. Regression analysis explains the behavior of a dependent variable (such as cost) in terms of one or more independent variables. Answer (D) is incorrect. A product's contribution margin is the difference between sales and variable costs.

14.2.5. The simple economic production lot size model will only apply to situations in which the production

A. Rate equals the demand rate.

B. Rate is less than the demand rate.

C. Rate is greater than the demand rate.

D. For the period covered equals the projected sales for the period.

Answer (C) is correct. *(CMA, adapted)*

REQUIRED: The situation in which the simple economic lot size model applies.

DISCUSSION: This model is the same as the basic EOQ model, with the production quantity (lot) substituted for the EOQ and the cost of a production run for the order cost. In the basic model, the production rate (or time to fill an order) is deemed to be instantaneous, but demand is assumed to occur at a constant rate over some period of time.

Answer (A) is incorrect. Production (or resupply) is assumed to be instantaneous. Answer (B) is incorrect. Production (or resupply) is assumed to be instantaneous. Answer (D) is incorrect. The purpose of the basic model is to adjust production to match demand. This answer choice implies that production is given.

14.2.6. A decrease in inventory order costs will

A. Decrease the economic order quantity.

B. Increase the reorder point.

C. Have no effect on the economic order quantity.

D. Decrease the carrying cost percentage.

Answer (A) is correct. *(CMA, adapted)*

REQUIRED: The effect of a decrease in inventory ordering costs.

DISCUSSION: The basic EOQ equals the square root of a fraction consisting of a numerator equal to the product of twice the unit periodic demand and the variable cost per order and a denominator equal to the periodic carrying cost. Thus, a decrease in inventory order costs (numerator) decreases the EOQ.

Answer (B) is incorrect. The reorder point is based on lead time, not the EOQ model. Answer (C) is incorrect. The EOQ should decline. Answer (D) is incorrect. The carrying cost percentage always is identical to the ordering cost percentage in accordance with the fundamental calculus underlying the EOQ model.

14.2.7. An increase in inventory carrying costs will

A. Decrease the economic order quantity.

B. Increase the safety stock required.

C. Have no effect on the economic order quantity.

D. Decrease the number of orders issued per year.

Answer (A) is correct. *(CMA, adapted)*

REQUIRED: The effect of an increase in inventory carrying costs.

DISCUSSION: The basic EOQ equals the square root of a fraction consisting of a numerator equal to the product of twice the unit periodic demand and the variable cost per order and a denominator equal to the periodic carrying cost. Thus, an increase in carrying costs (denominator) decreases the EOQ.

Answer (B) is incorrect. The safety stock is not a factor in the EOQ calculation. Management reduces safety stocks when inventory carrying costs increase. Answer (C) is incorrect. The EOQ declines. Answer (D) is incorrect. Orders increase. The average order size and average inventory held are smaller.

14.2.8. When the economic order quantity (EOQ) decision model is employed, the <List A> are being offset or balanced by the <List B>.

	List A	List B
A.	Ordering costs	Carrying costs
B.	Purchase costs	Carrying costs
C.	Purchase costs	Quality costs
D.	Ordering costs	Stockout costs

Answer (A) is correct. *(CIA, adapted)*

REQUIRED: The true statement about cost relationships in the EOQ.

DISCUSSION: The objective of the EOQ model is to find an optimal order quantity that balances carrying and ordering costs. Only variable costs should be considered. The EOQ is the point where the ordering cost and carrying cost curves intersect. It corresponds to the minimum point on the total inventory cost curve.

Answer (B) is incorrect. Purchase costs are not directly incorporated into the EOQ model. Answer (C) is incorrect. Neither purchase costs nor quality costs are incorporated into the EOQ model. Answer (D) is incorrect. Stockout costs are not directly incorporated into the EOQ model.

14.2.9. One of the elements included in the economic order quantity (EOQ) formula is

A. Safety stock.

B. Yearly demand.

C. Selling price of item.

D. Lead time for delivery.

Answer (B) is correct. *(CIA, adapted)*

REQUIRED: The element to include in the EOQ calculation.

DISCUSSION: The basic EOQ formula is used to minimize the total of inventory carrying and ordering costs. The basic EOQ equals the square root of a fraction consisting of a numerator equal to the product of twice the unit periodic demand and the variable cost per order and a denominator equal to the unit periodic carrying cost.

Answer (A) is incorrect. The safety stock is not included in the basic EOQ formula. Answer (C) is incorrect. The selling price of the item is not included in the basic EOQ formula. Answer (D) is incorrect. The lead time for delivery is not included in the basic EOQ formula.

14.2.10. Which one of the following items is not directly reflected in the basic economic order quantity (EOQ) model?

A. Interest on invested capital.

B. Public warehouse rental charges.

C. Setup costs of manufacturing runs.

D. Quantity discounts lost on inventory purchases.

Answer (D) is correct. *(CMA, adapted)*

REQUIRED: The item not reflected in the basic EOQ model.

DISCUSSION: The basic EOQ model minimizes the sum of order (or setup) and carrying costs. Included in the formula are (1) annual demand, (2) ordering (or setup) costs, and (3) carrying costs. Carrying costs include (1) warehousing costs, (2) property taxes, (3) insurance, (4) spoilage, (5) obsolescence, and (6) interest on invested capital. The cost of the inventory (including quantity discounts lost) is not a component of the EOQ model.

Answer (A) is incorrect. Interest on invested capital is considered in the basic EOQ model. Answer (B) is incorrect. Public warehouse rental charges are considered in the basic EOQ model. Answer (C) is incorrect. Setup costs of manufacturing runs are considered in the basic EOQ model.

14.2.11. The economic order quantity formula assumes that

A. Purchase costs per unit differ due to quantity discounts.

B. Costs of placing an order vary with quantity ordered.

C. Periodic demand for the good is known.

D. Erratic usage rates are cushioned by safety stocks.

Answer (C) is correct. *(CPA, adapted)*

REQUIRED: The assumption underlying the EOQ formula.

DISCUSSION: The EOQ formula is

$$EOQ = \sqrt{\frac{2OD}{c}}$$

If: O = ordering cost per purchase order
D = periodic demand in units
c = periodic carrying costs per unit

A change in unit demand will cause a change in the economic order quantity. All other values are given and assumed to be constant. The simplest form of the EOQ model is based on the assumption that demand is known and that usage is uniform throughout the period.

Answer (A) is incorrect. Unit purchasing costs are constant. Answer (B) is incorrect. The costs of placing an order are deemed to be constant. Answer (D) is incorrect. The usage rate is assumed to be uniform, full replenishment of the inventory is deemed to occur instantly when the last inventory item is used (no stockouts occur), and no safety stock is necessary.

14.2.12. The calculation of an economic order quantity (EOQ) considers

A. The purchasing manager's salary.

B. A corporate charge for advertising expenses.

C. The shipping costs to deliver the product to the customer.

D. Capital costs.

Answer (D) is correct. *(CMA, adapted)*

REQUIRED: The true statement about the calculation of the EOQ.

DISCUSSION: The determination of the EOQ balances the variable costs of ordering and carrying inventory. Factors in the equation include (1) the cost of placing an order, (2) unit carrying cost, and (3) annual demand in units. Carrying costs include (1) storage costs, (2) handling costs, (3) insurance, (4) property taxes, (5) obsolescence, and (6) the opportunity cost of investing capital in inventory. Thus, the return on capital that is forgone when it is invested in inventory should be considered.

Answer (A) is incorrect. The purchasing manager's salary is a fixed cost. The EOQ model includes variable costs only. Answer (B) is incorrect. Advertising is not an ordering or carrying cost. Answer (C) is incorrect. The cost of shipping to customers is a selling expense.

14.2.13. The following graph shows four cost curves:

- An annual inventory carrying cost curve
- An annual order cost curve
- An annual inventory total cost curve
- A fixed cost curve with respect to order quantity

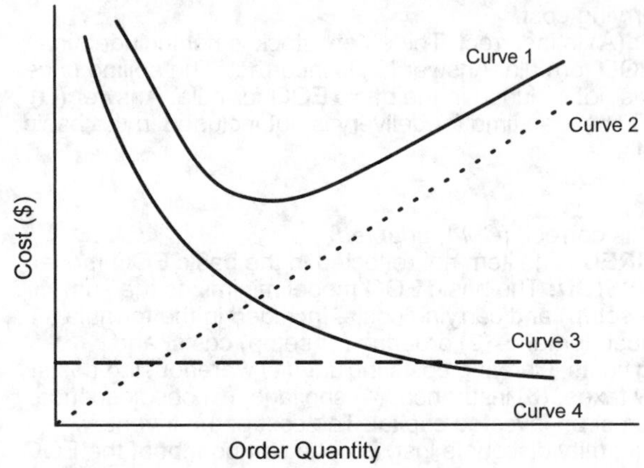

Which of the curves is the annual inventory carrying cost curve?

A. Curve 1.

B. Curve 2.

C. Curve 3.

D. Curve 4.

Answer (B) is correct. *(CIA, adapted)*

REQUIRED: The annual inventory carrying cost curve.

DISCUSSION: Annual inventory carrying costs (Curve 2) are a linear function of the amount of inventory carried. As the quantity ordered increases, so does the annual total carrying cost and the amount of average inventory.

Answer (A) is incorrect. Curve 1 has a minimum point. Thus, it must be the annual total cost curve for carrying inventory. Answer (C) is incorrect. Fixed costs (Curve 3) do not change with the amount of inventory held. Answer (D) is incorrect. Annual order costs (Curve 4) are inversely related to the order quantity and continually decline.

14.2.14. The economic order quantity is the size of the order that minimizes total inventory costs, including ordering and carrying costs. If the annual demand decreases by 36%, the optimal order size will

A. Decrease by 20%.

B. Increase by 20%.

C. Increase by 6%.

D. Decrease by 6%.

Answer (A) is correct. *(CIA, adapted)*

REQUIRED: The effect on the optimal order size if annual demand decreases.

DISCUSSION: If demand decreases by 36%, that is, from 100% to 64%, the EOQ decreases to 80% of its former value. Thus, it decreases by 20%.

$$Q_1 = \sqrt{\frac{2 \times a \times 0.64D}{k}} = \sqrt{0.64\left(\frac{2aD}{k}\right)} = 0.8Q$$

Answer (B) is incorrect. The new EOQ decreases to 80% of its former value. Answer (C) is incorrect. The EOQ decreases. Answer (D) is incorrect. The new EOQ decreases to 80% of its former value.

14.2.15. Which of the following is not considered a cost of carrying inventory?

A. Shipping and handling.

B. Property tax.

C. Insurance.

D. Depreciation and obsolescence.

Answer (A) is correct. *(CIA, adapted)*

REQUIRED: The item not considered a cost of carrying inventory.

DISCUSSION: Inventory shipping and handling costs are classified as ordering costs, not carrying costs.

Answer (B) is incorrect. Property tax is an inventory carrying cost. Answer (C) is incorrect. Insurance is an inventory carrying cost. Answer (D) is incorrect. Depreciation and obsolescence is an inventory carrying cost.

14.2.16. Given the EOQ model below, the optimal order quantity is

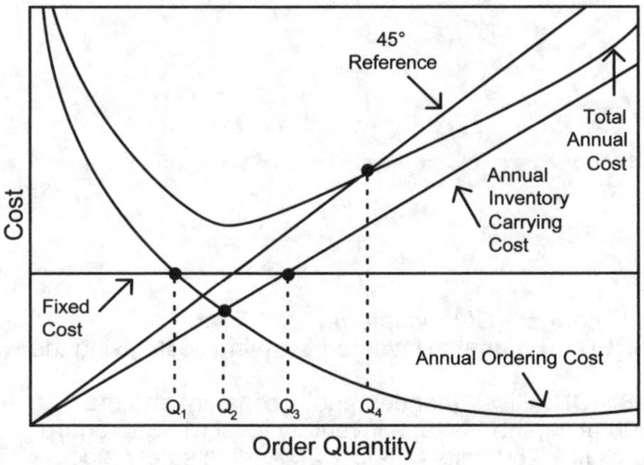

A. Q_1

B. Q_2

C. Q_3

D. Q_4

Answer (B) is correct. *(CIA, adapted)*

REQUIRED: The optimal order quantity given the EOQ model.

DISCUSSION: The objective of the EOQ model is to find an optimal order quantity that balances carrying and order costs. Only variable costs should be considered. The EOQ is the intersection of the order cost and carrying cost curves. It corresponds to the minimum point on the total inventory cost curve.

Answer (A) is incorrect. Fixed costs have no effect on EOQ. Answer (C) is incorrect. Fixed costs have no effect on EOQ. Answer (D) is incorrect. The intersection of the total annual cost line and the 45° reference line is meaningless.

14.2.17. The economic order quantity, Q, is the size of the order that minimizes total inventory costs. These costs, which are composed of ordering and holding costs, can be computed using the following expression:

$$TC = \frac{Qs}{2} + \left[\frac{D}{Q}\right]p + F$$

If: TC = total inventory costs
Q = size of each order
D = annual demand in units
F = fixed costs of ordering
p = variable cost of placing one order
s = holding cost per year for one unit of inventory

The following inventory information is available for an organization:

Annual demand (D)	20,000 units
Variable cost of placing one order (p)	$100
Holding cost per unit (s)	$ 1
Economic order quantity (Q)	2,000 units
Fixed cost of ordering (F)	$ 0

If the organization decides to order 4,000 units at a time rather than 2,000 units, by how much will its total inventory costs change?

A. $500 increase.

B. $1,000 increase.

C. $1,000 decrease.

D. $900 increase.

Answer (A) is correct. *(CIA, adapted)*

REQUIRED: The change in total inventory costs.

DISCUSSION: When the order size is 2,000 units, the variable inventory costs are $2,000 {[(2,000 units × $1) ÷ 2] + [(20,000 units ÷ 2,000 units) × $100]}. When the order size is 4,000 units, the variable inventory costs are $2,500 {[(4,000 units × $1) ÷ 2] + [(20,000 units ÷ 4,000 units) × $100]}. The increase in inventory costs is $500 ($2,500 – $2,000).

Answer (B) is incorrect. A $1,000 increase omits the change in the number of orders. Answer (C) is incorrect. Increasing the order size increases total costs. The EOQ is 2,000 units. Answer (D) is incorrect. A $900 increase results from an order size of 5,000 units.

Questions 14.2.18 and 14.2.19 are based on the following information. Based on an EOQ analysis (assuming a constant demand), the optimal order quantity is 2,500. The company desires a safety stock of 500 units. A 5-day lead time is needed for delivery. Annual inventory carrying costs equal 25% of the average inventory level. The company pays $4 per unit to buy the product, which it sells for $8. The company pays $150 to place a detailed order, and the monthly demand for the product is 4,000 units.

14.2.18. Annual inventory carrying costs equal

A. $750

B. $1,250

C. $1,750

D. $2,250

Answer (C) is correct. *(CIA, adapted)*

REQUIRED: The annual inventory carrying costs using the EOQ model.

DISCUSSION: Given that demand is constant and the EOQ is 2,500 units, the average inventory level without regard to safety stock is 1,250 units (2,500 ÷ 2). Adding safety stock results in an average level of 1,750 units (1,250 + 500). Given also that (1) annual carrying costs are 25% of average inventory and (2) unit cost is $4, total annual carrying cost is $1,750 [(1,750 units × $4) × 25%].

Answer (A) is incorrect. The amount of $750 results from subtracting instead of adding the cost of carrying safety stock. Answer (B) is incorrect. The amount of $1,250 ignores safety stock. Answer (D) is incorrect. The amount of $2,250 results from double counting the cost of carrying safety stock.

14.2.19. Total inventory order costs per year equal

A. $1,250

B. $2,400

C. $2,880

D. $3,600

Answer (C) is correct. *(CIA, adapted)*

REQUIRED: The total inventory order costs using the EOQ technique.

DISCUSSION: Total annual demand is 48,000 units (4,000 per month × 12). Thus, total annual order costs equal $2,880 [(48,000 units ÷ 2,500 EOQ) × $150 cost per order].

Answer (A) is incorrect. The amount of $1,250 equals the annual carrying cost of the average inventory, excluding safety stock. Answer (B) is incorrect. The amount of $2,400 assumes an EOQ of 3,000 units. Answer (D) is incorrect. The amount of $3,600 assumes an EOQ of 2,000 units.

Questions 14.2.20 and 14.2.21 are based on the following information. Ryerson Computer Furniture, Inc. (RCF) manufactures a line of office computer chairs. The annual demand for the chairs is estimated to be 5,000 units. The annual cost to hold one unit in inventory is $10 per year, and the cost to initiate a production run is $1,000. There are no computer chairs on hand, and RCF has scheduled four equal production runs of computer chairs for the coming year, the first of which is to be run immediately. RCF has 250 business days per year, sales occur uniformly throughout the year, and production start-up is within one day. RCF is considering using the following formula for determining the economic order quantity (EOQ):

$$EOQ = \sqrt{\frac{2aD}{k}}$$

If: *a = cost to initiate a production run per purchase order*
D = annual unit demand
k = cost of carrying one unit per year

14.2.20. The number of production runs per year of computer chairs that would minimize the sum of carrying and setup costs for the coming year is

A. 1

B. 2

C. 4

D. 5

Answer (D) is correct. *(CMA, adapted)*

REQUIRED: The number of production runs that minimizes the sum of setup and carrying costs.

DISCUSSION: The EOQ minimizes the sum of carrying and setup costs. The EOQ is the amount at which carrying costs are equal to setup costs. Thus, entering the data into the EOQ formula results in the following:

$$EOQ = \sqrt{\frac{2 \times \$1{,}000 \times 5{,}000}{\$10}} = 1{,}000 \text{ units}$$

If each lot consists of 1,000 units, five production runs per year are needed to meet the 5,000-unit demand. At this level, setup costs are $5,000 (5 × $1,000). Carrying costs also equal $5,000 ($10 per unit carrying cost × average inventory of 500 units). Accordingly, total costs are minimized at $10,000.

Answer (A) is incorrect. A single production run indicates an EOQ of 5,000 units. The carrying costs of $25,000 [$10 × ($5,000 ÷ 2)] exceed the $1,000 of setup costs. Answer (B) is incorrect. Two production runs correspond to an EOQ of 2,500 units and an average inventory of 1,250 units. The resulting $12,500 of carrying costs exceed the $2,000 of setup costs. Answer (C) is incorrect. Four production runs correspond to an EOQ of 1,250 units and an average inventory of 625 units. The resulting $6,250 of carrying costs exceed the $4,000 of setup costs.

14.2.21. If RCF does not maintain a safety stock, the estimated total carrying costs for the computer chairs for the coming year based on their current schedule is

A. $4,000

B. $5,000

C. $6,250

D. $12,500

Answer (C) is correct. *(CMA, adapted)*

REQUIRED: The estimated total annual carrying costs assuming no safety stock is held.

DISCUSSION: Given four production runs and an annual demand of 5,000 units, each production run must generate 1,250 units. Inventory totals 1,250 units at the completion of each run but declines to zero just prior to the next run. Thus, the average inventory is 625 units (1,250 ÷ 2), and the total carrying cost is $6,250 (625 units × $10).

Answer (A) is incorrect. The cost of maintaining an average inventory of 625 units is $6,250. Answer (B) is incorrect. The amount of $5,000 is based upon an EOQ of 1,000 units and an average inventory of 500 units. Answer (D) is incorrect. The amount of $12,500 is based on the maximum inventory level.

14.3 Other Inventory Control Methods

14.3.1. Companies that adopt just-in-time purchasing systems often experience

A. A reduction in the number of suppliers.

B. Fewer deliveries from suppliers.

C. A greater need for inspection of goods as the goods arrive.

D. Less need for linkage with a vendor's computerized order entry system.

Answer (A) is correct. *(CMA, adapted)*

REQUIRED: The true statement about companies that adopt just-in-time (JIT) purchasing systems.

DISCUSSION: The objective of JIT is to reduce carrying costs by eliminating inventories and increasing the deliveries made by suppliers. Ideally, shipments of raw materials are received just in time to be incorporated into the manufacturing process. The focus of quality control under JIT is the prevention of quality problems. Quality control is shifted to the supplier. JIT companies typically do not inspect incoming goods; the assumption is that receipts are of perfect quality. Suppliers are limited to those who guarantee perfect quality and prompt delivery.

Answer (B) is incorrect. More deliveries are needed. Each shipment is smaller. Answer (C) is incorrect. In a JIT system, materials are delivered directly to the production line ready for insertion in the finished product. Answer (D) is incorrect. The need for communication with the vendor is greater. Orders and deliveries must be made on short notice, sometimes several times a day.

14.3.2. Which of the following is a characteristic of just-in-time (JIT) inventory management systems?

A. JIT users determine the optimal level of safety stocks.

B. JIT is applicable only to large companies.

C. JIT does not really increase overall economic efficiency because it merely shifts inventory levels further up the supply chain.

D. JIT relies heavily on good quality materials.

Answer (D) is correct. *(CIA, adapted)*

REQUIRED: The characteristic of JIT inventory management systems.

DISCUSSION: Poor quality materials cause major problems in a JIT system. No safety stock is on hand to replace defective materials. Substandard materials cause major production disruptions and defeat the purpose of lowering cost and lead time while increasing product quality.

Answer (A) is incorrect. Safety stocks are not held in JIT systems, the goal of which is to minimize inventory by ensuring that materials arrive just in time for production. Safety stocks raise inventory levels and increase the risk of defective materials through obsolescence and potential damage during storage. Answer (B) is incorrect. Many smaller entities are adopting JIT with favorable results. They may implement JIT more readily because they can more easily redefine job functions and retrain workers. Answer (C) is incorrect. The close coordination required between suppliers and customers usually leads to overall inventory reductions throughout the production-distribution chain.

14.3.3. Bell Co. changed from a traditional manufacturing philosophy to a just-in-time philosophy. What are the expected effects of this change on Bell's inventory turnover and inventory as a percentage of total assets reported on Bell's balance sheet?

	Inventory Turnover	Inventory Percentage
A.	Decrease	Decrease
B.	Decrease	Increase
C.	Increase	Decrease
D.	Increase	Increase

Answer (C) is correct. *(CPA, adapted)*

REQUIRED: The expected effects of changing to JIT.

DISCUSSION: A JIT system is intended to minimize inventory. Inventory should be delivered or produced just in time to be used. Thus, JIT increases inventory turnover (cost of sales ÷ average inventory) and decreases inventory as a percentage of total assets.

Answer (A) is incorrect. Changing to JIT will result in increased inventory turnover. Answer (B) is incorrect. Changing to JIT will increase inventory turnover and decrease inventory as a percentage of total assets. Answer (D) is incorrect. One of JIT's advantages is less stored raw materials inventory, resulting in decreased inventory as a percentage of total assets.

14.3.4. A manufacturing company is attempting to implement a just-in-time (JIT) purchase policy system by negotiating with its primary suppliers to accept long-term purchase orders which result in more frequent deliveries of smaller quantities of raw materials. If the JIT purchase policy is successful in reducing the total inventory costs of the manufacturing company, which of the following combinations of cost changes would be most likely to occur?

	Cost Category to Increase	Cost Category to Decrease
A.	Purchasing costs	Stockout costs
B.	Purchasing costs	Quality costs
C.	Quality costs	Ordering costs
D.	Stockout costs	Carrying costs

Answer (D) is correct. *(CIA, adapted)*

REQUIRED: The combination of cost changes.

DISCUSSION: The objective of a JIT system is to reduce carrying costs by eliminating inventories and increasing the deliveries made by suppliers. Shipments should be received just in time to be used in the manufacturing process. This system increases the risk of stockout costs because the inventory buffer is reduced or eliminated.

Answer (A) is incorrect. The supplier may seek a concession on the selling price that increases purchasing costs, but the manufacturer's stockout costs increase. Answer (B) is incorrect. The cost of quality is not necessarily affected by a JIT system. Answer (C) is incorrect. Fewer purchase orders are processed by the manufacturer, so the ordering costs are likely to decrease. However, the cost of quality is not necessarily affected by a JIT system.

14.3.5. Which changes in costs are most conducive to switching from a traditional inventory ordering system to a just-in-time ordering system?

	Cost per Purchase Order	Inventory Unit Carrying Costs
A.	Increasing	Increasing
B.	Decreasing	Increasing
C.	Decreasing	Decreasing
D.	Increasing	Decreasing

Answer (B) is correct. *(CPA, adapted)*

REQUIRED: The changes in costs most conducive to switching to a JIT ordering system.

DISCUSSION: A JIT system is intended to minimize inventory. Thus, if inventory carrying costs are increasing, a JIT system becomes more cost-effective. Moreover, purchases are more frequent in a JIT system. Accordingly, a decreasing cost per purchase order is a reason to switch to a JIT system.

Answer (A) is incorrect. Switching to a JIT system should be considered when ordering costs decrease. Answer (C) is incorrect. Switching to a JIT system should be considered when carrying costs increase. Answer (D) is incorrect. Switching to a JIT system should be considered when carrying costs increase and ordering costs decrease.

14.3.6. In a just-in-time production system, costs per setup were reduced from $28 to $2. In the process of reducing inventory levels, it was found that there were fixed facility and administrative costs that previously had not been included in the carrying cost calculation. The result was an increase from $8 to $32 per unit per year. What were the effects of these changes on the economic lot size and relevant costs?

	Lot Size	Relevant Costs
A.	Decrease	Increase
B.	Increase	Decrease
C.	Increase	Increase
D.	Decrease	Decrease

Answer (D) is correct. *(CPA, adapted)*

REQUIRED: The effect of a JIT production system on economic lot size and relevant costs.

DISCUSSION: The economic lot size for a production system is similar to the EOQ. For example, the cost per set-up is equivalent to the cost per order (a numerator value in the EOQ model). Thus, a reduction in the setup costs reduces the economic lot size as well as the relevant costs. The fixed facility and administrative costs, however, are not relevant. The basic EOQ model includes variable costs only.

Answer (A) is incorrect. Relevant costs are reduced. Answer (B) is incorrect. The economic lot size is reduced. Answer (C) is incorrect. Relevant costs include the reduction in setup costs, resulting in a lower lot size.

14.3.7. In a JIT costing system, manufacturing overhead applied should be charged to

A. Materials.

B. Cost of goods sold.

C. Finished goods.

D. Work-in-process.

Answer (B) is correct. *(Publisher, adapted)*

REQUIRED: The account to which overhead applied is charged to in JIT systems.

DISCUSSION: A JIT system usually has no work orders. Thus, items such as direct labor and manufacturing overhead cannot be easily charged to specific jobs. Direct labor and overhead often are expensed directly to cost of goods sold. Year-end adjusting entries are required to allocate direct labor and overhead to the work-in-process and finished goods.

Answer (A) is incorrect. Overhead is not debited to materials. Answer (C) is incorrect. Overhead is not charged directly to finished goods. Instead, finished goods are adjusted to include their share of overhead at the end of a period. Answer (D) is incorrect. Overhead is not charged directly to work-in-process. Instead, work-in-process is adjusted to include its share of overhead at the end of a period.

14.3.8. A company uses a planning system that focuses first on the amount and timing of finished goods demanded and then determines the derived demand for raw materials, components, and subassemblies at each of the prior stages of production. This system is

A. An economic order quantity model.

B. Materials requirements planning.

C. Linear programming.

D. Just-in-time purchasing.

Answer (B) is correct. *(CIA, adapted)*

REQUIRED: The planning system that calculates derived demand for inventories.

DISCUSSION: Demand-dependent goods are components of other goods. Their demand is driven by the demand for the final goods of which they are a part (this is called derived demand). Materials requirements planning (MRP) is a push system; i.e., the demand for raw materials is driven by the forecasted demand for the final product as programmed into the system.

Answer (A) is incorrect. The EOQ model focuses on the trade-off between carrying and ordering costs. Answer (C) is incorrect. Linear programming is a decision model concerned with allocating scarce resources to maximize profit or minimize costs. Answer (D) is incorrect. JIT is a decentralized demand-pull system. It is driven by actual demand.

14.3.9. A company produces two components: A-1 and A-2. The unit throughput contribution margins for A-1 and A-2 are $150 and $300, respectively. Each component must proceed through two processes: Operation 1 and Operation 2. The capacity of Operation 1 is 180 machine hours, with A-1 and A-2 requiring 1 hour and 3 hours, respectively. Furthermore, the company can sell only 45 units of A-1 and 100 units of A-2. However, the company is considering expanding Operation 1's capacity by 90 machine hours at a cost of $80 per hour. Assuming that Operation 2 has sufficient capacity to handle any additional output from Operation 1, the company should produce

	Units of A-1	Units of A-2
A.	180	0
B.	45	100
C.	45	75
D.	0	60

Answer (C) is correct. *(Publisher, adapted)*

REQUIRED: The optimal product mix given expanded capacity.

DISCUSSION: A-1's throughput contribution margin per unit of the scarce resource (the internal binding constraint) is $150 ($150 UCM ÷ 1 machining hour). A-2's throughput contribution margin per unit of the scarce resource is $100 ($300 UCM ÷ 3 machine hours). Consequently, the company should produce as much A-1 as it can sell (45 units). If the company adds 90 machine hours to increase the capacity of Operation 1 to 270 hours (180 + 90), it cannot produce additional units of A-1 because the external binding constraint has not been relaxed. However, it can produce additional units of A-2. Given that the UCM per machine hour of A-2 is $100 and that the cost is $80 per hour, adding capacity to Operation 1 is profitable. Thus, the company should use 45 machine hours to produce 45 units of A-1. The remaining 225 machine hours (270 – 45) should be used to produce 75 units (225 ÷ 3 hours) of A-2. The latter amount is within the external binding constraint.

Answer (A) is incorrect. The company can sell only 45 units of A-1. Answer (B) is incorrect. The company can produce only 75 units of A-2 if it produces 45 units of the more profitable A-1. Answer (D) is incorrect. The company should produce as much of A-1 as it can sell.

14.3.10. Key Co. changed from a traditional manufacturing operation with a job-order costing system to a just-in-time operation with a backflush costing system. What are the expected effects of these changes on Key's inspection costs and recording detail of costs tracked to jobs in process?

	Inspection Costs	Detail of Costs Tracked to Jobs
A.	Decrease	Decrease
B.	Decrease	Increase
C.	Increase	Decrease
D.	Increase	Increase

Answer (A) is correct. *(CPA, adapted)*

REQUIRED: The effects of changing to a JIT operation with backflush costing.

DISCUSSION: In a JIT system, materials go directly into production without being inspected. The assumption is that the vendor has already performed all necessary inspections. The minimization of inventory reduces the number of suppliers, storage costs, transaction costs, etc. Backflush costing eliminates the traditional sequential tracking of costs. Instead, entries to inventory may be delayed until as late as the end of the period. For example, all product costs may be charged initially to cost of sales, and costs may be flushed back to the inventory accounts only at the end of the period. Thus, the detail of cost accounting is decreased.

Answer (B) is incorrect. With less raw materials inventory, the detail of costs tracked to jobs will decrease as well. Answer (C) is incorrect. Inspection costs also will decrease as a result of greater reliance on the supplier. Answer (D) is incorrect. Under a just-in-time inventory management system, both inspection costs and the detail of costs tracked to jobs decrease.

14.3.11. A major justification for investments in computer-integrated manufacturing (CIM) projects is

A. Reduction in the costs of spoilage, reworked units, and scrap.

B. Lower carrying amount and depreciation expense for factory equipment.

C. Increased working capital.

D. Stabilization of market share.

Answer (A) is correct. *(CIA, adapted)*

REQUIRED: The major justification for investments in CIM.

DISCUSSION: Automating and computerizing production processes requires a substantial investment in fixed assets and an increase in risk because of greater fixed costs. CIM also requires an increase in software costs and extensive worker retraining. However, the costs of labor, spoilage, rework, and scrap are reduced. The qualitative advantages of CIM are (1) increased flexibility, (2) shorter manufacturing lead time, (3) quicker development of new products, (4) better product delivery and service, (5) faster response to market changes, and (6) improved competitiveness.

Answer (B) is incorrect. An increase in fixed assets results in a higher carrying amount and depreciation expense. Answer (C) is incorrect. Working capital normally is reduced as investments change from current to fixed assets. Answer (D) is incorrect. Actual or potential market share changes may be reasons for investments in CIM.

Questions 14.3.12 through 14.3.14 are based on the following information. Rosecrans Manufacturing produces kerosene lanterns. The company can sell all of its output. Each unit sells for $120, and direct materials costing $48 per unit are added at the start of the first operation. Other variable costs are immaterial. Production data for one of its products is presented below:

	Operation 1	Operation 2	Operation 3
Total capacity per year	200,000 units	150,000 units	180,000 units
Total output per year	150,000 units	150,000 units	150,000 units
Fixed cost of operations	$1,200,000	$1,800,000	$2,250,000

14.3.12. Rosecrans hires additional workers at a cost of $50,000 per year to expedite setups and materials handling in the constraint operation. As a result, the annual output of the constraint increases by 500 units. The change in operating income attributable to the increase in workers is

A. $50,000

B. $36,000

C. $(14,000)

D. $(20,000)

Answer (C) is correct. *(Publisher, adapted)*

REQUIRED: The change in operating income.

DISCUSSION: Operation 2 is the constraint because it is functioning at its capacity. The incremental annual throughput margin (revenues – direct materials costs) from adding workers to Operation 2 is $36,000 [500 units × ($120 unit price – $48 direct materials per unit)]. Because the cost of the additional workers is $50,000, the change in operating income is $(14,000).

Answer (A) is incorrect. The incremental cost is $50,000. Answer (B) is incorrect. The incremental throughput margin is $36,000. Answer (D) is incorrect. The amount of $(20,000) is based on the assumption that an additional $12 per unit of fixed costs will be applied.

14.3.13. Tullahoma Company has offered to perform the Operation 2 function on 1,000 units at a unit price of $40, excluding direct materials cost. Chattanooga Company has offered to perform the Operation 1 function on 1,000 units at a price of $7, excluding direct materials cost. Chickamauga Company has made an offer to perform the Operation 1 function on 5,000 units at a unit cost of $5 (excluding direct materials cost). Which of these mutually exclusive offers is acceptable to Rosecrans?

A. Tullahoma's offer.

B. Chattanooga's offer.

C. Chickamauga's offer.

D. None of the offers should be accepted.

Answer (A) is correct. *(Publisher, adapted)*

REQUIRED: The acceptable offer, if any.

DISCUSSION: Tullahoma's offer should be accepted because its cost is $40,000 (1,000 units × $40), and the increase in throughput margin is $72,000 [1,000 units × ($120 unit price – $48 direct materials per unit)]. Thus, the relevant cost of Tullahoma's offer is less than the incremental throughput margin. Tullahoma's offer effectively increases the capacity of the constraint operation. Chattanooga's and Chickamauga's offers should both be rejected because, even though their $7 and $5 unit costs are less than the $8 unit operating cost (excluding direct materials) for Operation 1 ($1,200,000 fixed costs ÷ 150,000 units), they will result in the incurrence of additional costs with no increase in throughput margin, given that Operation 2 is already producing at its 150,000-unit capacity.

Answer (B) is incorrect. Chattanooga's offer will result in the incurrence of additional costs that merely add capacity to a non-bottleneck constraint. Answer (C) is incorrect. Chickamauga's offer does nothing to address the constraint operation. Answer (D) is incorrect. Tullahoma's offer will result in improved throughput margin.

14.3.14. Operation 1 produces 500 unsalable units and Operation 2 also produces 500 unsalable units. The relevant cost of the unsalable units to Rosecrans is

A. $24,000

B. $60,000

C. $84,000

D. $120,000

Answer (C) is correct. *(Publisher, adapted)*

REQUIRED: The relevant cost of the unsalable units.

DISCUSSION: The cost of the unsalable units in Operation 1 consists solely of the wasted direct materials because idle capacity is available to replace the defective units. As a consequence, Operation 1 can still transfer the maximum 150,000 units that Operation 2 can process, and no throughput margin is lost. The cost of the unsalable units in Operation 1 is thus $24,000 (500 units × $48 direct materials). In Operation 2, however, the lost throughput margin is an opportunity cost because no idle capacity exists to replace the defective units. The cost of the unsalable units in Operation 2 is $60,000 {(500 units × $48 direct materials) + [500 units × ($120 unit price – $48 direct materials cost)]}. Thus, the total relevant cost of the unsalable units is $84,000 ($24,000 + $60,000).

Answer (A) is incorrect. The direct materials cost of 500 units equals $24,000. Answer (B) is incorrect. The lost throughput margin and wasted direct materials cost of 500 units equals $60,000. Answer (D) is incorrect. The lost throughput margin and wasted direct materials cost of 1,000 units equals $120,000.

14.3.15. Increased competition, technological innovation, and a shift from mass production of standardized products to custom-produced products in many industries have increased the need for productivity improvement and flexibility of production systems. In response to these demands, organizations have increased their reliance on automation and the use of advanced technologies in their operations. Which of the following is an example of the use of automation and advanced technologies?

A. Flexible manufacturing system (FMS).

B. Just-in-time (JIT) system.

C. Master budgeting system (MBS).

D. Economic order quantity (EOQ).

Answer (A) is correct. *(CIA, adapted)*

REQUIRED: The example of the use of automation and advanced technologies.

DISCUSSION: Flexible manufacturing is the capacity of computer-controlled machinery to perform many different programmed functions. Eliminating machine setup time, strengthening control, and automating handling processes permits the efficient production of small numbers of different products by the same machines. Accordingly, output can be more accurately matched with consumer tastes, and long production runs of identical goods can be avoided. An FMS consists of two or more computer-controlled machines linked by automated handling devices such as robots and transport systems.

Answer (B) is incorrect. A JIT system involves the purchase of materials and production of components immediately preceding their use. Answer (C) is incorrect. A master budget is the detailed financial plan for the next period. Answer (D) is incorrect. The EOQ is the quantity that minimizes total costs.

14.3.16. Traditionally, large manufacturers have believed that economies of scale gained through large production runs of like, or similar, products are the best way to keep production costs down and remain competitive. Select the most appropriate response to whether this theory is still valid.

A. Yes, larger economies of scale continue to accrue from ever larger production runs.

B. Yes, lower-per-unit costs for standard products continue to guarantee a competitive advantage.

C. No, economies of scale can no longer be gained from long production runs.

D. No, production flexibility and diversity of products are needed to remain competitive.

Answer (D) is correct. *(CIA, adapted)*

REQUIRED: The most appropriate evaluation of the belief that economies of scale are the best means of reducing costs.

DISCUSSION: Global competition and more rapidly changing consumer tastes are (1) lessening the need for long production runs and (2) increasing the need for diversity of products and flexibility of manufacturing. The economies of scale concept is being replaced by economies of scope. They result when flexible manufacturing methods (use of computerized machines to perform many programmed functions) permit the economical output of small numbers of many different products with the same machines.

Answer (A) is incorrect. Economies of scale cannot continue to be achieved if the products are not salable. Answer (B) is incorrect. Economies of scale cannot continue to be achieved if the products are not salable. Answer (C) is incorrect. Economies of scale still can be achieved from long production runs if the goods are salable.

14.4 Reorder Points, Safety Stock, Stockout Cost

14.4.1. What are the three factors a manager should consider in controlling stockouts?

A. Carrying costs, quality costs, and physical inventories.

B. Economic order quantity, annual demand, and quality costs.

C. Time needed for delivery, rate of inventory usage, and safety stock.

D. Economic order quantity, production bottlenecks, and safety stock.

Answer (C) is correct. *(CIA, adapted)*

REQUIRED: The three factors a manager should consider to control stockouts.

DISCUSSION: The cost of carrying safety stock and the cost of stockouts should be minimized. Safety stock is the extra stock kept to guard against stockouts. It is the inventory at the time of reordering minus the expected use while new inventory is in transit. Thus, delivery time, rate of use, and safety stock are considerations in controlling stockouts.

Answer (A) is incorrect. Carrying costs, quality costs, and physical inventories are inventory-related concepts that do not relate directly to stockouts. Answer (B) is incorrect. The order quantity, annual demand, and quality costs are not direct concerns. Answer (D) is incorrect. Production bottlenecks result from a stockout. They are not a method of control. Also, EOQ is irrelevant to stockouts.

14.4.2. In computing the reorder point for an item of inventory, which of the following is used?

I. Cost
II. Usage per day
III. Lead time

A. I and II.

B. II and III.

C. I and III.

D. I, II, and III.

Answer (B) is correct. *(CPA, adapted)*
REQUIRED: The item(s) used in computing the reorder point for inventory.
DISCUSSION: The reorder point is the amount of inventory on hand indicating that a new order should be placed. It equals the sales per unit of time multiplied by the time required to receive the new order (lead time).

14.4.3. A company manufactures banana hooks for retail sale. The bill of materials for this item and the parts inventory for each material required are as follows:

Bill of Materials		
Raw Material	Quantity Required	On Hand
Wooden neck	1	0
Wooden base	1	0
Swag hook	1	300
Wood screws	2	400
Foot pads	4	1,000

An incoming order calls for delivery of 2,000 banana hooks in 2 weeks. The company has 200 finished banana hooks in current inventory. If no safety stocks are required for inventory, what are the company's net requirements for swag hooks and screws needed to fill this order?

	Swag Hooks	Wood Screws
A.	1,500	1,400
B.	1,500	3,200
C.	1,700	3,600
D.	1,800	3,600

Answer (B) is correct. *(CIA, adapted)*
REQUIRED: The net requirements needed to fill an order.
DISCUSSION: The entity needs 1,800 banana hooks (2,000 – 200) and therefore 1,800 swag hooks (1 × 1,800) and 3,600 wood screws (2 × 1,800). Given that 300 swag hooks and 400 wood screws are on hand, 1,500 swag hooks (1,800 – 300) and 3,200 wood screws (3,600 – 400) must be obtained.
Answer (A) is incorrect. The amount of 1,400 wood screws assumes that one wood screw is used per banana hook. Answer (C) is incorrect. The amounts of 1,700 swag hooks and 3,600 wood screws are needed if no banana hooks are in current inventory. Answer (D) is incorrect. The amount of 1,800 swag hooks is needed if no swag hooks are in current inventory. Also, 3,600 wood screws are needed if no banana hooks are in current inventory.

14.4.4. The elapsed time between placing an order for inventory and receiving the order is

A. Lead time.

B. Reorder time.

C. Stockout time.

D. Stocking time.

Answer (A) is correct. *(CMA, adapted)*
REQUIRED: The period between placing an order for inventory and receiving that order.
DISCUSSION: The time between placing an order and receiving that order is the lead time. The basic EOQ formula assumes immediate replenishment. In practice, time elapses between ordering inventory and its arrival. Lead time therefore must be considered in determining the order point (level of inventory at which a new order should be made).
Answer (B) is incorrect. Reorder time is not a meaningful answer. Answer (C) is incorrect. Stockout time is not a meaningful answer. The safety stock is the quantity of inventory that should be on hand when a new order arrives. Answer (D) is incorrect. Stocking time is the time to transfer inventory to its place of use once it has been received by the purchaser.

14.4.5. When a specified level of safety stock is carried for an item in inventory, the average inventory level for that item

A. Decreases by the amount of the safety stock.

B. Is one-half the level of the safety stock.

C. Increases by one-half the amount of the safety stock.

D. Increases by the amount of the safety stock.

Answer (D) is correct. *(CMA, adapted)*

REQUIRED: The effect on the average inventory level of carrying safety stock.

DISCUSSION: Given no safety stock, the average inventory is 50% of the EOQ. For example, if the EOQ is 500, the average inventory is 250. The entity has 500 units immediately after a purchase and zero immediately before the receipt of the next purchase (replenishment is assumed to be instantaneous). However, safety stock increases the average inventory by the amount of the safety stock. The modified EOQ model assumes that safety stock is never used. Thus, given a safety stock of 100, the average inventory level increases to 350. Inventory is 600 units immediately upon receipt of a purchase and 100 units immediately before the receipt of the next purchase.

14.4.6. Which of the following is not a typical characteristic of a just-in-time (JIT) production environment?

A. Lot sizes equal to one.

B. Insignificant setup times and costs.

C. Push-through system.

D. Balanced and level workloads.

Answer (C) is correct. *(CPA, adapted)*

REQUIRED: The item not typically a characteristic of a just-in-time (JIT) production environment.

DISCUSSION: In a JIT system, minimization of inventory is a goal because many inventory-related activities are nonvalue-added. Moreover, it is a pull system; items are pulled through production by current demand, not pushed through by anticipated demand. Thus, one operation produces only what is needed by the next operation, and components and raw materials arrive just in time to be used. To implement this approach and to eliminate waste, the factory is reorganized to permit what is often called lean production.

Answer (A) is incorrect. Under a JIT/lean production system, production of custom goods in small lots becomes more feasible. Answer (B) is incorrect. Reduced setup times and costs are benefits of JIT/lean production. Answer (D) is incorrect. Balanced and level workloads become easier to maintain in a JIT/lean production environment.

14.4.7. As a consequence of finding a more dependable supplier, Dee Co. reduced its safety stock of raw materials by 80%. What is the effect of this safety stock reduction on Dee's economic order quantity?

A. 80% decrease.

B. 64% decrease.

C. 20% increase.

D. No effect.

Answer (D) is correct. *(CPA, adapted)*

REQUIRED: The effect of the safety stock reduction on the EOQ.

DISCUSSION: The variables in the EOQ formula are periodic demand, cost per order, and the unit carrying cost for the period. Thus, safety stock does not affect the EOQ. Although the total of the carrying costs changes with the safety stock, the cost-minimizing order quantity is not affected.

14.4.8. Canseco Enterprises uses 84,000 units of Part 256 in manufacturing activities over a 300-day work year. The usual lead time for the part is 6 days; occasionally, however, the lead time has gone as high as 8 days. The company now desires to adjust its safety stock policy. The increase in safety stock size and the likely effect on stockout costs and carrying costs, respectively, would be

A. 560 units, decrease, increase.

B. 560 units, decrease, decrease.

C. 1,680 units, decrease, increase.

D. 2,240 units, increase, decrease.

Answer (A) is correct. *(CMA, adapted)*

REQUIRED: The increase in safety stock and the likely effect on stockout costs and carrying costs.

DISCUSSION: Given use of 84,000 units over 300 work days, the average rate is 280 units per day. Increasing the safety stock by a 2-day supply (8 days – usual 6-day lead time) increases inventory by 560 units (280 units × 2 days). The additional inventory should decrease stockout costs and increase inventory carrying costs.

Answer (B) is incorrect. Carrying costs increase with the increased inventory size. Answer (C) is incorrect. The entity is already carrying a 6-day supply of safety stock (280 units × 6 days = 1,680 units). The only additional units needed are for 2 extra days. Answer (D) is incorrect. The number of 2,240 units equals an 8-day supply, not the increase in safety stock. Also, stockout costs decrease and carrying costs increase.

Questions 14.4.9 through 14.4.11 are based on the following information. The diagram presented below represents the economic order quantity (EOQ) model.

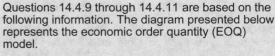

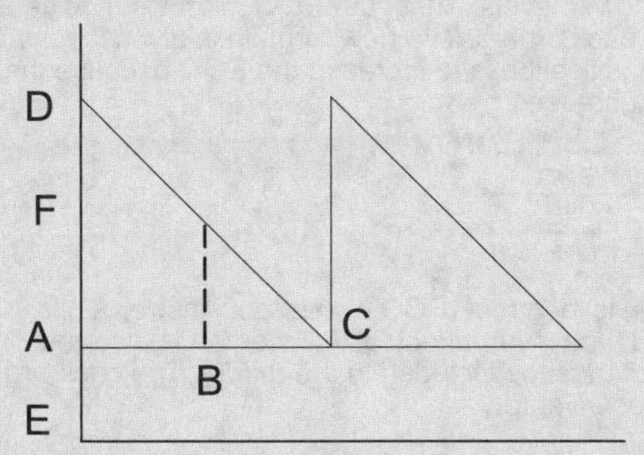

14.4.9. Which line segment represents the reorder lead time?

A. AB.

B. AE.

C. AF.

D. BC.

Answer (D) is correct. *(CMA, adapted)*
REQUIRED: The line representing the reorder lead time.
DISCUSSION: Time is represented by the x-axis and the quantity of inventory by the y-axis. The reorder lead time is represented by the line BC.
Answer (A) is incorrect. AB is the time between receipt of the last order and the placing of the next order. Answer (B) is incorrect. AE is the safety stock. Answer (C) is incorrect. AF is the quantity of inventory used during the reorder lead time.

14.4.10. Which line segment identifies the quantity of safety stock maintained?

A. AB.

B. AE.

C. AC.

D. EF.

Answer (B) is correct. *(CMA, adapted)*
REQUIRED: The line segment representing the quantity of safety stock maintained.
DISCUSSION: The y-axis represents quantities of inventory. Safety stock is represented by the line AE.
Answer (A) is incorrect. AB is the time between the receipt of the last order and the placing of the next order. Answer (C) is incorrect. AC is the EOQ. Answer (D) is incorrect. EF is the reorder point (the quantity available when an order is placed).

14.4.11. Which line segment represents the length of time to consume the total quantity of materials ordered?

A. DE.

B. BC.

C. AC.

D. AD.

Answer (C) is correct. *(CMA, adapted)*
REQUIRED: The line representing the time to consume all the materials ordered.
DISCUSSION: Time is represented by the x-axis. The line segment AC depicts the time to consume an entire order (to reduce the inventory to the safety stock).
Answer (A) is incorrect. DE is the total inventory just after an order received. Answer (B) is incorrect. BC is the reorder lead time. Answer (D) is incorrect. AD is the quantity ordered.

14.4.12. To determine the inventory reorder point, calculations normally include the

A. Ordering cost.

B. Carrying cost.

C. Average daily usage.

D. Economic order quantity.

Answer (C) is correct. *(CPA, adapted)*
REQUIRED: The item needed to calculate the reorder point.
DISCUSSION: The reorder point is the amount of inventory on hand indicating that a new order should be placed. It is calculated with the following equation:

(Average daily demand × Lead time in days)
+ Safety stock

Answer (A) is incorrect. Cost is not a factor in the reorder-point calculation. Answer (B) is incorrect. Cost is not a factor in the reorder-point calculation. Answer (D) is incorrect. The economic order quantity determines order size and can be used to determine the number of orders per period, but it is not used to calculate the reorder point.

14.4.13. If back orders can be taken (at an added cost per item back ordered),

A. EOQ will decrease.

B. EOQ will increase.

C. Lead time will decrease.

D. No change will occur. Back orders do not affect the EOQ model.

Answer (B) is correct. *(CIA, adapted)*

REQUIRED: The effect of providing for back orders in the EOQ model.

DISCUSSION: A back order is a sale made when the item is not in stock. If back orders are possible, inventory can be maintained at lower levels. Thus, the EOQ model is modified for the cost (b) of back orders. The new formula is given below. The effect of the modification is to increase the EOQ because the denominator decreases.

$$\sqrt{\frac{2aD}{k\left(\frac{b}{b+k}\right)}}$$

Answer (A) is incorrect. EOQ increases. Answer (C) is incorrect. Lead time is not affected. Answer (D) is incorrect. The back-order cost must be included in the model. The back-order system replaces inventory.

14.4.14. A company experiences both variable usage rates and variable lead times for its inventory items. The probability distributions for both usage and lead times are known. A technique the company could use for determining the optimal safety stock levels for an inventory item is

A. Queuing theory.

B. Linear programming.

C. Decision tree analysis.

D. Monte Carlo simulation.

Answer (D) is correct. *(CMA, adapted)*

REQUIRED: The quantitative technique used to determine safety stock given variable usage rates and lead times.

DISCUSSION: Simulation is a method for experimenting with mathematical models using a computer. Monte Carlo simulation generates the individual values for a random variable. A random number generator is used to produce numbers with a uniform probability distribution. The second step of the Monte Carlo process then transforms the random numbers into values consistent with the desired distribution. The performance of a model under conditions of uncertainty may be investigated by randomly selecting values for each of the variables in the model based on the probability distribution of each variable and then calculating the value of the solution. Advantages of Monte Carlo simulation are that time can be compressed, alternative policies can be considered, and complex systems can be analyzed.

Answer (A) is incorrect. Queuing theory is used to minimize the costs of waiting lines. Answer (B) is incorrect. Linear programming is used to minimize a cost function or maximize a profit function given constraints. Answer (C) is incorrect. Decision trees are diagrams that analyze sequences of probabilistic decisions, the events that may follow each decision, and their outcomes.

14.4.15. Each stockout of a product sold by A.W. Inn Co. costs $1,750 per occurrence. The carrying cost per unit of inventory is $5 per year, and the company orders 1,500 units of product 24 times a year at a cost of $100 per order. The probability of a stockout at various levels of safety stock is

Units of Safety Stock	Probability of a Stockout
0	.50
100	.30
200	.14
300	.05
400	.01

The optimal safety stock level for the company is

A. 0 units.

B. 100 units.

C. 300 units.

D. 400 units.

Answer (D) is correct. *(CMA, adapted)*

REQUIRED: The optimal level of safety stock.

DISCUSSION: The total expected cost of safety stock equals the sum of the expected annual (1) stockout cost and (2) carrying cost. Annual expected stockout cost equals the cost per occurrence ($1,750), times the probability of a stockout per cycle, times the number of cycles (24). Annual expected carrying cost of a safety stock equals the unit carrying cost ($5) times the number of units. Thus, a safety stock of 400 units has the lowest total expected cost.

Units Held	Carrying Cost	Expected Stockout Cost Per Cycle	Expected Stockout Cost for 24 Cycles	Total Expected Cost
0	$ 0	$875.00	$21,000	$21,000
100	500	525.00	12,600	13,100
200	1,000	245.00	5,880	6,880
300	1,500	87.50	2,100	3,600
400	2,000	17.50	420	2,420

Answer (A) is incorrect. A safety stock of 0 units has a total expected cost of $21,000. Answer (B) is incorrect. A safety stock of 100 units has a total expected cost of $13,100. Answer (C) is incorrect. A safety stock of 300 units has a total expected cost of $3,600.

14.4.16. Arnold Enterprises uses the EOQ model for inventory control. The company has an annual demand of 50,000 units for part number 191 and has computed an optimal lot size of 6,250 units. Per-unit carrying costs and stockout costs are $13 and $3, respectively. The following data have been gathered in an attempt to determine an appropriate safety stock level:

Units Short Because of Excess Demand during the Lead Time Period	Number of Times Short in the Last 40 Reorder Cycles
200	6
300	12
400	6

The annual cost of establishing a 200-unit safety stock is expected to be

A. $2,600

B. $4,040

C. $4,260

D. $5,200

Answer (B) is correct. *(CMA, adapted)*

REQUIRED: The annual cost of establishing a given safety stock.

DISCUSSION: The annual cost consists of the carrying cost of the 200 units of safety stock at $13 each, or $2,600, plus the stockout costs incurred when 200 units are insufficient. The stockout cost per unit is $3. The excess demand has been 100 units (300 – 200) greater than the proposed safety stock 30% of the time (12 ÷ 40). The cost per stockout was $300 (100 × $3). Demand has exceeded the safety stock by 200 units (400 – 200) 15% of the time (6 ÷ 40). The cost per stockout was $600 (200 × $3). Given 30% and 15% probabilities of $300 and $600 stockout costs, respectively, the expected stockout cost for a 200-unit safety stock for one reorder cycle is $180 [($300 × 30%) + ($600 × 15%)]. Thus, the annual expected stockout cost for a 200-unit safety stock is $180 times the number of reorder cycles per year, or $1,440 [(50,000 ÷ 6,250 EOQ) × $180]. The annual cost of a 200-unit safety stock is $4,040 ($2,600 + $1,440).

Answer (A) is incorrect. The amount of $2,600 is the carrying cost of the safety stock. Answer (C) is incorrect. The amount of $4,260 is the annual cost of establishing a 300-unit safety stock. Answer (D) is incorrect. The amount of $5,200 is the annual cost of establishing a 400-unit safety stock.

14.4.17. Huron Corporation purchases 60,000 headbands per year. The average purchase lead time is 20 working days, safety stock equals 7 days normal usage, and the corporation works 240 days per year. Huron should reorder headbands when the quantity in inventory reaches

A. 5,000 units.

B. 6,750 units.

C. 1,750 units.

D. 5,250 units.

Answer (B) is correct. *(CMA, adapted)*

REQUIRED: The reorder point in units.

DISCUSSION: The reorder point is the quantity on hand when an order is placed. With a 20-day normal lead time, a 7-day safety stock, and use of 250 units per day (60,000 units ÷ 240 days), an order should be placed when 27 days of inventory is on hand, a total of 6,750 units (250 units × 27 days).

Answer (A) is incorrect. An inventory of 5,000 units does not allow for safety stock. Answer (C) is incorrect. An inventory of 1,750 units covers only safety stock. Answer (D) is incorrect. An inventory of 5,250 units includes only 1 day of safety stock.

STUDY UNIT FIFTEEN
PROBABILITY AND STATISTICS

Probability theory is a method for mathematically expressing assurance about the occurrence of a chance event under conditions of risk.

Statistics applies to information calculated from sample data. A **parameter** is a numerical characteristic of a population computed using every element in the population. For example, the mean and the mode are parameters of a population. A **statistic** is a numerical characteristic of a sample computed using only the elements of a sample. For example, the mean and the mode are statistics of the sample.

A **probability distribution** specifies the values of a random variable and their respective probabilities. Certain standard distributions occur frequently and are useful in business. If the relative frequency of the values of a variable can be specified, the variable is a **random variable**. A variable is **discrete** if it can assume only certain values in an interval, for example, the number of customers served. A random variable is **continuous** if no gaps exist in the values it may assume.

Objective probabilities are calculated from either logic or actual experience, and **subjective probabilities** are estimates, based on judgment and past experience. The sum of the probabilities of all possible events is 1.0. Accordingly, the probability of an event varies from 0 to 1. A probability of 0 means the event cannot occur, and a probability of 1 means the event is certain to occur. Values between 0 and 1 indicate the likelihood of the event's occurrence. For example, the probability that a fair coin will yield heads is 0.5 on any single toss. Two events are **mutually exclusive** if they cannot occur simultaneously and **independent** if the occurrence of one has no effect on the probability of the other.

Descriptive statistics summarize large amounts of data. Measures of central tendency and measures of dispersion are such summaries. **Measures of central tendency** are values typical of a set of data. The **mean** is the arithmetic average of a set of numbers, the **median** is the 50th percentile, and the **mode** is the most frequently occurring value. **Measures of dispersion** indicate the variation within a set of numbers. The **variance** is the average of the squared deviations from the mean. It is found by (1) subtracting the mean from each value, (2) squaring each difference, (3) adding the squared differences, and (4) dividing the sum by the number of data items. The **standard deviation** is the square root of the variance.

Inferential statistics provides methods for drawing conclusions about populations based on a sample. **Statistical sampling** (1) randomly selects items and (2) uses a statistical method to evaluate the results (including measuring sampling risk). It is important because measuring the entire population is usually inefficient. The **central limit theorem** states that regardless of the distribution of the population from which random samples are drawn, the shape of the sampling distribution of $\overline{x}$ (the mean) approaches the normal distribution as the sample size is increased. The **normal distribution** is the most important and useful of all probability distributions. It has a symmetrical, bell-shaped curve centered about the mean. About 68% of its area (or probability) lies within plus or minus 1 standard deviation of the mean, and 95.5% lies within 2 standard deviations. The **standard normal distribution** has a mean of 0 and variance of 1. All normal distribution problems are first converted to the standard normal distribution to permit use of standard normal distribution tables.

The basic steps in a statistical **sampling plan** are to (1) determine objectives, (2) define the population, (3) determine acceptable sampling risk (precision or confidence interval), (4) calculate the sample size using standard tables or formulas, (5) select the sampling approach, (6) take the sample, and (7) evaluate the results.

For decisions involving risk, **expected value** is a rational means for selecting the best option. The expected value equals the sum of the products of (1) the probability of each outcome and (2) its payoff. It is the long-term average payoff for repeated trials.

QUESTIONS

15.1 Basic Concepts

15.1.1. To assist in an investment decision, Gift Co. selected the most likely sales volume from several possible outcomes. Which of the following attributes would that selected sales volume reflect?

A. The midpoint of the range.

B. The median.

C. The greatest probability.

D. The expected value.

Answer (C) is correct. *(CPA, adapted)*

REQUIRED: The attribute reflected by the selected sales volume.

DISCUSSION: Probability is important to management decision making because of the uncertainty of future events. Probability estimation techniques assist in making the best decisions in the face of uncertainty. Consequently, the most likely sales volume is the one with the greatest probability.

Answer (A) is incorrect. The midpoint of the range is the point halfway between two points. Answer (B) is incorrect. Half the values are greater and half are less than the median. Answer (D) is incorrect. The expected value is a weighted average using probabilities as weights.

15.1.2. Probability (risk) analysis is

A. Used only for situations involving five or fewer possible outcomes.

B. Used only for situations in which the summation of probability weights is less than one.

C. An extension of sensitivity analysis.

D. Incompatible with sensitivity analysis.

Answer (C) is correct. *(CPA, adapted)*

REQUIRED: The correct statement regarding probability (risk) analysis.

DISCUSSION: Probability (risk) analysis is used to examine the array of possible outcomes given alternative parameters. Sensitivity analysis answers what-if questions when alternative parameters are changed. Thus, risk (probability) analysis is similar to sensitivity analysis: both evaluate the probabilities and effects of differing inputs or outputs.

Answer (A) is incorrect. Probability analysis can be used when many outcomes are possible. Answer (B) is incorrect. The sum must equal one. Answer (D) is incorrect. Probability analysis enhances sensitivity analysis.

15.1.3. The probability of the simultaneous occurrence of two mutually exclusive events is

A. The probability that both events will occur.

B. The probability that one will occur given that the other has occurred.

C. The probability that two independent events will occur.

D. Zero.

Answer (D) is correct. *(Publisher, adapted)*

REQUIRED: The definition of mutually exclusive events.

DISCUSSION: Mutually exclusive events cannot occur simultaneously. The usual example is that heads and tails cannot both occur on a single toss of a coin.

Answer (A) is incorrect. Joint probability is the probability that both events will occur. Answer (B) is incorrect. Conditional probability is the probability that one will occur given that the other has occurred. Answer (C) is incorrect. Two independent events may both occur.

15.1.4. Joint probability is the probability that

A. Two or more events will all occur.

B. One event will occur given that another has occurred.

C. One event has no effect on the probability of a second event.

D. Mutually exclusive events will occur.

Answer (A) is correct. *(Publisher, adapted)*

REQUIRED: The definition of joint probability.

DISCUSSION: Joint probability is the probability that two or more events will occur. The joint probability for two events equals the probability of the first event times the conditional probability of the second event.

Answer (B) is incorrect. Conditional probability is the probability that one event will occur given that another has occurred. Answer (C) is incorrect. Events are independent if one event has no effect on the probability of a second event. Answer (D) is incorrect. Two mutually exclusive events cannot both occur.

15.1.5. Conditional probability is the probability that

A. Two or more events will all occur.

B. One event will occur given that the other has occurred.

C. One event has no effect on the probability of a second event.

D. Mutually exclusive events will occur.

Answer (B) is correct. *(Publisher, adapted)*

REQUIRED: The definition of conditional probability.

DISCUSSION: Conditional probability is the probability that one event will occur given that another has already occurred.

Answer (A) is incorrect. Joint probability is the probability that two or more events will occur. Answer (C) is incorrect. Events are independent if one event has no effect on the probability of a second event. Answer (D) is incorrect. Mutually exclusive events cannot both occur.

15.1.6. A warehouse contains records from both the retail and the wholesale divisions of the client company. Upon inspecting the contents of one randomly selected box, the auditor discovers that they do not match the label. On average, errors of this kind have occurred in 6% of retail boxes and 2% of wholesale boxes. Unfortunately, the part of the label indicating the division of origin is illegible. The auditor does know that two-thirds of the boxes in this warehouse come from the wholesale division and one-third from the retail division. Which of the following can be concluded?

A. The box is more likely to have come from the retail division.

B. The box is more likely to have come from the wholesale division.

C. The proportion of retail boxes in the warehouse is probably much larger than the auditor thought.

D. The proportion of wholesale boxes in the warehouse is probably much larger than the auditor thought.

Answer (A) is correct. *(CIA, adapted)*

REQUIRED: The true probabilistic statement.

DISCUSSION: Two-thirds of the boxes are from the wholesale division. Of these, 2% are mislabeled. Thus, about 1.33% (66 2/3% × 2%) of all the boxes are mislabeled and originated in the wholesale division. One-third of the boxes are from the retail division. Of these, 6% are mislabeled. Accordingly, about 2% (33 1/3% × 6%) of all the boxes are mislabeled and originated in the retail division. The probability is about 60% [2% ÷ (1.33% + 2%)] that the box came from the retail division.

Answer (B) is incorrect. The box is more likely to have come from the retail division. Answer (C) is incorrect. The contents of any one box are an insufficient basis for a conclusion about the population of boxes in the warehouse. Answer (D) is incorrect. The contents of any one box are an insufficient basis for a conclusion about the population of boxes in the warehouse.

15.1.7. Events are independent when

A. Their joint probability is zero.

B. Their joint probability is one.

C. The conditional probability of each event is its unconditional probability.

D. They are mutually exclusive.

Answer (C) is correct. *(Publisher, adapted)*

REQUIRED: The definition of independent events.

DISCUSSION: Conditional probability is the probability that one event will occur given that another has already occurred. Events are independent when the occurrence of one does not affect the probability of the other. Accordingly, two events are independent if the conditional probability of each event is its unconditional probability.

Answer (A) is incorrect. Events are independent when their joint probability equals the product of their individual probabilities. Answer (B) is incorrect. Events are independent when their joint probability equals the product of their individual probabilities. Answer (D) is incorrect. Events are mutually exclusive if their joint probability is zero.

15.1.8. Which one of the following is a correct rationale for using a nonparametric statistic rather than a more conventional statistic?

A. It is not known how the variable being tested is distributed.

B. The event or difference to be tested is fairly small, and therefore you need a more sensitive test.

C. The sample was not drawn randomly.

D. The variable being tested is measured on a continuous scale.

Answer (A) is correct. *(CIA, adapted)*

REQUIRED: The reason for using a nonparametric statistic.

DISCUSSION: Nonparametric statistics is usually defined to include methods that are not related to population parameters or are not based on rigid assumptions about the distribution of the population. For example, chi-square tests of goodness of fit are nonparametric procedures.

Answer (B) is incorrect. Nonparametric tests are usually less sensitive than conventional statistics. Answer (C) is incorrect. Proper inferences from nonparametric tests also require random samples. Answer (D) is incorrect. Nonparametric tests are more appropriate than parametric tests for variables measured by rankings or categories but not usually for continuous variables.

15.1.9. A company uses two major material inputs in its production. To prepare its manufacturing operations budget, the company has to project the cost changes of these material inputs. The cost changes are independent of one another. The purchasing department provides the following probabilities associated with projected cost changes:

Cost Change	Material 1	Material 2
3% increase	.3	.5
5% increase	.5	.4
10% increase	.2	.1

The probability that there will be a 3% increase in the cost of both Material 1 and Material 2 is

A. 15%

B. 40%

C. 80%

D. 20%

Answer (A) is correct. *(CIA, adapted)*

REQUIRED: The probability of joint increases.

DISCUSSION: The joint probability of occurrence of two independent events equals the product of their individual probabilities. The probability that the cost of Material 1 will increase by 3% is .3. The probability that the cost of Material 2 will increase by 3% is .5. The probability that both will occur is .15 (.3 × .5).

Answer (B) is incorrect. The average of the probabilities of a 3% increase in the costs of Material 1 and Material 2 is 40%. Answer (C) is incorrect. The sum of the probabilities of a 3% increase in the costs of Material 1 and Material 2 is 80%. Answer (D) is incorrect. The difference between the probabilities of an increase in the costs of Material 1 and Material 2 is 20%.

15.1.10. A company with 14,344 customers determines that the mean and median accounts receivable balances for the year are $15,412 and $10,382, respectively. From this information, the auditor can conclude that the distribution of the accounts receivable balances is continuous and

A. Negatively skewed.

B. Positively skewed.

C. Symmetrically skewed.

D. Evenly distributed between the mean and median.

Answer (B) is correct. *(CIA, adapted)*

REQUIRED: The conclusion drawn from information about the mean and median of accounts receivable.

DISCUSSION: The mean is the arithmetic average, and the median corresponds to the 50th percentile. Thus, half the values are greater and half are smaller. The auditor can conclude that the distribution is positively skewed because the mean is greater than the median and the distribution is continuous.

Answer (A) is incorrect. The mean is greater than the median and the distribution is continuous, so the distribution is positively skewed. Answer (C) is incorrect. The distribution is symmetrically skewed if the mean, median, and mode (the most frequently occurring value) were equal. Answer (D) is incorrect. Distributions spread evenly between two values are uniform distributions.

15.1.11. Thoran Electronics Company began producing pacemakers last year. At that time, the company forecasted the need for 10,000 integrated circuits (ICs) annually. During the first year, the company placed orders for the ICs when the inventory dropped to 600 units so that it would have enough to produce pacemakers continuously during a 3-week lead time before delivery of new ICs. Unfortunately, the company ran out of this IC component on several occasions, causing costly production delays. Careful study of last year's experience resulted in the following expectations for the coming year:

Weekly Usage	Related Probability of Usage	Lead Time	Related Probability of Lead Time
280 units	.2	3 weeks	.1
180 units	.8	2 weeks	.9
	1.0		1.0

The study also suggested that usage during a given week was statistically independent of usage during any other week, and usage was also statistically independent of lead time. If the company reorders integrated circuits when the inventory has dropped to a level of 700 units, the probability that it will run out of this component before the order is received is

A. .0008

B. .1040

C. .0104

D. .896

Answer (C) is correct. *(CMA, adapted)*

REQUIRED: The probability of a stockout if an order is placed when inventory has dropped to a given level.

DISCUSSION: Based on the given data, weekly usage must be either 280 or 180 units, and the lead time must be either 3 or 2 weeks. Whenever the lead time is 2 weeks, no stockout will occur because usage will be, at most, 560 units (280 units × 2 weeks). Thus, one condition of a stockout is a lead time of 3 weeks. A second condition of a stockout is that usage equals 280 units for at least 2 of the 3 weeks; if usage is 280 units for only 1 week, the total usage during the lead time will be only 640 units [(2 × 180) + 280]. The probability of a 3-week lead time is given as .1. Given that weekly usage is independent of lead time and of prior weeks' usage, the probability that usage will be 280 units for at least 2 weeks is the sum of the probabilities of the following combinations of events:

Week 1	Week 2	Week 3	Probability
280	280	280	.2 × .2 × .2 = .008
280	280	180	.2 × .2 × .8 = .032
280	180	280	.2 × .8 × .2 = .032
180	280	280	.8 × .2 × .2 = .032
			.104

The probability of both a 3-week lead time and usage in excess of 700 units is therefore .0104 (.1 × .104).

Answer (A) is incorrect. The percentage of .0008 is the probability that lead time will be 3 weeks and that usage will be 280 units each week. Answer (B) is incorrect. The percentage of .1040 is the probability of usage in excess of 700 units, given a 3-week lead time. Answer (D) is incorrect. The percentage of .896 is the probability of usage less than 700 units, given a 3-week lead time.

15.1.12. Which of the following statements is true concerning the appropriate measure of central tendency for the frequency distribution of loss experienced shown below?

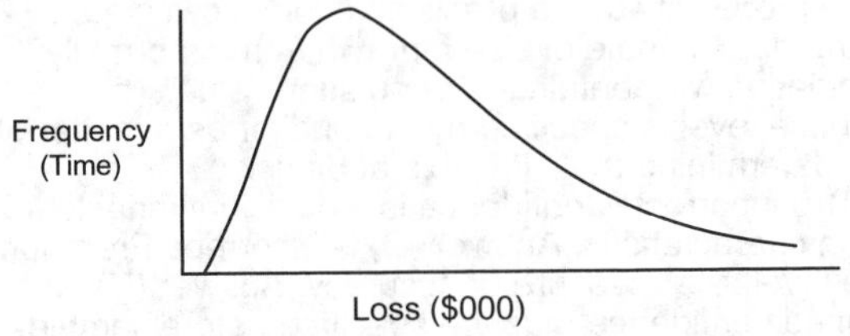

A. The mean, median, and mode are equally appropriate because the distribution is symmetrical.

B. The mode is the most appropriate measure because it considers the dollar amount of the extreme losses.

C. The median is the most appropriate measure because it is not affected by the extreme losses.

D. The mean is the best measure of central tendency because it always lies between the median and the mode.

Answer (C) is correct. *(CIA, adapted)*

REQUIRED: The appropriate measure of central tendency.

DISCUSSION: Measures of central tendency are the mode, the median, and the mean. The mode is the most frequently occurring value, the median is the value above and below which half of the events occur, and the mean is the average or the arithmetic mean. The median is the best estimate of the central tendency for this distribution because it is not biased by extremes. The given frequency distribution of loss is skewed by the extremely high losses. The median, which consists of absolute numbers of events, is unaffected by the magnitude of the greatest losses.

Answer (A) is incorrect. The example is an asymmetrical distribution. When the distribution is perfectly symmetrical, these three values are identical. Answer (B) is incorrect. The mode does not consider the extreme losses. It is simply the most frequently occurring value. Answer (D) is incorrect. In this situation, the median lies between the mean and the mode. This distribution is skewed to the right because of the very high loss values. Consequently, the mean is to the right of both the mode and the median.

15.1.13. In sampling applications, the standard deviation represents a measure of the

A. Expected error rate.

B. Level of confidence desired.

C. Degree of data variability.

D. Extent of precision achieved.

Answer (C) is correct. *(CIA, adapted)*

REQUIRED: The definition of the standard deviation.

DISCUSSION: The standard deviation measures the variability within a population. The following is the formula for the standard deviation of a population (σ = the standard deviation, x_i = an observation, μ = the mean, and N = the number of items in the population):

$$\sigma = \sqrt{\frac{\Sigma(X_i - \mu)^2}{N}}$$

Answer (A) is incorrect. The expected error rate is associated with attribute sampling. Answer (B) is incorrect. The desired confidence level is determined by the auditor's judgment. Answer (D) is incorrect. The extent of precision achieved in variables sampling is computed using the standard deviation.

15.1.14. Which of the following is not a measure of dispersion of a random variable?

A. Range.

B. Median.

C. Variance.

D. Standard error of the mean.

Answer (B) is correct. *(CIA, adapted)*

REQUIRED: The statistical measure not a measure of dispersion.

DISCUSSION: Measures of dispersion indicate the amount of variation within a set of numbers. Measures of central tendency, however, describe typical items in a population. The median, a measure of central tendency, is the halfway value when the raw data are arranged in numerical order from the lowest to the highest.

Answer (A) is incorrect. The range is the difference between the largest and the smallest values. Answer (C) is incorrect. The standard deviation is the square root of the variance. Answer (D) is incorrect. The standard error of the mean is the standard deviation of sample means.

15.1.15. Auditors employ confidence levels in the context of audit sampling. In a given sample plan, the confidence level

A. Is a decision variable that the auditor specifies after considering the economic consequences of drawing the wrong conclusion as a result of sampling risk.

B. Is a characteristic of the audit population and is not under the direct control of the auditor.

C. Is essentially a measure of the accuracy of the sample results obtained after the sample has been selected and tested.

D. Is not normally specified before the sample size is determined. Rather, it is computed once the sample has been selected and tested.

Answer (A) is correct. *(CIA, adapted)*

REQUIRED: The true statement about confidence levels.

DISCUSSION: In principle, given repeated sampling and a normally distributed population, the confidence level is the percentage of all the precision intervals that may be constructed from simple random samples of size n that will include the population value. In practice, the confidence level is regarded as the probability that a precision interval calculated from a simple random sample of size n drawn from a normally distributed population will contain the population value. The desired confidence level is specified by the auditor as a matter of judgment after determining the allowable audit risk.

Answer (B) is incorrect. Confidence is a decision variable, not a population characteristic. Answer (C) is incorrect. Precision, not confidence level, is a measure of accuracy. Answer (D) is incorrect. Planned confidence must be specified before sample size can be computed.

15.1.16. The principle stating that the distribution of the sample means from any underlying population is approximately normal when the sample size is large ($n \geq 30$) is the

A. Central limit theorem.

B. Sample mean theorem.

C. Maximum likelihood theorem.

D. None. The given statement is not true.

Answer (A) is correct. *(Publisher, adapted)*

REQUIRED: The principle stating that the distribution of the sample means is normal.

DISCUSSION: Given a large enough sample size, the central limit theorem states that the probability distribution of sample means generated from any underlying probability distribution is approximately normal. The mean of this distribution is the true population mean, and the variance is $\sigma^2 \div n$.

Answer (B) is incorrect. No such theorem exists. Answer (C) is incorrect. Maximum likelihood is a form of estimation that finds the value that maximizes the joint probabilities of all random variables sampled. Answer (D) is incorrect. The statement is true.

15.1.17. In audit sampling contexts, precision is

A. A characteristic of the population at hand and is not under the direct control of the auditor.

B. A measure of the accuracy with which one has generated sample estimates. Desired precision must be established before the sample is obtained and evaluated.

C. Evaluated independently of reliability in a given sample.

D. Important for evaluating variables samples, but not attributes samples.

Answer (B) is correct. *(CIA, adapted)*

REQUIRED: The definition of precision.

DISCUSSION: The precision or confidence interval (allowance for sampling risk) is an interval around the sample statistic that is expected to contain the true value of the population. Precision is a variable in the sample size formula and must be estimated prior to calculating the sample size. The estimated precision interval is based upon a point estimate of the population value and the tolerable rate (for attribute sampling) or the tolerable misstatement (for variables sampling) determined by materiality considerations. The achieved (computed) precision interval is a function of population size and standard deviation, sample size, and specified confidence level.

Answer (A) is incorrect. Precision is under the auditor's control. Answer (C) is incorrect. Precision and reliability are interdependent. Answer (D) is incorrect. Precision also applies to attribute samples.

15.1.18. An auditor wishes to determine whether the finished goods perpetual inventory records are being properly updated for completed production. To accomplish this, the auditor traces inventory quantity and cost records from production reports to perpetual inventory records, using an appropriate sample size based on a 95% confidence level, estimated error rate of 4%, and desired precision of ±2%. If the error rate in the sample is, as expected, 4%, and 2,000 production reports were posted to perpetual inventory records during the year, the auditor can be 95% sure that the number incorrectly posted was

A. At least 100.

B. At least 80.

C. Between 60 and 140.

D. Between 40 and 120.

Answer (D) is correct. *(CIA, adapted)*

REQUIRED: The number of errors in the inventory records.

DISCUSSION: The probability is 95% that the number of errors is between 2% (4% – 2%) and 6% (4% + 2%) because the precision is ±2% and the sample error rate equals the expected rate of 4%. Consequently, the range in terms of inventory records is between 40 [(4% – 2%) × 2,000] and 120 [(4% + 2%) × 2,000].

Answer (A) is incorrect. Using the complement of the confidence level instead of the error rate results in 100 (2,000 × 5%). Answer (B) is incorrect. The actual number of errors will be more or fewer than 80 (2,000 × 4%). Answer (C) is incorrect. For the number of errors to lie between 60 and 140, the complement of the confidence level is used instead of the estimated error rate.

15.1.19. An auditor has taken a large sample from an audit population that is skewed in the sense that it contains a large number of small dollar balances and a small number of large dollar balances. Given this, the auditor can conclude

A. The sampling distribution is not normal; thus, sampling based on the Poisson distribution most accurately defines the nature of the population.

B. The sampling distribution is normal; thus, the Z-score value can be used in evaluating the sample results.

C. The sampling distribution is not normal; thus, attribute sampling is the only statistical tool that can appropriately be used.

D. The sampling distribution is normal; thus, attribute sampling is the only statistical tool that can appropriately be used.

Answer (B) is correct. *(CIA, adapted)*

REQUIRED: The conclusion about a skewed population.

DISCUSSION: The central limit theorem states that, regardless of the distribution of the population from which random samples are taken, the shape of the sampling distribution of the means approaches the normal distribution as the sample size increases. Thus, Z-values (the number of standard deviations needed to provide specified levels of confidence) can be used. Z-values represent areas under the curve for the standard normal distribution.

Answer (A) is incorrect. The sampling distribution is normal (a continuous distribution). The Poisson distribution approaches the binomial distribution (a discrete distribution) for large samples and thus is related to attribute sampling, a method applicable to binary propositions, e.g., error rates. Variables sampling is appropriate for population values. Answer (C) is incorrect. The sampling distribution can be normally distributed given a large enough sample size. Moreover, attribute sampling is not appropriate for estimating population values. Answer (D) is incorrect. Variables, not attribute, sampling is appropriate in this context.

15.1.20. Compared with the standard deviation of the population, the standard deviation of the sampling distribution of the mean (standard error of the mean) is

A. Larger.

B. Smaller.

C. The same.

D. Indeterminate.

Answer (B) is correct. *(Publisher, adapted)*

REQUIRED: The relationship between the standard error of the mean and the standard deviation of the population.

DISCUSSION: The standard deviation of the distribution of sample means (standard error of the mean) is always smaller than the standard deviation of the population (σ). It equals the standard deviation of the population divided by the square root of the sample size ($\sigma \div \sqrt{n}$). The lower number also makes intuitive sense because extreme values of a population are typically excluded because of the averaging process in calculating a sample mean.

15.1.21. Given a normally distributed population with an unknown mean (μ) but a known standard deviation (σ) of 10, the standard error of the mean for a sample size of 100 is

A. 10

B. 100

C. 1

D. .1

Answer (C) is correct. *(Publisher, adapted)*

REQUIRED: The standard error of the mean.

DISCUSSION: The formula for the standard error of the mean is the standard deviation of the population divided by the square root of the sample size ($\sigma \div \sqrt{n}$). Consequently, the standard error of the mean is 1($10 \div \sqrt{100}$).

Answer (A) is incorrect. The amount of 10 is the population standard deviation. Answer (B) is incorrect. The amount of 100 is the sample size. Answer (D) is incorrect. The amount of .1 equals σ divided by n.

15.1.22. When a decision maker is faced with a decision and the probabilities of various outcomes are known, the situation is said to be decision making

A. Under risk.

B. Under uncertainty.

C. Under certainty.

D. Through satisficing.

Answer (A) is correct. *(CIA, adapted)*

REQUIRED: The condition in which a decision maker is faced with a decision and the probabilities of various outcomes are known.

DISCUSSION: Decision making under risk involves multiple possible future states of nature for each choice. The decision is under risk if a probability distribution for these states is known. Thus, the states of nature are mutually exclusive, and the sum of their probabilities equals 1.0. Risk increases as the variability of outcomes becomes greater. But the terms risk and uncertainty often are treated as synonyms.

Answer (B) is incorrect. Under uncertainty, the probabilities of the possible states of nature are unknown. Answer (C) is incorrect. Under certainty, the outcome of each decision choice is known. Its probability is 1.0. Answer (D) is incorrect. Satisficing decisions are satisfactory or sufficient but not optimal.

15.1.23. Decision makers are normally confronted with a choice among feasible choices. Their decisions often have to be made under conditions of risk or uncertainty, that is, with less than complete and accurate knowledge of the outcome for each alternative. Which of the following is true?

A. Under conditions of risk, there is only one potential outcome for each alternative.

B. Under conditions of uncertainty, the first task is to determine the expected value of each of the multiple outcomes.

C. Under conditions of risk, decisions are solely based on the decision maker's experience and intuition.

D. Under conditions of uncertainty, the first task is to establish subjective probabilities of occurrence for the multiple outcomes.

Answer (D) is correct. *(CIA, adapted)*

REQUIRED: The true statement about making decisions.

DISCUSSION: Probability is objective or subjective. Objective probabilities are calculated using logic or experience. Subjective probabilities are estimates, based on judgment of the likelihood of future events. In business, subjective probability can indicate the degree of confidence a person has in an outcome. Under conditions of uncertainty, objective probabilities cannot be determined. A decision maker first must establish subjective probabilities and then proceed as though under conditions of risk.

Answer (A) is incorrect. Under both risk and uncertainty, multiple outcomes are possible for each occurrence. Certainty exists when only one outcome is possible. Answer (B) is incorrect. Calculation of expected values is dependent upon probabilities. Answer (C) is incorrect. Decision makers also may rely on probabilistic information under conditions of risk.

15.1.24. Managers have varying attitudes regarding risk. A risk-neutral manager

A. Avoids risk.

B. Has a linear utility function.

C. Tends to choose options that involve large variations of actual monetary returns about expected monetary values.

D. Tends to choose options that have very little variation about expected monetary returns.

Answer (B) is correct. *(Publisher, adapted)*

REQUIRED: The characteristic of a risk-neutral manager.

DISCUSSION: A risk-neutral manager neither seeks nor avoids risk. (S)he chooses investments for which the expected monetary values equal the manager's subjectively perceived utility values (expressed in utils, an arbitrary measure). Thus, the decision maker has a linear utility function. The monetary amounts and utils have a constant or directly proportional relationship. Accordingly, (s)he is indifferent to risk.

Answer (A) is incorrect. A risk-averse manager avoids risk. Answer (C) is incorrect. A risk-seeking manager tends to accept greater variability of returns. Answer (D) is incorrect. A risk-averse manager tends to choose options that have very little variation about expected monetary returns.

15.1.25. A risk-averse manager

A. Neither seeks nor avoids risk.

B. Has a linear utility function.

C. Tends to choose options that involve large variations of actual monetary returns about expected monetary values.

D. Tends to choose options that have very little variation about expected monetary returns.

Answer (D) is correct. *(Publisher, adapted)*

REQUIRED: The definition of a risk aversion.

DISCUSSION: The risk-averse decision maker avoids risk. (S)he prefers a certain return on investments to the risk involved in other investments with potentially large gains but also large losses. The utility function for the risk-averse manager increases at a decreasing rate. Accordingly, the utility of a gain is lower than the disutility of a loss of the same absolute amount.

Answer (A) is incorrect. A risk-neutral manager neither seeks nor avoids risk. Answer (B) is incorrect. A risk-neutral manager has a linear utility function. Answer (C) is incorrect. A risk-seeking manager tends to choose options that involve large variations of actual monetary returns about expected monetary values.

15.1.26. Following is a table of probabilities for two separate product lines, X and Y:

Probability	X profit	Y profit
.20	$500	$ 50
.70	300	400
.10	600	800

The product line to obtain maximum utility for a risk-averse decision maker is

A. X because it has the higher expected profit.

B. Y because it has the higher expected profit.

C. Y because it has the higher dispersion.

D. X because it has the lower dispersion.

Answer (D) is correct. *(CIA, adapted)*

REQUIRED: The product line that provides maximum utility for a risk-averse decision maker.

DISCUSSION: The risk-averse decision maker avoids risk. (S)he prefers a certain return on investments to the risk involved in other investments with potentially large gains but also large losses. The utility function for the risk-averse manager increases at a decreasing rate. Accordingly, the utility of a gain is lower than the disutility of a loss of the same absolute amount. The expected value (mean) of X is $370 [(.2 × $500) + (.7 × $300) + (.1 × $600)]. The expected value (mean) of Y also is $370 [(.2 × $50) + (.7 × $400) + (.1 × $800)]. However, X is less risky than Y based on a variance criterion (sum of the products of the squared deviations from the mean and their respective probabilities). Thus, a risk-averse decision maker prefers X because it has less variation in its possible outcomes.

Variance of X

$.2 \times (\$500 - \$370)^2 + .7 \times (\$300 - \$370)^2 + .1 \times (\$600 - \$370)^2 = \$12,100$

Variance of Y

$.2 \times (\$50 - \$370)^2 + .7 \times (\$400 - \$370)^2 + .1 \times (\$800 - \$370)^2 = \$39,600$

Answer (A) is incorrect. The expected values of X and Y are equal. Answer (B) is incorrect. The expected values of X and Y are equal. Answer (C) is incorrect. A risk-seeking decision maker prefers Y.

15.1.27. A risk-seeking manager

A. Neither seeks nor avoids risk.

B. Has a linear utility function.

C. Tends to choose options that involve large variations of actual monetary returns about expected monetary values.

D. Tends to choose options that have very little variation about expected monetary returns.

Answer (C) is correct. *(Publisher, adapted)*

REQUIRED: The definition of a risk-seeking manager.

DISCUSSION: A risk-seeking manager chooses risk. A risk seeker prefers investments that have the potential for large gains although large losses may be possible. The utility function for the risk seeker increases at an increasing rate; i.e., riskier investments are appealing.

Answer (A) is incorrect. A risk-neutral manager neither seeks nor avoids risk. Answer (B) is incorrect. A risk-neutral manager has a linear utility function. Answer (D) is incorrect. A risk-averse manager tends to choose options that have very little variation about expected monetary returns.

15.1.28. Assume a linear utility for money and a risk-neutral decision maker. From the payoff table below, one can conclude that the utility of Alternative A is

	State of Nature		
	S1	S2	Expected Profit
Alternative A:	100	200	$160
Alternative B:	140	40	$ 80

A. $300

B. High.

C. Exactly twice that of B.

D. Approximately twice that of B.

Answer (C) is correct. *(CIA, adapted)*

REQUIRED: The utility of an action given a linear utility for money, a risk-neutral decision maker, and a payoff table.

DISCUSSION: Under the linearity assumption for the utility of money, each additional dollar has constant utility. Risk neutrality implies that the utility of a gain (profit) equals the disutility of a loss of the same magnitude. The conclusion is that a profit of $160 has exactly twice the utility of a profit of $80 although the utility function of the decision maker is not known.

Answer (A) is incorrect. Utility is measured in utils, not dollars. Answer (B) is incorrect. A conclusion that the utility is high requires a judgment about the utility function of the decision maker, which is unknown. Answer (D) is incorrect. The linearity assumption leads to exact statements, not approximations.

15.1.29. Statistical quality control often involves the use of control charts whose basic purpose is to

A. Determine when accounting control procedures are not working.

B. Control labor costs in production operations.

C. Detect performance trends away from normal operations.

D. Monitor internal control applications in computer operations.

Answer (C) is correct. *(CMA, adapted)*

REQUIRED: The purpose of statistical quality control charts.

DISCUSSION: A statistical control chart is a graphic aid for monitoring the status of any process subject to random variations. The chart consists of three horizontal lines plotted on a horizontal time scale. The vertical scale represents the appropriate quantitative measure. The center line represents the average or mean value for the process being controlled. The other two lines are the upper control limit and the lower control limit. The processes are measured periodically, and the values are plotted on the chart. If the value is within the control limits, no action is taken. If the value is outside the limits, the process is considered out of control, and an investigation is made for possible corrective action. Another advantage of the chart is that it makes trends visible.

Answer (A) is incorrect. Quality control applies directly to product quality, not accounting procedures. Answer (B) is incorrect. Quality control applies directly to product quality, not labor costs. Answer (D) is incorrect. Quality control applies directly to product quality, not computer operations.

15.1.30. The statistical quality control department prepares a control chart showing the percentages of defective production. Simple statistical calculations provide control limits that indicate whether assignable causes of variation are explainable on chance grounds. The chart is particularly valuable in determining whether the quality of materials received from outside vendors is consistent from month to month. What is the best term for this chart?

A. C chart.

B. P chart.

C. R chart.

D. X-bar chart.

Answer (B) is correct. *(CIA, adapted)*

REQUIRED: The statistical quality control chart described.

DISCUSSION: A P chart is based on an attribute (acceptable or not acceptable) rather than a measure of a variable, specifically, the percentage of defects in a sample.

Answer (A) is incorrect. A C chart also is an attribute control chart. It shows defects per item. Answer (C) is incorrect. An R chart displays the range of dispersion of a variable, such as size or weight. Answer (D) is incorrect. An X-bar chart plots the sample mean for a variable.

15.2 Probability Distributions

15.2.1. A quantitative technique useful in projecting a firm's sales and profits is

A. Probability distribution theory.

B. Gantt charting.

C. Learning curves.

D. Queuing theory.

Answer (A) is correct. *(CMA, adapted)*

REQUIRED: The quantitative technique useful in projecting sales and profits.

DISCUSSION: Probability distribution theory can be used to project sales. It is a mathematical method for making decisions about the likelihood of future events (such as sales) in the face of uncertainty. Various estimates of sales (generated from the sales force) can be weighted with different probabilities.

Answer (B) is incorrect. A Gantt chart is a bar chart used to measure progress toward a goal. Answer (C) is incorrect. A learning curve measures the benefit of experience in the early stages of a new task. Answer (D) is incorrect. Queuing (waiting-line) theory is used to determine the optimum balance between the cost of providing service to reduce waiting lines and the cost of allowing waiting lines to exist when items in the queue arrive at random.

15.2.2. Which of the following is an attribute of a probability distribution?

A. The total probability associated with all possible occurrences is zero.

B. It can be modeled by means of a formula or graph that provides the probability for every possible outcome.

C. Only one outcome is possible.

D. It applies to a discrete random variable only.

Answer (B) is correct. *(Publisher, adapted)*

REQUIRED: The attribute of a probability distribution.

DISCUSSION: In a probability distribution, the probability of any random event is between 0 (no chance) and 1 (certainty). The total probability of all possible random events must equal 1. Also, a probability distribution models a random variable through the use of a formula or graph that provides the probability of each value of the random variable.

Answer (A) is incorrect. The total probability is 1.0. Answer (C) is incorrect. If only one outcome is possible, the variable is not random but constant and known with certainty. Answer (D) is incorrect. The random variable may be discrete or continuous.

15.2.3. Which of the following is a discrete probability distribution?

A. Chi-square.

B. Normal.

C. Poisson.

D. Exponential.

Answer (C) is correct. *(Publisher, adapted)*

REQUIRED: The discrete probability distribution.

DISCUSSION: The Poisson distribution is a discrete distribution that measures finite events over a time interval or an area. It is similar to the binomial distribution when the sample is large, and the product of the probability of (1) observing a desired event and (2) the sample size is small.

Answer (A) is incorrect. A continuous probability distribution describes a random variable that may assume an infinite number of values. For example, an interval of time may be divided into ever smaller fractional units. The chi-square distribution is a continuous probability distribution. Answer (B) is incorrect. A continuous probability distribution describes a random variable that may assume an infinite number of values. For example, an interval of time may be divided into ever smaller fractional units. The normal distribution is a continuous probability distribution. Answer (D) is incorrect. A continuous probability distribution describes a random variable that may assume an infinite number of values. For example, an interval of time may be divided into ever smaller fractional units. The exponential distribution is a continuous probability distribution.

15.2.4. The binomial distribution is best described as one in which

A. Each outcome has the same probability.

B. Each event has only two possible outcomes.

C. Sampling occurs without replacement.

D. The curve is symmetrical and bell-shaped.

Answer (B) is correct. *(Publisher, adapted)*

REQUIRED: The definition of a binomial distribution.

DISCUSSION: The binomial distribution often is used in quality control. It gives the probability of each possible combination of trial results when each trial has only two possible outcomes.

Answer (A) is incorrect. In a uniform distribution, all outcomes are equally probable. Tossing one die is an example of an event with a uniform distribution. Answer (C) is incorrect. Sampling without replacement occurs in a hypergeometric distribution. Answer (D) is incorrect. A normal distribution is symmetrically bell-shaped.

15.2.5. What is the primary difference between a discrete and a continuous distribution?

A. One is not a legitimate probability distribution.

B. Continuous distributions always are symmetric, but discrete distributions are not.

C. Continuous distributions describe ranges in which any possible value has a probability of occurrence, but discrete distributions assign probabilities only to a finite number of values within a range.

D. Continuous distributions model finite random variables only, but discrete distributions may model any variable.

Answer (C) is correct. *(Publisher, adapted)*

REQUIRED: The primary difference between a discrete and a continuous distribution.

DISCUSSION: A continuous distribution of a random variable may have an infinite number of values. On a graph, (1) the total area is defined by its curve and the x-axis equals 1.0, and (2) the area between any two points equals the probability that the random variable is between those points. Discrete distributions model only random variables with a finite number of values, for example, the number of customers entering a store during a time period.

Answer (A) is incorrect. A discrete and a continuous distribution are probability distributions. Answer (B) is incorrect. Continuous probability distributions need not be symmetric. Answer (D) is incorrect. Continuous probability distributions model random variables that may take on an infinite amount of values.

15.2.6. A hypergeometric distribution can best be described as one in which

A. Each outcome has the same probability.

B. Each event has only two possible outcomes.

C. Sampling occurs without replacement.

D. The curve is symmetrical and bell-shaped.

Answer (C) is correct. *(Publisher, adapted)*

REQUIRED: The best description of a hypergeometric distribution.

DISCUSSION: The hypergeometric distribution is similar to the binomial distribution. It is used for sampling without replacement. When the size of the population is not large relative to the sample, the probability of a certain outcome is related to what occurred in preceding trials. The number of similar outcomes has a hypergeometric probability.

Answer (A) is incorrect. In a uniform distribution, each outcome has the same probability. Answer (B) is incorrect. An event in a binomial distribution has but two possible outcomes. Answer (D) is incorrect. A normal distribution is symmetrical and bell-shaped.

15.2.7. A Poisson distribution is best described as one used

A. To assess the probability that a certain event occurs a certain number of times in a given interval of time or space.

B. To assess the probability of observing an occurrence at least as long as a specified time interval.

C. When small samples of less than 30 are examined, and the underlying population is assumed to be normal.

D. To test the fit between the actual data and the theoretical distribution.

Answer (A) is correct. *(Publisher, adapted)*

REQUIRED: The best description of a Poisson distribution.

DISCUSSION: A Poisson distribution models the number of times a specified event occurs over a period of time or over a certain area or volume. It is similar to the binomial distribution when the sample is large and the product of the probability of (1) observing a desired event and (2) the sample size is small.

Answer (B) is incorrect. An exponential distribution is used to assess the probability of observing an occurrence at least as long (e.g., life of a fuse, engine, etc.) as a specified time interval. Answer (C) is incorrect. Student's t-distribution is used when small samples of less than 30 are examined and the underlying population is assumed to be normal. Answer (D) is incorrect. The chi-square distribution tests the fit between the actual data and the theoretical distribution.

15.2.8. A producer of salad dressing is using queuing analysis to determine how many mechanics should be available to adjust machinery in its large filling department. Similar high-speed filling machinery is operated simultaneously on each of 13 separate production lines. Machine adjustment failures occur randomly through time such that the length of time between failures has an exponential distribution. The number of adjustment failures occurring during an 8-hour shift in the above situation is best modeled by a

A. Normal distribution.

B. Binomial distribution.

C. Poisson distribution.

D. Uniform distribution.

Answer (C) is correct. *(CMA, adapted)*

REQUIRED: The distribution used in queuing analysis.

DISCUSSION: Queuing theory examines the costs of waiting lines and of servicing them. The Poisson distribution is used in queuing theory because more than one event usually occurs in a given period of time. If λ is the value of the mean in this distribution (the average number of occurrences of an event in the given interval of time or space), k is the number of occurrences, and e is the natural logarithm (2.71828...), the Poisson distribution is defined as

$$f\ (k) = \frac{\lambda^k e^{-\lambda}}{k!}$$

Answer (A) is incorrect. The normal distribution has a symmetrical, bell-shaped curve. Answer (B) is incorrect. The binomial distribution is a discrete distribution in which only two outcomes are possible. Answer (D) is incorrect. All outcomes are equally likely in the uniform distribution.

15.2.9. Which of the following is a continuous distribution?

A. Poisson.

B. Exponential.

C. Binomial.

D. Hypergeometric.

Answer (B) is correct. *(Publisher, adapted)*

REQUIRED: The continuous distribution.

DISCUSSION: A continuous probability distribution describes a random variable that may assume an infinite number of values. For example, an interval of time may be divided into ever smaller fractional units. The exponential distribution is related to the Poisson distribution. It is a continuous distribution used to assess the probability of observing an occurrence with a length of time greater than a specified time interval.

Answer (A) is incorrect. The Poisson distribution is a discrete probability distribution. Answer (C) is incorrect. The binomial distribution is a discrete probability distribution. Answer (D) is incorrect. The hypergeometric distribution is a discrete probability distribution.

15.2.10. The exponential distribution is best described as one used

A. To assess the probability that a certain event will occur a certain number of times in a given interval of time or space.

B. To assess the probability of observing an occurrence at least as long as a specified time interval.

C. When small samples of less than 30 are examined, and the underlying population is assumed to be normal.

D. To test the fit between the actual data and the theoretical distribution.

Answer (B) is correct. *(Publisher, adapted)*

REQUIRED: The best description of an exponential distribution.

DISCUSSION: The exponential distribution is related to the Poisson distribution. It is a continuous distribution used to assess the probability of observing an occurrence with a length of time greater than a specified time interval. A common use of the exponential distribution is in modeling the length of life of electronic components, engines, etc. Thus, the probability that a time unit will exceed a prespecified time unit is calculated.

Answer (A) is incorrect. A Poisson distribution is used to assess the probability that a certain event will occur a certain number of times in a given interval of time or space. Answer (C) is incorrect. Student's t-distribution is used when small samples of less than 30 are examined, and the underlying population is assumed to be normal. Answer (D) is incorrect. The chi-square distribution tests the fit between the actual data and the theoretical distribution.

15.2.11. Student's t-distribution is best described as one used

A. To assess the probability that a certain event will occur a certain number of times in a given interval of time or space.

B. To assess the probability of observing an occurrence at least as long as a specified time interval.

C. When small samples of less than 30 are examined and the underlying population is assumed to be normal.

D. To test the fit between the actual data and the theoretical distribution.

Answer (C) is correct. *(Publisher, adapted)*

REQUIRED: The best description of Student's t-distribution.

DISCUSSION: Student's t-distribution is a special distribution used when only small samples are available and the population variance is not given. It is bell-shaped and symmetric like a normal distribution, but typically flatter with more variation. A small sample is usually deemed to be less than 30. For samples larger than 30, the t-distribution gives results similar to those provided by the standard normal distribution.

Answer (A) is incorrect. A Poisson distribution is used to assess the probability of a certain event's occurrence in a certain number of times in a given interval of time or space. Answer (B) is incorrect. An exponential distribution is used to assess the probability of observing an occurrence at least as long as a specified time interval. Answer (D) is incorrect. The chi-square distribution tests the fit between the actual data and the theoretical distribution.

15.2.12. Separate statistical samples of invoice payments in each of 15 branch offices of your company show a number of errors. In determining whether the quality of performance among the 15 offices is significantly different from overall quality, which of the following statistical distributions should you assume to be most applicable?

A. Poisson distribution.

B. Chi-square distribution.

C. Hypergeometric distribution.

D. Binomial distribution.

Answer (B) is correct. *(CIA, adapted)*

REQUIRED: The distribution used to ascertain whether the differences between samples are statistically significant.

DISCUSSION: The chi-square distribution is used to examine the fit between actual data and the theoretical distribution. It tests the probability that a particular sample was drawn from a particular population. The chi-square statistic (χ^2) equals the sample variance (s^2), multiplied by its degree of freedom ($n - 1$), and divided by the hypothesized population variance (σ^2). Because quality may be defined as involving few errors and consequently a small variance, the variance of the samples of each office can be tested.

Answer (A) is incorrect. The Poisson distribution is a special case of the binomial distribution used especially in queuing analysis. Answer (C) is incorrect. The hypergeometric distribution is similar to the binomial distribution. It involves sampling without replacement. Answer (D) is incorrect. The binomial distribution applies to binary situations, e.g., a yes or no, error or no error basis.

15.2.13. A normal distribution is best described as one in which

A. Each outcome has the same probability.

B. Each event has only two possible outcomes.

C. Sampling occurs without replacement.

D. The curve is symmetrical and bell-shaped.

Answer (D) is correct. *(Publisher, adapted)*

REQUIRED: The definition of a normal distribution.

DISCUSSION: The normal distribution is the most significant probability distribution. In sampling, it describes the distribution of the sample mean regardless of the distribution of the population, given that the sample is large (typically greater than 30). It has a symmetrical, bell-shaped curve centered around the sample mean.

Answer (A) is incorrect. In a uniform distribution, each outcome has the same probability. Answer (B) is incorrect. In a binomial distribution, each event has only two possible outcomes. Answer (C) is incorrect. Sampling occurs without replacement in a hypergeometric distribution.

15.2.14. An internal auditor is interested in determining if there is a statistically significant difference among four offices in the proportion of female versus male managers. A chi-square test is being considered. A principal advantage of this test compared with a t-test in this circumstance is that

A. Generally available software exists for the chi-square test.

B. The chi-square can both detect a relationship and measure its strength.

C. The chi-square can be applied to nominal data.

D. The chi-square is a parametric, and therefore stronger, test.

Answer (C) is correct. *(CIA, adapted)*

REQUIRED: The principal advantage of the chi-square test over the t-test.

DISCUSSION: The chi-square test is used to determine the fit between actual data and the theoretical distribution. Thus, it tests whether the sample is likely to be from the population, based on a comparison of the sample variance and the population variance. The chi-square test is appropriately applied to nominal data. Nominal data simply distinguish one item from another, e.g., male from female. The chi-square statistic equals the product of (1) the sample variance and (2) the degrees of freedom (number in the sample – 1), divided by the population variance. This calculated value is then compared with the critical value in the chi-square table.

Answer (A) is incorrect. Software for the t-test is widely available. Answer (B) is incorrect. The chi-square test cannot measure the strength of a relationship. Answer (D) is incorrect. The chi-square test is nonparametric. Thus, it is applied to problems in which a parameter is not calculated.

15.3 Hypothesis Testing

15.3.1. Hypothesis testing includes all but which of the following steps?

A. Sample data are generated, and the hypothesis is formulated.

B. The probability of the hypothesis given the sample data is computed.

C. The hypothesis is rejected or not rejected based upon the sample measure.

D. The standards are adjusted.

Answer (D) is correct. *(Publisher, adapted)*

REQUIRED: The item not a part of hypothesis testing.

DISCUSSION: Adjusting standards is the final step in the control loop. It is not a step in hypothesis testing.

Answer (A) is incorrect. The first of the four steps is to formulate the hypothesis. Answer (B) is incorrect. In the third step, the conditional probability that (1) the hypothesis is true, given the observed evidence, and (2) the sample results actually occurred, is computed. Answer (C) is incorrect. In the fourth step, the hypothesis is rejected if its probability is smaller than some subjective fixed level of probability.

15.3.2. An audit of accounts payable was made to determine if the error rate was within the stated policy of 0.5%. One hundred of the 10,000 accounts payable transactions were randomly selected using a 95% confidence level. No errors were found. With 95% certainty, one can conclude that the sample results

A. Indicate another sample is needed.

B. Prove there are no errors in accounts payable.

C. Indicate the null hypothesis is false.

D. Fail to prove the error rate is above 0.5%.

Answer (D) is correct. *(CIA, adapted)*

REQUIRED: The sound conclusion if a sample contained no errors.

DISCUSSION: The null hypothesis is that the error rate is equal to or less than 0.5%. Given that no errors were found, no basis for disproving the null hypothesis is presented.

Answer (A) is incorrect. The sample is adequate. Answer (B) is incorrect. Even an examination of all 10,000 transactions would not necessarily prove that no errors exist in accounts payable. Answer (C) is incorrect. The null hypothesis has not been disproved.

Questions 15.3.3 and 15.3.4 are based on the following information. JR Smythe, the manager for a company that manufactures custom desks, is designing a series of statistical tools to be used in the measurement and control of costs. The desks are accounted for on a job costing basis.

15.3.3. Smythe's production management has expressed the concern that the average per-unit cost to manufacture desks has increased. In developing a statistical test to determine whether the average cost has increased, Smythe constructs a hypothesis about the difference in means that will imply

A. A two-tailed test.

B. A single-valued test.

C. An operating characteristic test.

D. A one-tailed test.

Answer (D) is correct. *(CMA, adapted)*

REQUIRED: The true statement about a test to determine average unit cost.

DISCUSSION: One possible hypothesis to be tested is whether the mean has increased, that is, greater than a certain value. The alternative hypothesis is that the average per-unit cost is equal to or less than the former estimate. Consequently, a one-tailed test is appropriate because it determines whether the new average is in the upper tail of the distribution.

Answer (A) is incorrect. If a two-tailed test is constructed, the hypothesis may be rejected if the sample value is in the upper or lower tail of the distribution. Answer (B) is incorrect. A single value is not a probability distribution. Answer (C) is incorrect. Operating characteristic test is a not a meaningful term.

15.3.4. In developing Smythe's statistical tests, a null hypothesis is formulated. This testing procedure can lead to the wrong decision (e.g., Type I or alpha error, Type II or beta error). What decision is wrong?

A. To reject the null hypothesis that the cost has not increased when the cost in fact has increased.

B. To reject the null hypothesis that the cost has not increased when the cost in fact has not increased.

C. To accept the null hypothesis that the cost has increased when the cost in fact has increased.

D. To reject the null hypothesis that the cost has increased when in fact the cost has not increased.

Answer (B) is correct. *(CMA, adapted)*

REQUIRED: The wrong decision when testing a null hypothesis.

DISCUSSION: Wrong decisions are of two types: Type I (alpha or incorrect rejection error) and Type II (beta or incorrect acceptance error). To reject the hypothesis that the costs have not increased when in fact they have not increased is a Type I error. It is also incorrect to accept the hypothesis that costs have not increased when in fact they have increased, a Type II error.

Answer (A) is incorrect. To reject the null hypothesis that the cost has not increased when the cost in fact has increased is an appropriate decision. (The question calls for a wrong decision.) Answer (C) is incorrect. To accept the null hypothesis that the cost has increased when the cost in fact has increased in an appropriate decision. Answer (D) is incorrect. To reject the null hypothesis that the cost has increased when the cost in fact has not increased is an appropriate decision.

15.3.5. A company is producing a machine part that must have a diameter of 1.000 inches ± .010. Historical records show that the mean diameter of all parts produced since the project began has been 0.995 inches. A sample of five observations (0.985, 1.015, 1.012, 0.988, 0.980, with a mean of 0.996) will be

A. Rejected by a quality control system that uses a mean chart ($\bar{x}$ chart) only.

B. Accepted by a quality control system that uses a mean chart ($\bar{x}$ chart) only.

C. Accepted by a quality control system that uses a range chart (R chart) only.

D. Accepted by a quality control system that uses both mean and range charts.

Answer (B) is correct. *(CIA, adapted)*

REQUIRED: The true statement about acceptance or rejection of a machine part using a range or mean chart.

DISCUSSION: The sample has a mean of 0.996. Because the mean of the sample must be between 0.990 and 1.01 (1.000 inches ± .010), the sample is accepted if a mean ($\bar{x}$) chart is used. A mean chart displays central tendencies, but a range chart displays an acceptable high-low range.

Answer (A) is incorrect. The sample is accepted if a mean ($\bar{x}$) chart is used. Answer (C) is incorrect. Each observation is outside the required range, so the sample is rejected if a range chart is used. Answer (D) is incorrect. Each observation is outside the required range, so the sample is rejected if a range chart is used.

Questions 15.3.6 through 15.3.12 are based on the following information. The ABC Organization has specified that the mean number of calories in a can of its diet soda is 1 or less. A consumer testing service examined nine cans with the following amounts of calories: .9, .95, 1.0, 1.05, .85, 1.0, .95, .95, and .9. The mean of these observations is .95. The sum of the squared deviations from the mean is .03. Assume the underlying population is approximately normal.

15.3.6. What is the sample standard deviation?

A. .0577

B. .0612

C. .0316

D. .00375

Answer (B) is correct. *(Publisher, adapted)*

REQUIRED: The sample standard deviation.

DISCUSSION: The sample mean is the sum of the observations divided by the sample size. The sample mean is represented by the symbol $\bar{x}$. The following is the sample variance (s^2): $\Sigma(x_i - \bar{x})^2 \div (n - 1)$. The sample standard deviation(s) is the square root of the variance. Thus, the sample variance is .00375 [.03 ÷ (9 – 1)], and the sample standard deviation is .0612 ($\sqrt{.00375}$).

Answer (A) is incorrect. The ratio of .0577 results from using n, not n – 1, in the denominator. Answer (C) is incorrect. The ratio of .0316 equals .03 divided by .95. Answer (D) is incorrect. The ratio of .00375 is the variance.

15.3.7. If μ is the true mean calories of all diet sodas produced by ABC, what hypothesis should be tested to determine whether its claim is valid?

A. H_o: $\mu = 1$
H_a: $\mu \neq 1$

B. H_o: $\mu \leq 1$
H_a: $\mu > 1$

C. H_o: $\mu = 1$
H_a: $\mu > 1$

D. H_o: $\mu = 0$
H_a: $\mu < 1$

Answer (B) is correct. *(Publisher, adapted)*

REQUIRED: The hypothesis to be tested to determine whether the advertising claim is valid.

DISCUSSION: ABC asserts that its diet soda has, on the average, no more than 1 calorie. Thus, a possible null hypothesis is H_o: $\mu \leq 1$. The alternate hypothesis is that the mean is greater than 1, that is, H_a: $\mu > 1$. Because the null hypothesis cannot be rejected if the test statistic is in the left-hand tail of the distribution, the test is one-tailed.

Answer (A) is incorrect. The null hypothesis supported by the sample, which had a mean of .95, is that the population mean is equal to or less than 1 calorie. The alternate hypothesis therefore cannot be 1. Answer (C) is incorrect. The null hypothesis is that the population mean is equal to or less than 1 calorie. Answer (D) is incorrect. The null hypothesis is that the population mean is equal to or less than 1 calorie. The alternate hypothesis therefore cannot be less than 1.

15.3.8. The appropriate means for testing the hypothesis is

A. A z-statistic.

B. A t-statistic.

C. An F-statistic.

D. A Q-statistic.

Answer (B) is correct. *(Publisher, adapted)*

REQUIRED: The appropriate statistic to test the hypothesis.

DISCUSSION: The t-statistic is appropriate for tests of hypotheses based on small samples. It measures how the sample mean differs from the hypothesized true mean in terms of standard deviations. The formula is

$$t = \frac{\bar{x} - \mu}{s \div \sqrt{n}}$$

If $\bar{x}$ = *sample mean*
μ = *hypothesized true mean*
s = *sample standard deviation*
n = *sample size*

Answer (A) is incorrect. The z-statistic is appropriate when the standard deviation of the population is known or a large sample (n > 30) permits a reasonable approximation of the population standard deviation. Answer (C) is incorrect. The F-statistic tests differences in variances. Answer (D) is incorrect. Q-statistic is not a meaningful term.

15.3.9. The value of the t-statistic is

A. –2.45

B. –.05

C. 2.45

D. 4.65

Answer (A) is correct. *(Publisher, adapted)*

REQUIRED: The value of the t-statistic.

DISCUSSION: Given that $\bar{x}$ equals .95, the hypothesized value of the true mean is 1, the sample standard deviation equals .0612, and the sample size is 9, the value of the t-statistic is

$$t = \frac{.95 - 1}{.0612 \div \sqrt{9}} = \frac{-.05}{.0612 \div 3} = \frac{-.05}{.0204} = -2.45$$

Answer (B) is incorrect. The value of –.05 is the difference between the sample mean and the hypothesized true mean. Answer (C) is incorrect. The value is negative. Answer (D) is incorrect. The value is negative.

15.3.10. The appropriate number of degrees of freedom for the t-statistic is

A. 8

B. 9

C. 0

D. 1

Answer (A) is correct. *(Publisher, adapted)*

REQUIRED: The appropriate number of degrees of freedom for the t-statistic.

DISCUSSION: The degrees of freedom associated with the test statistic equals the sample size minus the number of parameters tested. Measurements of calorie content were made for nine cans of diet soda, so the sample size was nine. The only parameter tested is μ, the mean calorie content of the diet sodas. Accordingly, the number of degrees of freedom is 8 (9 – 1).

Answer (B) is incorrect. The sample size is 9. Answer (C) is incorrect. One parameter is tested. Answer (D) is incorrect. One parameter is tested.

15.3.11. The following data are from a table of critical values of t:

d.f.	$t_{.10}$	$t_{.05}$	$t_{.025}$
5	1.476	2.015	2.571
6	1.440	1.943	2.447
7	1.415	1.895	2.365
8	1.397	1.860	2.306
9	1.383	1.833	2.262

The value of t defining the rejection region for testing the hypothesis that ABC's soda has no more than 1 calorie per can, assuming a 95% confidence level, is

A. 2.306

B. 1.86

C. 1.833

D. 2.262

Answer (B) is correct. *(Publisher, adapted)*

REQUIRED: The value of t defining the rejection region for testing the hypothesis at a 95% confidence level.

DISCUSSION: The rejection region is determined by the value of t at the appropriate degrees of freedom and the specific level of confidence. Choosing a 95% level of confidence means that the value of t restricts the probability of a Type 1 error (rejecting the null hypothesis when the null hypothesis is true) to 5%. The rejection region is defined by this value. Thus, the null hypothesis is rejected if the t-statistic calculated from the formula is equal to or greater than the t-value from a table of t-values. The t-value correlates the appropriate degrees of freedom (n – 1) and the appropriate probability of making a Type 1 error (.05). Given with 8 degrees of freedom (a sample size – 1), the appropriate rejection region is defined by a t-value of 1.86. Thus, a calculated t-statistic equal to or greater than 1.86 permits rejection of the null hypothesis H_o: $\mu \leq 1$.

Answer (A) is incorrect. The value of 2.306 is for a confidence level of 97.5%. Answer (C) is incorrect. The value of 1.833 is for 9 degrees of freedom. Answer (D) is incorrect. The value of 2.262 is for 9 degrees of freedom and a confidence level of 97.5%.

15.3.12. What conclusion can be drawn with 95% confidence?

A. The manufacturer's claim can be rejected.

B. The manufacturer's claim cannot be rejected.

C. No decision is possible based on current information.

D. All sodas have at most 1 calorie.

Answer (B) is correct. *(Publisher, adapted)*

REQUIRED: The conclusion with 95% confidence.

DISCUSSION: The critical value of t is 1.86, and the calculated t-statistic is –2.45. Thus, the 5% rejection region is to the right of the t-value of 1.86. Because the computed value is less than (to the left of) 1.86 in this one-tailed test, the null hypothesis cannot be rejected.

Answer (A) is incorrect. The null hypothesis cannot be rejected. Answer (C) is incorrect. The null hypothesis cannot be rejected. Answer (D) is incorrect. Some sodas have more than 1 calorie.

15.3.13. In a large computer manufacturer, there has been much concern about the consistency across departments in adhering to new and unpopular purchasing guidelines. An auditor has a list that rank-orders all departments according to the percentage of purchases that are consistent with the guidelines and indicates which division the department is from. The auditor performs a t-test for differences in means on the average rank of departments in divisions A and B to see if there is any difference in compliance with the policy and finds that division A (which has more departments) has a significantly higher (i.e., better) average rank than division B. Which one of the following conclusions should be drawn from this analysis?

A. Division A is complying better with the new policy.

B. A random sample of departments should be drawn and the analysis recalculated.

C. A t-test is not valid when the tested groups differ in size.

D. A t-test is inappropriate for this data and another type of analysis should be used.

Answer (D) is correct. *(CIA, adapted)*

REQUIRED: The true statement about application of a t-test to rank-ordered data.

DISCUSSION: For large distributions, the t-distribution is almost the same as the standard normal distribution. Accordingly, it is used for small samples for which the sample (not the population) standard deviation is known. A t-test is not valid when used with ordinal-level data. A t-test by definition is an application of parametric statistics. Nonparametric (distribution-free) statistics is applied to problems for which rank order, but not a specific distribution, is known.

Answer (A) is incorrect. A t-test is not valid given these facts. Answer (B) is incorrect. The auditor already has a list of the entire population, and no sampling is needed. Answer (C) is incorrect. A t-test can be used with groups that differ in size.

15.3.14. A consultant is reviewing the age composition of the employees of Giant National Bank as part of a study of the bank's hiring policies. A recent industry report shows that the percentage of workers over 50 years of age in individual banks is normally distributed and has an arithmetic mean of 10%. Using a t-test and a 95% confidence level, the consultant tested the hypothesis that no difference exists between the employees' age composition of Giant and that of other banks. A random sample of 100 Giant employees included four persons over 50 years of age. The calculated t-value was 4.0. How should the consultant interpret this t-value?

A. Four percent of Giant's employees are over 50 years old.

B. Because a t-value of 4.0 is considered small, no significant difference exists between the number of people over 50 years of age employed by Giant and by other banks.

C. Because a t-value of 4.0 is considered large, the risk is less than 5% that the sample result would have occurred if the number of Giant's employees over age 50 were identical to that of other banks.

D. Because a t-value of 4.0 is considered large, there is a 95% likelihood that the number of Giant's employees over age 50 does not differ from that of other banks.

Answer (C) is correct. *(CIA, adapted)*

REQUIRED: The interpretation of the calculated t-value.

DISCUSSION: Student's t-distribution is used when (1) confidence intervals for a population are required, (2) the sample is small (usually less than 30), and (3) the population is assumed to be approximately normal. For this two-tailed t-test, the null hypothesis is that no difference exists between the age composition of Giant's employees and that of employees at other banks. It is accepted when the calculated t-statistic is less than the t-value found in the table for (1) the desired level of confidence and (2) the appropriate degrees of freedom. The null hypothesis is rejected when the t-value calculated is greater than the value found in the table. A t-value of 4.0 is large. Consequently, it most likely exceeds the critical value of t found in a standard table, and the null hypothesis (H_o: $\mu = 10\%$) can be rejected.

Answer (A) is incorrect. The t-value is not a percentage. It is a variable with a probability distribution similar to the standard normal distribution except that its shape is dependent upon the number of degrees of freedom. When the size of the sample is large (more than 30), the values associated with the standard normal and t-distributions are the same. Answer (B) is incorrect. A t-value of 4.0 is large. Answer (D) is incorrect. A t-value of 4.0 means that the null hypothesis can be rejected.

15.4 Expected Value

15.4.1. A vendor offered Wyatt Co. $25,000 in compensation for losses resulting from faulty raw materials. Alternatively, a lawyer offered to represent Wyatt in a lawsuit against the vendor for a $12,000 retainer and 50% of any award over $35,000. Possible court awards with their associated probabilities are as follows:

Award	Probability
$75,000	0.6
$0	0.4

Compared with accepting the vendor's offer, the expected value for Wyatt to litigate the matter to a verdict provides a

A. $4,000 loss.

B. $8,000 gain.

C. $21,000 gain.

D. $38,000 gain.

Answer (A) is correct. *(CPA, adapted)*

REQUIRED: The expected value for Wyatt to litigate the matter to a verdict.

DISCUSSION: If the award is $75,000, Wyatt's net recovery is $43,000 {$75,000 – $12,000 retainer – [($75,000 – $35,000) × 50%]}. If the award is $0, Wyatt's net loss is the $12,000 retainer. The expected value is therefore $21,000 [($43,000 × .6) + (–$12,000 × .4)]. Compared with accepting the vendor's offer, litigation entails an expected loss of $4,000 ($21,000 – $25,000 settlement offer).

Answer (B) is incorrect. An $8,000 gain results if no contingent fee is charged. Answer (C) is incorrect. The expected value of litigating is $21,000. Answer (D) is incorrect. A $38,000 gain equals $63,000 ($75,000 – $12,000) minus the vendor's $25,000 offer.

15.4.2. Which tool would most likely be used to determine the best course of action under conditions of uncertainty?

A. Cost-volume-profit analysis.

B. Expected value (EV).

C. Program evaluation and review technique (PERT).

D. Scattergraph method.

Answer (B) is correct. *(CPA, adapted)*

REQUIRED: The most likely used tool to determine the best course of action.

DISCUSSION: Expected value analysis provides a rational means for selecting the best alternative in decisions involving risk. The expected value of an alternative is found by multiplying the probability of each outcome by its payoff and summing the products. It represents the long-term average payoff for repeated trials.

Answer (A) is incorrect. CVP analysis uses deterministic rather than probabilistic estimates of prices and costs to describe the effects of changes in prices, costs, sales mix, and production levels. Answer (C) is incorrect. PERT is a technique for controlling complex projects by developing network diagrams. It uses probabilistic time estimates. Answer (D) is incorrect. Scatter diagrams may be used to demonstrate correlations. Each observation creates a dot that pairs the x and y values. The linearity and slope of these observations are related to the coefficient of correlation by the previously stated rules.

15.4.3. Dough Distributors has decided to increase its daily muffin purchases by 100 boxes. A box of muffins costs $2 and sells for $3 through regular stores. Any boxes not sold through regular stores are sold through Dough's thrift store for $1. Dough assigns the following probabilities to selling additional boxes:

Additional Sales	Probability
60	.6
100	.4

What is the expected value of Dough's decision to buy 100 additional boxes of muffins?

A. $28

B. $40

C. $52

D. $68

Answer (C) is correct. *(CPA, adapted)*

REQUIRED: The expected value of Dough's decision.

DISCUSSION: The expected value is determined by multiplying the probability of each outcome by its payoff and summing the products. If Dough sells 60 boxes of muffins, the profit will be $20 [(60 boxes × $1 profit) – (40 boxes × $1 loss)]. If Dough sells 100 boxes, the profit will be $100 (100 boxes × $1 profit). The expected value is

60 boxes:	$20 × .6 =	$12
100 boxes:	$100 × .4 =	40
		$52

Answer (A) is incorrect. The difference between selling 100 boxes and selling 60 boxes is $28. Answer (B) is incorrect. The expected value of selling 100 boxes is $40. Answer (D) is incorrect. The expected value is $52.

15.4.4. Under frost-free conditions, Cal Cultivators expects its strawberry crop to have a $60,000 market value. An unprotected crop subject to frost has an expected market value of $40,000. If Cal protects the strawberries against frost, then the market value of the crop is still expected to be $60,000 under frost-free conditions and $90,000 if there is a frost. What must be the probability of a frost for Cal to be indifferent to spending $10,000 for frost protection?

A. .167

B. .200

C. .250

D. .333

Answer (B) is correct. *(CPA, adapted)*

REQUIRED: The probability of a frost to cause Cal to be indifferent.

DISCUSSION: The expected value of each outcome can be determined through the following payoff table:

	Buy Protection	Don't Buy Protection	Probability
Frost	$80,000 ($90,000 – $10,000)	$40,000	X
No frost	$50,000 ($60,000 – $10,000)	$60,000	(1 – X)

Thus, expected value (buy protection) = $80,000X + $50,000 (1 – X)
= $80,000X + $50,000 – $50,000X
= $30,000X + $50,000

Expected value (don't buy protection) = $40,000X + $60,000 (1 – X)
= $40,000X + $60,000 – $60,000X
= $60,000 – $20,000X

Cal will be indifferent for spending $10,000 for frost protection if the expected value of "buy protection" equals the expected value of "don't buy protection."

Therefore, $30,000X + 50,000 = $60,000 – $20,000X
$30,000X + $20,000X = $60,000 – $50,000
$50,000X = $10,000
X = $10,000 ÷ $50,000
X = 0.200

Answer (A) is incorrect. At a .167 probability of frost, Cal would not spend the $10,000. Answer (C) is incorrect. Cal should spend the $10,000 at a frost probability level of .250. Answer (D) is incorrect. Cal should spend the $10,000 at a frost probability level of .333.

Questions 15.4.5 through 15.4.7 are based on the following information. A beverage stand can sell either soft drinks or coffee on any given day. If the stand sells soft drinks and the weather is hot, it will make $2,500; if the weather is cold, the profit will be $1,000. If the stand sells coffee and the weather is hot, it will make $1,900; if the weather is cold, the profit will be $2,000. The probability of cold weather on a given day at this time is 60%.

15.4.5. The expected payoff if the vendor has perfect information is

A. $3,900

B. $2,200

C. $1,360

D. $1,960

Answer (B) is correct. *(CMA, adapted)*

REQUIRED: The expected payoff if the vendor has perfect information.

DISCUSSION: The vendor would like to sell coffee on cold days ($2,000) and soft drinks on hot days ($2,500). Hot days are expected 40% of the time. Hence, the probability is 40% of making $2,500 by selling soft drinks. The chance of making $2,000 by selling coffee is 60%. The payoff equation is:

Exp. payoff with perf. info. = Prob. hot (Payoff soft drinks) + Prob. cold (Payoff coffee)
= .4($2,500) + .6($2,000)
= $2,200

Answer (A) is incorrect. The most the vendor can make is $2,500 per day. Answer (C) is incorrect. The least the vendor could make by having perfect information is $2,000 on cold days. Answer (D) is incorrect. The least the vendor could make by having perfect information is $2,000 on cold days.

15.4.6. The expected payoff for selling coffee is

A. $1,360

B. $2,200

C. $3,900

D. $1,960

Answer (D) is correct. *(CMA, adapted)*

REQUIRED: The expected payoff for selling coffee.

DISCUSSION: The expected payoff calculation for coffee is

Expected payoff = Prob. hot (Payoff hot) + Prob. cold (Payoff cold)
= .4($1,900) + .6($2,000)
= $1,960

Answer (A) is incorrect. The least the company can make by selling coffee is $1,900. Answer (B) is incorrect. The most the company can make by selling coffee is $2,000. Answer (C) is incorrect. The most the company can make by selling coffee is $2,000.

15.4.7. If the probability of hot weather, given a hot weather forecast, is 50%, how much would the vendor be willing to pay for the forecast?

A. $600

B. $300

C. $1,000

D. $500

Answer (B) is correct. *(CMA, adapted)*

REQUIRED: The amount the vendor should be willing to pay for a forecast.

DISCUSSION: If the weather is hot and coffee is served, the vendor earns $1,900. If the vendor knows the weather will be hot, (s)he would sell soft drinks and make $2,500, a $600 increase. Thus, the vendor should be willing to pay up to $600 for perfect information regarding hot weather. However, if the forecasts are only 50% accurate, the information is not perfect. Accordingly, the vendor should be willing to pay only $300 (the $600 potential increase in profits × 50%) for the sometimes accurate forecasts.

Answer (A) is incorrect. The vendor would pay $600 for perfect information, but the forecasts are only 50% accurate. Answer (C) is incorrect. The most the vendor could profit from perfect information on hot days would be $600 ($2,500 – $1,900). Answer (D) is incorrect. Perfect information is worth $600, but information that is 50% accurate warrants only a $300 payment.

15.4.8. Which one of the following statements does not apply to decision tree analysis?

A. The sum of the probabilities of the events is less than one.

B. All of the events are mutually exclusive.

C. All of the events are included in the decision.

D. The branches emanate from a node from left to right.

Answer (A) is correct. *(CMA, adapted)*

REQUIRED: The statement not applicable to decision tree analysis.

DISCUSSION: In a decision tree, the events following from a decision are mutually exclusive. Also, all possible events are included. Thus, the sum of the probabilities of the events is 1.0.

Answer (B) is incorrect. With respect to decision trees, all of the events are mutually exclusive. Answer (C) is incorrect. With respect to decision trees, all of the events are included in the decision. Answer (D) is incorrect. With respect to decision trees, the branches emanate from a node from left to right.

15.4.9. Management of a company has asked the internal auditing department to assist in determining whether a new automated system should be implemented and whether the supporting software should be developed in-house, purchased, or leased. This will require evaluating a sequence of alternatives, each of which will result in different outcomes. The most effective tool the company can use to evaluate these choices would be

A. Ratio analysis.

B. Payoff tables.

C. Queuing theory.

D. Decision tree.

Answer (D) is correct. *(CIA, adapted)*

REQUIRED: The most effective tool to evaluate the choice of whether to develop, lease, or purchase software.

DISCUSSION: A decision tree is used when the most beneficial series of decisions is to be chosen. The decision maker should know the (1) possible decisions for each decision point, (2) events that might follow from each decision, (3) probabilities of these events, and (4) quantified outcomes of the events.

Answer (A) is incorrect. Ratio analysis considers only one part of the decision to be made. Ratio analysis is used to analyze costs and efficiencies. Answer (B) is incorrect. Payoff tables are used to assess a decision. Answer (C) is incorrect. Queuing theory is an approach to minimizing the costs of waiting lines.

15.4.10. A company is evaluating the following information in an effort to determine which of two products, A or B, it should manufacture during the coming year. Disregard income tax effects.

Product A		Product B	
Expected Sales	Probability (Units)	Expected Sales	Probability (Units)
7,000	.60	9,000	.75
8,000	.40	10,000	.25
	1.00		1.00

	Product A	Product B
Selling price	$ 20	$ 15
Variable cost per unit	$ 10	$ 8
Annual fixed manufacturing costs (all cash)	50,000	40,000
Annual company non-manufacturing expenses (all cash)	20,000	20,000

The company is considering engaging a market research firm to better estimate its sales. Assuming that the research firm can estimate sales with 100% accuracy, what is the value of this perfect information to the company?

A. $750

B. $2,100

C. $4,750

D. $6,850

Answer (B) is correct. *(CIA, adapted)*

REQUIRED: The value of perfect information to the company.

DISCUSSION: The expected values of making A and B are $4,000 and $4,750, respectively.

	Product A		Product B	
Units	7,000	8,000	9,000	10,000
Revenues	$140,000	$160,000	$135,000	$150,000
Variable costs	(70,000)	(80,000)	(72,000)	(80,000)
Contribution margin	$ 70,000	$ 80,000	$ 63,000	$ 70,000
Other costs	(70,000)	(70,000)	(60,000)	(60,000)
Profit	$ 0	$ 10,000	$ 3,000	$ 10,000
× Probability	× .6	× .4	× .75	× .25
= Expected value	$ 0	$ 4,000	$ 2,250	$ 2,500

The expected value of perfect information is the expected value of the decision made with perfect information ($6,850) minus the expected value of the preferred action made with existing information ($4,750), or $2,100.

(1) Possible sales estimates and related profits:

Case	Estimate	Product Made	Profit
1	A, 7,000; B, 9,000	B	$ 3,000
2	A, 8,000; B, 9,000	A	10,000
3	A, 7,000; B, 10,000	B	10,000
4	A, 8,000; B, 10,000	A or B	10,000

(2) Expected value with perfect information:

1	.6 × .75 = .45 ×	$ 3,000	=	$ 1,350
2	.4 × .75 = .30 ×	10,000	=	3,000
3	.6 × .25 = .15 ×	10,000	=	1,500
4	.4 × .25 = .10 ×	10,000	=	1,000
				$6,850

Answer (A) is incorrect. The amount of $750 is the expected value of A minus the expected value of B. Answer (C) is incorrect. The amount of $4,750 is the expected value of B. Answer (D) is incorrect. The amount of $6,850 is the expected value with perfect information.

Questions 15.4.11 and 15.4.12 are based on the following information.

Bilco Oil Company currently sells three grades of gasoline: regular, premium, and regular plus, which is a mixture of regular and premium. Regular plus is advertised as being at least 50% premium. Although any mixture containing 50% or more premium gas could be sold as regular plus, it is less costly to use exactly 50%. The percentage of premium gas in the mixture is determined by one small valve in the blending machine. If the valve is properly adjusted, the machine provides a mixture that is 50% premium and 50% regular. Assume that, if the valve is out of adjustment, the machine provides a mixture that is 60% premium and 40% regular.

Once the machine is started, it must continue until 100,000 gallons of regular plus have been mixed. Cost data available:

Cost per gallon -- premium	$.32
-- regular	$.30
Cost of checking the valve	$80.00
Cost of adjusting the valve	$40.00

Subjective estimates of the probabilities of the valve's condition are estimated to be

Event	Probability
Valve in adjustment	.7
Valve out of adjustment	.3

15.4.11. The conditional cost of not checking the valve when it is out of adjustment is

A. $80

B. $200

C. $120

D. $320

Answer (B) is correct. *(CMA, adapted)*

REQUIRED: The conditional cost of not checking the valve when it is out of adjustment.

DISCUSSION: The conditional cost is the difference between the cost of the fuel if the valve works properly ($31,000) and the cost if it does not ($31,200), a difference of $200.

100,000 × $.30 × .5	=	$15,000
100,000 × $.32 × .5	=	16,000
Cost when in adjustment		$31,000
100,000 × $.30 × .4	=	$12,000
100,000 × $.32 × .6	=	19,200
Cost out of adjustment		$31,200

Answer (A) is incorrect. The amount of $80 is the cost of checking the valve. Answer (C) is incorrect. The amount of $120 is the expected cost of checking and adjusting the valve. Answer (D) is incorrect. The amount of $320 equals the conditional cost of not checking the valve when it is out of adjustment, plus the cost of checking the valve, plus the cost of adjusting the valve.

15.4.12. Using the criterion of minimum expected cost, the valve should not be checked unless the probability that the valve is out of adjustment falls in the range of

A. 13 – .2499 inclusive.

B. 25 – .3799 inclusive.

C. 38 – .4999 inclusive.

D. 50 – 1.00 inclusive.

Answer (D) is correct. *(CMA, adapted)*

REQUIRED: The range of probability that justifies checking the valve.

DISCUSSION: Given that P is the probability of maladjustment, the expected cost of not checking a maladjusted valve is $200P*. The cost of checking is $80, and the expected cost of a needed adjustment is $40P. If the expected cost of not checking is equated with the expected cost of checking and adjusting ($200P = $80 + $40P), P is .5. The cost of checking the valve assuming a 50% chance of adjustment is $100 [$80 + ($40 × .5)]. The expected cost of not checking is $100 ($200 × .5). For any value of P greater than .5, the expected cost of not checking exceeds the expected cost of checking the valve, so .5 is the lowest value of P for which the valve should be tested.

*The expected cost of not checking a maladjusted valve is the difference between the cost of the fuel if the valve works properly ($31,000) and the cost if it does not ($31,200), a difference of $200.

100,000 × $.30 × .5	=	$15,000
100,000 × $.32 × .5	=	16,000
Cost when in adjustment		$31,000
100,000 × $.30 × .4	=	$12,000
100,000 × $.32 × .6	=	19,200
Cost out of adjustment		$31,200

Answer (A) is incorrect. For example, if P is .25, the cost of checking the valve is $90, which is more costly than the $50 cost of not checking it. Answer (B) is incorrect. For example, if P is .38, the cost of checking the valve is $95.20, which is more costly than the $76 cost of not checking it. Answer (C) is incorrect. For a value of P less than .5, checking the valve is more costly than not checking it.

15.4.13. A firm must decide whether to introduce a new product A or B. There is no time to obtain experimental information; a decision has to be made now. Expected sales can be classified as weak, moderate, or strong. How many different payoffs are possible in a decision tree under these circumstances?

A. Two.

B. Three.

C. Five.

D. Six.

Answer (D) is correct. *(CIA, adapted)*

REQUIRED: The number of different payoffs possible in a decision tree.

DISCUSSION: A decision tree displays (1) the possible decisions, (2) the events or states of nature that might follow from each decision, (3) the probabilities of these events, and (4) the quantified outcomes (payoffs) of the events. Given two possible decisions (A or B) and three events (low, medium, or high demand) that might follow each decision, six outcomes or payoffs are possible.

Answer (A) is incorrect. Two equals the number of decisions. Answer (B) is incorrect. Three equals the possible states of nature. Answer (C) is incorrect. Five equals the sum of two decisions and three states of nature.

15.4.14. The legal department of a firm prepared the following decision tree for a possible patent infringement suit.

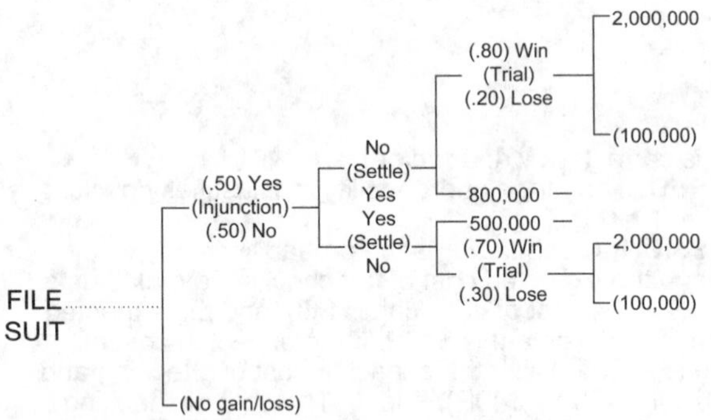

Based on the decision tree, the firm should

A. Not file the suit.

B. File suit; settle if injunction granted.

C. File suit; settle if injunction not granted.

D. Carry suit to trial.

Answer (D) is correct. *(CIA, adapted)*

REQUIRED: The action that should be taken based on the decision tree.

DISCUSSION: To solve this problem, expected outcomes for all possibilities must be computed. If the suit is filed, and an injunction granted, the following expected outcomes exist:

$$\begin{aligned} E(\text{Trial}) &= 0.5 \times [(0.8 \times \$2{,}000{,}000) + (0.2 \times -\$100{,}000)] \\ &= \$790{,}000 \\ E(\text{Settle}) &= 0.5 \times \$800{,}000 \\ &= \$400{,}000 \end{aligned}$$

If the suit is filed, but the injunction is not granted, the following expected outcomes exist:

$$\begin{aligned} E(\text{Trial}) &= 0.5 \times [(0.7 \times \$2{,}000{,}000) + (0.3 \times -\$100{,}000)] \\ &= \$685{,}000 \\ E(\text{Settle}) &= 0.5 \times \$500{,}000 \\ &= \$250{,}000 \end{aligned}$$

All outcomes are positive, so the suit should be filed. Moreover, because the expected outcomes are greater, the suit should be taken to trial.

Answer (A) is incorrect. Not filing results in no gain. Answer (B) is incorrect. Going to trial always has a higher expected value than settlement. Answer (C) is incorrect. Going to trial always has a higher expected value than settlement.

15.4.15. A local charitable organization orders and sells Christmas trees to raise funds. It wants to know the optimal quantity to order. Any merchandise not sold will be discarded without scrap value. This is an example of a single-period inventory model that is solved using

A. Economic order quantity (EOQ).

B. Payoff tables.

C. Materials requirements planning (MRP).

D. Game theory.

Answer (B) is correct. *(CIA, adapted)*

REQUIRED: The quantitative method for solving a single-period inventory model.

DISCUSSION: Payoff table analysis is appropriate for single-period inventory. A payoff table performs the same function as a decision tree by relating possible decisions, events that follow those decisions, and the quantified outcomes (payoffs) of the events.

Answer (A) is incorrect. EOQ models assume a nearly constant demand. Answer (C) is incorrect. MRP applies to dependent-demand inventories. Answer (D) is incorrect. Game theory is a mathematical approach to decision making in which each decision maker considers the action of competitors.

STUDY UNIT SIXTEEN
REGRESSION ANALYSIS

Correlation analysis measures the strength of the linear relationship between two or more variables. Correlation between two variables is represented by plotting their values on a graph to form a scatter diagram. If the points tend to form a straight line, correlation is high. The **coefficient of correlation** ($-1.0 \le r \le 1.0$) measures the relative strength of the linear relationship. The **coefficient of determination** (r^2) is the coefficient of correlation squared. It is the portion of the total variation in the dependent variable (y) explained by the regression equation.

Regression analysis extends correlation to find an equation for the linear relationship among variables. The behavior of the dependent variable (such as a cost) is explained in terms of one or more independent variables (such as a cost driver or drivers). Thus, regression analysis determines functional relationships among quantitative variables. The following is the simple regression equation:

$$y = a + bx + e$$

If: y = dependent variable
a = y-axis intercept (fixed cost in cost functions)
b = slope of the regression line (variable cost in cost functions)
x = independent variable
e = error term (the residual or disturbance term)

The **high-low method** is used to generate a regression line by basing the equation on only the highest and lowest of a series of observations. **Forecasts** are the basis for business plans, including budgets. Many quantitative methods are used to project the future from past experience. Examples of forecasts include sales projections, inventory demand, cash flow, and future capital needs. Computer models often are used in the forecasting process to simulate real-world conditions.

QUESTIONS

16.1 Correlation Analysis

16.1.1. Correlation is a term frequently used in conjunction with regression analysis and is measured by the value of the coefficient of correlation, r. The best explanation of the value r is that it

A. Is always positive.

B. Interprets variances in terms of the independent variable.

C. Ranges in size from negative infinity to positive infinity.

D. Is a measure of the relative relationship between two variables.

Answer (D) is correct. *(CMA, adapted)*

REQUIRED: The best explanation of the coefficient of correlation (r).

DISCUSSION: The coefficient of correlation (r) measures the strength of the linear relationship between the dependent and independent variables. The magnitude of r is independent of the scales of measurement of x and y. The coefficient lies between –1.0 and +1.0. A value of zero indicates no linear relationship between the x and y variables. A value of +1.0 indicates a perfectly direct relationship, and a value of –1.0 indicates a perfectly inverse relationship.

Answer (A) is incorrect. The coefficient is negative if the relationship between the variables is inverse. Answer (B) is incorrect. The coefficient relates the two variables to each other. Answer (C) is incorrect. The size of the coefficient varies between –1.0 and +1.0.

16.1.2. Quality control programs employ many tools for problem definition and analysis. A scatter diagram is one of these tools. The objective of a scatter diagram is to

A. Display a population of items for analysis.

B. Show frequency distribution in graphic form.

C. Divide a universe of data into homogeneous groups.

D. Show the vital trend and separate trivial items.

Answer (A) is correct. *(CIA, adapted)*

REQUIRED: The objective of a scatter diagram.

DISCUSSION: The objective of a scatter diagram is to demonstrate correlations. Each observation is represented by a dot on a graph corresponding to a particular value of x (the independent variable) and y (the dependent variable).

Answer (B) is incorrect. The objective of a histogram is to show frequency distribution in graphic form. Answer (C) is incorrect. The objective of stratification is to divide data into homogeneous groups. Answer (D) is incorrect. Regression analysis is used to find trend lines.

16.1.3. If the coefficient of correlation between two variables is zero, how might a scatter diagram of these variables appear?

A. Random points.

B. A least squares line that slopes up to the right.

C. A least squares line that slopes down to the right.

D. Under this condition, a scatter diagram could not be plotted on a graph.

Answer (A) is correct. *(CPA, adapted)*

REQUIRED: The scatter diagram if the coefficient of correlation is zero.

DISCUSSION: Each observation creates a point that represents x and y values. The collinearity of these relationships and slope of the observations are visible. If the coefficient of correlation is zero, there is no relationship between the variables, and the points will be randomly distributed.

Answer (B) is incorrect. It describes a direct (positive) relationship. Answer (C) is incorrect. It describes an inverse (negative) relationship. Answer (D) is incorrect. The points could be plotted on a scattergram, although it would have no meaning other than to confirm the lack of linear relationship between the variables.

16.1.4. In regression analysis, which of the following coefficients of correlation represents the strongest linear relationship between the independent and dependent variables?

A. 1.03

B. –.02

C. –.89

D. .75

Answer (C) is correct. *(CIA, adapted)*

REQUIRED: The correlation coefficient with the strongest relationship between independent and dependent variables.

DISCUSSION: A coefficient of –1.0 signifies a perfect inverse relationship, and a coefficient of 1.0 signifies a perfect direct relationship. Thus, the higher the absolute value of the coefficient of correlation, the stronger the linear relationship. A coefficient of –.89 suggests a very strong inverse relationship between the independent and dependent variables.

Answer (A) is incorrect. A coefficient of 1.03 is impossible. Answer (B) is incorrect. A coefficient of –.02 is very weak. Answer (D) is incorrect. A coefficient of .75 is .25 from the maximum, whereas –.89 is only .11 from the minimum.

16.1.5. Using regression analysis, Fairfield Co. graphed the following relationship of its cheapest product line's sales with its customers' income levels:

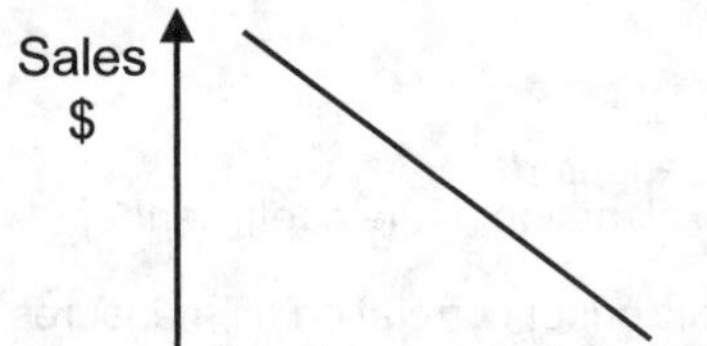

If there is a strong statistical relationship between the sales and customers' income levels, which of the following numbers best represents the correlation coefficient for this relationship?

A. –9.00

B. –0.93

C. +0.93

D. +9.00

Answer (B) is correct. *(CPA, adapted)*

REQUIRED: The correlation coefficient for this relationship.

DISCUSSION: The coefficient of correlation measures the relative strength of the linear relationship. The range of the coefficient (r) is –1.0 through +1.0. The value of –1.0 indicates a perfectly inverse linear relationship between x and y (i.e., as x increases, y decreases), a value of zero indicates no linear relationship between x and y, and a value of +1.0 indicates a perfectly direct relationship between x and y. Because Fairfield's sales decrease as income levels increase, the inverse linear relationship is very strong. This inverse relationship is best represented by –.93.

Answer (A) is incorrect. This figure falls outside of the coefficient of correlation's range. Answer (C) is incorrect. This figure represents a direct relationship between x and y. Answer (D) is incorrect. This figure falls outside of the coefficient of correlation's range.

16.1.6. The coefficient of correlation between direct materials cost and units produced is nearest

A. –0.75

B. 0.50

C. 0.0

D. 1.00

Answer (D) is correct. *(CIA, adapted)*

REQUIRED: The coefficient of correlation between direct materials cost and units produced.

DISCUSSION: The coefficient of correlation measures the relative strength of the linear relationship between two variables. It varies from –1.00 for a perfectly inverse relationship to 1.00 for a perfectly direct relationship. The number of units produced is strongly and directly related to direct materials cost. Thus, a coefficient of 1.00 best indicates the relationship.

Answer (A) is incorrect. A negative correlation coefficient indicates an inverse relationship between two variables. Answer (B) is incorrect. A correlation coefficient of 0.50 indicates some relationship between the two variables but not one as strong as that between direct materials and units produced. Answer (C) is incorrect. A value of zero indicates no linear relationship between the two variables.

16.1.7. To determine the best cost driver of warranty costs relating to glass breakage during shipments, Wymer Co. used simple linear regression analysis to study the relationship between warranty costs and each of the following variables: type of packaging, quantity shipped, type of carrier, and distance shipped. The analysis yielded the following statistics:

Independent Variable	Coefficient of Determination	Standard Error of Regression
Type of packaging	0.60	1,524
Quantity shipped	0.48	1,875
Type of carrier	0.45	2,149
Distance shipped	0.20	4,876

Based on these analyses, the best driver of warranty costs for glass breakage is

A. Type of packaging.

B. Quantity shipped.

C. Type of carrier.

D. Distance shipped.

Answer (A) is correct. *(CPA, adapted)*

REQUIRED: The best driver of warranty costs for glass breakage.

DISCUSSION: The best cost driver (independent variable) is the one that is most closely related to the incurrence of the cost. This is indicated by a high coefficient of determination (the proportion of the total variation of the dependent variable, or warranty costs, explained by the regression equation) and a low standard error of regression (the tightness of fit between the raw data and the regression equation). For glass breakage, the type of packaging is the best cost driver because it has both the highest coefficient of determination and the lowest standard error of regression.

Answer (B) is incorrect. Quantity shipped has a lower coefficient of determination and a higher standard error of regression than type of packaging. Answer (C) is incorrect. Type of carrier has a lower coefficient of determination and a higher standard error of regression than type of packaging. Answer (D) is incorrect. Distance shipped has a lower coefficient of determination and a higher standard error of regression than type of packaging.

16.1.8. The internal auditor of a bank has developed a multiple regression model which has been used for a number of years to estimate the amount of interest income from commercial loans. During the current year, the auditor applies the model and discovers that the r^2 value has decreased dramatically, but the model otherwise seems to be working okay. Which of the following conclusions are justified by the change?

A. Changing to a cross-sectional regression analysis should cause r^2 to increase.

B. Regression analysis is no longer an appropriate technique to estimate interest income.

C. Some new factors, not included in the model, are causing interest income to change.

D. A linear regression analysis would increase the model's reliability.

Answer (C) is correct. *(CIA, adapted)*

REQUIRED: The implication of the decrease in r^2.

DISCUSSION: The coefficient of determination (r^2) is the amount of variation in the dependent variable (interest income) that is explained by the independent variables. In this case, less of the change in interest income is explained by the model. Thus, some other factor must be causing interest income to change. This change merits audit investigation.

Answer (A) is incorrect. Cross-sectional regression analysis is inappropriate. The auditor is trying to estimate changes in a single account balance over time. Answer (B) is incorrect. Regression analysis may still be the most appropriate methodology to estimate interest income, but the auditor should first understand the factors that may be causing r^2 to decrease. The reason may be a systematic error in the account balance. Answer (D) is incorrect. Linear regression models are simpler models, but the auditor should be searching for a systematic error in the account balance or applying a more complex model.

16.1.9. A firm regressed overhead on units produced over the past year and found a coefficient of determination equal to 0.85 with a U-shaped residual error pattern. It is reasonable to conclude that the relationship between overhead and units produced is

A. Weak.

B. Causal.

C. Nonlinear.

D. Linear.

Answer (C) is correct. *(CIA, adapted)*

REQUIRED: The relationship between overhead and units produced.

DISCUSSION: A coefficient of determination measures the proportion of the total variation in y that is explained or accounted for by the regression equation. In this case, the relationship is strong because 85% of that variation is explained. However, the relationship is curvilinear because the residual error pattern is U-shaped. The residual error pattern consists of the plots of the estimates of the error term in the linear regression equation.

Answer (A) is incorrect. The relationship is strong (coefficient of determination = .85). Answer (B) is incorrect. Regression analysis measures the strength of the relationship among variables, but it does not establish causation. Answer (D) is incorrect. The U-shaped residual error pattern reflects a nonlinear relationship.

16.1.10. An auditor asks accounting personnel how they determine the value of the organization's real estate holdings. They say that valuations are based on a regression model that uses 17 different characteristics of the properties (square footage, proximity to downtown, age, etc.) to predict value. The coefficients of this model were estimated using a random sample of 20 company properties, for which the model produced an r^2 value of 0.92. Based on this information, which one of the following should the auditor conclude?

A. The model's high r^2 is probably due in large part to random chance.

B. 92% of the variables that determine value are in the model.

C. The model is very reliable.

D. This sample of properties is probably representative of the overall population of company holdings.

Answer (A) is correct. *(CIA, adapted)*

REQUIRED: The true statement about a regression model.

DISCUSSION: The coefficient of determination (r^2) always approaches 1.0 as the number of variables in the regression approaches the number of observations in the sample (even if the predictors are unrelated to the dependent variable). This model has a very large number of predictors for the small sample size.

Answer (B) is incorrect. The true model is unknown. Accordingly, the conclusion that 92% of the variables that determine value are in the model cannot be drawn. Answer (C) is incorrect. The model has too many predictors for the small sample size. Answer (D) is incorrect. A high r^2 can occur in a bad sample with a bad model just as easily as in a good sample and a good model.

16.1.11. Sago Co. uses regression analysis to develop a model for predicting overhead costs. Two different cost drivers (machine hours and direct materials weight) are under consideration as the independent variable. Relevant data were run on a computer using one of the standard regression programs, with the following results:

Machine hours	Coefficient
y-intercept	2,500
b	5.0
r^2 = .70	
Direct materials weight	
y-intercept	4,600
b	2.6
r^2 = .50	

Which regression equation should be used?

A. y = 2,500 + 5.0x

B. y = 2,500 + 3.5x

C. y = 4,600 + 2.6x

D. y = 4,600 + 1.3x

Answer (A) is correct. *(CPA, adapted)*

REQUIRED: The regression equation.

DISCUSSION: The simple regression equation is y = a + bx, given that y is the dependent variable, a is the y-axis intercept, b is the slope of the regression line, and x is the independent variable. The coefficient of determination (r^2) is the appropriate tool for determining which cost driver to use because the value of r^2 indicates the proportion of the total variation in y that is explained by the regression equation. Since machine hours has a higher r^2 than direct materials weight, the coefficients for machine hours are the better choice to predict costs. Consequently, the regression equation is y = 2,500 + 5.0x.

Answer (B) is incorrect. The equation y = 2,500 + 3.5x incorrectly multiplies the slope by r^2. Answer (C) is incorrect. Machine hours has a higher r^2 than direct materials. Answer (D) is incorrect. The machine hours coefficients should be used to predict overhead costs.

16.1.12. If regression analysis is applied to the data shown below, the coefficients of correlation and determination will indicate the existence of a

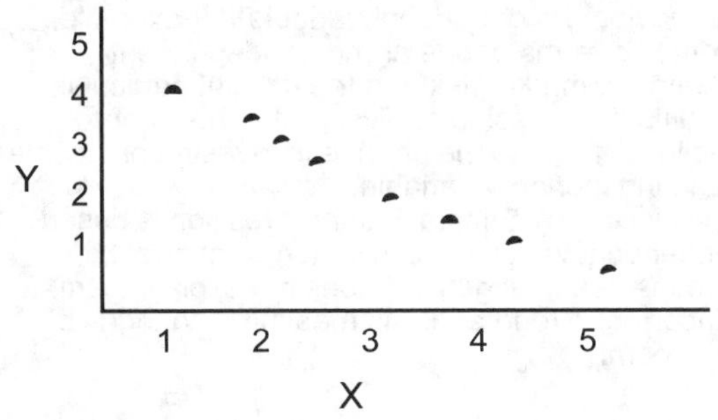

A. Low linear relationship, high explained variation ratio.

B. High inverse linear relationship, high explained variation ratio.

C. High direct linear relationship, high explained variation ratio.

D. High inverse linear relationship, low explained variation ratio.

Answer (B) is correct. *(CIA, adapted)*

REQUIRED: The implications of the scatter diagram regarding the coefficients of correlation and determination.

DISCUSSION: The coefficient of correlation measures the degree and direction of the linear relationship between two or more variables. The relationship is from perfectly inverse (–1) to perfectly direct (1). If no relationship exists, the coefficient of correlation is 0. The coefficient of determination is the portion of the variance of the dependent variable explained by the independent variable. It equals the coefficient of correlation squared (r^2). Given that the plotted points are almost in a straight line with a negative slope, the coefficient of correlation is almost –1, and the coefficient of determination is nearly +1.

16.2 Regression (Least Squares) Analysis

16.2.1. Multiple regression differs from simple regression in that it

A. Provides an estimated constant term.

B. Has more dependent variables.

C. Allows the computation of the coefficient of determination.

D. Has more independent variables.

Answer (D) is correct. *(CPA, adapted)*

REQUIRED: The difference between multiple and simple regression.

DISCUSSION: Improved accuracy of forecasts may often be achieved by regressing the dependent variable on more than one independent variable. The usual multiple regression equation is linear and is in the following form when y is the dependent variable; a is the y-axis intercept; x_1, x_2, etc., are the independent variables; b_1, b_2, etc., are the coefficients of the independent variables; and e is the error term:

$$y = a + b_1x_1 + b_2x_2 + ... + e$$

Answer (A) is incorrect. Both equations have a constant y-axis intercept. Answer (B) is incorrect. Both equations explain the behavior of a single dependent variable. Answer (C) is incorrect. The coefficient of determination (r^2), or the coefficient of correlation squared, may be interpreted as the proportion of the total variation in y that is explained or accounted for by the regression equation. Thus, r^2 may be calculated for both simple and multiple regressions.

16.2.2. Simple linear regression is a method applied when the underlying relationship between two variables is believed to be linear. The least squares process estimates this hypothesized true relationship by minimizing the sum of squared errors of the observations in a sample about a fitted line. Which equation represents the underlying true relationship between variables?

A. $y = a + x$

B. $y = a + bx$

C. $y = a + bx + e$

D. $y = a + bx^2 + e$

Answer (C) is correct. *(Publisher, adapted)*

REQUIRED: The equation for the true relationship between variables.

DISCUSSION: The equation is based on application of regression analysis to observations of the independent variable x and the dependent variable y. The result equates y (the dependent variable) with the sum of a (the y-intercept), bx (b is the slope and x is the independent variable), and e (an error term). The error term indicates the degree of uncertainty.

Answer (A) is incorrect. An error term should be included. Answer (B) is incorrect. An error term should be included. Answer (D) is incorrect. A simple regression should be a linear function.

16.2.3. The auditor wishes to determine if the change in investment income during the current year was due to (a) changes in investment strategy, (b) changes in portfolio mix, or (c) other factors. Which of the following analytical review procedures should the auditor use?

A. Simple linear regression that compares investment income changes over the past 5 years to determine the nature of the changes.

B. Ratio analysis that compares changes in the investment portfolio on a monthly basis.

C. Trend analysis that compares the changes in investment income as a percentage of total assets and of investment assets over the past 5 years.

D. Multiple regression analysis that includes independent variables related to the nature of the investment portfolio and market conditions.

Answer (D) is correct. *(CIA, adapted)*

REQUIRED: The analytical procedure for determining the reason for the change in investment income.

DISCUSSION: Regression analysis develops an equation to explain the behavior of a dependent variable (for example, investment income) in terms of one or more independent variables (for example, market risk and the risks of particular investments). Multiple regression analysis is the best approach. It allows the auditor to regress the change in investment income on more than one independent variable.

Answer (A) is incorrect. Simple linear regression is based on just one independent variable. Answer (B) is incorrect. Ratio analysis measures changes but does not explain them. Answer (C) is incorrect. Trend analysis measures changes but does not explain them.

Questions 16.2.4 through 16.2.8 are based on the following information. The usual formula for the simple regression equation is $y = a + bx + e$.

16.2.4. The dependent variable is

A. a.

B. y.

C. b.

D. x.

Answer (B) is correct. *(Publisher, adapted)*

REQUIRED: The symbol for the dependent variable in the regression equation.

DISCUSSION: The dependent variable in the regression equation is the item to be estimated (or calculated or predicted), i.e., y. In regression analysis, the objective is to predict a value of one variable (dependent) in terms of the values of one or more other variables (independent).

Answer (A) is incorrect. Variable a is the y-axis intercept. Answer (C) is incorrect. Variable b is the slope of the line. Answer (D) is incorrect. Variable x is the independent variable.

16.2.5. The y-axis intercept is

A. a.

B. b.

C. x.

D. e.

Answer (A) is correct. *(Publisher, adapted)*

REQUIRED: The symbol for the y-axis intercept in the regression equation.

DISCUSSION: The y-axis intercept is equal to a in the equation. If the relevant range includes zero volume, a is a fixed cost in the usual cost function. It is the expected value of y when x is zero, provided that it is within the relevant range of the sample. The relevant range of the regression analysis is the portion of the least squares line between the minimum and maximum values of the independent variable. The predictive ability of regression should be limited to this region.

Answer (B) is incorrect. Variable b is the slope of the line. Answer (C) is incorrect. Variable x is the independent variable. Answer (D) is incorrect. Variable e is the error term.

16.2.6. The slope of the line is

A. y.

B. b.

C. x.

D. e.

Answer (B) is correct. *(Publisher, adapted)*

REQUIRED: The symbol for the slope of the line in the regression equation.

DISCUSSION: The slope of a line is a constant equal to the proportionate change along the y-axis for each change along the x-axis. Thus, in a regression equation, slope is the variable portion of the total cost in the cost function, i.e., the change in cost that occurs for each one-unit change in activity.

Answer (A) is incorrect. Variable y is the dependent variable. Answer (C) is incorrect. Variable x is the independent variable. Answer (D) is incorrect. Variable e is the error term.

16.2.7. The independent variable is

A. a.

B. y.

C. b.

D. x.

Answer (D) is correct. *(Publisher, adapted)*

REQUIRED: The symbol for an independent variable in the regression equation.

DISCUSSION: The independent or explanatory variable (x) is the variable that is permitted to change. These changes are used to predict values of the dependent variable (y).

Answer (A) is incorrect. Variable a is the y-axis intercept. Answer (B) is incorrect. Variable y is the dependent variable. Answer (C) is incorrect. Variable b is the slope of the line.

16.2.8. The error term is

A. a.

B. y.

C. b.

D. e.

Answer (D) is correct. *(Publisher, adapted)*

REQUIRED: The symbol for the error term in the regression equation.

DISCUSSION: The error term in the equation is e. The error term is usually assumed to have a mean of zero in linear regression, thereby permitting calculations using the formula $y = a + bx$.

Answer (A) is incorrect. Variable a is the y-axis intercept. Answer (B) is incorrect. Variable y is the dependent variable. Answer (C) is incorrect. Variable b is the slope of the line.

16.2.9. Which equation represents the least squares estimates of the relationship between variables? Let ^ denote a least squares estimate of a value.

A. $y = \hat{a} + \hat{b} + x$

B. $\hat{y} = \hat{a} + \hat{b}x + e$

C. $\hat{y} = \hat{a} + \hat{b}x$

D. $y = \hat{a} + \hat{b}x^2$

Answer (C) is correct. *(Publisher, adapted)*

REQUIRED: The equation for a least squares estimate.

DISCUSSION: The least squares estimate has no provision for the error term. The error term is incorporated in the standard error of the estimate. An estimate of y is based on estimates of both a and b. Least squares estimates are deterministic, not probabilistic, estimates of the variable, so no error term should be included.

Answer (A) is incorrect. Variable b is the slope of the line. Answer (B) is incorrect. The equation should include no error term. Answer (D) is incorrect. The estimated relationship should be linear.

16.2.10. In determining cost behavior in business, the cost function is often expressed as $y = a + bx$. Which one of the following cost estimation methods should not be used in estimating fixed and variable costs for the equation?

A. Graphic method.

B. Simple regression.

C. High- and low-point method.

D. Multiple regression.

Answer (D) is correct. *(CMA, adapted)*

REQUIRED: The cost estimation method that should not be used to generate a function expressed as $y = a + bx$.

DISCUSSION: Regression analysis can be used to find an equation for the linear relationship among variables. However, multiple regression is not used to generate an equation of the type $y = a + bx$ because multiple regression has more than one independent variable. In other words, a multiple regression equation would take the form $y = a + b_1x_1 + b_2x_2 + b_3x_3 + \ldots$.

Answer (A) is incorrect. The graphic approach can be used to estimate a linear function. Answer (B) is incorrect. Simple regression, which is based on one independent variable, is the best means of expressing a linear cost function. Answer (C) is incorrect. The high-low method, although unsophisticated, can often give a good approximation of a linear cost function.

16.2.11. Autocorrelation or serial correlation

A. Defines the portion of the variance explained by the independent variable.

B. Means that observations are not independent.

C. Means that independent variables are correlated with each other.

D. Is the failure of random samples to represent the population.

Answer (B) is correct. *(Publisher, adapted)*

REQUIRED: The true statement about autocorrelation.

DISCUSSION: Autocorrelation and serial correlation are synonyms meaning that the observations are not independent. For example, certain costs may rise with an increase in volume but not decline with a decrease in volume.

Answer (A) is incorrect. The coefficient of determination is the portion of the variance explained by the independent variable. Answer (C) is incorrect. Multicollinearity means that independent variables are correlated with each other. Answer (D) is incorrect. Bias is the failure of random samples to represent the population.

16.2.12. Multicollinearity occurs when

A. A portion of the variance is explained by the independent variable.

B. Observations are not independent.

C. Independent variables are correlated with each other.

D. A random sample fails to represent the population.

Answer (C) is correct. *(Publisher, adapted)*

REQUIRED: The definition of multicollinearity.

DISCUSSION: Multicollinearity is the condition in which two or more independent variables are correlated. Thus, multicollinearity occurs only in multiple regression equations.

Answer (A) is incorrect. The coefficient of determination is the portion of the variance explained by the independent variable. Answer (B) is incorrect. Autocorrelation means that observations are not independent. Answer (D) is incorrect. Bias is the failure of random samples to represent the population.

16.2.13. Bias occurs when

A. A portion of the variance is explained by the independent variable.

B. Observations are not independent.

C. Independent variables are correlated with each other.

D. The parameters obtained from random sampling fail to represent the population.

Answer (D) is correct. *(Publisher, adapted)*

REQUIRED: The definition of bias.

DISCUSSION: Bias is the condition in which the random sample has failed to represent the population and therefore does not estimate the true parameters of the underlying data. For example, if the mean of random samples does not on average represent the true population mean, the sample mean is biased.

Answer (A) is incorrect. The coefficient of determination is the portion of the variance explained by the independent variable. Answer (B) is incorrect. Auto or serial correlation means that observations are not independent. Answer (C) is incorrect. Multicollinearity means that independent variables are correlated with each other.

16.2.14. The confidence interval for the value of y in the simple linear regression equation represents

A. A measure of variability of the actual observations from the least squares line.

B. A range of values constructed from the regression equation results for a specified level of probability.

C. A variability about the least squares line that is uniform for all values of the independent variable in the sample.

D. The portion of the variance explained by the independent variable.

Answer (B) is correct. *(Publisher, adapted)*

REQUIRED: The definition of confidence interval.

DISCUSSION: The confidence interval is a range of values constructed from the regression results that is expected to contain the true population value. It equals the estimate of y plus or minus the number of standard errors of the estimate appropriate for the desired level of confidence (probability that the interval contains the true value). Calculating the interval involves adjusting the mean for the standard deviation and the appropriate probability distribution.

Answer (A) is incorrect. The standard error of the estimate is a measure of variability of the actual observations from the least squares line. Answer (C) is incorrect. Constant variance is a variability about the least squares line that is uniform for all values of the independent variable in the sample. Answer (D) is incorrect. The coefficient of determination is the portion of the variance explained by the independent variable.

16.2.15. In a simple linear regression model, the standard error of the estimate of y represents

A. A measure of variability of the actual observations from the least squares line.

B. A range of values constructed from the regression equation results for a specified level of probability.

C. A variability about the least squares line that is uniform for all values of the independent variable in the sample.

D. The portion of the variance explained by the independent variable.

Answer (A) is correct. *(Publisher, adapted)*

REQUIRED: The definition of the standard error of the estimate.

DISCUSSION: The standard error of the estimate is variance of actual observations from the regression line. It is calculated based on the sample drawn from the population. If y_i is a data point, $\hat{y}$ is the estimate of y from the regression equation, n is the sample size, and s is the standard deviation of the sample, the standard error may be stated as follows for a simple linear regression:

$$s = \sqrt{\frac{(y_i - \hat{y})^2}{n-2}}$$

Answer (B) is incorrect. A confidence interval is a range of values constructed from the regression equation results for a specified level of probability. Answer (C) is incorrect. Constant variance is a variability about the least squares line that is uniform for all values of the independent variable in the sample. Answer (D) is incorrect. The coefficient of determination is the portion of the variance explained by the independent variable.

16.2.16. All of the following are assumptions underlying the validity of linear regression output except

A. The errors are normally distributed and their mean is zero.

B. Certainty.

C. The variance of the errors is constant.

D. The independent variables are not correlated with each other.

Answer (B) is correct. *(CMA, adapted)*

REQUIRED: The assumption that does not underlie linear regression.

DISCUSSION: Users of linear regression assume that (1) no changes occur in the environment, (2) errors are normally distributed with a mean of zero, (3) the variance of the errors is constant, and (4) the independent variables are not correlated. However, regression is only a means of predicting the future. Certainty cannot be achieved.

16.2.17. Constant variance means

A. A measure of variability of the actual observations from the least squares line.

B. A range of values constructed from the regression equation results for a specified level of probability.

C. A variability about the least squares line that is uniform for all values of the independent variable in the sample.

D. The underlying assumptions of the regression equation that are not met.

Answer (C) is correct. *(Publisher, adapted)*

REQUIRED: The definition of constant variance.

DISCUSSION: Constant variance is a uniform deviation of points from the regression line. This uniformity is based on the assumption that the distribution of the observations and errors is not affected by the values of the independent variable(s).

Answer (A) is incorrect. The standard error of the estimate is a measure of variability of the actual observations from the least squares line. Answer (B) is incorrect. A confidence interval is a range of values constructed from the regression equation results for a specified level of probability. Answer (D) is incorrect. Constant variance is one of the basic assumptions underlying regression analysis.

16.2.18. If the error term is normally distributed about zero,

A. The parameter estimates of the y-intercept and slope also have a normal distribution.

B. The estimate of the slope can be tested using a t-test.

C. The probability that the error term is greater than zero is equal to the probability that it is less than zero for any observation.

D. All of the answers are correct.

Answer (D) is correct. *(Publisher, adapted)*

REQUIRED: The true statement(s) about an error term normally distributed about zero.

DISCUSSION: This ideal situation permits t-tests (based on the t-distribution) to be performed to evaluate the significance of the estimates. For example, a confidence interval may be constructed around the estimate of the slope (b) of the regression line using the critical value of the t-statistic (based on the specified confidence level, sample size, and degrees of freedom) and the standard error of b. In other words, the interval equals b plus or minus the t-value times the standard error of b. If this interval does not include zero, the conclusion is that (1) the true slope is not zero and (2) the estimate is statistically significant (not affected solely by random factors).

Answer (A) is incorrect. The y-intercept (a) and the slope (b) are assumed to be normally distributed. Answer (B) is incorrect. The t-distribution may be used in hypothesis testing of the estimate of the slope. Answer (C) is incorrect. The mean of the error term is assumed to be zero.

16.2.19. Omaha Sales Company asked for a CPA's assistance in planning the use of multiple regression analysis to predict district sales. An equation has been estimated based upon historical data, and a standard error has been computed. When regression analysis based upon past periods is used to predict for a future period, the standard error associated with the predicted value, in relation to the standard error for the base equation, will be

A. Smaller.

B. Larger.

C. The same.

D. Larger or smaller, depending upon the circumstances.

Answer (B) is correct. *(CPA, adapted)*

REQUIRED: The relationship of the standard error associated with the predicted value to the standard error for the base equation.

DISCUSSION: The standard error associated with a predicted value is always larger because it considers two types of error. It contains the standard error of the estimate, the variability of the y values about the least squares line. But it also contains a measure (standard error of the base equation) of the extent to which the least squares line does not exactly represent the true relationship between x and y.

16.2.20. When the relationship between the independent and dependent variables is not expected to remain constant, an appropriate method of analysis is

A. Cluster analysis.

B. Simple linear regression.

C. Curvilinear regression.

D. Simplex linear programming.

Answer (C) is correct. *(CIA, adapted)*

REQUIRED: The analytical method used when the relationship between the independent and dependent variables is not expected to be constant.

DISCUSSION: Simple regression analysis involves one independent variable. Multiple regression has two or more. If the relationship among the variables can be described by a straight line, the regression is linear. Otherwise, the regression is curvilinear. Linear regression is appropriate when the relationship among the variables is constant for all variables, and curvilinear regression is used when it is not. For example, rainfall may increase crop yields up to a certain point, but excessive rain may have the opposite effect.

Answer (A) is incorrect. Cluster analysis is not meaningful in this context. Answer (B) is incorrect. A straight line indicates a constant relationship. Answer (D) is incorrect. Linear programming optimizes a revenue or cost function subject to resource constraints. The simplex method is an algorithm for finding the optimal solution.

16.2.21. An auditor used regression analysis to evaluate the relationship between utility costs and machine hours. The following information was developed using a computer software program:

Intercept	2,050
Regression coefficient	.825
Correlation coefficient	.800
Standard error of the estimate	200
Number of observations	36

What is the expected utility cost if the company's 10 machines will be used 2,400 hours next month?

A. $4,050

B. $4,030

C. $3,970

D. $3,830

Answer (B) is correct. *(CIA, adapted)*

REQUIRED: The expected utility cost.

DISCUSSION: If y is the dependent variable (utility cost), a is the y-intercept (fixed cost), b is the regression coefficient, and x is the independent variable (machine hours), the following is the basic equation for a simple regression:

$$y = a + bx$$

The expected utility cost is $4,030 [$2,050 + (.825 × 2,400)].

Answer (A) is incorrect. The amount of $4,050 equals the intercept plus 10 times the standard error. Answer (C) is incorrect. The amount of $3,970 results from using the correlation coefficient instead of the regression coefficient. Answer (D) is incorrect. The amount of $3,830 equals expected utility cost minus $200.

16.2.22. A company uses regression analysis in which monthly advertising expenses are used to predict monthly product sales, both in millions of dollars. The results show a regression coefficient for the independent variable equal to 0.8. This coefficient value indicates that

A. On average, every additional dollar of advertising results in $0.8 of additional sales.

B. Advertising is not a good predictor of sales because the coefficient is so small.

C. When monthly advertising is at its average level, product sales will be $800,000.

D. The average monthly advertising expenditure in the sample is $800,000.

Answer (A) is correct. *(CMA, adapted)*

REQUIRED: The meaning of the coefficient value.

DISCUSSION: In the standard regression equation y = a + bx, b represents the change in the dependent variable corresponding to a unit change in the independent variable. Thus, it is the slope of the regression line.

Answer (B) is incorrect. The absolute size of the coefficient bears no necessary relationship to the importance of the variable. Answer (C) is incorrect. To predict a specific value of sales, the value of the independent variable is multiplied by the coefficient. The product is then added to the y-intercept value. Answer (D) is incorrect. A regression coefficient cannot indicate the average monthly advertising expenditure.

16.3 Separating Fixed and Variable Costs

16.3.1. Thompson Company is in the process of preparing its budget for the next fiscal year. The company has had problems controlling costs in prior years and has decided to adopt a flexible budgeting system this year. Many of its costs contain both fixed and variable cost components. A method that can be used to separate costs into fixed and variable components is

A. Trend analysis.

B. Monte Carlo simulation.

C. Dynamic programming.

D. Regression analysis.

Answer (D) is correct. *(CMA, adapted)*

REQUIRED: The method used to separate costs into fixed and variable components.

DISCUSSION: The basic regression formula ($y = a + bx$) explains the behavior of a dependent variable (y) in terms of an independent variable (x). Fixed cost (a) corresponds to the value of y when x (the measure of activity) is zero. The coefficient of x is the variable cost.

Answer (A) is incorrect. Time series or trend analysis uses regression to find trend lines in data (e.g., sales or costs) for forecasting purposes. Answer (B) is incorrect. Monte Carlo simulation involves adding random numbers to otherwise deterministic models to simulate the uncertainty in real-world situations. Answer (C) is incorrect. Dynamic programming is used for problems that involve probabilistic variables and time-staged decisions, that is, decisions affected by previous decisions. It involves an iterative formulation of problems. A decision tree with probabilities for each branch illustrates a time-staged decision process that could be evaluated with dynamic programming.

16.3.2. The management of an airline is interested in the relationship between maintenance costs and the level of operations of its aircraft. Using regression analysis on cost and activity data collected over 12 months, the relationship below was estimated.

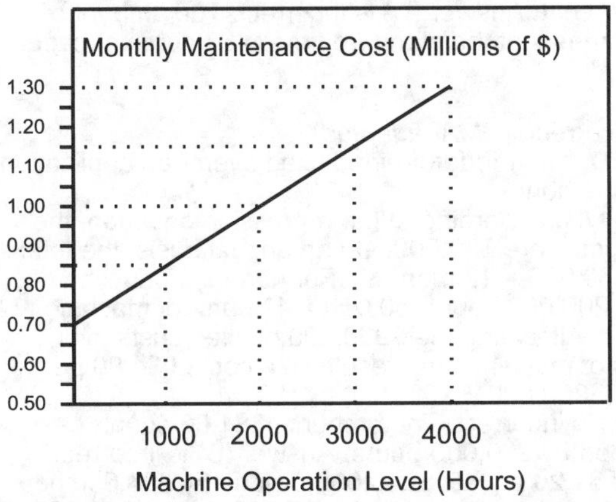

The estimated increase in the monthly maintenance cost for each additional hour of operation is

A. $150 per hour.

B. $300 per hour.

C. $450 per hour.

D. $850 per hour.

Answer (A) is correct. *(CIA, adapted)*

REQUIRED: The estimated increase in the monthly maintenance cost for each additional hour of operation.

DISCUSSION: The change in monthly maintenance cost per hour of operation is the slope of the cost function.

$$\frac{\$1,000,000 - \$850,000}{2,000 - 1,000} = \$150 \text{ per hour}$$

Answer (B) is incorrect. The amount of $300 per hour equals $1,150,000 minus $850,000, divided by 1,000 hours. Answer (C) is incorrect. The amount of $450 per hour equals $1,300,000 minus $850,000, divided by 1,000 hours. Answer (D) is incorrect. The amount of $850 per hour equals $850,000 divided by 1,000 hours.

16.3.3. Given actual amounts of a semivariable cost for various levels of output, which of the following will give the least precise mathematical measure of the fixed and variable components but be easiest to compute?

A. Bayesian statistics.

B. High-low method.

C. Scattergram approach.

D. Least squares method.

Answer (B) is correct. *(Publisher, adapted)*

REQUIRED: The quantitative method that most easily but least precisely separates fixed and variable costs.

DISCUSSION: The high-low method uses only two observations, a representative high point and a representative low point, to determine the slope of the line defining the relationship between activity and the variable cost. Thus, it is susceptible to error but is easy to compute.

Answer (A) is incorrect. Bayesian statistics is a method that bases future probabilities on past probabilities and occurrences. Answer (C) is incorrect. A scatter diagram may be used to estimate correlations, but it is not a mathematical approach. Answer (D) is incorrect. The least squares method is much more precise than the high-low method.

Questions 16.3.4 and 16.3.5 are based on the following information. The Mulvey Company derived the following cost relationship from a regression analysis of its monthly manufacturing overhead cost.

$$C = \$80{,}000 + \$12M$$

If: C = monthly manufacturing overhead cost
M = machine hours

The standard error of the estimate of the regression is $6,000. The standard time required to manufacture one six-unit case of Mulvey's single product is 4 machine hours. Mulvey applies manufacturing overhead to production on the basis of machine hours, and its normal annual production is 50,000 cases.

16.3.4. Mulvey's estimated variable manufacturing overhead cost for a month in which scheduled production is 5,000 cases will be

A. $80,000

B. $320,000

C. $240,000

D. $360,000

Answer (C) is correct. *(CMA, adapted)*

REQUIRED: The estimated variable manufacturing overhead for a month given production volume.

DISCUSSION: Each case requires 4 hours of machine time. Thus, 5,000 cases require 20,000 hours (5,000 cases × 4 hours). At $12 per hour, the variable costs total $240,000 ($12 × 20,000 hours).

Answer (A) is incorrect. The amount of $80,000 equals the fixed cost. Answer (B) is incorrect. The amount of $320,000 equals the total cost. Answer (D) is incorrect. The amount of $360,000 assumes that the standard time is 6 hours per case.

16.3.5. Mulvey's predetermined fixed manufacturing overhead rate would be

A. $1.60 per machine hour.

B. $1.20 per machine hour.

C. $4.00 per machine hour.

D. $4.80 per machine hour.

Answer (D) is correct. *(CMA, adapted)*

REQUIRED: The predetermined fixed overhead application rate per machine hour.

DISCUSSION: According to the regression equation, the monthly fixed costs are $80,000. On an annual basis, the total is $960,000 ($80,000 × 12 months). For normal production of 50,000 cases, 200,000 hours (50,000 × 4 hours) of machine time is required. Allocating the $960,000 of fixed costs over 200,000 hours of machine time results in a cost of $4.80 per machine hour ($960,000 ÷ 200,000).

Answer (A) is incorrect. The amount of $1.60 equals $320,000 divided by 200,000 hours. Answer (B) is incorrect. The amount of $1.20 equals $240,000 divided by 200,000 hours. Answer (C) is incorrect. The amount of $4.00 equals $80,000 divided by 20,000 hours.

16.3.6. A corporation wishes to determine the fixed portion of its maintenance expense (a semivariable expense), as measured against direct labor hours, for the first 3 months of the year. The inspection costs are fixed; the adjustments necessitated by errors found during inspection account for the variable portion of the maintenance costs. Information for the first quarter is as follows:

	Direct Labor Hours	Maintenance Expense
January	34,000	$610
February	31,000	$585
March	34,000	$610

What is the fixed portion of maintenance expense, rounded to the nearest dollar?

A. $283

B. $327

C. $258

D. $541

Answer (B) is correct. *(Publisher, adapted)*

REQUIRED: The fixed portion of expense as measured against direct labor hours.

DISCUSSION: The high-low method can be used to determine the fixed and variable cost components of a mixed cost. The variable cost is found by dividing the change in total cost (TC) by the change in activity, e.g., DLH. The fixed cost is found by substituting the variable cost into either of the activity or cost functions. Alternatively, the fixed cost is the cost given a zero level of activity.

Variable portion = Change in TC ÷ Change in DLH = $25 ÷ 3,000 = $.00833

Fixed portion = Total cost – Variable portion
Fixed portion = $585 – (31,000 × $.00833) = $327
Fixed portion = $610 – (34,000 × $.00833) = $327

Answer (A) is incorrect. Variable cost for January or March equals $283. Answer (C) is incorrect. Variable cost for February equals $258. Answer (D) is incorrect. Variable cost for February and March equals $541.

16.4 Other Forecasting Methods

16.4.1. To facilitate planning and budgeting, management of a travel service company wants to develop forecasts of monthly sales for the next 24 months. Based on past data, management has observed an upward trend in the level of sales. There are also seasonal variations with high sales in June, July, and August, and low sales in January, February, and March. An appropriate technique for forecasting the company's sales is

A. Time series analysis.

B. Queuing theory.

C. Linear programming.

D. Sensitivity analysis.

Answer (A) is correct. *(CIA, adapted)*

REQUIRED: The appropriate forecasting method.

DISCUSSION: In time series analysis, the dependent variable is regressed on time (the independent variable). The secular trend is the long-term change that occurs in the series. It is represented by a straight line or curve on a graph. Various methods include seasonal variations in this forecasting model, but most adjust data by a seasonal index.

Answer (B) is incorrect. Queuing theory minimizes the sum of the costs of waiting in line and servicing waiting lines. Answer (C) is incorrect. Linear programming optimizes a given objective function subject to constraints. Answer (D) is incorrect. Sensitivity analysis studies the effects of changes in one or more variables on the results of a decision model.

16.4.2. What are the four components of a time series?

A. Trend, cyclical, seasonal, and irregular.

B. Alpha, cyclical, seasonal, and irregular.

C. Alpha, cyclical, seasonal, and repetitive.

D. Trend, cyclical, seasonal, and repetitive.

Answer (A) is correct. *(CIA, adapted)*

REQUIRED: The four components of a time series.

DISCUSSION: Time series analysis or trend analysis relies on past experience. Changes in the value of a variable (e.g., unit sales of a product) may have several possible components. In time series analysis, the dependent variable is regressed on time (the independent variable). The secular trend is the long-term change that occurs in a series. It is represented by a straight line or curve on a graph. Seasonal variations are common in many businesses. A variety of methods include seasonal variations in a forecasting model, but most methods adjust data by a seasonal index. Cyclical fluctuations are variations in the level of activity in business periods. Although some fluctuations are beyond the control of the entity, they need to be considered in forecasting. They are usually incorporated as index numbers. Irregular or random variations are any variations not included in the other categories. Business can be affected by random happenings, e.g., weather, strikes, or fires.

16.4.3. The four components of time series data are secular trend, cyclical variation, seasonality, and random variation. The seasonality in the data can be removed by

A. Multiplying the data by a seasonality factor.

B. Ignoring it.

C. Taking the weighted average over four time periods.

D. Subtracting a seasonality factor from the data.

Answer (C) is correct. *(CMA, adapted)*

REQUIRED: The means by which seasonality can be removed from time series data.

DISCUSSION: Seasonal variations are common in many businesses. Various methods exist for including seasonal variations in a forecasting model, but most divide by a seasonal index. Seasonal variations can be removed from data by using a weighted average of several time periods instead of data from individual periods.

Answer (A) is incorrect. Adding or subtracting a seasonality factor to a forecast based on trend analysis is a means of adjusting for seasonality. Answer (B) is incorrect. Seasonality factors cannot be ignored. They are reflected in the data and must be considered for a model to be accurate. Answer (D) is incorrect. The seasonality adjustment for a single season's data may be an increase or a decrease.

16.4.4. Violation of which assumption underlying regression analysis is prevalent in time series analysis?

A. Variance of error term is constant.

B. Error terms are independent.

C. Distribution of error terms is normal.

D. Expected value of error term equals zero.

Answer (B) is correct. *(Publisher, adapted)*

REQUIRED: The assumption frequently violated in time series analysis.

DISCUSSION: Time series analysis is a regression model in which the independent variable is time. In time series analysis, the value of the next time period is frequently dependent on the value of the time period before that. Thus, the error terms are usually correlated or dependent on the prior period. Thus, they are characterized by autocorrelation (serial correlation).

16.4.5. An internal auditor for a large automotive parts retailer wishes to perform a risk analysis and wants to use an appropriate statistical tool to help identify stores that are at variance with the majority of stores. The most appropriate statistical tool to use would be

A. Linear time series analysis.

B. Cross-sectional regression analysis.

C. Cross tabulations with chi square analysis of significance.

D. Time series multiple regression analysis to identify changes in individual stores over time.

Answer (B) is correct. *(CIA, adapted)*

REQUIRED: The best statistical tool for identifying deviations from the majority.

DISCUSSION: Time series data relate to a given entity over a number of prior time periods. Cross-sectional data, however, relate to different entities for a given time period or at a given time. Thus, cross-sectional regression analysis is the most appropriate statistical tool because it compares attributes of all stores' operating statistics at one moment in time.

Answer (A) is incorrect. Linear time series analysis is inapplicable. It is a simple model that compares data for an individual store over time. Answer (C) is incorrect. Cross tabulations have to be built on a model of expectations. Unless the model is built, the analysis is not useful. Answer (D) is incorrect. The objective is to compare stores at one moment in time. Multiple regression time series analysis compares the performance of an individual store over a period of time.

16.4.6. The moving-average method of forecasting

A. Is a cross-sectional forecasting method.

B. Regresses the variable of interest on a related variable to develop a forecast.

C. Derives final forecasts by adjusting the initial forecast based on the smoothing constant.

D. Includes each new observation in the average as it becomes available and discards the oldest observation.

Answer (D) is correct. *(CIA, adapted)*

REQUIRED: The item best describing the moving-average method of forecasting.

DISCUSSION: Simple moving-average is a smoothing method that uses the experience of the past N periods (through time period t) to forecast a value for the next period. Thus, the average includes each new observation and discards the oldest observation. The forecast formula for the next period (for time period t+1) is the sum of the last N observations divided by N.

Answer (A) is incorrect. Cross-sectional regression analysis examines relationships among large amounts of data (e.g., many or different production methods or locations) at a moment in time. Answer (B) is incorrect. Regression analysis relates the forecast to changes in particular variables. Answer (C) is incorrect. Under exponential smoothing, each forecast equals the sum of the last observation times the smoothing constant, plus the last forecast times one minus the constant.

16.4.7. As part of a risk analysis, an auditor wishes to forecast the percentage growth in next month's sales for a particular plant using the past 30 months' sales results. Significant changes in the organization affecting sales volumes were made within the last 9 months. The most effective analysis technique to use would be

A. Unweighted moving average.

B. Exponential smoothing.

C. Queuing theory.

D. Linear regression analysis.

Answer (B) is correct. *(CIA, adapted)*

REQUIRED: The most effective method of forecasting the percentage growth in next month's sales.

DISCUSSION: Under exponential smoothing, each forecast equals the sum of the last observation times the smoothing constant, plus the last forecast times one minus the constant. Thus, exponential means that greater weight is placed on the most recent data, with the weights of all data falling off exponentially as the data age. This feature is important because of the organizational changes that affected sales volume.

Answer (A) is incorrect. An unweighted moving average does not give more importance to more recent data. Answer (C) is incorrect. Queuing theory minimizes the cost of waiting lines. Answer (D) is incorrect. Linear regression analysis determines the equation for the relationship among variables. It does not give more importance to more recent data.

16.5 Multiple Calculations

Questions 16.5.1 through 16.5.4 are based on the following information.

Below is an examination of last year's financial statements of MacKenzie Park Co., which manufactures and sells trivets. Labor hours and production costs for the last 4 months of the year, which are representative for the year, were as follows:

Month	Labor Hours	Total Production Costs
September	2,500	$ 20,000
October	3,500	25,000
November	4,500	30,000
December	3,500	25,000
Total	14,000	$100,000

Based upon the information given and using the least squares method of computation with the letters listed below, select the best answer for each question.

If: a = Fixed production costs per month
b = Variable production costs per labor hour
n = Number of months
x = Labor hours per month
y = Total monthly production costs
$\sum$ = Summation

16.5.1. The equation(s) required for applying the least squares method of computation of fixed and variable production costs can be expressed as

A. $\sum xy = a\sum x + b\sum x^2$

B. $\sum y = na + b\sum x$

C. $y = a + bx^2$
$\sum y = na + b\sum x$

D. $\sum xy = a\sum x + b\sum x^2$
$\sum y = na + b\sum x$

Answer (D) is correct. *(CPA, adapted)*

REQUIRED: The equation(s) expressing the relationship between fixed and variable costs.

DISCUSSION: The least squares method of computing fixed and variable production costs minimizes the sum of the squares of the vertical deviation from the points to a line depicted on a scatter diagram. The least squares equation minimizes the deviation from the expected linear relationship to provide the closest approximation of the relationship of fixed and variable production costs.

Answer (A) is incorrect. One of the equations is omitted. Answer (B) is incorrect. One of the equations is omitted. Answer (C) is incorrect. The first equation should be $\sum xy = a\sum x + b\sum x^2$.

16.5.2. The cost function derived by the simple least squares method

A. Is linear.

B. Must be tested for minima and maxima.

C. Is parabolic.

D. Indicates maximum costs at the function's point of inflection.

Answer (A) is correct. *(CPA, adapted)*

REQUIRED: The characteristic of the cost function derived by the least squares method.

DISCUSSION: The cost function derived by the least squares method is linear, containing both fixed and variable elements. Although it is useful over the relevant range, it is probably not completely accurate.

Answer (B) is incorrect. Using calculus to test for minimum and maximum points is not appropriate in a linear function. Answer (C) is incorrect. The function is not curvilinear. Answer (D) is incorrect. If maximum costs are at the function's point of inflection, the relationship is curvilinear.

16.5.3. Monthly production costs can be expressed

A. $y = ax + b$

B. $y = a + bx$

C. $y = b + ax$

D. $y = \sum a + bx$

Answer (B) is correct. *(CPA, adapted)*

REQUIRED: The equation for monthly production costs.

DISCUSSION: The least squares method of computation results in an equation with a dependent variable (y), a constant (a), plus a variable coefficient (b), and an independent variable (x). Thus, $y = a + bx$ expresses total monthly production cost (y) in terms of fixed cost (a) plus the variable cost (b) times the activity level (x).

Answer (A) is incorrect. Variable b is the coefficient of x. Answer (C) is incorrect. Variable b is the coefficient of x. Answer (D) is incorrect. The summation symbol should be omitted.

16.5.4. Using the least squares method of computation, the fixed monthly production cost of trivets is approximately

A. $100,000

B. $25,000

C. $7,500

D. $20,000

Answer (C) is correct. *(CPA, adapted)*

REQUIRED: The fixed monthly production cost.

DISCUSSION: Using the least squares method, the fixed monthly production cost is the constant. It can be calculated by substituting into the equations below.

$$a = \bar{y} - b\bar{x} \qquad b = \frac{\sum xy - n\overline{xy}}{\sum x^2 - n\bar{x}^2}$$

x	y	xy	x²
2,500	$ 20,000	$ 50,000,000	6,250,000
3,500	25,000	87,500,000	12,250,000
4,500	30,000	135,000,000	20,250,000
3,500	25,000	87,500,000	12,250,000
14,000	$100,000	$360,000,000	51,000,000

$\bar{x} = 3{,}500$; $\bar{y} = \$25{,}000$; $n = 4$

$$b = \frac{\$360{,}000{,}000 - (4 \times 3{,}500 \times \$25{,}000)}{51{,}000{,}000 - (4 \times 3{,}500^2)} = \$5$$

$$a = \$25{,}000 - (3{,}500 \times \$5) = \$7{,}500$$

Answer (A) is incorrect. The amount of $100,000 is $\sum y$. Answer (B) is incorrect. The amount of $25,000 is $\bar{y}$. Answer (D) is incorrect. The amount of $20,000 equals total cost for September.

Questions 16.5.5 through 16.5.12 are based on the following information.

Armer Company is accumulating data to be used in preparing its annual profit plan for the coming year. The cost behavior pattern of the maintenance costs must be determined. The accounting staff has suggested that linear regression be employed to derive an equation in the form of y = a + bx for maintenance costs. Data regarding the maintenance hours and costs for last year and the results of the regression analysis are as follows:

	Hours of Activity	Maintenance Costs
January	480	$ 4,200
February	320	3,000
March	400	3,600
April	300	2,820
May	500	4,350
July	320	3,030
August	520	4,470
September	490	4,260
October	470	4,050
November	350	3,300
December	340	3,160
Sum	4,800	$43,200
Average	400	3,600

Average cost per hour (43,200 ÷ 4,800) = $9

a coefficient	684.65
b coefficient	7.2884
Standard error of the a coefficient	49.515
Standard error of the b coefficient	.12126
Standard error of the estimate	34.469
r^2	.99724
t-value a	13.827
t-value b	60.105

Single-Tailed Values of t

Degrees of Freedom	$t_{.100}$	$t_{.05}$	$t_{.025}$	$t_{.01}$
8	1.40	1.86	2.31	2.90
9	1.38	1.83	2.26	2.82
10	1.37	1.81	2.23	2.76
11	1.36	1.80	2.20	2.72
12	1.36	1.78	2.18	2.68
13	1.35	1.77	2.16	2.65
14	1.35	1.76	2.15	2.62

16.5.5. The statistic used to determine whether the estimate of the slope is significantly different from zero is the

A. Coefficient of determination.

B. Standard error of the a coefficient.

C. Standard error of the estimate.

D. t-value of b.

Answer (D) is correct. *(Publisher, adapted)*

REQUIRED: The statistic used to determine whether the slope is significantly different from zero.

DISCUSSION: The t-value of b (the slope of the line of the equation) states how far removed the estimate of b is from zero in terms of standard deviations, given the assumption that the true value of b is zero. The greater the t-value of b, the greater the probability that zero is not the true value.

Answer (A) is incorrect. It is the portion of total variance explained by the independent variable. Answer (B) is incorrect. It describes the variance of the constant term a. Answer (C) is incorrect. It measures the variability of the actual values around the least squares line.

16.5.6. If Armer Company uses the high-low method of analysis, the equation for the relationship between hours of activity and maintenance cost is

A. y = 400 + 9.0x

B. y = 570 + 7.5x

C. y = 3,600 + 400x

D. y = 570 + 9.0x

Answer (B) is correct. *(CMA, adapted)*

REQUIRED: The high-low equation for the relationship between hours of activity and maintenance cost.

DISCUSSION: The high-low method compares the highest and the lowest activity levels with the highest and lowest maintenance costs. The difference establishes the coefficient of x. Thus, b is 7.5 [($4,470 – $2,820) ÷ (520 hr. – 300 hr.)], and the constant term a is $570 [$4,470 – ($7.5 × 520 hr.)].

16.5.7. Based upon the data derived from the regression analysis, 420 maintenance hours in a month would mean the maintenance costs would be budgeted at

A. $3,780

B. $3,461

C. $3,797

D. $3,746

Answer (D) is correct. *(CMA, adapted)*

REQUIRED: The budgeted maintenance cost at the given activity level.

DISCUSSION: Substituting the given data into the regression equation results in a budgeted cost of $3,746 (rounded to the nearest dollar).

$y = a + bx$
y = 684.65 + 7.2884(420)
y = $3,746

16.5.8. Assume the t-value of b is 3.0 and maintenance costs are expected to increase as hours of activity increase. If the null hypothesis is that b is zero, is the estimate of b significantly different from zero?

A. No, with 95% confidence.

B. No, with 99% confidence.

C. Yes, with 95% confidence.

D. Yes, because the estimate of b is positive.

Answer (C) is correct. *(Publisher, adapted)*

REQUIRED: The interpretation of the t-value.

DISCUSSION: If the null hypothesis is that the true value of b is zero, the formula below indicates how much the observed estimate of b differs from zero in terms of standard deviations.

$$\frac{b - 0}{\text{Standard deviation of b}}$$

The greater the difference, the lower the probability that the true value of b equals zero. A t-table may be used to find the critical t-value needed to assure the desired level of confidence. The absolute value of the statistic derived from the formula must be equal to or greater than the value from the t-table. Because the null hypothesis that b is zero implies a two-tailed test (the alternate hypothesis is that b is not zero), at a 95% confidence level, the appropriate t-value is found in the $t_{.025}$ column [(1.0 – .95) ÷ 2] and the 10 degrees of freedom row (n – 2 parameters tested = 12 – 2). Because 3.0 (the given t-value) is greater than 2.23, the upper critical value for this two-sided test, confidence is at least 95% that the estimate of b differs from zero.

Answer (A) is incorrect. The null hypothesis can be rejected with 95% confidence. Answer (B) is incorrect. The null hypothesis can be rejected with 95% confidence. Answer (D) is incorrect. Variable b may be negative.

16.5.9. The coefficient of correlation for Armer's regression equation for the maintenance activities is

A. 34.469 ÷ 49.515

B. 99724

C. $\sqrt{.99724}$

D. $(.99724)^2$

Answer (C) is correct. *(CMA, adapted)*

REQUIRED: The coefficient of correlation for the maintenance activities.

DISCUSSION: The coefficient of correlation determines the relative strength of the relationship between two variables. It equals the square root of r^2 (the coefficient of determination). Given that r^2 is .99724, the coefficient of correlation is the square root of .99724.

Answer (A) is incorrect. The number 34.469 is the standard error of the estimate, and the number 49.515 is the standard error of a. Answer (B) is incorrect. The number .99724 is r^2. Answer (D) is incorrect. The square root of r^2 should be taken.

16.5.10. Armer can be 95% confident that what interval contains the true value of the marginal maintenance cost?

A. $7.02 – $7.56

B. $7.17 – $7.41

C. $7.07 – $7.51

D. $6.95 – $7.62

Answer (A) is correct. *(CMA, adapted)*

REQUIRED: The 95% confidence interval for the marginal maintenance cost.

DISCUSSION: Marginal maintenance cost is the coefficient of b ($7.2884). The 95% confidence interval for a two-tailed test may be constructed using the single-tailed value of t. The interval is two-tailed because both ends of the possible range are of concern. Thus, the $t_{.025}$ column is used because 2.5% of the distribution [(1.0 – .95) ÷ 2] is in each tail. The number of degrees of freedom equals n (the number of time periods) minus the number of parameters estimated (a and b) in the least squares equation. Thus, the appropriate t-value at 10 degrees of freedom (12 – 2) in the $t_{.025}$ column is 2.23. The standard error of the b coefficient is $.12126, and the 95% confidence interval is $7.2884 plus or minus $.2704098 ($.12126 × 2.23). The interval is therefore $7.02 ($7.2884 – $.2704098) to $7.56 ($7.2804 + $.2704098).

Answer (B) is incorrect. The interval of $7.17 – $7.41 is based on a t-value of 1.0. Answer (C) is incorrect. The interval of $7.07 – $7.51 is based on a t-value of 1.81. Answer (D) is incorrect. The interval of $6.95 – $7.62 is based on a t-value of 2.76.

16.5.11. Refer to the information on the preceding page(s). The percentage of the total variance that can be explained by the regression equation is

A. 99.724%

B. 69.613%

C. 12.126%

D. 99.862%

Answer (A) is correct. *(CMA, adapted)*

REQUIRED: The percentage of total variance explained by the regression equation.

DISCUSSION: The percentage of the total variance that can be explained by the regression equation is r^2, or the coefficient of determination. It is expressed as the percentage of the total variance that is equal to one minus the proportion of the total variance not explained. The given value of r^2 is .99724, or 99.724%.

Answer (B) is incorrect. The percentage of 69.613% equals the standard error of the estimate divided by the standard error of a. Answer (C) is incorrect. The percentage of 12.126% is the standard error of b. Answer (D) is incorrect. The percentage of 99.862% is the square root of r^2.

16.5.12. Refer to the information on the preceding page(s). At 400 hours of activity, Armer management can be approximately two-thirds confident that the maintenance costs will be in the range of

A. $3,550.48 – $3,649.52

B. $3,551.70 – $3,648.30

C. $3,586.18 – $3,613.83

D. $3,565.54 – $3,634.47

Answer (D) is correct. *(CMA, adapted)*

REQUIRED: The 66 2/3% confidence interval for actual average maintenance costs.

DISCUSSION: A 66 2/3% confidence interval can be established by adding and subtracting approximately one standard error of the estimate to or from the predicted value of maintenance costs. When activity is 400 hours, the predicted maintenance cost is $3,600 [$684.65 + ($7.2884 × 400)]. The standard error of the estimate is given as $34.469. The 66 2/3% confidence interval is therefore $3,600 ± $34.469, or $3,565.54 to $3,634.47.

Answer (A) is incorrect. The range of $3,550.48 – $3,649.52 is based on the standard error of a. Answer (B) is incorrect. The range of $3,551.70 – $3,648.30 adds (subtracts) the sum of the standard error of the estimate and the t-value of a. Answer (C) is incorrect. The range of $3,586.18 – $3,613.83 adds (subtracts) the t-value of a.

STUDY UNIT SEVENTEEN
LINEAR PROGRAMMING

Linear programming (LP) optimizes an **objective function**. Thus, it maximizes a revenue or profit function or minimizes a cost function, subject to constraints. For example, these may be resources or levels of production or performance. In a business application, LP is used to plan resource allocations.

The conditions that restrict the optimal value of the objective function are **constraints**. A **shadow price** is the amount by which the value of the optimal solution changes if a one-unit change is made in a **binding** constraint. A **nonbinding** constraint has excess capacity because the optimal solution does not use all of the given resource. The shadow price for a nonbinding constraint is zero. The calculation of shadow prices is a simple example of **sensitivity analysis**, a procedure to test the responsiveness of the solution indicated by a model to (1) changes in variables, (2) other decisions, or (3) errors. The unknowns used to formulate the objective function and the constraints are decision **variables**. Their values are limited by the constraints. Values that are fixed for purposes of solving the model (but not permanently) are (1) **cost or profit coefficients** for the objective function, (2) **technical coefficients** for the constraints, and (3) the **constants** on the right-hand side of the constraints. When the number of constraint equations equals the number of variables, a unique solution exists. When the number of variables exceeds the number of constraint equations, infinite solutions usually exist. Values of the variables are the outputs of LP. The constraint equations usually reflect the types of input or types of resources being allocated, e.g., available machine hours or materials.

Methods of solving LP problems include the following:

- The **graphical method** is the easiest, but it is limited to problems with two variables.
- The **algebraic method** uses trial and error. Pairs of constraints are solved algebraically to find their intersection. The values of the decision variables then are substituted into the objective function and compared to find the best combination. The basic rule is that the optimal solution is at the intersection of two or more constraint equations. All intersections therefore can be calculated and each solution evaluated in the objective function to determine which solution is optimal.
- The **simplex method** is the most common. It is an algorithm to move from one corner solution to a better corner solution. When a better solution cannot be found, the optimal solution has been reached. The simplex method relies on matrix algebra. The constraint equations are arranged in a matrix of coefficients and manipulated as a group with matrix algebra. Almost all practical applications of LP use computers. Most computer facilities have an LP package based on the simplex algorithm.

QUESTIONS

17.1 Linear Programming (LP) Concepts

17.1.1. An investment company is attempting to allocate its available funds between two investment alternatives, stocks and bonds, which differ in terms of expected return and risk. The company would like to minimize its risk while earning an expected return of at least 10% and investing no more than 70% in either of the investment alternatives. An appropriate technique for allocating its funds between stocks and bonds is

A. Linear programming.

B. Capital budgeting.

C. Differential analysis.

D. Queuing theory.

Answer (A) is correct. *(CIA, adapted)*
REQUIRED: The method of allocating funds.
DISCUSSION: LP is used to plan resource allocations to optimize a given objective function subject to certain constraints. Thus, the maximum investment is constrained by a 70% limit on either investment choice and a minimum required return.
Answer (B) is incorrect. Capital budgeting is used to analyze and evaluate long-term capital investments. Answer (C) is incorrect. Differential analysis is used for decision making when differences in costs (revenues) for two or more options are compared. Answer (D) is incorrect. Queuing theory is used to minimize the sum of the costs of waiting lines and servicing waiting lines when items arrive randomly and are serviced sequentially.

17.1.2. Linear programming is an operations research technique that allocates resources. Mathematical expressions are used to describe the problem. The measure of effectiveness that is to be maximized or minimized is the

A. Constraints.

B. Set of decision variables.

C. Objective function.

D. Derivative of the function.

Answer (C) is correct. *(CMA, adapted)*
REQUIRED: The measure of effectiveness to be maximized or minimized.
DISCUSSION: The objective function in an LP model represents the outcome to be optimized, e.g., total contribution margin, operating income, or total cost.
Answer (A) is incorrect. Constraints are the resource limitations and other conditions within which the objective function is to be optimized. Answer (B) is incorrect. Variables are the unknowns used to formulate the objective function and constraints. Answer (D) is incorrect. Derivative of the function is a calculus term that is irrelevant in this context.

17.1.3. The constraints in a linear programming model are

A. Included in the objective function.

B. Costs.

C. Scarce resources.

D. Dependent variables.

Answer (C) is correct. *(CIA, adapted)*
REQUIRED: The nature of constraints.
DISCUSSION: LP models are used to maximize or minimize an objective function subject to constraints. Constraints are mathematical statements expressed as equalities or inequalities. They describe conditions, usually resource limitations, to which values of the variables are subject. These constraints must be specified before an LP problem can be solved.
Answer (A) is incorrect. The objective function consists of the variables to be optimized. Answer (B) is incorrect. Costs are included in the objective function. Answer (D) is incorrect. The constraints are given and are independent.

17.1.4. A company manufactures three products at its highly automated factory. The products are very popular, with demand far exceeding the company's ability to supply the marketplace. To maximize profit, management should focus on each product's

A. Gross margin.

B. Segment margin.

C. Contribution margin ratio.

D. Contribution margin per machine hour.

Answer (D) is correct. *(CMA, adapted)*
REQUIRED: The measure used to determine the profit maximizing output.
DISCUSSION: When demand far exceeds a company's ability to supply the marketplace, management will want to maximize its profits per unit of scarce resource. If the scarce resource is raw materials, the products that provide the greatest contribution margin per unit of raw materials are the products to emphasize. If machine hours are the constraint, profits are maximized by emphasizing the contribution margin per machine hour.

Questions 17.1.5 through 17.1.7 are based on the following information. Manders Manufacturing Corporation uses the following model to determine its product mix for metal (M) and scrap metal (S).

$$\text{Max } Z = \$30M + \$70S$$

$$\text{If: } \begin{aligned} 3M + 2S &\leq 15 \\ 2M + 4S &\leq 18 \end{aligned}$$

17.1.5. These mathematical functions are an example of a(n)

A. Simulation model.

B. Linear programming model.

C. Economic order quantity model.

D. Present value model.

Answer (B) is correct. *(CMA, adapted)*

REQUIRED: The model using maximization and constraint functions.

DISCUSSION: LP is used to maximize a revenue or profit function or minimize a cost function, subject to constraints such as limited resources. It often is used for planning scarce resource allocations. The optimization, or objective, function (Max Z = $30M + $70S) indicates that an entity wants to maximize its contribution margin on two products. The two constraint functions suggest that either the scarcity of resources or a lack of demand limits the amount of each product that can be produced.

Answer (A) is incorrect. A simulation model is a method of experimenting with models using a computer. It does not necessarily use maximization and constraint functions. Answer (C) is incorrect. The EOQ is based on a single equation that includes a square root. Answer (D) is incorrect. The present value model is based on a single equation that incorporates a rate of return.

17.1.6. The two inequality functions are

A. Contributions.

B. Shadow points.

C. Objectives.

D. Constraints.

Answer (D) is correct. *(CMA, adapted)*

REQUIRED: The term for inequality functions.

DISCUSSION: The restrictions on the optimal value of the objective function in LP are constraints. They are depicted by inequalities.

Answer (A) is incorrect. Contributions to revenue are included in the objective (maximization) equation. Answer (B) is incorrect. A shadow point, or shadow price, is the amount by which the value of the optimal solution of the objective function changes if a one-unit change is made in a binding constraint. Answer (C) is incorrect. Objectives are the components of the objective (maximization) equation.

17.1.7. The point at which M equals 2 and S equals 3 would

A. Minimize cost.

B. Lie in a corner.

C. Be a feasible point.

D. Be the optimal solution point.

Answer (C) is correct. *(CMA, adapted)*

REQUIRED: The true statement about a given point in an LP model.

DISCUSSION: The point at which M equals 2 and S equals 3 is a feasible point. It does not violate either constraint function. A graph of the constraints depicts whether the point is in a corner. Because it is not, it cannot be the optimal solution point. In an LP problem, the optimal solution is in a corner in the feasible area. Thus, all that is known about the point is that it is within the feasible area.

Answer (A) is incorrect. Costs are not included in the equations. Answer (B) is incorrect. The point is not in a corner. Answer (D) is incorrect. The point cannot be the optimal solution point unless it is a corner point.

17.1.8. The procedure employed to solve linear programming problems is

A. Calculus.

B. Simulation.

C. Expected value.

D. Matrix algebra.

Answer (D) is correct. *(CMA, adapted)*

REQUIRED: The procedure used to solve LP problems.

DISCUSSION: Matrix algebra is a method of manipulating matrices (rectangular arrays) formed from the coefficients of simultaneous linear equations. Similar rectangular arrays can be combined to form sums and products. Matrix algebra is used to solve LP problems, assuming a computer application is not available. This use of matrix algebra is the simplex method.

Answer (A) is incorrect. Calculus is used to find maxima and minima. Answer (B) is incorrect. Simulation is used to experiment with mathematical models. Answer (C) is incorrect. Expected value is a probabilistically weighted average of possible outcomes.

17.1.9. To solve a linear programming problem, slack, surplus, and artificial variables must be employed. A slack variable represents

A. Opportunity costs.

B. Unused capacity.

C. Outside variables with high cost.

D. The variable with the most negative value.

Answer (B) is correct. *(CMA, adapted)*

REQUIRED: The definition of a slack variable.

DISCUSSION: A slack variable represents unused capacity using the simplex method. Because LP formulations often are stated as inequalities, unused capacity is possible even at the optimal production level. To convert inequalities of the ≤ type to equalities, slack variables are added to account for the unused capacity. If an inequality is of the ≥ type, a surplus variable is subtracted. If a surplus variable is used, a second variable (an artificial variable) is added to prevent violation of the nonnegativity constraint.

Answer (A) is incorrect. Opportunity costs are the benefits forgone by using a scarce resource in a given way. Answer (C) is incorrect. A slack variable has a payoff or cost coefficient of zero. Answer (D) is incorrect. A slack variable has a payoff or cost coefficient of zero.

17.1.10. In linear programming, the shadow price refers to the

A. Measurement of the value of relaxing a constraint in a problem with dual variables.

B. Marginal change in profit associated with a change in the contribution margin of one of the variables.

C. Unused capacity available once the optimal solution is obtained.

D. Solution variable that is located outside the feasible area.

Answer (A) is correct. *(CMA, adapted)*

REQUIRED: The definition of a shadow price.

DISCUSSION: A shadow price is the amount by which the value of the optimal solution of the objective function changes if a one-unit change is made in a binding constraint. The calculation of shadow prices is an example of sensitivity analysis, a procedure that tests the responsiveness of a solution to changes in variables.

Answer (B) is incorrect. The change is in the limited resource, not in the contribution margin of one of the variables. Answer (C) is incorrect. Shadow prices relate to binding constraints, not nonbinding constraints. The shadow price of unused capacity, a nonbinding constraint, is zero. Answer (D) is incorrect. A shadow price is the benefit of moving the feasible area.

17.1.11. Shadow prices in linear programming solutions are ordinarily considered to be the same as

A. Relevant costs.

B. Differential costs.

C. Alternative costs.

D. Opportunity costs.

Answer (D) is correct. *(CIA, adapted)*

REQUIRED: The equivalent of shadow prices.

DISCUSSION: A shadow price is the amount by which the value of the optimal solution of the objective function in an LP problem changes if a one-unit change is made in a binding constraint. The calculation of a shadow price is a simple example of sensitivity analysis. An opportunity cost is the maximum benefit forgone by using a scarce resource for a given purpose. It is the benefit from the next best use of that resource. Thus, shadow prices and opportunity costs are related concepts.

Answer (A) is incorrect. Relevant costs are expected future costs that vary with the decision made. They are reflected in the objective function and constraints of LP problems. Answer (B) is incorrect. A differential cost is the net relevant cost. Answer (C) is incorrect. The term alternative costs is seldom used in either managerial (cost) accounting textbooks or in the literature on decision theory.

17.1.12. Sensitivity analysis in linear programming is used to

A. Test the accuracy of the parameters.

B. Develop the technological matrix.

C. Determine how the optimal solution will react to changes in parameters.

D. Develop objective function coefficients.

Answer (C) is correct. *(CMA, adapted)*

REQUIRED: The purpose of sensitivity analysis in an LP application.

DISCUSSION: Sensitivity analysis in an LP application determines how the optimal solution changes if an objective function coefficient, the limiting value of a resource constraint, or a constraint coefficient is varied. It also considers the effect of adding a new variable or constraint.

Answer (A) is incorrect. The accuracy of the parameters cannot be tested as a part of the model. The intent is simply to measure the effect of a variance from the assumed parameters. Answer (B) is incorrect. The technological matrix is developed by production managers or engineers and is an input to the model. Answer (D) is incorrect. Objective function coefficients are treated as given in the model. Sensitivity analysis can be used to determine the effect of changes in the coefficients.

17.1.13. Given the basic equations for the maximization of profits in a linear programming model, what quantitative technique is ordinarily employed to arrive at an optimal solution?

A. Regression analysis.

B. Markov analysis.

C. Monte Carlo analysis.

D. Simplex method analysis.

Answer (D) is correct. *(CPA, adapted)*

REQUIRED: The usual method of solving LP problems.

DISCUSSION: The simplex method is the method most commonly used to solve LP problems. It is an algorithm used to move from a possible solution to a better solution. The mathematical constraint equations are arranged in a matrix of coefficients and manipulated as a group by means of matrix algebra. Because of its complexity when numerous products and constraints are involved, the simplex method is used primarily with computers.

Answer (A) is incorrect. Regression analysis measures the relationship among variables. Answer (B) is incorrect. Markov analysis is used in decision problems in which the probability of the occurrence of a future state depends only on the current state. Answer (C) is incorrect. Monte Carlo analysis is used in a simulation to generate random values for a variable.

17.1.14. Given below is the final solution for which type of problem?

X_1	8	0	1	.5	–.055	0
X_2	4	1	0	–.5	.111	0
C_i -Z_j		0	0	–20	–6.67	0

A. Linear programming.

B. Markov absorbing chain.

C. Material requirements planning.

D. Two-line, three-server queuing system.

Answer (A) is correct. *(CIA, adapted)*

REQUIRED: The type of problem represented by the given solution.

DISCUSSION: The matrix given is the final solution of a simplex tableau. The simplex method is the method most commonly used to solve LP problems. It is an algorithm used to move from a possible solution to a better solution. The mathematical constraint equations are arranged in a matrix of coefficients and manipulated as a group by means of matrix algebra. The simplex method is used primarily with computers.

Answer (B) is incorrect. A sequence of events (a Markov chain) is an absorbing chain if it can reach a state that never changes. An example is the completion of a project. Answer (C) is incorrect. Material requirements planning is used to manage inventory. It treats inventory as directly dependent upon short-term demand for the finished product. Answer (D) is incorrect. Queuing theory is used to minimize the costs of waiting lines.

17.1.15. A transportation model is a special case of the

A. Markov model.

B. Linear programming model.

C. Dynamic programming model.

D. Critical path method.

Answer (B) is correct. *(CMA, adapted)*

REQUIRED: The model of which the transportation model is a special case.

DISCUSSION: The transportation model is a special type of LP. It involves physical movement of goods from sources of supply to destinations. The objective function includes the transportation cost of each item from each source to each destination. The constraints are the output for each supply point and the demand by each destination.

Answer (A) is incorrect. A Markov model is used in decision problems in which the probability of the occurrence of a future state depends only on the current state of nature. Answer (C) is incorrect. Dynamic programming is used for problems that involve time-staged decisions such as decisions affected by previous decisions. Dynamic programming ordinarily is used for much smaller problems than those addressed by LP. Answer (D) is incorrect. The critical path method is a means of managing large construction projects by focusing on the longest path in a network.

17.2 Graphs

Questions 17.2.1 through 17.2.8 are based on the following information.

Hale Company manufactures Products A and B, each of which requires two processes, polishing and grinding. A requires 2 hours of both grinding and polishing and B requires 4 hours of grinding and 2 hours of polishing. The contribution margin is $3 for Product A and $4 for Product B. The graph to the right shows the maximum number of units of each product that may be processed in the two departments.

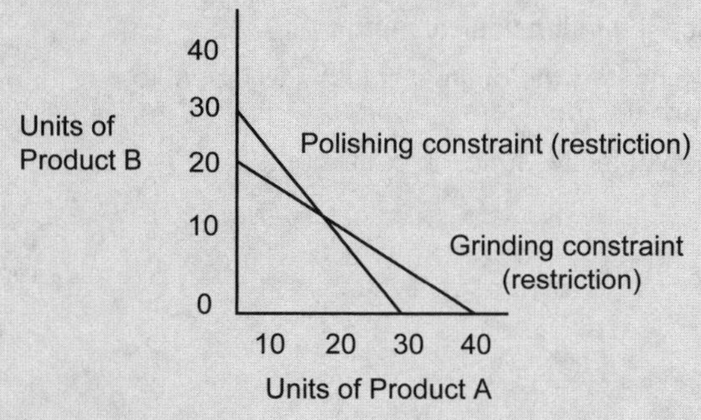

17.2.1. Considering the constraints (restrictions) on processing, which combination of Products A and B maximizes the total contribution margin?

A. 0 units of A and 20 units of B.

B. 20 units of A and 10 units of B.

C. 30 units of A and 0 units of B.

D. 40 units of A and 0 units of B.

Answer (B) is correct. *(CPA, adapted)*

REQUIRED: The profit maximization point in the graph.

DISCUSSION: To determine the profit maximization point on an LP graph requires the examination of each of the corner points on the feasible region. For 0 units of A and 20 units of B, the contribution margin is $80 (20 units × $4 UCM). At 20 units of A and 10 units of B, the CM is $100 ($60 CM for A + $40 CM for B). At 30 units of A and 0 units of B, the CM is $90 (30 units × $3 UCM). Thus, the product mix at 20 units of A and 10 units of B maximizes the contribution margin.

Answer (A) is incorrect. The CM is $80. Answer (C) is incorrect. The CM is $90. Answer (D) is incorrect. The points representing 40 units of A and 0 units of B and 30 units of B and 0 units of A lie outside the feasible region.

17.2.2. What is the polishing constraint?

A. $2A + 4B \leq 80$

B. $2A + 2B \leq 60$

C. $40A + 20B \leq 20$

D. $30A + 30B \leq 30$

Answer (B) is correct. *(Publisher, adapted)*

REQUIRED: The equation of the line representing the polishing constraint.

DISCUSSION: The polishing constraint on the graph consists of a line from 30B to 30A. Thus, the limitation imposed by polishing is 30A, 30B, or some combination of the two. Given that A and B both require 2 hours of polishing, 60 hours of polishing capacity must be available. Thus, $2A + 2B \leq 60$.

Answer (A) is incorrect. The grinding constraint is $2A + 4B \leq 80$. Answer (C) is incorrect. The constraint coefficients are the amounts of resources used per unit of output, not the maximum units that can be produced. Answer (D) is incorrect. The constraint coefficients are the amounts of resources used per unit of output, not the maximum units that can be produced.

17.2.3. What is the grinding constraint?

A. $30A + 30B \leq 30$

B. $2A + 4B \leq 80$

C. $40A + 20B \leq 20$

D. $2A + 2B \leq 60$

Answer (B) is correct. *(Publisher, adapted)*

REQUIRED: The equation of the line depicting the grinding constraint.

DISCUSSION: The grinding constraint is a line from 20B to 40A. Thus, if B alone is produced, the output is 20 units. If A alone is produced, the output is 40 units. Also, A requires 2 hours of grinding and B requires 4 hours. Only 80 hours of grinding capacity are available (20 units of B × 4 hours). Thus, the constraint is $2A + 4B \leq 80$.

Answer (A) is incorrect. The constraint coefficients are the amounts of resources used per unit of output, not the maximum units that can be produced. Answer (C) is incorrect. The constraint coefficients are the amounts of resources used per unit of output, not the maximum units that can be produced. Answer (D) is incorrect. The polishing constraint is $2A + 2B \leq 60$.

17.2.4. What is the slope of the polishing constraint?

A. 1/1

B. 4/3

C. 1/2

D. –1/1

Answer (D) is correct. *(Publisher, adapted)*

REQUIRED: The slope of the polishing constraint.

DISCUSSION: The slope equals the change in vertical distance divided by the change in horizontal distance. The polishing constraint line decreases by 1 unit vertically as it moves to the right (increases) horizontally by 1 unit. Thus, the slope is –1/1.

17.2.5. Constraint lines in linear programming usually have a negative slope. Which is an example of a constraint line that does not have a negative slope?

A. $2X + 7Y \leq 40$

B. $7X + 2Y \leq 40$

C. $X + Y \leq 40$

D. $Y \leq 40$

Answer (D) is correct. *(Publisher, adapted)*

REQUIRED: The constraint line that does not have a negative slope.

DISCUSSION: Each of the constraint lines given as answer choices is downward sloping (i.e., they connect between the y axis and x axis) except $Y \leq 40$. When this inequality is changed to an equality, its graphic depiction is a horizontal line (its slope is equal to 0).

17.2.6. What is the slope of the grinding constraint?

A. –1/1

B. –1/2

C. –2/1

D. 1/2

Answer (B) is correct. *(Publisher, adapted)*

REQUIRED: The slope of the grinding constraint line.

DISCUSSION: The grinding constraint line runs from 20B to 40A, decreasing 1 unit vertically for every 2 units of horizontal increase. Accordingly, the slope is –1/2.

Answer (A) is incorrect. The slope of the polishing constraint is –1/1. Answer (C) is incorrect. The inverse of the slope of the grinding constraint line is –2/1. Answer (D) is incorrect. The slope is negative.

17.2.7. What is the slope of the objective function?

A. –1/1

B. –3/3

C. –3/4

D. 3/4

Answer (C) is correct. *(Publisher, adapted)*

REQUIRED: The slope of the objective function.

DISCUSSION: The objective function consists of a series of parallel lines outward from the origin having the same profit potential. Given that each A generates $3 of UCM, and each B produces a $4 UCM, the entity is indifferent between producing 4A and 3B. On this graph, such a line connects 30B and 40A. The change is $3 vertically downward for every $4 horizontal increase, for a slope of –3/4.

Answer (A) is incorrect. The slope of the polishing constraint is –1/1 . Answer (B) is incorrect. The slope of the polishing constraint is –3/3. Answer (D) is incorrect. The slope is negative.

17.2.8. Which amounts of A and B lie on the same objective function line?

	A	B
A.	40	20
B.	20	40
C.	30	30
D.	40	30

Answer (D) is correct. *(Publisher, adapted)*

REQUIRED: The points on the objective function line.

DISCUSSION: The entity should be indifferent between producing 4A and 3B. This relationship may be depicted by a line from 30B to 40A. Each combination represented by a point on this line provides a contribution margin of $120.

Questions 17.2.9 and 17.2.10 are based on the following information.

A company produces two products, X and Y, which use material and labor as inputs. Fixed amounts of labor and material are available for production each month. In addition, the demand for Product Y each month is limited; Product X has no constraint on the number of units that can be sold.

A graphical depiction of these production and demand constraints is presented in the opposite column.

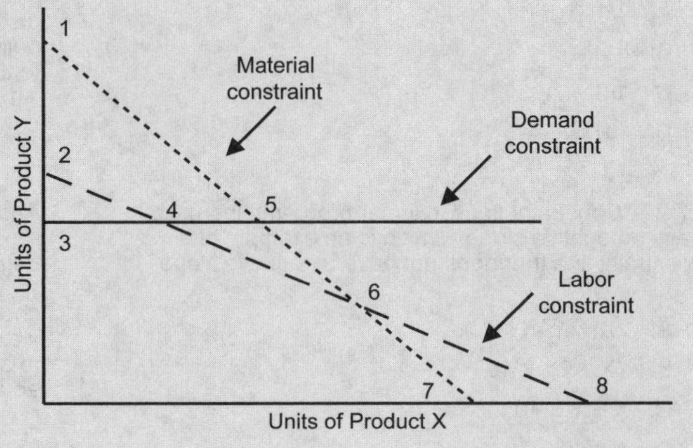

17.2.9. The feasible solution region is bounded by the lines connecting points

A. 3, 4, 6, and 7.

B. 1, 5, 6, and 8.

C. 2, 4, 5, 6, and 8.

D. 3, 5, 6, and 7.

Answer (A) is correct. *(CIA, adapted)*

REQUIRED: The points bounding the feasible region.

DISCUSSION: A model consisting of a system of functions may be used to optimize an objective function. If the functions in the model are all linear, the model is an LP model. LP is used to determine optimal resource allocation. Several methods are used to solve LP problems. The graphical method is limited to simple problems. The given graph consists of three lines, each representing a production constraint. The lines connecting points 3, 4, 6, and 7 bound the feasible solution region. Product mixes of X and Y that are outside this boundary cannot be produced or sold because the demand constraint (line 3,4), the labor constraint (line 4,6), and the material constraint (line 6,7) are binding.

Answer (B) is incorrect. Points 1, 5, and 8 are outside the boundary. Answer (C) is incorrect. Points 2, 5, and 8 are outside the boundary. Answer (D) is incorrect. Point 5 is outside the boundary.

17.2.10. If a series of profit lines for X and Y are drawn on the graph, the mix of X and Y that will result in the maximum profit can be determined from

A. The last point in the feasible solution region touched by a profit line.

B. Any point on the boundary of the feasible solution region touched by a profit line.

C. The first point on the feasible solution region boundary that intersects a profit line.

D. Any point on the demand constraint that intersects a profit line.

Answer (A) is correct. *(CIA, adapted)*

REQUIRED: The means of determining the mix of X and Y that results in the maximum profit.

DISCUSSION: A profit line has negative slope because the profit from sale of one product increases as the profit from sale of the other product declines. Moving the profit line rightward (while maintaining its slope) to the last point in the feasible region determines the solution.

17.2.11. When using the graphic method of solving a linear programming problem, which of the following is depicted on the graph?

	Line of Best Fit	Optimal Corner Point
A.	No	No
B.	No	Yes
C.	Yes	No
D.	Yes	Yes

Answer (B) is correct. *(CPA, adapted)*

REQUIRED: The element(s) of an LP graph.

DISCUSSION: The graphic solution to an LP problem depicts the area of feasible combinations of activity given the constraints. Any point along a constraint line has the same characteristics. Thus, a point represents the line. The extreme point of the feasibility region is the optimal solution.

17.2.12. The graphic method as a means for solving linear programming problems

A. Can be used given more than two restrictions (constraints).

B. Is limited to situations having two restrictions (constraints).

C. Is limited to situations with one restriction (constraint).

D. Cannot be used with any restrictions (constraints).

Answer (A) is correct. *(CPA, adapted)*

REQUIRED: The true statement about constraints in graphic solutions of LP problems.

DISCUSSION: LP problems assume linearity of relationships, and the solutions may be examined by plotting a solution (feasibility) region on a graph. The solution region is bounded by the constraint lines. The objective function also is a linear relationship that may be plotted on the graph. Thus, multiple relationships and multiple constraints may be examined.

Answer (B) is incorrect. More than two restrictions (constraints) are possible. Answer (C) is incorrect. No graph is needed if only one restriction exists. The optimal solution is either all of one product, item, etc., or all of another unless the slope of the constraint line equals the slope of the objective function. Answer (D) is incorrect. All LP problems have constraints.

17.3 Formulation

Questions 17.3.1 and 17.3.2 are based on the following information.

Keego Enterprises manufactures two products, boat wax and car wax, in two departments, the Mixing Department and the Packaging Department. The Mixing Department has 800 hours per month available, and the Packaging Department has 1,200 hours per month available. Production of the two products cannot exceed 36,000 pounds. Data on the two products follow:

	Contribution Margin (per 100 pounds)	Hours per 100 Pounds	
		Mixing (M)	Packaging (P)
Boat wax (B)	$200	5.0	3.6
Car wax (C)	150	2.4	6.0

17.3.1. The objective function for the linear program Keego should use to determine the optimal monthly production of each wax is

A. Z = 150B + 200C

B. 2B + 1.5C ≥ 36,000

C. 2B + 1.5C ≤ 36,000

D. Z = 200B + 150C

Answer (D) is correct. *(CMA, adapted)*

REQUIRED: The objective function.

DISCUSSION: The objective function is the equation to maximize the contribution margin. Given that each 100 pounds of boat wax contributes $200 and each 100 pounds of car wax contributes $150, the goal is to maximize the total of these amounts. If B equals the units of boat wax, C equals the units of car wax, and Z is the total contribution margin, the objective function is Z = $200B + $150C.

Answer (A) is incorrect. The coefficients of B and C are reversed. Answer (B) is incorrect. The coefficients should be stated in dollar amounts, not as proportions, and 36,000 equals maximum production in pounds. Answer (C) is incorrect. The coefficients should be stated in dollar amounts, not as proportions, and 36,000 equals maximum production in pounds.

17.3.2. The mixing constraint for the Keego linear program is

A. 2.4M + 6P ≤ 36,000

B. 5B + 2.4C ≥ 800

C. 5B + 2.4C ≤ 800

D. 5B + 2.4C = 800

Answer (C) is correct. *(CMA, adapted)*

REQUIRED: The mixing constraint.

DISCUSSION: The Mixing Department has only 800 hours available per month, a limitation (constraint) on production. Thus, the total mixing time is less than or equal to 800 hours. Every 100-pound batch of boat wax (B) requires 5 hours of mixing time, and every 100-pound batch of car wax (C) requires 2.4 hours of mixing time. Accordingly, the constraint equation is 5B + 2.4C ≤ 800.

Answer (A) is incorrect. The amounts of 2.4M and 6P equal hours per unit of car wax, and 36,000 equals maximum production in pounds. Answer (B) is incorrect. Total mixing time is equal to or less than 800 hours. Answer (D) is incorrect. Total mixing time is equal to or less than 800 hours.

Questions 17.3.3 through 17.3.6 are based on the following information.

Merlin Company has excess capacity on two machines, 24 hours on Machine 105 and 16 hours on Machine 107. To use this excess capacity, the company has two products, known as Product D and Product F, that must use both machines in manufacturing. Both have excess product demand, and the company can sell as many units as it can manufacture. The company's objective is to maximize profits.

Product D has an incremental profit of $6 per unit, and each unit utilizes 2 hours of time on Machine 105 and then 2 hours of time on Machine 107. Product F has an incremental profit of $7 per unit, and each unit utilizes 3 hours of time on Machine 105 and then 1 hour of time on Machine 107. Let D be the number of units for Product D, F be the number of units for Product F, and P be the company's profit.

17.3.3. The objective function for Merlin Company is

A. $P = 4D + 4F \leq 40$

B. $P = 2D + 3F \leq 24$

C. $P = 2D + F \leq 16$

D. P = $6D + $7F

Answer (D) is correct. *(CMA, adapted)*

REQUIRED: The objective function.

DISCUSSION: The objective function is to be optimized. Because the purpose is to maximize the total contribution margin, the function equals (1) an unknown number of units of D at a unit contribution margin of $6 plus (2) an unknown number of units of F at a unit contribution margin of $7 (P = $6D + $7F).

17.3.4. The optimal number of units for Product D can be solved by calculating

A. $2D + 3F \leq 24$

B. $2D + F \leq 16$

C. $2D + 3(16 - 2D) \leq 24$

D. $2(16 - F) + 3F \leq 24$

Answer (C) is correct. *(CMA, adapted)*

REQUIRED: The equation that must be solved to determine the optimal number of D to produce.

DISCUSSION: The constraint equations for machine hours are $2D + 3F \leq 24$ hours and $2D + F \leq 16$ hours. Because these equations involve two unknowns (D and F), they may be solved simultaneously. Solving for F in the second equation produces $F \leq 16 - 2D$. Substituting this result into the first equation gives $2D + 3(16 - 2D) \leq 24$.

Answer (A) is incorrect. The two equations must be solved simultaneously. Answer (B) is incorrect. The two equations must be solved simultaneously. Answer (D) is incorrect. Product D does not equal 16 – F.

17.3.5. The equations $2D + 3F \leq 24$, $D \geq 0$, and $F \geq 0$ are

A. Objective functions.

B. Inequalities.

C. Deterministic functions.

D. Constraints.

Answer (D) is correct. *(CMA, adapted)*

REQUIRED: The term for equations of the type given.

DISCUSSION: The objective function (P = $6D + $7F) is to be maximized subject to the given constraint functions. The following are the constraints: (1) the 24 hours limitation for Machine 105, (2) the 16 hours limitation for Machine 107, (3) the nonnegative production assumption for Product D, and (4) the nonnegative production assumption for Product D.

Answer (A) is incorrect. Objective functions are those that management is attempting to optimize. Answer (B) is incorrect. Inequalities refer to equations that do not balance. These can balance. Answer (C) is incorrect. Deterministic functions are those with known (determinable) variables.

17.3.6. A feasible solution for Merlin Company is

A. D = 2 and F = 8.

B. D = 6 and F = 4.

C. D = 12 and F = 0.

D. D = 8 and F = 3.

Answer (B) is correct. *(CMA, adapted)*

REQUIRED: The feasible solution.

DISCUSSION: This problem can be solved either graphically or by trial and error. The graphical approach involves drawing the constraint lines on a graph and defining the feasible region. An easier approach is to solve the problem by trial and error. Whether the production levels violate the constraint functions below can be determined for each answer. Only answer (B) does not violate the constraints.

$$2D + 3F \leq 24$$
$$2D + F \leq 16$$

Answer (A) is incorrect. D = 2 and F = 8 violate the Machine 105 constraint. Answer (C) is incorrect. D = 12 and F = 0 violate the Machine 107 constraint. Answer (D) is incorrect. D = 8 and F = 3 violate both constraints.

17.3.7. A firm must decide the mix of production of Product X and Product Y. There are only two resources used in the two products, resources A and B. Data related to the two products are given in the following table:

	Products	
	X	Y
Resource A	3	7
Resource B	2	1
Unit profit	$8	$6

What is the appropriate objective function to maximize profit?

A. 3X + 7Y

B. 2X + Y

C. 8X + 6Y

D. 5X + 8Y

Answer (C) is correct. *(CIA, adapted)*

REQUIRED: The appropriate objective function to maximize profit.

DISCUSSION: The objective function is the function to be optimized. To maximize profits on the sales of two products (X and Y), based on profits per unit ($8 and $6, respectively), the objective function is 8X + 6Y.

Answer (A) is incorrect. The function of 3X + 7Y is a constraint. Answer (B) is incorrect. The function of 2X + Y is a constraint. Answer (D) is incorrect. The function of 5X + 8Y is the sum of the constraints.

17.4 Calculations

17.4.1. The Mix and Match Company has two products, Product X and Product Y, that it manufactures through its production facilities. The contribution margin for Product X is $15 per unit, whereas Product Y's contribution is $25. Each product uses Materials A and B. Product X uses 3 pounds of Material A, and Product Y uses 6 pounds. Product X requires 6 feet of Material B and Product Y uses 4 feet. The company can only purchase 600 pounds of Material A and 880 feet of Material B. The optimal mix of products to manufacture is

	Product X		Product Y
A.	146 units	and	0 units
B.	0 units	and	100 units
C.	120 units	and	40 units
D.	40 units	and	120 units

Answer (C) is correct. *(CMA, adapted)*

REQUIRED: The optimal mix of products.

DISCUSSION: The objective function ($15X + $25Y) is to be maximized subject to the two constraint functions (Material A: 3X + 6Y ≤ 600 and Material B: 6X + 4Y ≤ 880). One way to solve this problem is to graph the constraint lines and determine the feasible area. The optimal production level is at a corner of the feasible area. The corners can be determined algebraically. If X equals 0, Y equals 100 in the first constraint equation (assuming it is stated as an equality) and 220 in the second. If Y equals 0, X equals 200 in the first equation and 146 in the second. Thus, the maximum units of X and Y that can be produced are 146 and 100, respectively. Substituting into the objective function yields these results:

($15 × 146) + ($25 × 0) = $2,190
($15 × 0) + ($25 × 100) = $2,500

A third feasible solution is to produce nothing (X = 0, Y = 0). This solution obviously yields a CM of $0. The fourth corner is the intersection of the two simultaneous constraint equations.

$$\begin{aligned} 3X + 6Y &= 600 \\ 6X + 4Y &= 880 \\ \hline 2 \times (3X + 6Y) &= 2 \times 600 \\ 6X + 4Y &= 880 \\ \hline 8Y &= 320 \\ Y &= 40 \text{ and } X = 120 \end{aligned}$$

This solution results in a CM of $2,800 [(120 × $15) + (40 × $25)].

Answer (A) is incorrect. The 146 units of X and 0 units of Y yield a CM of $2,190. Answer (B) is incorrect. The 0 units of X and 100 units of Y yield a CM of $2,500. Answer (D) is incorrect. Producing 120 units of Y violates the constraint for Material A.

Questions 17.4.2 through 17.4.5 are based on the following information.

The Marlan Company has just begun producing metal trays and storage devices. It began operations with five metal-forming machines and five metal-cutting machines rented for $300 each per month. Each machine is capable of 400 hours of production per month. No additional machines can be obtained.

Linear Programming Formulation

Maximize Z = $4T + $7S			
Subject to:	T + 2S	≤	2,000
	2T + 2S	≤	2,000
	T	≥	800
	T,S	≥	0

If: T = number of trays produced
S = number of storage devices produced
Z = contribution margin

	Machine Hours per Unit		
	Trays	Storage Devices	Total Available Machine Hrs./Mo.
Metal-cutting	1	2	2,000
Metal-forming	2	2	2,000

Expected costs and revenues are as follows:

	Trays	Storage Devices
Selling price per unit	$18.00	$27.00
Variable cost per unit	14.00	20.00

Demand for the storage devices is unlimited, but no more than 800 trays can be sold per month.

Marlan must operate within the specified constraints as it tries to maximize the contribution margin from this new operation. Marlan intends to operate at the optimal level (OP) on the graph below.

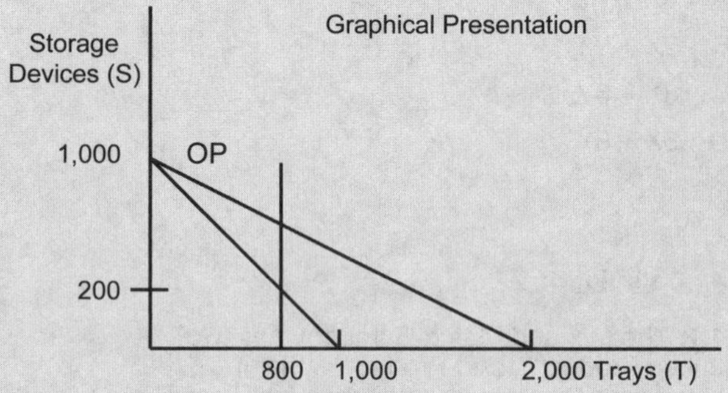

17.4.2. If the selling price of storage devices is lowered from $27 to $23, the maximum total contribution margin Marlan can earn will

A. Decrease by $3,800.

B. Decrease by $4,000.

C. Increase by $4,000.

D. Decrease by $3,200.

Answer (D) is correct. *(CMA, adapted)*

REQUIRED: The change in total CM given a change in selling price.

DISCUSSION: At the optimal point (point OP), 1,000 storage devices and no trays are produced. The result is a CM of $7,000 ($7 UCM × 1,000 storage devices). Lowering the price of storage devices reduces their UCM to $3 ($23 – $20). Because trays have a UCM of $4 ($18 – $14), as many as possible should be made when the UCM of storage devices is $3. This option maximizes the UCM per machine hour available for metal forming (the more restrictive of the metal working constraints). Thus, the maximum number of trays (800) is produced. Only 400 metal-forming hours are available [2,000 – (2 × 800)], so 200 storage devices are made. CM is $3,800 [($4 × 800) + ($3 × 200)], and the total CM decreases by $3,200 ($7,000 – $3,800).

Answer (A) is incorrect. The amount of $3,800 is the CM. Answer (B) is incorrect. The amount of $4,000 is the CM for 1,000 trays. Answer (C) is incorrect. The amount of $4,000 is the CM for 1,000 trays.

17.4.3. Marlan has just realized that a material needed for the production of both products is in short supply. The company can obtain enough of this material to produce 1,200 trays. Each tray requires 2/3 as much of this material as the storage devices. Which of the following constraints will incorporate completely and correctly this additional information into the formulation of the problem?

A. T ≤ 1,200

B. 2/3 S ≤ 1,200

C. T + 2/3 S ≤ 1,200

D. 2/3 T + 1 S ≤ 800

Answer (D) is correct. *(CMA, adapted)*

REQUIRED: The constraint required to express the change in available material.

DISCUSSION: Each question is to be treated independently. Thus, the decision to produce no trays is irrelevant. This material constraint limits trays and storage devices. Either 1,200 trays or 800 (1,200 × 2/3) storage devices or some combination can be produced. Thus, the constraint is

$$2/3T + 1S \leq 800$$

17.4.4. The maximum amount Marlan should be willing to spend on advertising to increase the demand for trays to 1,000 units per month is

A. $0

B. $600

C. $1,400

D. $5,400

Answer (A) is correct. *(CMA, adapted)*

REQUIRED: The maximum amount to spend on advertising to generate targeted demand.

DISCUSSION: If the optimal point is 1,000 storage devices and zero trays per month, trays should not be produced. Given unlimited demand for storage devices, advertising results in no marginal benefit.

17.4.5. If one metal-forming machine is returned to the rental agency and the rent can be avoided on it, Marlan's total profit will

A. Be unaffected.

B. Increase by $300.

C. Decrease by $1,100.

D. Decrease by $1,400.

Answer (C) is correct. *(CMA, adapted)*

REQUIRED: The effect on total profit of returning one machine.

DISCUSSION: Each metal-forming machine provides 400 hours of production per month, which generates 200 storage devices. Returning one machine therefore means that CM is reduced by $1,400 (200 units × $7). But cost is reduced by the $300 rent savings, so total profit decreases by $1,100.

Answer (A) is incorrect. Profit decreases. Answer (B) is incorrect. The amount of $300 is the rent saved. Answer (D) is incorrect. The amount of $1,400 is the decrease in CM.

17.4.6. When using the simplex method to solve a linear programming problem for the maximization of contribution margin, the optimal solution has been reached when the values in the index row of the matrix are

A. All zero.

B. All negative or zero.

C. Equal to zero when added across.

D. Equal to a positive value when added across.

Answer (B) is correct. *(CPA, adapted)*

REQUIRED: The nature of the values in the index row when the optimal solution is found.

DISCUSSION: Each item in the index row ($C_j - Z_j$) gives a measure of the direction and amount of the change in the objective function value resulting from a change in the solution. If the index row has positive or zero elements (nonnegative), the solution can be improved. Each item in the C_j row is the coefficient of a variable. A coefficient is the amount by which the value of the objective function increases if the variable increases by one unit. Each item in the Z_j row is the amount by which the value of the objective function decreases as a result of increasing the variable by one unit. This decrease (an opportunity cost) is caused by the change in the use of constraint resources. In a maximization problem, the optimal solution is found when each C_j item is equal to or less than the corresponding Z_j item. In a minimization problem, the foregoing also is true but with signs reversed.

Answer (A) is incorrect. The formula of $C_j - Z_j = 0$ is true only for basic variables. The variables not in the solution have positive or negative values. Answer (C) is incorrect. The answer of equal to zero when added across is nonsensical. Answer (D) is incorrect. The answer of equal to a positive value when added across is nonsensical.

Questions 17.4.7 through 17.4.10 are based on the following information. Milligan Company manufactures two models, small and large. Each model is processed as follows:

	Machining	Polishing
Small (X)	2 hours	1 hour
Large (Y)	4 hours	3 hours

The available time for processing the two models is 100 hours a week in the Machining Department and 90 hours a week in the Polishing Department. The contribution margin expected is $5 for the small model and $7 for the large model.

17.4.7. How is the objective function (maximization of total contribution margin) expressed?

A. 5X + 7Y

B. 5X + 7Y ≤ 190

C. 5X(3) + 7Y(7) ≤ 190

D. 12X + 10Y

Answer (A) is correct. *(CPA, adapted)*

REQUIRED: The objective function for the two models.

DISCUSSION: The objective function is the formula for the maximum total contribution margin. Given that each X produces a $5 CM, and each Y produces a $7 CM, the total CM is 5X + 7Y.

Answer (B) is incorrect. The objective function is not a constraint equation. Answer (C) is incorrect. The objective function is not a constraint equation. Answer (D) is incorrect. The unit CMs for X and Y are $5 and $7, respectively.

17.4.8. How is the restriction (constraint) for the Machining Department expressed?

A. 2(5X) + 4(7Y) ≤ 100

B. 2X + 4Y

C. 2X + 4Y ≤ 100

D. 5X + 7Y ≤ 100

Answer (C) is correct. *(CPA, adapted)*

REQUIRED: The constraint equation for the Machining Department.

DISCUSSION: The Machining Department has a total of 100 hours available each week. Each X requires 2 hours of time, and each Y requires 4 hours. Accordingly, the total time taken by production is 2X + 4Y, which must be equal to or less than the 100 hours available.

Answer (A) is incorrect. Unit CMs are not used in constraint equations. Answer (B) is incorrect. The hours available are omitted. Answer (D) is incorrect. Unit CMs are not used in constraint equations.

17.4.9. How is the restriction (constraint) for the Polishing Department expressed?

A. 5X + 7Y

B. 5X + 7Y ≤ 90

C. 2X + 4Y ≤ 100

D. X + 3Y ≤ 90

Answer (D) is correct. *(Publisher, adapted)*

REQUIRED: The constraint equation for the Polishing Department.

DISCUSSION: The Polishing Department has a total of 90 hours available each week. Each X requires 1 hour of time, and each Y requires 3 hours of time. Thus, the constraint is that X + 3Y must be equal to or less than 90.

Answer (A) is incorrect. The objective function is 5X + 7Y. Answer (B) is incorrect. Unit CMs are not used in constraint equations. Answer (C) is incorrect. The machining constraint is 2X + 4Y ≤ 100.

17.4.10. How many slack variables are needed for the simplex tableau?

A. None.

B. One.

C. Two.

D. Three.

Answer (C) is correct. *(Publisher, adapted)*

REQUIRED: The number of slack variables needed for the simplex tableau.

DISCUSSION: The simplex method requires a slack variable to transform each inequality constraint into an equality. Thus, two slack variables are needed, one for each of the two inequality constraints.

Answer (A) is incorrect. Two slack variables are needed. Answer (B) is incorrect. One objective function is stated. Answer (D) is incorrect. Two constraint equations and one objective function are stated.

Questions 17.4.11 through 17.4.13 are based on the following information. The final tableau for a linear programming profit maximization problem is presented below.

	X_1	X_2	X_3	S_1	S_2	
X_1	1	0	4	3	–7	50
X_2	0	1	–2	–6	2	60
	0	0	5	1	9	1,200

17.4.11. X_1, X_2, and X_3 represent products, slack variable S_1 relates to square feet (in thousands) of warehouse capacity, and slack variable S_2 relates to labor hours (in hundreds). The amount of X_1 that should be produced to maximize profit is

A. 60

B. 50

C. 1

D. 0

Answer (B) is correct. *(CPA, adapted)*

REQUIRED: The amount of X_1 to produce to maximize profit.

DISCUSSION: X_1 and X_2 are the products in the solution. Product X_3 is not included because its column does not contain a 0 and 1. The rows and columns for X_1 and X_2 but not X_3 form an identity matrix, so X_3 is not a basic variable. Accordingly, using the solution values in the right-hand column, the value of the objective function is

$$50\ X_1 + 60\ X_2 = 1{,}200$$

Answer (A) is incorrect. The amount of X_2 is 60. Answer (C) is incorrect. The 1 in the X_1 column means that X_1 is a basic variable. Answer (D) is incorrect. The 0 in the X_1 column means that X_1 is a basic variable.

17.4.12. The contribution to profit of an additional 100 hours of labor will be

A. 9

B. 2

C. 1

D. –7

Answer (A) is correct. *(CPA, adapted)*

REQUIRED: The contribution to profit of an additional 100 hours of labor.

DISCUSSION: The number 9 in the S_2 column (the slack variable in the labor constraint equation) is a Z_j value (the decrease in the value of the objective function from subtracting one unit of the resource). However, assuming operation within the range in which this shadow price is valid, 9 also is the amount by which the objective function increases as the result of increasing the labor constraint by one unit (100 hours).

Answer (B) is incorrect. The 2 in the S_2 column means that production of X_2 increases by 2. Answer (C) is incorrect. The Z_j value for S_1 (square feet) is 1. Answer (D) is incorrect. The decrease in production of X_1 is –7.

17.4.13. An additional 1,000 square feet of warehouse space will

A. Increase X_1 by 3 units and decrease X_2 by 6 units.

B. Decrease X_2 by 6 units and increase X_1 by 2 units.

C. Decrease X_1 by 7 units and increase X_2 by 2 units.

D. Increase X_1 by 3 units and decrease X_2 by 7 units.

Answer (A) is correct. *(CPA, adapted)*

REQUIRED: The effect of an additional 1,000 square feet of warehouse space.

DISCUSSION: If the square footage constraint is increased by one unit (1,000 sq. ft. of warehouse space), the effect is to increase profit by 1, to decrease production of X_2 by 6, and to increase production of X_1 by 3.

Answer (B) is incorrect. X_1 increases by 3 units. Answer (C) is incorrect. Increasing the labor constraint by one unit should decrease X_1 by 7 units and increase X_2 by 2 units. Answer (D) is incorrect. X_2 decreases by 6 units.

Questions 17.4.14 and 17.4.15 are based on the following information. Patsy, Inc., manufactures two products, X and Y. Each product must be processed in each of three departments: machining, assembling, and finishing. The hours needed to produce one unit of product per department and the maximum possible hours per department are provided below.

	Production Hours per Unit		Maximum Capacity
Department	X	Y	in Hours
Machining	2	1	420
Assembling	2	2	500
Finishing	2	3	600

Other restrictions follow:

$X \geq 50$
$Y \geq 50$

17.4.14. The objective function is to maximize profits if profit equals $4X + $2Y. Given the objective function and constraints, what is the most profitable number of units of X and Y, respectively, to manufacture?

A. 150 and 100.

B. 165 and 90.

C. 170 and 80.

D. 200 and 50.

Answer (C) is correct. *(CPA, adapted)*

REQUIRED: The most profitable product mix.

DISCUSSION: The optimal point is at a corner solution on a graph of the constraint equations and the objective function. The corner points define the feasibility space. Assuming the answers given contain the optimal solution, each should be evaluated by substituting the appropriate number of hours to eliminate the nonfeasible choices. Thus, 170 units of X and 80 units of Y should be produced [Profit = ($4 × 170) + ($2 × 80) = $840].

Answer (A) is incorrect. Profit is $800 [($4 × 150) + ($2 × 100)]. Answer (B) is incorrect. The assembling constraint is violated [(2 × 165) + (2 × 90) = 510]. Answer (D) is incorrect. The machining constraint is violated [(2 × 200) + (1 × 50) = 450].

17.4.15. How many constraints exist in Patsy's LP problem?

A. None.

B. Two.

C. Three.

D. Five.

Answer (D) is correct. *(Publisher, adapted)*

REQUIRED: The number of constraints.

DISCUSSION: Each of the three departments is subject to a capacity constraint, and X and Y are subject to minimum production constraints. Accordingly, the problem has five constraint equations.

Answer (A) is incorrect. Five constraints are given. Answer (B) is incorrect. Two equals the minimum production constraints. Answer (C) is incorrect. Three equals the capacity constraints.

STUDY UNIT EIGHTEEN
OTHER QUANTITATIVE APPROACHES

This study unit is an overview of some other quantitative approaches that have been tested on professional examinations.

Simulation is a computerized means of experimenting with logical and mathematical models when problems cannot be solved by known methods. It is an organized trial-and-error approach using a model of the real world to obtain information. Simulation is a five-step procedure involving (1) defining objectives, (2) formulating the model, (3) validating the model, (4) designing the experiment, and (5) performing the simulation and evaluating the results using appropriate statistical methods.

Queuing (waiting line) theory is a group of mathematical models for systems involving waiting lines. In general, a system consists of a queue (waiting line) and a service facility. The basic costs are (1) the cost of providing service (facility costs and operating costs) and (2) waiting cost (cost of idle resources). Queuing theory minimizes the total cost of the system, including service and waiting costs, for a given rate of arrivals.

Network models aid the planning and control of large-scale projects. Three common methods are Gantt (bar) charts, PERT, and CPM. A **Gantt chart** divides a project into activities. The start and completion times for each activity are estimated, and a bar chart is prepared showing each activity as a horizontal bar along a time scale. **Program Evaluation and Review Technique (PERT)** diagrams show each activity as a line between events. A sequence of lines shows interrelationships among activities. A PERT diagram includes probabilistic time estimates and identifies the critical path. The **Critical Path Method (CPM)** is a subset of PERT that uses deterministic time and cost estimates, including crash efforts and costs.

Learning curves reflect the increased rate at which people perform tasks as they gain experience. The time required to perform a given task becomes progressively shorter. This method applies only in the early stage of production or any new task. Ordinarily, the curve is expressed as a percentage of reduced time to complete a task for each doubling of cumulative production.

Other basic quantitative methods are matrix algebra, calculus, and game theory. **Matrix algebra** is an efficient method of manipulating multiple linear equations. The primary business application of **differential calculus** is to identify the maxima or minima of curvilinear functions. **Integral calculus** permits computation of the area under a curve. **Game (or decision) theory** is a mathematical approach to decision making when confronted with an enemy or competitor. Game theory classifies games according to how many players participate and the sum of the results. Games are classified according to the number of players and the algebraic sum of the payoffs.

The final subunit contains questions about the tools used in the **total quality management** approach covered in Study Unit 12.

QUESTIONS

18.1 Introduction to Quantitative Methods

18.1.1. Which is the false statement about quantitative methods?

A. Quantitative models are usually oversimplifications.

B. It is impossible to include all relevant variables in each model, and the methods may not be justifiable on a cost-benefit basis.

C. Every decision may be modeled mathematically and always permits a deterministic solution.

D. Behavioral issues should not be taken into account in analyzing quantitative methods.

Answer (D) is correct. *(Publisher, adapted)*

REQUIRED: The false statement about quantitative methods.

DISCUSSION: Including all relevant variables in a mathematical model is virtually impossible. Thus, the model must be evaluated regarding behavioral issues and other considerations.

Answer (A) is incorrect. Mathematical models are usually oversimplifications of the real world. To perform the calculations, assumptions must be made. Answer (B) is incorrect. Some relevant variables may not be quantified and are therefore not included. Also, the methods can be very complex and costly. Thus, cost-benefit analysis may not justify the use of some quantitative methods. Answer (C) is incorrect. Every real-life decision situation may be modeled mathematically under certain assumptions, and a deterministic solution may be achieved.

18.1.2. Variables that are important to the decision-making process but are out of the control of the decision maker, e.g., economic conditions, are considered to be

A. Exogenous variables.

B. Decision variables.

C. Performance criteria.

D. Constraints.

Answer (A) is correct. *(CMA, adapted)*

REQUIRED: The term for variables that are outside the control of the decision maker.

DISCUSSION: Exogenous or input variables are outside the control of the decision maker. Exogenous means "originating externally." These variables influence the decision model (system) but are not influenced by it.

Answer (B) is incorrect. At least one of the decision variables in a model must be under the decision maker's control. Thus, at least one variable cannot be exogenous. Answer (C) is incorrect. Performance criteria are the means of measuring the results of a decision after the fact. Answer (D) is incorrect. Constraints are limitations (constants, not variables) that must be considered as part of the decision process.

18.1.3. A company is deciding whether to purchase an automated machine to manufacture one of its products. Expected net cash flows from this decision depend on several factors, interactions among those factors, and the probabilities associated with different levels of those factors. The method that the company should use to evaluate the distribution of net cash flows from this decision and changes in net cash flows resulting from changes in levels of various factors is

A. Simulation and sensitivity analysis.

B. Linear programming.

C. Correlation analysis.

D. Differential analysis.

Answer (A) is correct. *(CIA, adapted)*

REQUIRED: The method used to evaluate cash flows from the purchase of a machine.

DISCUSSION: Simulation describes the behavior of a real-world system over time. It ordinarily uses a computer program to perform the simulation computations. Sensitivity analysis examines how outcomes change as the model parameters change.

Answer (B) is incorrect. Linear programming is a method for optimizing a given objective function subject to certain constraints. Answer (C) is incorrect. Correlation analysis is a statistical procedure for studying the relation between variables. Answer (D) is incorrect. Differential analysis is used for decision making that compares differences in costs (revenues) of two or more options.

18.1.4. Which of the following is not true about simulation models?

A. They are deterministic in nature.

B. They may involve sampling.

C. They mathematically estimate what actual performance would be.

D. They emulate stochastic systems.

Answer (A) is correct. *(CIA, adapted)*

REQUIRED: The false statement about simulation models.

DISCUSSION: Simulation experiments with logical or mathematical models using a computer. The simulation procedure has five steps: (1) define the objectives, (2) formulate the model, (3) validate the model, (4) design the experiment, and (5) conduct the simulation and evaluate the results. A simulation uses the laws of probability to generate values for random variables. Thus, simulation models are probabilistic, not deterministic.

Answer (B) is incorrect. Simulation modeling samples the operation of a system. Answer (C) is incorrect. Simulation models mathematically estimate what performance would be under various conditions. Answer (D) is incorrect. Simulation models are by definition stochastic or probabilistic models.

Questions 18.1.5 and 18.1.6 are based on the following information. A computer store sells four computer models designated as P104, X104, A104, and S104. The store manager has made random number assignments to represent customer choices based on past sales data. The assignments are shown below.

Model	Random Numbers
P104	0-1
X104	2-6
A104	7-8
S104	9

18.1.5. The probability that a customer will select model P104 is

A. 10%

B. 20%

C. 50%

D. Some percentage other than those given.

Answer (B) is correct. *(CMA, adapted)*

REQUIRED: The probability that a customer will select model P104.

DISCUSSION: Ten random numbers have been assigned. Of these, two (0 and 1) have been assigned to model P104. Thus, there are two chances out of ten, or 20%, that a customer will select that model.

Answer (A) is incorrect. The probability of selecting S104 is 10%. Answer (C) is incorrect. The probability of selecting X104 is 50%. Answer (D) is incorrect. The correct percentage is among the responses given.

18.1.6. In running a simulation of the computer demand, the following numbers are drawn in sequence: 2, 8, and 6. The simulation indicates that the third customer will purchase.

A. Model P104.

B. Model X104.

C. Model A104.

D. Model S104.

Answer (B) is correct. *(CMA, adapted)*

REQUIRED: The model that will be purchased by the third customer when the numbers drawn are 2, 8, and 6.

DISCUSSION: The third customer is simulated by the third number drawn. Therefore, the third customer's purchase is represented by the number 6. The numbers 2 through 6 correspond to model X104. Thus, the third customer is expected to purchase model X104.

Answer (A) is incorrect. Model P104 corresponds to numbers 0 and 1. Answer (C) is incorrect. Model A104 corresponds to numbers 7 and 8. Answer (D) is incorrect. Model S104 corresponds to number 9.

18.1.7. Quick Response Plumbing (QRP), a wholesale distributor, supplies plumbing contractors and retailers throughout the Northeast on a next-day delivery basis. QRP has a centrally located warehouse to accept receipts of plumbing supplies. The warehouse has a single dock to accept and unload railroad freight cars during the night. It takes 5 hours to unload each freight car. QRP's prior records indicate that the number of freight cars that arrive in the course of a night range from zero to five or more, with no indicated pattern of arrivals. If more than two freight cars arrive on the same night, some freight must be held until the next day for unloading. QRP wants to estimate the wait time when more than two freight cars arrive in the same night. The appropriate technique to analyze the arrival of freight cars is

A. Integer programming.

B. Linear programming.

C. Sensitivity analysis.

D. Monte Carlo simulation.

Answer (D) is correct. *(CMA, adapted)*

REQUIRED: The appropriate method to analyze the arrival of freight cars, given no indicated pattern of arrivals.

DISCUSSION: Monte Carlo simulation generates the individual values for a random variable, such as the arrival of freight cars. A random number generator is used to produce numbers with a uniform probability distribution. The second step of the Monte Carlo process transforms the random numbers into values consistent with the desired distribution. The performance of the model then may be investigated by randomly selecting values for each of the variables in the model based on the probability distribution of each variable and calculating the value of the solution. If this process is performed many times, the distribution of results from the model is obtained.

Answer (A) is incorrect. Integer programming is a variation of linear programming that applies to problems in which some variables have discrete, noncontinuous values. Answer (B) is incorrect. Linear programming optimizes a function, subject to constraints. Answer (C) is incorrect. Sensitivity analysis involves making several estimates of key variables and recalculating results based on the alternative estimates.

18.1.8. Probability (risk) analysis is

A. Used only when the sum of probabilities is less than one.

B. Used only for situations involving five or fewer possible outcomes.

C. Incompatible with sensitivity analysis.

D. An extension of sensitivity analysis.

Answer (D) is correct. *(CPA, adapted)*

REQUIRED: The description of probability (risk) analysis.

DISCUSSION: Probability (risk) analysis is used to examine the array of possible outcomes given alternative parameters. Sensitivity analysis answers what-if questions when alternative parameters are changed. Thus, risk (probability) analysis is similar to sensitivity analysis. Both evaluate the probabilities and effects of differing inputs or outputs.

Answer (A) is incorrect. The sum must equal one. Answer (B) is incorrect. Probability analysis can be used when many outcomes are possible. Answer (C) is incorrect. Probability analysis enhances sensitivity analysis.

18.1.9. A construction firm is in the process of building a simulation model for cost estimation purposes. Management has identified all relevant variables and relationships and gathered data on past projects. The next step should be model

A. Implementation.

B. Design.

C. Validation.

D. Experimentation.

Answer (C) is correct. *(CIA, adapted)*

REQUIRED: The next step in developing a simulation model.

DISCUSSION: The first step in designing a simulation model is to define the objectives of the project. The second step is to formulate the model, that is, to determine the variables to be included, their behavior, and their interrelationships in precise logical and mathematical terms. The third step is to validate the model. Some assurance is needed that the results of the experiment are realistic. For example, if the model gives results equivalent to what actually happened, the model is historically valid. Some risk remains, however, that changes could make the model invalid for the future.

Answer (A) is incorrect. Implementation of the simulation follows validation. Answer (B) is incorrect. The model already has been formulated (designed). Answer (D) is incorrect. Experimentation is sampling the operation of the model after validation and before full implementation.

18.1.10. A firm is attempting to estimate the reserves for doubtful accounts. The probabilities of these doubtful accounts follow a transition process over time. They evolve from their starting value to a changed value. As such, the most effective technique to analyze the problem is

A. Markov chain analysis.

B. Econometric theory.

C. Monte Carlo analysis.

D. Dynamic programming.

Answer (A) is correct. *(CIA, adapted)*

REQUIRED: The most effective method for analyzing a problem involving changing probabilities.

DISCUSSION: A Markov chain is a series of events in which the probability of an event depends on the immediately preceding event. An example is the game of blackjack in which the probability of certain cards being dealt is dependent upon what cards already have been dealt. In the analysis of bad debts, preceding events, such as collections, credit policy changes, and writeoffs, affect the probabilities of future losses.

Answer (B) is incorrect. Econometrics forecasts the effects of different economic policies and conditions. Answer (C) is incorrect. Monte Carlo analysis is a simulation method that uses random-number procedures to create values for probabilistic components. Answer (D) is incorrect. Dynamic programming is a problem-solving approach that divides a large mathematical model into a number of smaller, manageable problems.

18.2 Queuing Theory

18.2.1. A company has several departments that conduct technical studies and prepare reports for clients. Recently, there have been long delays in having these reports copied at the company's centralized copy center because of the dramatic increase in business. Management is considering decentralizing copy services to reduce the turnaround and provide clients with timely reports. An appropriate technique for minimizing turnaround time and the cost of providing copy services is

A. Queuing theory.

B. Linear programming.

C. Regression analysis.

D. Game theory.

Answer (A) is correct. *(CIA, adapted)*

REQUIRED: The method for minimizing turnaround time and the cost of providing copy services.

DISCUSSION: Queuing theory is a group of mathematical models for systems involving waiting lines. In general, a queuing system consists of a waiting line and a service facility (e.g., a copy center). The objective is to minimize total costs, including both service and waiting costs (turnaround time), for a given rate of arrivals.

Answer (B) is incorrect. Linear programming optimizes a given objective function subject to constraints. Answer (C) is incorrect. Regression analysis estimates the relation among variables. Answer (D) is incorrect. Game theory is an approach to decision making that considers the actions of competitors.

18.2.2. Queuing models are concerned with balancing the cost of waiting in the queue with the

A. Cost of providing service.

B. Number of customers in the queue.

C. Average waiting time in the queue.

D. Usage rate for the service being rendered.

Answer (A) is correct. *(CMA, adapted)*

REQUIRED: The true statement about the objective of queuing models.

DISCUSSION: Queuing (waiting-line) models minimize, for a given rate of arrivals, the sum of (1) the cost of providing service (including facility costs and operating costs) and (2) the cost of idle resources waiting in line. Waiting cost may be a direct cost if paid employees are waiting or an opportunity cost in the case of waiting customers. This minimization occurs at the point at which the cost of waiting is balanced by the cost of providing service.

18.2.3. The operating condition that cannot be identified by using a queuing model is the

A. Average percentage of time that a service facility is idle.

B. Probability of a specified number of units in the queue.

C. Actual amount of time each unit spends in the queue.

D. Average number of units in the system and the mean length of the queue.

Answer (C) is correct. *(CMA, adapted)*

REQUIRED: The operating condition that cannot be identified by using a queuing model.

DISCUSSION: Queuing models determine the operating characteristics of a waiting line. They include (1) the probability that no units are in the system, (2) the average units in the line, (3) the average units in the system, (4) the average time a unit waits, (5) the average time a unit is in the system, (6) the probability that a unit must wait, and (7) the probability of a given number of units in the system. However, the actual time spent in the queue cannot be determined from the model.

Answer (A) is incorrect. The queuing model calculates the average percentage of time that a service facility is idle. Answer (B) is incorrect. The queuing model calculates the probability of a specified number of units in the queue. Answer (D) is incorrect. The queuing model calculates the average number of units in the system and the mean length of the queue.

18.2.4. A bank has changed from a system in which lines are formed in front of each teller to a one-line, multiple-server system. When a teller is free, the person at the head of the line goes to that teller. Implementing the new system will

A. Decrease the bank's wage expenses because the new system uses fewer tellers.

B. Decrease time customers spend in the line.

C. Increase accuracy in teller reconciliations at the end of the day because fewer customers are served by each teller.

D. Improve on-the-job training for tellers because each will perform different duties.

Answer (B) is correct. *(CIA, adapted)*

REQUIRED: The effect of implementing the new queuing system.

DISCUSSION: When all customers must wait in a single queue (line), a decrease in waiting time is possible given multiple servers. An added effect is to increase customer satisfaction.

Answer (A) is incorrect. The number of employees is unlikely to change due to the new system. Answer (C) is incorrect. Assuming a Poisson process, the number of customers per teller does not change. Answer (D) is incorrect. Tellers' duties do not change, so on-the-job training does not improve.

18.2.5. The drive-through service at a fast-food restaurant consists of driving up to place an order, advancing to a window to pay for the order, and then advancing to another window to receive the items ordered. This type of waiting-line system is

A. Single channel, single phase.

B. Single channel, multiple phase.

C. Multiple channel, single phase.

D. Multiple channel, multiple phase.

Answer (B) is correct. *(CIA, adapted)*

REQUIRED: The type of waiting-line system described.

DISCUSSION: The drive-through represents a single queue (channel). Because this waiting line has three services in series, it is multiple phase. Another example is the typical factory assembly line. This terminology (channel, phase), however, is not used by all writers on queuing theory.

Answer (A) is incorrect. Service by one ticket-seller at a movie theater is an example of a single-channel, single-phase system. Answer (C) is incorrect. Supermarket checkout lines are a common example of multiple single-phase servers servicing multiple lines. Answer (D) is incorrect. An example of a multiple-channel, multiple-phase system is a set of supermarket checkout lines, each of which is served in sequence by a cashier and a person who packs grocery bags.

Questions 18.2.6 through 18.2.8 are based on the following information.

A bank has two drive-in lanes to serve customers, one attached to the bank itself, the second on an island. One teller serves both stations. The bank is interested in determining the average waiting times of customers and has developed a model based on random numbers. The two key factors are the time between successive car arrivals and the time customers wait in line.

Assume that the analysis begins with cars just arriving at both service windows, both requiring 3 minutes of service time. Car 1 is at the attached window, and car 2 is at the island window. A car will always go to the window attached to the bank unless that window has more cars waiting than the island window. The lone teller will always serve the car that arrived first. If two cars arrive simultaneously, the one at the attached window will be served before the one at the island.

Based on a known probability distribution, the bank assigns random numbers to arrival and service times:

Random #	Time between Arrivals	Random #	Service Time
1	1 minute	1, 2	1 minute
2, 3	2 minutes	3	2 minutes
4, 5, 6	3 minutes	4, 5, 6	3 minutes
7, 8	4 minutes	7, 8, 9	4 minutes

The bank then selects random numbers for the next two cars:

Random Numbers Selected

	Arrival	Service
Car 3	#3	#7
Car 4	#7	#8

18.2.6. The arrival time follows which probability distribution?

A. Binomial.

B. Chi-square.

C. Poisson.

D. Exponential.

Answer (C) is correct. *(CIA, adapted)*

REQUIRED: The probability distribution of the arrival time.

DISCUSSION: Queuing models assume that arrivals follow a Poisson process in which (1) the events (arrivals) are independent, (2) any number of events must be possible in the interval of time, (3) the probability of an event is proportional to the length of the interval, and (4) the probability of more than one event is negligible if the interval is sufficiently small. If λ is the average number of events in a given interval, k is the number of events, and e is the natural logarithm (2.71828...), the probability of k is

$$f(k) = \frac{\lambda^k e^{-\lambda}}{k!}$$

Answer (A) is incorrect. The binomial distribution is a discrete distribution in which each trial has just two outcomes. Answer (B) is incorrect. The chi-square distribution is a continuous distribution used to measure the fit between actual data and the theoretical distribution. Answer (D) is incorrect. Service time has an exponential distribution. This distribution gives the probability of zero events in a given interval, i.e., the probability of a specified time between arrivals.

18.2.7. The time that car 3 will have to wait to be serviced (not including its own service time) is

A. 0-2 minutes.

B. 3 minutes.

C. 4 minutes.

D. 5+ minutes.

Answer (C) is correct. *(CIA, adapted)*

REQUIRED: The time that car 3 must wait to be serviced (not including its own service time).

DISCUSSION: Car 1 is at the attached window and requires 3 minutes to service. Car 2 must wait for car 1 to be serviced (3 minutes in the queue + 3 minutes to be serviced = 6 minutes). Car 3 arrived at the attached window 2 minutes after cars 1 and 2. It must wait 1 minute for car 1 to be serviced and 3 minutes for car 2 to be serviced, a waiting time of 4 minutes.

18.2.8. The time that car 4 will have to wait to be serviced (not including its own service time) is

A. 0-2 minutes.

B. 3 minutes.

C. 4 minutes.

D. 5+ minutes.

Answer (C) is correct. *(CIA, adapted)*

REQUIRED: The time that car 4 must wait to be serviced (not including its own service time).

DISCUSSION: Car 4 arrives at the just-vacated island window 4 minutes after car 3. It must wait 4 minutes for car 3 to be serviced.

18.2.9. A post office serves customers in a single line at one service window. During peak periods, the rate of arrivals has a Poisson distribution, with an average of 100 customers per hour, and service times that are exponentially distributed, with an average of 60 seconds per customer. From this, one can conclude that the

A. Queue will expand to infinity.

B. Server will be idle one-sixth of the time.

C. Average rate is 100 customers per hour.

D. Average customer waiting time is 2.5 minutes.

Answer (A) is correct. *(CIA, adapted)*
REQUIRED: The conclusion about a queuing model.
DISCUSSION: One hundred customers arrive in line per hour, and only 60 are serviced per hour. Accordingly, the queue expands indefinitely (to infinity) during peak periods.
Answer (B) is incorrect. Insufficient information is given to determine overall idle time. The question gives only peak period data. Answer (C) is incorrect. Peak customer service is only 60 per hour. Answer (D) is incorrect. Insufficient information is given to determine average customer waiting time. The question gives only peak period data.

18.3 Network Models

18.3.1. A bank is designing an on-the-job training program for its branch managers. The bank would like to design the program so that participants can complete it as quickly as possible. The training program requires that certain activities be completed before others. For example, a participant cannot make credit loan decisions without first having obtained experience in the loan department. An appropriate scheduling technique for this training program is

A. PERT/CPM.

B. Linear programming.

C. Queuing theory.

D. Sensitivity analysis.

Answer (A) is correct. *(CIA, adapted)*
REQUIRED: The appropriate scheduling method.
DISCUSSION: PERT/CPM is a network model for scheduling interrelated time series activities and identifying any critical paths in the series of activities. The critical path is the longest path through the network.
Answer (B) is incorrect. Linear programming is a mathematical method for maximizing or minimizing a given objective function, subject to certain constraints. Answer (C) is incorrect. Queuing theory is used to minimize the costs of waiting lines when items arrive randomly at a service point and are serviced sequentially. Answer (D) is incorrect. Sensitivity analysis is a method for studying the effects of changes in one or more variables on the results of a decision model.

18.3.2. PERT and the critical path method (CPM) are used for

A. Determining the optimal product mix.

B. Project planning and control.

C. Determining product costs.

D. Determining the number of servers needed in a fast food restaurant.

Answer (B) is correct. *(CMA, adapted)*
REQUIRED: The reason for using PERT and CPM.
DISCUSSION: PERT (Program Evaluation and Review Technique) and CPM are used in the planning and control of a complex system or process. Each diagrams the time relationships between the events or subprojects to identify those having a direct effect on the completion date of the project as a whole.
Answer (A) is incorrect. Linear programming can determine product mix. Answer (C) is incorrect. Product costs are determined by cost accounting. Answer (D) is incorrect. Queuing theory determines the number of servers needed in a restaurant.

18.3.3. The primary difference between PERT and CPM is that

A. CPM uses probabilities on the activity times and PERT does not.

B. PERT considers activity costs and CPM does not.

C. PERT can assign probabilities to activity times and CPM does not.

D. CPM considers activity costs and PERT does not.

Answer (D) is correct. *(CMA, adapted)*
REQUIRED: The primary difference between PERT and CPM.
DISCUSSION: CPM is a subset of PERT. Like PERT, it is a network method. Unlike PERT, it uses deterministic time and cost estimates. Its advantages include cost estimates, crash times, and crash costs. These estimates allow the project manager to estimate the costs of completing the project if some activities are completed on a crash basis.
Answer (A) is incorrect. A less significant difference between PERT and CPM is that PERT uses probabilistic estimates of completion times. CPM times are deterministic. Answer (B) is incorrect. CPM but not PERT uses activity costs and considers crash times. Answer (C) is incorrect. A less significant difference between PERT and CPM is that PERT uses probabilistic estimates of completion times. CPM times are deterministic.

18.3.4. PERT is widely used to plan and measure progress toward scheduled events. PERT is combined with cost data to produce a PERT-Cost analysis to

A. Calculate the total project cost inclusive of the additional slack time.

B. Evaluate and optimize trade-offs between time of an event's completion and its cost to complete.

C. Implement computer-integrated manufacturing concepts.

D. Calculate expected activity times.

Answer (B) is correct. *(CMA, adapted)*

REQUIRED: The true statement about PERT-Cost analysis.

DISCUSSION: Combining PERT with cost data permits decisions as to whether the benefits of earlier completion of a project justify the additional costs of completion. For this purpose, activity times and costs must be estimated for both normal and crash efforts.

Answer (A) is incorrect. Slack time is an inherent part of the noncritical paths on PERT projects. Answer (C) is incorrect. PERT-Cost can be used without computerization. Answer (D) is incorrect. Costs are not needed for these calculations.

18.3.5. A Gantt chart

A. Shows the critical path for a project.

B. Is used for determining an optimal product mix.

C. Shows only the activities along the critical path of a network.

D. Does not necessarily show the critical path through a network.

Answer (D) is correct. *(CMA, adapted)*

REQUIRED: The true statement about a Gantt chart.

DISCUSSION: A Gantt or bar chart is sometimes used in conjunction with PERT or CPM to show the progress of a special project. Time is on the horizontal axis, the length of a bar equals the length of an activity, and shading indicates the degree of completion. However, the Gantt chart is not as sophisticated as PERT or CPM. It does not reflect the relationships among the activities or define a critical path.

Answer (A) is incorrect. The critical path is not shown on a Gantt chart. Answer (B) is incorrect. Linear programming is used to determine an optimal product mix. Answer (C) is incorrect. A Gantt chart shows the activities to be completed but not their sequencing.

18.3.6. In the Program Evaluation Review Technique (PERT), slack is the

A. Uncertainty associated with time estimates.

B. Path that has the largest amount of time associated with it.

C. Excess time available in the completion of the project after crashing the critical path.

D. Number of days an activity can be delayed without forcing a delay for the entire project.

Answer (D) is correct. *(CMA, adapted)*

REQUIRED: The meaning of slack in a PERT analysis.

DISCUSSION: The critical path is the longest path in time through the network. That path is critical because, if any activity on the critical path takes longer than expected, the entire project is delayed. Paths that are not critical have slack time. Slack is the number of days an activity can be delayed without forcing a delay of the entire project.

Answer (A) is incorrect. Uncertainty is reflected in the use of probabilistic estimates of completion times. Answer (B) is incorrect. The path with the largest amount of time associated with it is the critical path. Answer (C) is incorrect. Slack exists for some activities whether or not the critical path is crashed.

18.3.7. The process of adding resources to shorten selected activity times on the critical path in project scheduling is called

A. Crashing.

B. The Delphi technique.

C. Material-requirements planning.

D. A branch-and-bound solution.

Answer (A) is correct. *(CIA, adapted)*

REQUIRED: The process of adding resources to shorten selected activity times on the critical path.

DISCUSSION: When making a cost-time trade-off, the first activity to be crashed (have its completion time accelerated) is on the critical path. To select an activity on another path does not reduce the total time of completion. The activity chosen should have a completion time that can be accelerated at the lowest possible cost per unit of time saved.

Answer (B) is incorrect. The Delphi technique is a qualitative forecasting approach. Answer (C) is incorrect. Material-requirements planning is an inventory model. Answer (D) is incorrect. A branch-and-bound solution is an integer programming solution.

18.3.8. Which of the following terms is not used in project management?

A. Dummy activity.

B. Latest finish.

C. Optimistic time.

D. Lumpy demand.

Answer (D) is correct. *(CIA, adapted)*

REQUIRED: The term not used in project management.

DISCUSSION: Project management applies to managing teams assigned to special projects. Lumpy demand is periodic demand for a product or service that increases in large, lumpy increments.

Answer (A) is incorrect. A dummy consumes no time but establishes precedence among activities. It is used specifically in project management. Answer (B) is incorrect. The latest finish is the latest that an activity can finish without causing delay in the completion of the project. Answer (C) is incorrect. Optimistic time is the time for completing a project if all goes well.

18.3.9. California Building Corporation uses the critical path method to monitor construction jobs. The company is currently 2 weeks behind schedule on Job #181, which is subject to a $10,500-per-week completion penalty. Path A-B-C-F-G-H-I has a normal completion time of 20 weeks, and critical path A-D-E-F-G-H-I has a normal completion time of 22 weeks. The following activities can be crashed:

Activities	Cost to Crash 1 Week	Cost to Crash 2 Weeks
BC	$ 8,000	$15,000
DE	10,000	19,600
EF	8,800	19,500

California Building desires to reduce the normal completion time of Job #181 and, at the same time, report the highest possible income for the year. California Building should crash

A. Activity BC 1 week and activity EF 1 week.

B. Activity DE 1 week and activity BC 1 week.

C. Activity EF 2 weeks.

D. Activity DE 1 week and activity EF 1 week.

Answer (D) is correct. *(CMA, adapted)*

REQUIRED: The activity that should be crashed (sped up at additional cost) to maximize income.

DISCUSSION: Activities that are to be crashed in a CPM problem should be on the critical (longest) path. Thus, activity BC should not be selected because it is not on the critical path. To finish activity BC 2 weeks early does not reduce the total time to complete the project. Thus, the only feasible choices are DE and EF on the critical path. The total cost to crash DE and EF for 1 week each is $18,800 ($10,000 + $8,800), which is less than the cost to crash either activity for 2 weeks. Thus, DE and EF should be crashed for 1 week each because the total cost is less than the $21,000 ($10,500 × 2) 2-week delay penalty.

Answer (A) is incorrect. BC is not on the critical path. Answer (B) is incorrect. BC is not on the critical path. Answer (C) is incorrect. Crashing activity EF 2 weeks costs $19,500, which exceeds the cost of crashing DE 1 week and EF 1 week.

18.3.10. When using PERT (Program Evaluation Review Technique), the expected time for an activity when given an optimistic time (a), a pessimistic time (b), and a most likely time (m), is calculated by which one of the following formulas?

A. (b – a) ÷ 2

B. (a + b) ÷ 2

C. (a + 4m + b) ÷ 6

D. (4abm) ÷ 6

Answer (C) is correct. *(CMA, adapted)*

REQUIRED: The formula for calculating the expected time for an activity when using PERT.

DISCUSSION: PERT analysis includes probabilistic estimates of activity completion times. Three time estimates are made: (1) optimistic, (2) most likely, and (3) pessimistic. These estimates are assumed to approximate a beta probability distribution. PERT approximates the mean of the beta distribution by dividing the sum of (1) the optimistic time, (2) the pessimistic time, and (3) four times the most likely time by six.

Answer (A) is incorrect. The most likely time estimate should be in the formula. Answer (B) is incorrect. The most likely time estimate should be in the formula. Answer (D) is incorrect. All time estimates are not weighted equally.

18.3.11. In a PERT network, the optimistic time for a particular activity is 9 weeks, and the pessimistic time is 21 weeks. Which one of the following is the best estimate of the standard deviation for the activity?

A. 2

B. 6

C. 9

D. 12

Answer (A) is correct. *(CMA, adapted)*

REQUIRED: The standard deviation for the completion time of a PERT project given an optimistic time and a pessimistic time.

DISCUSSION: PERT approximates the standard deviation by dividing the difference between the pessimistic and optimistic times by 6. The basis for this approximation is that various probability distributions have tails that are about plus or minus 3 standard deviations from the mean. Accordingly, the estimated standard deviation is 2 weeks [(21 weeks – 9 weeks) ÷ 6].

Answer (B) is incorrect. The approximate number of standard deviations in various probability distributions is 6. Answer (C) is incorrect. The pessimistic time is 9. Answer (D) is incorrect. The optimistic time minus the pessimistic time is 12.

18.3.12. A PERT network has only two activities on its critical path. These activities have standard deviations of 6 and 8, respectively. The standard deviation of the project completion time is

A. 7

B. 10

C. 14

D. 100

Answer (B) is correct. *(CMA, adapted)*

REQUIRED: The standard deviation of the project completion time.

DISCUSSION: The standard deviation of the project completion time is the square root of the sum of the variances (squares of the standard deviations) of the times for activities on the critical path. The standard deviation of the project completion time (time for the critical path) is therefore the square root of $(6^2 + 8^2)$, or 10.

Answer (A) is incorrect. The mean of the standard deviations is 7. Answer (C) is incorrect. The sum of the standard deviations is 14. Answer (D) is incorrect. The sum of the variances is 100.

Questions 18.3.13 and 18.3.14 are based on the following information. The PERT network diagram and corresponding activity cost chart for a manufacturing project at Networks, Inc., is presented below. The numbers in the diagram are the expected times (in days) to perform each activity in the project.

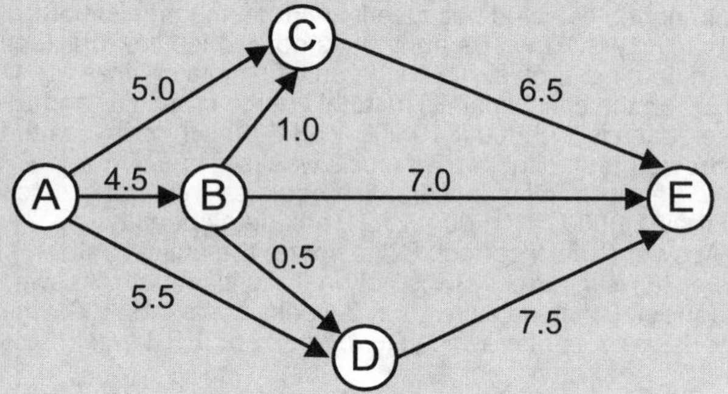

Activity	Normal Cost	Crash Time (Days)	Crash Cost
AB	$3,000	3.50	$4,000
AC	5,000	4.50	5,250
AD	4,000	4.00	4,750
BE	6,000	5.00	7,000
CE	8,000	5.00	9,200
DE	6,000	6.50	6,750
BC	2,500	.50	3,500
BD	2,000	.25	2,500

18.3.13. The expected time of the critical path is

A. 12.0 days.

B. 13.0 days.

C. 11.5 days.

D. 12.5 days.

Answer (B) is correct. *(CMA, adapted)*

REQUIRED: The expected time of the critical path.

DISCUSSION: The critical path is the longest path. The longest path in the diagram is A-D-E, which requires 13 days (5.5 + 7.5) based on expected times.

Answer (A) is incorrect. The days required for A-B-C-E equal 12.0 days. Answer (C) is incorrect. The days required for A-B-E and for A-C-E equal 11.5 days. Answer (D) is incorrect. The days required for A-B-D-E equal 12.5 days.

18.3.14. To keep costs at a minimum and decrease the completion time by 1 1/2 days, Networks, Inc., should crash activity(ies)

A. AD and AB.

B. DE.

C. AD.

D. AB and CE.

Answer (A) is correct. *(CMA, adapted)*

REQUIRED: The activity(ies) that can be crashed by a specified number of days at the least cost.

DISCUSSION: The critical path (A-D-E) requires 13 days. However, to decrease completion time to 11.5 days, paths A-B-C-E (4.5 + 1.0 + 6.5 = 12 days) and A-B-D-E (4.5 + .5 + 7.5 = 12.5 days) must also be shortened. Thus, A-D-E must be reduced by 1.5 days, A-B-C-E by .5 day, and A-B-D-E by 1.0 day. The only way to decrease A-D-E by 1.5 days is to crash activity AD (5.5 expected time – 4.0 crash time = 1.5 days). Crashing DE results in a 1.0-day saving (7.5 – 6.5) only. Crashing AB is the efficient way to reduce both A-B-C-E and A-B-D-E. The incremental cost of crashing AB is $1,000 ($4,000 crash cost – $3,000 normal cost). The alternatives are more costly.

Answer (B) is incorrect. Crashing DE saves only 1.0 day (7.5 – 6.5) and does not reduce A-B-C-E. Answer (C) is incorrect. Crashing AD does not reduce A-B-C-E or A-B-D-E. Answer (D) is incorrect. AB and CE are not on the critical path.

18.3.15. The following information applies to a project:

Activity	Time (days)	Immediate Predecessor
A	5	None
B	3	None
C	4	A
D	2	B
E	6	C, D

The earliest completion time for the project is

A. 11 days.

B. 14 days.

C. 15 days.

D. 20 days.

Answer (C) is correct. *(CIA, adapted)*

REQUIRED: The earliest completion time.

DISCUSSION: The two paths through the network are A-C-E (5 + 4 + 6 = 15 days) and B-D-E (3 + 2 + 6 = 11 days). The critical or longest path is A-C-E. Thus, the earliest completion time is 15 days.

Answer (A) is incorrect. The shortest time to completion is 11 days. Answer (B) is incorrect. The completion time of a path to completion is not 14 days. Answer (D) is incorrect. The sum of all of the activity times is 20 days.

18.3.16. The Gantt chart below shows that the project is

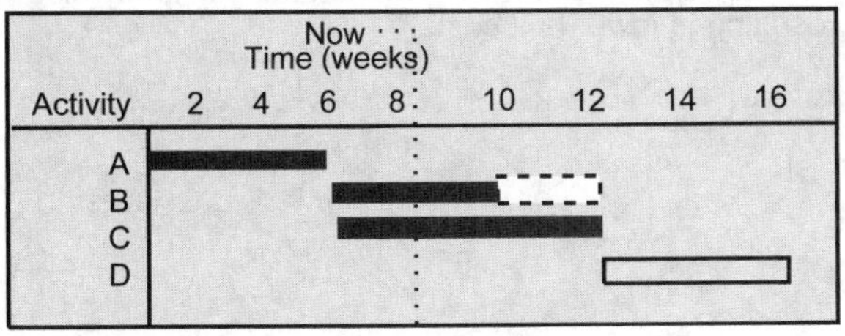

A. Complete.

B. Ahead of schedule.

C. On schedule.

D. Behind schedule.

Answer (B) is correct. *(CIA, adapted)*

REQUIRED: The status of a project according to the Gantt chart.

DISCUSSION: Assuming that (1) each of the bars represents the expected time necessary to complete an activity and (2) the shaded regions represent the portions completed, activity A has been completed as scheduled, and activities B and C are ahead of schedule. Consequently, the project is ahead of schedule.

18.4 Learning Curves

18.4.1. An entity received a request for a competitive bid for the sale of one of its unique boating products with a desired modification. The entity is now in the process of manufacturing this product but with a slightly different modification for another customer. These unique products are labor intensive and both will have long production runs. Which one of the following methods should be used to estimate the cost of the new competitive bid?

A. Expected value analysis.

B. Learning curve analysis.

C. Regression analysis.

D. Continuous probability simulation.

Answer (B) is correct. *(CMA, adapted)*

REQUIRED: The method of estimating the cost of a product similar to a product now in process.

DISCUSSION: Learning curves reflect the increased rate at which people perform tasks as they gain experience. The time required to perform a given task becomes progressively shorter as the workers better learn their jobs. Ordinarily, the curve is expressed as a percentage of reduced time to complete a task for each doubling of cumulative production. This methodology is appropriate when submitting a bid for a product for which the firm already has experience. The experience should lead to shorter production time and lower costs.

Answer (A) is incorrect. Expected value analysis selects the best alternative for decisions involving risk by multiplying the probability of each outcome by its payoff, and summing the products. Answer (C) is incorrect. Regression analysis is used to find an equation for the linear relationships among variables. Answer (D) is incorrect. Simulation would not be appropriate when a single project is being bid upon.

18.4.2. Which of the following may be scheduled in production planning by the use of learning curves?

A. Purchases of materials.

B. Subassembly production.

C. Delivery dates of finished products.

D. All of the answers are correct.

Answer (D) is correct. *(CIA, adapted)*

REQUIRED: The use(s) of learning curves.

DISCUSSION: Learning curves describe the increase in production efficiencies resulting from experience. Labor assignments benefit from applications of learning curves to labor-hour budgets. Materials purchases result in efficiencies in the EOQ if the adjustments in production efficiency, reflected in the learning curve, are used in ordering. Subassembly production and delivery dates of finished products each can be more efficiently scheduled if learning curve efficiencies are considered during planning.

18.4.3. If a firm is considering the use of learning curve analysis in the determination of labor cost standards for a new product, it should be advised that this technique ordinarily is most relevant to situations in which the production time per unit decreases as additional units are produced and the unit cost

A. Decreases.

B. Does not change.

C. Increases or decreases in an unpredictable manner.

D. Increases slightly.

Answer (A) is correct. *(CPA, adapted)*

REQUIRED: The situation where learning curve analysis is ordinarily most relevant.

DISCUSSION: The learning curve is a cost function showing that the time required for production and therefore the average cost per unit decrease as production rises.

Answer (B) is incorrect. As production increases, efficiency also increases, resulting in lower unit costs. Answer (C) is incorrect. The unit cost decreases in a predictable manner. Answer (D) is incorrect. As production increases, efficiency also increases, resulting in lower unit costs.

Questions 18.4.4 through 18.4.6 are based on the following information. LCB, Inc., is preparing a bid to produce engines. The company has experienced the following costs:

Cumulative	Total Cumulative Costs	
Units Produced	Materials	Labor
10	$ 60,000	$120,000
20	120,000	192,000
40	240,000	307,200

At LCB, variable overhead is applied on the basis of $1.00 per direct labor dollar. Based on historical costs, LCB knows that the production of 40 engines will incur $100,000 of fixed overhead costs. The bid request is for an additional 40 units; all companies submitting bids are allowed to charge a maximum of 25% above full cost for each order.

18.4.4. LCB's rate of learning on the 3-year engine contract is

A. 64%

B. 100%

C. 80%

D. 62.5%

Answer (C) is correct. *(CMA, adapted)*

REQUIRED: The learning curve percentage.

DISCUSSION: The cumulative average unit labor cost for 10 units was $12,000 ($120,000 ÷ 10). The cumulative average unit labor cost for 20 units (a doubling of production) was $9,600 ($192,000 ÷ 20). The cumulative unit average for the next doubling was $7,680 ($307,200 ÷ 40). Because $9,600 is 80% of $12,000 and $7,680 is 80% of $9,600, an 80% rate of learning occurred.

Answer (A) is incorrect. The percentage of 64% equals $307,200 divided by $480,000 (4 × $120,000). Answer (B) is incorrect. The percentage of 100% implies that no learning occurred. Answer (D) is incorrect. The percentage of 62.5% equals $120,000 ÷ $192,000.

18.4.5. The maximum bid price that LCB could submit to the Department of the Navy for the 40 units is

A. $760,800

B. $608,640

C. $885,800

D. $708,640

Answer (C) is correct. *(CMA, adapted)*

REQUIRED: The maximum bid price that could be submitted for the production of 40 units.

DISCUSSION: The company is permitted to bid 25% above full cost (including fixed overhead). Given a learning curve of 80% and a cumulative average unit labor cost for 40 units of $7,680 ($307,200 ÷ 40), the additional labor costs for the next 40 units can be determined. Cumulative average unit labor cost for 80 units is estimated to be $6,144 ($7,680 × 80%). Estimated total labor cost for 80 units is $491,520 (80 units × $6,144). Thus, the incremental labor cost of the last 40 units is expected to be $184,320 ($491,520 – $307,200). Variable overhead is $1 per direct labor dollar, or $184,320. Adding $240,000 for materials and $100,000 for fixed overhead results in a full cost of $708,640 ($184,320 DL + $184,320 VOH + $240,000 DM + $100,000 FOH). Consequently, the bid price should be $885,800 ($708,640 full cost × 125%).

Answer (A) is incorrect. The amount of $760,800 equals 125% times $608,640, which is full cost without including $100,000 fixed overhead. Answer (B) is incorrect. The amount of $608,640 is full cost without including $100,000 fixed overhead. Answer (D) is incorrect. The amount of $708,640 equals full cost. The maximum bid price equals full cost times 125%.

18.4.6. In order to ensure that the company would not lose money on the project, LCB's minimum bid for the 40 units would be

A. $760,800

B. $608,640

C. $885,800

D. $708,640

Answer (B) is correct. *(CMA, adapted)*

REQUIRED: The minimum bid to ensure that the company will not lose money on the contract.

DISCUSSION: The company is permitted to bid 25% above full cost (including fixed overhead). Given a learning curve of 80% and a cumulative average unit labor cost for 40 units of $7,680 ($307,200 ÷ 40), the additional labor costs for the next 40 units can be determined. Cumulative average unit labor cost for 80 units is estimated to be $6,144 ($7,680 × 80%). Estimated total labor cost for 80 units is $491,520 (80 units × $6,144). Thus, the incremental labor cost of the last 40 units is expected to be $184,320 ($491,520 – $307,200). Variable overhead is $1 per direct labor dollar, or $184,320. Adding $240,000 for materials and $100,000 for fixed overhead results in a full cost of $708,640 ($184,320 DL + $184,320 VOH + $240,000 DM + $100,000 FOH). However, that amount includes $100,000 of fixed overhead that would presumably not increase as a result of the production. Thus, if the company obtains the contract at a price of $608,640 ($708,640 – $100,000), it will break even. The minimum bid is therefore $608,640: the incremental cost of labor, variable overhead, and raw materials.

Answer (A) is incorrect. The amount of $760,800 equals 125% times $608,640, which is the full cost without including the fixed cost. Answer (C) is incorrect. The amount of $885,800 equals the maximum bid. Answer (D) is incorrect. The amount of $708,640 includes $100,000 of fixed costs.

18.4.7. A company has developed a learning (improvement) curve for one of its newer processes from its accounting and production records. Management asked internal audit to review the curve. Which of the following events tend to mitigate the effects of the learning curve?

A. Labor costs incurred for overtime hours were charged to an overhead account.

B. The number of preassembled purchased parts used exceeded the plan.

C. Newly developed processing equipment with improved operating characteristics was used.

D. All of the answers are correct.

Answer (D) is correct. *(CIA, adapted)*

REQUIRED: The event(s) that tend(s) to mitigate the effects of the learning curve.

DISCUSSION: The learning curve is developed with a plan for all factors of production. Any changes in the skill level of workers, processing equipment, parts used, or method of labor cost allocation makes the predetermined learning curve less useful.

18.4.8. Given demand in excess of capacity, no spoilage or waste, and full use of a constant number of assembly hours, the number of components needed for an assembly operation with an 80% learning curve should

I. Increase for successive periods.
II. Decrease per unit of output.

A. I only.

B. II only.

C. Both I and II.

D. Neither I nor II.

Answer (A) is correct. *(CPA, adapted)*

REQUIRED: The relationship between the number of components needed in an assembly operation and the operation's learning curve.

DISCUSSION: Learning curves reflect the increased rate at which people perform tasks as they gain experience. An 80% learning curve means that the cumulative average time required to complete a unit (or the time required to produce the last unit) declines by 20% when unit output doubles in the early stages of production. Thus, as the cumulative average time per unit (or the time to complete the last unit) declines, the number of units produced per period of time increases. As more units are produced, more components are needed for production. But the number of components per unit of output is not affected by an increase in output.

Answer (B) is incorrect. The number of components needed per unit of output produced should be constant, assuming no spoilage or waste. Answer (C) is incorrect. The number of components needed per unit of output produced should be constant, assuming no spoilage or waste. Answer (D) is incorrect. The number of components needed increases for successive periods for an assembly operation with an 80% learning curve.

Questions 18.4.9 and 18.4.10 are based on the following information.

Moss Point Manufacturing recently completed and sold an order of 50 units that had costs as shown in the next column.

The company has now been requested to prepare a bid for 150 units of the same product.

Direct materials	$ 1,500
Direct labor ($8.50 × 1,000 hours)	8,500
Variable overhead (1,000 hours × $4.00)*	4,000
Fixed overhead**	1,400
	$15,400

*Applied on the basis of direct labor hours.
**Applied at the rate of 10% of variable cost.

18.4.9. If an 80% learning curve is applicable, Moss Point's total cost on this order would be estimated at

A. $26,400

B. $32,000

C. $38,000

D. $41,800

Answer (A) is correct. *(CMA, adapted)*

REQUIRED: The total cost of a new order given a learning curve percentage.

DISCUSSION: Assuming that the cumulative average time model applies, an 80% learning curve means that the cumulative average time per unit (and labor cost, given a constant labor rate) declines by 20% each time unit output doubles in the early stages of production. The first lot size was 50 units, which was produced at a total cost of $15,400 ($1,500 for materials and $13,900 for labor and overhead). Materials costs are strictly variable and should remain proportional to production. The labor ($8,500) and variable overhead ($4,000) costs (labor-related), however, will be affected by the learning curve. The average cost per lot for labor and variable overhead after 100 units have been produced should be 80% of the costs of the first lot of 50 units. Thus, the average labor and variable overhead cost per 50-unit lot will be $10,000 ($12,500 × 80%). If production doubles again (to a total production of 200 units or four lots of 50 each), the cumulative average cost for labor and variable overhead will be $8,000 per lot ($10,000 × 80%). Given four lots of 50 each, at an average cost of $8,000 per lot, the total cost for labor and variable overhead must be $32,000. Adding $6,000 for raw materials ($1,500 per 50-unit lot) gives a total variable cost of $38,000 for 200 units. Fixed overhead is 10% of total variable cost, so total cost is $41,800. The total cost for the last 150 units is $26,400 ($41,800 – $15,400).

Answer (B) is incorrect. The amount of $32,000 is the total cost for labor and variable overhead for 200 units. Answer (C) is incorrect. The amount of $38,000 is the total variable cost for 200 units. Answer (D) is incorrect. The amount of $41,800 is the total cost for 200 units.

18.4.10. If Moss Point had experienced a 70% learning curve, the bid for the 150 units would

A. Show a 30% reduction in the total direct labor hours required with no learning curve.

B. Include increased fixed overhead costs.

C. Be 10% lower than the total bid at an 80% learning curve.

D. Include 6.40 direct labor hours per unit at $8.50 per hour.

Answer (D) is correct. *(CMA, adapted)*

REQUIRED: The true statement about the bid for an incremental 150 units given a 70% learning curve effect.

DISCUSSION: The sum of the direct labor hours for the initial lot of 50 units was 1,000. A second lot of 50 would reduce the cumulative hours per lot to 700 (70% × 1,000 hours). A doubling to four lots would reduce the cumulative hours per lot to 490 (70% × 700 hours). Thus, for an output of 200 units, the total hours worked would be 1,960 (4 lots × 490 hours). Subtracting the 1,000 hours required for the first 50 units from the 1,960-hour total gives 960 hours for the last 150 units. Dividing 960 hours by 150 units produces a per-unit time of 6.4 hours.

Answer (A) is incorrect. With no learning curve effect, estimated total hours would be 4,000 instead of 1,960, a change of more than 50%. Answer (B) is incorrect. Fixed costs applied per lot would decline because they are based on labor hours, which are declining. Answer (C) is incorrect. Due to the cumulative nature of a learning curve, a 10% change in the learning curve does not result in a 10% change in direct labor costs. Given an 80% learning curve, estimated total hours would be 2,560 instead of 1,960.

18.4.11. The average labor cost per unit for the first batch produced by a new process is $120. The cumulative average labor cost after the second batch is $72 per product. Using a batch size of 100 and assuming the learning curve continues, the total labor cost of four batches will be

A. $4,320

B. $10,368

C. $2,592

D. $17,280

Answer (D) is correct. *(CMA, adapted)*

REQUIRED: The total labor cost assuming the learning curve continues.

DISCUSSION: The learning curve reflects the increased rate at which people perform tasks as they gain experience. The time required to perform a given task becomes progressively shorter. Ordinarily, the curve is expressed in a percentage of reduced time to complete a task for each doubling of cumulative production. One common assumption in a learning curve model is that the cumulative average time (and labor cost) per unit is reduced by a certain percentage each time production doubles. Given a $120 cost per unit for the first 100 units and a $72 cost per unit when cumulative production doubled to 200 units, the learning curve percentage must be 60% ($72 ÷ $120). If production is again doubled to 400 units (four batches), the average unit labor cost should be $43.20 ($72 × 60%). Hence, total labor cost for 400 units is estimated to be $17,280 (400 units × $43.20).

Answer (A) is incorrect. The cost of the items in the fourth batch equals $4,320. Answer (B) is incorrect. The amount of $10,368 is based on the assumption that the cumulative average unit labor cost is reduced by the learning curve percentage with each batch, not each doubling of output. Answer (C) is incorrect. The amount of $2,592 represents the labor cost of 100 units at the unit rate expected after another doubling of production to eight batches.

18.5 Matrix Algebra

18.5.1. A company has two production and two service departments. Each service department provides service to the two production departments and to the other service department. In allocating service department costs, the company would like to account for the service provided by each service department to the other. To do so, it could use

A. Matrix algebra.

B. Regression analysis.

C. Game theory.

D. Sensitivity analysis.

Answer (A) is correct. *(CIA, adapted)*

REQUIRED: The quantitative method used for applying the reciprocal method of service cost allocation.

DISCUSSION: Matrix algebra is a method for solving a set of simultaneous equations. Matrices consisting of the coefficients of the variables of the equations may be manipulated by addition, subtraction, multiplication, and inversion. Because the two service departments simultaneously provide services to each other, recognition of these reciprocal services requires solution of a set of simultaneous equations.

Answer (B) is incorrect. Regression analysis is a statistical procedure for estimation of the relation between variables. Answer (C) is incorrect. Game theory is a mathematical approach to decision making that considers the actions of competitors. Answer (D) is incorrect. Sensitivity analysis is a method of studying the effects of changes in one or more variables on the results of a decision model.

18.5.2. For a given matrix A, a unique inverse matrix A^{-1} exists. Multiplication of the matrix A^{-1} by the matrix A will produce

A. The matrix A.

B. Another inverse matrix.

C. The correct solution to the system.

D. An identity matrix.

Answer (D) is correct. *(CPA, adapted)*

REQUIRED: The product of multiplying a matrix by its inverse matrix.

DISCUSSION: In matrix operations, ordinary division is not possible. Instead of division, multiplication by an inverse matrix is used. By definition, a matrix times its inverse results in an identity matrix. This operation is similar to dividing one number or one variable by itself and obtaining one. An identity matrix is a matrix with zeros in all elements except the principal diagonal, which contains ones.

18.5.3. Consider the two equations below.

$$7x + 8y = 39$$
$$4x - 3y = 21$$

The matrix algebra representation of the two equations is

A. $\begin{bmatrix} 7 & 8 \\ 4 & -3 \end{bmatrix} \begin{bmatrix} x \\ y \end{bmatrix} = \begin{bmatrix} 39 \\ 21 \end{bmatrix}$

B. $\begin{bmatrix} 7 & 8 \\ 4 & -3 \end{bmatrix} [\, x \;\; y \,] = \begin{bmatrix} 39 \\ 21 \end{bmatrix}$

C. $\begin{bmatrix} 4 & 7 \\ -3 & 8 \end{bmatrix} \begin{bmatrix} x \\ y \end{bmatrix} = \begin{bmatrix} 39 \\ 21 \end{bmatrix}$

D. $\begin{bmatrix} x \\ y \end{bmatrix} \begin{bmatrix} 7 & 8 \\ 4 & -3 \end{bmatrix} = \begin{bmatrix} 39 \\ 21 \end{bmatrix}$

Answer (A) is correct. *(CIA, adapted)*

REQUIRED: The matrix algebra representation of two equations.

DISCUSSION: Matrix algebra is an efficient method of manipulating multiple linear equations. Matrices can be added and subtracted if they are of the same dimensions. They can be multiplied if they conform, that is, if the number of columns in the first equals the number of rows in the second. Using the multiplication rule, the matrices in the correct answer can be transformed back into the given equations.

Answer (B) is incorrect. The two matrices on the left-hand side do not conform. Answer (C) is incorrect. The coefficient matrix is incorrect. Answer (D) is incorrect. The columns of the first matrix do not equal the rows in the second.

18.5.4. The Apex Fertilizer Company is planning a new formulation to appeal to the increasing market of herb growers. Each unit of the product will require 3 pounds of chemical A, 1 pound of chemical B, and 4 pounds of chemical C. The per-pound costs of chemical A are \$7.95; chemical B, \$3.28; and chemical C, \$6.14. Which of the following matrix algebra formulations will lead to the cost of one unit of the new fertilizer?

A. $[\, 7.95, 3.28, 6.14 \,] \begin{bmatrix} 3 & 0 & 0 \\ 0 & 1 & 0 \\ 0 & 0 & 4 \end{bmatrix}$

B. $\begin{bmatrix} 7.95 \\ 3.28 \\ 6.14 \end{bmatrix} [\, 3, 1, 4 \,]$

C. $\begin{bmatrix} 7.95 \\ 3.28 \\ 6.14 \end{bmatrix} \begin{bmatrix} 3 \\ 1 \\ 4 \end{bmatrix}$

D. $[\, 3 \;\; 1 \;\; 4 \,] \begin{bmatrix} 7.95 \\ 3.28 \\ 6.14 \end{bmatrix}$

Answer (D) is correct. *(CIA, adapted)*

REQUIRED: The matrix used to determine the unit cost.

DISCUSSION: The objective is to multiply the number of pounds of each material by the cost of each material and add the products.

$$(3 \times 7.95) + (1 \times 3.28) + (4 \times 6.14)$$

The items in each row (horizontal) of the first matrix are multiplied by the items in the second matrix's column (vertical). The products are then added. When the 1-by-3 matrix is multiplied by a 3-by-1 matrix, the result is a 1-by-1 matrix representing the cost. Thus, the dimensions of the matrix resulting from multiplying two matrices are equal to the number of rows in the first and the number of columns in the second.

Answer (A) is incorrect. A 1-by-3 matrix times a 3-by-3 matrix results in a 1-by-3 matrix, i.e., 3 separate numbers. Answer (B) is incorrect. A 3-by-1 matrix times a 1-by-3 matrix results in a 3-by-3 matrix, i.e., 9 numbers. Answer (C) is incorrect. A 3-by-1 matrix times a 3-by-1 matrix results in a 3-by-1 matrix, i.e., 3 numbers.

18.5.5. Presented below is a system of simultaneous equations.

$S_1 = 98{,}000 + .20S_2$ or $S_1 - .20S_2 = \$\ 98{,}000$
$S_2 = 117{,}600 + .10S_1$ or $S_2 - .10S_1 = \$117{,}600$

This system may be stated in matrix form as

A. $\underset{A}{\begin{bmatrix} 1 & -.20 \\ -.10 & 1 \end{bmatrix}} \underset{S}{\begin{bmatrix} S_1 \\ S_2 \end{bmatrix}} = \underset{B}{\begin{bmatrix} \$\ 98{,}000 \\ \$117{,}600 \end{bmatrix}}$

B. $\underset{A}{\begin{bmatrix} 1 & \$98{,}000 & 1 \\ -.20 & \$117{,}600 & -.10 \end{bmatrix}} \underset{S}{\begin{bmatrix} S_1 \\ S_2 \end{bmatrix}} = \underset{B}{\begin{bmatrix} \$\ 98{,}000 \\ \$117{,}600 \end{bmatrix}}$

C. $\underset{A}{\begin{bmatrix} 1 & S_1 & 1 \\ -.20 & S_2 & -.10 \end{bmatrix}} \underset{S}{\begin{bmatrix} S_1 \\ S_2 \end{bmatrix}} = \underset{B}{\begin{bmatrix} \$\ 98{,}000 \\ \$117{,}600 \end{bmatrix}}$

D. $\underset{A}{\begin{bmatrix} 1 & 1 & S_1 \\ -.20 & -.10 & S_2 \end{bmatrix}} \underset{S}{\begin{bmatrix} S_1 \\ S_2 \end{bmatrix}} = \underset{B}{\begin{bmatrix} \$\ 98{,}000 \\ \$117{,}600 \end{bmatrix}}$

Answer (A) is correct. *(CPA, adapted)*

REQUIRED: The matrix form of simultaneous equations.

DISCUSSION: The requirement is to multiply matrix A times matrix S to equal matrix B. In matrix multiplication, rows are multiplied by columns. In answer (A), for example, multiplying the first row of A times the first (and only) column of S results in

$$1 \times S_1 + (-.20) \times S_2$$

Multiplying the second row in A times the only column in S gives

$$(-.10) \times S_1 + 1 \times S_2$$

The result is the original equations:

$$S_1 - .20S_2 = \$\ 98{,}000$$
$$S_2 - .10S_1 = \$117{,}600$$

Answer (B) is incorrect. The amounts of $98,000 and $117,600 are constants, not coefficients. Moreover, the columns of A do not equal the rows of B. Answer (C) is incorrect. S_1 and S_2 are variables, not coefficients. Moreover, the columns of A do not equal the rows of B. Answer (D) is incorrect. S_1 and S_2 are variables, not coefficients. Moreover, the columns of A do not equal the rows of B.

18.6 Calculus

18.6.1. Financial statements of a number of companies are to be analyzed for potential growth by use of a model that considers the rates of change in assets, owners' equity, and income. The most relevant quantitative technique for developing such a model is

A. Correlation analysis.

B. Differential calculus.

C. Integral calculus.

D. Program Evaluation and Review Technique (PERT).

Answer (B) is correct. *(CPA, adapted)*

REQUIRED: The quantitative method for analyzing rates of change.

DISCUSSION: Differential calculus identifies the maxima or minima of nonlinear functions. In business and economics, they are the points of revenue (profit) maximization or cost minimization. The derivative of a function measures the slope or rate of change of that function. Maxima or minima occur where the slope is equal to zero. Thus, to measure rates of change, differential calculus is the appropriate method.

Answer (A) is incorrect. Correlation analysis measures relationships among two or more variables. Answer (C) is incorrect. Integral calculus is customarily used in business applications to identify the area under a probability curve. Answer (D) is incorrect. PERT examines complex projects for processes that are critical to the timely completion of the entire project.

18.6.2. What process is used when calculus is employed to determine a firm's maximum profit for a given revenue function?

A. Integration.

B. Differentiation.

C. Operations research.

D. Regression analysis.

Answer (B) is correct. *(CIA, adapted)*

REQUIRED: The process used when calculus is used to determine a firm's maximum profit.

DISCUSSION: Differential calculus identifies the maxima or minima of nonlinear functions. The derivative of a function measures the slope or rate of change of that function. Maxima or minima occur where the slope is equal to zero. A maximum exists when the second derivative of the function is negative.

Answer (A) is incorrect. Integral calculus computes the area under a curve. It finds antiderivatives. The first derivative of the integral is the function that was integrated. Answer (C) is incorrect. Operations research is a broad term for the application of scientific and quantitative methods to the understanding of systems, especially human-machine systems used in business. Answer (D) is incorrect. Regression analysis creates an equation to explain the variation in a dependent variable caused by changes in one or more independent variables.

18.6.3. An internal auditing department developed the formula, Total audit cost (TC) = $a + bX + cX^2$, with X equaling internal audit resources. The director wanted to minimize TC with respect to X. The appropriate technique to use is

A. Linear programming.

B. Least squares.

C. Differential calculus.

D. Integral calculus.

Answer (C) is correct. *(CIA, adapted)*

REQUIRED: The appropriate method of solving the equation.

DISCUSSION: Differential calculus identifies the maxima or minima of curvilinear functions. These points occur where the slope is zero. A minimum exists when the second derivative of the function is positive.

Answer (A) is incorrect. The formula is nonlinear with no stated constraints. Answer (B) is incorrect. Least squares is related to regression analysis. Answer (D) is incorrect. Integral calculus applies to areas and volume.

18.6.4. Which of the following statements about marginal costs is correct?

A. Marginal cost equals the derivative of the total cost function.

B. Marginal cost increases as output quantity increases.

C. Marginal cost decreases as output quantity increases.

D. Marginal cost increases when total cost increases.

Answer (A) is correct. *(CIA, adapted)*

REQUIRED: The true statement about marginal costs.

DISCUSSION: Marginal cost is the incremental cost incurred to produce one additional unit of output. The derivative of the total cost function is the change in total cost per unit change in output quantity. Accordingly, it equals marginal cost. As marginal cost increases or decreases, the derivative (slope) of the total cost function increases or decreases.

Questions 18.6.5 through 18.6.8 are based on the following information. Redler Company manufactures and sells an industrial strength cleaning fluid. The equations presented below represent the revenue (R) and cost (C) functions for the company if x is stated in terms of thousands of gallons of fluid.

$$R(x) = -\$100 + \$26x - \$0.05x^2$$
$$C(x) = \$50 + \$8x + \$0.01x^2$$

18.6.5. The function that represents the marginal cost to manufacture 1 gallon of cleaning fluid is

A. $\$8x + \$0.01x^2$

B. $\$8 + \$0.01x$

C. $\$8 + \$0.02x$

D. $\$8 \div \$0.02x$

Answer (C) is correct. *(CMA, adapted)*

REQUIRED: The function representing the marginal cost to manufacture 1 gallon of product.

DISCUSSION: The marginal cost function is the derivative of the total cost function. The basic formula for the derivative is

$$f'(Ax^n) = nAx^{n-1}$$

If: A = the constant, or number of x's
x = the variable being differentiated
n = the exponent of the independent variable

Thus, the derivative of the cost function is

$$f'(\$50 + \$8x + \$0.01x^2) = f'(\$50) + f'(\$8x) + f'(\$0.01x^2)$$
$$= 0 + \$8 + \$0.02x$$
$$= \$8 + \$0.02x$$

Answer (A) is incorrect. The cost function without the constant is $\$8x + \$0.01x^2$. Answer (B) is incorrect. The first derivative of $\$0.01x^2$ is $\$0.02x$. Answer (D) is incorrect. The derivative of the entire equation is the sum of the derivatives of the individual elements.

18.6.6. The quantity of cleaning fluid that should be produced to maximize revenue is

A. 520,000 gallons.

B. 260,000 gallons.

C. 160,000 gallons.

D. 150,000 gallons.

Answer (B) is correct. *(CMA, adapted)*

REQUIRED: The quantity of product to be sold to maximize revenue.

DISCUSSION: A maximization problem is solved by setting the first derivative of the revenue function equal to zero and solving for x. The first derivative of the revenue function is 26 – .1x. Thus,

$$.1x = 26$$
$$x = 260$$

Selling 260,000 gallons of cleaning fluid would maximize revenues.

Answer (A) is incorrect. The amount of 520,000 gallons assumes the first derivative is 26 – .05x. Answer (C) is incorrect. The amount of 260,000 gallons maximizes revenue. Answer (D) is incorrect. The amount of 150,000 gallons is the profit-maximizing amount.

18.6.7. The quantity of cleaning fluid that should be produced to maximize profit is

A. 520,000 gallons.

B. 260,000 gallons.

C. 160,000 gallons.

D. 150,000 gallons.

Answer (D) is correct. *(CMA, adapted)*

REQUIRED: The production level at which profit is maximized.

DISCUSSION: Profit is equal to the revenue function minus the cost function (–\$100 + \$26x – \$0.05x^2) – (\$50 + 8x + \$0.01x^2)]. It is not necessary to combine terms. The profit maximum is the first derivative of this profit function (26 – .1x) – (8 + .02x), or 18 – .12x. This derivative is set equal to zero and solved for x, or 150. Thus, producing 150,000 gallons of cleaning fluid will maximize profit.

Answer (A) is incorrect. The amount of 520,000 gallons is the quantity that maximizes revenue if the first derivative of the revenue function is 26 – .05x. Answer (B) is incorrect. The amount of 260,000 gallons is the quantity of product to be sold to maximize revenue. Answer (C) is incorrect. The amount of 150,000 gallons is the profit-maximizing production.

18.6.8. What would the profit (loss) be if the company manufactured and sold 300,000 gallons of cleaning fluid?

A. \$3,200,000

B. \$(50,000)

C. \$(3,350,000)

D. \$(150,000)

Answer (D) is correct. *(CMA, adapted)*

REQUIRED: The amount of profit (loss) generated given productivity and sales.

DISCUSSION: This question is easily solved by substituting 300 for x in the two provided equations.

$$\text{Revenue} = -\$100 + (\$26 \times 300) - (\$.05 \times 90{,}000)$$
$$\text{Cost} = \$50 + (\$8 \times 300) + (\$.01 \times 90{,}000)$$

The cost equation is subtracted from the revenue equation to determine profit or loss per gallon of x.

$$[-\$100 + \$7{,}800 - \$4{,}500 - (\$50 + \$2{,}400 + \$900)]$$
$$\text{Profit} = \$3{,}200 \text{ (revenue)} - \$3{,}350 \text{ (costs)}$$
$$= \$(150)$$

Because x is stated in thousands of gallons, the total loss is \$150,000.

Answer (A) is incorrect. The amount of \$3,200,000 equals total revenues. Answer (B) is incorrect. The amount of \$(50,000) equals fixed costs. Answer (C) is incorrect. The amount of \$(3,350,000) equals total costs.

18.6.9. The mathematical notation for the total cost for a business is $2X^3 + 4X^2 + 3X + 5$, if X equals production volume. Which of the following is the mathematical notation for the marginal cost function for this business?

A. $2(X^3 + 2X^2 + 1.5X + 2.5)$

B. $6X^2 + 8X + 3$

C. $2X^3 + 4X^2 + 3X$

D. $12X + 8$

Answer (B) is correct. *(CPA, adapted)*

REQUIRED: The formula for the marginal cost function.

DISCUSSION: The total cost function is $2X^3 + 4X^2 + 3X + 5$. Production volume equals X. The marginal cost function notation is determined by taking the first derivative of the total cost function notation. The derivative of a function is found using the formula $n(x^{(n-1)})$. The coefficient of the term is multiplied by the exponent, and the exponent is reduced by one. All constants are dropped. The marginal cost function is therefore $6X^2 + 8X + 3$.

Answer (A) is incorrect. The total cost function is $2(X^3 + 2X^2 + 1.5X + 2.5)$. Answer (C) is incorrect. The constant is omitted. Answer (D) is incorrect. The second derivative is $12X + 8$.

18.6.10. To find a minimum-cost point given a total-cost equation, the initial steps are to find the first derivative, set it equal to zero, and solve the equation. Using the solution(s) so derived, what additional steps must be taken, and what result indicates a minimum?

A. Substitute the solution(s) in the first derivative equation; a positive solution indicates a minimum.

B. Substitute the solution(s) in the first derivative equation; a negative solution indicates a minimum.

C. Substitute the solution(s) in the second derivative equation; a positive solution indicates a minimum.

D. Substitute the solution(s) in the second derivative equation; a negative solution indicates a minimum.

Answer (C) is correct. *(CPA, adapted)*

REQUIRED: The subsequent steps in differential calculus and interpretation of results.

DISCUSSION: The steps in differential calculus are to (1) calculate the first derivative, (2) set the first derivative equal to zero and solve the equation, and (3) calculate the second derivative to determine whether it is positive or negative. If the second derivative is positive, it is a minimum. If the second derivative is negative, it is a maximum. The second derivative of a function is the derivative of the first derivative of a function.

Answer (A) is incorrect. The substitution must be in the second derivative. Answer (B) is incorrect. The substitution must be in the second derivative. Answer (D) is incorrect. A negative solution indicates a maximum.

18.6.11. The mathematical notation for the total cost function for a business is $4X^3 + 6X^2 + 2X + 10$, if X equals production volume. Which of the following is the mathematical notation for the average cost function for that business?

A. $12X^2 + 12X + 2$

B. $2X^3 + 3X^2 + X + 5$

C. $.4X^3 + .6X^2 + .2X + 1$

D. $4X^2 + 6X + 2 + 10X^{-1}$

Answer (D) is correct. *(CPA, adapted)*

REQUIRED: The formula for average cost function.

DISCUSSION: The average cost function equals the total cost function divided by production volume. The total cost function is $4X^3 + 6X^2 + 2X + 10$. X is the production volume. Dividing the total cost by X gives the average cost of

$$4X^2 + 6X + 2 + 10X^{-1}$$

Answer (A) is incorrect. The first derivative is $12X^2 + 12X + 2$. Answer (B) is incorrect. Dividing by 2 results in $2X^3 + 3X^2 + X + 5$. Answer (C) is incorrect. Dividing by 10 results in $.4X^3 + .6X^2 + .2X + 1$.

18.6.12. The mathematical notation for the average cost function for a business is $6X^3 + 4X^2 + 2X + 8 + 2/X$, if X equals production volume. What is the mathematical notation for the total cost function for the business?

A. $6X^4 + 4X^3 + 2X^2 + 8X + 2$

B. $6X^2 + 4X + 2 + 8X^{-1} + 2X^{-2}$

C. $12X^2 + 8X + 4 + 16X^{-1} + 4X^{-2}$

D. $18X^2 + 8X + 2 - 2X^{-2}$

Answer (A) is correct. *(CPA, adapted)*

REQUIRED: The formula for the total cost function.

DISCUSSION: Total cost is average cost times production volume. The average cost function is $6X^3 + 4X^2 + 2X + 8 + 2X^{-1}$. Production volume equals X. Thus, multiplying the given average cost function by X results in the total cost function: $X[6X^3 + 4X^2 + 2X + 8 + 2X^{-1}] = 6X^4 + 4X^3 + 2X^2 + 8X + 2$.

Answer (B) is incorrect. Dividing by X results in $6X^2 + 4X + 2 + 8X^{-1} + 2X^{-2}$. Answer (C) is incorrect. Dividing by .5X results in $12X^2 + 8X + 4 + 16X^{-1} + 4X^{-2}$. Answer (D) is incorrect. The first derivative is $18X^2 + 8X + 2 - 2X^{-2}$.

18.6.13. A second derivative that is positive and large at a critical point (i.e., within the relevant range) indicates an

A. Important maximum.

B. Unimportant maximum.

C. Important minimum.

D. Unimportant minimum.

Answer (C) is correct. *(CPA, adapted)*

REQUIRED: The interpretation of a large positive second derivative at a critical point.

DISCUSSION: A positive second derivative indicates that the function is a minimum. The critical point implies an important minimum. The point is critical in the context of the problem, not in the mathematical sense.

Answer (A) is incorrect. A negative second derivative indicates a maximum. Answer (B) is incorrect. A negative second derivative indicates a maximum. Answer (D) is incorrect. The minimum is important.

18.7 Game Theory

18.7.1. The marketing department of your company is deciding on the price to charge for a key product. In setting this price, marketing needs to consider the price that a major competitor will charge for a similar product because the competitor's price will affect the demand for your company's product. Similarly, in setting its price, the competitor will consider what your company will charge. An appropriate mathematical technique for analyzing such a decision is

A. Game theory.

B. Probability theory.

C. Linear programming.

D. Sensitivity analysis.

Answer (A) is correct. *(CIA, adapted)*

REQUIRED: The mathematical approach to analyzing the price to charge given the existence of competition.

DISCUSSION: Game theory is a mathematical approach to decision making when confronted with an enemy or competitor. Games are classified according to the number of players and the algebraic sum of the payoffs. In a two-person game, if the payoff is given by the loser to the winner, the algebraic sum is zero and the game is called a zero-sum game. If it is possible for both players to profit, however, the game is a positive-sum game. Mathematical models have been developed to select optimal strategies for certain simple games.

Answer (B) is incorrect. Probability theory is used to express quantitatively the likelihood of occurrence of an event. Answer (C) is incorrect. Linear programming optimizes an objective function subject to constraints. Answer (D) is incorrect. Sensitivity analysis studies the effects of changes in variables on the results of a decision model.

18.7.2. Only two companies manufacture Product A. The finished product is identical regardless of which company manufactures it. The cost to manufacture Product A is $1, and the selling price is $2. One company considers reducing the price to achieve 100% market share but fears the other company will respond by further reducing the price. Such a scenario would involve a

A. No-win strategy.

B. Dual-win strategy.

C. One win-one lose strategy.

D. Neutral strategy.

Answer (A) is correct. *(CIA, adapted)*

REQUIRED: The effect of a price war.

DISCUSSION: If both firms reduce the selling price of Product A, neither will gain sales, and the resultant price war will cause both entities to earn lower profits. This outcome is inevitable when reduced profit margins do not result in a significant increase in sales. The effect is a no-win strategy.

18.7.3. The procedure for choosing the smallest maximum alternative loss is

A. Deterministic decision making.

B. Maximax.

C. Expected value decision making.

D. Minimax.

Answer (D) is correct. *(CMA, adapted)*

REQUIRED: The procedure for choosing the smallest maximum alternative loss.

DISCUSSION: In game theory, the minimax decision criterion selects the strategy that minimizes the maximum possible loss. It is a method used by a risk-averse player. The maximin criterion, which chooses the strategy with the maximum minimum payoff, gives the same results as the minimax procedure.

Answer (A) is incorrect. Deterministic decision making is based upon fixed (nonprobabilistic) inputs into the decision process. Answer (B) is incorrect. Maximax is a criterion that maximizes the maximum possible profit. Answer (C) is incorrect. Expected value decision making is a risk-neutral process that selects the strategy that should maximize value in the long run.

18.7.4. The decision rule that selects the strategy with the highest utility payoff if the worst state of nature occurs is the

A. Minimize regret rule.

B. Maximize utility rule.

C. Maximin rule.

D. Maximax rule.

Answer (C) is correct. *(CIA, adapted)*

REQUIRED: The rule that selects the strategy with the highest utility payoff if the worst state of nature occurs.

DISCUSSION: The maximin rule determines the minimum payoff for each decision and then chooses the decision with the maximum minimum payoff. It is a conservative criterion adopted by risk-averse players, that is, those for whom the disutility of a loss exceeds the utility of a gain having the same absolute value.

Answer (A) is incorrect. The minimize regret rule selects the action that minimizes the maximum opportunity cost. Answer (B) is incorrect. The maximize utility rule is not a decision rule. Answer (D) is incorrect. The maximax rule selects the choice that provides the greatest payoff if the most favorable state of nature occurs.

18.7.5. Your company (Company Y) has decided to enter the European market with one of its products and is now considering three advertising strategies. This market currently belongs to Company X. Company X is aware that your company is entering the market and is itself considering steps to protect its market. An analyst for your company has identified three strategies Company X might develop and has shown the payoffs for each in the tables below.

Net Payoff Company X
(in $000,000)

Company Y \ Company X	1 Take No Action	2 Extensive Advertising	3 Extensive Advertising & Price Reduction
1 Limited Advertising	–1	1	2
2 Extensive Advertising	–3	0	1
3 Extensive Advertising & Price Reduction	–2	½	–2

Net Payoff Company Y
(in $000,000)

Company Y \ Company X	1 Take No Action	2 Extensive Advertising	3 Extensive Advertising & Price Reduction
1 Limited Advertising	1	–1	–2
2 Extensive Advertising	3	0	–1
3 Extensive Advertising & Price Reduction	2	–½	2

The analyst has formulated this problem as a

A. Zero-sum game.

B. Cooperative game.

C. Prisoner's dilemma.

D. Game against nature.

Answer (A) is correct. *(CIA, adapted)*

REQUIRED: The type of game illustrated.

DISCUSSION: Game theory is a mathematical approach to decision making when confronted with an enemy or competitor. Games are classified according to the number of players and the algebraic sum of the payoffs. In a two-player game, if the payoff is given by the loser to the winner, the algebraic sum is zero, and the game is a zero-sum game. However, if it is possible for both players to profit, the game is a positive-sum game. In this situation, the sum of the payoffs for each combination of strategies is zero. For example, if X takes no action and Y chooses limited advertising, X's payoff is –1 and Y's is 1.

Answer (B) is incorrect. In a cooperative game, the players are permitted to negotiate and form binding agreements prior to the selection of strategies. In addition, in such games, the payoffs in one or more of the cells will not sum to zero. Answer (C) is incorrect. The prisoner's dilemma is a special outcome of a partly competitive game. In these games, each player has a strategy that dominates all others, and the outcome of each player's choice of the dominant strategy is less favorable to both players than some other outcome. Answer (D) is incorrect. Games against nature are formulations of problems in which only one player chooses a strategy, and the set of outcomes and payoffs is not influenced by the selection.

Questions 18.7.6 through 18.7.8 are based on the following information. A bank plans to open a branch in one of five locations (labeled L1, L2, L3, L4, L5). Demand for bank services may be high, medium, or low at each of these locations. Profits for each location-demand combination are presented in the payoff matrix.

Payoff Matrix

Location	L1	L2	L3	L4	L5
Demand:					
High	15	21	17	26	29
Medium	12	8	14	10	4
Low	7	–2	4	–3	–6

18.7.6. If the bank uses the maximax criterion for selecting the location of the branch, it will select

A. L1.

B. L2.

C. L3.

D. L5.

Answer (D) is correct. *(CIA, adapted)*

REQUIRED: The location selected assuming a maximax criterion.

DISCUSSION: Under the maximax criterion, the decision maker selects the choice that maximizes the maximum profit. The maximum profits for the five locations are

Location	L1	L2	L3	L4	L5
Maximum Profit	15	21	17	26	29

The location with the greatest potential profit is L5.

Answer (A) is incorrect. L1 is the choice based on the maximin criterion. Answer (B) is incorrect. L2 is the choice based on the minimax regret criterion. Answer (C) is incorrect. L3 is the choice based on the Laplace criterion.

18.7.7. If the bank uses the minimax regret criterion for selecting the location of the branch, it will select

A. L1.

B. L2.

C. L3.

D. L5.

Answer (B) is correct. *(CIA, adapted)*

REQUIRED: The location selected using the minimax regret criterion.

DISCUSSION: Under the minimax regret criterion, the decision maker selects the choice that minimizes the maximum regret (opportunity cost). The maximum regret for each location is determined from the opportunity loss matrix (see Discussion of the next question). The maximum regret for each location is the highest number in each column as indicated below.

Location	L1	L2	L3	L4	L5
Maximum Regret	14	9	12	10	13

The location with the minimum regret is L2. If demand is low, L2 has a payoff of –2, but L1 has a payoff of 7.

Answer (A) is incorrect. L1 is the choice based on the maximin criterion. Answer (C) is incorrect. L3 is the choice based on the Laplace criterion. Answer (D) is incorrect. L5 is the choice based on the maximax criterion.

18.7.8. If, in addition to the estimated profits, management of the bank assesses the probabilities of high, medium, and low demands to be 0.3, 0.4, and 0.3, respectively, what is the expected opportunity loss from selecting location L4?

A. 5.50

B. 7.90

C. 7.50

D. 5.00

Answer (A) is correct. *(CIA, adapted)*

REQUIRED: The expected opportunity loss from selecting location L4.

DISCUSSION: The opportunity loss matrix is as follows:

Location	L1	L2	L3	L4	L5
Demand: High	14 = 29–15	8 = 29–21	12 = 29–17	3 = 29–26	0 = 29-29
Medium	2 = 14–12	6 = 14–8	0 = 14–14	4 = 14–10	10 = 14–4
Low	0 = 7–7	9 = 7–(–2)	3 = 7–4	10 = 7–(–3)	13 = 7–(–6)

The expected opportunity loss from selecting location L4 is 5.50 [(3 × 0.3) + (4 × 0.4) + (10 × 0.3)].

Answer (B) is incorrect. The expected opportunity loss from selecting location L5 is 7.90. Answer (C) is incorrect. The expected opportunity loss from selecting location L2 is 7.50. Answer (D) is incorrect. The expected opportunity loss from selecting location L1 is 5.00.

18.7.9. Under conditions of risk, the rational, economic decision maker will use which one of the following decision criteria?

A. Maximax.

B. Minimum regret.

C. Laplace.

D. Expected monetary value.

Answer (D) is correct. *(CMA, adapted)*

REQUIRED: The decision criterion used by a rational decision maker under conditions of risk.

DISCUSSION: A rational economic decision maker (one completely guided by objective criteria) uses expected monetary value to maximize gains under conditions of risk because (s)he is risk-neutral (the utility of a gain equals the disutility of a loss of the same absolute amount). Expected value is the long-term average payoff for repeated trials. The best choice is the one having the highest expected value (sum of the products of the possible outcomes and their respective probabilities).

Answer (A) is incorrect. Maximax is adopted by risk seekers. Answer (B) is incorrect. The minimum regret criterion is used by a player who wishes to minimize the effect of a bad decision in either direction. Answer (C) is incorrect. The insufficient reason (Laplace) criterion applies when the decision maker cannot assign probabilities to the states of nature resulting from a decision.

18.8 Quality Tools

18.8.1. A manufacturer mass produces nuts and bolts on its assembly line. The line supervisors sample every n^{th} unit for conformance with specifications. Once a nonconforming part is detected, the machinery is shut down and adjusted. The most appropriate tool for this process is a

A. Fishbone diagram.

B. Cost of quality report.

C. ISO 9000 audit.

D. Statistical quality control chart.

Answer (D) is correct. *(Publisher, adapted)*

REQUIRED: The most appropriate tool for a process that shuts down and adjusts machinery once a nonconforming part is detected.

DISCUSSION: Statistical quality control is a method of determining whether the shipment or production run of units lies within acceptable limits. It is also used to determine whether production processes are out of control. Statistical control charts are graphic aids for monitoring the status of any process subject to random variations.

Answer (A) is incorrect. A fishbone diagram is useful for determining the unknown causes of problems, not routine mechanical adjustments. Answer (B) is incorrect. The contents of a cost of quality report are stated in monetary terms. This tool is not helpful for determining when to adjust machinery. Answer (C) is incorrect. An ISO 9000 audit focuses on the quality of the organization's total process, not the routine adjustment of machinery.

18.8.2. Quality Company produces a component of a machine. The target value for a key dimension of the component is 100 millimeters (mm). The quality loss per unit if the key dimension is measured at precisely the upper or lower specification limit (100 mm ± 1 mm) is estimated to be $10. The following are the measures of a sample of four units:

Unit	Measurement
1	99
2	101
3	99.5
4	100.5

The Quality Company produces 1,000 of the components. Based on the sample, the estimated quality loss is

A. $625

B. $6,250

C. $10,000

D. $25,000

Answer (B) is correct. *(Publisher, adapted)*

REQUIRED: The estimated quality loss.

DISCUSSION: The quality loss constant (k) in the Taguchi quality loss function equation is $10 [$10 loss at the specification limit ÷ (1 mm)²]. Accordingly, the quality loss for the sample may be determined as follows:

Unit	Measurement in mm	Actual – Target (x – T)	$(x-T)^2$	$k(x-T)^2$
1	99	–1	1	$10.00
2	101	+1	1	10.00
3	99.5	–.5	.25	2.50
4	100.5	+.5	.25	2.50
			2.50	$25.00

The average per unit quality loss for the sample is $6.25 ($25 ÷ 4). Consequently, the total estimated loss for 1,000 components is $6,250.

Answer (A) is incorrect. The amount of $625 equals $0.625 times 1,000 units. Answer (C) is incorrect. The amount of $10,000 equals $10 times 1,000 units. Answer (D) is incorrect. The amount of $25,000 is based on the total loss for the sample ($25), not the unit average loss ($6.25).

Questions 18.8.3 and 18.8.4 are based on the following information. An organization has collected data on the complaints made by computer users and has categorized the complaints in the Pareto diagram below.

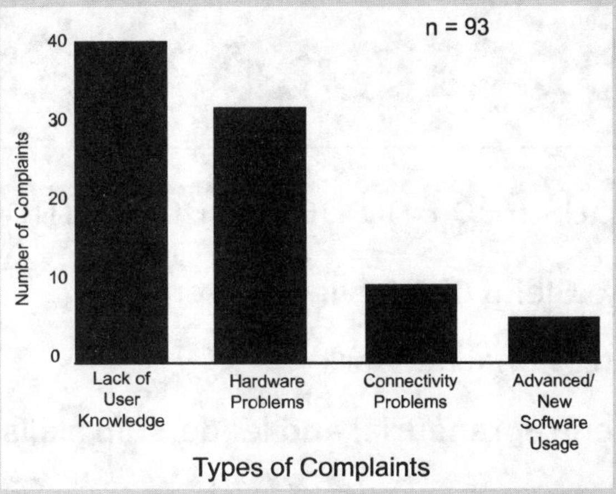

18.8.3. Using the information collected, the organization should focus on

A. The total number of personal computer complaints that occurred.

B. The number of computer complaints associated with connectivity problems and new software usage.

C. The number of computer complaints associated with the lack of user knowledge and hardware problems.

D. The cost to alleviate all computer complaints.

Answer (C) is correct. *(CIA, adapted)*

REQUIRED: The organization's focus based on the data.

DISCUSSION: Complaints based on lack of user knowledge and hardware problems are by far the most frequent according to this chart. Consequently, the company should devote its resources primarily to these issues.

Answer (A) is incorrect. More detailed information is not available. The Pareto diagram does not focus on the total quantity of computer complaints. Answer (B) is incorrect. Complaints about connectivity and software are infrequent. Answer (D) is incorrect. Cost information is not provided.

18.8.4. The chart displays

A. The arithmetic mean of each computer complaint.

B. The relative frequency of each computer complaint.

C. The median of each computer complaint.

D. The absolute frequency of each computer complaint.

Answer (D) is correct. *(CIA, adapted)*

REQUIRED: The information provided by the chart.

DISCUSSION: This Pareto diagram depicts the frequencies of complaints in absolute terms. It displays the actual number of each type of complaint.

Answer (A) is incorrect. A Pareto diagram does not display the arithmetic mean of the variable being measured. Answer (B) is incorrect. While relative frequencies can be estimated by visually examining the heights of the bars, a Pareto diagram does not calculate or display them precisely. Answer (C) is incorrect. Medians of each type of complaint are not displayed in a Pareto diagram.

JOIN THE MILLIONS WHO
HAVE SUCCEEDED WITH GLEIM
Become a Campus Rep and be a leader among your peers.
EARN a complete Gleim CPA Review System
GROW your professional network
ENHANCE your entrepreneurial and leadership skills
GLEIM
2018 EDITION
CPA REVIEW
FEBRUARY 2018
GLEIM® CPA REVIEW
GLEIM OFFERS EXAM PREP MATERIALS FOR CPA, CMA, CIA, AND EA.
Gleim.com/CampusRep | 800.874.5346 | campus.rep@gleim.com

APPENDIX A
SUBUNIT CROSS-REFERENCES TO COST/MANAGERIAL ACCOUNTING & QUANTITATIVE METHODS TEXTBOOKS

This section contains the tables of contents of current textbooks with cross-references to the corresponding study units and subunits in this study manual. The texts are listed in alphabetical order by the first author. As you study a particular chapter in your textbook, you can easily determine which subunit(s) to study in your Gleim EQE material.

Professors and students should note that, even though new editions of the texts listed below may be published as you use this study material, the new tables of contents usually will be very similar, if not the same. Thus, this edition of *Cost/Managerial Accounting Exam Questions and Explanations* will remain current and useful.

If you are using a textbook that is not included in this list or if you have any suggestions on how we can improve these cross-references to make them more relevant/useful, please submit your request/feedback at www.gleim.com/crossreferences/MAN or email them to MANcrossreferences@gleim.com.

COST/MANAGERIAL ACCOUNTING

Blocher, Stout, Juras, Smith, and Cokins, *Cost Management: A Strategic Emphasis*, Eighth Edition, McGraw-Hill/Irwin, 2019.

Braun and Tietz, *Managerial Accounting*, Fifth Edition, Prentice Hall, 2018.

Datar and Rajan, *Horngren's Cost Accounting: A Managerial Emphasis*, Sixteenth Edition, Pearson, 2018.

Garrison, Noreen, and Brewer, *Managerial Accounting*, Sixteenth Edition, McGraw-Hill/Irwin, 2018.

Gordon, *Managerial Accounting: Concepts and Empirical Evidence*, Sixth Edition, McGraw-Hill, 2004.

Hansen and Mowen, *Cornerstones of Cost Management*, Fourth Edition, Cengage Learning, 2018.

Hilton, Maher, and Selto, *Cost Management: Strategies for Business Decisions*, Fourth Edition, McGraw-Hill/Irwin, 2008.

Hilton and Platt, *Managerial Accounting: Creating Value in a Dynamic Business Environment*, Eleventh Edition, McGraw-Hill/Irwin, 2017.

Horngren, Burgstahler, Schatzberg, and Sundem, *Introduction to Management Accounting*, Sixteenth Edition, Prentice Hall, 2014.

Horngren, Harrison, and Oliver, *Financial & Managerial Accounting*, Third Edition, Prentice Hall, 2012.

Kinney and Raiborn, *Cost Accounting: Foundations and Evolutions*, Ninth Edition, Cengage Learning, 2013.

Lanen, Anderson, and Maher, *Fundamentals of Cost Accounting*, Fifth Edition, McGraw-Hill/Irwin, 2017.

Maher, Stickney, and Weil, *Managerial Accounting: An Introduction to Concepts, Methods, and Uses*, Eleventh Edition, Cengage Learning, 2012.

Miller-Nobles, Mattison, and Matsumura, *Horngren's Financial & Managerial Accounting*, Sixth Edition, Prentice Hall, 2018.

Needles, Powers, and Crosson, *Managerial Accounting*, Tenth Edition, Cengage Learning, 2014.

Vanderbeck and Mitchell, *Principles of Cost Accounting*, Seventeenth Edition, Cengage Learning, 2016.

Warren, Reeve, and Duchac, *Financial & Managerial Accounting*, Fourteenth Edition, Cengage Learning, 2018.

Warren, Reeve, and Duchac, *Managerial Accounting*, Fourteenth Edition, Cengage Learning, 2018.

Weygandt, Kieso, and Kimmel, *Managerial Accounting: Tools for Business Decision Making*, Eighth Edition, John Wiley & Sons, 2017.

Wild, Shaw, and Chiappetta, *Financial and Managerial Accounting: Information for Decisions*, Seventh Edition, McGraw-Hill/Irwin, 2018.

Wouters, Selto, Hilton, and Maher, *Cost Management: Strategies for Business Decisions*, International Edition, First Edition, McGraw-Hill Higher Education, 2013.

Zimmerman, *Accounting for Decision Making and Control*, Ninth Edition, McGraw-Hill, 2017.

QUANTITATIVE METHODS

Anderson, Sweeney, Williams, Camm, Cochran, Fry, and Ohlmann, *An Introduction to Management Science: Quantitative Approaches to Decision Making*, Fifteenth Edition, Cengage Learning, 2019.

Anderson, Sweeney, Williams, Camm, Cochran, Fry, and Ohlmann, *Quantitative Methods for Business*, Thirteenth Edition, Cengage Learning, 2016.

Heizer, Render, and Munson, *Operations Management: Sustainability and Supply Chain Management*, Twelfth Edition, Pearson, 2017.

Krajewski, Malhotra, and Ritzman, *Operations Management: Processes and Supply Chains*, Twelfth Edition, Pearson, 2019.

COST/MANAGERIAL ACCOUNTING

Blocher, Stout, Juras, Smith, and Cokins, *Cost Management: A Strategic Emphasis*, Eighth Edition, McGraw-Hill/Irwin, 2019.

Part One: Introduction to Strategy, Cost Management, and Cost Systems
- Chapter 1 - Cost Management and Strategy - SU 1
- Chapter 2 - Implementing Strategy: The Value Chain, the Balanced Scorecard, and the Strategy Map - 9.2-9.3, 5.1
- Chapter 3 - Basic Cost Management Concepts - 1.1-1.5
- Chapter 4 - Job Costing - SU 2
- Chapter 5 - Activity-Based Costing and Customer Profitability Analysis - SU 3
- Chapter 6 - Process Costing - SU 10
- Chapter 7 - Cost Allocation: Departments, Joint Products, and By-Products - SU 11

Part Two: Planning and Decision Making
- Chapter 8 - Cost Estimation - 13.1
- Chapter 9 - Short-Term Profit Planning: Cost-Volume-Profit (CVP) Analysis - SU 4
- Chapter 10 - Strategy and the Master Budget - 5.1-5.2
- Chapter 11 - Decision Making with a Strategic Emphasis - SU 8
- Chapter 12 - Strategy and the Analysis of Capital Investments - SU 13
- Chapter 13 - Cost Planning for the Product Life Cycle: Target Costing, Theory of Constraints, and Strategic Pricing - 8.1, 14.3

Part Three: Operational-Level Control
- Chapter 14 - Operational Performance Measurement: Sales, Direct-Cost Variances, and the Role of Nonfinancial Performance Measures - 5.4, 7.1-7.3, 7.5
- Chapter 15 - Operational Performance Measurement: Indirect-Cost Variances and Resource-Capacity Management - 5.4, 7.4, SU 11
- Chapter 16 - Operational Performance Measurement: Further Analysis of Productivity and Sales - 5.4, 7.1-7.5, 7.7
- Chapter 17 - The Management and Control of Quality - SU 12

Part Four: Management-Level Control
- Chapter 18 - Strategic Performance Measurement: Cost Centers, Profit Centers, and the Balanced Scorecard - 9.2-9.3
- Chapter 19 - Strategic Performance Measurement: Investment Centers and Transfer Pricing - 9.4
- Chapter 20 - Management Compensation, Business Analysis, and Business Valuation - 9.2

Braun and Tietz, *Managerial Accounting*, Fifth Edition, Prentice Hall, 2018.

Chapter 1 - Introduction to Managerial Accounting - SU 1
Chapter 2 - Building Blocks of Managerial Accounting - 1.1-1.5
Chapter 3 - Job Costing - SU 2
Chapter 4 - Activity Based Costing, Lean Operations, and the Costs of Quality - SU 3, SU 12, 14.3
Chapter 5 - Process Costing - SU 10
Chapter 6 - Cost Behavior - SU 1
Chapter 7 - Cost-Volume-Profit Analysis - SU 4
Chapter 8 - Relevant Costs for Short-Term Decisions - SU 8
Chapter 9 - The Master Budget - SU 5
Chapter 10 - Performance Evaluation - 9.1-9.3
Chapter 11 - Standard Costs and Variances - SU 7
Chapter 12 - Capital Investment Decisions and the Time Value of Money - SU 13
Chapter 13 - Statement of Cash Flows - N/A
Chapter 14 - Financial Statement Analysis - N/A
Chapter 15 - Sustainability - N/A

Datar and Rajan, *Horngren's Cost Accounting: A Managerial Emphasis*, Sixteenth Edition, Pearson, 2018.

Chapter 1 - The Manager and Management Accounting - 1.1
Chapter 2 - An Introduction to Cost Terms and Purposes - 1.1-1.5
Chapter 3 - Cost-Volume-Profit Analysis - SU 4
Chapter 4 - Job Costing - SU 2
Chapter 5 - Activity-Based Costing and Activity-Based Management - SU 3
Chapter 6 - Master Budget and Responsibility Accounting - SU 5, 9.1-9.3
Chapter 7 - Flexible Budgets, Direct-Cost Variances, and Management Control - SU 5, 7.1-7.3
Chapter 8 - Flexible Budgets, Overhead-Cost Variances, and Management Control - SU 5, 7.1, 7.4-7.6
Chapter 9 - Inventory Costing and Capacity Analysis - SU 6, SU 14
Chapter 10 - Determining How Costs Behave - 1.3, 4.3, SU 16
Chapter 11 - Decision Making and Relevant Information - SU 8
Chapter 12 - Strategy, Balanced Scorecard, and Strategic Profitability Analysis - SU 9
Chapter 13 - Pricing Decisions and Cost Management - SU 4, 8.4, 9.4
Chapter 14 - Cost Allocation, Customer-Profitability Analysis, and Sales-Variance Analysis - 7.5, 11.1-11.2
Chapter 15 - Allocation of Support-Department Costs, Common Costs, and Revenues - SU 11
Chapter 16 - Cost Allocation: Joint Products and Byproducts - 11.3-11.8
Chapter 17 - Process Costing - SU 10
Chapter 18 - Spoilage, Rework, and Scrap - 12.2-12.4
Chapter 19 - Balanced Scorecard: Quality and Time - 9.3, 12.1
Chapter 20 - Inventory Management, Just-in-Time, and Simplified Costing Methods - 10.2, SU 14
Chapter 21 - Capital Budgeting and Cost Analysis - SU 13
Chapter 22 - Management Control Systems, Transfer Pricing, and Multinational Considerations - 8.2, 9.4
Chapter 23 - Performance Measurement, Compensation, and Multinational Considerations - 8.2, SU 9

Garrison, Noreen, and Brewer, *Managerial Accounting*, Sixteenth Edition, McGraw-Hill/Irwin, 2018.

Prologue - Managerial Accounting: An Overview - SU 1
Chapter 1 - Managerial Accounting and Cost Concepts - 1.1-1.5
Chapter 2 - Job-Order Costing: Calculating Unit Production Costs - 2.1, 2.3-2.4
Chapter 3 - Job-Order Costing: Cost Flows and External Reporting - 2.2, 2.5
Chapter 4 - Process Costing - SU 10
Chapter 5 - Cost-Volume-Profit Relationships - SU 4
Chapter 6 - Variable Costing and Segment Reporting: Tools for Management - 1.4, 6.1-6.2
Chapter 7 - Activity-Based Costing: A Tool to Aid Decision Making - SU 3
Chapter 8 - Master Budgeting - SU 5
Chapter 9 - Flexible Budgets and Performance Analysis - 5.4
Chapter 10 - Standard Costs and Variances - SU 7
Chapter 11 - Performance Measurement in Decentralized Organizations - 9.1, 9.4
Chapter 12 - Differential Analysis: The Key to Decision Making - 8.1-8.4, 11.6
Chapter 13 - Capital Budgeting Decisions - SU 13
Chapter 14 - Statement of Cash Flows - N/A
Chapter 15 - Financial Statement Analysis - N/A

Gordon, *Managerial Accounting: Concepts and Empirical Evidence*, Sixth Edition, McGraw-Hill, 2004.

Chapter 1 - Managerial Accounting: Conceptual Framework - 1.1-1.2
Chapter 2 - Profit Planning: An Overview - SU 4
Chapter 3 - Cost Accumulation and Measurement - SU 2, SU 10
Chapter 4 - Standard Cost System - SU 7
Chapter 5 - Cost Allocation Issues - 11.1-11.6
Chapter 6 - Activity Based Costing/Management - SU 3
Chapter 7 - Pricing Decisions - 4.6-4.7
Chapter 8 - Financial Performance Measures - 9.2-9.3
Chapter 9 - Nonfinancial Performance Measures and Firm Strategies - 9.2-9.3
Chapter 10 - Transfer Pricing - 9.4
Chapter 11 - Budgeting for Current Operations and Cash Flows - SU 5
Chapter 12 - Capital Budgeting - SU 13
Chapter 13 - Postauditing Capital Investments - N/A
Chapter 14 - Management Accounting Systems as Agents of Organizational Change - N/A

Hansen and Mowen, *Cornerstones of Cost Management*, Fourth Edition, Cengage Learning, 2018.

Chapter 1 - Introduction to Cost Management - 1.1
Chapter 2 - Basic Cost Management Concepts - 1.2-1.3, 1.5
Chapter 3 - Cost Behavior - 1.4
Chapter 4 - Activity-Based Costing - SU 3
Chapter 5 - Product and Service Costing: Job-Order System - SU 2
Chapter 6 - Process Costing - SU 10
Chapter 7 - Allocating Costs of Support Departments and Joint Products - SU 11
Chapter 8 - Budgeting for Planning and Control - SU 5
Chapter 9 - Standard Costing: A Functional-Based Control Approach - 7.1-7.4
Chapter 10 - Decentralization: Responsibility Accounting, Performance Evaluation, and Transfer Pricing - SU 9
Chapter 11 - Strategic Cost Management - SU 9
Chapter 12 - Activity-Based Management - SU 3
Chapter 13 - The Balanced Scorecard: Strategic-Based Control - 9.3
Chapter 14 - Quality and Environmental Cost Management - SU 12
Chapter 15 - Lean Accounting and Productivity Measurement - 7.7
Chapter 16 - Cost-Volume-Profit Analysis - SU 4
Chapter 17 - Activity Resource Usage Model and Tactical Decision Making - SU 8
Chapter 18 - Pricing and Profitability Analysis - 4.6-4.7
Chapter 19 - Capital Investment - SU 13
Chapter 20 - Inventory Management: Economic Order Quantity, JIT, and the Theory of Constraints - SU 14

Hilton, Maher, and Selto, *Cost Management: Strategies for Business Decisions*, Fourth Edition, McGraw-Hill/Irwin, 2008.

Part I: Setting the Strategic Foundation: The Importance of Analyzing and Managing Costs
Chapter 1 - Cost Management and Strategic Decision Making: Evaluating Opportunities and Leading Change - N/A
Chapter 2 - Product Costing Systems: Concepts and Design Issues - 1.1-1.5
Chapter 3 - Cost Accumulation for Job-Shop and Batch Production Operations - SU 2
Part II: Activity-Based Management
Chapter 4 - Activity-Based Costing Systems - SU 3
Chapter 5 - Activity-Based Management - SU 3
Chapter 6 - Managing Customer Profitability - SU 3
Chapter 7 - Managing Quality and Time to Create Value - SU 12
Part III: Process Costing and Cost Allocation
Chapter 8 - Process-Costing Systems - SU 10
Chapter 9 - Joint-Process Costing - 11.3-11.8
Chapter 10 - Managing and Allocating Support-Service Costs - 11.1-11.8
Part IV: Planning and Decision Making
Chapter 11 - Cost Estimation - 4.2, SUs 15-18
Chapter 12 - Strategy, Balanced Scorecards, and Incentive Systems - 9.1-9.3
Chapter 13 - Cost Management and Decision Making - SUs 8-9
Chapter 14 - Strategic Issues in Making Long-Term Capital Investment Decisions - SU 13
Chapter 15 - Budgeting and Financial Planning - SU 5

Part V: Evaluating and Managing Performance: Creating and Managing Value-Added Effort
Chapter 16 - Standard Costing, Variance Analysis, and Kaizen Costing - SU 7
Chapter 17 - Flexible Budgets, Overhead Cost Management, and Activity-Based Budgeting - SU 5
Chapter 18 - Organizational Design, Responsibility Accounting, and Evaluation of Divisional Performance - 9.1-9.3
Chapter 19 - Transfer Pricing - 9.4
Chapter 20 - Performance Measurement Systems - 9.2-9.3

Hilton and Platt, *Managerial Accounting: Creating Value in a Dynamic Business Environment*, Eleventh Edition, McGraw-Hill/Irwin, 2017.

Chapter 1 - The Changing Role of Managerial Accounting in a Dynamic Business Environment - 1.1
Chapter 2 - Basic Cost Management Concepts - 1.1-1.5
Chapter 3 - Product Costing and Cost Accumulation in a Batch Production Environment - SU 2, SU 3
Chapter 4 - Process Costing and Hybrid Product-Costing Systems - SU 10
Chapter 5 - Activity-Based Costing and Management - SU 3
Chapter 6 - Activity Analysis, Cost Behavior, and Cost Estimation - 6.1-6.3, SUs 15-18
Chapter 7 - Cost-Volume-Profit Analysis - SU 4
Chapter 8 - Variable Costing and the Costs of Quality and Sustainability - 6.1
Chapter 9 - Financial Planning and Analysis: The Master Budget - SU 5
Chapter 10 - Standard Costing and Analysis of Direct Costs - SU 7
Chapter 11 - Flexible Budgeting and Analysis of Overhead Costs - SU 5, 7.4
Chapter 12 - Responsibility Accounting, Operational Performance Measures, and the Balanced Scorecard - 9.1-9.3
Chapter 13 - Investment Centers and Transfer Pricing - 9.3-9.4
Chapter 14 - Decision Making: Relevant Costs and Benefits - SU 8, SU 17
Chapter 15 - Target Costing and Cost Analysis for Pricing Decisions - 8.4
Chapter 16 - Capital Expenditure Decisions - SU 13
Chapter 17 - Allocation of Support Activity Costs and Joint Costs - SU 11
Appendix I - The Sarbanes-Oxley Act, Internal Controls, and Management Accounting - N/A
Appendix II - Compound Interest and the Concept of Present Value - 13.4-13.5
Appendix III - Inventory Management - SU 14

Horngren, Burgstahler, Schatzberg, and Sundem, *Introduction to Management Accounting*, Sixteenth Edition, Prentice Hall, 2014.

I: Focus on Decision Making
Chapter 1 - Managerial Accounting, the Business Organization, and Professional Ethics - 1.1-1.2, 1.6
Chapter 2 - Introduction to Cost Behavior and Cost-Volume Relationships - SU 4
Chapter 3 - Measurement of Cost Behavior - SUs 15-18
Chapter 4 - Cost Management Systems and Activity-Based Costing - SU 3
Chapter 5 - Relevant Information for Decision Making with a Focus on Pricing Decisions - 8.4
Chapter 6 - Relevant Information for Decision Making with a Focus on Operational Decisions - SU 8, SU 14
II: Accounting for Planning and Control
Chapter 7 - Introduction to Budgets and Preparing the Master Budget - SU 5
Chapter 8 - Flexible Budgets and Variance Analysis - 5.4, SU 7
Chapter 9 - Management Control Systems and Responsibility Accounting - 9.1-9.3
Chapter 10 - Management Control in Decentralized Organizations - 9.4
III: Capital Budgeting
Chapter 11 - Capital Budgeting - SU 13
IV: Product Costing
Chapter 12 - Cost Allocation - SU 11
Chapter 13 - Accounting for Overhead Costs - 7.4
Chapter 14 - Job-Costing and Process-Costing Systems - SU 2, SU 10
V: Basic Financial Accounting
Chapter 15 - Basic Accounting: Concepts, Techniques, and Conventions - N/A
Chapter 16 - Understanding Corporate Annual Reports: Basic Financial Statements - N/A
Chapter 17 - Understanding and Analyzing Consolidated Financial Statements - N/A

Horngren, Harrison, and Oliver, *Financial & Managerial Accounting*, Third Edition, Prentice Hall, 2012.

Chapter 1 - Accounting and the Business Environment - N/A
Chapter 2 - Recording Business Transactions - N/A
Chapter 3 - The Adjusting Process - N/A
Chapter 4 - Completing the Accounting Cycle - N/A
Chapter 5 - Merchandising Operations - N/A
Chapter 6 - Merchandise Inventory - N/A
Chapter 7 - Internal Control and Cash - N/A
Chapter 8 - Receivables - N/A
Chapter 9 - Plant Assets and Intangibles - N/A
Chapter 10 - Current Liabilities and Payroll - N/A
Chapter 11 - Long-Term Liabilities, Bonds Payable, and Classification of Liabilities on the Balance Sheet - N/A
Chapter 12 - Corporations, Paid-In Capital, and the Balance Sheet - N/A
Chapter 13 - Corporations: Effects on Retained Earnings and the Income Statement - N/A
Chapter 14 - The Statement of Cash Flows - N/A
Chapter 15 - Financial Statement Analysis - N/A
Chapter 16 - Introduction to Managerial Accounting - SU 1
Chapter 17 - Job Order and Process Costing - SU 2, SU 10
Chapter 18 - Activity-Based Costing and Other Cost Management Tools - SU 3
Chapter 19 - Cost-Volume-Profit Analysis - SU 4
Chapter 20 - Short-Term Business Decisions - SU 8
Chapter 21 - Capital Investment Decisions and the Time Value of Money - SU 13
Chapter 22 - The Master Budget and Responsibility Accounting - 5.1-5.2, 9.1-9.2
Chapter 23 - Flexible Budgets and Standard Costs - 5.4, SU 7
Chapter 24 - Performance Evaluation and the Balanced Scorecard - 9.3, 9.5

Kinney and Raiborn, *Cost Accounting: Foundations and Evolutions*, Ninth Edition, Cengage Learning, 2013.

Chapter 1 - Introduction to Cost Accounting - 1.1
Chapter 2 - Cost Terminology and Cost Behaviors - 1.1-1.5
Chapter 3 - Predetermined Overhead Rates, Flexible Budgets, and Absorption/Variable Costing - SUs 5-6, 7.4
Chapter 4 - Activity-Based Management and Activity-Based Costing - SU 3
Chapter 5 - Job Order Costing - SU 2
Chapter 6 - Process Costing - SU 10
Chapter 7 - Standard Costing and Variance Analysis - SU 7
Chapter 8 - The Master Budget - 5.1-5.2
Chapter 9 - Break-Even Point and Cost-Volume Profit Analysis - SU 4
Chapter 10 - Relevant Information for Decision Making - SU 8
Chapter 11 - Allocation of Joint Costs and Accounting for By-Products - SU 11
Chapter 12 - Introduction to Cost Management Systems - N/A
Chapter 13 - Responsibility Accounting and Transfer Pricing - SU 9
Chapter 14 - Performance Measurement, Balanced Scorecards, and Performance Rewards - 9.3
Chapter 15 - Capital Budgeting - SU 13
Chapter 16 - Managing Costs and Uncertainty - 14.3
Chapter 17 - Implementing Quality Concepts - SU 12
Chapter 18 - Inventory and Production Management - SU 14
Chapter 19 - Emerging Management Practices - N/A

Lanen, Anderson, and Maher, *Fundamentals of Cost Accounting*, Fifth Edition, McGraw-Hill/Irwin, 2017.

Chapter 1 - Cost Accounting: Information for Decision Making - 1.1-1.2
Chapter 2 - Cost Concepts and Behavior - 1.2-1.5
Chapter 3 - Fundamentals of Cost-Volume-Profit Analysis - SU 4
Chapter 4 - Fundamentals of Cost Analysis for Decision Making - SU 6
Chapter 5 - Cost Estimation - 4.3, SUs 15-18
Chapter 6 - Fundamentals of Product and Service Costing - SU 10
Chapter 7 - Job Costing - SU 2
Chapter 8 - Process Costing - SU 10
Chapter 9 - Activity-Based Costing - SU 3
Chapter 10 - Fundamentals of Cost Management - SU 7, 11.1
Chapter 11 - Service Department and Joint Cost Allocation - SU 11
Chapter 12 - Fundamentals of Management Control Systems - N/A
Chapter 13 - Planning and Budgeting - SU 5

Chapter 14 - Business Unit Performance Measurement - 9.1-9.3, 9.5
Chapter 15 - Transfer Pricing - 9.4
Chapter 16 - Fundamentals of Variance Analysis - SU 7
Chapter 17 - Additional Topics in Variance Analysis - SU 7
Chapter 18 - Performance Measurement to Support Business Strategy - N/A

Maher, Stickney, and Weil, *Managerial Accounting: An Introduction to Concepts, Methods, and Uses*, Eleventh Edition, Cengage Learning, 2012.

Part One - Overview and Basic Concepts
Chapter 1 - Fundamental Concepts - SU 1
Chapter 2 - Measuring Product Costs - SU 2, SUs 6-7, SU 10
Chapter 3 - Activity-Based Management - SU 3
Part Two - Managerial Decision Making
Chapter 4 - Strategic Management of Costs, Quality, and Time - SU 4, 12.1
Chapter 5 - Cost Drivers and Cost Behavior - 1.4, SU 3
Chapter 6 - Financial Modeling for Short-Term Decision Making - SU 8
Chapter 7 - Differential Cost Analysis for Operating Decisions - N/A
Chapter 8 - Capital Expenditure Decisions - SU 13
Part Three - Motivating Managers to Make Good Decisions
Chapter 9 - Profit Planning and Budgeting - SU 5
Chapter 10 - Profit and Cost Center Performance Evaluation - 9.1-9.3
Chapter 11 - Investment Center Performance Evaluation - SU 4, SU 9
Chapter 12 - Incentive Issues - N/A
Chapter 13 - Allocating Costs to Responsibility Centers - SU 9, SU 11

Miller-Nobles, Mattison, and Matsumura, *Horngren's Financial & Managerial Accounting*, Sixth Edition, Prentice Hall, 2018.

Chapter 1 - Accounting and the Business Environment - N/A
Chapter 2 - Recording Business Transactions - N/A
Chapter 3 - The Adjusting Process - N/A
Chapter 4 - Completing the Accounting Cycle - N/A
Chapter 5 - Merchandising Operations - N/A
Chapter 6 - Merchandise Inventory - N/A
Chapter 7 - Internal Control and Cash - N/A
Chapter 8 - Receivables - N/A
Chapter 9 - Plant Assets, Natural Resources, and Intangibles - N/A
Chapter 10 - Investments - N/A
Chapter 11 - Current Liabilities and Payroll - N/A
Chapter 12 - Long-Term Liabilities - N/A
Chapter 13 - Stockholder's Equity - N/A
Chapter 14 - The Statement of Cash Flows - N/A
Chapter 15 - Financial Statement Analysis - N/A
Chapter 16 - Introduction to Managerial Accounting - SU 1
Chapter 17 - Job Order Costing - SU 2
Chapter 18 - Process Costing - SU 10
Chapter 19 - Cost Management Systems: Activity-Based, Just-In-Time, and Quality Management Systems - SU 3, 12.1, 14.3
Chapter 20 - Cost-Volume-Profit Analysis - SU 4
Chapter 21 - Variable Costing - 6.1-6.2
Chapter 22 - Master Budgets - 5.1-5.2
Chapter 23 - Flexible Budgets and Standard Cost Systems - 5.4, SU 7
Chapter 24 - Responsibility Accounting and Performance Evaluation - 9.1-9.3
Chapter 25 - Short-Term Business Decisions - SU 8
Chapter 26 - Capital Investment Decisions - SU 13

Needles, Powers, and Crosson, *Managerial Accounting*, Tenth Edition, Cengage Learning, 2014.

Chapter 1 - Managerial Accounting and Cost Concepts - 1.1-1.5
Chapter 2 - Costing Systems: Job Order Costing - SU 2
Chapter 3 - Costing Systems: Process Costing - SU 10
Chapter 4 - Value-Based Systems: Activity-Based Costing and Lean Accounting - SU 3, 14.3
Chapter 5 - Cost-Volume-Profit Analysis - SU 4
Chapter 6 - The Budgeting Process - SU 5
Chapter 7 - Flexible Budgets and Performance Analysis - 5.4, 9.1-9.3
Chapter 8 - Standard Costing and Variance Analysis - SU 7
Chapter 9 - Short-Run Decision Analysis - SU 8
Chapter 10 - Capital Investment Analysis - SU 13
Chapter 11 - Pricing Decisions, Including Target Costing and Transfer Pricing - 5.5, 9.4
Chapter 12 - Quality Management and Measurement - SU 12
Chapter 13 - The Statement of Cash Flows - N/A
Chapter 14 - Financial Statement Analysis - N/A

Vanderbeck and Mitchell, *Principles of Cost Accounting*, Seventeenth Edition, Cengage Learning, 2016.

Chapter 1 - Introduction to Cost Accounting - SU 1
Chapter 2 - Accounting for Materials - SU 2, 7.2, SU 10
Chapter 3 - Accounting for Labor - SU 2, 7.1, 7.3, SU 10
Chapter 4 - Accounting for Factory Overhead - 7.4
Chapter 5 - Process Cost Accounting--General Procedures - SU 10
Chapter 6 - Process Cost Accounting--Additional Procedures; Accounting for Joint Products and By-Products - SU 11
Chapter 7 - The Master Budget and Flexible Budgeting - 5.1-5.3
Chapter 8 - Standard Cost Accounting--Materials, Labor, and Factory Overhead - 7.1-7.4
Chapter 9 - Cost Accounting for Service Businesses and the Balanced Scorecard - 9.2
Chapter 10 - Cost Analysis for Management Decision Making - SU 4, SUs 8-9

Warren, Reeve, and Duchac, *Financial & Managerial Accounting*, Fourteenth Edition, Cengage Learning, 2018.

Chapter 1 - Introduction to Accounting and Business - N/A
Chapter 2 - Analyzing Transactions - N/A
Chapter 3 - The Adjusting Process - N/A
Chapter 4 - Completing the Accounting Cycle - N/A
Chapter 5 - Accounting for Merchandising Businesses - N/A
Chapter 6 - Inventories - N/A
Chapter 7 - Internal Control and Cash - N/A
Chapter 8 - Receivables - N/A
Chapter 9 - Long-Term Assets: Fixed and Intangible - N/A
Chapter 10 - Liabilities: Current, Installment Notes, and Contingencies - N/A
Chapter 11 - Liabilities: Bonds Payable - N/A
Chapter 12 - Corporations: Organization, Stock Transactions, and Dividends - N/A
Chapter 13 - Statement of Cash Flows - N/A
Chapter 14 - Financial Statement Analysis - N/A
Chapter 15 - Introduction to Managerial Accounting - SU 1
Chapter 16 - Job Order Costing - SU 2
Chapter 17 - Process Costing Systems - SU 10
Chapter 18 - Activity-Based Costing - SU 3
Chapter 19 - Cost-Volume-Profit Analysis - SU 4
Chapter 20 - Variable Costing for Management Analysis - SU 6
Chapter 21 - Budgeting - SU 5
Chapter 22 - Evaluating Variances from Standard Costs - SU 7
Chapter 23 - Evaluating Decentralized Operations - 9.4
Chapter 24 - Differential Analysis and Product Pricing - 8.1, 8.4-8.5
Chapter 25 - Capital Investment Analysis - SU 13
Chapter 26 - Lean Manufacturing and Activity Analysis - 14.3

Warren, Reeve, and Duchac, *Managerial Accounting*, Fourteenth Edition, Cengage Learning, 2018.

Chapter 1 - Introduction to Managerial Accounting - 1.1-1.5
Chapter 2 - Job Order Costing - SU 2
Chapter 3 - Process Cost Systems - SU 10
Chapter 4 - Activity-Based Costing - SU 3
Chapter 5 - Cost-Volume-Profit Analysis - SU 4
Chapter 6 - Variable Costing for Management Analysis - 6.1
Chapter 7 - Budgeting - SU 5
Chapter 8 - Evaluating Variances from Standard Costs - SU 7
Chapter 9 - Evaluating Decentralized Operations - 9.4
Chapter 10 - Differential Analysis and Product Pricing - 8.1, 8.4-8.5
Chapter 11 - Capital Investment Analysis - SU 13
Chapter 12 - Lean Manufacturing and Activity Analysis - 14.3
Chapter 13 - Statement of Cash Flows - N/A
Chapter 14 - Financial Statement Analysis - N/A

Weygandt, Kieso, and Kimmel, *Managerial Accounting: Tools for Business Decision Making*, Eighth Edition, John Wiley & Sons, 2017.

Chapter 1 - Managerial Accounting - SU 1
Chapter 2 - Job Order Costing - SU 2
Chapter 3 - Process Costing - SU 10
Chapter 4 - Activity-Based Costing - SU 3
Chapter 5 - Cost-Volume-Profit - SU 4
Chapter 6 - Cost-Volume-Profit Analysis: Additional Issues - SU 4
Chapter 7 - Incremental Analysis - 8.1
Chapter 8 - Pricing - 4.6-4.7
Chapter 9 - Budgetary Planning - SU 5
Chapter 10 - Budgetary Control and Responsibility Accounting - 5.3, 9.1
Chapter 11 - Standard Costs and Balanced Scorecard - SU 7, 9.3
Chapter 12 - Planning for Capital Investments - SU 13
Chapter 13 - Statement of Cash Flows - N/A
Chapter 14 - Financial Statement Analysis - N/A

Wild, Shaw, and Chiappetta, *Financial and Managerial Accounting: Information for Decisions*, Seventh Edition, McGraw-Hill/Irwin, 2018.

Chapter 1 - Accounting in Business - N/A
Chapter 2 - Analyzing for Business Transactions - N/A
Chapter 3 - Adjusting Accounts for Financial Statements - N/A
Chapter 4 - Accounting for Merchandising Operations - N/A
Chapter 5 - Inventories and Cost of Sales - N/A
Chapter 6 - Cash and Internal Control - N/A
Chapter 7 - Accounting for Receivables - N/A
Chapter 8 - Accounting for Long-term Assets - N/A
Chapter 9 - Accounting for Current Liabilities - N/A
Chapter 10 - Accounting for Long-Term Liabilities - N/A
Chapter 11 - Corporate Reporting and Analysis - N/A
Chapter 12 - Reporting Cash Flows - N/A
Chapter 13 - Analysis of Financial Statements - N/A
Chapter 14 - Managerial Accounting Concepts and Principles - SU 1
Chapter 15 - Job Order Costing and Analysis - SU 2
Chapter 16 - Process Costing and Analysis - SU 10
Chapter 17 - Activity-Based Costing and Analysis - SU 3
Chapter 18 - Cost Behavior and Cost-Volume-Profit Analysis - SU 4
Chapter 19 - Variable Costing and Analysis - SU 6
Chapter 20 - Master Budgets and Performance Planning - 5.1-5.3
Chapter 21 - Flexible Budgets and Standard Costs - 5.4, SU 7
Chapter 22 - Performance Measurement and Responsibility Accounting - 9.1-9.3
Chapter 23 - Relevant Costing for Managerial Decisions - SU 8
Chapter 24 - Capital Budgeting and Investment Analysis - SU 13

Wouters, Selto, Hilton, and Maher, *Cost Management: Strategies for Business Decisions*, International Edition, First Edition, McGraw-Hill Higher Education, 2013.

Part 1: Setting the Strategic Foundation: The Importance of Analyzing and Managing Costs
- Chapter 1 - Cost Management and Strategic Decision Making: Evaluating Opportunities and Leading Change - N/A
- Chapter 2 - Product Costing Concepts and Systems - 1.1-1.5
- Chapter 3 - Cost Estimation - 4.3, SUs 15-18

Part 2: Activity-Based Management
- Chapter 4 - Activity-Based Costing Systems - SU 3
- Chapter 5 - Customer Profitability and Activity-Based Management - SU 3, SU 11
- Chapter 6 - Managing Quality and Time to Create Value - SU 12

Part 3: Planning and Decision Making
- Chapter 7 - Cost Management and Short-Term Decision Making - SUs 8-9
- Chapter 8 - Strategic Investment Decisions - SU 13
- Chapter 9 - Budgeting and Financial Planning - SU 5

Part 4: Product Costing and Cost Allocation
- Chapter 10 - Job and Order Costing - SU 2
- Chapter 11 - Joint Product and Process Cost Systems - SU 10, 11.3-11.8
- Chapter 12 - Managing and Allocating Support Service Costs - 11.1-11.2

Part 5: Performance Measurement and Management
- Chapter 13 - Analysis and Management of Cost Variances - SU 7
- Chapter 14 - Organizational Design, Responsibility Accounting, and Evaluation of Divisional Performance - 9.1-9.3
- Chapter 15 - Transfer Pricing - 9.4
- Chapter 16 - Strategy, Balanced Scorecards, and Incentive Systems - 9.1-9.3

Zimmerman, *Accounting for Decision Making and Control*, Ninth Edition, McGraw-Hill, 2017.

- Chapter 1 - Introduction - SU 1
- Chapter 2 - The Nature of Costs - 1.4-1.5, 16.3
- Chapter 3 - Opportunity Cost of Capital and Capital Budgeting - SU 13
- Chapter 4 - Organizational Architecture - 9.2-9.3
- Chapter 5 - Responsibility Accounting and Transfer Pricing - SU 9
- Chapter 6 - Budgeting - SU 5
- Chapter 7 - Cost Allocation: Theory - SU 11
- Chapter 8 - Cost Allocation: Practices - SU 11
- Chapter 9 - Absorption Cost System - 6.2-6.3
- Chapter 10 - Criticisms of Absorption Cost Systems: Incentives to Overproduce - SU 6
- Chapter 11 - Criticisms of Absorption Cost Systems: Inaccurate Product Costs - SU 6
- Chapter 12 - Standard Costs: Direct Labor and Materials - 7.1-7.3
- Chapter 13 - Overhead and Marketing Variances - 7.4-7.6
- Chapter 14 - Management Accounting in a Changing Environment - 12.1

QUANTITATIVE METHODS

Anderson, Sweeney, Williams, Camm, Cochran, Fry, and Ohlmann, *An Introduction to Management Science: Quantitative Approaches to Decision Making*, Fifteenth Edition, Cengage Learning, 2019.

Chapter 1 - Introduction - 18.1
Chapter 2 - An Introduction to Linear Programming - 17.1
Chapter 3 - Linear Programming: Sensitivity Analysis and Interpretation of Solution - 17.3-17.4, 18.1
Chapter 4 - Linear Programming Applications in Marketing, Finance, and Operations Management - 17.1
Chapter 5 - Advanced Linear Programming Applications - 17.3-17.4
Chapter 6 - Distribution and Network Models - 17.3-17.4, 18.3
Chapter 7 - Integer Linear Programming - 17.1
Chapter 8 - Nonlinear Optimization Models - 18.3
Chapter 9 - Project Scheduling: PERT/CPM - 18.3
Chapter 10 - Inventory Models - SU 14
Chapter 11 - Waiting Line Models - 18.2
Chapter 12 - Simulation - 18.1
Chapter 13 - Decision Analysis - SU 15, 17.1, 18.7
Chapter 14 - Multicriteria Decisions - 16.5
Chapter 15 - Time Series Analysis and Forecasting - SU 16
Chapter 16 - Markov Processes - 18.1
Chapter 17 - Linear Programming: Simplex Method (online) - SU 17
Chapter 18 - Simplex-Based Sensitivity Analysis and Duality (online) - SU 17
Chapter 19 - Solutions Procedures for Transportation and Assignment Problems (online) - SU 17
Chapter 20 - Minimal Spanning Tree (online) - N/A
Chapter 21 - Dynamic Programming (online) - SU 17

Anderson, Sweeney, Williams, Camm, Cochran, Fry, and Ohlmann, *Quantitative Methods for Business*, Thirteenth Edition, Cengage Learning, 2016.

Chapter 1 - Introduction - N/A
Chapter 2 - Introduction to Probability - 15.1
Chapter 3 - Probability Distributions - 15.2
Chapter 4 - Decision Analysis - SU 15, 17.1
Chapter 5 - Utility and Game Theory - 18.7
Chapter 6 - Time Series Analysis and Forecasting - SU 16
Chapter 7 - Introduction to Linear Programming - 17.1
Chapter 8 - Linear Programming: Sensitivity Analysis and Interpretation of Solution - 17.3-17.4, 18.1
Chapter 9 - Linear Programming Applications in Marketing, Finance, and Operations Management - 17.1
Chapter 10 - Distribution and Network Models - 17.3-17.4, 18.3
Chapter 11 - Integer Linear Programming - 17.1
Chapter 12 - Advanced Optimization Applications - 17.4
Chapter 13 - Project Scheduling: PERT/CPM - 18.3
Chapter 14 - Inventory Models - SU 14
Chapter 15 - Waiting Line Models - 18.2
Chapter 16 - Simulation - 18.1
Chapter 17 - Markov Processes - 18.1

Heizer, Render, and Munson, *Operations Management: Sustainability and Supply Chain Management*, Twelfth Edition, Pearson, 2017.

Part I: Introduction to Operations Management
- Chapter 1 - Operations and Productivity - 7.7, 10.2
- Chapter 2 - Operations Strategy in a Global Environment - N/A
- Chapter 3 - Project Management - N/A
- Chapter 4 - Forecasting - SU 16

Part II: Designing Operations
- Chapter 5 - Design of Goods and Services - N/A
- S5 - Sustainability in the Supply Chain - N/A
- Chapter 6 - Managing Quality - SU 12
- S6 - Statistical Process Control - SU 15
- Chapter 7 - Process Strategy - N/A
- S7 - Capacity and Constraint Management - N/A
- Chapter 8 - Location Strategies - N/A
- Chapter 9 - Layout Strategies - N/A
- Chapter 10 - Human Resources, Job Design, and Work Measurement - N/A

Part III: Managing Operations
- Chapter 11 - Supply Chain Management - N/A
- S11 - Supply Chain Management Analytics - N/A
- Chapter 12 - Inventory Management - SU 14
- Chapter 13 - Aggregate Planning and S&OP - N/A
- Chapter 14 - Material Requirements Planning (MRP) and ERP - 14.3
- Chapter 15 - Short-Term Scheduling - N/A
- Chapter 16 - Lean Operations - 14.3
- Chapter 17 - Maintenance and Reliability - N/A

Part IV: Business Analytics Modules
- A - Decision-Making Tools - SU 15, 17.1, 18.7
- B - Linear Programming - SU 17
- C - Transportation Models - N/A
- D - Waiting-Line Models - 18.2
- E - Learning Curves - 18.4
- F - Simulation - 18.1

Krajewski, Malhotra, and Ritzman, *Operations Management: Processes and Supply Chains*, Twelfth Edition, Pearson, 2019.

- Chapter 1 - Using Operations to Create Value - N/A
- Suppl. A - Decision Making - N/A

Part I: Managing Processes
- Chapter 2 - Process Strategy and Analysis - N/A
- Chapter 3 - Quality and Performance - SU 12
- Chapter 4 - Capacity Planning - SU 9
- Suppl. B - Waiting Lines - N/A
- Chapter 5 - Constraint Management - 17.1
- Chapter 6 - Lean Systems - 14.3
- Chapter 7 - Project Management - N/A

Part II: Managing Customer Demand
- Chapter 8 - Forecasting - SU 16
- Chapter 9 - Inventory Management - SU 14
- Suppl. C - Special Inventory Models - N/A
- Chapter 10 - Operations Planning and Scheduling - N/A
- Suppl. D - Linear Programming - 17.1
- Chapter 11 - Resource Planning - N/A

Part III: Managing Supply Chains
- Chapter 12 - Supply Chain Design - N/A
- Chapter 13 - Supply Chain Logistic Networks - N/A
- Chapter 14 - Supply Chain Integration - N/A
- Chapter 15 - Supply Chain Sustainability - N/A

APPENDIX B
COST AND MANAGERIAL ACCOUNTING GLOSSARY

This appendix presents a selection of key definitions. For important additional definitions, see the glossary related to activity-based costing in Appendix C.

Students should be aware that terminology varies somewhat among authoritative sources and from textbook to textbook. Compare, for example, the definition of cost allocation given on page 512 with the definitions of allocation and tracing in an ABC context provided in the glossary in Appendix C.

Abnormal spoilage is spoilage that is not expected to occur under normal, efficient operating conditions. Abnormal spoilage is typically treated as a period cost (a loss) because of its unusual nature.

Absorption (full) costing treats all manufacturing costs as product costs, i.e., both variable and fixed costs are included in product costs. [Contrast with *Variable (direct) costing*.]

Activity-based costing (ABC) is a refinement to an existing (job or process) costing system. Where traditional costing systems accumulate overhead in a single indirect cost pool and allocate the same amount to every unit of output, ABC involves the creation of multiple indirect cost pools based on the various activities that support the production process. A different allocation rate is computed for each pool. With increasing automation, overhead costs have come to make up an increasingly larger proportion of total manufacturing costs; ABC was devised to address this costing challenge.

Activity drivers are cost drivers used in activity-based costing (ABC) to allocate amounts accumulated in activity cost pools to next-stage cost objects. (Compare with *Resource drivers*.)

Actual costing is the most accurate method of accumulating costs. However, it is also the least timely and most volatile method. After the end of the production period, all actual costs incurred for a cost object are totaled; indirect costs are allocated. (Contrast with *Normal costing* and *Extended normal costing*.)

Applied (absorbed) overhead is manufacturing (factory) overhead that has been allocated to products, usually on the basis of a predetermined rate. Overhead is over- or underapplied (absorbed) when overhead charged is greater or less than actual overhead incurred, respectively.

Appraisal costs are the costs of quality that are incurred to detect nonconformance of products or services with specifications or customer needs. They include the costs of inspection and testing of materials, product acceptance (sampling of finished goods), process acceptance (sampling of goods in process), equipment used in measurement, packaging inspection, supervising appraisal, and outside endorsements.

Avoidable costs are those that may be eliminated by not engaging in an activity or by performing it more efficiently. (Contrast with *Committed costs*.)

Backflush costing is often used with a just-in-time (JIT) production system. It delays costing until goods are finished. Standard costs are then "flushed" backward through the system to assign costs to products. The result is that detailed tracking of costs is eliminated. The system is best suited to companies that maintain low inventories because costs then flow directly to cost of goods sold.

Balanced scorecard approach uses multiple measures to evaluate managerial performance. A typical balanced scorecard classifies objectives and the measures of progress toward them into four perspectives on the business: financial, customer satisfaction, internal business processes, and learning and growth. The scorecard allows a determination as to whether a manager is achieving certain objectives at the expense of others that may be equally or more important.

Benchmarking (also called competitive benchmarking or best practices) compares one's own product, service, or practice with the best known similar activity. The objective is to measure the key outputs of a business process or function against the best and to analyze the reasons for the performance difference.

Breakeven point is the output at which total revenues equal total costs.

Budget variance (also known as the flexible-budget variance or spending variance) is the difference between actual and budgeted fixed manufacturing overhead in a four-way analysis of overhead variances. In three-way analysis, the spending variance combines the variable overhead spending variance and the fixed overhead budget variance. In two-way analysis, the budget (flexible-budget or controllable) variance is that part of the total manufacturing overhead variance not attributed to the production volume variance.

Budgeting is the formal quantification of management's plans. Budgets are usually expressed in quantitative terms and are used to motivate management and evaluate its performance in achieving goals. In this sense, standards are established.

Byproducts are one or more products of relatively small total value that are produced simultaneously from a common manufacturing process with products of greater value and quantity (joint products).

Capital budgeting plans expenditures for assets, the returns on which are expected to continue beyond 1 year. Capital budgeting decisions are long-term and relatively inflexible.

Carrying cost is the cost of storing or holding inventory. Examples include the cost of capital, insurance, warehousing, breakage, and obsolescence.

Chief financial officer (CFO) is the senior manager who has oversight of the entity's financial activities, for example, the controllership and treasury functions, the internal audit activity, management of risks, and tax planning.

Coefficient of correlation measures the degree to which any two variables are related. The coefficient of correlation can be used to determine how a security performs against its benchmarks or how securities behave against other securities within a portfolio.

Committed costs result when a going concern holds fixed assets (property, plant, and equipment). Examples are insurance, long-term lease payments, and depreciation. They are by nature long-term and cannot be reduced by lowering the short-term level of production. (Contrast with *Avoidable costs.*)

Common cost is the shared operating cost of a cost object (plant, facility, activity, etc.) used by two or more entities.

Computer-integrated manufacturing (CIM) systems automate the design, engineering, production, and accounting functions. A **computer-assisted design (CAD)** system is used to design products that are tested using a **computer-assisted engineering (CAE)** system. They are manufactured using a **computer-assisted manufacturing (CAM)** system that consists of machinery controlled by computers, possibly including some applications of robotics. These functions are linked by an information system. For a specific type of CAM, see *Flexible manufacturing systems*.

The **constant gross-margin percentage NRV method** for allocating joint costs is based on using the same gross margin percentage for all of the products.

Contribution margin is calculated by subtracting all variable costs of the product or service from sales revenue. Variable costs include both variable cost of goods sold and variable selling and administrative costs. Fixed costs are then subtracted to arrive at variable-basis operating income. (Contrast with *Gross margin*.)

Controllable costs are directly regulated or significantly influenced by management of a given responsibility center within a given time span. (Contrast with *Fixed costs*, which are not controllable in the short run.)

Controllable variance in two-way analysis is the part of the total manufacturing overhead variance not attributable to the volume variance.

Controller (or comptroller) is a financial officer having responsibility for the accounting functions (management and financial) as well as budgeting and internal control.

Conversion costs are direct labor and manufacturing overhead, i.e., the costs of converting raw materials into finished goods. (Compare with *Prime costs.*)

Cost. In SMA 2A, the IMA defines cost as follows: "(1) In management accounting, a measurement in monetary terms of the amount of resources used for some purpose. The term by itself is not operational. It becomes operational when modified by a term that defines the purpose, such as acquisition cost, incremental cost, or fixed cost. (2) In financial accounting, the sacrifice measured by the price paid or required to be paid to acquire goods or services. The term 'cost' is often used when referring to the valuation of a good or service acquired. When 'cost' is used in this sense, a cost is an asset. When the benefits of the acquisition (the goods or services) expire, the cost becomes an expense or loss."

Cost accounting includes (1) managerial accounting in the sense that its purpose can be to provide internal reports for use in planning and control and in making nonroutine decisions and (2) financial accounting because its product costing function satisfies requirements for reporting to shareholders, government, and various outside parties.

Cost allocation is the process of assigning and reassigning costs to cost objects. It may also be defined as a distribution of costs that cannot be directly assigned (traced) to the cost objects that are assumed to have caused them. In this sense, allocation involves choosing a cost object, determining the direct and indirect costs assignable thereto, deciding how costs are to be accumulated in cost pools before allocation, and selecting the allocation base. Allocation is necessary for product costing, pricing, investment decisions, managerial performance evaluation, profitability analysis, make-or-buy decisions, etc.

Cost behavior is the relationship between costs and activities. It is the amount of change in a cost related to the activity level. A cost's behavior can be fixed, variable, or mixed (semivariable).

Cost center is the simplest of the four types of responsibility center. Management is accountable for costs only.

Cost driver "is a measure of activity, such as direct labor hours, machine hours, beds occupied, computer time used, flight hours, miles driven, or contracts, that is a causal factor in the incurrence of cost to an entity" (SMA 2A).

Cost objects are the intermediate and final dispositions of cost pools. Intermediate cost objects receive temporary accumulations of costs as the cost pools move from their originating points to the final cost objects. Final cost objects, such as a job, product, or process, should be logically linked with the cost pool based on a cause-and-effect relationship.

Cost of goods manufactured (COGM) is equivalent to a retailer's purchases. It equals all manufacturing costs (direct materials, direct labor, and manufacturing overhead) incurred during the period, plus beginning work-in-process (BWIP), minus ending work-in-process (EWIP). COGM is the amount transferred to finished goods.

Cost of goods sold (COGS) equals beginning finished goods (or merchandise) inventory, plus cost of goods manufactured (or purchases), minus ending finished goods (or merchandise) inventory.

Cost pools are accounts in which a variety of similar costs with a common cause are accumulated prior to assignment to cost objects on some common basis. The overhead account is a cost pool into which various types of overhead are accumulated prior to their allocation. Under ABC, a cost pool is established for each activity.

Cost-volume-profit (breakeven) analysis is a means of predicting the relationships among revenues, variable costs, and fixed costs at various production levels. It allows management to discern the probable effects of changes in sales volume, sales price, costs, product mix, etc.

Customer profitability analysis assigns revenues and costs to major customers or groups of customers rather than to organizational units products, or other objects. The results may direct organizational resources toward more profitable uses.

Differential (incremental) cost is the difference in total cost between two decisions.

Direct cost is one that can be specifically associated with a single cost object in an economically feasible way.

Direct costing. See *Variable costing.*

Direct labor costs are wages paid to labor that can feasibly be specifically identified with the production of finished goods or the rendering of services.

Direct materials costs are the costs of raw materials that can feasibly be specifically identified with the production of finished goods or the rendering of services.

Direct method of service cost allocation apportions service department costs directly to production departments. It makes no allocation of services rendered to other service departments.

Discretionary costs are characterized by uncertainty about the relationship between input (the costs) and the value of the related output. They tend to be subject to periodic (e.g., annual) outlay decisions. Advertising and research costs are examples. (Contrast with *Engineered costs.*)

Dividend growth model estimates the cost of common stock as equal to the next expected dividend per share divided by the market price, plus the expected constant growth rate.

Economic order quantity (EOQ) model determines the order quantity that minimizes the sum of ordering costs and carrying costs.

Economic value added (EVA) is a variation of residual income that defines the variable in specific ways. One version of EVA equals after-tax net operating profit minus the product of the weighted-average cost of capital (WACC) and operating capital. The WACC is an after-tax average of the costs of all sources of funds, equity as well as debt, used by the firm. Moreover, certain adjustments may be made in measuring net operating profit, e.g., amortizing R&D expense over a period of years. Operating capital equals total assets minus current liabilities.

Efficiency variances compare the actual use of inputs with the budgeted quantity of inputs allowed for the activity level achieved. When the difference is multiplied by the budgeted rate per unit of input, the resulting variance isolates the cost effect of using more or fewer units of input than budgeted.

Electronic data interchange (EDI) is the communication of electronic documents directly from a computer in one entity to a computer in another entity, for example, to order goods from a supplier or to transfer funds. EDI was developed to enhance just-in-time (JIT) production systems.

Engineered costs are costs having a clear relationship to output. Direct materials cost is an example. (Contrast with *Discretionary costs.*)

Equivalent unit of production (EUP) is a set of inputs required to manufacture one physical unit. Calculating equivalent units for each factor of production facilitates measurement of output and cost allocation when work-in-process exists under a process costing system.

Executional cost drivers capture a firm's operational decisions on how best to employ its resources to achieve its objectives. Executional drivers are determined by management policy, style, and culture. Examples are workforce involvement, existence of a quality assurance program, capacity utilization, relations with suppliers, etc. Together with structural cost drivers, executional cost drivers are an integral part of activity-based costing.

The **estimated net realizable value method** for allocating joint costs is a variation of the relative sales value method. The significant difference is that, under the estimated NRV method, all separable costs necessary to make the product salable are added in before the allocation is made.

Extended normal costing charges all product costs (direct materials, direct labor, manufacturing overhead) based on normalized (budgeted) rates. (Contrast with *Actual costing* and *Normal costing.*)

External failure costs are the costs of quality that are incurred when products and services do not conform with specifications or customer needs after delivery. They include the costs of recalls, lost sales, returns and allowances, product liability, warranties, and reduced market share. (Compare with *Internal failure costs.*)

Financial%%Leverage is the change in earnings resulting from a change in net operating income. The assumption is that firms with higher debt will have more financial leverage.

Fixed costs remain unchanged in total within the relevant range for a given period despite fluctuations in activity. Fixed costs per unit change as the level of activity changes.

Flexible budget is a series of budgets prepared for many levels of activity so that actual performance can be compared with the appropriate budgeted level.

Flexible manufacturing systems (FMSs) use computerized methods to reduce setup or change overtimes and facilitate the production of differentiated products in small numbers. The shift in emphasis is from mass production of a few products to a job-shop environment in which customized orders are manufactured. Automation allows for better quality and scheduling, rapid changes in product lines, and lower inventories and costs. (See *Computer-integrated manufacturing.*)

Full product cost is the long-term total cost of making and selling a product. It includes the costs of all business functions.

Full costing. See *Absorption costing.*

Gross margin (profit) is the difference between revenues and the full absorption cost of goods sold. It should be contrasted with contribution margin (Revenues – Variable costs).

The **high-low method** estimates the fixed and variable components of a mixed cost. The variable component is estimated by dividing the difference between the highest total cost and the lowest total cost by the difference between the highest activity and the lowest activity. The fixed component can be estimated as the difference between high total cost and the product of the variable component and either high or low activity. (Contrast with the *Regression method.*)

Imputed costs are properly attributable to a cost object even though no transaction has occurred that would be routinely recognized in the accounts. They may be outlay costs or opportunity costs but, in either case, they should be considered in decision making. An example of an imputed cost is the profit lost as a result of being unable to fill orders because the inventory level is too low.

Incremental (differential) cost is the difference in total cost between two decisions.

Indirect costs cannot be specifically associated with a given cost object in an economically feasible way. They are also defined as costs that are not directly identified with one final cost object but that are identified with two or more final cost objects or with at least one intermediate cost object.

Internal failure costs are the costs of quality that are incurred because of nonconformance of products and services with specifications or customer needs. These costs are identified before delivery to outside parties. They include the costs of scrap, rework, downtime, design modifications, and repeat testing. (Compare with *External failure costs*.)

Internal rate of return (IRR) is an interest rate calculated so that the net present value of the investment is zero.

Investment center is one of the four types of responsibility center. Management is accountable for revenues (markets), costs (sources of supply), and invested capital.

Job costing is appropriate when products or services have individual characteristics or when identifiable groupings are possible, e.g., batches of certain styles or types of furniture. The unique aspect of job costing is the identification of costs to specific units or a particular job. (Compare with *Process costing*.)

Joint costs are incurred in the production of two or more products by a common process from a common input up to the point at which the products become separable (the split-off point). Hence, they are irrelevant to the timing of sales. (Contrast with *Separable costs*.)

Joint products are two or more separate products produced by a common manufacturing process from a common input. The common (joint) costs of two or more joint products with significant values are customarily allocated to the joint products.

Just-in-time (JIT) production systems are based on a demand pull philosophy. Purchases of materials and output depend on actual customer demand. Inventories are reduced greatly or eliminated, a few suppliers must reliably deliver small amounts on a frequent basis, plant layouts must become more efficient, a zero defects policy is established, and workers must be able to perform multiple tasks, including continuous monitoring of quality.

Kaizen is the Japanese term for continuous improvement. Kaizen budgeting incorporates expectations for continuous improvement into budgetary estimates. Kaizen costing determines target cost reductions for a period, such as a month. Thus, variances are the differences between actual and targeted cost reduction. The objective is to reduce actual costs below standard costs. The cost-reduction activities associated with the Kaizen approach minimize costs throughout the entire product life cycle. Thus, it has the advantage of being closely related to the entity's profit-planning procedures.

Learning curve analysis reflects the increased rate at which people perform tasks as they gain experience.

Life-cycle costing accounts for all product costs in the value chain from research and development and design of products and processes through production, marketing, distribution, and customer service. It focuses on minimizing locked-in costs, for example, by reducing the number of parts, promoting standardization of parts, and using equipment that can make more than one kind of product.

Linear-cost functions are those that change at a constant rate (or remain unchanged) over the short run. Fixed cost in total, variable costs in total, and variable cost per unit are linear-cost functions.

Managerial accounting primarily concerns the planning and control of organizational operations, considers nonquantitative information, and is usually less precise than cost accounting.

A **manufacturing cell** is a group of all of the machines and workers needed to produce a certain product.

Manufacturing cycle efficiency is the quotient of the time required for value-added production divided by total manufacturing lead (cycle) time. Lead time is the time elapsed from when an order is ready for production until it becomes a finished good.

Manufacturing (factory) overhead (indirect manufacturing costs) consists of all costs other than direct materials and direct labor that are associated with the manufacturing process. It includes both fixed and variable components.

Margin of safety is the excess of budgeted revenues or unit sales over the breakeven point.

Marginal cost is the sum of the costs necessary to effect a one-unit increase in the activity level.

Mix variances measure the effects of changes in the proportions of various inputs, e.g., different mixes of direct materials or labor.

Mixed (semivariable) costs combine fixed and variable elements.

Net present value (NPV) is the difference between the present value of the net cash inflows and net cash outflows.

Normal capacity is the long-term average level of activity that will approximate demand over a period that includes seasonal, cyclical, and trend variations. Deviations in a given year will be offset in subsequent years. (Compare with *Practical capacity* and *Theoretical capacity*.)

Normal costing applies overhead based on predetermined rates and the actual usage of the base used to assign the costs.

Normal spoilage is the spoilage that occurs under normal operating conditions. It is essentially uncontrollable in the short run. Normal spoilage arises under efficient operations and is treated as a product cost.

Operating leverage is the change in operating income resulting from a change in sales. The assumption is that firms with greater fixed costs will have higher contribution margins and more operating leverage.

Operation costing is a hybrid of job costing and process costing systems. It is used by companies that manufacture goods that undergo some similar and some dissimilar processes. Operation costing accumulates total conversion costs and determines a unit conversion cost for each operation. However, direct materials costs are charged specifically to products as in job costing systems.

Opportunity cost is the maximum benefit forgone by using a scarce resource for a given purpose. It is the benefit, for example, the contribution to income, provided by the best alternative use of that resource. (Contrast with *Out-of-pocket costs*.)

Out-of-pocket (outlay) costs require negative cash outflows (expenditures) currently or in the near future. (Contrast with *Opportunity cost*.)

Outsourcing is the acquisition of products and services from sources outside the organization instead of producing them internally.

Partial productivity is ordinarily calculated as output divided by a single input.

Payback period is the number of years required to complete the return of the original investment.

Period costs are charged to expense as incurred and not to a particular product. They are not identifiable with a product and are not inventoried. Period costs may be classified as either revenue expenditures or capital expenditures. Revenue expenditures, e.g., advertising and officers' salaries, are charged to the income statement in the period the costs are incurred because they usually do not benefit future periods. Capital expenditures, e.g., those for depreciable assets, are initially recorded as assets and then expensed as they are consumed, used, or disposed of.

Periodic inventory systems rely on physical counts to determine quantities.

Perpetual inventory records provide for continuous record keeping of the quantities of inventory (and possibly unit costs or total costs). This method requires a journal entry every time items are added to or taken from inventory.

The **physical unit method** for allocating joint costs employs a physical measure, such as volume, weight, or a linear measure.

Practical capacity is the maximum level at which output is produced efficiently. It usually results in underapplied overhead. (Compare with *Normal capacity* and *Theoretical capacity*.)

Prevention costs are the costs of quality that are incurred to avoid defects in products or services. They include the costs of quality engineering, design engineering, employee training, quality planning and reporting, new materials, preventive maintenance, quality audits, and quality circles.

Price (rate) variance equals the difference between the actual and standard price of an input, multiplied by the actual quantity.

Prime costs are the costs of direct materials and direct labor.

Process costing should be used to assign costs to similar products or service units that are mass produced on a continuous basis. Costs are accumulated by process or department rather than by jobs, and unit costs are established by measuring output for a specified period and dividing into the process costs. Process costing is an averaging process that calculates the average cost of all units. (Compare with *Job costing*.)

Process reengineering involves analysis of business processes that results in radical change rather than incremental improvement. Redesign of processes is intended to result in elimination of unnecessary steps, reduction of circumstances in which mistakes can occur, cost minimization, quicker response times, and better quality.

Process value analysis is a systematic understanding of the activities involved in making a product or rendering a service. It identifies those that add value and those that may be eliminated.

Product (inventoriable) costs are incurred to produce units of output and are deferred to future periods to the extent output is not sold (kept on hand for sale in future periods). They are expensed in the period the product is sold. Hence, product costs are those that can be associated with specific revenues. Examples are direct materials, direct labor, and manufacturing (not general and administrative) overhead.

Productivity is the relationship of input and output.

Profit center is a responsibility center in which management is responsible for both revenues and costs. A profit center has the authority to make decisions concerning markets (revenues) and sources of supply (costs).

Quality costs are costs of conformance (prevention and appraisal) and nonconformance (internal failure and external failure) with quality standards.

Quantity (usage) variance is an efficiency variance for direct materials.

Rate variance is a price variance for direct labor.

Reciprocal method uses simultaneous equations to allocate each service department's costs among the departments providing mutual services before reallocation to other users.

The **regression (scattergraph) method** of estimating a cost function is quite complex and determines the average rate of variability of a mixed cost. (Contrast with the *High-low method*.)

Relative sales value method is used to allocate joint costs at split-off to joint products based upon their relative proportions of total sales value. If a product is not salable at the split-off point, its net realizable value (NRV) may be used to approximate its relative sales value. One variant of this method is the constant gross margin percentage method. Still another way to allocate joint costs is by physical quantities.

Relevant costs are those expected future costs that vary with the action taken. All other costs are assumed to be constant and thus have no effect on (are irrelevant to) the decision. (Contrast with *Sunk cost*.)

Relevant range is the range of activity within which assumed cost relationships are deemed to be true. For example, given a cost function assumed to be linear, variable unit costs are constant and fixed costs are constant in total. In this range, the incremental cost of one additional unit is also constant.

Residual income is the excess of the return on an investment over a targeted amount equal to an imputed interest charge on invested capital. The rate used is ordinarily the weighted-average cost of capital. Some enterprises prefer to measure managerial performance in terms of the amount of residual income rather than the percentage return on investment (ROI). The principle is that the enterprise is expected to benefit from expansion as long as residual income is earned. Using a percentage ROI approach, expansion might be rejected if it lowered ROI even though residual income would increase. (See *Economic value added*.)

Resource drivers are cost drivers used in activity-based costing (ABC) to allocate amounts incurred by various resources to activity cost pools.

Responsibility accounting is a means of managerial control that entails assignment of responsibility, determination of performance benchmarks, evaluation of performance, and distribution of rewards. In a traditional system, responsibility defined in financial terms is assigned to the head of an organizational unit. In a modern system, the emphasis shifts to processes and teams, and multiple, dynamic performance measures are established that relate to process efficiency and output, e.g., cycle time, on-time delivery, quality, and unit cost.

Responsibility centers include, in increasing order of complexity and scope of management responsibility, cost centers, revenue centers, profit centers, and investment centers.

Return on investment (ROI) equals income divided by investment. ROI is a measure of managerial performance that is sometimes called the accounting rate of return. "Income" and "investment" are defined in a variety of ways.

Revenue center is a responsibility center in which management is accountable for revenues only.

Rework consists of units that do not meet standards of salability but can be brought to salable condition with additional effort. The decision to rework or discard is based on whether the marginal revenue to be gained from selling the reworked units exceeds the marginal cost of performing the rework.

Sales mix variance measures the effect on the contribution margin of a change in the projected proportions of the different products or services composing an entity's total sales.

Sales quantity variance is the product of the difference between actual and budgeted units sold and the budgeted weighted-average unit contribution margin for the budgeted sales mix.

The **sales-value at split-off method** for allocating joint costs is based upon each of the joint products' relative proportion of total sales value ultimately attributable to the period's production.

Sales volume variance is the sum of the sales mix and sales quantity variances. It is the difference in the contribution margin attributable to the difference between actual sales and budgeted sales.

Scrap consists of raw materials left over from the production cycle but still usable for purposes other than those for which it was originally intended. Scrap may be sold to outside customers, usually for a nominal amount, or may be used in a different production process.

Sensitivity analysis uses trial-and-error to determine the effects of changes in variables or assumptions on final results. It is useful in determining whether expending additional resources to obtain better forecasts is justified.

Separable costs are those incurred beyond the split-off point and identifiable with specific products. (Contrast with *Joint costs.*)

Spending variance is a manufacturing overhead variance. For variable overhead, it is the difference between actual costs and the product of the actual activity and the budgeted application rate. For fixed overhead, the spending (also known as the budget) variance is the difference between actual and budgeted fixed costs. In three-way analysis, the two spending variances isolated in four-way analysis are combined. In two-way analysis, the two spending variances and the variable overhead efficiency variance are combined.

Split-off point is the stage of production at which joint products become separately identifiable.

Standard cost is a predetermined unit cost. Standard cost systems isolate deviations (variances) of actual from expected costs. Standard costs can be used with job costing and process costing systems.

Step-cost functions are nonlinear cost functions. These costs are constant over small ranges of output but increase by steps (discrete amounts) as levels of activity increase. They may be fixed or variable. If the steps are relatively narrow, these costs are usually treated as variable. If the steps are wide, they are more akin to fixed costs.

Step-down method of service department cost allocation is a sequential (but not a reciprocal) process. These costs are allocated to other service departments as well as to users. One common starting point is the service department that renders the greatest percentage of its services to other service departments.

Structural cost drivers are organizational factors that determine the economic structure driving the cost of a firm's products. They reflect a firm's long-term decisions, which position the firm in its industry and marketplace. They are: the firm's scale of operations; the experience level of the firm; the level of technology used within the firm; and the complexity of the firm's operations. Together with executional cost drivers, structural cost drivers are an integral part of activity-based costing.

Sunk cost is a past cost or a cost that the entity has irrevocably committed to incur. Because it is unavoidable and will therefore not vary with the option chosen, it is not relevant to future decisions. (Contrast with *Relevant cost.*)

Supply chain is the flow of services, goods, and information, beginning with initial suppliers and concluding with final transfer to ultimate customers. The supply chain may encompass more than one firm.

Target costing is the practice of calculating the price for a product by adding the desired unit profit margin to the total unit cost. It is an adjunct concept of target pricing.

Theoretical (ideal) capacity is the maximum capacity assuming continuous operations with no holidays, downtime, etc. (Compare with *Normal capacity* and *Practical capacity.*)

Theory of constraints is an approach to continuous improvement (reducing operating expenses and inventory and increasing throughput) based on a five-step procedure: (1) identifying constraints, (2) exploiting the binding constraints, (3) subordinating everything else to the decisions made in the second step, (4) increasing the capacity of the binding constraints, and (5) repeating the process when new binding constraints are identified.

Total productivity (also called total factor productivity) equals the quantity of output divided by the cost of all inputs.

Total quality management (TQM) is an approach to quality that emphasizes continuous improvement, a philosophy of "doing it right the first time," and striving for zero defects and elimination of all waste.

Transfer price is the price charged in an intracompany transaction.

Transferred-in costs are those incurred in a preceding department and received in a subsequent department in a multi-department production setting.

Treasurer has the responsibility for safeguarding financial assets (including the management of cash) and arranging financing.

Value-added costs are the costs of activities that cannot be eliminated without reducing the quality, responsiveness, or quantity of the output required by a customer or the organization.

Value chain is the set of successive functions by which the firm increases the utility of its products or services to consumers. These functions are R&D, design, production, marketing, distribution, and customer service.

Variable costs are operating expenses that vary directly and proportionately with activity. A change in a cost driver results in a proportionate change in a total variable cost. In the long-run, all costs are variable.

Variable (direct) costing considers only variable manufacturing costs to be product (inventoriable) costs. Fixed manufacturing costs are considered period costs and are expensed as incurred. (Contrast with *Absorption costing*.)

Variance analysis concerns the study of deviations of actual costs from budgeted amounts.

Volume (idle capacity or production volume) variance is the amount of under- or overapplied fixed manufacturing overhead. It is the difference between budgeted fixed manufacturing overhead and the amount applied based on a predetermined rate and the standard input allowed for actual output. It measures the use of capacity rather than specific cost outlays.

Waste is the amount of raw materials left over from a production process or production cycle for which there is no further use. Waste is usually not salable at any price and must be discarded.

Work-in-process (manufacturing) account is used to accumulate the costs of goods that have been placed in production but have not yet been completed.

Yield variances determine the effect of varying the total input of a factor of production (e.g., direct materials or labor) while holding constant the input mix (the proportions of the types of materials or labor used) and the weighted-average unit price of the factor of production.

APPENDIX C
ACTIVITY-BASED COSTING GLOSSARY

This appendix presents a glossary of activity accounting terms developed by the Consortium for Advanced Management, International (CAM-I). The approach of the CAM-I is more complex than that found in most cost/managerial accounting textbooks. It provides a coherent and comprehensive set of terms for ABC/M. However, readers should understand that textbook usage in this field is nonstandard. Accordingly, this book attempts to provide a sense of the range of terminology used in practice.

ABC model. A representation of resource costs during a time period that are consumed through activities and traced to products, services, and customers or to any other object that creates a demand for the activity to be performed.

ABC system. A system that maintains financial and operating data on an organization's resources, activities, drivers, objects, and measures. ABC models are created and maintained within this system.

Activity. Work performed by people, equipment, technologies, or facilities. Activities are usually described by the "action verb-adjective-noun" grammar convention. Activities may occur in a linked sequence and activity-to-activity assignments may exist.

Activity analysis. The process of identifying and cataloging activities for detailed understanding and documentation of their characteristics. An activity analysis is accomplished by means of interviews, group sessions, questionnaires, observations, and reviews of physical records of work.

Activity-based budgeting (ABB). An approach to budgeting in which a company uses an understanding of its activities and driver relationships to quantitatively estimate work load and resource requirements as part of an ongoing business plan. Budgets show the types, number, and cost of resources that activities are expected to consume, based on forecasted workloads. The budget is part of an organization's activity-based planning process and can be used in evaluating its success in setting and pursuing strategic goals. (See *Activity-based planning*.)

Activity-based costing (ABC). A methodology that measures the cost and performance of cost objects, activities, and resources. Cost objects consume activities and activities consume resources. Resource costs are assigned to activities based on their use of those resources, and activity costs are reassigned to cost objects (outputs) based on the cost objects' proportional use of those activities. Activity-based costing incorporates causal relationships between cost objects and activities and between activities and resources.

Activity-based management (ABM). A discipline focusing on the management of activities within business processes as the route to continuously improve both the value received by customers and the profit earned in providing that value. ABM uses activity-based cost information and performance measurements to influence management action. (See *Activity-based costing*.)

Activity-based planning (ABP). Activity-based planning (ABP) is an ongoing process to determine activity and resource requirements (both financial and operational) based on the ongoing demand for products or services by specific customer needs. Resource requirements are compared with resources available, and capacity issues are identified and managed. Activity-based budgeting (ABB) is based on the outputs of activity-based planning. (See *Activity-based budgeting*.)

Activity dictionary. A listing and description of activities that provides a common/standard definition of activities across the organization. An activity dictionary can include information about an activity or its relationships, such as activity description, business process, function source, whether value-added, inputs, outputs, supplier, customer, output measures, cost drivers, attributes, tasks, and other information as desired to describe the activity.

Activity driver. The best single quantitative measure of the frequency and intensity of the demands placed on an activity by cost objects or other activities. It is used to assign activity costs to cost objects or to other activities.

Activity level. A description of how elastic or sensitive an activity is to changes in the volume, diversity, or complexity of a cost object or another activity. Product-related activity levels may include unit-level, batch-level, product-sustaining, and facility-sustaining activities. Customer-related activity levels may include customer, market, channel, and project levels.

Allocation. A distribution of costs using calculations that may be unrelated to physical observations or direct or repeatable cause-and-effect relationships. Because of the arbitrary nature of allocations, costs based on cost causal assignment are viewed as more relevant for management decision-making. (Contrast with *Tracing* and *Assignment*.)

Assignment. A distribution of costs using causal relationships. Because cost causal relationships are viewed as more relevant for management decision-making, assignment of costs is generally preferable to allocation techniques. (Synonymous with *Tracing*. Contrast with *Allocation*.)

NOTE: In this book, *assignment* is used as a broad term encompassing both allocation and tracing.

Attributes. A label used to provide additional classification or information about a resource, activity, or cost object. Used for focusing attention and may be subjective. Examples are a characteristic, a score or grade of product or activity, or groupings of these items, and performance measures.

Best practices. A methodology that identifies the measurement or performance by which other similar items will be judged. This methodology is used to establish performance standards and to aid in identifying opportunities to increase effectiveness and efficiency. Best practices methodology may be applied with respect to resources, activities, cost object, or processes.

Bill of activities. A listing of activities required by a product, service, process output, or other cost object. Bill-of-activity attributes could include volume or cost of each activity in the listing.

Bill of resources. A listing of resources required by an activity. Resource attributes could include cost and volumes.

Capacity. The physical facilities, personnel, and processes available to meet the product or service needs of customers. Capacity generally refers to the maximum output or producing ability of a machine, a person, a process, a factory, a product, or a service. (See *Capacity management.*)

Capacity management. The domain of cost management that is grounded in the concept that capacity should be understood, defined, and measured for each level in the organization to include market segments, products, processes, activities, and resources. In each of these applications, capacity is defined in a hierarchy of idle, nonproductive, and productive views.

Constraint. A bottleneck, obstacle, or planned control that limits throughput or the use of capacity.

Cost center. A subunit in an organization that is responsible for costs.

Cost driver. Any situation or event that causes a change in the consumption of a resource, or influences quality or cycle time. An activity may have multiple cost drivers. Cost drivers do not necessarily need to be quantified; however, they strongly influence the selection and magnitude of resource drivers and activity drivers.

Cost driver analysis. The examination, quantification, and explanation of the effects of cost drivers. The results are often used for continuous improvement programs to reduce throughput times, improve quality, and reduce cost.

Cost element. The lowest level component of a resource, activity, or cost object.

Cost management. The management and control of activities and drivers to calculate accurate product and service costs, improve business processes, eliminate waste, influence cost drivers, and plan operations. The resulting information will have utility in setting and evaluating an organization's strategies.

Cost object. Any product, service, customer, contract, project, process, or other work unit for which a separate cost measurement is desired.

Cost object driver. The best single quantitative measure of the frequency and intensity of demands placed on a cost object by other cost objects.

Cost pool. A logical grouping of Resources or Activities aggregated to simplify the assignment of resources to activities or activities to cost objects. Elements within a group may be aggregated or disaggregated depending on the informational and accuracy requirements of the use of the data. A modifier may be appended to further describe the group of costs, i.e., activity cost pool.

Cross-subsidy. The inequitable assignment of costs to cost objects, which leads to overcosting or undercosting them relative to the amount of activities and resources actually consumed. This may result in poor management decisions that are inconsistent with the economic goals of the organization.

Direct cost. A cost that can be directly traced to a cost object because a direct or repeatable cause-and-effect relationship exists. A direct cost uses a direct assignment or cost causal relationship to transfer costs. (See also *Indirect cost, Tracing.*)

Enterprise-wide ABM. A management information system that uses activity-based information to facilitate decision making across an organization.

Hierarchy of cost assignability. An approach to group activity costs at the level of an organization where they are incurred, or can be directly related to. Examples are the level where individual units are identified (unit-level), where batches of units are organized or processed (batch-level), where a process is operated or supported (process-level), or where costs cannot be objectively assigned to lower level activities or processes (facility-level). This approach is used to better understand the nature of the costs, including the level in the organization at which they are incurred, the level to which they can be initially assigned (attached), and the degree to which they are assignable to other activity or cost object levels, i.e., activity cost, cost object cost, or sustaining cost.

Indirect cost. A resource or activity cost that cannot be directly traced to a final cost object because no director repeatable cause-and-effect relationship exists. An indirect cost uses an assignment or allocation to transfer cost. (See *Direct cost, Support costs.*)

Intermediate cost objects. Objects that temporarily accumulate costs as the cost pools move from their originating points to the final cost objects.

Life cycle cost. A product's life cycle is the period that starts with the initial product conceptualization and ends with the withdrawal of the product from the marketplace and final disposition. A product life cycle is characterized by certain defined stages, including research, development, introduction, maturity, decline, and abandonment. Life cycle cost is the accumulated cost incurred by a product during these stages.

Pareto analysis. An analysis that compares cumulative percentages of the rank ordering of costs, cost drivers, profits, or other attributes to determine whether a minority of elements have a disproportionate impact, for example, ascertaining that 20% of a set of independent variables is responsible for 80% of the effect.

Performance measures. Indicators of the work performed and the results achieved in an activity, process, or organizational unit. Performance measures are both nonfinancial and financial. Performance measures enable periodic comparisons and benchmarking.

Process. A series of time-based activities that are linked to complete a specific output.

Profitability analysis. The analysis of profit derived from cost objects with the view to improve or optimize profitability. Multiple views may be analyzed, such as market segment, customer, distribution channel, product families, products, technologies, platforms, regions, manufacturing capacity, etc.

Resource driver. The best single quantitative measure of the frequency and intensity of demands placed on a resource by other resources, activities, or cost objects. It is used to assign resource costs to activities, cost objects, or other resources.

Resources. Economic elements applied or used in the performance of activities or to directly support cost objects. They include people, materials, supplies, equipment, technologies, and facilities. (See *Resource driver, Capacity.*)

Support costs. Costs of activities not directly associated with producing or delivering products or services. Examples are the costs of information systems, process engineering, and purchasing. (See *Indirect cost.*)

Surrogate <item> driver. A substitute for the ideal driver but closely correlated with the ideal driver, if <item> is *Resource, Activity,* or *Cost object*. A surrogate driver is used to significantly reduce the cost of measurement while not significantly reducing accuracy. For example, the number of production runs is not descriptive of the materials disbursing activity, but the number of production runs may be used as an activity driver if material disbursements correlate well with the number of production runs.

Sustaining activity. An activity that benefits an organizational unit as a whole but not any specific cost object.

Target costing. A target cost is calculated by subtracting a desired profit margin from an estimated or a market-based price to arrive at a desired production, engineering, or marketing cost. This may not be the initial production cost but one expected to be achieved during the mature production stage. Target costing is a method used in the analysis of product design that involves estimating a target cost and then designing the product/service to meet that cost. (See *Value analysis.*)

Tasks. The breakdown of the work in an activity into smaller elements.

Tracing. The practice of relating resources, activities, and cost objects using the drivers underlying their cost causal relationships. The purpose of tracing is to observe and understand how costs are arising in the normal course of business operations. (Synonymous with *Assignment*. Contrast with *Allocation.*)

Unit cost. The cost associated with a single unit of measure underlying a resource, activity, product, or service. It is calculated by dividing the total cost by the measured volume. Unit cost measurement must be used with caution because it may not always be practical or relevant in all aspects of cost management.

Unit of driver measure. The common denominator between groupings of similar activities. Example: 20 hours of process time is performed in an activity center. This time equates to a number of common activities varying in process time duration. The unit of measure is a standard measure of time such as a minute or an hour.

Value-adding/Nonvalue-adding. Assessing the relative value of activities according to how they contribute to customer value or to meeting an organization's needs. The degree of contribution reflects the influence of an activity's cost driver(s).

Value analysis. A method to determine how features of a product or service relate to cost, functionality, appeal, and utility to a customer (i.e., engineering value analysis). (See *Target costing.*)

Value chain analysis. A method to identify all the elements in the linkage of activities a firm relies on to secure the necessary materials and services, starting from their point of origin, to manufacture, and to distribute their products and services to an end user.

APPENDIX D
THE IMA STATEMENT OF ETHICAL PROFESSIONAL PRACTICE

The Institute of Management Accountants (IMA) published a revised Statement on Management Accounting, *IMA Statement of Ethical Professional Practice*, effective July 1, 2017. The Statement contains four overarching principles, four specific standards, and a section of guidance on resolving ethical issues.

The memory aid for the four **principles** is HFOR (honesty, fairness, objectivity, and responsibility). The memory aid for the four **standards** is CCIC (competence, confidentiality, integrity, and credibility). The final section, **Resolving** Ethical Issues, is especially significant and has been the subject of many CMA examination questions. Common questions ask for the individual to whom a problem should be reported.

NOTE: The IMA has an ethics hotline for members who wish to discuss ethical conflicts. It is reached at 1-800-245-1383.

The Statement is printed below and on the following page in its entirety.

IMA STATEMENT OF ETHICAL PROFESSIONAL PRACTICE

Members of IMA shall behave ethically. A commitment to ethical professional practice includes overarching principles that express our values and standards that guide member conduct.

Principles

IMA's overarching ethical principles include: Honesty, Fairness, Objectivity, and Responsibility. Members shall act in accordance with these principles and shall encourage others within their organizations to adhere to them.

Standards

IMA members have a responsibility to comply with and uphold the standards of Competence, Confidentiality, Integrity, and Credibility. Failure to comply may result in disciplinary action.

I. COMPETENCE

1. *Maintain an appropriate level of professional leadership and expertise by enhancing knowledge and skills.*
2. *Perform professional duties in accordance with relevant laws, regulations, and technical standards.*
3. *Provide decision support information and recommendations that are accurate, clear, concise, and timely. Recognize and help manage risk.*

II. CONFIDENTIALITY

1. *Keep information confidential except when disclosure is authorized or legally required.*
2. *Inform all relevant parties regarding appropriate use of confidential information. Monitor to ensure compliance.*
3. *Refrain from using confidential information for unethical or illegal advantage.*

III. INTEGRITY

1. *Mitigate actual conflicts of interest. Regularly communicate with business associates to avoid apparent conflicts of interest. Advise all parties of any potential conflicts of interest.*
2. *Refrain from engaging in any conduct that would prejudice carrying out duties ethically.*
3. *Abstain from engaging in or supporting any activity that might discredit the profession.*
4. *Contribute to a positive ethical culture and place integrity of the profession above personal interests.*

IV. CREDIBILITY

1. *Communicate information fairly and objectively.*
2. *Provide all relevant information that could reasonably be expected to influence an intended user's understanding of the reports, analyses, or recommendations.*
3. *Report any delays or deficiencies in information, timeliness, processing, or internal controls in conformance with organization policy and/or applicable law.*
4. *Communicate professional limitations or other constraints that would preclude responsible judgment or successful performance of an activity.*

Resolving Ethical Issues

In applying the Standards of Ethical Professional Practice, the member may encounter unethical issues or behavior. In these situations, the member should not ignore them, but rather should actively seek resolution of the issue. In determining which steps to follow, the member should consider all risks involved and whether protections exist against retaliation.

When faced with unethical issues, the member should follow the established policies of his or her organization, including use of an anonymous reporting system if available.

If the organization does not have established policies, the member should consider the following courses of action:

- *The resolution process could include a discussion with the member's immediate supervisor. If the supervisor appears to be involved, the issue could be presented to the next level of management.*
- *IMA offers an anonymous helpline that the member may call to request how key elements of the* IMA Statement of Ethical Professional Practice *could be applied to the ethical issue.*
- *The member should consider consulting his or her own attorney to learn of any legal obligations, rights, and risks concerning the issue.*

If resolution efforts are not successful, the member may wish to consider disassociating from the organization.

IMA Ethics Helpline Number for callers in the U.S. and Canada:

(800) 245-1383

In other countries, dial the AT&T USA Direct Access Number

from www.att.com/esupport/traveler.jsp?tab=3, then the above number.

INDEX